Islam in the World Today

ISLAM
IN THE WORLD TODAY

*A Handbook of Politics, Religion,
Culture, and Society*

EDITED BY
WERNER ENDE AND UDO STEINBACH

CORNELL UNIVERSITY PRESS
ITHACA AND LONDON

This book is published with the kind support of the Robert Bosch
Foundation.

Originally published as *Der Islam in der Gegenwart,* 5th edition, edited
by Werner Ende and Udo Steinbach, copyright © Verlag C.H. Beck
oHG, München, 2005.

English translation first published 2010 by Cornell University Press

Printed in the United States of America

Library of Congress Cataloging-in-Publication Data

Islam in der Gegenwart. English.
    Islam in the world today : a handbook of politics, religion, culture,
and society / edited by Werner Ende and Udo Steinbach.
        p. cm.
    Includes bibliographical references and index.
    ISBN 978-0-8014-4571-2 (cloth : alk. paper)
    1. Islam—20th century.   2. Islam—21st century.   3. Islam—History.
4. Islam and state.   5. Civilization, Islamic.   I. Ende, Werner, 1937-
II. Steinbach, Udo.   III. Title.
    BP161.2.D46613   2010
    297—dc22   2009039910

Figure credits: Figs. 1, 3, 6, 7, 8, 14, 15: M. Scharabi, private collection.
Fig. 2: *Al-Qahira fi alf ʿam,* 1969. Fig. 4: Naguib, 1980. Fig. 5:
Abu-Lughod, 1971. Fig. 9: Jadarji, *Hiwar* 24–25 (1966). Fig. 10:
Gutbrod and Partners, Architects. Fig. 11: Scharabi, 1974. Figs. 12, 13:
Azzam/Corm/Scharabi.

Cloth printing   10 9 8 7 6 5 4 3 2 1

CONTENTS

PREFACE

The present volume is a translation from the German of the fifth edition of *Der Islam in der Gegenwart*, published in Munich in 2005.

The first edition appeared in 1984, at a time when the world was still under the impact of the revolution in Iran, in which mobilization of the masses by a (Shi'a) Islamic cleric played the decisive role. The revolution was the climax of a development that was described as "re-Islamization," for lack of a more precise term. In their foreword to the 1984 edition, the editors wrote that re-Islamization "was essentially concerned with reinstating Islam as the basis of the political, social, and economic order of the 'Muslim world.'" Although this was a very general description of the phenomenon, it reflected the editors' wish to provide comprehensive information about the forms in which the Islamic religion is manifested in the politics and society of states where Muslims live as a majority or a significant minority. The volume was intended to be different from the mass of publications that focus primarily on political Islam (issues such as fundamentalism, Islamism, and the like) and that attempt to analyze its roots and background, determine its significance in the context of the modern history of the Islamic world, classify it in relation to comparable phenomena in other parts of the "Third World," and give it a theoretical superstructure in terms of social and political science. While the 1984 edition of *Der Islam in der Gegenwart* sought to take account of religious and theological developments, it did not prioritize them. Where they are referred to in the present volume, it is mainly to help explain political and social developments. The same applies in relation to Islam as an element of the pattern of language, literature, and the arts in those parts of today's world where it has influence.

Habent sua fata libelli. It is evident that the two decades between the initial publication of *Der Islam in der Gegenwart* and the fifth edition could not pass without having their effect on the work. The trend toward re-Islamization became a broad political and social tendency. Chapters on new topics such as "Islamic economics" and the position of women had to be incorporated. Following the terrorist attacks of September 11, 2001, Islamist groups and movements had to be identified and described, and there was also the need to devote more attention to the social situation of Muslim communities in Europe and the United States.

The editors' concern in the present volume is to provide a manual rather than an academic monograph. The different contributions do not necessarily offer new insights but are intended to present the current state of research and knowledge clearly and factually. The book is designed for lay readers with a personal or professional interest in the Muslim world, as well as students seeking an introduction to the problems of modern Islam. We have therefore tried our best to ensure that the topics are comprehensibly presented, keeping specialist jargon to a minimum and limiting endnotes to strictly necessary information. The same applies to the bibliographical references. The different essays are intended to outline the current state of research on specific topics, but we have avoided going into detail about overly specialized aspects. While sources in English take priority in this American edition, we have included some important works in German and other languages. References to German works in the endnotes have obviously been retained.

Given the broad sweep of topics covered here, we could hardly hope to achieve a complete picture. This is particularly true of the essays in the historical section, which trace the development of Islam from its origins to the present day. It was also necessary to define the main emphasis of the cross-sectional articles that present different aspects of present-day Islam, and of the analyses by country. This meant, for example, that the single case study of Indonesia has to suffice as an illustration of the combination of Islamic teaching with pre-Islamic and non-Islamic local tradition which is so characteristic of the everyday life of Muslims in the wide area spanning the Maghreb in the west, Indonesia in the east, sub-Saharan Africa in the south, and Central Asia in the north. In presenting the analysis of Islam in individual countries, we focus on those that are of particular importance in the Muslim world, either by virtue of their size or because they demonstrate special developments of some kind. By the same token, in considering the situation of Muslim migrants in Europe, we can provide detailed analysis only of particularly significant cases. Inevitably there is some overlapping, and we had to accept a few minor gaps in content as well.

With respect to transliteration, we had to compromise between academic desirability and the need to be accessible to a broad range of readers. In general, the transliteration is based on that used in the *International Journal of Middle East Studies* (*IJMES*), a quarterly journal published by Cambridge University Press. With the exception of ʿayns and hamzas, diacritical marks have been omitted. Some names appear as they have come to be used in the Western media (although we occasionally had to distinguish between French- and English-based spelling). Terms that have become established in African, Asian, and Western languages, and names of Arabic origin, are generally supplemented in the text by the correct Arabic transcription. In the case of Ottoman words, it was sometimes necessary to compromise between the correct philological transliteration and the modern Turkish spelling. In most instances the correct transliteration is appended at the place where the relevant name or term first appears in a chapter or section.

Verses from the Qur'an are referenced by the number of the sura, followed by a colon, and then the verse number (e.g., 2:100 for sura 2, verse 100). The verse numbers are based on the official Egyptian edition of the Qur'an. English quotations from the Qur'an rely entirely on Marmaduke Pickthall's translation, *The Meaning of the Glorious Koran*.

Explicit mention should be made of the general problem of statistical data on the distribution of Muslim populations and the proportion of Muslims in given populations (see the introductory remarks to the contribution by Peter Heine and Riem Spielhaus, Part One, chapter V). The difficult situation of sources, and the contradictory, sometimes vaguely formulated information in the sources used, have made it impossible to achieve definitive coherence in the present volume; in a number of cases it is more a matter of approximation. In fact this is an insoluble problem, and any attempt to produce perfectly accurate figures would be rather misleading. (A recent valuable publication of the Pew Research Center, *Mapping the Global Muslim Population*, Washington, D.C., October 2009, came too late to be incorporated here.)

The editors and authors of this volume thank the Robert Bosch Foundation for its generosity in funding the American edition of this book. English is becoming increasingly dominant in the humanities (including Islamic studies). While this has enhanced the capacity for international communication, it has also resulted in a tendency for scholars of Islam to become less aware of academic publications in languages other than English. The result is that an area of study that is basically multicultural and multilingual is becoming impoverished. Germany and German-speaking countries are known for their long, important tradition of "classical" historical-philological work in Islamic studies. This tradition reaches back into the nineteenth century and is still making significant contributions to research today. Compared to this, the concern with contemporary Islam and the modern Muslim world in Germany has lacked the historical depth and broad scope of the Anglo-Saxon tradition. Since the early 1970s, however, German-speaking academics have made considerable efforts to link up with the international research in this field. The present volume is designed to record in a nutshell the many and varied ways in which academics in Germany are working on topics related to the Muslim world over a wide range of disciplines, from historical-philological Islamic studies to ethnology, political and social sciences, and economics.

ACKNOWLEDGMENTS

We gratefully acknowledge the assistance of many individuals who contributed to the realization of this project. In particular we thank the translators, who skillfully mediated between somewhat unwieldy academic texts in German and the demands of English-language readers.

Peter Potter, Ange Romeo-Hall, and Amanda Heller not only managed the complex process of translating and publishing this sizeable volume but also took care of countless details regarding language style and professional editorial requirements. We thank Dina Dineva for her excellent preparation of the indexes.

In addition, we are indebted to Axel Havemann of Freie Universität Berlin (Free University Berlin) and Frank Babing of Humboldt-Universität zu Berlin (Humboldt University Berlin), who assisted us in solving technical challenges with which we would not have been able to cope by ourselves.

WERNER ENDE AND UDO STEINBACH

Berlin, August 2009

Translated by Karen Margolis

ISLAM IN THE WORLD TODAY

Part One

Historical Expansion,
Political and Religious History

I

The World of Islam

A Brief Historical Survey

(Heribert Busse)

1. The Prophet Muhammad and the Emergence of Islam

Islam, at present the religion of more than 1 billion people all over the world, emerged on the Arabian Peninsula in the early decades of the seventh century, at a time when decisive changes were taking place in world history. In Europe, the unrest owing to the migration of populations gave way to the kingdoms of the Goths, the Lombards, and the Merovingians. Muhammad's contemporary on the papal throne was Gregory I, called Gregory the Great (ca. 540–604), who reorganized ecclesiastical institutions, fought remnants of paganism in Italy, and made a name for himself as the author of homilies and Bible commentaries that were considered exemplary for many centuries. Byzantium had to defend itself on two fronts, in Syria and Mesopotamia versus the Sassanid Empire, its hereditary enemy, and in the Balkans against the Avars, pressing in from the steppe. It assumed the tradition of Rome and carried on the Greek-Hellenistic culture; Christianity had been made the state religion by Theodosius I (379–395) and had become the mainstay of state and society. Persia was ruled by the Sassanids, who saw themselves as heirs of the Achaemenid Empire and protectors and modernizers of Zoroastrianism. In the north they were in direct contact with China, which after unification under the Tang dynasty had expanded its power throughout all of Turkistan. The Arabs still lived according to the traditions of a tribal society that had become semi-settled. In South Arabia the Himyarite kingdom had collapsed in the first half of the sixth century; it was initially succeeded by Ethiopia, which also attempted to expand its influence all the way to Mecca. But then the Sassanids appeared on the scene and established themselves in South Arabia, which played an important role as the hub of trade with India and Africa.

Mecca lay beyond the horizons of the major powers at the time, but it was tied to them in manifold ways. The city was situated on the trade route that led from South Arabia to the Fertile Crescent, reaching the Mediterranean Sea in Gaza. Mecca was ruled by the Quraysh; its businessmen played a leading role in transit trade. There is an echo of it in the Qur'an: "For the taming of Quraysh / For their taming (We cause) the caravans to set forth in winter and summer. / So [as thanks] let them worship the Lord of this House [i.e., the Ka'ba], / Who hath fed them against hunger and hath made them safe from fear" (sura 106: 1–5, "The Quraysh"). Mecca lived off long-distance trading, and the Ka'ba, the most significant shrine of heathen Arabia, provided the security that was absolutely essential for it. The city, with the neighboring Plain of 'Arafat, was the site of the annual pilgrimage festival (hajj), which was combined with a highly frequented market. Christianity had not yet gained a firm foothold in Arabia. South of Mecca, at the border of present-day Yemen, lay Najran, where there was a large, ethnically diverse Christian community. Christian anchorites had settled in the desert; isolated Christians also lived in the few cities; and Christian traders and adherents of other religions certainly visited the annual market in Mecca. Legend has it that the apostle Bartholomew preached in Arabia, although organized missionary work had not yet begun there, outside the borders of the Byzantine Empire. Only in the north, in present-day Jordan and Syria, were there Christian Arab tribes with their own church hierarchy. Arab Christianity mirrored the different denominations of the Christian heartland, whereby the two main forms of Eastern Christianity, Monophysitism and Nestorianism, considered heretical by the Greek Orthodox and Roman Church, certainly had the upper hand.

Judaism had been more widespread than Christianity in Arabia for centuries. That was true for South Arabia, and also for the Hejaz (Hijaz). There were Jewish communities in the towns of Wadi al-Qura, stretching in a southeastern direction from Tabuk to Medina. Very little is known of these Jews, whether they were immigrants or Arabs who had adopted Judaism. They were, in any case, strongly Arabized, living in tribal organizations and engaged in agriculture and handicraft. Their role in the emergence of Islam can hardly be overestimated. The same is true of Christianity, with its different denominations. Muhammad drew from both sources, whereby he learned to see Judaism from a Christian perspective. Opinions differ with regard to the part that each of these faiths played in the formation of Islam, but one can say without qualification that Islam would have been inconceivable without the preliminary work of these two religions on the Arabian Peninsula. Muhammad had definitely at least heard of Zoroastrianism, the state religion of Persia, but it hardly influenced emerging Islam. Manichaeism, by contrast, did leave its mark, as well as, perhaps, the flourishing Baptist sects in southern Mesopotamia. Finally it should not be overlooked that pagan traditions also live on in Islam, such as the hajj celebrated in Mecca, in which the ritual was retained in its original form and merely reinterpreted in a monotheistic sense.

The Arab world was in a period of religious upheaval when Muhammad began his work. He was born in 570 in Mecca into the Hashim family, an impoverished branch of the Quraysh. According to tradition it was the "year of the elephant," named after Abraha, the Ethiopian governor of South Arabia, who in that year is said to have advanced toward Mecca with an army that included a war elephant. The undertaking, which from the later perspective of the Muslims was directed chiefly against the Ka'ba, failed. The episode has been eternalized in the Qur'an, sura 105, "The Elephant." God protected his shrine, although at that time it had not yet been purged of idolatry. The purification was to be reserved for Muhammad, not the Christian Abraha. It appears to be historically certain, however, that the Ethiopian advance actually took place about two decades earlier than assumed by Muslim tradition.

Muhammad's father, according to tradition named 'Abdallah, "servant of Allah" (it later became the preferred name of Muslim converts), died before the birth of the Prophet. The child was raised by his uncle Abu Talib. As a young man Muhammad worked in the service of the wealthy widow Khadija, owner of a commercial house that engaged in long-distance trade with Syria and Egypt. Khadija later became his first wife. From this marriage came Fatima, the only one of the Prophet's children who survived him. Her marriage with 'Ali—Muhammad's cousin and son of his foster father Abu Talib—produced two sons, Hasan and Husayn, progenitors of today's numerous sayyids or sharifs (Arab. sing. *sharif*), whose genealogy traces back to the founder of Islam. After Khadija's death in 619, Muhammad remarried several times, usually for political reasons. Khadija can lay claim to the honorary title of being the first Muslim woman. There are numerous traditional stories about how Muhammad first confided in Khadija and was encouraged by her in his conviction of having received revelations and was referred to her cousin Waraqa ibn Nawfal, who knew the scripture of the Christians and may even have been a Christian himself.

Muhammad was raised in a pagan environment. In the Qur'an it says: "Did He [Allah] not find thee wandering and direct (thee)?" (sura 93:7, "The Morning"). From his early childhood on he was a God-seeker, open to all stimuli that rushed in on him from several directions. He is said to have traveled with a trading caravan to Egypt and Syria, but definitive information about that is lacking. In Bosra (near the southern border of present-day Syria) he allegedly met with the monk Bahira, who recognized in a vision that he would be the future prophet of the Arabs and taught him about faith in the one God. The call to prophethood is said to have come to him on Mount Hira', near Mecca, where he retreated each year to meditate and practice asceticism. As the "Prophet and Messenger of Allah," as he later called himself, he saw himself in the succession of a long series of prophets, most of them also known in the Bible. His aim at first was less to found a new religion than to create a book that corresponded to the Scripture of the Jews and Christians and would bring the revelation to the Arabs "in plain Arabic speech" (sura 26:195), which had been withheld from them. In terms of content, the Qur'an follows the Old Testament in many points with its untiring campaign against polytheism. Muhammad was beholden to the message of the New Testament and Christianity with his eschatological sermon on the Last Judgment, but he denied not only the doctrine of the divine nature of Jesus but also the fact that he died on the cross (see sura 4:157), which are central points of the Christian creed, as well as the dogma of original sin committed by our ancestors in paradise and inherited by humankind. This means that Islam rejects the Christian dogma of redemption: that God immolated his only son to remove the sins of the world. According to Islam, redemption occurred when God revealed himself to humankind, showing them the way to salvation. This is, by the way, much nearer to Judaism than to Christianity. The gulf between Islam and Christianity is irreconcilable. For Muhammad, Jesus was a human being, a servant and messenger of God like himself, and thus a Muslim in the strict sense of the word. Muslims believe that Christianity was distorted by the apostle Paul; some of them ascribe this distortion to Emperor Constantine I, who in truth did nothing more than issue the famous edict of toleration of Christianity in 313, and who did not receive baptism until he was on his deathbed. Similar charges of distorting Scripture were voiced against the Jews; as viewed by Muhammad, Abraham was in fact the first Muslim (sura 2:131). Islam shares with Judaism and Christianity the principles of social commitment, care for the needy, and the obligation to act ethically. The Qur'an includes a list of commandments and prohibitions (sura 17:22–39) that closely corresponds to the Ten Commandments promulgated in Exodus 20, which are holy to both Christians and Jews.

In response to his sermon and his call for moral renewal, Muhammad encountered fierce resistance in Mecca from the wealthy merchant class, who feared that Islam would bring the downfall of the shrine that guaranteed the prosperity of the city. The new doctrine also questioned the traditional social order, and the new form of the community of believers (Arab. *umma*) displaced the tribal order, ultimately making it obsolete. The adherents of the Prophet were at first limited to his family and closest acquaintances. After that it was predominantly the poor and desperate who joined him. In view of the constantly growing antagonism in Mecca, Muhammad soon felt forced to seek help from outside the city. He dispatched a group of followers to Abyssinia, and he himself initiated negotiations with the residents of Taif (al-Ta'if), near Mecca. In the end negotiations were successful with a group of pilgrims from Yathrib (Medina) who had adopted Islam and were seeking an arbitrator to settle disputes that had broken out in the city between the different tribes and groups. In summer 622 Muhammad left his native city in fear for his life and settled in Medina. This resettlement was referred to by Muslims from then on as the *hijra*, or emigration, and was later declared the beginning of a new calendar. It marked a new stage of development for the Islamic community. Muhammad had changed from being the leader of a persecuted minority into a politician and then a statesman. The so-called Charter of Medina, the details of which are still disputed among scholars, was an instrument with which Muhammad ended the internal chaos and at first integrated non-Muslims, including the large Jewish community that had been living in Medina since time immemorial. The Jews were organized into several tribes, of which three played an important role. Soon after Muhammad's arrival in Medina, conflicts were sparked that ended with the expulsion of some of the Jews from the city, while others were killed in a massacre that the Prophet had not ordered but had in fact condoned.

With the elimination of the Jews, the political community had been transformed into a purely religious one based on Islam. It was made up of participants of the *hijra,* the *muhajirun,* who had either accompanied Muhammad from Mecca to Medina or had followed him there over the course of time, and native Medinans, the "helpers" (*ansar*), some of whom had joined Islam prior to Muhammad's arrival in the city. In addition to securing the internal situation, Muhammad also strove to win over the Meccans to his cause. He may have been motivated by thoughts of returning to his home, from which he had been expelled along with the believers. This could also be explained from a religious perspective by his conviction that the Ka'ba was originally a monotheistic shrine, founded or rebuilt by Abraham (see sura 2:125–127) and desecrated through the idolatry of the Meccans, and that it needed to be returned to its original purpose (see sura 9:17–18). Focus on the Ka'ba found symbolic expression in the changing of the direction of prayer (*qibla*). Instead of Jerusalem, which had been declared the direction of prayer in Medina in order to win over the Jews, the direction was changed to the Ka'ba in Mecca (see sura 2:142–145). This served to declare the city with its shrine to be the spiritual center of Islam.

Elevating Mecca, that is, the Ka'ba, to the *qibla* marked the final break from Judaism. But just as Judaism had been a religion with a militant component, now the Muslims took to fighting, first for the sheer necessity of securing the upkeep of the impoverished *muhajirun,* and then for the possession of the shrine in Mecca and the right to return to their former residences, whence they had been expelled by the heathens (see sura 22:38–41). A series of skirmishes and battles in the surroundings of Medina ensued, with varied outcomes. A siege of Medina by the Meccans ended with their withdrawal. Muhammad's attempt a short time later to visit the shrine in Mecca led to the famous Treaty of al-Hudaibiyya, named after a tree on the outskirts of Mecca where the pact was made. In 630 Mecca fell to Islam without a struggle. Muhammad is said to have destroyed the idols in and around the Ka'ba with his own hands, reestablishing the monotheistic cult introduced by Abraham. He treated his enemies magnanimously, thereby facilitating their conversion to Islam. Soon the larger part of the Arabian Peninsula had been won over by Islam. Shortly before his death Muhammad led a campaign into Byzantine territory. Later conquests outside Arabia could then be interpreted as having been planned by the Prophet on divine orders. At the height of his success he allegedly sent letters to the rulers of the surrounding empires—the Byzantine emperor, the King of Kings of Persia, and the Negus of Abyssinia—demanding that they surrender and convert to Islam. Nothing illustrates how Islam aspired to world domination better than this legend.

The Qur'an (*qur'an*), meaning "recitation" or "reading," is the most significant legacy of the Prophet. It gives Islam a scripture comparable to the Bible. In sura 9:111 the Qur'an is put on a par with the Torah and the Gospel. Of course it differs from the Gospel on an essential point: the Gospel reports on Jesus, while according to Islam, the Qur'an contains the word of God in its purest form. As Jesus is the incarnation of God according to Christian belief, "begotten, not made," according to the Nicene Creed, the Muslims consider the Qur'an to be the verbalization of Allah, so to speak, the uncreated word of God according to Sunni belief. It developed in stages over the course of more than three decades; at the death of the Prophet it existed in a scattered form written down on papyrus, bone, and other writing materials. Muslims assume that it took on its present form under Caliph 'Uthman (r. 644–656), whereas recent Western research adduces arguments in favor of a much longer development. Divided into 114 suras that are arranged by decreasing length, it describes the decisive stages of the history of salvation from the creation of the world to the appearance of Islam, albeit not thematically ordered and fractured in many ways. Eschatology is a large focus, including judgment and reward and punishment in the hereafter. In addition to the narrative passages, there are prayers and especially rules that regulate the lives of believers down to many details. They became the foundation of the Islamic catalog of basic duties incumbent on the faithful. They are referred to as religious practice or worship (*'ibadat*) and are listed in five categories, also called the "pillars" (*arkan*) of Islam: (1) profession of faith (*shahada*); (2) ritual prayer (*salat*), to be done five times per day; (3) fasting during the month of Ramadan (*sawm*); (4) alms tax (*zakat*); and (5) pilgrimage to Mecca (*hajj*), which should be made at least once in a lifetime. The dietary laws, including the prohibition on wine (sura 5:90) and pork (sura 2:173) which are characteristic of Islam, belong to the area of ritual purity. As to financial transactions, Muhammad definitively banned the charging of interest (see sura 2:275–277). Questions of family and inheritance law are dealt with in relative detail in the Qur'an.

The Qur'an is the most reliable evidence about Muhammad's life and the substance of his doctrine. Just as Jews distinguish between written and oral Torah, in Islam as well, in addition to the Qur'an, there is the hadith, referring to the "sayings" or "tales" (Arab. *hadith*) about the Prophet, his actions, his statements, and his behavior on certain occasions. The hadiths were initially passed on in oral tradition and later put into writing. Some of them are equated with Qur'anic statements (*hadith qudsi,* divine sayings). Similar to the Christian apostles with respect to Jesus, the companions of the Prophet (*ashab* or *sahaba*) played an important role as eyewitnesses to Muhammad's actions in establishing the early Islamic community and are included in the tradition of the hadiths as warrantors. This also applies to women, in particular the wives of the Prophet, as they would have been the ones who knew him best. The hadith has become a means of manifesting the Prophet beyond his death. Hadith recitation offers pious Muslims information about Muhammad and his doctrine, and keeps the Prophet as a person alive beyond his death. The Qur'an, by contrast, is the word of God, which gained a worldly existence through the mouth of the Prophet. Its recitation makes God's presence real for believers. Like reciting the Eucharist for Christians, recitation of the Qur'an is a way for Muslims to be close to God.

The religious community in Medina became the nucleus of the Islamic state. As God is the legislator, customs and usages (*'urf*) that did not form part of the religious heritage were measured by the divine laws and declared forbidden if they contradicted them. In contrast to Christianity, which evolved outside the polity and grew into the state only secondarily—thus the independence of the two never disappeared from consciousness—Islam established a state around the religious nucleus. According to a strict interpretation the state is identical to the religious community (*umma*) and its institutions. In principle there is no dualism of church and state in Islam. Even if there are theorists in the Islamic world today who question Muhammad's intention to found a state in the modern sense of the word and postulate such a dualism, one does better justice to the historical evidence by understanding the Islamic community of Medina as an entity in which religion and state were merged into an inextricable unity.

The prerequisites for Islamic international and martial law were also laid down in Medina. The Prophet eradicated paganism using the force of arms whenever he encountered resistance; pagans had a choice only between Islam and death. As to the "people of the book," namely, Jews and Christians, who had divine scriptures, he felt sufficiently obliged to tolerate them, on the condition, however, that they submitted to Islamic rule. Muslims are called upon in the Qur'an to fight against those "who have the book." If they submitted, a peace treaty (*sulh*) was concluded with them. They were not expected to accept Islam, but had to pay tribute, that is, the poll tax (*jizya*) (sura 9:29). In addition, farmers had to pay the land tax (*kharaj*). Jews and Christians were granted freedom of worship provided that Muslims did not take offense; for example, Christians were not allowed to show the cross in public. Synagogues and churches remained in the possession of the Jews and Christians, who were allowed to do everything necessary for their repair and preservation but were forbidden to build new ones. If they offered any armed resistance, however, the Muslims were free to do as they pleased—kill them or enslave them and convert their synagogues and churches into mosques, use them for other purposes, or destroy them.

In the course of later conquests, these "privileges," so to speak, were extended to the Zoroastrians; when Islamic rule was established in India, it was expanded by necessity to the Hindus because of the sheer mass of subjects. With respect to civil rights, the "people of the book" remained outside the Islamic state. Because the Muslims were the constitutive people, the "people of the book" were not citizens—and thus not second-class citizens, as is often claimed. The communities had their own administrations and were, in a sense, independent states in a contractual relationship (*dhimma*) with the Islamic state. They were "people of the covenant" (*ahl al-dhimma,* a status that could be terminated if violated. They were exempt from military service because as nonbelievers they were considered unfit for service. From the perspective of Muslims, they enjoyed the protection of the Islamic state. The war (*jihad*) against nonbelievers outside the sway of Islam, to be fought according to rules laid down in the Qur'an and hadith, is a strictly Islamic matter. Muslim theologians even expressed the opinion that jihad should be financed through taxes paid by the people of the book. From the perspective of Muslim theorists as it developed in the Middle Ages, the world was divided into the Territory (literally "House") of Islam (*dar al-islam*), where Muslims rule, and the Territory of War (*dar al-harb*). War must be fought against the nonbelievers until they submit. If they are superior in strength, a truce can be agreed on, like the cease-fire (*hudna,* calm) the Prophet had agreed to with the Meccans at al-Hudaibiyya. The Muslims can break the truce, normally concluded for a period of ten years, without previous notice if they feel they are in a position to resume fighting.

The system outlined here was established in Medina and expanded and refined in the course of the conquests. Today it is still (or again) being propagated by Muslim fundamentalists ("Islamists") as ideal. It would be inaccurate to characterize the attitude toward the people of the book as one of true tolerance. In reality it is a toleration or forbearance, granted in a consciousness of the absolute superiority of Islam and tied to hopes that the people of the book will ultimately accept Islam. The Muslims were not disappointed in their hopes. Anatolia, Syria, Mesopotamia, Egypt, and other regions were once almost exclusively Christian, but now Christians have become a minority or disappeared entirely. The reasons for this development are manifold. Islamization was without a doubt fostered by the fact that Eastern Christianity was split into divergent denominations. Also, since Islamic legislation in matters of inheritance favored conversion, Islam was the religion of the victors, and little aid came from the West. Judaism held its ground incomparably better; Islam confronted the Jews' own consciousness of superiority, which was stronger than that of the Muslims. Also Judaism, which is fostered within the bosom of the family, offered less of a target than the strictly organized Christian churches, with their tendency to show a public presence. Judaism is a matter of birth, an incomparably stronger bond than the *character indelebilis* (indelible mark) impressed on the soul of Christians when they are baptized. In addition, the Jews were accustomed to living as a minority in hostile surroundings, for more than a millennium already at the time Islam appeared on the scene. In India, Hinduism resisted

Islam, particularly in the center and in the south, although the subcontinent had been under Islamic rule for several centuries. Obviously Mughal rule was more tolerant than the Islamic government had been in preceding periods and in other parts of the world.

2. The Four "Rightly Guided" Caliphs: The First Wave of Conquests

Muhammad died after a short illness on June 8, 632, at the age of sixty-three. Because he left no stipulations about his successor and his prophetic function could not be inherited, conflict soon arose, which escalated into fundamental disputes and finally to the schism of Islam. The Sunni majority, later on called *ahl al-sunna wa-l-jama'a*—that is, those who follow the practice introduced by Muhammad and decide on the basis of consent of the community when no precedent is known—spoke out for the selection of the caliph (*khalifa*, "successor" or "deputy") from the Quraysh tribe, the Meccan "nobility." According to the Shi'a, the "party (*shi'a*) of 'Ali," Muhammad was on the way from Mecca to Medina, returning from the "farewell pilgrimage" in March 632, when at the pond of Khumm he appointed 'Ali, his cousin and son-in-law, Fatima's husband, to be his successor. As the Shi'a later taught, the blood descendants of Muhammad inherited his prophetic charisma and thus were particularly called upon to lead the community. Extremist Shi'ites even went so far as to deify 'Ali or one of his progeny.

Abu Bakr emerged as the victor from the rivalries that broke out after Muhammad's death. He was a loyal follower of the Prophet from the very beginning, and he was Muhammad's father-in-law through his daughter 'A'isha. He ruled for only two years (632–634), most of which time was spent defeating the Arab tribes which had risen up after Muhammad's death. As it soon turned out, these campaigns were the prelude to widely expanding conquests, since Abu Bakr proved able to direct the forces northward, thereby initiating a movement that would profoundly change the political system around the world. Islam, on the one hand a religion of peace (*salam*), had possessed a strong militant element since the founding of the community in Medina, and the political situation was generally favorable for a move beyond Arabia. Byzantium and the Sassanid Empire had been weakened by prolonged fighting. The Sassanids had decisively defeated the Byzantines in 614 and advanced to the Mediterranean Sea. Not until a decade and a half later was Emperor Heraclius able to turn the tide of fate. In 629 he triumphantly returned the cross to Jerusalem that had been carried off by the Sassanids. On the way there, according to Arab tradition, he received the famous letter from Muhammad demanding that he surrender and accept Islam. In retrospect Muslim historiographers have declared that the conquests started when Abu Bakr dispatched four emirs (Arab. sing. *amir*). The number four expresses a claim to universal dominion. By the time Abu

Bakr died in August 634, victorious battles had taken place in Iraq and Syria, and vast areas of Palestine had been occupied. Only the coastal cities and Jerusalem continued to resist.

The undertaking that Abu Bakr had begun was carried further by 'Umar ibn al-Khattab (r. 634–644), whom Abu Bakr had designated to be his successor. He led the military operations from Medina and was able to reap what Abu Bakr had sown. Two crucial battles were fought under 'Umar, first in Syria in August 636 at the Yarmuk River (which flows into the Jordan River south of the Sea of Galilee). After this defeat the Byzantines were forced to cede Syria and Palestine. The way to Egypt was thus opened up for the Arabs. The second decisive battle took place at al-Qadisiyya in Iraq, southwest of Hira. The Arabs were victorious in the face of Sassanid superiority in terms of numbers and equipment. The victory paved the way to the Iranian heartland. Yazdegerd III, the last significant Sassanid King of Kings, was defeated in the battle of Nahavand (south of Hamadan); he fled and was murdered by his own people around 640.

In Syria the conquests at the northern border came to a standstill, so Byzantium, now limited in Asia to a region that, generally speaking, was identical to present-day Turkey, was given a reprieve. Through the occupation of Syria and Palestine, Egypt was cut off from its land connection to Byzantium and, after back-and-forth fighting, became Muslim spoils.

'Umar's achievements as a strategist corresponded to the skill he showed in organizing the new empire. He entrusted the most respected companions of the Prophet (*ashab*) with positions of leadership and took harsh disciplinary measures against arbitrary army generals. The conquered provinces were secured by setting up garrison towns (*amsar*). That is how the cities of Kufa (near present-day al-Najaf) and Basra in Mesopotamia developed, as well as al-Fustat (the tent) in Egypt, the precursor to present-day Cairo. The financial administration was organized in the *diwan*, which was responsible for paying stipends and pensions to Muslims, especially the soldiers. Regarding the administration of justice, the establishment of judges (*qadi*) is attributed to 'Umar, who is also said to have expanded Islamic criminal law and supplemented the catalog of duties incumbent on Muslims in some points. By introducing a new calendar that started after the *hijra*, which is still used today in the Islamic world, he clearly demonstrated the continuity between the original community in Medina and the new Islamic empire. By taking on the title "Prince of the Believers" (*amir al-mu'minin*), he combined the authority of a traditionally elected Arab tribal chieftain with that of his position as leader of a community joined in faith.

After ruling for ten years, 'Umar died in November 644 at the hand of a murderous discontented slave. Shortly before his death he allegedly appointed a panel of six electors to regulate his succession. The lot fell to 'Uthman (r. 644–656). A wealthy businessman and son-in-law of the Prophet he had participated in the emigration to Abyssinia. The campaign of conquest that Abu Bakr had started and 'Umar continued on a large scale came to a standstill, although one cannot forget that Iran was conquered once and for all during ʿUthman's reign, and movements got under way from Egypt that were to have far-reaching consequences. From here, two routes were open to the further advance of the Arabs: to move up the Nile or along the North African coast. On their way up the Nile they encountered the Christian kingdom of Nubia, with its center in Dongola. Battles ensued that went unfavorably for the Arabs and ended with a settlement, for which Muhammad's cease-fire with Mecca served as a justification for the temporary halting of hostilities. The treaty with the Nubians is referred to in Arab historiography by the Latin term *pactum* (*baqt*). It remained in force until 1315, when the Mamluks of Egypt were able to expand their sphere of influence in the south beyond Aswan. The Christian kingdom of Alwa, bordering Dongola to the south, was conquered in 1504 by the Funj, herders from the south whose rulers had been converted to Islam.

After temporarily stopping in the south, the Arabs concentrated their efforts in Egypt on advancing along the Mediterranean coast. Here they were more successful, since Byzantine rule in North Africa had never really penetrated the country and found no resonance among the Berbers. After the first raids, which began in 647, it took almost until the end of the century before the Arabs managed to advance all the way to the Atlantic coast and defeat the Berbers once and for all. From a camp set up in Tunisia in 662 the conquerors developed the city of Kairouan (Qayrawan), which was to become a cultural center of Islam in North Africa.

The advance to North Africa and the defeat of Sassanian Iran marked the end of the first wave of conquests. ʿUthman was not adept at domestic policy. As an Umayyad he represented the interests of a widely branching and influential Meccan family whose members had adopted Islam very late and had only loose connections with the original community in Medina. As caliph he promoted members of his immediate family, giving them key positions in the provinces; apart from that he reserved a disproportionate share of the spoils for himself and his kin. In such a situation it was inevitable that the cohesiveness of the Islamic community would be put to the acid test. Malcontents set off from all directions for Medina, where they took up positions around the house of the caliph and presented their charges, especially that of nepotism and dissipating the state coffers. After prolonged negotiations, one group pushed its way into the house and murdered the caliph. Troops that Muʿawiya, the Umayyad governor of Syria, had allegedly sent to Medina to protect the caliph came too late and could not prevent the tragedy.

The assassination of ʿUthman marked a turning point in the history of early Islam. The direct aftermath in the form of civil wars would long continue to occupy the Islamic state. In response to the murder of the caliph, voices calling for vengeance grew louder. But initially agreement was reached in Medina on the election of a successor. The caliphate was awarded to ʿAli (r. 656–661), who had already been a member of the electoral council installed by 'Umar. His election was challenged by Mu'awiya because it came to pass by a minority vote without the participation of the notables in the provinces. 'Ali was closely tied to Muhammad in many ways, as has been noted repeatedly. Although Shi'i tradition views some things about him through rose-colored glasses, it does appear certain that he was a talented and energetic man. He had been caught up in profound disputes with his three predecessors, in which theological problems played an important role. According to the Shi'i interpretation—which was not declared until later, of course—the first three caliphs were usurpers who wrongfully kept 'Ali from attaining the caliphate to which he was entitled immediately following Muhammad's death.

Right after 'Ali assumed his position, fronts formed with different goals. The main issue was how to assess the murder of 'Uthman and adequately punish the perpetrator. It was a decision of far-reaching consequences that 'Ali gave up Medina as the state seat and settled in Kufa, where he had strong support. Medina was thus no longer the center of the Islamic state, and as it turned out, this change was final. The first attempt to remove the caliph from his position by force of arms originated in Medina, where the old companions of the Prophet feared for their influence in the community. Under the pretext of taking vengeance for the murder of 'Uthman, which 'Ali supposedly was not pursuing strongly enough, the Medinans went to battle. Under the leadership of Talha and Zubayr, they were accompanied by 'A'isha, Muhammad's influential widow. 'Ali emerged victorious from the fight that ensued in southern Mesopotamia, which came to be known as the "Battle of the Camel" owing to the camel on which 'A'isha observed the skirmish.

Mu'awiya also supported the call for vengeance for his murdered relative 'Uthman. 'Ali took the offensive in opposing him. In summer 657 he and his troops encountered Mu'awiya's army near Siffin, on the upper Euphrates, east of Aleppo. After days of back-and-forth fighting, both sides agreed to decide the matter through arbitration. Although the arbitrators convened over several days in different places, they could not come to a conclusive decision; in the end, however, Mu'awiya emerged the victor because his power in Syria remained untouched.

Agreeing to arbitration brought nothing but disadvantages for 'Ali, who now was faced with a new enemy of threatening strength, the Kharijites. These were people from among his own followers who rejected the arbitration for theological reasons and thus "seceded" (or "went out," Arab. *kharaja*) from his army, which explains their name. They fought many battles against the caliph and developed into a sect of their own with a puritanical orientation, which later splintered into several groups. The most significant of these, the Ibadis, continues today to live in Oman and North Africa. The fact has fallen virtually into oblivion that in their heyday the Kharijites formed the third major Islamic denomination, after the Shi'a, who were able to assert themselves unchallenged, and the Sunna, who were always in the majority. From a political perspective, they differed from both the Sunna, which retained the caliphate of the Quraysh, and the Shi'a, which viewed the caliphate as hereditary among the descendants of Muhammad, in their emphasis on the theological and moral qualities of the leader of the Islamic community. They felt that the best Muslim should become the caliph, "even if he were an Abyssinian slave."

3. The Arabian Dynasty of the Umayyads: The Second Wave of Conquests

To achieve their objective the Kharijites did not shrink from murder. 'Ali was assassinated at the hand of a Kharijite at the gate to the mosque of Kufa in January 661, which cleared the way for Mu'awiya (r. 661–680) and the Umayyads. Now Syria became the nucleus of the empire that extended from the Atlantic to eastern Iran, connecting areas that had been separated as if by an iron curtain for centuries by the border between the Sassanid Empire and Byzantium. Syria was the natural center of this polity. The Arabian Peninsula, particularly the Hejaz, the cradle of Islam, fell back into the state of political uneventfulness in which it had existed prior to Muhammad's activities. Medina became the "sulking corner" of the pious who could not come to terms with the changed situation and countered the political dynamism of the Umayyads in Syria with the ideal of conservative Islamic piety. As they saw it, Mu'awiya's coming to power brought the series of "rightly guided caliphs" to an end. Instead of the closest companions of the Prophet, the new leaders of the Islamic community were men who had accepted Islam after the conquest of Mecca for opportunistic reasons, rather than out of inner conviction.

The Umayyad dynasty was Arab-dominated, and Muhammad's original idea of Islam as a religion of the Arabs still had force. Whereas 'Umar had "purged" the Hejaz of non-Muslims and advanced the principle that Christian Arabs should convert to Islam, the Umayyads made being an Arab a condition for conversion. In order to satisfy the requirement, non-Arabs had to join an Arab tribe, thereby acquiring the status of a "client" (Arab. *mawla*, pl. *mawali*). But even that was actually not desirable, since the Islamic state was to be supported by a people composed of true Arabs. Muslims were the only ones permitted to bear arms, and they were not to pursue any employment but would instead be supported as warriors by the tribute and taxes paid by the subjects. The goal of conquests was not conversion of the conquered but the establishment of Islamic rule.

The central problem of the Umayyads was finding a balance between the particularistic tribal interests and the demands of a centralized state, as well as asserting the dynastic principle. Mu'awiya succeeded during his lifetime in having homage paid to his son Yazid (r. 680–683). Right after Yazid took power, resistance developed on the Arabian Peninsula and in other parts of the empire. The first to lay claim to the caliphate was 'Ali's son Husayn. With a host of followers he advanced to Iraq, where 'Ali had already sought the support of his followers, and he fell at Karbala (near Kufa) following a short battle with the troops sent by Yazid. The circumstances of his death have been imaginatively conceived by Shi'i propaganda, and the anniversary is celebrated, on the tenth of Muharram, as a holiday. In Iran, southern Iraq, and many other areas with a Shi'i population, this event is traditionally commemorated with the *ta'ziya*, a kind of passion play, combined with parades through the streets and self-flagellation by the participants as penitence for Husayn's having been forsaken by his followers.

The martyr's death of Husayn brought an end for the time being to the Shi'a's hopes of gaining power. His brother Hasan renounced all political activities and died in Medina as a pensioner of the Umayyads. After Husayn's death 'Abdallah ibn al-Zubayr appeared as a pretender to the throne. His claims were based on the same stance that his father, Zubayr, had endorsed on the side of Talha in the resistance against 'Ali. At the Battle of the Camel, 'Abdallah had fought on the side of his father. Now he succeeded in gathering large sectors of the Islamic world behind him. In Mecca he ruled as a counter-caliph and managed to stay in power for twelve years, since the Umayyads had been weakened by internal strife. The unity of the dynasty could not be reestablished until the reign of Caliph 'Abd al-Malik (685–705). He ended the civil war and instituted a number of administrative reforms. Arabic was made the official language in place of the national languages, the coinage was Arabized and Islamized, and magnificent buildings were erected in the main cities of the empire. In Jerusalem he followed in the footsteps of King David, adorning the Temple Mount with splendid buildings which were understood to be the restituted, albeit Islamized, Temple. When Muslim tradition subsequently made the Haram al-Sharif the destination of Muhammad's nocturnal journey (*isra'*) and the location of his ascension (*mi'raj*; see sura 17:1), Jerusalem was promoted to being the third holy city of Islam, after Mecca with the Ka'ba and Medina with the Prophet's tomb.

The end of the civil wars and the continued consolidation of the dynasty under 'Abd al-Malik's son Walid (705–715) led to a new wave of conquests after the Arab expansion had come to a halt around the middle of the seventh century and the attempts by the early Umayyads to conquer the Byzantine heartland brought no results. Under Tariq ibn Ziyad the Arabs ventured across the Strait of Gibraltar (Jabal Tariq) to Spain in 711. The Visigoths had been weakened by internal turmoil, and they lacked strong allies. Consequently almost all of the Iberian Peninsula fell relatively quickly to the Arabs. Only in the north did Asturias remain, which became the point of departure of the Reconquest. It began practically at the same moment that the Arabs took possession of Spain, so their thrust toward southern France and the occupation of Narbonne and Toulouse could not hold for long. Reinforcement of the Carolingians brought the Arab advance in France to a halt (at the Battle of Tours and Poitiers in 732) and ushered in a countermovement, in the course of which the Franks crossed the Pyrenees and established the Spanish March, creating a base that served to intensify the Reconquest.

North Africa later became a base for Arab moves into southern Europe. Starting out from Tunis, the Aghlabids conquered Sicily (which was not regained from the Arabs until the Norman invasion) beginning in 827, and then invaded Italy. In Bari an Arab emirate was able to hold its own for three decades (841–871), and in 868 Malta was conquered. Marauding Arab bands established themselves in the Alps and became a threat along the routes connecting Italy with central Europe.

At about the same time that the Arabs crossed the Strait of Gibraltar in the west, they pressed forward from eastern Iran toward Transoxania and took Bukhara and Samarkand after prolonged battles. This laid the foundation for the conquest of Central Asia and the Islamization of the Turks. These successes were possible not least because China had been weakened by internal turmoil and could not assert its supremacy in the remote parts of Turkistan.

From southern Iran the Arabs pressed forward through Baluchistan as far as the Indus Valley and founded the emirate of Multan in 711, which was to become the nucleus of Islamic India. It would take a long time, however, before the Ghaznavids operating from Afghanistan set their sights in the first half of the eleventh century on India and, in the aftermath of a series of advances that started out as nothing more than raids, an Islamic state emerged that covered large parts of northern India and served as a foundation for the continued—mostly peaceful—expansion of Islam into southern and eastern Asia.

The new beginning in the early eighth century culminated in the caliphate of 'Umar ibn 'Abd al-'Aziz (717–720), 'Abd al-Malik's nephew, also called 'Umar II to distinguish him from 'Umar ibn al-Khattab. His name is connected to the regulations that affected the legal status of non-Muslims living in the Islamic state. These statutes, which are theoretically still valid today and can be put back in force at any time, are attributed to 'Umar I, the second of the "rightly guided caliphs," because of their fundamental significance. 'Abd al-Malik's son Hisham (724–743) was one last energetic Umayyad ruler. He led annual campaigns against Byzantium and continued the struggle against the Turks in Central Asia. But internal unrest announced that the end of Umayyad rule was in the offing. The Shi'a rose up again in Iraq, the Kharijites were fomenting unrest, a Berber uprising in North Africa could hardly be suppressed, and the Abbasid propaganda in Khurasan found resonance among the Arab tribes settled there. In November 749 homage was paid to the Abbasid Abu l-'Abbas as caliph in Kufa. He persecuted the Umayyads without mercy. Marwan II, the last Umayyad caliph (744–750), was defeated by Abbasid troops in January 750 in northern Mesopotamia; he fled and was murdered in Egypt. 'Abd al-Rahman, a grandson of Hisham, escaped to Spain and founded a successor kingdom that reached its peak in the caliphate of Córdoba and survived into the eleventh century.

4. The Abbasid Empire and Islam as a World Religion: Political Divisions Based on Religious Dissent

The movement that brought Umayyad rule to an end had emerged in Iraq and was initially very successful in eastern Iran under the propagandist Abu Muslim. It took advantage of the discontent that could be felt throughout the empire and gave especially the Shi'a reason to be hopeful. The caliphate was passed on, however, not to a descendant of 'Ali, as the Shi'a had hoped, but to the family of the Abbasids, descendants of 'Abbas, an uncle of the Prophet. The Abbasids observed strict Sunni practices, and the Umayyads were systematically denigrated. With the exception of 'Umar II they were now considered nonbelievers and were referred to not as caliphs but as "kings," that is, as wrongful rulers who governed autonomously, not according to divine law. In contrast to them, the Abbasids claimed to continue the politics of the four "rightly guided caliphs." Moreover, they raised chiliastic expectations, as can be inferred from their selection of throne names. Here, too, demands were later scaled down a notch, and they were content to have the throne names express their close ties to the divine mission.

The new rulers transferred the center of the empire to Iraq, which caused bitter resentment in Syria. Caliph Mansur (754–775) founded Baghdad as the new capital, which he gave a name rich in associations: "city of peace" (Madinat al-salam). In the center of the city, which lay west of the Tigris, stood the mosque with the caliph's palace. The almost circular form of the city, with its gates pointing in the four cardinal directions, symbolized a cosmic reference and the claim to universal rule. Its position at the junction of important trade routes helped Baghdad quickly grow to a notable size and become the economic and cultural center of the empire. River navigation on the Tigris linked it with the Persian Gulf, whence it had trade relations with East Africa and India and further connections to the South Seas and East Asia. Goods and cultural assets were brought from these distant regions to the center of the empire, and Islam pressed forward along the trade routes into areas that lay beyond the political and military sphere of influence of the Abbasids. Whereas the path to Europe through the Christian states was obstructed for Islam, it encountered cultures in Africa and South and Southeast Asia that were less dismissive of foreign ideas. Islam had a particularly easy time in places where its acceptance brought links to a culture that was higher or thought to be higher.

By granting full equality to the *mawali*, non-Arabs who had converted to Islam and who played an important role in the victory of the Abbasids, Islam stepped beyond its ethnic fetters and became a real world religion. Islamization of the conquered regions now progressed rapidly, especially in

Persia, where Zoroastrianism had lost strength and disappeared entirely by the end of the tenth century, except in some limitrophe areas. By contrast, the exclusively Christian regions—Syria, Mesopotamia, and Egypt—continued to offer strong resistance to Islamization. Arabic, however, the language of the victors, rapidly gained ground in the conquered territory with a largely Aramaic-speaking population. It was asserted as the colloquial language, and it gained a foothold in Christian liturgy as well. The Copts in Egypt were also affected by the Arabization, while the Berbers in North Africa were able to hold their own to a large extent, though after considerable resistance most of them accepted Islam, albeit without being totally Arabized in terms of language. The Arabic alphabet, however, had a greater influence than Arabic as the language of the Qur'an, and older alphabets were pushed out wherever a majority of the population professed their faith in Islam. The alphabet spread from the Persians to the Turks of Central Asia, although it was even less suited for the Turkish language than for Persian. With the acceptance of Islam and adoption of the Arabic alphabet, the vocabulary of Persian and Turkish became greatly influenced by Arabic, especially in the areas of religion and material culture. Persian also had considerable impact on Turkish, since it was from Iran that Islam reached the Turks.

As it is important for Muslims to profess the right faith and act in compliance with the religious prescriptions covering nearly all spheres of life, the development of religious law, the shari'a, was particularly significant. In principal the caliph was the highest authority in all legal matters. Eventually four sources of law were recognized: the Qur'an, the Sunna (the mode of conduct of the Prophet as it was passed down in the hadith), consensus (*ijma'*, the joint opinion of the legal scholars), and analogical reasoning (*qiyas*). As the empire expanded and Islam spread into areas with very diverse conditions, a certain flexibility was assured through the development of four schools of law (Arab. *madhhab*, pl. *madhahib*) over the course of the eighth century. They were named after their founders: Ahmad ibn Hanbal (Hanbalis), Abu Hanifa (Hanafis), Muhammad ibn Idris al-Shafi'i (Shafi'is), and Malik ibn Anas (Malikis). It goes without saying that like all believers, the caliph too was subject to the religious law and had very little leeway for making independent decisions. The theologians (*'ulama'*)—or, strictly speaking, the lawyers (*fuqaha'*)—were the appointed interpreters of religious law. The formation of the four schools marked the end of legal development, and "the Gate of Independent Reasoning" (*bab al-ijtihad*) based on the Qur'an and the other sources mentioned earlier was closed. There was, however, no codification of the law. In assessing this fact one should bear in mind that the revealed texts offered only the rudiments of a legislative code. This contributed to allowing theologians to expand and permanently secure their influence in state and society. They became the true leaders, and so it was possible for the community to survive when the caliphate ultimately vanished.

Harun al-Rashid (786–809) became quite well known in Europe, although he was not one of the truly great Abbasids. He is said to have had diplomatic relations with Charlemagne. Charlemagne fought with little success in Spain, where the Umayyads—not the Abbasids—ruled, and the time of the Crusades, when reference was freely made to the great Carolingians as pioneers for the Christian cause, still lay in the distant future. Ma'mun (813–833) was especially important from a cultural perspective. He founded an academy in Baghdad and had significant scientific works of Hellenistic heritage translated into Arabic with the help of Christian scholars. Based on the translations, Arabic sciences continued to develop on their own and achieved a high standard in a wide range of areas. Much of this knowledge was later passed on to Europe and had a prolonged impact there.

Because the Umayyads continued to rule in Spain, from the very beginning the Abbasid dynasty covered only part of the Islamic world. The geographic expansion of the empire led almost inevitably to some provinces becoming independent; the governors saw their offices as family property and recognized the caliph in name only. More dangerous than the purely politically motivated independence efforts in the provinces were the religiously grounded uprisings and secessionist movements of various Shi'a sects, which did not acknowledge the caliphate at all and installed Alid counter-caliphs (who were alleged or actual descendants of 'Ali). After Husayn's defeat in 680, his descendants by no means abandoned their claims. But divisions soon arose over how the succession should be regulated, and later there was a tendency to want to let the series of hereditary "imams" (Arab. sing. *imam*) come to an end and regulate the leadership of the community in some other way. The first division came after the death of Husayn's son Zayn al-'Abidin ("Adornment of the Worshippers") in about 712. One branch recognized Zayn al-'Abidin's son Zayd as the rightful successor, while the other branch acknowledged Muhammad al-Baqir ("Revealer of Knowledge"). The Zaydis represented a moderate Shi'i standpoint. The imam had to come from the family of Muhammad, and he was also expected to be familiar with theological scholarship; that is, personal qualifications were required of him. The Zaydiyya found followers in particular at the peripheries of the empire, at the Caspian Sea and in Yemen. In South Arabia they succeeded in the early tenth century in founding a state, which survived despite many threats until 1962.

More radical than the Zaydis, and for the Abbasids more threatening, were the Isma'ilis. They were descendants of Isma'il, a son of Ja'far al-Sadiq ("the Truthful," d. 765) and grandchild of the aforementioned al-Baqir (d. 731). After Isma'il's death (760), Ja'far had designated not his son Muhammad but Isma'il's brother Musa al-Kazim ("the One Who Swallows His Anger") to be his successor. Isma'ili doctrine is strongly influenced by gnostic elements, going so far as to deify the imam and, through its expectation of the return of the imam as the Mahdi (Arab. *mahdi*, lit. "guided by God"), propagate messianic ideas. In its early manifestations it was extremely militant. Specially trained and selected missionaries (sing. *da'i*) spread the message, sometimes very successfully. In the early tenth century, 'Ubayd

Allah, from Syria, claimed to be of Alid descent and was acknowledged by his followers as the Mahdi. He conquered North Africa and made the newly founded Mahdia (south of Tunis) his capital. The dynasty founded by 'Ubayd Allah was named the Fatimids, after Fatima, Muhammad's daughter and ancestor of the Alids. When Egypt was conquered in 969, the route to Syria and the Arabian Peninsula opened up for the Fatimids. The advance northward marked the beginning of close relations between Syria and Egypt, which continued, with a short interruption during the time of the Crusades, until the sixteenth century and experienced a final echo as the United Arab Republic (1958–1961).

Lasting evidence of the Fatimid dynasty is the city of Cairo (al-Qahira, "the Powerful") as the capital together with the old city of al-Fustat, and al-Azhar ("the Radiant"), a theological institute established to preserve and spread Isma'ili doctrine, which continued as a Sunni university after the end of the Fatimids. Based in Egypt, the Isma'ilis strengthened their propaganda in the eastern Islamic world, but internal splintering soon occurred. The Druze came from among the followers of Caliph al-Hakim (996–1021), who pursued eccentric policies and died under inexplicable circumstances. Their center is today in Lebanon, with smaller communities in Syria (Hauran) and present-day Israel (Carmel).

Of greater significance than the secession of the Druze was a division that ensued after the death of Caliph Mustansir (1036–1094). One group followed Mustansir's son Nizar and developed into the extremist sect of the Assassins, with their main base in Iran and a branch in Syria. Both existed as militant groups into the thirteenth century, and their activities, which in fact included assassinations, wreaked havoc in the Islamic world, including the Crusader states. Their western name (from the French *assassin*) derives from their use of hashish in their religious exercises (Arab. *hashshash*). The Nizaris continue to live in Syria, eastern Iran, India, and East Africa today, albeit lacking any political ambitions. The other group followed Mustansir's son Musta'li, who ruled as caliph until 1101. This group was less militant than the Assassins and was able to survive the decline of the Fatimids, existing to the present day in their center in Yemen and in India (Bombay) as the Bohras. Their imam is the famous Aga Khan.

At about the same time as the Fatimids, the Qarmatians rose up on the east coast of the Arabian Peninsula and in the Syrian desert. They were a social revolutionary sect following extreme Shi'i doctrine, whose connections to Isma'ili Shi'a, however, are disputed. In any case they do not appear to have cooperated with the Fatimids. A Qarmatian state was established on the eastern Arabian coast with its center in Bahrain, from whence they forayed into Arabia and countries to the north. The plundering of Mecca in 930 and the theft of the Black Stone of the Ka'ba, which was hidden and not returned until a quarter century later, is symbolic of their break with established Islam. The state declined in the late eleventh century, though its ideas continued to thrive in Bahrain for a long time.

Less radical than the Isma'ilis and its splinter groups were the Twelver Shi'a. They recognized not Isma'il but his brother Musa al-Kazim (d. 799) as the legitimate imam, from whom the imamate was always passed down from father to son. According to Twelver Shi'a doctrine, almost all the imams in the series of twelve had died a violent death, either in the struggle against the caliphs or as their prisoners, ever since Husayn preceded them as a martyr. Their burial places have become important Shi'i shrines. Al-Kazimiyah (today a suburb of Baghdad), one of the most celebrated Shi'i pilgrimage sites, is the burial place of Musa al-Kazim and his grandson Muhammad al-Jawad ("the Generous," d. 835), the ninth imam. Muham-mad al-Mahdi (or al-Muntazar, "the Awaited One"), the twelfth imam in the series, disappeared mysteriously in Samarra (between Baghdad and Tikrit) in 874. According to the Twelver Shi'i faith he went into occulta-tion (*ghayba*) and led the community from there, at first through "em-issaries" (*safir*) and then, when no one else laid claim to this function, through theologians acting as the appointed interpreters of the doctrine. An independent legal system developed which was at variance with that of the Sunnis, especially by virtue of the fact that it accepts *ijtihad,* or truth-finding based on independent reason, without question. The *mujtahid* is authorized to use *ijtihad*. The ayatollah has the highest theological author-ity; he is never formally elected but receives his office through acclama-tion by theologians. The Shi'ites go their own way also in Qur'an exegesis (*tafsir*), as the selection of 'Ali, which is not expressly mentioned in the Qur'an, is based on a Qur'an passage. Theologians were given the task of leading the community until the awaited imam returns from his occultation at the end of time, leading believers to victory over the infidels and to the Last Judgment. This idea makes the Shi'i denomination less militant, as the struggle for the rightful cause does not take place until the imam returns from occultation. In the meantime it is permitted, if circumstances make it necessary, to resort to dissimulation (*taqiyya*) about one's faith. It is thus not imperative in achieving salvation to emulate the suffering of the imams. Ayatollah Khomeini broke with this quietist tradition and demanded "the governance of the faqih" (*velayat-e faqih*), also the title of one of his books (published in English in 1981), and to assert it in the Iranian Revolution in 1979.

Twelver Shi'a found supporters among the Buyids, who ruled Persia and Iraq from 934 to 1055 and southern Iran until 1062. After the conquest of central and western Iran, they spread to Mesopotamia and brought the caliphate under their control with the conquest of Baghdad in 945. They turned the caliphs into puppets but let the caliphate in principle remain. Consequently Twelver Shi'a was able to organize quietly under the protec-tion of the Buyids. The foundations for Shi'i theology were laid by a number of notable scholars. When, five centuries later, Twelver Shi'a was declared the state religion of Persia, it was possible for the Twelver Shi'is to build on the foundations laid by the Buyids.

5. The Turks: Assertion of Sunni Orthodoxy

The Buyids, who were Persians, replaced the Arabs as rulers and played an important role in politics, but only for a short time. The future belonged to the Turks, and this situation would continue for a long time, extending into the twentieth century. From the time the Abbasids took power, Turks had made up part of the mercenary troops and thus came into contact with the religion and culture of Islam. The Turks from the Central Asian steppe had been introduced to Sunni Islam from Iran and had become acquainted with the Hanafi school of law; this was to determine their religious affiliation to the present day, with very few exceptions. After the Turkish Ghaznavids had succeeded in founding a state with its center in present-day Afghanistan in the late tenth century, the Seljuqs under Toghril Beg took all of Iran in the first half of the eleventh century. In 1055 they captured Baghdad and brought an end to Buyid rule. The situation for the Abbasids hardly changed, however, since they remained just as powerless under the Seljuqs as they had been under the Buyids.

In a further advance westward the Seljuqs experienced a decisive victory over the Armenians in 1071 near Manzikert at Lake Van. The battle marked a turning point in the history of the Near and Middle East. The destruction of Greater Armenia opened the way for the Turks into Anatolia, which had been blocked to the Arabs for centuries. The Armenians found a new home in Cilicia in the kingdom of Lesser Armenia. It offered important support for the Franks during the Crusades and survived until 1375, when it was destroyed by the Mamluks invading from Syria. The kingdom of the Rum-Seljuqs (Rum originally meaning Eastern Rome) developed around Konya (Iconium). Only Trebizond (Trabzon) and the northwestern part of Anatolia remained under Byzantine rule.

In Syria the Seljuqs were able to press forward to the Mediterranean, driving out the Fatimids; with Palestine they also took Jerusalem. In addition to the deadly threat to Byzantium, this was what directly triggered the Crusades. Because the Turks viewed themselves as the guardians of rigid Sunni orthodoxy and were less liberal toward the Christians than the Fatimids had been, the opinion spread in Europe, certainly not without tendentious propaganda, that Muslims were going to destroy the Christian sanctuaries and prevent Christian pilgrims from venerating the holy places. The papal call for "armed pilgrimage" found a great echo, and Jerusalem was conquered in 1099 after a short siege, although by that time the Fatimids had already regained possession of the city.

The Great Seljuq Empire reached as far as present-day Afghanistan. By the end of the eleventh century the empire broke up into individual states, most of which were ruled by *atabegs*, guardians and tutors appointed for Seljuq princes. In the early twelfth century 'Imad al-Din Zengi, the *atabeg* of Mosul, conquered Aleppo and fought from northern Syria against Byzantines and Franks. The conquest of Edessa (Urfa) led to the Second Crusade,

but the Franks could not regain Edessa. It was Egypt that delivered the
decisive strike against the Crusaders; the Ayyubids, a family of warriors of
Kurdish descent whose home was Tikrit, toppled the Fatimids in 1169 and
assumed rule of Egypt. The famous Saladin (Salah al-Din, r. 1169–1193)
took Jerusalem in 1187, thereby ushering in the end of Frankish rule in the
eastern Mediterranean. With the conquest of part of Syria, he reestablished
pre-Seljuq and pre-Crusade conditions and also spread out onto the Arabian
Peninsula.

Ayyubid rule, however, was not granted longevity. The last Ayyubids
used purchased slaves (Mamluks), mostly of Turkish descent, to serve as
mercenaries. They took over the government themselves in 1250. Egypt
now entered a long period of stable political conditions. The Mamluks
eliminated the final remnants of Crusader rule by conquering Acre in 1291;
from Syria they pushed forward to Cilicia, where they annihilated Lesser
Armenia. In the south they defeated the Nubian kingdom of Dongola,
thereby overcoming the barriers that had prevented Islam from moving
up the Nile since the early Islamic period. Through its position as a transit
country for the spice trade between the South Seas and Europe, Egypt enjoyed an economic heyday until the end of the fifteenth century, when the
Portuguese appeared on the scene. Theology, mysticism, and belles lettres
were able to develop in great richness under the favorable conditions. Numerous buildings in Cairo, Damascus, and Jerusalem are reminders today
of the high standard of Mamluk architecture.

While this was going on in the Middle East, Islam peacefully progressed
southward from North Africa through the Sahara. Ghana, Songhai (Mali),
and Kanem (Chad), the countries at the end of the trade routes through the
Sahara, accepted Islam in the tenth and eleventh centuries. The reform movement of the Almoravids (1061–1147), which emerged under the Berbers, expanded its sphere of influence throughout all of African Islam. It propagated
a return to original Islam and, as its name (*al-murabitun,* from Arab. *ribat,*
frontier outpost) implies, it was originally organized in belligerent religious
communities at the borders of Islam. The Berber principalities of Morocco
and western Algeria were conquered under Yusuf ibn Tashufin, founder of
the dynasty. This paved the way to invade Spain, where the Umayyad dynasty had ended in 1031 and numerous petty states (*muluk al-tawa'if*) had
emerged. For the most part they became part of the Almoravid spoils; at the
same time, the Christian Reconquest was pushing forward from the north
and east. The Almoravids soon had to give way to the Almohads, the "(true)
believers in the oneness of God" (*al-muwahhidun*), as opposed to the an-
thropomorphism of the Almoravids. They adhered to a form of puritanism,
but at the same time they allowed freedom of philosophical speculation, so
that well-known philosophers such as Ibn Tufayl (Abubacer) and Ibn Rushd
(Averroës) could represent doctrines that also became known in Europe and
would long continue to stir emotions. The Almohads took Marrakech in
1147, succeeding the Almoravids in North Africa and Spain. They were

able to hold their ground in Spain until 1269. The Nasrids of Granada were the only ones to resist the Christian reconquerors. After the fall of Granada in 1492, the Christian rulers succeeded in moving from Spain to North Africa, which they declared a Crusade. In back-and-forth fighting with the Muslims, they foreshadowed what the southern European powers would accomplish in the nineteenth century.

6. The Mongols and the Timurids: The End of the Caliphate

In the early thirteenth century the Khwarezm shahs—that is, the rulers of present-day Khiva, south of the Aral Sea—took advantage of the Seljuqs' weakness to bring the entire region of eastern Islam from India to Anatolia under their control. But the Mongols were ready and waiting; they set off from their home at Lake Baikal and had already expanded their campaigns of conquest beyond China when they conquered Transoxania in 1220 and forced the last Khwarezm shah, Jalal al-Din Mingubirti (1220–1231), to flee. From Transoxania they forayed and plundered their way through Iran. In 1258 they took Baghdad, killing the Abbasid caliph Musta'sim (1242–1258). This marked the end of the Abbasid caliphate in Baghdad. After the failed reconquest of Baghdad, a sideline in Cairo carved out a shadowy existence that was established for the sole purpose of legalizing the Mamluk government. When the Ottomans took Egypt in 1517, that caliphate, too, ceased to exist. From then on "caliph" (*khalifa*) was no more than an honorary title.

The destruction of the Abbasid caliphate is just one aspect from which to view the relationship of the Mongols to Islam. But they also contributed to spreading Islam to areas that had previously been out of its reach. The Mongol Empire extended from China to beyond southern Russia. Genghis Khan (d. 1227) was succeeded by his son Ögödei, who resided in China. Although the Mongol rulers in China ultimately did not accept Islam but instead became Buddhists, there was nevertheless a constant flow of Muslims from the western regions to China. Consequently Islam, which had previously been widespread only in the coastal cities through trade, was strengthened and became a significant factor in China's religious history. The other areas of the Mongol Empire were distributed so that Genghis Khan's son Jochi and his descendants received the western part, that is, southern Russia and western Turkistan. The Mongol line in southern Russia gave rise to the Golden Horde, whose state played a very important role in nascent Russia. The Golden Horde's conversion to Islam in the early fourteenth century led to alienation from the population. The rise of Poland and Lithuania in the fifteenth century sealed the fate of this state, in which Mongols and Turks had melted into the people referred to as Tatars. The Tatar khanates of Kazan and Astrakhan emerged, as well as khanates in the Crimea and Siberia. The Giray khans in the Crimea stood their ground against Russia until into the eighteenth century; the Crimean khanate thus proved to be the longest lasting of the numerous successor states to the Mongol Empire.

Genghis Khan's son Chagatai and his descendants, who ruled Transoxania and eastern Turkistan, wavered for a long time between Islam and their traditional paganism. Not until the early fourteenth century did Islam assert itself, though the eastern regions of this kingdom did not follow suit. Mongolia thus remained outside the Islamic world. Hulagu, a son of Genghis Khan's fourth son, Tolui, established the Ilkhanid state in Iran. His descendants were quickly persuaded to adopt the Iranian culture. After having long wavered between Buddhism and Christianity, they finally decided on Islam, the religion of their host country. Ghazan Khan (1295–1304) converted and created a legislative code in which the traditional law of the Mongols was reconciled with Islamic regulations. Just a few decades after Ghazan's death, the Ilkhanate Empire, which had encompassed Iran, Iraq, the Caucasus, and Anatolia, disintegrated into rival small states that were first reunited under Timur (1370–1405).

Timur was part of a family that claimed to be descended from Genghis Khan. From modest beginnings he succeeded in gathering the support of the great Mongol-Turkish tribal systems of the decaying Mongol Empire. From his base in Transoxania, he initiated campaigns that led to southern Russia, Anatolia, and India, aiming to reestablish the Mongol Empire. These undertakings with disproportionately large armies were by their nature, however, purely raid and plunder actions that brought unspeakable misery to the ravaged areas and resulted in the loss of many lives. In particular the Christian population suffered from them. Even though the Eastern churches also suffered great losses through Islam, they had so far been able to survive and to some extent even experience a belated heyday, as demonstrated by the "Syrian Renaissance." But Timur's campaigns gave Christianity in those regions the finishing blow; only meager remnants of the once flourishing church life remain in the Middle East, and in some areas it has been extinguished entirely.

Timur died just as he was about to start a campaign to China. He had divided the empire among his sons and grandsons. A vibrant Islamic culture developed in the successor states, especially in eastern Iran and in Transoxiana, where Timur himself had already assembled the cultural elite in Samarkand. These successor states soon had to give way to greater power structures. The Timurid Babur (d. 1530) took refuge in India and founded the dynasty of the Mughal emperors, which lasted until 1858 and played an important role in establishing Islam in India.

7. The Islamic World from the Sixteenth Century to the Present

The Timurid dynasty was the last political system on Islamic soil that was based on the rule of the peoples of the steppe, clinging to their traditions.

The future belonged to other groups with other ideals. The introduction of firearms brought profound changes to the political map, in the Near and Middle East as well. In the early sixteenth century there were three major powers: the Ottoman Empire at the Mediterranean, the Safavid kings in Iran, and the Mughal emperors in India. In some respects they anticipated the modern Islamic world, or at least had a lasting influence in shaping it. The religious picture that the Islamic world offers today is a direct consequence of political developments since the sixteenth century.

The Safavid dynasty grew out of a Sufi (*sufi*) order that had emerged in eastern Anatolia and northwestern Persia and had already played a political role under Timur. Sunni in the beginning, it turned to Twelver Shi'a (*imamiyya*) and was at the same time transformed into a militantly messianic movement. In the early sixteenth century, Shaykh Isma'il conquered a region that by and large corresponds to present-day Iran; in the east it also encompasses parts of present-day Afghanistan. Repeated attempts by the Safavids to incorporate Iraq permanently into their empire were thwarted by the Ottomans. Shah Isma'il (1505–1524) made Twelver Shi'a the state religion, asserting this by force despite some resistance. The Sunnis were persecuted, and many theologians emigrated to the Ottoman Empire, whose ruling class was hostile to the Shi'a. People of other faiths were able to subsist in the Safavid state only on the peripheries and in small groups. The Turks in Azerbaijan, too, were converted to Shi'i Islam, representing an exception among Turkish-speaking peoples, the vast majority of whom are staunch adherents of Sunni Islam. Theologians of Arab descent from the Shi'i centers of learning in Iraq were brought into the country; continuing the work of earlier scholars, they developed a doctrine of imposing consistency. Qom near Tehran, location of the shrine of Fatima al-Ma'suma ("the sinless Fatima"), sister of Ali ibn Musa al-Rida (the eighth imam, who was buried at Mashhad), emerged as a center of religious learning and has lost nothing of its importance to this day. There was, however, a deeply rooted rivalry between secular government and religious authority, between crown and turban, which mirrored the antagonism of Sufi quietism versus militant Shi'i extremism. Whereas in the early decades of Safavid rule the king went so far as to claim that he was the living emanation of the godhead, the leading theologians (ayatollahs and *mujtahids*) dreamed of a theocratic government and regarded themselves as the representatives of the twelfth imam dwelling in occultation. It was not until Shah 'Abbas I (1588–1629), the most able of all Safavid rulers, that a greater separation of the two spheres gained ground.

The Safavid state was originally organized in tribal orders of the Turkish Qızılbash ("redheads," because of the color of their headgear), the belligerent supporters of the Safavid cause. Shah 'Abbas I transformed it into a centralized state with an Iranian-Islamic character, created a mercenary army, and made Isfahan the capital. He embellished it with magnificent buildings and founded institutes of higher learning, which gave rise to the wordplay

"Isfahan nisf-i jahan" (Isfahan is half of the world). Decline set in quickly, however. In the first half of the eighteenth century the country became easy prey to Afghan tribes, which could never have conformed to Safavid religious policies. The empire founded by Nadir Shah (1736–1747) ultimately emerged from the turmoil, extending as far as the Indus. Nadir Shah's attempt to replace Safavid Shiʿa with a more moderate course failed. Behind it were efforts to make a pact with the Ottomans, strict Sunnis who had long been enemies of Shiʿi Iran. In the end, Nadir Shah was assassinated by enemies of his domestic policy. The dynasty collapsed, and the Zands (1750–1794) took over in Shiraz and Isfahan. The rulers did not call themselves "shah" but were content with the title *wakil,* "representative" of the Safavid pretender who was waiting for his opportunity to return to the throne.

The Qajars, who ultimately took power in 1779 and made Tehran their capital, oriented themselves toward the Safavid state, but they called an end to expectations of Safavid restoration and crowned their own heads. Since the beginning of the nineteenth century, Iran had been caught in the tension between England's and Russia's policies toward the Middle East, as the two powers pursued conflicting interests in the region and continued to intervene in the country's fate. The Qajars failed in their plans to reform their state according to Western models and became increasingly dependent on the Western powers. As the power of the crown diminished, the influence of the Shiʿi clergy grew. They were financially independent because of wealthy endowments and knew how to garner the support of the people, who had long since become firmly anchored in the Shiʿi faith. The clergy also played an important role in the contention over a constitution which started in 1905. Consequently a clause was inserted in the constitution that served to ensure that state legislation would be enacted in keeping with the laws of Islam. Under the Pahlavi dynasty, which succeeded the Qajars in 1925, that was no longer an issue. The Pahlavis attempted to adopt Western technology and modern forms of production. They fought illiteracy in rural areas and revived Old Iranian state traditions, claiming they were in harmony with Islam; formally they ruled in the name of the hidden imam. The encroachment on the rights of the clergy, which emphatically resisted the land reform, and general discontent with the shah's policy led to revolution in 1979 and the proclamation of the "Islamic Republic of Iran." While some democratic institutions of Western character do exist, this does nothing to alter the fact that in the Islamic state the sovereign is God, not the people, and legislation has to agree with the precepts of Islam.

Whereas Iran was able to assert its political independence despite the internal weakness of its changing regimes, and despite massive pressure from Russia and England, the situation in India developed very differently. The Mughal Empire got caught up in battles with internal and external enemies and also had to deal with the European colonial powers that had established a foothold in India. Dangers from within threatened from the Hindu population, which always outnumbered the Muslims. After Emperor

Akbar (1556–1605) tried to establish the "Divine Faith" (*din-i ilahi*) as a settlement between Islam and Hinduism, religious tolerance came to an end under the zealous Muslim Aurangzeb (1658–1707). External dangers also threatened from Afghanistan, where, after Nadir Shah, the Durrani kings (1747–1842) and then the kings of the Barakzai tribe set up a state, invaded India again, and defended themselves successfully against attacks from Iran and India.

The landing of Vasco da Gama in Calicut in 1498 marked the beginning of the European penetration of India. The rivalry between France and England was decided in England's favor in 1757 at the Battle of Plassey, and the 1763 Treaty of Paris put an end to French ambitions in India. From 1774 on, British governors-general were installed, and the British East India Company built up its territorial rule, which expanded from Bengal to other areas. In the nineteenth century, efforts were begun to Anglicize the Indian educational system and open up work options for the Christian mission. As part of the cultural legacy of the Islamization of India, which came from Iran, Persian had previously been made the official administrative language of the Mughal Empire; in 1836 it was replaced by English. As a result of this and other measures, an uprising of the Indian troops, in cooperation with the disempowered Indian upper classes, took place in northern India in 1857. The mutiny was crushed, followed by the liquidation of the East India Company. The office of the governor-general was transformed into that of a viceroy, which meant that the rule of the Mughal emperors had come to an end. In 1877 India was declared an empire, and Queen Victoria adopted the title Empress of India. The viceroyalty existed until 1947, ending with the independence of India and the creation of the states of India and Pakistan.

For historical reasons Muslims were in the majority in the northwestern part of the Indian subcontinent as well as in Bengal and Assam in the east; there were scattered Muslim minorities down to Kerala and Madras in the south. Moreover, the Muslim population was (and is) divided into Sunnites and Shi'ites, Sufi orders and sectarian groups, and subject to influences from Iran and Afghanistan. The attitude of Muslims towards Hindus, in their eyes idolaters (*mushrikun*) in the true sense of the word, was characterized by hatred and contempt; the same applied for the attitudes of Hindus toward Muslims. The opposition between the two groups, which had been bridged by the Mughal emperors through clever religious policies, led in the agitated nationalist atmosphere to riots and persecution; more than 6 million Muslims (dubbed *muhajirun* after Muhammad's *hijra*) fled to Pakistan and Bengal, and nearly the same number of Hindus from those regions fled into the territory of the Indian Union.

The modern state of Pakistan is the first and so far only Islamic state whose borders were drawn according to the creed of the majority of its inhabitants. This was the work of Muhammad 'Ali Jinnah (1876–1948). After the First World War he had fought in the Khilafat movement, which, following the downfall of the Ottoman Empire, aimed at preserving the caliphate as a political no less than a spiritual institution, considered to be the very essence of Islam. 'Ali Jinnah later broke with the Indian nationalists and was active in promoting the foundation of an independent Muslim state. In light of the problem innate to Islam regarding the true nature of the community (*umma*), it is small wonder that the part which Islam had to play in the constitution of Pakistan was under dispute from the beginning, in a process that progressed slowly but surely. In 1977 all political parties not adhering to the principles of Islam were outlawed; a 1984 referendum confirmed the politics of Islamization; in 1988 the shari'a was proclaimed to be decisive in judicial matters. It should also be noted that Islamist movements such as that of the Taliban (Arab. *taliban*, students [of the Qur'an], from Arab. sing., *talib*) originated in Pakistan, that border disputes with India remain unsettled, and that Pakistan is a nuclear power.

Pakistan's annexation of Bengal, which was inhabited predominantly by Muslims, proved not to be tenable in the long term. It was only natural that Bangladesh seceded from Pakistan in 1971. As socialist-oriented policies were implemented, the Islamic clauses in the constitution that had remained valid throughout the period in which Bangladesh belonged to Pakistan were abandoned, but Bangladesh nevertheless views itself as an Islamic state and is seen as such by the Islamic world. Owing to its separation from Bangladesh, Pakistan lost its status as the leading country in the Islamic world in terms of population. This position went to Indonesia, where about 87 percent of the population, a total of over 210 million, profess their faith in Islam. Recently, however, a growing trend can be observed toward secularizing the state and declaring religion to be a private matter.

The Ottoman Empire is in many respects the most significant of the aforementioned three political entities. Its origins lie in a small frontier state in northwest Anatolia, one of the numerous successor states that emerged after the fall of the Rum-Seljuqs. It was founded by Osman I (r. 1281–ca. 1324); there is little historically confirmed information on his life and activities. In his wars with neighboring Byzantium he was supported by Turcoman fighters (mujahidin) who streamed to the border from farther east. In the middle of the fourteenth century, the Ottomans crossed the Dardanelles at Gallipoli and settled in, taking advantage of the disunity of the Slavs in the Balkan states. Serbia, which had only recently won a hard-fought struggle for its independence from Byzantium, was defeated in the famous Battle of Kosovo in 1389 and came more and more under Turkish control. Bulgaria became a Turkish province in the late fourteenth century. The conquests in the Balkans were consolidated into the province of Rumelia (from Rum, i.e., eastern Rome), and the capital was moved from Brusa (Bursa) to Adrianople (Edirne). Bayezid I (r. 1389–1402) had the caliph of Cairo grant him the title of sultan, but he lost Anatolia to Timur. In the course of reestablishing Ottoman rule, the small Turkish states in Anatolia were defeated one after the other and incorporated into the Asian part of the Ottoman Empire, the province of Anatolia. Mehmed II (r. 1444–1446 and 1451–1481) succeeded in conquering the long-isolated Constantinople in 1453. It became the capital (Istanbul), and the Ottoman Empire succeeded Byzantium. The empire of Trebizond (Trabzon), which had been founded in 1204, surrendered in 1461.

Although the Ottomans failed to conquer Rhodes (the island did not fall until 1522) and immediately withdrew from Otranto (Italy) after Mehmed's death, the foundations for further conquests had been laid. The sixteenth century was the empire's golden age. Starting in 1516 Mesopotamia, Syria, and Palestine, as well as Egypt, were conquered. Ottoman rule also extended to the Arabian Peninsula, including the sacred places of Islam, which earned the Ottoman sultan the title "Servant of the Two Sanctuaries" (*khadim al-haramayn*). From Hejaz the Ottomans continued to advance until they reached South Arabia. From Egypt they attacked North Africa; only Morocco always remained outside of the Ottoman sphere of influence. Parallel to the incorporation of the Arab provinces, further conquests took place in the Balkans and in Iraq under Suleiman the Magnificent (r. 1520–1566), also called "the Lawgiver" (*qanuni*) because he created a code of general law for the empire. The kingdom of Hungary was brought down in 1526 in the Battle of Mohács, and in 1529 the first siege of Vienna followed.

The nature of the Ottoman Empire was that of a military state. It rose owing to a strictly led army and an efficient administration, inspired by the notion of war against the nonbelievers (Arab. *jihad*) and the creation of a state in the service of Islam. The backbone of the army and the civil service was made up of freed slaves of Christian background who were rounded up in the Christian provinces of the empire in the regularly conducted "gatherings" (*devshirme*) and trained for the various services according to their respective aptitudes. The Ottomans were tolerant of non-Muslims within the scope of Islamic requirements, so Jews who had been expelled from Spain during the Christian Reconquest were willingly taken in and could live freely. The adherents of religions and denominations acknowledged in Islam as "people of the book" (*ahl al-kitab*) were organized into "nations" or religious communities (*millet*) and were represented by their respective chief (*mutran*, "patriarch" or "bishop") before the Sublime Porte. While this at first looks favorable, the result was fragmentation and a loss of strength of the religious communities.

Advantages for minorities, whether real or fictitious, contrasted with disadvantages for Muslims of non-Turkish descent. The conquered Arab—that is, predominantly Islamic—provinces of the empire in the sixteenth century were in practice not treated any differently than the Christian provinces in the Balkans (Rumelia), which had been conquered earlier and thus served as a kind of model for Islamic parts of the empire that came later. As Muslims, the Arabs correctly saw themselves as having higher status than the non-Muslims, but the Turks remained the privileged constitutive people. The provinces were administered by governors who rotated at regular intervals and later, as the empire was in its decline, took advantage of their short terms in office to add to their personal wealth by pillaging the province entrusted to them. Islamic institutions were misused, and they decayed; the cultural treasures collected over centuries were transferred to Constantinople. This is why the most significant Arab manuscripts and works of art can be found today in libraries and museums in Istanbul. Nevertheless, a high-ranking, especially courtly literary culture with a strong Arab-Persian component developed, which mirrored the original acculturation of the Turks on Iranian soil. This culture radiated from the court in Istanbul particularly to the Balkans, where Persian poetry was cultivated until the beginning of the nineteenth century.

Militarily and in terms of foreign policy the Ottomans never did have any sweeping success in their confrontation with the European powers. They were not in a position to exploit Europe's internal weakness and had no eye for the fact that over time the political and economic situation had changed globally to their disadvantage. The war that started in 1683 with the second siege of Vienna ended in 1699 with the Treaty of Karlowitz, according to which the Ottomans had to cede vast regions to Austria, Poland, and Venice. This was the beginning of the Ottoman decline. The Greek war of independence from 1821 to 1829 weakened the position of the Ottomans in the Balkans; it took less than a century for them to be pushed out almost entirely.

The countries bordering the eastern coast of the Mediterranean Sea had been a transit region for European trade with the East for centuries. Ever since the European discovery of the Americas and the circumnavigation of Africa, however, the Mediterranean had retained only secondary importance. Trade with East Africa and South Asia no longer had to go through Islamic, that is, Ottoman territory. This too contributed to the decline of Arab countries. Egypt lost its leading position in trade with the East, and Iraq became nothing more than a province on the periphery. In 1571 the Ottomans lost their supremacy in the Mediterranean in the naval battle of Lepanto. Subsequently the semi-independent Barbary States emerged in Tripoli, Tunis, and Algiers, which subsisted primarily on piracy. This ended in the early nineteenth century with the presence in the Mediterranean of naval forces of the neighboring European states. In 1830 the French invaded Algiers; in 1882 Tunis was compelled to recognize the French protectorate; in 1904 France and Spain marked off their spheres of interest in Morocco; and in 1912 the Italians established their rule over Cyrenaica and Tripolitania.

The position of the Ottoman Empire had been thoroughly shaken by the losses it suffered in the nineteenth century. Reforms were planned and to some extent implemented to counter this decline, but they were also and especially due to pressure from the Western powers, which for various reasons felt the need to defend their interests. Among these reforms was the Règlement Organique, which had been introduced after the massacre of Christians in Syria and Lebanon in 1860. It provided for far-reaching co-determination by the Western powers and formed the rudiments for the later creation of

the state of Lebanon. The Ottoman constitutional and administrative reforms (Tanzimat) in the period from 1839 to 1876 were supposed to, for
example, ensure equality for non-Muslims and grant them full civil rights,
eliminating the poll tax (*jizya*) and including them in the military draft. The
masses could not grasp this break with the traditional regulations of Islam.
Pious Muslims believed that they should take the law into their own hands if
the state did not follow Islamic precepts. The massacres of Armenians prior
to the First World War must be judged in this light. The violence continued
during the First World War, when Armenians, whether rightly or wrongly,
were accused of collaborating with the Russian enemy and fell victim to a
persecution that has been termed genocide by less benevolent observers.

The Young Turk movement held that the reforms instituted by the government did not go far enough. Its goal was to create a Turkish nation-state
with a purely Turkish population. Sometimes in cooperation with the Young
Turks and sometimes independently, national forces among the Arabs began
to stir. Their goal was the creation of an Arab state that would be a home
to all Arabs. When Turkey entered the First World War on the side of the
European Central Powers, the Allies made promises to the Arabs in order to
persuade the Arabs to side with them against the Ottomans. These efforts
were directed particularly at the sharif of Mecca, Husayn ibn ʿAli (believed
to be a descendant of the prophet Muhammad), the supposed head of the
future Arab state. At the same time, however, England and France had divided up the later Mandate territories among themselves in the Sykes-Picot
Agreement of 1916, which was diametrically opposed to the promise made
to the Arabs. On top of everything else, British foreign secretary A. J. Balfour issued, "on behalf of His Majesty's government," the famous declaration of November 11, 1917, that was understood by Zionists as assurance
of the founding of a Jewish state in Palestine.

Of all these plans, projects, and dreams, all that had been realized by
the end of the First World War and the collapse of the Ottoman Empire
was the creation of a Turkish nation-state. Mustafa Kemal Pasha (Atatürk)
broke radically with Islamic-Arab traditions. Sultanate and caliphate were
abolished, and a republican constitution was introduced; religion and state
were separated, the outcome of which, however, was that matters pertaining
to religion were de facto put under state control. Free exercise of religion
seems to be restricted even for Muslims, and it cannot be denied that the
situation of Christians of different denominations has been aggravated. In
this context one has to remember that, for example, most of the Christians
of Tur Abdin, the region around Mardin in the southeast, once a flourishing
Aramaic-speaking community with numerous churches and monasteries,
left the country in the past several decades.

With respect to the Arabs, instead of the dreamed-of Arab union there
were individual states whose borders were drawn at European conference
tables, sometimes with a ruler and sometimes according to manmade structures such as the railway line between Aleppo and Mosul, which became

Turkey's southern border, and without regard for historically and numerically significant ethnic groups such as the Kurds, who found themselves
scattered over present-day Turkey, Iran, and Iraq. Natural living spheres
were mangled, and state institutions were created that operated contrary to
tradition. Sharif Husayn, "King of the Arabs," was forced out of the Hejaz
in 1924–1926 by the Saudis (Arab. Al Saʿud), who as adherents of Wahhabism propagated a pure Islam purged of all added ingredients. He died
in exile in 1931. The French, who were not ready to tolerate a monarchi-
cal government within their sphere of influence, chased Husayn's son Faysal
(d. 1933) out of Damascus, where he had asserted his claims. He established
a kingdom in Iraq in 1921 with British support, which was replaced by the
republic in 1958. With British approval, ʿAbdullah, Husayn's second son,
established the Hashemite emirate, later the kingdom of Transjordan (Jordan). In 1948 the state of Israel was founded by consensus of the United
Nations and against the united resistance of the Arabs.

It was the aftermath of the Second World War and the end of the Mandate in Syria and Palestine that finally brought most Arab states full independence. The Arab League (1945) was envisioned as a step toward
achieving Arab unity. There have also been alliances between individual
states, mostly of short duration, such as the United Arab Republic joining Egypt and Syria from 1958 to 1961. A dozen such projects since 1945
can easily be listed, though most never got past the planning stage. Beyond
Arab unity, efforts to bring together the entire Islamic world are viewed as a
provisional substitute for the long-lost unity of the caliphate. The first organization of this kind was founded by the Saudis in 1926 in Mecca under the
name Islamic World Congress (Muʾtamar al-ʿalam al-islami), an ambitious
substitute for the failed Arab empire under the sharif of Mecca (who also asserted claims to the caliphate). The idea was brought up again after 1949 by
Pakistan, which then claimed to lead the Islamic world. Later, in 1962, the
Saudis—having become rich through oil, professing the Wahhabiyya as the
"pure doctrine," and acting as guardians of the holy sites with a constantly
growing stream of pilgrims—founded a new organization under the name
League of the Islamic World (Rabitat al-ʿalam al-islami). Under the patronage of the League, and with Saudi financing, an organization to propagate
Islam in the non-Islamic countries was founded; mosques have been built at
many locations, including Rome, for example, to demonstrate the Islamic
presence and to underline the age-old striving of Islam to spread its message
throughout the world.

A major concern of Islamic thought has become how to cope with tensions
ensuing from the coexistence of Islam and the modern world, enhanced by
the problem of national identity and of determining an appropriate form of
government. Suggested solutions vary greatly and range from radical separation of religion and state to Islamic fundamentalism and the reestablishment
of the supposedly ideal situation of original Islam with the goal of universal domination. A phenomenon of its own is the Ahmadiyya, a messianic

movement named after its founder, Mirza Ghulam Ahmad (1835–1908), which originated in India in the late nineteenth century. Contrary to the dogma that revelation ended with Muhammad, "the Seal of the Prophets" (khatam al-anbiya'), Mirza Ghulam Ahmad claimed to be a prophet and also the Mahdi, sent to lead humankind into the Golden Age, which according to general Islamic belief precedes the Last Judgment. When Pakistan was founded, the main branch moved from Qadian in India to Rabwah ("refuge on high ground," given to Jesus and his mother; see sura 23:50), southwest of Lahore. Rejecting the idea of jihad as a means to promote Islam, the Ahmadiyya launched missionary activities all over the world, translating the Qur'an into the local vernacular and founding schools and hospitals after the Christian model. For this and other things, such as their critical attitude toward the 'ulama', whom they accused of ignoring the "supreme realities of Islam," the Ahmadiyya was declared a non-Muslim community by Pakistani authorities in 1984 and subjected to persecution and punishment. Consequently, it moved its headquarters from Rabwah to London.

This is certainly not all there is to Islam. In addition to Shari'a-Islam, which is totally oriented toward the law, as it is represented by theologians and Muslim political theorists, there is also a traditional religiousness that is influenced, among other things, by mysticism and is realized in Sufism. Its aim is the union with God, the *unio mystica,* which also has a long and rich tradition in Christianity. Sufism goes back to the early period of Islam. It has developed since the twelfth century into a popular movement with an extensive catalog of associations in the form of the often strictly hierarchical Sufi orders, with cloister-like institutions. This form of Islam has reached a broad range of social strata. Sufism has become a truly missionizing movement and has contributed greatly to the spread of Islam, especially among Turks and Persians, but also in Africa and South Asia. Sufis are pious in the context of mysticism and satisfy the duties placed on them by Islam. For them the form of Islamic government has no primary significance; fundamentalism is a concept that they reject.

Islam thus takes manifold forms and was very flexible in its golden age. Otherwise it would not have developed into a world religion.

Translated by Allison Brown

II

SUNNI ISLAM

(Bernd Radtke)

The Arabic word *sunna* means "tradition," "custom." A Sunni (Arab. *sunni*) is a person who strives to live and act according to customs and tradition. The substance of the customs consists of the sayings and teachings that were passed down from the Prophet Muhammad. Emulating the Prophet is the goal of every pious Muslim; and every pious Muslim will claim that his customary practice and the doctrine he believes in are the true sunna of the Prophet. In this way a Shi'i, too, can be considered a Sunni, which is why it is necessary to define the concept of sunna precisely in a narrow sense and from a historical perspective.

1. Historical Outline

The opposition between Sunni and Shi'i Islam in the Islamic world is the outcome of a process that developed over centuries. Although the core of Sunna and Shi'a already existed in the seventh century, one can speak of Sunni Islam and Shi'i Islam only from the ninth century onward.

The unity of believers ended in 656 with the murder of 'Uthman ibn 'Affan, the third successor of the Prophet Muhammad as leader of the community and the Islamic political system. 'Ali ibn Abi Talib, son-in-law of the Prophet, who was chosen in Medina to be 'Uthman's successor, did not enjoy the support of the entire community, as was the case with his predecessors Abu Bakr (632–634), 'Umar ibn al-Khattab (634–644), and the murdered 'Uthman (644–656). Mu'awiya ibn Abi Sufyan, governor of Syria from the clan of the Umayyads, challenged 'Ali, demanding revenge for the death of his relative 'Uthman. The Umayyads, a patrician house from Mecca, had long been engaged in bitter resistance to the Prophet Muhammad. A second adversary to the caliph 'Ali emerged from among his former supporters who had abandoned his camp because they disapproved of 'Ali's behavior in the conflict with Muʿawiya. They were referred to as "those who go out," the "seceders" (Arab. *khawarij,* sing. *khariji*), or "Kharijites." The military conflict between ʿAli and Muʿawiya ended in a stalemate; but ʿAli was assassinated in 661, allowing his rival to rule relatively unchallenged as caliph starting in that year. The caliphate remained with the Umayyads until 750.

The Umayyad caliphs had to assert themselves continually against open rebellion throughout their entire dynasty, especially after the death of Muʿawiya in 680. Descendants of the caliph ʿAli kept rising up against the Umayyads, whom they referred to as usurpers. Their followers called themselves "the party of ʿAli" (Arab. *shiʿat ʿAli*). Their views developed into what from the tenth century onward formed the core of Shiʿi doctrine. In the opinion of this group, leadership of the Islamic polity had to remain in the hands of a member of the family of the Prophet Muhammad, who were seen as bearers of a special God-given charisma.

The Kharijites stood in sharpest contrast to the party of ʿAli and the rest of the Islamic community. In their eyes it was not being a descendant of the Prophet, nor possessing the personal charisma of a leader, that authorized someone to lead the community, but solely his morality. Some groups of Kharijites developed what seemed to be an almost ludicrous moral rigorism that in the end let them decline into an insignificant marginal group in the Islamic world.

The masses of pious Muslims who disapproved of Shiʿi and Kharijite extremism and could be characterized as "moderates" adopted a stance that ranged from neutral to rejecting toward the Umayyads but was not openly rebellious. Among them were the intellectual progenitors of the later Sunna. Hasan al-Basri, who died in 728, could be considered a typical representative of this group.

The Umayyad dynasty succumbed to the storm of opposition in 750 and was replaced by the dynasty of the Abbasids. These descendants of ʿAbbas, an uncle of the Prophet, knew how to take advantage of various forms of discontent—religious, national, social—through clever propaganda to bring Umayyad rule to an end, in which they received support from non-Arab troops of eastern Iranian descent. They maintained the caliphate until 1258. The Abbasids transferred the capital of the Muslim empire from Damascus to Baghdad and increasingly brought non-Arabs into the government administration, especially Persians, who up to then had been excluded from leadership in the polity. Through the class of state secretaries of Iranian descent (Arab. *kuttab,* sing. *katib*) that was developing, elements of Iranian political and intellectual tradition found their way into the previously Arab-dominated Islamic world. The heritage of Greek antiquity also entered the Islamic world through translations from Greek and Syrian, which had been commissioned by Abbasid caliphs in the ninth century.

The theologians and jurists (Arab. *ʿulamaʾ,* sing. *ʿalim*) who were taught in the tradition of the moderates, whose circles cultivated what was genuinely Islamic-Arabic knowledge, stood in competition with the *kuttab* for influence in leading and structuring the Islamic polity. The *kuttab* put the case for a more autocratic concept of caliphate and state, thereby approaching Shiʿi tendencies—as did, for example, the Persian Ibn al-Muqaffaʿ (executed 759), who was secretary to the second Abbasid caliph, Mansur (754–775), and is also considered one of the creators of Arab prose. In contrast, the ʿulamaʾ fought for a more constitutional concept of state. For them the decisive criterion for the weals and woes of the state was to be found not in the person who ruled but in obeying and applying the religious principles of the holy book, the Qurʾan, and the tradition (sunna) practiced and recognized in the community.

The struggle between the two positions, which continued for almost a century, was decided in the years following 850 with the victory of the ʿulamaʾ, whose "Sunni" doctrine then became officially recognized in the caliphate. Only from this point on can one speak of a "Sunni caliphate."

The victory of the ʿulamaʾ was accompanied, however, by an external loss of power of the Abbasid caliphate, which then culminated in 945, when the Sunni caliphate came under the influence of the Shiʿi dynasty of the Buyids, who had served in Baghdad as majordomos of a sort for the Abbasids. In the same century, the provinces at the peripheries of the caliphate—Spain, North Africa, eastern Iran—started gaining independence under local, mostly non-Arab dynasties. A counter-caliphate of extreme Shiʿi provenance emerged in the second half of the tenth century in Egypt under the dynasty of the Fatimids, which propagated subversive propaganda against the Sunni caliphate of the Abbasids.

Coming to the aid in the eleventh century of Sunni Islam, which was being pressured from all sides, were the Turks from Central Asia. In 1055 they eliminated the Shiʿi Buyids as Abbasid majordomos and initiated a Sunni counteroffensive by founding institutions of higher education. These academic institutions were called Nizamiyya, after their initiator, the vizier Nizam al-Mulk. The most outstanding representative of the Sunni ʿulamaʾ who taught at these schools was the Persian Abu Hamid Muhammad al-Ghazali (d. 1111).

The Mongol invasion in the thirteenth century, which brought the destruction of Baghdad and thus the end of the Abbasid caliphate (1258), was stopped by the Sunni Turkish Mamluks, who ruled Egypt and Syria from the mid-thirteenth to the early sixteenth century. The Mamluk dynasty then fell in 1517 to the Sunni Turkish Ottomans, whose state lasted into the twentieth century. Perhaps the most significant intellectual of the Mamluk period was the Syrian Ibn Taymiyya (d. 1328), whose writings have had a great influence in modern times.

2. Theology

Islam is a religion of law. God revealed his will to his last and greatest prophet, Muhammad. It is laid down in the holy book, the Qurʾan, partly in the form of laws. These eternal, holy, and divine laws must be applied in a world, in a community, in order for Islam to exist as a religion. Islam is therefore never solely a private affair between an individual and his God, but always also a matter of the public, society, and the state. The perspectives according to which society is structured and decisions are made as to who should exercise authoritative functions in it must therefore be of crucial significance to a Muslim. This is particularly the case in ascertaining how a person is to behave if the leader of the state does not comply with the divine laws, as the application of these laws determines the well-being of the Muslim as a member of the community, outside of which—to use Christian terminology—there is no salvation. If the leader of the polity is not living in harmony with divine law, must pious Muslims say that divine will is also expressed in sinful governance, or do they have the right, even the duty, to rebel against the sacrilegious authority?

This had to ignite questions as to the freedom of action of the individual and the origins of evil, and it is precisely these two questions that mark the beginning of Muslim theological discourse. The way the Umayyads led the Islamic polity met with rejection by many and was viewed as contradictory to divine law and tradition as endowed by Muhammad—whether rightfully or wrongfully is not the issue here. The Umayyads, however, asserted that the leadership of the state had been entrusted to them by divine destiny, and for that reason resistance to their authority was tantamount to resisting God's will. The resistance to this self-legitimation of their power came from the predecessors of the later Shi'a, on the one hand, and from the Kharijites, on the other. But the Umayyads' demand for recognition of their power as God-given found only limited approval in the circles of the moderates as well, since the gap between the reality of the actions of Umayyad caliphs and the demands of divine law was all too obvious.

The prolonged discussion that took place in moderate circles on the relationship between divine omnipotence and human freedom of action started, of course, with arguments based on statements in the Qur'an, which, however, does not take any clear-cut position: on the one hand, the Qur'an emphasizes divine omnipotence, but on the other hand, human beings are given responsibility for their actions, for which they will someday reap either a divine reward in paradise or eternal punishment in hell. Both standpoints—that which focuses more on God's omnipotence and that with more of an eye toward human accountability—could be proved legitimate according to the Qur'an. The former position is referred to in Islamic theological literature as Jabarite and the latter as Qadarite, but I will refrain from explaining the two terms in detail here. In many respects the views of Hasan al-Basri (d. 728) were qadarite, emphasizing free will and human responsibility. Hasan was less a theologian than an ascetic and revivalist preacher. The mystical movement views him as one of its progenitors. Hasan appealed to the people to do penance and practice self-discipline; he also condemned the encroachments of the political rulers but rejected open rebellion. Basra,

Hasan's hometown, seems to have played a particularly important role in the development of dogmatic, legal, and mystical schools. There, but also in the other urban centers of the Islamic world such as Kufa, Medina, and Damascus, discussion circles of pious, often ascetic members of the community formed as early as the seventh century, in which dogmatic, legal, and mystical problems were discussed.

Among those in these discussion circles were members of a sect called the Murji'a. They were generally on amicable terms with the Umayyad dynasty since they rejected judging the fate of a sinner—including an Umayyad caliph who sinned—and left the decision up to God alone. This posture also explains their name: *murji'a* can mean "those who postponed," that is, those who put off the decision on a Muslim's redemption or damnation until the Last Judgment. One adherent of this sect was Abu Hanifa (d. 767), founder of the Hanafi school of law.

The Murji'ite position of not ostracizing sinners from the community of salvation of the Islamic polity as long as they do not openly apostatize from Islam already included the core of the later Sunni doctrine of justification through faith alone (*sola fide*). This declares that all Muslims, insofar as they are committed to the principles of the Islamic religion and act accordingly, will still be able to partake of paradise, meaning eternal bliss, despite any transgressions of divine law. Great sinners spend only a certain amount of time in hell, but through intercession by the Prophet Muhammad are redeemed from there by God. It cannot be overlooked that this view could foster a somewhat lax morality, in contrast to the moral rigorism advocated by Hasan al-Basri and the circles around him, which made heavy demands on human actions without offering any certainty of one day being rewarded. While the Murji'ite attitude may have concealed the dangers of an all too great certainty of mercy ("despite my sins I belong to the Islamic community of salvation and am thus certain of God's mercy"), the views of Hasan and the Qadarites could also lead to an exaggerated feeling of self-assurance. This was felt, recognized, and opposed, for example, by some mystics who stood in the spiritual tradition of Hasan al-Basri.

The Abbasids, who superseded the Umayyad dynasty in 750, were initially supported by the moderate 'ulama', since they demonstrated their willingness to lead the Islamic polity according to divine law and the customs and traditions of the pious, thereby satisfying the main demand of the moderates. They lost the support of the 'ulama', however, when they elevated the doctrine of a certain theological, scholastic movement, the Mu'tazilites, to state dogma. This occurred in the period from 833 to 850, referred to by the moderate 'ulama' as *mihna* (test). An exponent of the moderates at this time was Ahmad ibn Hanbal (d. 855), founder of the Hanbali school of law, named after him.

The Mu'tazilites, intellectual heirs of the Qadarites, introduced Greek concepts into Islamic theological discussion for the first time. Their doctrine can be summarized in five main points, of which only the first two played a major role in the debate. The first point in Mu'tazilite dogma is *tawhid,* which can be translated as "monotheism" or "consciousness of divine oneness." Mu'tazilite *tawhid* says that God's essence is unique and indivisible. The attributes (Arab. *sifat*) ascribed to God in the Qur'an must be viewed as identical with God's essence in order to rule out any and every element of multiplicity. Thus God knows or speaks through himself, through his essence, not through an attribute of "knowing" or "speaking" that would be apart from him. Because the Qur'an is considered the word of God, God's speech (Arab. *kalam Allah*), one must ask how to view this "speaking" of God that was revealed in time, that appeared in creation. Did the Qur'an present God's speech itself, and was it therefore eternal and divine in its form that appeared in time? Or was it only a manifestation of the uncreated, divine quality of "speech" that appeared in time? Because of their doctrine of divine qualities, the Mu'tazilites had to decide on the createdness of the Qur'an. The doctrine of the createdness of the Qur'an was raised to the status of state dogma in 833 by the Abbasid caliph Ma'mun (813–833). This was directed against the legitimation of the moderate 'ulama', who originally supported the Abbasids. The 'ulama' saw themselves as the appointed interpreters and preservers of the eternal divine law that is revealed in the Qur'an. If the source of their legitimation, the Qur'an, were questioned, if it were to lose its divine—that is, eternal—quality, then the power and influence of the 'ulama' in shaping the Islamic polity would also be jeopardized. The dogma of the createdness of the Qur'an was therefore adamantly rejected by the 'ulama'.

The second point of Mu'tazilite doctrine, *'adl* (justice) describes God's relationship to human beings. God cannot be unjust, because injustice would be contrary to his essence. He will therefore be just to human beings, as he promised, or threatened, in the Qur'an; that is, he will reward or punish in accordance with the deeds of the individual, who is responsible for them. It is inconceivable for God to be arbitrary. Evil in the world emerged through human beings, not God. And they are accountable for their actions. If individuals are responsible for their deeds, then they must also be given a certain freedom of action; that is, the works of divine omnipotence must be at least limited within the realm of human actions.

The creeds (Arab. *'aqa'id,* sing. *'aqida*) that emerged in the ninth and tenth centuries within the moderate group, which can now be referred to as Sunna (the reason will be explained in the next section), deviate in characteristic points from Mu'tazilite doctrine. For example, they emphasize the predetermination of all things through God, including human action. Human accountability thus appears less significant.

Sunni Islam, which was consolidating in the second half of the ninth century, found a *fidei defensor,* a defender of the faith, in the early tenth century in the person of Abu l-Hasan al-Ash'ari (873–935). At first a student of Jubba'i (d. 915), a Mu'tazilite, and therefore an outstanding expert on Mu'tazilite thought and dogmatics, he went through a kind of conversion around 912–915 and from then on viewed himself as an adherent of the doctrine of Ahmad ibn Hanbal. Al-Ash'ari renounced the substance of Mu'tazilite thought, but he retained the Mu'tazilite method of argumentation that is characterized as dialectic (Arab. *kalam*). Because he thus did not deny his entire Mu'tazilite heritage, the Sunni 'ulama' long treated him and his successors with suspicion.

Al-Ash'ari opposed Mu'tazilite doctrine on four main points. First, he declared his belief in the uncreatedness of the Qur'an. Second, the Mu'tazilites interpreted the anthropomorphisms that appear in the Qur'an as metaphors. For example, they understood the "hand of God" as the attribute of mercy. Al-Ash'ari countered this with the notion that Qur'anic anthropomorphisms should be accepted without asking how, without being able or permitted to use human reason to make statements about them. This "not asking how" regarding divine attributes was referred to as *bi-la-kayf*. Third, the beatific vision of God that is promised to believers in the Qur'an was interpreted by Mu'tazilites in such a way that believers would see God not with their real eyes but with their hearts as the site of knowledge. Al-Ash'ari insisted on the interpretation of viewing God with one's own eyes, but again in the sense of "not asking how." The fourth and last point concerns human action. Qadarites and, following them, Mu'tazilites ascribed to human beings a capacity to act (*istita'a*) that is preexistent to the individual actions taken, deriving human free will and human responsibility from this. Al-Ash'ari—and even precursors such as the non-Mu'tazilite theologian Dirar ibn 'Amr (d. ca. 800), the theosophist Hakim al-Tirmidhi (d. ca. 910), and others—spoke of the creation (*khalq*) of human actions through God and their acquisition (*kasb, iktisab*) by human beings on the basis of the capacity to act (*al-istita'a ma'a l-fi'l*) that exists only during the respective action. This reveals a basic concept of Ash'arite-Sunni thought: creation, including human beings, is directly "with God" in every moment, is created in every moment by God. What individuals think they see as eternal laws of creation—we would speak of laws of nature—are in reality nothing but an expression of God's custom of creation (*'adat al-khalq*), which God in his omnipotence can break off at any moment. Breaking the customary course of creation (*khariq al-khalq, khariq al-'ada*), which for God is just one option of creation, is experienced by human beings as a miracle.

Al-Ash'ari lived in the center of the caliphate in Basra and Baghdad. His contemporary Maturidi (d. 944) lived and worked at the periphery of the Islamic world in Transoxania. Like al-Ash'ari, Maturidi tried to integrate rational methodology into Sunni theology. His teachings differ in some points from those of al-Ash'ari; he spoke, for instance, of a capacity to act that precedes action, following a Qadarite-Mu'tazilite tradition. Maturidi sympathized with the Hanafi school of law, while al-Ash'ari saw himself as a follower of the Hanbali school.

In the subsequent period Sunni theology was the domain of al-Ash'ari's adherents and successors. For the tenth and eleventh centuries the following persons should be mentioned: Baqillani (d. 1013); Ibn Furak (d. 10150);

Isfara'ini (d. 1027); Baghdadi (d. 1037); Qushayri (d. 1072), who was also known as a writer on mystical subjects; and al-Juwayni (d. 1085), who taught in Nishapur at one of the aforementioned Sunni Nizamiyyas.

Al-Juwayni's student Abu Hamid Muhammad al-Ghazali (1058–1111) is certainly one of the most outstanding personalities of Islamic intellectual history. He was born in eastern Persia, in Tus (near present-day Mashhad), studied in his hometown as well as in Gorgan at the Caspian Sea and in Nishapur under al-Juwayni. He became a professor at the Baghdad Nizamiyya in 1091, but an internal crisis led to his abandoning his position in 1095. From then on he devoted himself to a mystical, ascetic life until his death in 1111.

In his autobiography *Deliverance from Error* (*Al-Munqidh min al-dalal*), al-Ghazali left us a description of his efforts to compile the most important intellectual political positions of his time and the critical discussion of them. Discussion of extreme Shi'i propaganda is included, as is discussion of Greek philosophy. Greek sciences and philosophy had been received by the Islamic world from early times, especially since the early ninth century. In addition to Islamic theology and scholasticism, which made use of some Greek concepts but whose subject matter remained Islamic, an Islamic philosophy of Greek provenance also took shape, the most outstanding representatives of which were Kindi (d. 870), Farabi (d. 950), and Ibn Sina (Avicenna, d. 1037). Al-Ghazali wrote a refutation of the doctrine of the Islamic philosophers who followed Greek philosophy (*Tahafut al-falasifa*), but he did take up some of their Neoplatonic concepts—just as al-Ash'ari before him had rejected essential points of Mu'tazilite doctrine while adopting its methodology. We will encounter something similar again with respect to the Hanbali theologian Ibn Taymiyya. Through al-Ghazali, Neoplatonic concepts that had previously been foreign to Sunni theology were introduced into it.

Al-Ghazali saw the corruption of his colleagues, the Sunni 'ulama', and it was hard for him to bear. He observed their submissiveness toward the authorities, their hypocrisy, and their striving for secular power and recognition. Personalities such as Ahmad ibn Hanbal, who despite massive state efforts to exert pressure during the period of the *mihna* had remained steadfast and true to his convictions, were in fact rare exceptions. The hunger of the 'ulama' for secular recognition by the political rulers, whose violence all too often was not legitimated by divine law, of which the 'ulama' claimed to be the guardians, must have seemed a dangerous aberration to al-Ghazali. He then discovered the true God-given doctrine and practice among the mystics of Islam, the so-called Sufis. He followed their practice in the last decade and a half of his life and attempted to understand and reconcile their doctrine with Ash'arite dogmatics. His greatest work, *The Revival of the Religious Sciences* (*Ihya' 'ulum al-din*), is evidence of that. Prior to al-Ghazali there had been similar attempts to present mystics using Ash'arite concepts, such as Kalabadhi's in the late tenth century, but none was as convincing or vigorous as al-Ghazali's.

In a time of intense external threats through the Mongol invasion in the thirteenth century, the Hanbali theologian Ahmad ibn Taymiyya appeared on the scene in Syria. He and his student Ibn Qayyim al-Jawziyya (d. 1350) were initially met with harsh rejection. Ibn Taymiyya's criticism was directed against phenomena that were deviations from what he considered to be original Islam. This included especially the theosophical mysticism of Ibn al-ʿArabi (d. 1240) and his students, as well as forms of traditional piety such as worshipping the graves of people who had a reputation for holiness. Ibn Taymiyya found neither saint veneration nor the teachings of Ibn al-ʿArabi to be a custom of original Islam, so he considered them damnable innovations. Ibn Taymiyya's position on mysticism was not that of an absolute adversary, however. He accepted a lot, in particular from mystics of the early period, and even some aspects of the mysticism of Ibn al-ʿArabi. Ibn Taymiyya, who was not permitted to assert his views during his lifetime and suffered severe persecution by the established powers (he died in the prison of the citadel of Damascus) first had a public impact through Muhammad ibn ʿAbd al-Wahhab (1703–1792), the intellectual progenitor of modern Saudi Arabia.

3. Law

In moderate circles, aside from questions of dogma and religious practice, legal questions were also raised, which is self-evident considering the public nature of the Islamic religion. In the course of the eighth century a number of schools of law were established in the urban centers under the influence of outstanding personalities. The school of Abu Hanifa was set up in Kufa in Iraq, that of Malik ibn Anas in Medina, and that of Awzaʿi in Syria. These eighth-century institutions are referred to as the old schools of law. Characteristic of this time is the lack of generally recognized standards such as legal sources and standards of jurisprudence. While the Kufa school of law tended to allow great latitude to the personal rationale (Arab. *raʾy*) of administrators of the law, in Medina there was greater reliance on the city's traditional legal customs, on which there was general agreement. The legal sources were the Qurʾan and a municipal and school tradition that was gradually forming. The latter was referred to as "sunna" in the eighth century. There was therefore a sunna of the school in Medina, a sunna of the school in Syria, and others.

Standardization of legal sources was asserted through the efforts of Shafiʿi (d. 820). The doctrine of *usul al-fiqh*, the roots or foundations of the law, which was developed by Shafiʿi, aimed at replacing personal decisions, *raʾy*, in favor of "objective" criteria. The four roots of law demanded by Shafiʿi were: (1) Qurʾan; (2) sunna; (3) *consensus doctorum* (Arab. *ijmaʿ*); and (4) analogical reasoning (Arab. *qiyas*). There was no longer any place for personal opinion, or *ra'y,* in this system. The concept of sunna also took on a new meaning through Shafi'i. Whereas earlier the sunna was understood to be the legal custom or tradition of the local school of law, Shafi'i demanded that every sunna be recognized only if it could be proved to be the genuine traditional sunna of the Prophet. Through and after Shafi'i the sunna of a city or local school of law became the sunna of the Prophet, which was now also considered divinely inspired. The sunna of the Prophet acquired the character of the eternal, timeless standard, whereas in the eighth century, for example, legal rulings were still made that consciously contradicted the decisions of the sunna of the Prophet.

A sunna of the Prophet was considered normative if it had been passed down through a certain chain of warrantors that had to trace all the way back to the Prophet. A tradition that relayed the actions, demands, or teachings of the Prophet is called hadith. A hadith is made up of two parts: the *isnad,* the chain of warrantors tracing back to the Prophet, and the *matn,* the reported sunna of the Prophet. The criterion for authenticity is not the substance, the *matn* of the hadith, but the *isnad,* which should have only irreproachable warrantors and should not contain any chronological contradictions. *Isnad* literature developed into the very comprehensive biographical literature in Arabic.

The traditions on the teachings and actions of the Prophet that were viewed as authentic were consolidated starting in the ninth century into six canonical collections. The two most important ones are those of Bukhari (d. 870) and Muslim (d. 875). The problem of historical authenticity of the canonical collections, which is of great interest to Western scholars, is one of the most difficult questions facing Islamic scholarship and has yet to be resolved. Are the hadiths simply ninth-century projections onto Muhammad, or do we really have authentic reports, at least in part, about him?

The demand for an *isnad* dating back without any gaps all the way to the Prophet led to another demand: the recognition of all companions of the Prophet (*sahaba*) as authorities, which in turn entailed the recognition of all of the first four caliphs—Abu Bakr, 'Umar, 'Uthman, and 'Ali—as rightly guided (*rashidun*). Their ranking was appraised according to when they appeared chronologically. Both views constituted and still constitute a sharp contrast to Shi'i doctrine. Accepting all companions of the Prophet as transmitters of the sunna, which the Shi'a also view as sacred, is untenable for the Shi'a, as in their eyes many of the companions of the Prophet disrespected 'Ali and were thus guilty of a serious offense and therefore of having sinned. The Shi'a also cannot accept the fact that Abu Bakr was given precedence over 'Ali. Both of these—recognition of all companions of the Prophet and recognition of the first four caliphs as rightly guided—are essential points in the creeds of the moderates in the ninth century.

The Shafi'i doctrine of *usul al-fiqh* asserted itself over the course of the ninth century. The old schools of law of the eighth century either underwent a transformation or disappeared entirely, such as the Awzaʿi school in Syria. The four remaining schools still exist today:

1. The Hanafi school of law, originally in Kufa, of which Abu Hanifa (d. 767) is considered the founder. In addition to the four legal foundations demanded by Shafiʿi (Qurʾan, sunna, *ijmaʿ,* and *qiyas*), the Hanafis recognize two other juristic practices: the customary *raʾy,* or personal opinion, of their school from time immemorial, and the *istihsan,* the preference for a particular solution as appropriate with respect to the society. The Hanafi school of law is widespread mostly in Turkey, in Central Asia, and on the Indian subcontinent.
2. The Maliki school of law emerged from the old school of Medina, with Malik ibn Anas (d. 796) recognized as its founder. In addition to the four *usul al-fiqh* of Shafiʿi, the Malikis make use of one additional criterion for finding justice, the *istislah* (considering what is deemed proper in the public interest in making a legal judgment). This school can be found in North, West, and Central Africa and was the authoritative school in Spain before the Christian Reconquest.
3. Those who chose to use only the four *usul al-fiqh* demanded by Shafiʿi formed the Shafiʿi school of law. It is widespread in East Africa, southern Arabia, and Southeast Asia.
4. The use of rational methodology in jurisprudence is limited in the Hanbali school of law even more so than in the Shafiʿi school. The Hanbali school even largely rules out analogical reasoning (*qiyas*), the fourth basis of law according to Shafiʿi. This school views its founder to be Ahmad ibn Hanbal, author of the *Musnad,* a collection of roughly eighty thousand hadiths, which is considered of equal value to the six aforementioned canonical hadith collections. Ahmad ibn Hanbal was the bitter adversary of Muʿtazilite dogmatics during the *mihna* of the ninth century.

The Zahiri school, which was established in the second half of the ninth century, went even further than the Hanbalis in its rejection of rational methodology. The Zahiris accepted only literal meanings. It found very few adherents, however, and soon died out.

In the second half of the ninth century and the first half of the tenth, what we have come to call Sunni Islam emerged from the constitution of the four schools of law, the related canonization of the hadith, the development of a specific dogmatics, and political developments (in which the moderate ʿulamaʾ emerged victorious from the *mihna,* so the Islamic community was now to be led and organized according to their views). The Arabic word *sunni,* in its meaning as an adherent of Sunni Islam, was first documented in the second half of the tenth century.

It would represent a total misunderstanding of Islamic reality if I were not to mention here that Islamic law, the shariʿa (to use the common term), was at no time used absolutely in jurisprudence. The tension between an ideal shariʿa and actual legal reality is one of the main problems in Islamic history. The weakness of the shariʿa in dealing with today's legal reality is due not least to the fact that the forms of jurisprudence remained stuck in the ninth century, when the collection of legal sources was declared complete and their contents were recognized as sacrosanct. The weakness of the shari'a also comes, however, from the vulnerable position of those who supported it in public. Always at the mercy of the despotism of those in power, they were often all too rash in their willingness to succumb to the demands of the rulers. Exceptions such as Ahmad ibn Hanbal and Ibn Taymiyya were rare.

The question as to who is called upon to lead the Islamic community found two extreme solutions with the Shi'a and the Kharijites. The Shi'i solution turned legitimacy into a question of blood descent, whereas for the Kharijites the question was a purely moral one. The Sunni solution represents a compromise: on the one hand, the leader of the state should come from the Quraysh tribe, the tribe of the Prophet, thereby being related to him to at least some degree; on the other hand, the leader should be elected by a council (Arab. *shura*) of respected men and confirmed by an oath of allegiance (*bay'a*). The leader of the community, the caliph (*khalifa*), is required to act according to the principles of the sunna, that is, according to the rules established by the 'ulama'. He is not an authority who can determine justice as he sees fit but merely a servant of the divine right administered by the 'ulama'.

From the eleventh century on, the Sunni doctrine of law was forced to cope—worth mentioning in this context is the author al-Mawardi (d. 1058)—with the fact that the legitimate Abbasid caliph no longer had sufficient external power to assert the shari'a politically, since the power was de facto in the hands of "secular" dynasties such as the Buyids, Ghaznawids, and Seljuqs. The Abbasids had to make do by turning the "secular" dynasties into vicarious agents of the caliphs, thereby helping them gain a certain degree of legitimation.

4. Mysticism

Some members of pious circles in the first centuries of Islam strove for more profound piety by internalizing the demands of the shari'a and living an ascetic lifestyle. Ascetic, mystical ambitions can be traced back to the time of the Prophet. It should be noted that these cults were in no way antinomian. Such antinomian traits did appear, however, with people who were called *sufiyya* (sing. *sufi*). *Sufi* is a derivative of *suf*, "wool," and alludes to the dress of the individuals; it may also have been originally a derisive name.

The original *sufiyya*—there is evidence of their existence since the middle of the eighth century—seem to have paid homage to a kind of emotional religiosity. They used to put themselves into special moods by listening to music or poetry. They were opposed by members of the ascetic, mystical sect. These *viri religiosi*, or devout worshippers (Arab. *nussak*, *'ubbad*, sing. *nasik*,

'abid), formed their own science in the eighth and ninth centuries, which
they called *'ilm al-batin*, "internal knowledge," in contrast to jurisprudence
(*fiqh*) and hadith, which were referred to as "external knowledge" (*'ilm al-
zahir*). The substance of the "internal knowledge" was the inner experiences
and instructions for a psychagogia, the leading of the soul. The beginnings
of this kind of science had already been demonstrated by Hasan al-Basri.
Fully developed, it could be recognized in the ninth century in Muhasibi
(d. 857), who like many of these devout worshippers came from 'ulama'
circles. In the course of the ninth century, this psychagogia was joined
by cosmological speculation, anthropology, and dogmatic debate. As in
other circles, here too the relationship of divine omnipotence and oneness
(Arab. *tawhid*) to human action played a central role in the debates of
the devout worshippers. Their solution aimed for the total suppression of
human independence and complete devotion to God, experienced as the
only real actor. Evidence of these debates includes the writings of Junayd
ibn Muhammad in Baghdad (d. 910) and Hakim al-Tirmidhi (d. ca. 910)
in Transoxania.

In the course of the second half of the ninth and first half of the tenth
centuries, the designation *sufiyya*, which up to then had been the name
of a marginal group, spread to the devout worshippers as well. The reasons for this are not clear. Regional differences evidently existed, since the
name *sufi* was still largely unknown in the eastern part of the Islamic world
around 900.

From the tenth century on, the entire mystical movement was called "Sufism" (Arab. *tasawwuf*). In Sufi textbooks that could be regarded as classical, which were written after the middle of the tenth century, distinctions
were no longer made between the originally separate *sufiyya* and devout
worshippers. A devout man such as Fudayl ibn 'Iyad (d. 803), referred to
in tenth-century creeds as an authority of Sunni 'ulama', became a progenitor of the *sufiyya* in Sufi literature. As authors of classical Sufi textbooks
of the tenth and eleventh centuries, Kalabadhi (d. 990 or 994), Abu Nasr
al-Sarraj (d. 988), Sulami (d. 1021), and Qushayri (d. 1072), who was also
an Ash'arite theologian, should be mentioned.

Because of the antinomian elements adopted from the original *sufiyya*,
which by far did not find approval among everyone, the *sufiyya* sometimes
suffered persecution by the state with the tacit consent of the 'ulama'. This
persecution did not harm the movement, however.

The *tasawwuf* enjoyed great encouragement through the authority of al-
Ghazali, mentioned earlier in another context. Al-Ghazali did not bring any
fundamental innovation to the *tasawwuf*, as there were devout worshippers in the ninth century who were models for his efforts to bring together
shari'a and inwardness, *'ilm al-zahir* and *'ilm al-batin*, and he was familiar
with their works. Nevertheless, the concepts and ideas of Greek philosophy
that were introduced into the mystical movement through al-Ghazali were
indeed new. The concepts of the worshippers and the systematic theologians

of the tenth and eleventh centuries came from the Islamic tradition, dogmatics, the shariʿa, and the hadith.

From the demand to see God's work in all things and heed his commandments in all actions by suppressing one's own ego as much as possible and the wanting that derives from it (as in the *tawhid* doctrine of the classical *tasawwuf*), it is just a small step to the statement that God is everything. But this step was first taken in the thirteenth century by Ibn al-ʿArabi (d. 1240) of Spain. His doctrine of the oneness of being (Arab. *wahdat al-wujud*) had a major impact on the further development of Islamic mysticism. The harshest adversary of Ibn al-ʿArabi and especially of his students was the aforementioned Ibn Taymiyya, whose criticism had no effect in his time.

There were always outstanding personalities to inspire the training of students. No information is available about firm organizational forms of mystical schools in the early centuries of Islam. One eleventh-century author counted twelve major schools that existed in his time. They seem to have exhibited theoretical currents more than set organizational forms. The mystical schools started acquiring such forms of organization, which we call orders (Arab. *tariqa*, pl. *taraʾiq* or *turuq*), in the thirteenth century. A number of orders were established, some of which still exist today. In the late Middle Ages they had much political influence, for example, in the emergence of the Safavid state in Iran and in the Ottoman Empire.

The mystical path is fundamentally open to every Muslim. Everyone—even if, especially in modern times, through the leadership of a shaykh—can rise to higher (according to the *sufiyya*) forms of religious knowledge, which are promised to the novice as one of the fruits of the path. The Shiʿa, for whom religious authority and knowledge must always be tied to a blood relationship tracing back through the imams to the Prophet Muhammad, were and still are opposed to this "democratic" understanding of knowledge of the Sufis. Shiʿa is an old and yet always a new adversary of Sufism, as the aftermath of the Iranian Revolution of 1978–79 has shown. The Shiʿization of Persia after 1500 following the Safavid conquest also did not help promote the Sunni Sufis, who were organized in orders that were then oppressed. Some survived, but only because they Shiʿized themselves. The thought and culture of the Sufis, however, had already influenced the general intellectual culture of Iran to such a great extent, even before the Safavid dynasty, especially through the medium of the great Persian poetry, that it remains one of its entrenched components to the present day.

Research on the exoteric history and the history of ideas of non-Persian Sunni mysticism from the thirteenth century to today is still in its infancy. It can generally be said that the theosophical teaching system of Ibn al-ʿArabi had a great influence. Order activity was definitely stimulated in the eighteenth and nineteenth centuries. English-language literature even speaks of a neo-Sufism; whether this is factual shall be left open for now. Especially modern *sufiyya* often refer to their mystical doctrine and practice as *tariqa muhammadiyya*, "Muhammad's path." But even for the oldest *sufiyya* the life (*sira*) and deeds (*sunna*) of Muhammad were their model. The *sufiyya* were not merely to emulate him (*imitatio Muhammadi*) with their body and soul but also strive to have Muhammad always in their thoughts and feelings. This visualization could become so intense that they imagined they saw before their eyes the physical Muhammad himself, who came to them with advice and instruction. They were and are, in contrast to the Wah-habis, convinced that even after his death Muhammad continues to live on in a human form. The corresponding theory cannot be explained in detail here. In this extreme manifestation the practice of obeying the sunna of the Prophet turned away from the tradition of the book and returned to the Prophet himself.

Translated by Allison Brown

III

SHIʿI ISLAM

(Werner Ende)

1. Twelver Shiʿa

Roughly 10 to 15 percent of the present Muslim population worldwide belongs to the religious denomination of Shiʿi Islam. The Twelver Shiʿa (Arab. *ithna ʿashariyya*) are by far the largest Shiʿi sect. Their main communities have for centuries been in southern Iraq, in Iran including Azerbaijan, and in some regions of the Indo-Pakistan subcontinent (for example, Lucknow). There are also significant religiously and politically active Twelver Shiʿa minorities in Afghanistan, Lebanon, Bahrain, and the coastal regions of the Arab Gulf states.

Within the Shiʿa as a whole, this group is theologically somewhere between the Zaydiyya, whose teachings are, all things considered, closest to those of the Sunna, and special groups referred to by the Twelvers themselves as "exaggerators" (*ghulat*). These are characterized by more or less obvious deification of their imams and an extreme esoteric interpretation of the Qurʾan (*taʾwil*).[1]

The name "Twelver" refers to the series of twelve leaders (imams, Arab. sing. *imam*) from the family of the Prophet Muhammad (d. 632), who according to the beliefs of adherents of this denomination were appointed by God. This series begins with ʿAli ibn Abi Talib (d. 661), the cousin and (through his marriage with Muhammad's daughter Fatima) son-in-law of the Prophet. Other designations for the Twelvers are Imamiyya (in reference to the central role of the imamate in their doctrine) and Jaʿfariyya (owing to the special status of the sixth imam, Jaʿfar al-Sadiq, in shaping this doctrine). Consciously emphasizing their quantitative inferiority relative to the Sunni community, apologists for the Twelver Shiʿa like to use the epithet "the special" or "the elite" (*al-khassa*) to refer to their own group, whereas they refer to the Sunnites with the expression "the (common) people" (*al-ʿamma*). Sunni polemics refer to the Twelvers—together with all other Shi'a—as "rejectors" (*rafidi,* pl. *rawafid*). A corresponding polemical Shi'i term for the Sunna is *nasibi* (pl. *nawasib*), roughly meaning fanatic adversary of 'Ali (and therefore of the Shi'a). This expression is supposedly derived from the "appointment" (Arab. *nasb*) of Abu Bakr as leader of the community after the death of Muhammad. In the interest of interdenominational peace and potential rapprochement, most Shi'i and Sunni authors now refrain from using such polemical characterizations. These, however, have their roots in early Islamic history. Not only did they appear in heresiographical and other theological and juristic sources on both sides, but also they were used as a matter of course for centuries in poetry and fiction (sometimes referring to different groups on the respective other side).

The emergence of the Shi'i denomination in Islam can be traced back to the dispute in the early Islamic community over who would assume the leadership following the death of Muhammad. It seems that Muhammad, who had no surviving sons, had not made any provisions on this matter. That is at least what the Sunna still believe today. In the absence of 'Ali, who according to tradition made the arrangements for the Prophet's funeral, Abu Bakr was selected, one of the earliest followers of Muhammad. It is difficult for today's historical-critical research to verify the actual events of the time. What follows is essentially a presentation of what the Twelver Shi'a consider to be the historical truth.

a. The Shi'i View of History

The Twelver Shi'a have common ground with the other Shi'i sects and schools (some of which no longer exist) in their conviction that it was God's will that 'Ali ibn Abi Talib should have been the Prophet's first successor (or caliph, from Arabic *khalifa;* see, for example, sura 2:30 and 38:26) to lead the community (or, from a later perspective, the state). Particularly significant for reasoning in this matter are the statements referring to 'Ali that Muhammad made on his way to Medina, on the return journey from his last pilgrimage to Mecca in March 632 at the pond of Khumm (Arab. *ghadir Khumm*), especially the sentence "Of whomsoever I am master [Arab. *mawla*], 'Ali is his master." In commemoration of this event, which is extremely significant in the Shi'i understanding of history, Twelver Shi'ites celebrate the annual Ghadir festival ('*id al-ghadir*), which has been an official holiday in Iran for centuries. In addition to this pronouncement at Ghadir Khumm, Shi'i tradition has passed down many sayings of the Prophet (hadiths, from Arab. sing. *hadith*), in which 'Ali and the later imams are referred to as the leaders of the community and the highest authorities on Islamic doctrine after Muhammad. For example: "I am leaving behind among you two precious things (Thaqalayn): the Book of Allah and my 'Itrah [kinsfolk], my Ahl al-Bayt [household]. As long as you adhere to them you will never go astray after me." In the Shi'i faith, the "kinsfolk" and "household" clearly refer to 'Ali and his progeny according to a number of Qur'an verses, especially

33:33 and 42:23. The related historical and theological justification is the result of a later development over centuries.[2]

The Sunna have a different interpretation of the Qur'an verses and corresponding hadiths that the Shi'a cite as evidence. To the extent that the Sunna even recognize these hadiths as authentic, as with that of Ghadir Khumm, their interpretation negates Shi'i claims.

Under both Abu Bakr (r. 632–634) and 'Umar (r. 634–644), 'Ali apparently assumed neither military (with one exception under 'Umar) nor civilian positions. The number of his supporters with respect to his claim to the caliphate was very small—especially according to the Shi'i faith. The terms "Shi'a" and "Shi'i" were derived from the Arabic name for the partisans of 'Ali, *shi'at 'Ali* (Party of 'Ali). Here too, later Shi'i doctrine used the Qur'an to justify its standpoint toward or its understanding of history. The Qur'anic verse 37:83, in which the word *"shi'a"* appears: "And lo! of his [i.e., Noah's] persuasion [or party, *shi'a*] verily was Abraham" is considered proof for the special place of this true community of Islam in divine providence, that is, proof of its existence before Muhammad appeared and of its relationship to the patriarchs (in the Muslim faith, prophets) of the Old Testament.[3]

A typical example is the interpretation given to a Qur'anic verse that seems to contradict the strict monotheism of Islam and thus continues to interest theologians. Sura 2:34 says that God commanded the angels to prostrate themselves before Adam. In Shi'i tradition this verse assumes a more profound meaning that eliminates all doubt that it is associated with hadiths about the preexistence of Muhammad, 'Ali, Fatima, Hasan, and Husayn, that is, their creation long before Adam. When God created Adam, he placed these five into Adam's loins. The command to the angels to prostrate themselves before Adam was thus a test of their obedience to God and at the same time a sign of their deference to Muhammad, Fatima, and the first three imams. One of the best-known Shi'i hadiths is about 'Ali having the same status relative to Muhammad as Aaron has vis-à-vis his brother Moses (see sura 25:35 and Exodus 4:14–16).

Opinions quickly diverged within the Shi'i realm regarding which descendants of 'Ali were supposed to, or actually did, assume leadership of the community, and which special, more or less superhuman qualities these leaders and theological authorities possessed. All Shi'i sects believe that God himself decided and announced to the early community through Muhammad who was to be the first successor to the Prophet in leading the community, namely, 'Ali, thus voiding the selection of Abu Bakr. Present-day Sunni theorists like to refer to the democratic aspect of selecting rulers in early Islam by consultation (Arab. *shura*); any suggestion, however, that this pertains also to the legitimacy of 'Ali's imamate is absurd from a Shi'i perspective.

Since most of the companions of the Prophet did not support 'Ali's leadership claim, thereby disobeying God's will, according to Shi'i interpretation they committed a serious sin. Writings on the wrongdoings of these companions of the Prophet, including some of the Prophet's wives, make up a significant part of Shi'i literature. In later centuries it became common to follow any written or verbal mention of their names with a disparaging epithet. This custom was consciously promoted (or initiated) by Shi'i dynasties as a demagogical means in the struggle against Sunni communities or states, such as by the Safavids in their conflict with the Ottomans. In contrast to the practice in the early centuries of Islam, it also became frowned upon to name Shi'i children after these "renegade" companions of the Prophet—that is, to name girls 'A'isha (the widow of the Prophet who went to battle against 'Ali in the "first civil war" of Islam) and to name boys Abu Bakr, 'Umar, 'Uthman, and so on. Whereas Shi'i modernists generally avoid those epithets or else speak out openly against this custom, even today one generally does not come across the names of the "renegade" companions of the Prophet among Shi'ites.

Among the few companions of the Prophet who, according to Shi'i tradition, remained loyal to 'Ali—and thus to true Islam—are Abu Dharr al-Ghifari, 'Ammar ibn Yasir, Salman al-Farisi, and Miqdad ibn 'Amr. Especially the first three play an important role in the consciousness of most pious Shi'ites to the present day. Abu Dharr is considered a brave pioneer of the principle of social justice, 'Ammar is referred to as a historical witness for the justification of *taqiyya* (discussed later in this chapter), and Salman al-Farisi, a man from Iran who is said to have come as a slave to Medina and to the house of the Prophet and became a Muslim, is regarded especially among religious Persians as evidence of the early connections between their country and Islam.

Sunnites reject the Shi'i rebuke of a majority of the companions of the Prophet. They view 'Ali as one of the most meritorious comrades-in-arms of Muhammad and the fourth and last of the "rightly guided" caliphs highly esteemed by him. After 'Ali's death the hereditary rule of the Umayyad dynasty was established, which also in Sunni opinion deserves criticism from a religious point of view (even if the Sunnites do not claim that the regime was generally un-Islamic, as Shi'ites do).

In historic terms, treating 'Ali as equivalent to the first three caliphs is the result of a certain "Shi'ization" of the Sunni view of history. To be sure, Sunnites by no means accept the Twelver Shi'i view that 'Ali's three predecessors were ultimately usurpers. Shi'a and Sunna have a very different picture of early Islamic history and its religious significance. Total agreement cannot be reached despite all efforts toward rapprochement.[4]

The dispute on the religious and political leadership of the community, which lies at the roots of the denominational rift between Shi'a and Sunna, led in the subsequent period to more or less different developments in their respective legal systems (especially in matrimony and inheritance law) and to different religious practices. But also within the Shi'a, that is, the religious, political school that wanted to keep the leadership of the Islamic community as a whole (*umma*) within the family of the Prophet's lineage, schisms emerged shortly after 'Ali's death (661). These led in turn to further special developments in religious law and practice. The point of departure of the intra-Shi'i schisms was, first of all, the question of who was considered a member of the Prophet's family (*ahl al-bayt*). Originally it was widely believed that potentially every descendant of 'Ali could assert a claim to the imamate. Being descended from his marriage with Fatima was definitely not as significant as it later appeared from a Twelver Shi'i view. (After Fatima's death, 'Ali had a son with a woman from the clan of the Banu Hanifa, whom many believers considered the rightful imam after Husayn's death.)

b. The Imamate Doctrine

The decisive criterion for belonging to the Twelver Shi'a is recognition of their imam succession and acknowledgment of the absolute authority of the imams for the true understanding of Islam. From the perspective of historical-critical research, the imam succession of the Twelvers is no more "logical" or justifiable than that of the other Shi'i groups. In contrast to these other factions and splinter groups, the Twelver Shi'i sect has had relatively great political success (and has survived to the present), which has afforded it the opportunity to establish its theology and jurisprudence firmly and record it in comprehensive sources. This literature presents the imam succession of the Twelvers, of course, as God-given and thus the only correct one. The Twelver Shi'a also have extensive heresiographical literature, which attempts to distinguish the background and doctrine of their own community from that of the other groups that also view themselves as Shi'a. Table 1 lists the imam succession of the Twelvers.

According to Twelver Shi'a doctrine, the twelfth imam has not died but continues to live in hiding through a divine miracle. He in particular but the other imams as well have a number of honorary epithets. Pious Shi'ites follow the mention of the name of any imam with the phrase *'alaihi al-salam* (peace be upon him), a greeting that is mainly used by Sunnites in connection with mention of the name of Jesus ('Isa).

Aside from 'Ali and (for a short time and limited range) Hasan, the elder of 'Ali's two sons from his marriage with Fatima, none of the imams of Twelver Shi'a had military or political power. The imams' claims to political power continued to exist, but according to the Twelver faith, the imamate is not at all dependent on the actual exercise of power. The fact that the second imam, Hasan ibn 'Ali, ceded the caliphate (in terms of political and military power) to the first Umayyad caliph, Mu'awiya, who was and still is hated by the Shi'a, therefore cannot be interpreted—according to Twelver Shi'i doctrine—as his having abdicated the imamate. It is not least this separation of spiritual and secular power in the imamate doctrine of the Twelvers that has guaranteed the sect's flexibility and thus its ability to survive all hazards.

Table 1. The Imam Succession of the Twelver Shiʿa

Name and Epithet	Died	Place of Burial
1. ʿAli ibn Abi Talib "Amir al-muʾminin" (Commander of the Faithful)	661	Najaf, Iraq
2. al-Hasan ibn ʿAli "al-Mujtaba" (the Chosen One)	669	Medina, Hejaz
3. al-Husayn ibn ʿAli "Sayyid al-shuhadaʾ" (Lord of the Martyrs)	680	Karbala, Iraq
4. ʿAli "Zayn al-ʿAbidin" (Adornment of the Worshippers)	714	Medina
5. Muhammad "al-Baqir" (the Revealer or Splitter of Knowledge)	733	Medina
6. Jaʿfar al-Sadiq (the Truthful One)	765	Medina
7. Musa "al-Kazim" (One Who Swallows His Anger)	799	Kazimiyyah, near Baghdad, Iraq
8. ʿAli "al-Rida" (Pers. "Riza") (Pleasing [to God])	818	Tus (Mashhad), Iran
9. Muhammad "al-Jawad al-Taqi" (the Generous One, the Pious One)	835	Kazimiyyah
10. ʿAli "al-Hadi al-Naqi" (the Guide, the Pure One)	868	Samarra, Iraq
11. al-Hasan "al-Zaki al-ʿAskari" (the Pure One, Citizen of a Garrison Town)	874	Samarra
12. Muhammad "al-Mahdi al-Muntazar" (the Awaited Mahdi, the Rightly Guided One)		

The crucial function of the imams thus lies in the spiritual leadership of the community. Their supreme task is to maintain the community in a world of enemies, and even expand it under conditions of more or less intense persecution through "secular" rulers. The majority of believers are convinced that all the imams—except for the twelfth, who is still alive—died as a martyr for their faith. This is not the view of all Shiʿi theological authorities, especially with regard to the death of the sixth imam, Jaʿfar al-Sadiq, but corresponding corrective statements have done little to change the deeply rooted beliefs of the masses. The death of the grandson of the Prophet, the third imam, Husayn, in a battle against a far superior army of Umayyads near Karbala on the Euphrates in 680 plays a particularly significant role in the Twelver conception of history.[5]

The imamate doctrine of the Twelvers—apart from the speculations about the twelfth, the Mahdi—was essentially already developed at the time of Jaʿfar al-Sadiq (d. 765). This doctrine is based on the belief that the Islamic community always needs an infallible leader inspired by God to keep adherents from going astray. God's quality of goodness implies that that this leader exists at all times. After the Prophet Muhammad, the imams are these leaders. God gave them theological and moral infallibility (*ʿisma*). They differ from Muhammad—who according to the general Islamic view was the final "seal" of the prophets—essentially only in that they received no revelations. But they have full knowledge of the Jewish and Christian books of revelation and are the only ones aside from the Prophet Muhammad who possess absolute authoritative knowledge of the Qurʾan, in both the external and the esoteric meanings of the text. Their knowledge of the visible and hidden things (including the past and the future) corresponds to that of the Prophet. Each obtains this special knowledge from his respective predecessor in the final moments of his life. The succession as a rule goes from the father to one of his sons (not necessarily the eldest); the succession from Hasan to his younger brother Husayn is the only deviation from this rule. There can be only one imam at any particular point in time: during the lifetime of the predecessor, the next imam (whom God has long since determined) is "silent." It is possible for the imam to assume his position even as a minor, as demonstrated by the ninth imam, Muhammad al-Jawad, who was only seven years old when his father died.

This important decision that was made with regard to Muhammad al-Jawad proved to set a promising precedent when in 874 the eleventh imam, Hasan al-ʿAskari, died in the residential and garrison town of Samarra in Iraq as a quasi-prisoner of the Abbasid caliph al-Muʿtamid. Shiʿi sources concede that a majority of the community did not know of any son of the eleventh imam, much less that this son was designated to be the successor to the imamate. Amid the confusion of the community—a confusion that led to numerous splinter groups with respect to the question of Hasan al-ʿAskari's successor—one group finally asserted the claim that an underage son named Muhammad existed.[6] They said that the eleventh imam kept his existence hidden even from most of his own followers in order to protect him from persecution by the Abbasids. Still a boy at the time, he was translated by God into a mysterious occult state (*ghayba*) in the year his father died. From 874 to 941 the twelfth imam was supposedly in contact with the community through four emissaries. But since then even this indirect contact had been cut off, although the twelfth imam had allegedly been seen from time to time by certain people and appeared in dreams to many pious men and women, and was said to have been in Mecca during the annual pilgrimage. In the nineteenth century some individuals in Iran claimed to be authorized messengers from the imam, but none of them succeeded in being acknowledged generally.

The Twelver Shiʿa have focused on the twelfth and final imam with respect to their chiliastic ideas of a messiah and eschatological ruler or Mahdi. According to these views, which were already well developed in Islam in the ninth century, the Mahdi will appear one day and break the rule of the usurpers and tyrants, establishing a kingdom of justice. The twelfth imam is the messiah, the rightly guided and rightly guiding one, the ruler of time. Anticipation of this Mahdi has had significant consequences for the political actions of the Twelver Shi'a, in the subsequent period and right up to the present day.

c. Hadith and Theology

The central status of the imams in the historical view of the Twelver Shi'a corresponds to the authority of their reports (*akhbar*) for the religious doctrine of their community. They are viewed (contrary to the evidence of the companions of the Prophet who opposed 'Ali and of later, non-Shi'i tradition) as certification of the authenticity of what the Shi'a recognize as the hadith of the Prophet or its binding commentary. The imam hadith is the historical continuation of the Prophet hadith. It presents a source of religious insight—especially for the deeper understanding of the Qur'an according to the Shi'i faith—that is not accessible to the Sunnites. This hadith corresponds to the Shi'i judgment of the conduct of most of the companions of the Prophet. In contrast to it, the consensus (*ijma'*) of the early Islamic community, which for Sunnites is so important in deciding all matters, thus receded far into the background.

Distinctions are made, theoretically, between the Prophet hadith and the imam hadith, and it is true (also theoretically) that to the Prophet hadith is attributed greater authority. Within individual subject areas for which they serve as evidence, however, the two kinds of hadith are not listed separately in the canonical hadith collections of the Twelver Shi'a. Most theological discourse on Twelver Shi'a doctrine treats the two types of hadith as having de facto equal ranking.

Like the Sunna, the Twelver Shi'a also assume that Prophet hadiths were falsified or fabricated in the early Islamic dispute between the different factions. But while the Sunnites view this as a practice especially of the Shi'a, Twelver Shi'ites believe that this falsification was promulgated largely by their adversaries, namely, the companions of the Prophet who opposed 'Ali and later by the Umayyads and their (alleged) mercenary writers such as Abu Hurayra (d. ca. 678). As with the Sunna, the Shi'a have also developed a "critical" study of hadiths with the aim of compiling hadiths of the Prophet that support their own doctrine and attempting to substantiate them with imam hadiths. This hadith research was the main outcome of the phase immediately following the period in which the community was led directly by the imams. The fact that a dynasty of Shi'i rulers of Iranian descent, the Buyids, actually ruled the Abbasid Empire from 945 to 1055 (without eliminating the Sunni caliphate) created favorable external conditions for the activities of a series of scholars who even today are considered in a sense the "Church Fathers" of Twelver Shi'i Islam. In addition to the writers of what is referred to as the "four fundamental works," this includes Shaykh Mufid (d. 1022), al-Sharif al-Radi (d. 1015), and his brother al-Murtada (d. 1044).

The Twelver Shiʿa correlative to the Sunna's six canonical hadith collections is their "four fundamental works" (*al-usul al-arbaʿa*). These are:

1. *Al-Kafi fi ʿilm al-din* by Kulayni (or Kulini; d. 940)
2. *Man la yahduruhu al-faqih* by Muhammad ibn Babuyah al-Qummi, called al-Saduq (d. 991)
3. *Tahdhib al-ahkam* by Muhammad al-Tusi, referred to as Shaykh al-Taʾifa (d. 1067/68)
4. *Al-Istibsar* by the same author

Nahj al-balagha (Peak of Eloquence), a collection of sermons, prayers, proverbs, and the like attributed to the first imam, ʿAli ibn Abi Talib, has special significance among Shiʿi (imam) hadith literature. This work, which is esteemed also in the Sunni sphere not least for its literary brilliance, was compiled in the tenth century by al-Sharif al-Radi. Quotations from *Nahj al-balagha* can still be found today in the literature of the Islamic peoples. Similarly, numerous pieces from *Sahifa sajjadiyya,* a collection of prayers attributed to the fourth imam, ʿAli Zayn al-ʿAbidin (with the epithet "al-Sajjad," roughly "the Prostrating One"), have made their way into many Sunni prayer books.

After the Buyid dynasty, during the period of Sunni restoration under the Seljuq sultans, the religious studies of the Twelver Shiʿa continued to develop. Among the great achievements of this epoch are the Qurʾan commentary by Tabarsi (d. 1153?) and the *Tajrid* by Nasir al-Din Tusi (d. 1273), which marked the beginning of the dogmatics of the Twelver Shiʿa.

In the fourteenth and fifteenth centuries there was, on the one hand, a merging of Shiʿi theology and the virtually pantheistic mysticism of the Sunni Muhyi al-Din ibn al-ʿArabi (d. 1240)—especially in the works of Haydar al-Amuli (d. after 1385)—while on the other hand, jurisprudence was developed further, and Twelver Shiʿi doctrine was defended over Sunni criticism in extensive apologetic works such as *Minhaj al-karama* by ʿAllama al-Hilli (d. 1326). The harshest and most comprehensive Sunni riposte to this work was the *Minhaj al-sunna* by Ibn Taymiyya (d. 1328).

The aspects of the Twelver Shiʿa school of thought concerned with mystic gnosticism and philosophical theory, which is most pronounced in the writings of Mulla Sadra Shirazi (d. 1640), has remained vital to the present day within the milieu of the Shiʿi dervish orders in Iran.

Three very significant hadith collections were compiled in the seventeenth and eighteenth centuries, in which the material of the four fundamental works was passed down and in part supplemented with other material, reorganized, and expanded through introductions, commentaries, and the like. These works are the *Wafi* by Muhsin Fayd Kashani (d. 1680), *Wasaʾil al-shi'a* by al-Hurr al-ʿAmili (d. 1692), and *Bihar al-anwar* by Muhammad Baqir al-Majlisi (d. 1699).

The four fundamental works and these later hadith collections have influenced all of Twelver Shiʿi spiritual life continuously up to the present day. The Qurʾan commentaries rely largely on them.[7] Neither the speculative theology and philosophy of the Twelver Shiʿa nor their jurisprudence can be understood without constant reference to the historical tradition laid down in these works. It must of course be taken into account that despite all attempts to scrutinize the material critically (as Kulayni did), the voluminous hadith material in these writings contains numerous inconsistencies regarding statements by the Prophet and the imams, leading to a centuries-old dispute within Twelver Shiʿa as to how to treat these statements.

Having been influenced by Muʿtazili theology, the "Church Fathers" of the Buyid dynasty introduced rationalistic principles for assessing the Prophet hadiths and especially the imam hadiths (the so-called *akhbar*). There was controversy on this method very early on, which led to the rejection of many *akhbar* as apocryphal (and therefore unsuited, for example, as a basis for legal rulings). A traditionalist school, the Akhbariyya, opposed it, saying that reason had been made the standard by which to judge the applicability of hadiths. This school gave the *akhbar* of the imams a certain precedence over the Qurʾan and the Prophet hadiths by declaring the *akhbar* that were recognized as authentic by the "Church Fathers" to be the sole key to understanding the Qurʾan and the Prophet hadiths. The Akhbariyya rejected any further rationalistic classification and interpretation of the material in the four fundamental works.

They opposed the use of *ijtihad* with respect to the hadith. *Ijtihad* is a method of independent truth-finding based on reason wherever hadiths recognized as authentic appear to be incompatible with each other or in contradiction with statements of the Qurʾan. This is the method used by opponents of the Akhbariyya, namely, the Usuliyya or Mujtahidiyya, who finally prevailed after centuries of conflict. They of course admit that not every individual believer has the ability to apply *ijtihad,* not even everyone educated in theology. Instead they emphasize that application of a principle of independent, rational, scientific decision making in questions of hadith (and thus of Twelver Shiʿi law) requires comprehensive, intensive training. Only then can one become *mujtahid* (that is, a religious scholar authorized to apply *ijtihad*). Of course, only very few have the intellectual qualifications to achieve this status. According to Usuliyya doctrine, common believers who wish to avoid errors and worse in their religious practice and general lifestyle are obliged to obey a *mujtahid* of their choice. Followers of the Akhbariyya, by contrast, counter this view by saying that all believers who are familiar with the tradition of the imams are in a position to satisfy their religious duties without further education or constant guidance. And anyone who does not feel capable of resolving an apparent contradiction between two hadiths should refrain from making a decision. They say that both applying *ijtihad* on one's own and following (*taqlid*) a *mujtahid* are forbidden.

Through the work of some outstanding theologians in the seventeenth and eighteenth centuries, the Akhbariyya gained ground vis-à-vis the Usuliyya, which had predominated up to then. Its influence diminished starting in the late eighteenth century, however, and today only remnant communities still exist (especially in the area of Khorramshahr-Abadan and in Bahrain).

The victory of the Usuliyya fostered the formation of a religious establishment composed of *mujtahids* within Twelver Shi'a, for which the term "clergy" is definitely appropriate. But the distinctions among the different levels of clergy in the hierarchy are not clear-cut, in contrast to the situation, for example, in the Roman Catholic Church. For most simple theologians (at least in Iran) the term *mulla* or *akhund* is common today. Among *mujtahids,* who are often given an honorary title such as *hujjat al-islam* (authority [for the doctrine] of Islam), some acquire another, higher title, namely, that of an *ayatullah* ([miraculous] sign of God). The highest *mujtahid,* called the *marjaʿ al-taqlid* (highest theological authority providing orientation for believers), is accordingly also called *al-ayatullah al-ʿuzma* (lit.: greatest of the ([miraculous] signs of God). When a *marjaʿ*—such as Khomeini—is also referred to as "imam," this has nothing to do with putting him on a par with the twelve imams. The word *imam* (lit.: prayer leader) in this context means roughly "highest (political and) religious leader." As such, the *marjaʿ al-taqlid* is only a "deputy" of the (twelfth, hidden) imam (*naʾib al-imam*).

Titles such as *ayatullah* or *marjaʿ al-taqlid* are not formally granted. In fact, they cannot be granted, since there is no institution that could do that. These are instead honorary titles that are offered to a *mujtahid* from the community of believers and somehow accepted by other *mujtahids,* if he (through numerous writings, successful training of many students, exemplary lifestyle, or the like) has achieved an outstanding reputation. Many *ayatullahs* are sayyids, that is, they come from families that pride themselves on being descendants of the Prophet Muhammad (and thus are closely related to the imams).

d. Orthodoxy and Popular Faith

The *mujtahids* naturally see themselves as preservers of the Twelver Shiʿi orthodoxy. They stand in opposition to numerous forms of popular faith. In their efforts to draw as many believers as possible to their side, however, *mujtahids* are often prepared not merely to refrain from criticizing unorthodox ideas and practices but even to justify them. In doing this they are motivated in part by their rivalry with other *mujtahids* for power and influence.

Through popular Twelver Shiʿi literature for purposes of entertainment and edification, the legends in the classical hadith collections and Qurʾan commentaries about the pre-Islamic prophets and Muhammad and the imams have become widely known and elaborated upon. According to that popular tradition the martyr's death of the imams was already proclaimed to Adam, Noah, Moses, and Jesus, and they used moving words to express their infinite sadness about this future event—especially the struggle and death of Husayn ibn ʿAli at Karbala.

In Twelver Shiʿi popular faith and in the corresponding writings, the worshipping of Fatima plays a role that is in some ways suggestive of Mary worship in the Catholic realm. Fatima is often compared with Maryam (Mary), the mother of Jesus. She also plays an essential role in the passion plays during the month of Muhammad, in which the history of the suffering of the imams (here again, especially the events at Karbala) and the other martyrs of the Shiʿa are dramatically presented.

These passion plays contain numerous legends and fantastic elaborations, and even totally invented hadiths.[8] Many orthodox Twelver Shiʿi theologians judge the passion plays and the processions that precede them with skepticism or even outright rejection. But they have not been able (and have not made any definitive attempt) to prohibit these plays or revise them in the sense of orthodox doctrine. The same applies to their ambivalent attitude regarding the self-flagellation and self-inflicted injuries with chains and swords (as a sign of mourning for the martyred imams), which for centuries have been a firmly established part of the Muharram celebrations.[9]

The religious excitement of hundreds of thousands of devout Shiʿites in the annual mourning events of Muharram (*taʿziya*) has proved to be an extremely effective means of spreading or sustaining Shiʿi ideas among the masses and mobilizing these people against alleged or actual enemies of Shiʿi Islam. The Iranian Revolution of 1978–79 proved to be an impressive example. To be sure, arousing the pious can also lead to incidents that are not desirable for the ʿulamaʾ (and the respective government) anywhere that *taʿziya* events take place in the proximity of Sunnites. In India and Pakistan, for example, interdenominational conflicts continue to occur at times whenever Sunnites feel provoked by the (sometimes only presumed) cursing of companions of the Prophet which becomes especially loud here and there in the Muharram processions.

In Twelver Shiʿi doctrine the only true believers are those who know and accept the imam of their time (since 874, that is, the twelfth, hidden imam). The imams can intercede with God on behalf of the members of their community. Visiting their graves is a meritorious deed that brings blessings. Rejection of the grave-worshipping cult (and even destruction of mausoleum domes), which under the influence of the Salafiyya movement has gained followers in vast regions of the Sunni world, is untenable for the Twelver Shiʿa. Destruction of the domes atop the graves of the imams in Medina by the Wahhabis (starting in 1804 and again in 1926) has not been forgotten to this day in the Shiʿi world and continues to give Shiʿi dignitaries occasion to request at least partial restoration from the Saudi Arabian government. A visit (*ziyara*) to the graves of the imams (such as that of ʿAli al-Rida (Persian: Reza) in Mashhad, the only imam of the Twelvers who was buried on Iranian soil) does not relieve believers of their duty in orthodox Twelver Shiʿa to make a pilgrimage (hajj) to Mecca, but in the consciousness of popular piety it is considered to be at least comparable. The graves of the countless descendants of the imams (Persian: *imam-zadah*) are the objects of worship. In Iran this applies largely to the grave of Fatima, sister of the eighth imam, ʿAli al-Reza, called Hazrat-i Maʿsuma (roughly "the Sinless One"), in Qom (an early Shiʿa center in Iran), Hazrat-i ʿAbd al-ʿAzim near Tehran, Shah Chiragh in Shiras, and Shah Niʿmatullah Wali near Kerman.

Most Shiʿi pilgrims to Mecca end their pilgrimage with a visit to the Baqiʿ al-Gharqad cemetery in Medina, in order to visit the graves of the four imams and other members of the house of the Prophet buried there. The pilgrims from Iran especially try to include a *ziyara* to the graves of the imams in Iraq either before or after the pilgrimage. Significant pilgrimage sites have emerged around the shrines of the imams buried there. Karbala and Najaf in particular are surrounded by extensive cemeteries because for centuries the bodies of pious Shiʿites who wanted to be interred near ʿAli and Husayn have been brought there for burial. Furthermore, it often happens that Shiʿites settle near a pilgrimage site when they are old in order to spend the last years of their life in the "neighborhood" (*mujawara*) of an imam and to be buried there. Najaf and Karbala especially are also considered centers of theological scholarship, where students and scholars gather from throughout the Shiʿi world.

For centuries most leading theologians at the Shiʿi pilgrimage sites in Iraq (so-called *ʿatabat*) were Iranians or closely related to the renowned scholar families of Iran. This dominance of Iranians, which has only recently declined in Iraq for political reasons, is historically connected to the fact that the Twelver Shiʿa sect of Islam (as well as other Shiʿa groups) found followers in Iran very early on. On top of that, in Iran—as in no other Islamic country—Twelver Shiʿa has officially been the ruling denomination (since the early sixteenth century). Nevertheless, the widespread view in popular Western and Sunni Muslim depictions that Twelver Shiʿa is something like the Iranian variant of Islam is a distortion of the facts. Shiʿi Islam emerged in the seventh century in the Arab environment of the Hejaz and Iraq. Into the sixteenth century the Shiʿi groups in Iran were a minority among the Sunna. The historical turning point favoring the Shiʿa came with the victory of the tribes of Turkish descent, which had followed the leader of an extreme Shiʿi order. The tenets of faith of this order, the Safawiyya, conflicted on essential points with those of Twelver Shiʿa orthodoxy. This pertains especially to the idea propagated in the Safawiyya of the divine nature of the leader of the order. In 1501, after the conquest of Tabriz and the accession of Ismaʿil, the leader of the order, to the throne as the shah of Iran, he declared the Twelver Shiʿa to be the official ruling denomination in the country. Subsequently the Safavid dynasty, which developed from the leadership of the Safawiyya, knew how to tame or eliminate the fanatic, extreme Shiʿi tribes to whom they owed their victory. To legitimize their actions, the Safavids relied on orthodox Twelver Shiʿa scholars whom they had called upon to come to the country from Arab centers of the Twelvers, especially from Lebanon and Bahrain. Thus, even after 1500, theologians of Arab descent (particularly from the Jabal ʿAmil in southern Lebanon and from Bahrain) helped shape the development of Twelver Shiʿi doctrine in Iran. Over centuries a kind of Twelver Shiʿi intellectual aristocracy emerged, often through marriage, from a number of Arab-Iranian theologian families. They have considerable religious and political influence on their communities in Iran, Iraq, and Lebanon. The Sadr family, for example, originally came from southern Lebanon. In the twentieth century it played, and still plays, a role in these three countries.[10]

The "Iranian heritage" in Twelver Shiʿa—predominantly in Iran, but to some extent also indirectly in the Arab world—can best be observed in popular ideas and customs, as well as in the way ritual duties are carried out. It might be correct to claim that the extreme circumspection shown by pious Twelver Shiʿites in everyday life with respect to the rituals of purity prescribed in Islam has something to do with the corresponding Zoroastrian teachings. Many rulers of Iran in the Islamic period, and up to the present day, have drawn remarkable ties between Old Iranian and Islamic-Shiʿi ways of portraying themselves and in their historical legitimation, in their names, titles, and their court ceremony, but only to a limited extent does this involve the doctrine and self-image of the Twelver Shiʿa.

e. The Twelvers, the Mahdi, and Secular Power

> Lying with their foreheads on the sacred ground of the graves that are places of mercy; crying, constantly carrying the death of their masters on their bodies; disguising their convictions in the face of persecution; paying keen attention to the emotions of the soul left dissatisfied by official Islam and exploiting the propaganda that treads lightly but is as artful as it is untiring; working at princely courts with refined, crafty diplomacy; bringing a martyr's death to foreign "heretics" in their zeal for their own martyrs; steering brutal forces toward their aims in the war camps of world conquerors—that is the Shiʿa.[11]

In its idea of the twelfth imam as the awaited messiah and Mahdi, Twelver Shiʿa is very closely tied to the doctrine which holds that until he returns from occultation, all political rule—even that of a ruler committed to Twelver Shiʿa—can be legitimate only to a certain degree.[12] The attitude of the believers toward that kind of rule depends on whether and to what extent it respects the principles of (Twelver Shiʿi) Islam. Whether or not this is the case is decided—at least theoretically—by Shiʿi scholars. To that extent they have an authority that carries directly into the political sphere. The notion of concrete guardianship by the highest *mujtahids,* however, developed only gradually and was never free of controversy even among theologians (there was always a quietist, even "royalist" faction). Not until the twentieth century did it lead to clear-cut demands with respect to control functions of the most qualified legal scholars. Up to now the most extreme form of this idea has been described in the doctrine of Khomeini as the direct exercise of power by the best-qualified legal scholars (Pers. *wilayat-i faqih*) as deputies for the twelfth imam, the Mahdi. This institution was also incorporated into the 1979 constitution of the Islamic Republic, but it has meanwhile also been criticized by some Shi'i theologians with respect to the interpretation by Khomeini and his followers.

Khomeini tried to derive his doctrine from the tradition of the Shi'i concept of the state. In the writings of the "Church Fathers" of the tenth and eleventh centuries, however, this doctrine had not yet been formulated. Instead they had to draw their conclusion from the fact that all imams starting with the fourth—in particular Ja'far al-Sadiq, the sixth—had adopted a quietist position. Since the return of the twelfth imam was long in arriving, the community had to come to terms with the persisting reality of illegitimate rule. Their legal scholars thus had to decide to what extent a Twelver Shi'ite could be allowed to serve a ruler—whether Sunni or Shi'i—who was illegitimate (in view of the absence of the twelfth imam). A distinction had to be made between an illegitimate but just ruler and an illegitimate and at the same time unjust ruler. The scholars' response must be viewed within the context of the concrete historical situation in which it was formulated: it ranged from strict rejection of any cooperation whatsoever to the decision that Twelver Shi'a could serve even an unjust illegitimate ruler if this were beneficial in safeguarding or strengthening the Twelver Shi'a community as a whole. Under certain conditions this service could even be obligatory.

In fact Twelver Shi'ites have assumed high governmental positions not only under rulers of their own denomination but also under Sunnites. Within this context it proved advantageous that the scholars of Twelver Shi'a developed a specific doctrine of permission to conceal their own convictions consciously (*taqiyya* or *kitman*). *Taqiyya* is permitted, and urgently necessary, to maintain one's personal safety in a hostile environment or to protect the Twelver Shi'a community and its interests.

Khomeini tried to repress the trend toward quietism. He assumed that the occultation of the twelfth imam could not mean that the laws of Islam would not apply until he returned. He felt that the present-day Islamic world was characterized precisely by the far-reaching repression of the shari'a. In this situation he viewed revolution as a duty. The goal of this revolution had to be to establish a true Islamic order as it had existed during the reign of the imam 'Ali (656–661). In Khomeini's view, the government of this Islamic state would have to be controlled by a recognized, just legal scholar (*faqih*) or a council of such scholars. With respect to their *function* of exercising government authority and as masters of jurisprudence, according to Khomeini, these scholars do not differ fundamentally from prophets or the imams. In *this* quality they are their successors and heirs.

Khomeini substantiated his arguments with a very broad interpretation of sura 4:60 and a statement by Imam Jaʿfar al-Sadiq. According to these sources, it is clearly forbidden for believers to turn to idols (*taghut*) in deciding their controversial affairs. This includes any representative of the illegitimate state authority, as Jaʿfar al-Sadiq is supposed to have said regarding a specific case. Khomeini clearly identified regimes such as that of the Shah with *taghut,* thereby declaring obedience to this or any similar regime to be a kind of idolatry.[13]

With this interpretation, and at the same time attempting to limit the legitimate sphere of application of *taqiyya,* Khomeini helped a militant fundamentalism achieve a breakthrough unprecedented up to that time in Twelver Shiʿa. Its long-term impact in both Shiʿi and non-Shiʿi spheres cannot yet be assessed conclusively.[14]

The Shiʿi fundamentalism represented by Khomeini is also characterized by a conspicuous (at least verbal) commitment to the socially oppressed. It shares this commitment with Shiʿi modernism, which has been influenced by intellectuals educated in the West. Large portions of the "left wing" of the Islamic revolutionary movement in Iran and corresponding Twelver Shiʿa movements in Iraq, Lebanon, and elsewhere have declared their support for this Shiʿi fundamentalism. One of the ideological cult figures of this faction was ʿAli Shariʿati, an Iranian religious sociologist who died in England in 1977. His writings often refer to Abu Dharr al-Ghifari, a companion of the Prophet and follower of ʿAli, as a pioneer of an independent, authentic (Shiʿi) Islamic socialism.[15]

The discrepancy between Khomeini's understanding of Islam and of the Shiʿa, on the one hand, and Shariʿati's, on the other, is obvious. In the fervor of the revolution it was at times repressed. The resulting contrasts in practical political questions have meanwhile come to the surface (see the chapter on Iran by Udo Steinbach in this volume).

2. The Zaydis

Virtually all adherents of the Zaydiyya live in northern Yemen. Until its unification with South Yemen they constituted about 50 percent of the population of the Arab Republic of (North) Yemen. From 897 to 1962 they ran a religious state in this country under the rule of imams. The Zaydi reign that was established in the region south of the Caspian Sea in 864 ended in 1126.

The history of the Zaydi imamate in Yemen begins with Yahya ibn al-Husayn, the leader of a small Zaydi community in Medina who settled in Saʿda (North Yemen) in 897. Under the epithet "al-Hadi" he set up an independent imamate and started to spread the Zaydi sect among the tribes. Since then the Zaydiyya has had a definitive influence on the political history of Yemen, although Sunni dynasties ruled over great portions of the country into the sixteenth century. After that, the imams were forced (for a time) to accept the supremacy of the Ottomans. Until the revolution in 1962, non-Zaydis in the direct sphere of influence of the imams were rarely able to assume higher-level political and administrative positions. Admittedly, the loyalty that Zaydi tribes showed the imams had to be coerced again and again. The actual power of the imams was often enough limited to a tight radius around their residences.

The Zaydiyya traces back to Zayd ibn 'Ali, a great-grandson of 'Ali ibn Abi Talib and son of the fourth imam, 'Ali Zayn al-'Abidin. Zayd fell in 739–40 in Kufa (Iraq) during an uprising against the Umayyads. He was the author of theological writings, but the Zaydi doctrine named after him was first distinguished from that of other Shi'i factions and made into a system in and of itself by later leaders of the movement, especially al-Qasim ibn Ibrahim (d. 860). The faction within the Zaydiyya that was founded by al-Qasim is the only one that still exists today, namely, in Yemen. The discussion that follows deals only with this faction and not with the other early Zaydi groups and their doctrine.

Of all the Shi'i communities that continue to exist today, it is the Zaydiyya that has most common ground with the Sunna. Its imamate doctrine and its jurisprudence (*fiqh*) differ greatly from that of the Twelver Shi'a and even more so from that of the Seveners and the *ghulat*. According to Zaydi doctrine, a candidate for the position of imam needs to satisfy a number of important qualifications.

He must be part of the *ahl al-bayt,* though it is irrelevant if his descendants trace back to Hasan or Husayn ibn 'Ali. (The imams of Yemen were mostly Hasanids.) A strict hereditary succession is rejected. The decisive criterion is the ability and readiness of the imam to fight for and defend his rule with force. For this reason, in contrast to the doctrine of the Twelvers, a child cannot hold an imamate. Also, the Zaydiyya adopted neither the doctrine of a messiah imam and eschatological ruler (*mahdi*) nor that of his temporary occultation (*ghayba*) and anticipated later return.

The series of Zaydi imams was not interrupted, but has continued to the present day. On the one hand, Zaydi political law concedes that there can be a time without a recognized, de facto ruling imam—an important stipulation in view of the situation in Yemen since 1962. On the other hand, according to Zaydi doctrine there can be several imams appearing at the same time. The ousting of one imam by a counter-imam is accepted, but a deposed imam can regain his position if he succeeds in turn in ousting the rival or rivals.

It was therefore impossible for a firm dynastic tradition to develop, and consequently there has not been a continuous succession of imams. In accordance with the idea of an imam who actively fights under all circumstances, *taqiyya* is rejected. Instead the imam and all Zaydis have the duty, always and openly, to "enjoin the right and forbid the wrong" ("al-amr bi-l-ma'ruf wa-l-nahy 'an al-munkar," sura 9:71). Furthermore, Zaydi imams are required to be very knowledgeable about theology and to have a literary education. As a result, numerous theological treatments and literary works (including poetry) by Zaydi rulers in Yemen have been passed down.

Deficient military prowess, violation of religious and moral standards, commission of crimes, grave gaps in knowledge that are brought to light, and the like can lead to the deposition of an imam. It is obvious that among the Zaydis the office of the imamate is a simple divine right but does not have an unchangeable character.[16] If it should happen that an imam satisfies his two main duties to very different degrees, his recognition as a full imam can be denied or revoked, that is, he can be considered only a "war imam" or a "knowledge imam." Below the status of imam there are other Zaydi authorities, such as the *da'i,* who can assert a claim to the imamate and must then fight for recognition.

As could be expected from such a matter-of-fact, practical political imamate doctrine, faith in the imams' ability to perform miracles does not play any essential role for the Zaydis. Mysticism and mystical orders are largely rejected, although the ascetic trait of Sufism did attract some Zaydis. With regard to law, the Zaydiyya do not offer a clear-cut picture. They support the claim of their scholars (of course including, first and foremost, the imams) to use *ijtihad.* The decisions of individual teachers of law are sometimes closer to the views of Sunni authorities than to those of other Zaydis. This has contributed to the fact that in present-day Yemen, many Zaydi and Sunni (Shafi'i) believers are willing to pray in the same mosque behind a single prayer leader.

The Zaydi picture of early Islamic history is not characterized by the degree of irreconcilability that we find with the Twelvers. Although Zaydis insist that 'Ali was the most worthy candidate for the imamate, they do not refer to the first three caliphs as usurpers. Of course in certain situations, such as when mobilizing the Zaydi tribes against foreign Sunnites, Zaydi imams did not balk at designating the latter as nonbelievers and calling for jihad against them. This was also the case in battles against the Ottomans (1872–1914) and agitation of the "royalists" in the civil war from 1962 to 1967 (or 1970) against the Egyptians. Such calls for jihad were, in principle, not directed against the native Sunnites, provided they did not support the foreigners.

Even today the Alids (descendants of 'Ali) play a leading role in public life. They make up the influential social stratum of the Sayyids (*sada*). Zaydi scholars cultivate their works in sayyid circles, and at the same time, many sayyids are judges and hold important administrative positions. The stratum of the Zaydi *sada* in Yemen consists of roughly sixty clans. They can all potentially lay claim to the imamate. In recent history, however, only three of them have brought forth or asserted imams (apart from one counter-imam from the Wazir family in 1948), namely, the Daylami, Sharaf al-Din, and Hamid al-Din families. The imams of the twentieth century came from the last-named family: Mansur (r. 1890–1904), Yahya (r. 1904–1948, after

1926 with the additional title of king), Ahmad (r. 1948–1962), and Badr (reigned for only a few days in September 1962).

The republic that was established as the form of state in 1962 is incompatible with the traditional approach of the Zaydi imamate.[17] Nevertheless, tribal rivalries and other factors led some Zaydi tribes to support at least temporarily the republican central government, made up primarily of Shafi'is, in the civil war (1962–1970).[18] This certainly has nothing to do with recognizing the legitimacy of the republican leaders in a *religious* sense. The same is true for the situation since 1970, but at least there we find rudiments for a reform of Zaydi politics in the sense of accepting certain principles of a republic.[19]

After the unification of North and South Yemen in 1990, however, the question of reestablishing a Zaydi imamate has been pushed even further into the background. In the future it would be asserted as at most, if at all, a religious, political authority for the Zaydi minority in Yemen, not as the position of a ruler for the entire country. It is also by no means certain that this imamate would again fall into the hands of the Hamid al-Din family, and, with regard to the Zaydi community, it is completely out of the question that it could use the archaic, absolutist methods of the imams Yahya and Ahmad.

Translated by Allison Brown

IV

REVIVALIST MOVEMENTS IN ISLAM FROM THE EIGHTEENTH TO THE TWENTIETH CENTURY AND THE ROLE OF ISLAM IN MODERN HISTORY

Anticolonialism and Nationalism

(Rudolph Peters)

1. Revivalist Movements from the Eighteenth to the Mid-Nineteenth Century

One characteristic common to most revealed religions is that reform is usually depicted as the return to roots and origins, that is, to a pure form of the religion based on the revealed texts and the doctrines of the respective founders. The Christian Reformation of the sixteenth and seventeenth centuries is only one example of this phenomenon. There has been no major movement within Islam comparable to the Reformation. Nevertheless, over the course of Islamic history there have frequently been spiritual currents claiming to represent an original and pure Islam against the prevailing "depraved" form of the religion, and these currents have often had close ties to political movements. For reasons that have yet to be fully explained, the eighteenth and nineteenth centuries were particularly fruitful ground in this regard. During this period a number of reform thinkers attempted to revive Islam, and several of them established religious-political movements in the process. These figures are important insofar as many of their ideas inspired the Islamic modernism that arose in the second half of the nineteenth century.

Such religious strivings and movements are usually classified as "fundamentalism." This is not incorrect as long as we bear in mind that there is an enormous difference between Islamic and Christian fundamentalism. As the central elements of Christian fundamentalism are strict scripturalism and the rejection of biblical criticism, most Muslims can be called fundamentalist in this sense.

Islamic fundamentalism, however, means more than this. It designates intellectual currents and strivings that conceive of God in more transcendental than immanent terms, that attribute enormous significance to the unity of Islam and condemn its (contemporary) plurality, that are concerned with the authenticity of Islam and resist external influences, and finally that regard all believers as equal before God and are thus averse to hierarchies.

As with other monotheistic religions, a tension exists in Islam between those who emphasize the otherness of God and his existence separate from creation and those who insist that creation is a part of God himself and that God manifests himself everywhere. The first tendency is evident in the scripturalist-influenced understanding of Islam by scholars (Arab. *'alim*, pl. *'ulama'*). If God is separate from creation, then humans can attain knowledge of God and his commandments only through the divine revelation received by Muhammad, that is, through the Qur'an and the sunna, as the latter has been passed on in the hadith (Arab. *hadith*), whereby it is regarded as mediated revelation. In contrast, most mystics believe that God resides in his creation and that it is possible to have contact with him directly through mystical experience.

Since its establishment in the seventh century, Islam has spread over an enormous territory. Regional influences on Islam in the form of local customs and traditions have been so powerful that we can speak of an Indonesian, an African, and a Turkish Islam with their respective characteristics. Apart from these territorial distinctions, however, differences in doctrine also exist. There are Sunnites and there are Shi'ites; Sunnites have four different legal schools (Arab. *madhahib*, sing. *madhhab*) as well as different orders within the mystical tendency. The fundamentalists strive to overcome these distinctions and divisions and to unite all Muslims in a single faith, in a single doctrine and religious practice. This can occur, however, only if the authentic tradition of Islam (Arab. *sunna*) is retained and foreign influences (Arab. *bid'a*) are rejected.

Together with the notion of the equality of all believers, these are the basic characteristics of fundamentalist thought. This does not mean, though, that all fundamentalists have a completely identical approach. Classifying the ideas of an author or a school of thought as fundamentalist is not an absolute judgment but a conditional one. By this I mean that Islamic fundamentalism is not a precisely determined and clearly delineated standpoint but rather a counter-position in relation to the ideas of other thinkers. When we designate the authors and movements examined in this section as fundamentalist, this does not mean that they all professed the same doctrine. As will become apparent, a great diversity of ideas existed. What these authors do share is the fact that they would rank higher on a "fundamentalist evaluation scale" than most of the other contemporary thinkers within the Islamic mainstream.

There are a number of quite specific doctrines encountered in most fundamentalist writings, and these are derived from the basic problems that characterize fundamentalism. The first and, with regard to later developments, crucial doctrine is that appropriately qualified scholars are allowed to interpret the Qur'an and the hadith independently (*ijtihad*) and are not obligated to adhere exclusively to the views of one legal school. In contrast to this, according to the doctrine that gradually prevailed in Islam beginning in the tenth century, everyone, regardless of how well educated he might be, was required to follow the doctrines of earlier scholars in his legal school (Arab. *taqlid,* to imitate).

This first doctrine (*ijtihad*) is in fact closely related to all of the basic characteristics of fundamentalism. The connection between *ijtihad* and authenticity is quite obvious. For fundamentalists, *ijtihad* means turning directly to the sources of Islam in order to ascertain God's commandments as reliably as possible, that is, as they have been revealed by the Prophet Muhammad. In contrast, the obligatory observance of the doctrine of *one* legal school introduces an element of intellectual comprehension, which can be mistaken. For believers, this represents an obstacle in their striving to identify the authentic precepts, the knowledge of which can be obtained only through the mediation of the Prophet. Furthermore, these legal schools arose only in the third century of Islam and were thus not part of the pure Islam of the first generation of Muslims. They also continue to be one of the reasons for discord among Muslims because they all follow different obligatory doctrines.

The relation between *ijtihad* and the fundamentalist's transcendental conception of God is somewhat more complicated. As we have seen, transcendence in this context means that humans can experience God's commandments only through the revelations received by the prophets. Thus prophets constitute the sole connecting link between the creator and humanity. A Muslim can be a true believer only if he follows and obeys Muhammad. Precisely because fundamentalists believe that any other path leading to God is impossible, they also strictly condemn the idea that the founders of legal schools, as saints, had direct access to divine knowledge and were therefore infallible or virtually infallible—a conception that adherents of *taqlid* have often used to justify their position.

It is frequently asserted that fundamentalists are intransigent opponents of mysticism. This, however, is incorrect. As we will see, there have been fundamentalist movements that practiced mysticism—or, to put this differently, there have been mystical orders that had a fundamentalist doctrine. Nevertheless, it is correct that in general, fundamentalists have taken a firm stance against what they regarded as the excesses of mystical teachings and practices, without, however, condemning mysticism itself.

An important object of their attacks was the doctrine of the oneness of existence (Arab. *wahdat al-wujud*), which had been initially formulated by Ibn al-ʿArabi (d. 1240) and was very popular in mystical circles. This doctrine stated that nothing exists except God and that as a consequence the entire universe—including humans—was consubstantial with God. Such a conception could lead to polytheistic ideas and contradicted the fundamentalists' conception of divine transcendence. What fundamentalists regarded as even more important, however, was the fact that precisely this doctrine was used as a justification for unlawful endeavors (that is, those violating the shariʿa). It was argued that if the ultimate aim of the mystical way had actually been attained and a person was now one with God, that person would no longer be obligated to follow religious laws that were binding only for common mortals.

Further objects of critique were those rituals and practices by mystical orders that fundamentalists believed contradicted the sunna. These included ecstatic rituals such as dancing in combination with music (which many Muslims believe to be forbidden) as well as practices such as devouring living snakes and burning coals or piercing the body with knives and other sharp objects.

The veneration of saints is also a part of mysticism. The founders and important shaykhs (Arab. sing. *shaykh*) of most orders are regarded by many Muslims as saints (Arab. sing. *wali*); that is, it is believed that because of their piousness, God gave them the power to perform miracles as a way of honoring them. Furthermore, it is widely held that believers could request that these holy men act as mediators with God. This belief was accompanied by rituals such as visiting graves, burning candles, and other pious acts. Fundamentalists usually take offense at the veneration of saints. They condemn the rituals and celebrations associated with this as contradicting the sunna. In addition, they regard this kind of veneration of saints as incompatible with their monotheistic understanding that God is the only permissible object of veneration and prayer. Since many saints are venerated only locally, fundamentalists believe that these different cults promote the continuation of divisions among Muslims and obstruct unity. Finally, most fundamentalists criticize the idea that saints are capable of acting as intermediaries to God (Arab. *tawassul,* mediation). The belief that humans, however extraordinary their talents might be, can successfully act as mediators implies that one can place such people between oneself and God, which, fundamentalists argue, is incompatible with God's transcendence and with the idea of the equality of all believers.

This latter point—the equality of all believers before God—has assumed various forms. Fundamentalist authors often emphasize precepts of moderation that can be found in the Qur'an and the sunna. These forbid male followers from using gold plates and cups or wearing gold jewelry and silk robes, and exhort them not to treat other men with exaggerated respect, for example, by kissing their hand or by addressing them with extravagant honorific titles.

The fundamentalist teachings that I have described here were not new or original to the eighteenth century. The fundamentalist tradition itself is significantly older. Most of these views can be traced back to the well-known theologian and legal scholar Ibn Taymiyya (d. 1328) and his student Ibn Qayyim al-Jawziyya (d. 1350); both were well known for their numerous treatises on a wide variety of religions issues. Later fundamentalists and even modernist authors have frequently referred to them to support positions on legal methodology (for example, the issue of *ijtihad* and *taqlid*), the condemnation of practices by certain mystical orders, the critique of the veneration of saints, and the issue of mediation.

Fundamentalism is often regarded as identical with conservatism. This is not correct. Conservatism endeavors to maintain the existing order and opposes any changes to that order. The central reason for the existence of fundamentalism is the rejection of the existing order as inconsistent with the pure and original principles of Islam. Fundamentalism seeks change, in the sense of shaping society according the example of the sunna of the Prophet. This explains why fundamentalist movements are frequently action-oriented and tied to political movements. In societies where the political and religious domains are not clearly separate, political and social opposition is usually expressed in the form of religious opposition. The call for the application of true Islamic precepts based exclusively on the Qur'an and the sunna is attractive to those who disapprove of the existing political and socioeconomic order and who would like to change that order into something better.

For this reason fundamentalists often find themselves opposed to their environment and in particular to the conservative 'ulama'. Such opposition has at times turned into armed conflict. In these cases fundamentalists have sought refuge in the teaching of jihad, or holy war, despite the fact that their opponents were nominally Muslim. In such instances opponents were declared apostates and infidels, against whom a war had to be waged to compel them to become true Muslims.

The following section focuses on four fundamentalist authors from the eighteenth century and the first half of the nineteenth. Their significance derives not only from the essential spiritual and at times political role they played in their own era but also from the influence they have exerted on contemporary Islamic thought.

Muhammad ibn 'Abd al-Wahhab (1703/4–1792)

One of the best-known fundamentalist movements—and one that is still significant today—was founded by Muhammad ibn 'Abd al-Wahhab. It is usually called the Wahhabite movement after its founder. This name, however, is rejected by the movement's followers, who call themselves *muwahhidun,* believers in the unity of God.

Muhammad ibn 'Abd al-Wahhab was born in the small provincial town of 'Uyayna in Najd, the central part of the Arabian Peninsula. After studying in Mecca, Medina, Basra, and possibly other cities of the Middle East, he settled again in Najd in 1739 and began teaching. His ideas, however, brought him into conflict with the religious establishment in Huraimala, where he now lived. He was forced to leave and return to his city of birth, 'Uyayna. There he was able to persuade 'Uthman ibn Mu'ammar, the ruler of the city, to support his ideas. Together they destroyed the domes of several sacred tombs and felled several trees that were revered by local inhabitants. Ibn Mu'ammar began to issue Qur'anic punishments for crimes, a custom that had fallen out of practice. This sudden eruption of religious enthusiasm unsettled the local population, in particular the clans of the area. They threatened to stop paying tribute and to prevent merchants from crossing their territory if Ibn Mu'ammar continued these policies. Ibn Mu'ammar ultimately relented, and Ibn 'Abd al-Wahhab was forced to leave in 1743 or 1744.

Wahhab traveled to Dir'iyya, which was also located in Najd and was ruled by the Sa'ud family. Some time later he established contact with the emir, Muhammad ibn Sa'ud, who realized that a partnership with Ibn 'Abd al-Wahhab might be advantageous. The two men entered into a formal relationship through mutual oaths in 1745. Ibn 'Abd al-Wahhab promised not to abandon the emir (Arab. *amir*), who swore in turn that he would govern in accord with the strict rules of Islamic law as interpreted by Wahhab.

One Wahhabite doctrine of crucial significance in this context was the demand that anyone who did not adhere to the strict principles of monotheism—for example, by performing certain acts of religious devotion at saints' graves—be regarded as an infidel (Arab. *kafir*), against whom war had to be waged. Because such practices were part of the popular religion and were widely performed, this meant that war could be carried out against virtually all Muslims until they had accepted the Wahhabite form of monotheism and also accepted the rule of the emir from the Sa'ud family. At the same time, Saudi warriors could believe that they had satisfied their religious obligations and would be admitted directly to paradise if they died on the battlefield.

This alliance of religious enthusiasm and the striving for worldly gain proved successful, as had been the case eleven centuries earlier. By the time Ibn 'Abd al-Wahhab died in 1792, the Sa'udi dynasty ruled over most of the Arabian Peninsula. Mecca was conquered in 1803 (and again in 1806), Medina in 1805. During these years the Sa'udi state was at the peak of its power; its armies attacked cities outside the Arabian Peninsula, including Damascus and Karbala. Saudi expansion, however, alarmed the Ottoman Empire. The Ottoman sultan (Arab. *sultan*) wanted to remove this threat but was incapable of defeating the Sa'udi armies on his own. He requested that Muhammad 'Ali, the Ottoman governor in Egypt, assume this commission. In a war that lasted seven years, Egyptian soldiers ultimately pushed back the Sa'udi forces. In 1818 they conquered the city of Dir'iyya, the capital of the Sa'udis, and destroyed it, marking the end of the first Sa'udi state. Over the course of the nineteenth century, the Sa'udis—together with the descendants of Ibn 'Abd al-Wahhab—ruled over a principality of varying size in Najd. In the 1920s they conquered the Hejaz and established the Kingdom of Saudi Arabia. The spiritual power in Saudi Arabia is still to a significant degree in the hands of the Ibn 'Abd al-Wahhab family.

At the center of the Wahhabite doctrine is the declaration of the unity of God (Arab. *tawhid*). According to Wahhabites, this term has two implications: the recognition of God's sovereignty over the universe and the awareness that God is the sole permissible object of prayer and reverence. As we have seen, Wahhabites condemn every form of popular religious behavior that they regard as incompatible with this second point and thus as a sign of polytheism (Arab. *shirk*). Central points of contention between Wahhabites and their opponents usually include whether a person—alive or dead—is capable of serving as an intermediary to God for another person; whether visiting graves (with the intention of obtaining mediation with God through the dead) is permitted; and whether this kind of conduct is identical with disbelief and polytheism.

Wahhabites insist that legal practices must follow the Qur'an and the sunna. Although they regard themselves as Hanbalites, they argue that the "gates of the *ijtihad*" are not closed. Legal scholars with sufficient prerequisites can thus continue to practice *ijtihad* and interpret the Qur'an and the hadith. This form of *ijtihad* is not completely unrestricted, however, as was the case for the founders of the different legal schools during the initial centuries of Islam. Today only a limited form of *ijtihad* is permitted— "*ijtihad* mixed with *taqlid*," as one Wahhabite scholar has called it. By this the Wahhabites mean that qualified scholars can select from the doctrines of the different legal schools those rules that best accord with the Qur'an and the sunna, and that it is not necessary for them to follow the conceptions of a particular school. In practice, though, the Wahhabites adhere to the Hanbalite *madhhab*.

There are nonetheless several Wahhabite principles that deviate from the prevailing Hanbalite doctrine and can thus be designated as specifically Wahhabite. For instance, the Wahhabites regard smoking as a punishable offense and thus place tobacco and alcoholic beverages on the same level. They believe that beard cutting and using a rosary (*subha*) contravene the sunna of the Prophet and are thus prohibited. They argue that everyone has the duty to participate in communal Friday prayers (*salat*), and reject the position that the community as a whole can be excused from this obligation if a sufficient number of people actually take part. Finally—and this has enormous political consequences—they believe that everyone who does not participate in the *salat* and pays no alms tax (*zakat*) is an infidel and can be killed for it. This contradicts the view of the majority of Muslim scholars, who argue that this is the case only if the person accused has explicitly rejected his or her obligation to participate in the *salat* and to pay the *zakat*.

Shah Wali Allah al-Dihlawi (1703–1762)

In contrast to his Arab contemporaries, the Indian Muslim scholar Shah Wali Allah never lived to see his ideas become the spiritual foundation of a political state. This may have been related to the fact that Shah Wali Allah's ideas were not as implacably severe as those of Ibn 'Abd al Wahhab. The latter emphasized the unity of God and attacked anyone who did not share this conviction; Shah Wali Allah, in contrast, moved the unity of Islam and all Muslims into the foreground and sought to reconcile opposing positions. Despite these differences, however, the two men shared a number of ideas.

These similarities in approach were not entirely coincidental. Both scholars studied in Medina at approximately the same time, and we know that they were affiliated with teachers who belonged to the same intellectual circle. Although the predominant ideas of this group have not yet been investigated in detail, it can be said that it was usually hadith scholars who addressed this issue to keep the sunna alive and that they were concerned with questions such as the unity of Islam and the unity of God.

Except for his stay in Mecca and Medina, which lasted somewhat longer than a year, Shah Wali Allah spent his entire life in northern India, the India of the Mughal emperors. The empire, which had blossomed under Sultan Aurangzeb (r. 1658–1707) and expanded territorially, had encountered difficulties after the sultan's death. Internally it suffered from dynastic confusion; externally it was threatened by Hindus such as the Marathas, who conquered a large portion of Mughal territory, as well as by incursions from neighboring Muslim rulers such as the Iranian Nader Shah.

Shah Wali Allah was well aware of the weaknesses that had befallen Indian Islam. An important part of his writings addresses this issue and can be read as an attempt to remedy the situation. At the center of his thought was the conviction that recovery could come only by adhering to the sunna, the definitive guide for human conduct. Following the example of his teachers in Medina, he dedicated much time to studying the hadith, which is apparent in most of his writings. Another indication of his search for the sources of Islam is his translation of the Qur'an into Persian, the cultural language of Indian Muslims—despite the traditional opposition to translations of the Qur'an. His aim here was to spread knowledge about the Qur'an so that non-Arab Muslims could recognize that it contained more than merely Arabic formulas that were passed on in prayer and on other occasions without any real comprehension.

The attempt to return to the original sources also meant that Shah Wali Allah rejected the prevailing doctrine that the "gates of *ijtihad*" were closed. Like Ibn ʿAbd al-Wahhab, he insisted that a limited form of *ijtihad* could still be practiced by qualified legal scholars. They should select from the positions of the different legal schools those that best complied with the Qur'an and the sunna.

Indian Islam had always had a special character. It was syncretistic to a certain degree. Many Hindu customs had assumed a superficial Islamic coloring and were also practiced by Muslims. Shah Wali Allah's enthusiasm for the purity of Islam moved him to sharply criticize these customs as polytheism. Nevertheless, he did not go so far as Ibn ʿAbd al-Wahhab, who condemned all forms of saint veneration and grave-worshipping cults.

These moderate positions certainly arose from his desire to unite all Muslims. Behind many of his stances we can recognize his zealousness in this regard. He was more interested in bringing Muslims together harmoniously than in driving them apart. Thus he declared all legal schools to be fundamentally equal. Like Abu Hamid Muhammad al-Ghazali (d. 1111), he worked assiduously to bridge the chasm between law-oriented Islam and mystical Islam. He severely criticized the unlawful orientation of many mystical orders and insisted that obedience to the precepts of Islamic law was a prerequisite for adhering to mysticism. He was himself a mystic and attempted to demonstrate the fundamental similarity in the actions and perspectives of the different orders.

Shah Wali Allah was primarily a scholar and teacher. Several of his works demonstrate his interest in politics, although he was not politically active himself except for occasional writings, in which he offered political advice to statesmen. Nevertheless, at the beginning of the nineteenth century, approximately half a century after his death, his ideas became the ideological platform for an action-oriented religious-political movement, the Tariqa-yi muhammadi. The movement was led by Saiyid Ahmad Barelwi (1786–1831) and supported by two scholars, Shah Isma'il and Shah 'Abd al-'Aziz, the former a grandson, the latter the husband of a granddaughter, of Shah Wali Allah.

This movement was a further reaction to the weakness of Indian Islam at the time. But whereas Shah Wali Allah had sought to overcome this situation from his desk, the leaders of the Tariqa-yi muhammadi were more interested in action. They traveled throughout the entire country to recruit people for their ideas and to build up an organization. In essence they propagated the ideas of Shah Wali Allah in a militant form. This was a consequence of political developments after Shah Wali Allah's death. The memory of Aurangzeb remained alive during Shah Wali Allah's lifetime, and he had been able to believe that his ideal, the purification and revival of Islam, could still occur within the Mughal Empire. By the beginning of the nineteenth century, however, the power of the Mughals had disappeared. Through treaties and conquests the British had brought all of India under their control. The Mughal Empire continued to exist as an ally of the British, but its sultans were now merely paid puppets. For this reason the leaders of the new movement had no illusions about a pure and strong Islam arising on the basis of the Mughal Empire. They strove to create a new and pure Islamic state.

Beginning around 1824 the movement attempted to implement this ideal. The location for the proposed state was the Sikh territory of northwestern India. The Sikhs ostensibly were oppressing the Muslims living there, and these Muslims were to be liberated. Following this liberation, a truly strong Islamic state was to be established, which would serve as a base for the expansion of the movement through all of India.

To prepare for this, messengers were sent throughout the entire land. They now not only preached a return to the purity of Islam through the rejection of practices such as the veneration of saints, grave-worshipping cults, and customs of Hindu origin, but also proclaimed that under certain circumstances jihad, or holy war, was the duty of all Muslims. They aggressively sought to recruit volunteers. Although it is unlikely that there actually were organizational ties between the Tariqa-yi muhammadi and the Arab Wahhabites, the similarities between the ideas of these two movements are astounding. It is thus not surprising that the British at the time designated members of the Tariqa-yi muhammadi as Wahhabites.

In 1830 the movement began to battle the Sikhs. The war did not last long. Local Muslims showed little inclination to join the fight for an Islamic state, in particular after Saiyid Ahmad Barelwi began to levy taxes on them as prescribed by Islamic law. In response, the tribes abandoned their support of the movement. As a result the Sikhs defeated the Tariqa-yi muhammadi in 1831. Saiyid Ahmad Barelwi and Shah Isma'il were killed in the battle. Although the main part of the movement was defeated, the movement itself did not cease to exist at this time. Its members continued to harass the British, who were not able to suppress the movement completely until 1883.

Muhammad ibn 'Ali al-Shawkani (1760–1832)

Yemen has been somewhat neglected in terms of cultural history. Its peripheral location, its rugged mountains, and the fact that its rulers and many of its inhabitants belonged to a smaller Shi'a sect, the Zaydiyya, have resulted in a certain isolation. Although the Turks conquered Yemen in the sixteenth century, the influence of the Sublime Porte was always weak to ineffective, particularly in the interior of the land.

The rise of the Yemeni scholar Muhammad ibn 'Ali al-Shawkani is characteristic of this isolation. He never left his homeland during his entire life, not even for a pilgrimage to Mecca. In a description of his life he reports that this was the result of excusable circumstances: his parents had not permitted him to leave his home city of Sanaa (San'a'), and he was subsequently too preoccupied with learning and teaching. After he learned everything there was to learn in Sanaa and studied with all the available teachers there, he began to read books on his own, rather unusual behavior in a culture that attached great importance to the old saying "A man without a teacher is taught by the devil."

Until the age of thirty-five Muhammad ibn 'Ali al-Shawkani led the introspective life of a scholar, devoting his time to reading, teaching, and writing. In 1795 the imam of Yemen, al-Mansur bi-llah, appointed him senior judge of Sanaa, a post he occupied until his death. The fact that he was selected for such a high position despite his unorthodox ideas was perhaps a result of the contemporary political situation. Yemenite imams followed the Zaydiyya legal school and originally ruled over primarily Zaydi territories. In the eighteenth century under the dynasty of the Qasimi imams, the central government expanded its power to the south, where the majority of the population was Shafi'i. The appointment of al-Shawkani, who did not adhere to the Zaydiyya or any of the other established legal schools but was more inclined in general toward Sunni legal doctrine, was probably an attempt to overcome the ideological resistance of Shafi'i territories to Zaydi rule.

Originally an adherent of the Zaydiyya legal school, al-Shawkani came to believe before his thirtieth birthday that adherence to a single legal school contradicted true Islam. He argued instead that it was necessary to study the Qur'an and the hadith and to follow strictly the sunna of the Prophet. In his view *ijtihad* was the duty of everyone with sufficient knowledge. By "sufficient knowledge" he meant knowledge of a brief textbook in each of the five branches of scholarship that were required for practicing *ijtihad*. He rejected the claim that only a restricted form of *ijtihad* was permitted. In his view it was necessary to obey the precepts of the Qur'an and the sunna, independent of how these had been interpreted by scholars over the course of history. Thus his conception of *ijtihad* was significantly more radical than that of Ibn 'Abd al-Wahhab and Shah Wali Allah. Nevertheless, the practical implications of this radical approach appear to have been minor; there were probably only limited differences between al-Shawkani's position and the prevailing doctrine.

As the imam's secretary, al-Shawkani engaged in correspondence with the head of the Sa'udi state between 1807 and 1813. He was familiar with the teachings of the Wahhabites, and his general view of them was positive, as he himself was also an opponent of venerating saints and making pilgrimages to graves of the dead. Nevertheless, he did not share the Wahhabite view that anyone who did not participate in public Friday prayers was an infidel and could be killed.

Muhammad ibn 'Ali al-Sanusi (1787–1859)

Like Ibn 'Abd al-Wahhab, Muhammad ibn 'Ali al-Sanusi—the fourth fundamentalist thinker we will examine in this section—was the founder of an action-oriented movement. In contrast, however, to the Wahhabites, who were organized as a state, the Sanusiyya was principally a mystical order. Only after the death of its founder and under external influences did it become a state. The Sanusi movement is ideologically important because it illustrates how mysticism and fundamentalist thought can coexist.

The rise of al-Sanusi indicates that he was a cosmopolite, at least within the scope of the Islamic world. His life exhibited a certain restlessness that is frequently encountered in those Muslim scholars of the past who traveled from place to place in search of knowledge, complying with the Prophet's command to go in quest of knowledge even as far as China.

Born in the west Algerian city of Mostaganem, al-Sanusi traveled to Fez in 1804 to complete his studies at the theological college of al-Qarawiyyin. He remained there until 1819, initially as a student and later as an instructor. During those years he became an expert in the various branches of Islamic scholarship and was introduced into several mystical orders. The intellectual climate in Fez at the time must have been stimulating. During the first decades of the nineteenth century two mystical reformers—al-Tijani (1737–1815) and al-Darqawi (1761–1823)—played a significant role in the intellectual and political life of Morocco. The decision by Sultan Suleiman (r. 1793–1822) to accept and apply Wahhabite doctrine—through which he hoped to control the power of the mystical orders—must have led to fierce disputes. Although al-Sanusi never addressed these schools of thought and disputes in his own writings, he was probably influenced by the cultural atmosphere of Fez during this time.

He left Fez in 1819 and traveled around Algeria for several years before departing for Mecca in 1822. Stopping initially in Cairo to study and teach at Al-Azhar University, he arrived in Mecca in 1825, where he remained for fifteen years. His stay in Mecca was of central importance to his spiritual development. Here he not only encountered a number of important Islamic scholars but also had contact with the Moroccan mystic Ahmad ibn Idris (1760–1837). Recognizing how close Ahmad ibn Idris's ideas were to his own, he began to regard the latter as his intellectual mentor.

In 1840 al-Sanusi returned to North Africa. From Cairo, where he again remained for some time, he traveled to Tunisia and from there eastward to Cyrenaica. A number of his followers in Cyrenaica had begun to establish a *zawiya*, a base of the order consisting of a mosque, a school, and guest rooms. This became the core from which the Sanusi order quickly expanded over the following years. Although al-Sanusi also was active in the Hejaz for approximately eight years (1846–1854) in an attempt to expand his order there, Cyrenaica and its Saharan hinterland were the territories in which the main activities of the order occurred.

Through the establishment of additional *zawiyas* among the Bedouins, the order created religious centers where the latter could be educated and where disputes could be settled according to Islamic law. The Bedouins valued these services, and many tribes requested that *zawiyas* be established in their territory. In this way members of the order, the Ikhwan (lit. brothers), who lived in these *zawiyas* were able to spread the Sanusi conception of a pure Islam among the Bedouins, who until this time had been only nominally Muslim. A number of these *zawiyas* were located strategically along trans-Saharan trade routes. They also served as resting places for caravans and as marketplaces, which strengthened the order economically. The Sanusiyya were able to expand their influence to the south along these trade routes. One indication of this development was the fact that in 1858 al-Sanusi moved the headquarters of the order from Baida'in Cyrenaica to Jaghbub, several hundred kilometers southeast.

As a thinker al-Sanusi was interested not merely in mysticism. His central focus was the purification of Islam. He wrote several treatises on legal methodology, in which he emphasized the value of studying the hadith. His position on the issue of *ijtihad* and *taqlid* was similar to that of Ibn 'Abd al-Wahhab and Shah Wali Allah. He insisted that unrestricted *ijtihad* was no longer permitted. This did not mean, however, that the conceptions and

rules of a certain *madhhab* had to be accepted blindly. If one was sufficiently familiar with the basic branches of Islamic scholarship, one could
independently follow the Qur'an and the hadith and interpret both. In doing
so, however, one had to adopt the methodological rules of one of the legal
schools. Al-Sanusi argued that such an approach would ensure that the precepts of the Qur'an and the sunna were respected.

By the time al-Sanusi died in 1859, his order had attained a broad influence. There were *zawiyas* in the Hejaz and in Egypt. The center of his order,
however, was in Libya and in the Saharan territories. Led by al-Sanusi's son
and later by his grandson, the order gradually assumed the character of a
state. It was more or less recognized as such by Ottoman Turks (who ruled
the coastal strip of Libya); for example, the Sanusis were allowed to negotiate with Ottoman authorities in the name of the Bedouins of the hinterland.
The process of state building intensified when the Sanusis began to engage
in military opposition to French expansion into the Sahara and, beginning
in 1912, to the Italian occupation of Libya. The Sanusis were ultimately defeated by the Italians. After the Second World War, however, an independent
kingdom of Libya was established, and one of al-Sanusi's grandsons was
proclaimed its monarch.

2. Islam and the West: Religious Developments during and after the Colonial Era

Beginning in the second half of the nineteenth century, the history of Islam
became inextricably tied to the history of Western expansion. Western control of the Islamic world and the indigenous reaction to it were the central
factors that shaped modern Islam. The military and technical superiority of
the West and its growing political and cultural influence have affected most
Muslim thinkers in the modern era. The essential theme of contemporary
Muslim thought is the position of Islam in regard to the West. Most of
the issues addressed by modern Muslim thinkers touch either directly or
indirectly on the question of whether the intellectual products of the West
should be rejected or accepted.

The spread of European colonial rule over the Islamic world was a process that lasted for more than a hundred years, from the late eighteenth
century to the end of the First World War. Beginning in the final decades
of the nineteenth century, this process accelerated. The European powers
quickly appropriated almost the entire Islamic world. Those territories that
were left uncolonized either were regarded as worthless in economic or strategic terms—for instance, the interior of the Arabian Peninsula—or were
controlled by one or several European powers indirectly, for example, the
Ottoman Empire or Iran.

By the end of the eighteenth century there was already a sense, at least in
the Ottoman Empire, that "something had gone wrong" with the Islamic

world, that it had fallen behind the West militarily and politically. This problem was regarded as a military one, requiring a technical solution. Redress was sought through reform of the army and officer training by Western experts. As a result of increased contact with Europe during the nineteenth century, individual Muslims realized that military reforms alone would not be sufficient and that reforms on a greater scale were necessary. In many of the Islamic countries that were still independent at the time, the governments began to work out reform programs, primarily in the realms of legislation, administration, and education. In conjunction with this, there was also a growing stratum of officers, government officials, and teachers who called for reforms according to Western models and whose influence on their respective governments grew. At the same time, Western influence became increasingly apparent through the rise in trade and the growing presence of foreigners.

Religious reactions to these developments varied. There were preachers who fulminated against everything Western and designated all reforms as *bid'a,* that is, as changes of questionable character. They represented only a small minority. The majority of religious dignitaries were either silent about the reforms or tacitly attempted to undermine them. Very few attempted to integrate these reforms into an overarching Islamic context. Men such as Khayr al-Din al-Tunisi (1810–1889) and Rifa'a Rafi' al-Tahtawi (1801–1873) sought to prove that Islam was open to reforms. They were exceptions, however.

In the territories directly subject to colonial rule, primarily in India and Algeria, the situation was somewhat different. Here the colonial administrations carried out reforms themselves. The French occupation of Algeria began in 1830 and was completed only in 1848, following the defeat of the resistance movement led by 'Abd al-Qadir. After this, French access to the country was so firmly established—not only in terms of security but also in terms of education and culture—that there was no maneuvering room for the development of a nontraditional Islam. In India, which had been subject to the British Raj since the first decades of the nineteenth century, the cultural and religious climate was much more open. Several Muslim thinkers who were convinced that it was senseless to resist the British rulers—as the rebellion of 1857 (the Mutiny), in their view, had demonstrated—attempted to make the best of the situation and initiated pro-British Islamic reformism.

After the Russian conquest of large parts of Muslim Central Asia, the French occupation of Tunisia (1881), the British occupation of Egypt (1882), and the establishment of tighter financial control over the Ottoman Empire by the European powers, most Muslim thinkers realized that European colonialism functioned globally and was very dangerous. On the political level there was a wave of pan-Islamic sentiment that was cleverly exploited by Ottoman sultan Abdülhamit II (r. 1876–1909). Although most tradition-conscious 'ulama' rejected the claims to the caliphate of the Ottoman sultans, the latter had used the title of caliph since the end of the eighteenth century. In doing so they expected the European powers to recognize them as the protectors of all Muslims regardless of where they lived—a policy that resembled the claims of France and Russia with respect to Christians in the Ottoman Empire. In 1876 this policy was included in Article 4 of the Ottoman Constitution: "His Majesty the Sultan, under the title 'Supreme Caliph,' is the protector of the Muslim religion." Aided by the fact that the influence of pan-Islamism had been starkly exaggerated in Europe—as an organized political movement, pan-Islamism existed only rudimentarily—and that pan-Islamic agitators were suspected of being involved in every local rebellion in the colonized territories of the Islamic world, the Ottoman sultan was able to enhance his standing vis-à-vis the European powers through this policy. Ottoman pan-Islamism, however, was fundamentally defensive and did not aim at territorial expansion.

The spread of pan-Islamic sentiment was the expression of a comprehensive and deep-seated movement triggered by the confrontation between Islam and Western colonialism. Because the division between colonizer and colonized was also characterized by the religious distinction between Christian and Muslim, Islam—or, better, being Muslim—acquired a new dimension. It became an integral component of a cultural identity that had to be defended against the culture of the rulers. To be Muslim was no longer (only) a way of believing in God and finding a meaning in life. For many it also became a political stance: they were Muslims in a willful and conscious way and were thus oppositional Muslims.

For Muslims, the necessity of defending their cultural identity arose not only from the contemporary situation of being subjected to colonial rule but also from direct attacks on this identity. The notion of the comprehensive and substantive superiority of European Christians, of the white man and his culture, had developed as a natural consequence of colonial expansion. Notions such as the *mission civilisatrice* of the West and the white man's burden were invoked to justify European political rule over non-European peoples. To emphasize the necessity of European intervention, non-European peoples, cultures, and religions were portrayed as inferior and backward. This was particularly true of Islam and Muslims.

The negative image of Islam was composed of a number of elements that were diametrically opposed to the values fostered by the European bourgeoisie of the nineteenth century. Thus Islam and Muslim society were described as rigid and unalterable, incapable of progress. Islam as a religion was regarded as irrational, an obstacle to the search for truth and the striving for scientific knowledge. Because of the doctrine of jihad, Muslims were considered bellicose and fanatical. The belief in divine omniscience and predestination were seen as a source of Muslims' resignation to fate and the reason why they did not attempt to improve their situation. Muslim men were said to be sensuous and debauched, and the institution of the harem was regarded as proof of this. It was argued that the acceptance of polygamy and the frequent repudiation of wives led to the lack of a secure and healthy family life—another factor that ostensibly contributed to the weakening of Muslim society. Finally, from a Western perspective, Islamic governments were necessarily autocratic and despotic. These are a few of the numerous prejudices about Islam that were common in the West—and to some extent still are.

Muslims responded to these intellectual attacks in two different ways. The first response was defensive: they agreed with the accusations but claimed at the same time that the arrangements or precepts in question had emerged through a false interpretation and a distortion of the true and ideal Islam. The second response was more confident: it consisted of uncompromisingly defending Islam as it was, especially the points of criticism, although it did not deny the necessity of purifying Islam. The different responses to the Western critique of polygamy in Islam were characteristic. The Egyptian lawyer and defender of women's rights Qasim Amin (1863–1908) agreed completely with the Western critique of polygamy but argued that it was also forbidden by the Qur'an, which he attempted to demonstrate through a comparison of two Qur'anic passages: "And if ye fear that ye will not deal fairly by the orphans, marry of the women, who seem good to you, two or three or four; and if ye fear that ye cannot do justice (to so many) then one (only)" (sura4:3) and "Ye will not be able to deal equally between (your) wives, however much ye wish (to do so)" (sura 4:129). In response to objections that polygamy was affirmed by both the sunna and established practice, Qasim Amin insisted that the most that could be said was that polygamy was permitted but not recommended. In such a case, he continued, a ruler could declare a practice illegal if the public interest demanded its abolition—which Qasim Amin believed was the case with polygamy. In contrast, Muhammad Rashid Rida (1865–1935) defended polygamy, insisting it was a widely known fact that men throughout the entire world were polygamous by nature. He argued that in the West men were hypocritically compelled to have only one legal wife while they simultaneously kept one or more mistresses; the Islamic precepts, he contended, were more natural and beneficial to both parties: the husband could follow his natural essence, and all of his wives possessed legal status. In addition, polygamy offered a solution when a wife was childless or ill. Through marriage to a second wife, the husband could ensure his progeny without having to repudiate his first wife.

In this way Islam became for many Muslims primarily—or even exclusively—something they regarded as an essential aspect of their cultural identity which had to be defended against external attacks, rather than a form of religious belief, the discovery of the meaning of life, or an ideal social order. To fulfill this new role, Islam had to become something they could be proud of. But how could they be proud of Islam, given the contemporary weakness and subservience of the Islamic world? One solution was to shift the focus back to the past glory of medieval Islamic civilization. The other solution—which is of greater significance for the modern era—arose from discussions about the causes of the backwardness of the Islamic world in comparison to the West.

As noted earlier, this discussion had begun early, that is, before the establishment of colonial rule. The issue initially appeared to be of a purely technical nature. Gradually, however, Muslims realized that it was necessary to view the problem in a broader framework. The strength of the West could not be attributed solely to its technological advances but was also the result of its political institutions, laws, and values, for example, innovation and the entrepreneurial spirit, which ostensibly were more in vogue in the West than in Islamic countries. The role that religion had played in these developments, however, remained an open question. Had Islam been an obstacle to progress, as many Western thinkers claimed? It was not surprising that Muslim intellectuals answered this question in the negative, arguing that in the early Middle Ages the Islamic world had been significantly more developed economically and culturally than Christian Europe.

According to a number of Muslim thinkers, the scales had now tipped in favor of the West because Muslims had deviated from true and authentic Islam. This idea was not entirely new. Over the course of Islamic history, strict adherence to the sunna had always been regarded as the source of human and social prosperity as well as political strength. If these now had been lost, it was essential that Muslims be persuaded to live again according to the sunna. A problem arose here, however, because both the sunna and the idea of the true and authentic Islam were open to interpretation.

Like fundamentalists of the eighteenth and early nineteenth centuries, these new thinkers turned to the sources to determine what true and authentic Islam was. For this reason they had to reject the duty of *taqlid,* that is, blind adherence to a legal school, and insist that they were justified in exercising *ijtihad,* the free interpretation of the Qur'an and the hadith. To this extent their conception conformed to the fundamentalist stance. This similarity, however, was merely formal; that is, they agreed only in terms of the procedure for determining what should be considered pure Islam. There were many differences in their respective interpretations. Whereas the "old" fundamentalists' system of reference had been exclusively Islamic, these new thinkers had become acquainted with Western thought and were influenced to a certain degree by it. For them the notion of *ijtihad* acquired a new dimension. Instead of merely being a means for increasing the authenticity of Islam, it now became a method of purposive interpretation, a means for adapting Islam to the new situation.

The insistence on practicing *ijtihad* and the condemnation of *taqlid* were also ideologically significant. This stance was supposed to demonstrate that Islam was not a religion of stagnation and ossification but rather one capable of change and development. This was of essential importance in an era in which the central slogans—at least in the West—were progress, development, and change. Thus the call for *ijtihad* was not only an initial step on the way to reform but also a component in the ideological battle between Islam and the West.

For these new thinkers at the end of the nineteenth century, the reform of religion was the lever for producing social and political change. This meant, on the one hand, purifying Islam of all forms of behavior and belief that belonged to the realm of popular religion such as the veneration of saints and the ecstatic conduct of the Sufi orders, as well as superstition and magic; on the other hand, it also meant searching for general principles and interpreting those principles in terms of the public interest, *maslaha*. In the process, many Western values of the nineteenth century were tacitly appropriated and, so to speak, "Islamified." In this way a form of Islam was created that was acceptable to the Europeanized elite. They no longer had to be embarrassed about their religion. On the contrary, they could be proud of it since it affirmed most of the basic values they had learned to esteem.

The reform of Islam as a means for strengthening Muslim society, however, required a strategy. The new interpretations and conceptions had to spread throughout society. For this reason, reform thinkers attributed great importance to education and expended much time and energy on practical plans to improve the educational system. Characteristically they concentrated especially on higher education, convinced that ideas would more or less trickle down from the elite to the common people as a matter of course. This was also characteristic of their scripturalism. For these reformers Islam was first and foremost a matter of words, texts, and interpretations. As a consequence, they approached the issue more intellectually than emotionally.

Most books on modern Islam provide an extensive treatment of Islamic reform. This focus is justified if we consider the influence of Islamic reform on political elites and leading members of the Islamic world. This emphasis, however, should not conceal the fact that for a very long time these reformers and their supporters remained only a small minority among the large majority of traditional 'ulama' who ruled the religious institutions.

The following section investigates in more detail three pioneers of this reform. They have been selected not only because they significantly influenced later Muslim thinkers but also because they can be seen as representatives of three different currents of reform. Sir Saiyid Ahmad Khan represented a reform of Islam based on an uncritical appropriation of Western thought and Western institutions. Jamal al-Din al-Afghani stands for Islamic resistance to colonialism. Muhammad 'Abduh represents the most successful type of reform, a new interpretation of Islam that owed much to Western conceptions but nevertheless maintained a certain distance from them and corresponded thoroughly to the taste of the liberal and nationally conscious elite.

Sir Saiyid Ahmad Khan (1817–1898)

It is not surprising that India was the first country where ideas about the reform of Islam were expressed. These initial impulses for reform arose in part from the fact that India was colonized at a relatively early date. By

1820 British colonial rule extended across all of India. As a result, Indian Muslims had access to the West and to Western ideas earlier than Muslims in other regions of the Islamic world. Ahmad Khan can be regarded as the father of Islamic reform, even if later reform thinkers distanced themselves from his thought because of his expressly pro-British stance.

Ahmad Khan was born in Delhi to a family with close ties to the still existent Mughal court. He obtained a basic religious education before going to work at the age of twenty for the East India Company, which ruled over India at the time. After working as a staff member for an Islamic court, Ahmad Khan was appointed judge. This left him time for scholarly activities. He studied religion and Islamic history and wrote several treatises on various religious and historical subjects. These writings were rather conventional, except they revealed a certain influence from the Indian fundamentalist school of Shah Wali Allah.

The Indian Rebellion of 1857 (the Mutiny) came as an enormous shock for Ahmad Khan. Muslim and Hindu soldiers, or sepoys, of the East India Company rebelled against the British, and the uprising subsequently spread throughout the land. Through draconian measures the British were finally able to suppress the rebellion, although they suffered heavy casualties in the process. While both Muslims and Hindus had taken part in the rebellion, British punishments were directed solely at the Muslim population, which was subsequently disadvantaged in terms of government appointments and senior posts. The primary reason for this was that the British suspected the rebellion might have been an attempt by the Mughal elite to shake off the British yoke and reestablish its old rule. This was also the beginning of a consistent British colonial policy of divide and rule. This new policy toward Indian Muslims primarily affected the upper and middle classes.

The rebellion itself and the ensuing events were crucial for Ahmad Khan's development. Throughout the rebellion he had sided with the British, and after the rebellion had been suppressed he was even more convinced than before that the future of India was closely tied to the British presence. For this reason he dedicated the bulk of his activities over the subsequent decades to improving relations between Indian Muslims and the British. He hoped in this way to improve the fate of the Muslim upper and middle classes.

Ahmad Khan published several books and articles that pursued a dual aim. First, he attempted to convince the British that Muslims had been neither the main culprits in the rebellion nor (as one English author had titled his work on the subject) "bound in conscience to rebel against the queen." Second, he sought to enlighten his fellow Muslims on precisely this point and to dissuade them from what he considered the unjustified and dangerous belief that Islam demanded hostility toward and war against the British. To this end he developed a completely new interpretation of the Islamic duty of jihad, the duty to engage in a holy war, which I will examine in a moment. Characteristic of Ahmad Khan was the stance he took in a separate treatise on the issue of whether Muslims were permitted to dine with Christians, a question that Indian Muslims had usually answered in the negative. Ahmad Khan's response was, of course, an unqualified yes.

During this time he also composed a commentary on the Bible, a plan that he pursued in order to become more familiar with Christianity. He rejected strict Muslim doctrine, according to which the texts of previous revelations—as we know them today—had been distorted or corrupted (*tahrif*). Through a comparison of the Bible and the Qur'an he sought to establish the basic relatedness of Islam and Christianity.

In 1869–70 Ahmad Khan lived for approximately a year and a half in England. This visit had an enormous influence on his ideas. Until that time he had attempted to promote reconciliation and political rapprochement between Indian Muslims and the British. After his trip to Europe he sought to persuade his fellow Muslims not only to be loyal to the British Raj but also to take up Western culture. He was so impressed by England that he is reputed to have said, "All good things, spiritual and worldly, which should be found in man have been bestowed by the Almighty on Europe, especially on England" (cited in Baljon 1949, 107). During his stay he wrote home, "I can truly say that the natives of India, high and low, merchants and petty shopkeepers, educated and illiterate, when contrasted with the English in education, manners, and uprightness, are as like them as a dirty animal is to an able and handsome man" (cited in Smith 1969, 11).

Through his own activities and the support of the British—he received a knighthood for his services to the empire—Ahmad Khan was recognized as one of the significant leaders of the Indian Muslim community. After his return from Europe he assumed political posts and began editing the journal *Tahdhib al-akhlaq* to spread his ideas. One of his ideals, to which he dedicated great energy, was the establishment of a university for Indian Muslims, where they could become familiar with European science and culture. These efforts were crowned with success when the Mohammedan Anglo-Oriental College in Aligarh was opened in 1878. The college was modeled on Oxford and Cambridge; English was the official language of instruction.

In his intellectual activities in the realm of religion Ahmad Khan consciously pursued two objectives. First, he sought to create a form of Islam that was acceptable to young Muslims with a European education, since he feared that otherwise they would turn away from Islam and become either Christians or atheists. Second, he sought to defend Islam against attacks by European thinkers, in particular by orientalists. The result was an Islam permeated with nineteenth-century philosophical concepts—primarily "reason" and "nature"—and robbed of the sharp edges that unsettled Europeans.

Muslim opponents designated Ahmad Khan and his supporters "Naycharis," a term derived from the English word "nature." This reflected the preeminent position that the concept of nature occupied in Ahmad Khan's thought. In contrast to traditional Islamic theology, which recognized no natural laws but merely customs of God, from which he could deviate,

Ahmad Khan supported the view that natural laws were firm and unchanging. He insisted that there could be no contradiction between these laws and the Qur'an, as God's word (the Qur'an) corresponds unconditionally to his actions (nature). Drawing on earlier rationalist currents in Islam (for instance, the Mu'tazila), he attempted to demonstrate that sections of the Qur'an that had traditionally been interpreted as references to supernatural phenomena could also be understood in a completely naturalist way. For example, he argued that the word *jinn,* which appears repeatedly in the Qur'an and was usually understood as "spirit," really refers to savages dwelling in the mountains and wilderness. According to Ahmad Khan, Islam was not only a natural religion but also a rational religion, and he attempted to demonstrate that there were good reasons for all of its precepts. He argued that the prohibition on pork, for example, was necessary to maintain the moral purity of humans, since pigs have bad habits that run counter to human ethics.

Although Ahmad Khan greatly esteemed reason, he did not regard it as sufficient to guide humanity. Like medieval Islamic philosophers, he taught that revelation was at least equally important. He accepted the doctrine that the Qur'an contains the direct word of God. As a consequence, he could not use critical-historical analysis or philological textual criticism to analyze the words of the Qur'an. His position was less strict with the hadith. While devout scholars rejected only certain hadiths because of errors in the *isnad* (chain of transmission), Ahmad Khan also rejected hadiths on the basis of content, accepting only a small number of them as authentic.

In creating this new form of Islam, Ahmad Khan insisted on the right to *ijtihad* and rejected *taqlid.* His *ijtihad* served not only to demonstrate that Islam was a natural religion grounded in reason but also to defend Islam against European attacks and accusations. Thus he addressed a number of issues that had repeatedly been the object of European ideological attacks, for example, the doctrine of jihad, the status of women, the keeping of slaves, physical punishment, and the prohibition on interest. Ahmad Khan regarded his new interpretation of the duty of jihad as an important dimension of a policy of reconciliation between Indian Muslims and the British. According to classical doctrine, jihad was a war that was fought to expand the territory of the Islamic state or to defend that territory from attack. In the first case it was the collective duty of all members the community, from which they could be exempted if a sufficient number of men participated in the jihad; in the defensive case it was the individual duty of all people living in the territory under attack. In his new interpretation Ahmad Khan examined the relevant parts of the Qur'an and concluded that jihad was a duty only when Muslims were oppressed in their capacity as believers and prevented from performing their religious duties. In his opinion, living under foreign, non-Muslim rule was not sufficient ground for jihad because jihad was a religious concept that could not be used for mere political objectives. The effects of these positions were far-reaching. Beneath the surface this meant that politics and religion were conceived as two separate realms—a position completely foreign to orthodox tendencies in Islam.

Ahmad Khan's views on the status of women in Islam were less sensational. He considered the segregation of women to be permissible and even beneficial. He also argued that polygamy was permitted, but only as an exception when the first wife was ill or unable to bear children. Ahmad Khan also wrote a separate treatise on the issue of slaveholding in Islam. On the basis of a completely novel interpretation of the Qur'an, he concluded that the acquisition of slaves had already been forbidden during the Prophet Muhammad's lifetime.

According to Islamic penal law a number of crimes were supposed to be punished by beatings and mutilation. Under certain circumstances, theft was punished by the amputation of a hand. Through an intellectual exegesis on the relevant sections of the Qur'an, Ahmad Khan came to the conclusion that Islam offered a choice between physical punishment and imprisonment for such crimes; if a country could afford the luxury of a prison system, the latter alternative had to be adopted. With regard to the prohibition of interest in the Qur'an, Ahmad Khan argued that the Qur'anic verses on the subject (sura 2:275ff.) had to be read in the context of the previous verses, which made it clear that collecting interest was forbidden only in the case of poor debtors, not wealthy ones.

Although Ahmad Khan's ideas were never completely accepted, they were nevertheless extremely important insofar as they stimulated discussion about the position of Islam within a society undergoing a rapid process of transformation as a consequence of colonial influence. His very pro-British stance provoked resentment, however, initially among those Muslims who yearned for the old days of Mughal rule, but later among those who began to develop nationalist thinking as well.

Jamal al-Din al-Afghani (1838/39–1897)

If Ahmad Khan's position can be described as a strategy of defeat, then Jamal al-Din al-Afghani's position should be called a strategy of defense. Although there were certain similarities in their respective conceptions of Islam, their stances toward Europe and European colonialism were diametrically opposed. While Ahmad Khan sought reconciliation between Indian Muslims and the British, Jamal al-Din al-Afghani dedicated almost his entire life to the battle against European colonial expansion in the Islamic world.

Despite the efforts of several biographers, we still know little about many areas of Jamal al-Din al-Afghani's life. This is also true of his innermost thoughts and convictions. Overall he was an enigmatic person, not least as a result of the many mysteries that he himself initiated. The best known of these is his place of birth. He called himself al-Afghani and implied that he had been born in Afghanistan. Historians, however, have now proved that he was in fact born in or near the Iranian city of Asadabad. The reason for this deception was that Jamal al-Din's birth in Iran points to his Shiʿa descent, which he wanted to conceal because he spent almost his entire life in predominantly Sunni countries. For this reason he preferred to be regarded as a Sunni Afghan.

Jamal al-Din's great restlessness is one of the reasons why it is difficult to determine the course of his life more precisely. In the first thirty years of his life he traveled to India, Hejaz, Iraq, and possibly Istanbul. He lived for a time in Afghanistan, where he served as an adviser to the emir and tried to persuade him to adopt a firm anti-British stance. After his expulsion in 1868 he traveled to Istanbul via Bombay and Cairo. In Istanbul he had contact with several Ottoman reformers. After giving a public lecture on the relation between religion and philosophy that was considered heretical, he was expelled again owing to pressure from religious authorities. This time he traveled to Cairo, arriving in 1871. His stay in Egypt, which lasted eight years, was one of the most fruitful periods of his life. Together with his supporters and students, including Muhammad ʿAbduh (discussed later in this chapter) and Saʿd Zaghul (who became the best-known political leader in Egypt after the First World War), he played an important role in Egyptian politics of this era.

The 1870s were a decade of unrest in Egypt. During these years Western influence on the Egyptian economy, state finances, and politics grew rapidly. Deficit spending, poor control of state finances, and the scheming of creditors led to insolvency in 1876 and the introduction of a British-French commission that was supposed to supervise Egyptian state finances. This meant increased foreign intervention in Egyptian politics aimed at protecting the interests of the primarily British and French stockholders. When Khedive Ismaʿil (r. 1863–1879) exhibited reservations about working with the foreign powers, the latter ensured that he was replaced by his son Tawfiq (r. 1879–1892).

These developments strengthened Jamal al-Din's anticolonial sentiments. Together with his students he attempted to spread his ideas through public talks—he was a skillful and powerfully eloquent speaker—as well as through newspaper articles and personal discussions. His students also began to write newspaper articles. Because of his uncompromising stance regarding foreign intervention, Jamal al-Din was expelled yet again, this time by Khedive Tawfiq.

Jamal ad-Din spent the next three years relatively quietly in India. He published several articles and a treatise titled *The Truth about the Neichari Sect and an Explanation of the Neicharis* (also known as *The Refutation of the Materialists*, after the title of the Arabic translation). This treatise was a critique of Ahmad Khan and sought to refute the latter's doctrine of nature. While Ahmad Khan was not mentioned by name, the work was in fact an attack on his political positions. Through the treatise Jamal al-Din sought to brand Ahmad Khan a heretic and cast a shadow over the man and his views, thereby discrediting him with his own people, the Indian Muslims.

In 1882 Jamal al-Din traveled from India to Europe, where he spent the next seven years of his life. He visited Paris, London, and St. Petersburg, occupied with (often fanciful) political plans. When Muhammad 'Abduh—who had been expelled from Egypt for his participation in the 'Urabi rebellion (discussed later in this chapter)—came to Europe, the two founded the journal *Al-'Urwa al-wuthqa* (The Firmest Bond; see sura 2:256 and 31:22) to spread their ideas in the Islamic world. Eighteen volumes of the journal were published between March and October 1884. The British banned the journal in Egypt and India because of its pan-Islamic and anticolonialist stance. Nevertheless it found many readers and was quite influential among educated, reform-oriented people in the Islamic world.

In 1899 Jamal al-Din was invited to Tehran by Shah Nasir al-Din (r. 1848–1896), to whom he had provided a number of diplomatic services. Shortly after his arrival he realized that he would not, as he had hoped, be offered an important post and that he had no influence on the Iranian government. Thus he was forced to search for an alternate means of attaining his pan-Islamic reform goals. As in Egypt, he assembled a number of young intellectuals, with whom he discussed not only his reformist and anti-British plans but also the possibility of toppling the shah's autocratic regime.

The shah quickly learned of these meetings and decided to banish Jamal al-Din from Tehran to the city of Qom. Jamal al-Din was able to elude the shah's soldiers and sought refuge in the shrine of Shahzadeh 'Abd al-'Azim, south of Tehran. Many people came to visit him there and listen to his flaming lectures against the regime, until the shah decided in early 1891 to violate the sacred nature of the shrine and to have Jamal al-Din arrested by his cavalry. He was immediately deported to Iraq, which was Ottoman territory at the time.

From Iraq and later from London, where he arrived in 1892, Jamal al-Din continued his oppositional activities, sending militant letters to his friends in Iran as well as to religious dignitaries. He called upon the latter to take action against increasing foreign interventions in Iran's economic and political sovereignty. A tobacco concession that the shah had recently granted to a British company became a symbol of foreign interference, and Jamal al-Din focused his efforts on actions that were supposed to encourage resistance to this concession. These activities contributed to the waves of protest that overwhelmed the country between 1891 and 1892 and finally led to the revocation of the concession.

In London he received an invitation from Sultan Abdülhamit II to live as his guest in Istanbul. Jamal al-Din probably hoped that the sultan wanted to secure his services to implement a pan-Islamic foreign policy. It is unlikely, however, that this was actually the sultan's intention. There are indications that Abdülhamit wanted to have Jamal al-Din near him in order to better monitor his activities. The sultan was apparently concerned that Jamal al-Din might be involved in plans to establish an Arabic caliphate that would threaten the integrity of the Ottoman Empire. Whatever the cause might have been, Jamal al-Din was never appointed to any important post in Istanbul. He died of cancer of the jaw in 1897, having spent the final years of his life virtually a prisoner. There were several petitions to allow him to leave the country, but the sultan denied them.

It is not easy to provide an overview of Jamal al-Din's thought. He was more a political activist than a systematic thinker. In his few publications and in the statements recorded by his biographers and acquaintances there are many contradictory assertions. Several of these can be attributed to changes of opinion resulting from certain developments in histhinking, as is probably inevitable over the course of approximately forty years. But there are also contradictions that cannot be resolved in this way. These can usually be explained by the fact that Jamal al-Din was a political tactician who wanted to attain certain objectives and who subordinated his words and writings to these objectives. This would explain, for example, why he called for national unity in India on the basis of language in 1882 and harshly attacked this kind of unity two years later in *Al-'Urwa al-wuthqa,* arguing that nationalism of this form would seriously weaken the only true unity, Islamic unity. Jamal al-Din certainly understood that in India national unity was a stronger force against British colonialism and that a call for religious solidarity in India would have divided anticolonial forces. The situation was different in the Middle East. There the Muslims constituted the overwhelming majority, and the idea of Islamic unity could represent a significantly more powerful force than that of national unity.

Jamal al-Din also tended to adjust the expressions he used and the thoughts he supported according to his audience. This might have been due to the influence of Islamic philosophy on his education. Islamic philosophers have often defended the position that their ideas are appropriate only for the select few, while the vast majority of people must make do with the religion alone, and that words and expressions should be chosen accordingly. Jamal al-Din, for example, expressed himself much more freely in his response to Ernest Renan's famous lecture "L'Islamisme et la science," which had been published in a French journal, than he usually did elsewhere. He even agreed with Renan that Islam, like most other religions, had obstructed the progress of science, a view he would never have supported in a Muslim environment.

Jamal al-Din wanted the Islamic world to be powerful again so that it could resist the continuous colonial expansion of the Europeans. This motive predominated throughout his entire life and his entire thought. Experiences from his youth—he had probably witnessed the brutal suppression of the Indian Rebellion of 1857 by the British—may have contributed to this stance. He believed that the power of Europe was based in action, entrepreneurial spirit, and rationalism, and that these virtues had contributed to the development of European science and technology. Thus for Jamal al-Din and his compatriots, Europe was Janus-faced. It stood for aggressive colonial conquest and at the same time for economic and technological progress, military and political strength, free political institutions, and modern education. Muslims, in other words, could learn much from Europe.

Yet, according to Jamal al-Din, Muslims should not uncritically adopt European technology and European institutions. Europe should not be imitated blindly. Attention should always be paid to the compatibility of such technology and institutions with Islam. Nevertheless, he insisted that the virtues and values that constituted the basis of European strength were also present in Islam. In his eyes, however, contemporary Islam was corrupt and full of superstition and scholastic casuistry. Through the practice of *ijtihad* and the renewed illumination of the sources, the true basis of Islam could again be set free, and Islam could be cleansed of inauthentic excesses.

Thus in his view true Islam was in essence a rationally oriented religion, that is, a religion that accorded with human reason and stimulated the use of reason. The sources of Islam should be interpreted rationally, and if some texts appeared to contradict reason, they should be interpreted symbolically. True Islam was never opposed to the search for the truth and to the cultivation of science. In fact, he argued, the Qur'an itself referred to various modern scientific and technological discoveries such as electricity and railroads.

According to Jamal al-Din, industriousness and the entrepreneurial spirit were also essential traits of true Islam. Fatalism and idleness, so often regarded as typical Islamic characteristics, had nothing to do with the real Islam. God had said, "Allah changeth not the condition of a folk until they (first) change that which is in their hearts" (sura 13:11). In his view this passage was fundamental to a true understanding of Islam.

Jamal al-Din also contended that there was no reason to reject technology and science. The spread of the European sciences, he argued, owed much to Islamic thinkers of the past. In the Middle Ages, Europe had borrowed from the achievements of Islamic philosophy and science. Thus when the Muslims appropriated technology and science from the West, they were merely reappropriating what was rightfully theirs.

As we have seen, Jamal al-Din strove for Islamic unity as a means to counter European colonialism. This unity was not necessarily political. Unity of the *umma*, the Islamic community, was supposed to be a unity of the heart, a state of mind. The different governments and political leaders in the Islamic world should act in the spirit of cooperation to resist the attacks of European powers. This pan-Islamic stance, however, limited its own capacity to propagate reforms. To win the support of the largest possible group, Jamal al-Din had to dilute his declarations about a new interpretation of Islam so that they appeared to be orthodox. Nevertheless, pan-Islamism never became a mass movement. Like other reformers of his era, Jamal al-Din preferred to negotiate with governments and elites to achieve his objectives.

Jamal al-Din was hardly a systematic thinker. His significance lies not so much in the work he left behind as in the influence he exerted on a younger

generation of reform-oriented Muslim intellectuals through personal relationships. He showed them that Islam was capable of change and development, and he opened their eyes to the dangers of European colonialism.

Muhammad 'Abduh (1849–1905)

Muhammad 'Abduh can be regarded as Jamal al-Din's preeminent student.
Despite the close student-teacher relationship, however, and the friendship
and ties that lasted for more than a decade, there were essential differences
between the two men, their ideas, and their careers. Jamal al-Din was an
impulsive man who tended toward sudden and often unexpected actions, a
combative political activist, and a cosmopolite whose home was the entire
Islamic world. Muhammad 'Abduh, in contrast, was a modest person. He
did not believe in sudden change and in his later life kept his distance from
politics. He was aware that reform would take time, and he was prepared to
work patiently for long-term change. He was a widely traveled man, but not
entirely voluntarily. He always felt connected to his native Egypt.

Muhammad 'Abduh was born in the Nile Delta in 1849. His father was a
farmer with moderate landholdings, and there was a tradition of education
in his family. After completing a basic education—learning the Qur'an by
heart—he was sent to the mosque school in Tanta in 1862. His experiences
there certainly contributed to the awakening of his later interest in issues of
education, for in Tanta he became acquainted with all the negative aspects
of traditional Islamic education. The students were required to memorize all
kinds of difficult texts, regardless of whether they understood the content.
Instructors were not generally very helpful; their pedagogy was limited to
rattling off incomprehensible subject matter, and students were not permitted to ask any questions. Disappointed by his experiences in Tanta, Muhammad 'Abduh left a short time later and returned home with the intention
of becoming a farmer like his father. His uncle Shaykh Darwish al-Khidr
introduced him to mysticism, which Muhammad 'Abduh found much more
interesting than the dry scholasticism he had attempted to master in Tanta.
He was introduced by his uncle into the Shadhiliyya order. As a result of this
new interest in religion, his uncle was also able to persuade him to return
to Tanta to resume his studies. Muhammad 'Abduh remained in Tanta until
1866 and then traveled to Cairo to study at Al-Azhar University. He was
still a student when Jamal al-Din arrived in Cairo in 1877. When the young
'Abduh learned that Jamal al-Din was in Cairo, he visited him together
with several friends. He was immediately impressed with the way Jamal
al-Din spoke about religion. This encounter was the beginning of a close
relationship. Through Jamal al-Din, 'Abduh was introduced to Islamic philosophy, a discipline that was not part of the curriculum at Al-Azhar, as
well as to European philosophical literature.

After completing his studies in 1877, 'Abduh began to teach at Al-Azhar
and at the Dar al-'ulum, a kind of teacher-training seminar. When the new

khedive expelled Jamal ad-Din in 1879, however, his friend and companion 'Abduh was considered a security risk for the government, and he was banished to his home village. He did not remain there long, as Riyad Pasha, an influential statesman who had been Jamal al-Din's patron, arranged for him to return to the capital. 'Abduh was not allowed to teach, but he was named coeditor of the government gazette *Al-Waqa'i' al-misriyya,* a position that he held until 1882.

His tenure as editor was a time of great political unrest in Egypt, including the 'Urabi Revolt, a movement of officers and later also civilians against the Turco-Circassian political and military elite in Egypt and against foreign intervention. The tumultuous events surrounding the revolt ultimately led to the British military occupation of the country to protect the interests of foreign stockholders and the empire's lines of transportation, specifically the Suez Canal. 'Urabi and his supporters were condemned in summary trials and expelled. While 'Abduh had not always condoned 'Urabi's tactics and methods and had often voiced his criticism, he remained tied to the movement, whose general objectives he had supported in his journal. After the British occupation he was brought before a tribunal and banished. He initially traveled to Beirut before joining up with Jamal al-Din in Paris at the beginning of 1884. Together they edited *Al-'Urwa al-wuthqa.* At the end of 1884 he returned to the Middle East through North Africa, settling again in Beirut, where he worked as a teacher until his banishment was lifted in 1888 and he was able to return to Egypt.

In Egypt he adapted himself to the realities of the British occupation and abandoned politics. He became a friend of Lord Cromer, the British consul-general in Egypt and the actual ruler of the country. One of the reasons he adopted this position was his belief that Egypt had much to learn from the West and that the presence of the British could be useful in this regard. Later on practical considerations also came into play. After he fell out of favor with the khedive, he was dependent on British support to retain his position and to implement his plans.

'Abduh would have liked to resume teaching in Egypt, but this was not permitted because the authorities feared that he would infect his students with latitudinarian ideas. Instead he was appointed a judge at one of the local courts and later was promoted to appellate court judge. In 1899 he was appointed to the highest religious office in Egypt, that of the mufti. In the same year he became a member of the Legislative Council, an advisory body composed primarily of government appointees. He held both positions until his death in 1905.

During the final seven years of his life 'Abduh focused his energies on two issues: the reform of the educational system—in particular Al-Azhar University, which he thought should become the intellectual center of reform—and reform of the shari'a courts. He was the driving force in many of the committees responsible for these realms and also published a number of reports and recommendations. His endeavors led to several successes, if not to everything he had hoped for. 'Abduh concentrated his practical and intellectual activities on initiating a general religious awakening in Islam, which he believed was the only way to strengthen the Islamic world in other areas as well. In his own words, his objective was

> the correction of the articles of belief and the removal of the mistakes which have crept into them through misunderstanding of the basic texts of the religion in order that, when once the beliefs have been made free of harmful innovations, the activities of Muslims may, as a result, be made free from disorder and confusion, the conditions of the individual Muslims may be improved, their understanding enlightened by the new sciences, both religious and secular, and the wholesome traits of character developed; and that this desirable state may communicate itself through the individuals to the nation as a whole. (cited in Adams 2000, 110)

'Abduh believed that living according to the true precepts of Islam was the key to the well-being of humans, as individuals and as a society, because the way of life taught by Islam was not only pleasing to God but also the best way to ensure social stability and the progress of the community. According to 'Abduh, the search for the true Islam was a necessary prerequisite for the general spread of this way of life. Thus the search served another aim as well, that is, the unification of Muslims, since unsubstantiated religious practices and false religious doctrine such as the exaggerations of the Sufi order and the extreme fervor of the sects had divided Muslims, and this division was one of the reasons for their decline.

Unity also played a role in 'Abduh's thought in a different context. The influence of European civilization and technology had become increasingly apparent over the course of the nineteenth century. Many Muslims, in particular those from the upper classes, had felt the attraction of Europe and had also been more or less Europeanized. This number steadily increased through the introduction of an educational system based on a European model. At the same time, European political and economic institutions as well as European-inspired laws were introduced. As a result, a deep chasm emerged in the Islamic world between the Europeanized elite and these Europeanized realms on the one hand and the vast majority of the population and traditional institutions on the other. One of 'Abduh's goals was to bridge this chasm.

To achieve this he sought a middle course. He condemned as *taqlid* the uncritical appropriation of everything European as well as the blind acceptance of traditions. Thus, like Jamal al-Din, he tried to demonstrate that true Islam contained the basis for these new and apparently foreign laws and institutions and that the values of nineteenth-century European civil society were in fact those of Islam as well. In this way he sought to justify Europeanization through Islam itself.

The central concept of all these projects and thoughts was that of the true Islam. For this reason 'Abduh dedicated great energy to elucidating his understanding of authentic Islam. His works in this realm exhibit a certain eclecticism based on a broad knowledge of Islamic and European culture. He was influenced by many conflicting currents of Islamic thought: Islamic philosophers, the Mu'tazila, al-Ghazali, and the neo-Hanbali fundamentalist school of Ibn Taymiyya. The influence of European authors, including Darwin, Spencer, Comte, Guizot, and Renan, is also evident in 'Abduh's writings.

This eclecticism and his tendency to avoid taking unambiguous positions on controversial theological issues—for example, the question of whether or not the Qur'an was created—allowed 'Abduh to develop a form of Islam that was acceptable to everyone, and in particular, however, to the Europeanized elite. For their sake he did confront several philosophical issues that were debated during his lifetime, for instance, the relation of reason and religion or science and religion—an issue that Ahmad Khan had addressed earlier.

'Abduh's positions were not in fact fundamentally different from those of Ahmad Khan. Like the latter, he emphasized that Islam was a religion that appealed to reason and that the Qur'an called upon humans to use their reason. In the old dispute about the relation between reason and revelation, 'Abduh argued that humans were able to use reason to prove the existence of God as well as the necessity of prophets and revelation. Since reason has shown that Muhammad was a prophet and that the Qur'an was a divine revelation, the content of the Qur'an and the hadith had to be recognized as such, even if that content appeared at times to exceed reason. If, as occurred sometimes, they seemed to contradict reason, then the hadith should be given preference and the texts should be interpreted symbolically to resolve the apparent contradiction.

In the relation of religion and science, 'Abduh recognized the idea of natural laws, albeit with the reservation that God remained the original ground of all occurrences. According to 'Abduh, the Qur'an could not contradict natural laws since God had—as he put it once—given us two books, the one created (nature) and the other revealed (the Qur'an). Science, the study of nature, was commendable not only as an aim in itself but also as a way of deepening human understanding of God.

Drawing upon the Mu'tazila, he attempted to read the Qur'an accordingly and to explain away anything that appeared supernatural. Thus he denied the reality of magic, to which many Qur'anic verses appeared to refer. He argued that the *jinn* mentioned in the Qur'an were microbes—a resourceful solution to a problem that Ahmad Khan had sought to resolve before him.

In the realm of the methodology of religious laws, 'Abduh's ideas corresponded almost completely to those of eighteenth- and nineteenth-century fundamentalists. He rejected *taqlid,* arguing that those sufficiently educated were permitted—or, better, were obligated—to practice *ijtihad.* One new element in his thought, however, was the important consequence that he drew from the traditional distinction between those parts of the shari'a concerned with religious duties (*'ibadat*) and those concerned with the relations of humans to one another (*mu'amalat*). He claimed that in the former realm precepts existed in a clear and unambiguous form in the Qur'an and the hadith and were thus unalterable. In regard to the latter realm, he argued that the Qur'an and the hadith contained only general principles that could be interpreted according to concrete circumstances in such a way that they were socially and ethically beneficial (*maslaha*). This was the operational realm of reason.

Here, however, 'Abduh offered less concrete solutions. In regard to polygamy and slavery he once cautiously wrote that in the present day it could be demonstrated that these institutions were not essential aspects of Islam and for this reason could be altered according to the circumstances. He defended physical punishment for purely pragmatic reasons: while detention might work as a deterrent in Europe, it could not have this effect in poorer countries such as Egypt since criminals there might prefer their prison cells to their own impoverished housing.

In his official post as state mufti he was obligated to follow the regulations stipulated in the existing legal codes. As a man of great religious repute, however, he was often asked for advice in religious matters by private citizens, even in foreign countries. Several of the fatwas (Arab. sing. *fatwa*) that he wrote in response are quite well known, for example, one arguing that it was permissible for a Muslim to wear a European-style headdress or another arguing that Muslims were allowed to draw interest on postal savings accounts.

3. The Twentieth Century: Battle for the Islamic State

Over the course of the nineteenth century the foundations were laid for a new form of Islam adapted to the needs of a rapidly changing society. The three thinkers examined in the previous section contributed to these developments. They wrote on many different subjects, attempting to reinterpret Islam and to reform Islamic society. Conspicuously absent in their work, however, was the attempt to establish a purely Islamic state that was supposed to incorporate the unity of religion and politics. This is precisely what has become one of the most distinctive characteristics of contemporary Islamic thought.

In 1924 the Turkish nationalist leader Mustafa Kemal, later called Atatürk (1881–1938), eliminated the caliphate, which had continued to exist as a purely spiritual office—that is, as the office of religious leadership for all Muslims—for two years after the founding of the Turkish Republic and the abolition of the sultanate. As we have seen, the conscious connection of the Ottoman sultanate to the idea of the spiritual leadership of the Islamic world, symbolized by the title "caliph," occurred at a relatively late date. This idea gained influence at the beginning of the twentieth century, which meant that the subsequent abolition of the caliphate caused great alarm in the Islamic world. Several congresses were held to examine the possibility of establishing a new caliphate. The issue, however, was intertwined with contradictory dynastic interests, and practical steps toward a new caliphate were never undertaken.

In 1925, when discussions of this issue reached their apex, a book published in Egypt led to sharp conflicts. The author of the book, 'Ali 'Abd al-Raziq (1886–1966), was a judge at a shari'a court and had studied at Al-Azhar University as well as at Oxford for a year. The book was titled *Islam and the Foundations of Governance* (*Al-Islam wa-usul al-hukm*); its main thesis was that neither in the Qur'an nor in the hadith was the caliphate designated as a necessary institution. 'Abd al-Raziq argued that Muhammad's mission had been a purely spiritual one and that his political actions were significant only for his own era and had nothing to do with the essence of Islam. God had left the domain of worldly governance and worldly interests completely to human reason.

Although this approach reflected the prevailing situation in almost every country of the Islamic world, the publication of the book triggered a storm of protest because there was an enormous difference for most 'ulama' between accepting an existing de facto situation and declaring this situation to be correct on the basis of Islamic theory and thus recognizing it de jure. As a result of opposition to the book, a tribunal of renowned shayks at Al-Azhar condemned 'Ali 'Abd al-Raziq and declared him unfit to hold public office. He was dismissed from his post as judge and lived as a recluse until his death in 1966.

'Ali 'Abd al-Raziq belonged to Muhammad 'Abduh's school of thought, as did surprisingly one of his best-known opponents, Muhammad Rashid Rida (1865–1935), who had been 'Abduh's closest colleague for many years. Rashid Rida founded the influential Islamic journal *Al-Manar*. He was less attracted to 'Abduh's freethinking and modernist interpretations than to his search for a pure Islam grounded solely in original sources. Rashid Rida was greatly influenced by the fundamentalists of the eighteenth and nineteenth centuries; it was no coincidence that he was well disposed toward the Sa'udi state on the Arabian Peninsula.

Rashid Rida had himself published a treatise on the issue of the caliphate in 1922, when the leader of the Turkish Republic had stripped the sultan of his political power. In 1925, after the publication of 'Ali 'Abd al-Raziq's book, he contributed fervently to the debate in *Al-Manar*. He insisted that the concept of Islam was indissolubly attached to the notion of a political community. In his view no genuinely Islamic society could exist without a caliph. He argued that the main responsibility of such a caliph, in addition to protecting Muslims, was to issue legislation by *ijtihad*, which should be done in consultation with a body of experienced men, guardians and interpreters of the law. Rashid Rida argued that new men should be trained for this, since none of the existing 'ulama' was suited for such a task.

In Rashid Rida's view, the Ottoman sultanate-caliphate had been only a "caliphate of necessity," since the Ottoman sultan, who did not know Arabic, was not in a position to practice *ijtihad*. He was also not a descendant of the Quraysh clan, which orthodox Muslims regarded as a prerequisite for becoming a lawful caliph. Nevertheless, it had been necessary to tolerate the Ottoman caliph because there had been no better alternative, and he had in fact been able to protect Muslims. Now that the Ottoman caliphate had ceased to exist, Rashid Rida argued that Muslim representatives should assemble to elect a new caliph, since he was convinced that no one was currently suited for the authentic caliphate. He hoped, however, that this would change in the future.

At the time when Rashid Rida presented his thoughts to the public, European colonial expansion had reached its apex in the Islamic world. Nevertheless, the internal decline of colonialism had already begun. In many territories colonial subjects had started to organize and to oppose colonial oppression. Almost nowhere, though, did Islam play a crucial role as an ideology of anticolonial resistance. The endeavors of Jamal al-Din and Rashid Rida had little effect. The new political forces fighting for independence were grounded ideologically in secular nationalism and liberal European ideas such as democracy and constitutional government.

If these opponents of colonialism were Muslims (and not, for example, Christians), they were so in a rather ambiguous and vague way. 'Abduh had demonstrated that there was in fact no contradiction between Islam and modern civilization and that Islam included most of the values that were regarded as components of European civilization. The new political elite went further and claimed that the two were completely consubstantial. Islam had been absorbed, so to speak, into modern thought and implemented a number of universal values, such as the equality of humanity, democracy, tolerance, intellectual freedom, rationality, and progress. At the same time—although few of the elite admitted it openly—their own political practices were actually based on the separation of religion and politics. For them, Islam played little if any role in politics. If it was mentioned at all, then it was usually as a secularized Islam as a component of national history and culture stripped of its religious substance so that even Christians could consent to it.

Like Jamal al-Din al-Afghani before them, nationalist leaders assumed a contradictory stance toward the West. Although they did in fact fight the West and attempted to liberate their countries from colonial oppression, they also continued to regard the West as the fountainhead of their own political ideals. This stance implied a certain contradiction, and this contradiction became the target of attacks from new political movements that claimed to be based solely on Islam and can be designated as "neo-fundamentalist" for this reason.

The rapid social and economic reforms brought about by colonialism and the compulsory integration into the global market did not affect all social classes of the Islamic world in the same way. Although small groups from the upper and middle classes had benefited from the new developments, much of the population had not. As a result of the introduction of wage labor, the proletarianization of large parts of the ruralpopulace, the dissolution of village communities, and the flight from rural areas in connection with Westernization which permeated almost all realms of society, many Muslims felt uprooted, like strangers in their own homeland. They yearned for a society of small, well-ordered communities in which everyone had his or her own place, people took care of one another, and everyone felt secure. Since the West and the Westernized elite were held responsible for these negative developments—not entirely without reason—there were calls for a program to rectify their detrimental effects, drawn from indigenous sources, that is, from Islam. Thus it was only natural that the ideal of an Islamic state and a true Islamic society was regarded as precisely what people yearned for.

Beginning in the 1930s and 1940s several neo-fundamentalist movements arose in different parts of the Islamic world. The best known of these are the Society of Muslim Brothers (Jamʿiyyat al-Ikhwan al-Muslimin) in Egypt and Syria and the Jamaʿat-i Islami among Indian Muslims. These movements addressed the sense of dissatisfaction with social and economic developments and the animus against the West and Westernized elites, claiming to offer a concrete and realistic program as an alternative to the existing situation. They worked for an Islamic society and an Islamic state that were supposed to be based on the example of the Islamic community during the lifetime of Muhammad and his first followers, the "rightly guided caliphs." Thus they turned to the past to find a solution to contemporary problems. They claimed that their ideal society could be attained by following the sunna of the Prophet and the first generation of Muslims.

These movements are not only based on the yearning for an idealized past; they are also rooted in anti-Western sentiment. They are directed in principle against Western political, cultural, and economic hegemony. For this reason, neo-fundamentalists are more radical than nationalist political leaders, who in fact opposed only the political presence of the West. Neo-fundamentalist movements reject all ideologies that they maintain were introduced by the West. They are opposed to nationalism because it keeps Muslims separated, whereas Islam is able to unite them and give them back their strength. Neo-fundamentalists criticize the principle of democracy because they believe it has led to exaggerated individualism and social chaos (two phenomena that many Muslims perceive in their own social environment and feel have undermined their sense of belonging). Islamic state reform, they claim, is neither democratic nor dictatorial but rather assumes a middle position and includes the best of both systems. In the same way they speak of an Islamic economy that is neither capitalist nor socialist.

The objective of these neo-fundamentalist organizations is to establish an Islamic state. This has brought them into conflict not only with Western colonial powers but also with the governments and the political establishments of their own countries, especially after decolonization had begun and independent states were founded in the Islamic world. In their view these states are ruled by godless regimes and heathen cliques that have removed Islam from its rightful place in politics; they are enemies against whom jihad—which the neo-fundamentalists have declared a "permanent revolution"—must be waged.

After the Muslim world had attained its political independence, an increasing number of Muslims realized that most Islamic countries, despite formal independence, continued to be ruled by the West. Through the consolidation of mass communications, Western cultural influence has become increasingly visible. For many Muslims the image of the West has been defined by popular television programs such as *Dallas, Charley's Angels,* and *Kojak.* At marketplaces and in businesses a wide variety of Western products often displace local goods. This—along with the growing chasm between developed and underdeveloped countries, between Westernized elites and the vast majority of the population—provides fertile ground for Islamic neo-fundamentalist organizations.

Translated by Tom Lampert

V

The Distribution of Muslims throughout the World

Figures and Information on the Present Situation

(Peter Heine and Riem Spielhaus)

Dealing with demographic statistics is always difficult. They are invariably connected with too many concrete political implications. The problems are well known and apply also to demography in the Third World. According to the Old Testament, God punished David for having a census taken (2 Samuel 24). Mistrust, fear, and various notions of prestige also lead today to imprecise answers being given in censuses.[1] Yet even in countries with elaborate systems for registering vital statistics, figures relating to the size of the Muslim population are not necessarily reliable. This is due especially to the fact that data on religious affiliation are collected only in exceptional cases if at all. In addition, in Europe and North America one can rely only on estimates that are based on insufficient data from the immigrants' countries of origin and that also have the inherent problem of neo-ethnicization. In such cases all immigrants from countries that are predominantly Muslim are usually defined as Muslim; the actual religion or religious practice of the individuals is not taken into account.[2]

In addition to individual reasons for giving false information in demographic surveys, serious distortions arise because of political and economic motives. Population figures can be used as arguments in the granting of humanitarian aid or development projects. In some countries the population share of a religious community can also play a role in filling important offices. In Europe and the United States, estimates of the Muslim population are similarly exaggerated by Islamic organizations and critics of Islam alike in order to enhance their own importance, either with the argument of representing a quantitatively significant community or in warning against a great threat. So the problems are numerous. Provided the available data are taken with a grain of salt, they can nevertheless give an impression of the respective magnitude of the Muslim population. If these data are compared with the demographic data from the first edition of this book, the sometimes substantial population growth in recent years is astounding. This growth has to do with the fact that the average age in some of the countries included in this chapter is decreasing rapidly. The ten-to-twenty-four age group in many of the countries constitutes up to 60 percent of the total population. This growth will continue in the coming years and will have considerable social, economic, and political consequences.

The fundamental question arises as to who is to be considered a Muslim. This question has caused headaches especially in the regions where adherents of an animistic or ancestor worship form of religion turn to Islam. In theory, the question at what point someone is a Muslim is easy to answer, and Muslim theologians and legal experts have established clear guidelines in this regard: whoever professes faith in one God and recognizes Muhammad as the messenger of God is a Muslim, or even more generally, whoever considers himself or herself to be Muslim is one. In this way theorists avoid the problem of minorities and sects in Islam. In practice, however, this definition largely breaks down. Developments in the religious history of Islam, and not only on the peripheries, have shown that a consensus among Muslims about who is a Muslim is not as easy to reach as appears to be the case in theory. Just to give one example, the Ahmadiyya, a particularly active group in western Europe and West Africa, refers to itself as the "Ahmadiyya Movement in Islam," yet some time ago the Pakistani parliament declared that the group does not belong to the community of Muslims.

If we are dealing with a political and legal framework, that is, one that is defined or at least definable, the problem with respect to the so-called peripheries of Islam becomes incomparably more complicated. Let us look at the situation in West Africa. In some regions the beginnings of Islam can be traced back to the ninth century; cities such as Timbuktu and Djenné were centers of Islamic study throughout the Middle Ages. It nevertheless cannot be assumed that these regions are Islamic or that the majority of people living there are Muslims. Islam, substrate religions, and to some extent also Christian ideas have in many cases led here to a syncretism that often has strange effects. For example, some members of the Bariba tribe living in northern Benin today observe the Islamic commandment to fast during the month of Ramadan, although they are not Muslims.[3] Yet Muslims also demonstrate social and religious behavior that the Moroccan world traveler Ibn Battuta found reason to criticize back in the fourteenth century.[4] These and similar practices have since time immemorial prompted zealots and reformers to try to form or reform West African Islam the way they came to know the religion in the core countries.[5] Thus the question as to when syncretistic ideas become Islamic ones and at what point someone can be considered a Muslim can hardly be answered in those cases. The situation of Muslim minorities in western Europe and the Americas is similarly complex. The problems have to do not with an Islamic-legal evaluation, however, but with perceptions of oneself and others. Ever since the existence of Muslims in Western societies has been on the security policy agenda, demographic data have taken on a disproportionate significance. The consequence of this is often a kind of stereotyping that can be characterized as "ummatization."[6] This term denotes the perception of Muslim minorities as a homogeneous group, neglecting all national, ethnic, and social differences. Religious affiliation alone is ascribed a dominant identity-building function.

Muslim demographers are familiar with this problem. They know that especially in the peripheral regions of Islam, many Muslims have only a rudimentary knowledge of the most important principles of their religion. Nevertheless, they include these people in their calculations.[7]

The spread of Islam as a religious and cultural system proceeded in a very different way. The conversion of non-Muslims to the religion of the Prophet from Mecca was and is based on a diverse combination of motives, of which direct coercion may play a role in only the rarest of cases. Instead the warning in the Qur'an, "la ikraha fi l-din" (There is no compulsion in religion, sura 2:256), led in general to a large degree of tolerance being shown people of other faiths. Of course this is in contrast to the fact that Islam was brought to many parts of the world through belligerent conquests.

These campaigns of conquest under the green flag of the Prophet have not spread Islam in a "holy war with fire and sword," as they are often presented, but served instead to spread a kind of state structure and the pursuit of economic and political interests, as well as accommodating the pugnacity of Arab, Berber, and Turkish tribes. They only secondarily had to do with spreading Islam as a religion.

The acceptance of Islam as a religion by residents of the conquered regions was only very rarely pushed by the Muslim rulers. Often the opposite was the case, since the conversion of non-Muslims to Islam meant that the Islamic states would lose tax revenue. It may well be that the Christianization of vast territories, such as the Byzantine Empire, was hardly as extensive as some church historians would like us to believe, or it may be that the wish to open up diverse advantages by adapting to the ruling class's religion was overpowering, but in any case the fact remains that many non-Arabs adopted Islam. This Islamization was not a sudden occurrence, however, but a centuries-long process that viewed Islam as presenting an advantage, if only because a re-Christianization or re-Judaization was interpreted as apostasy and punishable by death.

In addition to adapting to the political situation, another motive for conversion from the mid-eighth century on that should not be underestimated was the dominance of the Islamic cultural system at that time as a whole.

Despite the belligerent expansion of the Islamic *state,* the spread of the Islamic *religion* proceeded by and large without coercion or violence. The regions of the world in which, in quantitative terms, the largest communities of Muslims live today or in which Islam was most successful in its missionizing efforts were introduced to the religion of Muhammad through a totally different medium.

Trade was one important, if not the most important, element of economic life in Islamic countries. Muslim rulers had attempted since time immemorial to maintain an exchange of goods even with states outside the *dar al-Islam*. Trade lay primarily in the hands of Muslim businessmen, although the share of Jewish subjects of the Muslim rulers was certainly substantial, at least in the Middle Ages. Building on the existing trade routes, a complex network of trade relations developed, which went far beyond exchanging goods but also included money and credit transfers, not to mention the exchange of economic information.

The occupation of trader was and is viewed as extremely honorable in Islamic countries, as the Prophet himself was also a trader, and emulating him in all aspects of life is judged as meritorious. It is not surprising, then, that there were many pious men among the Muslim traders who tried to observe strictly the Qur'an and the sunna. Travel conditions in the Middle Ages demanded a certain form of long-distance trade. Businesspeople who traded wares across great distances had representatives at the distant trading centers. These affiliated traders were often relatives who stayed there for many years, doing business for the colleagues who remained at home. The other option was for a trader with a large stock of goods to make the journey himself, thus, under certain circumstances, having to spend many years living in a non-Muslim country. Both cases made it more difficult to satisfy religious duties than in the core countries of Islam. There was a lack of schools, mosques, and all the religious and legal institutions that a pious Muslim needed from time to time. And so it seemed the obvious solution for these traders to establish those religious facilities where they were. Consequently, at the main trade centers in West Africa, on the Indian subcontinent, and in Sri Lanka, Muslim communities whose members were initially exclusively foreign Muslims emerged, complete with mosques, schools, and courts. This gave the native population an opportunity to take note of Islamic religious practices for the first time.

There were several factors leading to the great success of Islam. The Muslim traders had extensive administrative expertise and as a rule could write and, of course, do arithmetic. Their knowledge in many fields was far superior to that of the people around them. And they were part of a culture that was considered superior. Owing to the special economic and legal circumstances in medieval West Africa, for example, Muslim traders had extraordinarily close contact with the local chiefs and kings. Where more complex forms of rule existed, their special administrative skills helped them supplement their trading activities through appointment to positions in the administrations of such kingdoms as scribes and the like.[8] This put them in a position to exert considerable influence on a ruling house. Medieval sources on West Africa frequently reported about successful attempts by Muslim traders to persuade native rulers to convert to Islam.[9] Here it turned out to be beneficial that Islamic doctrine is basically not all that complex;introducing a non-Muslim into the foundations of Islam requires no special knowledge reserved for religious functionaries. Once the rulers had been won over for Islam, it was often a necessary consequence that the rest of the population also adopt the new religion, even if at times this Islamization was initially very superficial. The animistic elements in Islam, which have certain parallels to the indigenous religions of West Africa, also facilitated the acceptance of Islam.[10] The tolerance that Islam shows in matters of faith also had a favorable impact:

> Consequently as long as traditional beliefs can be adjusted in such a way, that they fall into places within a Muslim schema in which the absoluteness of Allah remains unquestioned, Islam does not ask his new adherents to abandon their accustomed confidence in all their mystical forces. Far from it. In the voluminous store-house of angels, jinns and devils, whose number is legion, many of these traditional powers find a hospitable home; and passages from the Quran are cited to justify their existence as real phenomena.[11]

The tradition of the Arab and Berber traders, who spread Islam in West Africa, was adopted by the Hausa people, who then in turn passed Islam on in a similar way.

The spread of Islam to the East proceeded largely as it had in West Africa, through peaceful means. Here too it was primarily resident Muslim traders who formed both small and larger communities in the port cities of the Indonesian islands and China. Whereas in West Africa the spread of Islam was evidently accomplished almost exclusively at the hands of "laypeople," and not until the present time has it been carried out by professional missionaries, in East Asia outright missionizing efforts began as early as the fifteenth century. Also, the flexibility in the dogmatic structure of Islam led to the integration of many aspects of the autochthonous forms of religion, giving Islam in these countries an individual character.

After the largely unorganized form of Islamization in the early period of Islam, this task was increasingly assumed by brotherhoods. These were tightly structured organizations that were strongly influenced by mysticism, which had been gaining power and influence throughout the *dar al-Islam* since the eleventh century. There emerged on a large scale religious functionaries who did this work as their profession, something that had not been very widespread up to that time in the Islamic religion. They assumed the task of missionizing, which had previously taken a more casual form, and now carried it out systematically by founding centers in areas that had hardly been Islamized at all and engaging in their missionary efforts from those bases.

It is certainly no coincidence that, in regions of the world in which Islam had only recently become the most significant religion, the brotherhoods had a strong impact in determining the face of religious life. They were also responsible for intensifying and firmly establishing Islam on the peripheries, where it had in some ways been superficial. They replaced some of the syncretistic elements of this form of Islam, which had come from the substrate religions, with mystical elements they understood to be genuinely Islamic.

The brotherhoods, with their relatively simple systems, also offered new Muslims the opportunity for strong emotional experiences similar to those they knew from their former religions, whereas the relatively reserved and formal religious practice of Sunni Islam offers fewer options in that regard. In addition, the brotherhoods offered a system of social relationships to the new Muslims, who as individuals had largely abandoned not only their traditional religion, such as ancestor worship, but also their old social system.

Although Islam had viewed itself from its very beginnings as a world religion, for centuries it had not organized missionary activities as Christianity had done from the outset. To be sure, various heretical Islamic groups engaged in broad-based organized missionizing, although these targeted only Sunni Muslims. From their strictly ordered, hierarchically structured headquarters they attempted to spread a specific form of Islam throughout the entire Muslim world. But even this formal attempt did not initially lead to the spread of missionizing ideas to people of other faiths in the sense of a long-term planned action. An organized Islamic mission did not develop until after it confronted the numerous Christian missionary movements and societies that emerged in the age of colonialism and whose activities also targeted Muslims. With the spread of pan-Islamic ideas, a feeling of solidarity also emerged with Muslims who were exposed to the Christian missionizing efforts in Africa and Asia, as well as in the Mediterranean core countries of Islam. Since Christian missionizing went hand in hand with the growing influence of the colonial powers in the *dar al-Islam,* many Muslims saw this as a causal relationship, and they believed that countermissionizing could also be a way to fight colonialism.

In the years prior to the First World War, plans were therefore forged in Cairo and Istanbul to establish a Muslim missionary society, which ultimately led to the founding in 1912 of a school in Cairo for Muslim missionaries, run by the Society for Propagation and Guidance. Muslims from the diaspora received preferential treatment in the missionary school, as they were then to spread Islam in their home regions. The school also had the task, however, of intensifying the knowledge of Islam in the core countries of the religion and to drive back popular Islam and in this way put Muslims in a position to have stronger arguments for defending themselves against Christian missionaries. But the school was closed when the First World War broke out.[12] Its functions were taken over by Al-Azhar University in Cairo, where, in addition to the curriculum that was required for all Al-Azhar students, pupils from the Islamic peripheries received a different, special education that would prepare them for their later work. These efforts to win over students from Sub-Saharan Africa, the Indian subcontinent, and the islands of Indonesia have called attention to the fact that Egypt is viewed as the large, central Islamic country and Cairo as the capital, as it were, of the *dar al-Islam.*

The Society for Propagation and Guidance has now concentrated its efforts on improving religious knowledge, especially among young Muslims in the Arab-Islamic core countries. It supports official efforts to intensify the spread of Islamic ideas in a variety of ways. In comparison with Christianity, however, the volume of officially organized missionary work is still very low, which certainly has to do with the lack of highly developed hierarchical structures in Sunni Islam. The Shiʻi minority of Islam, by contrast, has developed much stronger missionary activities as a result of its long tradition and the fact that its organization has a more hierarchical basis.

In recent times another aspect must be added to the previously mentioned factors influencing the spread of Islam: the migration of large Muslim ethnic groups. Whether voluntarily or involuntarily, numerous Indian and Indonesian Muslims emigrated, according to their respective colonial rulers, as cheap labor to East and South Africa, the Caribbean, and South America. Massive waves of Syrian and Lebanese Muslims fled from economic and political oppression in their homelands in the late nineteenth century to North and South America and West Africa. And finally, the need for labor in the industrial countries of western and northern Europe brought large numbers of Muslims to European conurbations in response to the shortage of workers in the 1960s due to the cold war. Statistics in these industrial countries often calculate the size of the Muslim populations according to the nationality of the immigrants and not by their actual beliefs.

The Muslim countries—that is, states in which the Muslim share of the total population is clearly more than 50 percent—have formed a loose affiliation called the Organization of the Islamic Conference (OIC), which has become increasingly active.[13] Their General Secretariat in Jidda, which organizes and coordinates the conferences, reported thirty-nine member states at the 1979 summit conference in Pakistan. This figure had increased to fifty-seven member states in 2008. There were also five states with observer status.[14] In this context it should be noted that among the OIC member countries are also countries such as Gabon, whose population, according to the OIC office, is 65 percent Christian,[15] and countries such as the Republic of Senegal, whose former president Léopold Sédar Senghor can hardly be considered a Muslim.[16] These two examples alone clearly show that the definition of "Islamic states" poses similar problems as the question of who is a Muslim. Is it a matter of the Muslim share of the population, the legal system, or the country's self-description?

We understand "Muslim states" to mean all those states that Muslims regard as *dar al-Islam* (house of Islam). This does not mean that all citizens of a particular country are Muslim. From a Muslim point of view all member countries of the OIC are part of the *dar al-Islam*. According to ancient ideas Muslims should not live in the *dar al-harb* (house of war), that is, outside the *dar al-Islam*. Only in part as a consequence of Muslims migrating to non-Muslim countries, a new concept has developed: the *dar al-ʻahd* (house of contract),[17] where Muslims are free to practice their religion. This has also led to a new type of Islamic jurisprudence, the *fiqh al-aqalliyyat*.[18]

We have already discussed both the problem of counting Muslim minorities in Europe and the Americas and that of the reliability of demographic data either from countries whose systems for registering vital statistics are largely still being established or from countries in which the population share of individual groups is frequently directly proportional to their political influence. The absolute figures listed in the table at the end of the chapter are therefore estimates from which projections were made for 2004, insofar as data were available.

Statistics regarding the proportional size of the Muslim population relative to the total population of the respective countries are likely to be more interesting. In numerous cases the Muslim population is made up of a wide range of ethnic groups. The political problems that arise among these groups cannot be prevented despite their common religion.

The population figures and percentages listed here are often premised on different ethnic groups in the total population of the respective countries. They are based on data from the *World Population Data Sheet* of the Population Reference Bureau (Washington, D.C., 1992), the *Demographic Yearbook* of the United Nations (1993), and various editions of the *Nahost Jahrbuch* of the German Orient Institute (DOI), edited beginning in 1987 by Thomas Koszinowski and Hanspeter Mattes. Wherever available, data from official sources were included. (See the table for data about countries not included in this discussion.)

Africa

Algeria: Ninety-nine percent of the population of Algeria is Muslim. The vast majority are Sunni adherents of the Maliki school of law; some Ibadis live in the Mzab region and in the country's major cities. Seventy-five percent of the population are Arabs; the rest are Berbers.

Benin: Sixteen percent of the inhabitants of Benin are viewed as Muslims. They are predominantly members of the ethnic groups of the Yoruba, Bariba, Fulani, and Songhai. As far as definitions are at all possible, they are Sunnis belonging to the Maliki school of law. The most significant brotherhoods are the Tijaniyya and the Qadiriyya. *Burkina Faso:* Forty-three percent of the population is Muslim, belonging to the Mossi, Fulani, and Mandingo ethnic groups. They are all Sunnis of the Maliki school of law.

Cameroon: Cautious estimates hold that 20 percent of the population is Muslim. Other estimates speak of as much as 55 percent. The main ethnic group is the Fulani. The Sunni Maliki school of law is predominant, although there has been some Wahhabi (Hanbali) influence. The most powerful brotherhood is the Tijaniyya.

Chad: Half the population of Chad is Muslim. In terms of ethnicity, the Muslims belong to the Arab tribes, the Darfur, Maba, and Tebu. The vast majority are Sunna of the Maliki school of law.

Comoros: Half of the population of this group of islands is Muslim. A majority belongs to the Shafiʻi school of law. The main ethnic groups are various Bantu groups from the East African coast, Arabs, and Madagascans.

Congo, Democratic Republic of the (formerly Zaire): Two percent of the population is Muslim. A majority are Sunna of the Shafiʻi school of law. The most important brotherhood is the Qadiriyya. There are strong networks between Muslims in Congo and Muslims in Zanzibar.

Djibouti: Ninety-four percent of the population is Muslim. The vast majority is Sunni. Their affiliation with a school of law corresponds to their ethnic affiliation. Somali and Afar, who together make up 60 percent of the total population, are Shafiʻis. Twenty-three percent are Asian, most of whom are Hanafis, aside from some Shiʻa.

Egypt: Ninety-two percent of the Egyptian population is Muslim. In Upper Egypt most adhere to the Sunni Maliki school of law; in Lower Egypt the Shafiʻi legal school predominates. Owing to the Turkish influence starting in 1517, however, numerous areas of law are regulated in accordance with Hanafi law.

Eritrea: It is estimated that 50 percent of the total Eritrean population are Sunni Muslims. They are primarily from the Tigre and Afar tribes. Muslims live predominantly in the plains of the eastern and western parts of the country, whereas the highlands are inhabited mostly by Christians.

Ethiopia: Fifty-two percent of the Ethiopian population is Muslim. Most are members of the Oromo, Somali, and Afar tribes. Depending on the region, they are Sunni adherents of the Hanafi, Maliki, or Shafiʻi schools.

Gambia: Ninety percent of the Gambian population is Muslim, from the ethnic groups of the Mandingo, Fulani, Wolof, Soninke, and Diola. They are Sunni adherents of the Maliki school of law. The most significant brotherhoods are the Qadiriyya and the Tijaniyya.

Ghana: Twenty percent of Ghana's population are Muslims. They belong to the Mole-Dagbane, Akan, Yoruba, and Hausa ethnic groups and are Sunni Muslims adhering to the Maliki school of law. The two most influential brotherhoods are the Tijaniyya and the Qadiriyya. The Ahmadiyya mission has also recently increased its efforts in this West African country.

Guinea: Seventy percent of the population is Muslim, especially from the Fulani, Susu, and Mandingo ethnic groups. They are Sunni adherents of the Maliki school of law. The most widespread brotherhood is the Qadiriyya.

Guinea-Bissau: At least one-third of the population is Muslim. The main ethnic groups are the Fulani and the Mandingo. All of them are Sunni adherents of the Maliki school of law.

Ivory Coast: Twenty-five percent of the population are Muslims. Most belong to the ethnic groups of the Mandingo, Mossi (Mole-Dagbane), Senufo, Soninke, and the nomadic Fulani. They are by and large Sunnis of the Maliki school of law. The Muslims are organized in religious brotherhoods, especially the various offshoots of the Tijaniyya and the Qadiriyya orders.

Kenya: According to some estimates 10 percent and according to others up to 30 percent of the population profess the Islamic faith. The dominant ethnic groups are the Bantu, Somali, and Asians. The most widespread school of law is the Shafi'i school, and the main brotherhood is the Qadiriyya.

Liberia: Twenty percent or, according to other estimates, as much as 45 percent of the population is Muslim. The strongest ethnic group among the Muslims is the Mandingo. As everywhere else in West Africa, here as well the predominant legal school is the Sunni school of the Malikis.

Libya: Ninety-eight percent of the population is Muslim, the vast majority of which is Arab and about 5 percent of which is Berber. Among the latter the main ethnic group is the Ibadis, whereas the rest of the population are Sunnis of the Maliki school of law. About one-third of the population belongs to the Sanusiyya brotherhood.

Madagascar: Seven percent of the population is considered Muslim. The main ethnic groups are the Bantu, Arabs, and Malays. Corresponding to the different immigration waves of Muslims, there are Sunna from the Shafi'i and Hanafi schools of law, as well as adherents of Twelver Shi'a.

Malawi: Twelve percent of the population is Muslim; most are members of the central Bantu and Asian ethnic groups. A majority are Shafi'i Muslims. There is also a Twelver Shi'i minority.

Mali: Seventy-five percent of the population is Muslim, especially from the ethnic groups of the Mandingo, Fulani, Berbers, and Songhai. They are Sunna of the Maliki school and organized primarily in the Tijaniyya brotherhood.

Mauretania: Ninety-six percent of the Mauretanian population is Muslim. Most by far are Sunna belonging to the Maliki school, regardless of whether they are Mauri (defined as Hassaniyya speakers), Tukulor, or Fulani. Brotherhoods, in particular the Qadiriyya, are very significant.

Mauritius: Seventeen percent of the island population is Muslim. A vast majority are of Asian descent and either Sunna of the Hanafi school or Twelver Shiʿa.

Morocco: Ninety-five percent of the population is Muslim, the vast majority Sunna belonging to the Maliki school of law. Moroccan "popular Islam" is strongly influenced by a Berber element and therefore plays a special role in the country.

Mozambique: Fourteen percent of the population is Muslim. Most belong to the Yao, a central Bantu group, and are Sunna of the Shafiʿi school of law.

Niger: Eighty-five percent of the population is Muslim. The predominant ethnic groups are the Hausa, Songhai, Fulani, Kanuri, and Berbers. The vast majority are Sunna adherents of the Maliki school of law and organized in the Tijaniyya and Qadiriyya brotherhoods.

Nigeria: Roughly 50 percent of the population is Muslim. The main ethnic groups are the Hausa, Fulani, Yoruba, Kanuri, and Nupe. The northern part of the country has been more strongly Islamized. The Muslims are Sunna of the Maliki school of law.

Senegal: Ninety percent of the population is Muslim. Senegal is therefore, after Gambia, the most intensively Islamized country in West Africa. The Islamized groups are predominantly Wolof, Fulani, Serer, and Tukulor. All are Sunna of the Maliki school of law. As elsewhere in West Africa, the Muslims here are organized in brotherhoods, the largest being the Tijaniyya. The Muridiyya branch of the Qadiriyya has considerable influence, especially economically.

Seychelles: Fourteen percent of the population are Muslims. Most of them are immigrants from Asian countries (largely Sunna).

Sierra Leone: Forty percent of the population of Sierra Leone is Muslim. The main ethnic groups are the Temne, Mende, and Mandingo. They are almost entirely Sunna adherents of the Maliki school of law. The most widespread brotherhood is the Tijaniyya.

Somalia: Ninety-eight percent of the population is Muslim, especially northeast Bantu, Arabs, and Asians of different schools of law.

South Africa: Two percent of the population is Muslim. Most are immigrants from Asian countries, such as the so-called Cape Malays.

Sudan: Seventy-two percent of the population, mainly in the northern part of the country, is Muslim. The Islamic minorities there are Arabs, Beja,

Hausa, and Nubians. A majority of them are Sunni Muslims adhering to the Maliki school, although Hanafi law is also used in some legal fields. The brotherhoods exercise great influence, especially the Qadiriyya, the Shadhiliyya, and the Majdhubiyya.

Tanzania: About one-third of the Tanzanian population professes the Islamic faith. Most are Bantu and, in particular on the island of Zanzibar, Arabs who immigrated from Hadramawt. There is also a large group of immigrants from Iran, India, and Somalia. The most widespread school of law is that of the Shafi'is. The most powerful brotherhood is the Shadhiliyya.

Togo: Twelve percent of the population is Muslim, generally Fulani, Hossi, and Hausa. The most common school of law is that of the Malikis. The most important brotherhood is the Tijaniyya.

Tunisia: Ninety-two percent of the Tunisian population are Muslims. They are generally Sunna of the Maliki school, and there are also some Hanafis. In addition, several thousand Ibadis live on the island of Djerba. The most important brotherhoods are the Shadhiliyya and the Tijaniyya.

Uganda: Six percent of the Ugandan population is Muslim. A majority are Asian immigrants (a large number had been driven out in the 1990s); there are also members of the African groups of the Busoga and Mbale. Sunna make up a vast majority of the Muslims. Among the Asians there is an appreciable number of Shi'a.

West Sahara: One hundred percent of the population is Muslim. They are Sunna belonging to the Maliki school. The most widespread brotherhoods are the Tijaniyya and the Qadiriyya.

Zambia: One percent of the population are Muslims, the vast majority of whom are Asian immigrants, and among them most are Shi'a. The African Muslims are predominantly immigrants from Malawi.

Looking at the regional distribution of the Muslim population in Africa, one can say that Islamization increases in intensity from south to north. From another perspective, Islam is advancing on the continent from north to south. It is reasonable to assume that the degree of Islamization of a country correlates with the length of time Islam has had to gain influence in a certain region or among a certain ethnic group.

The other major region in which Islam plays a substantial role is Asia.

Asia

Afghanistan: Ninety-nine percent of the Afghan population is Muslim. Eighty percent profess the Sunni Islamic faith. This includes primarily the population groups of the Pashtuns, the vast majority of the Tajiks, as well as Uzbeks and Turcomans. Among them the most widespread school of law is the Hanafi. The 19 percent who are Shi'a are divided between the ethnic groups of the Mongolian Hazaras and some Pamiris (mountain Tajiks). Most of them are adherents of Twelver Shi'a. Only in the province of Badakhshan are there also adherents of the Isma'iliyyah.

Azerbaijan: Over ninety percent of the inhabitants are adherents of Shi'i Islam. Small minorities of Sunni Azeri and Tatars also live here, and 3 percent are Dagestani.

Bahrain: Ninety-five percent of the population is Muslim. The vast majority of the Arab segment are Sunni of the Maliki school, and a small portion are adherents of the Hanbali school of law. Most Shi'a are inhabitants of Persian or Indo-Pakistani descent. All together, about 70 percent of the Muslim population is Shi'i. Most of them are Twelver Shi'a, though a small group belongs to the Shaykhiyya.

Bangladesh: Eighty-seven percent of the population is Muslim. A majority belongs to the Bengali ethnic group. Ninety percent of the Muslims are Sunna of the Hanafi school, and the rest are adherents of Twelver Shi'a.

Cambodia: Three percent of the population is Muslim, most of which, as far as is known, is Sunni, although there are also some Shi'a. The largest ethnic group of Muslims are the Cham, followed by the Malays.

China: Two percent of the population is Muslim. There are regional centers in the provinces of Qinghai with a Muslim share of 99 percent, Xinjiang with an 80 percent Muslim share, and Gansu with a 65 percent Muslim share. The Muslims are predominantly from the ethnic minorities of the Uighurs, Kirghiz, Kazakhs, Tajiks, and Uzbeks. There are also some Chinese Muslims, the Hui, most of whom are Sunna.

Gaza/West Bank: Eighty percent of the population is Muslim, belonging especially to the Hanafi and Shafi'i schools of law. In recent years the influence of the Hanbali school of Islam has increased considerably.

India: Twelve percent of the Indian population profess to be adherents of Islam. Approximately 90 percent of that group are Sunna belonging to the Hanafi school of law. There are also some Shafi'is. About 10 percent are Shi'a, most of whom belong to the Twelvers, but there are also some Bohras and some small Isma'iliyyah sects.

Indonesia: This is the country with the greatest number of Muslims, corresponding to 80–85 percent of the total population according to official figures, but only 73 percent according to unofficial data. The largest ethnic groups are the Javanese with 45 percent of the total population, the Sundanese with 14.5 percent, and Madurese and Malays with 7.2 percent each. The vast majority are Sunna of the Shafiʿi school. As a result of syncretism, a majority of Indonesian Muslims have turned toward more mystical forms of religion.

Iran: Ninety-eight percent of Iranians are Muslims. The state religion is Twelver Shiʿa. Most Kurds (6 percent of the total population) and Baluchis (4 percent of the total population) are Sunni Muslims.

Iraq: Ninety-six percent of Iraqis are Muslims. The population in the north of the country—largely Kurds, Arabs, and Turks—are mostly Sunni of the Hanafi and Shafiʿi schools of law. In the south a majority are Twelver Shiʿa, and most are Arabs. The most significant Shiʿi shrines in Iraq are visited by numerous believers of other nationalities.

Israel: Fourteen percent of the population of Israel is Sunni Muslim of the Shafiʿi school of law.

Jordan: Ninety-six percent of the population of Jordan are Sunni Muslims. The vast majority belong to the Shafiʿi school of law, although there are also some Hanbalis and Malikis.

Kazakhstan: Fifty-three percent of the population are Kazakhs, most of whom are Sunni Muslims. There are also Uzbek, Tatar, and Uighur minorities that can be assumed to be Muslims. It can be assumed that about 47 percent of the total population of Kazakhstan are Muslims.[19]

Kuwait: All Kuwaiti citizens are Muslim. The Arabs are Sunna of a moderate Wahhabi sect. Non-Kuwaiti inhabitants, for example, in Kuwait City, make up three-quarters of the total population, however. The vast majority of Iranians and Asians living in Kuwait can be considered Shiʿa. They make up approximately 30 percent of the Muslims. There are also Christians, Hindus, Sikhs, and Parsi, who together with the followers of other beliefs constitute up to about 15 percent of the people living in the country.

Kyrgyzstan: Fifty-two percent of the population are Kyrgyz and 13 percent Uzbeks. There is also a Tatar minority. About 75 percent of the total population of Krygyzstan are considered Sunni Muslims.

Laos: One percent of the population is considered Muslim. The religious situation is comparable to that in Cambodia.

Lebanon: Defining the share of Muslims among the total population of the state of Lebanon is a political issue because government offices are distributed according to a proportionality rule based on religion and denomination. This rule has been questioned. Censuses have not been conducted for decades for political reasons. About 60 percent of the present Lebanese population is presumably Muslim. A bare majority are Sunna of the Shafi'i school of law. The number of Shi'a, however, is only slightly lower. Lebanon is the main place of residence of the Druze, a religious community that is not Muslim but which developed from Shi'i Islam.

Malaysia: Fifty-eight percent of the population are Malays and thus Muslim. Except for a small minority of adherents of the Hanafi school of law (mostly Muslims of Indian descent), Malaysian Muslims are Shafi'i Sunna.

Maldives: The entire population of the Maldives is Muslim. The inhabitants are Sunna and observe the Maliki school of law.

Mongolia: Ten percent of the population are Muslims, most of whom belong to various Turcoman tribes. A majority are Sunna of the Hanafi school of law.

Myanmar (Burma): Four percent of the population is Muslim, far more than half of whom are of Indian origin. One-third are native Arakanese. Two percent of the Muslims are Chinese.

Oman: The entire population of Oman is Muslim. Eighty-five percent—15 percent of whom are nomadic—are Arabs. Descendants of African slaves, Baluchis, and Indo-Pakistanis are minorities dispersed throughout the country. A large majority (75 percent of the total population) are Ibadis. The largest Ibadi population in the Islamic world is found in Oman. Barely a quarter of the inhabitants are Sunna, and there are also some Twelver Shi'a.

Pakistan: Ninety-seven percent of the population of Pakistan is Muslim. Eighty percent of that group are Sunna of the Hanafi school of law, and barely 20 percent profess the Twelver Shi'a faith. The Ahmadiyya movement in Islam, which is undertaking considerable missionary efforts, especially in West Africa and Europe, originated in Pakistan. In the country of origin its members are subjected to harsh political pressure.

Philippines: Five percent of the population of the Philippines is Muslim, primarily within the ethnic groups of the Maguindanao, the Maranao, and the Tausug in the southern Philippines. Most are Sunna of the Shafi'i school of law.

Qatar: All the citizens of Qatar are Muslim. They are Wahhabi and thus adhere to the Hanbali school of law. Arabs are the predominant ethnic group. Descendants of African slaves as well as Persian, Indian, and Pakistani minorities have also been integrated into the society.

Saudi Arabia: All Saudi citizens are Muslim, as no non-Muslims are granted citizenship. The vast majority are Sunnis (Wahhabis) of the Hanbali school of law. A large group of Twelver Shiʿa lives in the eastern part of the country, and there are Zaydis and Ismailis in the south. Apart from about 500,000 Tihami, Arabs are the main ethnic group.

Singapore: Fifteen percent of the population are Muslims. They are largely of Malay background, though a considerable percentage of the population is of Indian descent, and some of the population of Chinese descent are also Muslims. A majority are Sunnis of the Shafiʿi school of law.[20]

Sri Lanka: Eight percent of the population are Muslims, mostly Tamils. A clear majority are Sunnis of the Shafiʿi school of law.

Syria: Eighty-seven percent of the population is Muslim. The vast majority are Arabs. Other ethnic groups living in Syria are Kurds and Turks. Sixty-eight percent are Sunna of the Shafiʿi school of law, 12 percent are Alavis (Alavites), 2 percent Druze, and 1 percent Ismailis.

Tajikistan: Sixty-five percent of the inhabitants are Tajiks, who speak a language largely corresponding to Persian, and 25 percent are Turkic-speaking Uzbeks. Like the Tatar and Kyrgyz minorities, most of them are Sunni Muslims.

Thailand: Almost 4 percent of the Thai population are Sunni Muslims. Most of them live in the three southern provinces of Yala, Pattani, and Narathiwat.

Turkey: Ninety-eight percent of the population of Turkey is Muslim. A vast majority are Sunna of the Hanafi school of law. There are also some Twelver Shiʿa and Alevis (Turk. Alevi).

Turkmenistan: Seventy-two percent of the population are Turcomans, a majority of whom view themselves as Sunni Muslims. The same is true for the 9 percent who are Uzbeks. There are also smaller groups of Muslim Kazakhs, Tatars, and Baluchis.

United Arab Emirates: Ninety-seven percent of the UAE—that is, the emirates of Abu Dhabi, Dubai, Sharjah, Ajman, Umm al-Quwain, Raʾs al-Khaimah, and Fujairah—are Muslims, most of whom are Sunnis of the Maliki and Hanbali schools of law. A small number, mostly Persians and Indians, are adherents of Twelver Shiʿa. About 10 percent of the population is still nomadic. Because of the large number of guest workers, the UAE is the country with the lowest share of native population in the world.

Uzbekistan: Sixty-nine percent of the population are Uzbeks, 5 percent are Tajiks, 4 percent Kazakhs, 2 percent Karakalpaks, and there are also Tatar and Kyrgyz minorities. The vast majority are adherents of Sunni Islam.

Yemen: Ninety-nine percent of the population is Muslim. In the north of the country a good half of the Muslims belong to the Zaydis (a Shi'i group), in addition to another roughly 50,000 Ismailis. The remaining Yemenites are Sunnis of the Shafi'i school of law. In terms of ethnicity, most of them are Arabs. In addition there are descendants of African slaves and Tihami, also originally from Africa. In the south, most of the Muslims belong to the Shafi'i school, except for the few Shi'a, most of whom are of Indian origin. The majority of the southern population are members of the various Arab tribes. There are also substantial minorities from Somalia and India, not all of whom are Muslim.

When speaking of the "Islamic world," one usually imagines the Near and Middle East. This derives from the fact that this is the region in which Islam developed, in which the most significant religious and intellectual historical developments for this religion occurred, and which still today is the site of the places where Islamic intellectual life and religious developments—as well as Islam's exchange with the modern world—are particularly fostered. Furthermore, the main languages of the region—Arabic, Turkish, and Persian—are the main cultural languages of Islam.

Such a view reveals a large degree of ethnocentrism, however, since this is the region that had and still has the most intensive contact with Europe from historical, political, and cultural perspectives. For this reason it is important to bear in mind that—in quantitative terms—the largest Muslim population is found in the Indian and Indonesian sphere, even if up to now this region has not exerted a very strong influence on the Near and Middle East and is often considered to be on the fringes. The fact that impulses for change may also originate from this region is apparent from the significance of the Pakistani al-Mawdudi, one of the main proponents of a return to and reinterpretation of Islamic sources.

Europe

A large number of Muslims also live in Europe, among them both adherents of Islam who have been settled in certain regions or countries for centuries and recent immigrants, who usually left their Islamic-influenced countries of origin as guest workers or refugees and are developing their own, sometimes subcultural structures here. In western European countries the attention paid to immigrant Muslims has grown immensely in recent years, and discussion about foreign nationals has been transformed largely into a discussion about Muslims.[21]

While the Muslim minorities in Finland and Poland, for example, have undergone a long process of assimilation in many respects and become integrated with their non-Muslim environment, one must ask if new immigrants will also be prepared to go through such a development. This is one of the crucial questions with an eye toward social peace—in the broadest sense—in the industrial countries of western Europe. Today people are also increasingly asking to what extent Europe needs to adapt to the newly arriving religious groups.[22]

Albania: Seventy percent of Albanians are Muslims. These are predominantly Sunnis of the Hanafi school of law. The Bektashi order used to play a significant role.

Austria: The proportion of Muslims in the total population in Austria has more than doubled in recent years to about 4 percent. According to census figures, that corresponds to 339,000 people. Roughly 60,000 Muslims have been naturalized since the 1990s. Most of them came from Turkey and Bosnia. The largest group of Muslims still consists of those with Turkish citizenship.

Bosnia-Herzegovina: Forty-four percent of the population is Muslim of the Hanafi school of law.

Bulgaria: Twelve percent of the Bulgarian population is Muslim. In terms of ethnic affiliation they are mostly Turks and Sinti. They are all Sunnis, adhering especially to the Hanafi school of law. Since 1989 there has been some emigration of Bulgaria's Muslims to Turkey.

Cyprus: Twenty-three percent of the population, especially in the north of the island, are Sunni Muslims, especially Hanafis. In terms of ethnic affiliation they are Turks.

France: Estimates range from 3.65 to 6 million people in France with a Muslim background, or 6–10 percent of the total population. About three-quarters of them came from the countries of the Maghreb, 315,000 from Turkey, and 250,000 from West Africa. Because all people of immigrant background who are born in France have the right to French citizenship, estimates tend to fluctuate greatly. The number of Muslims in France with French citizenship is higher than the number of those without a French passport.[23]

Germany: A government report from 2007 estimates 3.4–3.6 million people with a Muslim background in Germany, constituting roughly 3.8 percent of the total population. Through the end of 2005 somewhat more than 1 million people from countries with a Muslim majority had received German citizenship. At that time there were 1,764,041 people registered in Germany with Turkish citizenship and 188,197 from Bosnia-Herzegovina. Roughly 200,000 foreign nationals in Germany carried a passport from an

Arab country, the largest groups among these being Moroccans and Palestinian refugees. An estimated 2.4 million Muslims in Germany are Sunnis. The figures for Alevites range from 400,000 to 600,000. Their proportion among all people of Turkish descent in Germany is presumably higher than in Turkey, their country of origin. The number of Shiʻa living in Germany is estimated at 125,000. According to their own data, there are about 60,000 Ahmadis living in Germany.[24]

Greece: Two percent of the population is Muslim, comprising especially those of Turkish descent and Pomaks and Albanians. Recently immigrated Muslims make up an extremely small minority. Their main settlement area is Thrace. They are predominantly Sunnis of the Hanafi school.

Macedonia: Thirty-four percent of the population are Muslims, of whom 25 percent are Albanians and 3.8 percent Turks; there are also Muslim Roma and Slavs.

Netherlands: Statistics Netherlands (Centraal Bureau voor de Statistiek [CBS]) estimated the number of Muslim inhabitants of the Netherlands in 2006 at a total of approximately 857,000 individuals, divided according to countries of origin as follows: Turkey, 325,000; Morocco, 260,000; and the former Dutch colony Surinam, 34,000.[25]

Russia: Religious affiliation in Russia can be specified only in connection with ethnic affiliation. The importance of Islam for individuals and groups remains unclear, though a revitalization of many religions, among them Islam, can be observed in Russia. It can be assumed that Tatars make up 3.8 percent of the total population, Bashkirs 1 percent, and Chechens and Ingushetians 1 percent. The classification of other ethnic groups, such as Uzbeks, Kazakhs, and Tajiks, cannot be determined with certainty. Estimates for the total percentage of Muslims in Russia range from 10 to 15 percent.

Serbia and Montenegro: About 19 percent of the population is Muslim, especially Bosnians (i.e., Muslim Slavs), Albanians, and Roma. The vast majority are Sunni Muslims of the Hanafi school.

The Americas

Finally, Australia-Oceania and the Americas must be mentioned. Whereas there are only about 120,000 Muslims living in the former region, the number of adherents of Islam in the latter is significantly larger.

Islam went through tumultuous developments among African Americans in the 1920s in North America, in which the Nation of Islam, also called the Black Muslims—which was long led by Elijah Muhammad and subsequently by Louis Farrakhan—was a major topic of discussion. A far greater number of Muslims in the United States are descendants of Arab immigrants. This is true also for most Muslims in South America, many of whom left their homes, primarily in Syria and Lebanon, especially in a major wave of emigration in the late nineteenth century. Another group of Muslims in this region is made up of Asians, in particular from India and Indonesia, who were brought here for work purposes by the colonial rulers in England and the Netherlands. In some cases an astounding symbiosis with the resident population developed.

Canada: One-half of 1 percent of the Canadian population are Muslims from a wide range of countries of origin.

Guyana: Ten percent of the population are Muslims. They are almost exclusively immigrants from Asian countries, the largest group of which are Shi'a.

Surinam: Twenty percent of the population are Muslims, of whom the vast majority are Asian immigrants, most of them Shi'a.

Trinidad and Tobago: Seven percent of the total population is Muslim. Here as in other Caribbean countries, most Muslims are Asian immigrants, among whom the Shi'a are the predominant group.

United States of America: Similar to the situation in most European countries, in the United States as well only estimates of the number of Muslims are available, and these vary greatly: some Muslim groups report the number of Muslims in the United States as 6–7 million. In spring 2007 the Pew Research Center presented the results of a quantitative survey of American Muslims, estimating 2.35 million Muslims living in the United States. All schools of law are represented, though the strongest is the Hanafi school. Most immigrant Muslims come from southern or central Asia (33 percent), followed by Arabs (25 percent). African American Muslims make up 30 percent of the total number of Muslims in the United States.[26]

Table 2. Muslim Population in Selected Countries of the World (2004)

	Absolute Numbers in Thousands	% of Total Population		Absolute Numbers in Thousands	% of Total Population
I. AFRICA					
Algeria	32,000	99	Chad	4,650	50
Benin	1,100	16	Comoros	300	50
Burkina Faso	5,700	43	Congo R	60	1
Burundi	60	1	(Brazzaville)		
Cameroon	3,200	20	Congo DR	566	2
Central African	260	7	(formerly Zaire)		
Republic			Djibouti	700	94

Table 2. *(continued)*

	Absolute Numbers in Thousands	% of Total Population		Absolute Numbers in Thousands	% of Total Population
I. AFRICA *(continued)*					
Egypt	66,000	92	Morocco	29,000	95
Eritrea	2,200	50	Mozambique	2,500	14
Ethiopia	37,000	52	Niger	10,000	85
Gambia	1,400	90	Nigeria	67,000	50
Ghana	4,100	20	Senegal	9,540	90
Guinea	6,300	70	Seychelles	14	14
Guinea Bissau	460	35	Sierra Leone	2,300	40
Ivory Coast	4,300	25	Somalia	7,840	98
Kenya	3,200	10	South Africa	880	2
Liberia	700	20	Sudan	27,400	72
Libya	5,400	98	Tanzania	12,400	35
Madagascar	1,200	7	Togo	650	12
Malawi	1,400	12	Tunisia	8,100	92
Mali	8,700	75	Uganda	1,500	6
Mauretania	2,800	96	West Sahara	300	100
Mauritius	200	17	Zambia	100	1
II. ASIA					
Afghanistan	28,000	99	Malaysia	15,000	58
Armenia	200	6	Maldives	300	100
Azerbaijan	7,600	93	Mongolia	250	10
Bahrain	670	95	Myanmar	1,980	4
Bangladesh	128,000	87	(Burma)		
Bhutan	60	3	Oman	2,600	100
Brunei	300	67	Pakistan	145,000	97
Cambodia	400	3	Philippines	4,100	5
China	26,000	2	Qatar	600	100
Gaza/West Bank	2,900	80	Saudi Arabia	24,100	100
Georgia	470	10	Singapore	700	15
India	201,700	12	Sri Lanka	1,500	8
Indonesia*	190,000	80–85	Syria	15,000	87
Iran	65,300	98	Tajikistan	63,000	95
Iraq	23,200	96	Thailand	2,500	4
Israel	940	14	Turkey	70,000	98
Jordan	5,300	96	Turkmenistan	5,100	89
Kazakhstan	7,000	47	United Arab	3,780	97
Kuwait	2,300	85	Emirates		
Kyrgyzstan	3,750	75	Uzbekistan	20,000	80
Laos		1	Yemen	19,200	99
Lebanon	2,500	60			
III. EUROPE					
Albania	2,170	70	Greece	200	2
Austria	340	4.2	Italy	600	1
Belgium	310	3	Macedonia	700	34
Bosnia-	1,700	44	Netherlands	857	4.4
Herzegovina			Norway	40	1
Bulgaria	900	12	Russia	~10,000	10–15
Croatia	60	1	Serbia and	1,900	19
Cyprus	210	23	Montenegro		
France	3,650	6	Spain	400	3
Germany	3,400	3.8	Sweden	250	3
Great Britain	2,600	5	Switzerland	300	4

Table 2. *(continued)*

	Absolute Numbers in Thousands	% of Total Population		Absolute Numbers in Thousands	% of Total Population
IV. THE AMERICAS					
Australia-Oceania	120		Trinidad and	90	7
Canada	160	0.5	Tobago		
Guyana	80	10	United States	2,300	1
Surinam	80	20	Venezuela	70	0.3

Note: Estimates that assumed a higher birthrate especially among Muslims in minority situations projected 1.2–1.3 billion Muslims in the world at the turn of the millennium.

* See also Vincent J. H. Houben, "Southeast Asia and Islam," in *Islam: Enduring Myths and Changing Realities,* edited by Aslam Syed, *in Annals of the American Academy of Political and Social Science* 588 (Thousand Oaks, Calif.: Sage, July 2003), 149–170.

Translated by Allison Brown

Part Two

The Political Role of Islam in the Present

I

The Intra-Islamic Discussion
on a Modern Economic and Social System

(Johannes Reissner)

Part of the Prophet Muhammad's legacy was his conscious intervention into the existing social and economic system of the early-seventh-century Arabian Peninsula. The best-known examples are the compulsory tax for the poor paid by every Muslim (Arab. *zakat*) and the Qur'an's ban on charging interest, yet there are many more. Islamic law developed at a later stage comments on many areas of economic life, and the religious endowments (Arab. *awqaf*, plural of *waqf*) are an institution created by Islam which is still of great economic and social significance in some countries of the Islamic world to this day. The Qur'an and the sunna, and the examples set by the first Muslims, offer many viewpoints on social and economic ethical issues. Finally, medieval Islam also experienced a wide-ranging discussion between ascetic mystics and urban merchants about the religious value of business activities and profit making. Although there is no standard set of Islamic teachings on the economy and social system for one to refer to, there have been many efforts at creating such a theory on the basis of elements of Islamic social ethics and rulings under Islamic law. This process was initiated by the ideological debate over capitalism and communism and by the specific conditions of economic and social developments in the Islamic countries.

Despite the diversity of development in the countries of the Islamic world since the mid-nineteenth century, there are common denominators: the problem of the supremacy of Europe and the industrialized nations within the imperialist system, and the later economic and technological dependence on those industrialized nations. This meant that the Islamic countries were more strongly integrated into the world market, and the capitalist sector was extended into the individual national economies. In the last decade of the twentieth century, the countries of the Islamic world were steamrollered by globalization, the "second wave of structural homogenization in the global system,"[1] in which there are striking similarities in the reactions to the two waves, owing to the structural equivalences between imperialism and globalization. The following periods of intra-Islamic discussion on economic and social theory can be distinguished:

1. Pre–World War I: acknowledgment of social problems and isolated references to Islamic concepts.
2. Post–World War I: beginning of the discussion of "Islam and socialism" and initial attempts toward creating Islamic economic and social theories.
3. Post–World War II: development of Islamic economic theory and discussion of specific efforts toward constructing an independent form of socialism.
4. Post–cold war: gradual reduction of the felt need to create an Islamic economic and social system, balanced by a trend toward integrating Islamic economic practices, such as alms giving and interest-free banking, into general business life.

What remains is the fundamental aim of ethically guided economic activity.

1. Social Problems and the Term "Socialism"

As early as the late nineteenth century, the representatives of secular nationalist ideologies—Turkish and Arab—were already debating issues of economic and social life and even socialism. The Arabic term for socialism, *ishtirakiyya,* presumably derived from the form *ishtirak-i emwal,* meaning "commonality of ownership" and found in nineteenth-century Turkish literature, was mainly used in Egypt, where the rather short-lived Blessed Socialist Party (Al-Hizb al-ishtiraki al-mubarak) was formed in 1908.[2] Two years later Hüsein Hilmi founded the Ottoman Socialist Party (Osmanlı Sosyalist Fırkası) in Istanbul. It was primarily the writings of the Cairo-based Lebanese Christian Shibli Shumaiyil (1853–1917) and the Egyptian Coptic Salama Musas (1887–1958) that contributed to the spread of socialist ideas. Salama Musas's 1913 book *Socialism (Al-Ishtirakiyya)* demonstrates extensive knowledge of socialist theories, including Marxism.[3]

There was no comparable level of activity in the discussion of social questions among the Islamic reformers. They certainly did acknowledge the issue, however. One indication of this is a series of essays by Muhammad ʿAbduh in 1880–81 dealing with the economic and social behavior of Egypt's new capitalist class.[4] Another is the fact that many of the reformers were active in Muslim charitable organizations, which had been formed in Syria, Lebanon, and Egypt in the second half of the nineteenth century. Jamal al-Din al-Afghani even wrote an early commentary on the subject of Islam and socialism in the 1890s, which was, however, not published until 1931. The text not only refers to "workers' rights" (*huquq al-ʿummal*)—and is an early example of the use of the term "working class" (*tabaqat al-ʿummal*)—but also contains basic elements that were to determine later Islamic economic theories. These include, for example, references to the Prophet's companion Abu Dharr al-Ghifari, who had demanded that the later Ummayad caliph Mu'awiya should restrict luxuries among the new ruling class, and who became something of an early hero of Islamic or Arab socialism in later texts. The main element contained in this early commentary, however, is the interpretation of the term *ishtirakiyya* in the sense of its Arabic roots, as an ultimately morally justified sharing of the property of the rich with the poor.[5]

2. The Ideology of Cooperation

The 1917 October Revolution in Russia brought a certain caesura, which extended to the Islamic world. The Justice Party (*Hizb-i 'adalat*) was formed in Iran that year, the first openly communist party in the Islamic world. In 1924 it was followed by the Syrian-Lebanese Communist Party. Muhammad 'Abduh's most prominent student, Rashid Rida, welcomed Bolshevism to a certain extent, stating that it was on the side of the oppressed, which included the Muslims, but adding that Bolshevism and Islamic law were not compatible.

In 1929 the Syrian Muhsin al-Barazi published his Paris dissertation *Islamisme et socialisme,* going into detail on the subject of the relationship between Islam and socialism for the first time. His conclusion was that although Islam and socialism are incompatible, Islam does have the social well-being of the Muslim community as its goal. The text also contains the initial seeds of what would later become the very frequently expressed idea that the economic and social theory of Islam lay somewhere between capitalism and socialism. With regard to the history of ideas, the interesting thing about this work is that it denies that very quality to many aspects of the teachings and history of Islam subsequently cited as evidence for the existence of Islamic socialism.

One term that had gained considerable importance for Islamic social theories since the 1920s was *ta'awun*. It signified cooperation in the concrete sense of cooperative organizational forms as well as the idea of all members of society working together for the common good. In Egypt it was primarily Yahya al-Dardiri who had discussed the ideas of Charles Fourier and Friedrich Wilhelm Raiffeisen in detail in the *Journal of Young Muslim Men* (*Majallat al-shubban al-muslimin*) in 1929–1931. He had gone beyond purely apologetic statements that Islam encourages cooperation, and had made specific suggestions for setting up cooperatives in Egypt, following Raiffeisen's example. The Muslim Brotherhood, founded in 1928 by Hasan al-Banna, had its own companies run on a cooperative basis.

In the Arab and India-Pakistan regions, it was primarily Muslim reformers and members of religious-political organizations such as the Muslim

Brotherhood that dealt with questions of Islamic economic and social theory between the two world wars.[6] The Sunni *'ulama'* reacted to the discussion of economic and social systems relatively late, as the *Journal of al-Azhar University* (*Majallat al-azhar*), the most famous Islamic university in Cairo, shows. In 1938 (volume 9) the journal contained an essay titled "Socialism in Islam" ("Al-Ishtirakiyya fi l-islam"). Despite the progressive-sounding title, the content of the essay is limited to pointing out various rulings on *zakat*. A year later the journal published an essay on Western socialism and Islamic cooperation, while later articles up to 1950 preferred terms such as "cooperatism" (*ta'awuniyya*) or "system of cooperation" (*nizam al-ta'awun*) to describe Islamic economic and social theory. As late as 1947, the head of al-Azhar, Muhammad al-Shinawi, rejected any similarity between Islam and either capitalism or socialism in the university's journal (volume 19).

3. "Islamic Socialism"

At the end of 1949 the Syrian Muslim Brothers formed the Islamic Socialist Front (al-Jabha al-ishtirakiyya al-islamiyya).[7] This organization and the burgeoning public proclamation of socialism within Islam laid the foundations for acceptance of the terms "socialism" and "Islam" in combination. The specific measures that the Muslim Brothers called for under "Islamic socialism" at the time broadly correspond with the minimum of what is now expected of a welfare state. There were two reasons for calling for social reforms in the name of "Islamic socialism." First, non-Islamic socialist movements such as the Ba'th Party were gaining more and more ground. The second aim, in view of the cold war and the broad efforts toward a policy of neutrality essentially also shared by the Muslim Brothers, was to use the term "Islamic socialism" to present Islam as an autonomous "third way."

A new situation came about when democratic and cooperative socialism was made the official ideology in Egypt under Gamal Abdel Nasser (Jamal 'Abd al-Nasir) at the end of 1957 and the first steps were taken toward nationalization in the United Arab Republic (i.e., Egypt and Syria) in 1961. To justify these measures as legitimate under Islam, Egyptian propaganda made use of the book *The Socialism of Islam* (*Ishtirakiyyat al-islam*), first published in 1959 and written by the long-standing leader of the Syrian Muslim Brothers, Mustafa al-Siba'i. Al-Siba'i protested at this use of his book, as the Muslim Brothers had been embroiled in a bitter conflict with Nasser since 1954.

The discussion of Islam and socialism reached a climax in the 1960s. Although there had been several previous works on the subject, such as Saiyid Qutb's book *Social Justice in Islam* (*Al-'Adala al-ijtima'iyya fi l-islam*), which was also translated into English, there was a veritable flood of literature on socialism, Arab socialism, and Islam in the 1960s. This literature can be roughly divided into the following groups. First, there was the literature by those authors who actually wanted to establish some form of socialism and attempted to legitimize it by references to social aspects of the history of the Arabs and Islam. Second, there were those—mainly in and around the Muslim Brotherhood—who applied the term "socialism" to social aspects of Islamic teachings in an apologetic manner, but they essentially meant a capitalist welfare state and sharply condemned concrete efforts toward socialism in the Arabic countries.[8] The third group is made up of several authors who attempted to found an Islamic economic theory solely on the basis of the shariʿa, ignoring the discussions for and against socialism. One interesting example is the book *The Economic System in Islam* (*Al-Nizam al-iqtisadi fi l-islam*), written by the founder of the Islamic Liberation Party (Hizb al-tahrir al-islami), Taqi al-Din al-Nabhani, and published as early as 1953.

The socialism debate died down in the 1970s. Experiments in Islamic socialism had not brought the promised benefits, and the term "socialism" had become less attractive. After Nasser's death in 1970, the ideological conflict between "progressive" and "reactionary" Arab states was soothed with the aid of Saudi Arabian petrodollars. In 1975, following decades of discussion about the possibility of Islamic banks that would work on an interest-free basis, the Islamic Development Bank (al-Bank al-islami li-l-tan-miya) was formed under the auspices of the International Islamic Conference (Organization of the Islamic Conference, Munazzamat al-muʾtamar al-islami).[9] It is primarily an institution for the distribution of oil monies to poor Islamic countries.

One experiment of historical interest is Libya's variant of Islamic socialism under Muammar el-Qaddafi (Muʿammar al-Qadhdhafi). During the "cultural revolution" in 1973 Qaddafi continued to embellish his brand of socialism with apologetic Islamic trimmings similar to those the Muslim Brothers and related theorists had used. In his *Green Book* (*Al-Kitab al-akhdar*), first published in 1977, however, the chapter titled "The Solution of the Economic Problem: Socialism" does not mention Islam directly at any point. Although Qaddafi may well regard his economic and social theory as Islamic to some extent, it is just as certain that many Muslims do not share this opinion.

After the 1979 revolution in Iran, a number of Islamic principles were anchored in the constitution of the Islamic Republic. A lively discussion developed on the "Islamic economy," and Shiʿi economic theories boomed. The best-known book on the subject was written before the revolution: *Our Economy* (*Iqtisaduna*) by the Iraqi scholar Muhammad Baqir al-Sadr.[10] The Islamic economic theories of the first president of the Islamic Republic of Iran, Abu l-Hasan Bani Sadr, and the militant Islamic organization the People's Mujahidin (*mujahedin-e khalq*) were under a more "leftist" socialist influence. The latter regarded a theosophically broadly interpreted profession of God's unity (*tawhid*) and implicit ontological unity as the basis for social unity in the sense of a classless society.[11] A considerable number of texts on the Islamic economic system have also been written by revolutionary clerics. There are collections of sermons on the subject on the market by the political leaders Sayyid ʿAli Khamenei and ʿAli Akbar Rafsanjani. Despite the dictum attributed to Ayatollah (Ayatullah) Khomeini that the economy is for donkeys to worry about, conferences were held on his economic policy, at which many relevant and controversial issues were discussed under the protection of his name.

4. Basic Theological Positions and Societal Ideals

In this section, following a historical overview of the discussion about Islam and economic systems, I provide a systematic survey of the key aspects of what is currently regarded as Islamic economic theory. An ideal guide is the book *The System of Islam: The Economy (Nizam al-islam: al-iqtisad)*, published in 1972 and written by Muhammad al-Mubarak (d. 1981), who was a member of the Syrian parliament for the Islamic Socialist Front in 1949 and later taught in Medina. His clear presentation, partly based on similar earlier works,[12] represents the overall consensus on basic issues among all those convinced of the existence of a specifically Islamic economic and social theory superior to capitalism and socialism.[13]

Essentially the economic theories are normative and share certain basic methodological characteristics. Theological constructions, ethical demands, concrete rulings, and—where they are of use—examples from the history of Islam are allotted the same normative power to determine reality. They are regarded as a reality of Islam, all on an equal level.

Economic activity is placed within a theological framework in that man, as the Qurʾan states in several instances (sura 2:30, 6:105, 26:62, 35:39, and 57:7), is seen as God's representative on earth. The earth is provided for his use, and all efforts at making a living benefit from God's benevolence. Unlike in capitalism, economic activities and profit making in Islam are not a means in themselves. Rather the aim is to secure a living so that man can satisfy God by doing good, thanking him for his benevolence, observing both his laws and human laws, and helping one's fellow man.

Muhammad al-Mubarak emphasizes Islam's positive attitude toward all economic activity. Unlike in Christianity, he states, work is not seen as punishment for Adam's original sin. This emphasis on the positive position must be regarded in the light of the common European charge that Islam has a characteristic attitude of fatalism which is opposed to economic activity. As early as the 1930s, Muslim activists in fact preached a work ethic quite similar to the Protestant work ethic described by Max Weber.

By giving economic activity a theological aim, Muhammad al-Mubarak also rejects any kind of materialism, dismissing both capitalism and socialism. The authors who referred to "socialism in Islam" also repeatedly distanced themselves from socialism itself, stating that its only goal was to meet material needs, and that it usually brought revolution (*thawra*) or even anarchy (*fawda*). Unlike socialism, these authors state, Islam fights not merely for the well-being of a single class, the working class, but for that of society as a whole. It seeks a just balance between rich and poor, they comment, as the poor in Islam have a legal right (*haqq*) to the property of the rich. Although Muhammad al-Mubarak also referred to the working class in political speeches, as Jamal al-Din al-Afghani did many years previously, it is not acknowledged in his theoretical presentations of Islamic economic theory; the Islamic concept of the worker, according to Muhammad al-Mubarak, refers to any person who works.

The goal of Islamic social teachings is not just class harmony but harmony itself. This is evident even from terms such as "Islamic cooperatism" (*ta'awuniyya islamiyya*) and especially in the concept of "mutual social responsibility" (*al-takaful al-ijtima'i*). Mustafa al-Siba'i, in an already renowned book, had brought together all aspects of Islam with any hint of "social characteristics," elevating them to elements of the "socialism of Islam."[14] The principle of economic equality of all people is not acknowledged. Although some reformers, as well as Qaddafi, have attributed to Islam a demand for equal economic opportunity, authors and scholars in general maintain that all are equal before the law. What they mean is Islamic law, shari'a. As long as Muslims follow the law and fulfill the many moral obligations of Islam, it is held, they will achieve a united and harmonious society. Again, this indicates that Islamic economic theory is above all a matter of social ethics.

5. The Doctrine of Property

There is general agreement on the basic principle that God is the ultimate and actual owner of all things; nevertheless, very different conclusions are drawn from this principle. Al-Bahi al-Khuli writes, for example, in his book *Socialism in Islamic Society: Between Theory and Practice* (*Al-Ishtirakiyya fi l-mujtama' al-islami, baina l-nazariyya wa-l-tatbiq*)—a typical work of the Nasser era praising the socialist character of Islam—that man is only a trustee (*wakil*) of the property entrusted to him. Taqi al-Din al-Nabhani, in contrast, derives from this principle that man does have a legal right to property (*haqq al-milkiyya*) but does not hold any actual ownership (*milkiyya fi'liyya*). Muhammad al-Mubarak in turn argues that original property (*milk asli*) is commonly owned by all, but must de facto generally be private property, as man is solely responsible to God. Whatever the scholars argue, theoretically there can be no private property as we understand it, according to Islamic belief; yet most regulations come down to it in reality. It is private property that is tied to the general good by regulations on its legal acquisition (*kasb*) and its use (*tasarruf*). There are certainly differences between Sunni and Shi'i Islam and within the Islamic schools of thought when it comes to the details of the legal regulations concerning permitted and forbidden types of acquisition and use of property. Muhammad al-Mubarak's summary can nevertheless serve as an overview.

Legal acquisition of property is possible, first, through one's own efforts (*juhd*) such as paid labor, crafts, trading, or hunting. Unlike other scholars, Muhammad al-Mubarak does not include making use of fallow land and mining minerals as sources of private property; in his opinion the only possible result in these cases is common property. The second permitted type of acquisition is on the basis of a legal regulation (*hukm al-shar'*) without exerting one's own effort, such as in the case of inheritance, women's legal right to maintenance in keeping with their social status, or the right of the poor to *zakat.*

Prohibited types of acquisition are: (1) taking another's property without a legal right to it, that is, all types of theft, be it of private or common property; (2) gambling; (3) accepting money for forbidden activities such as prostitution and fortunetelling or as a result of bribery; and (4) charging interest. It is important thatinterest, the prohibition of which is regarded as a characteristic of Islamic economic theory and has become the linchpin of the increasingly common practice of "Islamic banking," is embedded in the central concept of justice as a prohibited type of acquisition.[15] As to the use of property, the principle applies that neither any other individual nor the community may be harmed. The fundamental connection of property or ownership to the general good is expressed in a number of prohibitions such as the aforementioned ban on unjust acquisition, and in commandments on dealing with property.

6. Tax for the Poor and Alms

The prohibitions against certain practices of capitalist economies are accompanied by a number of commandments, the most important of which is that of *zakat,* one of every Muslim's five fundamental duties. The prevailing opinion is that this is not just a form of alms for the poor but a tax to be paid annually. Paying this tax is one of the *'ibadat,* that is, duties to God, and every Muslim must do so (*fard al-'ayn*). The only difference in opinion between the schools of thought is on the question whether the mentally ill have to pay it. According to Islamic law, Muslims must pay a 10 percent *zakat* on field crops, grapes, and dates, or 5 percent if these crops are artificially irrigated; there are rather complicated rules for camels, goats, and sheep, and a 2.5 percent *zakat* is charged for gold, silver, and trade goods. The state treasury (*bait al-mal*) administers the money collected, to which the following persons are entitled according to the Qur'an (sura 9:60): (1) the poor and needy, meaning those with no income whatsoever, and those whose income is inadequate; (2) those who collect and administer the *zakat;* (3) those engaged in "winning hearts," which means giving money to unbelievers out of the *zakat* in order to make it easier for them to covert to Islam, and also giving it to Muslims for improving themselves in the practice of their religion; (4) those buying the freedom of prisoners or slaves; (5) debtors unable to pay their debts, mainly because of accidents or natural disasters; (6) those who work for Islam; and (7) travelers in need of protection and support.

Some of these categories have been subject to very wide-ranging interpretation. Muslim apologetics have not only seen them as anticipating the modern welfare state but also praised them as an incarnation of the ideal of social justice realized by Islam. This is no more than rhetoric, however, as shown by the example of Saudi Arabia, where the *zakat* is a legal requirement. The discussion on the reintroduction of the *zakat* in Pakistan has demonstrated that the individual *zakat* regulations are clear and simple only in the general descriptions of Islamic economic theory. Reintroducing the *zakat* also means emphasizing the difference between Muslims and non-Muslims, as it can be paid only by Muslims.

Along with the legal duty to pay the *zakat,* Muslims have a religious and moral duty to give alms to the poor (*sadaqa*). Verse 177 of the second sura of the Qur'an makes it clear that giving money to relatives, orphans, the poor, travelers, and those who ask for it is just as much a part of Muslim piety as belief in God, the Day of Judgment, the angels, and the Qur'an, performing prayers, and paying the *zakat*. Alms have also been praised as a key social aspect of Islam, and many of those who referred to "Islamic socialism" were accused of propagating "alms socialism." Muhammad al-Mubarak, like Mustafa al-Siba'i before him, treats *zakat* and alms as institutions of "mutual social responsibility" (*al-takaful al-ijtima'i*). He also places religious endowments (*awqaf*) in this category, emphasizing endowments for founding schools, hospitals, and orphanages. *Kaffara,* or payment to atone for a sin which applies to no other person (such as breaking a fast), which usually consists of feeding the poor, is also described as a social institution within Islam. Finally, Islamic inheritance law has also been interpreted in this sense—that is, Muslims are allowed to pass on one-third of their property for good works, writes Mustafa al-Siba'i *(al-takaful al-ijtima'i)*—and the Qur'anic regulation that one-fifth of war spoils must be given to the Prophet and to the poor and orphans has been emphasized as unique.

7. The Role of the State

The basic task of the state in Islamic society is to ensure the application of shari'a. In business life—according to Muhammad al-Mubarak—this means that the principle of the free economy applies within the limits set by shari'a. The state's task, he explains, is to monitor the legality of acquisitions and the use of property, the payment of suitable wages, the conclusion of correct contracts, and so on. As the key institutions of this task, Muhammad al-Mubarak lists the *hisba,* that is, the office of the market inspector, who was often also chief of police in the Middle Ages, and the office of the judge (*qada'*). The state, however, may intervene in the sphere of business not only in the event of violations of the law but also in emergency situations that threaten the common good. It is thus possible for the state to set wages and prices, force individuals to perform certain types of work, or confiscate property in return for compensation. Islamic economic theorists generally admit that the state has a right to nationalize (*ta'mim*) foreign property and restrict land ownership (*tahdid al-milkiyya*), but they seldom agree on the details of the matter. Because of the semi-feudal conditions still prevalent in many countries in the Islamic world, the issue of restricting or even abolishing landownership plays a very significant role in the discussion of socialism.

According to Islamic doctrine, the state also intervenes in economic life by fulfilling public tasks and providing public services. Muhammad al-Mubarak does not detail which areas fall under the heading of "public services" (*al-khidma al-'amma*). Although he does emphasize that students often received support from the state in medieval times, he does not explicitly posit the existence of a publicly funded education system. Finally, the state has the role of administering the state treasury. This consists of the collected taxes and the movable and immovable assets jointly owned by Muslims. The taxes also include the poll tax (*jizya*) paid by non-Muslim subjects—usually Christians and Jews—in order to guarantee the protection (*dhimma*) of their lives, personal liberty, and property by the Muslim state. In the theoretical descriptions of Islamic economic theory, this tax is frequently listed as a matter of course, although it no longer exists in reality. In his work on the economic system in Islam, Taqi al-Din al-Nabhani even goes so far as to declare legitimate only those payments to the state recognized by Islamic law, rejecting taxes (*dara'ib*), be they direct, indirect, or progressive, as they are levied in most countries in the Islamic world.

8. Theory and New Practices

An essay in the journal of al-Azhar University from 1951 (volume 23) states that Islam encourages private property, that the Islamic economy is capitalist (*iqtisad ra'smali*) in nature, and that economic activities are based in Islam, as in capitalism, on the objective of personal well-being, the means of competition, and the condition of freedom. The author adds, however, that the creation of property under these conditions in Islam does not hold absolute validity, as there is also a moral factor. The title of the essay is "Socialism in Islam." This is a fitting description of the core of what the theorists still offer as the "Islamic economic system" to the present day: a capitalist market economy oriented toward the general good by means of several regulations under Islamic law and many moral rules. Most general economic theories are at a certain distance from reality owing to their overwhelmingly normative character—not least because the major part of these rules and regulations is borrowed from precapitalist, preindustrial society. There is very little discussion of the specific conditions; the general economic theories scarcely address problems of industrialization, urbanization, rural exodus, unemployment, and the like.

It appears as if the end of the East-West conflict as a clash between competing systems has also taken the pressure off Muslims to assert Islam as a superior alterative to capitalism and communism by formulating an Islamic economic system. Independently of the extent to which the ideological claim to an autonomous Islamic economic system may have been retained, niches of Islamic business practice have appeared in the Islamic world, which has been subject to processes of globalization since the 1990s in particular. One visible sign of this involves the developments in Islamic banking. According to estimates dating from August 2004, international Islamic banking is worth some $250 billion and is growing at an annual rate of 15 percent.[16] It is now of interest not only to the rich but also to the emerging Muslim middle class; it has been known for some time that the generally rather traditional middle class makes use of local and regional Islamic banking institutions.[17] Islamic banking has reached dimensions that make it attractive for Western banks (for example, the German Commerzbank) to launch their own "Islamic banking" products—a striking illustration of the niche character of Islamic economic practices in the world market.

The developments in Islamic banking deserve particular attention as an indicator of a new type of Islamists, namely "upwardly mobile pragmatists who combine the ability to learn with cultural confidence."[18] They take their orientation from the independent national and regional structures within the capitalist global economic system, which demands entrepreneurial qualities, knowledge of economic policy, and international connections. They have their own international publicity and media system.[19] The range of Internet sites available under the keyword "Islamic banking" reveals lively conference activities on related subjects and problems. It is not so much the countries with "conspicuous" Islamist profiles that are active in this area but rather centers in the smaller states on the Persian Gulf and in Malaysia, Turkey, and London.

This development should be understood not merely as a product of the increased diversity of forms of present-day Islam but also and more precisely as a sign of functional differentiation within practicing Islam. These are constructive ways of arranging oneself with respect to globalization processes, the second wave of homogenization in the global market after imperialism, in the name of Islam. They are no longer mere reactions but elements of previous reactions to the "assault of the West"; that is, elements of the previously formulated autonomous Islamic economic and social theory are being practiced in part in new situations. The focus of discussion is less on the theoretical aspects than on moral and ideological ones. The central category is justice. Not only is it used to raise social demands, but also in its name Islamist movements and regimes in particular condemn the unjust world order dominated by the West.

The ebbing of the discussion on Islamic economic theory since the end of the East-West conflict, accompanied by a wide adoption of Islamic economic practices, is linked to the emergence of the discussion of state and society in the 1990s. "Democracy," "participation," "the rule of law," and "civil society" became the core terms and can be subsumed under the ideal of justice. It is unlikely that the increase in Islamic business practices occasionally presented as an alternative to globalization will create more justice in Muslim societies, but the ideal will continue to exert a powerful appeal.

Translated by Katy Derbyshire

II

ISLAMIC ECONOMICS IN PRACTICE

Interest-Free Financial Management

(Volker Nienhaus)

The Qur'an and the sunna contain the basic elements of Islamic business ethics, which have been further formulated and specified on an institutional basis by traditional Islamic law (shari'a). These business ethics have influenced the economic behavior of individual Muslims, on the one hand, and led to the evolution of specific forms of economies (for example, religious endowments, educational and social institutions run by mosques), on the other.

This chapter does not deal with such practical implementations of the traditional economic theory developed by Islamic theologians and legal scholars.[1] Instead it covers the contemporary theoretical development of modern Islamic economics and, above all, approaches to putting that theory into practice.[2] Today's theory does not deal with instructions on correct behavior for individual Muslims so much as it focuses on institutions and rules within society designed to allow the realization of Islamic values in economies that are becoming increasingly complex and rely on an increasing division of labor. Practical applications of Islamic economics can be found mainly in the financial sector, where institutions (banks, investment companies, insurance companies) have been founded since the mid-1970s that offer their customers all the standard financial services, but on the basis of interest-free transactions. Most of these Islamic financial institutions operate within secular economies based on interest.

In some Islamic countries these microeconomic efforts are supported on a macroeconomic level by governments and central banks (particularly in Sudan, Bahrain, and Malaysia). By contrast, the policy of a comprehensive "Islamization" of the economy initiated in three countries in the 1980s has since come to a standstill in Iran, been displaced by economic crises, trading sanctions, and civil war in Sudan, and was never implemented to a great extent in Pakistan, where it was in fact revoked by the country's financial sector. Contrary to the hopes of many Islamic economists, no social welfare systems have been set up on the basis of *zakat*. Only a handful of states have set rules for this "welfare donation," one of the highest religious duties for Muslims. It is generally left to the individual to decide how much and how frequently to pay.

It is thus justified to focus a discussion of Islamic economics in practice on private as well as state efforts to establish and develop an interest-free financial system.

1. Basic Concepts

The central aspect of the efforts toward establishing an interest-free financial system is the discussion surrounding the correct interpretation of the ban on *riba* (interest) and on the correct application and development of traditional Islamic contract law.[3]

a. Prohibition of Riba (Interest Ban)

The Qur'an forbids Muslims from charging *riba* for loans of money. For advocates of Islamic banking, this means that a lender may not demand any advantages from the borrower other than the guaranteed repayment of the sum loaned, regardless of the success of the venture. The purpose of the loan (whether for consumption or investment) is irrelevant. In contrast, profits from trade and from leasing goods are generally allowed. Purely financial transactions (not based on trading or leasing activities) are permitted if the party providing the capital bears the accepting party's risk and the financing agreement stipulates shared profit and loss.

b. Interest-Free Banking Practices

The interest-free techniques used by Islamic banks can be reduced to two basic types: financial transactions on the basis of profit-sharing practices (financing agreements specifying shared profit and loss) and trading transactions on the basis of markup practices (purchase and lease agreements with fixed markups). There are also interest-free securities, which can be traded on capital markets. There is much controversy over which practices are permissible, and not all banks use all instruments; the specific form of instruments with the same name can also differ significantly from one bank to another. Finally, the catalog of possible financing instruments is continually being expanded by financial innovations.[4]

Profit-and Loss-Sharing Financing and Profit-and Loss-Sharing Deposits
The fact that all interest from loans is prohibited does not mean that the productivity of capital in conjunction with business activities is denied or that

investors providing companies with money to finance productive activities have no chance to obtain payment for their loans.

Financial transactions are permissible in which investors participate in the success of the company or project wholly or partly financed by the investment, provided the investor shares not only the positive results (profit) but also any possible negative outcome (loss), thus balancing the chance of profit against a risk of loss. The Islamic alternative to interest-bearing monetary loans is financing on the basis of profit sharing (profit and loss sharing, PLS). Investors and capital recipients agree that the investor will receive a certain share of the profit made by the (co-)financed company or project in return for providing financial means (liquidity); as this share is set in terms of percentages, its absolute level is unknown in advance and becomes clear only after the conclusion of the financed project. Should a loss be incurred, the investors have to bear a share of the sum equal to their share of capital invested in the undertaking.

In the case of profit-sharing finance, the creditor-debtor relationship with interest payments independent of success is replaced by a partnership with payment for each partner depending on the success of the project. (Partners may also be groups of individuals.) Forms of partnership are distinguished according to whether both partners provide capital and have a right to manage the project (Arab. *musharaka*) or only one partner invests capital and the other works with it (Arab. *mudaraba*).

What makes the profit-sharing principle particularly attractive from the point of view of Muslim theorists (and perhaps also for those in need of capital)—that is, the bank's participation in the entrepreneurial (yield) risk—makes this instrument difficult from the bank's point of view.

- In order to gain a reliable idea of the anticipated profit of a financial transaction, the bank requires qualified and expensive staff capable of evaluating investment plans and market expectations on a sound basis.
- Despite all evaluations, the bank does not know the precise level of profits or the profitability of its capital investment in advance. This insecurity is increased the longer term and more innovative a project is.
- As the profit share is set only in percentage terms, the bank has to protect itself from incidents of manipulation or window-dressing as well as management errors, which could cause the absolute profit level and thus the bank's share to be lower than expected. This requires not only considerable expenditure on protection and supervision on the part of the bank but also the disclosure of internal data by the financed company and certain co-determination possibilities in important decisions for the bank, which is of little appeal to companies.

By contrast, the principle of profit and loss sharing is relatively easy to apply in the deposit business. The bank's customers do not receive fixed interest payments for money held in PLS accounts (savings or investment accounts) but instead get a share of the profit (or loss) made by the bank or by a pool combining the customers' deposits, which is then used to finance projects. As the bank cannot guarantee in principle full repayment of the funds it receives, the monies paid in by the customers are not deposits in the strict sense, although Islamic banks generally do use this term.[5]

Markup Financing

Islamic banks would have to live with the problems of PLS financing were there no other option for financing business ventures. There is a clear alternative, however, considering that

- Companies generally take out loans with conventional banks not for liquidity purposes but to purchase goods (raw materials, pre-production goods, machinery, systems, and so on).
- Interest is prohibited on monetary loans, but trading is expressly allowed, and there are no objections to leasing out material goods.

Instead of lending the financial means required to purchase the goods they need, the banks provide the business ventures with the goods themselves. Islamic banks can buy the required goods on behalf of their customers and then sell them in turn to the customers at a previously agreed-on fixed markup (Arab. *murabaha*) or lease them (Arab. *ijara*).[6] The markup financing sector plays a dominant role in the practice of Islamic banks, as it ensures a fixed (safe) income that the bank can plan in advance.

There is some debate over the permissibility of purchase deals in which the object to be purchased does not yet exist. Traditional Islamic law recognizes two different types of contracts in which goods that have yet to be produced and must be delivered as of a set date in the future are paid for in advance by the purchaser, thus providing financing for their production.[7] These are:

- *salam* for agricultural goods that can be determined by type and amount of a standard quality (generic goods)
- *istithna'* for goods made according to the purchaser's specifications

Although these contracts legally cover the purchase of generic goods or goods manufactured to order, they strongly display the economic characteristics of financing contracts. These types of contracts are the subject of controversial discussion among scholars of Islamic law, as there is uncertainty as to the vendor's future ability to fulfill the agreement, and also because the price determination includes either considerable speculative elements or a very close resemblance to interest-bearing loans. Despite these concerns, both types of contract are becoming increasingly popular with Islamic banks (at first mainly in Malaysia, but now also in the Arab region) owing to their more clearly financing character and the greater flexibility they offer in terms of contract goods and conditions. It is becoming more common for them to take the place of *murabaha* constructions, which presuppose the existence of trade goods and are thus suitable for financing businesses (particularly in the service sector) to only a limited extent.

The aforementioned financing practices on the basis of purchase or lease contracts assume that the bank's customer actually intends to use the physical goods forming the basis of the contract for business purposes. In the practice of Islamic financing, however, techniques have emerged for situations in which this is by no means the case. Material assets frequently play only a formal role; shari'a-compliant profits are instead derived from permissible trading activities through an ingenious combination of purchase, sale, or lease contracts, while the substance of the agreements is clearly interest-analog financing. These constructions, referred to as *tawarruq* or commodity *murabaha,* are used for both deposits and financing activities.[8]

De facto interest-bearing fixed deposits are constructed in such a way that Customer C pays $100 into his or her account with Bank B. No deposit agreement is made through this payment, however; instead the payment puts in motion a complex set of contractual mechanics, whereby all the following agreements are concluded almost simultaneously:

- In an initial agreement, B purchases metal at the current market price from Commodity Trader T1 on the metal exchange, as an agent of C, at the value of the payment ($100).
- In a second agreement, C sells this metal to B, whereby B agrees to pay only the purchase price to C at a future date (e.g., in one year), and the purchase price consists of the current market value of the metal ($100) plus a fixed profit for B (e.g., $10). The customer's payment is thus factually equivalent to a time deposit with a fixed interest rate (in this example 10 percent); the transaction, however, is based not on purely financial agreements but on trading contracts, thus making it shari'a compliant.
- In a third agreement, B sells the metal in turn directly to Commodity Trader T2 at the current market price ($100). The bank thus has access to the liquid funds paid in by C.

If we turn this construction around, it can also be seen as an interest-bearing loan in the factual sense:

- Bank B purchases metal in cash at the current market price from Commodity Trader T2 for a sum specified by Customer C ($100).
- B sells the metal to C, who will pay the initial price ($100) plus a profit for B (e.g., $10) to B at a future date (e.g., in one year).
- C commissions B to sell the metal directly to Commodity Trader T1 at the current market price ($100) for immediate payment. C receives the market price ($100) from T1 on the date of sale and has to pay the market price plus profit (a total of $110) to B at a future date (in one year). In factual

terms this is equivalent to a loan with an interest rate of 10 percent. Bank
B, however, does not pay the loan to Customer C but uses it to purchase the
metal for C from T2, which C in turn sells to T1 (through the bank as agent)
to gain the required liquidity.

Such constructions, which are strongly reminiscent of old legal tricks and
evasions of the law, have always been controversial among Islamic legal
scholars and economists. This has not prevented the shari'a boards—composed of high-profile shari'a experts—of many Islamic banks in the Gulf
region or of the Malaysian central bank from declaring these questionable
practices permissible.

Through the use of *tawarruq, salam,* and *istithna'* agreements, Islamic
banks are coming closer and closer to emulating the instruments of conventional financial institutions. The differences between Islamic financial
institutions and their conventional competitors (or models?) are steadily
dwindling and losing their ideologically persuasive force—much to the regret of those Islamic economists who maintain that an Islamic financial system should not deal with the same ventures of the same customers according
to the same economic criteria, solely on a different legal basis, but rather
believe in the construction of a financial sector that promotes development
and encourages business potential.

c. Interest-Free Securities

Companies and states can cover their financing needs not only through
banks but also by issuing securities. Shares are now accepted as securities
representing part ownership of a company, although they have no historical
predecessors in Islamic law. Shareholders do not receive fixed interest but
share in the company's profit through dividends. But they also bear a risk if
the company's share price falls in the event of losses.

Most companies in the Islamic world are not, however, joint-stock companies, and even those few that take the legal form of joint-stock companies
make only very restricted use of the instrument of share issues. On the one
hand, issuing shares alters the owner structure, while on the other hand,
investors expect compensation for share price and dividend risks, which can
often make financing by means of shares an expensive method. As the state
is also one of the largest consumers on the capital market and is unable to
issue shares, Islamic economists began looking for alternatives analogous to
fixed-interest state bonds or corporate bonds early on. Several types of securities with fairly fixed yields and costs (Islamic bonds)—called *sukuk*—have
been developed in recent years.[9] They are basically constructed as follows:

- A capital seeker (company or state) combines several of its income-yielding
  assets into a single economic entity. It generally transfers these to a special
  purpose vehicle, or SPV.

- The claims to the yields from these assets (e.g., rental income or trading profits) are securitized.
- The securitized claims are offered on the capital market by the SPV as standard securities (with a specific nominal value, a fixed term and a fixed share of the yield from the asset pool, and so on).
- If the assets on which the securities are based have been transferred to an SPV, this company uses the income from floating the securities to pay the original owner for the transfer of the assets.
- For securities with fixed terms, the issuer is expected to repurchase them at the end of the term. If an SPV was involved, this company receives the funds for the repurchase of the securities by (re-)selling the transferred objects to the original owner.

The subscribers to or holders of the securities receive a fixed share of the yield for the length of the fixed term. In principle the absolute level of this sum may vary. Such yield-sharing securities, however, are given the character of fixed-interest securities by the fact that there are generally leasing, rental, or acceptance contracts for the assets covering the entire term of the security and thus ensuring fixed yields.[10] Depending on the type of income-yielding asset pool, bonds are referred to as *mudaraba, musharaka, ijara, murabaha, salam,* or *istithna'* bonds.

The profit-sharing securities originally provided for the payment of yields from "genuine" market transactions. In the case of profit-sharing state bonds, this meant that the asset pool had to consist of state properties or institutions that make money from the sale of services to third parties, for example, infrastructural items such as bridges, which charge tolls for use, or state-owned power companies, which sell electricity to private consumers. Early writings on Islamic economics emphasized as a particular advantage of an Islamic system the idea that only such productive activities of the states could be financed through the financial markets; there were no suitable instruments for financing general (unproductive) state budget deficits, which were regarded as undesirable. This restriction no longer applies, in view of the possibility of issuing *sukuk* certificates via SPVs. The state can ultimately transfer any amount of assets to an SPV and rent them back from it—even if there is no actual demand for these assets other than from the state. In such a case, the level of the rental or leasing payments is not determined by the market-valued use of the assets themselves but is calculated on the basis of the yield rates (interest) on the capital market. In cases in which nothing changes in the actual use of assets, and the yield value of the securities is determined by the yield rates or interest level on the capital market rather than the conditions on the market for the assets, *sukuk* certificates do not transfer market-led rights of usufruct. Instead a financing instrument is constructed which dispenses with feedback to real or market-based investment income at its economic core. The possibility of designing such securities undermines the claim made by Islamic economists that the financial sector in an Islamic system is always so closely linked with the real economy that it is impossible for the financial sector to assume an uncontrolled existence of its own, thereby threatening stability.[11]

The separation of the issued securities from real market conditions has also attracted attention and criticism from Islamic legal scholars, not (usually) members of the boards in those financial institutions that have developed these types of *sukuk*. At the beginning of 2008 the Accounting and Auditing Organization of Islamic Financial Institutions was prompted to publish a resolution of criteria for *sukuk* to be traded on security markets.[12] This includes, for example, the criterion that *sukuk* should be repurchased not at a nominal value at the end of their term but rather, for instance, on the basis of the market value of the assets in question.

d. Takaful: Islamic Alternatives to Insurance

Insurance was long regarded as impermissible in the Islamic world because it was seen as a violation of the ban on speculation and gambling. Insurance contracts were regarded as a kind of bet between the insurer and the insured party on the occurrence of a future case of damage. Not until the mid-1980s did Islamic legal scholars clarify that the idea of mutual support in the event of damages to objects or persons by no means fundamentally contradicted principles of Islamic law, as there were examples of such mutual benefit communities in early Muslim times. In contrast to modern insurance companies, mutual benefit associations do not sell the risk for the payment of a premium to another institution (the insurance company) but retain the risk, shared among the members of the group. The basic principle of insurance permissible under Islam—referred to as *takaful*—is broadly equivalent to mutual insurance in the West, which has all but disappeared from the market through conversions to joint-stock companies. Instead of the insurance premium, the members pay contributions into a risk pool, from which their claims are reimbursed in the event of damage. These contributions to the risk pool belong to those who pay them in rather than to the insurance company.

In Islamic law the contributions are seen not as analogous to a purchase price in a bilateral contract for (insurance) services but rather as a kind of unilateral donation (*tabarru'*). With this kind of contract, the inherent uncertainty over the monetary value of services rendered and the expected reciprocal services provided by the recipient of the donation are acceptable. Nor is it objectionable that the donation is not solely charitably motivated but carried out in anticipation of services received in return (compensation in the event of damages). There are now Islamic property insurance policies (general *takaful*) and life insurance policies providing financial security for surviving family members (family *takaful*) based on these principles. The policies must ensure in particular that the portion of contributions designated for building capital is strictly separated from the risk pool and invested in a shari'a-compliant way (i.e., observing the ban on *riba*).

The conceptual difference between a conventional insurance policy and *takaful* is particularly clear when it comes to the treatment of surpluses or deficits in the risk pool: if the total claims do not exhaust the contributions paid into the risk pool, the contributors have a right to repayment of the surplus (or in some cases a right to form reserves for future claims); if the claims exceed the volume of contributions, the members of the community are obliged (at least in principle) to pay the excess. In the case of conventional insurance policies by contrast, surpluses in the risk pool are converted to profit for the insurance company, which also has to cover claims exceeding the premium income out of its own resources.

In practice the *takaful* model has hardly ever been implemented in its pure form (i.e., as a self-organized mutual benefit association) anywhere in the Islamic world. First, corporate law in most Islamic countries does not provide a basis for mutual insurance policies or similar cooperative models.[13] Second, it is presumably virtually impossible either to raise the necessary capital to cover risks solely through members' contributions from day one, or to start out with such a large number of members that the necessary contributions do not exceed a calculable and affordable level for each individual. The existing *takaful* undertakings therefore have a hybrid structure, combining elements of Western insurance companies with elements of mutual insurance models. A *takaful* undertaking is initiated by a joint-stock company, which works as a *takaful* operator (TO) on behalf of the members of the mutual benefit association, assuming the management of the contracts, risks, and assets in return for a fee.[14] Moreover, although the TO does not assume risks on behalf of the mutual benefit association, it does make interest-free credit (*qard*) available in the event that the total claims exceed the contributions and the reserves in the risk pool. The members of the association have to repay this credit out of their future contributions.

It is conceptually controversial whether the TO grants this interest-free loan at its own discretion or has a legal obligation to do so. Even if such an obligation could not be derived from Islamic law, however, it does exist in almost all countries in the form of a requirement on the part of the state insurance regulators before a license may be granted. The probability that the *qard* facility will be used is particularly high in the initial years of a *takaful* undertaking, when the reserves in the risk pool are still being built up. Despite the conceptual differences, state regulators generally treat *takaful* undertakings in an analogous manner to conventional insurance companies, at least with regard to the required minimum capital for the TO. In fact in certain situations the conceptual difference would have no practical consequences. For example, if deficits occur in the risk pool of only one *takaful* undertaking and the members of the association may change undertakings at short notice (e.g., after one year for property insurance), they are highly likely to do so if they expect that a larger portion of their future contributions will be used not to cover current risks but to repay a *qard* facility for past claims. A different *takaful* undertaking with a more positive claims record would be more likely to provide a higher countervalue for their contributions. It is also conceivable that deficits in the risk pool might be repeated, meaning not only that the repayment of the *qard* facility would have to be postponed but also that more and more members would leave owing to the even greater credit repayment burden on future contributions. As a consequence, the TO's claim to repayment of the *qard* facility would be practically impossible to assert. If we consider that such situations are possible, the conclusion is not simply that the TO must have sufficient capital resources equivalent to those of insurance companies explicitly assuming risks in return for premiums. The question also arises as to whether the conceptual difference between conventional and Islamic insurance companies is as fundamental as it is often presented in textbooks. This issue is all the more relevant in that the TO not only initiates the foundation of a *takaful* undertaking but also can make all business decisions at its own discretion. Although the members of the association have to bear their own risks in principle, they have no more influence over their calculation and management than holders of conventional insurance policies, who are thus in a significantly more comfortable position in that they have "sold" their entire risk to the insurance company.

2. The Practice of Islamic Banks

As indicated previously, banks are not the only Islamic financing institutions; there are also investment companies, building and savings associations, cooperative credit unions, and insurance companies. Nevertheless, the Islamic financial sector is dominated by banks, and the discussion in this section therefore refers only to banking.

a. Origin and Development

One of the first experiments with interest-free financial institutions took place in Egypt from the mid-1960s to the early 1970s.[15] Following the first leap in oil prices, the Islamic Development Bank (IDB) was set up in Jidda in 1975. It is run by governments of Islamic countries as a nonprofit international institution for development cooperation. That same year also saw the foundation of the first private Islamic commercial bank by local tradesmen in Dubai; additional Islamic banks and investment companies were founded in the Gulf region, Sudan, and Egypt from 1977 on. More and more Islamic financial institutions have been set up in non-Arab countries of the Muslim world since the 1980s (including Turkey, Bangladesh, and Malaysia).

A number of national governments have actively supported the development of an Islamic banking system, first by initiating a complete Islamization of their banking systems (from the mid-1980s to 2002 in Pakistan, as well as in Sudan and Iran), and second by instituting a "dual banking system," in which conventional banks have the opportunity to set up "Islamic windows" separate from their conventional operations (from 1993 on in Malaysia).

In the 1990s the number of Islamic banks continued to rise, including several new high-capital banks in the Gulf region. The existing banks continued to grow—often at above-average rates. Since the 1990s there have also been more and more Islamic financial institutions (banks, insurance companies, building and savings associations, investment companies, and so on) in non-Muslim countries, including Thailand, the Philippines, South Africa, Russia, Britain, and the United States.[16]

From the mid-1990s on, conventional banks have shown increased interest in the Islamic market. Both local Arabic and internationally operating conventional banks have adopted Islamic products, set up special Islamic departments, or founded subsidiaries operating as independent Islamic financial institutions (e.g., HBSC, Citibank, UBS). The range of Islamic financial services and techniques also broadened considerably in the 1990s. Financial engineering in the Islamic banking sector has mainly been driven by Western banks and the Islamic windows of conventional banks in Malaysia.

The first decade of the twenty-first century initially saw sustained high growth and a further differentiation of the product range of Islamic banks and financial service providers, and of the supporting infrastructure. Institutions were founded to deal specifically with credit and risk ratings, standardization of bookkeeping and accounting regulations, and the regulating of Islamic financial institutions by central banks. In addition, an increasing number of companies have been using Islamic financing techniques to finance, for example, large real estate and infrastructure projects—more frequently with financing volumes above the billion-dollar level—and the start-up capitalization of newly founded Islamic banks has reached previously unknown levels. In 2008 the Noor Islamic Bank in Dubai and the Al Hilal Islamic Bank in Abu Dhabi started with approximately $1 billion each.

The Islamic banking system has gained international recognition after several decades' development. One indication is that international institutions such as the World Bank and the International Monetary Fund and also central banks of secular states are attempting to gain a deeper understanding of the specific characteristics of Islamic banking and to take them into account in the supervision and regulation of banks (for example, in conjunction with the Basel II recommendations). The European central banks have also abandoned their long-standing restrictive stance toward Islamic banks. In 2004 Britain granted a license for the foundation of the first Islamic bank in Europe (Islamic Bank of Britain) and altered its tax legislation to remove an existing double tax burden on real estate purchases financed by Islamic techniques (the combination of two purchase contracts). The British government also declared its intention to make London an international hub of Islamic finance. Within a few years an additional four Islamic investment banks had been licensed there. The French government also expressed a desire to make the country more attractive to Islamic financial products and financial institutions—in the interest of both the Muslims in France and the country's economic relations with the Muslim world.

b. Quantitative Dimension

In 2007 the Islamic Research and Training Institute (IRTI) of the Islamic Development Bank and the Islamic Financial Services Board (IFSB) published an extensive study on the long-term prospects of the Islamic financial sector.[17] The study takes a critical look at various estimates of the quantitative dimension of the Islamic financial sector (on the basis of statistics for 2005). All estimates suffer from the fact that there are no reliable primary data available for key subsectors. For instance, most bank balance sheets and national statistics do not state the financial volume of the Islamic departments of conventional banks or of Islamic products offered by conventional financial institutions. Moreover, there is scope for discussion about whether Islamic funds should be fully or only partially included in the volume of the Islamic financial sector, as these funds do mobilize customer monies in a shari'a-compliant manner but invest them from a large to an overwhelming extent in conventional shares traded on Western stock exchanges (which fulfill pragmatic criteria for shari'a compliance) for want of "genuine" Islamic investment forms. One must therefore take into account considerable margins of error for all estimates.[18]

- On the basis of the IRTI/IFSB study, and adopting the common assumption of annual growth rates between approximately 15 and 20 percent, one may assume that more than three hundred Islamic financial institutions were operating in mid-2008 in approximately seventy Muslim and non-Muslim countries.[19]
- The total assets of the Islamic financial sector amount to between $500 and 700 billion.
- Just under 90 percent of this volume is divided roughly equally between Islamic banks and Islamic windows of conventional banks.
- Islamic funds and securities flotations *(sukuk)* have a share of around 10 percent.
- A small but fast-growing volume is contributed by Islamic insurance policies *(takaful* and re-*takaful).*
- The assets managed by banks and insurance undertakings are occasionally boosted by the addition of capitalization of the shari'a-compliant stock exchanges in Muslim countries (mainly the Gulf states and Malaysia), amounting to some $300 billion.

The growth of the Islamic financial sector in recent years is due not only to internal growth of "purely" Islamic financial institutions but also, to an increasing extent, to the establishment of Islamic windows in conventional banks or the complete transformation of conventional institutions into Islamic banks, particularly in the Gulf region. The oil price boom (up to the end of 2008) prompted this growth of the Islamic financial sector in the Gulf region in particular, where two new Islamic "mega-banks" were founded in 2008 with equity of approximately $1 billion each.

These figures on the quantitative dimension are based on the situation before the outbreak of the global financial crisis in fall 2008. The numerical values of market shares, market capitalizations, and the like no doubt looked different at the end of 2008 compared to the middle of that year. The Islamic banks, however, had previously been spared major setbacks, mainly because, on the one hand, they were unable to purchase the particularly loss-creating types of securities owing to their nonconformance with shari'a, and, on the other hand, their stock portfolios contain neither bank shares nor shares in companies with particularly high levels of third-party financing (which were hit first and hardest by the credit crunch), for the same reason. In view of the rapidly spreading global recession, however, and the falling price of oil, it seemed highly unlikely that the Islamic financial sector would remain entirely unaffected by crises.

In some Gulf states the governments had already announced, as a protective measure, that deposits in Islamic banks were safe. This was in clear contradiction of the concept of profit-and-loss-sharing investment accounts but may have been a justifiable emergency measure in view of the systematic crisis. High-profile shari'a experts supported this measure, on the basis of a remarkable argument: although it is not permissible for the bank to guarantee deposits, it does not contradict Islamic law if a third party does so. It is certainly admitted that this contravenes the spirit of PLS investment accounts, but the argument is that this is to be blamed not on the guarantor but on the holder of the investment account if he or she actually makes use of this guarantee without need.

c. Business Practice

Most Islamic banks have a shari'a board, on which experts assess the compatibility with Islamic law of the financial techniques and contractual structures used by the bank.[20] Whereas a consensus has at least been reached on the form and permissibility of "classic" financial techniques within the Islamic schools of jurisprudence, opinions on new types still diverge. In order to avoid different interpretations and applications of Islamic law for financial innovations, a national shari'a board was set up at the Malaysian central bank to issue binding legal opinions for all Islamic financial institutions in the country.

In the deposits sector, Islamic banks tend to pay yield rates for customer deposits into profit-and-loss-sharing accounts (referred to as investment accounts) that follow interest development in the conventional sector of the economy.[21] Islamic banks can achieve this alignment by building up or drawing on reserves depending on the market situation, and thus reducing or raising the profit to be shared with the accountholders. By building up or drawing on "profit equalization reserves," these PLS accounts become very similar in terms of economic characteristics to conventional interest-based bank deposits, a fact that has repeatedly provoked criticism.

In the financing sector, the dominant activity has always been short-term trade financing with fixed markups for the bank. Medium- and long-term financing projects are rarely carried out.[22] A key reason for this preference lies in the term structure of the deposits. Most accountholders prefer short-term investment forms (e.g., time deposits with a term of thirty days). Banks can allocate loans with longer terms to only a very limited extent out of monies available on a daily or monthly basis. Maturity transformations are more difficult for Islamic banks than for conventional institutions because they cannot simply fall back on the interbank market or central bank loans in the event of unexpected liquidity needs, as these options incur interest in conventional systems; interest-free alternatives are not yet available in most countries.[23] Independent of the term, it is noticeable that profit and loss sharing is not a significant portion of most banks' financing operations. Eighty percent and more of financing transactions use techniques that ensure safe yields for the banks *(murabaha, salam, istithna', tawarruq, ijara)*. In some banks the percentage of profit-and-loss-sharing transactions has risen in recent years; this does not mean, however, that these banks are actually prepared to bear a greater amount of economic risk on behalf of independent enterprises. First of all, banks use *musharaka* agreements to finance projects of companies in which they hold a significant share of equity so that they can thus (co-)determine the companies' business policies. Second, *murabaha* agreements are being replaced by *musharaka* or *mudaraba* constructions for short-term trading financing. The risk entered into by the bank is minimal in such transactions, provided the conditions for further sale (including prices and expected yields) are set before acquisition of the commodity itself.

Since about 2000, law firms, corporate advisers, and financial engineers of Western and Islamic banks have developed a broad range of innovative financial techniques, which have at least been approved by the shari'a boards of individual Islamic financial institutions. These newer (and not yet generally accepted) financial innovations include, for example:

- shari'a-compliant securitization
- shari'a-compliant indexation
- shari'a-compliant acquisition finance
- shari'a-compliant hedging
- Islamic money market instruments
- shari'a-compliant profit rate swaps
- Islamic real estate investment trusts (I-REITs)
- shari'a-compliant forward exchange transactions

Many financial innovations make extensive use of special purpose vehicles (SPVs), which can make the structures extremely complex in terms of contractual design and documentation and the applicable corporate and tax law. They require specific legal and market knowledge, which leads to higher costs in comparison to techniques for analogous purposes in the conventional sector.

Moreover, a not unproblematic practice appears to be emerging in the field of assessing shariʿa compliance, which involves dismantling complex structures by means of (sometimes several) SPVs into simpler segments, each of which is then subjected to a separate compliance examination. It is easy to lose sight of the shariʿa quality of the arrangement as a whole through this process, which allows financial engineers to create overall structures out of several shariʿa-compliant segments, with which almost any financial technique in the conventional interest-based system can be emulated, even if the result violates the principles and intentions of shariʿa. The long-standing controversy over *tawarruq,* which have a simple structure in comparison to many other recent financial innovations in the Islamic sector, shows that such a risk of overemphasis on the form and neglect of the substance of agreements is all too real.

On the one hand, the more that conventional instruments can be emulated in the Islamic financial sector, the more efficient (in the conventional sense) the sector becomes, and the simpler it is to integrate the sector into global financial markets and network it with the conventional mainstream. On the other hand, it thereby becomes increasingly difficult to pinpoint substantial distinctive features and differences in the Islamic financial system. In this context there has been a remarkable change in the terminology. Whereas previously the adjective "Islamic" was applied to specific financial techniques and products, it is now standard practice to refer to them as "shariʿa compliant." The ideological undertone of "Islamic" has thus been replaced by a reference to a formal legal system. This matter has also been addressed by Islamic economists, for whom the term "Islamic" signifies ideas for social and economic reform and a stronger orientation toward development. It is no surprise that bankers have little understanding of this view. It remains to be seen which position will take hold among shariʿa experts in the long term.

3. Institutional Infrastructure of the Islamic Finance Sector

Up to the mid-1990s there was neither an effective representation of the joint interests of Islamic banks nor effective institutions accompanying their operations in interest-based economies. This situation has since changed. On the one hand, a tendency has emerged toward standardizing Islamic financial products and rules for monitoring and regulating Islamic banks.

On the other hand, Islamic banks can now make use of specialized services from ratings agencies, index publishers, and financial brokers.

a. The Accounting and Auditing Organization of Islamic Financial Institutions

The Accounting and Auditing Organization of Islamic Financial Institutions (AAOIFI) was founded in Bahrain in 1991.[24] Its original objective was to develop standards for accounting, balancing, and auditing, for management and ethics, and particularly for the application of shariʿa in the financial world, and to recommend these measures to Islamic financial institutions. By mid-2008 AAOIFI had 155 members from forty countries, including banks, investment companies, insurance companies, and the central banks or banking regulatory authorities of Bahrain, Palestine, Indonesia, the Maldives, Syria, and Qatar, along with consulting and auditing companies. AAOIFI has succeeded in building a respected international reputation and developing thirty standards on shariʿa issues, twenty-three on accounting principles, five on auditing, six on corporate structure and management, and two on professional ethics, which are used on a voluntary basis by numerous Islamic financial institutions. In recent years AAOIFI has additionally gained recognition from the relevant authorities for banking supervision and regulation in nine countries, which have declared its standards binding; other countries have used them as guides for their own regulations. The use of uniform standards in more and more countries increases not only the transparency and comparability of Islamic financial practices but also the ease of cross-border networking between Islamic financial institutions and products. This is an important step toward overcoming the fragmentation of the Islamic financial sector and developing a global market with greater volume and more possibilities for division of labor and specialization. As a relatively new service, AAOIFI also offers contract certification, examining and certifying the conformity of financial contracts between Islamic financial institutions and their customers with international shariʿa standards.

b. Islamic Financial Services Board

Whereas the AAOIFI standards are primarily aimed at financial institutions operating on the market, the recommendations of the Islamic Financial Services Board (IFSB), established in Kuala Lumpur in 2002 and active since 2003, are directed at central banks and regulatory authorities.[25] The objective is to contribute to the solidity and stability of the Islamic financial sector by means of internationally applicable regulation and supervision standards. In mid-2008 the 164 members (21 full members, 21 associate members, and 122 members with observer status) were made up of 41 central banks and supervisory authorities of Islamic and non-Islamic countries, 6 international organizations (including the Asian Development Bank, the World Bank and

International Monetary Fund, and the Bank for International Settlements), and 117 market players from 33 countries. Standards have been determined on issues of risk management, appropriate capital endowment, corporate structure and management, reporting obligations, and bank supervisory authorities, with additional standards at the consultation stage. The IFSB has gained a lofty reputation in the Islamic financial sector and among central banks and supervisory authorities, not only in the Muslim world, and has played a key role in integrating the Islamic financial sector into the global financial system.

c. International Islamic Financial Market

Founded in 2001 and operating in Bahrain since 2002, the International Islamic Financial Market (IIFM) is another institution for promoting international trading in shari'a-compliant securities and diversifying investment options for Islamic banks.[26] The founding members of the IIFM were the Islamic Development Bank; the central banks of Bahrain, Sudan, and Indonesia; the Ministry of Finance of Brunei; and the Malaysian regulatory authority for the offshore financial market in Labuan (Labuan Offshore Financial Services Authority, or LOFSA). Since its foundation the IIFM has also attracted a number of market players and has a membership of about forty institutions. It focuses on the clarification and international standardization of demands made of shari'a-compliant security flotations and trading in these securities required from the point of view of Islamic law, particularly with regard to documentation, structure, and contract design.[27] For this purpose the IIFM develops "master agreements" for shari'a-compliant types of securities and techniques, particularly for risk management (hedging), for liquidity management, and for the money market business (Islamic *repos,* treasury *murabaha* contracts), which require product innovations on the one hand and on the other hand reduce transaction costs by setting standards, thereby achieving broader international market acceptance so as to promote the growth of a global Islamic financial market.

d. Liquidity Management Center

The Liquidity Management Center (LMC)[28] was founded in 2002 by the Islamic Development Bank and three private Islamic banks,[29] with the support of the central bank of Bahrain. Its objective is to help create a type of interest-free capital market, which enables the Islamic banks to manage their liquidity more efficiently. For this purpose a (secondary) market was to be set up for trading in high-quality, shari'a-compliant securities, particularly *sukuk.*[30] Islamic financial institutions holding more liquidity than profitable investment possibilities of their own in the short term can purchase *sukuk* certificates, which offer a minimum profitability. In the opposite case of a liquidity shortage, *sukuk* can be sold from the institution's own stock.

In order for such a liquidity management model to work on the securities market, a sufficient volume of suitable securities has to be issued (primary market), which are then traded on a secondary market. On the primary market, the LMC is actively involved in constructing and issuing *sukuk* certificates from state institutions (particularly the Bahraini government) and private companies. On the secondary market, the LMC offers various services (including price information and registration of sale and purchase offers).

Out of the total volume of new *sukuk* issues outside of Malaysia,[31] only 6.2 percent were administered by the LMC. This low share and the sustained low volume of secondary market sales via the LMC,[32] along with the fast development of the *sukuk* market in Dubai (see the section on Dubai later in this chapter), indicate that the LMC is likely to be of only local significance in the long term.

e. International Islamic Rating Agency

The International Islamic Rating Agency (IIRA) was founded in Bahrain in late 2002, funded by the Islamic Development Bank, four private Islamic banks, and two ratings agencies from Malaysia and Pakistan.[33] Its task is to assess the creditworthiness of market-listed companies, Islamic banks, and security issues, particularly in terms of shari'a compliance. Since its founding almost all conventional rating agencies have also adopted this task; the IIRA, however, has a unique feature in that it also and particularly rates the shari'a quality of its customers' institutions and/or security issues (Shari'a Quality Rating, SQR). This does not mean that the IIRA voices an opinion on the decisions or legal positions (fatwas) of Islamic banks' shari'a boards. Instead it examines in what way such decisions and positions are taken into account in a bank's business processes. Moreover, it judges the shari'a quality of its products, its personnel, or the observation of AAOIFI standards in its accounting. The IIRA's shari'a board consists of nineteen of the best-known shari'a experts in the Islamic financial world, almost all of whom are on the shari'a boards of several Islamic financial institutions. As of mid-2008 SQRs had been completed for only one *takaful* operator and one Islamic investment fund and were valid for one year; agreements on future SQRs were made with two banks at the end of 2007 and the beginning of 2008. The *takaful* operator's SQR classification was withdrawn in 2008 as it failed to renew the rating agreement.

f. Dubai International Financial Centre

In recent years Dubai has been endeavoring—in competition with Bahrain—to become an international financial hub between New York and London in the West and Hong Kong and Tokyo in the East, through which the Arab financial markets—particularly those of the Gulf Cooperation Council

(GCC) states—are developed and integrated into the global money and capital market. In particular, it aims to

- offer attractive investment opportunities in the region for Arab capital—not least in conjunction with major privatization programs in most Arab states
- build up the underdeveloped insurance markets
- create "the" global center for Islamic finances

The Dubai International Financial Centre (DIFC) was founded for this purpose, commencing operations in 2004.[34] The DIFC is a "free zone" with a modern infrastructure and generous tax advantages for service companies and financial institutions. In contrast to other tax oases and free zones, the DIFC does not have particularly lax tax regulations, but it does have clear laws applicable to all companies within the zone, which are also subject to internationally recognized standards and regulations for accounting and corporate governance.

As a supervisory authority for the financial market, the Dubai Financial Services Authority (DFSA) was established in 2004 and is responsible for financial institutions and the capital market—in both the conventional and the Islamic sector.[35] Companies may operate as purely Islamic financial institutions or as Islamic windows of conventional institutions. The DFSA is also responsible for overseeing (domestic and foreign) Islamic investment funds and Islamic real estate investment trusts (I-REITs), and for the issuance of Islamic securities (particularly *sukuk*). The DFSA generally requires the Islamic financial sector to follow the AAOIFI accounting rules, for example, and some regulations are based on IFSB standards (provided such standards exist). In the Islamic market segment, the DFSA (in contrast to Pakistan and Malaysia) does not lay down material standards with regard to the shari'a compliance of specific techniques or products; such decisions are reserved for the respective shari'a boards of the individual financial institutions. The DFSA does, however, require that suitable internal systems for examining and securing shari'a compliance (in line with the position on Islamic law of the respective shari'a boards) function within the financial institutions.

To accelerate the development of the financial market, the Dubai International Financial Exchange (DIFX) was opened in September 2005. This exchange, focusing on the Middle East and the Indian subcontinent, operates on the basis of rules similar to those of leading international exchanges such as in London, New York, and Hong Kong. The DIFX has become the world's largest trading exchange for *sukuk* outside of Malaysia, issued not only by companies from the region but also in North America, Europe, India, and Australia. Out of a global total value for issued *sukuk* of $88 billion (2007 listed value), $13 billion were traded at DIFX.[36] The DFSA and the Securities and Exchange Commission of Malaysia (SEC) have concluded an agreement on the mutual recognition of standards and regulations for *sukuk* certificates issued on the DIFX or the Kuala Lumpur exchange, which can now be traded on the other exchange without major additional red tape.

g. Islamic Stock Exchange Indexes

Since the early 2000s, Dow Jones & Company has offered a continually expanding family of now more than fifty Islamic market indexes (as of March 2008).[37] These indexes depict the performance of shares, compiled into regional or industry-based groups and considered shari'a compliant by a council of high-ranking international Islamic legal experts.[38] Shares can be included in an Islamic index if the companies fulfill several conditions:

- The companies may not carry out any activities or produce products that are banned or undesirable (industry filter). This excludes companies producing alcohol and pork products, as well as those offering conventional financial services and entertainment services (particularly movies, music, gambling, and pornography) and producing tobacco products or armaments.
- Financial statistics are prepared for the remaining companies, and those companies with interest-based third-party financing or income from interest that is considered too high are excluded (financial filter). Permissible factors are (1) debts, (2) cash balances and interest-bearing securities, and (3) receivables for sales and services of less than 33 percent of market capitalization (flexible twelve-month average).[39]

The numerical limits for interest-related financial data are set on a pragmatic (or random) basis and cannot be derived from principles of Islamic law, and they have already been changed (relaxed) to some extent. The use of such measures is due to the fact that there currently are not sufficient investment opportunities for Islamic capital that adhere strictly to all shari'a requirements, on either national or international markets.

The Financial Times Group has also constructed a family of Islamic indexes using a very similar technique (in conjunction with Yasaar Research).[40] The FTSE Shari'a Global Equity Index Series is distinguished from the competition by a more conservative approach to financial filtering, in which the debts, cash balance, interest-bearing securities, and receivables are related not to the higher market capitalization, which varies according to price movements, but to the balance sheet total.[41] Other Islamic indexes are run by MSCI Barra, Global Investment House, and for *sukuk*, HBSC along with DIFX.[42]

h. Legal and Corporate Consultancies, Rating Agencies, Media

Another sign that the Islamic financial sector has become part of the global financial world is the fact that in recent years, not only have numerous internationally operating conventional banks and insurance companies taken up activities in the Islamic financial sector, but so have a large number of well-known (mainly British) law firms, corporate consultancies, rating agencies, and auditing companies as well. These include, for example:

- Law firms such as Clifford Chance, King & Spalding, Lovells, Norton Rose, and Simmons & Simmons, whose skills are in particular demand for structuring complex finances (especially security flotations) that fulfill the requirements of Islamic and international law.[43]
- Corporate consultancies and auditing companies acting as advisers and auditors for Islamic financial institutions such as Ernst & Young,[44] KPMG,[45] and McKinsey.
- Rating agencies such as Moody's, Standard & Poor's, and Fitch Ratings,[46] which not only apply their rating methods to Islamic financial institutions and securities with some degree of adaptation but also publish risk and market analyses.

It is also worth mentioning that more and more specialized print and electronic media are becoming established and are reporting regularly on Islamic financial markets, for instance, the magazines *Islamic Banker, New Horizon, Islamic Business and Finance,* and *Middle East Insurance Review Incorporating Global Takaful,* the annual *Islamic Finance Review* from *Euromoney,* and online services such as *Islamic Finance News* and industry information from *Zawya.*

i. Training, Education, and Research

One of the greatest problems facing the fast-expanding Islamic financial sector is the lack of qualified staff on all levels.[47] Among other things, this leads to headhunting and disproportional rises in wages and salaries.

Alongside a flood of specialist conferences and seminars on individual aspects of the Islamic financial sector and internal training and advanced education programs in the Islamic financial institutions and regulatory bodies, there are two initiatives worth mentioning for their more comprehensive approach.

- In 2006 the central bank of Malaysia founded the International Centre for Education in Islamic Finance (INCEIF) with an endowment of 500 million ringgit (approximately $135 million), devoted to the development of qualified personnel and specialists for the Islamic financial sector in Malaysia and beyond.[48] In the interest of achieving as broad a range as possible, INCEIF uses Web-based distance learning methods. The first and still most important program is the Chartered Islamic Finance Professional Programme (CIFP). INCEIF, which has the status of a private university, also offers academic degree programs: a master's and a Ph.D. in Islamic finance.

- The Bahrain Institute of Banking and Finance (BIBF), in existence since 1981, has offered a wide range of seminars and courses for the Islamic financial sector at its Center for Islamic Finance since 1997, including professional diplomas and a master's in Islamic finance. In competition with Malaysia to some extent, the central bank of Bahrain and several commercial banks jointly founded a Waqf Fund in 2006 to carry out public relations work on popularizing the Islamic financial sector and particularly to strengthen the BIBF's training capacity in this area. The $4.6 million start-up capital provided by the central bank was to be increased through contributions from Islamic financial institutions.[49]

Both the INCEIF and the BIFB were developing their own master's programs in conjunction with Western universities, in which Islamic finance would play a major role. In addition, an increasing number of universities in Islamic countries have been offering degree programs (bachelor's, master's, and Ph.D.) or at least modules on Islamic finance in existing programs.

There is a particular shortage of shariʿa experts with sound knowledge of the financial markets. This has led to both an extreme accumulation of board memberships for the big names—who are practically indispensable, particularly because of their effect on marketing—and to exorbitant fees for these individuals.[50] As the established shariʿa experts are not necessarily interested in expanding their numbers in the near future, and it is therefore difficult for newcomers to get a foot in the door, Malaysia, for example, restricts the number of memberships on shariʿa boards for any one individual. In view of the growing number of Islamic financial institutions, this measure may provide effective help for newcomers, who can bring fresh perspectives and ideas.

To promote research and the education of new shariʿa experts, in 2008 the central bank of Malaysia initiated the International Shariʾah Research Academy for Islamic Finance (ISRA) as an independent organization under the roof of INCEIF.[51] Shortly after being founded, this academy was already very active, with the aims of:

- Achieving a high-level position for applied shariʿa research through its own and commissioned studies in the field of Islamic finance.
- Enlarging the pool of shariʿa experts through various talent promotion programs, stipends, and mentor programs.
- Creating forums for the discussion of relevant shariʿa issues with representatives of the financial sector and with (shariʿa) scholars on the regional and international level.
- Promoting (international) harmonization and mutual recognition of techniques and instruments of Islamic finance, including through translations and interdisciplinary expert councils.

In line with this fourth aim, the ISRA has started publishing a very useful collection of fatwas from various institutions in the Arab world and

Malaysia concerning financial issues on its website in both the original languages and English translation.

4. The Islamic Finance Sector in Selected Countries

Whereas in most states in the Muslim world Islamic banks operate within interest-based financial systems, six states have actively forwarded the establishment of a more comprehensive Islamic financial sector, in differing forms and with differing methods and outcomes. These states are Pakistan, Sudan, Iran, Malaysia, Bahrain, and more recently Dubai. A more comprehensive Islamic financial sector requires interest-free banking techniques and securities, and also shari'a-compliant monetary policy instruments and an interest-free interbank market. In order to discuss issues of systematic workability of an interest-free financial system on more than an abstract level, one can look to these countries for empirical evidence of macroeconomic problems.

Whereas the governments of most other Muslim states and almost all Western states took a distanced to skeptical stance on Islamic financial systems until well into the 1990s, this attitude has altered fundamentally since then.

More and more Muslim countries have welcomed Islamic financial institutions (including Saudi Arabia, Qatar, and Indonesia) or allowed initial bank foundations (for example, Morocco and Syria). And states with Muslim minorities have also adopted an increasingly positive basic stance toward Islamic finances, for instance, Britain, which has not only granted licenses to five Islamic financial institutions and altered its tax regulations to enable Islamic real estate financing but also repeatedly announced its intention of making London the Western hub of the Islamic financial sector. France has also become more involved in this sector, with growing interest registered from Luxembourg, although Germany took no concrete steps following several initial high-profile events. In Asia, the Islamic financial sector is actively supported by the Singapore authorities, but growing interest can also be observed in China (Hong Kong) and Japan.

As it would be impossible even to sketch the worldwide developments in this single chapter, the discussions that follow deal solely with those countries that have taken special routes toward the introduction of an Islamic financial system (Pakistan, Iran, Sudan, and to some extent Malaysia), or where pioneering conceptual work has been undertaken in specific financial sectors (Malaysia, Bahrain, Dubai), which other countries now also make use of.

a. Pakistan

The founding of Pakistan in 1947 was intended to establish a "Muslim nation-state" on the Indian subcontinent. Legislative authority is vested in the democratically elected parliament of the Islamic Republic of Pakistan; Islamic institutions (such as the Council of Islamic Ideology and the Federal Shariʿat Court) have no legislative powers of their own. Although they can call attention to conflicts between Islamic law and parliamentary legislation and suggest solutions, the final decision is reserved for the parliament.

Islamization of the Economy "from Above"

Only thirty years after the founding of the Pakistani state, concrete steps were taken under the military government of General Muhammad Zia-ul-Haq (Ziya' al-Haqq) to enforce Islamic regulations more strongly in economic life from 1977 on. The "Islamization" of the economy took place first in the levy sector by means of state organization of *zakat,* and second in the financial sector by means of an elimination of interest in banking transactions.[52]

- In 1979 and 1980 the operations of several specialized banks and investment societies were converted to an interest-free basis.
- In 1980 a decree was passed on the founding and operation of *mudaraba* societies, in which one party functioning as a project manager carries out a profit-oriented project with the capital provided by the other parties through the purchase of mudaraba certificates.
- In 1980 a legal basis was created for Participation Term Certificates (PTCs), which were first issued in 1981. PTCs are profit-sharing bonds with a term of five to ten years, which were intended to replace interest-bearing industrial bonds.
- In 1981 special departments were set up at all five nationalized commercial banks, in which customers could deposit funds into profit-and-loss-sharing accounts; no interest is paid, but accountholders do receive a share of the bank's profit or loss from transactions financed out of the PLS funds. From mid-1985 all previously interest-bearing accounts were converted into PLS accounts.
- In 1982 the banks were allowed to provide companies with operating capital on the basis of *musharaka* agreements.
- In mid-1984 the central bank published a list of twelve types of financing techniques that it considered permissible under Islamic law, which was declared binding for banks' financing operations as of April 1, 1985.

This list of permissible financing instruments differed in several respects from those used by Islamic banks in other countries.[53] It contained the following:

- As instruments for financing by lending: (1) interest-free loans with cost-oriented fees, (2) interest- and fee-free loans (Arab. *qard hasan*).
- As instruments (primarily) of trade-related modes of financing: (3) the purchase of goods and further sale with markups, (4) the purchase of commercial

bills with markdowns, (5) the purchase of property with buyback agreements, (6) leasing, (7) hire purchase, (8) development of property in return for fees.

- As instruments of investment-type modes of financing: (9) *musharaka* (profit and loss sharing), (10) capital participation, (11) the purchase of profit-sharing securities (PTCs, *mudaraba* certificates), (12) rent-sharing.

The Islamization of the banking sector came to a preliminary completion in 1985. The financial system, however, was by no means entirely Islamized by that point, as not only were foreign transactions still based on conventional interest-bearing methods, but also government bonds were exempted from the interest ban.

Un-Islamic Practices in the "Islamized" Banking Sector

Following Zia-ul-Haq's death in a plane crash in August 1988, his successors Benazir Bhutto and Nawaz Sharif showed no signs of wanting to continue or complete the Islamization of the economy. A judgment by the highest shari'a court (Federal Shari'at Court) at the end of 1991, however, put the subject back on the political agenda. Following wide-ranging consultations with Islamic scholars, economists, bankers, lawyers, and civil servants, the court declared on November 14, 1991, that twenty-two of Pakistan's economic laws contravened Islamic law and had to be changed or else they would become invalid as of July 1, 1992. The shari'a court particularly emphasized that any form of interest was inadmissible and that the practice of Pakistani banks did not take the interest ban into sufficient account.[54]

This criticism of "un-Islamic" banking practices may be surprising to the extent that the banks were restricted to the list of permissible types of financing issued by the central bank. The criticism referred, first, to the fact that the banks made excessive use of those financing types (especially items 3, 4, and 5 in the foregoing list) that are most similar to interest-based transactions. Second, there was also criticism of the banks' practice of combining two types of financing instruments originally conceived for different purposes (items 3 and 5) and of making this a standard technique in the financing sector, that is, the purchase and further sales of goods with markups and the purchase of assets with buyback agreements.

- The first type of financing was intended to correspond to *murabaha* financing by Islamic banks in the Arab world: Customer A asks Bank B to purchase certain goods from Supplier C and to sell them to him in turn with a markup for later payment.
- The second transaction type, the purchase and buyback of assets, involves only Customer A and Bank B; the central bank's list does not explicitly mention any difference between the purchase and buyback prices. Such transactions are useful, for instance, for securing debts, particularly in the case of longer-term financing projects (e.g., real estate); the purchase and buyback can take place at different points in time at identical prices.

The standard technique used by Pakistani banks—with which approximately 80 percent of their financing business was carried out—consisted of the bank purchasing assets from customer A (e.g., his goods in stock) and immediately selling them back to him with a markup.[55] This practice is in the tradition of the legal tricks and loopholes developed in classic Islamic law for bypassing the interest ban. The shari'a court rejected it as un-Islamic.

The government showed no intention of changing this status quo. On the one hand, it stated, it was not clear what type of interest was banned, while on the other hand, there were no workable alternatives; commissions were to be formed to deal with these issues again. In view of the previous intensive discussions on the "correct" interpretation of the interest ban in Pakistan (and elsewhere), and the conceptual and practical efforts toward genuine alternatives to the criticized loophole operations, this reaction only superficially concealed the lack of political will to Islamize the financial sector consistently.

While the government initially remained passive, various banks challenged the shari'a court judgment before the supreme court (Shari'a Appellate Bench of the Supreme Court). In May 1992, only a matter of weeks before the un-Islamic business laws were to become invalid, the government also went before the appellate bench, not seeking an extension of the deadline but applying for a repeal of the shari'a court judgment. The supreme court then suspended the judgment until it reached its own verdict, which was not announced until seven years later. In this verdict of December 23, 1999, the Shari'a Appellate Bench confirmed the 1991 shari'a court judgment and overruled the appeals and objections on the part of the banks and the government.[56] The legislation incompatible with Islamic law was to lose its legal force as of June 30, 2001, at the latest. The court called for a Commission for the Transformation of the Financial System (CTFS) and task forces to plan and carry out the transformation process.

The government, newly installed after General Pervez Musharraf's military putsch in October 1999, initially conformed with the supreme court ruling. The CTFS was established at the central bank, one task force was formed in the Ministry of Finance for eliminating interest in the government's financial transactions, and another was formed in the Ministry of Justice for adapting the legal system. The CTFS presented a first interim report in October 2000 and a second in May 2001, containing a draft directive for the Islamization of the finance sector, followed by a final report in August 2001. The commission investigated interest-free banking techniques—by that time practiced by numerous Islamic banks in other countries—and other banking services and capital market instruments, all in great detail. It also made proposals on how a ("genuine") Islamic banking system might be publicized among banks and other financial market players and to the general public.

From Complete Islamization to a Parallel System

Shortly before the incompatible laws were due to become invalid at the end of June 2001, the finance minister announced a number of measures for eliminating *riba* and promoting an Islamic banking system in his budget speech for 2001–2, delivered in mid-June 2001.[57] In particular, the measures were intended to create a legal framework for encouraging banks and other financial institutions to offer Islamic banking products alongside their conventional operations. Those at the highest political level decided in September 2001 to pursue a strategy of step-by-step (and long-term) transformation to an interest-free banking system rather than a complete Islamization by means of legislation.[58]

In practice this meant the official recognition of a conventional banking system in Pakistan (which had never actually been abolished), and thus also the formal end of the "complete" Islamization of the financial sector. Pakistan has passed to a mixed financial system in which the Islamic sector plays only a quantitatively and structurally subordinate role. In this system:

- Commercial banks working on a conventional basis can establish subsidiaries for their shari'a-compliant transactions.
- Conventional banks can set up specific branches offering only Islamic banking products.
- New commercial banks can be established, working solely according to Islamic principles.

Since 2002 a system has been developing in Pakistan that displays similarities with Malaysia's dual banking model, and in which experiences of financial market innovations in Bahrain (both discussed later in this chapter) serve as orientation.

Whereas the government had accepted the principle of the supreme court verdict of mid-2001 (although it altered its Islamization strategy significantly), it was principally disputed by the United Bank Ltd. (at that time a state institution), owing to procedural and case errors. The supreme court upheld the appeal in a very brief verdict of June 24, 2002, revoked the 1991 and 1999 judgments, and passed the case back to the shari'a court for renewed processing.[59] The 2002 verdict is of less significance for the actual development of Islamic banking in Pakistan than for the legitimization of the new policy of gradual Islamization by means of a parallel system with both a conventional and an Islamic sector. Along with the previous verdicts, it also cancels their threatened consequences—particularly the invalidation of numerous "un-Islamic" business laws—thus providing the necessary time to build an Islamic financial sector gradually.

Growth and Differentiation of the Islamic Sector

The new strategic direction for Islamic banking coincided with a fundamental change in the structure of the entire financial sector in Pakistan, focusing on restructuring and privatizating the banking sector. The "second-generation" financial sector reforms are outlined in the central bank's

Financial Sector Roadmap for 2005–2010.[60] Plans to expand the Islamic financial sector include:

- Improving the legal framework for Islamic transactions.
- Developing new instruments for indirect monetary policy and extension and intensification of the financial markets on the basis of *musharaka, mudaraba, salam,* and leasing.
- Promoting secondary markets for shari'a-compliant securities.
- Modifying general accounting and publicity rules in line with AAOIFI recommendations to make the unique nature of Islamic transactions sufficiently clear and transparent.
- Assessing tax laws and modifying them if necessary to avoid disadvantages for Islamic financing methods.

As the first experiment in Islamic banking in Pakistan failed as a result of the insufficient shari'a compliance of banking practices, it is logical that the central bank has initially concentrated on securing shari'a quality and consistency in the second attempt. It has set up a multitiered shari'a compliance structure designed to establish customer trust in the Islamic system. Its core is an Islamic Banking Department (IBD), which was founded within the central bank in September 2003 for the development and promotion of the shari'a-compliant financial sector.

- One of the first steps was the establishment of a shari'a board at the central bank in October 2003, which not only advises the central bank itself but also has the final decision in differences of opinion between Islamic banks and the central bank over the shari'a compliance of specific products and practices. The composition of the board is of some interest. The central bank was of the opinion that a board made up solely of Islamic legal scholars is not suitable for taking all complex legal, technical, and economic aspects of the financial sector into appropriate account, and therefore decided that the board should be composed of two Islamic scholars, one auditor, one lawyer, and one banker.
- In the first half of 2004, guidelines were passed containing minimum requirements for securing shari'a compliance for Islamic banks and their branches. These include the appointment of at least one shari'a adviser, who must fulfill the suitability criteria set by the IBD. These guidelines have since been revised.
- In April 2005 the central bank published nine basic Islamic financing techniques authorized by its shari'a board, along with sample agreements for each. Deviations are permitted, provided they have been approved by the bank's shari'a advisers. Orientation to standard techniques and sample agreements is intended to contribute to basic harmonization regarding shari'a compliance and improved transparency in the financial sector. The list of

standard techniques and sample agreements was extended by several new financing types in 2008.[61] It includes four participatory,[62] five trading-based,[63] and three other financing techniques,[64] interest-free loans *(qard)*, and a sixth trade-based type of financing *(tawarruq)*, permissible only in exceptional cases and with prior permission. This list is not comprehensive either, however; Islamic banks many also use other financing techniques, provided these are approved by their shariʻa advisers.

Further measures toward securing shariʻa quality include, for example, shariʻa inspections of Islamic financial institutions by the central bank, procedural rules on informing the central bank of new financial products offered by Islamic banks, and structured meetings of shariʻa advisers. As Pakistan's Islamic financial sector is also open to foreign banks and is part of a global financial market, the central bank has been attempting in recent years to introduce international accounting standards (AAOIFI), and to use internationally recognized regulation standards (IFSB) as orientation for its guidelines, for instance, on risk management. And since Pakistan is one of the few countries with special legislation and regulations for microfinance institutions, the central bank also passed guidelines for Islamic microfinancing in 2007.

The first license for a commercial Islamic bank under the new system was granted to Meezan Bank Ltd., which commenced operations in 2002. By the end of 2007 the number of purely Islamic banks had risen to six; twelve conventional banks had also set up a total of 289 Islamic branches. The banks and branches were concentrated in just under fifty towns and were not present in rural areas. The Islamic share of the total banking sector had climbed to 4.1 percent of deposits and 3.6 percent of financing and investments. A market share of 5 percent was expected by mid-2008,[65] with a further rise to 12 percent over the next five years.[66]

Pakistan learned from its mistakes and adopted international best practice as guidance for its second attempt at establishing an Islamic financial sector. It is worth noting that in her speeches the governor of the central bank repeatedly referred to ideas of participatory financing, risk sharing, and financing for groups outside of established business circles.[67] The current practice, however, by no means meets these ideals. In Pakistan as elsewhere, the dominant financing techniques are risk-free and similar to loans; the Islamic banks and Islamic branches of conventional banks are present only in towns, not in rural areas; and financing for new entrepreneurs is unlikely to be more common with the Islamic banks, which are often targeted at lucrative submarkets, than with the conventional banks operating across the country. It is questionable whether the central bank can counter these tendencies on a sustainable basis with "market-compliant regulations." It would be a pioneering success if it did manage to bring the often purported development-promotion potential of a "correctly understood" Islamic banking system to fruition in Pakistan.

b. Iran

In the early phase of the Islamic Revolution, far-reaching measures were introduced to nationalize service and industrial companies and gain government control of the economy, which were, however, originally led by the situation rather than by ideology.[68] More than twenty years after the revolution, attempts began to reverse these developments.

Between State and Market Economy

As the revolution leader Ayatollah Khomeini himself had not developed any economic concepts and considered practical economic issues rather insignificant, from the 1980s on ideology tended to be based mainly on the work of the highly regarded theologian Muhammad Baqir al-Sadr, who had been executed in Iraq in 1981. In his main work *Our Economy* (1961) he develops ideas that can hardly be regarded as a draft for a functioning economic system but were used in everyday policy to justify state interventions (e.g., regulations, price controls, credit rationing, subsidies, foreign trading licenses, control of currency exchange, and the like) and nationalization. In view of the ongoing war against Iraq, this dirigiste policy was widely accepted.

The lack of efficiency of this particular form of statist economy became impossible to ignore after the end of the war with Iraq in 1988, prompting a change in the orientation of economic policy toward the strengthening of private initiative and a reduction of state interventionism. The changes in course started in Khomeini's lifetime, but it was not until after his death and the election of Ali Akbar Hashemi Rafsanjani as president and head of government (1989–1997) that the new policy took shape. His successor, Muhammad Khatami (1997–2005), continued the reform policy in the same basic direction.[69] Conservative religious circles, however, repeatedly blocked privatization, liberalization, and deregulation measures. After Mahmoud Ahmadinejad took office as president and head of government in August 2005, conflict-oriented policies led not only to isolation on the foreign policy stage and international economic sanctions against Iran but also to backward steps in economic reform. The fourth Five-Year Plan (2005–2009) displayed strongly populist characteristics, envisaging redistribution of oil income in favor of the poorer segments of the population by means of social programs and subsidies (amounting to 25 percent of the gross national product).[70] A rise in redistribution expenditures, accelerating inflation, and a prescribed interest cut have reinforced the exodus of capital.

A redistribution component has also been integrated into privatization policy.[71] Following an alteration of Article 44 of the constitution, in mid-2006 the Supreme Leader of the Islamic Revolution, Ayatollah Khamenei, announced the privatization of 80 percent of state-owned companies over the coming ten years (with a few exceptions in the oil, infrastructure, and financial sectors). First of all, the country's least developed regions would receive approximately 30 percent of the privatization revenues. Second, between 40 to 100 percent of the shares in a number of profitable small companies would benefit the poorest segments of the population by means of holding companies or investment funds (referred to as "justice shares").

At the beginning of 2008 it was announced that the country would be opened up for foreign investors as part of the privatization policy. Foreigners would be permitted to purchase up to 100 percent of privatized state-owned companies in the future, provided the proportion of foreign-owned companies did not exceed 35 percent of any industry. Whether this was merely a tactical move to ward off feared American military intervention and undermine sanctions, or a key step toward an open market economy, remained to be seen, as did the reaction of possible investors, increasingly from Russia and China.

Structure of the Banking System

After the 1979 revolution all commercial banks were nationalized and foreign ownership of banks was banned. The number of banks fell significantly through mergers, particularly the number of commercial banks, from thirty-six to six. Reforms in the 1990s and early 2000s aimed primarily at increasing the efficiency of banking regulation and monitoring by the central bank, and rarely at strengthening the private sector or intensifying or creating competition in the financial sector.[72] Changes only became apparent in mid-2008.

The structure of the banking system has changed little since the banks were nationalized. The most important developments in the early years of the twenty-first century were the registration of six small private banks and the licensing of a state post office bank. The private banks took up positions in market niches where they played a role in financing the private sector. In early 2008, 16 percent of the receivables in the banking sector came from financing and participations in the nonpublic sector, and 19 percent of the deposits in the nonpublic sector were held by private banks and credit institutions.[73] The growth in deposits with private banks is due mainly to their offering higher rates of return than the state banks, and to increased trust in the private sector. The privatization of most major state banks has been announced several times in the past, and appeared to be taking concrete form, at least for two of these banks (Bank Saderat and Bank Mellat), by 2009.

The financial sector nevertheless remains dominated by the state banks, which are all thoroughly undercapitalized and inefficient by international standards. The central bank pursues a dirigiste lending policy—as under the shah—with finance lines for high-priority sectors (up to 2005) and subsidized financing costs. In nonprivileged sectors, loans are rationed or not available. For a long time the state-controlled and subsidized loan allocation was concentrated on a relatively small number of major companies in priority sectors (particularly agriculture). At the end of 2005 Ahmadinejad ruled that up to 35 percent of bank loans were to be awarded to small and medium-sized enterprises (with up to fifty employees).[74]

There is little to no competition among banks, and the bank supervisory authority is weak, concentrating primarily on maintaining regulations rather than banks' risk management. A reform toward a risk-oriented supervision of the banks is overdue, and a necessary prerequisite for effective liberalization and privatization of Iran's financial sector. Despite the lack of competition, the banks' profitability is low, which is partly due to the numerous interventions by the central bank, inefficient management methods, and politicized loan allocation with relatively high losses and frequently negative real interest rates in times of rising inflation.

Along with the licensed banks, a large number of small, informal bank-like financial institutions and credit cooperatives operate on the local level in Iran. In addition, some of the charitable trusts (*bonyadha*), which are part of the revolutionary establishment and are in some cases very large, carry out bank-like transactions. These institutions, which have been authorized by the interior ministry, do not have to disclose their finances and are not under the control or regulation of the central bank.[75] Monetary policy is dominated by direct intervention, with a lack of market-based instruments. There is no interbank market, as the commercial banks can rely on relatively cheap overdraft facilities (with de facto interest) from the central bank in the case of liquidity shortages.

Financial Techniques

The Law on Interest-Free Banking was passed in 1983, forming the basis of interest-free transactions for the commercial banks from March 1984, regulating relations among the commercial banks, and providing the central bank with new instruments for a far-reaching selective control of lending.

The law provides for types of transactions and practices that appear to be of doubtful permissibility under Islamic law outside of Iran.[76] These include:

- negotiation of (trade) bills
- charging processing fees proportionate to the loan amount
- the possibility of excluding the bank from bearing losses in *mudaraba* and *musharaka* transactions
- guaranteeing minimum yields for bank deposits

In addition, all other financial techniques used by Islamic banks outside Iran can also be employed in the country (sometimes under different Iranian names). The central bank regularly publishes data on the use of the various techniques in the banking sector.[77] Whereas 51 percent of financing transactions at commercial banks and 70 percent at specialized banks were carried out through installment purchase techniques, this figure was only 11 percent for private banks and credit institutions. These institutions are dominated by partnership and profit-sharing techniques (particularly *mozarebeh*, or civil partnerships, and legal partnerships), which account for 69.5 percent, whereas these types of financing make up only 20 percent of commercial banks' transactions and 14 percent for the specialized banks.

The few innovations in financial techniques include various types of participation papers, which are issued by the government or the central bank to finance the state budget or to intervene in the open market.

- To finance infrastructure projects, Government Participation Papers (GPPs) were introduced in 1998. The buyers of GPPs purchase temporary part-ownership of the financed infrastructure objects for the term of the paper (generally five years). The government promises to pay a yield on expiry of the paper, which corresponds to that of the infrastructure objects and should be at least equal to the rate of return in the private sector. As the buyers are granted part-ownership not of specific infrastructure projects but of a pool of projects, the government can control the GPPs' rate of return by specifying the projects in this pool and by fixing the (calculatory) fees for the projects that it or other state institutions pay for using these projects. GPPs are thus de facto securities with fixed yields, with economic characteristics corresponding to those of fixed-interest securities (with a single interest payment on expiry).
- Central Bank Participation Papers (CBPPs), launched in 2001, were designed to become the most important instrument of indirect monetary policy. These are papers with fixed nominal values (1, 2, 5, and 10 million rials), fixed terms (six or twelve months), and a previously determined rate of return. The yield is based on the central bank's claims against the government for financing a pool of infrastructure projects for the state. It is obvious that the CBPPs' fixed rates of return have nothing to do with market yields but are the result of political decisions. Moreover, considering that the central bank itself is a state institution asserting claims against another state institution—the government—the CBPPs are hardly substantially interest-free. The CBPPs form the core of an open-market policy for controlling liquidity in the economy, which, however, seems to be of questionable effectiveness in view of the many direct interventions by the central bank.[78]

The practice of Islamic banking in Iran has attracted substantial criticism.

- In theory, the returns from deposits on profit-sharing accounts depend on the bank's profit and are therefore not determined in advance. In actual fact, however, accountholders in Iran can rely on safe and fixed returns. The return is announced in advance and realized by the bank management's either increasing (if the actual returns are above the expected level) or decreasing (if the returns are below expectations) so-called profit equalization reserves, depending on the state of its operations, which lowers or raises the profit shares due the accountholders. This method of stabilizing returns, however, is common practice for Islamic banks in other countries, and profit equalization reserves are accepted by shari'a boards, AAOIFI, and the IFSB.

- The methods for calculating rates of return and profit sharing have never been made public. No meaningful profit and loss calculations have been published, and there have never been clear calculations of profit ratios for public sector financing. The central bank sets both the minimum profit rates to be paid to the accountholders by the banks and also the maximum loan costs to be paid to the banks by borrowers, varying according to sector.
- Political pressure on the banks has repeatedly led to a very high concentration of loans being granted to a small number of public enterprises (of very questionable solvency).
- The extensive regulations have prevented effective competition among the banks and have also frequently resulted in negative real returns on deposits and thus capital exodus, real estate speculation, and investment in foreign currency and gold.
- The concentration of loans to a small number of sectors and large borrowers has created a financing gap for small and medium-sized enterprises; this gap is filled by an informal system of moneylenders and bazaar traders on the one hand and credit cooperatives and *qarz-al-hassaneh* (Arab. *qard hasan*) funds on the other. The financing costs in this sector are significantly higher than those of the licensed banks. The government did not address the problems of financing small and medium-sized enterprises until the Fourth Five-Year Plan (2005–2009).
- The interventionist system with unrealistic real rates of return and financing costs encourages indirect transactions and evasion of regulations: it can be very lucrative to borrow from the state banks at low or even negative interest rates and use these funds more or less legally for profitable financing operations in the informal financial sector.
- There has been a redistribution from creditors to borrowers via the banking system; since the revolution, average returns for bank deposits have been well below the inflation rate, causing losses in purchasing power for savers. The financing costs in the priority sectors have also often been well below the rate of inflation and returns on deposits, leading to capital waste and tantamount to deposit holders' subsidizing borrowers.

In contrast to Pakistan, there has not yet been a comprehensive reform of the Iranian financial sector. The numerous unique traits of Iranian banking law—regarding both the commercial banks' permissible transactions and the relationship of the commercial banks to the central bank—and the still existing dominance of the state banks imply that the Iranian interest-free banking system cannot serve as a model for other Islamic countries.

c. Sudan

Colonel Jaʿfar al-Numairi came to power through a military coup in 1969. He was formally elected president of Sudan in 1971 and confirmed in office in 1977 and again in 1983. After his second reelection, Numairi began

Islamizing the country, including its economy. As a reaction, civil war with non-Muslim population groups broke out again in the south. Numairi was toppled by a military coup in 1985; the civilian government formed in 1986 was then toppled by another military coup under General 'Umar Hasan Ahmad al-Bashir in 1989. In 1993 Bashir formally dissolved the military government and took office as president, confirmed by (undemocratic) elections in 1996. Bashir had supported Iraq in the 1991 Gulf War, thus isolating the country on the international stage. The United Nations imposed sanctions against Sudan in 1996 owing to involvement in terrorist activities, which were revoked in 2001. The United States imposed comprehensive economic, trade, and financial sanctions in 1997. The armed conflict in the south of the country, which was a great drain on the economy, was ended by a peace treaty in 2005, whereas the conflict in Darfur has continued despite a treaty signed in 2006.

Macroeconomic Background

Sudan's economy is extremely dependent on the agricultural sector, which is subject to major fluctuations as a result of weather conditions. Despite the discovery of oil and the beginning of oil exports in recent years, the economic situation has not changed significantly. The economy is also under pressure from internal conflicts and the U.S. sanctions. Other characteristics of the Sudanese economy are high foreign debt, a very low per capita income level, and widespread state interventionism in conjunction with heavy bureaucracy.

Since the 1990s Sudan has been working toward macroeconomic stabilization of its fragile economy, with the support of the International Monetary Fund (IMF).[79] The country's banks were very small, and the banking system was thus strongly fragmented. Up to the end of the 1990s, the central bank (Bank of Sudan) pursued a very strict and interventionist credit policy. In addition, the Sudanese financial system was characterized by a lack of indirect monetary policy instruments, an underdeveloped banking supervisory system, and insufficient accounting rules. At high rates of inflation, the real financing costs were often negative, which led to grave errors in managing capital investments, to which the central bank reacted with more and more financing guidelines and special conditions for various sectors of the economy. During the first half of the 1990s Sudan's relations with the IMF continuously deteriorated. In 1997 a threatened expulsion was narrowly avoided as the country began to fulfill its payment obligations to the fund and to design and implement its first program for macroeconomic stabilization and liberalization of the financial sector jointly with the fund. Several other programs followed. Sudan managed to reduce its budget and payment balance deficits, and the inflation rate fell from over 100 percent in 1996 to under 10 percent by 2000. A plan for stabilizing the financial sector, essentially drawn up by the IMF, was implemented in the late 1990s and extended into a more comprehensive program of liberalization and efficiency increases for the financial sector in the year 2000.[80] The measures included stricter bank supervision, higher capital requirements for banks, the introduction of new monetary policy instruments, and the development of an interbank market. Interestingly, neither Sudan nor the IMF ever questioned the compliance with Islamic principles or the use of interest-free finance techniques during this or later reforms supported by the IMF.

Islamic Banking in Sudan

The Faisal Islamic Bank of Sudan (FIBS) was founded in 1977 on the basis of a specific law granting it far-reaching tax privileges and exemptions from the foreign currency control rules. The bank, which started operating in 1978, registered high growth rates for deposits, above-average profits, and a strong rise in equity in its initial years. The success of the FIBS prompted further establishment of Islamic banks, often with close links to political groups through both their ownership and their customers. The FIBS, for example, had links to the National Islamic Front; the Sudanese Islamic Bank, founded in 1982, was linked to the Khatmiyyah (Khatmiya) Sufi order and the Democratic Unionist Party; and the Tadamon Islamic Bank, opened in 1983, was connected with the Muslim Brotherhood.[81] The Tadamon Islamic Bank later became one of Sudan's most successful banks, whereas the FIBS lost significance.

The Islamization of the banking system began in 1983 with a law requiring the use of Islamic financing techniques in all banks from September 1984 on. The management of most of the previously conventional banks, however, made only nominal use of the new instruments without changing banking practices significantly. Following the fall of Numairi, many of these banks returned to their previous practices. The Islamization process was intensified, however, under Bashir from 1989 on. The ban on interest, relaxed in 1987 by the authorization of "compensatory rates" for loans and deposits, was reinforced again. From 1992 the Islamic principles for interest-free financial transactions were extended from the banking sector to the entire Sudanese financial system. In addition, there was criticism of the banks' *murabaha* practice at the time, as it often operated without predetermined profit markups for the bank or with flexible repayment schemes. In such arrangements the financing costs depend on the credit period, which contradicts the conditions for *murabaha* agreements according to Islamic law and is equivalent to an interest-based loan owing to the time factor in the calculation of the financing costs. A fatwa was issued by the central bank's shari'a council (Higher Shari'a Board for the Banking System and Financial Institutions) in 1993 to put a stop to this practice. The shari'a board and the central bank itself have formulated repeated fatwas and regulations, especially since 2005, with the aim of adapting the Islamic financial system to recognized standards (particularly those of AAOIFI and IFSB).[82]

The key goals of the reform program for the financial sector, implemented with the support of the IMF from 2000 on, were the expansion and strengthening of the private banking sector, including through the privatization of a state bank; a switch to more participatory financial techniques (profit and loss sharing); a reduction of the percentage of agreements with fixed markups; and the development of instruments for an indirect, market-oriented central bank monetary and credit policy (open market transactions with new types of securities) rather than the previously dominant direct bureaucratic intervention.[83]

A problem specific to the Sudanese economy because of its strong dependence on agriculture is the development of suitable shariʿa-compliant financing techniques for the agricultural sector. This calls for instruments for advance financing of agricultural production (farming and livestock). *Murabaha* agreements are not suitable for this purpose, as they require the existence of tradable products. The only current alternatives are *musharaka* partnerships and *salam* financing.

- In the case of *musharaka* partnerships, both partners have to participate in financing and managing a project. Small-scale farmers are unlikely to be capable of contributing financial means, and banks are unlikely to have the necessary expertise for managing agricultural projects.
- In the case of *salam* financing, the bank enters into a high level of risk on volatile agricultural markets, as it bears the price risk for marketing the pre-financed agricultural products without appropriate instruments for diversifying risks, since there are no commodity futures exchanges in Sudan.

The example of the reluctance to use Islamic financial techniques in the agricultural sector owing to the lack of futures exchanges demonstrates that the problems of an Islamized financial sector cannot be solved by individual measures (such as increasing the legal precision of *salam* agreements). Rather, what is needed is a comprehensive overhaul of the country's financial infrastructure, which is possible only as a long-term process over a number of years. This includes:

- Strengthening the independence of the central bank by law.
- Developing an interbank market.
- Creating a stricter bank supervisory body, including regulation of financial institutions without banking licenses.
- Obliging the banks to apply the accounting standards developed by AAOIFI.
- Formulating and implementing central bank instructions on corporate governance, transparency, and reporting.
- Fast restructuring of banks in financial need and rectifying the banks' general undercapitalization.
- Strengthening the banking sector through capital increases, fusions, and privatizations.
- Reducing the share of irredeemable debts in bank balance sheets, which amounted to a quarter of all loans in 2007.[84]

New Interest-Free Central Bank Instruments
Apart from Iran, Sudan is the only country with a fully Islamized financial sector. In contrast to Iran, the Sudanese banking sector is organized on a more decentralized and (at least potentially) more competitive basis, although it is still dominated by a small number of large state banks. Instruments of indirect monetary policy and those for the development of interest-free interbank markets are thus highly relevant within the system. The new monetary policy instruments are, in particular:

- "financing windows" for the purpose of liquidity management and credit management
- *musharaka* certificates for purposes of controlling money supply and financing state budgets
- a system of minimum rates for profit sharing and markups, as a replacement for conventional interest policy[85]

Financing windows provide liquidity and financial titles to the banks as required.

- Beginning in 2000 banks became able to bridge short-term gaps in liquidity through a Liquidity Deficit Financing Window. This kind of overdraft facility was free of charge for a maximum of one week. If extended (which was not desirable from a monetary policy point of view), it became very expensive. This instrument was abandoned in 2005. Instead banks may now sell investment certificates to the central bank in the event of liquidity shortages, which the central bank may later resell to the banks.
- The central bank can use an investment financing window to close financing gaps, either in the economy as a whole or in priority sectors or projects. The Bank of Sudan offers commercial banks funds on the basis of *mudaraba* or *musharaka* partnerships, which the banks can use for profitable financing activities either in any area or in specifically agreed-upon areas.[86] By means of the investment window, the central bank can continue its previous policy of selective credit management even under the conditions of an interest-free economy. As the economy is gradually transformed into a market-led system, however, structural management instruments should be used less and less.

For the management of liquidity across the whole of the economy, the central bank can make use of open market operations. By selling securities, it removes liquidity from the economy, expanding liquidity by purchasing securities. In contrast to interest-bearing open market papers, suitable securities used in an Islamic system of open market operations have to be interest-free and covered by real assets.

- Central Bank Musharaka Certificates (CMCs) were developed by the Bank of Sudan in 1998 for the purpose of short-term liquidity management. These

certificates were very liquid papers with a nominal value of 1 million Sudanese dinars (SDD) with no maturity date, which were traded solely between
the central bank and the commercial banks. The papers' current value was
calculated quarterly, on the basis of the profits resulting from the shares in
commercial banks held by the central bank. These shares formed the real
asset coverage for the CMCs. As they did not fulfill expectations, the CMCs
were liquidated in 2004, and the shares held by the central bank were returned to the commercial banks. Central Bank Ijarah Certificates (CICs)
were introduced to replace them in 2005.

- Government Musharaka Certificates (GMCs) and Government Investment
Certificates (GICs) were developed as interest-free financing instruments
for state budget deficits. In principle, these papers could also be used for
open market operations. Introduced in 1999, the GMCs have a volume
of 500 million SD and a term of one year, and are sold in tranches at auction. The buyers of GMCs share in the profit of state companies, which
provide the real asset cover. GICs were introduced in 2003, with longer
terms offering buyers the prospect of an income not subject to strong
fluctuation.

In conventional systems, financing costs are influenced by interest policy.
In Sudan, minimum rates for markups and profit sharing are set for this
purpose.

- In the case of *murabaha* agreements, the financing costs depend on the bank's
fixed markups. Up to the mid-1990s the central bank prescribed minimum
markups for the commercial banks, differing according to the sector of the
economy in question. Since 1998 these rates have been standardized and
lowered in stages.
- In the case of *musharaka* partnerships, financing costs depend on the percentage of profit the bank receives from the enterprise. Up to 1998 the central
bank set minimum profit share rates; this instrument was then abolished.

Rather than a robust economy with dynamic growth, Sudan has a fragile
one subject to strong fluctuation. This presents every financial system with
serious challenges, but particularly an Islamic one, which

- operates against the heritage of an inefficient banking system with strong
central bank interventionism, influencing the behavior of businesspeople, deposit accountholders, and consumers, but also state bureaucracies and bank
managers
- has some way to go before completing its structural reforms (strengthening private banks, developing interbank markets, establishing a legal
framework)
- remains cut off from international financial markets to all intents and
purposes

- has only recently begun implementing its central bank instruments, with no other financial market products yet in existence
- has no flanking infrastructural institutions (such as futures exchanges) or benchmarks for market profitability, which are available in almost other Islamic countries with mixed financial systems

It remains to be seen whether a functioning and competition-led system of Islamic financial markets (including securities and interbank markets) can be formed under such difficult conditions in the coming years.

d. Bahrain and Dubai

Since the end of the 1990s the government of Bahrain has been undergoing serious attempts to make the country a center of the Islamic financial world by promoting both Islamic banks and Islamic capital markets in diverse ways. Although the first Islamic commercial bank was founded in Dubai in 1975, the government has only recently taken the initiative toward promoting the country's Islamic financial sector and establishing a leading role for Dubai in competition with Bahrain.

The Islamic Financial Sector in Bahrain
The country's first Islamic bank—the Bahrain Islamic Bank—was founded in 1978. By mid-2008 the number of Islamic banks had climbed to 26 compared to 89 conventional banks,[87] with a consolidated balance sheet of $21.1 billion and thus just under 7.8 percent of the total balance sheet of the banking sector.[88] In addition, 19 of 35 companies in Bahrain's insurance sector operate according to Islamic principles (*takaful* undertakings), and 57 of 135 local investment funds are classified as Islamic.[89] Bahrain is thus the state with the largest number of Islamic financial institutions.

The central bank began establishing a transparent and consistent regulation regime for this complex Islamic financial sector in the late-1990s. It was a pioneer in the regulation of *takaful* undertakings in the Arab region, and since 2006 has been attempting to adapt the Basel II regulations to the Islamic financial sector, also using IFSB standards as a guide.

Development of Islamic Securities in Bahrain
Bahrain has played a pioneering role in the development of the Islamic financial system, particularly with regard to shari'a-compliant securities.

- The first steps toward creating tradable Islamic securities were taken in the mid-1980s by combining assets in a pool, issuing standardized ownership certificates, and selling these to investors, who were given the option of selling the certificates back to the pool. This was the beginning of the now very common *sukuk* certificates.
- This option was designed to create a liquid market. The pool concept was quickly picked up by Islamic financial institutions and used to construct

extensive international consortium loans on the basis of *murabaha* agreements in external relationships to the financed company and *mudaraba* agreements in internal relationships among the financing banks.[90] It was not possible, however, to securitize these loans, that is, to transform them into securities, and thus no corresponding market formed.

- The pool idea has been used for the construction of numerous Islamic investment funds. Particularly for private investors, investment funds are an alternative to credit in bank accounts: with investment certificates they purchase a share of ownership of profitable assets or a claim to a share in the returns of financed projects, whereby the returns must be the result of transactions that are permissible under Islamic law. Investment certificates are traded on the capital market and may vary in market value.

In the early 2000s the Central Bank of Bahrain (CBB), originally the Bahrain Monetary Agency (BMA), was increasingly active in the development of the Islamic financial sector, with the expressed goal of making Bahrain the international center of the Islamic financial world.[91] The BMA developed new financing instruments and promoted institutions to support Islamic financial institutions and markets.[92]

- In June 2001 the central bank began to issue monthly *sukuk* as shari'a-compliant treasury bills with three-month terms (a total of eighty-six flotations by June 2008). These *sukuk* certificates are based on *salam* agreements, in which Party A sells Party B a certain amount of precisely described goods for delivery on a later date, for which Party B pays the purchase price immediately. This purchase price is below the expected sale price of the goods as of the date of delivery. In the case of *sukuk al-salam* agreements, the central bank sells the banks, for example, a certain amount of aluminum, which has to be supplied in three months. In return the banks pay a price on the date of purchase which is below the anticipated sales price of the aluminum on the date of delivery. At the same time, the banks charge the central bank with selling the aluminum, whereby the central bank proposes to the banks a sale price that anticipates a profit on the entire transaction corresponding to that of interest-bearing money market papers. Formally, the banks as purchasers of the *sukuk al-salam* bear the delivery risk (should the government be unable to supply the aluminum on the due date) and the price risk (should the government be unable to sell the aluminum at the proposed price); in actual fact these risks are unlikely to be greater than the country risk entailed by conventional treasury bills, which depends on the government's financial status. The *sukuk al-salam* are interest-free money market papers that the Islamic banks can use for their microeconomic liquidity management and the central bank for its macroeconomic equivalent.
- Since September 2001 the central bank has issued *ijara sukuk* with terms between three and ten years and differing volumes, at irregular intervals. These display all the key characteristics of government bonds. They are based on

state assets such as buildings, infrastructural items, and production facilities, which are precisely specified and made legally independent. Investors can gain part-ownership in this pool of assets by purchasing an *ijara* certificate. The users of the assets in the pool pay long-term fixed rents or leasing fees, in which the certificate holders participate. *Ijara sukuk* thus generate a fixed yield across their terms. The standard *sukuk* can be traded on the capital market during their terms, whereby the price may be above or below the nominal value, depending on alternate investment opportunities. Long-term *ijara sukuk* are designed to offer Islamic financial institutions secure medium- to long-term investment opportunities, with yields that can be used as benchmarks for pricing other financial products.

• Since 2005 the central bank has also issued monthly short-term *ijara sukuk* with a term of six months. Like the long-term *ijara sukuk,* these are based on leasing agreements, but they serve similar liquidity management and benchmarking purposes as *sukuk al-salam.*

At the end of the second quarter of 2008, 74.5 percent of the total outstanding government bonds (amounting to 705 million Bahraini dinar, or just under $2 billion) were in the form of Islamic securities (72 percent *ijara sukuk,* 2.5 percent *sukuk al-salam*).[93]

Key Institutional Infrastructure in Bahrain

The central bank has been actively involved in the foundation of several of the key infrastructural institutions in the Islamic financial sector detailed in the foregoing—for example, the IIFM, LMC, IIRA, AAOIFI, and IFSB—and has made major contributions to their efficacy and success through its own measures.[94] For instance, the central bank's *sukuk* issues have played a significant role in the development of the Islamic capital market, and the binding requirement of AAOIFI standards has been key in establishing accounting and management rules, thus supporting the international comparability of business figures and the globalization of Islamic financial markets.

The financial and regulatory techniques used in Bahrain and the shariʿa interpretation on which they are based are likely to be accepted to a greater extent in the Persian Gulf region than the alternatives developed in Malaysia (discussed in the next section). In addition, the volume of internationally placed Islamic loans from public and private issuers is increasing sharply, putting Bahrain in a good position to become the center of the international Islamic financial market for a time.[95] In recent years, however, Dubai has become a serious competitor to Bahrain in the Gulf region.

Expanding Islamic Stock Exchanges in Dubai

Although Dubai has always been an important regional center for the Islamic financial system, this sector has developed an extraordinary dynamic only in recent years, through major support from the state and the ruling family. The locations of this dynamic are first the Dubai International Financial Center (DIFC), established not merely for Islamic finance in 2004 and including the Dubai Financial Services Authority (DFSA) and the Dubai International Financial Exchange (DIFX, discussed earlier), and second the Dubai Financial Market (DFM).[96]

The DFM was established in 2000 as a conventional stock exchange and converted into an Islamic exchange with its own shariʿa board in 2007.[97] This means that the main trading business is in shariʿa-compliant securities, and there is a strict distinction (via separate accounting and income statements) between these transactions and those involving other stocks. For new security flotations, the DFM will check shariʿa compliance on the basis of AAOIFI standards and classify them accordingly to provide investors with reliable criteria for decision making. Trading in securities that do not fulfill the shariʿa criteria may be continued, but the resulting returns (which account for less than 2 percent of the exchange's total profits) are to be used for charitable purposes.

Not only do the DFM and DIFX have up-to-the-minute trading technologies, but also they can offer investors a solid supervisory and regulatory system, including recognized procedures for checking shariʿa compliance of shares, *sukuk* certificates, and other securities. The rapid growth of the Islamic segment of the Dubai capital market was promoted by the oil boom of recent years, with rising state investment expenditure and the resulting extensive construction work in the Gulf region in general and in Dubai in particular.

Whereas Bahrain has many more Islamic banks than Dubai (twenty-six compared to six as of 2009), the Dubai stock exchange is considerably larger and above all much more active than that in Bahrain. With an overall market capitalization of $136 billion in Dubai and $28 billion in Bahrain in 2007, more than 105 billion shares with a value of over $100 billion were traded in Dubai, whereas in Bahrain this figure was only 851 million shares with a value of $1 billion.[98] Thus there has been a certain division of labor in recent years between the two most active locations of Islamic finance in the Gulf region: Bahrain has been the center for Islamic banking and Dubai that for shariʿa-compliant securities. Developments in the United Arab Emirates may, however, change this situation in the near future.

Islamic "Mega-Banks" in Dubai and Abu Dhabi

The Noor Islamic Bank (NIB) commenced operations in Dubai at the beginning of 2008.[99] With 3.2 billion AED (approximately $900 million) in authorized capital, held in equal parts by the state and Dubai's ruling family, NIB exceeded all other existing Islamic financial institutions in terms of financial status at the start of operations.[100] This new quantity has given rise to a new quality: with this volume of capital, it seemed probable that NIB would achieve its ambition of becoming one of the ten largest financial institutions in the world by 2015. The capital was planned for use in a rapid international expansion strategy, including in non-Islamic countries (particularly in western and eastern Europe and Southeast Asia).[101] The bank planned to purchase holdings in other banks or to take them over as a whole, and—in the case of conventional banks—convert them to Islamic techniques and products as necessary.

In reaction to Dubai's initiative, the ruler of Abu Dhabi announced the foundation of an even larger Islamic bank with capital of 4 billion AED (approximately $1.1 billion). Al Hilal Islamic Bank was opened in June 2008.[102] It planned to focus its activities not on international business but mainly on the Gulf region.

Mega-banks with initial capitalization of around $1 billion do of course have the potential to shift market shares within the Islamic financial world. In order to make a sustainable profit, however, they need a clear expansion of the Islamic financial sector as a whole, which is probably possible only at the cost of the conventional sector. Since the existing range of products and services is unlikely to be sufficient for this purpose, we can expect financial innovations from the new Islamic mega-banks in many areas. It remains to be seen how the conventional banking sector in the Gulf states will react to these perspectives. On the one hand, it still plays the dominant role in and has profited from the oil boom, but on the other hand, Islamic financial institutions are becoming increasingly popular with the rulers of the Gulf states.

e. Malaysia

Malaysia is more densely populated than the Gulf states (approximately 27 million inhabitants), with an economy in dynamic growth. While Muslim Malays make up the majority of the population (57 percent), they are mainly employed in the public sector and agriculture, whereas trade and industry are dominated by ethnic Chinese (25 percent). The Malaysian government has been promoting the development of an Islamic financial sector since the 1980s, although it has never pursued the objective of complete Islamization (such as in Pakistan and Sudan, for example). Malaysia is interested in creating a parallel system in which the Islamic sector exists alongside the conventional sector, with the two cooperating. The central bank published its long-term aims and strategies on the development of the Islamic (and conventional) financial sector in its 2001 Financial Sector Master Plan.[103] Along with opening up markets for international investment and further differentiation, this plan provides for more innovative Islamic financial products and techniques, as well as improvements in the regulatory and infrastructural frameworks. The goal was to raise the market share of Islamic financial institutions significantly, from approximately 10 percent to 20 percent by 2010. The stated long-term objective was to place Malaysia in a leading position in the international Islamic financial services market.

The development of the Islamic financial sector in Malaysia can be roughly divided into three phases:

- The starting phase in the 1980s, when the first Islamic bank was founded and developed its first range of Islamic financial products, and the construction of the first interest-free securities launched the development of the Islamic capital market.
- The growth phase in the 1990s, when the number of market players and Islamic financial products increased significantly, and important regulatory conditions were created.
- The globalization phase in the early 2000s, in which the further differentiation of the Islamic financial sector as well as its international opening and positioning have been pushed on the basis of the master plan for the development of the financial sector.

Islamic Banks, Windows, and Subsidiaries

Following the 1983 Islamic Banking Act, which laid the legal foundations, the Bank Islam Malaysia Berhad (BIMB) was founded the same year.[104] In its first ten years the BIMB developed and introduced over twenty Islamic financial products and interest-free financing techniques for various customer groups and needs.

In order to expand the Islamic financial sector as quickly as possible after this successful introductory phase, the government did not initially promote the foundation of purely Islamic banks but encouraged all existing conventional banks to set up separate "Islamic windows" during the growth phase from 1993 on. This approach, which was unprecedented in the Islamic world, had a number of advantages:

- With the setting up of Islamic windows in existing banks, a large number of new market players was created, achieving a critical mass for the Islamic financial sector in a short time.
- The conventional banks' reputation was at least partly transferred to their Islamic windows, prompting rapid acceptance of Islamic products.
- The Islamic windows could use the existing infrastructure of the conventional banks, significantly reducing initial investments for expanding the Islamic sector.
- Most conventional financial institutions were (and still are) owned and run by non-Muslims (especially ethnic Chinese); setting up a large number of new Islamic banks under Muslim control, consciously separated from the conventional financial sector, would have incurred a risk of unwanted religious or ethnic tensions. The dual finance system with Islamic windows, in contrast, enabled cooperation between Muslims and non-Muslims.

By the end of 1993 the central bank had granted twenty-one financial institutions authorization to set up Islamic windows. This, however, was merely the first step. The second step was taken in 1996, when the central bank created the possibility for conventional banks to set up not just Islamic windows but entire Islamic branches. The third step in 2005 was to create the legal basis for converting the Islamic windows (or branches) into legally independent Islamic subsidiaries within the banking groups. Foreign investors may also hold up to 49 percent of the capital of these subsidiaries.

While Islamic windows, branches, and subsidiaries aim to integrate conventional banks into the Islamic financial sector, the sector itself has also been expanded by the foundation of new, independent Islamic banks.

- In the wake of the Asian crisis in the late 1990s, Malaysia also saw restructuring in the banking system. During the fusion of three banks, the Islamic sections were extracted and merged into a new, exclusively Islamic bank, the Bank Muamalat Malaysia Berhad, which commenced operations in 1999.
- In the course of the liberalization of the financial sector from 2004 on, licenses were granted to three Islamic commercial banks founded with international capital, which are subsidiaries of Islamic banks in the Gulf region: the Kuwait Finance House (2005), Al-Rajhi Banking and Investment Corporation (2007), and Asian Finance Bank (2007), a joint venture of the Qatar Islamic Bank, RUSD Investment Bank (Saudi Arabia), and Global Investment House (Kuwait).

The range of services offered by Islamic banks has extended further and further, consisting by 2009 of around sixty financial products and services, from various deposit forms through numerous financing techniques for general and specific purposes, to shari'a-compliant credit cards.[105] During the implementation of the Financial Sector Master Plan, the Islamic banking sector has increased in terms of weight and quality. The number of Islamic banks rose from two in 2001 to eleven commercial and investment banks in 2007.[106] The share in the banking sector's total assets increased from 8.2 percent to 12.8 percent, the share of the total banking sector financing from 6.5 percent to 14.0 percent, and the share in the total deposits in the banking sector from 9.5 percent to 14.0 percent.[107]

Capital and Money Market

An Islamic banking system can work efficiently only if the financial institutions in particular are in a position to transform terms and diversify risks. This means, first, that banks can generate longer-term financing out of short-term deposits, which requires them to be able to raise liquidity quickly if needed, and second, that they have a broad range of alternatives with differing risk characteristics for investing customer monies. Banks tend to use securities for both these purposes, which are traded on an organized capital market. The expansion of the Malaysian Islamic banking sector thus simultaneously favored and required the development of an Islamic capital market with a large volume and complex structure. After shari'a-compliant types of securities had been developed both in the private sector and by the state (finance ministry and central bank) in the 1980s and 1990s, the Islamic capital market was restructured in the early years of the twenty-first century and soon opened up to international investors. The Islamic and conventional capital markets are linked in various ways. First, there are a number of private and state stakeholders active as issuers and/or subscribers of securities on both sub-markets. Second, the Islamic shares market is a (relatively pragmatically defined) subset of Malaysia's shares market as a whole.

The 2001 Capital Market Master Plan Malaysia states the further-reaching objective of developing Malaysia into the center of an international Islamic capital market.[108] The proposed measures include designing innovative financial market products, particularly for improved risk management; expanding the technical and legal market infrastructur; training qualified staff; and enhancing the regulatory and tax parameters.

The development of the Islamic capital market began in parallel with the development of Malaysia's Islamic banking sector.

- Since 1983 the government has been able to issue interest-free state bonds (Government Investment Issues, or GIIs).[109] These GIIs offer subscribers returns set by the central bank and can also be used for liquidity management.[110] The range of monetary policy instruments for banks' liquidity has been continuously expanded. An innovative step within the Islamic world was the establishment of the Islamic Interbank Money Market (IIMM) in 1994. Twelve different financial security types are traded on this interbank market for short-term capital, including GIIs and Mudaraba interbank investments (MII), Bank Negara monetary notes-i (BNMN-i), sell and buy back agreements (SBBA), Islamic private debt securities (IPDS), Islamic accepted bills (IAB), and Islamic negotiable instruments (INI).[111]
- In the 1990s and early 2000s a wealth of further financial instruments have been developed in Malaysia, suitable mainly for risk management purposes. These include various types of derivatives: futures, options, foreign exchange swaps, Islamic profit rate swaps, Islamic hedge funds, and the like. The shari'a compliance of many of these arrangements is still controversial. By 2009 only two derivative products had been authorized for trading on the stock exchange (Bursa Malaysia): crude palm oil futures and single stock futures for shari'a-compliant shares.[112]
- Following initiatives by the BIMB in the early 1980s, the Securities and Exchange Commission of Malaysia (SEC) produced its first list of shari'a-compliant shares in 1997, which is updated twice a year. Shares traded on the Kuala Lumpur exchange are regarded as shari'a-compliant if they come from companies whose core operations are not banned or undesirable, and whose turnover and sales from banned activities (for example, production of alcohol, gambling, interest-based financial services) or undesirable operations (production and sale of tobacco products) remain below pragmatic cut-off levels (of 5, 10, 20, or 25 percent, depending on the level of

impermissibility).[113] According to these criteria, 843 of 988 listed securities were declared shari'a-compliant in May 2008. Hence, 85 percent of companies are regarded as shari'a-compliant, accounting for about two-thirds of total market capitalization (571 billion RM) as of June 2008.[114]

- On this basis, Islamic share indexes were then developed: the first in 1996 by RHB Unit Trust Management Bhd., followed by further indexes in 1999, namely the Dow Jones Islamic Market Index (DJIM), the Kuala Lumpur Shari'a Index (KLSI) from Bursa Malaysia and the FTSE Global Islamic Index Series from the FTSE Group.[115] In the subsequent period the number of stockbrokers specializing in trading with shari'a-compliant shares and funds investing their subscribers' capital in such shares leaped.[116] By mid-2008, 136 of 530 unit trust funds were shari'a-based; with a net asset value of 18 billion RM, they administer 11 percent of all assets in Malaysian investment funds.[117]

- While this segment of the Islamic capital market is de facto based on a subsection of the conventional shares market, the development of Islamic bonds in the form of *sukuk* certificates is founded on innovative financial techniques. The first *sukuk* issue by a Malaysian company took place in 2001. The Malaysian government issued its first global sovereign *sukuk* with a five-year term in 2002. In recent years *sukuk* have become the favored form of bonds. In 2007—the last year before the global financial crisis—three-quarters of newly issued bonds in Malaysia were *sukuk* (121 billion RM), and the value of the outstanding *sukuk* represented 35 percent of all bonds.[118]

- A change in legislation in 2005 gave the government greater flexibility for developing new types of securities based on leasing assets. In 2006 the central bank introduced a new monetary policy instrument, issuing Sukuk Bank Negara Malaysia Ijarah (SBNMI), which are also designed as a benchmark for other short to medium-term Islamic bonds. SBNMIs are also traded on the IIMM.

In recent times, Malaysia has seen increased discussion of Islamic venture capital undertakings and shari'a-compliant microfinance institutions.

Supervision, Regulation, Human Capital

The Malaysian banking and insurance sector is subject to supervision by the central bank (Bank Negara Malaysia, BNM), whereas the Securities Commission Malaysia (SC) is the supervisory authority for the capital market.[119] In the interest of more effective supervision and regulation, and to increase the efficiency of the financial sector as a whole, these two authorities have created special organs and additional institutions.

- To standardize shari'a interpretations by Islamic financial institutions, a national shari'a council (National Syariah Advisory Council on Islamic Banking and Takaful, NSAC, also Shari'a Advisory Council, SAC) was founded within the central bank in 1997 as the highest authority on issues of Islamic financial law.

- A special subdivision for cases of Islamic economic law (*mu'amalat*) was set up in 2008 within the commercial division of the high court.
- To train management staff for the Islamic financial sector, the central bank founded the International Centre for Leadership in Finance (ICLIF) in 2003.[120] It also set up the International Centre for Education in Islamic Finance (INCEIF) in 2006 to qualify staff for all levels of the fast-expanding Islamic financial sector and to promote academic study of the Islamic financial system. This center offers not only a practice-based training program for Chartered Islamic Finance Professionals (CIFP) but also a university-level master's in Islamic finance and a Ph.D. program.[121]
- To promote a new generation of shari'a scholars, the central bank set up a stipend program and a program funding shari'a research projects in 2005.[122] In 2008 it also established the International Shari'a Research Academy for Islamic Finance (ISRA) under the roof of INCEIF.[123]
- In 2006, during the period of liberalization and international opening of the Malaysian financial markets, the Malaysia International Islamic Financial Center (MIFC) was jointly initiated by the regulatory institutions (BNM, SC, LOFSA, Bursa Malaysia) and the Islamic financial sector (banks, insurance companies, capital market service providers).[124] Its goal is to position Malaysia globally as a dynamic and innovative international center of the Islamic financial sector. The MIFC focuses Malaysia's long-standing competence, making it accessible for international players hoping to make Malaysia a platform for their Islamic financial activities. One of its main tasks is to promote the new opportunities for international Islamic banking, insurance, securities, and currency operations in Malaysia, and provide information on legal conditions—particularly new types of licenses for International Islamic Banks (IIB) and International Takaful Operators (ITO)—and tax incentives. A further innovation is that offshore banks may now open operational offices in Labuan for transactions in international currencies.

Conceptual Criticism

In the mid-1990s Malaysia constructed the most complex Islamic financial system in the Muslim world, with its interbank money market and the broad range of Islamic securities on both participation and loan bases. The Malaysian concept of an Islamic financial sector has prompted great interest in the rest of the Muslim world, but also a great deal of stark criticism. This criticism focuses on two types of contracts that are often used for interest-free bank financing in Malaysia, the basis of almost all interest-free bonds.

In line with the growing skepticism toward *tawarruq*, the Arab world is taking an increasingly critical view of the widespread Malaysian practice of *bayʿ al-ʿinah,* a purchase transaction linked with a direct repurchase of the object by the seller.[125] The fact that *bayʿ al-ʿinah* is considered shariʿa compatible in Malaysia is due to the specific interpretation of a Shafiʿi legal position.[126] Formally or generally, there is no objection to the purchase and repurchase of objects; such a contract becomes a problem only if it is used for a prohibited purpose, in this case granting an interest-bearing loan.

Bayʿ al-ʿinah is used not only for financing through banks, however, but also for structuring securities. If a company prefers to finance a project by issuing bonds via the capital market rather than through a bank loan, it can specify certain assets—for example, its machinery—and assign a plausible value to these items. If it were issuing an interest-bearing bond, these assets would only serve as security; in the case of issuing an Islamic bond, however, the assets must change ownership so that the subscribers of the bond do not earn banned interest payments but receive permissible trading profits. In order to ensure this, the company securitizes claims against itself at the level of the value of the specified assets. The claims are thus covered by real values and can be traded like the objects themselves. Each of these claims has a specific nominal value and a due date; in addition, the company undertakes to repurchase its own claims on the due date at the nominal value. No regular payments on the part of the company—as in the case of sale and lease-back transactions, or *ijara sukuk*—are charged. The Malaysian structure creates shariʿa-compliant asset-covered bonds on the basis of a purchase contract with repurchase guarantee (*bayʿ al-ʿinah*) with a fixed nominal yield on issue. The securities' yield results from the difference between the nominal value or later purchase price and the lower issue rate paid by the purchaser.[127]

In Malaysia it is permissible for the initial purchaser of such a bond to resell the bond on the stock market (secondary market). The shariʿa compliance of these transactions is debatable, however, if the sale price of a claim or a bond (*bayʿ al-dain*) to a third party deviates from the nominal value of the claim.[128] The fact that the bond is based on real assets cannot remove these doubts, which are primarily linked to the fact of the flotation below the nominal value and the repurchase guarantee at said value.

In the Arab region shariʿa-compliant instruments for risk-free financing with guaranteed yields are constructed differently through capital markets: *sukuk* certificates, considered acceptable, are based not on *bayʿ al-ʿinah* agreements but on *murabaha* or *ijara* constructions. The most important difference is that the value of the *sukuk* derives from the yield potential of the assets on which they are based (trading profits, rent income, and so on),[129] thus enabling a flotation at a price above the nominal value, whereas the value of Malaysian Islamic bonds is ultimately based only on the repurchase promise at the nominal value given by the issuer, and the issue price necessarily *below* the nominal value reflects the scarcities on the (conventional) money and capital market.

Both types of securities are very close to interest-based financing techniques in economic terms, but they incur higher legal and administrative costs ("technical" transaction costs). These are lower for the Malaysian Islamic bonds, but the shari'a compliance ("ideological" transaction costs) of the latter is higher. Market players in Islamic countries can thus choose among three techniques with equal economic outcomes but differing cost characteristics:

- interest-bearing bonds with the lowest technical and highest ideological transaction costs
- Islamic bonds with medium technical and medium ideological transaction costs
- *sukuk* with the highest technical and the lowest ideological transaction costs

Given the debates in AAOIFI detailed earlier, it appears likely that the third variety will become increasingly accepted in the future.

5. Closing Remarks

In reaction to the crisis beginning in 2008 in the conventional financial sector, an increasing number of voices have maintained that such a crisis would not be possible in an Islamic system. This position is based, first, on the allegedly close link between the financial sector and the real economy. In my discussion of Islamic financing techniques I have expressed my doubts about this position. Second, this claim of superiority is founded on the idea that Islamic banking is in essence a financial system with a strong ethical basis. This position is also difficult to accept per se in view of the actual practice of Islamic banks: it is hard to present as a particularly ethical characteristic the fact that certain business areas in conjunction with gambling, alcohol, pork, and so on are avoided. Moreover, Islamic banks tend not to participate in business risks, and they finance for the most part the same types of projects for the same customer groups at similar conditions as conventional banks; the differences are more in the form than in the substance of the activities. Ethical considerations may play a role in individual financing decisions; yet this is not an exclusive systemwide characteristic of the Islamic financial sector but can also be observed in some segments of the conventional sector.

The Islamic financial system has become established and demonstrated its ability to function and survive on an economic level in mixed systems. It has yet to be proved, however, whether fully Islamized systems can function. Pakistan has returned to a mixed system; the state banks continue to dominate the financial sector in Iran; and in Sudan the establishment of market structures and the reduction of direct central bank intervention have only recently begun. In the two countries with the furthest-developed Islamic financial sectors—Bahrain and Malaysia—mixed systems are in place, in which conventional banks and capital markets not only set benchmarks for the Islamic sector but also represent a continual challenge for the efficiency of interest-free techniques. It remains to be seen whether the Islamic financial system will gain additional market shares at the cost of the conventional sector in the competition between the two systems, and how Islamic financial institutions will solve the conflict between economic efficiency and ideological objectives.

Translated by Katy Derbyshire

III

Developments in Law

(Hans-Georg Ebert)

In the countries of Asia and Africa in which the Islamic religion has a presence, specific legal systems have formed on the basis of these countries' historical, political, social, and religious development, taking account of imposed norms and principles. The majority of these are fully able to regulate relationships among people (private law), as well as the individual's relationship to state authority and relationships among state bodies (public law). At the same time, national legal systems reflect various local, regional, and Islamic characteristics that overlap and cannot be reduced to Islamic law, or shari'a. As in Western countries, the state in Islamic countries has made inroads into ever more areas of life through laws and regulations, and has thus, wittingly or unwittingly, made legal interactions more complicated. Today, classification into various branches of law largely follows the Western model, but such classification can also be derived in principle from the "classic" legal compendiums, which originated mainly between the ninth and fourteenth centuries CE. As will be shown, recognition of the divine character of shari'a by no means requires renunciation of national legislation. Islamic law, however, provides a certain framework that limits the legislature's freedom and subordinates it to a canon of values geared primarily toward justice ('adala) and performance of good works (ihsan). Without doubt, the efforts at Islamization by individuals, groups, and states in recent decades have gradually influenced the legislative processes in all Islamic countries, in different ways. This has led and is leading, however, not to a one-sided Islamization of the entire corpus of law but rather to debates on various Islamic legal precepts, and has pointed up domestic conflicts between the actors involved in legislation and implementation of law. The prospects for legal development in the Islamic world cannot be reduced to their religious aspects. They result instead from a multitude of internal and external factors, which have taken on a special character in the course of globalization and the legal processes that accompany it. New areas of law (such as intellectual property law) require new solutions that take account of international norms and standards. Thus the discourse on content, sources, and methods of law in the Islamic world has taken on great social significance.[1]

1. The Law of Islamic Countries: Sources and Methods

a. Islamic Law

The development of the Islamic religion starting in the seventh century CE occurred in conjunction with the gradual establishment of political systems on the Arabian Peninsula. Islam as a religion of state and law was obliged to regulate relations between people and to create a functioning administration. In addition to the revelations, Muhammad's ad hoc decisions at first formed a sufficient basis for this. After the Prophet's death in 632, however, the situation changed: in order to govern the expanding state system legitimately, it was necessary not only to *build upon* that which already existed but also to *extend* it. With recourse to the Prophet's sayings and acts (Arab. sing. *hadith*), and through the editing of the Qur'an under the caliph 'Uthman (d. 656), important conditions were created for solving conflicts in the Islamic community.[2] With increasing temporal distance from the lifetime of the Prophet, and through territorial expansion, the basis for decisions had to be objectified. Thus Islamic jurisprudence (*fiqh*) developed consistently with the collection, and later the written recording, of the Prophet's sayings and acts; according to the latest research, this process can be assumed to have already begun by 700.[3] In the spiritual centers of the Islamic caliphate, specific legal views crystallized and were consolidated by the tenth century as so-called legal schools (sing. *madhhab*), which were named for the founders of the schools. Four of these Sunni schools predominate to this day: the Hanafi, Maliki, Shafi'i, and Hanbali legal schools. Fiqh (in the sense of jurisprudence) and theology now became independent fields within Islamic scholarship.[4] In addition to the normative description of the different branches of law (*furu' al-fiqh*), there emerged a systematic study of legal sources (*usul al-fiqh*), established by Muhammad ibn Idris al-Shafi'i (d. 820), which, in addition to the Qur'an and the sayings and acts, included the consensus (*ijma'*) of scholars of Islamic law and religion (*'ulama'*), as well as analogy (*qiyas*). There was, however, no agreement among adherents of the various schools regarding either individual legal norms (with the exception of the few Qur'anic rules that required no interpretation) or sources of law, to say nothing of their differences with Shi'a and other non-Sunni views. These differences quite significantly affect the character of *fiqh*. They are seen as legitimate and refute the thesis of the monolithic structure of Islamic law. The existence of these legal schools, accepted to this day, may have made the independent creation of law (*ijtihad*) more difficult, but it did not prevent it within the schools. The "classic" *fiqh* texts underscore this thesis.[5] They are also an important source in modern times, when Islamic law is relied on for application because of gaps in the law or lack of codification. In addition, legislators refer to these works in cases involving formal or substantive application of shari'a today. It is obvious that in this way, quite different things may be declared to be "Islamic law."

b. "Western" Law

Shari'a is not based solely on conditions prevailing in pre-Islamic Arabia; it was also influenced by Muslim contact with non-Muslims. The adoption of ancient Near Eastern, Jewish, Persian-Sassanid, Roman, and Byzantine legal ideas can be seen in various legal concepts, not least in the "practical" questions of administration. The geopolitical changes in the process of European-Christian expansion, the caliphate's crisis-prone situation, and developing trade relations influenced contacts between Muslims and Christians. The Islamic concept of the ruler's prescriptive authority (*siyasa shar'iyya*) at first provided enough leeway to proclaim "new" norms for which there was no direct basis in Islamic legal sources. Starting in the sixteenth century, the Ottoman sultans were forced to grant European merchants privileges through treaties. Such later treaties ("capitulations") gave foreigners special legal status in the territories of the Ottoman Empire and remained at least partially in force until their complete elimination in Egypt, through the 1937 Treaty of Montreux. Napoleon's Egyptian campaign in 1798 symbolized a decisive turning point in the erstwhile broad legal autonomy of the Islamic region. The West's technical and technological superiority subsequently also had an effect on the field of law, since modernization in some areas of the Islamic world, driven by internal and external forces, also made legal reforms necessary. Technical and infrastructural changes and new requirements in education, trade, and the world of work stimulated interest in "Western" legal concepts. The European powers promoted this process with their colonial policies, above all through efforts to eliminate obstacles to their economic activities. The French legal system, built on the principles of personal equality and economic freedom, found increasing regard in the Islamic world: the five bodies of law (Code Civil, Code de Commerce, Code Pénal, Code de Procédure Civile, and Code d'Instruction Criminelle, from 1804–1810) form a pillar of the national legal systems of numerous Islamic countries to this day, even if France's direct colonial influence did not endure.

These legal reforms took hold in the Ottoman Empire, which—weakened by its conflicts with the European powers—attempted, by adopting French law, to counteract its gradual social decline (commercial law code, 1850; penal code, 1858; code of commercial procedure, 1861; code of criminal procedure and code of civil procedure, 1879).[6] No general elimination of shari'a norms was intended; specific Islamic legal precepts were anchored in the field of criminal law, and in the law of obligations the Hanafi interpretation predominated, with the Ottoman civil code, the *mecelle* (discussed later in this chapter). Personal status laws (in the sense of family, personal, and inheritance law) remained uncodified (at least until 1917) and, with a few exceptions, informed by Islamic law. Not until the reforms under Mustafa Kemal Atatürk in the 1920s were Islamic provisions eliminated in favor of European legal norms.

A similar development took place in Egypt. The creation in 1876 of so-called Mixed Courts (*mahakim mukhtalita*), responsible for conflicts in which foreigners were involved, went hand in hand with the adoption of French-inspired laws (civil, commercial, maritime trade, penal, and codes of commercial and criminal procedure).[7] From 1883 on these laws were applied to Egyptians, in slightly altered form, by the so-called Native Courts (*mahakim ahliyya*). In Egypt, too, the authority of shari'a in the areas of family, personal, and inheritance law was not affected.

On the Indian subcontinent the British rulers favored a comparable strategy. The Islamic provisions of personal status continued to apply to Muslims, as affirmed by the Shariat Act of 1937. Islamic penal norms were eliminated in 1862 with the Indian Penal Code and the Code of Criminal Procedure. In other areas of law, the common law prevailed.[8] Thus in parts of the Muslim world the monopoly of Islamic law was broken, in some branches of law, in favor of a combination of "Western" norms and *fiqh* provisions. To this day, this combination—in different gradations—predominates.

c. Customary Law

As in other legal systems, unwritten law is also part of the various legal systems in the Islamic world by virtue of its practice and acceptance. In the context of shari'a, some special characteristics should be noted. Customary law (*'urf*), that is, regional or tribal customs and traditions (*'adat*), has been integrated, in part, into the corpus of Islamic law through the system of Islamic legal sources. The Hanafi and Maliki schools of law, in particular, "Islamized" customary norms because of their reference to the legal opinions of scholars as well as the benefit (*maslaha*) to the community.[9] But the scholarly consensus was also able to lend customary law Islamic legitimacy. Yet customary law can certainly contradict or modify Islamic provisions, though theoretically on condition that shari'a and *qanun* (law in the substantive sense) may not be violated as a result (as in the Shariat Act of 1937). Thus studies on Bedouin tribal law, for example, show that norms of penal or treaty law can contradict shari'a but are nevertheless applied by Muslim actors. In the Islamic regions of Asia and Africa that are particularly influenced by non-Islamic cultures, customary law provides a useful opportunity to preserve non-Islamic legal traditions.[10] In Indonesia, the term *adat* is used for all noncodified law, and in this interpretation includes Islamic provisions.

d. Methods of Lawmaking

With the help of the tools provided by Islamic legal sources, the rules of individual areas of law can be established and actions legally judged. The study of Islamic sources of law developed within the various schools of law and therefore—like the study of branches of law—is implemented in different ways.[11] The theory of "closing the gates of *ijtihad*," based on the development of the schools of law, has often been described in scholarship on the Orient, but it contradicts the actual process of law creation and the partial adaptation of Islamic norms to social needs. Muslims themselves have emphasized the historical conditionality of Qur'anic precepts in the doctrine of the circumstances of revelation (*asbab al-nuzul*). Referring to values that are to be protected by shariʿa (religion, life, property, family, reason), to the "aims of shariʿa" (*maqasid al-shariʿa*), or to ethical principles of law (such as the principle that necessity permits exceptions, under Qur'an 2:173), reform-oriented Muslims seek to demonstrate the ability of *fiqh* to evolve.

On the one hand, the Islamic countries face the fundamental question of how to translate Islamic law into national law, taking into account society's changing need for regulation. On the other hand, national legislators must respond to Islamic laws that conflict with their interests but, because they are rooted in the Qur'an, cannot readily be abolished through law. An important means of establishing Islamic law in adapted form is codification (*taqnin*), that is, compiling the main Islamic legal precepts for a branch of law into a code structured according to the Western model, which is then adopted and implemented by the state through a formal process. Such a law can use the differences (sing. *ikhtilaf*) among the various schools of law and other approaches (such as that of the Twelver Shiʿa) by choosing suitable doctrines (*takhayyur*), in eclectic fashion, and combining them into a "new Islamic law" (*talfiq*). Numerous examples of this can be found, in particular in the area of personal status laws.[12] State lawmaking opens up manifold possibilities for de facto abrogation of substantive Islamic law—codified or uncodified—through formal law (procedural law) or for influencing the applicability of subjective law. The spectrum of methods in this regard is great; they range from changing optional rules into obligatory ones, to cooperation between government bodies or courts in implementing subjective law or court decisions, to applying legal devices (*hiyal*) that already served to circumvent Islamic precepts in medieval commercial law. Codification of various areas of law in Islamic countries has left some gaps in the law that cannot, or cannot only, be ascribed to a lack of meticulousness on the part of lawmakers, but are intended from the start to provide room for varying interpretations. First, the intention can be to defuse conflicts between advocates and opponents of Islamization or "Westernization" of law; second, medium- or long-term changes can initially be realized by way of rules of procedure, relevant legal opinions, and high court decisions. This method of "legislative silence"[13] includes scholars of Islamic law and religion in the process of normative change, without, however, calling into question the state's sovereign rights. The interpretation of Islamic legal precepts is hardly uniform and is subject to social change, for example, through the reinterpretation of repudiation (*talaq*) as divorce with the cooperation of the courts, or the "obligatory will" as a representation that does not exist in Sunni Islamic law (stirpital succession). Overall, an increasing accumulation of laws can be discerned in all branches of law in the Islamic world. National legal systems, especially in the Islamic world, are oriented toward regional role models (especially Egypt), so in some areas (law of obligations and inheritance law, among others), a surprising legal uniformity can be found.

2. Constitutional Law

a. Legal History and Legal Situation

Constitutional law, in the sense of a supreme law, arises neither historically nor conceptually from Islamic legal concepts but is modeled on the European legal tradition. Independently of this, Muslim scholars have striven to find the roots of a fundamental law of the state in Islamic tradition in order to manifest legitimacy in this regard. The so-called Constitution of Medina (*sahifa*)—which emerged around the year 624—is often perceived (even terminologically) as the first Islamic constitution, although it contains only certain elements regarding the coexistence of Muslims and Jews. The Shi'a, in addition, refer above all to commands of the first imam (the fourth caliph, in the Sunni tradition), 'Ali ibn Abi Talib (d. 661), who set down principles of government in an epistle to his Egyptian governor.[14] Furthermore, the Qur'an (especially 4:58 and 4:59, as well as 3:159 and 42:38) is cited for consultation (*shura* in Arabic), and the sunna for proof of the Islamic legitimacy of a constitution. Inspired by European models and with direct European cooperation, the constitution of Tunisia of April 26, 1861, brought into force by the country's bey after prior confirmation by Napoleon III, became the first constitutional document in the Islamic world. The installation of a French protectorate in Tunisia in 1881, however, soon brought an end to this constitution. The first constitution of the Ottoman Empire, of December 23, 1876 (Fundamental Law, *qanun-i esasi*), modeled on the Belgian constitution, had already been suspended by 1878. Not until 1908 did the Young Turk movement succeed in reintroducing it. The first republican constitution in Kemalist Turkey, of April 20, 1924, still contained a provision that Islam was to be the state religion (Article 2). This was eliminated, however, on April 9, 1928. Although Egypt was formally part of the Ottoman Empire in the nineteenth century, the first advisory bodies developed there under British influence, taking up the Islamic *shura* concept. The first written constitution, adopted on February 7, 1882, called *al-la'iha al-asasiyya* and containing only the rules for the Chamber of Deputies, would be revoked upon British occupation in 1882 and replaced on May 1, 1883, with a new basic document, *al-qanun al-nizami*. Not until the constitution of independent Egypt on April 19, 1923, did a new phase of constitutional law begin in the Arab-Islamic world, illustrated outwardly by the term *dustur* (constitution), borrowed from the Persian language and used to this day.[15] The constitutional movement in Iran (*mashrutiyat*) in the late nineteenth and early twentieth centuries—supported by some of the Twelver Shi'a clergy—led to the signing of a Constitution Law (*qanun-e asasi*) on December 30, 1906, and a Supplemental Constitution Law (*motammem-e qanun-e asasi*) on October 7, 1907. The latter document contained two provisions that still appear in similar form in some of the basic laws of Islamic countries. Under Article 1, Twelver Shi'a was proclaimed the state religion, and according to Article 2, a council of five Islamic Shi'a scholars was to examine the conformity of laws passed by parliament with the principles of Islam.

The national independence of most of the Islamic countries following World War II encouraged the adoption of constitutions, which, however, often changed rapidly, were replaced by new ones, or were limited in effect by emergency laws. In the 1950s and 1960s, modernization and the search for a "third way" between Western capitalism and eastern European socialism, as well as an ideological and political alternative, were determining factors in constitutions and constitutional projects; but by the 1970s the failure of this concept was already apparent, which led to a push to revive Islamic values and legal concepts. The constitution of the Islamic Republic of Iran of November 15, 1979,[16] in particular, affirmed the view that the thesis of the priority of shari'a was in no way opposed to a constitution in which the basic order of the state and the rights of its citizens were anchored. Not an elected head of state (president), however, but a Shi'a scholar was to stand at the head of this state (*velayat-e faqih*). The Arab countries Saudi Arabia and Oman refrain from using the term *dustur*, and instead use the terms *al-nizam al-asasi li-l-hukm* or *al-nizam al-asasi li-l-dawla*, in order not to call outwardly into question the validity of Islamic law. Both documents, however, may be characterized as constitutions in content. Thus a broad consensus exists in the Islamic world regarding the necessity and usefulness of such documents. The current constitutional documents of the Islamic countries, as well as aspects of their constitutional history, are available both in text versions and on the Internet.[17] In connection with efforts at democratization, imposed constitutions aim to help overcome political deficits and instabilities (e.g., Afghanistan, December 2003; Law of Administration for the State of Iraq, March 8, 2004; Constitution of the Republic of Iraq, October 15, 2005).

b. Shari'a-Relevant Characteristics of Constitutions of Islamic Countries

Constitutional assertions about Islam—apart from general phrases—can be classified into three main areas: state religion, lawmaking, and *shura*. Most of the constitutions of Islamic countries recognize Islam de jure or de facto as the state religion (*din al-dawla*); the term does not come directly from Islamic tradition but bears a relationship to European constitutional history. European secularization, however, has no comparable parallels in the Islamic world. The thesis sought by many Muslims regarding the unity of state and religion in Islam (*al-islam din wa-dawla*) was and is by no means uncontroversial, and thus does not result in a uniform Islamic theory of the state. A state religion means, first of all, the privileging of a religion or religious community. Historically, the unequal treatment of Muslims and non-Muslims goes back to the status of adherents of so-called religions of the book (*ahl al-kitab*). Jews, Christians, and other recognized religious minorities enjoyed rights, but not equal rights. Residues of this concept can be detected to this day in many areas of law (the prohibition on marriage between a Muslim woman and a non-Muslim man; the exclusion of non-Muslims from legal succession; the prohibition on "deserting the Islamic faith," *irtidad*). In the allocation of public offices, too, religious considerations can be decisive: thus even in republican forms of government the head of state is a member of the Muslim faith, and higher public offices are allocated on the basis of religious considerations (for example, in Egypt and Jordan). Yet, as the example of Lebanon shows, this need not necessarily be tied to the establishment of a state religion.

By anchoring Islam in the constitution as the state religion, the state declares itself the custodian of religion and feels called upon to make decisions on Islamic matters and to supervise the activities of legal and religious scholars. The observance of religious ritual (*'ibadat*) enforced by the state, and the publicly fostered propagation of Islam (*da'wa*) inwardly and outwardly, above all satisfy the state's need for legitimacy. The forms differ from country to country, but they include primarily the construction and upkeep of mosques and Qur'an schools; observance of fasting and prayer periods and religious regulations regarding food, drink, and clothing; encouragement of pilgrimages; logistical support in collecting the charity tax; administration of religious endowments (*awqaf*); and the use of state media for religious purposes. Numerous Islamic countries couple assertion of a state religion with constitutional establishment of freedom of religion or belief as the outward side, and/or freedom of faith or ritual as the inward side. The wording is oriented toward Western models but can also be traced back to Qur'anic sources (2:256, 16:125). In fact, in evaluating freedom of religion and faith in the Islamic world, it is above all necessary to analyze the political situation. It is not shari'a but primarily a lack of democracy in addition to social deficiencies that prevent the implementation of constitutional provisions. Thus, not establishing Islam as a state religion (such as in Turkey, Indonesia,[18] Lebanon, Sudan,[19] and Syria[20]) does not automatically result in a greater degree of religious freedom.

In the constitutions of some Arab-Islamic countries, the role of shari'a in the legislative process is codified. The Egyptian constitutional amendment of May 22, 1980 (Article 2), under which "the principles of Islamic shari'a shall be the main source of legislation," sparked discussion of a resulting Islamization of the laws. Nevertheless, various Egyptian courts—including the Constitutional Court in 1985—have determined that all laws adopted before 1980 remain in force.[21] Yet the Constitutional Court was granted the right to examine whether new laws conform to the principles of Islamic law. Similar wording in other constitutions (Yemen, Libya, Oman, Qatar, Saudi Arabia) is based mainly in a population structure that—aside from foreign guest workers—is almost exclusively Muslim.

Consultation (*shura*) is described in the "classical" sources not as a concrete institution but as a general method going back to Muhammad and the companions of the Prophet (*sahaba*). The decision (*hukm*) of the ruler, however, outweighs consultation. The return to the "true" and "authentic" sources of Islam stimulated by the reformists of the nineteenth and twentieth centuries led to a redefinition of *shura* as an expression of democratic participation within the framework of shari'a. In the constitutions of Islamic countries, the *shura* concept is anchored as both a general state principle and a concrete institution (parliament, "upper house," and the like). Countries such as Libya, with its specific system of a People's Congress, or the individual emirates in the UAE, with their respective consultative bodies, also see themselves as implementing the *shura* principle. The *majles-e shoura-ye eslami* provided for in the constitution of the Islamic Republic of Iran considers itself the country's parliament. The changes in the Gulf region since the 1990s have been accompanied by the formation of consultative bodies, which have been, or are supposed to be, gradually transformed into parliamentary bodies. In these countries consultation is also part of the tradition of the political culture. Thus on March 1, 1992, under Article 68 of the Basic Order, the Saudi king decreed an "Order on the Consultative Council" (*nizam majlis al-shura*).[22]

3. Criminal Law

a. Criminal Law in the Context of Shari'a

In the areas to which the Islamic religion spread, a system of norms was developed—building on what was already there—in order to investigate and prosecute (law of criminal procedure), punish criminal acts (criminal law), and carry out sentences (corrections law). Unlike in modern European criminal law, however, these areas could not be separated from one another, according to shari'a, but instead form a unit in three or four separate areas. The usual classification into a general and a special category within criminal law is not developed in Islamic law, nor is a criminal prosecution authority, in the form of the state prosecutor. In Islamic criminal law (*al-'uqubat*), criminal statutes (*jinayat*), which were adopted in altered form from pre-Islamic customary law, confront the elements of crimes and the punishments established by the Qur'an and sunna. While the former have mainly a private law character (*haqq al-'ibad*), the divine character is dominant in the latter (*haqq Allah*). As in personal status law, criminal accountability is determined not by a person's age but by biological maturity. Only people who are *baligh* (of legal age in the sense of biological sexual maturity) can be held criminally liable. They are punishable, however, only if in full possession of their mental faculties (*'aqil*). Conditional criminal accountability cannot be directly derived from Islamic sources. The following discussion describes, with necessary brevity, the field of Islamic criminal law.[23]

1. *Hadd* offenses. The expression refers to the limits (*hudud*, sing. *hadd*) that God places on humankind, which they may not overstep. The crimes and punishments established in this way are based on Qur'anic statements that are made more precise in the sunna and received an interpretation specific to the legal schools in the *furu' al-fiqh* works. Therefore punishments for the same offense may differ. Differences can also be found in regard to criminality outside of Islamic territorial sovereignty and to prosecution of non-Muslim perpetrators. The Hanafi legal school considered these problems in detail for practical reasons (especially because of commercial contacts) and established exemption from *hadd* punishment for acts committed outside Islamic rule.[24] Because this area involves primarily "divine law," remorse (*tawba*) can serve to exempt one from *hadd* punishment. For the Hanafis, however, this applies only to brigandage and apostasy. The *hadd* offenses are the following:

- Illicit sexual relations, that is, sexual relations outside of a legal marriage (*zina*, fornication), under Qur'an 24:2–3, 17:32, and 4:15. The perpetrator— man or woman—is punished by stoning, if he or she has already had sexual relations in a legal marriage; if the perpetrator has not had such relations, he or she receives one hundred lashes. The procedural rules in this regard, however, make punishment possible in few cases—generally only where there has been a confession—since the act must be substantiated by four male Muslim witnesses. In addition, statutes of limitation are short (generally only one month). In case of doubt (*shubha*), a *hadd* punishment cannot be applied.
- False accusations of fornication (*qadhf*) under Qur'an 24:4. The slanderer— that is, one who cannot prove his accusation—receives eighty lashes. In contrast to the other *hadd* offenses, however, this one requires an application by the slandered person, so that, at the same time, a personal legal claim is manifest.
- Consumption of intoxicating beverages (*shurb al-khamr*), under Qur'an 2:219, 4:43, and (the definitive prohibition) 5:90–91. The punishment is forty or eighty lashes, depending on the legal school (Hanafi, Maliki: eighty). More than in the case of almost any other *hadd* crime, the prohibition on alcohol has come to the attention of a broader public through contact with the non-Islamic world, although consumption of alcohol was and is socially and culturally acceptable in only a few regions of the Islamic world.

- Theft of valuable objects (*sariqa*) under Qur'an 5:38. The thief's right hand, and for recidivists the left foot, is to be amputated. This punishment can be imposed and carried out, however, only if the stolen object had a minimum value (dependent on time and place) and was adequately protected. Thus pickpocketing is not considered a *hadd* offense.
- Highway robbery (*qat' al-tariq; muharaba*) under Qur'an 5:33. Various offenses are included in the crime of highway robbery, starting with brigandage. The brigand is jailed. If he has committed a robbery, his right hand *and* left foot are amputated. In case of intentional killing, the brigand himself is killed. If he has committed robbery and murder, the penalty is execution and crucifixion.

In addition to the *hadd* offenses, whose description in Islamic legal literature is largely consistent, others often classified as such are revolt against state authority (*baghy*) under Qur'an 49:9, and apostasy from the Islamic faith (irtidad) under Qur'an 2:217, 4:137–138, and 5:21. The killing of rebels and apostates particularly involves political-governmental interests.

2. *Qisas* (retaliation) offenses. Crimes against life and limb are fundamentally oriented toward the pre-Islamic principle of *talion* (repaying like with like: *mumathala*); limits, however, are established in the Qur'an (2:178–179, 17:33) and sunna that modify the principle of private revenge. Only for intentional (*'amdan*) unlawful killing or injury can the injured person himself or the heirs to the person killed carry out retaliation, after a judicial determination of guilt. It is possible to refrain from punishment, as well as to avoid it through a settlement (*sulh*) for specified blood money. A precondition for retaliation is the equality of perpetrator and victim, which, according to prevailing doctrine, is not the case between men and women, freemen and slaves, the healthy and the disabled, and—with the exception of the Hanafi—between Muslims and non-Muslims.[25] Thus this form of punishment has largely been rolled back in the Islamic context.Nevertheless, Bedouin customary law shows that the practice of retaliation cannot be ascribed generally to Islamic sources.

3. *Diya* (blood money). This punishment also applies to crimes against life and limb, and is employed when retaliation is prohibited because the preconditions (equality; unintentional act) are not met, or the person or persons entitled to it prefer(s) blood money to *qisas* punishment. Such renunciation is considered creditable and thus reflects a characteristic of Islamic criminal law. Both the amount of the blood money and the number of those obligated to pay differ depending on the crime. While for intentional or quasi-intentional (*shibh al-'amd*) killing—that is, killing by means that would not usually lead to death—full blood money (traditionally measured in the Arab milieu according to the value of a certain number of camels) and an additional atonement (*kaffara*) under Qur'an 4:92 are due, this blood money is reduced for unintentional killing. Only for an intentional act is the tribe (*'aqila*)—reduced over time to the male, patrilineal

relatives—freed from the obligation to pay; the blood money is the obligation of the perpetrator alone. The rules for bodily injury are largely based
on this system. Compensation for the loss of body parts or functions can
arise from the usually applicable rules or through judicial decision.

4. *Ta'zir* offenses. The so-called corporal chastisement crimes all involve
offenses related to a sin (*ma'siya*) for which none of the aforementioned
punishments or atonement is designated.[26] This definition points to the
Qur'anic principle "to ordain what is right and forbid what is wrong" (*al-
amr bi-l-ma'ruf wa-l-nahy 'an al-munkar;* 3:104, 3:110, 3:114, 7:199). The
punishments are, in the Islamic view, not absolute and unchangeable, but
are considered to be entrusted to the judge or ruler. They can extend to any
of the foregoing offenses that, because they lack the preconditions, are not
punishable by *hadd, qisas,* or *diya* (for example, certain forms of fornication; theft of objects not appropriately protected) or—in most cases—are
not "analogous" to the crimes listed (breach of trust, defamation, bribery,
gambling, usury, trespass, bearing false witness, refusing to testify, consum-
ing forbidden food, cruelty to animals,[27] as well as embezzlement, property
damage, fraud). *Ta'zir* can also be interpreted as a supplementary punishment or, as developed by the Maliki school, a way to "protect society"
(as a security measure against persons considered dangerous). Against the
background of *siyasa* authority, the result is extensive power on the part of
the ruler, who is obliged to establish crimes and punishments in detail. Only
stoning and amputation of limbs are not permitted. Otherwise, as long as
the principle is observed that a *ta'zir* punishment may not be more severe
than a comparable *hadd* punishment, any physical punishments, imprisonment, and asset forfeitures may be imposed, as well as censure, warning,
public proclamation, or removal from office. The field of *ta'zir* thus opens
up to the respective legislator the opportunity to codify general and special
provisions of criminal law in accordance with the needs of society.

b. Legal History and Legal Situation

Criminal law in the Islamic world was characterized, until well into the
nineteenth century, by the coexistence of Islamic legal rules as interpreted
by the various legal schools, on the one hand, and regionally valid norms
with an urban, rural, or Bedouin background, on the other. Customary law
and the rulers' regulations were supposed to preserve the general, peaceful order. The Islamic value system was accepted without alternative, and
thus the *hadd* punishments were legitimized—if they were applicable. This
changed only upon contact with Europe and the advance of European colonialism into the areas in which the Islamic religion prevailed. The European
Enlightenment brought about a fundamental reform and humanization of
criminal law. The principle *nulla poena sine lege* (no punishment without
law), as well as the separation of investigative and prosecutorial authorities
from the courts, signified a new orientation. Hence Islamic criminal law

contradicted basic European bourgeois values in theory and practice. Consequently, the Europeans (in part in alliance with Muslim reformists) sought to replace Islamic criminal laws with European laws, or at least to declare the former inapplicable to non-Muslims. The Ottoman criminal law code of 1858, structured according to the French model, which was also applied in Egypt starting in 1863, was still overloaded with Islamic provisions; but the Indian Penal Code and Code of Criminal Procedure of 1862 marked the beginning of a radical criminal law reform in the Islamic world, although Islamic criminal law was not entirely supplanted de facto. In the territory of what is now Indonesia, a criminal code for Europeans was promulgated by the Dutch colonial administration in 1867 and one for Indonesians in 1873. The criminal code of 1918 (modeled on the Dutch criminal code of 1886), still in effect today in altered form, overcame this legal division, while a planned new version was supposed to include Islamic references.[28] The changes in criminal law introduced in connection with the restructuring of the Egyptian court system in the late nineteenth century already pointed to the modernization of criminal law on the European, and especially French, model that would emerge a few decades later. The French legal trisection of criminal acts into crimes, misdemeanors, and infractions became the basis for most of the criminal codes in the Islamic world, as expressed, for example, in the Turkish criminal code of 1926 (on the Italian model),[29] the Iranian criminal code of 1926,[30] and the Egyptian criminal code of 1937.[31] The British-Indian model was adopted in 1899 in Sudan, with some changes, and also in Zanzibar and the East African protectorates. Finally, it attracted interest in Kuwait in 1956 (in the Sudanese variant).

The national independence of Islamic countries forced the rapid adoption of codes of criminal law and procedure, which largely displaced Islamic law.[32] Only remnants remained in effect, such as the prohibition against alcohol in the Gulf Emirates, which was affirmed by the British. Also striking was and is the wealth of additional and supplementary laws, of which it is difficult to gain an overview. Even in Saudi Arabia, numerous crimes are regulated by law, even though the rules for *hadd, qisas,* and *diya* crimes can be gathered from the *fiqh* works, predominantly those of the Hanbali school.[33]

The Islamization tendencies since the 1970s have left sometimes contradictory marks on criminal law, if not to an extent that would allow us to expect a general Islamization of this area of law in the future. Some Islamization projects even failed from the start, as in Egypt in 1982,[34] or proved to be more like token laws to legitimize the political leadership. The so-called "Islamic legislation" in Libya from 1971 to 1974—relevant to the area of criminal law because of laws on *hadd* punishments—was considered a supplement to the criminal code of 1953. Except for punishments for consumption of alcohol, however, the physical punishments provided for were applied only in exceptional cases (as in 2002).[35] Neither did Pakistan's Hudood Ordinance of 1979 abrogate the existing criminal code, but instead supplemented it with *hadd* punishments. In the 1987 criminal code of the UAE, Article 1 stipulated punishments under shari'a for *hadd, qisas,* and *diya* offenses. To this extent, the law is understood to be a codification of *ta'zir* crimes.

The discourse on the Islamization of criminal law was sparked in particular by relevant laws in two Islamic countries, Sudan and Iran. With the "September laws" of 1983, Sudan adopted a criminal code oriented around the taxonomy of the 1974 law but at the same time containing provisions of Islamic criminal law. Corporal punishments—especially whipping—were added to the other punishments. The 1991 criminal code—adopted first by Sudan's six northern Islamic states—affirmed the *hadd* corporal punishments. It did not base this, however, on the views of a particular legal school but instead joined various views into a "new" Islamic law. In addition, certain offenses, such as *zina* and consumption of alcohol, are punished differently or not at all in the north and the south.[36] The Islamization policies of the religiously legitimized regime of the Islamic Republic of Iran were aimed at applying Islamic criminal law. By 1982–83 four laws had already gone into force, temporarily at first; they were synthesized in 1991, with the exception of the *ta'zir* rules. The reform of 1996 added the area of *ta'zir*. Islamic punishments are listed individually, but the legislature provided for modifications and, especially in the revision of 1996, replaced whipping in some cases with a fine.[37] As in Saudi Arabia (and despite different legal situations), reports emerge constantly from Iran and Nigeria (the northern Islamic states) about the actual imposition of Islamic corporal punishments. Human rights organizations have called attention to such practices and court decisions.

c. Problematic Areas for Criminal Law in the Islamic World

Without doubt, the discussion on the application or introduction of criminal law norms from the *fiqh* is critically important. Although the majority of Muslims generally, and legal and religious scholars in particular, acknowledge the legal relevance of shari'a, there are varying views of the necessity and feasibility of criminal laws under changed internal and external social and political conditions. The methods of modifying *hadd, qisas,* and *diya* rules or entirely eliminating them are as varied as they are contradictory. From the sources themselves, procedural rules can be developed that limit or prevent the application of substantive norms. Far more sweeping, however, is the approach of interpreting Islamic criminal law in a historical context and inferring the elimination of Islamic punishments in fact (*ijtihad*) from changes in social conditions.

Islamic criminal law is no longer able, in the twenty-first century, to do justice to generally accepted human rights principles or modern criminological insights. In addition to deterrence, retribution, and atonement, education and correction of the perpetrator has more and more come to the fore as a goal of punishment. In addition to protecting the community from further crimes, rehabilitating the perpetrator is increasingly attracting interest. The deficits of Islamic criminal law in this regard are becoming apparent and have led the majority of Islamic states, despite their commitment to Islam, to refrain from such codification. Nevertheless, it may be expected that a more or less formal relationship to shari'a will remain even in criminal law, and that in some countries, Islamic legal rules will continue over the long term to be considered valid and applicable. Islamist commentators, however, should not be the only ones taken into account. The problems with criminal law in Islamic countries cannot be reduced to shari'a. Instead it appears that dictatorial regimes abuse criminal law to persecute and sometimes brutally repress political opponents, in the process referring to Islamic legal concepts such as rebellion or apostasy (though as *hadd* punishments they are controversial). Human rights violations through extensive expansion of special and military courts, the use of methods that interfere with free will (torture, threats against family members, and so on), disregard for defense and appeal opportunities, imposition of the death penalty, and the like are found in most Islamic countries, sometimes under the mantle of fighting terror. So-called honor killings, that is, killings of women for supposed violations of family honor, are connected with concepts of Islamic values. Such cases have been reported in many Islamic countries—including Egypt, Jordan, Pakistan, Syria, and Turkey—which does not mean they are not happening elsewhere. The regimes refer to French laws, since the Code Pénal of 1810 provided for mitigation of punishment for such crimes (which applies to this day in most Arabic countries and Iran, to the point of exemption from punishment), but this cannot be taken as a justification.[38] In many Islamic countries homosexual behavior is prohibited, and in some cases—as in Iran (Articles 108–134)—punishable by death, although it is not clearly defined as a *hadd* offense.[39] Criminal prosecution of violations of the Islamic dress code for women (such as in Iran and Saudi Arabia) is based on traditions that recall the powers of the state-appointed *muhtasib* (market supervisor) in Ottoman and pre-Ottoman times. In some Islamic regions (especially in Africa) "female circumcision" continues to be practiced, and not only by Muslims, although it has officially been prohibited to some extent, as in Egypt in 1996 and 1997. This genital mutilation has been internationally condemned but is not punishable in Sudan to this day.[40]

4. Personal Status Laws

a. Legal History and Legal Situation

The phrase "personal status law" in this context includes the areas of family, personal, and inheritance law.[41] This area is more influenced by shari'a than any other branch of law, without being homogeneous in the Islamic world as far as the degree and content of this influence. The differences range from legal neglect of Islamic rules in Turkey, through the extensive adoption of

Swiss law in 1926 and its revision on November 22, 2001[42] (though illegal "imam marriages" are entered into, without official registration), to continued applicability of Islamic legal norms through recourse to the "classic" *fiqh* works (Saudi Arabia). It is clear from the terminology that personal status laws have undergone changes over time: the expressions *munakahat* (marriage law) and *fara'id* (inheritance law) are barely used in modern statutes, having been replaced by the terms *ahwal shakhsiyya* (personal status), *qanun al-usra* (family law), and *al-mawarith* (inheritance law).

Until the nineteenth century, matters of personal status were left to the respective religious communities and were grounded in an accepted inequality of citizens based on religious affiliation. With the Tanzimat reforms in the Ottoman Empire, introduced in 1839, this inequality was abolished under French influence, but the responsibility of religious communities for the areas of family and inheritance law was not called into question. No thoroughgoing secularization occurred, so that no body of laws comparable to the French Code Civil could emerge in the Ottoman heartland or its dependent territories. The shari'a courts, which continued to be responsible for all matters of personal status, had to orient themselves around the *fiqh* works. A codification (and thus the establishment of specific norms) in this area of law was not achievable at first. Only after changes in the Egyptian court system as a result of European pressure could such a codification become reality: in 1875 Muhammad Qadri Pasha (d. 1888) compiled the *Kitab al-ahkam al-shar'iyya fi l-ahwal al-shakhsiyya wa-l-mawarith,* a Hanafi compilation comprising 647 articles, which, while it never attained the force of law, serves to this day in Egypt and the successor states of the Ottoman Empire as a source of legal orientation or to fill gaps in the law if no other laws have been enacted.[43] In places where the Twelver Shi'a are found, there were similar, though less successful, efforts to codify the legal substance of the personal status laws. The Ottoman Family Law Code of October 25, 1917, first introduced the process of codification of personal status laws. This Ottoman legal code forms to this day the basis of law, in barely altered form, for Muslims in Lebanon (though not, however, for the Druze) and in Israel. As in other areas of law, the formation of nation-states provided a stimulus to codification of family and inheritance law. Here, too, Egypt was a pioneer, with its two family law codes of 1920 and 1929 (effective as version 100/1985). Laws on legal succession and bequests followed in 1943 and 1946.

After World War II many Arab states enacted personal status laws, including inheritance law. They are based above all on the Egyptian example, as well as on the laws of the regionally dominant legal schools (such as the Maliki in the Maghreb) and utilize the instruments for adaptation to changed social conditions discussed earlier. Comparable laws were created with the codifications in Syria in 1953, Tunisia in 1956, Morocco in 1957–58, Iraq in 1959, Jordan in 1976, Algeria in 1984, Kuwait in 1984, Libya in 1984 (without inheritance law), Sudan in 1991, Yemen in 1992, Oman in

1997, Mauritania in 2001, and the UAE in 2005; they are, however, hardly uniform in extent or content.[44] Differences may also be seen in the opportunities for non-Islamic communities (especially Christians and Jews) to shape their personal relationships to law autonomously, that is, to have recourse to specific laws or internal religious rules. While in the area of family law such separate religious law is accepted in some countries with significant native non-Muslim populations (Egypt, Iraq, Jordan, Lebanon, Morocco, Sudan, Syria), in inheritance law we may observe broad countrywide application of the relevant Islamic legal norms (exceptions include Lebanon, Sudan, and, with some restrictions, Morocco). Thus non-Muslims are also subject, at least in part, to Islamic legal requirements.

In many Islamic countries the authority of shariʿa courts or the shariʿa chambers of national courts extends to personal status law, while in other (nonreligious) areas of law, civil courts dominate. Outside the Arab world, the first complex Islamic law on personal status, structured according to a Western model, emerged between 1928 and 1935 in the form of the Iranian civil code. This law was changed following the Islamic Revolution in Iran and supplemented with additional laws, overall worsening the legal status of women.[45] On the Indian subcontinent, the English colonial administration traditionally pursued a legal policy of religious classification of personal status matters, which was continued after the founding of the states of India, Pakistan, and (since 1971) Bangladesh. Aside from some provisions applicable throughout the country (such as the Special Marriage Act of 1872, in the 1923 version), the application of Islamic legal norms to Muslims in Pakistan is determined by the Muslim Personal Law (Shariat) Application Act of 1937, the Dissolution of Muslim Marriages Act of 1939, the Special Marriage Act of 1954, and the Muslim Family Law Ordinance of 1961. This orientation was intensified by the Enforcement of Sharia Act 1991.[46] The legal system, described as Anglo-Muhammadan law, displays formal and substantive differences from "classical" *fiqh*. In Indonesia an initially secular draft of the Law on Marriage of 1974 was brought into line with Islamic legal precepts through the intervention of Muslim forces. This process of increased reference to shariʿa continued with President Suharto's signing of the Kompilasi Hukum Islam in June 1991. In addition to family law regulations, the Kompilasi Hukum Islam contains regulations on inheritance law, donations, and the religious endowment (*waqf*).[47]

b. Marriage and Its Effects

From the Islamic point of view, marriage (*zawaj* or *nikah*) is not a sacrament, even if religious ceremonies—with regional differences—are observed, but rather a (civil) contract (*ʿaqd*) concluded on the basis of offer and acceptance as part of a negotiation. This contract must generally be witnessed by two male Muslims. In the "classical" view it need not be written; today, however, this is required in all Islamic countries, and these contracts are registered with the relevant offices and authorities. This guarantees that the contract can be proved and violations of marriage law more easily recognized and punished. Yet marriages that evade state registration continue to be entered into, with the involvement of only legal and religious scholars (*'urfi* marriages). Such marriages sometimes prove to be disguised prostitution and are evidence of ongoing social problems.

The rules on personal status have been made more precise in recent years, in part as a result of new technical capabilities. The marriage contract can include the actual marriage certificate, or it can be structured as a type of additional contract between the spouses. In addition to the marriage dower (*mahr* or *sadaq*), it contains agreed-upon conditions that may not, however, contradict legal or Islamic precepts. There is consensus among Muslims on these essentials. The marriage dower, which can be due either at the consummation of the marriage or, depending on the contract, at a later date (for example, in case of divorce or death), is determined very differently in different regions: it varies from a more symbolic payment (in some Maghreb regions) to a sum that far exceeds the average income (together with the cost of the wedding). The latter often makes marriage, which is recommended in the Qur'an (4:3 and 24:32), difficult or prevents it altogether. As a result, the number of marriages to foreigners has grown, so that some Islamic countries have attempted to moderate the problem by law (by stricter licensing procedures in Libya, Saudi Arabia, and Syria), the establishment of a maximum limit on costs (Pakistan), or low-interest loans to men interested in marrying (UAE).

The capacity to marry in the Islamic sense does not initially require attaining the age of majority in personal matters (*bulugh*, age of consent), which is based on the criterion of actual biological maturity. Consummation of the marriage, however, is permitted only upon attainment of this maturity. The majority of Islamic countries deviate from these rules by establishing not only biological sexual maturity but also concrete age limits for marriage.[48] Although the minimum age of marriage is in many cases lower for women than for men, and the relevant courts can permit earlier marriage, in general an increase in the minimum age of marriage can be observed (despite contrary examples such as Yemen, 1999). This "reform" takes account of changes in social and economic conditions. A woman's declaration of willingness to marry is generally not sufficient; the participation of a male Muslim guardian (*wali al-nikah*) is necessary (the woman's father, grandfather, or another male patrilineal relative). He usually also signs the marriage contract (often in the bride's absence).[49] Only the Hanafi school of law allows a woman of the age of consent to conclude a marriage contract without the participation of a guardian, and even this is not common. The guardian may not force his ward to marry or refuse to permit a marriage without a comprehensible reason. In case of a conflict, the judge must decide (see, for example, Article 10 of the Law on Personal Status in Oman).

The practice of polygamy (*ta'addud al-zawjat*), tolerated by shari'a (Qur'an 4:3, 4:128) and limited, in contrast to the pre-Islamic period, to four wives, confronts changes in social conditions in today's Islamic world, as well as the influence of monogamous, Christian culture. At the heart of polygamy historically was the problem of caring for destitute women, given a lack of social networks, and not the idea, popular especially in the West, of oriental sensuality in a "harem." Today the extent of polygamy varies greatly. In some countries on the Gulf, figures as high as 10 percent of total marriages have been estimated.[50] In most Islamic countries, however, the proportion is very low, and tending to shrink further. Nevertheless, while polygamy is limited in most Islamic countries, it still does occur. Aside from Turkey, Tunisia is the first and so far the only Arab country in which polygamy has been abolished by law, with the justification that the spirit of Islam requires equal treatment of wives, but treating the wives equally is no longer possible today. Nevertheless, many countries have, in their relevant laws, required the participation of a court or notary, making it possible to investigate whether equal treatment seems feasible, whether the first wife has been sufficiently informed of her husband's intention to enter into a second marriage and, if necessary, agreed to it, and whether a particular social situation or some other reason such as the wife's infertility justifies polygamy. This improves the woman's legal status. Given the lack of social welfare systems, though, problems are evident. Wives are repudiated so that husbands can enter into new marriages (see the example of South Yemen). Absolute obstacles to marriage render the match null and void (*batil*). Relative, temporary reasons to rule out marriage, which may be corrected, create a defective (*fasid*) marriage. The differences are not, however, always apprehended in shari'a with systematic correctness. Absolute obstacles to marriage are relationships by blood (*qaraba*), affinity (*musahara*), and milk (*rida'*), a relationship believed to exist on the basis of a common wet nurse (limited today to direct offspring). The common practice of marriage between cousins (so-called *bint al-'amm* marriage), however, is legally valid (*sahih*). Marriage between a male Muslim and a member of a religion of the book (Christians, Jews) is permitted, according to Sunni doctrine, but marriage of a female Muslim to a non-Muslim is forbidden, with reference to Qur'an 2:221. Such inequality not infrequently contradicts constitutional principles, but—in view of the religious upbringing of children conceived in such a relationship—continues to be adhered to. The marriage contract, in the Sunni view, may not in principle be time-limited. Only the Twelver Shi'a accept so-called temporary marriages (*mut'a;* in Persian, *sighe*), which may be entered into with Muslims as well as Christians or Jews. Although temporary marriage can never entirely rebut the accusation of legalized prostitution, it continues to be widespread in some Shi'a regions, though the trend is decreasing (see Iranian civil code, Articles 1075–77).[51]

Spouses are obligated to respect each another and prevent harm to the family together. Their rights and duties are based on the respective roles of men and women in society. The man's general function of protecting and caring for his wife results in particular in a duty to be entirely responsible for his wife's upkeep (*nafaqa*), including food, clothing, medical care, shelter, and other necessities of life. The amount of support required depends on the married couple's social standing. The wife must in particular carry out domestic duties and be "obedient" to her husband, in accordance with Islamic tradition. Leaving the marital home on her own (for example, to take a job) was, and to some extent is to this day, considered a violation of this duty of obedience. Given economic exigencies, however, women today are forced more than ever before to contribute to the family's financial survival through income from employment. Heretofore accepted norms and principles are thus losing their significance. In most modern family law codifications, the Islamic precept of strict separation of property applies. In Indonesia, however, the laws of 1974 and 1991, based on local tradition, for the first time established a law of matrimonial property.

c. Divorce

In regard to divorce law, too, the family law codifications in Islamic countries are based on shari'a, without, however, adopting unchanged the "classical" precepts of any one legal school. The main form of divorce described in the *fiqh* books, the one-sided repudiation of the wife by the husband (*talaq*) under Qur'an 2:226–237 and 65:1–6, is included conceptually in the laws but is connected with a range of effectiveness criteria in order to limit its arbitrary character. Aside from consideration of defects of a personal nature (such as mental deficiency, lack of intent, or drunkenness), which are also present in the legal works, we find above all changes in traditional practices through procedural routes, by way of judicial participation (Algeria, Tunisia) or confirmation (Jordan, Morocco, Syria), or at least through official certification and notice to the wife (Egypt). It is obvious that this improves the woman's legal status. If no judicial participation is provided for, and the woman therefore has no opportunity to demand a *talaq* herself, some Islamic countries (Iran, Iraq, Jordan, Morocco, Syria) consider a repudiation power conferred by the husband on his wife in the marriage contract to be legitimate, and even recommended.[52] A repudiation is followed by a three-month waiting period (*'idda*) for the woman or, in case of an existing pregnancy, up to the delivery, during which time she may not enter into another marriage. At the same time, the repudiating husband has the right to "call back" the wife to the marriage (*talaq raj'i*) if he has not repudiated her for the third time. Only after the waiting period is over is the repudiation irreversible (*talaq ba'in*).

A limit on the practice of repudiation by men is also created by establishing compensation for women over and above support during the waiting period. Especially in the Maliki legal school, the grounds for a judicial divorce action by a woman are established; for this reason, some codifications are based on this interpretation. Harm or injury (*darar*) caused to the wife (or husband), but also a quarrel or insurmountable difference of opinion between spouses, is accepted in many Islamic countries as a basis for such an action. According to the Egyptian example, two arbiters (*hakaman*) must be appointed before the divorce judgment in order to try to bring about reconciliation. If this does not succeed, the judgment can be (irreversibly) rendered. Long absence (such as a long prison sentence) or a missing husband, nonpayment of support, or a medical defect (such as impotence) can lead to judicial dissolution of the marriage.

In recent years women in the Islamic world have increasingly been taking the opportunity under Islamic law to buy their way out of marriage through a compensation payment to the husband (especially by forgoing unpaid portions of the marriage dower), *khul'*. Egyptian lawmakers have even gone a step further: if the wife forgoes all legal claims to property, the court can end the marriage even against the will of the husband, after an attempt at reconciliation (Article 20 of Law No. 1/2000).[53] Other ways to dissolve a marriage mentioned in the codifications can be classed as subtypes of *talaq* or judicial divorce. The relatively high divorce rates in some Islamic countries sometimes stand in stark juxtaposition to inadequate social security systems and lax treatment of financial claims on the part of divorced wives or children in need of support.

d. Kinship and Guardianship

A child's descent (*nasab*) from its father is based in some Islamic countries on its conception in a legal marriage. The child's mother is of course the woman who bore it. The child's religious affiliation depends on the father. The child of a divorced or widowed woman can also be legitimate (in regard to its father) if it is born within a specified period following divorce or death. Thus, given the lengthy maximum periods for pregnancy specified in the *fiqh* books (up to four years!), if a child is born within a period of one year after dissolution of the marriage (Egypt, Jordan, Kuwait, Libya, Morocco, Syria, Tunisia), it is considered to be descended from the husband. The question of descent touches on the problems of family planning and abortion, which, as became clear during the discussions at the Cairo World Population Conference in 1994, are fiercely debated in the Islamic world. The Arab countries have the highest fertility rates in the world.[54] Only in Turkey and Tunisia, however, is abortion not a criminal offense, and even there only if social justifications are present and under certain conditions, although a point of departure is offered by the Islamic concept of the "breathing in of the soul" (usually 120 days after conception). Cultural traditions and to some extent political ambitions on the part of states (striving for a larger population) have so far prevented regulations from loosening any further.

Adoption (*tabannin*) is not accepted in Islamic law, in accordance with Qur'an 33:4–5 and 33:37. Among the Islamic countries that refer to shari'a in personal status law, only Tunisia has legalized adoption, in 1958. Yet acknowledgment (*iqrar*) of paternity can have an adoption-like effect. The regulations on acknowledgment, going back to the Qadri Pasha Codification (Article 350), make legitimate descent possible even if, consciously or unconsciously, a new affiliation can arise.[55]

Children have a claim to support (*nafaqa*) from their father. As in the case of support for wives, this depends on local and temporal custom. The Maghreb countries include mothers with property in the support obligation, in accordance with Maliki doctrine. The age limit for support depends today above all on the child's ability to find a source of income. Thus the claim to support can be extended because of the requirements of study and training. Children require a female custodian until a point generally set in the Sunni *fiqh* works at seven years for boys and the attainment of puberty for girls; she is responsible for care of the child. This right of care (*hadana*) is first of all the mother's obligation or (if the mother is not able) that of the closest adult female relative. In the interests of the child, modern codifications have adapted the age limits to new social conditions. In case of divorce, the mother retains the right of care in principle, but she can lose this right, under shari'a, if she changes her residence or enters into a new marriage.

From a multitude of published court decisions and changes in laws in recent years, it becomes clear that today, happily, the welfare of the child (*maslaha*) has increasingly taken center stage. Thus not only can actual care of the child be temporally extended, but also a right of visitation (*haqq al-ru'ya*) can be established for both parents (see Article 20 of Egyptian law 25/1929 in versions 100/1985 and 1/2000). Also, statements on joint care of the child by both spouses in an existing marriage (Algeria, Libya, Morocco, Oman, Tunisia) underscore a partial change of opinion on the structure of family relations. Until they reach majority, minors (as well as the incapacitated) require a legal representative (*wilaya*) in property matters; this is generally the father or the closest adult male relative. This legal guardian (*wali*) is authorized to appoint a testamentary guardian (*wasi*). The separation of *hadana* and *wilaya* makes it difficult to assign the duty of care for property to the mother. Nevertheless, with the help of legal tricks (such as through interpretation of the thesis that the mother provides care at the father's behest), the father's powers can be judicially assigned to the mother, if the child's welfare requires it.[56] Majority (*bulugh*), which coincides with the capacity to marry and the age of criminal liability and with the duty to fulfill ritual commandments, must be distinguished from the capacity to conduct business in property matters, which is connected, according to shari'a, with the capacity to handle property responsibly. Almost all Islamic countries have abandoned this criterion, however, in favor of a concrete age determination (ranging from fifteen years of age in Yemen to twenty-one years of age in Egypt; generally regulated in the civil codes).[57]

e. Inheritance and Bequests

Inheritance law in Islamic countries is based almost entirely on shari'a, so that for Muslims (with a few exceptions) the rules and principles laid down in the Qur'an (4:7–12, 4:33, 4:176, 2:180–182, 5:106) and sunna continue to apply, in codified or noncodified form. Efforts were made in the Ottoman Empire, through the Land Law of 1858 and especially the law of February 21, 1912, which applies to this day in some eastern Arab countries, to exempt state land (*miri* land) and foundation land. Nevertheless, Islamic rules predominate, with very few modifications.[58]

According to Islamic interpretation, four duties, to be observed in sequence, are connected to a person's legacy, which includes all items of property and rights to assets: the costs of burying the deceased, the decedent's debts, the bequests, and finally legal succession. The main reasons for inheritance are marriage and blood relationship. Only those alive at the time of succession are entitled to inherit. Muslims and non-Muslims are by law not mutually entitled to inherit, but most likely a Muslim can effectively stay a bequest in favor of a non-Muslim. This bequest (*wasiyya*) may not exceed one-third of the property (after deduction of burial costs and debts) without the agreement of the other heirs, and may not be made for the benefit of one of those entitled to inherit, although Sunni countries (such as Egypt) also take advantage of the Twelver Shi'a rule under which a bequest of a maximum of one-third of the property is effective for everyone. Because Islamic legal succession has no concept of representation, a so-called obligatory will has been introduced, especially in the Arab world, to take account at least of children of deceased descendants. Dispositions made on a person's deathbed (*marad al-maut*) are generally considered to protect the rights of creditors and heirs as bequests. Legal succession (*mawarith*) is based on recognition of classes of inheritance, with significant distinctions between Sunni and Shi'a doctrine. It is therefore understandable that in areas in which Sunnis and Shi'a both live (Iraq, Lebanon, Pakistan), only general rules of inheritance law are codified in order to make legal succession possible according to the respective interpretations.

The principle by which female heirs are entitled to half the inheritance of the male heirs of the same rank is breached only in rare cases. The entire system of Islamic legal succession ensures that neither fathers nor mothers, sons nor daughters, husbands nor wives can be excluded, but rather—depending on constellation—each receives a specified share. The "Qur'anic," or quota, heirs of the first class of heirs receive established quotas (*fara'id;* hence the "classical" term for Islamic inheritance law, *al-fara'id*). Qur'anic heirs are above all those people who, in pre-Islamic times, were not entitled to inheritance, or were only secondary: husbands, wives, fathers, mothers, grandfathers, grandmothers, daughters, daughters of sons, full sisters, half-sisters on the father's side, half-siblings on the mother's side. The shares for these heirs, however, can be reduced or eliminated, given certain familial conditions (especially where male descendants exist). Substitute rights to inheritance in the second class are also possible. In normal cases the individual rules are structured such that a large share of the estate falls to the heirs of the second class. These so-called agnates (*'asaba*) include not only the male descendants, ascendants, and collateral relatives of the testator of the male line but also some female relatives (daughters, daughters of sons, full sisters, half-sisters on the father's side), that is, those who would inherit if there were no sons, sons of sons, full brothers, and half-brothers on the father's side of the testator of the first class. The second-class heirs receive the remainder (following satisfaction of the first class), whereby descendance comes before ascendance, which comes before collateral relatives, and closer relatives completely exclude more distant ones. People related to the testator through one or more women (so-called cognates) are taken into account in the Hanafi school as a third, subsidiary class; in the Maliki view (as in the Maghreb countries), in contrast, they are not entitled to inherit. In calculating the share of the inheritance, increases and reductions in the quota are possible if several Qur'anic heirs are involved. Many specific cases are described in the *fiqh* books, which, however, often have merely theoretical significance.

The system of bequests and legal succession under shari'a is able, in both codified and noncodified form, to solve even complicated inheritance cases. Nevertheless, to this day many problems can be found with its practical implementation. The splitting of property on the basis of nonexistent universal succession and the rules on classes of heirs and bequests is one of them, especially in countries with little usable agricultural land and large areas of desert.[59] The abovementioned Ottoman law of February 21, 1912, was supposed to minimize this problem. Often, actions are taken in this regard to circumvent it (gifting or sale during one's lifetime, creation of a religious foundation, and so on), or rules of inheritance are consciously ignored. Even though Islamic law takes account of women in inheritance law (with half the inheritance share), the realization of these rights is hardly to be taken for granted. Women often forgo the property to which they are entitled as a result of familial pressure, or are forced to accept inferior payments. Because of the national applicability of some inheritance law codifications, even non-Muslims are subject to Islamic law. A last-minute conversion to Islam on the part of the testator, however, as well as—in the case of Shi'a in Iran, for example—by an heir, distorts the legal succession because of mutual exclusion of inheritance or preferential treatment of Muslims. It is clear that theory and reality, especially in inheritance law, can diverge greatly.

5. Civil, Commercial, and Economic Law

a. Legal History and Legal Situation

Property law in Islamic countries can be based on shari'a to only a limited extent today, as a system of Islamic legal norms corresponding to the requirements of modern economic life is only partly available. The particular orientation of Islamic law toward contract law, however, and the regulations and principles exemplified by contracts of sale, do provide some basis for civil law codifications. At the same time, since the prohibition on risk taking (*gharar*) in Qur'an 2:219, 5:90–91, and 4:29, as well as the much-discussed prohibition on interest (*riba*) under Qur'an 2:275, 2:278–280, 3:130, 4:160, and 30:39, must be taken into account, from the start, circumventions and legal tricks have enjoyed, and continue to enjoy, great importance.[60] The Ottoman *mecelle*, the civil code, was enacted between 1869 and 1876 on the basis of Hanafi legal doctrine; it also contained rules of civil procedure.[61] To this day its effect goes beyond the Turkish heartland (in Turkey, in any case, the Swiss civil code was largely copied in 1926), since some of its principles were incorporated into civil codes that continue in force today (Iraq, Jordan, UAE).[62] The economic and political encroachment of the European powers on large parts of the Islamic world led to increasing adoption of the French Code Civil, whose rules had an influence, direct or indirect, on the civil codes of the Islamic countries (with a few exceptions). In Egypt this process occurred through the elimination of the capitulations and the creation of a national judicial system in 1949. This was linked with the adoption of a new, uniform civil code. Under the guidance of 'Abd al-Razzaq al-Sanhuri (d. 1971), a model civil code (no. 131/1948) was enacted; it was based on French law but also codified some Islamic legal concepts. This Egyptian civil code was taken into account in the codification of civil law in numerous Islamic countries: Syria, 1949; Iraq, 1951; Libya, 1954; Kuwait, 1961 and 1980; Qatar, 1971; Somalia, 1973; Algeria, 1975; Jordan, 1976; Afghanistan, 1977; Sudan, 1979 and 1984; UAE, 1985; Yemen, 1992 and 2002; Bahrain, 2001. It was adopted almost unchanged in Syria, Libya, Somalia, and Algeria.[63] In this way a remarkable uniformity of civil law has emerged in large parts of the Islamic world.

Al-Sanhuri's ten-volume commentary on civil law, *Al-wasit fi sharh al-qanun al-madani al-jadid,* has a significance that extends far beyond Egypt. It serves to this day as an important source in resolving civil law problems in the Islamic countries just mentioned. In commercial law, too, rules from French law were adopted extensively. The Ottoman commercial code of 1850 and the commercial code enacted for so-called Native Courts in Egypt in 1883 marked off the outlines of the fundamental orientation of commercial and corporate law in many Islamic countries, still recognizable today, in accordance with the French Code de Commerce. Changes in economic demands in recent years have led to the enactment of new commercial, corporate, and commercial agency laws or to changes in laws, for example, in Egypt (new commercial code, 1999), Algeria, Bahrain, Jordan, Kuwait, Morocco, Oman, UAE, and Yemen.[64] In addition, the tendency toward economic globalization requires reformation of copyright law and commercial remedies. On the one hand, some Islamic countries are attempting, through investment promotion laws, to create special customs zones, liberalization of the market, and so on, in particular to encourage foreign investment. On the other hand, Islamic financial institutions (banks, investment companies) in some countries (Pakistan, Iran, Egypt, the Gulf states) are aimed at attracting new customers and externally demonstrating the observance of Islamic law.

b. Civil Law

The overwhelming influence of French law in the development of the civil law codes in Islamic countries does not contradict shariʻa, in the view of many Muslim scholars of law and religion, because, first of all, certain principles of French law are already recognizable in Islamic law, and second, the laws clearly take account of specific Islamic legal concepts. Konrad Dilger has shown, in regard to the Egyptian civil code—and therefore with relevance, with some modifications, to the codes of those sharing the Egyptian legal system—the most important Islamic influences in the Egyptian laws of obligations and property.[65] Specifically, these involve the following legal concepts:

- Limited legal capacity (*naqis al-ahliyya*), depending on "ability to distinguish" (*tamyiz*) under Articles 46 and 110.
- Transfer of debt (*hawalat al-dain*) under Articles 315–322.
- Gifting (*hiba*) under Articles 486–504.
- Immediate acceptance of an offer among those present in a contractual negotiation, including by telephone (*majlis al-ʻaqd*), under Article 94.
- Sale below value in a deathbed situation under Articles 477–478.
- The possibility that the heirs of a deceased tenant or leaseholder may dissolve a rental or lease agreement that survives the death of the party under Article 601.
- A common wall (*haʼit mushtarik*) on the border between two properties under Articles 814–818.
- The lease of land in exchange for a portion of the harvest (*muzaraʻa*) under Articles 619–627.
- Leaseholding (*hikr*) of *waqf* (endowment) land for a maximum of sixty years under Articles 999–1014.
- The right of preemption (*shufʻa*) for buildings under Articles 935–948.

In addition, some Islamic legal concepts (such as, for example, the right to withdraw from a contract until the object of the contract has been viewed) have been adapted to modern requirements. Thus under Article 419 the illustration and description of the item being sold in the contract is enough to obtain sufficient knowledge of it.

Rules are also found in the civil codes, however, that cannot be directly traced to shariʻa. The difference between a natural person (*shakhs tabiʼi*) and a legal person (*shakhs iʼtibari*)—for example, in the Egyptian civil code,

Articles 29–53—cannot be directly derived from the theory of divine and human legal rights. Neither can statutes of limitations, which are common and indispensable today, be derived from shariʿa. Immaterial damages, in contravention of Islamic views, are generally taken into account in civil codes (see Article 222 of the Egyptian civil code; Article 293 of the civil code of the UAE).[66] On the issue of freedom of contract, shariʿa provides a sophisticated picture. While most legal scholars start from a limited number of types of contracts (only the Hanbalis accept a freedom of type in fact), they nevertheless agree in permitting clauses as subsidiary agreements that do not contravene Islamic law. Thus there is the possibility of perceiving "new" types of contracts—such as leasing or insurance contracts—as Islamically correct. Life insurance contracts, too, are now considered legitimate in most Islamic countries, although they are rejected as aleatory contracts by some ʿulamaʾ.[67] The civil codes' stipulations on interest, in contrast, are less uniform. The Egyptian law, which is based on the principle of proportionality of performance and consideration, establishes a legal interest rate of 4 percent, or 5 percent in commercial matters (Article 226). Contractual interest can be agreed upon up to 7 percent (Article 227).[68] Interest (*fawaʾid*) based on a loan is permitted in Egypt (Article 542); in the UAE, by contrast, charging interest on loans is prohibited by the civil code (Articles 710–721). The commercial code of 1993, however, allows interest of up to 12 percent in commercial matters.[69]

c. Commercial and Economic Law

The entire complex of commercial and economic law in Islamic countries cannot, of course, be dealt with in detail here.[70] This discussion will, however, illuminate certain specific aspects that characterize this area of law and are connected to an extent with Islamic legal concepts. While in the area of civil law, as we have seen, interest is sometimes prohibited, in commerce (especially international commerce), doing business with interest is tolerated, with a few exceptions. Since the early 1970s, however, some Islamic forces and regimes have increasingly brought pressure to "Islamize" the economic system—that is, to organize the banking and insurance sectors, in particular, on an interest-free basis. This field of "Islamic banking" has proved perfectly capable of existence and growth.[71] Such banks and investment companies are active even in non-Islamic countries. The establishment of an "interest-free savings bank" in a small Egyptian town in 1963, and the opening of the Islamic Development Bank in Jidda, Saudi Arabia, in 1975, paved the way for this sector,[72] which was significantly encouraged by the Islamization policies in Pakistan under Muhammad Zia-ul-Haq beginning in 1979 and Iranian financial policies starting in the mid-1980s. The business practices of Islamic financial institutions can be summarized as belonging to three basic types: *musharaka* (financial partnership with profit and loss sharing), *mudaraba* (commendum; provision of capital with no influence on business management), and *murabaha* (markup sale).[73]

Murabaha financing is undoubtedly the central aspect of "Islamic banking." The investment associations (*sharikat tawzif al-amwal*) created in Egypt in the 1980s on the basis of transferable *mudaraba* certificates—set up mainly with money transfers from Egyptian guest workers in the Gulf states in mind—at first discredited this form of investment owing to numerous irregularities; in principle, however, these investment associations can be successful economic actors. "Islamic banking" is thus emerging step by step from its niche status and developing into an accepted form of banking.

The harmonization of intellectual property and copyright law with international standards (for example, TRIPS, the Agreement on Trade-Related Aspects of Intellectual Property Rights), made necessary by the intensification of international commerce, has been promoted in many Islamic countries since the 1990s through membership in the World Trade Organization and new laws or changes in laws.[74] Legislators start with the assumption that, while shariʿa contains no independent theory of intellectual property, protection of such property can be derived from the early writings of Islamic legal scholars and various legal opinions.[75] In commercial agency law a tendency is emerging, especially in the Arab countries, to privilege native agents (sing. *wakil*) by law as both individual retailers and commercial representatives. Thus the termination of such a contract is possible only through compensation for harm caused to the agent; the same is true of short-term contracts that are not renewed. Such a rule is included in Egypt's commercial code. Commercial representatives must be distinguished from "sponsors" (sing. *kafil*) or service representatives (*wakil al-khidmat*), a familiar feature in commercial relations with public offices, especially in the Gulf states. These legal concepts, however, have no direct basis in Islam but result from the state's interest in involving nationals in business through protectionist rules.[76] Islamic countries often prefer the establishment of joint ventures with firms from Western industrialized countries, in order to acquire capital and know-how. With the growth of international interdependence and new forms of telecommunication, methods have developed for monetary transactions by which significant sums can be transferred, bypassing the financial and economic monitoring authorities. Nevertheless, transfers oriented around the Islamic legal concept of debt transfer (*hawala*), without the use of banks, carries with it the danger of misuse and creation of an Islamic "shadow economy."

Translated by Belinda Cooper

IV

THE STATUS OF ISLAM AND ISLAMIC LAW
IN SELECTED COUNTRIES

1. Turkey

(Ursula Spuler-Stegemann)

a. The Current Situation

After decades of decline (1923–1950), Islam underwent a resurgence in Turkey (1950–1980) and has now grown into the dominant political force in the country. The republic on which Mustafa Kemal Atatürk left such an indelible mark continues to have a secular constitution, and religion is still denied access to the legislature, but religious forces have gained such importance institutionally and in terms of their impact on the masses that many believe Turkey is in the midst of a transition to a fundamentalist state. Others wonder with increasing concern just how long the military will passively watch this development, which it in fact originally encouraged itself. There is also growing hope that Turkey's desire to join the European Union will force the Islamic government to adapt European democratic and human rights standards permanently.

Nevertheless, buzzwords such as "re-Islamization," "restoration," and "fundamentalism" do only limited justice to the current status of Islam in Turkey. There is much more at stake, and it is of an entirely different nature. Turkey is a nation-state in search of an identity, and it has increasingly found this identity in Islam and the revival of the Islamic community of faith, the *umma* (Turk. *ümmet*), of which it is a part. The process has involved a fundamental restructuring of the state. While religious forces claim that they will continue to adhere to the secular principle, their de facto goal is to reactivate the basic tenets of the Ottoman Empire—albeit in a modern guise. The most significant component of this search for identity—and the source of much antagonism—is easily identified: 99.2 percent of the Turkish population are officially regarded as Muslims. The rest consist primarily of various Christian denominations and smaller minorities of Jews, Arab Alawites (also called Nusayris), and Kurdish Yezidis.

Most Turks are Sunnis. In the late 1980s and early 1990s people first became aware of the fact that at least 15 percent of the population are Alevis,[1] who constitute an independent religious community.[2] The majority of Alevis define themselves as "Islamic," but they have a distant relationship to majority Sunni Islam and the Shi'a.

With an estimated 76 million inhabitants in 2007, Turkey has a larger population than any of the other countries bordering on the Mediterranean, including Egypt, France, Italy, and Spain. Demographic developments are easily retraced: in 1927 Turkey had just 13.6 million inhabitants; in 1960, 27.7 million; and in 1980, 44.7 million. By 2006 the gross national product had increased to the equivalent of approximately $4,100 per capita. On January 1, 2005, currency reform went off without a hitch: 1 million old liras were exchanged for 1 YTL (Yeni Türk Lirasi, or new Turkish lira). The inflation rate, which had skyrocketed to 156 percent in 1994, fell to just under 10 percent in late 2006 and was running at 10.5 percent in March 2008. The phase of expansion starting just after the economic crisis of 2001 has continued, but at a slower pace.

Turkey is also the only large state inhabited by Muslims that is located partially on European soil. The fact that traffic signs at Istanbul intersections point to both "Avrupa" (Europe) and "Asya" (Asia) is more than mere symbolism. A key component of Turkey's self-image is its function as a bridge between the two continents. As a NATO member state since 1952, Turkey is firmly allied with the West and dependent on Western countries both as economic partners and as a source of technological development. Yet Islam binds it to the Arab states of North Africa and the Middle East. Beyond the Arab League, these bonds extend to Iran and the Central Asian Turkic republics of Kazakhstan, Kyrgyzstan, Turkmenistan, and Uzbekistan, which gained independence after the dissolution of the Soviet Union. Islam also links Turkey to Shi'ite-dominated Azerbaijan. Traditional linguistic, cultural, and religious ties spawn many related activities, often with strong competition between Turkey and Iran. This divide between material ties to the West and intellectual affinity with the Islamic world has continued to shape Turkey into the present. At the same time, the country is making substantial efforts to meet the "Copenhagen criteria" defined in 1993 in order to become a full member of the European Union.

Furthermore, Turkey is experiencing a wave of rampant racist nationalism. Hitler's *Mein Kampf* became a best-seller and something of a cult book in the country, especially among young Turks. On August 22, 2007, publishers were prohibited from printing and selling the book, though this had to do with problems over publishing rights rather than the publishers' better judgment.[3] Books by authors such as Eşref Günaydın, who specializes in theories of Jewish-Kurdish plots, and Söner Yalçın, a great promoter of anti-Jewish conspiracy theories, have flooded the market, together with a large number of overtly anti-American publications.[4]

For years a central topic in the Turkish media has been the denial of the Armenian genocide.[5] Only 65,000 Armenians currently live in Turkey (compared with 30,000 in Germany and 400,000 in France). The debate on the Armenian question in the German Bundestag and the memorial celebration in April 2005 provoked indignation in Turkey and resulted in an inflamed nationalism that generally tended to strengthen bonds among Turks. Invoking the idea of an *umma,* Prime Minister Recep Tayyip Erdoğan exploited the situation in order to overcome ethnic differences and consolidate his position of power. This nationalist sentiment led to demonstrations in commemoration of former interior minister Talat Pasha, who had ordered the expulsions of Armenians in April 1915. By contrast, when one of the top contemporary Turkish poets, Orhan Pamuk, mentioned the murder of 30,000 Kurds and 1 million Armenians, he was hauled into court for "insulting Turkishness, the Turkish Republic, and the Grand National Assembly" (Article 301 of the Turkish penal code). He received death threats, and his books were burned in public.[6] The proceedings against him were dropped on January 22, 2006, and in October the same year Pamuk was awarded the Nobel Prize for Literature. On January 19, 2007, however, the Armenian editor of the magazine *Agos,* Hrant Dink, was murdered. At the time of his death several court cases were pending against him for critical statements he had made about the genocide of the Armenians. A large number of people turned out for his funeral, but Erdoğan was not among them, having chosen to attend the opening of a tunnel instead. The hatred toward everyone who violates Turkish nationalist feelings has also spilled over to Germany. Nationalism, with all its imagined enemies, has resulted in previously inconceivable commonalities between religious groups of various hues on the one hand and members of Erdoğan's AKP (Adalet ve Kalkınma Partisi) party, Alevis, left-wingers, Kurds, and nonreligious right-wing nationalists on the other. A political storm is brewing whose potential should not be underestimated.

Turkey has created a legal framework for improving the protection of human rights, and it has even established its own human rights ministry, but reforms have slowed down since the progress initially made at the urging of the EU. There continue to be human rights violations and infringements of the constitution, about which the government remains silent.[7] Freedom of opinion and freedom of the press are still in jeopardy; in 2006, seventy-two journalists critical of the state were charged with crimes under Article 301 of the Turkish penal code, and thirty-five under Article 216 ("inciting the population to hatred and hostility").[8] After repeatedly announcing its intention to loosen Article 301, parliament approved amendments in early May 2008, but critics see these as mere "cosmetic surgery." Although guaranteed by the constitution, freedom of religion exists more or less on paper only.[9] The state's onesided support of Sunni Islam isolates the Alevis and special Alevi groups such as the Tahtacı, who demand the right to religious and cultural autonomy. Non-Islamic minorities continue to be subject to discrimination.[10] On a positive note, in late February 2008 parliament passed the Foundation Act, which had been delayed by former president Ahmet Necdet Sezer, returning to these minorities the property confiscated by the state in 1974. The state continues, however, to use military force to fight the Kurdish independence campaign. Prisoners are still tortured, and the torturers are rarely punished. It was not until the West stepped up pressure on Turkey that the country granted Kurds cultural rights such as the unrestricted use of their language, but in practice these rights are being implemented at a very slow pace.

b. The Historical Background

The Ottoman Empire

After the conquest of Cairo in 1517, the Ottoman sultans claimed the title of caliph, the sole ruler of all Sunni Muslims. But it was not until the eighteenth century that they began using this office as a political tool in an attempt to reverse the decline of their empire. Serving as the *şeyh-ül-islam* (Arab. *shaykh al-islam*), the mufti of Istanbul (Arab. *mufti,* Turk. *müftü*) embodied the actual power in the state, holding a position comparable to that of the pope.[11] On the one hand, the mufti served and was on the payroll of the sultan, who appointed him directly (as was otherwise the case only with the Grand Vizier). On the other, as the highest-level religious authority the mufti was required to pass judgment on whether the sultan was living and acting in accordance with Islam, and to ensure that state law conformed to shariʿa. Although the mufti was a member of the palace staff, he even had the power to depose the sultan on religious grounds (though this rarely occurred owing to power relations). From the Ottoman Empire the modern Turkish Republic inherited this institutional separation between the state power of the sultan and the religious power of the *şeyh-ül-islam.*

The disempowerment of this central religious authority began in the nineteenth century. The *şeyh-ül-islam* was removed from the Sublime Porte and relegated to the *fetvahane* (fatwa department), which was under the sole control of the Grand Vizier. The pious foundations, which had previously been the most important source of funding for the clergy, were taken away from them and nationalized. The first public schools were built and placed under the supervision of a newly founded Ministry of Education, along with the higher religious schools known as madrasas (from Arab. sing. *madrasa*). Within the framework of administrative reform in the Tanzimat period (1839–1876) Turkey adopted European laws, and the *şeyh-ül-islam* was no longer able to influence further developments.

The Period after the First World War

The Ottoman Empire's debacle in the First World War, combined with the military, technical, and economic superiority of the Christian West, caused many to blame Islam for all the failures of the past as a hopelessly backward religion. Mustafa Kemal Pascha, who emerged as victor in the war of independence (1919–1922) and whom parliament later (1934) awarded the honorific title Atatürk (father of the Turks), saw it as a top priority to constitute the new Turkish nation-state as a secular republic based on European models and to liberate it from the chains of backward-looking religious functionaries. The reform process that began in Turkey in 1923 lasted for more than a decade, and it transformed religion into a matter of purely private piety, albeit less so in tradition-bound rural areas than in the cities.

In November 1922 the caliph, Sultan Mehmed VI, was ousted by parliament and left the country. Parliament elected Abdülmecid II as his successor but awarded him only the office of caliph. When the republic was proclaimed on October 29, 1923, the sultanate was abolished, and the sultan was replaced by the state president, who was elected by the National Assembly and invested with substantial powers, including supreme command of the military. To jettison the baggage of the Ottoman tradition, Ankara was made the capital of the new republic. In a session there on March 3, 1924, the National Assembly abolished the caliphate and expelled Abdülmecid (d. 1944) from the country.

On March 3, 1924, the office of the *şeyh-ül-islam* was replaced by the Directorate of Religious Affairs (Diyanet İşleri Reisliği). Its responsibilities were restricted to monitoring religious literature and overseeing theological offices and professions.

The *şeriat* courts were dissolved on April 8, 1924, and all jurisdiction was transferred to the Justice Ministry. In 1926 the Swiss civil code was introduced in place of the previous civil law, which was partially rooted in shari'a.

With the nationalization of the 479 madrasas still in existence on March 3, 1924, the entire school system was effectively placed under the control of the Ministry of Education, which introduced the principle of coeducation in 1925. European languages replaced both Arabic, the language of the Qur'an and religious scholarship, and Persian, the language of court poetry, in school curricula. Religion classes were phased out in high schools in fall 1924, in middle schools in 1927, in urban elementary schools in 1930, and in village schools in 1938.

In 1924 most of the clergy (Turk. *ulema*, from Arab. *'ulama'*) went into retirement. The only theological faculty in the country, which was founded in Istanbul in 1924 with 284 students, was converted into an oriental studies department at the faculty of philosophy in 1933. It had only twenty students and just a single Arabic instructor.

Mosque staff (imams and preachers) were trained in so-called İmam-Hatip classes at state schools, but these classes were discontinued in 1932 owing to a lack of demand. Most mosques were closed over time and fell into decay, while others were converted into museums such as the Hagia Sophia (1934) in Istanbul or put to other uses.

On November 30, 1925, the convents (*tekke*) and mausoleums (*türbe*) of the powerful dervish orders (Turk. *tarikat*, Arab. *tariqat*) were closed, as they were considered hotbeds of reaction. Their shayks were retired or banished from the country. The Hat Law, passed on November 25, 1925, banned turbans and fezzes and required men to wear European headwear. In 1934 honorific titles such as effendi, bey, and pasha were abolished, and a ban was imposed on wearing clerical attire in public.

Many important shari'a reforms concerned women. In 1925 polygamy was prohibited, and it became easier for women to get a divorce. A law proclaimed on February 17, 1926, made civil marriages mandatory, but even today the state has been unable to eliminate religious marriages (so-called imam marriages) completely.[12] In the period between 1930 and 1934 women were first granted the right to vote and finally the right to run for office. In 1925 Turkey introduced the European (Gregorian) calendar and, in 1935, made Sunday the weekly holy day, thereby eliminating the most important underpinning of the Muslims' Friday sermons. Other than the adoption of the international number system on May 20, 1928, the most effective measure taken by the state to roll back the influence of religion was script reform on November 11, 1928, which replaced Arabic Ottoman script with the Latin alphabet, which remains standard in Turkey today. As early as mid-1929, books and magazines were printed in Latin script only. This reorientation process was supported by an urgently needed literacy campaign, as only 17.4 percent of men and 4.7 percent of women could read and write in 1927. These measures enabled Turkey to emancipate itself from the Islamic cultural community, since young people were now no longer able to read traditional writings. These writings were replaced by modern literature in all areas of life, largely adopted from Europe or influenced by the national state ideology.

All of this was possible even though Article 2 of the 1924 constitution enshrined Islam as the state religion. But in 1928 this article was struck down and not replaced. It was not until 1938 that the gap was filled by a series of state norms describing the state as secular. The most important reforms implemented by Atatürk, who died in 1938, are set forth in Article 174 of the 1982 constitution and continue to provide a foundation for the Republic of Turkey today.[13]

Developments after the Second World War

Islam's renaissance began after Atatürk's successor İsmet İnönü established the current multiparty system in 1946. Many groups competing with what had previously been the country's sole political party—Cumhuriyet Halk Partisi (CHP, Republican People's Party)—were able to win votes from the conservative segment of the population, which carried on the legacy of Islam. In 1950, for instance, the opposition Demokrat Partisi (DP, Democratic Party) under Adnan Menderes won a parliamentary majority in what many religious Turks saw as a key turning point in the country's history. The return to religion was fueled by a fear of the Soviet Union, which was seeking to expand its influence as one of the victors of the Second World War. Islam was offered as a counterweight to godless Soviet communism.

In the course of these changes religious instruction was reintroduced, initially as an elective in primary schools and then, in 1982, as a mandatory course in all schools. In 1949 a new theological faculty was inaugurated in Ankara and enrolled eighty students. State Qur'an courses flourished, as did the illegal courses offered by many religious groups. Mosque associations sprang up in great numbers throughout the country, and they refurbished old buildings and built new ones. The state now had ever greater difficulty controlling these developments.

In 1949 the destruction of busts of Atatürk by followers of the Ticaniye order (Arab. Tijaniyya) resulted in the issuance of laws designed to protect secularism and Atatürk's memory. The Milli Selamet Partisi (MSP, National Salvation Party) became the first political group with Islamic and anti-European tendencies to participate in coalition governments (1974, 1975, and 1977). Necmettin Erbakan, a member of the Nakşibendiye order (Arab. Naqshbandiyya), was the head of this party and the deputy prime minister. Like most other party leaders, he survived the military's attempt to ban political parties in 1980 and went on to become secretary-general of the fundamentalist Refah Partisi (RP, Welfare Party), founded in 1983. Even so, in accordance with Articles 86–88 of Party Law 18,027, passed on April 23, 1983, all political parties are obliged to recognize secularism and refrain from pursuing religious goals in the legal system, politics, business, and the social sector.

In the 1983 elections, 45.15 percent of the vote went to Turgut Özal's Anavatan Partisi (ANAP, Motherland Party). In the ensuing period Özal, who also had family ties to the Nakşibendiy order, provided considerable support for Sunni Islam, not least through his personal religious activities.[14]

Following its electoral victory in late 1991 under Süleyman Demirel, the conservative Doğru Yol Partisi (DYP, True Path Party) formed a coalition government with the Sosyaldemokrat Halkçı Parti (SHP, Social Democratic Party), led by Erdal İnönü. This coalition was reconstituted in 1993 by Prime Minister Tansu Çiller (DYP), with Demirel serving as president. Early elections were held in December 1995, from which the Islamist Refah Partisi (RP, Welfare Party) emerged victorious.[15] Its chairman, Necmettin Erbakan, became prime minister in 1996 but was forced to step down just one year later under pressure from the military. Nevertheless, during his short time in office he succeeded in installing many of his followers in the civil service and important positions of power. The Turkish constitutional court banned his party on January 16, 1998, and in a ruling confirmed by the European Human Rights Organization in Strasbourg, Erbakan and six other leading functionaries received occupational bans for several years. The legal successor of the RP was the Fazilet Partisi (FP, Virtue Party), which had a nearly identical political platform. After Mesut Yılmaz (ANAP) was toppled in 1998, the newly formed, short-lived coalition government that he had led was replaced on January 11, 1999, by a minority government (Demokratik Sol Parti [DSP] with Milliyetçi Hareket Partisi [MHP] and ANAP) under long-serving Social Democrat Bülent Ecevit. During Ecevit's term a dramatic governmental, economic, and financial crisis shook Turkey, culminating in "Black Wednesday" on February 19, 2001. On account of Ecevit's grave illness, new elections were announced in July 2002. This period was characterized by a struggle between the military and the government over issues such as the treatment of Islamic groups, which saw the balance of power shifting increasingly in their favor. When the constitutional court banned the FP on June 22, 2001, new parties were founded in the usual manner, but this time the FP split into the Saadet Partisi (Felicity Party)—Erbakan's wing—and a "reform wing" that was led by Recep Tayyip Erdoğan and adopted the name Adalet ve Kalkınma Partisi (AKP, Justice and Development Party). Because of Turkey's unusual election system, the AKP was able to take power on November 3, 2002, after winning just 34.2 percent of the vote, while the Saadet Partisi was consigned to permanent irrelevance. Abdullah Gül was initially appointed prime minister. Because of a prison sentence that Erdoğan had received for quoting a religious poem as mayor of Istanbul, constitutional amendments were required before he could accept a parliamentary mandate and later the office of prime minister. While it is true that the AKP's leaders come from Necmettin Erbakan's Milli Görüş movement, the AKP is not a successor party in the sense of Saadet Partisi. Rather it has attempted to accomplish its goals in a pragmatic way. In contrast to Erbakan's ideology, the AKP has opened up to the West, but it maintains close ties to the Islamic world and has shown the way for Islam's further integration into Turkish society. For the first time ever, a Turkish party often described as Islamic-conservative, moderate Islamist, and occasionally even merely conservative held the majority of seats in parliament.[16]

After a period marked by careful strategizing and a willingness to compromise with orthodox Kemalist forces, Prime Minister Erdoğan took an increasingly confrontational course. He announced his candidacy for the office of departing president Sezer in April 2007, but he was forced to abandon these plans after demonstrations by the secular middle classes. His party fellow, Foreign Minister Abdullah Gül, ran instead.[17] Despite renewed mass demonstrations that were the largest non-state protests in Turkish history (and included many women), and despite warnings from General Chief of Staff Yaşar Büyükanıt, Gül insisted on running and was ultimately elected by parliament on August 26, 2007, after early elections on July 22.

The AKP scored an overwhelming victory at these elections, taking 46.58 percent of the vote. Because of Turkey's complex electoral law, which favors the strongest party, the AKP won the absolute majority and secured 341 out of a total of 549 parliamentary seats. The "time-honored, senile"

CHP, noticeably weakened, won 112 seats, and the nationalist MHP 70. The other parties did not clear the 10 percent hurdle but were represented by some of the twenty-six independents.

The AKP's success is attributable to a number of factors: positive economic developments; support by Kurds and members of non-Islamic minorities who hope for greater security and rights as a result of EU demands; and backing from a new post-Kemalist generation that is frustrated and on the lookout for new alternatives. The failures of the old political elite have been all too obvious: their stodgy coalition governments, bent on preserving their own power, disregarded the people's needs and hardships. In addition, they saddled the country with catastrophic inflation. In contrast, well-trained male and female members of the AKP canvassed villages and impoverished regions throughout the year, listening to the people's worries and promoting their party. The headscarves worn symbolically by the wives of AKP leaders may have aroused fears among secular groups, but they signaled to the tradition-bound majority that their religion was once again respectable, even in the highest echelons of government.[18]

With the National Security Council restricted in its capacity to act and the armed forces temporarily tied up in northern Iraq, the AKP's determined efforts to install Gül as president and its attempt, albeit unsuccessful, to abolish the headscarf ban at universities threw down the gauntlet to both the judiciary and the military. The AKP began progressively filling positions in the state apparatus and the media with its members.

The military, a staunch champion of Atatürk's reforms, has repeatedly taken control of the state (1960, 1971, 1980), in each case after a period of roughly ten years in which religious groups managed to increase their power. The military apparently hoped for increased stability by promoting Islam, which it regarded as a counterweight to revived left-wing forces. But Islam evolved into a highly efficient, internally nuanced state enterprise, a "Sunni republic" with a shrinking democratic correlative. This put the secular bastions of the judiciary and the military are anxiously on their guard. Attorney General Abdurrahman Yalçınkaya, whom Sezer appointed in 2007, filed a petition with the court of appeals in mid-March 2008 to ban the governing AKP, citing violations of the secular principle and the no longer guaranteed separation of the legislative, executive, and judiciary. The simple majority, secured by the vote of a single constitutional judge, was not enough to pass the ban. Yalçınkaya also pursued an occupational ban for Erdoğan and many AKP representatives.[19]

c. Religion and Politics

Ever since the elimination of the harsh and often abused Paragraph 163 from the penal code in April 1993, the Islamists who once fought the "atheist" state from the underground have been prosecuted in court only for egregious violations of the secular principle or criminal offenses.[20] Islamists have successfully used a variety of opportunities to infiltrate parties and state institutions, even without concealing their religious identities.

Political parties have adopted ideologies that attempt to integrate Islam into Turkish society. The best-known school of thought is the Türk-İslam Sentezi (Turkish-Islamic Synthesis), which aims to combine 2,500 years of Turkishness, 1,000 years of Islam, and 150 years of Western alignment. Its intellectual pioneers and supporters included the conservative members of Aydınlar Ocağı (Intellectuals' Club), who offered concrete proposals on how to frame the constitution and body of laws. Necmettin Erbakan's Islamist parties propagate the idea of a "just order" (*adil düzen*) and hope to tap into the pool of potential left-wing voters by using the vocabulary of socialism. Islamic liberalism (*islami liberalizm*), an ideology that arose in the early 1990s, was even accepted by many fundamentalists, who interpret democracy and the multiparty system as an "un-Islamic" form of government. Strong nationalism is currently a part of diverse political currents.

Even if official recognition is yet to come, the traditional popular orders (*tarikat*) and religious communities (*cemaat*) are firmly established in Turkish society. They include the Nakşibendi, Qadiri (Qadiriyya), Mevlevi, and Rufai; the Halveti with their Cerrahi branch; the Işıkçı and Süleymancı; the Nurcu with their radical anti-Western and antigovernment Med-Zehra group (also called Hizb-i Kuran, or Party of the Qur'an); as well as the Aczmendi. The most powerful and influential group is the Fethullahçı,[21] who, though highly problematic, are perceived by many as "liberal conservatives." They call themselves Fethullah Hocanın Talebeleri (Students of Fethullah Gülen), and their worldview blends "neo-nationalism, neo-Ottomanism and Nurcu ideology." Their *dershaneler* (houses of learning) and *ışık evleri* (houses of light) train an elite religious cadre.[22] A large number of parliamentary representatives, members of government, provincial governors, and administration officials belong to these religious groups; it is only the military that has managed to keep them at bay. They are otherwise a firm fixture of Turkish society, many of which have reorganized into associations and foundations with innocuous names. They have their own universities, run private schools, offer remedial courses for school students, and own their own retail chains and other companies. In addition to marketing religious music, they own publishing houses and large daily papers such as *Türkiye, Zaman,* and *Tercüman,* as well as numerous magazines. They operate private radio and television stations that broadcast to regions as distant as the Turkic republics of Central Asia.[23] They are also active in social welfare and health care.

The most important Islamic human rights organization is Mazlumder (İnsan Hakları ve Mazlumlar için Dayanışma Derneği, or Organization of Human Rights and Solidarity for Oppressed People). Founded in 1991, it distributes humanitarian aid in Turkey and abroad. Islamic NGOs hold international conferences devoted to planning the future and are present at all levels.

d. State Support of Islam

Article 10 of the 1982 constitution grants all citizens of the state equal rights irrespective of their religious affiliation. It expressly forbids privileged treatment of individual groups or classes. Nevertheless, the state promotes only one religion, Sunni Islam, which has in fact assumed the role of a state religion in Turkey. Islam is supported by four main institutions: the National Ministry of Education, the Ministry of Religion, the Directorate of Religious Affairs, and the Directorate of Foundations.

The Ministry of Education

In accordance with the constitution, the Millî Eğitim Bakanlığı (MEB, National Ministry of Education) has exercised a monopoly on education since 1924, including religious instruction and university theology studies. The General Directorate of Religious Education (Din Eğitimi Genel Müdürlüğü) at the MEB is responsible for personnel, textbooks, and curricula. Article 24 of the 1982 constitution regulates religious instruction, stating: "Education and instruction in religion and ethics shall be carried out under state supervision and control. Instruction in religious culture and ethics is a mandatory subject in primary and secondary schools. Religious education and instruction can take place outside these schools upon special request and, in the case of minorities, upon the request of their representatives."

According to these constitutional provisions, textbooks must bear the description "Din Kültürü ve Ahlak Ahlâk Bilgisi" (Religious Culture and Ethical Knowledge). A portrait of Atatürk adorns the flyleaf, along with the Turkish national flag and the lyrics of "Independence March," the Turkish national anthem. The last page shows a map of Turkey with all its provinces, often followed by a map of "the Turkish World," extending from central Europe and the Middle East to the Turkic republics of Central Asia and the Republic of Sakha (Yakutia). The textbooks are supposed to convey national values such as pride in being a Turk and good citizenship; they also provide an in-depth understanding of the "perfect religion of Islam." They offer information on the differences between Sunnis and Shi'ites, as well as on Christianity and other religions. The primary goal of religious instruction is to strengthen national and religious unity.

The need for professional staff to run mosques has grown with the renewed importance of religion. Fifty students graduated from the first ten-month İmam-Hatip courses in 1949. İmam-Hatip schools were introduced in 1951 to train students for the professions of imam and preacher. Since that time the number of students attending these schools has exploded. In 1997 the compulsory age for primary school was raised from five to eight, and in 1998 junior high schools were eliminated. Children can now switch to general or vocational-technical secondary schools, and İmam-Hatip schools are included among these. The religious schools offer the same curricula as their secular counterparts, but they are also required to teach

Arabic, the Qur'an, and basic courses on Islam, with an additional year of study planned.

According to the Ministry of Education, there were 445 İmam-Hatip secondary schools during the 2005–6 school year, attended by a total of 43,726 students (of whom 29,837 were girls). There were also seven Anadolu İmam-Hatip schools with 23,288 students (14,655 girls), which offer better foreign language programs. İmam-Hatip graduates still account for only around 7 percent of the 1.95 million Turkish high school graduates. Although the numbers temporarily declined, they returned to holding steady. Nevertheless, there are many more graduates than can be accepted for theological studies or enter religious professions. For this reason, many study other subjects or enter the mid-level civil service, which they are infiltrating on a large scale as a religious bloc.

Like other vocational centers, the İmam-Hatip schools were placed on an equal footing with general secondary schools in 1990, but even afterward, general high school students were given preferential treatment when applying to universities because of different methods of evaluating university admission exams. On May 13, 2004, the AKP won out against the CHP in the area of university reform, abolishing this unequal treatment and making it easier for graduates of İmam-Hatip schools to gain access to universities. In 2005 only 28 percent profited from these reforms.[24]

The one way to change this situation would be to reform the YÖK (Yüksek Öğretim Kurulu, Council on Higher Education), a constitutionally mandated institution that was founded by the military in 1982 and placed under the control of the president. The YÖK, of which the military is a member, has the authority to oversee curricula and coordinate university finances and staff planning. It is therefore also able to appoint professors and deans. There have been repeated bloody student protests against this all-powerful, rigid body, including one in early November 2004. Reforming the YÖK is essential if independent academic work is to be sustained.

Theological faculties have expanded as rapidly as the İmam-Hatip school system. With the conversion of the Higher Islamic Institutes (Yüksek İslam Enstitüleri) in the period after 1959, they increased in number to eight by 1982. In the 2003–4 academic year, 7,423 students were enrolled at the twenty-three theological faculties at Turkey's fifty-three poorly equipped state universities. Of these students, 3,475 were women and 3,948 men.[25] In addition, Turkey has several military academies and twenty-four state-accredited private universities that are run by foundations and are quite expensive to attend. Some of the Turkish theologians affiliated with the "Ankara School" have recently published works that take a critical academic approach to Qur'an exegesis. Previously unheard of in the Muslim world, such criticism has caused observers to prick up their ears. The results of their study of the hadiths were eagerly awaited.[26]

The headscarf ban in state educational institutes, public offices, and parliament has always had tremendous symbolic importance as a sign of state secularism. This explains the great stir caused by the resolution on a general amnesty that was passed by the Turkish parliament the night of February 23, 2005. The amnesty applied to all students who had been expelled from the university over the previous five years without being allowed to take their final examinations, most for wearing headscarves. President Ahmet Necdet Sezer vetoed the resolution, but his veto was over-ridden by 349 votes—more than the required three-fifths majority—and he was ultimately forced to approve it. Nevertheless, the YÖK kept up its resistance, even after the headscarf ban was abolished on February 2, 2008. Once again tens of thousands took to the streets, but the protests were relatively limited.[27]

The Ministry of Religious Affairs

By creating the office of a state minister of religious affairs, Recep Tayyip Erdoğan elevated Islam to governmental status. Of all people it was the religious representative of the state, Mehmet Aydın of Izmir University, who explained in early April 2005 that with the exception of financing, he planned to liberate the Directorate of Religious Affairs (DİB) from its dependence on the government in order to achieve the required separation of religion and state powers. In the future the DİB would make personnel decisions on its own, and the president would be appointed by the *ulema* rather than by the state—in much the same way as the DİB's High Council. These changes had the potential to make the institution comparable to the office of the *şeyh-ül-islam* in the Ottoman Empire. By early May 2008, however, the plans had not yet been realized.

Mehmet Aydın also complained that he was unable to send enough religious attachés to Europe because of their poor foreign language skills. Many critics have described the activities of these attachés as nothing more than "proselytizing."[28] The Turkish state was able to establish two endowed professorships for Islamic studies at the Protestant Theological Faculty of the Johann Wolfgang von Goethe University in Frankfurt am Main; The holders of these chairs have the authority to administer exams. Additional professorships are planned for other German universities.

The Directorate of Religious Affairs

The Directorate of Religious Affairs (Diyanet İşleri Başkanlığı, DİB) is head-quartered in Ankara and subject to the control of the prime minister. It was established as a state body by Article 154 of the 1961 constitution, which was adopted in Article 136 of the 1982 constitution. Law 1,327, passed on September 20, 1971, awarded civil service status to its central staff. According to its constitutional mandate, the DİB, "is obliged to work for national solidarity and unity and, in accordance with the secular principle, to refrain from taking political positions."

Specifically, the ban on taking political positions means that the DİB is not allowed to criticize state legislation and the constitution publicly from the perspective of Islamic law. Nevertheless, the DİB has evolved from a supervisory authority for Islamic activities into a powerful institution that promotes Islam in Turkey. It does so by means of a secular state that is actually supposed to be religiously neutral—a highly problematic development for many experts on constitutional law.[29]

The DİB's responsibilities include issuing fatwas (from Arab. pl. *fatawa*); formulating, translating, and censoring religious works; publishing official sermons; promoting religion in Turkey and abroad; supporting and paying the salaries of mosque staff in Turkey and abroad; supervising Qur'an courses and training course instructors; organizing pilgrimages (hajj and *'umra*); and building and managing its own mosques.

Ali Bardakoğlu became president of DİB in November 2002. The directorate's budget for 2005 amounted to 1,126,041,000 YTL, with a total of 2 billion YTL earmarked for 2008.[30] Personnel costs of the 88,563 employees accounted for 79 percent of all expenses.[31] More than 50,000 graduates of İmam-Hatip schools work at its 78,608 mosques, most of which were established by the congregations themselves with the support of foundations and local associations. The DİB provides them with an official text for Friday sermons. For a time Kocatepe Camii, completed in 1987, was the largest newly built mosque in Turkey, offering seating for 24,000, but it was surpassed by the Sabancı mosque in Adana, built in 2000, which can accommodate 25,000. The Muslim World League (Rabitat al-'alam al-islami), which supports the foundation of mosques worldwide, has invested a large sum in a mosque built in the parliamentary park. According to the DİB, in 2007, 155,285 students took part in its 4,322 Qur'an courses, which run over several months.[32] Only 17,891 of them were boys.

After the previous president of the DİB had disclosed plans to open up the organization carefully to women, in July 2004 Bardakoğlu announced that six hundred vacant positions would be filled by female applicants in a process of "positive discrimination." At the same time there was also talk of increasing the number of established positions by fifteen thousand. Some 2,700 women were hired in 2006. Eighty-one muftis in the various provinces have fatwa authority and can thus issue religious opinions on Islamic law. There were also plans to have women installed as deputy muftis, but they would be responsible only for issues involving women and families. Furthermore, women serving as imams are already allowed to lead Friday prayers in services for their sex. Under certain conditions they can preach to both men and women, and in extreme emergencies to men alone.[33] The DİB's prestigious administration building houses an ultramodern library containing around 4.5 million books and a bookstore. Aside from the Qur'an, the library holds works of the classical religious tradition, as well as Islamic studies literature and modern writings, including anti-Christian works. It also collects the four periodicals published by the DİB: an internal monthly magazine that can viewed on the Internet, the Turkish-language *Diyanet Europa-Zeitschrift,* a children's magazine, and an academic quarterly.

The DİB's foreign activities are focused primarily on organizing pilgrimages to Mecca, where it has its own pilgrims' stations. A source of dissatisfaction for many Turks has been Saudi Arabia's practice of allowing only 1 percent of the population of each Islamic country to take part in hajj. This translated to 96,442 Turkish pilgrims in 2004. The DİB also sends one commissioner to each of the five Turkic republics in Central Asia, looks after religious education there, and ensures that one "large mosque in the Ottoman style" is built in each country. It distributes copies of the Qur'an on a massive scale, printing a total of 5.225 million copies between 1983 and 1992. The DİB is responsible for all religious agencies abroad. For instance, in early 2007 it dispatched eight hundred Turkish imams to perform four years' service at the German mosque associations of the Türkisch Islamische Union der Anstalt für Religion (Turkish Islamic Union for the Office of Religious Affairs) that are affiliated with the DİB. These imams are subordinate to the religious attachés of the Turkish general consulates, who are also responsible for the content of Friday sermons.[34] Despite its activities abroad, the DİB has always responded with annoyance to Western offers to send humanitarian aid to Turkey (including offers from the German Red Cross and other aid organizations after earthquakes), since it regards them as an attempt to proselytize in the country.

The information presented here emphasizes the enormous quantitative expansion that the DİB, once a small agency under Atatürk, has undergone ever since it was put in charge of mosque staff in 1950. But we must also examine two important qualitative changes aside from its constitutional status and expanded powers as the central state body supporting Islam.

First, the generously endowed Turkish Religious Foundation (Türkiye Diyanet Vakfı, TDV) was established at the General Directorate of Foundations by the 1975 Foundation Law, which was supplemented by a special resolution in 1986. The sole purpose of this foundation is to provide financial support for the DİB's undertakings. Since 1991 the president of the DİB has simultaneously served as president of this foundation. Thanks to this new authority, not only has he been able to determine how TDV money is allocated to staff positions, mosque construction, and so on, but also, in a pragmatic way, he has been able to use the freedoms offered by the Foundation Law to bring nearly all the Islamic factions and groups in Turkey under his control. This was demonstrated most clearly to outsiders by the creation of a nearly complete network of religious bookstores in all large Turkish cities. They carry the books of 354 different Turkish religious publishers, although most of the houses put out only a few titles. In addition to the Qur'an, commentaries on the Qur'an, the *Islam Ansiklopedisi,* classical works, fatwa collections, and edifying literature, these stores sell dervish writings, which are still officially banned, and works by the Nakşibendi shaykhs Mehmed Zahid Kotku and Esat Coşan. Books by the antisecular, anti-Jewish, and anti-Christian female preacher Emine Şenlikoğlu, who was sentenced to prison for "religiously misleading the youth," have gone through up to fifty printings. The shelves also hold 130 works by Bediüzzaman Said Nursi and additional publications by Nurcu authors, as well as numerous writings by Fethullahçı founder Fethullah Gülen. Works by the leading authorities on contemporary political Islam—including two Egyptians, Hasan al-Banna and Sayyid Qutb, as well as the Pakistani Abu l-Aʿla Maududi—are openly displayed, along with pamphlets railing against Christian missionaries, Jehovah's Witnesses, Jews, Bahai, and Alevis. The offerings include much-coveted videos by Algerian and Iranian fundamentalists and radical Turkish preachers; religious posters and magazines; as well as cassettes of Qurʾan readings, Sufi music, and Arabic courses. A few of these publications openly advocate shariʿa, particularly the separation of the sexes in society, and vehemently attack the secular principle. Notably absent are the Qurʾan interpretations of the murdered writer Turhan Dursun or the anti-fundamentalist books of authors such as Ruşen Çakır. The TDV's expanded interest in publishing and the book market shows how the DİB, even in its highest echelons, has been infiltrated by members of fundamentalist groups such as Süleymancı, who make no secret of their religious affiliations.

Second, on the basis of the resolution of January 30, 1992, the High Council of the DİB reconstituted the Executive Committee of Religious Affairs (Din İşleri Yüksek Kurulu) after a thirteen-year hiatus. The council members, including a woman for the first time, are high-ranking DİB dignitaries and respected theology professors who meet regularly under the chairmanship of the DİB's president to frame religious policy at the highest level, particularly by issuing fatwas. The most important development is that the executive committee, which is directly elected by imams and theologians for a period of seven years, cannot be constituted or dissolved by state authorities. It therefore represents the first high-ranking religious committee independent of the state since the republic was founded.

The fatwas issued by the High Council serve the purpose of elucidating issues for the Islamic community. They offer paradigmatic rulings on religious questions based on an *ijmaʿ*, the consensus of the *ulema*. The resolutions serve as "proper guidance" (*irşât*) for the faithful throughout the Turkish Muslim world. Delegations from within Turkey and abroad regularly visit the DİB department responsible for fatwas in order to keep up to date and receive definitive instructions. The fatwas and rulings, which are issued on the basis of the Qurʾan, the sunna, and the Hanafi school of law, are not always consistent with the fundamental principles of the modern state and its legislation. The DİB has gone beyond merely managing religion on behalf of the state and has made Turkish Islam largely autonomous again, as in the days of the *şeyh-ül-islam*.

It is impossible to predict what basic changes the planned reforms of the DİB will bring. These were still largely unrealized as of early 2008.

The General Directorate of Foundations
All Turkish foundations serve public purposes. They are constituted as independent legal bodies based on the founder's intention, which finds expression

in the foundation's stated aims. Recognized objects of funding are instruction and education; art and culture; health care, sports, and social welfare; businesses and commerce; national defense; and the promotion of religion. Foundations are administered by the state or, in the case of private sponsorship, are regularly audited by the Ankara-based Directorate of Foundations (Vakıflar Genel Müdürlüğü, VGM), which, with its large staff, acts as a kind of general accounting office.[35]

One of the VGM's most important duties is the upkeep of all important buildings, including non-Islamic facilities. Today three-quarters of all foundations serve diverse religious purposes, such as building İmam-Hatip schools and mosques, stocking libraries, organizing book fairs, awarding grants and scholarships, and supporting pilgrimages. Of particular importance is the funding provided for the DİB's activities by Türkiye Diyanet Vakfı. Foundations that support science, health care, and the social welfare system (charity for widows and the poor), as well as those that found kindergartens and community centers, are often religious in nature or have been set up especially by religious groups, including fundamentalists, to finance their organizations. Furthermore, foreign capital is allowed to flow into such foundations. "Turkified" in this manner and subject to nearly no controls, it is used to fulfill the foundation's purpose.[36]

"The religious directorate has its own holdings, like the army. These ensure that the religious foundation affiliated with the Directorate (Diyanet Vakfı) has the necessary funds to operate printing shops and research institutes for Islamic history and Islam in the present."[37] As a result, nearly all religious groups benefit from the state support of foundations (legal recognition and tax advantages). State funds have also been directed to foundations within the framework of the Fak-Fuk-Fon Foundation Law for the support of the poor (from Fakir Fukara Fonu, meaning Fund for the Poor). If the founder's original intention can no longer be fulfilled, the remaining assets are usually distributed to poor relief, which is one of the five pillars of Sunni Islam.

e. The Alevis

As a non-Sunni religious community, the Anatolian Alevis have no place in the state ideology.[38] In this regard they resemble the Kurdish ethnic group. Their teachings do not recognize Sunnis or Shi'ites, and until recently they were the targets of pogroms.[39]

The broader public was first made aware of the Alevis by a series of articles written by Fuat Bozkurt, who earlier, in 1982, published a collection of sacred Alevi texts called *Buyruk* (The Commandment). The series, which caused quite a stir in Turkey, first ran in *Sabah* (January 22–February 9, 1990) and was then continued in *Cumhuriyet* (May 6–21, 1990).[40] Ever since, in a kind of self-discovery process, Alevi writers have published a large number of books about their community in order to preserve their religion and culture, which is passed down almost exclusively as an oral tradition.[41]

Although the DİB had previously denied the existence of the Alevis, it has more recently evoked an Islamic unity that includes them, and has even offered Alevis positions in its organization, provided they take part in the state (Sunni) educational program for theologians. As indicated by their name, the Alevis are "followers of ʿAli," Muhammad's son-in-law, whom they hold in special regard. The majority go out of their way to emphasize their affiliation with Islam, but with the exception of the profession of faith, which was expanded by the Shiʿites, they reject the five pillars of Islam as mere external duties and regard shariʿa as transcended with admission into the religious community. The "autonomous individual" is the center of their teachings. The Bektaşi order, with which they share many articles of faith, is regarded as a nationalist group, but it does not have high political visibility.

The Alevis, some of whom are Kurds, have founded a growing number of associations. At a delegates' meeting in Ankara in December 1994 they resolved to form a central council in which their religious leaders, science board, and youth and women's organizations are represented. This council intended to start up a private radio and TV station and a central magazine to work against the uncontrolled proliferation of articles by its own members, who on occasion have written too candidly about conflicts with orthodox Islam. The Alevis emphasize the large contribution they have made to Turkish culture, particularly in poetry and music, and expressly demand recognition as equal citizens and taxpayers.

The Turkish state is unwilling to accept the Alevis as an autonomous "religious community." It continues to prohibit them from using "Alevi" or "Bektaşi" in the names of their organizations. When the Alevis applied for a building permit for a *cemevi* (religious community center) in Çankaya in the government district of Ankara, the state obtained an expert opinion from the DİB and then turned down the building project. In February 2005 the Alevis' lawsuit was dismissed with the argument that the Alevis claimed to be Muslims, and the small mosques (*mescit*) and Friday mosques (*cami*) were the only acceptable places of prayer in Islam. At the same time, the Alevis have built a growing number of *cem* centers but called them "cultural houses" or "sites of encounter." According to Alevi estimates, there were between forty-five and fifty such assembly buildings in 2005 in addition to other community meeting places.[42]

The government has agreed to put Alevi teachings on religious curricula in the schools, but the Alevis argue that the new educational material has been tailored to the government's political interests and to unified Sunni Islam. This material is therefore unacceptable to them and even worse than the previous situation.[43]

The various Alevi groups and organizations demand:

- Express recognition of freedom of opinion and freedom of faith.
- Implementation of the secular principle.

- A new structure for the DİB compliant with Article 136 of the constitution, with a special department for the Alevis and a say in all other departments.
- One-third of DİB's budget for "religious services" in accordance with Article 10 of the constitution.
- Abolition of mandatory religious instruction.
- Establishment of *cemevleri* with material state support—that is, the religious community centers typical of the Alevis—instead of additional mosque buildings in their villages.
- An end to the policy of *sünnileştirme,* or "Sunnification."
- Withdrawal of the defamatory statements made against them.
- Their own radio and TV broadcasting times.

The Cem Vakfı, headed by İzzettin Doğan, is attempting to unify the various Alevi traditions and wields great influence in Turkey. The international conference it held on August 31, 2002, was attended by over 1,200 academics and religious functionaries from all over the world, who came to discuss the future of Alevism. The participants included 600 religious dignitaries, both *dedeler* (from Turk. sing. *dede,* grandfather) and *babalar* (from Turk. sing. *baba,* father). One key issue was the education of the *dede,* since traditional knowledge, which had previously been handed down in "holy families," is no longer sufficient to allow these leaders to supervise the constantly growing communities. In addition, the knowledge of their ancestors, which may have been scant in many areas, no longer meets the demands of the current age. The Cem Vakfı, which puts out its own series of publications, regards the Alevis as an Anatolian form of Islam and as an Alevi-Islamic religious community.

The Alevis are champions of secular government and traditionally support left-wing parties. Prime Minister Erdoğan long refused to receive the leaders of organizations such as Cem Vakfı and Alevi-Bektaşi Federasyonu, so the advances he made in early 2008—in the form of a dinner invitation— met with distrust among many Alevi organizations, whose cultural centers are still not recognized.[44] Many decided not to attend. The Directorate of Religious Affairs has started sending *dedeler* to Alevi-Bektaşi communities abroad, but the Alevis continued to take a skeptical view of Erdoğan and his government.

f. Outlook

Turkey is currently a testing ground that will show whether an Islamic country with a religiously based government can develop a secular conception of democracy, not only recognizing the full range of human rights but also enforcing them in a functioning legal system. Turkey has so far been unable to complete its transformation into a secular state. Rather it has accorded Islam a firm position in government. It has supposedly granted the still existent, powerful Directorate of Religious Affairs freedom, but it continues to give it state funding. At the time of publication, the nationalism that has swept through all ethnic groups in Turkey remained an important yet unpredictable factor that may bring unholy, fragile alliances in the future.

For some, the reforms in Turkey are happening much too quickly; the general population and the administrators are having difficulty adapting to them, and as a result, they are becoming increasingly skeptical about EU membership. Others are hoping that the EU will put sustained pressure on Turkey to implement the required standards quickly, and many see the country's initial efforts in this regard as a sign of positive things to come. Whatever the case, it is imperative that the measures taken to fulfill EU requirements not become a case of one step forward and two steps back. Numerous reforms have been tackled, but not all are positive. The process is far from over. Turkey is in transition, and we must wait to see which way the pendulum ultimately swings.

Translated by Adam Blauhut

2. Iran

(Udo Steinbach)

a. Early Historical Background

With the collapse of the Sassanid Empire (642 CE), Islam began spreading across the Iranian highland. And although this process initially occurred rather slowly, Iran's contribution to the history and culture of Islam during the High Middle Ages was substantial and in some ways decisive.

A crucial event in the history of Iran was the introduction of Twelver Shi'a Islam as the country's official religion by the founder of the Safavid dynasty, Shah Isma'il I.[1] Reigning from 1501 to 1524, Isma'il was from a family that had headed a mystical (initially Sunni) order for some two hundred years. This order had been named after its founder, Shaykh (Arab. *shaikh*) Safi al-Din (d. 1334) and had its seat in Ardabil in northwestern Iran.

Up to the fifteenth century, the Iranian highland was predominantly Sunni territory. In all likelihood the Safavid order first turned toward Shi'a at this time. And although only a small segment of the population was Shi'a when Ismail died in 1524 (today some 85 percent of the population are Shi'a), the religious and political measures he took affected the country's history in a variety of ways.

- Orientation toward Shi'a Islam significantly contributed to the development of a national feeling among Iranians, and to the country's policies toward its neighbors. As of the sixteenth century, Iran assumed an independent role in religious and political matters.[2] This enabled it to hold out against the expansion of the Ottoman Empire and escape the intrusion of colonial powers, in particular of England and Russia, or at least to avoid coming under their direct rule and administration.

- Iran remains the only country in modern history where Shiʿa Islam (Arab. *shiʿa*) has evolved into the dominant religious and political force within an Islamic political system. As a consequence, the relationship between religion and the political situation at any given time has been of a different nature than in Sunni countries. This stems from the fact that Shiʿi theologians acknowledge to only a limited extent—or even regard as unlawful—secular power exercised by an individual who is not actually considered to have legitimacy under Shiʿa Islam.[3] This stance and the fact that Shiʿi theologians have always enjoyed an excellent social status and a high degree of financial independence meant that from the start there was a constellation of factors that made conflict at times inevitable. Since its early days—when the Safavids first brought in religious scholars (mostly from Arab countries) to establish the theological foundations for disseminating the teachings of orthodox Twelver Shiʿa Islam—to the time of Ayatollah Khomeini's conflict with Shah Muhammad Reza Pahlavi, the clergy's relations with the different regimes have gone through several stages. These have ranged from providing religious and political support for an individual regime, to protesting against the intervention of outside powers and all too close relations to foreign—in particular Western—countries, to offering open resistance to a "corrupt system." Such resistance had its most militant spokesman in Khomeini, though it should also be noted that in only a few instances have Iranian Shiʿi theologians taken a united theological or political stance against secular power in its concrete manifestations.

The revolution in Iran, which began as a more secular social and political protest in 1977 and evolved into an "Islamic Revolution" in the course of 1978, had complex causes.[4] Although it was not until the clergy took over—led by Ayatollah Ruhollah al-Musavi al-Khomeini (1902–1989) from the Iraqi city of Najaf and, as of 1978, from Paris—and began mobilizing the masses, especially the lower classes, that the revolution actually gained momentum.[5] The protest of the clergy was sparked by the shah's attempt to reduce its influence and structure modernization on the separation of state and religion. These efforts, along with the way mass mobilization was implemented, the quality (or lack thereof) of the clergy's relations to the leaders of the nonreligious opposition, and ultimately its dilemma after the revolution succeeded, were all significant for the clergy's political and social role, a role that had been in the making since the nineteenth century.

b. The Role of the Clergy in the Nineteenth and Twentieth Centuries

The complexity of the relations between the Shiʿi clergy and secular forces in Iran first became apparent in the course of the nineteenth century. Prior to this period the Safavids (who reigned until 1722) had successfully taken measures to avoid conflict with the clergy. Two factors ultimately contributed to the clergy's ever more open resistance to the Qajar dynasty (in power from 1779 to 1924): on the one hand, there were the mounting efforts of Russia and England to intervene in Iranian politics, concentrated primarily on obtaining control of the country's economy; on the other hand, there was the Qajars' autocratic exercise of power. Opposition escalated into an uprising when the Persian government granted a British company exclusive rights to produce, sell, and export tobacco (1890). At the peak of the protest movement, which had spread to ever wider segments of the urban population by 1891, Ayatollah Mirza Hasan al-Shirazi issued his famous fatwa banning the use of tobacco. As a result the government felt obliged to retract the concession.[6]

The Tobacco Protest can be seen as the prelude to a far-reaching protest movement, one that eventually led to the introduction of the constitution in 1906–7. While the unrest was initially an expression of objections to the meddling of foreign powers in the country's economy and finances, demands became more radical as protests escalated, culminating in the call for a constitution and a parliament. Ultimately the pressure was so great that the shah was forced to yield to these demands (1906).[7]

Developments between 1890 and 1911, in the final years of the constitutional era, were marked by the close alliance of the clergy (or a part of it) with urban, liberal and/or nationalistic middle-class groups and the *bazaris* (merchants). This alliance resulted from their shared concerns about the regime, whereby it was the clergy's involvement in the protest movement that was responsible for the mobilization of broad segments of the population. Both the bourgeoisie and the clergy aspired to resist the West's mounting influence, which in view of the regime's weaknesses seemed almost unavoidable. Since many of the mullas were from bourgeois or petit-bourgeois families and had close ties to city bazaars and guilds, they were well suited to act as spokesmen for the urban population who felt threatened, in particular in their positions in business and banking. Indeed, both the urban middle class and the majority of the clergy advocated—albeit for different reasons—limiting the absolutist authority of the Qajar rulers.

Nevertheless, this alliance was only seemingly stable, since it was not long until, in addition to their shared concerns, differences surfaced with regard to the country's modernization. The role of the *'ulama'* in the protest movement against the Qajar regime had been, at least partially, determined by the fear of losing its privileges (for example, in the educational system), a fear first felt during the rather hesitant reform efforts in the last decades of the nineteenth century. With the victory of the constitutionalists, the *'ulama'* faced a dilemma: on the one hand, it found the movement's ideological point of departure, namely the sovereignty of the people, unacceptable (according to the concepts of Shi'a Islam, only a prophet or an imam may delegate sovereignty); on the other hand, it was convinced that the despotic rule of the Qajars could be held in check only by a constitution, as the latter would make governing dependent on the people's consent.[8] The outcome was a compromise in the constitution, one reflecting the powerful role of the clergy in the movement. Article 1 of the supplement (October 7, 1907) declares the official state religion to be Twelver Shi'a Islam, and Article 2 prescribes the creation of a body of at least five clerics who are to review the laws enacted by parliament and ensure that they are not at variance with the tenets of Islam.

The political role of the *'ulama'* in twentieth-century Iran was enshrined in the 1906–7 constitution. Moreover, the fact that clerics were elected to the country's first parliament actually reinforced the position of religious leaders as representatives of the people—from a religious and historical standpoint, a right the clergy had always felt it was entitled to anyway. The role of the clergy emerged even more clearly in a third phase of modern Iranian history, when the Qajars were overthrown and Reza Khan pronounced himself shah, that is, during the transition from the Qajar to the Pahlavi dynasty (October 1923 to December 1925). Plainly impressed by events in neighboring Turkey (which had proclaimed itself a republic in October 1923), Reza Khan, who was prime minister at the time, began toying with the idea of following suit. Most of the high clergy, however, who observed these tendencies with growing distrust and displeasure, came out in favor of preserving the monarchy. In 1924 Reza Khan gave up the idea of establishing a republic; instead he sought an alliance with the clergy—now with the goal of legitimizing his own takeover.[9]

From this point on the clergy's actual influence on the country's policies varied. In any case, the good relationship between Reza Khan (now Reza Shah) and the clergy did not last long. From the start, the new ruler's modernization efforts, inspired by Kemal Atatürk, were doomed to encounter resistance from the *'ulama'*. A large number of measures caused dispute: these included everything from reforming the educational system, to extending the state's decision-making powers and suspending clerics from military service, to reducing further the application of religious law, increasing the supervision of religious schools, introducing Western clothing and banning the veil, strengthening the control of the authorities over religious foundations, and establishing the faculty of theology as one of four founding faculties of the secularly oriented University of Tehran.

After Reza Shah's abdication, which was forced by Great Britain in 1941, the clergy began to participate actively—not least through the different parties emerging at the time—in political events. For a while, several leading clerics collaborated closely with the National Front under Muhammad Musaddiq (Mossadegh).[10]

In the early 1960s the confrontation between the shah and the clergy escalated. This was caused, on the one hand, by the beginning of land reform, which the clergy saw not only as the regime's attempt to increase its power but also as an attempt to undermine further the clergy's financial independence.[11] On the other hand, the intention of the shah to improve women's social and legal status, specifically by granting them the right to vote and to run for office (1962), touched on a sensitive topic for the clergy, for until then Islamic law had—for the most part—applied to such issues. (In 1967 another step toward improving women's legal status and reducing gender inequality before the law was taken when the Family Protection Act was ratified. It made divorce more difficult for men while facilitating it for women, as well as allowing them to receive custody of their children.) In 1963 unrest broke out in Tehran, Shiraz, and other cities. The clergy played an active role in these events, and indeed it was in this context that the name of Ayatollah Khomeini first appeared as a radical spokesman of a group of clerics impatient for more political power.[12] Owing to the suppression of these 1963 uprisings (Khomeini was exiled in 1964, first to Turkey and then later to Najaf, Iraq) and the regime's growing bureaucratization, as well as its economic and political consolidation from the mid-1960s to the mid-1970s, the clergy were no longer able to play a visible role in politics. Behind the scenes, however, in the face of growing despotism and corruption, and increasing influence from abroad (especially in the 1970s), a number of clerics undoubtedly stepped up their efforts to find a new theologico-political justification for their role in society.[13] Khomeini, who enjoyed greater religious freedom in Najaf than his colleagues back in Iran, delivered his radical concept of *velayat-e faqih* (governance by the religious jurist) to the public for the first time in 1970.[14]

c. The Basis of Clerical Power

The status of Shi'i clerics in Iranian society has always been based on the scope of their functions in private and public life. Arising from their authority as "sources of emulation," these functions usually include administering the wealth put in their care, supervising the affairs of the socially disadvantaged (such as widows and orphans) with whom they have been entrusted, collecting and managing charitable donations, notarizing documents, allocating funds from a variety of sources to religious schools (Arab. sing. *madrasa*) and other religious beneficiaries (mosques, scholarship holders, and so on), as well as assuming a large number of administrative tasks. Of course one central duty has always been to protect Islamic law. Every attempt to restrict its application or to replace it with a secular code of law created by the state—including the attempt to introduce a constitution—has initially aroused the clergy's distrust or even disapproval.

In fact under the shah, the state steadily reduced the clergy's sphere of influence, a sphere religious leaders felt to be rightfully theirs. All the same, the state succeeded in having only a limited impact on religious life. For instance, the classical tradition of religious education remained largely unaltered. The place of theological instruction was the madrasa, which had developed as a center of Islamic scholarship in the early Middle Ages and spread during the Safavid era. And although the Pahlavi regime influenced the curriculum, much of the content and style of instruction had hardly changed over the centuries. The simple village cleric (*akhund*) received his education at such a school, as did the *mujtahid* (a theologian authorized to exercise *ijtihad*). Official control over the material actually taught, especially with regard to oppositional religious-political propaganda, remained largely ineffective.[15]

The second decisive factor for the status of the clergy was (and still is) its considerable wealth and hence high degree of financial independence from secular authorities.[16] Its most important sources of income included fees for the aforementioned clerical and legal services and activities, earnings from religious foundations, and religious taxes (*khums*). True, as the legislature increasingly curbed the role of clerics, their incomes also declined. Nevertheless, even in Pahlavi Iran, clerical wealth was considerable, and it enabled the clergy to perform its many public duties. Moreover, a number of prominent clerics earned rather substantial amounts from business activities of their own. Private donations, especially from *bazaris,* also contributed to the affluence of leading clerics. In fact, throughout the protest movements of the nineteenth and twentieth centuries, financial interests recurrently motivated the clergy to form alliances with large landowners and bazaar merchants. Hence the period of protest from 1960 to 1963, which was related to the impending land reform and other of the shah's reforms, known collectively as the White Revolution, was based on an alliance between the clergy and big landowners. At the outset of the Islamic Revolution in Iran (1977–78), the clergy and bazaar merchants once again joined forces—despite their different motivations—against the regime.

Qom is the religious center of Shi'i Iran. The city's significance is closely related to the history of the Shi'a in Iran. The sister of the eighth imam ('Ali al-Reza), Fatima (Hazrat-e Ma'suma), is buried there. Under the Safavids the city experienced a time of prosperity and expansion. With its countless mosques and madrasas, libraries, and social facilities, the city played a key role in religious life. During the nineteenth and twentieth centuries, however, it also became a major hotbed of tension between the clergy and secular regimes.[17]

Relations between the clergy and the country's rulers took on a special quality for another reason as well: the holiest Shi'i sites, the cities of Najaf and Karbala, with their shrines to the first imam ('Ali) and the third imam (Husayn), were both located *outside* Iran. This meant not only that Iranian rulers could banish unwanted clerics to these locations, but also that oppositional clerical leaders could agitate from abroad (for instance, during the constitutional revolution before World War I) against whichever Iranian regime was in power. Khomeini, as already mentioned, was able to announce his concept of *velayat-e faqih* to the public from the Iraqi town of Najaf around 1970. Since his concept of religious rule implied overthrowing the existing dynasty, it could only be demanded from abroad. Since the fall of Saddam Hussein's Ba'th regime, Iran's religious-political leadership attempts to exert greater influence over these holy sites in Iraq.

d. Islam in the Islamic Republic of Iran

In the early 1970s Shah Muhammad Reza Pahlavi left no doubt about his aspirations to separate religion and politics.[18] Although he did not dare to offend the clergy directly (but instead occasionally visited mosques, such as the Holy Shrine in Mashhad, to display his respect for religion), he sought to diminish its influence in all matters of public concern. In this context his policies involved two particularly significant elements.

- The accelerated pace of economic development and social upheaval since the early 1970s also sought to undermine the importance of religion as a central social factor. Directing the energies of Iranians toward processes of development and modernization seemed well suited to relegating Islamic traditions to the background.
- Reorientation toward pre-Islamic times that is, to the Achaemenid and the Sassanid empires—sought to reduce the dominant role of Islam in the Iranian identity. Reza Shah had already taken recourse to such tactics when he adopted Pahlavi as a family name. In other words, allusions to great historical figures were used to justify ongoing developments and legitimize the shah's leading role in them. As time passed, it would make Islam seem like a relic from a mere episode in Iranian history and an obstacle to progress. This was an assault on the position of Islamic scholarship in the political-social system.

These processes were accompanied by a whole range of symbolic events, all of which may be considered of equal consequence in this context: the coronation of the shah (1967), the festivities marking the 2,500th anniversary of the founding of the Persian monarchy (1971), and the introduction of a calendar calculated on that basis.[19]

At first the revolution in Iran had little to do with these developments. As 1978 progressed, however, the role of the clergy in the protest movement, in particular that of Khomeini, grew dramatically, though it was not until the massacre at Jaleh Square in Tehran (Black Friday, September 8, 1978) that a threshold was crossed—and those who wanted to topple the monarchy assumed leadership. Vague ideas of what the new order might be after the fall of the shah tended to revolve around Khomeini's concept of the "Islamic Republic," the actual content of which was unknown to many of the different oppositional groups.[20]

Ultimately it was the clergy who, by mobilizing the masses, and in particular the lower classes, delivered the decisive blow to the shah. Since there was no longer a legal political opposition that could make itself heard by parliamentary means, pulpits became platforms for encouraging protest and resistance against the regime. Despite all official bans, the masses could also be called from those pulpits into the streets at any given moment.

Moreover, the religious language used by the clergy gave the ubiquitous secret police almost no legal grounds to intervene. Nonetheless, listeners understood its symbolism and the allusions to political grievances without their being spelled out. In their minds and hearts they converted what was said into political messages. While the government could control, and if necessary discontinue, all other information channels of political dissent, the mosque remained the one place from which Khomeini could spread his message, even when he was in Najaf or Paris.

Of course the response to the clergy was strongest where social injustices were the most glaring. Communication with their followers remained intact, for although discontent and dissent against the shah's autocratic rule and misdirected economic measures were mounting among much of the middle class, its relationship to religion had relaxed. The essentially secular attitude and political ideas of the middle class were the outcome of an almost century-long process of Westernization.[21]

Hence the clergy were primarily able to mobilize the inhabitants of those districts of the big Iranian cities, in particular Tehran, where living conditions were (and still are) wretched. The residents of these slums had originally left rural areas for financial reasons, expecting to find employment in the city. Wrested away from traditional social structures and extremely impoverished, they increasingly found in religion a refuge, a hope. The mulla spoke their language. Thus it was no coincidence that the issue of improving the situation of the "downtrodden" (*mustaz'afan*) was central to the socio-political propaganda of the religious opposition.[22]

The fall of the shah (January 16, 1979), the return of Khomeini to Iran (February 1, 1979), the resignation of Shapour Bakhtiar, the last prime minister under the Pahlavi dynasty (February 12, 1979), and the referendum approving the Islamic Republic (March 30, 1979) were by no means the deliberate stages of a well-planned march from monarchy to a new and clearly defined Iran that would be unmistakably structured around Islam. In 1979 Khomeini declared that the Islamic Republic would have nothing in common with a Western democracy. And so initially two levels of state authority existed alongside each other: the formal level, represented by the appointment of Mehdi Bazargan as prime minister; and the informal level of the Revolutionary Council, and of the revolutionary committees and courts, all of which operated in the background. In reality, however, the authority was Khomeini, who with his charisma could reverse just about any governmental decision.[23]

Decisive for the Islamization of the political system was the appointment of an Assembly of Experts. It was assigned the task of drafting a new constitution for the Islamic Republic (August 1979).[24] Of the seventy-three members, fifty-five were clerics (most of whom belonged to the Islamic Republic

Party, IRP) or had close ties to the clergy. At one end of a very diverse spectrum were the secularists, and at the other, those advocating an "Islamic order" based on the principles of the "governance of the religious jurist" (*velayat-e faqih*). Muhammad Beheshti, who had helped make the IRP the strongest political party in Tehran, gradually became the driving force behind the Islamization of the constitutional debate.

The constitution, which was approved by referendum on December 2, 1979, reflects the essential elements of the Shi'i understanding of state and governance.[25] Article 12 explicitly declares Twelver Shi'a Islam (Ja'fari ithna 'ashari) Iran's official religion. Central to the political order is the Supreme Faqih. According to the constitution, the clergy is to govern state institutions, and Islamic law is to form the basis of the legal system, restricting individual rights and liberties to what is permissible in Islam. A Council of Guardians (Shura-ye negahban) consisting of twelve clerics has the power to overrule all laws of the *majlis* (the National Assembly) that conflict with Islamic law or the basic principles of the constitution. Article 4 determines that all laws and regulations related to civil, penal, financial, economic, administrative, cultural, military, and political matters—as well as all other fields—are to be based on Islamic criteria.

The constitution outlines in detail the qualifications required for the position of Supreme Faqih, as well as his rights and powers.[26] In Article 5 leadership of the community devolves "in the absence of the Lord of the Age"—the *vali-ye 'asr* or Imam Mahdi—to the "just and pious person who is aware of contemporary problems, courageous, and has executive skills." Moreover, the majority of the people should have a high opinion of him as leader. If such a person cannot be found, leadership of the community is then to devolve to a leadership council whose members are experts on religious law. Articles 107 through 112 regulate the selection of these *faqihs,* that is, the members of the Assembly of Experts (*majles-e khobregan*). The Supreme Faqih's extensive powers include appointing the following: legal specialists to the Council of Guardians, the top jurists of the judiciary, the commander-in-chief of the army, the supreme commander of the Revolutionary Guard Corps (*pasdaran*), the majority of the members on the Supreme Council for National Security, and—upon its recommendation—the chief commanders of the other branches of the military forces. The Supreme Faqih also approves the candidates for the office of president of the Islamic Republic and dismisses the president if he is declared incompetent by parliament or if the Supreme Court finds him guilty of neglecting his duties.

The transition from the autarky of Ayatollah Khomeini, the charismatic Supreme Faqih of the Islamic Revolution, to his successors, all of whom lacked his religious authority and political charisma, made it necessary to change the constitution.[27] A commission was formed that concluded its deliberations on July 28, 1989. That same day—which was also the date of the presidential elections—the amendments were put to a popular vote and approved with a majority of 97.3 percent.

First and foremost these amendments were the pragmatic response to past experiences and new developments. On the one hand, they effected a centralization of power on the level of the executive, which manifested itself most visibly in the consolidation of the offices of president and prime minister; from this point on, all executive power was in the hands of the president. With respect to the status of the Supreme Faqih, it meant that Khomeini's successors could hardly assume the superior position he had held as "Islamic Leader." Important in this context was the enshrinement in the constitution of the Expediency Council (also known as the Council for the Discernment of the System's Expediency, Majma'-e Tashkhis-e Maslahat-e Nezam). Khomeini had created this council in the winter of 1988 with the intention of facilitating intervention if the parliament and the Council of Guardians were unable to reach consensus on a law. After the constitution was amended, this council became an organ empowered to advise and thus influence the Supreme Leader (*rahbar*), though in addition to consulting the council, the Supreme Leader was now also allowed to present it with any issue he deemed worthy of discussion.

The fact that the Supreme Leader no longer had to be a *marja' al-taqlid* (one of the highest clerics) also significantly altered the overall structure of the constitutional system. A bipolar distribution of power emerged. Ultimately, how well the system works depends to a great degree on the quality of relations between the two poles of leadership—and this includes their personal relationship.

How problematic the differentiation between *velayat-e faqih* and *marja'iyya* (highest clerical function) could be for the Supreme Leader became evident in December 1994, when Ayatollah 'Ali Khamenei aspired to succeed the Grand Ayatollah (*al-ayatullah al-'uzma*) 'Ali Araki, whose death on November 30, 1994, had left the position of *marja'iyya* vacant. Khamenei's application sparked a lively debate, the central argument against him being that he lacked the necessary theological expertise for the office. Prominent clerics in Lebanon and Iraq came out in favor of Grand Ayatollah 'Ali al-Sistani from Najaf; in Iran several influential ayatollahs backed the Grand Ayatollah Hossein Ali Montazeri, the archrival of Khamenei. The former was well advised when, in a speech on December 14, 1994, he put an end to the controversy by withdrawing from the race.[28]

Contrary to predictions of the early demise of mulla rule, the office has been able to consolidate its powers substantially over the years, and by early 2009 displayed—despite considerable internal problems—relative stability. The reasons for this are many. A propaganda apparatus—with the Ministry for National Guidance (Vezarat-e irshad) at its center—disseminates basic Islamic principles and codes of behavior to the country's most outlying regions while promoting the image of the Islamic Republic abroad. Over the years, state control (that is, control by the clergy) over the mass media has enabled the widespread mobilization of the masses, in particular the lower classes. Mobilization has also been effected by the press, which—despite

considerable resistance—has largely been brought into line with the regime, as well as by the flood of publications on Islam (as understood by the
mullas), on the Islamic Republic, and on prominent spiritual leaders (first
and foremost, of course, Khomeini). Friday prayers and sermons, as well
as annual ideological preparations and pilgrimages to Mecca, are central
to the government's mobilization efforts.[29] And it goes without saying that
Tehran plays a special role in these activities. In addition, leading figures
from the regime take turns speaking (as both clerics and politicians) on
university campuses about the problems and issues in the Islamic Republic,
and by doing so communicate their methods for developing the state, society, foreign relations, and more. Above and beyond all propaganda and
mass mobilization efforts, however, a repressive apparatus has guaranteed
that the principles of the Islamic Republic are observed. Noteworthy in this
context is the Revolutionary Guard Corps. Founded as the new regime's
security force in 1979, the *pasdaran* has been continually expanded, especially since the outbreak of the Iran-Iraq War (September 1980). Meanwhile
it has become a full-fledged army that no longer simply maintains domestic
order and stability but is—alongside the regular army—a central division
of Iran's military forces. Its existence is also enshrined in the constitution
(Article 150).

The establishment of an "Islamic system" has had drastic consequences
for the Iranian legal system as well.[30] Article 4 of the constitution—which
declares Iran a country in which all laws and legal norms are based on Islam
and hence are to be interpreted accordingly—has meant the systematic Islamization of the state. This has, of course, primarily affected codes related
to penal, family, and personal status law.

Initially the highest decision-making body within the judiciary was the
High Council of the Judiciary (Article 157; 158). It consisted of five members, namely the president of the Supreme Court and the prosecutor general,
who were both appointed by the Supreme Faqih, as well as three judges who
were nominated by the judiciary itself. Internal friction, however, did not
make the High Council very efficient. When the constitution was amended,
collective leadership was abandoned and the office of the head of the judiciary created, with a single person occupying the position by appointment of
the Supreme Leader; the judiciary itself and/or other bodies were no longer
entitled to nominate candidates.

The Iranian judiciary's jurisdiction covers two realms: ordinary jurisdiction, which consists of civil and criminal courts, in which investigations
are conducted with the aid of public prosecutors, the police, and security
authorities; and revolutionary jurisdiction, in which the judiciary initially
collaborated with revolutionary prosecutors and was assisted in its investigations by its own institution until 1994. After the ratification of a law
introducing both general and revolutionary courts in July 1994, all public
prosecutors, including revolutionary prosecutors, were dismissed. Now revolutionary courts are also forced to rely on the investigations of the ordinary

judiciary and security authorities; they no longer have revolutionary prosecutors and/or their own apparatus at their disposal. The jurisdiction of the revolutionary courts includes offenses violating the internal and external security of Iran, financial crimes such as usury and hoarding basic commodities, as well as crimes involving drugs and alcohol or smuggling. In 1987 Khomeini also established the Special Court for the Clergy to investigate offenses and crimes committed by clerics.

The most important laws reforming the penal code were enacted in 1982–83.[31] They involved the law on *hudud* and *qisas,* the one on *diya,* and two others, the more recent of which was ratified on August 9, 1983, called the law on *ta'zirat* (discretionary punishment). To a certain extent these laws closed the gap that had resulted when Khomeini declared that the secular laws passed under the shah were no longer applicable. Remarkable in this context (and repeatedly emphasized in the European press) was the reintroduction of corporal punishment. In many cases, where the law had stipulated a maximum prison sentence of two years, it now prescribed flogging. Ultimately, in August 1982 the new Criminal Procedure Code was adopted, creating a court structure compatible with the basic principles of Islamic judiciary law. Most important, this new system was based on the Islamic principle that verdicts were to be delivered by a single judge instead of a panel of judges. In 1996 the penal code was reformed further. With regard to corporal punishment, it should be noted that the head of the judiciary also issued a directive asking judges no longer to impose stoning as a penalty; instead they were to convert such punishments into a prison sentence or other penalty. In January 2003 another important reform reinstituted the examining magistrate, which became the court of first instance. It could decide if and where a case should be tried. This enabled the greater specialization of criminal courts and reduced the workload of trial judges.

After the revolution, family and personal status codes also underwent Islamization. The area of greatest contention was the Family Protection Act, which contained provisions on possible grounds for divorce, consequences of divorce, and divorce proceedings. In several ways these provisions infringed upon Islamic principles and so conflicted with Article 4 of the constitution. Although this act, which originated under the shah, was not formally repealed, essential elements of it were regarded as no longer applicable, at the very latest after Khomeini's speech on August 23, 1982, in which he demanded that all laws violating the shari'a be thrown "in the trash." Other legislative measures adopted afterwards underscored this position. Since 1998, however, a number of important reform ideas have been implemented: for instance, bride payments were adjusted to inflation (1998); laws on divorce were altered to benefit women (2001); the legal age of marriage for girls was raised (2002); and age equality was established for boys and girls in child custody cases (2003). Overall we may speak of a trend toward reforming family law, a trend that was pursued with renewed vigor in particular under President Sayyid Ahmad Khatami (1997–2005).

In fact, general discussion of legal reforms became quite common. In some instances people even began voicing their ideas on constitutional structure, the inequality of *diyat* (pl. of *diya*) for women and religious minorities, as well as the position of the *vali-ye faqih.*

Over and beyond the legal realm, efforts were and still are being made to subject private and public life to "Islamic morals." Participation in communal prayers, the ban on alcoholic beverages and drugs, and punishment of illicit sexual intercourse are some of these areas. The most visible for the public is the rigorous enforcement of "Islamic" dress for women,that is, the *hijab,* which actually means headscarf, though it is often interpreted as a covering for the entire body, with the exception of the face and hands. Harsh punishments are meted out for infractions. In addition, there is gender segregation in schools and other public places. At the end of the day, the position of women deteriorated even further because of the pressure exerted on them to quit their jobs. Islamic rulers stress the role of the woman in the family as formulated in the lengthy preamble to the constitution.[32]

Islamic principles also determine the attitude of the regime toward minorities. In the case of religious—that is, non-Islamic—minorities, the regime differentiates between Muslims and non-Muslims. Tolerated religions have a status similar to that of "persons enjoying protection and safety" (Arab. *dhimmi*). This affects everything from personal status rights to the limited "participation" of "tolerated" minorities in political life, especially in parliament. Yet the Bahai sects, which first emerged in the nineteenth century, do not fall into the category of *dhimmi.* In the eyes of the regime, as their persecution over the years demonstrates, they are not worthy of tolerance because their followers are seen as apostates of Islam.

Early on, the extreme belief in community consensus and the exclusivity of "Islamic citizenship" in the Islamic Republic created a barrier between a large number of minorities and the central government. From August 1979 onward, Khomeini categorically rejected all demands for autonomy, and this was the case even though diverse ethnic groups, in particular the Kurds, had expected their demands to be fulfilled after the fall of the centralized Pahlavi regime.

Since the shah's economic policies had been one of the central causes of revolt against his regime, Khomeini devoted his first programmatic declarations to formulating new "Islamic" priorities for economic policies (infrastructure, agriculture, and so on).[33] Abolhassan Bani Sadr, the first president of the Islamic Republic, can be viewed as one of the leading theorists of an "Islamic" economic system. In 1983 all banks were forced to implement the so-called—and rather controversial—Islamic ban on interest payments. A group of pragmatic clerics who advocated the continuance of traditional economic practices and ethics encountered opposition from a faction that vehemently championed a "socialist" reformation of the economy under Islamic auspices. This group demanded the widespread redistribution of land to farmers and the nationalization of industry and of foreign and domestic trade. So long as Ayatollah Khomeini was alive, it was strictly forbidden to take out foreign loans or to become involved in (Western-controlled) international financial organizations.[34]

Implementation of the "Islamic system" has also had a lasting impact on Iran's foreign policies. From the start the constitution laid out that the Islamic Republic was to support the "downtrodden." As early as 1979, when very few were calling for a universal Islamic revolution, many were already demanding active support for all "downtrodden" Muslims. More concretely, the focus was on the situation of the Shi'a in Iraq and Bahrain, as well as of Muslims resisting the Soviet occupying forces in Afghanistan. Iraq's attack on Iran in September 1980 and the widespread support of it by the majority of Arab regimes contributed to a radicalization of relations between Tehran and almost every other Islamic country in the region. In mid-1982, when the Iranian government decided—after beating back the Iraqi invasion—to continue the battle as a holy war until the downfall of the "satanic" Saddam Hussein, the war acquired a new dimension. At the same time, voices from Tehran, in particular Khomeini's, began articulating the desire to liberate all Muslims in the Middle East, which meant overthrowing all oppressors (that is, the existing regimes, which were seen as having no legitimacy to rule). The idea was to liberate Karbala and then move on to Jerusalem.[35] Although Iran's troops had not had any resounding successes at the front, revolutionary forces in Tehran were involved in countless—partially subversive—activities aimed at exerting pressure on a number of existing orders. The most spectacular was Iran's intervention in Lebanon, which occurred directly through the deployment of *pasdaran,* and indirectly through support for the radical wing of the Shi'a and the buildup of the Hizbullah.[36] This not only raised the status of the hitherto subordinate Lebanese Shi'a but also altered the regional balance. In a speech on July 20, 1988, Khomeini declared the United Nations Security Council's adoption of Resolution 598, which formed the basis for the cease-fire in the Iran-Iraq War, "more bitter than poison."[37]

The decree (fatwa) to kill the British author Salman Rushdie because of his allegedly blasphemous depiction of the Prophet Muhammad and Qur'anic revelation also derived from the notion of the Islamic community (*umma*), a notion that is incompatible with the modern idea of the nation-state.[38]

e. Friction and Differences within the Clerical Establishment

The war against Iraq and its objectives caused deep schisms between individual members and differing clerical-political schools of thought within the Islamic regime. The 1982 decision to continue the war was pushed through with Khomeini's explicit approval and despite the opposition of a group that was against taking the war into Iraqi territory. More generally, the split between the Hujjatiyye and the Maktabi is relevant in this context.[39] No matter how fuzzy the line between the two may seem, differences are easily discerned: while the former faction strives for a radical Islamization in both cultural and legal spheres but opposes extensive social and socioeconomic reforms, the latter focuses precisely on the idea of revolutionizing society and the economy.

The rift between the Hujjatiyye and the Maktabi reveals that the ideological basis of the Islamic Republic was at no time monolithic. The Islamic Republican Party (IRP), founded in 1979, was dissolved in 1988 after becoming incapacitated by internal party strife between leftist and rightist factions. Two political associations resulted from the IRP's collapse: the leftist-Islamic Militant Clerics' League (*majma'-e ruhaniyun-e mobarez,* MRM) and its conservative counterpart, the Association of Combatant Clergy (*jame'eh-ye ruhaniyat-e mobarez,* JRM). By 2008 the most illustrious members of the JRM included the "Leader of the Islamic Revolution" 'Ali Khamenei, as well as former parliamentary presidents 'Ali Akbar Nateq Nouri and Hashemi Rafsanjani. In addition, the majority of the Council of Guardians and the Assembly of Experts are members of the JRM. Support is also particularly strong among higher-ranking officers and the top squads of the Revolutionary Guard Corps, as well as diverse intelligence and security agencies. Ideologically, the JRM champions the Islamic-theocratic components of the system; it accords them greater priority than the constitution or the sovereignty of the people.

Left-wing Islamists can be separated into three groups that cooperate with one another, the most important being the aforementioned MRM. It includes some radical—especially anti-American—members but also many liberal ones, including former minister of culture Muhammad Khatami, who was elected president of the republic in May 1997. Initially left-wing Islamists pursued a strict policy of economic austerity. They subjected the economy to rigorous state controls and advocated exporting the revolution. After being driven out of power in 1992, they altered their restrictive approach to domestic and cultural policies. As of 1997 they backed the constitutional state, the basic concepts of civil society, and the gradual opening of the system. A few months before the presidential election in 1997, "democratically reformed" left-wing Islamists and technocratic right-wing modernists agreed to form a coalition. Their joint candidate, Khatami, won the election in May 1997.

Although the opening of the system under Khatami was limited, a counterpublic was able to establish itself in the print media. Here intellectual discussions were almost free of taboos, and the political bastions of the conservatives—the judiciary, security agencies, and/or Revolutionary Guard—were relentlessly criticized. A critical public discourse gradually evolved that reassessed the relationship of Islamic tradition to the dominant theocratic form particular to Iran since 1979 on the one hand and Western modernity with its concepts of democracy, due process, and human rights on the other.[40]

Abdolkarim Soroush, a leading thinker of these critical intellectuals, represented the conviction, for instance, that the clerical nomenclature has unacceptably reduced religion to only one interpretation and in doing so has transformed Islam into an ideology with fascistic tendencies, from which a large majority of the Iranian people have turned away. As an alternative, Soroush propagated the idea of a religious-democratic government in which liberal-pluralistic conceptions of order are reconciled with a religious worldview. Other liberal thinkers who have regarded the system and its diverse implications critically include Sa'id Hajaryan, Mohsen Kadivar, Mashaallah Shams al-Wa'izin, Akbar Ganji, Yusuf Eshkevari, Habibollah Payman, Hashem Aghajari, Ebrahim Yazdi, 'Ali Reza 'Alawi-Tabari, Mohsen Sazegara, Mujtahid Shabistari, and Grand Ayatollah Husain 'Ali Montazeri.

The political system, like its ideological basis, also exhibits differentiations at the center of power, and these can affect matters in a number of directions.[41] Basically a strong dualism marks the state and social structure of the Islamic Republic as well as its balance of powers. This dualism has existed from the start, laid out in November 1979 in the constitution, which contains both republican-democratic elements and theocratic-Islamic elements. Unresolved—and increasingly acute—has been the dilemma resulting from this dual source of political authority. On the one hand, there is the president and a parliament directly elected by the people, and on the other, there is the legitimate Supreme Leader with the state and revolutionary institutions he controls. The authority of the president is still greatly exceeded by the authority of the Supreme Leader. This situation is also a consequence of Article 56 of the constitution, which states that sovereignty derives not from the people but from God or from the Hidden Imam as his rightful representative. Thus the Supreme Leader can appoint people to key positions or dismiss those holding them. In addition, he may nominate the six clerical jurists on the twelve-member Council of Guardians.

During the almost ten years of reform from 1995 to 2005, the Council of Guardians—as the quasi–upper house of parliament—played a decisive role in hindering reforms.[42] Significant reform laws were blocked or watered down into compromises, and this eventually damaged the reputation of reform president Muhammad Khatami. Prior to the parliamentary elections on February 20, 2004, the Council of Guardians used its constitutional right to nominate candidates on the basis of their loyalty to the system and theory of rule. From over eight thousand applicants, it rejected the candidacy of more than three thousand, most of whom were reformers. From 1998 until early 2003 the judiciary shut down more than ninety reformist newspapers, and a large number of critical journalists, student leaders, theologians, writers, intellectuals, lawyers, and even high officials from the executive and government administration who were associated with President Khatami were arrested and convicted on flimsy political charges. The fact that former president Akbar Hashemi Rafsanjani, who became chair of the Expediency Council since 1997 and initially supported Khatami, switched to the conservatives in 1999, and then attempted to foil Khatami's plans for reform, put an additional strain on the reform process. Ultimately this imbalance of power as laid out in the constitution between the Supreme Leader and the president has proved insurmountable, as have the complexity and diversity of the different centers of power, the majority of which are predominantly conservative and—like the judiciary, the Council of Guardians, the Expediency Council, the Assembly of Experts, the Revolutionary Guard Corps, and revolutionary foundations—represent veto powers and political enclaves.

More than thirty years after the revolution, the rulers of the Islamic Republic find themselves in a cul-de-sac from which there is no easy way out.[43] In this situation, one that is particularly frustrating for many young people, as was seen clearly in the presidential election campaign of June 2009 and the popular uprising that broke out in its aftermath, the call for the separation of religion and state—for a long while rather sporadic and faint—is becoming more audible.[44]

With Mahmoud Ahmadinejad's election in 2005, political fronts hardened and critical viewpoints were often suppressed. In December 2006 elections were held for the Assembly of Experts, whose eighty-six clerical members may appoint and supervise Iran's Supreme Leader. Former president Rafsanjani, considered a pragmatic man, was able to assert himself against Muhammad Taghi Mesbah Yazdi, who was well known for his fundamentalist behavior and as Ahmadinejad's spiritual "mentor." After the death of Ayatollah ʿAli Meshkini, who had been chairman of the Assembly of Experts by seniority, Rafsanjani was elected to chair the Assembly in September 2007, by a majority vote of 41 to 30. Although his election had no immediate impact on the repressive atmosphere of Ahmadinejad's government, that government's hold on power was shaken in 2009 when enormous crowds took to the streets in support of the reform presidential candidate Mir Hossein Mousavi, both before the election and, especially, after the dubious announcement that Ahmadinejad had won.

Translated by Catherine Kerkhoff-Saxon

3. Afghanistan

(Abbas Poya)

a. The Islamization of Afghanistan

Ten years after the death of the Prophet the Muslim army, though greatly outnumbered and inferior in military terms, defeated the armies of the Persian Empire in the year 642, thus putting an end to the Sassanid dynasty.

Arab invaders conquered the city of Merv (in present-day Turkmenistan) with no major resistance, going on to use it as their main supply camp, and advanced farther and farther toward Central Asia and modern Afghanistan. The first Arab Muslims reached Kabul as early as the year 664. This foray was less a war of conquest, however, than a raid, and proved costly for the Arabs, with the people of Kabul attacking and massacring the small Arab-Islamic troop. The Arab army repeatedly launched new attacks with the aim of conquering Kabul, Kandahar, and the regions to the south. The entire operation was coordinated from Basra, the seat of the Iraqi governor-general, Hajjaj ibn Yusuf (d. 714). By the end of the seventh century, Islam had extended its presence across Sistan,[1] Khurasan,[2] and the Oxus to Central Asia. The southern regions of present-day Afghanistan, however, remained untouched by Islamic influences for another two centuries.[3]

At the time of the first Muslim advances, numerous local natural religions were competing with Buddhism, Zoroastrianism, and Hinduism in the territory of modern Afghanistan. Buddhism was the dominant religion, as traces from Herat in the west to Balkh in the north, Jalalabad in the southeast, and Bamiyan in central Afghanistan indicate. The two monumental Buddha statues (53 and 35 meters high) in Bamiyan, which were almost entirely destroyed by the Taliban in March 2001, were regarded as the largest Buddha sculptures in the world, documenting a deeply rooted Buddhist history in Afghanistan. Zoroastrianism was also practiced in some regions, particularly in the north. In the southern and southeastern areas, which were mainly controlled by the Hindu rulers in Kabul and Baghram, the population was under Hindu influence. There were also Nestorian Christians and Jewish communities.[4]

The Islamization of Afghanistan took place particularly through the efforts of sects regarded by dominant orthodox Islam as heretical and were persecuted in the core areas of the Islamic empire, such as the Kharijites (*kharijiyya, khariji,* pl. *khawarij*) and Qarmatians (*qarmatiyya, qarmati,* pl. *qaramita*). Locally influenced Kharijite sects were formed in Balkh and Sistan, and a militant Kharijite movement came about in the valley of Hari Rud and the town of Gardez as late as the tenth century.[5] The Qarmatians, adherents of an Isma'ili sect, had many followers, including in the region of present-day Afghanistan. The Karramiyya sect, which held that belief (*iman*) came about by reciting the testimony of faith a single time and required neither inner conviction nor outward deeds, was also present in the region. Thus no single concept of Islam managed to establish itself in these territories for many years. Alongside Sunni orthodoxy, which was represented by the official religion of the local rulers, various syncretist mystic sects competed for favor among the population.

It was only the Ghaznavids who were able to Islamize the present Afghan territory almost entirely. Under their rule people were forcibly converted; numerous raiding wars were carried out, mainly in India; and Hindu temples were destroyed or turned into mosques. Simultaneously the sciences, literature, and the arts blossomed. Under Mahmud (998–1030), the empire produced the philosopher and doctor Avicenna (Ibn Sina), the polyhistor Biruni, and the poet Firdausi. As chance would have it, the descendants of the inhabitants of the mountain region of Ghor east of Herat later inherited the empire itself, having been converted to Islam by Mahmud, the founder of the Ghaznavid Empire. The Ghorids continued the Ghaznavid tradition of raids into India, repeatedly destroying Buddhist and Hindu shrines, in the attempt to spread Islam as the Ghaznavids had before them.

When the Mongol invasion arrived in Central Asian regions from 1220 on, the feuding local principalities were too weak to put up effective resistance to the new conquerors. The Mongols caused great damage to the region's cultural legacy. In later years, however, they adopted the conquered region's culture and religion and helped rebuild them. Probably the best known and most colorful of the Mongolian rulers was Timur (Tamerlane, r. 1388–1405), who left a trail of destruction on his many raids through Central Asia to Egypt, India, and Russia. His son Shah Rukh Mirza (r. 1405–1447) attempted to repair his father's destruction, promoting the sciences, literature, the arts, and architecture. In his more than forty years in power, which were marked by the influence of his educated wife, Gauharshad (d. 1457), the empire and particularly its capital, Herat, blossomed again. The artistic and architectural subtleties still visible in surviving buildings from this time testify to a highly cultured society.

By the sixteenth and seventeenth centuries, the territory of present-day Afghanistan no longer produced great rulers. The region was divided by strong dynasties that had formed in the neighboring countries in the meantime. The northern part of Afghanistan was ruled by Uzbek princes, descendants of the great dynasty of the Shaibanids. The Shaibanid Empire had come about in Central Asia in the early sixteenth century and had extended its territories to Khorasan for a time before its collapse. The southern and southeastern parts of Afghanistan were controlled by the Moguls, the descendants of Timur in northern India and Kabulistan. Kabul remained a part of their empire and was the Mogul rulers' summer residence. West Afghanistan with the city of Herat, the cultural center of the Khorasan region, was under Safavid rule. This Iranian dynasty attempted to establish the Twelver Shiʿa in all areas under its influence. These activities led to the formation of large Shiʿa-influenced groups in the regions around Sistan, Herat, and Kandahar.[6]

b. Islam in the Afghan Nation-State

The history of present-day Afghanistan begins with the rule of Ahmad Shah Durrani (r. 1747–1772), although his empire extended beyond the boundaries of modern Afghanistan, in the west to Mashhad and Nishapur, in the north to Bukhara and Samarkand, and in the south to Sindh.[7] Durrani, the Pashtun general of the Iranian ruler Nadir Shah (r. 1736–1747), secured the support of several influential army officers, and especially leaders of the Pashtun clans, after the king's death. He later became known as the founder of Afghanistan, Ahmad Shah Baba (father of the nation), a title that only King Zahir (d. 2007) has borne since, on his return from Italian exile to the Islamic Republic of Afghanistan.[8] Ahmad Shah Durrani made Kandahar, the center of the Pashtun region, his capital. It was his son Timur (r. 1773–1793) who relocated the capital to Kabul, although the Pashtuns remained in power in Afghanistan. The Tajik Habibullah II, known as Bača-i Saqau (son of the water-carrier), managed to interrupt Pashtun rule for a mere nine months in 1929. Although the Pashtun rulers had difficulties maintaining control over the country's non-Pashtun clans, their main problem was uniting the various Pashtun clans under their rule. Soon after Timur's death, competition for dominance broke out among the clans. The Saduzai dynasty, founded by Ahmad Shah Durrani, lost power to the Muhammadzai. Dust Muhammad Khan (r. 1826–1839) gained control over Kabul, founding the Muhammadzai dynasty. He had trouble, however, bringing the whole of the country under his control and legitimizing himself as its ruler. It was not until the ascension of the "Iron Emir" 'Abdurrahman (r. 1880–1901) that a brutal policy of oppression broke the resistance of other Pashtun clans and ethnic minorities and consolidated the Muhammadzai dynasty's power. The Muhammadzai retained power over the country until the military coup by the pro-Soviet People's Democratic Party of Afghanistan (PDPA) in 1978. The last king from the Muhammadzai family was Zahir Shah (r. 1933–1973), who was dethroned by another member of the family, Muhammad Daoud (Da'ud, r. 1973–1978). Daoud proclaimed a republic but fell victim to the brutal putsch organized by left-wing forces.

As an identity factor uniting almost all ethnic groups in Afghanistan, Islam has always played a key role in the country's political rule, with its strong ethnic and tribal characteristics. The rulers have always had to ensure that their policies and practices were seen as conforming to Islam. The *'ulama'* determined the compliance of the ruler with Islam. It was therefore absolutely essential for rulers to secure their goodwill, although the *'ulama'* have always remained independent of financial payments from rulers. The Iron Emir, for instance, was able to carry out his policy of oppression in the name of Islam. Legitimized by *'ulama'* fatwas (Arab. *fatawa,* sing. *fatwa*), he brutally put down religious and ethnic minorities, not merely continually violating the most elementary of human rights but even seizing religious foundations (Arab. *awqaf*) in one campaign, all with the endorsement of the *'ulama',* who remained loyal to the government.[9] The more reformist King Amanullah (r. 1919–1929), in contrast, failed to gain the support of the *'ulama'* for his liberal course. He was dethroned after only ten years by the same religious dignitaries who had initially legitimized his rule. After a visit to Europe, accompanied by his wife dressed in Western clothing, he informed the Grand Assembly (Loya Jirga) of his plans to transform the country from a traditional to a modern society. The religious representatives, including

the extremely influential Fazl ʿUmar Mujaddidi, known as Hazrat-i Shur
Bazar, rejected these plans, calling them un-Islamic. The subsequent popular
uprising against Amanullah's modernization project ultimately led to his
downfall.[10] The role of Islam as a political legitimization factor in Afghanistan is also illustrated by the fact that the country's Islamic nature has been
emphasized in every constitution that Afghanistan has had in its recent history, even that of the Communist Muhammad Najibullah. Two important
factors continue this tradition. First, the Islamic nature of the country and
the president cannot be ignored in present-day Afghanistan, despite all the
atrocities experienced by the Afghans under the Islamist Taliban and mujahidin; and second, an internationally recognized Islamic Republic has been
founded for the first time in the country's history.

Afghanistan's official Islamic school of thought has always been Hanafi
Sunni Islam, the denomination shared by the large ethnic groups of the Pashtuns, Tajiks, and Uzbeks and several smaller groups such as the Nuristanis
and Turcomen. It was hoped that Afghanistan's Sunni character would set
the country off against its stronger Shiʿa neighbor, Iran. All constitutions to
date have allotted a central role to the Hanafi Sunni school of jurisprudence,
which forms the basis of justice and in which the head of state has to profess
his belief. In the Islamic Republic of Afghanistan, however, the absolute
sovereignty of Sunni Islam has been relativized, and Shiʿa Muslims now
have the option of acting according to their own understanding of jurisprudence in the field of personal law. Afghanistan is home to both Twelver
Shiʿa (the majority) and Sevener Ismailis (a minority), together making up
over 20 percent of the country's population. Because of their strong presence in the public sphere over the past decades, and thanks to major support
from Iran since the outbreak of the Afghanistan conflict, the interests of the
Twelver Shiʿa can no longer be ignored. The Ismailis have been in a more
difficult position, rejected and discriminated against not only by the Sunni
majority but also by the Twelver Shiʿa. Traditionally the Sayyids of Kayan
have always maintained political and religious leadership over the Sevener
Shiʿa in Afghanistan. They are, however, increasingly coming to regard the
Aga Khan as their spiritual leader. Since the years of civil war and in the
Islamic Republic of Afghanistan they have been gradually gaining recognition within society, not least owing to generous donations and investments
from the Aga Khan.

There have also been non-Muslim minorities living in Afghanistan. The
Nuristanis in the East were adherents of natural religions up to the end of
the nineteenth century. Their territory was referred to as Kafiristan (land
of the unbelievers) up to their conversion, which did not take place until
1895. ʿAbdurrahman had them converted to Islam as a forcible response
to the efforts of several British missionaries to win the people of the region over to Christianity, and the territory was renamed Nuristan (land of
light). The number of Hindus and Sikhs living mainly in the urban centers of
Kabul, Jalalabad, Ghazni, and Kandahar up to the civil war was estimated

at approximately thirty thousand. The majority of them worked as traders. During the civil war many of them fled to India, some moving on from there to Europe and North America. There was also a small Jewish community in Afghanistan, living in small groups in the cities of Kabul, Herat, and Mazar-e Sharif. Their number was estimated at several thousand. After the state of Israel was founded, many Afghan Jews emigrated there. A large group of Afghan Jews made up of over two hundred families also now lives in New York City. There was allegedly only a single Afghan Jew living in Kabul in 2005.

Islam in Afghanistan is marked by diverse heterogeneous characteristics and features, some of which display traits of mysticism. One of the most important brotherhoods in Afghanistan is the Naqshbandiyya order. The order originated in Central Asia and is traced back to Muhammad Baha' ul-Din al-Naqshband (d. 1389). In Afghanistan it is mainly prevalent among the Tajiks in the cities but also has adherents among some Pashtun clans in the south and southeast. Since the end of the nineteenth century, the Naqshbandiyya order has been associated with the Mujaddidi family, which has been closely involved in politics on several occasions, including playing a leading role in the failure of Amanullah's modernization plans. The founder of another influential brotherhood, the Qadiriyya order, 'Abd al-Qadir al-Gilani (d. 1166), came from Baghdad. The brotherhood arrived in Afghanistan in the early twentieth century. In comparison to the Naqshbandiyya, the Qadiriyya order had fewer political ambitions, although several of its members later married into the Muhammadzai royal family, gaining particularly protected status. In contrast to these two orders, which were present in the capital city and directly or indirectly active in politics, the Cishtiyya order had its main adherents in and around Herat and was hardly politically active at all. The Chishtiyya brotherhood was founded by Mu'in ul-Din Muhammad Chishti (d. 1236) and prevalent mainly on the Indian subcontinent, whereas its influence in Afghanistan continually waned. The order only reappeared in public life during the resistance period, engaging in political activities in the Herat region with the *jam'iyyat-i islami* under its local leader, Isma'il Khan.

The dominant understanding of Islam is, however, orthodox and based on the shari'a. Hence the *'ulama'* play an important role in the opinion-forming process and the political orientation of the country's rulers. As in other Sunni countries, however, the Sunni *'ulama'* in Afghanistan have never been independent of the political rulers. Neither have the Shi'a *'ulama'* been able to organize independently, unlike Iranian scholars, for example. The Afghan *'ulama'* have always been dependent on financial support from the central government or local rulers, owing to the generally poor economic conditions in the country. In return, the ruling class has used its religious authority for its own political ends. The central political significance assumed by the *'ulama'* during the resistance against the Soviet usurpation, however, was a new phenomenon. The PDPA's seizure of power and the

outbreak of widespread civil war prompted the destruction of the old societal structures. The ensuing vacuum in the political leadership, which now
had to coordinate the "holy war" against the Russian usurpers, was filled
by the religiously influential *'ulama'*. Major financial and military support
from the United States and other countries merely strengthened the *'ulama'*
in their new position.

Islamic nationalism also evolved in the course of Afghanistan's history as
a nation-state. Under the influence of the pan-Islamic movement in the Arab
world and the nationalist movement in Turkey, the Young Afghan (*jawanan-
i afghan*) movement arose in the early twentieth century. Following the
death of the authoritarian 'Abdurrahman, his son Habibullah I (r. 1901–
1919) took a number of cautious steps toward normalizing the sociopolitical conditions in the country. During his time in office the Afghan traders,
politicians, and intellectuals who had fled the country because of 'Abdurrahman's repressive policies began to return. Mahmud Tarzi (1866–1935),
who had grown up abroad and not only picked up new political ideas there
but also recognized the important role of the press in societal change, was a
member of this new Afghan elite. Among other activities, he published the
fortnightly newspaper *News Lantern* (*Siraj al-akhbar*) between 1911 and
1918, in which he and his fellow intellectuals discussed their ideas on Islamic and Afghan identity, political liberty, and a modern society. These new
and hopeful intellectuals called themselves the Young Afghans. Amanullah
was very receptive to their ideas, particularly in his modernization policy.
After he was forced to abdicate under enormous pressure from the conservative *'ulama'*, the subsequent rulers rescinded all of Amanullah's modernist
changes inspired by the Young Afghans. Habibullah II (r. 1929) passed several political decrees immediately after taking power, including reintroducing compulsory veiling for women and closing girls' schools. Nadir Khan
(r. 1930–1933) was also compelled to grant Hanafi Sunni Islam a central
position in terms of policy and jurisdiction.

Several decades passed before the political elite returned to the ideas of
the Young Afghans in the 1960s, introducing a modern constitution in 1964
and establishing a modified and pragmatic understanding of Islam in comparison to the pan-Islamic version envisaged by the Young Afghans. This
practical understanding of Islam has prevailed to the present day and has
influenced President Hamid Karzai's style of government; Karzai's efforts to
integrate the *'ulama'* into state politics are not solely calculated power politics but also result from the country's traditional convictions.

c. The Role of Islam in the Afghanistan Conflict

April 27, 1978, saw the event known as the April Revolution (*inqilab-i
thawr*) in Afghanistan. The Marxist-Leninist People's Democratic Party of
Afghanistan (PDPA) staged a brutal putsch, murdering Muhammad Daoud,
who had himself gained power in 1973 through a military coup supported

by the PDPA. The PDPA, which consisted of a radical and mainly Pashtun wing, Khalq (People), and a comparatively moderate and mainly Farsi-speaking wing, Parcam (Flag), had the full support of the Soviet Union. Deep-seated differences of opinion emerged in the party virtually from the day it came to power, particularly between the two wings.[11] In September 1979 Muhammad Taraki, the first PDPA president from the Khalq wing, was killed by his power-hungry comrade and deputy Hafizullah Amin. Soviet soldiers invaded Afghanistan three months later, in December 1979. Strengthened by Soviet support and under the Soviet aegis, the Parcam wing ejected the Khalqis from key positions in the Kabul government. The leader of the Parcam wing, Babrak Karmal, became the new head of government. In 1986 the Soviet Union ordered more changes in Kabul. The previous head of the secret service, Najibullah, took over the country's political leadership, which he retained until the mujahidin seized power in 1992.

The phenomenon of Islamism developed in Afghanistan during the Soviet occupation, although its foundations were actually laid much earlier, during the "Decade of the Constitution" (*daha-i qanun-i asasi*) from 1963 to 1973.[12] The introduction of the constitution in 1964 and the subsequent widening of the scope for political activities had prompted young religious students at the University of Kabul to become involved in political activities along with several lecturers at the shari'a faculty. These activists with Islamist inspiration, some of whom called themselves the Young Muslims (*jawanan-i* musalman) and others the Islamic Community (*jam'iyyat-i islami*), were led by lecturers trained at al-Azhar University in Cairo and familiar with the Islamist ideas of the Muslim Brothers (*ikhwan al-muslimin*), most prominently Ghulam Muhammad Niyazi (d. 1978).[13] Their activities were initially focused on the Marxist groups Khalq, Parckam, Shu'la-i jawid (Eternal Flame), and Sitam-i milli (National Oppression), which were very active at the University of Kabul and in general among young people in the capital and in parliament. Very soon, however, the Islamists started to direct their activities against the political rulers, whom they declared responsible for the un-Islamic conditions in the country, which were far from meeting their expectations of an Islamic state. These activists included the university lecturer Burhanuddin Rabbani, the dignitary Sibghatullah Mujaddidi, and the students Gulbuddin Hekmatyar (Hikmatyar) and Ahmad Shah Mas'ud, who later became the leading cadre of the mujahidin during the resistance against the Soviet occupation.

The mujahidin groupings did not, however, share a common understanding of Islam. Their ideologies were influenced by various politically motivated movements in the Islamic world. On one side were the mystic orders of the Qadiriyya and Naqshbandiyya, which had become increasingly politicized in the course of the history of the nation-state. Two specific parties were connected to the mystic orders: the National Salvation Front (*jabha-i milli nijat*) under the command of Sibghatullah Mujaddidi, a member of the well-known Naqshbandiyya family, and the National Islamic Front (*mahadh-i milli-i islami*) led by Pir Saiyid Ahmad Gailani, who was also the spiritual leader of the Qadiriyya order. The links between the groups and the orders were, however, fairly nominal and not of a spiritual nature. They pursued a pragmatic approach to politics and were defined as royalists owing to their positive disposition toward the monarchy.

On the other side, the Islamic concepts of the Egyptian Muslim Brothers had a major influence within the mujahidin. The books of Hasan al-Banna (1906–1949), the founder of the Muslim Brotherhood, and Sayyid Qutb (1906–1966), the movement's great ideologist, were widely read across all mujahidin groupings. Alongside the works of the Indian-Pakistani legal scholar Abu l-A'la Maududi (1903–1979), their books formed the de facto ideological introduction, particularly for members of the Islamic Party (*hizb-i islami*), led by Hekmatyar, and the Islamic Community (*jam'iyyat-i islami*) under Rabbani's command. During the fight for independence, for strategic reasons the Islamic Community was in competition with the Islamic Party for sole claim to the Islamic position. The Islamic Community was, however, under the weighty influence of its charismatic military leader Mas'ud, who never presented himself as a religious fanatic but regarded himself as a fighter for independence. In the course of the resistance period the party increasingly distanced itself from extreme versions of Islam, propagating a more moderate form. Another mujahidin grouping with an Islamist background was the Islamic Union for the Liberation of Afghanistan (*ittihad-i islami bara-yi azadi-i afghanistan*), founded as late as 1980 and led by 'Abd al-Rasul Sayyaf. Because of its financial and ideological links to Saudi Arabia, this party was very close to Wahhabism (*wahhabiyya*). Two more Islamist parties operated from Pakistan: the Islamic Revolutionary Movement (*harakat-i inqilab-i is*lami), led by Maulawi Muhammad Nabi Muhammadi (d. 2002), and a second Islamic Party (*hizb-i islami*) under Maulawi Muhammad Yunus Khalis (d. 2006), who emerged from Muslim Brotherhood circles and was initially active alongside Hekmatyar in the other party of the same name.

The Islamic Revolution in Iran, which took place almost simultaneously with the PDPA's seizure of power and the flaring up of anti-Soviet resistance in Afghanistan, spurred on the Islamist movement in Afghanistan in particular. Iran had an especially large influence among the country's Shi'a population, the Hazara, not least as a result of the great respect that Afghanistan's Shi'a Muslims have for the Iranian *'ulama'*. Two organizations played a major role in the Shi'a resistance movement: the Revolutionary Council of Islamic Unity (*shura-yi inqilabi-yi ittifaq-i islami*) under the leadership of Saiyid 'Ali Bihishti (d. 1996), who trained as an ayatollah in Najaf, and the Islamic Movement (*harakat-i islami*), led by Shaykh Asif Muhsini, another ayatollah trained in Najaf. Despite their close religious links with Iran, the two parties pursued independent policies. The Organization of Victory (*sazman-i nasr*) under the command of 'Abdul-'Ali Mazari (d. 1995) and the Guardians of Islamic Jihad (*pasdaran-i jihad-i islami*) under the command of Shaykh Muhammad Akbari were very close to Iran in ideological and strategic matters—which did not prevent them from becoming embroiled in repeated bouts of infighting, like all other Afghan resistance groups. It was mainly these last two parties that joined to form the Unity Party (*hizb-i wahdat*) in 1989, in response to the exclusion of Shiʿa Muslims from the formation of an interim government from the ranks of the Sunni-influenced parties based in Pakistan, and under major pressure from Iran. This party, led by Mazari, constituted the Shiʿa front in the brutal fighting among the mujahidin in Kabul from 1992 to 1996.

The entire phase of the resistance against the Soviet usurpation was overshadowed by fratricidal war (*baradar kushi*), a recurring phenomenon in Afghan history.[14] The power-political interests in these conflicts outweighed the ethnic, religious, and ideological aspects by far. In this war within a war, every ethnic and religious group essentially waged war against every other, and even against its own people, in an attempt to defend or extend its field of influence. The fratricidal war reached its peak in the years 1992–1996, when practically the entire country's population, particularly in the capital, Kabul, was at war with one another. On the premise that control of Kabul meant control over the country as a whole, the power struggle among the mujahidin groups focused on the capital city. Whereas the great rivals Hekmatyar and Masʿud were concerned with gaining sole control of Kabul and thus central rule over Afghanistan, the Shiʿa Wahdat and the Uzbek Junbish-i milli-i islami (National Islamic Movement), a new player in the mujahidin alliance under the leadership of the former pro-communist general Abdul Rashid Dostum, hoped to secure seats in the future government through their presence in the capital.

By the time the Taliban made their first appearance in south Afghanistan in the summer of 1994, the mujahidin had long since lost their reputation as holy warriors fighting for Islam and in defense of the country. The Taliban brought the Pashtun territories in the south and southeast under their control with no significant resistance. Shortly afterwards, Yunus Khalis's Hizb-i islami closed ranks with the Taliban. Nabi Muhammadi's Harakat-i inqilab-i islami was already acting as the structural basis of the Taliban movement at that time; its members later became the main decision makers in the Taliban government and Taliban councils. In 1995 the Taliban advanced to the outskirts of Kabul, simultaneously conquering the well-armed and allegedly highly resistant stronghold of Ismaʿil Khan, the city of Herat. Faced with the rapidly advancing Taliban, the feuding mujahidin groups Hizb-i islami, Jamʿiyyat, Ittihad, Wahdat, Harakat, and Junbish now formed an alliance against them, putting a sudden end to their bitter infighting. The alliance was unable to hold Kabul, however, and withdrew ever farther to the north. It entrenched itself in the remote northern territories as the Northern Alliance, assisting the United States and its Western allies in expelling the Taliban at the end of 2001 without the participation of Hekmatyar's Hizb-i islami.

The magic formula which had enabled the Taliban movement to expand across the entire country within two years, conquering, expelling, or incorporating large mujahidin groups, was always Islam. The Taliban represent a literalist version of Islam, interpreting the text of the Qur'an and the sunna (the traditions of the Prophet) literally.[15] The Taliban (religious students) were formed in the religious schools (*madrasa*, pl. *madaris*) in the Pakistani provinces bordering Afghanistan which had come about under the ideological influence of the Deobandi school.[16] Most Taliban have attended only a madrasa, and have only fragmentary knowledge of the Qur'an. Their knowledge of the shari'a, which they intended to introduce in Afghanistan and use to establish a theocracy modeled on the early Islamic period, is of a purely superficial nature. In practice, their jurisprudence was more frequently based on the Pashtun code of honor and law (Pashtunwali) than on shari'a law.[17] There were, however, political and economic interests of international dimensions behind the movement. When the mujahidin no longer offered safety for the country or for the planned American oil deals after two years of brutal warfare, the Taliban were supposed to provide peace and security in Afghanistan, with major support from Pakistan and U.S. oil companies. In turn, many Muslim extremists from around the world made use of the peace forcibly imposed upon the country through violence and a rigid, puritan interpretation of Islam as an infrastructural basis for implementing their Islamist ideas. In the Taliban's Islamic Emirate of Afghanistan, they had the freedom to train their adherents on an ideological and military basis, preparing for the "Holy War" (*jihad*) against the "crusaders" and their allies. Their main objective was to threaten U.S. interests around the world. Saudi Arabia and other Arab countries, initially relieved that their own Islamist troublemakers had settled far away in Afghanistan, soon had to pay the price for their error of judgment.

Attacks on U.S. military institutions in Dhahran in eastern Saudi Arabia (1996) and the U.S. embassies in Dar es Salaam and Nairobi (1998) and their horrific consequences are described as the beginning of a state of quasi–world war. This development reached its zenith on September 11, 2001, when Islamist terrorists trained in Afghanistan flew hijacked passenger planes into the towers of the World Trade Center in New York City. Two daysearlier, on September 9, 2001, Mas'ud, the leader of the anti-Taliban alliance, had been assassinated. The internationally operating al-Qa'ida network (*al-qa'ida*), led by Osama bin Laden (b. 1959), was behind these and the previous attacks. The U.S. administration reacted extremely quickly, beginning to destroy the al-Qa'ida network's infrastructure in Afghanistan in an international alliance and with UN backing, putting an end to the Taliban regime that it had previously supported.

Once the Taliban had been quickly driven back by massive U.S. air attacks, Northern Alliance troops marched into Kabul in triumph. This time, however, they had to abide by the instructions of the Americans and their allies, who were no longer interested in an Islam-oriented government. At the Petersberg conference, Germany (November 27–December 5, 2001), the representatives of the mujahidin had to bow to the American dictates and agree on an interim government under the leadership of Hamid Karzai, a member of one of the most respected and influential Pashtun landowner families. With the support of U.S. and NATO peacekeeping troops, Karzai was expected to lead the feuding and poverty-stricken Afghan society to peace and stability. His course was initially supported and bolstered by various Afghan technocrats and intellectuals returned to Afghanistan from Europe and the United States, who formed a very close circle of government. Karzai set out to return the Afghan establishment to the traditional concept of Islam, which stands for Islamic ethics but not Islamic politics—much as, at the beginning of the twentieth century, the Young Afghans influenced the political elite with their ideas of Islam as a factor of identity but not a form of state.

d. The Position of Islam in Afghanistan's Constitutions

Initiated by the reformist king Amanullah, Afghanistan's first constitution came into effect in 1924. It was essentially modeled on the constitutional movement in Iran at the beginning of the twentieth century and the Turkish republican movement under Atatürk. The 1924 constitution was intended to introduce a modern constitutionalism in Afghanistan, but it was too closely tailored to the authority and inviolability of the monarch for this purpose. Although the constitution did have a certain modern and progressive character, it merely tolerated the religious and ethnic minorities, not granting them equal rights. On the one hand, all Afghan citizens (*atba‘*) were equal before the law, yet on the other hand, the constitution emphasized that the religion of the Afghan people was Islam and that the followers of other religions such as Jews and Hindus were under the full protection of the state.[18] This understanding of citizenship in the constitution can probably be ascribed to the then widely spread concept of *dar al-islam* versus *dar al-harb,* which regarded only Muslims as citizens of an Islamic state, including non-Muslims in the opposition camp and defining them as tolerated elements on Islamic territory. The constitution also specified that the shari‘a was the basis of all political and legal actions. In this case, however, the shari‘a denoted not a concept of Islam authorized by the *‘ulama’,* for whom the constitution did not foresee any political function, but the traditional Afghan understanding of Islam.

Nadir Khan's ascension to power in 1930 brought a conservative renewal of the constitution, revoking the liberal civil rights and the rights of minorities. The state religion was now no longer Islam but the more restricted Hanafi Sunni version of Islam. The domestic press was banned from contradicting Islam, while foreign press representatives were granted entry to the country only if they agreed to respect the religion and the government's practices. Non-Muslims were referred to with the term *ahl-i dhimma* (Arab.

ahl al-dhimma, people of the pact of protection), an outdated term that is not acceptable in the context of a modern state. Overall, this constitution displayed a markedly authoritarian and intolerant outlook. Following the murder of Nadir Khan and the enthronement of his son Muhammad Zahir in 1933, this authoritarian and intolerant constitution remained in force for another three decades.

In the wave of general liberation movements around the globe after World War II, particularly in the colonized countries, new political ideas and demands came to the fore in Afghanistan. There was an all-encompassing sense of an impending new era at this time. The Afghan parliament held contentious debates on political freedoms, civil rights, and limitation of the royal family's influence on politics; political activists wrote in the press on the subjects of the day; and numerous political groups were formed on an unofficial basis. Muhammad Yusuf (d. 1998), a politician who was not a member of the royal family, was appointed prime minister in 1963. From then up to the fall of the monarchy in 1973, a phase of democratization began which, as mentioned earlier, is known in Afghan history as the Decade of the Constitution. King Muhammad Zahir's new constitution was passed in 1964, a result of careful consideration that conformed to modern ideas of the democratic rule of law. The freedom of the individual, freedom of the press, and freedom to form political parties were all anchored in the constitutional text.[19] The Hanafi Sunni school of jurisprudence, however, once again remained the dominant version of law and Islam, in which the king had to profess his belief. The subsequent republican constitutions passed under Muhammad Daoud (1973–1978) and Najibullah (1986–1992) retained many elements of the 1964 constitution, although they did address women's rights more explicitly. The Afghan population paid little attention to these two constitutions, despite their progressive aspects, as they were used to legitimize coups d'état and thus the misuse of political power, which then led to brutal unrest in Afghanistan.

The constitution of the Islamic Republic of Afghanistan was passed by the traditional Afghan Grand Assembly (Loya Jirga) on January 4, 2004, following more than one and a half years of consultation and preparation. It promised the people democracy and observation of human rights. Women were explicitly granted equality with men before the law. For the first time in the history of Afghanistan, the Shi'a school of jurisprudence was recognized alongside its Sunni equivalent. The country's minorities were granted the right to maintain their languages. On the whole, the constitution thus contained many liberal rights. Nevertheless, it also emphasized the country's Islamic status much more strongly than previous constitutions. Like its neighbors Iran and Pakistan, Afghanistan was now an Islamic republic. The new emblem of Afghanistan depicted the *mihrab* (prayer niche) and the *minbar* (mosque pulpit), with the addition of the Islamic creed, the *shahada.* The constitution obliged the Afghan state to ensure that education complies with Islam and to abolish un-Islamic customs.[20]

These repeated oaths to Islam may be seen as a concession to the former mujahidin groups within the anti-Taliban alliance, but they also confirm the increased trend toward turning back to the roots of Islam which has been present in all Muslim countries since World War II—regardless of the fact that these roots now bring forth very different fruit, owing to the many unavoidable influences of modernity, and are thus different entities.

e. Closing Remarks

Several years have passed since the United States began its military campaign Operation Enduring Freedom (OEF), launched October 7, 2001, to neutralize the Taliban and al-Qaʿida activists. The coalition against terrorism has continued to work with the Northern Alliance, which played a pivotal role in many atrocities and the destruction of Kabul. As OEF was a matter of contention under international law from the very outset, the International Security Assistance Force (ISAF), founded on December 22, 2001, was set up to achieve international cooperation on the military front. ISAF was established in response to requests by the new Afghan government to the international community, and with the permission of the UN Security Council. In practice, however, the NATO-led ISAF constitutes a continuation and extension of OEF. On March 28, 2002, the UN also joined the peace and reconstruction process. The United Nations Assistance Mission in Afghanistan (UNAMA) has relied to a great extent on U.S. or ISAF support in reaching its goals, whereby the military operations have claimed many victims to date, prompting much discontent in the population. The officially announced goal of UNAMA and the international community was to establish democratic civilian structures and institutions based on the rule of law, including the 2004 constitution. The cooperation with past war criminals from the ranks of the former mujahidin and the continuing military violence, however, have shaken the population's faith in these objectives and institutions.

Translated by Katy Derbyshire

4. Russia, the Islamic Republics of the Caucasus, and Central Asia

(Rainer Freitag-Wirmingshaus)

Islam in the territory of the former Soviet Union experienced a twentieth-century history that was different and at times detached from that of the rest of the Islamic world. Together with the developmental processes following the disintegration of the Soviet Union, this has lent it the unique form it has today. It does not constitute a self-contained and homogeneous Islamic world within the areas in which it currently prevails in today's Community of Independent States (CIS). The term "Muslim" first of all refers only to the cultural classification of the various peoples living in that region. The diverse times and intensities of their Islamization in themselves have an effect to this day. This is true both of Muslims in the Russian Federation and the South Caucasus and of Muslims in Central Asia, which, with approximately 55 million people, is the largest contiguous region populated by Muslims, comprising the five post-Soviet successor states of Kazakhstan, Kyrgyzstan, Uzbekistan, Tajikistan, and Turkmenistan. Until the Russian conquest, the Muslims of the Caucasus and Central Asia considered themselves part of a Turkish-Persian cultural sphere, in which Islam formed a strong pillar of society. This changed when, in the nineteenth century, first the Caucasus and then Central Asia were incorporated into the Russian Empire. In the later Soviet Union, Islam's main concern was adapting to a hostile environment in order to survive. During this period, however, with the splitting of the Soviet multicultural state into republics, the seeds were planted for the birth of today's nation-states, which have been independent since 1991. In the current conflict-ridden process of becoming nations and states, the dynamic of deep-seated social change has also gripped Islam.

a. Historical Background up to the Soviet Period

In the pre-Islamic period, Central Asia was marked by religious pluralism. Zoroastrianism, Buddhism, Manichaeism, and Nestorian Christianity had brought forth great cultural centers.[1] Although the Arab conquerors had brought Islam to Central Asia within the first fifty years after the *hijra,* complete conversion here, as in the Caucasus, was a long process. In the ninth century, Islam became the dominant majority religion. During the following two centuries the cities were integrated into the network of Islamic culture. Islam was always more deeply rooted among the sedentary peoples and in the urban civilizations dominated by the *ulema* (Arab. *'ulama'*) than among the nomads. The tribal areas of the Kazakhs, Kyrgyz, and Turcomen, some of them not Islamized until the eighteenth century, preserved elements of the shamanist tradition, while proselytizing by the Sufi orders left its own mark on their Islam.

Most of the Muslims of Central Asia and the Caucasus belong to the Hanafi school of Islam. The most important exceptions are the Azerbaijani Shi'a and, in Central Asia, the Isma'ili community in Badakhshan in today's Tajikistan.[2] Unlike their neighbors, who are Turkic peoples, the Tajiks are Persian-speaking. While Turkic languages were always dominant in Central Asia, Persian prevailed as the language of literature. The language of religion was Arabic; later, Russian was added as a lingua franca.

In the tenth century, Central Asia was the second economic and cultural center of the Islamic world, next to the political center of the caliphate in

Iraq. Khorasan, in the northeast part of modern Iran, and Transoxania, the land between the Syr Darya and Amu Darya rivers, had come together. Central Asia was no longer considered the periphery but rather a region that was equal to and sometimes superior to the Islamic West, a center of Islamic intellectual development. The traditional connection between religious and secular forces was marked by tolerance. The empire of the Samanids, with its center in Bukhara, became the leading region of the Islamic world around the turn of the millennium. The economic basis for this cultural heyday was the trade in goods from the East. As a center of theology, natural sciences, and philosophy, it was the home of great figures such as the scientist and scholar al-Bukhari (d. 870), al-Biruni (d. 1050), and the philosophers al-Farabi (d. 950) and Ibn Sina (Avicenna, d. 1037); at the same time, Sufism experienced its high point in this region.

Through the invasion of the Mongols and the establishment of their empire, the eastern Islamic world was separated from the western; Transoxania, along with what is today Xinjiang in western China, formed the Chagatai Khanate. But under the Timurids in the fifteenth century, Samarkand became a glittering centerpiece once again. Only the colonial expansion of England and Russia would turn Central Asia into a marginal region within the Islamic world. After the sixteenth century, as a result of a worldwide shift in trade routes and the disintegration of the classic Silk Road, it fell into economic and cultural isolation and insignificance.

This was the situation the Russian conquerors found in the nineteenth century. Russian colonization did not change the situation. Its primary aim was economic exploitation. Unlike the Soviet power later on, tsarist rule left Islam untouched.

The first fierce resistance in the name of religion emerged in the Caucasus in the early nineteenth century. A central figure in the rebellion was the spiritual leader of the Naqshbandi order, Imam Shamil (1797–1871), who drove his murids into holy war against the conquerors. The tsarist army did not succeed in putting down the rebellion for twenty-five years (in 1859).

In Central Asia the Kokand Khanate was at first the center of resistance; following its defeat, this shifted to East Turkistan (Xinjiang). In Kazan, which had already been incorporated into the Grand Duchy of Moscow in the sixteenth century, the holy war was waged without weapons, by means of boycotts of military service and refusal to pay taxes. The Volga and Kazan Tatars were more heavily Russified and possessed a higher level of education than the Muslims of Central Asia. Under the Azerbaijanis, too, a secular intelligentsia emerged, encouraged by the oil boom in Baku in the late nineteenth century.

In response to the threat to religious and cultural identity, in the second half of the nineteenth century a broad Islamic reform movement developed. The Jadid movement (renewal, from Arab. *jadid,* new), supported by the Tatars and Caucasians, addressed itself above all to the educational system, on the basis of *usul-i jadid,* the new educational principles. Its most important representative, Ismail Gaspirali (Gasprinski, 1851–1914), was at the same time a pioneer of Turanism, which aimed at the political unification of all Turkic peoples. Determined resistance was offered by well-organized pan-Islamic groups, which joined together at secret congresses in 1905 and 1906 to form the Union of Muslims in Russia.

b. Islam in the Soviet Union

The Soviets cracked down much more harshly on Islam than on other religions because, on the one hand, they characterized it as especially backward, antisocial, and reactionary, and on the other, they feared it, recognizing its potential for resistance. They therefore sought to destroy the Islamic infrastructure.

Under Stalin's rule this oppression took on a militant character. With the introduction of the Soviet legal system, shari'a courts were eliminated.[3] As part of a campaign against Islam, foundation property was confiscated and Islamic educational institutions were closed. The *ulema* were persecuted, banished to work camps, or executed. By 1942 some 90 percent of the 26,000 mosques registered in 1917 had been closed or transformed into secular facilities and socially useful buildings such as schools, department stores, and the like. Another 25 percent of official mosques were closed under Premier Nikita Khrushchev between 1958 and 1964, and by 1980 there were only two hundred large mosques.[4]

The campaign against Islam banished Islamic piety and values from the public sphere. Through the elimination of religious education, the public teaching of Islamic knowledge was prevented. It was thus forced underground and depended on conveyance by word of mouth. The isolation from the rest of the Islamic world intensified the process.

Under Soviet rule, years of brutal repression alternated with periods of relative tolerance. The creation of an Islamic board—under strict state control—during World War II brought a degree of relaxation. Stalin needed the Muslims, and he placated them in 1942 by creating four Muslim directorates, in Tashkent, Baku, Buinaksk (Dagestan), and Ufa, and at the same time installing a spiritual hierarchy. The Spiritual Board of the Muslims of Central Asia and Kazakhstan in Tashkent supervised a limited number of officially approved mosques and was permitted to operate two madrasas for the education of the "official" *ulema*. But only a dozen students were admitted annually for Islamic training at the Mir-i Arab Madrasa in Bukhara and the Imam al-Bukhari Institute in Tashkent. The boards, however, which were subordinate to the highest monitoring organ, the Council for Religious Affairs of the Council of Ministers of the USSR, were never exclusively compliant instruments of the Soviet leadership. In fact their politics walked a fine line between acknowledgment of state power, on the one hand, and the attempt, on the other, to preserve Islam—between adaptation and cautious opposition. Following the attacks on Islam in the late 1920s and early

1930s, they had to find techniques and methods of surviving in a hostile system and to appear politically unthreatening. Distrust of the leadership of the religious board remained, for ultimately Islam could not be reconciled with the state ideology.

While atheist campaigns continued, some formal elements of Islamic custom could be maintained. One could now be a Muslim and an atheist at the same time. Existence as a Muslim remained an essential part of local and ethnic identity but was limited to customs and traditions, without any real religious connection or significance. One was a Muslim because one was Uzbek or Kyrgyz, regardless of whether one was a believer. The institutionalized Islam of the official clergy was able to carry out its functions, under permanent threat of penalties and the need to prove the theoretical and practical compatibility of communism with Islam; thus fatwas were issued freeing Muslims from fasting. At the same time, religious practices deeply rooted in society, such as burial rites, continued to be practiced even by party members. In the 1980s this was done by the intelligentsia more for nationalist than religious reasons, in order to demonstrate a degree of independence from Moscow.

The repressive mechanisms drove many *ulema* to the countryside. There the antireligious campaign was less successful; unofficial and illegal communities existed in many places. The mullas in the villages could be tracked down by the KGB only with difficulty. They had received their training not in madrasas but as oral traditions from their fathers and grandfathers, protected by the solidarity of their group. Wandering mullas crisscrossed Central Asia. The number of illegal clergy in this area of unofficial or "parallel" Islam, as it was called, soon exceeded those who were registered. In Tajikistan this number is estimated to have been around six thousand in 1960.[5] A considerable number of them came from the traditional religious dynasties; this was also true, however, of the official clergy. In 1963 there were only 325 officially registered houses of prayer in the Soviet Union but more than 2,000 unregistered ones, though these were found mainly in small communities in Uzbekistan and Tajikistan, generally with their own imams.[6] On Muslim holidays people met in the open. Syncretistic traditions such as pilgrimages to holy places were very popular and compensated for the closing of mosques. But even the official mosques were filled for religious festivals such as Qurban Bairam; many people observed Ramadan.

Independent Islam was largely represented by Sufism. This was difficult to contain outside the control of institutionalized Islam, and it could not be combated with the instruments of religious policy.[7] Among the most important orders were the Naqshbandiyya, founded by Baha'al-din Naqshband in the fourteenth century in a Persian-speaking environment in Bukhara, and the Yasawiyya, in the Turkish-speaking tradition, which goes back to Ahmad Yasawi (twelfth century). The Naqshbandiyya, which was able to spread throughout the entire Islamic world and has an especially strong influence in the northern Caucasus and Turkey, played a major role in the revolts of the *basmachi* (in Uzbek, "bandits"; Turk. *basmacı*)[8] against the Sovietization of Central Asia. Under Stalin they were a preferred target of persecution.

"Official" and "parallel" Islam should not, however, be seen as sectors separate from one another. The comparison undertaken by Western researchers in the 1980sbetween official Islam, embodied by the institutionalized clerical administration, and parallel Islam, represented by the Sufi orders, only partially reflects reality. The relative lack of knowledge of Islam in Central Asia and the mysterious synthesis of Soviet and Islamic culture—along with restriction to Soviet sources and the impossibility of empirical research—excited the imagination of many Western observers. The role of the Sufi shaykhs has been exaggerated. The destruction of Islam as a belief system had not left them unaffected. The first Western studies of the "forgotten Muslims" sometimes drew the premature conclusion that underground Islamic movements represented the greatest threat to the Soviet Union, and that they could ultimately have demolished it. Here the assessments of Soviet researchers had an influence: Islamic Sufi orders as a dangerous, conspiratorial force.

The three forms of Islam in Central Asia today—the conservative Islam of the *ulema*, Sufism, and radical Islam, which was added in the post-Soviet period—are not at all antagonistic. A believer can belong to *one* group but also to all three. Connections between *ulema* and Sufi shaykhs are common, and the Naqshbandiyya is closely linked to orthodoxy. The official muftis in Uzbekistan and Tajikistan are Naqshbandi; the spiritual leader of the Tajik opposition, Akbar Turajonzoda, belongs to the Qadiriyya order. The policy of official Islam was not the suppression of parallel Islam but rather its supervision. Conversely, parallel Islam was not in absolute opposition to the regime.

The religious leaders appointed by the government, like the unofficial ones, were an integral part of the special form of "Soviet" Islam. A characteristic of this Islam is the juxtaposition of multiple identities. It was and continues to be no problem to consider oneself an atheist and, at the same time, a Muslim, in the sense of an ethno-cultural classification. Thus, on the one hand, Muslims could in the past become communists, while on the other, communist leaders—of whom many were already practicing Muslims in private—could present themselves to the public as pilgrims to Mecca after the fall of communism.

In general, the intelligentsia viewed Islam as a national legacy more than a spiritual value. Islam became in a sense a way of life, a guide for daily living, instrumental in nature and basically secularist. Among other segments of the population, in contrast, it was seen as a system of religious, moral principles and daily ritual practices and, as such, as an alternative to the existing system. Today, radical, antisecular Islam can draw on this perception at a time when the post-Soviet states are seen as a continuation of the antireligious system. When it became clear, in the 1970s, that the Soviet ideology was bankrupt, a search began for alternative ideologies. This development was supported in the Brezhnev period by theology students sent to Islamic countries abroad, to friendly states such as Syria and Libya. The young *ulema* were loyal to the Soviet Union, but in the long run they contributed to reviving the importance of Islam. As early as the 1960s, Moscow needed the support of the Islamic world for its foreign policy and had to prove its tolerance of Islam.

Starting in the 1980s, its role in the Soviet Union was once again up for discussion. After seventy years of atheist rule the region was characterized by secularism. But surveys showed extensive religious activity among all social strata, including young people and the educated classes, closely connected with daily life and nationalist feelings.

The development that brought Islam back into the spotlight was spurred by both internal and external developments. In rural areas of Uzbekistan and Tajikistan, conservative movements and groups emerged that gathered around local authorities and took traditional religious texts as their point of reference. They were immediately and distrustfully branded Islamic fundamentalists by the Soviet press and persecuted by the state. The last Soviet anti-Muslim campaign under Mikhail Gorbachev once again pointed to Islam as an enemy of modernization and a gathering place for anti-Russian views. At the same time, thousands of young Muslims were forced to fight the Afghan mujahidin. Many were impressed by their devotion, and some joined them.

This was followed in 1988, in turn, by a wave of tolerance. The revival of Islam was encouraged by perestroika. Many of the parallel mullas left their jobs on the kolkhozes to practice their profession—this time in Islamic garb—in rebuilt or newly built mosques. It was hoped that a conciliatory policy would guide the awakening Islamic "threat" onto peaceful pathways. In the West, too, warnings were already being sounded about the threat to the stability of the Soviet Union from the high growth rate of the Soviet Muslim population, along with the importation of fundamentalist ideologies from Iran and Afghanistan. To prevent these ideas from filling the ideological vacuum, it was thought necessary to strengthen the Central Asian orthodoxy with official Islamic institutions. Propaganda was now expected to awaken pride in the special and unique Islamic traditions of Central Asia. Religious leaders were to act as a moral counterweight against social and economic disintegration, emphasizing the ethical values of Islam. To spread this message, editions of the Qur'an were now published again for the first time, and new mosques were built. The official hierarchy was given broader visibility and increased influence. The majority of Muslims, however, were skeptical of Gorbachev's reforms. They opposed the dissolution of the Soviet Union and were more or less surprised by independence. Islamic movements played no role in the collapse of the Soviet Union.

c. Islamic "Rebirth" in Central Asia

The effects of Soviet repression resulted in the destruction of the Islamic infrastructure, which manifested itself among the population in an astonishing lack of knowledge of the bases of Islamic doctrine. Soviet religious policies destroyed Islamic educational institutions and reduced Islam to customs and rites. People were isolated from modernizing forms of Islam. This led a Turkish newspaper of Islamic stripe to ask in despair whether it was easier "to squeeze water from a rock or explain Islam in Central Asia."[9] While the understanding of Islamic teaching is only rudimentary, a fragmentary system of religious ritual survived, detached from conscious penetration by faith, which was passed down through the generations as a historical and cultural legacy. The forms of unorthodox Islam, so-called popular Islam and the dervish system, together with the veneration and cult of holy places, proved resistant and served as the most important means of separating oneself from Soviet culture, thus contributing to the survival of Islamic identity. It was Islam that provided both support and protection in the individual's private sphere. The life cycle of birth, circumcision, marriage, and death was accompanied by Islamic rituals and festivities. The customs of everyday Islam ensured the continued existence of a Central Asian identity that was both religious and ethnic. The connection between religion, the patronage system, and guaranteed solidarity on the basis of the village community or the neighborhood communities typical of Uzbekistan and Tajikistan (*mahalla*) could here serve both as a means of control and as a defense mechanism.

The degree of piety varies from country to country and region to region. It is more marked in plains regions with sedentary populations than in mountainous areas with nomadic populations. Islam has its weakest roots in Turkmenistan. According to a survey in the early 1990s, Muslims in Central Asia considered themselves linked first and foremost with their families and neighborhoods (*mahalla*) as well as their regions, and secondarily with the Islamic community. In Uzbekistan approximately half of those surveyed identified themselves as devout Muslims, and in Kazakhstan even fewer. Nevertheless, 92 percent of all Uzbeks consider themselves Muslim. Over two-thirds observe Ramadan, but over 70 percent do not pray. Almost all Tajiks, too (95 percent), consider themselves Muslim, and the same is true of Kyrgyzstan (94.1 percent of all Kyrgyz, that is, 79.9 percent of the total population).[10]

The return to Islam that has been observed in public life since the 1970s, often described as a rebirth of Islam or a re-Islamization, is an attempt to affirm the native culture. Rebirth, however, and especially re-Islamization, are ambiguous terms, for no real de-Islamization had ever occurred, given the adaptability of popular Islam in combination with Sufi tradition.

A renaissance of Islam took place, at most, in the area of orthodox Islamic principles, since, as a result of the destruction of the Islamic educational system, religious education had taken place only through oral traditions in families or small groups of Sufis, so that it was primarily traditional elements that were passed on. The revival that now began, in the awareness that Bukhara and Samarkand had once been centers of Islamic scholarship, at first expressed itself in the rebuilding of a religious network.

In the 1990s the number of religious organizations in Kyrgyzstan, Uzbekistan, and Tajikistan rose steeply, along with the number of mosques. In 1997, 1,500 mosques already existed in Kyrgyzstan (the figure in 1987 was just 34), while in Uzbekistan the figure was 2,000 to 3,000, compared with 87 mosques in 1987.[11] In Tajikistan around a thousand new mosques were opened in 1990–1992.[12] Many of them were built through private initiatives. At the same time, Qur'an schools and Islamic centers were established, financed in part by Muslims abroad. After 1994 one can observe a degree of satiation, as both the number of mosques and mosque attendance fell slightly.[13]

d. Islam in the Caucasus and Russia

Azerbaijan

The development of the oil industry at the end of the nineteenth century contributed to the fact that Muslims in Azerbaijan—the only one of the three southern Caucasian countries with a Muslim population—are more strongly secularized than their fellows in Central Asia. The first opera house in the Muslim world was opened in Western-influenced Baku. The sources of this secularization are also connected with the Jadidism of the Caucasian Muslims and the necessity, for Azerbaijanis, of taking a position vis-à-vis Armenian nationalism. To this day—or perhaps especially today—national consciousness is far more strongly defined than identification with the Islamic community. The war with the Christian Armenians for Nagorno-Karabakh was never justified religiously in any way. Islam does form part of the national identity, but the majority of the population advocates strict separation of religion and politics. The status of Islam can be seen in the slogan "Turkism, Modernization, and Islam." It was the model during the short period of independence (1918–1920), and was taken up again by the nationalist Azerbaijan Popular Front, which governed in 1992–93. Here Islam has an important position, but is only in third place.

Some 87 to 92 percent of the population of roughly 8 million consider themselves Muslim, 65 to 75 percent of them Shi'a. Seven percent consider themselves fervent believers, and only 4 percent atheists.[14] Both sets of figures confirm the secular orientation of the majority of the population but also a rise in religiosity. The Shi'a form a majority in the regions of the south that border Iran, in the center, and in Baku, with the Sunni in the north and northwest. There is little evidence of difference between Sunni and Shi'a; often they pray together in the same mosques. This was not always the case. In the past, Azerbaijan was not infrequently a battleground for sectarian conflicts, with rulers of different orientations forcing their subjects to adopt their religion. It was only the conflict with Armenian nationalism in the early twentieth century that brought an end to religious disputes.

In the Soviet period Islam became privatized and withdrew into the most conservative institution in Azerbaijan, the arena of the family. Despite this retreat into a sphere of preservation of tradition, many Muslims grew up without a clear awareness of whether their ancestors were Shi'a or Sunni. Religion became a "secret matter," in line with the Shi'a tradition of *taqiyya,* denial of faith in hostile surroundings, which has deep historical roots here.[15]

Shi'a and Sunni are both subject to the Caucasian Muslim Board (in Azerbaijani, Qafqaz Müsälmanlari Idaräsi), as the old Soviet Muslim Spiritual Board of Transcaucasia (Zaqafqaziya Müsälmanlari Idaräsi) was renamed in 1989. Since 1980 it has been overseen by the Şeyhülislam Hacı Allahşükür Paşazadä, who has managed to survive every regime. The influence of his office has declined in favor of the unofficial clergy. This can be seen in the numerous pilgrimage sites, where large mosques have been erected with the help of donations and foreign money. The graves of saints already enjoyed great popularity among pilgrims in the Soviet period, and since independence they have experienced a renaissance. According to Paşazadä, of the five hundred mullas in the country, only fifty have a right to that title.[16] His claim to be the authority for all Shi'a in the region and all Sunni in the Caucasus is only theoretical. In reality his influence is limited, outside of Azerbaijan, to the Sunni Adjaris and the Shi'a Azeris in Georgia.[17]

In Azerbaijan, too, the building of numerous new mosques and the establishment of innumerable Islamic schools and an Islamic university are evidence of a revival of Islam. At the end of the Soviet period there were some two hundred mosques; in 2001 there were approximately 1,500, of which, however, only perhaps a thousand were supervised by the Board of Caucasian Muslims. The rest were unregistered.[18] The mosques are mainly financed by donations from the public; some were built with Iranian help.

Nevertheless, the rich religious culture of Shi'a Islam, as it exists in Iran, has so far experienced a certain renaissance only in the private sphere of the faithful. In the mid-1980s the number of mullas, still cut off from the Shi'a centers and scholarly institutions of Iraq and Iran, was estimated at fifty to seventy. Some of them were able to achieve positions of power, between 1988 and 1993, in the traditionally pious villages around Baku. In those years numerous Shi'a missionaries arrived from Iran, without, however, being able to achieve any great success. Iran could not serve as a model of a nation-state with an Islamic orientation because Azerbaijan lacked the necessary religious hierarchy as it existed in Iran. Nationalism in Azerbaijan was based on the idea of Turkism. This includes the fact that the Iranian state is seen as an oppressor of the Iranian Azeris.

The most important representative of an Iranian orientation is the Islamic Party, which was thought to have had some fifty thousand members at its founding in 1994. Because of the training of the Islamic Guards in Iran, it was banned and its leaders arrested. This further limited the already minor Iranian influence. Under the surface, however, the party continued to be active, especially among the 700,000 to 800,000 refugees from Armenia and Nagorno-Karabakh. It has been legalized again under more moderate leadership.

The connection between Islamic activities and social protest was clearly expressed in the summer of 2002 during the disturbances in Nardaran, the center of Shi'a agitation. There, Islamic rhetoric was combined with socioeconomic problems. This suggested the potential of Islam to become a focal point for the impoverished population. The politicization of Islam has clearly made the country's leadership nervous; as a result, their only reaction to the disturbances involved the use of the state security apparatus.[19]

Turkish influence is stronger than Iranian influence. This is primarily a question of political orientation but is also reflected in the religious arena. The semiofficial Turkish Diyanet Vakfı established a theology department and numerous schools similar to the Turkish *İmam-Hatip* schools. This is not unproblematic and has led in public to accusations that Sunni scholarly views dominate Shi'a doctrines. The order of the Fethullahçı (Nurculuk) of the preacher Fethullah Gülen is also affected by this. He was able to establish himself in Azerbaijan, but his theology department at the private Caucasus University was closed in 2002 after state intervention.[20]

Russian Federation

The approximately 20 million Muslims in the territory of the Russian Federation represent the second-largest religious community, after the Russian Orthodox Church. They do not form a homogeneous community, however, but live in all regions, with a splintered Islamic administrative structure consisting of some fifty regional and local mufti offices that often compete with one another. The main line of conflict runs between the Central Spiritual Board of Muslims and the Spiritual Board of Muslims of the European Part of Russia in Moscow, and the superregional Council of Muftis.[21]

Of the approximately forty Muslim peoples—mainly Turkic peoples and Caucasian ethnic groups—the Tatars, with 5.5 million, are the numerically largest nationality. The republics of Tatarstan and Bashkortostan in the Volga-Ural region, as well as the northern Caucasus, are the two areas with an overwhelmingly Muslim population. The two regions are extremely different in character. While the Tatars, like the Azerbaijani Muslims, have identified increasingly with Europe or European Russia—only here could the Jadid movement have emerged in the nineteenth century—Dagestan, which was Islamized more recently, was more closely linked to the Arab world. Nowhere did Russian colonization face such strong rejection as in the northern Caucasus. As the Chechen resistance shows, this is the case to this day.

Tatarstan and Bashkortostan are firmly integrated into Russia, while in contrast the northern Caucasus—which, in addition to Dagestan and Chechnya, includes the republics of Ingushetia, North Ossetia, Kabardino-Balkaria, Karachay-Cherkessia, Adygea, and the Russian regions of Stavropol and Rostov—has been considered since the Russian conquest to belong to the periphery. Dagestan is the republic most strongly influenced by Islam, primarily through the Sufi orders.[22] The organizational structure of so-called Muridism reached well into the Soviet Party bureaucracy. The Muslim leader Shamil's struggle in the nineteenth century against the Russian conquerors relied on the Murids; Sufism offered its ideology and the formal structure of the orders. With its strict discipline, Muridism became a political movement. The later mass deportations and liquidation of northern Caucasian Muslims under Stalin could do little harm to the orders as a point of reference for ethnic identity. Following independence, it was hoped that the social crisis could be overcome with the help of this identity. The orders' infrastructure was revived and strengthened. Today they largely cooperate with the state and partially dominate the religious administration.

The Caucasus—both the North Caucasus, belonging to Russia, and the South Caucasus—is the region in Europe with the greatest concentration of violent conflicts. This has an effect on the Russian public's image of Islam and Muslims. Since the end of the Soviet Union, the Caucasus—not least because of the Chechen war—has been equated with a crisis-prone Islamic periphery. The majority of Russians view Islam as an aggressive and fanatical religion.[23] Not just Chechens but Caucasians generally, as well as Central Asians who work in Russia as migrants—a million Muslims live in Moscow alone—suffer from this image and are subject to growing anti-Muslim racist sentiments. This can be seen especially in the wake of violent incidents connected to the war in Chechnya, such as the Moscow hostage drama in October 2002. Azerbaijanis and Tajiks suffer most from Islamophobia.[24]

In Russia, too, more and more young Muslims associate their religion with a sense of ethno-national solidarity. They are drawn to Islam in order to ensure their own ethnic identity and cultural distinctiveness, especially as Islam is the religion of a minority. According to Russian sociologists, in 1993 some 76 percent of Tatars defined themselves as religious;[25] in the North Caucasus this figure is most likely far higher.

But aside from these two main areas of distribution, Islam in general does not play a commensurate role in Russian public life. There is little awareness of the multi-religious character of the country that would accord with the realities. The lack of well-trained religion teachers has led to a relatively low level of Muslim culture. The attempts of foreign Islamic organizations to fill the vacuum have been more likely to discredit than to lead to more profound knowledge. The loyal Muslim centers have not yet expressed a comprehensive, convincing position on social and political issues.

Developments in Chechnya represent a special case. There, Islam became an ideological weapon owing to its deep roots in the struggle for independence. In the Sunni-influenced republic, the first president, Dzhokhar Dudayev, found support in the Qadiriyya order, although he was at first opposed to the instrumentalization of Islam in politics. Moscow's brutal warfare, however, helped bring about a turn toward extremism. In 1993

Dudayev was forced to seek cooperation with radical forces, and in the draft constitution Islam became the state religion. Political Islam spread at the expense of traditional Sufism, based in clan structures. In the course of the conflict, through volunteers from Islamic countries, foreign influence gained the upper hand, and in 1996 the so-called Wahhabis became the dominant political force.

e. Extremist Influences and "Wahhabism"

The reintegration of Central Asia and Azerbaijan into the Islamic world manifested itself in the new states' membership in the Organization of the Islamic Conference. Conversely, they were also now open to foreign influence. But the idea that the process of Islamic "rebirth" was initiated by other parts of the Islamic world misses the mark. Nor is the radicalization of political Islam merely the result of imports of ideologies from outside.

At first, support from the Islamic world was appreciated. In the early 1990s Saudi Arabia sent editions of the Qur'an and financed the rebuilding of mosques. Missionaries were welcomed, and foreign preachers arrived from the Gulf states, Saudi Arabia, Pakistan, Iran, and Turkey. But while they were informing simple believers that some of their customs did not correspond to "authentic" Islam, they quickly earned the displeasure of the governments, for they also brought with them fundamentalist ideas. In 1992–93 fifty Saudi missionaries were expelled from Uzbekistan. It need hardly be mentioned that the Chechen rebels were supported financially by various Arab sources.[26]

The importation of Islamic literature brought a degree of Islamic pluralism to Central Asia. Sects and groups appeared that had not previously existed there. Students gained the opportunity to study in Turkey, Egypt, and Pakistan. Travel costs to Mecca were sometimes paid by Saudi Arabia. Here, too, distrust ultimately prevailed. Early on, Uzbekistan ordered its students back from Turkey, and Kazakhstan later followed suit by recalling its students from Islamic institutions abroad.

At first it had been expected that Iran would attempt to export its Islamic Revolution. But Tehran realized early on that this was not a realistic prospect, if only because of the Sunni-Shi'a difference. In contrast, Turkish missionaries played a much larger role, and not only in Azerbaijan. A third of the missionaries working in Kyrgyzstan in 1999 came from Turkey (fifty-five, as against forty from Pakistan);[27] most were Nurcus from Fethullah Güllen's organization, which runs not only hundreds of schools in Central Asia but also businesses. Their newspaper, *Zaman,* was banned in Uzbekistan in 1994. The Turkish influence is also felt in the support for Sufi traditions, especially in Kazakhstan and Uzbekistan. At first this was welcomed by the Uzbek government, but later attempts to re-create Sufi orders were suppressed.

The revival of Islam is taking place against a backdrop of economic and social decline in a difficult transitional phase. The economic decline, the

slow pace of reform, the all-encompassing corruption, and the lack of freedom of opinion have increasingly destabilized all areas of life. Nevertheless, the majority of the population continues to trust the official religious
hierarchies. In general, radical missionaries in the early 1990s found little
response. The representatives of radical Islam are still a minority limited to
certain regions, but the trend is spreading.

No single theory can sufficiently explain this phenomenon of Islamism in
Central Asia. Many factors come together: the economic situation, traditional
patronage networks, external influences. Repressive measures on the part of
the government, especially in Uzbekistan, have driven even moderate forces
into the training camps of extremist organizations, whose sources of income
include not only foreign financing but also drug dealing and hostage taking.

In a region facing decline and a seventy-year history of suppression of
religion, religion is able to mobilize, as an ideology, when nationalism in the
new nation-states has been undermined as an identifying force by competing
subnational identities, while at the same time, the idea of liberal democracy
is nowhere able to fill the vacuum. This was seen for the first time in the
Tajik civil war (1992–1997), which claimed fifty thousand dead and drove
the country to ruin. Although one of the parties to the civil war was labeled
Islamist, and the conflict was characterized as a religious war, Islam was not
the cause of the conflict; the civil war was primarily a battle for dominance
between various regional groups and clans. Here it also became clear that
political Islam is effective when its supporters succeed in instrumentalizing it
for other partisan interests. In this case it was connected with the phenomenon of regionalism and the power interests of regional elites.

The political pressure on the population, shortages of land, environmental damage, unemployment, and the drug trade provide militant Islam a
point of entry at which it can agitate with its effective propaganda apparatus, starting in mosques and madrasas and led by orthodox, anti-Western
mullas. It joins with conservative neo-fundamentalism, which post-Soviet
society rejects along with Western values and lifestyles.

But Central Asia is not a potential Afghanistan, as is sometimes claimed.
On the one hand, although there are groups that question the secular state,
the actual threat is often overestimated. On the other hand, Islamism cannot
be viewed separately from the Taliban (Arab. sing. Talib) in Afghanistan or,
to a lesser extent, from the events in Chechnya. Developments there form
an external framework, expanded in the late 1990s by the connection to
al-Qaʿida.

Internationally this has led to an increasing tendency to view Islam in
the Caucasus and Central Asia within the context of security policy and
geopolitics. Attention is limited to Islamism or the "Islamic threat." Russia, China, and especially the United States have provided generous military
aid to combat rebels and terrorists, particularly since the start of the war
in Afghanistan, but these do not alleviate the serious economic, social, and
political problems.

The drastic event that startled both Moscow and the West was the August 1999 attack by rebels belonging to the Islamic Movement of Uzbekistan in the province of Batken in southern Kyrgyzstan, in the border region between Tajikistan, Kyrgyzstan, and Uzbekistan. The timing, which coincided with the renewed, spectacular appearance of Islamic rebels in the Caucasus, kindled a discussion of whether Islamism had shifted to the margins of the Islamic world. While several villages were occupied in Kyrgyzstan, an "independent Islamic state" was proclaimed in a small area of Dagestan, which served the Russian leadership as the trigger for the second war in Chechnya. The threatening scenario perceived at the time of Islamic networks based in difficult-to-monitor areas of Tajikistan and Afghanistan led the Muslim areas of the former Soviet Union to be viewed as increasingly endangered regions of global importance. The events following September 11, 2001, and the subsequent war in Afghanistan mark the high point of this development.

In any consideration of Islam in Central Asia, the focus is necessarily on Uzbekistan, the most populous and important country in the region. Because it lies centrally between the other states and Afghanistan, it has also played the most important role in the antiterrorism campaign. The center of radical political Islamism is the Fergana Valley, divided between Uzbekistan, Tajikistan, and Kyrgyzstan. It is a transit point for weapon and drug smuggling and is difficult to monitor. Following independence, the artificial borders of the republics, drawn in 1924, destroyed the natural integrity and the social and cultural unity of this area and allowed new minorities to emerge in the new states. The fertile Fergana Valley has always been the center of Central Asia and its most densely populated region, with 20 percent of the entire population of Central Asia. The center of activity in the Fergana Valley is above all Namangan, an Uzbek province, which suffers from heavy demographic pressure and chronic shortages of land. The mass of young people there, badly educated, especially in rural areas, and without work or prospects, represents a favorable recruitment pool for Islamist agitators.

The rudimentary knowledge of Islam creates a convenient vacuum into which political Islam, with its fundamentalist interpretations, can easily insert itself. Individual clergy preaching "pure Islam" had already appeared in the 1970s in the Fergana Valley. The first so-called Salafis demanded religious education;[28] not until the late 1980s did they make public political demands, in the period of perestroika and upheaval. Tape recordings of their sermons on traditional moral values, as elements of a puritanical and emphatically normative Islam, began to circulate. Until the end of the Soviet Union they were able to spread their influence underground. One of the most influential preachers was Muhammad Rustamov (1892–1989), known as Hindustani.[29] He had studied in Deoband and imported the ideas of the Deobandi movement to Central Asia; for this he spent fifteen years in prison in Siberia. The Deobandi school—founded in India in the nineteenth century as a Sunni revival movement—contributed a great deal to the revival of the idea of jihad in the twentieth century, and thus also to the jihadist orientation of the Islamic movement in Central Asia. In the late 1980s Deobandi schools in Pakistan granted young Muslims from Central Asia free education and stipends for travel to Pakistan. The Salafis were able to replace traditional, loyal imams and channel political mobilization. The positing of "pure Islam" is aimed mainly at popular Islam, linked to Sufism and considered un-Islamic, which had guaranteed the survival of Islamic traditions, especially in the Soviet period.

In the early 1990s radical groups in the Fergana Valley began to organize and propagate an Islamic state. In the generally chaotic, lawless situation, the Adolat group (Arab. 'adalat, justice), which exercised power in Namagan for a short time, utilized shari'a to fight crime. This met with a degree of approval. Apparently a segment of the Uzbek population saw and continues to see elements of shari'a as an answer to rising criminality;[30] this is also true of some of the official and unofficial clergy. In Chechnya, too, it was hoped that introducing Islamic law would ease a social situation that had spun out of control.

While the center of Islamic agitation is found in the Fergana Valley, religious developments have been different in each of the Central Asian states. In Kazakhstan, only the south, closest to the traditional sites of Islam and with a strong Uzbek minority, was a preferred target of foreign missionaries preaching radical Islamism. In general they have less chance in Kazakhstan, but here too, economic, social, and demographic pressures create favorable conditions for radical tendencies. While Islamism was only slowly perceived to be a threat in Kazakhstan, the least has been heard in this regard from Turkmenistan, where the state controls all social processes, although this was the country that maintained the best relationship with the Taliban.

In Russia, political Islam emerged with the establishment of the Islamic Revival Party in June 1990. The last anti-Islamic campaign in 1986, under Gorbachev, was aimed at so-called Wahhabi subversion. Since then all manifestations of radical political Islam have been subsumed under the term "Wahhabism"; both in Central Asia and in the Caucasus, Islamists are known as Wahhabis. This diffuse term—at first usually used to refer to Islamic critics of the official clergy—has become symbolic of the common Russian saying regarding the danger from the south, and is also often equated with Islamic terrorists in general. The term, with its allusion to the regime in Saudi Arabia, also suggests a degree of external control, although it has little to do with Wahhabism in the rest of the Islamic world. Wahhabism has become the fear-mongering label for any movement believed to be a threat, and thus a means to discredit it.[31]

This is above all true of the Islamic movements in the northern Caucasus. While Islam in Chechnya has become the ideological basis of the struggle for independence and national identity, Dagestan is considered the actual religious center of the Caucasus. In contrast to Chechnya, there is no comparable national movement in the multinational republic of Dagestan, and anti-Russian sentiments are less strongly marked. Caucasian Wahhabism is also a generational problem and not infrequently leads to a split in local Muslim religious communities. In the early 1990s hundreds of young men from Chechnya and Dagestan received religious instruction in madrasas in Uzbekistan and Tajikistan. Religious disagreements often divide tribes and families. While the older generation frequently identifies with a deformed Islam, the younger generation sees itself as the bearer of pure Islam. The mosque, with an attached gymnasium—a site of religious instruction and the practice of Eastern martial arts—became the most important meeting place. Solidarity and social involvement are the basic elements of the movement. While the fight against corruption and criminality is propagated, the relationship between organized crime and purist faith occupies a gray area. A great discrepancy exists between Islamic purism and the region's religious traditions, which were formed by the Sufi orders. The latter sustained the rebellions of the nineteenth century. Although the Wahhabis see themselves as part of an unbroken tradition of Muridism under the legendary shaykh Shamil, they oppose traditional popular Islam and its cult of saints. Yet there are elements that link the tradition of *ghazawat*, the fight against unbelieving aggressors, and strict obedience to shariʿa, which is also advocated by Sufi adherents. The generation of Chechen field commanders were influenced by their experiences in the Soviet army and the Afghanistan war. The militarization of society as a legacy of Soviet society, the role played by a conspicuous number of wrestlers and boxers in the movement, and the possibility of easily procuring weapons are elements that, in conjunction with traditional features such as codes of honor and blood feuds, highlight violence as a feature of post-Soviet society.[32]

In 1996, after the first Chechen war, which was lost by the Russians, Islam was proclaimed the state religion of the "Chechen Republic of Ichkeria," and shariʿa was introduced as the legal system on the model of Sudanese criminal law, although this was rooted in an Islamic legal school foreign to the northern Caucasus; the Muslim mountain peoples had mainly ordered their legal affairs in pre-Soviet times according to customary law (*adat*, Arab. *ʿadat*) rather than shariʿa.[33] At the time, this marked the victory of Islamic forces in the internal Chechen power struggle, which involved government and mafia structures and nationalist and Islamist elements. The actual strength and proliferation of radical Islamic forces among the population are not nearly as pronounced, however, as the events and the reactions to them might suggest.[34]

The Islamophobic presentation of the Chechen conflict to the Russian public reinforced the modern usage of the term "Wahhabism." The conflict was Islamized through military escalation. This contributed to the fact that in Chechnya, Islamic influences from outside could actually become a threat, through the establishment of extremely effective networks, thus turning Russia, in its own view, into a frontline state in the war against international terrorism. Native warlords such as Shamil Basayev and imported

Wahhabis such as Ibn al-Khattab, a member of the Chechen minority in Jordan, determined later developments. Their attacks on Dagestan triggered the second war, which ended terribly for the Chechens. Under the guise of fighting terrorism, Moscow's harsh policy of repression had a decisive effect on the development of jihad and martyrdom. The overused term "Wahhabism" became the collective term for all Islamic currents categorized as radical within the territory of the former Soviet Union.

f. Islamist Organizations in Central Asia

Islamic Revival Party

The first populist manifestation of Islamic fundamentalism in Central Asia in organized form was the Islamic Revival Party (IRP). It was established in Astrakhan in June 1990 for the entire union, at the initiative of Russian Muslims, with the goal of uniting all Muslims on Soviet territory. The movement united various streams of Islam and thus made a claim to representativeness that went beyond that of other groups. It included registered clergy from official Islam, as well as unofficial *ulema* and Sufi shaykhs. It was not interested in challenging the USSR. It identified with the Jadidists; the general orientation was traditionalist Sunni and antinationalist, and it thus stood in contrast to the trend of the times. The declarations of independence of the various Soviet republics caught it, like many others, unprepared. But it was not spared the effects of national divisions; its Tajik branch was excluded because of its alliance with nationalists.

Nevertheless, it was able to achieve significance only in Tajikistan. In 1995 the Islamic Revival Party of Tajikistan (Rastokhez) joined with democratic forces in establishing the United Tajik Opposition, under the IRP's leadership, which formed one side in the civil war against the communists. But its base did not go beyond regional clan relationships, and in some regions it was not represented at all.

Once the civil war ended, its participation in government and the integration of its fighters into the official security forces ushered in cooperation between secularists and Islamists. The party is represented in various government institutions through an agreement by which 30 percent of government positions are reserved for the opposition. Important parts of the peace agreement were never put into effect, however. The party's position was undermined by the government, and as a result it was marginalized. In parliamentary elections in 1999 it won only 8 percent of the vote and two seats. This not only led to tensions but also created an opening for more radical groups.

As a former party to the civil war, the IRP had fought for the creation of an Islamic state. Since the conclusion of the peace agreement in 1997, the party has undergone a process of differentiation. The realization that it had little political support from the public, and that the IRP—like the government, a party to the civil war—had thereby discredited itself with the public, triggered internal debates on the strategic priorities of the Islamic movement in Tajikistan and Central Asia. From the beginning the party was able to bring together at its head people as varied as Said Abdullo Nuri (1947–2006), a student of Hindustani, and Qazi Akbar Turajonzoda (b. 1954). The latter, who had been the grand mufti of the Tajik Muslims during the final years of the Soviet Union, became the IRP's poster boy owing to his moderate views and popularity abroad. Later he was excluded from the party because of his overly close relationship with other members of government in his function as first deputy prime minister.

The discussion is embedded in a secular-Islamic dialogue that forms an essential element of the peace process.[35] In the search for a compromise the IRP refrained, in the Commission for National Reconciliation, from questioning the secular nature of the state. In this way, for the first time a moderate Islamist school of thought emerged in Central Asia, and it is still distinguishing itself in terms of both content and organization. The IRP is the only legal party in Central Asia with a religious mandate. Through its integration into the government, it has succeeded in having an Islamic movement recognized as a legitimate actor in political life. It functions as a buffer between government, opposition members, and more radical Muslims. Through its legitimization, some of its Islamist ballast was discarded. While the public, international image of the leadership seems modern, its base consists of pious, uneducated rural Muslims. Officially it has distanced itself from radical organizations such as Hizb ut-Tahrir (Arab. Hizb al-Tahrir) and the Islamic Movement of Uzbekistan. Because it is not, however, a firmly established party with a strict agenda but has always been a conglomerate of various interests and ideas, from Islamists to pure opponents of the government, many no longer view it as an oppositional alternative.

The Islamic Movement of Uzbekistan

Best known internationally is a group of radical Islamists whose influence can actually be considered minimal. In conjunction with the anti-terror campaign under U.S. leadership and the war in Afghanistan (beginning in 2002), however, their most spectacular actions have attracted worldwide attention.

In September 2000 Washington added the Islamic Movement of Uzbekistan (IMU; in Uzbek, Özbekiston Islomiy Harakati) to its list of terrorist organizations. There was certainly reason for this: its close relationship to the Taliban and Osama bin Laden, the Uzbek leadership's claim to have sufficient proof of a large-scale conspiracy on the part of the IMU and the existence of a network of radical Islamists throughout Central Asia and the Caucasus, and the escalation of violence in Central Asia since 1999.

In early August 1999 some one thousand rebels infiltrated the Osh region in Kyrgyzstan from Tajikistan, occupied three villages, took one hundred hostages, and caused the flight of five thousand people. They were attempting to reach Uzbek territory in the Fergana Valley in order to establish an Islamic state that would comprise the districts of Andijan, Fergana, and Namangan in Uzbekistan and the Leninabad oblast in Tajikistan. The attacks on Uzbekistan and Kyrgyzstan came from Taliban territory and from the impassible mountain regions of Tajikistan and were part of a broad-based strategic coordination with the Afghan religious warriors. While their offensives were supported by the IMU, the IMU attacks benefited the Taliban, since the connection between warlords and the drug mafia created a courier system for Afghan opium through Central Asia to Russia and the West. A large portion of the IMU's funding comes from the heroin trade. Despite this connection—IMU fighters were trained in camps in Afghanistan and Pakistan—the operation was more a guerrilla uprising against the Uzbek regime than an act of transnational terrorism. The IMU was a product not only of the complicated developments in Tajikistan and Afghanistan but also of the repressive policies of the Uzbek state. The immediate aim of the operations, which were repeated in 2000 and 2001—in summer 2000 the IMU succeeded in coming within sixty kilometers of Tashkent—was the release of Muslims from prisons in Uzbekistan, where a wave of repression had begun after the 1999 attacks, leading to the disappearance of a number of religious leaders.

The mastermind of the attacks was thought to be the Uzbek Islamist Juma Namangoni, who was also believed to be responsible for bombings in Tashkent in February 1999 and had supposedly been deputy defense minister in the Taliban government. He had built a network of "sleepers" in the Fergana Valley and was thus able to create a movement that made the regime nervous, although it never posed a serious threat.

The origins of the IMU date back to the early 1990s, when a reawakened interest in Islam was accompanied by a rapid decline in government control of all areas of society. In the Fergana Valley, groups sprang up—often from illegal study circles that had already existed in the Soviet period—which derided local customs and traditions as un-Islamic. Attempts to form a legal Islamic party were blocked. In Namangan, however, small, informal Islamist groups took shape, such as Islom Lashkarlari (Soldiers of Islam) and Adolat, the nucleus of the future IMU. Adolat consisted primarily of associations (*futuwwat*) of young men with military experience who organized Islamic militias in the *mahallas* and attempted to fill the security vacuum using shari'a means. In 1991, under the leadership of twenty-four-year-old imam Tohir Yuldashev and the twenty-two-year-old Afghan fighter Namangoni, they occupied the city. They received financial support from the Pakistani secret service and from Saudi sources.[36] Adolat advocated Islamic puritanism, for example, urging women to wear the veil. It attempted to regulate public life on the basis of shari'a and spoke out against corruption and for social justice and equality. This enabled it to win a certain amount of admiration from older people. Adolat grew out of touch with the masses, however, through its emphasis on armed struggle and the strengthening of its military wing. (For this reason the Russian orientalist Vitaly Naumkin refers to its members as jihadis.)[37]

Following the takeover of Communist Party headquarters and the regional administration in Namangan, the movement felt strong enough to take up the fight against the regime of President Islam Karimov; it was defeated, however. Its leaders fled to Tajikistan, where they joined with Islamist forces to form the so-called Namangan Battalion. With the end of the civil war and the integration of the United Tajik Opposition into the government, Namangoni no longer had a part to play there. Nevertheless, he had been able to form the IMU in 1996 with the support of the United Tajik Opposition. The IMU rejected the Tajik cease-fire and aligned itself with the Taliban, while the IRP supported the Afghan Northern Alliance under Ahmad Shah Mas'ud.

Once the Taliban had taken control in Kabul, the IMU was able to become active in the Fergana Valley. In cooperation with al-Qa'ida, it found a secure hinterland in Afghanistan, with bases in Mazar-e Sharif and Kunduz and unhindered access to Tajikistan. The Taliban is believed to have given refuge to as many as three thousand IMU fighters, supposedly including Chechens and Uighurs. Many died in the Afghan war at the fall of Kunduz. The Uzbek government's claim that the IMU was destroyed in the Afghan war must, however, be taken with a grain of salt.

The IMU failed in its attempt to gain support for its jihad. Its greatest effect consisted in the fact that Islamic terrorism in Central Asia has influenced the international image of Islam in the region. The idea of a threat to Central Asia from Islamists seems to have taken shape with these events. The subsequent attacks in Uzbekistan that occurred repeatedly were characterized as an international terrorist plot, although they bore all the marks of an internal revolt. The danger exists, however, that international "jihadism" and the Islamic-nationalist struggles will merge with each other.

Hizb ut-Tahrir

Greater popularity than that of the IMU was enjoyed by Hizb ut-Tahrir (HT, Party of Liberation), the goal of which was the creation of a transnational caliphate in Central Asia, with Osh as its center. In the second half of the 1990s it was able to build up a network of party cells. The first reports of its activities came from Uzbekistan in the mid-1990s.[38] Following a wave of repression there after 1997, it spread to southern Kyrgyzstan, where the earliest cells emerged between 1997 and 1998 in Osh and Jalalabad. In 1998 a branch was formed in Tajikistan, and since 2000 it has also been active in southern Kazakhstan. Although its influence is often exaggerated, it has in fact been the most rapidly growing movement in recent years and is thought to have up to twenty thousand adherents in Central Asia.

The party, founded by a Palestinian member of the Muslim Brotherhood in 1952,[39] is a secret organization, structured as a cadre party and active in over forty countries, with a control center in London.[40] Little is known about its international organizational structure. Since the early 1980s its regional leaders have apparently been granted relative freedom of activity, depending on local conditions, as long as they adhere to the central ideological precepts.[41]

HT is less a religious organization than a political party whose ideology is based in Islam. Its rigid pyramidal organizational structure, with training programs and energetic recruitment practices, includes locally based units, regional organizational levels, and a superregional leadership. At the lowest level its organization consists of cells (*da'ira* or *halqa*), study groups of five to seven members; above these is a *mahalla* committee. The head of a cell (*mushrif*) gives its members new tasks each week; only he knows the next-higher organizational level, so there is little mutual acquaintanceship. The regional representative is chosen by a central political council at the international level. The party works mainly through the distribution of literature and flyers, which, however, reach few people. In Uzbekistan, one of its first underground publications has been making the rounds since 1995. Nevertheless, a mass movement cannot easily emerge through underground work, and the range of activities is generally narrowly limited.

Its declarations are primarily anti-Western, anti-Semitic, and anti-Shi'a.[42] The widespread view that HT rejects violence is misleading. Theoretically it rejects terrorism, and there has been no evidence that it has participated in violent acts.[43] Still, a degree of justification of violence can be found in its literature, and the party was involved, at least, in the coups d'état in Jordan in the 1960s and early 1970s. The doctrine that all Muslims will be joined in a new caliphate is characteristic of the party. The theoretical basis of its position is the historic example of the Prophet. It plans a peaceful political struggle to increase the number of its adherents and carry out a bloodless coup. Central Asia, Xinjiang, and later the entire *umma* will rise up after peaceful protests, overthrow the governments, and unite in a caliphate. Despite the propagation of this peaceful jihad, a battle for power is not ultimately ruled out. With the introduction of shari'a, all social and economic problems will be solved. Olivier Roy describes the party as neo-fundamentalist because it is less concerned with the definition of a genuine Islamic state than with the introduction of shari'a.[44] While HT rejects Western democracy as an anti-Islamic invention, it has, unlike the IMU and the Taliban, recognized the value of technology and uses it in spreading its message. It is less radical than the Taliban regarding women; they are granted a right to education.

Its absolutism and lack of realism give HT little chance of becoming a political force with a future. Of all the radical Islamic movements it has the most decidedly anachronistic goals. How, then, does it happen that a secretive pan-Islamic movement from the Middle East, which has little to say concretely about the specific problems of Central Asia, could become the most widespread underground movement in the region?

HT's backward-looking utopia is linked with appeals to social justice, which, given the economic, social, and moral decline in Central Asia, fall on fertile ground. Its supporters' motivations are based on a complex mix of psychological, political, and social factors. HT finds support above all in urban centers, at universities, and among the educated classes; it is not exclusively, however, a movement of intellectuals, but also has a social base among unemployed, uneducated young men. Because most have little religious grounding, it is relatively easy to recruit them. An important role is played by a sense of abandonment by the state and society. For those confronted with loss of social status, nonexistent prospects, lack of meaningful social activity, an obstructive system of corruption, and increasing repression, the idea of a lawful caliphate offers a way out of the grim reality. The vision of a just father figure resonates with patriarchal Central Asian societies. The answer to the chaotic introduction of a market economy, with its social consequences (for which, according to HT, godless regimes and the enemies of Islam—the United States and Israel—are responsible), is the distribution of what is produced nationally, as in the days of early Islam.

The success of HT is also a result of the fact that in Central Asia—unlike in Pakistan, for example, where its influence is minimal—it can act without competition. Dissatisfaction with the Uzbek system is the primary reason for its success. Because the government's repressive policies prevent any religious pluralism, conspiratorial groups such as HT are provided an ideal environment for their propaganda. Despite its estimated ten thousand members, HT in Uzbekistan is not a mass organization; it has nonetheless become the only serious political opposition, and its four thousand or more imprisoned members represent the largest proportion of political prisoners.[45] Among the population, its persecution by an unpopular regime lends it, to some degree, the role of martyr. On the one hand, it offers conservative young men a political and theological justification for male superiority in society. On the other hand, HT also recruits women whose husbands or sons are in jail. Persecution in Uzbekistan has led to the spread of its activities to Kyrgyzstan. Only about 10 percent of its supporters are Kyrgyz, but it could become a unifying force between Kyrgyz and Uzbeks in the Fergana Valley.

In Tajikistan some of its success is also based on dissatisfaction with the legal Islamic opposition, the IRP, and disillusionment over its peaceful course. HT was able to fill a protest niche that is conceded less and less to the legitimate opposition. The IRP changed from an armed opposition to a legal party involved in building the constitution. In contrast, the IMU, with its idea of jihad in its purest form, became part of the international militant Islamist movement, with links to the Taliban. It gained its greatest attention through operations that revealed the weakness of the Central Asian militaries. After September 11, 2001, the IMU lost influence, but HT gained in popularity. When distinctions are drawn between moderate, radical, and militant Islam, HT, in contrast to the IMU, is often characterized as radical but not militant. The IMU is more interested in short-term political goals, such as the overthrow of the Uzbek regime, while HT places emphasis on the utopian goal of creating a caliphate.

HT's links to the IMU, like its funding and the extent of its international support, remain unclear. The IMU's actions, however, have led HT to distance itself officially from it. While HT is often alleged to support the IMU and to cooperate with al-Qaʻida, there is no evidence of its involvement in violent acts, although it has, for example, welcomed suicide bombings against Israel.

HT's rapid rise was surprising; after the elimination of the IMU, radical Islam was not expected to have any further serious potential in Central Asia. Yet even though the ideology is based on imported ideas and not on an understanding of Islam rooted in Central Asia, its utopian visions have gained increasing popularity, even without a real conception of the structure of its caliphate. Although one often hears of the supposed infiltration of Central Asian elites and institutions, HT, as a relatively small radical organization with minimal influence outside a group of marginalized young men, still poses no immediate threat to the states of Central Asia. Nevertheless, their fears are not unjustified. One cannot rule out the possibility that HT might follow the call of other radical groups to armed uprising.

g. Government Islamic Policies

Seventy years of Soviet rule did not destroy Islam, but it had significant consequences for the secularization of society and political elites. Following independence, the increased interest in Islam, along with the appearance of Islamic groups, posed a challenge to the new nation-states. The rediscovered conviction of belonging to the Islamic cultural sphere did not, however, contribute to standardization in Central Asia. The new religious boards continue to be instruments of the state, which now happens to be the nation-state. Central Asia is not a monolithic bloc. Subnational structures, such as familial and tribal relationships, had an important function even during the Soviet period. In Tajikistan, after the dissolution of the Soviet Union this fragmentation almost destroyed the cohesion of the independent nation-state. Strong presidents and their control apparatuses cannot hide the fact that state structures in these transitional societies are still weak. In all the Muslim states of the former Soviet Union, society arose out of a combination of traditional Islamic values and norms, Soviet modernization, and Russian-Western culture. Among their characteristics are the masses' obedience to authority and the seamless transformation of party cadres into nationalist ruling elites. With its special relationship between traditionalism, modernization, and secularization, the post-Soviet national identity of Muslims in Central Asia represents a new phenomenon.

The nation-state subdivision of the spiritual administration in the new national states is tantamount to a nationalization of Islam. The Spiritual Board of Muslims of Kazakhstan and Central Asia in Tashkent, formerly responsible for all of Central Asia, was replaced by boards in each of the republics. Kazakhstan led the way in 1990; along with the establishment of an Islamic Institute in Almaty, this was also an expression of emancipation from the dictates of Tashkent.

The post-Soviet leaders attempted to compensate for their lack of legitimacy by turning to nationalism. This included holding up Islam as the embodiment of the nation's cultural heritage. Because nationalism related to the modern state is a new phenomenon in the region, today's leaders consciously draw on the Jadidist slogan that love of the fatherland comes from faith. "Secular" Islam is supposed to constitute the actual Islamic revival, within the framework of nation and state building.

In connection with the respective nationalisms of the titular nation, leaders fell back, for national identity formation, on cultural and religious symbols from the heyday of Central Asia's Islamic history. In Uzbekistan especially, this took place with the idea of undermining the opposition movements, which used Islam as a means of criticizing the regime. The great medieval Islamic scholars were honored as national heroes; Timur Lenk (Tamerlane, d. 1405) was hailed as a symbol of the unity of Islam and secular rule. Sufi traditions were celebrated as a national contribution to the spiritual development of mankind, and the Jadidist reform movement was portrayed as a countermodel to religious extremism. To separate themselves from extremism, and from variants such as Turkish or Iranian Islam, leaders attempted to create a national version of Islam in order to present it as an integral element of national identity, part of a state ideology that was supposed to fill the ideological vacuum left by the end of communism. In Uzbekistan and Kyrgyzstan the presidents swore their oaths not only on the constitution but also on the Qur'an, and a pilgrimage to Mecca is part of their obligatory program. The mufti is present in all the states at important official occasions, such as the swearing-in of the president.

The promotion of loyal state Islam is a continuation of the Soviet policy of employing religion in the service of the state. Leaders profess the secular separation of state and religion, but this is not connected with freedom of religion. With the exception of the Islamic Revival Party in Tajikistan, political parties with a religious orientation are prohibited. The Uzbek government propagates "good" Islam; "bad" Islam is Islam that is "misused" for political purposes and thus endangers stability. Outwardly, one can supposedly identify it through the wearing of a beard or veil. Nevertheless, its existence is useful, given reformist pressure from outside; the Islamic movement serves as a justification for repressive measures and the blocking of democratic reforms.

The national mufti offices, introduced in the early 1990s, are subordinate to the Committees or Councils for Religious Affairs. Non-Muslim communities are also subject to these bodies. The mufti office—only in Turkmenistan is it combined with the committee—is responsible for approving clergy members. In Uzbekistan the Committee for Religious Affairs, subordinate to the ministerial cabinet, supervises the Muslim Spiritual Board, which in turn monitors the clergy through official fatwas and prescribed Friday sermons.

Training to become an imam is provided by state-controlled organizations, first of all in madrasas, then in Tashkent at the Islamic al-Bukhari Institute and the Islamic University. The most important means of control is the duty to register religious organizations with the committee. The law on freedom of conscience and religious organizations of 1998 formally guarantees religious freedom, but thousands of mosques have been closed for failing to fulfill the requirements of registration. Religious literature is censored and missionary activities are prohibited. The last mufti from the Soviet era had to give up his office and go into exile after accusations of misappropriation of funds and Wahhabism. Since then, the official Muslim leadership has played only a subordinate role.

In Azerbaijan, too, despite constitutionally anchored religious freedom since 2001, religious communities of all denominations are subject to compulsory registration. A State Committee on Work with Religious Associations attempts to limit missionary activities—both Islamic and Christian—through strict conditions. Because the greater transparency being sought for activities emanating from mosques and holy places, and their stricter supervision, could not be achieved by the old structures, the authority of the Spiritual Leadership of Caucasian Muslims and the Şeyhülislam has been increasingly undermined by the committee. The direction of the restructuring has been against organizations with connections to the Gulf states or Iran.[46]

The stronger the dictates of the state, the less authority is enjoyed by the clergy, and the lower their degree of respect among the public. In Uzbekistan the extreme regulation of religious instruction has driven even orthodox education underground. There is no religious instruction in public schools; formal training occurs only to a limited extent in state-controlled institutions, and instruction in mosques can take place only with special permission for fear of Wahhabi imams. When religious instruction, despite prohibitions, takes place underground, the state has little control over what is taught. The limitations have revived an old tradition of learning, *hujra,* which was practiced during the Soviet period: instruction by imams in small groups or in the family. Thus government policies are creating fertile soil for Islamist agitation, since ignorance of religion gives groups such as Hizb ut-Tahrir a virtual interpretive monopoly over religious texts.

The state has succeeded, through its purge measures, in ending the tacit rapprochement between the religious hierarchy and the purists found toward the end of the Soviet period. Nevertheless, a definite result of the repeated waves of persecution, in which no distinction was made between radical and moderate believers, was to make political Islam the most important expression of growing opposition. Under the worsening conditions of a "merciless" market economy and the growth of impoverished sectors of the population with no prospects, along with brutal repression on the part of the regimes, a strengthening of radical Islamic currents is almost unavoidable. The main societal conflict today is between the Islamically tinged but fundamentally secular leadership elites and the representatives of political Islam. This ultimately leads to further delegitimization of the secular system. The strategy pursued by Islamic groups of offering Islamic alternatives to secular elites disavowed because of their repressive policies could thus be successful, at least in some regions. Persecution by the authorities creates martyrs and thereby strengthens their mythical aura. Foreign observers have long warned that repressive policies are counterproductive because they drive the public into the arms of the extremists.[47]

All Central Asian governments see political Islam as the main threat to their power. The emergence of the Islamists serves to justify the concept of "stability at any price," of which an authoritarian system is the best guarantee. It supports the leaders' more or less open arguments against democratic development, which maintain that it cannot counter the Islamic threat. In Uzbekistan all opposition—including non-Islamic opposition—was eliminated on this premise. The question whether, over the long term, this does not in fact breed instability or itself strengthen Islamic fundamentalism is ignored.

The unresolved relationship between state and religion will remain a conflict-provoking factor in Central Asia for a long time to come. The methods for controlling Islam carry on Soviet traditions but display national variations in the application and degree of the restrictions.[48] They appear most repressive in Uzbekistan, while in Kazakhstan and Azerbaijan they function more subtly. In Tajikistan, too, more liberal legislation often fails to prevent state encroachment. Tajikistan is the only country with a legal Islamist party, but the Islamic Revival Party never had a clear concept of an Islamic state. When it was integrated into the government in 1997, public support for political Islam as a solution to problems fell. While the peace agreement was celebrated by international observers as a unique compromise between secular and Islamic forces and as proof of the possibility that Islamic movements could play a constructive role, in practice it looks more like a victory for the secular forces. The supervisory structures for religion were not eliminated by integration; for example, a number of unregistered mosques were closed. Tajikistan has no mufti office, and responsibility lies with the state-controlled Islamic Center of Tajikistan. Here, too, the security forces play a central role in religious matters. Pointing to the activities of the banned Hizb ut-Tahrir, with its growing number of supporters—especially among Uzbeks in the northern part of the country and in Dushanbe—the Tajik leadership is attempting to sideline even moderate Islamists.

In Kyrgyzstan, HT has its greatest potential in the strongly Islamic-influenced south, with its large Uzbek minority. Kyrgyzstan is religiously fragmented, and a secular lifestyle is more widespread than in Uzbekistan. While foreign Islamic missionaries have been banned since 1999, new Christian groups are enjoying their greatest successes in Kyrgyzstan. Because of HT's activities, Kyrgyzstan's theoretically broad freedom of religion has been increasingly restricted, through the same methods as in the other countries. Kazakhstan has the most liberal policies; there Islam generally plays a smaller role. Until the late 1990s, when HT gained influence in the southern part of the country, where piety is greatest, no reason was seen to intervene.

As in many other contexts, Turkmenistan differs from its neighboring countries in its religious policies. There is no separation of state and religion in practice. President Saparmurat Niyazov, who died in 2006, introduced his own personalized pseudo-religion as the official ideology. Millions were spent on building new mosques, primarily to glorify the president. The Council on Religious Affairs is directly answerable to the president and supervises all religious activities.

Owing to lack of information, Western scholars generally have difficulty assessing the extent of the Islamist threat. There has so far been no real threat to Uzbekistan. The IMU's campaigns, however, strengthened the conviction, both in the United States and in Russia, that Uzbekistan represented an important barricade against Islamic fundamentalism. The Islamist threat as an alleged major danger to the security of Central Asia was exploited for propaganda purposes by both Moscow and Tashkent. For Russia, the "Islamist conspiracy" is proof of the necessity of a common struggle against transnational Islamist terrorism, from Chechnya to the Fergana Valley, and thus of a common security policy in Central Asia, which could be put to good use in reintegrating Russia's traditional sphere of influence. During his presidency Vladimir Putin made the fight against this new danger the most important theme of Russian policy in Central Asia and the Caucasus. The fact that this strategy did not entirely work was partly due to Tashkent, which viewed such attempts with distrust, until its break with the United States as a result of its bloody quelling of the revolt in Andijan in May 2005. It has since then accepted military assistance from the United States as well as from China, which fears Islamic extremism in the form of Uighur separatism.

Undoubtedly the involvement of the United States in Central Asia in the fight against international terrorism, for example, through the establishment of military bases in Uzbekistan (until 2005) and Kyrgyzstan (threatened with closure in 2009), acts as a provocation to Islamist zealots—especially against the background of the increase in anti-American resentment in connection with U.S. Middle East policy. Yet for a majority of the population of Central Asia, Islam does not represent the central factor in their lives. The tradition of secularism and the harsh struggle for survival undermine religious norms. A discrepancy still exists between attachment to Islam and a willingness to accept this as determining the form of the political system. Political Islam has not achieved, as it has in Afghanistan, a degree of effectiveness that would allow it to have a mobilizing effect based purely on its strength and symbolism, and it is still dependent on specific constellations of conflict. It is possible that it would have rapidly disappeared had it been channeled into a democratic political process. In general, there is no possibility for Islamists to come to power in the region. It is more likely that governments will continue to use Islamism as an excuse to prevent reforms, and in this way will improve conditions for the Islamists, maintaining a vicious cycle.

Translated by Belinda Cooper

5. The People's Republic of China

(Thomas Heberer)

China is the home of the largest Muslim minority population in East and Southeast Asia, totaling approximately 22 million Muslims. More Muslims live in China than in Malaysia or even in the majority of the countries in the Middle East.

With the advent of the reform policy at the end of the 1970s, more information on Islam, its development, and its problems has become available again. The information has also become more readily available with a growing independence movement that, on the one hand, is the consequence of a decades-long failed policy on minorities and development and, on the other hand, is linked to the hope of the Turkic peoples on the Chinese side of the border (East Turkistan), particularly among the Uighur people, in creating an independent state following the breakup of the Soviet Union and the creation of new nation-states in Central Asia (West Turkistan).

a. Islamic Ethnic Groups in China

There are no exact numbers for the size of the Muslim communities in China because data on religious affiliation are not published. Yet given the census data including Muslim nationalities, and taking into consideration an annual population growth rate of 1.5 to 2 percent, one can estimate that there would have been around 22 million Muslims in China in 2004, spread over ten nationalities (of fifty-six officially recognized).

Constituting a fifth of the total minority population, the Islamic population in China includes six Turkic groups (Uighur, Kazakh, Kirghiz, Uzbek, Tatar, Salar), two Mongolian groups (Bonan or Baoan, Dongxiang), an Iranian group (Tajik), and the largest group (Hui). The Hui people differ little in appearance and in language from the Han Chinese, who are in the majority. Whereas the other groups of peoples constitute for the most part separate ethnic groups concentrated in specific centers and having their own languages, the Hui are the product of extremely different migration patterns. They are defined more closely along religious lines than ethnic lines, with the spectrum ranging from assimilated urban-dwelling Hui to strict orthodox Muslims who avoid contact with non-Muslims. The Hui live in all

Table 3. Population Figures for Muslim Groups in China, Based on the 2000 Census

Nationality	Number of People	Percentage of All Minorities	Percentage of the General Population
Hui	9,816,800	9.39	0.79
Uighur	8,399,200	8.04	0.068
Kazakh	1,250,500	1.20	0.10
Dongxiang	513,800	0.50	0.04
Kirghiz	160,800	0.15	0.01
Salar	104,500	0.10	0.01
Tajik	41,000	0.04	0.00
Baoan	16,500	0.02	0.00
Uzbek	12,400	0.01	0.00
Tatar	4,890	0.00	0.00
Total	20,320,390	19.44	1.64

Source: Figures from *Zhongguo Minzu Bao* (Newspaper on China's Nationalities), January 7, 2003.

provinces, whereas the rest of the Muslim ethnic groups are concentrated in northwestern China.[1] Most of the Muslims in China are Sunnis and followers of the Hanafi school of legal thought, with the exception of a few Shi'ite Tajik. The Sunnis can be further broken down into Sufi and non-Sufi orders, of which the latter constitute nearly two-thirds.

b. History of Islam in China

Islam is said to have been officially introduced to China in 651. Caliph 'Uthman (r. 644–656) reportedly sent an envoy to the emperor Gaozong of the Tang dynasty (650–683) and achieved official toleration for Islam.[2] From then on, many thousands of Arabs and Persians began to arrive at southern China's port cities, and others came from Central Asia heading to northwestern Chinese trading centers. The Muslims who settled in China and married local women not only traveled by sea but also came by land. And quite often they were soldiers or mercenaries.

Up until the end of the Song dynasty (1279) the Muslim groups in China were able to develop without much challenge. Yet if it were not for the Mongolian rule (1271–1368), which upended China's insularity, it is highly unlikely that large swaths of China would have been converted to Islam. Thousands of Muslims from the regions conquered by the Mongols in Asia Minor and Central Asia were brought to China, including soldiers, scholars, craftsmen, artists, and religious leaders. They all had a stimulating effect on the Chinese culture. Nevertheless, the Mongolian rulers restricted the religious autonomy of their Muslim subjects. Kublai Khan released a decree that made it illegal to slaughter animals according to Islamic law, among other things.

The double-edged policy toward the Muslims, which was intended to be at the service of the court yet pursued a policy of discrimination that led to repeated rebellions, continued into the Ming dynasty. As one of the first moves during his reign, the first Ming emperor, Taizu (r. 1368–1398), prohibited the wearing of foreign clothing and use of foreign languages and names in order to eradicate the non-Chinese influence that had been supported by the Mongols. Instead of promoting intermarriage between the Mongols and their previous allies, the new policies placed an emphasis on intermarriage with Han Chinese. Muslims adopted Chinese names such as Ma (for Muhammad), Na (for Nasir), and Sai (for Sayyid). They began to wear Chinese dress and speak the local dialect. The only thing that remained relatively unchanged was their religion. The emperor made certain that the Muslim groups did not become closed communities and thus kept them dispersed by means of resettlement so as to maintain tighter control over them.

The number of Muslims grew as a result of intermarriages between the Han and the Muslim groups, adoption, and conversion, alongside immigration and expansion of the Chinese Empire toward Central Asia. The Qing dynasty of the Manchus (1644–1911) heralded the beginning of a phase of open suppression accompanied by rebellion after rebellion resulting in the deaths of millions. (There were ten major rebellions in the eighteenth and nineteenth centuries alone.)

Not only were the uprisings a product of massive resistance by the Hui against the new dynasty (the first major rebellion took place in 1648), but also there remained a potential for unrest in the Hui territories. Historical accounts from that period describe the Hui people as troublemakers, rebellious and violent. The emperor did not understand Islamic practices and regarded the Muslims as groups that defied public control, maintained their own private traditions and cohesiveness, and rejected imperial authority. He found his suspicions confirmed after a further revolt (1781–1784) incited by followers of the Jahriyya Sufi school. The followers of the "New Teaching" (discussed later in this chapter), which was introduced and spread by Mecca pilgrims, had previously fought bloody battles with adherents of the "Old Teaching," the Khafiyya Sufi, who were tolerated by the Qing dynasty. The suppression by the Qing rulers provoked the Jahriyya leaders to set off a "holy war" against the nonbelievers.[3]

The dissatisfaction was only augmented by the growing efforts at suppression and the attempts at sinicization made by the Qing rulers starting in the 1720s (the Chinese administrative structures replaced traditional Islamic administration, with the examinations for government officials now based on Confucianism) and restrictions on religious practice. (Traditional animal slaughter was banned in 1731, followed by bans on construction of new mosques and pilgrimages to Mecca.)[4] In addition, there were conflicts with Han immigrants over farmland, mines, and water usage rights, as the local Han-run administrations generally sided against the Muslim populace.

The sinicization efforts of this dynasty were hampered by the dispersal of the Hui throughout all provinces and larger cities, their living together in compact communities, and their feeling of superiority in terms of religion. These efforts were ratcheted up as the Qing dynasty began to weaken and in light of the social crisis in the first half of the nineteenth century and the major uprisings of the Nian and Taiping rebels (1850–1864), whereby the dissatisfaction among the Muslims erupted in Yunnan (1855–1873) and in northwestern China (1864–1877). The local Han populations were persecuted with much bloodshed. After the Qing put down these rebellions, they retaliated brutally. According to one estimate, the Chinese troops apparently massacred the Hui to such an extent that their numbers were reduced by 40 to 50 percent.[5] In the southwestern province of Yunnan alone, 5 million of its 8 million Hui inhabitants were killed during the uprisings and the subsequent quashing by the government. In Shaanxi nine-tenths of the Hui were murdered. The Qing government attempted to break down the cohesiveness of the Hui communities through deportation, expulsion from the cities, and a ban on large Hui settlements. Resentment, hate, and mistrust motivated by these actions remain even today as the result of collective memory. The Hui, however, had no sense of a national identity and solidarity, and this prevented them from ever banding together and taking up arms. J. N. Lipman attributes this to the topographic and ethnic diversity of the northwestern Chinese settlement area. The individual Hui communities were not concentrated in one region but rather lived in sparsely populated, isolated, and scattered communities that had little contact with one another.[6]

The defeat of the Chinese troops at the hands of the Arab army at the Talas River and the Arabs' subsequent advance into Central Asia in the eighth century are considered to mark the beginning of the proselytization of the Turkic peoples in Central Asia to Islam. The ruler of Kashgar and Khojan, Satok Bughra Khan, is said to have converted to Islam in the tenth century in what is now Chinese territory. In subsequent centuries Islam was spread to the Tatars (tenth century), the Uzbeks (thirteenth–fourteenth centuries), the Uighurs (fifteenth century), and the Kazakhs (sixteenth–seventeenth centuries).[7] Ethnic differences between the Turkic peoples in Xinjiang, especially the Uighurs and Kazakhs on the one side and the Hui on the other, prevented any cooperation that could have potentially resulted in the creation of a unified Islamic state in the nineteenth century. Nevertheless, many Hui escaped to what is now Xinjiang following the uprisings or because of famines or natural catastrophes. The hostilities rooted in their ethnic backgrounds did not pose a threat to the central government. On the contrary, the Hui acted as conveyors of elements of the Han Chinese culture and as middlemen between the Turkic and Han peoples. During the Qing dynasty, Hui people served as local government officials in Xinjiang, and they were generally stricter toward the Turkic people than the Han officials were.[8] The Turkic peoples, unlike the Hui, were subjected to little outside

influence until well into the twentieth century and did not incorporate themselves into Han Chinese society.

c. Special Characteristics of Islam in China

There are two main strains of Islam in China: the Islam of the Hui, arriving
in China by peaceful means through traders and merchants and partially
adapted to Confucian customs; and the Islam of the Turkic peoples, spread
to Central Asia in part by the sword. Whereas the Hui are seen by Han
Chinese primarily as a religious group, not an ethnic one, the Turkic peoples are defined more along the lines of ethnicity, and less so as a religious
grouping.

Religious Elements of the Hui

Since the eighteenth century, the northwestern Chinese Hui can be defined
as adherents of either *xinjiao* (New Teaching) or *laojiao* (Old Teaching,
Khafiyya). The majority follow the teachings of *laojiao* (with its three sub-
sects), meaning that its worshippers combine the preservation of traditional
practices with the adoption of Han Chinese influences in their orthodox
thought. The term "old" (*gedimu,* from Arab. *qadim,* old), referring to the
Hanafi school of thought, is juxtaposed with "new," from the Sufi reform
movement (Jahriyya).[9] Many of the Muslim communities abiding by the
"Old Teaching" had been assimilated into the Chinese culture, as can be
seen in their adoption of elements of ancestor worship, local spirit worship,
and Chinese funeral rituals.[10] The isolation of China's Muslims from the
Arab world also ties in to this.

The Mecca pilgrims brought the idea of "pure teaching" to China. This
new movement, referred to as *xinjiao,* which meant Jahriyya *tariqa* in the
eighteenth century and was considered an offshoot of the Yasawiyya, was
a Sufi school of thought that arrived in China from Central Asia. The Salar
people brought this teaching to the Hui. It is not a unified school of thought
but rather is subdivided into a number of sects and comprises a plethora of
practices such as ecstatic praying and dancing, divination, the tomb cult,
and the custom of removing shoes at funerals. Today there are still two
main groups of this movement in existence: the Jahriyya and the tomb cult.
The latter has ties to Chinese ancestor worship and the *qubba* cult from
Central Asia.[11] The *xinjiao* movement is more militaristic; during the Qing
dynasty it was already considered the main source of the unrest among the
Muslims.[12] Its followers rejected any form of sinicized Islam and called for
a return to spiritual foundations. The role of the mosques and the might of
the spiritual leaders were to be expanded. *Xinjiao* experienced strong pan-
Islamic periods over the course of its history.[13] Essentially it was a reaction
to the increase in Chinese interference in the religious and social lives of the
Muslims. There has been much bloodshed in interactions between the followers of the various teachings even to this day.[14]

The Hui had no institutionalized religious organization or structure and were organized in vastly self-sufficient communities. These communities gave birth to the *menhuan,* which were brotherhoods whose origins lie in a Sufi founding saint. These *menhuan* were basically a melding of Sufism with Chinese ancestor worship.[15]

In certain areas there was a great degree of synthesis with Han Chinese culture, for example, in terms of ancestor worship, spirit worship, funeral rites and dress, and Confucian ethics. Even the architecture of the mosques in many areas reflected the classical Chinese architectural style, and a system of schooling comparable to that of Han Chinese private schools was adopted in the mosques and used for educating imams.

Religious Particularities of the Turkic Peoples

The ethnic identity of the Turkic peoples is rooted in more than just Islam; nevertheless, religion has always been a crucial driving force for their survival. A distinction needs to be made, however, between the Kazakhs and Kirghiz and the Uighurs. The first two groups blend animistic and shamanistic practices with Islam and in turn are less radical in their religious beliefs, whereas the Uighurs tend to have stronger pan-Turkic and pan-Islamic influences.[16] Among the Turkic peoples in Xinjiang, Sufism plays an ever greater role. Today the Silk Road is witness once again to Muslims dancing the *dhikr,* which they also sometimes view as a war dance for their men.[17] Sufism has contributed to the survival of Islam in China because it does not implicitly require an imam to act as an intermediary between man and God, or even to lead prayers. Its believers can personally connect with God through meditation, yoga, and inner contemplation. For this reason its followers were able to continue practicing it in hiding, even in times of severe oppression. Yet in China as in other Islamic countries, Sufism encounters opposition from many orthodox Islamic institutions. Because the Sufi sects widely refuse to be subject to state control and their actions are considered unorthodox, there is unity in their rejection by most official Islamic representatives and those from the party-state.

Nevertheless, there are similarities between the Hui and the Turkic peoples. Both groups regard themselves a part of the *umma,* the greater community of Muslim believers, especially under conditions that appear to threaten the faith by processes of modernization and immigration. And it is not only the religious foundations and the religious ties of all Muslims in China that are identical. Quite often worshippers from the different ethnic groups will convene in the cities to pray together in a mosque, and some Sufi orders even include members of various ethnic groups. Localized acts of discrimination against Islamic communities quickly trigger the solidarity of Muslim groups from around the country. The return to the marketplace and entrepreneurship has nurtured the emergence of Muslim economic networks once again. Aside from their economic aspect, these networks also serve social and charitable purposes: they support mosques and Islamic schools and contribute to charitable organizations. Recent years have also seen the emergence of private institutions of learning and publishing houses for Muslims.[18]

d. East Turkistan (Xinjiang): Main Region of Conflict

Since the nineteenth century there have been attempts to create an independent state in Xinjiang. One main reason is the incursion of Russia (and China) into Central Asia, which resulted in a fragmentation of its peoples and groups through arbitrarily drawn borders. Aided by the British, the Russians, and the kingdom of East Turkistan, Yaqub Beg, an Uzbek khan, attempted to found an Islamic nation with its capital in Kashgar in the mid-nineteenth century. This region had been largely independent for nearly sixteen years until it was reconquered by the Chinese army in 1876–1878. The uprisings that reemerged following the Chinese Revolution in 1911 were part of an attempt to create an independent state. By the 1930s there were rebellions in eastern and southern Xinjiang aspiring to create an Islamic republic. At the end of 1933 the East Turkistan Republic was proclaimed in Kashgar. The help of the Soviet Union was eventually required to quash these rebellions. In return for this support Moscow availed itself of privileges and special rights. The Kazakhs revolted in 1944 with the support of the Soviet Union. In the same year that Chinese troops crushed this revolt, a new uprising resulted in the foundation of yet another East Turkistan Republic. Once again the Chinese communists had to rely on help from the Soviet Union to integrate Xinjiang into the People's Republic.[19] By the end of 1951 the new central government had crushed all forms of resistance in the region. The result was a mass exodus. Tens of thousands of Uighurs and other Turkic peoples are believed to have been executed.

Even to this day there are periodic uprisings motivated by the political and religious unrest in Xinjiang. The protests became more radical when the Central Asian countries gained independence from the former Soviet Union and state-led forces attempted to limit the influence of religion. According to the Chinese minister of public security there were twelve active separatist movements in the mid-1990s in Xinjiang. Ties to Turkey and the respective organizations in the Central Asian republics are known. The party leaders from Xinjiang described the situation in 1998 as extremely serious and critical.[20] In *Qiushi*, the theoretical journal of the Chinese Communist Party, an article marking the fortieth anniversary of the founding of the autonomous region points out that separatism and the fight against it have long existed in Xinjiang and will continue to do so. Furthermore, the author writes, this fight is "extremely harsh" and even "caustic,"[21] thus highlighting the threat of the separatist movement. In recent years the region has been constantly unsettled by bombings, guerrilla attacks, protests, and demonstrations and the repressive measures taken by the authorities in response to them.[22] The United States even demonstrated its willingness in 2002 to include the East Turkistan Islamic Movement on its list of international terrorist movements, despite initial reluctance.

China endeavored in 1996 to establish the Shanghai Cooperation Organization—which counts Russia, China, Uzbekistan, Kazakhstan, Kyrgyzstan, and Tajikistan as members—as a mechanism for fighting "separatism, terrorism, and religious extremism." The first joint military exercises carried out by several members of this organization took place in 2003 in Xinjiang, among other locations. The primary goal there was the "fight against terrorism." At the end of 2003 the Ministry for Public Security published a list proclaiming four organizations and eleven individuals to be terrorist organizations or persons involved in terrorism.[23] The publication of this list accompanied a request to the international community to support China in its fight against terrorism. Because no reliable evidence for the claim of terrorism has been put forth, it is suspected that Beijing is trying to justify its own actions in Xinjiang under the guise of fighting terrorism.

Yet at the same time, Beijing does fear protests from its Muslim population with regard to international events. The Islamic Association of China, the official umbrella organization representing Chinese Muslims nationwide, called for Chinese Muslims to refrain from organizing antiwar protest events during the Iraq War in March 2003. Chinese foreign policy, which rejects the war, is also said to be in the interests of the Muslims in China.[24] This call came in reaction to individual Muslim protests in various parts of China.

e. The Renaissance of Islam and the Growing Sense of Ethnicity in Xinjiang

At the beginning of the 1950s all Muslim organizations were consolidated under the state-controlled Islamic Association. It was intended to act as a link between religious believers and the state and monitor the inner workings of the various religious groups. By the end of the decade a ban had been placed on traditional associations such as Sufi brotherhoods and the previously mentioned *menhuan*. Eventually the mosques were either closed or destroyed during the Cultural Revolution. It became illegal to study the Qur'an and to perform circumcisions. And in some cases religious believers were even forced into pig breeding.

The introduction of the reform polices at the end of the 1970s heralded a "renaissance" of Islam in China. For example, a survey of villages in the Kashgar district (southern Xinjiang) in the 1990s revealed that more than 90 percent of the local population was regularly participating in religious activities, with the figures for rural areas being higher than those for urban areas. A study of Kazakh villages in the Yili district (northern Xinjiang) showed that even "activists" (of the Communist Party), "model workers," and officials were participating in religious activities. In Hui villages 70 to 80 percent of party members were actively religious by the mid-1980s, even though party members are strictly forbidden to practice any religion actively.

This fact was magnified by pressure religious believers placed on nonbelievers. Some believers would even refuse to shake hands with nonbelieving members of their own nationality, visit them on holidays or other festive days, or attend their funerals. Authorities complained that religious activities in southern Xinjiang were nearly out of control. It is said that there were only five thousand mosques in the Kashgar district in 1978. By the 1990s there were ten thousand (with all mosques doubling as schools for believers, that is, religious schools). By comparison the number of state schools dropped substantially.[25] From the Chinese point of view the magnitude of Islamic law (applied by the imams), Muslim (polygamous) marriages, and sermons against the planned birth policy had become alarming.[26]

Even the importance and prestige of the imams (Pers. *akhund,* teacher, cleric) had increased significantly. A survey of grade-school children in a locality in Xinjiang found, for example, that more than 60 percent of those polled listed *akhund* as their desired profession.[27] The *akhund* (*akhond*) generally play a greater role in Muslim communities than local party or government officials. His cooperation or approval is sought for all important municipal events (such as family planning, education, local elections, public safety), and local government offices often ask the *akhund* to communicate important political measures and decisions to worshippers following Friday prayer.[28]

The Chinese authorities assert that a "too liberal stance" toward Islam in recent years is to blame for the rise in separatist and Islamist movements. A growing number of Qur'an schools supposedly propagate blatant "separatist ideas," especially the independence of Xinjiang and the renewed foundation of an East Turkistan Republic. Tens of thousands of Muslim nationals have passed through these schools in recent years. The majority of the party members, cadre, and teachers have turned to Islam; the proportion of believers in these groups varies between 50 and 100 percent. In Kashgar four-fifths of all retired party functionaries pursued religious activities. A large number of these officials are even active as imams. The figures for teachers tell a similar story. To some degree young people attending school were awarded the title of "Three Goods" student (actually intended for students who, aside from being diligent in classwork, also excelled in serving socialism and the people) only if they would participate in the five prescribed daily prayers. In several learning institutions prayers were held on a regular basis, and there were readings from the Qur'an.[29]

Against this backdrop, measures limiting religious activities were decreed at the beginning of the 1990s. The "Provisional Regulations on the Administration of Religious Activities in the Xinjiang Uighur Autonomous Region" mandated that no one "is permitted to use religion to conduct activities aimed at opposing the leadership of the CCP [Chinese Communist Party], the socialist system, the democratic dictatorship of the people, Marxism-Leninism, and Mao Zedong Thought [i.e., the Four Basic Principles, which are anchored in the constitution], splitting the motherland, and destroying unity among all nationalities." In addition, "no one is permitted to use places for religious activities to organize secret ties, to incite people to create disturbances, or to invoke counterrevolutionary activities." Also "religious feudalist privileges" such as imposed taxes and financial apportionments, required work without pay or donations made against people's will, settling of disputes by religious leaders, missionary activities, private religious schooling, listening to foreign religious broadcasts, and contact with religious organizations outside China were strictly banned.[30] These "Provisional Regulations" required the religious leaders and clerics "to live in harmony on the basis of patriotism," educate religious believers in a manner conducive to the party, and keep the relevant organizations on temple and church activities informed on a regular basis. Once a year the activities and actions of this group of people are subject to monitoring, and appropriate measures are to be taken if punishment, praise, or correction is due. The running of Qur'an schools and religious education for persons under eighteen were prohibited.[31]

f. Beijing and Islam

Without doubt Beijing has been making efforts since the end of the 1970s to tone down policies targeted at Islam. Economic liberalization is only one aspect. Procuring investments and development aid from Islamic countries and the desire for foreign policy support from these nations are two additional reasons. Furthermore China is increasingly dependent on oil imports from Islamic countries to supply its demand for energy, and it is thus interested in maintaining good relations with these countries. Nevertheless, the liberalization policy led to new patterns of conflict. Inasmuch as the Islamic nationalities share the basic values of Islam and the Qur'an—which also is a reaction to the modernization process considered to come from outside (that is, from the Han Chinese) and perceived by some as of foreign origin, as well as the inundation of Muslim-inhabited areas by Han Chinese through immigration—the central government attempts to make use of Islam to promote its "law and order" thinking. D. E. MacInnis writes: "The moral principles of Islam which urge people to give up bad habits and practice good behavior are, objectively speaking, helpful, regardless of the motive of the speaker, in bringing bad social norms under control. Good social norms teach people to be good citizens and abide by the law."[32] Other observers detect an ambivalence in Islam toward economic development as on the one hand building confidence while on the other hand promoting an attitude "based on destiny."[33]

Yet as can be seen, the Muslim nationalities can be split into two main groups, one that appears to be essentially integrated into Chinese society (Hui and other non-Turkish Muslims) and another in which separatist tendencies are swelling (Turkic peoples). The latter group is a latent threat for China because without the loyalty of the Muslims, the west of China is a crisis zone in terms of strategic measures and policies. Furthermore there is one trait that both groups have in common: no other ethnic minority considers itself superior to the Han to the extent that some of the Muslim ethnic groups do, in particular those that also continue to view themselves as true believers and the Han Chinese as "idolaters" or "infidels." This also holds true for the Hui, who do actually regard themselves as part of the Chinese nation. As one Hui put it, the Han are "people lacking Arab and Islamic blood."[34] In turn, the Han Chinese regard the cultures of the Muslim minorities with scorn because they reject two pillars of Chinese cuisine (pork and alcohol) and use a "secretive language," Arabic, for their religion and they dismiss Confucian values such as ancestor worship.[35] The traditional view has been that anyone rejecting Confucian values was not part of (Chinese) civilization. If there is an ethically based (and Islamic) barrier for the Han in the eyes of the Turkic peoples, then in the eyes of the Hui it is primarily an Islamic one. Faithful Muslims are not capable of living as members of the social community because of the ban on patronizing Han restaurants, accepting invitations to dine with Han (because they consume pork), and drinking alcohol, in effect creating separate lifestyles and spheres of living. Therefore the assimilation policy with regard to Islamic nationalities is ultimately a failure.

A development transpired in May 1989 when, for the first time ever, members of all Islamic groups in China demonstrated together nationwide against a book on Muslim sexual customs, criticizing it as offensive to Islam. The book portrayed minarets as phallic symbols, Muslim graves and domes as the "mound of Venus," and pilgrimages to Mecca as "orgies," and it interpreted the taboo placed on the consumption of pork as sexually inspired. Three thousand Muslims took to the streets in Beijing, and in the Hui-dominated northwestern Chinese cities there were hundreds of thousands who demonstrated. The protests in the northwest in particular led to unrest, which the authorities met with moderate measures for fear of potentially escalating matters with a dictate from Beijing. The book was prohibited and destroyed, and the editors responsible for it were punished.

These types of protests are not new to China, yet they gained a new quality in 1989. First, all the Muslim nationalities were involved. Second, the radical fundamentalist actions taking place abroad (such as the death threats against Salman Rushdie) had their counterparts in China, giving Islam in China a new transnational dimension.[36] Third, the type and content of the protests indicated a radicalization of the Islamic movement in

China. Fourth, the state exercised extreme restraint out of national as well as international concerns and did not take action against the protests at any point. And finally, the Chinese Muslims realized that their success meant they could be a formidable force when acting in concert.

g. Conclusion

The broader picture indicates that the lines of conflict are growing. Not only are international constellations at work here. Social, political, and economic factors also play a role, such as the increasing disparities in the level of development between east and west China, insufficient rights of self-rule, unchecked levels of Han Chinese immigration, rigid population policies, and ecological destruction. Furthermore, there are cultural and re- ligious rifts (dissatisfaction over the interference in matters of religion and local traditions, contradictions between Confucianism and socialist-Islamic beliefs) that play out here too. This dissatisfaction is fueled further by the cultural colonialism reflected in education, which propagates the values of the Han Chinese while virtually ignoring the culture and history of the Mus- lim peoples, and in the job market, which demands a good command of the Chinese language and general behavior deemed acceptable by the Chinese people, just to name two examples. The titular nation of the Uighurs may be the nationality with the greatest numbers in Xinjiang, yet the Han Chi- nese dominate the more modern social sectors, such as science, technology, administration, the industrial workforce, and the military. The Han are the most important leaders and decision makers there (in the party, in the mili- tary), even though they are formally assigned a native-born person as an official superior.

The traditional stance of the state with respect to religion may also play a part here. Religions have always been suspect in traditional China. For one thing, the Chinese never developed their own version of a religion of redemption. For another, philosophical Confucianism put religion on a level with superstition. Religious practice was subjected to rigid control because religious activities often gave rise to parallel structures of power that were a threat to the state. If they were deemed to serve the principles of the state and remained loyal, they were tolerated; otherwise they were persecuted. The communists were able to latch on to this perception of re- ligion as something foreign, coming from without, a threat to the state that gained influence particularly in periods of internal weakness. Throughout the history of the republic, religion has been equated with superstition, just as religion has supported hostility toward the state. A big-character poster from the time of the Cultural Revolution stated that Muslims would no longer be able to mask themselves behind their religion. Words "muttered" in Arabic were considered anti-Chinese, so Muslims should not waste time in prayer either.[37] Although today's policy is more moderate, this sentiment continues to have the same effect.

It is not a likely scenario that China would experience a collapse as seen in the Soviet Union. The situation in the former USSR was very different. The creation of an independent East Turkistan would be possible only if extreme changes in domestic policy and massive support from abroad occurred. Those advocating independence, and who were encouraged by the success in Chechnya during the first war against Russia after the breakup of the Soviet Union, are also aware of that fact. For this reason Moscow's brutal hardline response to Chechnya was welcomed by Beijing, for if the Russian military were victorious, that would likely discourage any movement for independence by the Turkic people in China.

Xinjiang is of vital importance to China. In addition to having vast and valuable deposits of raw materials, it has converted Beijing into a regional player in Central and western Asia, in turn boosting China's geostrategic importance. If the political situation remains relatively steady, Beijing will quash any attempts to break free. Moreover, the supremacy of present-day China, unlike Russia, in terms of sheer numbers is too great to be weakened by the emergence of corrosion in domestic policy. Yet the political leadership lacks any empathy for the problems regarding nationalities and religions. On the fortieth anniversary of the founding of the Xinjiang Autonomous Region it declared: "Xinjiang would never have been liberated had it not been for the Communist Party. There would also not have been a new Xinjiang."[38]

The involvement of individual Uighurs in support of the Taliban regime in Afghanistan, in Chechnya, and for al-Qaʻida has gained some attention. These were, however, only small minorities, not mass movements. One factor here might also be the fact that Islam as it is practiced by the Uighurs draws strongly from elements of Sufism, and the Uighurs tend to reject radical Islamist forms of Islam. At the same time, Beijing exploited this development to criminalize and persecute other forces moving peacefully toward independence or even greater self-determination.[39]

It appears, however, that it would be nearly impossible to change policy on religion and nationalities (the latter referring in particular to the question of Islam) without the democratization of China from the ground up. There is no chance for a democratic policy on nationalities and religion in an authoritarian state. There may be attempts in particular by the Turkic people in Xinjiang—mainly the Uighurs—to break away from China. The matter is somewhat different for the Hui. The religious communities are at risk of declining because they make up only a small percentage of the overall population, and the pressure to modernize that engulfs them is tremendous. Where this is not the case, Islam becomes more radical, in part through antimodernization ideologies. For this reason, despite its weaknesses and partial splintering, Islam will remain a challenge for all of the Chinese leadership.

Translated by David Fenske

6. India

(Munir D. Ahmed)

Muslims make up the largest religious minority in the Republic of India, accounting for 12 percent of its population. Numbering more than 140 million, they are the largest Islamic minority in a non-Islamic state. They have always been a minority, even over the centuries when large parts of the Indian subcontinent were ruled by Muslim sovereigns and India was considered an Islamic state. In terms of ethnicity, around 80 percent of them are Indians whose ancestors converted over the course of time to Islam. The remaining 20 percent are descendants of immigrants who arrived in India in the wake of Muslim armies. These include Arabs, Persians, Afghans, and Turkish peoples who have nominally retained their ethnic identity but are otherwise fully integrated into Indian society.[1]

Remnants of Hinduism—including superstition and mythology—are a real part of Muslim society in India. Indeed for many converts, their status as Muslims has brought little in the way of change besides the designation itself. This was evident in the 1930s in Rajputana, for example, when Hindu zealots launched a successful campaign to win back farmers who had converted to Islam (the Shuddhi movement). These converts had remained Hindu in their way of life. With some caveats, this is more or less true for the majority of Indian Muslims. Many, for example, prefer local custom to Islamic law (shari'a) in inheritance matters in order to prevent female family members from inheriting property.

The Hindu caste system probably played a role in many decisions to convert. For low-ranking and disadvantaged castes, Islam must have seemed like a lifeline. Islamic society is egalitarian, even though in India it displays certain features of a caste system. The lines between its castes are not rigid, however, and can occasionally be crossed. More important, it has no untouchables or outcastes who are excluded from social interaction. Caste membership plays a role in forging family alliances, in part because of the sense of superiority associated with one's own caste or subcaste, but even more so in ensuring cohesion among kinship group, clan, and family. The general assumption is that marrying outside one's kinship group will result in social incompatibility. Even among castes that are considered of equal standing, unwritten yet fixed rules can still dictate or influence whether intermarriage is permitted. Many people refuse to give their daughters to members of other castes otherwise viewed as equal, although the men might well take women from that same caste as wives.[2]

The partition of India into the Union of India and Pakistan at Independence in 1947 represented a turning point for Muslims on the subcontinent. The call for a separate state was raised by the All India Muslim League (IML), which was the most significant albeit not the only Muslim party. Its political leadership had traditionally been held by individuals who believed in an integrated nation of all Indians and were thus natural allies of the Indian National Congress (INC). This viewpoint was shared by many Muslim scholars from Deoband who were engaged in active resistance to the colonial power. The political organization of Islamic clerics, the Jamʿiyyat ʿUlamaʾ-i-Hind (JUH), was also convinced that Muslims should join with the INC in the struggle for independence instead of undermining it by calling for a separate state.[3] For them, the partition of India and the founding of Pakistan represented a bitter setback. Millions of Muslims emigrated to Pakistan. Among them were those who had originally rejected the idea of a separate Islamic state.[4] These included the founder of the Jamaʿat-e-Islami (JI), Maulana Abu l-Aʿla Maududi, who opposed partition because the chance to Islamize India would thereby be lost. Following Independence, he had to move his residence to Pakistan. Similarly, the only recourse left to the Majlis Ahrar-i Islam, which had been engaged primarily in opposing the Ahmadiyya, was to move to Pakistan, where it continued to pursue political agitation with a religious gloss although it had to stop functioning as a political party.

a. Distrust of Muslims

Following Independence, Indian Muslims found themselves in a difficult situation owing to frequently raised doubts about their loyalty to the Union of India. These doubts were certainly based to some extent on Muhammad ʿAli Jinnah's "Two Nations Theory," which defined Muslims and Hindus as separate nations. Had not the overwhelming majority of Muslims in British-ruled India voted for a separate state? How could or should the memory of this be erased after Independence? For Hindu nationalists, it was clear that Muslims could never be loyal to the Union of India. As a result, Muslim clerics called upon their fellow believers to emigrate to Pakistan if they harbored any sympathies for the country. Those who did not were advised to break off relations with Pakistan, including family ties. By 1948 a conference held in Lucknow of all major Islamic organizations had already passed a resolution not to establish any separate Islamic political parties. The IML, whose leadership had relocated to Pakistan by that time, had discontinued its work in India anyway. Maulana Abu l-Kalam Azad, who as education minister was a member of the Indian government as well as vice president of the ruling INC party, appealed to his fellow believers to join the INC on the grounds that it alone could offer Muslims protection and security.[5] At the same time, the JUH decided to limit itself to addressing Muslim religious concerns and pursuing social welfare activities. For the first time it began offering membership to non-clerics, and also invited non-Muslim speakers to its meetings. Moreover, it broke off all ties to party offices located on Pakistani territory. In 1958 it called on Muslims not to make any political demands for the subsequent two to five years, but instead to concentrate on building up the country. To a large extent this call for political abstinence was heeded. The JI broke off from its mother party in Pakistan and decided to discontinue all political activity from that point on, including both passive and active participation in parliamentary elections.[6]

The question occupying Indian Muslims after Independence was that of their relationship to the Hindu majority with whom they lived together in a single state. Clerics compared the situation to the time of Muhammad, when the city-state of Medina was inhabited by both Muslims and Jews. The two communities had a written agreement (*mithaq madina*) stating that they were free to pursue their respective rites and obligations. Together they formed one nation (*qawm*) with Muhammad at its head. With reference to that period, there was talk in India of an "agreement" between the Hindu majority and the Muslim minority, namely the constitution, which stipulated that the state was secular and consequently neutral in religious matters. Secularism, however, was interpreted differently by different groups of Muslims. Some saw secularism as a negation of religion, and therefore unacceptable. Others held that religion was a personal matter for each individual, and as such something for secularism to respect. The third group, which included a conspicuously large number of clerics, was of the opinion that the secular state was legally bound to neutrality regarding religions, and that this offered the best chance for survival given the country's overwhelming Hindu majority.

Secularism was the object of passionate discussion among the Hindu population as well, particularly given the fact that Hindu fundamentalism, which had begun to form long before Independence, was anticipating new opportunities to spread. Like Islam, Hinduism addresses all aspects of life and originally knew no separation between religion and politics. The militant Rashtriya Swayamsevak Sangh (RSS) seeks to transform India into a Hindu empire. It rejects the idea of an integrated nation composed of different peoples and religious communities. As far as it is concerned, the Indian nation can consist only of Hindus, and those wishing to belong to it must accept Hinduism. Interestingly, Maududi, who would later call for Pakistan to become an Islamic state, had advised Hindus to establish the Union of India as a Hindu state. Asked what rights Muslims would have in this state, he responded that Muslims should be treated as a religious minority and that they should be satisfied with the rights designated for non-Hindus. Presumably he was unable to imagine that Hindu fundamentalism would one day go so far as to deny basic rights to religious minorities.

The greatest concern currently facing Indian Muslims is the frequent attacks by Hindu fanatics on their homes, businesses, places of worship, and cultural facilities. The worst massacre up to that time occurred in Gujarat in March 2002. It took the lives of more than one thousand Muslims and was not just tolerated but actively supported by the state government. An earlier massacre had taken place on December 6, 1992, in connection with the razing of the Babri mosque in Ayodhya. Fear of Hindu fundamentalism spread as a result. Other religious communities such as such as Sikhs, Christians, and Buddhists are also the objects of religious intolerance. But these groups are not the targets of fanatics as are Muslims, who are expected to suffer for what their ancestors supposedly inflicted on the Hindu population when they ruled India.[7]

b. Secularism and Muslims

The majority of Indian Muslims support secularism, although these supporters may be divided into two groups. The first is a product of the modern educational system; its adherents favor a new interpretation of Islam that allows it to adapt to the exigencies of modern life. Although commonly known as modernists on account of their affirmation of modern life, they seek hardly any radical reforms of Islamic doctrine. The second group is led by clerics, who exert a much greater influence over the masses than the modernists. When in doubt, Muslims traditionally turn to leading religious schools for support and advice in the form of a legal decision (fatwa). Recently, for example, many questions have been posed regarding sterilization (for men as well as women) as a means of family planning. The debate on whether insurance is permissible from a religious standpoint also arose from questions raised by concerned Muslims. This would indicate that Indian Islamic society continues to be religiously influenced. Muslims who set store by their religious traditions are prepared to accept new ideas and changes to their lifestyle only if such changes are found to be compatible with these traditions. The sole reason why clerics approve of the secularism underlying the Indian constitution is that it protects the interests of Muslims. It is what provides the guarantee that the Hindu majority cannot transform the country into a Hindu state, which might well have no place for Muslims. Apart from that, Islamic clerics in Pakistan and other Muslim states place secularism on a par with nonreligiosity.[8]

The clerics by no means constitute a homogeneous bloc. During British colonial rule they were divided into two major groups. Those who participated actively in the struggle for freedom and thus were viewed as rebels were known as "clerics of truth" (*'ulama'-i haqq*). The others were called "clerics of evil" (*'ulama'-i su'*) on account of their alleged collaboration with the rulers. The individual who coined these terms was none other than Abu l-Kalam Azad, who himself was later condemned as a collaborator on account of his ministerial position in Nehru's cabinet. In contrast to him, many clerics retained their independence by founding religious schools (madrasas), for which they did not seek support from the state. Nor did the constitution of the Union of India permit government support of religious instruction. They thus became the real leaders in the eyes of the Muslim population. Paradoxically, the secular nature of the state serves to strengthen the claims to leadership of those clerics who work outside the parliament and other state institutions. Parliamentary activity is reserved for others, generally from the modernist camp, who tend to do more harm than good in the name of Indian Muslims. Voters' trust in them has tended not to increase but rather to diminish over time. This has been evident in discussions on the necessity of adapting Islamic law (shariʿa) to the country's legal system, which is supported by the modernists but rejected by the clerics.

c. State Law and Shariʿa

Muslims are generally of the opinion that shariʿa covers all areas of life, and also that all Muslims should strive to base their lives on shariʿa. Indian Muslims view efforts to introduce shariʿa in Pakistan as important and worthy of emulation. Yet for them this can only be a dream, because the Indian constitution stands in the way. Personal law is the one area in which Muslims are allowed a separate legal system, and this does not correspond to shariʿa in all respects though inspired by it.[9] Having been formulated under colonial rule, the Muslim Personal Law (Shariat Act) of 1937 is unpopular with many people. But when a personal law code was introduced for Hindus (Hindu Code Bill of 1955) and the question arose whether the state should redraft the code for Muslims as well, there were vehement protests by Muslims. The Islamists held that the Hindu majority in parliament is not qualified to deal with shariʿa. For political reasons, therefore, the Indian government did not seek to standardize its personal law code for all citizens. One result of this debate, however, was to reveal that the modernists categorically rejected the Muslim Personal Law as backward. The radicals among them called for annulling the separate personal law code for Muslims, which they saw as an obstacle to integration into Indian society. They found the legality of polygamy for Muslims outdated because monogamy had long since become established. And they supported the advancement of women in society, which is possible within the framework of shariʿa only if some fundamental changes are made to it. To support their position, they drew attention to similar endeavors in other Islamic countries. But the Islamists stuck to their position that the secular Indian state is not entitled to make changes to the personal law code for Muslims. And they themselves saw no reason to do so.

Two written proposals were submitted by the modernist side to change the Muslim personal law code. Asaf A. A. Fayzi (Fyzee) suggested establishing a family law court with jurisdiction over matters of marriage and divorce. To limit abuses, he proposed a mandatory marital contract that specifies the partners' legally binding rights and obligations. Danial Latifi, by contrast, called for a general prohibition on both polygamy and divorce by repudiation, as well as on the veil. This posed a dilemma for the clerics. The JI appointed an expert commission and charged it with listing all the areas in which changes are necessary as well as feasible under shariʿa. The renowned Dar al-ʿulum theological college in Deoband sent a catalogue of queries to clerics and legal experts in order to gather their views and wishes regarding potential modifications to the personal law code. For their part, the clerics wanted parliament to accept without any restrictions the draft legislation proposed by the Muslim side.

This exchange intensified in 1985 in connection with the lawsuit brought by Shah Bano, a woman whose husband had left her after many years of marriage. He had divorced her by repudiation and based his rejection of her claim for maintenance on shari'a. Shah Bano went to court, and her claim was upheld. The court ordered that her divorced husband make payments of 25 rupees a month, a sum later raised to 179 rupees by the Supreme Court of Madhya Pradesh. The ex-husband's appeal based on the Muslim Personal Law was later rejected. In the eyes of the clerics, this constituted state interference in shari'a legislation. They organized street protests and compelled the state to back down.

In 1986 parliament passed the Muslim Women's Protection of the Right of Divorce Bill, which denied Muslim women the right to sue for maintenance on the basis of the Criminal Procedure Code.[10] In October 1993 the All India Muslim Personal Law Board, consisting of 151 public figures, announced the creation of Islamic courts (Arab. *qadi* courts), which can be used by Muslims for personal law issues. This was an attempt to prevent ordinary courts from interceding in family law for Muslims. It was prompted by a decision made previously by a committee of *ahl-i hadith* ("followers of the hadith," because they take it as their main source of law) denying the validity of three declarations of divorce pronounced in immediate succession; at most the three can be viewed as a single declaration, which can then be taken back.[11] Among Indian Muslims a consensus holds that while this means of divorce may not be entirely fair, it nevertheless effects a permanent separation.

This dubious victory by the clerics over the civil courts cannot hide the fact that their scope of influence in certain areas has been greatly limited by legislators. According to the Special Marriage Act of 1954, for example, Muslims of either sex can enter into marriage with members of other religions without either partner having to change his or her religion. Children of these marriages enjoy all the rights of those from marriages in which both partners are members of the same religion. They have full inheritance rights. According to this act, marriages are not subject to the inheritance rules of the spouses' respective religious communities. Spouses inherit from each other and may specify the other as sole heir. In the clerics' view this contradicts Islamic law, which prohibits marriage between a Muslim and a non-Muslim if the latter is not from a religion of the book. Furthermore, non-Muslims, whether male or female, may not inherit from a Muslim. They also consider it strictly forbidden for a Muslim woman to marry outside Islamic society. By passing the Special Marriage Act, legislators minimized the potential impact of the religious communities and clamped down on the sanctions imposed by them.

d. Changed Social Conditions

Islamic society in India faces serious problems and radical change. Cohesion in the Muslim community is crumbling to an ever greater degree. Many of the men with the most mobility and material means have emigrated to Pakistan or left India to pursue their fortunes in the Near East or the West. The resulting lacunae are visible everywhere. The fact that Muslim women are increasingly marrying non-Muslim men is ascribed not least of all to this phenomenon. In a few cases the bride's family succeeds in having the groom convert nominally to Islam in order to avoiding offending relatives' religious sensibilities and to ensure that the family's good name does not suffer. Statistics on mixed marriages are not available, but one may assume that they number in the hundreds of thousands. Children of these marriages generally distance themselves from both religious communities. Religious instruction is not allowed in the schools. Private instruction is generally not pursued either, including in families in which both parents are Muslims.

Urdu was traditionally the most common language in northern India and beyond, spoken by Muslims and Hindus alike. It was the nationalists who made Hindi the language of the liberation movement and subsequently the national language of India. For its part, Urdu became the language of the Pakistan movement and thus the language of Muslims. As far as the spoken idiom is concerned, there is not a large difference between Urdu and Hindi. Where the languages diverge, however, is in their written forms. Urdu uses an expanded Arabic-Persian script and Hindi the Devanagari script. After Hindi was declared the national language of India, Urdu fell into the category of minority languages. Numerous protests and lengthy parliamentary debates ensued before Urdu was declared one of the country's eighteen official languages. With the exception of Muslim schools in some states, Urdu is not taught in the educational system. As a consequence, the younger generation of Muslims can no longer read the books of their ancestors. The number of books published in Urdu is dropping off at a relentless rate. Muslim children are compelled to learn Hindi in the schools in order to prepare for positions in the civil service. This means that the number of people who read Urdu is constantly declining. (An estimate in 1992 suggested that only 10 percent of the 25 million Muslims in Uttar Pradesh, whose native language is Urdu, could actually read it.) Urdu continues as a spoken language, but it is unclear whether the script will survive.[12] The vocabulary of modern Urdu literature is taking an increasingly evident turn from Persian-Arabic to Sanskrit. Moreover, major Urdu authors are moving toward having their work published in Devanagari. Urdu forms the bridge to Pakistan, where, though not native, it serves as the national language.

In the area of education and training, a conspicuous decline is evident among Muslims.[13] To what extent this derives from the indisputable discrimination they face is an open question. The fact remains that their literacy rate—42 versus 54 percent for the overall population, and for women 11 versus 39.42 percent—is disproportionately low. (An exception seems to be Gujarat, where the Muslim literacy rate of 73 percent is higher than the overall population's 68.3 percent; Muslim women also outpace Hindu women there at 63.5 and 56 percent, respectively.) Does the higher level of illiteracy really derive from a lesser desire to learn on the part of Muslims, as is occasionally suggested, or do the reasons lie elsewhere, such as in a disturbed social symmetry? The upper and middle classes have been greatly reduced by emigration. Muslims are primarily engaged in farming, crafts, and the trades or are day laborers for whom the struggle to survive encourages an early decision to learn a trade. School enrollment takes place on a selective basis (Muslims make up on 2 percent of pupils although they constitute 12 percent of the population), and Muslims generally do not spend very many years at school. Moreover, they show a distinct preference for religious schooling, which usually starts at the local mosque and is then continued at madrasas, which private initiatives have established at an increasing rate since the Union of India was founded.[14] Education at these schools is not geared toward selecting a future occupation, and can also be discontinued at any time. Girls are largely excluded because they are prohibited from attending the boys' schools, and corresponding segregated institutions for them do not exist. The reason for the relatively low percentage of Muslims who hold university degrees (only 2 percent of engineers and 2.5 percent of physicians in India are Muslim) could be that they make up a disproportionately small share of the middle class; and as is well known, a society's middle class produces the majority of its university graduates. In contrast to the trajectory in Hindu society since Independence, which shows a strong increase in the size of the middle class, the Muslim middle class has grown by a barely perceptible degree. The lower middle class has taken a very long time to recover from the bloodletting following Independence. Only in the last few decades have its members acquired sufficient financial stability to consolidate and expand their position in society.

Sayyid Ahmad Khan (1817–1898), who can truly be described as a reformer on account of his educational writings, founded the Mohammedan Anglo-Oriental College in Aligarh in 1876 and sincerely attempted to raise awareness among Muslims that progress cannot be made without embracing the modern sciences. This college grew into today's Aligarh Muslim University, which is no longer a purely Islamic institute of higher education. It depends on financial support from the state and thus enjoys no appreciable academic freedom in religious matters. The situation was no different before Independence, which is why nationalist forces left the university in 1920 and founded the Jami'a Milliyya Islamiyya, which subsequently moved to Delhi and is now considered a prestigious university. After Independence, however, it had to relinquish its purely Islamic status. The third Islamic college in India was the Osmaniya University in the principality of Hyderabad. It too lost its Islamic character following Independence. Thus India's

Muslims were deprived of their "cadre training grounds" from which most of their leadership had emerged. This left only the religious educational centers, including the most famous college, Dar al-ʿulum in Deoband. It was founded in 1865 by Maulavi Abu l-Qasim Nanautawi to spread the scholarly tradition of Shah Wali Allah. Acquiring a reputation for rejecting colonial power, it became a refuge for nationalist clerics who stood side by side with the INC in the struggle for independence. In contrast to the majority of India's Muslims, these clerics opposed the call to partition the country. The majority of faculty and students at the Aligarh Muslim University, by contrast, supported the Pakistan movement. Many of them left India after Independence to settle in Pakistan.

e. Muslim Political Organizations

Following Independence, India's Muslims appeared to have no recourse but to follow the counsel of Abu l-Kalam Azad and forgo establishing separate political organizations. This was the logical consequence of the elimination of separate voting rights for Muslims. The renowned Muslim leader Rafiʿ Ahmed Qidwa'i, however, opposed Azad's counsel to join the INC; he considered Muslims' interests to be better protected if they were not bound to any political party. The JUH, which had ceased its own political activities, also took this line. It recommended that members weigh the interests of Muslim society—which could differ from region to region—and vote for the party that best represented them. The JI resolved to leave politics altogether, even deciding not to exercise either passive or active voting rights. On account of his prominent position in the government, Azad's counsel was generally followed, and many Muslims joined the INC. Though pleased with their support, the INC nevertheless feared that Muslims might pressure it by voting as a bloc. It therefore rejected all demands by Muslims from the very start. This prompted Sayyid Mahmud to call leading Muslim figures to a conference in 1963 to determine a future course of action. They decided to found a council (Majlis-i Mushawarat) which would meet for advisory purposes on a case-by-case basis. Though expressly declaring itself not a political party, the council did not refrain from advising Muslims to vote for parties willing to address their concerns in place of the INC. In Uttar Pradesh, where Muslims make up 15 percent of the population, a political party called Muslim Majlis was founded which won several provincial parliament seats in the 1969 elections. The ʿAwami Tanzim was founded in the state of Bihar and the Adam Sena and the Muslim League in Delhi. The most successful of these was the Indian Union Muslim League, which is native to southern India. In Kerala, where Muslims make up 19.5 percent of the population, they had four ministers in the coalition government in 1992. In this state 12 percent of civil service jobs and university admissions are reserved for Muslims. In Hyderabad, by contrast, the Majlis Ittihad al-Muslimin has declined to insignificance.

The break with the Congress Party, which had split in the meantime, came in 1975, when Prime Minister Indira Gandhi declared a state of emergency and thereby aroused the ire of many segments of society, including Muslims. The Muslims switched to the Janata Party (JP), which, although it had won the 1977 elections under the leadership of Jaya Prakash Narayan, was not able to meet their expectations. The Congress (I), as the party of Indira Gandhi was called after splitting from the INC, received support from the JUH, which played a substantial role in regaining Muslims for the Congress (I) and Gandhi's election victory in 1980 through a 1979 campaign to "save the state and people" (*mulk-o millat bachao tahrik*). Whether the 474 pogrom-like attacks against Muslims between 1980 and 1982 in different parts of the country were connected to the party's support for Mrs. Gandhi is difficult to ascertain, yet quite conceivable. It is well known that these attacks were politically as well as religiously motivated.[15] In 1983 elections for the provincial assembly of Assam led to severe unrest, in the course of which more than three thousand Muslims lost their lives. Since then there have been countless pogroms against Muslims, with the instigators making no secret of their long-term plans for India to become a Hindu state. Madhukar Dattatraya Deoras, known as Balasaheb, the head of the RSS, stated in 1984 that his party rejects a nation of different peoples; India is a Hindu nation, and anyone wishing to belong to it must profess Hinduism. There is also talk of accepting Muslim Hindus if they show no outward signs of Islam and integrate visibly into Hindu society. Those not willing to do so must emigrate to Pakistan.[16] Both these alternatives are unacceptable to Muslims. Giving up Islam is no more conceivable than leaving India. An Urdu poet expressed the sentiment in a two-line work: "We will live and die here, / for there will be no second emigration for us." Another slogan often cited by Muslims plagued with existential fears is "Qabristan ya Pakistan"—"Our choice lies between the graveyard and Pakistan."

Muslim society also includes elements who do not shrink from challenging the RSS. One example is the Kerala-based Islamic Sevak Sangh (ISS), which is considered an extremist organization and is said to be responsible for numerous local conflicts between Muslims and Hindus. It was banned in connection with the bloody Hindu-Muslim conflict over the Babri mosque in December 1992—together with the JI, which the authorities also designated a radical organization. On the Hindu side, the RSS and the Vishva Hindu Parishad (VHP), which had largely carried out the destruction of the mosque, were also banned. Shortly thereafter, however, a court revoked the ban on the RSS on the grounds that it had not been formally responsible for razing the mosque. It had welcomed the action, but it left the dirty work to the VHP. In actuality the VHP was created by the RSS to promote global Hinduism. In addition to destroying the Babri mosque, which, it claims, occupied the birthplace of the Hindu god Rama, it calls for converting another three thousand mosques throughout India into Hindu temples. Nevertheless, the role of the RSS in attacks on Muslims in many of the country's cities has remained unexamined, especially the massacres in Mumbai in December 1992 and January 1993 which claimed thousands of Muslim lives. Shortly thereafter a series of bombs exploded at the Stock Exchange, assumed to be perpetrated by Muslims seeking revenge. As usual the desire was to implicate Pakistan, but without presenting concrete evidence.

The Babri mosque conflict had an epilogue in Pakistan, where Hindu temples were destroyed in a number of cities, with human casualties as well. The Pakistani government was supposedly caught unawares by the destructive fury of the masses. It responded in a very hesitant manner, taking days to come to the assistance of besieged religious minorities. In addition to Hindu temples and Sikh *gurdwaras,* some Christian churches were also attacked. The government did, however, undertake to restore the destroyed houses of worship.

The Indian prime minister at the time, Narasimha Rao, promised that his administration would rebuild the Babri mosque at the same location. It was uncertain whether this would ever take place, as nothing was done toward this goal. Rao's cabinet colleague Arjun Singh was not even able to convince the central committee of the governing party that an apology should be made to Muslims as a gesture of reconciliation. Meanwhile, Hindu fundamentalists were laying all the preparations for building a temple to Rama. A temple was in fact erected, although it is not viewed as a replacement for the Babri mosque. Hope is thus ebbing on the part of Muslims who once placed their trust in secularism.

In May 1992 the All India Milli Council (IMC) was founded in Mumbai, viewing itself as a group of leading Muslim figures from throughout the country. In order to avoid sectarian conflicts, the *kalima* (creed) was declared the common denominator for membership. The IMC seeks to promote the lives, property, honor, and cultural identity of Muslims. It does not desire to be a political party, and is therefore active on a nonparliamentary basis. The question has been deliberately left open as to whether the IMC has taken the place of the All India Muslim Majlis Mushawarat (IMMM), which was accused of inaction.

The situation of Muslims in India has never been particularly pleasant.[17] Not only has their loyalty to the state been questioned, but also they have been accused of focusing more on the Islamic world, and especially Pakistan, than on India. It cannot be denied that Indian Muslims do in fact look to a greater degree toward the Islamic world, especially the Gulf states, which offer lucrative employment opportunities. Or they become involved in the Near East conflict on the side of the Palestinians. They register every tremor in the Islamic world at large. They view themselves as a part of the worldwide Islamic *umma,* although they are often denied entry to the corresponding bodies. On the basis of numeric strength—they are the fourth-largest Islamic community in the world—Morocco's King Hasan II invited India to participate in the OIC (Organization of the Islamic Conference) in Rabat in 1979. But instead of sending a representative of the Muslim population who would probably have been accepted, India sent its local ambassador, who, to top it off, was a Sikh. Pakistan's president Muhammad Zia ul-Haq took umbrage and triggered a row by leaving the conference site in protest. He wanted to prevent India in particular, and possibly other non-Muslim countries with sizable Muslim populations, from gaining entry to the OIC at a later date, including what was then the Soviet Union as well as China and Yugoslavia. While this prevented the OIC from swelling in size to become a twin of the Non-Aligned Movement, it also blocked a considerable number of Muslims, specifically those with minority status in their home countries, from exerting influence. Nevertheless, India's Muslims are represented in nongovernmental institutions, such as the Muslim World League, where they are active in a number of bodies, including the Islamic Jurisprudence Council and the Council for Mosques.

f. The Special Case of Kashmir

Kashmir is the only Indian state in which Muslims make up 80 percent of the population. Its permanent legal status is still disputed by India and Pakistan.[18] Pakistan does not recognize Kashmir's accession to the Union of India in the course of Indian independence, claiming that it took place unlawfully. The Hindu ruler at the time acted without determining the wishes of the people, and thus violated the principles of the independence agreement. Aware of this, the Indian government agreed at the UN to hold a plebiscite. This has yet to happen. As a consequence of the popular revolt (1947–1949) in which Pakistani military groups and fighters from tribal areas fought on the side of the Kashmiris, Kashmir was divided de facto along the cease-fire line between India and Pakistan but retained a special status in both countries. In Pakistan this state of affairs continues, although Azad Kashmir forms an independent administrative unit and is not a member of the federal state. Article 370 of the Indian constitution gave Kashmir the status of a state with special rights. The government of Kashmir moved toward a closer association with India, as desired by New Delhi. This was expressed in the state constitution of Kashmir that went into effect in January 1957. It declared Kashmir to be an integral part of the Union of India. Until that time Kashmiri delegates to the Indian parliament were elected indirectly via the Kashmiri Constituent Assembly. The Kashmiri head of state was called the president (*sadr-i riyasat*), and the head of government was given the title of prime minister (*wazir-e a'zam*). As part of the assimilation process with other Union states, these positions were renamed governor and chief minister. Since then Kashmir has been represented in the Indian National Assembly by delegates who are chosen directly by the people in general elections. India has come to view this as an agreement by Kashmir to join the Union of India, rendering a plebiscite on the issue superfluous. This view also appears to have gained considerable acceptance within the UN. At any rate, the UN resolution on the plebiscite is considered obsolete in some quarters.

Kashmiri Muslims form the largest self-contained Muslim population within the Union of India. They are able to practice their religion unhindered and need not take Hindu sensibilities into account. Cows are slaughtered in Kashmir, a practice that Hindus condemn and that regularly leads to bloody strife in other parts of India. At the same time, Islam as a religion is neither challenged nor required to prove itself on a daily basis in Kashmir. An intellectual dialogue with other religions and worldviews, which usually engenders new modes of thought, does not take place there. Instead Kashmir has acquired the reputation of being the state in the Indian Union most plagued by problems and political unrest. The worst local disturbances took place in December 1963, when a holy relic (*hazrat bal*) was stolen from a shrine near Srinagar. Political calculation presumably lay behind the theft. In any event, the turmoil led to polarization and division within the governing All Jammu and Kashmir National Conference (JKNC).

The JKNC, which later took the name National Conference (NC), is the most important party in Kashmir. It originated in the 1930s and rejects any sectarian affiliation. It was closely associated with the INC both during and after the struggle for independence. The Muslim National Conference (MNC), which was close to the IML and supported the latter's call to partition India, split off from it. It was in favor of Kashmir's joining Pakistan and formed the government in liberated Azad Kashmir. In the Indian part of Kashmir another splinter group formed, the Jammu and Kashmir Plebiscite Front (PF), which called for Kashmiri independence or the refusal to join either India or Pakistan. It was replaced by the more radical Jammu and Kashmir Liberation Front (JKLF), which together with other Muslim groups has led a popular insurgency since 1990. In contrast to the JKLF, the Hizb al-Mujahidin (HM) and al-Jihad are expressly Islamic groups that are fighting to establish an Islamic state in Kashmir. It is assumed that their efforts are supported by Pakistan and the Afghan mujahidin. At the Hazrat Bal mosque in September 1993, the All Parties Hurriyat Conference was held with the ʿAwami Majlis-i ʿAmal, Jamaʿat-e-Islami, Jammu and Kashmir Liberation Front, People's Conference, and Muslim Conference particpating. They agreed to coordinate efforts to hold the plebiscite. Because some of the participating parties rejected joining either India or Pakistan, a compromise was allowed by which the plebiscite would also offer the third option of an independent state of Kashmir.

Kashmir is increasingly becoming a survival issue for India. There are fears in New Delhi that a Kashmiri secession would trigger a chain reaction and encourage liberation movements in other parts of India to follow the path of resistance. In particular, it would fuel the armed rebellion by Sikhs fighting for an independent "Khalistan," all the more so because their home state of Punjab borders both Kashmir and Pakistan. In other parts of India this development could unleash a bloodbath between Muslims and Hindus that might prompt an exodus of Muslims from India. In all scenarios, secularism would suffer as the guiding principle of the constitution. The consequence would be Hindu Rashtra, or a Hindu polity as sought by the RSS. Given the increasing degree of fundamentalism among both Hindus and Muslims, which is not bringing the two religious communities closer together but rather goading them into conflict, it is questionable whether peaceful coexistence will be possible at all.

In the summer of 2004 India and Pakistan began holding comprehensive talks on bilateral issues at the undersecretary level. These negotiations were also expected to address the question of Kashmir, a reluctant concession made by India on account of ongoing struggles with the mujahidin since 1989. As an initial confidence-building measure, the parties agreed to institute bus service between Srinagar (India) and Muzaffarabad (Azad Kashmir). This is the first direct link between the two parts of Kashmir. The two sides were brought to this new course by the changing worldwide political situation as well as pressure from the United States.

g. Sects and Currents in Indian Islam

The majority (over 80 percent) of Indian Muslims are Sunnis, and of these the majority follow the Hanafi school of jurisprudence. There are also smaller groups of Shafi'is in southern India and a numerically insignificant number of Hanbalis. The so-called Wahhabis actually belong to the *ahl-i hadith*, who do not feel bound to any of the schools of law, calling themselves "non-imitators" (*ghayr muqallid*) and claiming the freedom to make independent theological and juridical decisions based on the sources of law.[19] In contrast to the Wahhabis on the Arabian Peninsula who follow the Hanbali school, they are closer in essence to the Hanafi school. They follow the path of Shah Wali Allah, the eighteenth-century reformer who sought to remove the remnants of Hinduism from Indian Islam. His teachings influenced nearly all the major Islamic movements in India in the nineteenth and twentieth centuries. These include the tradition of liberal Islam initiated by Sir Sayyid Ahmad Khan (whose adherents were denounced by enemies as Ničiri, or nature worshippers) as well as the Ahmadi movement, whose founder, Mirza Ghulam Ahmad from Qadian—which is why his followers are known as Qadianis—was close to the *ahl-i hadith* in his youth. Although he influenced a large segment of the educated classes, Ahmad Khan did not found any organized theological group or movement of his own.

Mirza Ghulam Ahmad, by contrast, organized the Ahmadiyya Jama'at, which the Pakistani parliament declared to be non-Muslim in 1974. Ahmadis have since been persecuted in Pakistan, and large numbers have therefore emigrated—including their leader Mirza Tahir Ahmad, who left the country secretly in 1984 to escape the threat of imprisonment and execution. He resided in London until his death in April 2003. He was said to have considered moving to Qadian (India), which is considered the eternal center of the Ahmadiyya Jama'at and where a small group of Ahmadis (called Darwish) were holding out. In December 1991 he visited Qadian for the traditional annual gathering, at which the local populace apparently received him with great enthusiasm and encouraged him to return. It is an open question whether the Indian government would have permitted him to do so, and how Hindu fundamentalists would have reacted. He also had to consider whether returning to his place of birth, which he and his family had had to leave in 1947, would have aroused suspicion in Pakistan. It would have called Ahmadi loyalty to Pakistan into question at a time when members were already being accused of collaborating with Israel and other enemies of Islam. Unlike in Pakistan, Ahmadis had not suffered persecution in India, from either Muslims or non-Muslims.

It is notable, albeit certainly not unusual owing to the minority status of Muslims in India, that Islamic subgroups do not engage in the violence that was virtually routine before Independence and continues to erupt in Pakistan to this day. The Shiʿa, who account for 15 to 20 percent of Muslims in India, continue to be the object of strong verbal attacks. Nearly 90 percent of Shiʿis adhere to the "Twelfth Imam" school, which has a history of militant action and does not shy from conflict. The Ismaʿilis and the Bohra-Khojas (see the section on Pakistan in this volume), by contrast, maintain a low profile more in keeping with their mercantile activities. A real war of words blazes among the different groups of Sunnis, especially between the Deobandis and Brailvis. The former are conservative but by no means regressive owing to their origins in the school of Shah Wali Allah. The Brailvis, by contrast, represent the epitome of popular Islam with a syncretistic mixture of superstition and saint worship. They consider themselves to be the true representatives of Islam, which for them is more than a mere religion. The fundamentalists have exploited this passion for their own purposes and have recruited many followers from their ranks.

It is remarkable that the very movement that in many parts of the world is seen as a driving force behind fundamentalism, namely the Tablighi Jamaʿat, was founded by Maulavi Muhammad Ilyas from the Deoband school.[20] He established it in the 1930s to remind Muslims of their obligation to follow conscientiously both the commandments and the injunctions of Islam. The original idea was not deliberately to create an organization, yet it has since grown into one capable of holding annual gatherings attended by millions in India, Pakistan, and Bangladesh. It sends volunteer missionaries (whence the name Tablighi Jamaʿat) to both domestic and foreign destinations for a few days or weeks every year. Out of this revival movement a worldwide organization has developed which is said to back many subversive activities by fundamentalists in Europe and the United States. In many countries it has already established missionary offices for the purpose of converting non-Muslims to Islam.

Islam is clearly on the retreat in India, although spectacular conversions to the religion took place some years ago by Dalits from the caste of untouchables. In 1981, 180 Dalit families from Meenakshipuram in the state of Tamil Nadu converted to Islam. They took on considerable hardships in the process. For example, they lost their rights to free schooling, college scholarships, eligibility for quotas in the civil service, cheap home-building loans, and government land grants. They relinquished all these privileges that membership in a scheduled caste had granted. As Muslims, they no longer belonged to this category and therefore did not enjoy state protection. But as one of their spokespersons put it, they no longer wished to be "second-class citizens," preferring slower progress in their new category to rapid advance with a second-class status. Hindu fundamentalists responded with threats and all kinds of violence to prevent more Dalits from following their example. They accused the Muslim community of having funded this action with petrodollars from the Gulf states. The impetus for converting Dalits in two villages came not from Muslims, however, but rather from the villagers themselves, who sought to leave the caste system after centuries of servitude. Conversion to Christianity, which Dalits had traditionally undertaken starting in the colonial period, had lost its attraction for a number of reasons. Following the angry response to their conversion to Islam, they appear to have been turning to Buddhism of late.

Statistics have not confirmed the notion that the average birthrate of Indian Muslims exceeds that of their Hindu neighbors. But the Bharatiya Janata Party (BJP) is predicting a nightmare for India, claiming that the Muslim population will quadruple by the middle of the twenty-first century and that a further partition will be demanded to found another Muslim state. The party goes on to argue that the only way to prevent this is to make India a Hindu state beforehand which no longer recognizes other nationalities or religious communities.

The Muslims of India are facing difficult times in which even a secular constitution may not be of much help.

Translated by Marlene Schoofs

7. Pakistan

(Khálid Durán and Munir D. Ahmed)

In contrast to countries such as Afghanistan or Malaysia, Pakistan and Bangladesh present Islam with a remarkable identity problem. Pakistan is a melting pot of the cultures of its neighbors. It stands, so to speak, with its back to India and its face to Arabia. The Indus, which flows roughly down its center from north to south, might be viewed in very general terms as a border between the Middle East and South Asia. The region has also been settled since ancient times (for some five to seven thousand years) by a river culture comparable to that of the Nile or the Euphrates, and which stands out from the cultures to the east and west.

After Hinduism arose in the Indian heartland (today's India), the areas
that are now Bangladesh and Pakistan became outlying regions or buffer
states. From a Hindu perspective they were already no longer quite "pure"
(*pak*), in fact barely tolerable at best. Thus the foundation was laid for a
type of perpetual revolt by these two territories against the Hindu heartland.
Hindu reform movements and Buddhism were therefore more readily received in what is today Bangladesh and Pakistan than in India itself, where
they originated. This tradition of resistance to Hinduism would later benefit
Islam. It is notable that at the actual sites of Muslim rule in India (Delhi and
its environs), most of the population remained Hindu, whereas far from
these administrative centers in the often neglected outer reaches of the Mughal Empire, the overwhelming majority took on the new faith.

a. The Question of Muslim Self-Image

This background is crucial for understanding the self-image of Muslims
in Bangladesh and Pakistan. Incursions by Arabs, Persians, Turks, and Afghans had a largely colonizing character, motivated less by a desire to spread
the faith than to plunder the fabulous treasures of India. For centuries the
Indian subcontinent was an El Dorado for Muslim adventurers from Baghdad, Bukhara, Ghazni, and Shiraz—comparable to the role of Latin America for the Spanish. This was generally encouraged by the populace of what
is today Pakistan; often it seemed as if they were waiting for warlords from
abroad—preferably with new ideologies—to launch campaigns against Hin-
dustan. By rejecting a Hinduism perceived as exploitative, inhumane, and
racist, they effectively often preferred to identify with alien intruders instead
of with their kinfolk whose Hindu arrogance was seen as intolerable. This
basic pattern underlies both the expansion of Islam and the particular form
it took on the subcontinent. And its main features persist unchanged to this
day. This applies in only qualified form to Bangladesh, however, because
foreign incursions there were not as marked as in Pakistan.

The Identity Problem for Pakistani Muslims
Muslims of foreign descent constitute a barely significant number in Bangladesh, whereas in Pakistan they may account for as much as 15 to 20 percent
of the population. Even with this figure, however, one cannot speak of contained settlement areas. Instead there are kinship groups of Arab, Persian, or
Central Asian–Turkish origin dispersed almost everywhere and interspersed
with inhabitants of Indian heritage. At the same time, Pakistanis in the various regions of the country are related to their respective neighbors beyond
the national borders. To the west of the Indus, Baluchis and Pashtuns are
related to their tribal cousins in Afghanistan and Iran—or are separated
from them by an extremely artificial border. In the two large regions east of
the Indus, namely Punjab and Sind, the populace has close ties to Hindus
and Sikhs in India. Here too the border was drawn arbitrarily, sundering

geographic, ethnic, and linguistic entities. For Baluchis and Pashtuns, it is a given that they belong to the Middle East. Their counterparts in Afghanistan and Iran are all Muslims, so except for the political question whether to secede from Pakistan and found an independent Baluchistan or Pashtunistan, they do not face any serious problems of identity.

By contrast, for the two populous provinces of Punjab and Sind (which account for over two-thirds of the country's population), the crisis of orientation triggered by the founding of Pakistan in 1947 continues to this day. The people there belong to the same kinship groups, clans, and tribes as those with a different faith on the other side of the border and with whom they lived together until the subcontinent was divided. Exclusively Muslim and Hindu areas arose only as a result of the population exchange between India and Pakistan. With respect to tradition, language, names, and social structures, Muslim Punjabis and Sindis have more in common with their Hindu relatives than with Arabs or Turks. Outsiders cannot distinguish their appearance, clothing, cuisine, or music from those of Hindus and Sikhs. Even the caste system persists in Muslim society, albeit in modified and milder form.

For the intellectual ruling class this creates a self-definitional dilemma which occasionally takes dramatic expression such as strenuous claims that the people differ entirely from Hindus and have nothing in common with them—that as Muslims they are united with their fellow believers on the Bosporus and in North Africa. Numerous authors, in particular Pakistan's national philosopher and poet Muhammad Iqbal (1879–1938), described Pakistanis as Arabs in the diaspora.[1] Muslim thinkers and politicians in the 1930s promoted the "two nations theory" in opposition to the pan-Indian nationalism supported by the Congress Party under Gandhi and Nehru. Advanced most prominently by the country's founder, Muhammad 'Ali Jinnah (1876–1948), this theory drew such a sharp distinction between the lifestyles of Hindus and Muslims on the subcontinent that it was no longer possible to view them as a single people; they resembled far more two contrasting nations.[2]

The Historical Identification of Islam with Political Power in Popular Consciousness

It is sometimes said that the "two nations theory" and the resulting "Islamic ideology of Pakistan" have no roots in the Muslim masses who coexisted peacefully with their fellow Hindu and Sikh villagers, and that the entire idea of Pakistan is the work of a rising Western-oriented Muslim middle class that saw little chance of advancement against the more strongly developed and educated class of Hindus. While this assessment may be valid to some extent, it is one-sided. It fails to take into account the psychological effect of centuries of Muslim rule on most of the uneducated classes as well. For Muslims, Islam and state power had become synonymous. The notion of Muslims as a "master race" was not simply invented by modernists inspired from afar by Hitler and Mussolini. Muslim farmers could well have enjoyed neighborly relations with Hindus, but they did so largely with a sense of superiority. When the empire came to an end, many nourished the proud memory of being a "warrior race." More than five hundred years of Muslim glory in India had ensured a rich trove of sagas. So although people of the same racial and linguistic groups lived alongside one another on largely peaceful terms, they aspired to mutually antagonistic models and heroes, and their experiences of history stood in conflict.

Muslims lived with the consciousness of the class on which the state was built, whereas for Hindus the Mughal Empire was as foreign a rule as British colonialism. This contrast was sharpened all the more by the fact that especially in Bengal, many members of the lowest Hindu castes converted to Islam and were thus upstarts and usurpers in the eyes of their Hindu compatriots. Converts from Brahmin and warrior castes, which were not unheard of, were viewed all the more so as collaborators, just as Hindus and Muslims alike later saw Christian converts as collaborating with British colonial power.

After the British supplanted Muslim imperial power (1857), humiliated Muslims were left with few alternatives except emigration or passive resentment. Tens of thousands left the country, the majority for Afghanistan, and many came to grief on account of the hardships. In general, however, they maintained their traditions outside the public realm—with the conservatism of those whose world is threatened by dissolution. The age of Islamic rule was gilded and romanticized in their memories and its restoration preached in messianic tones. Thus the synonymous nature of state rule and Islamic religion was an understanding shared by no small segment of the rural masses who were later to constitute the population of Pakistan.

This can also be seen in the images crystallizing in the fledgling state that were to become the symbols of Pakistani Islam. Both the most grandiose architectural monuments and the major theological centers were "left behind"; that is, they could not be taken along by the millions of Muslims who emigrated to Pakistan from India. Tellingly, no mosque or gravesite (not even the Taj Mahal) or shrine (not even Ajmer Sharif) enjoyed the same symbolic significance as the Red Fort in Delhi. The focal point of the collective consciousness of Pakistani Muslims was not the theological college of Deoband (one of the world's most important schools of orthodox Islam after Cairo's al-Azhar) but rather this symbol of the Mughal Empire.[3] The most coveted prize for Pakistani soldiers in the wars with India was to raise their flag with the crescent moon above the Red Fort, a heroic act anticipated in songs and poetry as well as in illustrations in school books.

Pakistan's "Muslim Nationalism"
Here too we see the conflict of identity in Pakistani Islam. On the one hand, Muhammad Iqbal glorified the Ka'ba in Mecca and the mosque (Mezquita) in Córdoba in his poetry, seeking if only intellectually to loosen ties with

India—setting an example in the process that is still pursued with great zeal. On the other hand, he and nearly all Pakistani Muslims felt a strong sense of independence within Islam, as well as pride—at times concealed or latent, at times also aggressively formulated—in their achievements within the worldwide Muslim community.

Understandably enough, intellectuals who had more contact with the rest of the Islamic world and who encountered little sympathy for or even downright rejection of their calls for pan-Islamic integration were more prone to emphasize the specific contributions made by Indo-Pakistani Muslims to Islamic culture. Especially in the Arab world, Pakistanis are often forced to realize that there can be hardly any talk of pan-Islamic equality and that their Islam is not fully recognized. They also discover that other Muslim peoples such as Moroccans, Turks, and even their neighbors the Afghans maintain a pronounced national identity within the international Muslim community—an identity reinforced by specific national forms of religious interpretation and practice. Not infrequently this experience triggers a radical reorientation among Pakistanis. For example, they consider their way of following Islam to be more correct, if not the most correct of all. Here the tendency arises to swing from one extreme to another, that is, from an irrational fixation with Arabia to a neofascist Islamic nationalism, such as when a religious scholar and major government official opines that true Islam is practiced only within the borders of Pakistan, whereas that practiced beyond *wagah* (the border with India) or *zahedan* (the border with Iran) is entirely an aberration. As in many other areas, one notes that Hindu ideas have crept unnoticed into the Muslim structure of thought. One's own territory is *pakistan* ("pure land," so to speak), whereas everything outside it is *napak* (impure). Accordingly, Pakistani Muslims often display a fractured relationship with Indians as well as with Arabs—and also, of course, with Iranians (except for Pakistani Shi'is).

It is also often the case that any given tendency finds its own protagonist, which in turn unleashes strong tensions. One group of Pakistani Muslims persists in blindly following the Middle East, lamenting that Pakistan cannot form a single state with Turkey because the troublemaker Iran lies in between. Another current of thought, itself divided into two groups, looks toward Indian Islam. The first of these subgroups is based on the nostalgia felt by Indian refugees for Lucknow and Hyderabad, that is, for the court culture of decadent Muslim principalities. The second is the Aligarh group, which consists essentially of rural nobility as well as officers and bureaucrats in today's Pakistan who attended the modern university of Aligarh in India. This seat of learning exerted a formative influence on the All India Muslim League party of founder Muhammad 'Ali Jinnah, and produced an educated class that, although it cannot be called enlightened in religious matters, has nevertheless adopted a comparatively liberal attitude toward religious practice and in many cases evokes aspects of the Freethinker movement. In political terms, Aligarh graduates have gravitated toward a type of "Muslim democracy," rather like Latin America's Christian Democrats, especially where the latter cooperate with military dictatorships, or at least where the line between their parties and those dictatorships is blurred.

In any event, the much-invoked spirit of Aligarh signals a continuation of that type of Muslim chauvinism which, although not unique in the world, is more evident in Pakistan than elsewhere. Even during the period of "Islamic social democracy" under Prime Minister Zulfikar 'Ali Bhutto, who was subsequently executed, it was possible for Kauthar Niyazi, the minister of religious affairs and a leading religious scholar, to call for all of Pakistan to be transformed into an Aligarh.[4] No religious criterion per se is operative here. Instead the aim is to preserve benefits for Muslims, specifically for Pakistani Muslims, as a privileged people. Aligarh, as a symbol of this loyalty, lies in India and thus ensures a sort of revanchism against the Hindus who would not have dared rebel had they not been provoked into doing so by the English.

Thus for all its orientation toward Arabia and for all its romantic idealization of the Muslim world community, Pakistani Islam is remarkably autarkic, or at least more so than many Pakistanis realize. As such, it contrasts with Islam in countries such as Nigeria or Indonesia. Indonesian Islam depends for its intellectual regeneration (or stagnation) to a large degree on Egypt's al-Azhar theological university, at which hundreds of the country's theologians are studying at any given time. Owing to the fame of al-Azhar, European commentators often consider it to be the most important spiritual center of Sunni Islam, at times even the Vatican of Cairo. In Pakistan, however, the name al-Azhar is not even familiar to all theologians, let alone to the general educated public. Yet it is hard to find anyone in the country who does not know the theological college of Deoband, which was founded in India in 1880. For Muslims on the subcontinent, Deoband is what al-Azhar is for Egypt and the surrounding African and Arab countries.

The term "Deobandi" describes a school of thought that set the tone among the Pakistani orthodoxy and created a political wing of the Jam'iyyat al-'Ulama'-i Islam, or JUI (though not all JUI members are Deobandis, and many Deobandi legal scholars are also no longer aligned with the JUI). At any rate, there are strong parallels between what the name Azhari means in the Sudan, for example, and the connotation of Deobandi in Pakistan.

The autarkic nature of Indo-Pakistani Islam is not restricted to its centers of learning but is reflected mainly and especially in the two greatest thinkers of recent centuries. Shah Wali Allah, who revitalized Islamic thought in Delhi in the eighteenth century, is even called the "national imam" of Indo-Pakistani Islam by one school of thought—albeit smaller than the Deobandi.[5] Written in the strenuous Arabic of Khorasan mystics, his main work, *Hujjat Allah al-Baligha*, is considered one of the highlights of Islamic intellectual history, equal to or even surpassing al-Ghazali's (d. 1111) *Ihya' 'Ulum al-Din*. According to 'Ubaid Allah Sindhi (d. 1945), the main proponent of this still vibrant current of thought, the elite of the Islamic empire emigrated to Delhi following the destruction of Baghdad. He likened that to the emigration of Greek scholars from Constantinople to Italy and the resulting Renaissance. According to this view, then, Delhi is the navel of the world—or at least of the Islamic world.

Just as they do with al-Azhar, most European depictions of Islamic revival also ascribe a central role to the Egyptian reform theologian Muhammad ʿAbduh (d. 1905). In doing so, they neglect the easily demonstrable influence exerted on him by the Indo-Muslim reformer Sayyid Ahmad Khan (1817–1898).[6] For Pakistanis, few of whom have heard of ʿAbduh, the question of comparison does not even arise. For them, Sayyid Ahmad Khan is the greatest reformer of the modern age and also the first intellectual trailblazer for the idea of Pakistan. Many Pakistanis, especially of the fundamentalist and orthodox persuasions, may reject Sayyid Ahmad Khan's Qurʾanic interpretations. But for most members of the educated class, he is the leading figure of modern Islamic intellectual history, more so than any Arab, Persian, or Turk. This autarkic quality becomes all the more evident when one considers that after Sayyid Ahmad Khan, it is the onetime Indian minister of education Abu l-Kalam Azad (1888–1958) who enjoys the greatest admiration as a Muslim thinker.[7] Again, this is not someone from outside the subcontinent but rather a Muslim who did not support the idea of Pakistan and who became something of a Martin Buber figure as an Indian nationalist. Azad's interpretive Urdu translation of the Qurʾan, which is deeply influenced by philosophical mysticism, is considered by most Pakistanis to be the best, although he was much maligned for remaining in the Indian government.[8] Thus the paradox arises that the Arabian orientation of Pakistani Muslims, which some Hindus at times have called paranoid and which many Arabs view with condescension, turns out on closer inspection to be the converse, namely, a religious independence from Arabia and an Islamic autonomy for which there are few parallels in the rest of the Islamic world.

b. The Variety of Islamic Movements and Sects

The Ismaʿilis

A pronounced phenomenon of Pakistani Islam is its sheer incalculable division into movements, schools of thought, sects, sub-sects, factions, and communities, including the numerous orders of Sufis associated with them. The fact that everything splits into subdivisions makes it difficult to talk about any religious majority in Pakistan.

It is nevertheless the case that around 75 percent of the population are Sunnis who at least nominally follow the Hanafi school of jurisprudence, although some are actually closer to the Hanbali school, and a few profess adherence to a lofty Islamic catholicism that transcends individual schools of law. The exact proportion of Shiʿa in the country is a subject of considerable debate. They themselves frequently say 20 percent, and the especially ambitious among them claim 30 percent. Sunni government officials, however, insist on a figure of 6.5 percent. A realistic estimate might be 15 percent or slightly more.[9] Like the Sunnis, however, the Shi'is are very divided. Of course, a large majority belong to the Twelver Shi'a and feel like Persians in the diaspora, as many Sunnis feel like Arabs in the diaspora. In addition, there are two groups of Isma'ilis, of which the followers of the Aga Khan (Khojas) are the larger, followed by the Bohras, led by Imam Burhanuddin (Burhan al-Din). Pakistan's founder, Jinnah, belonged to a branch of the Bohra Isma'ilis.

For the Aga Khan Isma'ilis, Pakistan has become their main homeland after many had to leave East Africa. Largely concentrated in Karachi, these Isma'ilis, as well as their fellow believers in East Africa and England, are descended from Hindu converts from Gujarat. Their primary center used to be Mumbai, while today it is Mumbai's offshoot, Karachi. In ethnic terms they belong to the same group as the Parsis and the Islamic Memon sect.

The Khojas, Bohras, and Memons are all close to their Hindu origins in terms of language and customs. Yet all three groups are equally clear about claiming Persian or Arab descent. Muslims in general view both the Memons and the Isma'ilis as heterodox. In the mid-nineteenth century, the Isma'ili heresy was no longer even considered part of the Muslim community. Reintegration was the lifelong mission of Sultan Muhammad Aga Khan (grandfather of Karim Aga Khan), who began to play a leading role among Muslim notables in India in 1906.[10] His work as an advocate for Muslim interests was pursued and strongly reinforced by a worldwide program of philanthropic activities headed by his successor, Karim Aga Khan, a Pakistani citizen.

This created a paradox whereby Isma'ilis are welcomed in Pakistani society with its sectarian tensions despite the fact that their religious practices continue to make them the most heretical of the major Muslim sects. Isma'ilis maintain their own houses of worship in Pakistan, known as "community houses" (sing. *jama'at khana*), in which the rites are held not in Arabic but in Gujarati. The Qur'an, too, is read in Gujarati. The five daily prayers have been reduced to three; women are not veiled (owing to a religious ruling, not to unsanctioned liberal views); and members generally marry only within their own community.

With respect to religious practice, Isma'ilis are therefore much further removed from orthodox Islam than the excommunicated Ahmadiyya groups, whose view of Islam is more formalistic in many respects than that of Ayatollah Khomeini. While all manner of hostility is directed against the Ahmadis as putative apostates (similar to the hostility toward Bahais in Iran), reserved judgment is exercised with the Isma'ilis as if a lost son were being granted time to return. Like the Ahmadis, the Isma'ilis have an effective system of social welfare which easily attracts the envy of other groups. The danger is even greater for Isma'ilis than for Ahmadis, because followers of the Aga Khan possess more wealth and are especially well represented among rich merchants and industrialists. Yet the Ahmadis have represented a greater source of friction because they have the highest levels of education (and lowest illiteracy rates) of all Pakistan's religious communities, and have therefore been feared as competitors for many coveted positions in science and government administration. By contrast, the Isma'ilis, like their "cousins" the Memons, showed little interest in anything but business and trade on into the 1960s. A Memon who returned to Karachi in 1969 with a doctorate from Germany was a sensation and had to show his diploma to all. As worthy as Karim Aga Khan's efforts to raise the level of education in his community may be, they also represent a real danger for the future. All toleration aside, comparisons between the dynamic Isma'ilis and the Jews have long been on the agenda.

Precise numerical figures for the Isma'ili community are especially hard to come by. In addition to the Gujarati Isma'ilis in Karachi, one would have to add some barely ten thousand inhabitants of the Hunza Valley in the Himalayas, who constitute a completely different population group. Whether the Isma'ilis really number over 2 million or not even 1 million they alone can say with any accuracy, although they have not been very forthcoming on this score. Their economic clout, however, is well out of proportion to their small share of the country's overall population.

The Twelver Shi'a

In contrast to the Isma'ilis, Pakistan's Twelver Shi'a are anything but a homogeneous community. They include nearly all the country's ethnic elements, because most regions have one or more Shi'i enclaves. A notable feature of Islam in Pakistan is that it was spread in many areas by Shi'i preachers (mainly Isma'ilis). It is a reasonable assumption, therefore, that the majority of the population of what is now Pakistan was Shi'i in past centuries. The converse development to that in Iran set in, however, as Afghan-Turkish warlords and the Mughal emperors then promoted Sunni Islam. Today's Isma'ilism is to some extent a surviving remnant of earlier times. It is also interesting from a religious-historical perspective in terms of reconstructing the first generations of converts to Islam, because many of its rituals simply replace Hindu with Islamic nomenclature. As an aside, the religious music of Pakistani Muslims in general can be used for this purpose as well. Among mystics in particular there is little Middle Eastern influence; formally speaking, their performances have remained Indian with virtually no changes, while only the content is now Islamic.

The Twelvers, by contrast, have taken an ever stronger Persian course over the centuries, a development that reached its climax in the identification by Pakistani Shi'a with Ayatollah Khomeini's regime in Iran. This may be due to the fact that the Shi'i ruling class is predominately of Iranian origin from a time when the Mughal Empire maintained close ties with Persia and when many Persian nobles acquired rank and status in India. Their descendants who emigrated to Pakistan continue to fill the upper echelons of officialdom, which means that the proportion of Shi'a in both the administration and the educational system is higher than their share of the overall population—a typical syndrome for Pakistani minorities if one recalls, for example, the Ahmadis before they were "excommunicated."

The relatively high proportion of Shi'a among immigrants from India, who settled predominantly in larger cities and particularly in Karachi, means that the Shi'a in Pakistan are mainly an urban phenomenon. This in turn contributes to the strife that takes lives almost every time the annual Shi'i religious processions are staged, specifically for Muharram. Several Karachi streets displayed nearly warlike scenes of destruction in 1981. With Sunnis already repelled by Shi'i reenactment of the martyrdom of Husayn (grandson of the Prophet), these processions additionally turned into pro-Khomeini demonstrations and provoked correspondingly robust reactions. Traditionally, however, it is by no means the case that the minority falls victim to the majority on such occasions. Instead the attacks have tended to be launched more often by the Shi'a, whose religious emotions are whipped up to ecstatic levels during the reenactment of their Passion.

A major new source of conflict resulted from the introduction in 1979 of *zakat,* which is a type of "church tax" required by the Qur'an. The Shi'a objected and held a mass demonstration in Islamabad on a scale never seen before by the military dictatorship and probably unprecedented among Shi'a in Pakistan. (Official estimates suggest 100,000 participants; the Shi'a themselves add a zero.) In their eyes, *zakat* is not a tax but a voluntary donation or alms. As an aid to understanding this issue, one might imagine the French state, for example, introducing a church tax without making a distinction between Catholics and Protestants.

Sunni-Shi'i Tensions

Relations between Shi'a and Sunnis in Pakistan are complex but display definite parallels to those between Catholics and Protestants in many European countries. The Sunni majority harbors strong prejudices against the Shi'a, whom they see as having deviated from or even distorted the true faith. In connection with the "excommunication" of the Ahmadis (1974), extreme orthodox and fundamentalist circles have often gloated over the prospect of the Shi'a being next in line. The aim of many Sunni fanatics is to have the Shi'a declared a non-Muslim minority as was done with the Ahmadis, or in other words to give them the same status as Christians, Hindus, and Parsis.

The Sunni masses view the Shi'a similarly to the way northern German Protestants view the country's Catholics. Sweeping generalizations such as "the Catholics are all wrong" are made in precisely the same form about the Shi'a. Their strict positions on religious issues, their formalism, and their strong group solidarity evoke suspicion and ill will on the part of Sunnis yet also admiration. They have succeeded in being viewed as especially fanatical and intolerant by a society in which many groups consider these properties to be virtues and vie with one another to display them. As in European countries (Germany, England, France, the Netherlands) where more people have converted from Protestantism to Catholicism than vice versa since the middle of the twentieth century, so too have more Sunnis become Shiʿi in Pakistan than the reverse.

Sunni Muslims in Pakistan, however, also made some attempts in the twentieth century to accommodate the Shiʿa where possible. For example, Sunnis generally saw no reason not to encourage tribute to the Prophet's family, whom they too revered, in order for the Shiʿa to feel at home. The sacred month of Muharram has been observed to such an increasing degree by Sunnis that foreign Sunnis might be led to believe they are in a predominantly Shiʿi country. This pan-Islamic promotion on the part of Sunnis has been given little credit by the majority of Shiʿa, however. Many Sunnis have been left with the impression that the more they attempt to accommodate the Shiʿa, the more the latter withdraw and harden their Shiʿi particularism.

Sunni sectarians subsequently showed that they could also embark on a course of confrontation. This happened, for example, when they introduced an "ʿUmar's Day" (*yawm-i ʿUmar*) in place of Muharram, which they still did not consider quite legitimate. ʿUmar al-Faruq, the second Islamic caliph (r. 634–644), is viewed by Shiʿa as a usurper and reviled. The introduction of *yawm-i ʿUmar* in 1970 was therefore an unbearable provocation. A failure to fraternize with Shiʿis also led to specifically Sunni names such as ʿUmar and Faruq becoming fashionable again among Sunnis after a long period in which "Shiʿi names" (such as Dilawar, Husayn, Farzand, and ʿAli, for example) were common. It was no coincidence that the head fundamentalist ideologue, the Indian-born journalist Maulana Abu l-Aʿla Maududi, named his son Faruq (as did his former comrade Kauthar Niyazi, who became a minister in Bhutto's government).[11] Naming in Pakistan is all too often an expression of loyalty to an extreme Sunni or a fanatic Shiʿi line. That was also one of many propaganda points used by fundamentalists against the subsequently executed prime minister Bhutto. His own—very Shiʿi-sounding—first name, Zulfikar ʿAli (Dhu l-fiqar is the name of the legendary sword of ʿAli ibn Abi Talib), could hardly be faulted on grounds of historical pedigree. But his giving the typically Shiʿi name Murtaza to both his private residence and his eldest son was taken as evidence that he had become Shiʿi because of the influence of his wife, who was of Iranian heritage.

The fact that Nusrat Bhutto, a Shiʿa, was able to succeed her husband as chair of the People's Party and enjoy great popularity in all regions of the country is again a hallmark of the religious situation in Pakistan. Political leaders who successfully represent the interests of the population at large and openly demonstrate that they place the concerns of Islam as a whole above their own denominational affiliation have often enjoyed special popularity. This was true of the Aga Khan and of Muhammad ʿAli Jinnah as well as of Jinnah's sister Fatima and Nusrat Bhutto, and also initially of the Shiʿi president General Yahya Khan before he lost the war against India. Opponents of erstwhile presidential candidate Fatima Jinnah as well as of Nusrat Bhutto did not dwell on their Shi'i religious affiliations but rather stressed the much graver objection that women should not hold any major positions of state.

Islamic consciousness in Pakistan thus fluctuates between violent confrontations involving Shi'a and Sunnis on the one hand and collective declarations of transcendent Islamic unity on the other. Since the time of the Mughal emperor Akbar, intellectual circles have displayed a certain *una sancta* tendency that was especially pronounced during the "Enlightenment" phase under the influence of British liberalism. It is also exemplified by the two most important religious reformers: Sayyid Ahmad Khan for the Sunnis and Sayyid Amir 'Ali for the Shi'a. *The Spirit of Islam,* Amir 'Ali's widely circulated major work, became a model of Shi'i readiness to compromise and had a lasting impact on leading cultural and political figures such as the raja of Mahmudabad, who although a Shi'a became the patron of numerous Sunni scholars.

The agreement in the early 1970s on religious instruction in schools also fits into this tendency toward pan-Islamic understanding. Pupils were to have a common curriculum through the eighth grade and only afterwards receive separate Sunni or Shi'i religious instruction. The agreement followed long years of bitter struggle that in many cases resulted in no instruction taking place at all. The laboriously achieved settlement was once again undermined by the Iranian Revolution and its effects on the Shi'i community in Pakistan.

In general it might be said of Pakistani Shi'a that their individual attitudes are a nuance sharper than those of their Sunni compatriots. Conservative religious Shi'a (who account for a larger share of their respective population than is the case for Sunnis) are usually more orthodox or fundamentalist, and more resistant to progress. For their part, liberal Shi'a normally leave their Sunni friends far behind and indulge in what for Pakistani conditions are veritably brazen Freethinker attitudes. Before Partition, the number of Muslims among members of the Communist Party of India was disproportionately high and dominated by Shi'a. The most famous of this very strong Freethinker current among Shi'i intellectuals was Josh Malihabadi,[12] the libertine poet-king of the Urdu language, whose work was banned by the military dictator Muhammad Zia ul-Haq.[13] From him comes the ironic statement that Islam, in particular the Shi'i variant, is like an incurable disease: if you catch it you can never get rid of it no matter how hard you try.

The Shi'i community in Pakistan is synonymous with a higher level of commitment to both political and religious matters. This commitment can be reactionary or revolutionary, orthodox or liberal, capitalist or socialist, but it is generally more strident than among Sunnis.

Popular Faith or "Unofficial" Islam as the Majority Religion

Among Sunnis in Pakistan, the difference—also observed elsewhere—between the "official" Islam of legal scholars and the "unofficial" counterpart of the masses is especially blatant. On the surface it appears to be a distinction between urban and rural Islam. Yet associations of legal scholars are also influential in many rural areas, while urban migration has brought the religion of the countryside into the cities.

Popular faith among the Pakistani masses, which is to say the majority religion, recalls in many respects the Catholicism of Mexico or of other Latin American regions whose predominantly indigenous populations have synthesized pre-Columbian and Christian customs to varying degrees. In general one could say that the core elements consist of certain ritualistic actions with a universal character. Parallels can also be drawn, for example, to popular religion in parts of Morocco with a Berber majority. In any case there is a focus on worshipping saints, usually mystics and preachers who had spread the faith in that particular region—and often been killed, that is, had become martyrs. Not infrequently their gravesites bear a closer resemblance to the temples of earlier religions than the standard models of contemporary houses of worship. Religious calendars revolve around the special days of these patron saints, which in Latin America are observed as a *feria,* in Islamic regions as a *mawsim* or *mawlid,* and in Pakistan as an *'urs.* By some reckonings, a certain number of pilgrimages to the grave of a local saint can be accorded a similar significance as a journey to Mecca.

On the occasion of an *'urs,* the faithful bring flowers to the grave of the "friend of God" (*wali*), spread a resplendent new cover (*chador*) over the grave, light candles and incense, and pray, sing, and dance. At the same time, a fair is held which can assume carnival-like features including the use of alcohol, drugs, and especially prostitutes. The saint's grave, at which prayers are offered primarily for love and children, is showered with donations. Over the centuries these have been used to expand and often lavishly decorate the associated buildings—in contrast to the mosques, which are usually very plain. Special attention is devoted to the gateway to the grave (*darwazah*), which can often be made of gold or silver. From the Mughal emperors to General Zia ul-Haq, rulers have engaged in pious acts such as donating a *darwazah* decorated with Qur'an verses to a famous shrine.

A shrine is also called a *darbar* (court), because here the saint holds court, so to speak, and grants an audience to the faithful. The most important shrine is Lahore's Data Ganj Bakhsh of the mystic 'Ali Hujwiri, who might be called the national saint of Pakistan. Other noteworthy examples include the gravesites of the mystic poet Shah 'Abd al-Latif Bhita'i and the Persian wandering preacher 'Uthman Marwandi, called La'l Shahbaz Qalandar, both of which are located in the southern province of Sind.

With the rise of the film industry, the cult of saints has effectively broken through to legitimacy thanks to the unstintingly commercial basis of Pakistani production. Films depicting tearful worshippers at graves and saints hearing their prayers quickly turned into box office hits and prompted more of the same, so much so that a certain type of scene became a set piece of stereotypical Pakistani film repertoires. Moreover, film actors chose La'l Shahbaz Qalandar to be the patron saint of their profession. Since then, attractive stars have regularly posed before the decorative arched gates of his tasteful mosque for a large number of magazines. Famous singers give free concerts during their visits, and there is no better way for fans to approach their idols than to participate in an *'urs.*

The fleeting prayer of a love-struck girl at this saint's grave became a popular song, and then—after being adapted in over thirty pop music versions and sung in all regional languages—became the country's greatest hit of the 1970s: "Dam-a-dam mast Qalandar" (roughly "Let Come What May, Qalandar!"). The Qalandars are one of the most extravagant fraternities of wandering dervishes who gather every year in Sind to perform ecstatic dances together. They reject all intellectual debate and speak solely of brotherly love, without making moralistic demands and without engaging in social causes. As far as they are concerned, nominal religious affiliation is ultimately irrelevant; at times they are even led by Hindus. Sinners are not rebuked but rather received with open arms. As a result, Qalandars have long exerted a special attraction for prostitutes, who can expect nothing in the way of spiritual guidance from urban legal scholars. The fact that the group's pious songs have become popular dance music at Pakistani discotheques is considered not a disgrace but rather a triumph.

Politicians have always had to take account of popular religion in Pakistan. One expression of this was the close friendship that former president Muhammad Ayyub Khan maintained for a long period of time with a highly revered popular saint.[14] Nevertheless, members of the ruling class have generally found it hard to overcome their doubts about what orthodox Islamic legal scholars denounce as a regression to paganism. The first politician to take the majority of the country's faithful deliberately into account and orient his policies exclusively toward them—which was very well received— was Zulfikar 'Ali Bhutto. By neglecting no opportunity to visit the graves of saints, participate in various *'urs,* and wherever possible donate a new chador and spread it over a grave with his own hands, he effectively became a practicing follower of "popular Islam." One of the favorite mystical songs from his home province of Sind was changed to refer to him ("Our Bhutto has entered the arena, now you will see how God helps his friend!"), and became a hit election campaign tune. An overwhelming success, it helped pave the way for the landslide in the first free election in 1970. General Zia ul-Haq later made similar concessions to popular Islam by helping to expand the "national shrine" of Data Ganj Bakhsh, for example, even though doing so ran completely counter to his fundamentalist views.

Although mystical popular Islam constitutes the majority religion in Pakistan, it is by no means a homogeneous phenomenon. The extremely high number of votes for the People's Party was the only unified demonstration of this popular faith, because for simple voters, and especially those in rural areas, the choice is not between belief and nonbelief or between Islam and communism but rather between two different ways of expressing Islam— the rigid formalism of the legal scholars, which they find alienating, versus the redeeming cult of saints, which reflects the depths of their being. Aside from this, there is nothing to serve as a common denominator for the amorphous mass of individual sects throughout the different parts of the country, with their disparate historical traditions and languages. It is possible to summarize only certain aspects of this popular religiosity, or only individual groups or classes of followers.

These include the mystic orders, which may well be more numerous in Pakistan than in other countries. The most common are probably the Qadiris, who have risen in prominence since the 1950s, when the patriarch of the founder's descendants, Shaykh 'Abd al-Qadir al-Jilani, immigrated to Pakistan from Baghdad. Of great importance also are the Naqshbandis, who are very close in outlook to the orthodox and who build a bridge between the Islam of the legal scholars and that of popular piety. The equally widespread Chishtis have a more pronounced mystical character. This picture is of course blurred by the many splinter and subgroups that often depart considerably from their "mother orders."

Some fraternities and grave cults have found organizational expression in an association of religious leaders (Jam'iyyat al-Mashayikh), which however does not include anything near the thousands of Sufi masters called *pir* ("wise one" or "elder," the Persian equivalent of the Arab. *shaykh*). The Jam'iyyat al-Mashayikh, which also sometimes acts to further political interests, does not come close to representing the entirety of popular Islam. The same is true for the clerics' party, the Jam'iyyat 'Ulama'-i Pakistan (JUP), which takes a more conciliatory approach toward popular faith than the orthodox Jam'iyyat 'Ulama'-i Islam (JUI). The JUP is essentially the political wing of the Brailvis, who are named after a theological seminar held in the city of Rae Bareli in present-day India and are sometimes described as a sect. They combine popular religion with the Islamic jurisprudence of legal scholars. In other words, Brailvi scholars approach popular Islam with an attitude of understanding and loving attention, but ultimately what they propagate is Islamic law. This can be seen in places such as the Indian Muslim community in South Africa, where the Brailvis play a prominent role. Because popular Islam is less prevalent there in recent contexts owing to a lack of saints' graves, the Brailvis in South Africa display a much more orthodox air. In essence they represent a stage in Islamic development that can also be seen in several other parts of the world. The Brailvis focus on the first stage after conversion and bring newcomers, who are still full of "pagan customs," a step closer to the Islamic law of Arabia. From a long-term perspective they actually contribute to a stricter orthodoxy, even though proponents of the latter are seldom capable of appreciating the Brailvis' role in spreading Islam but rather tend to reject it as syncretistic.

The Main Religious Centers: Karachi and Lahore

As political organizations, neither the Brailvis nor the strictly orthodox—the JUP and JUI—have succeeded in attracting more than a very small percentage of voters. Nor have the fundamentalists from the Islamic Party (Jama'at-i Islami, JI) managed to do better.[15] These three parties combined, each of which represents in its own way the Islam of the clerics, have never reached more than 11.3 percent in a national election. This, however, has a lot to do with regional affiliations. Orthodox Muslims in the JUI, for example, are concentrated in the northwest near their spiritual center, the theological college in Akora Khattak. Outside their home region they recruit supporters primarily from among Pashtun emigrants, of whom there are said to be more than a million in Karachi. While not dependent on refugees from India, the Brailvis and their JUP still see them as their main source of supporters. They are therefore centered in the refugee metropolis of Karachi. The same applies to the fundamentalists (JI), whose true population center has remained Karachi, although they also have found support among Punjabis and have established their main location (both party headquarters and their institute of religious learning) in Lahore.

As the country's largest city and commercial hub, Karachi has remained the most important religious center. Although most religions, denominations, sects, movements, and orders have houses of worship in Islamabad, the newer capital in the north, religious life has long remained sterile there. Karachi, by contrast, is a melting pot and bastion not only for Twelvers, Aga Khan and Bohra Isma'ilis, Memons, Brailvi Sunnis, and Jama'at-i Islami fundamentalists, but also for Parsis, Catholics who had settled previously in Goa, and a multitude of smaller Islamic sects and groups, some of which show a marked independence. Karachi may well be the only city in which one can find Dhikris, a small sect that displays remote parallels to the Yazidis or "devil worshippers" in Iraq and who otherwise inhabit only isolated desert areas of Baluchistan.[16] Other Muslims regard Dhikris as having a religion that is strange in the extreme. Here, too, there are calls to declare the group a non-Muslim minority. All in all, the Islamic landscape of Pakistan, and especially that of Karachi, appears an impenetrable thicket to fellow believers—particularly from countries with a relatively homogeneous religious profile such as Jordan or Tunisia.

Lahore, which is essentially the capital of the north and originally the cultural center of Pakistan, has lost some religious diversity compared to Karachi but remains bewildering enough. It continues to be marked by intellectual circles that often take the form of schools of religious thought. A prominent example centered on the modernist Ghulam Ahmad Parvez and his rich body of writing. His Sunday gatherings became a not insignificant institution for Westernized educated elites, earning him the nickname of "the bureaucrats' imam." Similar circles and debating clubs can be found across the entire political spectrum—from the far right to the extreme left. Some of these circles gather around individuals who are active in religious cultural institutions such as the Iqbal Academy, the 'Ulama'Academy, the Institute of Islamic Culture, and so on. Others take the form of literature circles (*halqa arbab-i dhawq*) or are connected with religiously oriented publications. In addition, associations such as the Educators' Club or the Pakistan Philosophical Society have become forums for religious discussion to a degree virtually unparalleled in the rest of the Islamic world and alien to most believers in the Middle East.

Religiously oriented circles, particularly in the upper classes, also coalesce around palm readers and clairvoyants, who in some cases exert extraordinary influence—including in political matters—and are generally frequented precisely by people with power. Often such clairvoyants are associated with one of the mystical fraternities and are revered by their clients as a *pir* or *murshid* (spiritual guide). The Sufi Zahir was especially influential in the 1970s and 1980s, attracting leading intellectuals and top politicians as disciples to his jewelry shop on Lahore's main shopping street. Though a mystic, Zahir shared a kinship bond with the fundamentalist Zia ul-Haq, as both were members of the Ara'in-baradari. Among Zahir's predictions that may have influenced policy decisions was the notion that sacrilege committed by the Russian people would earn them the fate of mass destruction. Zahir also predicted the growing prominence of neo-Sufi fraternities such as the Shadhilis, who began playing a role among the highly educated class previously exercised by the now prohibited Freemasons.

Islamism or Islamic Fundamentalism

For the fundamentalists of the Jama'at-i Islami, all of this is an outrage. Unable to appreciate the manifold forms of Sufism's spiritual exigencies, they do not offer anything comparable in its place. Their outlook is humorless and hostile to the arts, anti-intellectual, and exclusive. Like the orthodox, they stress the importance of shari'a, which has no resonance among the majority of Pakistanis and especially not among the illiterate rural masses. Whereas traditional orthodox Muslims view shari'a as strict adherence to a medieval way of life, fundamentalists actually see it as a true totalitarian system. Their system is based at least as much on modern examples as it is on precedents from the early period of Islam. Members of the Jama'at-i Islami thus rely heavily on a special nomenclature that enables them to view this longed-for totalitarianism as true self-expression instead of a poor imitation. Moreover, the fundamentalists have specific categories of first-, second-, and third-class citizens. Their party organization features a strict hierarchy of members, sympathizers, and hangers-on. As for society at large, they distinguish Muslims by degree of dependability, followed by non-Muslim minorities such as Christians and Parsis, and then Hindus a step further down. At the very bottom are groups excluded from Islam such as Ahmadis and Bahais. According to Islamic ideology, they are apostates subject to the death penalty.

There is not the slightest accommodation of political ideologies other than Islamism. Not only communism but also socialism and liberalism are viewed as subversive. Democracy and Western parliamentarianism are rejected. Women are excluded from political life and prohibited from entering certain professions such as the judiciary; and the entire educational system is strictly segregated by sex.

These sociopolitical ideas, as applied in Iran under Khomeini and to a considerable extent also in Pakistan from 1977 to 1988 under Zia ul-Haq, were formulated by Maududi in numerous Urdu writings, and subsequently translated into many languages and spread throughout the world by a modern public relations organization. The Jama'at-i Islami, which he founded, received ever more extensive funding from Saudi Arabia toward the end of the 1960s yet remained a cadre party for the urban petit bourgeoisie. It is strongly rejected by the majority of Pakistanis, who view it more in political than religious terms because its tenets do not accord with their usual conception of religion. Maududi's identification of religion and politics is shared at most by some of the orthodox, but not by the broad masses. To simple believers in Pakistan, the Jama'at-i Islami's doctrines and the lifestyle of its cadre appear to be Wahhabi. Wahhabism in Pakistan is associated with the fanatic fundamentalism advocated by Indian admirers of the Wahhabiyya Arab revival movement. Since that time "Wahhabi" has served as a term of abuse, with the rough meaning of someone who blasphemes or engages in sacrilege. Because the general populace in Pakistan are barely aware of the affinity between Wahhabism and Saudi Arabia, however, they have no trouble revering as saints the Arab rulers who protect the sites of pilgrimage.

The traditional orthodox are closer to the fundamentalists in many respects, although they reject them as upstarts lacking theological expertise. Only a few of the fundamentalists have gone through the grueling programs in Islamic law at orthodox educational institutes, which can often take decades. Instead, like Maududi himself, they pursue half-traditional and half-modern educational careers and generally are active in modern professions. Anxious to retain their privileges as protectors of tradition, orthodox legal scholars therefore view fundamentalist Islamic scholars as dangerous rivals and consider Maududi's claim to religious leadership presumptuous. Thanks to his better relations with Saudi Arabia, however, Maududi succeeded in being recognized as an authority in Islamic studies like no Pakistani ever before. Though lacking a good command of Arabic, Maududi managed to make Pakistanis respectable and to gain recognition for them as scholars, when previously their view of Islam had been considered heretical or at least eccentric in most Arab countries. Maududi was the first winner of the King Faisal International Prize for Service to Islam. Following his death in 1979, he was celebrated as a reviver (*mujaddid*) of Islam in the twentieth century. His reputation among conservative Muslims in many countries contrasts markedly with the flat rejection accorded him by the majority of his compatriots, for whom he was not a religious figure but a fascist party leader. Moreover, they have not forgotten that for a long period he was opposed to the idea of a Pakistani state.

Ahmadi Messianism and the Dispute over
a Legal Definition of "Muslim"

Until 1974 the Ahmadiyya were just one of a range of Islamic denominations in Pakistan.[17] This group was founded by the "Promised Messiah" Mirza Ghulam Ahmad (d. 1908) in the Indian town of Qadian, which is why its members are also known, albeit mainly by critics, as Qadianis. The Ahmadis claim to have derived their name not from that of their founder but rather from a promised status accorded him in the Qur'an. They themselves call their organization the Ahmadiyya Movement in Islam and view themselves more as a Muslim elite than as a new religion. Although they share some perspectives on sociology and religious history with the Bahais, their situation is different in so far as they have not themselves left Islam but instead were excluded from the Muslim community and declared a non-Muslim minority by a resolution passed in the Pakistan National Assembly. Although they view this as an injustice, the Ahmadis also see it as confirmation that the rest of the followers of Islam are no longer faithful, and that they themselves are the sole true community of the last age.

More so than other Muslim communities in Pakistan, the Ahmadis tend to double or triple their membership estimates. Their number may have exceeded 1 million in Pakistan, but the figure of 200 million they claim worldwide is certainly too high. They have set up their "capital," the Rabwah settlement, in a rural area between the cities of Lahore and Sargodha, where they have maintained their own jurisdiction for some time now under the head of their community. The name Rabwah was changed to Chanabnagwar by an act of the Provincial Assembly of the Punjab, against the will of the Ahmadiyya community. The third Khalifatul Masih (Successor to the Messiah), Mirza Nasir Ahmad, a grandson of the founder who was educated in England, contributed substantially to the countrywide anti-Ahmadi unrest of 1974 by virtue of his pretentious challenges to the orthodox. This agitation left the Bhutto government no choice but to abandon what were loyal supporters in the 1970 election. Many technocrats among the Ahmadiyya, including not a few high-level individuals, were compelled to emigrate as a result of the discriminatory measures they faced. Canada and Germany were the preferred destinations—as they were previously for the Catholic Goanese who saw their cultural existence threatened by the nationalization of mission schools under Bhutto. The most prominent representative of the Ahmadi elite was the nuclear physicist and Nobel Prize winner Abdus Salam ('Abd al-Salam), who directed an institute in Trieste (Italy) until his death in 1996.

Since the state of Pakistan was founded, the Ahmadiyya question has virtually monopolized its religious-political climate. The first time that martial law was imposed was in 1953, following organized acts of violence against the Ahmadis. On the surface the conflict seems to revolve around a theological dispute as to whether another prophet can follow Muhammad, the "Seal of the Prophets." Mirza Ghulam Ahmad claimed to be a "shadow prophet" and the fulfillment of the Qur'an, albeit without his own revelatory scripture. At the same time, however, he professed to incorporate in his person the return of both Jesus and the Muslim mahdi. These and other flights of fancy were controversial enough, but even more serious was the claim on the part of Mirza and his descendants, in the style of feudal lords, to religious-political leadership of all Muslims. They reinforced this aspiration by establishing missions in a large number of countries. Within Pakistan, the Jamaʿat-i Islami became the sworn enemy of the Ahmadiyya, all the more so given that the two hardly differ, especially in their social practices but also in their interpretation of Islam. The Ahmadis, too, are Hanafi Sunnis with strong Hanbali tendencies. In sociological terms, the Jamaʿat-i Ahmadiyya and the Jamaʿat-i Islami are hostile twins who have employed the same intensity and tactics in attempting to infiltrate the officer corps, as well as government administration and the universities.

In general, the foreign missions of the rigid Ahmadiyya movement have not been very successful, particularly in the Western Hemisphere. An exception is West Africa, where they have been able to gain a foothold primarily in Ghana as well as Nigeria. In many places their active missionary work has led Muslims and non-Muslims alike to overestimate considerably the strength of their community in Pakistan. Because their missionaries were the first Muslims to pose a serious challenge to Christian missions, the Ahmadiyya have acted as a type of religious catalyst. Muslim missionary activity today, especially in Africa, is spurred on by the Ahmadis as both an example to be emulated and a force to be countered. In addition, their network of foreign missions has proved helpful in assisting the many Ahmadis who have emigrated from Pakistan.

Like all the Islamic groups in Pakistan, the Ahmadiyya are divided. The smaller subgroup headquartered in Lahore, however, is of hardly any significance anymore. From the very beginning it resembled more a group of intellectuals around a publication, and thus stood firmly in Lahore's Muslim tradition. In Nigeria a group of converts declared itself independent but continued to use the Ahmadiyya name. Neither they nor the Pakistani Ahmadiyya should be confused with the Ahmadiyya found primarily in Egypt and Sudan, who take the form of a popular Sufi fraternity.

The "excommunication" of the Ahmadis by parliamentary resolution is unique in the history of Islam, and is viewed by many intellectuals, especially in Pakistan, as a dangerous precedent. Only very few members of the National Assembly viewed the issue in terms of religious conscience. Debate focused far more on finding the best tactical response to political pressure. The Islamists saw the coerced resolution as a triumph over the secularists. The question thereby raised for the Pakistani educated classes was not so much the extent to which Mirza Ghulam Ahmad's prophecies, generally derided for their faulty Arabic and awkward English, might be accepted as divine revelation. Far more central was a fundamental question recalling debate in Israel over the nature of Judaism, namely, "Who is actually a

Muslim?" The Islamists did not even deny the parallels to Zionism. In fact they sought precisely to emphasize that the state of Pakistan is an ideological creation. Decades of efforts to formulate a generally valid definition of "Muslim," however, have not yielded a consensus. For a large part of the educated classes, they have produced only an abiding unease of both a religious and a material nature.

c. "Islamization" as an Objective of the State

The seizure of power by General Zia ul-Haq in July 1977 opened a new chapter in the history of Pakistan, marked by the declared objective of the state to introduce an "Islamic system." Zia was by no means the first Pakistani head of state to place himself in the service of Islamization. Most of his predecessors had instrumentalized Islam for their own purposes, although it is notable that the founder, Muhammad 'Ali Jinnah, envisioned a liberal democratic state along the lines of Westminster. He died thirteen months after the state was founded, before the basic lines of the constitution had been laid.

Jinnah's successors allowed themselves to be led into a trap on the question of sovereignty. As far as the Islamists were concerned, sovereignty is owed not to the people but to God. National leaders did not accord this matter any great significance because it appeared to carry no practical consequences. They allowed the sovereignty of God (Allah) to be specified in the preamble, with the qualification that it is delegated by him to the state and the people within the limits prescribed by him. Respect is due to the Qur'an and the sunna of the Prophet Muhammad, which should serve as guidelines for passing legislation. A council was proposed to examine existing laws and to make recommendations for bringing them into conformity with the injunctions of Islam. There were also calls to establish an institute of research and teaching, which would help rebuild Islamic society. These concessions to the Islamists, who had succeeded in mobilizing demonstrations against the government in connection with the Ahmadiyya issue in 1953, were viewed as cosmetic features and not taken very seriously by those in power. By contrast, Maududi considered the constitution of 1956 to be a step toward Islamizing the state, because acknowledging the sovereignty of God means no more nor less than requiring the introduction of his law. This document was immediately known as the "Islamic constitution," although it remained in effect for only two years. In October 1958 it was abruptly repealed by the first military dictator, General Ayyub Khan, who wanted a constitution that was tailored to his own aspirations and that accommodated his idea of "basic democracy."

This constitution, which he announced in 1962, not only omitted all "Islamic paragraphs" but also removed the adjective "Islamic" from the country's name; it would now be called simply the Republic of Pakistan. The opposition, using this action as ammunition against his regime, organized demonstrations. Two years later Ayyub Khan was compelled to reintroduce the Islamic paragraphs and to restore the name Islamic Republic of Pakistan. Moreover, the Council of Islamic Ideology received constitutional status and was charged with serving parliament in an advisory capacity and evaluating prospective legislation for its accordance with Islamic teachings.[18] It was also given the task of recommending how existing laws could be brought into conformity with Islamic injunctions. In its zeal the Ayyub regime invented "Islamic ideology," which was occasionally called "Pakistan ideology," and which no authorized political party was permitted to contest. Its attempt to ban the Jama'at-i Islami, which had opposed the founding of Pakistan before Independence, was rejected by the Supreme Court precisely because this party had been in the vanguard of efforts to make Pakistan an Islamic state.

Following the secession of East Pakistan (thereafter Bangladesh) in 1971, Zulfikar 'Ali Bhutto became the president of what remained of Pakistan. His Pakistan People's Party (PPP) originally leaned to the left. But he did not want to leave the enthusiasm for Islam in the country unutilized, and therefore called for "Islamic socialism." Under pressure from the opposition and especially the Islamists, however, not much socialist content remained in the version of the constitution drawn up by his government in 1973.[19] At the same time, more Islamic provisions were added, and for the first time Islam was declared the state religion. In addition to the office of president, which the two earlier versions of the constitution had also stipulated could be held only by a Muslim, now the office of prime minister was subject to the same condition as well. To underscore his work in the service of Islam, Bhutto had parliament declare the Ahmadiyya a non-Islamic minority in 1974.[20] His predecessors had all hesitated to take this step in order not to encourage an ominous development. Since then the Islamists have called for excluding the Dhikris and Shi'a from Islam as well. After joining together into the Pakistan National Alliance for the March 1977 elections, the opposition parties responded to Bhutto's attempt to harness Islam in the service of his regime by taking the Qur'an as their election manifesto. They revealed his pseudo-Islamic actions as a sham and called for turning Pakistan into a true Islamic state.[21] Election fraud committed by the PPP government triggered mass demonstrations, which encouraged the head of the army, General Zia ul-Haq, to take power. It was therefore no coincidence that General Zia later used Islamic policy to consolidate his regime and legitimize his rule.[22]

Shortly after taking power, Zia announced that an Islamic system was to be introduced. The cornerstone of the Islamic state was presumably laid by his introduction of amputation as punishment for theft and robbery. Regulations on fornication, fornication-related libel, and theft of property rights as well as the prohibition on alcohol came into effect shortly thereafter on February 10, 1979. On the same date Shariat Benches were set up at all the high courts. In May 1980 a Federal Shariat Bench was formed, and later a Shariat Court was added to the Supreme Court. These were to be commissioned by the federal or provincial governments or petitioned by citizens to evaluate whether a given law conformed with Islamic injunctions. In addition, a permanent legal council was set up to advise on the Islamization of legislation. At the Qaʾid-i-Aʿzam University in Islamabad, a shariʿa faculty was established that subsequently became an Islamic university. At the same time, a fund was set up for the collection of *zakat,* primarily from bank accounts.[23] *Zakat* committees were appointed to distribute these monies to the needy; in the process they also helped establish a clientele for Zia throughout the country. His successors have since made enthusiastic use of this instrument, especially as these funds are distributed largely to their own supporters.

The Shiʿa rebelled against the collection and management of *zakat* by state offices. According to Twelver Shiʿi law (*fiqh jaʿfariyya*), such money has to be channeled to clerics, who are free to distribute it to the needy at their discretion. Several days of strikes and an unparalleled march on Islamabad succeeded in getting them exempted from mandatory payment of *zakat* to the state. What they did not manage, however, was to institute separate instruction for Shiʿi schoolchildren in "Islamic history and theology" (Islamiyat) as promised by Bhutto. Zia disregarded this agreement and declared that instruction in the subject had to be uniform. He did, however, assure Shiʿi representatives on July 6, 1980, that constitutional guarantees would be instituted for *fiqh jaʿfariyya,* though all this yielded was an amendment to an article of the constitution stating that *fiqh jaʿfariyya* should be applied to Shiʿa in matters of personal law, which was common practice anyway.

Presumably in order to legitimize his rule, Zia had a referendum held in December 1984 that asked whether voters agreed with his Islamization policy. Although voter participation reached barely 20 percent, Zia proclaimed that an overwhelming majority of the people had answered the question in the affirmative, and had therefore voted him into another five years of office. This curious presidential election was followed in February 1985 by a parliamentary election in which political parties were not allowed to participate. Even before the government was formed, with Muhammad Khan Junejo commissioned to do so, the 1973 constitution was resuscitated in a strongly modified form. At his opening speech to parliament on March 23, 1986, Zia called for continuing the policy of Islamization. Shortly thereafter two Islamist senators, evidently with the support of Zia, introduced a private Shariat Bill which was approved at that time by the Senate, although the Junejo government viewed it with reservations. The bill met with opposition in the National Assembly, so the government introduced its own legislation, a ninth amendment to the constitution, which rendered the Shariat Bill superfluous. It stipulated that Islamic injunctions as contained in the Qurʾan and the sunna of the Prophet form the supreme law and source of guidance for legislation enacted by the parliament and provincial assemblies and for policymaking by the government. It also stated that the Federal Shariat Bench was to extend its jurisdiction to fiscal legislation, and that it was authorized to declare the constitution or parts thereof invalid if they did not conform to Islamic doctrine. Although this was not enough for the Islamists, they voted with the government coalition that had formed in the meantime to accept the ninth amendment to the constitution. They held to their demand, however, that the Shariat Bill must also be passed, by which they sought to rescind the sovereignty of the constitution. Zia supported them in their efforts and encouraged them to apply pressure on the government, which in his opinion had been neglecting the policy of Islamization.

This was also one of the reasons he cited for dissolving the Junejo government on May 29, 1988. A few days later the Shariat Ordinance was decreed, which contained nearly everything that the Shariat Bill had sought. It had a limited lifespan, however, having to be issued anew every four months. Following Zia's death on August 17, 1988, his successor, Ghulam Ishaq Khan, extended its validity for another four months on October 15, 1988. But Benazir Bhutto, the daughter of Zulfikar 'Ali Bhutto, who had become prime minister in the meantime, was not willing to introduce the ordinance for adoption by the National Assembly, which meant that it lost its validity for good on February 15, 1989. Bhutto's actions in this regard prompted the opposition to brand her administration anti-Islamic. When President Ghulam Ishaq Khan dismissed her government on August 6, 1990, however, the reasons given did not include a failure to pursue Islamization.

The opposition party Islami Jumhuri Ittihad (IJI), which had gathered together nearly all the opponents of the PPP for the upcoming parliamentary elections in October 1990, campaigned with the promise to pass the Shariat Bill as one of its first actions after forming a government. Yet it redeemed this promise differently than anticipated by the Islamists. Instead of the Shariat Bill, the government of Muhammad Nawaz Sharif introduced its own proposed legislation to parliament, which was then passed by a majority. Sharif was already known for the remark that he wanted to pass a "nonfundamentalist" law. It is notable that this legislation, the Enforcement of Shariah Act (ESA, 1991), contrasted with the Shariat Bill by not infringing on the sovereignty of the constitution or transferring jurisdiction to the courts in place of parliament.[24] Nevertheless, it did raise shari'a to state law although the constitution had already designated it *the* source of guidance for legislation. Indeed this act was conspicuous for the fact that nearly all of its content already existed prominently in the constitution. Examples include requiring the state to take measures to introduce an "Islamic economic system" as well as appropriate steps to Islamize the judicial system. Although the Islamists had voted to adopt the ESA, they were dissatisfied in large part with it because it stated that the judicial system may not call into question parliamentary democracy or the existing system of government. It also stipulated that the constitutional rights guaranteed non-Muslims and women may not be violated.

The Islamists nevertheless viewed passage of the ESA as a preliminary victory because it contributed to the Islamization of the country. But they did not conceal their disappointment with the Sharif government, which they accused of having capitulated to criticism from abroad. Shortly thereafter the Jama'at-i Islami left the IJI to pursue the struggle for an Islamic state on its own, as its members put it. They contested the parliamentary elections in October 1993 as a "third power" alongside the People's Party and the Pakistan Muslim League (PML). The Pakistan Islamic Front (PIF) was created specifically for this reason, although it was actually a cover organization for the JI. Like the other Islamic parties, it did miserably in the elections. Its leaders' hope that the winner would need them as a coalition partner was not fulfilled. It then attempted to present itself as the only clean and democratic party in the country as well as the champion of Muslim freedom fighters' causes in Indian Kashmir and Afghanistan. A cautious attempt by the Benazir Bhutto government in the spring of 1994 to annul or mitigate the infamous stipulations of paragraph 295-C of the Pakistan Penal Code (PPC) of October 12, 1986, which forbids abusing the name of the Prophet Muhammad under penalty of death, was used by the Islamic parties as an occasion to mobilize against her government.

Paragraph 295-C has been applied to an increasing extent against non-Muslims. There have been several cases of Christians being charged under it. In at least one case the accused was sentenced to death, although the penalty was not carried out; and elsewhere several accused Christians were murdered by (supposedly or actually) angry Muslims. Originally this paragraph was created to punish the Ahmadis, whose profession of faith per se is considered an insult to the Prophet. By revering their own founder as a Prophet, Ahmadis are accused by their enemies of slandering Muhammad, who is held to be the last of the prophets. Created under Zia ul-Haq, this penal provision represented the high-water mark of the development set in motion by his ordinance of April 26, 1984. It prohibited Ahmadis, under penalty of up to three years in prison and/or a fine, from applying to other persons certain terms traditionally reserved for the caliphs, the companions of the Prophet Muhammad, and similar revered figures; from using the term "mosque" (*masjid*) for their houses of worship; and from using the Muslim call to prayer (*adhan*). They were also forbidden to call themselves Muslims or their religion Islam, to preach their faith, to do missionary work, to proselytize, or to violate the religious sensibilities of Muslims. Since then charges have mounted against Ahmadis for their use of the greeting "peace be upon you" (*as-salamu 'alaykum*). For a time the Ahmadis courted arrest by wearing the Islamic profession of faith, "There is no God but Allah, and Muhammad is His Prophet" (*la ilaha illa Allah wa-Muhammad rasul Allah*), in an attempt to demonstrate to the world the nonsensical quality of this regulation. This offense led to the courts sentencing thousands of Ahmadis to years in prison. In the meantime, the Ahmadiyya appear to have departed from this confrontational course, on which they can only lose. They are in the process of generating a new religious vocabulary to ensure the survival of their community in Pakistan. Thus far, however, they have strictly refused to accept the status of a non-Muslim religious community.

They reject participation in parliamentary elections, for example, although one seat was reserved for them in both the National Assembly and the Provincial Assembly of the Punjab. In fact, Islamization policy was the general basis on which separate election rights for Muslims and non-Muslims were introduced. Yet the advantage gained from having seats in parliament reserved for non-Muslims was more than overshadowed by the disadvantages entailed by separate election rights. Members of non-Islamic religious communities were seen by their compatriots as foreign elements, and their loyalty to the state and society was viewed as suspect.

Election rights were changed once again in 2002. All citizens, regardless of their religious affiliation, may now exercise both passive and active rights in general elections. At the same time, sixty seats are reserved for women and ten for non-Muslims, to be assigned by the elected parliamentarians. Independently of this provision, both women and non-Muslims may run in the general elections without reducing their respective quotas if elected.

The Muttahida Majlis-i 'Amal Pakistan (MMA), an electoral alliance of Jama'at-i Islami, Jam'iyyat al-'Ulama'-i Islam, Jam'iyyat-i 'Ulama'-i Pakistan, and three other religious parties, won 11.3 percent of the vote and became a vocal opposition to the regime of general Pervez Musharraf (1999–2008), but broke up before the 2008 elections. Musharraf's political and military support for the United States's "war on terrorism" sparked protests in all conservative factions of society, in particular among fundamentalists and Deobandis. The "Red Mosque" (Lal Masjid) in Islamabad, led by Abdul Aziz and Abdul Rashid Ghazi, became a centre of criticism and militancy. Army commandos stormed the mosque on July 10, 2007, killing Abdul Rashid Ghazi and dozens of his followers. Since then, Pakistan has witnessed a series of suicide bombings against security forces and politicians in cities such as Karachi, Lahore, and Islamabad. On December 27, 2007, former Prime Minister Benazir Bhutto was killed in such an attack at Liaquat Bagh in Rawalpindi.

Translated by Marlene Schoofs

8. Bangladesh

(Hans Harder)

a. Overview

Present-day Bangladesh was formed from the eastern wing of Pakistan in 1971–72 following a bloody war for independence. Yet to understand the country's recent history and the role of Islam in its development, attention must also be given to the 1947 partition of India and its period of existence as part of Pakistan.

Following Independence in 1947, British India was divided into two sovereign states: India and Pakistan. The pivotal reason behind drawing these borders was primarily the majority situation based on the demographics for religion. India received the territories with Hindu majorities and Pakistan the Muslim ones. The largest concentrations of Muslims, however, were clustered not in one contiguous territory but rather along the northwestern and northeastern borders of the subcontinent. For this reason Pakistan as it was created in 1947 formed a highly irregular entity: 1,500 kilometers of Indian territory divided West Pakistan, a vast region that was ethnolinguistically heterogeneous yet was more than 90 percent Muslim, from East Pakistan, a small, extremely populous area in the Ganges Delta that was nearly entirely Bengali yet also contained large percentages of non-Muslims (more than 30 percent by 1947). The western parts of Bengal, which had a Hindu majority, then became a state of the Indian Union called West Bengal. Until this point East Bengal had been a remote area relying predominantly on agriculture. The newly formed East Pakistan, which was a result of the partition of Bengal in 1947 following Independence, was now isolated from its urban and economic center, Kolkata; this caused the various religious minorities to emigrate in large numbers to the territories of their respective majorities.

The Bengalis formed the majority in Pakistan, yet they were vastly underrepresented in political bodies and suffered economic disadvantages. Moreover the government initially refused to recognize Bengali as the second official language after Urdu. This depreciatory attitude of the West Pakistanis toward the Bengalis, who on average are smaller built and have darker skin, can be traced back to the Turkish and Persian ruling classes' feeling of superiority over the local population in premodern times and during the Mughal Empire in particular. Furthermore, there were certain doubts as to the "Islamic character" of the Bengali language and Bengali Muslims in general, not to mention their loyalty to Pakistan. Yet the Bengali Muslims were the ones who had offered support in raising political will among Indian Muslims when the Muslim League was founded in Dacca in 1906, and in the following years the Pakistan movement was advanced here as enthusiastically as in other parts of India. Urdu and Persian were cultivated here only by groups of the privileged *ashraf* class; by the mid-twentieth century their status had dwindled in favor of Bengali.

The fact that Muhammad 'Ali Jinnah and other West Pakistani leaders after him opposed recognition of the Bengali language eventually led to the formation of the Bengali Language Movement. A protest organized by Bengali intellectuals and university students in Dacca on February 21, 1952, was broken up by force of arms; this date, which the UN declared International Mother Language Day, provided the first martyrs for the advancement of Bengali nationalism, and it became the crystallization point of the movement, in which the calls for secession gradually grew stronger in view of repeated disappointments. In 1970 the charismatic Bengali nationalist

Shaykh Mujibur Rahman won the Pakistan general elections together with his Awami League. These elections were annulled by the West Pakistani leaders and led to the Bangladesh Liberation War (*muktiyuddha*), or the Secession War of 1971, in which the Pakistani military responded using horrific means verging on a pogrom, which were also directed against the civilian Bengali population. The military support of India under Indira Gandhi eventually tipped the outcome in favor of Bangladesh.

The fledging state of Bangladesh presented itself with a decisively secular and socialist constitution that does not grant any religious group a political status and forbids religious-backed political parties under Section 38, which affected both the Jamaʿat-i Islami and the Muslim League. In 1976, following the murder of founder and president Mujibur Rahman and during the military rule of General Ziaur Rahman, the ban was lifted for parties with a religious orientation, and in 1988 Islam was declared the official religion during Muhammad Ershad's tenure. The Awami League unsuccessfully attempted to reverse this decision during its term in 1996–2001. From 2001 to 2006 an Islamist party, the Jamaʿat-i Islami, was part of the government.

b. The Islamization of Bengal

The Islam of Bangladesh appears at first glance to be more homogeneous than that of Pakistan or India. There are approximately 120 million Muslims living in Bangladesh (more than one-tenth of all Muslims in the world), and they are, with few exceptions, all Sunnis who adhere to the Hanafi school of legal thought. The number of Shiʿites is negligibly small, and groups such as the Ahmadiyya or Ismaʿiliyya are not very widespread, despite the impression evoked by recent attacks. Yet this homogeneous image is deceptive. When viewed more closely, numerous local religious groups, which are often little known, not to mention little studied, come to the surface even to this day. They are the products of the specific type of Islamization that transpired in Bengal.

The Islamization of Bengal took place gradually and over a long period of time, starting even before the Turk Bakhtiyar Khilji from Central Asia conquered the country and seized it from the Hindu Sen rulers in 1201. The process only gained speed in the sixteenth and seventeenth centuries during the Mughal Empire. By the beginning of the sixteenth century, the main channel of the Ganges had shifted eastward into what had previously been a heavily forested area of the delta, opening up new possibilities for agricultural use. The spread of Islam is viewed in conjunction with the clearing, cultivation, and settlement of this region, which was further advanced by land grants and other such means. Immigrants from the northwestern parts of South Asia as well as present-day Afghanistan and Iran spearheaded this settlement movement and brought with them the high form of Islam to the local populations, who were only superficially Hindus or animists. The persistence of large numbers of Muslims in the eastern part of Bengal is attributed to the collective, mostly only nominal conversion that took place in these newly formed village communities. For various ideological reasons other factors such as the conversions forced on the local populations by the Muslim rulers, a supposed social liberation from an oppressive Hindu society, and immigration from Islamic source countries are often underscored in this respect, but it is unlikely that they played a major role in terms of numbers.[1]

The Islam spreading through Bengal by these means served as a rural religion and was characterized strongly by elements of Sufism. The pioneers of this rural immigration, dubbed Sufi settlers by Richard Eaton, became saints in many places, and their shrines became places of worship (for example, Khan Jahan Ali in Bagerhat). Furthermore, they assumed the roles that the different folk deities had previously performed, such as providing protection from the wilderness and diseases. The teachings of the Bengali Sufis from the late Middle Ages were also infused to a great degree with yogic and tantric concepts as well as themes stemming from Hindu mythology. In this manner beliefs from Bengali folk religions, with their part Buddhist-Hindu, part local origins, were integrated into the Islam of Bengal.[2] Even to this day the mystic groups in particular show undeniable elements of Vishnuite and yogic-tantric concepts.

The early urban centers must be viewed differently. They were the venues where the religious movements came into close contact with national developments within Islam and thus were less inclined to adopt local forms of religion. The castes of *ashraf* (Arab. "noble person") and *atrap* (from Arab. *ajlaf,* "common person," "uneducated person"), which even today carry some relevance in Bangladesh, refer to the foreign or local origin of the classes in question, and in terms of religious observance, the latter caste was associated with deep-rooted local forms of Islam.

At the beginning of the nineteenth century, East Bengal came under the influence of Islamic reform movements. The victory of the British East India Company over the Nawab of Bengal in the battle of Plassey in 1757 and the ensuing loss of direction felt by a part of the Muslim population provided the backdrop for this growing influence. The renunciation of the "true belief" was in part made responsible for the situation, and there were calls for a renewed moral awakening that could be achieved by embracing the "fundaments" of Islam and rejecting the "Hinduized" practices of folk religions such as the worshipping of saints' tombs by numerous sects. The Fara'izi movement, founded in 1818 by Shariatullah (Shari'atullah, 1781–1840), a religious leader from Faridpur, played a more significant role in this respect than the Tariqat al-Muhammadiyya, which was mainly active in the northwestern part of the subcontinent and whose influence extended to the western parts of Bengal. Shariatullah was introduced to Wahhabism in 1799 while in Mecca. In Bengal he started a movement against practices in folk religions and sects of saint worship invoking concepts such as *shirk* (polytheism) and *bid'a* (sinful innovation). He declared British India to be the *dar al-harb* (house of war) and suspended the Friday and *ʿid* prayers. Printed in pamphlets on Islamic topics, his messages, in particular those that were written in Bengali, were circulated in the press and had a great impact on the East Bengali rural population. Shariatullah's son Dadhu Mian led the movement after his father's death and added an aspect of social revolution to his father's work. He was arrested in 1857 during the Indian Mutiny, thus ending the dynamic phase of the movement. Their reformist concepts, however, were adopted by various groups, and they retain their importance today as predecessors to later Islamist movements and as the original crystallization point of a distinct socioreligious identity, in particular for the rural Muslims of Bengal.[3]

c. Folk Islam and Sufi Traditions

Despite these attempts at reform, Sufism and folk Islamic beliefs remain widespread. The anniversaries of the death of local saints or *pirs*, which are referred to as *ʿurs* ("wedding day," referring to the union of the saint with God) in other parts of South Asia, remain popular national holidays. Many of the old groups practicing shrine worship are showing signs of bringing their beliefs up to date and reinterpreting them. The local patron of Sylhet, Shah Jalal Mujarrad, one of the early Sufis and purveyors of Islam in East Bengal, came from Yemen (other reports state that he came from Konya, Turkey), and even orthodox Muslims still worship at his shrine. There is, however, an increasing process of "purification" of devotional practices taking place. For example, the *sijda*, a bow performed with knees and head touching the ground before the saint's tomb, and *samaʿ*, which involves a dance performance with devotional songs at the shrine, are under scrutiny and are increasingly being sanctioned. The saint is transformed from a miracle-performing mystic to a historic pioneer of Islamization. Sects with lesser saints are being orphaned and the role of living *pirs* (spiritual leaders) is becoming more and more marginalized in society. Bangladeshi migrant workers in Saudi Arabia, the Gulf region, and Great Britain play a role in this context, exerting particularly strong influence in Sylhet, and even in the rest of Bangladesh, as they, after returning home, strive to implement the concepts of a purified Islam that they learned from their time spent abroad, as a result of a privileged economic position.[4]

In other areas the trend goes in a completely opposite direction. For example, many regions of Chittagong have been experiencing for several decades a veritable renaissance of sects practicing shrine worship and Sufi traditions infused with local beliefs. The role of the Maizbhandari movement deserves special mention in this respect. From the mid-nineteenth century onward a number of mystics venerated as saints toiled to create an eminent pilgrimage center, giving rise to the Maizbhandari *tariqa* (Sufi order). It is the only Bengali order of any prominence with firm roots that could assert itself alongside the orders of Chishtiyya, Qadiriyya, and Suhrawardiyya and spread across the borders of Bangladesh and into all of South Asia. This religious movement, which also continues to use Vishnuite and tantric-yogic images and has gained notoriety beyond its national borders, attained popularity mainly through its tradition of mystic songs (*mar'phati gan*). Owing to the Maizbhandari movement, other sects practicing shrine worship in Chittagong have also seen an improvement in their image. Old shrines are being revitalized and new ones are being built. Songs about saints in the Maizbhandari tradition are being dedicated to other Muslim and even Hindu saints.

There are a variety of groups in various parts of Bangladesh whose doctrines are often extremely independent—for example, the Sufi tradition of Mirzakhil (Chittagong), the groups of the extremely popular Atrasi Pir (in Faridpur, Dacca, the personal *pir* of the former head of state, president Mohammad Ershad), the Sufi Samrat ("Sufi ruler," in Dacca), and the Naqshbandi movement of Thakurgaon, to name a few.

Worthy of mention here are the Bauls, who form a closed, antiritualistic group of mystics living in both Bangladesh and West Bengal. They combine esoteric teachings intermixing Vishnuite, tantric, and Sufi thought and are considered to be an emblem of Bengali mystic folk belief and tradition since Rabindranath Tagore started to lend a sympathetic ear to this form of religion because of its mystic songs. In Bangladesh these mystics are simply and indistinctly referred to as *phakir* (fakir). Time and again Bauls presumed to be heretics are persecuted, often with violent means, by followers of orthodox Islam. At the same time there are also enormous undertakings to integrate one of the most prominent Baul spiritual leaders, Lalan Fakir, as a Sufi master in the Islamic canon of saints.[5]

d. Islamic Reform and Islamism

At the opposite end of the religious spectrum are groups that focus on providing access to Islam through its written documents instead of local traditions. It is often difficult to define boundaries because the Sufi movements in Bangladesh also develop and promote the writings of their teachings, and the attitude of modern "Islamic law" and the orthodoxy toward the representatives of the Sufi and folk religion groups ranges from friendly affection to harsh rejection. The same holds true for the Sunni madrasas in the country, which, depending on their dogma, provide greatly varying interpretations of sainthood, for example. Therefore the real antipode to Sufi Islam and folk Islam is the reformist, fundamentalist movements, which often represent an Islam with Wahhabi traditions and receive vast sums of financial assistance from Saudi Arabia. Many of the approximately 7,000 madrasas (as of 1998; compared to 66,000 primary schools and 13,000 secondary schools) in the country are maintained by this funding.

The most important popular movement from this end of the spectrum is the Tabligh-i Jama'at, which has also spread to other parts of South Asia and can boast a particularly large following in Bangladesh. Its members have a duty to participate actively in missionary work, and devotees are visited to encourage them to follow an inner mission and to remind them of the need to fulfill their religious duties. The followers of this movement are not involved in politics and are not recruited from a clearly defined political arena.

The Chhatra Shibir is the more radical and aggressive student wing of the Islamist party Jama'at-i Islami, which regained legal status in 1976. The Chhatra Shibir's sometimes bloody clashes with the student organizations of secular or left-wing parties are infamous, and the organization is also credited with active involvement in rioting directed against Hindus. Actions such as demands for protection money and torture methods in their struggle against their opponents are said to be common practices for the Chhatra Shibir. Yet this is the case with many other actors in the conflict-ridden and, in part, mafia-like student political scene in Bangladesh.

The majority of Biharis, who left Bihar, a state of the Indian Union, to settle in Bangladesh after Partition in 1947, are primarily followers of a strict form of Islam, members of the Jama'at-i Islami, and clear supporters of Pakistan and opponents of Bangladeshi nationalism. Many of them were active during the Liberation War in the al-Badr paramilitary organizations that targeted the Bengali intelligentsia with their acts of cleansing, among other methods, and greatly liquidated their numbers. Countless Biharis have emigrated to Pakistan in recent decades. Yet for those who stayed and in part are still living in camp settlements, the initial stigmatization has worn off, and their situation has improved.

There are many other Islamist organizations working only at the local level and with varying levels of outreach. Conflicts continue to arise between these organizations and groups observing folk religions as well as with aspects of the secular urban society and Western nongovernmental organizations. An organization called Sahaba Sainik Parisad entered the public spotlight when it issued a fatwa against the writer Taslima Nasrin and put a price on her head. Nasrin had taken a very critical stance on the position of women in Bangladesh and in Islam in general in her feminist writings. Most significantly in her novel *Lajja* (published in English as *Shame* in 1997), she had dared to side uncompromisingly with those who had been persecuted after riots directed against Bangladesh's Hindus broke out following the demolition of the Babri mosque in Ayodhya, India, in 1992. A publisher was put under pressure because he printed a short story by Selina Hossain that reportedly offended the feelings of Muslims because of its portrayal of a rape. Other events such as the celebration of Valentine's Day have also aroused unhappiness and demonstrations in recent years. The work of very visible foreign nongovernmental organizations carried out in Bangladesh has repeatedly evoked contempt from Islamist circles that consider efforts to improve the situation of women in particular (by providing them with microcredit to promote their economic independence through business projects or offering educational initiatives) to be inconsistent with Islam.

Yet the main political arm of Islamism is the Jamaʿat-i Islami. This party was originally an insignificant wing of the party founded by Maulana Abu l-Aʿla Maududi, which mainly operated out of West Pakistan. It was only in the 1960s that the Bengali wing of the Jamaʿat attained a position on the political stage that needed to be taken seriously. The creation of an Islamic government system in Bangladesh is its highest political goal. Prior to and during the Liberation War it opposed the calls for Bangladesh's independence in many areas and positioned itself alongside Pakistan. Deemed a collaborator, its leader, Ghulam Azam, spent much time as persona non grata and had to flee to West Pakistan to live in exile. His persona still pervades political discussions today. Not only was the rehabilitation of the Jamaʿat-i Islami in the independent state of Bangladesh sparked by economic need and the dependence on development aid and loans from Arab countries, whereby Saudi Arabia in particular set the recognition of Islam in public life as a major precondition for the aid, but also the military regime led by Ziaur Rahman and Mohammad Ershad sought the cooperation of the Jamaʿat to provide Islamic legitimacy to their rule both domestically and abroad. The Bangladesh National Party (BNP), led by Khaleda Zia, the widow of Ziaur Rahman, received the Jamaʿat's support in 1991, and after her party's victory she used her influence to call for a hardline stance toward "apostates" such as Taslima Nasrin. The Jamaʿat worked side by side with the BNP under Khaleda Zia in the government from 2001 until the end of her term and was replaced by the "caretaker government." Although they never won more than 12 percent of the vote in the elections and were able to pick up only a few seats in the parliament because of the majority voting system, the Jamaʿat knew how to influence the political debate to their advantage.[6]

More recently a wave of terror by Islamist groups such as the Jamaʿat al-Mujahidin Bangladesh has also stricken Bangladesh. The caretaker government responded with draconian measures (ordering the execution of a number of leaders in the spring of 2007) and announced as part of its political agenda that it would not provide Islamist terrorism and terrorism directed against India in Bangladesh with a base of operations.

It is difficult to expound quantitatively on these religious movements and modern, secular attitudes in present-day Bangladesh because specific characteristics can easily be found in several of them and their agendas are not always clearly defined.In many instances they are in gradual transition along a continuum. Nevertheless, a study conducted by Razia Akter Banu attempted just that, finding that the religious beliefs of Bangladeshi Muslims can be split into three types: modern, orthodox, and folk beliefs. In rural areas only 1 percent of the population practices a modern form of Islam, whereas 50 percent are orthodox believers and 48 percent observe folk beliefs. In an urban context 12 percent of those surveyed observe a modern form, 62 percent orthodox, and 25 percent folk beliefs.[7]

e. Islam and National Identity

Taking into account how Bangladesh was formed, we can see a certain level of tension between the models of how Islamic and Bengali groups identify themselves. In 1947 Pakistan, including its eastern wing, was set up to create a state of Indian Muslims as reflected by the majority situation on the basis of religion; with the independence movement and the Liberation War of 1971, however, a linguistic and ethnic Bengali identity emerged as a unifying factor. "Bengali Hindus, Bengali Christians, Bengali Buddhists, Bengali Muslims—we're all Bengali," proclaimed a widely displayed poster during the Liberation War. The difficulty when a national identity is redefined on the basis of a common language and culture is that there are also Bengalis living in Indian West Bengal. Thus the Bengali identity cannot be claimed by Bangladesh alone. In this respect, soon after Bangladesh gained independence, the ratio used for the partition of India reemerged as a factor defining identities: Islam became the majority religion of the population.

Bangladesh's cultural self-image alternates from broad (Bengali) to narrow (Bangladeshi) terms, the latter generally including Islam as a differentiating criterion. Complicating matters for a nationalism based purely on language and culture is that the Bengali identity was defined and brought to blossom in terms of culture by Bengali Hindus in Kolkata. For extended periods in the nineteenth century and even up to the beginning of the twentieth century, the Bengal renaissance had greatly influenced the national movements of the entire subcontinent and defined concepts of cultural heritage and national history.

Compensating trends in Bangladesh's cultural kitchen continue to resurface in an attempt to place the emphasis of the Bengali culture in Bangladesh and focus on the cultural industry of Bengali Muslims. Here, too, there emerges a difficulty for evaluating Bengali Islam, because the orthodox forms of this religion could be attributed for a long time to the urban and in part immigrant upper classes living in Bangladesh, while the rural population practiced an Islam imbued with folk beliefs and rich in local elements. The tension between loyalty to fundamental Islam and Bengali folk religions can still be felt even in academic debates. An affirmative analysis of medieval Muslim Bengali literature, which built greatly on local traditions, has been in the making for a long time, yet a consensus on the folk-religious traditions that continue to be practiced today has not been reached. Nevertheless, it appears to be noteworthy that brief statements issued by Bangladeshi embassies abroad underscore the "syncretistic" character of Bangladesh even in times when the Jama'at-i Islami is active in the government.

The Awami League, a party with a social democratic agenda, is generally credited with the efforts made to provide a balance between the different religious groups in Bangladesh. Excessive acts of violence by the Pakistani army and its backers, such as the al-Badr organizations, directed against Hindus in particular, have not been repeated to the same extent, yet discrimination and persecution at the local level continue to be reported. This is one of the factors contributing to the decreased number of Hindus in Bangladesh, which has seen a drop to only around 10 percent in recent years from 22 percent in 1951. There has been a gradual but steady emigration taking place in addition to the periodic surges of emigration during the partition of India and the Liberation War. The most overpowering reason for the Bangladeshi Hindus to emigrate, mainly to India, lies in the economic situation of the country. Significant numbers of Bangladeshi Muslims have become economic refugees, going, often illegally, to look for work in the urban centers of India or rural capitals of neighboring West Bengal.

A substantial number of Bangladeshis live primarily as migrant workers abroad—in the Arab countries, Southeast Asia, Japan, Great Britain (mainly London), the United States, and so on—and are subjected to a variety of conditions. Along with the nongovernmental organizations, they represent an enormous economic factor for the country. The effects of this process on the situation of Islam in Bangladesh have been the subject of only piecemeal investigations (see the foregoing discussion on Sylhet). We can expect to see that the future configuration of Islam and the nation itself in Bangladesh will also be defined by the Muslim immigrants and in that respect by developments in the Islamic world and various Islamic diasporas.

Translated by David Fenske

9. Southeast Asia

(Olaf Schumann)

a. Indonesia

The Republic of Indonesia is neither a secular state nor an Islamic state. After declaring independence on August 17, 1945, Indonesia established the ideology of Pancasila, the Five Principles or Pillars. (Indonesian and Malay terms in this section are written using the official orthography that both countries introduced in 1973.) The first principle states that all Indonesians believe in the "one and only divine lordship," according to the doctrine of one of the five recognized religions: (Sunni) Islam, Protestantism, Catholicism, Hinduism, and Buddhism. In this respect Indonesia is a "religious" nation, in which religious life is protected and backed by the state, yet the state has no right to intervene in the internal affairs of a religious community as set forth in the 1945 constitution, which also embodies the ideology of Pancasila in its preamble. The state considers the one and only divine lordship (Ketuhanan Yang Maha Esa) to be a matter of constitutional law in that it is not based on or legitimized by a religion and thus does not raise one religion to the status of a state religion. The state acknowledges that all of its citizens belong to one of these five state-sanctioned religions by their own free choice and that the state endeavors to protect religious life and religious observance in accordance with the various interpretations of these beliefs. The state guarantees freedom of worship without bias. Neither the state nor any of its bodies follows a particular theology, which makes it different from an "Islamic state."

Initially the 1945 constitution was intended to be provisional. After the internal political situation was stabilized and independence was recognized by the former colonial power, the Netherlands, under international law at the end of 1949, a freely elected body, the *konstituante,* was to draft the final constitution, and with it the finalized version of the state's ideological foundation. This *konstituante* was finally elected in 1955. The Islamist parties, which received 43.5 percent of the overall vote, sought to form a government, in which Islamic law, shari'a, was recognized as the foundation of the constitution. These parties advocated the dissolution of Pancasila because it did not grant special rights to any specific religious group. Although the election results did not place the Islamist parties in a position to implement their objectives, they were able to prevent the creation of a two-thirds majority, which would have been necessary for final recognition of Pancasila as a state-sanctioned ideology. After years of ineffectively debating this issue, the Indonesian president, Sukarno, issued a decree on July 5, 1959, in which he reinstated the 1945 constitution and its interpretation of Pancasila and dissolved the *konstituante.* All parties agreed to this decree by acclamation. The Indonesian government under General Suharto (starting in 1967) also embraced this decree. Thus the public debate on retaining Pancasila was officially put to rest; the internal discussions on the issue, however, are not over by far. Following Suharto's fall and the elections of 1999, several parliamentarians from small Islamic parties raised the issue again in parliament, although no changes were effected. Nevertheless, a veiled process of Islamization has been taking place through legislation.

The Indonesian leadership under Suharto attempted to anchor Pancasila gradually in both the constitution and society. In 1978 the People's Consultative Assembly approved a decision on Guidance to Understanding and Implementing Pancasila and called for political organizations to adopt Pancasila as an ideological basis in their respective structures.[1] In August 1981 an official statement was released announcing that any Indonesian who questions the 1945 constitution and thus the philosophy of Pancasila as worded in its preamble would be accused of subversion and should expect to receive the harshest of punishments for such crimes. At the same time, preparations were being made for a law, which was eventually passed in 1985, requiring all "social" organizations, including religious ones and churches, to embrace Pancasila in their structures as the sole basis of social and political life. It is, however, the interpretation as established in this "guideline" that was made legally binding, and not Pancasila itself.[2]

Indonesia is home to the world's largest Muslim community. According to official figures from 2005, Muslims made up approximately 87 percent—or, correcting for irregularities prevalent after the 1980 census, approximately 73 percent—of the 240 million people living in Indonesia.[3] Many belong to mystic brotherhoods. In 1973 all earlier Islamic parties, ranging from the "modernists" to the "traditionalist" Nahdlatul Ulama (NU), were consolidated into the United Development Party (Partai Persatuan Pembangunan, or PPP) as part of a political party reform. This party takes an ambivalent stance toward the 1945 constitution and Pancasila; at least that is the impression received by other political groups as well as the government and military. The PPP is determined to require all Muslims to abide by shariʿa as established through national law, if not through the constitution. Opponents consider these efforts to be nothing more than a new tactic in the attempt to achieve the old objective of creating an Islamic state, because once all Muslim Indonesians abide by shariʿa, it will not be possible to prevent changes to the constitution in the long run. As a union of all the Islamic parties from the days of the *konstituante,* the PPP also claims to speak for all Muslims in Indonesia and to represent them as a group, which is demonstrated by its use of the Kaʿba on its party flag. Yielding to pressures before the elections in 1987, the party replaced this symbol with the star that stands for the first pillar on the Pancasila coat of arms. The Islamists—that is, politicians from the *santri* (discussed later in this chapter)—have repeatedly professed their allegiance to Pancasila; even their representatives agreed to Sukarno's 1959 decree.[4] Yet they still point out that they accept Pancasila only because they interpret the first pillar in terms of the Islamic *tawhid,* the belief in the one and only divine lordship.

This line of argumentation is by all means legitimate because the first pillar does not contain any particular religious ideology in and of itself; instead each religious community must provide its own doctrine. Problems arise only when attempts are made to obligate other religious communities to abide by the Islamic interpretation too. This arouses the resistance not only of non-Muslims but also of Muslim nationalists who have refrained from calling for specific Islamic demands in the interest of all Indonesian people and therefore have often been inappropriately labeled "secular nationalists." They dispute the PPP's claim to speak for all Muslims.

Both the Islamists and the Pancasila supporters have set their sights on a specific understanding of unity. This fact sheds light on the great chasm that divides their respective worldviews and that is camouflaged by the quarrels in daily political life.

The Islamists consider the unity of the Islamic *umma,* the people of God, as a reflection of their commitment to the one and only divine lordship. The unity of the *umma* manifests itself in the shared commitment to and observance of law as the basis of social order. The Islamists trace these roots back to the revelation from God as received by the Prophet. Differences in laws between the various Islamic groups are acceptable as long as these differences are in the details. They are not acceptable in matters of principle.

In Indonesia this unity of the *umma* has advanced quite well in the past, according to the Islamists. The Shafi'i school of legal thought was adhered to, at least until the rise of the Islamic reform movements at the end of the nineteenth century. The Islamic sultanates had brought large swaths of present-day Indonesia under their control, especially Mataram, with its power center in Central Java. Mataram under Sultan Agung (r. 1613–1648), its most prominent ruler, even sallied forth to accept the ideological and territorial legacy of the last major Hindu empire of Majapahit (defeated in 1478 in a decisive victory by Raden Patah, the first Islamic prince of Java). It was only the intervention of the European colonial powers, in particular the Dutch, and their cooperation with traditional (*adat*-oriented) leaders that prevented Indonesia from being unified under the banner of Islam.[5] Later the opposition against the foreign rulers was led predominantly by the Islamic kingdoms or princes. The first nationalist organization in the twentieth century, Serikat Islam, even fought against Dutch rule under the banner of Islam.[6]

The Islamists claim, however, that the Dutch attempted to instigate discord among the Muslims by applying the divide-and-conquer approach. It was to be expected that the Dutch would try to set the various Islamic princes, or in more recent times the different Islamic organizations, in opposition to one another. More fatal were the Dutch attempts to undermine the legal unity of the Muslims, in particular by using the knowledge of the orientalist C. Snouck Hurgronje (d. 1936). The Dutch would support groups in the various courts or populations that abided by the *adat* (from Arab. *'ada*, tradition, custom) and its law, imposing Islamic law only as it fit in with the *adat*.

For this reason the Islamists felt that since before World War II they had been standing on the front lines opposite proponents of the *adat* who not only exerted a certain influence over the Dutch but also held considerable sway with the nationalists, albeit for other reasons.[7] Several of them were legal counselors who had received their training in the *adat* legal school founded by Cornelis van Vollenhoven, a legal scholar from Leiden, the Netherlands.[8] They focused on finding common basic structures in the different *adat* traditions that could then serve as the ideological foundation for the Indonesian constitution and its underlying legal system as an authentic Indonesian cultural legacy. As a result they championed a separation of religion and state, contrary to the Islamists, who maintained that religion, specifically Islam, and the state were intertwined.

The line of argumentation favored by the Pancasila supporters is also shouldered by a specific concept of how the unity of the Indonesian people and their cosmos should be defined. In particular, ancient Javanese traditions and mysticism come to the fore in this respect. The Pancasila supporters regard Islam as the destroyer of the ancient Hindu-based order. They maintain that Islam has been incapable of replacing the old order with a new one that makes the entire population "feel at home." Even within the Islamic community the tensions between the *santri* (San. *sastri*, scholar), that is, the advanced students of Islamic boarding schools (*pesantren*), and the *abangan* (the "red" or "brown" ones, the true Javanese) have been flaring up repeatedly over the years.[9] The reason behind the conflict is said to be the "Arabic" elements of Islam.

These elements originated with a particular group of Muslims, namely the Muslim Arabs, yet they are not any closer to the nature of eternal Islam than the Indonesian ones. Each community is expected to decide how Islam is incorporated into its respective cosmos, so that elements originating in other human contexts, such as the Arab ones, do not become a source of irritation as Islam becomes established in the Indonesian context. Islam can be seen as "tolerant" only when the teachings of Islam, such as the belief in the one and only divine lordship and the legal norms, have been adapted to the Indonesian way of thinking. Yet the *santri* and many Islamic politicians continually accuse representatives of this tolerant form of Islam of spreading heresy. This attitude exemplifies how the *santris*' concept of unity is limited to their own group and the convictions they entertain. This situation builds up tensions within the *umma* with the *abangan* and even the non-Muslim Indonesians that, in the end, make it impossible to unify the Indonesians under one nation.

According to Pancasila supporters, the history of the Serikat Islam also offers evidence of this fact. Once greater emphasis was placed on the Islamic character of the organization, in particular after the national congress that was held in 1921, which its founder H. O. S. Tjokroaminoto was not able to attend, this organization could no longer be the catchall for the nationalist groups. For this reason Sukarno, as one of the spokesmen for the nationalists, started drawing on the traditional Javanese philosophy of *gotong royong*, which is based on mutual assistance and solidarity, after first becoming active in politics in 1926. He combined it with socialist ideas and propagated the concept as the ideological foundation, based on justice and harmony, for the peaceful coexistence of all Indonesians. He thought that *gotong royong* should be revived after independence was achieved and believed that the kingdom of Ratu Adil, which many Indonesians longed for, would reemerge with its implementation.[10] In addition to its socialist elements, *gotong royong* contained democratic ones, including those typical of Indonesian as opposed to Western philosophy. It was thought that the concept of collective, unanimous decision making by *mufakat* (Arab. *muwafaqa*, consensus), which is also an expression of an all-inclusive unity, could be achieved through joint consultation, *musyawarat* (Arab. *mushawara*), allowing the participation of representatives from all groups.

There is also an affinity here for Islamic thinking, as reflected by the terms adopted from Arabic. Even though participation for Muslims in the *musyawarat* is limited to representatives of the *umma*, Sukarno's intentions were aimed at representatives of the entire nation (*bangsa*). For this reason none of the religions practiced in Indonesia can play a role in shaping the unity of the nation as long as one group alienates other groups through a dogmatic system or sociological stance. Sukarno stood together with his adherents proclaiming the motto of the national movement in 1928 at the Youth Congress in the oath "One country, one people, one language." The religious thread binding all Indonesians together can be found embedded in the empirical religions or, in historical terms, before them: it is the belief in the one and only divine lordship. This belief is merely expressed in more detail and in a different manner by the doctrines of the respective religions. Belief in a religion, not the observance of any one specific religion, was to define the nature of the Indonesians and to be espoused by the constitution. Every Indonesian should be free to practice his or her religion of choice.

In this respect Sukarno leaned toward separation of religion and state and held the opinion that Islam would also do best to modernize its teachings and its self-image. As a role model he pointed to Mustafa Kemal Atatürk with great admiration in this regard. Like Atatürk's "laicism," Sukarno's idea of the relationship between state and religion (and culture) was also not a secular, Western-style concept, despite accusations by Islamists, and despite how other groups of nationalists represented it.

This fact became evident when Sukarno presented his concept of Pancasila in the final months before the end of the Second World War. The negotiations on the constitution entered a crucial stage after the Japanese occupational forces had finally promised independence to the Indonesians and it was becoming more and more evident that the Japanese would be defeated. In a committee set up by the Japanese to prepare for Indonesian independence, Sukarno delivered his famous speech, "The Birth of Pancasila," on June 1, 1945, in which he summed up the "soul" that the constitution would reanimate in five principles:

1. *Ketuhanan Yang Maha Esa* (the one and only divine lordship)[11]
2. *Kemanusiaan yang adil dan beradab* (fair and civilized humanity)
3. *Persatuan Indonesia* (the union of Indonesia)
4. *Kerakyatan yang dipimpin oleh hikmat kebijaksanaan dalam permusyawaratan/perwakilan* (democracy guided by wisdom through consultation and [parliamentary] representation)
5. *Keadilan sosial untuk seluruh Rakyat Indonesia* (social justice for the whole of the people of Indonesia)

Sukarno saw these five principles as espousing the "unified, philosophical basis, the 'view of the world,' in which we all agree. I repeat, agree!"[12]

And this was actually the case. At a meeting on June 22, 1945, the Islamists advocated only one addition to the first principle, obligating all Muslims to adhere to shariʿa.[13] The remainder of the members accepted this addition as a concession. The document that was approved there and proposed as the preamble to the constitution was later called the Jakarta Charter.[14]

But history passed the Jakarta Charter by. It would have meant granting special status to one group of the population, that is, the Islamic community it specified. Independence was declared on August 17, 1945. One day later the committee set up by the Japanese to produce a constitution convened to pass the preamble, which did not include the proposed "seven words" establishing shari'a. It is still unclear to this day who was responsible for this exclusion. Clearly there was an underlying fear that separatist tendencies would emerge in the non-Muslim territories if the Jakarta Charter were to be adopted, inspired by fears of an Islamic state. In reaction to a proposition by a Hindu Balinese, the term "Allah" was eliminated from one line stating that independence had been achieved by the "mercifulness of Allah" and it was replaced with "Tuhan Yang Maha Kuasa" (the Almighty Lord).[15] Another section of the draft constitution was "de-Islamified" when Article 6, which required the country's president to be a Muslim, was also dropped. In the end one more event disappointed the hopes of the Islamists: the Ministry of Religion, set up in January 1946, also received directorates-general for the recognized non-Muslim religions, therefore making it no longer in charge only of Muslim affairs. This ministry would have given Muslims their anticipated permanent seat in the government.

Now the Pancasila supporters had gained the upper hand in the contest for the national ideology. One of their leading legal authorities was Raden Supomo, who was a follower of van Vollenhoven's school. He had played a major role in the formulation of the 1945 constitution and in the foundation of the Indonesian legal philosophy after independence. He died in 1958.

The Islamists did not acquiesce to this development. Their political wing resumed its cooperation with the national government only after the Allied forces took the stage in the fall of 1945 and the subsequent arrival of the Dutch forces spelled danger for the country's independence. In view of the Muslim majority in the country, the outcome of the first free elections, which were finally held in 1955, gave hope to the political wing for a mandate that would legally amend the constitution to bring it in line with Islamic doctrine.

The militant wing of the Islamists, however, attempted to achieve this goal through military means. While still fighting against the Dutch in guerrilla warfare, S. M. Kartosuwirjo launched an uprising against the national government in 1948 in West Java, which was inhabited by the Sundanese. He proclaimed the creation there of Darul Islam (Arab. *dar al-islam*), that is, the Islamic State of Indonesia, in 1949.[16] Until his capture in 1962, West Java was plagued by bloody guerrilla warfare waged between its "Islamic Army" and the national army. In 1950 a similar Darul Islam movement led by Kahar Muzakkar emerged in Sulawesi, claiming many civilian lives as well in the years that followed. The unrest in that region ended only in

1967. In 1959 a compromise was negotiated with Daud (Da'ud) Beureueh, the leader of the Islamic rebellion in Aceh (North Sumatra). Since then Aceh has been the only province in Indonesia that officially recognizes shari'a. In spite of that, the government has been working for years to revoke this special status. This has led to the formation of new guerrilla groups, similar to the jihad groups that periodically appear in other regions and incite local unrest. Toward the end of Suharto's rule and even later, there was new, heavy warlike fighting between the Indonesian military and the rebels, in particular because of the rich natural resources in Aceh. For the people of Aceh, the issue of shari'a is of secondary concern. It is primarily exaggerated by the power center in Jakarta to discredit the resistance movement of the people of Aceh.

The clashes with the militant Islamists have strained the Indonesian army. Now any attempt to create a special status for Islam in the nation incites a heavy-handed response. For this reason the military government under President Suharto held on tightly to Sukarno's decree from 1959 that established the 1945 constitution and Pancasila as the unalterable foundation of the Indonesian state, despite all other criticism of the former president. The government also did not permit the Masyumi Party, whose agenda followed the ideas of "Islamic revival" and which was banned under Sukarno in 1960, to regroup after the change of power in 1967, even though the Islamic forces had expected government approval because of the party's active support of the military during the anticommunist "purging" of 1965–66. When the Partai Muslimin Indonesia was eventually formed in early 1968, it was ordered to ban leading representatives of the former Masyumi from holding any position as a party official. In 1973 it was also part of the fusion that created the new unifying Islamic party, the Partai Persatuan Pembangunan.[17]

Particularly since the ban on the Masyumi Party, which leading Islamist intellectuals had belonged to, many of these scholars began to think that their goal of creating an Islamic state could not be achieved, at least not at present. Their political opponents had become restive, and the Muslim population in general reacted with either complacency or disfavor. This outlook led to an intensification of the *da'wa* (invitation to propagate and increase understanding of Islam) from the 1960s on. Expanding the Islamic school system and intensifying religious classes in Islam in the state schools, providing further education especially directed at women, and distributing materials for teaching and edification were actions intended to shore up the Islamic consciousness, in particular of the *abangan,* who were the main cause of the losses in the elections. In addition to the area of education, the social organizations of Muhammadiyah, an educational and charitable organization founded in 1912, received even more support, in particular for their hospitals and medical clinics.[18] As the Suharto government implemented the development plans it embarked on in 1969, large amounts of federal funding that had been earmarked for assisting religious projects were made available for this program. Furthermore, an extensive program to erect new mosques as well as to expand older ones was carried out.

The focus in the political sector is primarily directed at influencing legislation in line with Islamic doctrine, or at least taking Islamic beliefs into consideration. It is not a backdoor attempt to indoctrinate the state with Islamic thinking, as some claim; not even the Masyumi offered concrete ideas toward this end, although it did champion the foundation of an Islamic state. Strictly speaking, Islam is not merely a religion but also a way of life. For this reason the state needs to provide the means for its Muslim citizens to lead their lives according to their view of the world.

Shedding some light on this subject is the marriage law that was passed in the parliament in late 1973. The government's proposal originally intended to replace the various regulations that were a vestige of Dutch rule and differed for each group of the population with a standardized national marriage law. The Islamists viewed this move as a secularization of marriage and raised their voices in protest. The wording of the law that was finally passed defines marriage in terms of the belief in the one and only divine lordship, the first pillar of Pancasila, and declares that a marriage is legally binding "if it has been performed according to the laws of the respective religions and beliefs of the parties concerned," that is, the nuptial couple (Articles 1 and 2). Notwithstanding this, they also need to be registered under civil law. The national courts adjudicate matters involving non-Muslims, whereas Muslims must turn to the Islamic religious courts. According to this law, every decision issued by an Islamic court, for example, in matters of divorce, had to be approved by a national court.[19]

Not only were the Islamists pushing for national law to require that Muslim marriages be recognized by Islamic law, but also they were working to confine as much as possible the application of *adat* law to Muslims, at least in order to achieve a legal entity for the whole of the Islamic community in Indonesia based on shari'a. Depending on how the addition of "and beliefs" to the abovementioned Article 2 is interpreted, it is possible to measure the extent to which this goal was achieved. For Islamists, "beliefs" is merely a postscript to the interpretation of "religion." Other scholars, whose sympathies obviously lie with the government, preferred to interpret "belief" (*kepercayaan*) as a reference to traditional Indonesian religions. In this way there is then also room for *adat* law. In actual practice it is possible to perform a marriage according to *adat* law, giving the couple the choice of which law will be applicable. This path is chosen primarily by couples who are members of different religious communities, since the 1973 marriage law contains no provisions for interfaith marriages.

Broadly speaking, legislation continues to be the showplace for the fight against *adat* law, that is, the fight against traditional Indonesian religious orders. This fight reached its climax in March 1978, when the newly elected People's Consultative Assembly met to discuss a government proposal to declare the religious orders a legacy worthy of government funding and as defining the identity of the Indonesians. The proposal was approved, albeit without the votes of the PPP parliamentarians, who for the first time in the history of an independent Indonesia staged a walkout during the vote and denied themselves *mufakat* in the process. The religious orders were recognized as a cultural heritage of Indonesia in 1978; the Islamists, however, were concerned that these religious orders would be elevated to the status of a faith. If that were to be the case, a substantial number of *abangan* would likely join forces with the religious orders and secede from the Islamic group. The Islamists have attempted to prevent this development; yet their efforts have led to tensions with the government, since a fair number of its members belong to the religious orders.

For many years the PPP had used the Ka'ba as its party symbol. By so doing it laid claim to its organization's representing the entire Muslim community in Indonesia—a claim criticized even by several Muslim activists. For its opponents the party was sending a signal that it aligned itself with a center that lay outside Indonesia. It apparently did not want to incorporate itself into the unity of the Indonesian cosmos, a perception that was only underlined by the party's walkout during the vote on the religious orders in 1978. A survey from early 1981 published in the Indonesian weekly news magazine *Tempo* found that there were no longer any supporters of an Indonesian Islamic state, especially because this concept had been discredited throughout its history in Indonesia and by events in Iran, which were initially followed favorably.[20] Even the significance of the Jakarta Charter was not discussed publicly. Yet the events that unfolded with the marriage law show that it was not forgotten. It is supposed to be "the life goal of every Muslim to create an Islamic personality and society," even at the national level.[21] This goal is juxtaposed, however, with the deep disdain felt by the majority of Indonesians toward everything foreign, including all "Arab" elements of Islam. Yet it has not prevented the Islamists from declaring these "Arab features" to be "Islamic" and emphasizing them as elements of their own special identity, which clearly further engenders alienation from the masses. The Islamists still have not provided an answer to the question how their goal can be achieved in a manner suitable to Indonesia.

Discord between members of the former NU (Nahdlatul Ulama) and the former Partai Muslimin Indonesia within the PPP, which became evident around 1980 when the candidate lists were being assembled for the upcoming elections, led eventually to the NU's decision at a congress in Situbondo (East Java) in 1984 to secede from the PPP and return to its political agenda dating from 1926, the year of its founding. Abdurrahman Wahid ('Abd al-Rahman Wahid), son of the former minister of religious affairs Wahid Hasyim (Wahid Hashim) and grandson of NU cofounder Hasyim Asy'ari (Hashim Ash'ari), was elected chairman. The NU has defined itself as a social organization, not a political one. It maintained the traditions of the Ahl al-sunna wa-l-jama'a in matters pertaining to religion, but it recognized

Pancasila as the "sole basis" (*satu-satunya asas*) for its social activities, anticipating the 1985 law mandating that all "social" organizations embrace it as the sole basis of their social and political activities.[22] The NU no longer had a reason to back only the PPP, because the political organizations (or parties) had already been placed under the mandate of a similar law, and the NU would also have had to sacrifice its character as an exclusively Islamic party, at least formally. NU members were now able to be members of any party. Another reason why the NU base in particular became increasingly estranged from the PPP was the dominant role of the party officials. Because they lacked their own base among the people, they were subjected or exposed to the influences exerted by other forces in order to maintain their position. The price exacted for this meant alienation from the people and their problems.

Whereas Suharto's administration had promoted the anchoring of Pancasila in public life since the end of the 1970s, it had also increasingly solicited the sympathetic awareness of followers of the "Islamic revival" in the Muhammadiyah, the bureaucracy, and among intellectuals. The administration hoped for a sustainable basis that would support the implementation of its development plans through a coalition of all bureaucrats and the fundamentalists. At the same time, the "fanatical" groups in Islam, whose activities continue to be directed against the government, could be more easily isolated.

The rapprochement of the Islamic and state bureaucrats, represented primarily by the professional groups supporting the government (Golongan Karya, also known as Golkar), caused the PPP to lose ground increasingly even among the Islamists. A surprising development could be observed in the elections of June 1992. The PPP performed best in areas where representatives from the NU—that is, politicians who were responsible to their own base—headed its slate of candidates.

The administration's efforts to reach out to the Islamists were expressed in the greater accommodations that were being made to Islamic demands in legislation, for example. This became clear with Law 7/1989 on the Islamic Courts of Justice (Peradilan Agama). Islamic courts were granted greater independence from the national courts, which are under the control of the Justice Ministry, in particular in matters affecting marriage law, inheritance, and "pious foundations" (Arab. *awqaf,* pl. of *waqf*).[23] The country's Supreme Court was only the court of third instance. The main problem, however, was that the Muslims were increasingly being separated from other groups of the population in legal matters affecting important areas of social life. This law only made the unresolved matter of religious marriages for interfaith couples with Indonesian citizenship more complicated. Even the 1989 law on the national education system granted the Ministry of Religious Affairs, which generally represents Islamic interests in these cases, considerable influence in religious education at the state schools and non-Muslim confessional schools.[24]

To give their voice more sway, Muslim intellectuals supporting the "Islamic revival" planned the foundation of an Indonesian Association of Muslim Intellectuals (Ikatan Cendekiawan Muslim Indonesia, or ICMI). The government showed strong interest during the founding convention, leading to the election of the minister of science and technology, B. J. Habibie, who had been educated in Aachen and Munich, as its chairman. Both Emil Salim (Salim), minister of the environment, and the former student activist Nurcholish Madjid (Majid) joined the ranks of this foundation. Amien Rais, who had earned his doctorate in the United States and had also been influenced by the "fundamentalist" philosophies of Maududi and Sayyid Qutb, was the chairman of the People's Consultative Assembly and shortly thereafter the leader of the Muhammadiyah, holding both positions only briefly. The ICMI announced its goal of shaping Indonesian society to eschew a modern Islamic identity in the twenty-first century.[25]

Habibie's goal, which he pursued in the name of the ICMI and with the government's backing, was to fill positions in the national and state-controlled bodies and organizations as well as to make appointments in the government proportionately based on the statistics for religion, even though many Indonesians suspected these figures to have been manipulated, as the Muslim community was said to constitute 87 percent of the population. The destructive political situation that had occurred earlier at the time of the *konstituante* was repeating itself. Another Islamic organization was claiming to speak in the name of the entire Islamic community and to represent "its interests" without any form of legitimacy. Habibie began to succeed in his endeavors in 1993, when the government and parliament were formed on the basis of proportional representation using the official statistics for religion. The ICMI subsequently established chapters even in villages, increasingly giving the appearance that this organization was a political, Suharto-backed party under the president's patronage.

Suharto's fall in May 1998 closed the book on the political power of the ICMI. Habibie, the former vice president, assumed the presidency (until October 1999). He allowed reelections, in which the Islamist parties won a mere 16 percent of the vote. The "civil society" debate in Indonesia, which started in the 1980s and was mainly propagated by Muslim intellectuals who were in conflict with the authoritarian government, has undoubtedly raised awareness in the country of an obviously stronger sense of citizenship, as it was expressed in the first free elections since 1955. As the first freely elected Indonesian president, Abdurrahman Wahid ('Abd al-Rahman Wahid), NU chairman and major supporter of the creation of a civil society, repealed a number of repressive laws and made efforts to depoliticize the military. This led to his impeachment in July 2001, which was backed by the U.S. government. His successor, Megawati Sukarnoputri, was able to assuage further the atmosphere in the political arena, yet she was still powerless against the resurgence and actions of radical Islamist groups with international ties and backed by groups in the military, such as Laskar Jihad and Jama'a Islamiyya, which repeatedly carried out terrorist attacks not only in East Indonesia but also on Bali in 2002 and in Jakarta. Parliamentary elections held in April 2004 resulted in a distribution of seats for the Islamist parties that in general reflected the outcome from 1999, whereas the first directly elected president, retired general Susilo Bambang Yudhoyono, who was elected in September 2004 in a second round of voting, was seen as a politician with deep ties to Javanese traditions mixed with Islamic mysticism.

b. Malaysia

In contrast to Indonesia, Islam is the official religion *in* Malaysia, yet it is not the official religion *of* the state. That distinction goes back to the foundation of the Federation of Malaya in 1957 and it continued to be the case when, in 1963, Singapore (until its expulsion in 1965) and the British crown colonies of Borneo, Sarawak, and Sabah (previously British North Borneo) joined Malaya to form the new Federation of Malaysia. Yet Malaysia is still not an Islamic state because its constitution and legislation do not espouse shari'a. To understand the role Islam plays in contemporary Malaysia, it is necessary to consider the historical, economic, and ethnic developments that have played out on the Malay Peninsula since the fifteenth century. Malaya was never a great kingdom, unlike its close cultural and ethnic cousin Indonesia, with its predominant base in Java. Malaysia's geography—a landscape of jungle and mountains that divide the peninsula lengthwise—makes ties between the west and east coasts more difficult than ties to Sumatra on the other side of the Straits of Malacca and to the Indochinese peninsula.

The ruler of Malacca converted to Islam in 1413, leading to the subsequent Islamization of the most important trading centers on the coasts and rivers, whose shores and banks had witnessed the birth of the oldest states in Malaya. In particular after the Portuguese conquered Malacca in 1511, some of these river states became sultanates, of which nine managed to flourish relatively undisturbed by outside influences into the nineteenth century, apart from their need to fend off repeated incursions by Buddhist Siamese from the north.

Following the Anglo-Dutch Treaty of 1824 and the division of the spheres of interest between the British and the Dutch in Southeast Asia, the British took greater interest in Malaya, in particular because of its strategic position along the sea route to China. The district of Malacca and the islands of Penang and Singapore became a British crown colony. The British signed a treaty in 1874 with the nine sultanates in order finally to secure their cooperation in economic and strategic matters. The British, however, avoided intervening in the internal affairs of their new allies, in particular in cultural, legal, and religious matters. Islam was and still is the most important thread that bound and continues to tie a sultan to his subjects. In addition, according to Malay *adat*, subjects are to show absolute loyalty to the ruler according to a strict system of patronage.

The character of Islam in Malaya is strongly bound by tradition. Although the school of legal thought is officially Shafi'i, just as in Indonesia, *adat* law remains in place in many areas and determines the court ceremonial. The sultan is the head of Islam in his territory and appoints the judges (*kathi;* Arab. sing. *qadi*), legal counselors (*mufti*), and the imams. The religious tithes (Arab. sing. *zakat*) are managed by his servants. All legal matters are handled by the religious courts, whose close ties to the sultan's court substantiate the absolute rule of the princes. The constitution of Malaysia also stated that a sultan could not be charged under national law.[26]

In a number of Malay states there are Islamic religious councils (Majlis Ugama Islam), the oldest of which, the Council of Religion and Malay Custom (Majlis Ugama dan Ista'adat Melayu), was established in Kelantan in 1916.[27] These councils enjoy varying levels of authority in the different sultanates. They were set up to provide counsel to the ruler in all matters relating to religion or Malay custom and to bring both into harmony with the country's laws. These councils can offer legal advice (Arab. *fatawa,* sing. *fatwa*) and can manage the religious foundations (*wakaf,* Arab. sing. *waqf*). Often the cemeteries fall under their jurisdiction, and some are even in charge of subdividing housing areas (*mukim*) that belong to a mosque. And they also usually manage the religious tithes, in particular *zakat fitrah* (Arab. *zakat al-fitr* and *sadaqat al-fitr*) at the end of Ramadan. Furthermore, they often oversee—generally with the sultan's approval—the imams, *kathis,* and the mufti, who is the highest religious figure in any given state.

In addition to the Majlis Ugama, each state has a department for religious affairs that is primarily in charge of administering Islamic law, usually in close cooperation with the Majlis Ugama. This department deals mostly with family law, but it also registers Muslim marriages, divorces, and any annulments. The role of the Islamic courts and *kathis* is very narrow in contrast: they can preside only over crimes committed by Muslims, for which national law prescribes a maximum punishment of six months in jail or M\$1,000.[28]

Mystic orders have been widespread in the country for ages. These orders contribute their part toward conveying an antiquated impression of Islam in Malaysia through their strict discipline instilled by spiritual and physical exercises and their traditional views. On occasion their rejection of modern developments has led to acts of violence. Their followers, mostly farmers and fishermen, avoid the cities or have settled on the urban fringes grouped in a *kampung*. This mindset had also motivated the British to use foreign workers mainly from China, and to a lesser extent from southern India, to work on their rubber plantations and in their tin mines because they could not rely on the Malay workers. This laid the foundation for the problem that plagues Malaysia to this day: the tensions between the ethnic groups, specifically the native "sons of the earth" (*bumiputera*) and the immigrant "foreigners."

The British made efforts to preserve the special rights of the *bumiputera* with regard to land purchases. They also helped to set up a comprehensive school system with Malay as the language of instruction. Still the conservative stance of the Malays meant that the modernist ideas of the "Youth Group" (Kaum Muda) from the beginning of the twentieth century spread at a slow pace through the general population. These "youths" were exposed to the ideas propagated by Muhammad 'Abduh (1849–1905) and his school during their pilgrimage to Mecca, and after returning they attempted to promote a renewal of Islamic thinking in the schools. In Cairo several of them, together with Indonesian students, had attempted to found a pan-Malaya national Islamic-based movement. As in West Sumatra (Minangkabau), with its close cultural ties to Malaya, the "Old Group" (Kaum Tua) was forced onto the defensive, in particular in the western sultanates. Yet the beliefs of these "youths" found little resonance in the general population and remained predominantly limited to the intellectual, urban-dwelling, or aristocratic classes of society. In addition to these Malays, many followers of the "youths" were ethnic Arabs, ethnic Indians, or ethnic Indonesians— that is, foreigners. There was little motivation for an anticolonial movement because the British pursued a policy of nonintervention with respect to the internal affairs of the sultans. The Malays gradually became aware of their ethnic and religious identity after 1910, especially in contrast to the non-Malay ethnic groups. A "non-Muslim" Malay seems to be a contradiction in terms.

After the British announced the end of colonial rule, a debate began roiling in the Federated Malay States that has continued since 1945 over the requirements for citizenship of those already residing in the country. The Malays, who had banded together in the United Malays National Organization (UMNO) under Dato Onn ibn Jaafar (Ja'far) in 1946, opposed the British proposals that granted the right to citizenship for all who had been living in Malaya for the previous ten years. The Malayan Chinese Association (MCA), founded in 1949, became the voice of the ethnic Chinese in Malaya. After Tunku Abdul Rahman ('Abd al-Rahman), son of the sultan of Kedah, took the helm of the UMNO, there were moves to work together with the MCA. They formed an alliance in order to force the British to grant the country full independence as soon as possible. On August 31, 1957, they achieved their goal with the foundation of the Federation of Malaya. According to the constitution, citizenship is granted either by law, applying the principle of *jus soli;* by registration, for example, if one of the parents is or was a citizen; or by naturalization.[29] At the root of this conflict was the Malays' fear of becoming a minority in their own country if they were outnumbered by a strong base of immigrants, who, after all, remained loyal to their countries of origin. The option of dual citizenship for the ethnic Chinese was revoked only in 1974, when diplomatic ties were reinstated between Malaysia and the People's Republic of China. Up until that time there had been repeated incidents of racial rioting, the worst taking place on May 13, 1969, in the country's capital, Kuala Lumpur.[30]

The 1957 constitution, as well as the 1963 constitution of Malaysia, declares Islam the official religion in the country. In principle, however, there is freedom of religion. The constitution specifies, "Every person has the right to profess and practice his religion and, subject to Clause (4), to propagate it." The text of Clause 4 reads, "Federal law may control or restrict the propagation of any religious doctrine or belief among persons professing the religion of Islam."[31] Any offenses against this provision are tried by federal courts, not by religious (Islamic) courts. The religious communities were granted the right to establish their own schools. "But it shall be lawful for the Federation or a State to establish or maintain Islamic institutions or provide or assist in providing instruction in the religion of Islam and incur such expenditure as may be necessary for the purpose."[32]

Furthermore, the 1957 constitution states that English will be replaced by Malay as the official language following a transitional period of ten years. It also establishes the position of head of state, called the Yang di-Pertuan Agong. This person is elected for a period of five years by and from the ranks of the nine rulers who form the Conference of Rulers, roughly equivalent to a third chamber.[33] During his reign this sultan is not permitted to carry out his functions in his own state, with the exception of being the religious head of the Islamic community. As the head of state, he is head of Islam only in his own state, in the capital district of Kuala Lumpur, and in Penang and Malacca (formerly the Straits Settlements), which are not ruled by a sultan and in which Islam is not the official religion. He is not head of the greater Islamic *umma* in the federation. Sabah and Sarawak were included under this provision in 1963.

The two territories on Borneo, Sabah and Sarawak, did not adopt the provisions in the constitution declaring Islam the official religion and granting special protection and rights to the Islamic community when they joined the Federation of Malaysia, since the Muslims were only a minority there. The Malays in these territories were not considered *bumiputera;* the majority of the indigenous tribes continued to practice their tribal religions, or else they had become Christians. Therefore it was also decided that English would continue to be the official language indefinitely.[34]

In the 1970s a turn of events occurred in Sabah. Tun Mustapha ibn Harun (Mustafa ibn Harun), chief minister since 1967, was concerned that the future of the indigenous peoples in Sabah was running a course similar to that of the Malays in West Malaysia. Therefore one of his goals was the Islamization of the region. He intensified the educational and cultural program for Islam through the United Sabah Islamic Association (USIA). He allowed nearly 90,000 Muslim refugees from the southern Philippines to enter Sabah, where the total population was around 700,000, and as a result he greatly strengthened the Islamic element in the region. An amendment to the constitution of Sabah elevated the status of Islam to the official religion there in 1973, even though the Muslims still made up less than 40 percent of the population. Discrimination against non-Muslims was one reason why Mustapha ibn Harun was not reelected chief minister in 1975, despite his influential friends in Kuala Lumpur, such as Tunku Abdul Rahman, the premier, who stepped down in 1971.[35] The governments under Tun Abdul Razak ('Abd al-Razzaq) and later Dato Hussein (Husayn) Onn were more guarded in their actions and withdrew their support for ibn Harun after suspicions arose that he wanted to create an independent Islamic territory incorporating Mindanao and the Sulu Islands, too.

The United Sabah Party (Parti Bersatu Sabah, or PBS), led by the Catholic Joseph Pairin Kitingan, ruled in Sabah beginning in 1986, with the 1990 elections reconfirming its popular support. Through interfaith and interethnic cooperation the party made attempts to improve the infrastructure of Sabah, which is required to hand over the majority of its revenues to the federal government. After the PBS broke away from the UMNO-led National Front shortly before the 1990 elections, the leaders of the UMNO decided to found their first branch outside the peninsula. UMNO also attempted to undermine the cooperation efforts between Muslims and Christians within the PBS.[36] After 1977 similar trends to those seen in Sabah under Tun Mustapha began emerging in Sarawak as well. With its presence in Sabah, the UMNO was once again faced with the issue of deciding whether its own development would be hindered if it continued to limit its scope to the interests of the Malays. Its cofounder, Dato Onn ibn Jaafar, lost his party's confidence in 1951, when he proposed to open party membership to non-Muslims. Up until 1989 it was taken for granted that non-Malay Muslims wishing to join the UMNO would have to accept the Malay *adat*. This attitude could not hold up in terms of ethnic background, religion, or culture, at least in Sabah, if the UMNO harbored genuine hopes of taking root there.

There was early opposition to the exclusive fusion of Malay traditions and Islam. In 1955 a group of Qur'an- and Sunna-oriented *'ulama'* broke off with several followers and registered the Parti Islam Se-Malaya (Islamic Party of Malaysia, or PAS, from a previous name, Parti Agama Islam). Although it also supported Malay as the national language and the Malay culture as the founding element of the national culture, it viewed the UMNO agenda as *'asabiyya* (chauvinism) and in turn as un-Islamic. Generally speaking, the PAS was in opposition to the National Front. In the elections in Kelantan, however, it managed to win strong backing several times from 1990 on, allowing the party to implement shari'a rules in this state that were applied to non-Muslims too (for example, bans on alcohol and gambling, and limited freedom of movement for women). The UMNO and PAS were constantly at odds, in particular on the scope and objectives of the Islamization of Malaysian society which both sides propagate.[37]

Following ethnic clashes in May 1969, Malay students also began to reflect more and more on the universal values of Islam, which were, however, primarily available in English through the works of scholars with a "fundamentalist" orientation such as Maududi, Sayyid Qutb, and Murtada Mutahhari, to name a few. Of the youth organizations that emerged back then, the Malaysian Islamic Youth Movement (Angkatan Belia Islam Malaysia, or ABIM) is the most well known to have taken the stage. It was led by Anwar Ibrahim, who had held ministerial positions in Mahathir ibn Muhammad's cabinet and was eventually appointed deputy prime minister, until they broke off ties and Anwar was arrested in 1998.

The Movement for State Awareness (Aliran Kesadaran Negara, or Aliran), led by Chandra Muzaffar, began working in 1977 to challenge the efforts to Islamize Malaysian society and ignore the interests and fears of the minorities on the potential loss of their religious and cultural identity. This movement took as its goal promoting the "universal values of Islam" in an open, pluralist society—as represented by (modern) Malaysian society in contrast to the (traditional) Malay social community. This should be achieved by also incorporating values existing in other religions and cultures which may encourage a modern society.[38] Given this outlook, Aliran was deeply opposed to the administration's policies, laid down by Prime Minister Mahathir ibn Muhammad beginning in 1981. He attempted to bring the ethnic groups closer together through "national unity" (*perpaduan*), which he had outlined in his book *The Malay Dilemma*. He was aiming at a long-term program to bring Malay and Islamic values to the country for the other ethnic groups to adopt, similarly to what Tun Mustapha attempted in Sabah. The government-controlled media were placed in the service of this program. The opposition, however, had to contend with the threat of the Internal Security Act (ISA), which was initially passed in 1960 to combat communist rebels, and with the accusation of attempting to thwart the unity of Malaysia.

Although Tunku Abdul Rahman, the "Father of Malaysia," who died in 1990, was very responsive to the fears of the minorities, he welcomed in Kuala Lumpur in 1980 the launching of the Regional Islamic Da'wah Council of Southeast Asia and the Pacific, with the purpose of spreading Islam (*da'wa*), which received substantial support from the oil-rich countries in the Middle East. The participants agreed on the need to strengthen support for *da'wa* among all non-Muslims of this region. Apparently Abdul Rahman anticipated Islam's being particularly suitable for accelerating the unity among the peoples of the country and preventing future recurrences of the ethnic clashes from the past. He commented in his *Viewpoints:* "What I am really proposing to do, if our plan succeeds, is to ask the government to recognize the converts as Muslims and to give them the same privileges as those enjoyed by the Malays. Until this is done not many of them will embrace Islam."[39] The question was whether the anticipated integrating momentum could be gained as long as Islam was identified either directly or indirectly with Malay traditions and values.

The most dangerous problem facing Malaysia remains its race problem. Immediately following the riots in May 1969, the government at the time attempted to create a basis for solidarity throughout the entire nation by having the Yang di-Pertuan Agong proclaim Rukunegara (harmony in the nation) on the national holiday in 1970, which was a type of charter consisting of five principles, similar to the Indonesian Pancasila:

1. belief in the divine lordship (Kepercayaan kepada Tuhan)
2. loyalty to king and state (Kesetiaan kepada Raja dan Negara)
3. the supremacy of the constitution (Keluhuran Perlembagaan)
4. rule of law (Kedaulatan Undang-undang)
5. courtesy and morality (Kesopanan dan Kesusilaan)

Especially politicians in the opposition and civil rights groups such as Aliran moved to have Rukunegara made a part of the constitution of Malaysia.

Yet beginning in the early 1990s Rukunegara progressively slid into the background, making room for a heated debate on the Islamization of Malaysia and the establishment of an "Islamic society." There was even talk about the possibility of founding an Islamic state. This debate was publicized by the government-controlled media and shaped to a great extent by Anwar Ibrahim, who had been elected Mahathir ibn Muhammad's deputy in the UMNO and deputy prime minister in the government. He regarded the Treaty of Medina, which was drafted by Muhammad and the Arabs of Yathrib, as the "constitution" and considered it to be a model for creating a modern civil society (*masyarakat madani*). When he brought forward this idea in 1996 at a speech in Indonesia, the civil society debate came to a standstill there too. His close personal ties to several of the leaders in the PAS, the former opponent of the UMNO, helped to defuse the tensions between the UMNO and the PAS. Once talk about him as a potential successor to Mahathir ibn Muhammad as head of state spread, he also seemed to make efforts to rebuild confidence with non-Islamic groups starting in early 1994. Yet his colorful Islamist attitude and in turn the issue of loyalty to the UMNO or PAS were singled out as the undisclosed reasons why Mahathir distanced himself from Anwar after he was ousted from his political posts in 1998.

Nevertheless, the problem remains as to how the Malays should respond to such a change, that is, to the option of creating an Islamic state. What is therefore at issue is how the cultural and social changes in Malay society that are without doubt forthcoming will unfold. Creating an Islamic nation would require entirely new power structures and thus represent a radical break with Malay culture and the tradition of sultans as legal, *adat,* and community leaders. Mahathir's attempts to limit the power of the sultans altered little in the way of the people's fidelity to tradition. This may yet change. The main problem is that the modern idea of a state, even if it is to be an Islamic state, is not part of the tradition of Islam. Therefore their relationship to the modern state is of relatively little importance to the majority of Malays as long as they can live in peace in terms of both their Malay identity and their Islamic cultural and social identity under the protection of their ruler or another trusted authority, and *alongside* other ethnic groups.

In a calculated attempt to knock the wind out of his opponents' sails, the ones who accused him of not supporting national Islamic issues, Mahathir pointedly declared that Malaysia has always been an Islamic state and therefore does not need to become one. His statement surprised and angered opponents and allies alike, who wanted to know the basis for his reassessment. In the end there was a deep crisis of confidence in the UMNO and the country toward the administration, together with a growing indignation over new incidents of corruption, felt in particular by the non-Malays, who did not want to interfere in the internal cultural conflicts of the Malays, but who also did not want to be involved in these conflicts. The civil society debate was revitalized and with it the call to shelve the social privileges afforded the Malays too.[40]

Mahathir eventually decided to retire as prime minister in the fall of 2003 to avoid a repetition of the losses experienced in the elections in 1999. His highly respected successor, Abdullah Ahmad Badawi, captured a convincing electoral victory in the spring of 2004. The election outcome also showed voters' preference for a leader representing a moderate, tolerant, and modern form of Islam, as seen in Indonesia. The PAS, which had taken control of the government in Trengganu in 1999, not only lost in this state again but also nearly lost in its traditional heartland, Kelantan, to the UMNO-led National Front. The reason for its poor performance in the elections can be attributed to growing dissatisfaction with its continual strengthening of its policy of Islamization, a policy that cannot resolve the social problems in this particularly poor state. In 2005 there were 24 million people living in Malaysia, of whom 58 percent were Malays. Statistics were not available for other religions. Badawi increasingly bowed to pressure from Malay Islam groups during his tenure. For this reason interethnic tensions escalated once again, and calls for eliminating the discriminatory provisions for non-Malays became sharper. This trend was also reflected in the election outcome from the spring of 2008, dubbed a "political tsunami" by some politicians, in which five of the thirteen federal states of Malaysia were turned over to the opposition parties. Another astonishing result was the possibility of a merger between UMNO and PAS that surfaced in July 2008.

c. The Philippines

The Philippines is the third largest country in the Malay region and the only Asian country with a Christian (Catholic) majority. It had a population of approximately 87 million in 2005, with 83 percent practicing Roman Catholicism and 5 percent professing the Muslim faith.

The Spanish conquered Mindoro and the region around Manila in 1570–71. From there they repeatedly waged war against the sultans who had settled down on Mindanao and the Sulu Archipelago in the southern part of the present-day Philippines and were attempting to extend their territory to the islands lying to the north. They felt a cultural tie to the other Malay sultanates in the archipelago and on the Malay Peninsula. The Spanish and the Moros, as they had dubbed the Muslims, echoing the usage back in Spain, had been at war for three centuries. The Spanish brought Christianity to the territories they controlled and also demanded allegiance to the Spanish throne.

Though closely related, the independence-minded Moros to the south and the Filipinos to the north living under Spanish rule never developed a sense of common ground. The Spanish and the Filipinos regarded the Moros as uncivilized and backward in moral, social, and economic terms. The Filipinos and the Moros, who had finally lost their political independence in their defeat by the sultan of Sulu in 1876, rarely cooperated even after the nineteenth century, when the nationalist movements led by the Filipinos against the Spanish, and later against American colonialism beginning in 1898, gained momentum. The Moros tended to align themselves with the other Malay sultanates, with which they were connected by history, genealogy, and in particular religion.[41] They have never considered themselves part of the Philippines.

After having finally struck down the last revolt by the Moros and subjected them to Philippine authority, the Americans made efforts to improve the educational and economic situation of the Moros during their colonial rule from 1898 to 1946. In general, tensions between the Americans and the Moros eased. The Moros submitted petitions again and again, in which they sought guarantees espoused in the constitution that would anchor the protection of Islam and in turn prevent any bans on their customs and traditions, reserve the undeveloped land in Mindanao for the Moros, transfer political offices in Islamic territories to Muslim Filipinos, and protect the traditional position of the upper class, the *datus* and the sultans, from being changed.[42]

Although the Moros gained the support of the Americans with their proposals, they did not penetrate the Christian majority in the parliament in Manila and their lobby. The Christian Filipinos had inherited their stance from the Spanish and viewed Mindanao and the Sulu Archipelago as a colony. In particular, Mindanao received a surge of Christian settlers from the overpopulated northern islands that reversed the demographic composition within a few decades. For example, the province of Cotabatu, Mindanao, had a population that was 55 percent Muslim and 45 percent Christian in 1939; in 1948 it had changed to 35 percent Muslim and 65 percent Christian.

The situation took a turn for the worse in 1946 after independence. There were acts of violence, and the national government sympathized with the Christians. During the Mindanao-Sulu crisis at the end of the 1960s,[43] the Moros founded the Muslim Independence Movement (MIM, later changed to Mindanao Independence Movement), with the aim of creating an "Islamic Republic of Mindanao and Sulu." A group of students and intellectuals organized themselves into the Moro National Liberation Front (MNLF) to gain independence through acts of guerrilla warfare. President Ferdinand E. Marcos eventually declared martial law in October 1972 and admitted that the situation on Mindanao and Sulu had taken on the appearance of a civil war. Yet the situation in the southern Philippines was not the only reason for declaring martial law. Social revolutionary movements had started to take a stand against the failures of the nationalist movement. Similar to Malay nationalism, yet in contrast to the Indonesian national movement under Sukarno, the nationalist movement had, for the most part, not questioned the traditional power structures and, in particular, the power monopoly of the owners of haciendas. Thus the nationalist movement had relatively little impact in terms of social policy.

A short time later the president appointed a commission to examine the option of allowing Muslims to apply portions of civil law according to shariʿa within the framework of national law. The Code of Muslim Personal Laws of the Philippines was published in 1977 by presidential proclamation, stating that "the legal system of the Muslims in the Philippines as part of the law of the land" would be recognized. It did not include all of shariʿa, and it codified only personal law. Because there are also Muslim judges presiding over national courts who have no special knowledge of Islamic law, it was determined that ʿulamaʾ should assist them. A mufti was also to be appointed by the president and placed under the supervision of the Supreme Court.

This proclamation was followed in 1981 by a directive to create a ministry for Muslim affairs, which would also be in charge of finding ways to integrate Muslim Filipinos into the Philippine nation with the same rights as others while respecting their faith, their *adat,* and their traditional institutions, while working on improving their economic and educational situation.[44]

Despite these new administrative measures, matters came to a head owing to the military conflicts increasingly taking place in the south, accompanied by a general deterioration of the internal political situation in the 1970s. The international community also became aware of the events taking place there. The World Muslim Congress (Muʾtamar al-ʿalam al-islami) and other Islamic organizations repeatedly sent delegations to investigate the accusations of "genocide" in particular. Libya and Sabah especially provided their support during Tun Mustapha's presidency. Sabah had been ruled by the sultan of Sulu at various times (in title until 1878), and there were repeated speculations about Tun Mustapha's Islamization plans in Sabah (he himself was from Sulu) with the aim of uniting these territories into a new Islamic kingdom.

These plans for secession were only an illusion, however. They would have run into decisive resistance in Malaysia and the Philippines. The future of the Moros lies in the Philippines, and it is only their position in the constitution that is still open to debate. An agreement was signed in December 1976 by the Philippine government and MNLF representatives in Libya's capital, Tripoli, guaranteeing regional autonomy to the areas in the south primarily inhabited by Muslims; their governments would be placed under direct control of the president. Because of a lack of political backing for the opportunities it provided, this agreement never resulted in a satisfactory solution to the problem, which only worsened under the unguided agenda pursued by Corazon Aquino, who served as president from 1986 to 1992.

It is difficult for the Muslims to identify themselves as an integral part of the nation (*bangsa*) because of the persistent colonial mentality of the Christian Filipinos and the traditional definition of Philippine nationalism based on the interests of the Catholic upper class. "Integration" could mean "assimilation" in the terms of the nationalist aims often directed against them, resulting in a loss of identity. A sense of national identity has been emerging from their midst, one that is shaped by their experiences throughout history and strengthened by the influences of the "Islamic revival."[45] They regard themselves as the first population group in the Philippines to create an identity for protecting themselves from foreign influences. Nevertheless, they are prepared to join the modern Philippine nation as a cultural minority, as long as their rights and dignity are acknowledged as part of a pluralist society. Leading representatives of this minority have started to see themselves more often as Muslim Filipinos; use of the term "Moro" has been gradually diminishing because of the negative connotations. Yet only small groups of Christians have demonstrated their willingness to acknowledge the Muslims as part of the Philippine nation to date.

Negotiations between the government and the MNLF were only resumed under President Fidel Ramos (1992–1998). They were intended to discuss implementation of the Tripoli Agreement against the backdrop of the 1987 constitutional reform, which eventually ended in an agreement negotiated in Jakarta in 1996 and signed on September 2 of that year in Manila. Four provinces on Mindanao and Basilan were granted partial autonomy. Nur Misuari, leader of the MNLF, became their governor. The agreement met with strong reactions, however, from both Christians, who thought the compromises were too great, and Muslims, who had hoped for a more effective strengthening of their social organizations and, in particular, more legal securities in terms of their economic interests and landownership rights. The Moro Islamic Liberation Front (MILF), formed in 1984 by Salamat Hashim from groups within the MNLF and in protest against their leftist and socialist tendencies, refused to give its support and became entangled in an escalating battle with Philippine government forces.

More radical, and with indefinable goals, are the groups of Abu Sayyaf (meaning "sword-bearer" or "executioner") that have emerged since the early 1990s. Abdurajak Abu Bakar Janjalani, their founder, who was assassinated in 1998, was born in Basilan, the son of a Christian mother and a Muslim father. As a student in Saudi Arabia he was introduced to the *da'wa* movement. Many of his teachers there came from Pakistan. In the late 1980s he returned to Basilan, where he gathered his followers, after having traveled through Libya and Afghanistan, where he came into contact with mujahidin who had been trained by the CIA. They were schooled in the ways of unyielding anti-Western ("antimaterialistic") thinking and have carried out kidnappings (the kidnapping of tourists in Sipadan, Sabah, in 2000 was an especially big "triumph"), extortion and ransom demands, and brutal attacks on Christian and national institutions. Their actions are condemned by other Islamic organizations, including the MILF, as "ideologically, politically, psychologically, and culturally incorrect."[46]

Misuari was increasingly accused of opportunistic collaboration with his earlier enemies. After his loss of credibility and a failed attempt at revolt, he fled to Sabah in 2001, where he was arrested by the Malaysian police. The decision by Philippine President Gloria Arroyo and U.S. President George W. Bush to fight terrorism together after September 11, 2001, also resulted in the return of warlike conditions for the civilian population of Moroland, whose Muslim sector had been placing its hopes on closer ties between the MNLF and MILF since 2001 and in turn a strong negotiating position that would aim at a stable political solution, ending in effective autonomy as Bangsamoro (Moro Nation) if national independence is not possible.

d. Brunei

Negara Brunei Darussalam, the sultanate located on the northern coast of the island of Borneo, gained full independence in 1984, after being declared a British protectorate in 1888 and having accepted its first British resident in 1906. This British resident advised the sultan in all internal and foreign affairs with the exception of matters affecting the Islamic faith or the Malay culture and tradition (*adat*). In 1959 Brunei received its first written constitution, which replaced the British resident with a high commissioner and laid down plans for creating a legislative council. The high commissioner had the power to control decisions only in foreign affairs and defense, a restriction laid down by a further treaty in 1971. A new treaty was finally drafted in 1979 at the insistence of the British to provide full independence as soon as possible. On January 1, 1984, independence was then officially declared by Sultan Hassanal Bolkiah Mu'izzaddin Waddaulah (Hasan al-Bulqiyya Mu'izz al-Din wa-l-Dawla), the twenty-ninth sultan of Brunei. Soon afterwards Brunei became a member of various international organizations, including the Association of Southeast Asian Nations (ASEAN), the UN, and the Organization of the Islamic Conference.

The official territory of Brunei (5,765 square kilometers) is divided into two regions by the valley of Limbang, which belongs to Sarawak. As of 2004 Brunei had 372,000 inhabitants, of whom 67 percent were Malay (Muslim), 15 percent ethnic Chinese, and 5 percent members of various indigenous tribes; there are smaller numbers of Indians, Europeans, and others. Islam is the official religion, and the sultan is the head of the Muslim community. The observance of Christian (approximately 10 percent), Buddhist (approximately 13 percent), and folk religions, such as by the Murut and Iban, are tolerated, although they run into resistance on occasion. Bandar Seri Begawan is the capital; until 1970 it was called Bandar Brunei (Brunei Town). The sultan's family has become extremely wealthy since the discovery of oil off the coast of Brunei at the end of the nineteenth century. The wealth has been put toward development in the small country, particularly during the rule of Sultan Omar Ali Saifuddin ('Umar 'Ali Sayf al-Din, r. 1950–1967). Brunei has begun to display once again some of the same prestige and wealth it had once enjoyed when it ruled over the entire island of Borneo during the Middle Ages—one reason why the Europeans named the island after its capital.

Brunei, called Po-ni by the Chinese, had been an important entrepôt between China and the western half of the Malay archipelago centuries before the arrival of Islam. When the prince of Brunei married one of the daughters of the "sultan of Johor" (who was likely the sultan of Malacca),[47] he converted to Islam and imposed Malay *adat* and the Malay language on his court. His subjects, who had also converted to Islam, laid down their *adat* traditions and became "Malays," yet proportionately few ethnic Malays resettled in the sultanate. This led to the term "Malay," as elsewhere on Borneo, becoming synonymous with "Islam" or "Muslim," a fact that the members of indigenous animist tribes attempted to use to set themselves apart in cultural, religious, and particularly political respects. The first sultan's niece married an Arab from Ta'if, Sharif 'Ali, who became Brunei's third sultan under the name of Sultan Berkat (Barakat). He carried on the efforts to proselytize the population and tightened the reins on Brunei's administration, using Malacca as his model. He lent "Arab legitimacy" to the sultan's family.

By the time the Europeans arrived, Brunei ruled nearly the entire northern coast of Borneo and was able to extend its realm for a time to include the Sulu Archipelago and Mindanao too. Brunei ran into conflict with the Spanish after they founded Manila in 1570 and strove to expand their dominion to the south. Brunei encountered another competitor in the emerging sultanate on the Sulu Islands, which had even brought North Borneo (present-day Sabah) under its control for a while and triggered the conflict over Sabah between Malaysia and the Philippines that has lasted even to this day. The ever-increasing activities of pirates caused great instability, compelling the sultan of Brunei to transfer much of modern-day Sarawak to James Brooke, known as the White Raja, in a series of stages starting in 1841 to bring peace and development to the territory. In 1865 the sultan granted the American Trading Company a ten-year lease over North Borneo (Sabah), thus documenting the sultan's territorial claim to this region. It was later purchased by the Austrian consul, Baron von Overbeck, in 1875. A charter from 1877 closed the book on the sultan's control over this territory. As compensation he received a yearly stipend. In 1881 the rights to the company were transferred to Alfred Dent, Overbeck's British business partner, who, with the aid of a royal decree, established the British North Borneo Company. When the tribal leaders from the Limbang Valley asked the White Raja to liberate them from the sultan's mismanagement and oppression in 1890, Brooke decided to incorporate this territory with the Trusan Valley into the Fifth Division of Sarawak. The sultan unsuccessfully attempted to resist this move. His realm was then limited to the territory surrounding the capital, which was further divided into two entirely separate territories, one consisting mainly of farmers, fishermen, and hunters, and the other occupied by the royal family.

The efforts of Britain to reduce its imperial presence in Southeast Asia after World War II initially focused on the Malay Peninsula. The economic development and educational system were more advanced there than in its possessions in the northern part of Borneo and in Brunei. After the Federation of Malaya declared independence in 1957, the destiny of the three territories on Borneo required attention. In 1958 the British proposed the foundation of a "Federation of North Borneo" that would include Brunei, Sarawak, and Sabah as member states. But Sultan Omar Ali Saifuddin, who had decreed the first five-year plan for the development of Brunei in the 1950s, opposed the creation of this federation. His main concern was likely that Brunei's coffers would also have to finance the development of other regions inhabited primarily by non-Muslim peoples and ethnic Chinese. When Malay prime minister Tunku Abdul Rahman ('Abd al-Rahman) publicly announced in 1961 his idea of expanding the Federation of Malaya to include Singapore and the three territories on Borneo in a Federation of Malaysia, the sultan of Brunei gave his assent. He regarded it as a great step toward bringing together the culturally related Malay sultanates and as a guarantee that Islam would remain the official religion, something that would not have been the case in a "Federation of North Borneo." In addition, Malay was to become the national language of Malaysia.

The sultan realized, however, that he was facing agrowing opposition in internal affairs that received support from Indonesia and the Philippines, both of which were steadfast in their opposition to the Malaysia plan. There was also decisive and nearly unanimous resistance to the Malaysia plan in Sarawak and Sabah. The people there feared that implementing this plan would mean only that colonial powers would be transferred from the British to the Malays, who would plunder their natural resources without constraint.

Even relations with Singapore were ambivalent. On the one hand, the nationalists in the northern part of Borneo regarded Singapore's membership as a crucial counterweight to the dominating power of the Malays if Malaysia were actually to be founded. On the other hand, the island state was experiencing an economic recession with high unemployment levels, which meant that it would be faced with problems caused by the immigration of unemployed people, mainly Chinese, to Borneo.

The oppositional Brunei People's Party (Party Rakyat Brunei, or PRB) won fifty-four of the available fifty-five seats in the elections for the district councils in Brunei at the end of August 1962. This meant that the sixteen seats in the legislative council reserved for the district councils would be held by the PRB when the council was formed in September. The remaining members of the thirty-three-seat legislature were appointed by the sultan. The chairman of the PRB, Shaykh Ahmad M. Azahari (Ahmad Muhammad Azahari), requested that the sultan relinquish his absolute powers as ruler, implement democratic reforms to the government system, and strive for independence from the British as soon as possible in order to form a federation with Sarawak and Sabah. The northern part of Borneo would be permitted to join the federation only if it could improve its economic and political position and raise the general educational level to one comparable to that of the peninsula.

The sultan refused to yield to the PRB's demands, which only underlined the sultanate's isolation in the region and its limited sphere of interest. In December 1962 the Party Rakyat attempted to overthrow the government. Around the same time Azahari, who "happened" to be on a trip to Manila (a safe haven for him), named himself prime minister and appointed the sultan head of the "Federation of North Borneo." The revolt was toppled with the help of the British, the legislative council was disbanded, the Party Rakyat was banned, and its leaders were arrested—at least those who had not already fled the country. At the same time, a state of emergency was declared. Born in Labuan, Azahari, who was known in Indonesia as an active participant in the guerrilla actions directed against the Dutch in 1946–1949, took shelter in Indonesia under Sukarno.[48]

This solidified the sultan's position in internal affairs once again. Afterward no opposition could be formed to act against him, at least not in the sultanate. Sultan Omar, however, also objected to Brunei's accession to the Federation of Malaysia because he feared that too much capital might end up flowing into Kuala Lumpur and prevent him from assuming his "rightful" place beside the nine Malay sultans. In 1967 Sultan Omar abdicated to his then twenty-one-year-old son, Hassanal Bolkiah, who had been educated at Sandhurst, because he did not wish to bow to the pressure exerted by the British-backed politicians in his country who were calling for immediate democratization of domestic policies and independence after the sultan refused to join Malaysia. When Sultan Hassanal Bolkiah declared independence in 1984, his nation was still ruled under the absolute power of a sultan and had no controlling bodies that were democratically legitimized. The British government continued to guarantee Brunei's security.

Previously the sultan would delegate important government positions to four of the dignitaries from the former structure of the Malaccan government: the Pengiran Bendahara (prime minister and treasurer), the Pengiran

Digadong (finance minister), the Pengiran Pemancha (who, in a similar fashion to the *syahbandar,* was in charge of commercial and foreign affairs), and the Pengiran Temenggong (defense minister).[49] After the modernization of the cabinet in 1959, which continued to use the official titles of some of the former positions, the administration of religious affairs was delegated to the minister of religion in the cabinet, who is also in charge of administering the religious courts. In addition the sultan is advised by a council for religious affairs, which he appoints. Islam and Malay *adat* form a unity in both the interpretation of the law and legal practice. Because Malay *adat* requires absolute loyalty to the sultan, and Islam has lent religious legitimacy to his ruling position, the sultan is in essence the highest instance of appeal, deciding on the development and application of Islamic law. The provisions of the British protectorate fortified his position, as the British resident was not permitted to interfere in the administration of religious and cultural traditions. Nevertheless, legal authorities and judges saw a formalization here of what they considered to be traditional, if not already codified, Islamic law under the influence of the British legal system.

In this manner Islam and *adat* form the cultural basis and the ideological thread that binds ruler and people together. Therefore emphasis is laid on strengthening an Islamic awareness embedded in the Malay tradition and propagated in particular by the media and educational system in the official representation of the sultanate, in the various areas of internal development, and especially in education. For this reason reformist interpretations of Islam, and even "fundamentalist reinterpretations," receive little support, and there are constant warnings not to spread "misconceptions" in religious matters. Brunei's minister for religious affairs has concluded with his Indonesian and Malaysian counterparts at various meetings in recent years that the "Malay nations" should increase cooperation with regard to the *da'wa,* Islamic education (*tarbiya*), and the setting of dates for Islamic holidays, to name a few.

e. Singapore

The island of Singapura (Lion City) and its port city Temasek gained prominence as a pirate haven in precolonial times. Working on behalf of the British East India Company, Sir Thomas Stamford Raffles signed a treaty in 1819 with Hussein (Husayn), who was next in line to the throne in the sultanate of Johor, granting the British exclusive rights to develop a trading post and settlement there. This treaty transferred possession of Singapore to the British, who would group it together with the other British territories in Malacca and Penang (including Province Wellesley as part of Penang) in 1826 to form the Straits Settlements. In 1832 Singapore became the capital. It retained this position as a British administrative and trading center even after the Straits Settlements were removed from the authority of the India Office in 1867 and made directly answerable to the Colonial Office in London.

After World War II the other two Straits Settlements, along with the Federated and Unfederated Malay Sultanates, were incorporated in 1948 into the Federation of Malaya, which was eventually granted independence from Great Britain in 1957. Singapore continued to be directly administered as a crown colony owing to its status as a free port, and particularly because of problems with the ethnic makeup of its population and its large majority of ethnic Chinese. In 1957 Singapore became a member of the British Commonwealth with sovereignty in internal affairs. Independence from Great Britain was granted in 1963, when Singapore, Sarawak, Sabah, and the Federation of Malaya were united to form the Federation of Malaysia. Discord between Singapore's political leaders and the federal government in Kuala Lumpur resulted in Singapore's forced secession from the federation in 1965. Since then Singapore has endeavored to make its mark as an independent island nation in terms of politics, economy, and culture in the eyes of its neighbors.

The history of Singapore is also the history of its Muslim population, which is predominantly Malay. According to some estimates there were barely two hundred Malays living on the island when Raffles and Hussein signed their treaty. A steady stream of Chinese workers primarily—and to a lesser extent Indian and Arab traders—arrived in subsequent years, developing Singapore into the "new Malacca" as the administrative and trading center for the British. Malays came mainly from the Riau Archipelago and Malacca and later from other territories on the Malay Peninsula and Sumatra. Immigrants from Java and Bawean as well as from territories belonging to the Dutch East Indies were at times recorded as separate ethnic groups and at other times as Malays, especially when their families had lived on the island for several generations. The Malays made a distinction in ethnic grouping for the Indian Muslims and Arabs, many of whom considered themselves descendants of the Prophet (especially those from the southern Arabian Peninsula region of Hadramaut) and demanded special privileges and respect from the Muslim community as Sayyid family members. Although they set themselves apart in this manner, it did not hinder in particular Arabs, who ventured abroad without families, from marrying into upper-class Malay (or even Chinese) families.

The level of education of the Indian Muslims and Arabs was substantially higher than that of the Malays. By the end of the nineteenth century these groups, and a few Mecca pilgrims from Java and Sumatra who stayed on in Singapore, had already formed a modest intellectual elite that helped to spread to the archipelago Islamic reform ideas from the Orient. The magazine *Al-ʿUrwa al-wuthqa,* published by Jamal al-Din al-Afghani and Muhammad ʿAbduh, traveled to Indonesia via Singapore despite the restrictive measures imposed by Dutch colonial rule. Even *Al-Manar* was read in Singapore. A magazine titled *Al-Imam,* which was edited in Singapore, enjoyed short-lived popularity starting in 1906. It also published articles and fatwas (Arab. *fatawa*) that were translated from *Al-Manar.* Several madrasas (the so-called Islamic reform schools, that is, schools for reforming Islamic education) were also founded in Singapore, similar to those on Java and especially in Minangkabau (West Sumatra). Nevertheless, their influence on the Malay population in Singapore and on the peninsula appears to have been minimal. These areas embraced the traditional Qur'an schools.

Yet Malay students were the exception even in the British-run school system, and no attempts were made to increase their numbers there. Apart from a few farmers and fishermen, the Malays worked as craftsmen or simple clerks in trade or government administration, and in the twentieth century more often as members of the British armed forces. They may have been dependent on their employers, but they were independent in terms of other social ties. The concept of mutual assistance, which was a matter of course in their villages of birth through kinship ties, did not exist for the most part in Singapore.[50] And Malays very seldom joined together with other Malays to form associations in their professional lives. Although they did live in village-like communities (*kampung*) in Singapore, just like in their Malay or Indonesian homeland, their connecting thread was the tribal group, not the family. The center of social activity was the mosque. And this is where they selected the people who were to receive specific duties and roles within the local community. The criterion was primarily the degree of authority that a person exuded. Prestige was not a commodity to be purchased at will. For the majority of Malays this fact made it easy to move frequently from place to place. Social contact with other ethnic groups, even with other Muslims, was minimal. This idiosyncrasy in the Malays' traditional behavior may have contributed to their general absence from the political and economic stage, and even in matters of higher education, especially since there was no Malay aristocracy or elite in Singapore, as opposed to the peninsula, where the Malay elite was limited to members of the aristocracy.

Yet there was another reason why the Malay community lived in these communes. Whereas in the Malay sultanates the British were "indirectly" in charge of the rulers, whose position as head of the Islamic community in their respective country was expressly recognized and respected, the sultan of Johor no longer controlled Singapore after 1824. The Malays there were lacking a religious head and, with this position, a mediator who could represent their interests before the British colonial administration, as well as a central court to appeal to in matters affecting religious law. This situation resulted in the reliance on a *kathi* (judge, from Arab. *qadi*), whose verdict would be the mildest. After the British colonial administration named a protector for the Chinese community in 1877, a group of Muslims insisted on having a *kathi* in order to register marriages in the proper manner. This led to the enactment of the Mahomedan Marriage Ordinance of 1880, which granted the colonial administration the power to name *kathis*. Their activities would be limited to registering marriages and divorces within their own ethnic community. The colonial administration wanted to name *kathis* on the recommendation of the Islamic communities, forcing the Muslims to consult with one another more often. A Muslim Endowments Board was established in 1906 to administer the Muslim religious and charitable foundations.

Malay identity in Singapore was defined in general by isolation from other ethnic groups, and this attitude influenced the sense of community within the Islamic *umma*. Islam and the Malay language were the threads that bound the Malays together; both elements had an equal role in shaping their identity.

Because of its ethnic complexity, the Islamic community in Singapore can be viewed as an entity only with some reservations.[51] Singapore had a population of 4.4 million in 2004, of which 14 percent was Malay. No statistics were given for religious affiliation. In 1980, 16.3 percent of the population were Muslims. It is likely that these figures can be applied, more or less, to earlier periods too. In terms of ethnic groups, in 1980, 0.1 percent of Chinese, 99.4 percent of Malays, 21.8 percent of Indians, and 6.5 percent of "other" (including Arabs) were Muslim, which would mean 90.2 percent of Muslims in Singapore were Malays.[52] Even though the Malays were in the majority by far within the Islamic community, they did not assume a leading role in society, culture, or politics as the Arab and Indian Muslims did. For this reason the Malays were in a weak political, social, and economic position within Singaporean society in general and within the Islamic community in particular. The newspaper *Bintang Timur* described this situation with a play on words back in 1894: "Kenapa Melayu layu?" (Why are the Malays withering away like that?).[53]

Without a doubt, British policies on education played a role in this development, in addition to the previously mentioned attitude of the Malays. Because the British insisted that matters affecting Islam and Malay tradition were in the hands of the sultan and not the British when the treaty on colonial rule was drawn up with the Malay sultans, little of the British curriculum for Malay-language schooling was designed to separate the language of instruction from its Islamic content. This applied to Singapore, too, which led to minimal interest in these schools. But the Malays were not interested in the Islamic reform schools either, as mentioned previously. In general, all that remained for them were the Qur'an schools, which did not by any means prepare their students for advancement in public or economic life in Singapore.

Following the mutiny by Muslim Indian solders in 1915, which was actually instigated by German secret agents, the British colonial administration decided that it was again time to improve its contacts with the Muslims. The British set up the Muhammadan Advisory Board to present the different Islamic organizations and groups with a means to bring their issues before the government.

Finally after World War I a *kathi* managed to gain recognition owing to his personal authority as chief *kathi* and in essence as head of the entire Islamic community in Singapore. After his death the British instilled Imam

Haji Abbas ibn Taha (Imam Hajji ʿAbbas ibn Taha) as the first official chief
kathi in 1936. This appointment nevertheless carried the stipulation that all
marriages and divorces had to be registered in the proper manner. The British had already appointed a Malay to the municipal council in 1922.

Not until after World War II did the British realize that the Malays in
Singapore would continue to be a source of political and social instability
unless improvements were made in three old yet very important areas: family life, education, and political representation. These issues became para-
mount as the British intensified their efforts to end their colonial presence
in the Malay region and confronted Singapore's situation as a special case.
The first step was to separate the island nation from the other Straits Settlements, which in turn were incorporated with the sultanates into the Federation of Malaya in 1948.

A particularly critical area of Islamic law for the Malays turned out to
be the lax interpretation of marriage. In the early 1950s talks on setting up
a shariʿa court system were initiated with the aim of improving the organization of matters related to Islamic marriage and family issues.[54] After
receiving jurisdiction by enactment of the Muslims Ordinance of 1957, the
shariʿa court commenced activities in 1958. One of its first tasks was to
begin once again registering marriages and divorces, which could be done
only after thorough consultation. As a result, the divorce rate, for example,
was reduced to 17.5 percent in 1964 from 51.7 percent in 1957. Unlike in
neighboring countries, where ministries for religious affairs presided over
Islamic jurisdiction, in Singapore the Ministry for Social Affairs and Community Development was responsible for overseeing the shariʿa court.

The government led by Lee Kwan Yew of the People's Action Party (PAP)
implemented sweeping reforms in education after internal self-government
was granted in 1959. The prospect of full independence as part of the Federation of Malaysia gained momentum, as it appeared only a few years off,
and the Malays were not alone in feeling that they could finally progress
beyond their minority status on the political stage. The PAP-led government also regarded a rapid and effective development of a Malay-language
branch within the Singaporean educational system, which had been organized by the British on the basis of language (English, Chinese, to some
extent Tamil, and to a minimal degree Malay), to be an opportune starting
point for their accession to the federation. The PAP had already agreed to
the demand to make Malay the national language of the new federation and
Islam the official religion.

The short period between 1963 and 1965 when Singapore was part of
the Federation of Malaysia was a time filled with expectation for Singapore's Malays, because they now finally belonged to a privileged ethnic majority guaranteed protection by special provisions in the constitution, just
like the Malays in the other federal states. And just as in the other federal
states that were not ruled by a sultan, the Yang di-Pertuan Agong, the head
of state, who is elected for a period of five years by and from the ranks of

the sultanates, also assumed the role of head of the Muslim community in Singapore.

Yet the PAP, which was still the strongest force in Singapore, regarded the special rights granted to Malays with growing displeasure because these rights contradicted the party's agenda of creating a multiracial and multicultural society. When these provisions in the constitution were expressly dealt with by the Singapore Malay National Organization in 1964 and calls for their implementation were sent to Singapore, the PAP responded by convening its own Malay Convention, at which Lee Kwan Yew merely offered more support of education for the Malays.[55] Only the "multiracial" aspect of the school system, in which the different linguistic groups were administered separately, was to remain in place; access to schooling would remain unchanged.

Singapore's forced secession from the federation spearheaded by Tunku Abdul Rahman ('Abd al-Rahman) in 1965 meant that the Malays living on the island returned to their minority status. Yet this time they were fortified in their awareness of belonging to an ethnic majority to the north, although they had also been confronted with the mistrust that Singapore's government and the majority of the population harbored in terms of Malay national loyalty.

The employment situation of the Malays improved rapidly, and their options widened to include more than just menial jobs as a result of the immediate need to fight for their survival. The positions open to them were increasingly higher paid and in industry. And Malay women were more visible in the workforce as well.

In education, the Singapore Malay Teachers' Union (Kesatuan Guru-guru Melayu Singapura) had been calling, since 1968, for mandatory instruction in Islam for Malays, the founding of elite Malay schools, and the founding of a university with Malay as the language of instruction, which served as a reminder that Singapore's constitution had also established Malay as an official language. This was merely a formality, however, for the government backed a policy of bilingualism to promote international communication and to improve internal communication and integration between English and the ethnic mother tongue. And for Muslim Malays, their religious education—although religion was a compulsory subject, the choice of religion was left open to the students—was based on textbooks written in English and Malay.

The Council on Education of Muslim Children (Mendaki, which literally means "climb a mountain") began working in 1981 to improve the educational and professional prospects of young Malays, whose dropout rates remained much too high. It was funded by eight Islamic organizations and headed by the minister for social affairs and the environment, who was also the presiding minister for Islamic affairs.

The administrative and representational ties between Singapore's Muslim community and the Malaysian authorities were broken when Singapore seceded from the Federation of Malaysia. In particular Singapore's Muslims mourned the loss of the Yang di-Pertuan Agong as their community leader. A regional Islamic council was planned, which was supposed to assist this post. Singapore's parliament passed an Administration of Muslim Law Act (AMLA) to organize the administrative needs of the Islamic community in 1966. The Islamic Religious Council of Singapore (Majlis Ugama Islam Singapura, or MUIS) was created in 1968 in accordance with this new act.[56] It was also placed under the Minister of Social Affairs and the Environment. Its main role was to advise the president of the Republic of Singapore in matters affecting the Islamic community, effectively abandoning the Yang di-Pertuan Agong, the Islamic sultan. Its members were to be a chairman nominated by the president on recommendation of the minister and a minimum of seven additional members who would be recommended by Islamic organizations and nominated by the president. In addition, a mufti was appointed who was permitted to issue rulings only with approval of the fatwa council, as had been demanded back in the 1930s. Furthermore, the MUIS could issue documents on property holdings in inheritance cases, provided that the beneficiaries did not belong to the Shafi'i school of legal thought. A shari'a court system would handle cases for Shafi'i adherents.

In later years the MUIS transformed itself into a central administrative body that played a number of roles previously handled by various others, such as the administration of the *zakat;* issues involving pilgrimages to Mecca, in which nearly three thousand Muslims participate each year; and the construction of mosques in new residential areas, where the construction committees were no longer handled locally. These new mosques were also social and educational centers, allowing a new generation of Muslims to prosper.[57] Here they could overcome the ethnic isolation of the new apartment buildings, which had become intolerable, and trade the traditional orientation for one based on shari'a as a new expression of their identity. The MUIS also encouraged efforts to devise a standard syllabus for religious instruction in Islam.

A minister's proposal led to the founding of an Islamic Community Fund (Dana Masyarakat Islam) in 1985 to promote investments by Muslim businesspeople. It also collected financial support for Mecca pilgrims.

At the beginning of the 1980s the PAP-led government and a number of Islamic organizations began to increase cooperation efforts, in particular as a result of the work of the MUIS and Muslim parliamentarians in the PAP; the minister for Muslim affairs was also a member of the party. The government had set several priorities, which had also been valid during Singapore's fight for survival: (1) economic, technical, and technological development; (2) creation of a durable form of nationalism for all involved parties, one that respects the country's multiethnic, multicultural makeup yet does not afford a privileged status to specific ethnic groups; and (3) in this respect the favoring of English as a "neutral" language in public life.

As long as the Muslims work toward these priorities, they can be expected to achieve vast support in tackling their problems and integrate rapidly into Singapore's society.

f. Thailand

The population of the kingdom of Thailand was approximately 65.5 million in 2005. About 3.8 percent practice Islam in a country where Theravada Buddhism is the official religion. These figures include in particular ethnic Malays, but also immigrants from the ancient kingdom of Champa on the Indochinese peninsula as well as ethnic Chinese, ethnic Indonesians, and ethnic Indians from various regions. Approximately 800,000 Muslims live in the southern Thai provinces of Pattani, Yala, and Narathiwat, which used to form the heart of the Malay sultanate of Patani,[58] as well as Satun, which used to belong to the Malay sultanate of Kedah. They constitute approximately 73 percent of the population in these provinces. Despite the dismissive references to *khaek* (visitor, foreigner) often made by Thais, the Malays living here feel a connection and dedication to the dynasty and cultural heritage of the ancient Patani kingdom. With haunting memories of the long warlike clashes between Patani and the Thais still lingering, which were only underlined by the Thai government's policy of pushing cultural and linguistic unity, the Malays feared a loss of their identity and history. This fear led to the founding of resistance organizations. These ethnic Malays in southern Thailand will be the topic of further discussion here, as the other Muslims live scattered throughout the country. They are organized only in the larger cities and for the most part have already been assimilated into society.

Before the fifteenth century, the center of one of the oldest kingdoms on the Malay Peninsula had been Langkasuka, which was located near Patani. Even before the ascent of the kingdom of Srivijaya in the seventh century, its capital had established itself as a trading post for those on their way to China and was dominated by Indians from the subcontinent. The geographic location of the capital, situated to the south of the Kra Isthmus, played a substantial role in its history. Through it passed a trade route that connected the Strait of Malacca to the South China Sea.[59] Srivijaya ruled over this region for a long period, although it continued to pay tribute to the Chinese emperor. Suddenly Langkasuka disappeared in the early sixteenth century. Patani developed into a sultanate overshadowed by Langkasuka and leaped forward only when its ruler converted to Islam in 1457 under the influence of Malacca. Islam is said to have had its own traditions in Patani even before Malacca was founded. For this reason it is possible that Muslim traders from Pasai who were living there had performed the first conversions, which would explain Patani's reputation as the cradle of Islam in Southeast Asia. The region soon blossomed again into a trading center on the eastern coast. As it was the northernmost Malay kingdom, it was frequently attacked, and even at times captured, by the Thais to the north encroaching south-ward. Although Patani officially recognized Thai rule, recurring unrest led by Patani, and at times backed by Kelantan, Trengganu, and Kedah, caused these kingdoms to fall into the hands of Siam at various points in history. Generally these kingdoms were only required to pay tribute. Nevertheless, the king of Siam, who had founded a new dynasty in 1782 which continues to rule Thailand today, often intervened in the internal affairs of Patani and repeatedly demanded active support of his military endeavors, in addition to the annual tribute. Finally in 1816 King Rama II (r. 1809–1824) divided the territory of Patani into seven provinces, each with a raja, appointed by the king of Siam, in charge of their administration. The rajas were Malay aristocrats from Kedah or Kelantan who were in some manner related to the family of the sultan of Patani. With this move Patani ceased to exist as an administrative unit. The system of kinship ties that existed among the rajas in what was then the Patani kingdom were similar to those in other Malay kingdoms. It was in this manner that the raja of Patani province could act as representative of this kingdom's tradition at the end of the nineteenth century, when Siam endeavored again to implement an administrative re-form to promote greater centralized control and accelerate modernization. This reform was also necessary to fend off any colonial aspirations of the French to the east or the British to the west (Myanmar) and south (Malaya), who could have used the internal conflicts as a pretext to provide the "assis-tance" of a colonial administration in the last remaining sovereign kingdom on the Indochinese peninsula.

When King Chulalongkorn (Rama V, 1853–1910; his rule began in 1868) appointed Prince Damrong Rajanubhab to become minister of in-ternal affairs in 1892, he chose the right person to implement his reform plans ambitiously and effectively. The provinces were grouped together into "districts" (*monthon*) and were led by a royal commissioner. He was also responsible for expanding the school system, whose teachers were increas-ingly well trained Buddhist monks. From its very first king, the dynasty was particularly concerned with the reform and education of the monks, since religious laxity, among other things, was blamed for the demise of the Ayut-thaya kingdom. The reform of the taxation system was also a particularly radical change because the administration of taxes was no longer in the hands of province officials. Taxes had to be paid directly to the government, and the state officials would receive pay for their work. When the admin-istrative reform was implemented in 1902, it essentially disempowered the traditional upper class in the provinces, leading to massive social conflicts in many parts of the country.

Unrest also emerged in Patani, where Raja Tunku Abdul Kadir ('Abd al-Qadir) enjoyed the traditional loyalty of the Malays to their ruler. For one thing, the old system of taxation was not in harmony with the *adat*, because it passed through the regional aristocracy, meaning those from the same eth-nic group. For another, this system was an expression of the autonomy, even though limited, which the aristocracy along with their subjects enjoyed and was thus a guarantee of their social structure and independent identity in terms of culture and religion. It was now planned that Patani would be incorporated into Nakhon Si Thammarat (Ligor). It became evident that the administrative reform was meant to transform the Malay territory of Patani occupied by the military into the Siamese province of Pattani. The presence and arrogance of the foreign Siamese bureaucrats in the official posts and the linguistic difficulties in communication aggravated the pain over losing independence and the feeling of having no control over the social and cultural alienation taking place. The attempt by Tunku Abdul Kadir to launch a rebellion in 1903 ended in his stepping down and subsequent banishment. His hopes for British intervention were futile. The Malays in Patani had now fully lost their traditional leadership as well as the close ties with neighboring Malay sultanates. The aristocracy was not the only group with close ties of kinship. The *'ulama'* had also been fostering close contacts with one another over the centuries. The loss of these ties meant that hopes of effective support from neighbors and relatives were dashed, especially since Kedah, Kelantan, Trengganu, and even Perlis had success- fully aligned with the British. When the British and the Thais finally worked out a treaty in 1909, the Thais chose to abandon their dominion over the sultanates. Patani and a portion of Kedah were recognized by the British as belonging to Siam, a boundary that lasts even to this day. Patani itself was transformed once again into a *monthon* in 1906 and subdivided into four provinces (*changwat*), with a Thai as royal commissioner. The *changwat* of Saiburi was reshuffled, with one area being incorporated into Patani and another into Narathiwat.

These measures to simplify the administrative system were not limited to the areas of finance, the economy, and education. There were also re- forms effected in the judiciary. The role of the *'ulama'*, which was the second mainstay of Malay society alongside the aristocracy, was reduced to the application of Islamic law in matters affecting the family and inheritance disputes. Although the quarreling parties were allowed to seek out a *qadi*, a state judge had the right to validate or suspend the *qadi*'s verdict. The feel- ing of being neglected by the government and intentionally discriminated against as *khaek* led to a new protest movement in 1922. Sparking off this unrest was a law introducing compulsory schooling in 1921, which would also have required Malay children to attend state schools and use the Thai language. One of the leaders of these protests was the last raja of Patani, Abdul Kadir, who had established contacts with the Malay aristocracy and *'ulama'* in Patani from his exile in Kelantan and supported them both finan- cially and politically in their resistance to the Siamization of their homeland. Abdul Kadir met with the approval of the aristocracy and *'ulama'* in the Unfederated Malay States—with the exception of the previously mentioned four sultanates adjoining Thailand, plus Johor—who were afraid that the British might be planning a similar encroachment into the internal structure of their states, as the Thais had done in Patani. For this reason they also did not join the protectorate of the Federated Malay States established by the British in 1896, even after they had been granted independence from Siam in the Anglo-Siamese Treaty of 1909.[60]

In the end the government in Bangkok decided to change its policy toward the Malays in Patani out of fear that the nationalist movements in the Malay sultanates could spread into Patani. In a royal decree to the minister of internal affairs, King Vajiravudh (Rama VI) announced that:

- No new laws could be passed if they contradicted or harmed Islam.
- Taxes levied on the Malays could not be any higher than those in the Malay states.
- Only honest and well-behaved civil servants could be sent to Patani, and never one being transferred for disciplinary reasons.

Yet these accommodations were not intended to diminish the principle aim of the state, namely the development of a national identity with Thai as the national language and Theravada Buddhism as a cultural basis. There had to be a place for the minorities in this plan. There was no room for greater autonomy. For the Muslims there was still one pressing problem: there were no textbooks on Islam written in Thai, the Buddhist language of instruction at the state-run schools. Therefore the close ties between Islam and Malay remained intact.

The irreconcilable gap between the Thai-Buddhist (nationalist) and Malay-Islamic (secessionist) camps did not close even after the 1932 coup d'état that transformed Siam from an absolute monarchy to a constitutional monarchy, despite initial hopes to the contrary. At the outset Muslims living in Bangkok were also involved in these events; even Abdul Kadir's son Tengku Mahmud Mahyuddin (Mahmud Muhyi al-Din) came to Bangkok to announce that the Malays of Patani were now ready for cooperation under a democratic constitution with equal rights for all.

There was a fundamental dilemma, however, as the Malays realized in the elections of 1933: only one Malay representative from the province of Satun (which had formerly belonged to Kedah) was elected to the national parliament, while only Buddhist Thais were elected or were permitted to be elected in the entire region of Patani.[61] The Malays' rejection of the Siamese educational system only reinforced the illiteracy rate, and it prevented a Malay elite from receiving training, which would have effectively increased their representation in the political hierarchies.

The new situation involving the constitution now gave rise to a rapid transition. The Malay religious elite, that is, the 'ulama' and their students, seized the opportunity for meaningful participation in politics. By the 1937 elections Malay representatives had been assured a seat in parliament for the three provinces of Patani; yet this did not mean that the Malays had unconditionally resigned themselves to the new situation. Their participation was conditional: if it contributed to an improvement in the current situation, they would cooperate. They had not given up their hope for autonomy, and they homed in on the role and attitude of the former aristocracy, as they had done earlier. Their aspirations were pinned on Tengku Mahyuddin.

The national spirit of the movement of 1932 soon developed into one of chauvinism, and the programs aimed at the Siamization of society were resumed with new vigor. When Luang (a military title) Phibun Songkhram was appointed prime minister in December 1938, this heralded the advent of a completely new situation.[62] In the 1932 coup d'état he had represented the nationalist element; he had enjoyed a military elitist training and had developed a preference for authoritarian figures such as Mussolini and Hitler who based their concept of nationalism on the people and not the country. Thai nationalism—even the renaming of Siam to Thailand in 1939 was his doing—gained a character of populism under his reign.[63] The ethnic Chinese living in the country were the first to realize this. In the Sino-Japanese War, which broke out in 1937, he sided with Japan, setting the tone for Thailand's role in World War II in his cooperation with Dai Nippon (Great Japan): while Japan occupied the colonies of Western states in Southeast Asia, "Great Thailand" managed to reincorporate several regions on the Indochinese peninsula that it had staked claims on and ruled at times over the course of history, such as parts of Laos, Cambodia, and the Shan districts in Myanmar. In addition, the four northern Malay sultanates were occupied once again.

The policy of nationalist homogenization was implemented by propagating the use of Thai as the common language and the observance of Buddhism as an expression of genuine national identity. At the same time, there was a decree laying down the rules of cultural expression in personal lifestyles, including the adoption of Western attire such as pants, neckties, hats, and gloves or the adoption of the Western calendar as an expression of progress and civilization. The Malays would encounter problems if they wore their traditional attire. In addition, they lost the right secured under Chulalongkorn to bring cases involving family and inheritance law before a *qadi* according to Islamic law, even if still overseen by a state judge.

Tengku Mahyuddin saw in this tense situation an opportunity to revive Patani. He organized an underground Malay resistance movement with the help of the British to fight the Japanese—a special interest of the British—and the Thai occupational forces. He also appealed to the approximately three thousand Malays from Patani who were stranded in Mecca and were supposed to work as teachers backing Mahyuddin's cause and to fight for Patani's independence, which the British had envisioned as a "Malay Union" and in which the role of the sultans was still open for definition. Yet for the time being the British and the sultans still relied on each other, and the active role of Mahyuddin helped bring both sides closer together.

In early 1944 a group of 'ulama' led by Haji Sulong ibn Abdul Kadir (Hajji Sulung ibn 'Abd al-Qadir) emerged in Patani and offered mutual assistance in defense of obedience to shari'a. Tengku Abdul Jalal ('Abd al-Jalal), another Malay leader and parliamentarian, protested in a petition to Phibun Songkhram's government that the royal commissioner of Patani was profaning Islam; in particular he pointed to the forced prayer before statues of Buddha. The government's reply was succinct and gave a nod of approval to the royal commissioner's actions.[64] With that, Tengku Abdul Jalal joined forces with Tengku Mahyuddin and headed to Kelantan and the underground, where he would fight for the liberation of Patani alongside the anti-Japanese guerrilla fighters.

As the defeat of the Japanese in the Pacific war became more apparent, Phibun was overthrown in July 1944. The new government under Pridi Phanomyong, who had recently returned from the United States, also worked toward improving relations with the Malay minority. In early 1945 the Patronage of Islam Act was passed to signal that a part of Thailand's population in a specific region belonged to Islam and to provide a guarantee of support for this group in administering and practicing their religion. Accordingly the Malay schools and religious institutions were placed under protection by Thailand's administration. In addition a national Council of Islamic Affairs (Majlis Ugama Islam), headed by a *shaykh al-Islam* (*chularajmontri*), would be set up with branch offices in the relevant districts. Senator Chaem Phromyong was appointed *shaykh al-Islam*. The government recognized him as the spokesman for the Islamic community in Thailand and as an adviser to the king, who had been declared the supreme protector of all religious communities in Thailand.

The government also used this move to try to gain control of the Islamic institutions and their leaders by offering this protection. By making a show of interest in the complaints of Muslims, the government was attempting to attract the attention of the Malay population rallying behind Tengku Mahyuddin and his supporters, who were now demanding a national referendum to be held among the Malays in Thailand after the war was over.

Tengku Mahyuddin and the leaders of the Malay aristocracy, pinning their hopes on British support and the incorporation of Patani in the plans for a Malay Union, founded the Gabungan Melayu Patani Raya (Greater Patani Malayu Association, or GAMPAR) with this goal. Yet the 'ulama' were not content to remain inactive. Haji Sulong ibn Abdul Kadir, who in the meantime had been appointed president of the provincial office of Islamic affairs, joined with other 'ulama' in Patani to organize the Patani People's Movement (PPM), which sought to cooperate with GAMPAR. Tengku Mahyuddin did not receive British support as he had expected. On top of this, the borders between Thailand and Malaya from 1909 were sanctioned and the movement led by aristocrats was disavowed. The movement led by the religious elite therefore took over the fight for Patani's independence.

The Muslim Malays following Haji Sulong submitted a memorandum to the government in April 1947 proposing a seven-point program creating an autonomous region called Patani Raya, specifying:

1. A high commissioner should be appointed to have full rule over the region of Patani Raya without restrictions and with the power to substitute, furlough, or release all government officials working in that region; this person should be chosen from the region and directly elected by the people.
2. Eighty percent of the government officials should be Malay Muslims, in order to reflect the demographics of the nation.
3. Both Malay and Siamese would be the official languages.
4. The Malay language would be taught in grade schools.
5. Islamic law should be applicable in the region, including access to Islamic courts separate from and independent of the national legal system.
6. All tax revenues should be used for the exclusive benefit of the people of this region.
7. An Islamic Religious Council (Majlis Ugama Islam) for this province would receive full authority over legislation according to Islamic law for all matters affecting Islamic and Malay culture, under the supreme authority of the high commissioner, as mentioned in point 1.[65]

It is possible that Prime Minister Pridi and Haji Sulong made progress in the months that followed. Tengku Mahyuddin, who in the meantime had become director of the educational department in neighboring Kelantan, was apparently proposed as high commissioner. Pridi, however, had to flee the country in November 1947 after the coup d'état, taking with him Chaem Phromyong, the former *chularajmontri,* whom everyone admired. In January 1948 Haji Sulong was arrested with his son and several other leading *'ulama'* after they had called for a boycott of the elections slated for January 29, 1948, and had threatened to call for a *hijra:* a flat-out refusal to cooperate with the new government. The Islamic Council of Patani was also banned.

The situation continued to worsen when Phibun Songkhram seized power again in April 1948. After being accused of committing war crimes, he had disappeared from the political arena for a while at the end of World War II. Yet with the advent of the cold war, even his former enemies regarded him as a strong and useful person. The first communist guerrilla actions had already been carried out in Malaya. The British, who held the key to the solution for the Patani problem, relied on good relations with the Thai government. And the Thais were quick to justify their actions against the Malays, pointing to the dangers of communist infiltration in the south of the country. Haji Sulong was released again in 1952, and two years later he and his son Ahmad Tokmina disappeared under mysterious circumstances. There were rumors claiming that they were drowned by members of the police force.[66] Phibun's policy of forced assimilation had obviously failed.

Haji Sulong summed up the sentiment of the Malay Patanis, saying: "We Malays are aware that we came under Siam's rule because we were defeated. The expression 'Thai Islam' that the government of Siam announced to us reminds us of that defeat.... Therefore we call upon the government to refer to us as 'Malay Muslims' so we can distinguish ourselves from the Thai in the eyes of the international community."[67]

Even the "soft assimilation policy" that was reintroduced in 1957 after Phibun's departure did not produce any results. For the Malays the unity of cultural and religious tradition forms the basis of their identity and their solidarity with their political and religious leaders. In a like manner, the monarchy, Buddhism, and the bureaucracy in Thailand are also factors underpinning the integration of the nation. Because the traditional Islamic schools (*pondoks*) were the backbone of Malay education, the Thai administrations after Phibun's time attempted to bring the *pondoks* under their control by requiring them to abide by the mandatory curricula for private schools as well.[68]

As the traditional leaders became less influential, another group of Muslims gained in importance, namely, those who had studied at the university and learned about civil rights movements or Marxist or Islamist ("fundamentalist") liberation movements. They were able to give the Malay movement in Patani a new face. And they also gave the separatist organizations, which had been around for some time, a new character. These organizations included:

- The National Liberation Front of Patani (Barisan Nasional Pembebasan Patani, or BNPP). It was founded by Tengku Mahyuddin in Kelantan, and after Haji Sulong's arrest it gained greatly in popularity. It has been increasing its efforts to attract the interest of Saudi Arabia since 1977. Many Patanis study at Arab universities and receive posts in the Malay governments on the peninsula when they return. Its stated goal is to restore Patani to its former glory.
- The National Revolutionary Front (Barisan Revolusion Nasional, or BRN). With the goal of founding a "Republic of Patani" by force, tt has ties to communist groups on both sides of the border, which is why it has a relatively isolated position within the Patani liberation movements.
- The Patani United Liberation Organization (Pertubohan Persatuan Pembibasan Patani, or PPPP, also known by its English acronym, PULO). This organization was founded in 1968 with headquarters in Mecca. Its stated goal is to restore Patani as an autonomous Islamic region by means of guerrilla warfare. It is considered the most ambitious of the three organizations. It is likely that it is also being backed by several of the mystic orders (*tarekat*, Arab. *tariqat* or *turuq*) that also become actively involved whenever political or social tensions rise in the Malay region.[69]
- The Young Muslim Association of Thailand (Persatuan Belia Muslim Thailand, or YMAT). This association, which was founded in 1964, appears to

be modeled after the Malaysian ABIM. It is receptive to ideas of Islamic revival and is active in the *da'wa*. For this reason its range of action spread beyond southern Thailand to include northern and central Thailand.

• The United Front of Patani Mujahidin (Barisan Bersatu Mujahidin Patani) was founded in 1984. It is reported to have close ties to radical groups in Malaysia and Indonesia, such as the Jama'a Islamiyya, who are also said to be active in Moroland.

After days of unrest in 1975, the policies of subsequent Thai administrations have attempted to use diplomatic channels to persuade those countries and organizationsthat support the separatist movement, such as the Islamic Conference Organization (ICO), to change their minds, in addition to continuing military actions. The government has also attempted to win over the Muslim Malay minority in the south, occasionally using increased "appeals," such as measures directed against corrupt or high-handed government officials.

Since then the Thai governments have been attempting to regain the trust lost primarily through Phibun's policies by improving the educational system, which also supported the traditional *pondoks* as long as the use of Thai would be granted more freedom; by improving the options of further education for Muslims with insufficient language skills; and by making efforts to improve the economic situation of the Muslim Patanis, in particular those working in agriculture. At the national level efforts have been made to relativize the Theravada Buddhist character of the country, which the minority groups regard as exclusivist, and to highlight the religious pluralism in the country, for example, affording the king a more effective position than earlier as ruler and protector of the other religious communities too. At the same time, attempts have been made to bring together the disparate ethnic-based understandings of identity as perceived by the various Muslim groups—in addition to the Malays, the much smaller groups of ethnic Chinese, ethnic Indians, and Cham Muslims who fled Cambodia—in a common national identity founded in Thai Islam. The spacious Foundation of Islamic Center of Thailand in Bangkok was erected at the end of the 1970s with this aim.

In an effort to make concessions in the legal realm, Islamic law was introduced for family law and an offer of amnesty was made in the 1980s. Yet "confidence-building measures" were repeatedly forced out by the military, which increasingly acted as an occupying power with repressive means, similar to the Indonesian army in Aceh and Papua. This has provoked greater resistance, in particular since the end of the 1990s, which has manifested itself in more and more violent acts of terror owing to established contacts in international terrorist networks such as al-Qa'ida.[70]

Translated by David Fenske

10. Maghreb

(Franz Kogelmann)

a. The Maghreb as a Geographical and Cultural Unity

The Arabic term *maghrib* means the West, or Land of the Setting Sun. Today the name Maghreb usually signifies the three North African countries Morocco, Tunisia, and Algeria, which were all formerly under French domination; but this narrow definition was not always self-evident in the past. In fact Maghreb is generally taken to mean the region stretching from Tripolitania (the western part of Libya), across Tunisia and Algeria to Morocco. In present-day Arabic parlance, Maghreb is also an abbreviated form of *al-Maghrib al-aqsa*—the far West—meaning Morocco only. The Arab geographers of the Middle Ages were undecided as to whether the territory of present-day Mauritania, with its extensive arid regions, belonged to the Maghreb or sub-Saharan Africa (*bilad al-sudan*). Moroccan nationalists in the twentieth century never completely abandoned their historically grounded demands in relation to Mauritania, but they ultimately failed to reclaim the country for Morocco. Meanwhile, the Moroccan military asserted that nation's territorial claim to the former Spanish Western Sahara by force. The region has been occupied—in contravention of international law—since 1976.

In the course of its history the Maghreb was seldom ruled entirely by a single power, yet the region exhibits a series of common traits. In ethnic terms—with the exception of Mauritania, which has a considerable proportion of black African Muslims—most of the Maghreb's population are Islamized Berbers and Arabs.[1] Even today there are still small, autochthonous Jewish minorities. The trans-Saharan trade that once flourished in the Maghreb was an important basis for economic prosperity and the early development of nation-states and paved the way for lasting cultural influence on the regions south of the Sahara.

Another factor shared by the Maghreb countries is the epoch of foreign domination by Europeans. Aside from Libya (which is discussed separately in this book), a large part of the Maghreb was under French rule from the nineteenth century on, with the exception of the Spanish zones of influence in northern and southern Morocco and Spanish Western Sahara. The French occupation took various forms and varied as to duration and intensity in the different countries. The reactions to European hegemony and the configuration of the states after independence were correspondingly varied.

A glance at the official self-designations of the individual countries shows that they have little in common on the national constitutional level. Morocco calls itself a kingdom (*al-mamlaka al-maghribiyya*), Mauritania an Islamic republic (*al-jumhuriyya al-islamiyya al-muritaniyya*), Algeria a democratic people's republic (*al-jumhuriyya al-jaza'iriyya al-dimuqratiyya al-sha'biyya*), and Tunisia simply a republic (*al-jumhuriyya al-tunisiyya*).

The Maghreb states have many political and ideological differences, yet they still share a common series of problems today. For example, the decline in the prices of raw materials negatively affects their national trade balance. Weak economies, high population growth, a marked trend toward migration away from rural regions, and a high illiteracy level are accompanied by a variety of problems such as unemployment and a lack of prospects for young people. Added to this, atrophied political and social structures, frustrated political hopes, entrenched oligarchies, nepotism, rampant corruption, and the like furnish ample grounds for political radicalization. Moreover, the population in each of these countries often sees the security system that backs up state power as one of the few effectively functioning state institutions.[2]

Despite the struggles for regional domination, zones of influence, and raw materials, the Maghreb's political leaders have kept sight of their eventual goal of creating a league of nations based on a common economic area on the model of the European Union. In 1989, after several failed attempts, Libya, Tunisia, Algeria, and Mauritania combined to create the Arab Maghreb Union (*ittihad al-maghrib al-'arabi*). The projected free exchange of goods and personnel, however, seems to be making little progress, whereas cooperation on security policy is working quite efficiently. Special interests have impeded a lasting solution to the conflict around the former Spanish Western Sahara as well.

The most enduring features shared by the Maghreb states are their common language and religion. French still plays an important role in public life, the Berber languages are largely recognized officially, and in the southern region of Mauritania a number of Niger-Congo languages are spoken, yet Arabic is the official language. An active but only partially successful Arabization policy is being pursued in all the Maghreb countries.

In the Maghreb as in other regions, the image of Islam is marked by cultural diversity and a variety of individual ways of expressing faith; but the Muslim population of the region is largely unified in terms of adherence to a single school of law. Apart from an Ibadite minority, and followers of the Hanafite school of law whose presence is a relic of the Ottoman hegemony over large areas of the Maghreb, the overwhelming majority of Maghrebi Muslims can be counted as adherents of the Malikite school of law. The intellectual and cultural achievements of the Maghreb's most important centers of Islamic scholarship are still firmly rooted in the minds of the indigenous population. Over the centuries, the mosque-university in Fes, al-Qarawiyin, for example, and its counterpart in Tunis, al-Zaytuna, had a strong influence well beyond the region. Little is left of this splendor today. The mosque-universities have become part of the state education system, with responsibility for training the next generation of Muslim scholars to maintain the religious infrastructure.

A similar decline in importance can be seen at Chinguetti (Arab. Shinqit or Shinjit), a city in the Mauritanian part of the Sahara that has lost its former function as a bridge for the spread of Islam and the Arabic language in West Africa. This culture was initially fostered by the Sufi Brotherhoods (*tariqa;* pl. *turuq*), with their transnational networks; it was they who mounted the fiercest resistance to the threat of foreign rule in many regions of the Maghreb as colonialism began to invade and spread. In most cases, however, the Sufi Brotherhoods ended up cooperating closely with the European powers during the colonial era. After independence, nationalist leaders openly accused the brotherhoods of collaboration, and they were discredited for a long time. They still play a role in Maghrebi society today, but relatively little is known about their present social, political, or even economic influence.

b. The Influence of the Salafiyya Movement on Islam in the Maghreb

Although the impact of the Salafiyya movement varied in the different countries, we should not underestimate its influence on the political consciousness of Maghrebi Muslims. The Salafiyya originated in late-nineteenth-century Egypt as an Islamic reform movement in reaction to the direct confrontation between European powers and Muslim states. The movement's followers explained the Muslims' inferiority in relation to the West by arguing that the perception of Islam had become atrophied by inherited tradition. The Salafiyya was largely an urban phenomenon. One characteristic of the movement was—and still is—its fight against specific religious practices of the Sufi Brotherhoods.

Immediately after the First World War, followers of the Salafiyya movement began to establish so-called reform schools in the urban centers of the Maghreb. Their goal was a form of Islamic education, a reformed education system that would accord with the Salafiyya's concepts while simultaneously fitting with the needs of the times. The idea was to create a basis for reviving the strength of the Maghrebi Muslims.[3] A reformed education system was seen as the precondition for Muslims to be able to regain their rightful place in the world.

Tunisia

Tunisia was the first Maghreb country to have contact with the Salafiyya movement. One of the leading representatives of Salafiya reform Islam was 'Abd al-'Aziz al-Tha'alibi (1876–1944). By the beginning of the twentieth century, al-Tha'alibi was already in conflict with the religious establishment over questions of religious practice and Qur'an interpretation. His political career began with active involvement in the Young Tunisians' movement (1907–1912). The Destour Party (*hizb al-hurr al-dusturi;* roughly, Liberal Constitutional Party) was founded in 1920; it emerged from an alliance between Tunisians influenced by secular modernism and followers of the Salafiyya movement. In 1934 there was a decisive break between these two intellectual tendencies, and the Neo-Destour Party emerged victorious under the leadership of a French-educated politician, Habib Bourguiba (Habib

Bu Raqiba). The politics of independent Tunisia was strongly influenced by Bourguiba's secularization program, while the followers of the Salafiyya movement seem to have had a relatively minor influence.[4]

Algeria

The Salafiyya movement had a more lasting influence in Algeria.[5] The intense and sustained French influence on every area of life meant that the majority of Algerian Muslims were largely alienated from their own culture, language, and religion. Salafiyya followers focused specifically on combating the effects of the French policy of assimilation, and their campaign was particularly popular in Algeria. A fairly large sector of educated Muslims in Algeria seemed to want to clear the path to an independent, pervasive Islamic culture—of the kind influenced by Salafiyya reform Islam, of course. 'Abd al-Hamid ibn Badis (1889–1940) was a prominent figure in the establishment of the Salafiyya's ideology in Algeria; he and his comrades founded the Association of Algerian Muslim Scholars (*jam'iyyat al-'ulama' al-muslimin al-jaza'iriyyin,* often known by its French acronym, AUMA) in 1931. Although the association defined itself as purely religious and cultural, it developed into an important basis of the nationalist movement. The main demands of *jam'iyyat al-'ulama' al-muslimin al-jaza'iriyyin* were preservation of Islamic personal law, reform of the court system, separation of religion and state, restoration of the Islamic endowment system (*waqf;* pl. *awqaf*) to Muslim control, and abolition of all discriminatory measures against the Arabic language. These demands were never achieved under French rule. After the war of independence broke out in 1954, AUMA came out in solidarity—though rather hesitantly—with the National Liberation Front (Front de Libération Nationale, FLN). Finally, after independence, Algeria's new leaders appointed the general secretary of AUMA, Ahmad Tawfiq al-Madani, the first minister for Islamic endowments.

Morocco

After the First World War a group called the Neo-Salafiyya (*al-salafiyya al-jadida*) emerged in Morocco demanding direct, unlimited participation in shaping the country's social and economic affairs, and advocated new structures to achieve this. The Moroccan Salafiyya movement gained influence rapidly, partly because the two best-known Salafiyya representatives in Morocco, Abu Shu'ayb al-Dukkali (1878–1937) and his disciple Muhammad ibn al-'Arabi al-'Alawi (1880–1963) had long been integrated into the protectorate system at the highest level. Another factor was that the Neo-Salafiyya doctrine was part of the ideological basis of the country's nationalist movement.[6] A series of representatives of the nationalist movement were decisively influenced by Salafiyya reform Islam and retained their influence on the country's destiny even after national independence had been won. One example is Muhammad al-Makki al-Nasiri (1906–1994), who was minister for endowments, Islamic affairs, and culture in the 1970s.[7]

The most prominent and influential representative of the Moroccan Salafiyya movement was 'Allal al-Fasi (1907–1974). He was the longtime head of the Independence Party (*hizb al-istiqlal*), which was founded in 1943 and is still important today. Al-Fasi held a government post in independent Morocco's first cabinet—though only briefly—as minister for Islamic endowments. He analyzed the dilemmas of the Arab world in a book published in 1952, *Al-naqd al-dhati* (Self-Criticism), placing himself clearly in the tradition of the Salafiyya movement.[8]

Mauritania

There has been little research to date on the influence of Salafiyya reform Islam in Mauritania. On the one hand, we can infer from the strong presence of Sufi Brotherhoods in Mauritania that the ideas of the Salafiyya movement, which challenged specific Sufi practices, made little headway in the region. On the other hand, given its position as a bridge between sub-Saharan Africa and the Maghreb, Mauritania was hardly isolated from contemporary intellectual tendencies in Islam. In many cases this meant that the fierce, sustained resistance against foreign domination organized by the brotherhoods was transformed into close cooperation with the French colonial forces. Reform-oriented Muslims began criticizing this cooperation in the 1940s. Mauritanian centers of Muslim scholarship had a significant regional influence in French West Africa (Afrique Occidentale Française, AOF); this was encouraged by the French policy toward Islam. The French administration also tried to win direct influence over the education of Muslims. Under French rule, the Institut d'Études Islamiques in Boutlimit in southern Mauritania became the main authority for the graduation certificate for all the Écoles Franco-Arabes (French Arabic Schools) in French West Africa.[9] A leading figure whose reformist ideas made him influential in the development of Islam in the AOF region was Mukhtar Uld Hamidun, who worked at the Institut Français d'Afrique Noir (IFAN) in Dakar in 1940, and later at the Institut Mauritanien de Recherches Scientifiques in Nouakchott until the 1980s.[10] Another leader, Mahmoud Bâ, endeavored to realize his reformist ideas in the Senegal River region while the country was still under French hegemony. He tried to implement his ideals in the educational field through his organization, the Harakat al-Falah (Salvation Movement); but he had to wait until the end of French rule to establish schools on a major scale. By 1976 he had set up thirty schools in Mauritania alone. Shortly after the restoration of national independence, the first Mauritanian president, Mokhtar Ould Daddah, appointed Mahmoud Bâ inspector of Arabic teaching. He was a presidential adviser on educational affairs until 1978.[11]

c. Islam in the Constitutions of the Maghreb States

The role of Islam as an ideology in the national independence struggle in the individual Maghreb states took a variety of forms, but it represented an important mobilizing factor for the population, giving the people a sense of identity. Despite the many ideological differences in shaping national policy, in some way or other Islam is part of the constitution of all four states discussed here.[12]

Islam is the state religion in Tunisia, while at the same time Article 5 of the constitution guarantees freedom of religion. Islam is also the religion of the president. In Algeria the preamble to the constitution emphasizes Islam as one of the basic elements of national identity. Here again, the president has to be a Muslim; he is advised by an Islamic High Council. The state institutions are responsible for banning practices that contravene Islamic morality. The Islamic endowment system is also protected by law. Islam is the state religion in the religiously legitimated monarchy of Morocco. The king, as *amir al-mu'minin* (Commander of the Faithful), is also spiritual head of his Muslim subjects; but the state guarantees freedom of religious practice. The constitutions of Tunisia, Algeria, and Morocco do not mention Islamic law as the source of legislation. The constitution of Mauritania, however, states in its preamble that the fundamental principles of the Islamic religion (*ahkam al-din al-islami*) are the sole source of law (*al-masdar al-wahid li-l-qanun*): Islam is the religion of the people and the state. The Mauritanian constitution makes no reference to freedom of religious practice. It guarantees the validity of Islamic inheritance law and protection of the Islamic trust system. The president appoints a five-member Islamic High Council (*al-majlis al-islami al-a'la*) to advise him on questions of Islam and Islamic culture.

d. State Islamic Structures

Independently of the status of Islam in the different countries' constitutions, most present-day Muslim Arab states have a ministry responsible for maintenance and, above all, for tight state control of the religious infrastructure. This ministry is usually responsible for the Islamic endowment system as well.

Tunisia

Tunisia is one of the few Muslim states today with no remaining Islamic endowments.[13] Immediately after the restoration of national independence, Bourguiba's sweeping policy of secularization culminated in the abolition of the Islamic endowment system. The Tunisian legislature dissolved all the endowments in 1956–57. The state declared itself responsible for funding the entire religious infrastructure, and proceeds from the dissolution of the endowments reverted to the legal heirs under the relevant conditions of Islamic law. Aside from abolishing the endowment system, the state also organized the abolition of Islamic courts responsible for the personal legal affairs of Muslims. The Tunisian legislature extensively revised the country's personal law, which has since been the most "Westernized" in the whole Middle and

Near East. The state also put the entire Islamic educational system under its control and direction. This makes Tunisia one of the few present-day Muslim states without a special ministry of religious affairs. The state-controlled religious infrastructure is responsible to the prime minister and administered by two official bodies—the Office of the Mufti of the Republic (*dar al-ifta'*) and a directorate for places of worship (*idarat al-sha'a'ir al-diniyya*).

Algeria

The long period of French colonial domination in Algeria had far-reaching consequences for the Islamic endowment system. The colonial rulers integrated the Islamic endowments into the state sphere. Right up to the end of its hegemony, France rejected the demands of reform-orientated *'ulama'* for a separation of religion and state and the return of the Islamic endowments to Muslim control. The leaders who came to power after national independence in 1962 did not implement this demand either. Instead they established a ministry for Islamic endowments on the model of other Muslim states. This ministry had particular importance in a state that laid claim to so-called Islamic socialism as its national ideology, especially after Houari Boumedienne (Hawari Bu Madyan) took power.[14]

In line with its changing responsibilities, the ministry has had a series of different titles in the course of its existence. Founded originally as the Ministère des Habous, in 1970 it was renamed Ministère de l'Enseignement Originel et des Affaires Religieuses, in 1979 Ministère des Affaires Religieuses, and then Ministère des Affaires Religieuses et des Habous. From 1977 to 1979 the ministry was directly responsible to the president of the state.

The first minister for Islamic endowments, Ahmad Tawfiq al-Madani, was soon dissatisfied with his allotted scope of authority. At the beginning of 1963 he announced that his ministry would not be confined only to the religious infrastructure but planned to play an active role in the education of the Algerian people. The religious education system was eventually regulated by an order of January 11, 1964, and the ministry of endowments was made responsible for it. Although religion classes in public schools were a compulsory part of the curriculum from 1964 on, the ministry of endowments began setting up a parallel Islamic school system. The parallel structure was not legalized until 1971, however. Five years later this Islamic variant of the Algerian education system was integrated into the national education structure. In 1979 the state conclusively defined the ministry's political responsibility: it was to serve the implementation of national policy as defined by socialist principles and social justice rooted in Islam. The ministry's main responsibility was defined as religious education "dans ses dimensions idéologiques et morales."[15]

It was hardly surprising that the Islamic endowments were dropped from the ministry's title in 1970. Although a subdepartment of the ministry was charged with administration of Islamic endowments in 1980, the "nationalization" of the agriculturally utilizable endowment estates in the wake of the agrarian revolution launched in 1971 meant that the stock of endowed property overseen by the ministry had been severely reduced. By 1980 the only properties it directly administered were endowed buildings.

The agrarian revolution polarized Algerian society because its aim was to nationalize not only endowment estates but also large private landholdings, municipal land, and tribal land. In 1974 there were already demonstrations by young people inspired by Islam calling for an end to the redistribution of agricultural properties. In the following years there were clashes between rival student groups. A similar situation occurred in 1982, with internal conflicts in the student body. Student supporters of politicized Islam called, for instance, for lands confiscated during the agrarian revolution to be restored to their original owners. The state reacted with repression. Over a thousand people were arrested, including ʿAbbasi Madani, the future leader of the Islamic Salvation Front (Front Islamique du Salut, FIS).

Around the same time as the protest against the agrarian revolution, there was a building boom for mosques. As they were a key part of the religious infrastructure, the postcolonial state tried to exercise the tightest possible control over them all through a ministerial bureaucracy. Nevertheless, many of the mosques founded in the 1970s and 1980s evaded state control. Along with prestigious buildings that the governing politicians founded to underscore their religious legitimation, this period saw the emergence of a number of improvised people's mosques (*masajid al-shaʿb*), free mosques (*masajid hurra*), and private mosques. What they all share is that they tried to escape the grasp of the state, in terms of both the religious message propagated by their imams and the maintenance of the buildings.

During the 1980s the state reacted to the growth of autonomously administered mosques by trying to bring them under the control of the Ministry of Religious Affairs while making its own investment in the religious infrastructure. At that time, in fact, the government had begun to yield to the population's evident need for more mosques; but it was not in a position to staff them with enough personnel educated in state-controlled institutions. The ministry tried to circumvent the lack of suitable imams by licensing "free imams" in state-controlled mosques—then subsequently tried to halt this development, which ultimately contradicted the interests of the ruling power. The president of state from 1979 to 1992, Chadli Bendjedid (al-Shadhili Bin Jadid) also fiercely attacked this phenomenon in a keynote speech. He described the free imams as "harmful and stupid elements" who were using the mosques for destructive ends.

The 1980s, particularly after the riots of 1988, were ultimately marked by developments that culminated in rapid political liberalization, and especially in the Islamization of political discourse. After decades of one-party rule, at the beginning of the 1990s several parties were constituted whose goal was to establish an Islamic social order. The most successful and best organized of these was the Islamic Salvation Front (Front Islamique du Salut,

FIS; *al-jabha al-islamiyya li-l-inqadh*). Although the religious endowments are a genuine Islamic institution with a grand history, the FIS discussed the endowment system surprisingly little in its programs and publications. Islamic endowments were mentioned only in connection with the legal resources of the state.[16]

Contrary to the lack of the Islamic endowments on the agenda of the FIS, from 1991 the Algerian state tried to put the endowments system on a new legal basis, which was achieved by 2002 by means of several, sometimes mutually contradictory, measures. Law 91–10 of April 27, 1991, defines the general regulations on administration, organization, and preservation of Islamic endowments.[17] It emphasizes that the individual articles of the law are based on the provisions of Islamic law. The endowments nationalized during the agrarian revolution were to be returned to the ministry. But the legislators seem to have been overhasty in drawing up this new law on Islamic endowments. The regulation on the structure of private endowments was deleted in 2002, along with a series of complementary provisions relating to the economic exploitation of endowments. We can only speculate as to the motives for these modifications and the background behind the delay. The constant crises in domestic politics during the 1990s clearly played a decisive role here. But the state seems to have had insufficient information on the actual situation of the endowments; otherwise Law 01–07 of 2001, whose provisions included making a general inventory of the Islamic trusts, would have been superfluous.

Along with the legal principles, the legislature also issued a series of regulations for implementation and several ordinances relating to the religious infrastructure. One such regulation covers the building, administration, and responsibilities of mosques.[18] In each case, regardless of whether the mosque was founded by the state or by a private organization or individual, it is regarded as an Islamic endowment. As a house of God, it does not belong to anybody, yet it is under the sole authority of the state, which is responsible, among other things, for guaranteeing that the mosques are able to carry out their tasks independently in relation to spiritual life, social affairs, education, and training. The ministry is also responsible for appointing imams. A concluding legal order was issued in 2000 to regulate the central administration and organization of the Ministry of Religious Affairs and Islamic Endowments.[19] Meanwhile, further orders covered training of all employees within the religious infrastructure. From then on, the Qur'an school system was under the ministry's supervision and within its sphere of authority.

After evidently losing control of religious discourse in the 1980s, the state tried to regain the initiative in the 1990s. With the country in a situation comparable to civil war, it was forced to take urgent action. The Ministry of Religious Affairs and Islamic Endowments was made responsible for the Islamic education system, training of mosque personnel, administration and building of mosques, utilization of Islamic endowments, publication and distribution of Islamic writings, and so on. The state also tried to gain authority over religious content through a religious infrastructure controlled by the various ministry authorities. The ministry acted as a transmission belt for the state-sanctioned, proper understanding of Islam.

Morocco

In Morocco, the Ministry for the Endowment System and Islamic Affairs (*wizarat al-awqaf wa-l-shu'un al-islamiyya*) is the backbone of the country's religious infrastructure, presided over by the king as the spiritual head of state. Unlike in many other Muslim countries, in Morocco the restoration of national independence did not coincide with a rupture in the system of Islamic endowments or the nationalization of endowed properties. Basic reforms took place immediately after the French protectorate was established.[20] This key ministry for the endowment system was therefore distinguished by a high degree of continuity, both on the staff side—some of the ministers remained in office for up to twenty years—and in the way the religious infrastructure was administered. Alongside the ministers of the interior, foreign affairs, and justice, the minister of Islamic affairs was one of the *ministres de souveraineté,* meaning that he was appointed solely by the king.

Internal restructuring first took place in 1976. Two complementary portfolios covered the "spiritual" and "material" tasks of the ministry. The Office of Islamic Affairs deals with all the spiritual aspects of religious practice. In addition to spreading Islamic culture in Morocco and abroad, its activity ranges from recruiting competent imams and organizing the pilgrimage to Mecca to publication of religious tracts. The administration of endowed properties is organized separately. The ministry earns the funds for its activities to a certain degree from Islamic endowments. Under clearly defined preconditions, the legal reforms already implemented under French rule have enabled real estate from endowments to be incorporated into the free market. Aside from building mosques, the ministry is active in various ways in the real estate sector. There were plans during the 1970s to make endowed land part of a Moroccan "agrarian revolution," but this was never implemented.

In June 2000 there was public surprise at the announcement of a series of circular orders from the minister for endowments, 'Abd al-Kabir M'daghri (Madaghri) al-'Alawi. On June 5 he signed four orders that would have had a revolutionary effect on the development of the ministry and on the religious infrastructure; four days later he issued a fifth order annulling the previous four.

The first order called on the minister's representatives in the provincial administrations to appoint an administrator for each mosque to be answerable to him, and to organize literacy courses in the mosques under the guidance of the regional *'ulama'* council. The second order called for an increase in the number of mosques by fostering individual initiative and getting financial aid from patrons. The third would have opened the mosques to women—actually giving them an active role as preachers or jurists. Female representatives from civil society, that is, women activists, would also have been given access to mosques for their social work. The fourth circular order would have transferred almost the entire range of religious issues, which had been under the aegis of the Ministry of Islamic Endowments and Affairs up until then, to the authority of the fourteen regional *'ulama'* councils. These ministerial ordinances would have given the mosques the opportunity to become embedded in their natural sociocultural surroundings—under the supervision of the *'ulama'* councils and with responsibility for a great many social duties. The councils are associations founded in 1984 and organized on the national as well as regional level. Transferring all the assignments of the mosques to the *'ulama'* would have considerably upgraded the status of the councils' terms of reference and responsibility.

We can only speculate on the reasons for the sudden annulment of these reforms, which were thought to have originated in an initiative by the king to combat Islamism. In November 2002 this finally spelled the end of 'Abd al-Kabir M'daghri al-'Alawi's political career, which had spanned almost a quarter of a century. He was replaced by Ahmad al-Tawfiq, a brilliant intellectual and a member of the Bushishiyya Brotherhood. Tawfiq's main priority was the overdue reform of the country's religious institutions. The events of May 16, 2003, when Islamic suicide bombers attacked targets in Casablanca, shocked Moroccan society to the roots and speeded up reform measures. In December 2003 and in April of the following year, King Muhammad VI decreed laws that aimed at restructuring the Ministry of Endowments and Islamic Affairs on the one hand and, on the other, expanded the authority of the Supreme Council of Islamic Scholars (*majlis al-'ulama' al-a'la*) and its local branches. In a speech at the end of April 2004, the king emphasized the urgency of reforms in relation to religious institutions. The reform measures undertaken from then on ultimately stabilized the role of the religious establishment within the structures of the state and society, and were aimed at boosting the monarchy's religious legitimation.

Mauritania

The attribute "Islamic" in the official designation of Mauritania should not be taken to indicate a state legitimated by Islam. Rather it refers to the religion of the majority of the population and the function of Islam in unifying and fostering a sense of identity.[21] Despite the eminent importance of Sufi Brotherhoods for present-day Mauritania, immediately after national independence the brotherhoods were barely tolerated by the state leadership, and were scorned as heterodox and obscurantist. Yet the state absolutely came to rely on the support of the *turuq* network for implementing its political goals. For instance, the Niasse branch of the Tijaniyya Brotherhood played an important role after the conflict between Mauritania and Senegal

(1989–1992). The transnational activities of this Sufi brotherhood put it in a position to mediate between hostile population groups.

In the period immediately after the establishment of the state, the administration of Mauritania's religious infrastructure was carried out by a High Commission. The government later set up a ministry for religion that was always tied in with another portfolio—such as the Ministry of Justice or the Ministry of Culture. As in most Muslim states, the ministry was utilized to expand state control over all areas of religion. In 2003 the Mauritanian legislature declared mosques to be public buildings directly under state control. In addition, imams are required to refer exclusively to the doctrine of the Malikite school of law. The Institut d'Études Islamiques, originally set up in Boutlimit by the French colonial administration, moved to Nouakchott in 1978. Now called Institut Supérieur d'Études et de Recherches Islamiques (ISERI), it is integrated into the state education system and used for training imams and teachers of religion and Arabic. Islamic law plays an important role in Mauritania. Attempts to Islamize penal law as well were short-lived, however. International protests against the use of Islamic penal law in the 1980s led to the suspension of *hadd* sentences.

e. Islamism in the Maghreb

Since the 1970s the political opposition in the Maghreb has increasingly used Islamic rhetoric that challenges state leadership. Its leaders argue that Islamizing the public sphere would help solve the multitude of national problems. Although in many cases these Islamist movements have earned great merit (and can claim partial success) in fields like social work—an area where most contemporary Muslim states generally fail—their concrete political program barely goes beyond slogans such as "Islam is the solution" (*al-islam huwa al-hall*), or the call for application of shariʿa law (*tatbiq al-shariʿa*).

Personal law is a particularly sensitive topic in the individual states of the Maghreb. It is one of the few areas of national legislation where Islamic law is still valid. The rulers of the different countries have reacted to this challenge in widely differing ways. At times they have tried to manipulate the respective Islamic groups to maintain their own power. In Tunisia during the 1980s, the regime used the Mouvement de la Tendance islamique (MTI) to stem left-wing tendencies, until the movement itself fell victim to state repression. Its main theorist, Rashid Ghannouchi (Ghannushi), and other prominent figures were imprisoned and brought to trial. After the overthrow of Habib Bourguiba that same year, the regime briefly seemed more conciliatory and organized parliamentary elections. Although the law on political parties prohibited the formation of parties based on religion, the MTI reconstituted itself as the party of Tunisian renaissance (*hizb al-nahda al-tunisiyya*). But it was refused legal status, and from then on the

Tunisian regime persecuted the country's Islamist movement very severely. The regime partially yielded to the pressure to Islamize society, however, by emphasizing Islam as a basic element of Tunisian identity. It allowed state-conformist *ulama* to exercise more influence, or gave more public status to Islamic symbols.

In Algeria the political leadership's maneuvering against Islamist tendencies culminated in civil war in the 1990s. In 1988 the state reacted to violent unrest with political liberalization, which included allowing a series of Islamist movements to organize legally as parties. After the FIS registered success in the January 1992 parliamentary elections, the state leaders declared the elections null and void, plunging the Algerian nation into the most serious crisis since national independence. The struggle between the state and various armed Islamic groups escalated, and at times militant Islamists took control of some parts of the country, a situation in which the distinction between an "Islamic state"—whatever form that might take—and banditry was often blurred. The state may have largely defeated these armed groups in military terms—many of their leaders had gained fighting experience in the Afghan War (1979–1989)—while simultaneously giving Islam more scope in the public sphere; but the basic problems of the country have remained unsolved. To establish a sustainable *concorde nationale,* since 1999 Algeria's political leadership has developed various methods of keeping the wide range of militant Islamist movements in check. Over the years it has been fairly successful with security measures to isolate the *maquis* and legal provisions to reintegrate former Islamist fighters who renounced violence. But in 2007 a group calling itself al-Qa'ida in Islamic North Africa gained notoriety with a series of bomb attacks.

Unlike the governments in Tunisia and Algeria, the Moroccan monarchy can claim religious legitimacy; but this does not make it completely immune from attacks mounted by Islam. 'Abd al-Salam Yasin's epistle to the king, "Islam or the Flood" ("Al-islam aw al-tufan"), which described the monarch as a renegade, earned him several years' incarceration in a psychiatric hospital. But this did not stop the organization he founded, *jama'at al-'adl wa-l-ihsan* (Association for Justice and Welfare), from developing into one of the country's most influential Islamist movements. Today it has considerable mobilizing potential. Unlike the Party of Justice and Development (*hizb al-'adala wa-l-tanmiya*), led by 'Abdallah Binkiran and represented in parliament, Yasin's movement has been denied political recognition—sparing it the need for compromises required by the daily business of politics. The Moroccan state prosecuted Islamist movements particularly harshly after the suicide bomb attacks in Casablanca.

In Mauritania, oppositional Islamist tendencies have been discernible since the 1980s. The Party Law of 1991 prohibits political parties based on religion. The state reacted repressively to assassinations of French priests and Mauritanian politicians in 1993 with arrests, expulsion of foreigners, and bans on Islamist associations. Particularly since September 11, 2001, the state leadership has become more sensitive toward Islamist tendencies—above all under pressure from the United States. This has led to a ban on Islamist welfare organizations. Saudi institutions have been forced to shut down, Islamist press publications have been censored, and politicians suspected of Islamism have been arrested.

Translated by Karen Margolis

11. The Independent States of Sub-Saharan Africa

(Jamil M. Abun-Nasr and Roman Loimeier)

a. Introduction

According to recent estimates, around 365 million Muslims live in Africa, of whom 140 million live in the five northern countries—Egypt, Libya, Tunisia, Algeria, and Morocco—while 225 million live in sub-Saharan Africa, from Mauritania to Somalia and from the Republic of Sudan to South Africa.[1] In the past few decades the number of Muslims in sub-Saharan Africa has probably increased more than in any other region in the Muslim world. This is due to the rapid population growth of the existing Muslim societies as well as the conversion of members of indigenous African religions. The Christian churches in sub-Saharan Africa have also seen enormous growth in recent decades. In some regions, such as the East African hinterland of Tanzania or Kenya, Christians have grown in number even more than Muslims, whereas in other regions such as Mali, Niger, and Chad, the number of Muslims has increased disproportionally. In North Africa, however, the process of Islamization has reached its limits; the number of non-Muslims, particularly Coptic Christians, is probably barely over 6 million.

Despite the growth of Muslim populations in the countries of sub-Saharan Africa, in the years after independence Islam was mainly on the defensive in political life there. While most Muslims in West and East Africa supported their countries' nationalist movements, in most of the independent states of sub-Saharan Africa, Muslim leaders were largely politically marginalized. Since the 1980s, however, radical Muslim movements that are no longer willing to tolerate the political marginalization of Islam have developed in many of these countries. New Muslim leaders and groups have entered the political arena and are calling for a stronger role for Islam in political and social life. To date, however, the Muslim societies of sub-Saharan Africa—aside from a few exceptions such as Northern Nigeria—have not been overly influenced by the radical Islamic (Islamist) movements whose leaders in the Middle East and North Africa are demanding reorganization of their countries' political systems along Islamic lines. The established political forces

frequently describe these tendencies as "foreign to our country" and dominated by external interests, and they have failed to gain decisive social influence to date. The growth in numbers of Muslims in Africa and the claims
they are consequently making in the public arena in the various countries
raise the question as to why Islam in sub-Saharan Africa has not become the
basis of a kind of religiously legitimized nationalism on the model of Iran
or the Muslim Brotherhoods, and why no religiously legitimated political
movement in sub-Saharan Africa has been able to win political power up
till now.[2]

The political leaders who came to power in the North African countries and in sub-Saharan Africa after independence in the 1950s and 1960s
claimed the right to determine not only development plans and educational
policy but also their countries' course in the interests of political integration
and economic development. In this process the elites in North Africa aiming for change favored identification with Islam and those in sub-Saharan
Africa identification with their African cultural heritage. In Senegal, for
example, this was expressed by the concept of *négritude,* and in Ghana
by "African socialism." Ultimately the ideas these leaders nurtured for the
future of their states were based not on Islamic or African but on European
traditions of thought. To legitimize their political and economic agendas,
they fostered an image of society projected back into the precolonial past.
This was modeled on the "invention of tradition,"[3] begun in the colonial era
and continuing in the postcolonial period in relation to the development of
national identity. But the established traditional political and social institutions were still seen as obstacles in the path of the new nation-states. Although the established institutions were often tolerated in national planning
and development policies, some were destroyed, such as those in Guinea in
the Sékou Touré era.[4]

Radical Islamic movements have changed the political situation in the
Middle East and North Africa dramatically in the past few decades. They
have forced leaders of nations in these regions to rethink their position between aspirations for modernization and identification with Islam. Islam is
part of the national heritage in many sub-Saharan African countries—a fact
political leaders have to take into account. This applies not only to Somalia,
Djibouti, the Comoros, and Mauritania, where the population is wholly
Muslim, but also to the countries of sub-Saharan Africa with a large Muslim majority, such as Senegal, Gambia, Guinea (both Bissau and Conakry),
Mali, Niger, and Chad, as well as those countries where Muslims form a
considerable part of the population if not necessarily the majority, such as
Burkina Faso, Nigeria, Cameroon, Ethiopia, Eritrea, Kenya, Tanzania, and
Mozambique. Even in those countries of sub-Saharan Africa where Muslims constitute a more or less influential minority, political constellations
could develop that would give them national importance. This applies, for
example, to South Africa, Mauritius, Togo, Benin, and Ghana. Nevertheless, the political leaders in sub-Saharan Africa, even in the countries where

Muslims are in the majority, still seem capable of keeping extremist Muslim demands in check, even in cases such as the defeat of the fanatical Maitatsine movement in Northern Nigeria in the 1980s, which involved considerable bloodshed.[5] A bigger problem has emerged in recent years: the demand, particularly in Northern Nigeria, but also in other countries of sub-Saharan Africa, for the introduction of shari'a in the area of penal law.

The political significance of radical Islamic groupings is still at a low level. This seems related to the fact that in terms of religious consciousness, Muslims in sub-Saharan Africa were not influenced by the reformist Islamic Salafiyya movement. In the Middle East and North Africa the Salafiyya convinced Muslims that Islam could create a suitable basis for a modern nation-state. The leaders of modern radical Islam in North Africa and the Middle East propagated an ideology based on a few simplified principles of the Salafiyya's reformist teachings. The advocates of the Salafiyya, such as Muhammad 'Abduh in Egypt and Ibn Badis in Algeria, could not conceive that the manifest technological and social backwardness of their societies was related to Islam. They explained this backwardness as a result of deviations from "true" Islam by Islamic societies and their political elites—deviations that had developed over centuries and persisted through the force of tradition. But the representatives of the Salafiyya movement and its successors—especially the Egyptian Muslim Brotherhood—claimed that if Islam were "properly" understood, it could be a suitable basis for developing modern, socially progressive states. The reformist scholars shaped the idea in Muslim religious consciousness that "true" Islam was different from the image rooted in traditional Islamic law, and also different from the existing Islamic way of life.

Unlike in North Africa and the Middle East, Islam in sub-Saharan Africa was not reshaped into an abstract revolutionary ideology by reformist conceptions of the "true Islam," although reformist teaching was represented by a series of prominent figures who helped to found the modern African reformist traditions.[6] A notable example in East Africa was Shaykh al-Amin ibn 'Ali al-Mazru'i (1891–1949), who was *qadi* of Mombasa from 1932 and later chief *qadi* of Kenya. Shaykh al-Amin was inspired by the writings of the Salafiyya leaders Muhammad 'Abduh and Rashid Rida; in 1931 he founded the weekly magazine *Al-Islah* (Reform) to propagate reformist teaching. Although Shaykh al-Amin insisted on command of the Arab language as the precondition for building modern Islamic societies on the basis of reformist Islam, his magazine appeared in Arabic and Kiswahili. He also published a series of texts in Kiswahili in which he tried to convey Islamic teachings to Muslims from a reformist standpoint; and he began the project of translating the Qur'an into Kiswahili. The translation was completed in 1969 by Shaykh 'Abdallah Salih al-Farsi (1912–1982), his pupil and successor as leader of the reformist movement.[7]

Shaykh al-Amin was highly respected as a scholar, judge, and member of the Mazru'i family, which had politically dominated Mombasa in the past.

For a long time, however, the reformist teaching he represented had very little influence. It was not until the 1970s that a younger, more politically radical generation of Muslim reformers emerged in Kenya, Uganda, and Tanzania. Led by Shaykh ʿAbdallah Salih al-Farsi, the chief *qadi* of Kenya from 1968 to 1982, they made their name as *ansar al-sunna* (followers of the sunna). These reformers called for more consideration of Islamic norms in social and political life, and attacked the corruption of the political elites in their countries. The *ansar al-sunna* groupings also protested against specific Muslim practices in East Africa, such as the widely celebrated festival of *mawlid al-nabi* (the Prophet's birthday), the Sufi Brotherhoods' *dhikr* ceremonies, and the extravagant nature of burials, naming ceremonies, and weddings, which they criticized as *bidaʿ* (un-Islamic innovations). The *ansar al-sunna* were consequently described as *watu wa bidaʿa* (*bidaʿ* people), that is, people who constantly talked about the *bidaʿ*.

Criticism of the *mawlid al-nabi* festival and the Sufi Brotherhoods' *dhikr* is part of the reformist trend in East Africa increasingly supported by Muslims, especially in the cities, where modern Islamic schools are being set up. Often called *maʿahid* (institutes), these schools are supported by growing numbers of Muslims. The conflict between the generation of younger Muslim reformers and the established Muslim worthies, who frequently represent the religious policy of the state leadership, is also sparked by arguments about specific prominent symbols such as fixing the beginning of Ramadan, the month of fasting. The *ansar al-sunna* demand adherence to the date prescribed by Mecca (that is, by Saudi Arabia), whereas established religious leaders, such as the mufti of Zanzibar, insist that local sighting of the new moon should take precedence. The claim to leadership advanced by the different groupings ultimately seems to be a struggle for mastery of interpretation, which further exacerbates the conflict among Muslims in East Africa.

In West Africa, in the period immediately after the Second World War, the Muslim population included reformists of various stripes. Two groups were particularly active; they were described as "associations" because of their type of organizational structure. One of them, the Subbanu Association, known locally as the Wahhabiyya, had its head office in Bamako (Mali). Its leading figures were Muslims who had studied at al-Azhar University in Cairo in the 1930s and were influenced by contact with reform groups in Egypt. Lansiné Kaba, a Guinean scholar who wrote a detailed study of this association, said that the great majority of its members consisted of traders who acted as middlemen between the big European trading firms and the Africans. The association's religious activities consisted primarily of fostering the spread of reformist Islamic teaching and command of Arabic by founding modern Islamic schools. In the 1950s, in addition to Mali itself, the Subbanu Association had active members in Guinea, Sierra Leone, Ivory Coast, and Burkina Faso.[8] The followers of the Subbanu Association were a community distinguished by strict piety, with economic links beyond Mali's territorial borders. Since the 1980s a younger generation of Muslim reformers has emerged from the original Subbanu groups and has won supporters by setting up Islamic schools in the cities. Furthermore, in Mali, as in other parts of West and East Africa, there has been a latent conflict with the established representatives of local Sufi Brotherhoods, who call the Muslim reformers Wahhabis to discredit them as minions of Saudi Arabia.[9]

One of two most important reformist groups in West Africa emerged in Senegal and was led by Shaykh Abdoulaye Touré (1925–2005). Shaykh Touré, a member of a respected family of scholars from the Tijaniyya Brotherhood, was initially trained as a religious scholar. In 1952–53 he had the opportunity to go on a study tour to Algeria with a Senegalese student group. In Constantine, then one of the most important centers of the Islamic reform movement in North Africa, he met pupils of 'Abd al-Hamid ibn Badis (d. 1940), the founder of the Algerian Jam'iyyat al-'Ulama' al-Jaza'iriyyin al-Muslimin, who introduced him to the philosophical tradition of the Salafiyya at the Bin Badis Institute. On his return to Senegal in 1953, Shaykh Touré founded the Union Culturelle Musulmane (UCM; al-Ittihad al-Thaqafi al-Islami) with the goal of spreading reformist teachings in Senegal.[10]

From the eighteenth century on, Islamic reform in West Africa primarily meant the efforts of Muslim scholars to combat un-Islamic practices in their society and to impose observance of Islamic religious and legal norms as they understood them. These reformist efforts were promoted by religious scholars from the Qadiriyya and, from the nineteenth century on, by scholars from the Tijaniyya Brotherhood. Muslim civil rights movements on an equal footing with the French municipalities had already developed in Senegal from the mid-nineteenth century in the "Quatre Communes," the coastal areas of St. Louis, Dakar, Gorée, and Rufisque. They worked to secure a fitting place for Muslims in colonial society. With this goal they advocated modern education as well as recognition of Islamic personal law and closer relations with other parts of the Islamic world, especially through the pilgrimage to Mecca. They also emphasized the necessity of improving Arabic language teaching to help people learn to read the Qur'an on their own. This created the basis for the Islamic reform movement in Senegal to develop into a movement for education. Shaykh Touré took this somewhat further by stressing that the reform of Islam also required a reform of the institutional framework of Islamic societies.[11] Yet he failed to have much influence on other West African reformist leaders with his ideas on reform, which went beyond equating reform with purging local Islamic religious practice of apparently un-Islamic practices of faith.

In 1957 a congress held in Dakar recognized the Subbanu groups in Mali as a branch of the UCM. The congress resolved to establish new branches of the UCM in Ghana, Ivory Coast, Benin, Burkina Faso, and Guinea.[12] But the UCM, now supraregionally established, failed to develop into a pan–West African Islamic reform movement. In the context of the independence of the West African countries in 1960, the UCM had either already been destroyed in these countries (in Guinea by Sékou Touré and in Mali by Modibo Keita) or were forced to conform, as in Senegal under Léopold Sédar Senghor. It was not until the late 1970s that a second generation of Muslim reformers developed in Senegal. Though still based on the legacy of Shaykh Touré, these reformers abandoned their fierce rejection of the Sufi Brotherhoods, which were particularly strong in Senegal, and especially of the Muridiyya and Tijaniyya. In place of the struggle against the Sufi Brotherhoods, the new Senegalese reform groups, especially the Jama'at 'Ibad al-Rahman and Harakat al-Falah, stressed the unity of Muslims in the struggle against the secular state.[13] These reform groups simultaneously tried to build up their base in the population by setting up and running modern Islamic schools.

At around the same time this change in the reform movement occurred in Senegal, Abubakar Gumi (1922–1992) established the Jama'at Izalat al-Bid'a wa-Iqamat al-Sunna in Northern Nigeria. Immediately after its establishment in 1978 it began a fierce struggle against the two major Sufi Brotherhoods, the Tijaniyya and Qadiriyya. The rapid success of the 'Yan Izala, as the group was known in Northern Nigeria, was due not only to its dogmatic religious argumentation against so-called *bida'* but also to its opposition to a series of cost-intensive religious customs sanctioned by Sufi scholars and increasingly difficult to finance because of economic problems, particularly in the cities. In addition, in 1978 the 'Yan Izala started establishing a large number of new Islamic schools that enrolled girls and women and taught "marketable skills," meaning the "modern" subjects from the state school curriculum, alongside some subjects from the established canon of Islamic knowledge. The combination of religious, economic, and social reform initiatives in the 'Yan Izala's program explains its development in the 1980s in Northern Nigeria into the first reformist mass movement in sub-Saharan Africa.[14] But the 'Yan Izala's triumphal progress came to a halt in the 1990s, for several reasons. First, its spiritual leader, Abubakar Gumi, died in 1992, and without an adequate successor the organization disintegrated into several rival factions. Second, from the 1980s on, the Sufi Brotherhoods of the Tijaniyya and Qadiriyya were able to undermine the 'Yan Izala's religious standing by pointing out that their attacks on other Muslims led to conflict (*fitna*) among believers, which contributed to strengthening the Christians in Northern Nigeria. The Muslim split was apparent in the 1988 local government elections, when Christian politicians defeated the 'Yan Izala candidates in constituencies that actually had a majority of Muslim inhabitants. This political signal, and the great increase in Christian missionary activities from the 1980s on,[15] forced the 'Yan Izala to halt its struggle against the Sufi Brotherhoods at the beginning of the 1990s in the interests of Muslim unity.

The pacification of relations among Muslims in the 1990s occurred at a time of increasing tensions with Christian groups. These were expressed not only in the recurring riots in the north mentioned earlier but also in the debate that had reopened in 1999 on the introduction of shari'a penal law. In October 1999 the governor of the federal state of Zamfara, Ahmad Sani, decreed the introduction of shariʿa law (supplementary to Islamic personal law, which was already in force). This aroused attention on a national level because it represented a contravention of the Nigerian constitution, and therefore a direct challenge to President Olusegun Obasanjo, who had been democratically elected in 1998. Even so, shariʿa law was introduced in eleven other federal states of Northern Nigeria in 2000 and 2001. This was welcomed by broad sections of the Muslim population there as an attempt to bring order to the chaotic situation in the region.[16] The introduction of shariʿa law has been restricted mainly to symbolic measures such as separation of men and women in the public transport system. The death sentences against Muslim women for alleged adultery, which received worldwide publicity, were either not carried out or were revoked. Muslim scholars have characterized the introduction of shariʿa law as a politically motivated and therefore inadmissible maneuver.[17] Abolishing shariʿa law would be far more difficult than introducing it, however, not least because debates about shariʿa in Northern Nigeria are related to political power strategies and the political (and ultimately economic) marginalization of the Christians in the region.

To date, Muslim reformers in West and East Africa have succeeded in making only minor changes to the traditional principles of religious life in their societies. Although Salafiyya teachings are the starting point of their reformist efforts, they have not been able to fundamentally shake the strong social standing of the Sufi Brotherhoods. The religious practices they oppose have also retained their popularity. The only social field where they have had some degree of success is the modern educational system, which can be explained mostly in terms of the state's failure in this area. Given increasing urbanization and the decline of community structures, however, third- or fourth-generation Islamic reformism could develop into a more important social and political force in sub-Saharan Africa.

b. Islam and National Consciousness

In North Africa, national consciousness became linked with reformist Islam because European civilization was seen as a direct challenge to the Islamic culture and way of life in the region. The reformist teachings of the Salafiyya developed into a politico-religious response to the equation of Islamic culture with backwardness, and to the justification of colonial rule that claimed European superiority over Islamic culture. In sub-Saharan Africa, by contrast, Islam played merely a secondary, supportive role in the development of national consciousness. This meant that the expansion of European hegemony in the nineteenth century was opposed in the name of Islam.[18] The resistance struggle against the establishment of British rule in northern Somalia and Italian rule in the south of that country was fought mainly by the so-called dervishes led by Sayyid Muhammad ʿAbdille Hasan (d. 1920).[19]

Muslims sometimes also played an important role in the nationalist movements that led the struggle against colonial hegemony after the Second
World War. In Tanganyika urban Muslim groups led by Shaykh Hasan ibn
'Ameir (1880–1979) supported the movement led by Julius Nyerere, the
Tanganyika African National Union (TANU, originally the Tanganyika African Association), from the time of its establishment in 1954.[20] In West Africa, Subbanu reformers supported nationalist leaders such as Sekou Touré
in Guinea and Félix Houphouet-Boigny in Ivory Coast.[21] The emergence
of organized Muslim groups like the Subbanu Association and the Union
Culturelle Musulmane can also be seen as an aspect of the struggle against
colonial hegemony, because their activities were aimed not at reviving Islam
but at fighting the Sufi Brotherhoods, which were labeled "Marabuts," and
which the colonial rulers often acknowledged as religious representatives
of the Muslims in the territory under their rule. This meant that the Muslims supported nationalist leaders who were usually non-Muslims, and who
linked their countries' national identity with their African rather than their
Islamic cultural heritage.

Two contributory factors seem to explain why Islam did not play a decisive role in the formation of national consciousness in sub-Saharan Africa.
First, the colonial rulers basically emphasized the superiority of Europeans
over Africans, whether Muslim or not. Unlike in North Africa, where religion was the key, in sub-Saharan countries race was decisive for the demarcation between the European colonial administration elites and the indigenous
peoples. The legal regulations of Islam were integrated into the colonial
justice system in sub-Saharan Africa, but only insofar as they were part of
"native law and custom"—to quote the English terminology—and were not
"repugnant to good custom."[22] In the judicial and educational systems, as
in other areas, colonial policies reduced Islam to features that were adapted
to the various African communities. Islamic scholars were employed in administrative bodies and as judges. They were appointed on the basis of their
education and their reputation in their groups of origin, but not usually as
representatives of Islam. These policies did not lead to the disappearance
of Islamic exclusiveness in territories such as Zanzibar, Somalia, Northern
Nigeria, northern Cameroon, and Senegal, where the Muslims formed closed
societies and had a tradition of hegemony over non-Muslims. They did result, however, in the majority of the younger generation of sub-Saharan Muslims who grew up under colonialism developing an increased awareness of
the African component of their identity.

The second reason why Islam did not play an important role in the development of national consciousness in sub-Saharan Africa is related to the
collaboration between established Muslim families and the colonial authorities. To maintain their status as rulers within a limited framework, the emirs
in Northern Nigeria and northern Cameroon, and the sultan of Zanzibar,
were willing to accede to the political and economic interests of the British,
Germans, and French. And in Senegal, Guinea, and Mali, Muslim religious

leaders, especially the Marabuts—that is, the representatives of the Sufi Brotherhoods—were largely prepared to collaborate with the colonial authorities. This enabled them to consolidate, or even expand, their social influence and economic power.[23] This was particularly clear in Guinea, where some of the Marabuts originated from Mauritania and stressed their Arab or Berber origins. The collaboration between the Marabuts and the colonial authorities was fiercely attacked by nationalists and religious reformers. A circular letter from the Parti Démocratique de Guinée dated October 16, 1959, described the Marabuts as accomplices of colonialism and the Arabs as racists.[24] A novel by the Ghanaian writer Ayi Kwei Armah, *Two Thousand Seasons,* presents a similar picture of the Muslims from the north as exploiters of the Africans.[25] This is also reflected in the discourse of Zanzibar's African independence movement, the Afro-Shirazi Party (ASU), and in the anti-Moorish polemics in Senegal in the 1980s and 1990s.[26]

The recognition of Islam only in the context of its established and developed forms in Africa represented a kind of colonial construction of tradition that led to the emergence of the concept of "Islam noir" in the French colonial territories. Islam noir was seen as "tolerant" and "syncretic" in comparison to the ostensibly radical and racist "Islam arabe."[27] Despite ideas of this kind, the colonial authorities often regarded themselves consciously or subconsciously as successors to the Muslim dynasties that had ruled the Africans before them and had discovered the economic resources of sub-Saharan Africa and developed the region's political life. In European historical literature about Africa from the first half of the twentieth century, which was partly written by colonial officials, this viewpoint is reflected in the role the Muslims are supposed to have played in the creation of the African nation-states. The state system in Africa is traced back solely to the incursion of Arab or Berber groups from the north.[28] Given this conception of the political history of Africa and the cooperation between the old leading Muslim families and the colonial authorities, in determining their cultural identity the Africans initially reacted by dissociating themselves from Islam to some extent.

c. Islam and the New State System in Sub-Saharan Africa

The independent nation states in sub-Saharan Africa were—or still are—governed by heads of state who legitimate their authority by reviving the African cultural heritage and modernizing their societies. Socialism was propagated in several sub-Saharan countries as the safe fast track to modernization and economic development. Socialism was mainly presented as a social system with roots in precolonial (African) communal solidarity among members of the same group, and in collective utilization of the land. As a result, from an ideological standpoint, if not always in reality, the African leaders had an equal obligation to modernization and to African culture. In the 1960s, sub-Saharan Muslims found themselves at a disadvantage with regard to this double-edged political ideology and the structural framework that emerged from it. Their religious loyalty to the common Islamic world was in contradiction to their society's general ideological course. Their firm adherence to the Islamic education system in the colonial era had left them less prepared than other social groups for participation in building the new nation-states. This situation, as well as the fact that initially the consciousness of sub-Saharan Muslims was barely influenced by the Islamic reform movement, led to the development of two tendencies that can be seen as different aspects of the same defensive attitude toward the new political and social structures.

The basis of the first tendency is that the old Islamic ruling elites try to remain autonomous within the new states, for which exceptions are made in developing political structures and legislation. The defensive aspect of this tendency can be seen in the way these elites make no claims to co-determine the general political and economic development of their states in line with their Islamic convictions. Instead they try to use its remaining social influence in political life to ensure that national leaders take account of the religious and cultural specificities of their groups. To illustrate these relations we shall consider three examples, from Senegal, Northern Nigeria, and Zanzibar.

In Senegal, the Sufi Brotherhoods exercise great influence on political life, although their spiritual leaders, the Marabuts, remain formally outside of organized political groups. Around 95 percent of the Senegalese population is Muslim, and 90 percent of the Muslims are followers of the Sufi Brotherhoods. Three brotherhoods dominate the lives of Senegal's Muslims; their adherents are divided among the Muslim population as follows: the Tijaniyya 50 percent, the Muridiyya around 25 percent, and the Qadiriyya around 15 percent. There are also a few thousand members of the small Layènne Brotherhood, whose influence is confined to the Cap Vert region.[29] Reformist urban Muslims, who make up no more than 5 to 10 percent of the total Senegalese population, have attacked the superstition and blind obedience attributed to Sufi Brotherhood followers. At the beginning of the 1960s the Muslim prime minister, Mamadou Dia, helped by Muslim reformers, unsuccessfully attempted to limit the Marabuts' influence. By contrast, the (Catholic) president Léopold Senghor who dismissed Dia in 1962, and Senghor's successor, Abdou Diouf (1980–2000), who was a Muslim, were able to preserve their power in the framework of close cooperation with the Marabuts. It was only in the final years of Abdou Diouf's government that the ruling Socialist Party began to show signs of dissociating itself from the Marabuts.

The disproportional influence of the Murids as compared to the Tijaniyya, which had disintegrated into a large number of clans, resulted from the comparatively strong internal cohesion of the Murid clans and their economic power. Unlike the Tijaniyya, up to the present day the Murids acknowledge only one supreme religious leader, the Khalifa Général in Touba.

The Murid Marabuts developed an old custom whereby Qur'an students pledged to do unpaid service for their religious teachers into a comprehensive form of religious service by young adherents, the Talibé. The Talibé of the Murid Marabuts farmed their Marabuts' extensive peanut fields; after several years of unpaid work they were allotted their own plots of land. This meant that exceptionally close relationships developed over several generations between the Murids' religious leaders and their followers. Donal Cruise O'Brien, who published a study on this brotherhood in 1971, later observed that the Marabuts of the Murids used their collective strength to wring concessions from political leaders.[30] They used this strength particularly against measures that could have undermined their position, especially interventionary attempts by the state to regulate agriculture. At the end of the 1970s the Murid Marabuts even succeeded in achieving the dissolution of Senegal's largest peanut marketing organization, ONCAD.[31] In the 1980s and 1990s their extensive power, based on control of a large potential electoral bloc, prompted President Diouf, who had personal connections to the Tijaniyya Brotherhood, to introduce a program of state withdrawal from agricultural policy, on the one hand, and to disassociate himself increasingly from the great Marabut families on the other. As a result, in the 1993 elections the Khalifa Général of the Murids declined for the first time to make an electoral endorsement of the sitting president, and a phase of political reorientation began.[32] Abdou Diouf's attitude toward the Marabuts partly explains his electoral defeat and the democratic changeover of power in 2000. His successor, Abdoulaye Wade, the leader of the opposition Parti Démocratique Sénégalais (PDS), had close links to the Murid Brotherhood.[33]

Northern Nigeria provides the best example of a traditional Islamic enclave within a new African state. At the time of the British conquest at the beginning of the twentieth century, the most important part of Nigeria consisted of two large Islamic kingdoms, the caliphate of Sokoto and the emirate of Bornu. They had emerged at the end of the nineteenth century from the religious reform movement of Usman dan Fodio and his jihad against the Hausa principalities and the kingdom of Bornu. The Fulani, who constituted the majority of Usman dan Fodio's followers, formed the new ruling political class in the caliphate of Sokoto. But since the caliphate had a decentralized political structure from the beginning, a large number of dynasties of "emirs" developed over the years; their recognition of the key politico-religious authority of the sultan in Sokoto was often merely formal.[34]

During the British colonial era the emirs retained a considerable amount of their former political authority, as well as their status as guardians of Islamic tradition, whereas the sultan of Sokoto had to surrender his political power completely and was recognized only as the religious leader of the Northern Nigerian Muslims. In independent Nigeria, too, the emirs initially retained their traditional authority as part of the new state's accommodation toward the religious and political specificity of the north of the country. The emirs received the privilege of appointing representatives answerable to the village elders in the various districts of their respective territories. More-over, the emirs were granted large allowances by the state to enable them to retain the external symbols of their traditional authority, such as courtiers and ceremonial guards. But under the political leadership of Ahmadu Bello, a member of the family of the sultan of Sokoto who became prime minister of the region of Northern Nigeria in 1954, a series of sultans who opposed specific modernization measures were removed from office. From then on the emirs gradually lost their authority to the new political elite in the north, whose power base was in Kaduna, the capital city of Northern Nigeria. But it was not until the period of the military regimes which began in 1966 that the emirs finally became puppets of Nigeria's new political rulers. Some individual emirs, such as the emir of Kano, were able to retain a degree of influence over political events.[35]

The political survival of the emirs in Northern Nigeria in the period be-fore independence can be seen in terms of their religious and cultural im-portance for Muslims in Nigeria, alongside the fact that the emirs' interests were interwoven with those of big agricultural firms, traders, and politi-cians. Nonetheless, from the 1950s the emirs were under increasing pressure on two flanks: first, from the constantly growing numbers of immigrants to the Northern Nigerian cities from rural areas of the region and from the Christian south of the country; and second, from modernizing Muslim elites who administered the north as representatives of the Nigerian federal government and managed its economic development. The arrival in urban areas of large numbers of migrants from all parts of Nigeria has contrib-uted to a great change in the social composition of these areas. The popula-tion groups that traditionally inhabited the Northern Nigerian cities—the Hausa, Kanuri, and Fulani—have been joined in the cities by migrants from the "middle belt," that is, the largely non-Muslim regions on the Niger and Benue, as well as Yoruba and Igbo from the south. The cities have become increasingly cosmopolitan and now have sizeable Christian communities. The chaotic coexistence of these different groups, and conflicts over re-sources which are often inflamed by religion, are partly responsible for the riots and unrest in Northern Nigeria since the 1980s.

The development of Zanzibar offers another example of the attempt to preserve Muslim enclaves. As in Northern Nigeria, the British colonial powers in Zanzibar gave the sultan and the ruling Muslim elite, which was originally from Oman, a considerable degree of self-determination. After integration into the British Empire in 1891, Zanzibar had the status of a protectorate rather than a British colony; even if the British "resident" actu-ally determined the administration of the Protectorate of Zanzibar, in formal legal terms the ultimate authority lay with the sultan and his privy council. Islamic jurisdiction remained largely untouched. Even in the education sys-tem the local religious scholars were largely able to determine the curricular structure of the "government schools" established on the British model. The political stability of the elite that originated in Oman was so important to the British that in the 1920s and 1930s they protected the Omani plantation owners, who were threatened with financial ruin by their mainly Indian creditors. As a result, the feudal power structures were consolidated until the sultanate gained independence in 1963, although in the democratic elections of 1957, 1961, and 1963 the Afro-Shirazi Party under Abeid Amani Karume (d. 1972) consistently won a majority of votes. The continuing economic and political marginalization of the African population, however, led to increasing dissatisfaction with the existing regime.[36] The British withdrew, and Zanzibar gained independence on December 12, 1963. Only a month later, on January 12, 1964, there was a violent revolt against the sultan, during which not only was the sultan himself overthrown and expelled, but tens of thousands of Zanzibar citizens of Arab and Indian origin were killed or expelled as well. In the aftermath, Zanzibar joined the federation with Tanzania in April 1964 but largely retained its right to autonomy, and was ruled by a socialist regime led by Abeid Amani Karume.[37] Like other African heads of state in that period, Karume introduced a radical modernization program. He began by disassociating himself clearly from Zanzibar's Arab-Islamic roots and stressed the island republic's African identity.[38] After the elimination or marginalization of the old scholarly families and their socio-religious influence, toward the end of the 1960s Karume permitted a new start in Islamic education policy. Under his successors Islam became an important frame of reference for the discussion on Zanzibar's identity, partly because the country's increasingly complex economic and political links with Tanzania from the 1980s on led to the erosion of Zanzibar's autonomous status. Zanzibar's increasing integration into the social and political structures of Tanzania, in which Muslims played no role in authority, and the economic mismanagement by Zanzibar's government after the 1964 revolution motivated the emergence of a religious opposition which promulgated the island's "Islamic" identity and independence and condemned the Tanzanian federation as a Christian-dominated state system. The reversion to Islamic identity advanced by Muslim reform groups in Zanzibar is also supported by the Muslims on the Tanzanian mainland, who feel marginalized by the well-educated Christian elite trained in the missionary schools.[39]

The conflicts between reformist Muslim groups and the state in Zanzibar and Tanzania have assumed an additional aspect since the 1980s with the emergence of a debate about Muslim personal law. Many Muslims, particularly in Zanzibar, feared that their country would lose its last remaining rights of autonomy in the area of jurisprudence. As a result, they rejected the demands of Muslim women's associations that specific regulations of Islamic personal law which these associations define as impermissible discrimination against women should be adapted to current (Tanzanian) union law. The demand for adjustment of the national legal system is seen in Zanzibar not primarily as an argument about a particular interpretation of Islamic law but above all as an attempt to abolish the autonomy of "Islamic" Zanzibar.[40]

There are two dominant trends among sub-Saharan Muslims that determine their attitude toward the new political structures. The first, already described, is a tendency for Muslims in some regions to want to assert themselves within the postcolonial structures by means of enclaves and rights of autonomy. The second, and probably more important, tendency in the long term consists in the appearance of Islam as a personal religion without direct influence on political life. This is the dominant tendency among educated urban Muslims who have grown up since independence. It implies emphasizing the moral principles of Islam and the duty of strict adherence to the ritual commandments at the expense of the role of Islam as a basis for structuring social life.

This means that the revival of Islam and its increasing spread in sub-Saharan Africa, mentioned briefly at the beginning of this section, are occurring side by side with its restructuring in the form of a personal religion. Factors such as the modern school system and the socioeconomic development of African societies have played an important role in shaping this new course. These factors alone, however, do not seem to account fully for the emergence of this tendency. Modern schooling and socioeconomic change have had an influence on the Muslims in North Africa and the Middle East. In these regions, modernizing attempts by national leaders to separate religion and the state have provoked radical Islamist uprisings and protest movements whose leaders, like 'Abbas Madani in Algeria, have rejected a separation of this kind as a conspiracy against Islam.[41] In sub-Saharan Africa, however, this separation occurred without major resistance, except in regions where Islam was the basis for traditional enclaves.

The absence of serious opposition to this development is related to several historical features of the establishment of Islam in sub-Saharan Africa.[42]

Unlike in North Africa, Islam in sub-Saharan Africa was not spread by military conquest and did not result in Arabization. It appeared initially as the religion of foreign traders, and later as the religion of the rulers in countries where the majority of the population were non-Muslims up until the nineteenth and twentieth centuries. For this reason, Islam was established almost exclusively in the form of rites and legal regulations that were detached from the Arabian cultural context in which they originated, and even from their basis in religious philosophy. Islam in sub-Saharan Africa was thus "translated" into the various social contexts in different ways, and was very important as a symbol of its followers' social and political differentiation in relation to other Africans. But it was adopted selectively, adapted to the respective framework conditions, and developed further. The internal powers of integration of the sub-Saharan African societies—including those that displayed great enthusiasm for Islam—ensured that the cult practices and legal regulations of Islam that could ultimately be established in social life were adaptable to the African way of life and would not infringe on group solidarity. The basis for the selective adoption of Islam is shown clearly by the fact that among sub-Saharan Muslims, with the exception of so-called Arabs and Indian Muslims in East Africa, the regulations of Islamic law on the question of child custody and female inheritance rights, particularly in relation to real estate, have been set aside. Consequently, in large parts of sub-Saharan Africa, Islam remains a system of rites and legal regulations that were selectively adopted and integrated into the framework of traditional social structures. This created a dualism in the life of sub-Saharan Muslims that has been documented in written sources since the fourteenth century.[43]

This dualism gave African Muslims a double identity: a particular identity based on African social norms and institutions, and a universal one linked to the world of Islam, which was communicated by religious scholars and translated into the respective general social contexts. The dualism means that the Muslims of sub-Saharan Africa, unlike Muslims in societies whose traditional way of life is steeped in Islam, are prepared for adaptation to the modern world in relation to religious questions. As a result, in the context of the extensive modernization of the sub-Saharan African countries beginning in the twentieth century, with urbanization and social transformation on many different levels, Muslim reform movements have developed that advocate, for example, modern forms of education that are in no way contradictory to the content of state education. An important feature of the modern Islamic reformist and education movements is the translation of the "holy" texts from Arabic into the African languages. Translations of the Qur'an are available today in Wolof, Fulfulde, Bambara, Hausa and Yoruba, Kiswahili, Zulu, Amharic, Afrikaans, and Kikuyu.[44]

In addition to the Qur'an, many other religious texts are also being translated. This should give educated, often urban Muslims access to the sources of the religion independent of any established teachers of the faith (religious scholars and Marabuts). At the same time, established religious teachers are being criticized for representing religious obscurantism. In the reform-oriented milieus of African Muslim society there even seems to be a discernible turn toward a new understanding of faith. This is related to the sustained shakeup of the social influence of established religious representatives.

d. The Revival of Islam in Sub-Saharan Africa

The efforts of the African Muslim reform movement to revive Islam are not in contradiction to its selective adoption; nor do they appear to be aimed at constructing a state system on Islamic foundations. Their goal is rather to secure the influence of Muslims in the context of existing political and legal structures. This can be seen in the shari'a debate in Nigeria, and is also a key motif of the actions and discourse of the Islamic opposition in Zanzibar and Senegal. Moreover, the attempt to strengthen Islam seems linked to the fact that in many sub-Saharan African countries, the relation to African identity as a political ideology has lost much of its importance. This poses the question whether, in the African countries where Muslims are in the majority, Islam can be made into a national ideology that would replace African features of identity in an analogous way to the case of Algeria or Iran, for example. But an ideological transformation of this kind is not very likely, if only because Islam's links to African culture are not as close as to Arab culture.

The revival of Islam in sub-Saharan Africa is above all an urban phenomenon. It is being advanced mainly by the establishment of associations that foster cooperation among Muslims, set up modern Islamic schools, and take positions on social questions from an Islamic religious viewpoint. Associations like this exist today in almost all the major African countries. In the former French-occupied countries of West Africa, organizations such as the Jama'at 'Ibad al-Rahman in Senegal, the Communauté Musulmane de Ouagadougou in Burkina Faso,[45] and the Union Musulmane du Togo[46] developed out of the former Union Culturelle Musulmane. In Nigeria the 'Yan Izala, the Muslim Students' Society, and the Young Muslim Association, as well as Muslim women's movements such as the Federation of Muslim Women's Associations in Nigeria (FOMWAN), have emerged since the 1960s and 1970s.[47] In Kenya and Tanzania in the 1960s and 1970s a series of Islamic organizations arose that were loyal to the state; in the 1980s these gave rise to new, sometimes oppositional groupings such as the Mosque Council (Baraza la Miskiti), the Muslim Writers' Workshop (Warsha), the Association of the Imams (Jumuiya ya Maimamu) and the Association of Awakening (Jumuiya ya Uamsho), an umbrella organization of particularly radical Muslim groups, as well as a large number of Muslim school associations and professional associations.[48] The situation is similar in the Republic of South Africa, where the Muslims, while numerically weak, have disproportionate influence owing to their participation in the struggle against apartheid after the elections of 1994, although they make up a kaleidoscopic picture of widely different groups and orientations.[49] In South Africa, as in sub-Saharan Africa, the activities of Islamic reform movements often signify a deliberate reaction to the missionary efforts of the Christian churches. One example is the Islamic Propagation Center International, founded in Durban (Natal, South Africa) by Ahmed Deedat (1918–2005), who was of Indian origin. The organization runs forms of Islamic mission (da'wa) that are a mirror image of a pentecostal South African movement, Christ for All Nations, founded by Reinhard Bonnke. Ahmed Deedat accompanied this charismatic Christian organization on its "crusade" through Africa with his own Muslim missionary and counter-propaganda.[50]

The activities of these and other Islamic associations are now able to look back at a historical tradition of their own, with several generations of reformers in some cases; but it is still difficult to discern their real sociopolitical importance for the future development of African society. In general, one can characterize these new Islamic associations by saying that their activities implicitly represent a critique aimed at both the Europeanized African elite and the established Muslim religious leaders and scholars.

They are giving Islam a new and "popular" meaning by dissociating themselves from old local Islamic customs and systematically presenting Islamic teachings and the major commandments in African-language publications designed for ordinary people. But this remains confined to Islamic rites and moral principles.

Yet the activities of these new associations give Islam a stamp of modernity that enables the younger generation of Muslims to advocate seriously the old belief in the superiority of Islam vis-à-vis other religions, while simultaneously dissociating themselves from the historical configuration of Islam in Africa. In its modernist form, reduced to moral principles and ritual practices, Islam has a clear advantage over Christianity. Like Christianity, a renewed form of Islam is perceived and experienced as a living religion adapting to the modern world; but unlike Christianity, it does not carry the burden of identification with colonial hegemony. This allows the Muslims of sub-Saharan Africa to retain their bonds with the Arab Islamic world while simultaneously seeing themselves as Africans. The numerical growth of Islam in sub-Saharan Africa and the new kind of vigor with which it is represented will probably result in Muslims' being more able to assert themselves in public life in the future. But there is little likelihood that the revival of Islam in sub-Saharan Africa will effect its transformation into a militant political ideology.

Translated by Karen Margolis

12. The Islamization of Sub-Saharan Africa

(Hans Müller)

Islam was introduced to sub-Saharan Africa through two different routes: by land from the north through the desert and the Nile Valley, and by sea from the east via the Red Sea and the Indian Ocean. The population of this large and geographically diverse area across which Islam spread was—and still is—made up of many different peoples, large and small ethnic groups which are very diverse in terms of mentality, religion, language, culture, social life, economics, and political structure. But those who were responsible for the spread of Islam were also quite diverse in terms of their heritage, education, religious orientation, and economic interests. As a result, as Islam mixed with the various local religious, legal, and social worldviews and practices, surprisingly diverse forms and structures of Islamic society emerged in this part of the continent commonly referred to as "Black Africa" or "Tropical Africa."

Despite the widely varying forms of Islam found there, at a very general level a few characteristics of "Black Islam" can be discerned, and sub-Saharan Africa can be divided into several regions in which Islam developed along a

particular path that yielded relatively uniform Islamic relations. The regions
of western and central Sahel Sudan—stretching between today's Senegal and
Chad and extending into the forests to the south—can be summarized under
the abbreviated geographical name West Africa, despite the numerous differences within this broad area. A second region, Sudan, can be distinguished
to the east along the upper Nile Valley, encompassing approximately what is
today the country of Sudan. Northeast Africa, which includes Ethiopia and
northern Somalia along the eastern horn of the continent, will be addressed
as a third region, and a fourth is East Africa, reaching from southern Somalia to Mozambique and including the islands off the Indian Ocean coast. All
four regions have seen a multiphased course of Islamization over the past
centuries which has not yet come to an end.

a. West Africa

The first Muslims came to West Africa shortly after the Maghreb was conquered by the Arabs. They were Berber and later also Arab traders who
traveled along the old caravan trails from Morocco through the desert into
certain areas of Senegal and along the Niger bend, and then from Tunisia
and Libya into central Sahel Sudan to the west and east of Lake Chad.
They were principally interested in gold and slaves, for which they traded
luxury goods from the north and, even more important, salt—a resource
badly needed in Sudan—which they brought from deposits in the Sahara.
Their trading partners were those living in the towns and in small Black
African kingdoms in the savannahs south of the desert that would soon
become larger empires.

The history of the medieval Islamic Sudanese empires of Ghana (which
saw its golden age from the ninth to the eleventh centuries), Mali (thirteenth to fourteenth centuries), Songhai (eleventh to sixteenth centuries),
and Kanem Bornu (eleventh to nineteenth centuries), to name just the most
prominent ones, is relatively well known today from the accounts of Arab
geographers and travelers. This history allows us to discern several parallels
and similar developments in the spread of Islam across these empires, despite their recognizable differences. Traders from the north initially brought
Islam to the area and practiced it, but they were not particularly interested
in proselytizing. In the beginning they were primarily members of Kharijite
sects, and thereafter—at the latest following the violent spread of the Almoravid reform movement (1061–1147)—Sunnis of the Maliki *madhhab*.
The traders did not intend to settle permanently; they were looking for safe
havens. The princes sometimes allowed them to erect housing, warehouses,
and mosques in their own quarters, and they were treated well by the princes
because both sides profited from the relationship. The princes exploited the
traders' knowledge and skills—for example, in foreign trade as well as in
reading, writing, arithmetic, and languages—by employing some of them as
high-level administrators, particularly in finance.

The prestige enjoyed by the traders was extended to their religion as well, which was seen by some rulers and large segments of the urban elite not only as superior but also as a beneficial force that served to stabilize power structures. This was a major reason why they accepted Islam—or at least a few of its visible ritual customs, such as communal prayer on Fridays— while still rejecting Islamic law regarding inheritance, the family, and property. Initially they did not place an emphasis on converting the population, which meant that in both the towns and rural areas life did not change much for the common people. Islam was laid down like a veneer over the local animistic religion, which the rulers knew they had to respect if they did not want to risk uprisings among their subjects.

Of the basic Islamic obligations, one in particular seems to have appealed to some rulers, especially those of the Mali and Songhai empires: the pilgrimage to Mecca. The spectacular, elaborate pilgrimages of the Mali king Mansa Musa in 1324 and the Songhai ruler Askia Muhammad in 1496–97 became legendary across the Islamic world. Both rulers donated lavishly along the way and in Mecca, and they brought many theologians and scholars back home with them. Askia Muhammad even appointed a caliph for Sudan. They thereby turned towns such as Timbuktu, Djenne, Walata, and Gao into economic, intellectual, and cultural centers. Yet during their pilgrimages the West Africans became aware that the animistic-influenced Islam they practiced did not conform to the classical Islamic teachings. Upon their return, some of them enlisted the help of the newly immigrated scholars in their efforts to impose purer forms of the Islamic teachings.

Starting in the fourteenth and fifteenth centuries, black Muslim scholars and traders increasingly became the driving force behind Islamization in West Africa. In particular, Dyula traders and later Fulbe scholars and Hausa traders were prominent in the spread of Islam. But the special African imprint on the Islam that developed in the region can be attributed not only to them but also to the religious brotherhoods that gained a foothold in West Africa in the eighteenth century and spread widely in the nineteenth. Both the Qadiriyya and later the Tijaniyya, including their various offshoots, should be mentioned in this context. They came from the western Sahara (Mauritania) to West Africa, but they no longer followed the same mysticism characteristic of the North African brotherhoods. Instead they offered the wider population—which had become more Islamic by this time—a religious forum and leadership as well as social and political orientation. This in turn further contributed to the dissemination of Islam in the region.

Simultaneously with the spread of brotherhoods in West Africa—and in conjunction with this development—jihad movements sprang up in the eighteenth and nineteenth centuries. The cause of their rise is not always evident, but clearly many factors led to this development. The initiators and leaders of the jihad movements, mainly devout Fulbe scholars, were targeting not only animism but also Muslim rulers and groups whom they saw as not following the true Islamic teachings. The Fulbe were relatively light-skinned, nomadic cattle herders who had gradually expanded eastward starting in the eleventh century, sometimes peacefully and sometimes using force, from the territory that now comprises Senegal and Guinea; today they live in an area stretching from Senegal into the state of Sudan. Despite their pronounced pride in their race and a feeling of superiority over black farmers, some Fulbe groups settled in towns and rural areas and partially mixed with the local population. As a people they thus spread out over a large area and were usually a minority subject to the rule of a local sovereign. This certainly contributed to their openness to a strict form of Islam, which augmented their sense of superiority in relation to the animistic population around them. In various areas of West Africa, Fulbe leaders and scholars, some of whom had emerged from the brotherhoods, began calling themselves, or were called by their followers, imam (*almami,* Arab. *al-imam*), renovator (*mujaddid*), or even mahdi or caliph. Over the course of several holy wars they were able to overthrow their rulers and create new statelike formations that survived up until the colonial period, for example, Futa Toro (in today's northern Senegal), Futa Jallon (in Guinea and Senegal), Masina (in Mali and Burkina Faso), the Sokoto caliphate (the former Hausa city-states in Northern Nigeria and Niger), and Adamawa (in northern Cameroon).

When the French and British colonial powers moved into West Africa in the second half of the nineteenth century, a new phase of Islamization began. After the first violent clashes, the colonial authorities came to accept the Muslim leaders; the French accommodated the Marabuts of the large brotherhoods in Senegal and Mali, and the British the emirates of the Sokoto Empire. Despite differences in their administrative styles, both colonial powers used the existing political structures and Muslim organizations to stabilize their rule and to pacify the country. Because the colonial powers extended their reach southward into the forest areas of the Guineas, where Islam had not yet spread, Muslim traders and missionaries were able to gain new ground for Islam through already secured channels. The process of Islamization was also facilitated by several other factors. First, the colonial powers tried to restrain Christian missionary activity, which they often saw as a hindrance. Second, Muslims and animists alike saw Christianity as the religion of the despised colonial rulers. And third, Islam proved to be more compatible with animistic traditions, social relations, and beliefs than Christianity. These factors also played an important role later on in the postcolonial period.

b. Eastern Sudan

The Islamization of eastern Sudan took a very different course from that of West Africa. Eastern Sudan, also called Nilotic Sudan, stretches across the Upper Nile Basin and has at times had a historical reach—particularly in recent centuries—all the way to Lake Chad, where it shaped the fate of the Muslim Kanem-Bornu, Bagirmi, and Wadai empires, whose territories belong to what is today the state of Chad.

Shortly after the conquest of Egypt in the seventh century, Muslim Arabs undertook conquest expeditions southward along the Nile, where they were then held back by Christian states: from Maqurra (Makuria), with its capital, Dongola, and from 'Alwa, with its capital of Soba, near today's Khartoum. The Arabs conquered Dongola in 651–52 CE and entered a treaty with the Nubians establishing trade relations in which the latter were obliged to deliver certain goods annually, primarily slaves. The treaty allowed the Nubians to retain their independence as Christians and brought peace for the next six hundred years, during which the Arabs' Islamic influence remained minimal.

Islamization and Arabization increased only in the thirteenth and fourteenth centuries, when the Egyptian Mamluks undertook raids into Nubia, Arabic Bedouin clans migrated to the territory in search of better pastureland, and a short time later Islamic preachers and scholars arrived from the north and from Hejaz (Hijaz) and Yemen. The area south of Nubia, ruled by the Muslim convert dynasty of the Funj from their capital city of Sennar along the Blue Nile starting in the early sixteenth century, and parts of the Kordofan and Darfur regions to the west, converted to Islam, but areas farther south remained animist or partly Christian and divided among numerous peoples and clans. The Muslim missionaries who immigrated to the area, together with their local students, who soon established clerical families and grew in influence, propagated an Islam based in both law and mysticism. These leanings can be traced to the fact that they were largely legal scholars who followed the Malikite school of law but also often belonged to religious brotherhoods, in particular the Qadiriyya.

In the nineteenth century, during the Turkish-Egyptian reign, which also saw a boom in the slave trade and the hunt for slaves, the brotherhoods became more powerful, and new reform brotherhoods such as the Sammaniyya and the Khatmiyya sprang up. An increasingly wider segment of the population found refuge and direction in the brotherhoods during these troubled times. The highpoint of this development came in 1881, when Muhammad Ahmad, a legal scholar born in Dongola and belonging to the Sammaniyya order, declared himself a mahdi, opposed the Turkish-Egyptian government and its religious policies, brought about strict reforms, created a defiant state with its own army, and conquered Khartoum shortly before his death in 1885. His teachings also sparked conflicts with other religious orders that felt threatened by him, particularly the Khatmiyya. The Mahdists were overthrown by the British-Egyptian army in 1898, but their influence has continued up to the present, despite the fact that the British arbitrarily determined religious policy for many years and despite the very different governments in place since Sudan attained independence in 1956. In no other sub-Saharan African country is the question of further Islamization and Arabization so pressing and contentious as in Sudan. (For more, see the contribution on Sudan in this volume.)

c. Northeast Africa

Northeast Africa, the Ethiopian-Somalian realm, is also home to many different peoples who can be divided into a few large groups on the basis of their religion. To simplify radically, in the northern and mid-western highlands live Coptic-Monophysitic farmers, in the far plains of the coastal region live nomadic Muslims, and in the southwest live primarily animistic peoples. The Islamization of northeast Africa began in the port cities and was led by Muslim Arabic traders who came from the Arabian Peninsula in the seventh century and controlled the Red Sea. They and their descendants gradually moved inland and brought Islam to both the nomadic and settled peoples. Soon small Muslim statelike entities such as Ifat, Adal, Mora, Hubat, and Jidaya and farther south Fatajar, Dawaro, Hadiya, and Bali began to grow along the inland trade routes, primarily in the province of Shoa, where the capital Addis Ababa now lies. In the eastern part of Dawaro, since the twelfth century Muslim princes had been transforming the city of Harar into a religious, political, and economic center, a status the city still enjoys today.

The Muslims' expansion necessarily led to confrontations with the local Christian populations. The entire medieval history of northeast Africa is one of constant wars between these two religious rivals, who alternately captured and recaptured large areas from each other. One famous war was the jihad of Imam Ahmad ibn Ibrahim (1506–1543), who used his Afar and Somali warriors to battle not only Christians in their strongholds but also other Islamic sultanates. His victories and conquests did not last long, however.

The peoples in the western region were not the only ones subject to Islamization. Also affected were the nomadic tribes of the wide coastal region, all of whom are still Muslim and have been for a long time: the Bedja in the north in Eritrea and into what is today Sudan, where they reach all the way to the Nile; south of this the Afar (Danaqil), who reach down to Djibouti; and the Somali, who live along the Somali coast and reach deep inland, stretching all the way over the border into Kenya. With their gradual advance southward, the Somali drove out the animist people in the area, the Oromo (Galla), who moved westward and to the northwest and dispersed into many groups. Of these groups, over time some became Christian and others Muslim, such that today in southwest Ethiopia around the city of Jimma as well as in the north along the Sudanese border there are larger Muslim Oromo areas that have retained strong traces of animism.

Islam in northeast Africa, at least theoretically, largely follows the Shafiʿi school of religious law, and in the north also the Maliki school, but animistic beliefs, law, and practice as well as religious brotherhoods have always played an important role. Of the brotherhoods, first the Qadiriyya, followed later by the Tijaniyya, Mirghaniyya, and Ahmadiyya, played an important role in Islamization and are spread out in various areas across northeast Africa. In the west, the well-known Somali warrior and leader of the rigorous Salihiyya order, the "Mad Mullah" Muhammad ibn 'Abdallah Hasan ('Abdille Hassan, 1864–1920), posed a great challenge to the Christian colonizers and is considered the second national hero of the Somalis after Imam Ahmad ibn Ibrahim. (For more, see the contribution on the Horn of Africa in this volume.)

d. East Africa

As in northeast Africa, Islam arrived in East Africa by sea. Already in pre-Islamic times Arab traders from southern Arabia, in particular Hadhramaut, maintained close relations with the east coast of Africa. They further strengthened these relations in the Islamic centuries that followed, reaching all the way to India and China in cooperation, and in rivalry, with Indian and Indonesian seafarers. In contrast to their activities in northeast Africa, the Arabs limited their contact with this region to the coastline until well into the nineteenth century. They settled in strategic coastal areas and nearby islands that were accessible and easy to defend, some of which developed into significant trading posts or even city-states that lasted for varying periods of time.

Starting from Mogadishu and Barawa in today's Somalia, their settlements spread through Pate, Lamu, Malindi, and Mombassa in Kenya and Zanzibar and Kilwa in Tanzania to Sofala in Mozambique.

Interested in acquiring ivory, gold, slaves, ore, and certain plant products, the Muslim traders mixed with the native black Bantu peoples. This intercultural mixing, also with the presence of other immigrants to the area who belonged to various Islamic currents and thus often arrived as exiles, led to the emergence of what is called Swahili culture (from Arab. *sawahili,* coastal inhabitant). From this emerged the trade language Kiswahili, which is based on structures and elements of Bantu languages but also contains many Arabic words. Kiswahili is still the most developed and widespread of African languages in East Africa. Despite the strong sense of community among the Swahilis, which can be traced to a legend about the Persian, or more specifically Shirazi, origin of some of its dynasties—some Swahilis still proudly call themselves Shirazi—no state ever developed out of this community.

When Vasco da Gama arrived on the East African coast at the turn of the sixteenth century, the Muslims of East Africa entered a period of constant economic and military conflicts with the Christian Portuguese. From the second half of the seventeenth century on, Ibadi Arabs from Oman controlled a large part of the coast and the islands—without, however, particularly serving the interests of the Ibadiyya. Later, in the nineteenth century, they found themselves confronted with two other colonial powers when the

British and Germans arrived. But the British and German colonial policies, in particular the construction of railroads, brought them easier access to remote backcountry areas where they had long been capturing slaves. Thus Muslim traders primarily from the coast and the Indian subcontinent as well as Muslim servants of the colonial powers reached westward to lakes Victoria, Tanganyika, and Nyassa (Lake Malawi), thereby also bringing Islam to these areas. With the exception of the kingdom of Buganda (in today's Uganda) and the Nyamwezi and Yao clans (in southern Tanzania), Islam found relatively few followers here, however.

The Islamic brotherhoods, above all the Qadiriyya and the Shadhiliyya, first spread their reach wider in the colonial period, but their influence was limited to the coast and the islands. The coastal area and the islands of Zanzibar, Pemba, and the Comoros are the parts of the region where Muslims constitute more than half the population today.

Other than the four regions named, Muslims are also found in most other states in sub-Saharan Africa, but in much smaller numbers and usually limited to certain population groups. For example, the Muslim Cape Malays in South Africa were brought to the Cape as slaves, political prisoners, or exiles from the mid-seventeenth to the mid-eighteenth centuries by the Dutch from Dutch India. From 1860 on, other waves of Muslim and Hindu immigrants followed—this time as contract workers from South Asia who primarily came to Natal to work on sugar cane plantations. This, however, did not lead to a significant spread of Islam in the region.

Translated by Christina White

13. Horn of Africa

(Hans Müller)

The region known as the Horn of Africa covers four countries: Ethiopia, Somalia, Djibouti, and Eritrea. (There is some doubt about the inclusion of the "Republic of Somaliland" in the northern part of Somalia. Formerly British Somaliland, it declared independence in May 1991 but has not been internationally recognized.) Islam is the dominant religion today in the region as a whole, but its share of the population in the four countries varies considerably, from approximately 98 percent in Somalia to around 95 percent in Djibouti, around 50 percent in Eritrea, and an estimated 45 percent in Ethiopia. Monophysitic Coptic Christianity arrived in Ethiopia and Eritrea in the fourth century CE and is generally as strong as Islam there today. Traditional African religions are now found only sporadically in the Horn, but over the centuries they have influenced the existence of Islam and Christianity in many different ways.

The four states in the Horn of Africa have close ethnic, historical, and cultural ties; this gives them certain aspects in common, but there are also considerable differences. Ethiopia, a multiethnic country, is regarded as the oldest existing state in Africa, although its borders have changed over time. The other three states first developed in the colonial era and gained full independence fairly recently: Somalia in 1960, Djibouti in 1977, and Eritrea in 1993. The Horn of Africa has been a region of permanent crisis for centuries. A series of factors are responsible, including the large number of nomadic and sedentary peoples who live there and strive to secure their existence; the clash of Christianity, Islam, and traditional African religions and cultures; expansionist ambitions (especially of Ethiopian rulers); the intervention of European colonial powers; and periods of drought. The region has endured many domestic and interstate conflicts, sometimes with devastating consequences, especially in recent times. Here I mention the most important: the Eritrean war (1961–1991), the Tigre (Tigray) and Oromo war (1975–1991), the Ogaden war between Somalia and Ethiopia (1977–78), the civil war in Somalia beginning in 1988, and the Ethiopian-Eritrean border war (1998–2000).

These conflicts cannot be described as religious wars, but religious arguments and motifs have played a not insignificant role. Some of the countless "liberation movements," whether short-lived or longer lasting, have an explicitly Islamic character. In considering the situation of Islam today in the four states of the Horn, we must keep in mind that present conditions of life are extremely clouded and confused. The latest wars have created much misery, death, and destruction and have caused extensive population shifts. Hundreds of thousands of people have been forced to flee to other regions or to neighboring countries (including Sudan and Kenya), and have been resettled or dispersed; many live in camps or are permanently on the move, uprooted and divorced from their traditions and social environments. It remains to be seen what this means for the practice of religion in the region.

a. Somalia

The Republic of Somalia was created on July 1, 1960, by the unification of former Italian and British Somaliland. It was renamed the Democratic Republic of Somalia after a military coup in 1969. Islam is the state religion. Around 98 percent of the population are followers of Sunni Islam and the Shafiʿi school of law. Around 95 percent are ethnic Somali (more precisely, Somal; sing. Somali), with a common language and culture. This rare kind of unity should have been the ideal precondition for developing a stable, homogeneous state. Instead, in recent times the country indulged in a self-destructive civil war that, combined with famine and a refugee disaster, resulted in extensive international aid operations. The primary reasons for this instability are the composition of the Somali people and the aspirations of some of its political leaders.

Only around three-quarters of the Somali people live in Somalia itself. The territory occupied by Somali settlers and nomads is much bigger, reaching into southern Djibouti, eastern Ethiopia (the Ogaden), and northern Kenya. This situation has given nationalist Somali politicians a pretext to engage in repeated conflicts with neighboring countries and foster secessionist hopes there. In the mid-1980s over half the Somali population (of an estimated total of around 7 million) were nomads or semi-nomads; around a quarter were farmers or fishermen, and the rest lived in cities (although the urban share of the population has risen sharply since then).

The Somali people inside and beyond the country's borders form a segmented society with a democratic, egalitarian structure. Despite the ethnic, religious, and cultural homogeneity already mentioned, their specific social structure, tailored to nomadic life, has hindered the Somalis from establishing a stable political entity. The people are divided into two different lines of descent: the mainly nomadic Samaale—the "real Somali," who consist of the great clan confederations (clan families), the Darod (Darood), Hawiye, Dir, and Ishaq (Isaaq)—and in the south of the country the largely sedentary Sab, comprising the Digil and Rahanweyn lineages. Each of these six clan confederations consists of a whole series of clans divided into subclans and family and lineage groups. They provide the social context and represent the major organizational unit for their individual members. The small units may be rivals, and often permanent enemies, in the daily existential struggle for watering places and pastures, but they still have a sense of belonging. At least in less educated circles, they share the belief in their common descent from the Quraysh, the tribe of the Prophet Muhammad. This conviction, alongside obvious material and political interests, was the reason behind the popular support for Somalia's desire to join the Arab League in 1974.

Emphasis on the common bonds of all Somali and their shared Islamic tradition played a major role in the establishment of the state in 1960. It was important for integrating the two parts of the country into a unified state and was reflected in the new state's first constitution. Islam was declared the state religion, the president of state had to be a Muslim, all Muslim school pupils were to receive religious instruction, Islam was to be the main source of law, and all laws and ordinances had to accord with its general principles. This last point caused considerable problems in the sense that four different traditions of law had to be combined into a unified system of jurisprudence. The north had previously been governed by British law and the south by Italian law, alongside shari'a law and common law, which had operated throughout the whole country. The attempt to unify the law led to inevitable compromises that aroused fierce argument. But we should bear in mind that in Somalia, as in other states marked by nomadism, legislators in the cities have little influence on nomadic legal practice. Nomads regard freedom, self-determination, equality, and scant tolerance of any kind of authority as key elements of their way of life.

The political and legal situation in Somalia changed decisively in 1969, when Major General Muhammad Ziyad (Siad) Barre installed a military regime after a coup. Under Barre, the legal system was initially influenced by "Arab socialism" and the legal situation in Egypt, Sudan, and South Yemen. President Barre made many speeches asserting that the "scientific socialism" he propagated was in line with Islam, since both were mainly concerned with achieving justice. Islam remained the state religion, and Islamic law was given increased privileges over common law, but the Islamic clergy mounted considerable opposition to several new legal regulations. They protested in 1972, for example, when Somali was given official status as the written language and, after lengthy discussion, the Latin rather than the Arabic alphabet was declared binding; and especially in 1975, when family and inheritance law was recodified on the basis of the law of the People's Democratic Republic of Yemen (South Yemen). This essentially reinforced the position of women with regard to marriage, divorce, maintenance, and their relationship to their children. The dictator Barre, who had moved away from scientific socialism and toward the West, was overthrown in 1991. The constitution of 1979 was suspended, but in the country's chaotic situation it was not replaced, although drafts for a new one did exist.

With regard to religious institutions and practice, one should broadly distinguish between the cities, the agrarian settlements, and the nomads. Most of Somalia's big cities lie on the coast and have enjoyed relations for centuries with the world overseas, particularly the Arab world. The cities are where Arab traders and theologians live and where orthodox Islam, along with the religious orders, has its greatest influence. The majority of mosques and Qur'an schools are also located in the cities, and the educational level is higher there. Last but not least, the cities demonstrated the heaviest opposition to President Barre's socialist reforms and experiments. At the beginning of the 1970s Barre progressively reduced the rights and privileges of leading clergy. He accused them of serving capitalism and neocolonialism, and of representing a rich, privileged, and powerful class that basically betrayed Islam. Barre claimed that Islamic principles could be truly achieved only by scientific socialism. He demanded that religious leaders keep out of politics yet actively cooperate in building a socialist state. At the end of 1975 he ordered the execution of several clerics who protested in particular against plans to introduce equality for women in inheritance law. He also criticized the teaching methods and curricula of Qur'an schools and clerical educational institutes. Instead he tried to develop a modern, secular education system that would extend from primary school to university, including technical schools and adult education institutes, and would be open to all sectors of the population throughout the country—girls as well as boys. He wanted teaching on Islam to be integrated into this system. The project had very different levels of success in individual parts of the country.

The decisive issues for further development were the costly Ogaden war in 1977–78, which Somalia lost; the policy reversal of the Soviet Union (which was by then giving aid to Ethiopia); economic decline; and the growing protests of various clan and opposition groups against the president's dictatorial methods. Barre successively filled all the important posts in his regime with members of his own clan. The resulting widespread dissatisfaction and general insubordination culminated in civil war. Somalia's turn to the West, which had begun after the Ogaden war and led to its anti-Iraq position in the 1990 Persian Gulf crisis, brought the country increased support from Western nations and from Saudi Arabia, Kuwait, and the Islamic Development Bank (*al-bank al-islami li-l-tanmiya*). Islamic institutions also profited from this to some extent. But it was impossible to halt the inexorable ruin of the country.

Even apart from the chaos of war, the religious life of the nomads, particularly in northern and central Somalia, differs from that in the cities. The nomads cannot and do not want to fulfill basic Islamic duties to the same extent as their urban counterparts. Of course this does not prevent them from feeling that they are especially good Muslims. Constantly on the move with their herds, they live in small groups, although their clans are fairly large—over a hundred thousand members in some cases. Religious conditions in the individual groups vary considerably. Some of them do without any kind of religious ministry; others have religious teachers or preachers who move around with them, teach their children and sometimes act as a *qadi*. Yet others rely on traveling preachers visiting them from time to time. There are also some nomads with connections to a village or another kind of settlement that may have a small mosque, a *qadi*, and a Qur'an school. But nearly all of them feel bound to a religious order such as the Qadiriyya, the Ahmadiyya-Idrisiyya, or the Salihiyya, to name only the largest. Clans, sub-clans, or family groups generally adhere firmly to a specific order that provides them with preachers. The orders run small branches spread across the whole country, each in a specifically defined area. Branches have usually been set up after a pious member of the order has had a plot of building land allocated to him in the area owned by a clan or sub-clan and developed it with his followers, erecting a mosque and perhaps a Qur'an school. This would have put him in a client relationship to his benefactors. The founder of the branch was often highly respected and more revered after his death than the actual founder of the order, or even the Prophet himself. A pilgrimage to a founder's grave is often accepted entirely as a substitute for the pilgrimage to Mecca.

Important members of orders are not the only figures who can become saints for the Somali. In many cases (at least among the Samaale) they also award this status to the founders of their clans and clan families. The graves of these men are revered, surrounded by cemeteries, and visited regularly. Occasionally they are the scene of ceremonies derived from pre-Islamic customs, such as rainmaking sacrifices and rituals. Sometimes the *baraka*, the saint's powers of blessing, were passed on to his descendants, who became his successors, managed his grave, and worked and preached as *qadi*.

There are also saints who are not assigned to a specific group but are worshipped generally and may even date back to pre-Islamic times. Nearly all Somali—whether or not they follow the Salihiyya order—revere their national hero Muhammad ibn 'Abdallah Hasan (1864–1920) as a saint. (The British nicknamed Hasan the "Mad Mullah.") For twenty years he waged a jihad, an anticolonial struggle against the British, Italians, and Amhara. He was a powerful preacher and a notable poet whose poems still circulate among the people today.

Most of the population in the cities, savannas, steppes, and deserts, especially of northern and central Somalia, belong to the four main families of the Samaale clan: the Darod, Hawiye, Dir, and Ishaq families. In the south, the densely populated fertile valleys of the Juba and Shebelli rivers and the area between them are inhabited by settlers from the Digil and Rahanweyn lineages, mainly farmers and cattle breeders, known collectively as the Sab. The Samaale nomads regard them as inferior (that is, less noble than themselves). The Sab have intermarried with long-established Bantu and Oromo and migrants of various races, which has influenced their religious ideas. They are more differentiated than the Samaale. They speak a different Somali dialect, their social structure is more hierarchical and marked by their sedentary lifestyle, and their tribal structure is not as clear because of intermarriage with members of other peoples. Instead of their clan leaders, the Sab worship a large number of local saints with mystical powers, patron saints of the harvest, and other such figures. Their religious leaders have more influence than their Samaale counterparts on community politics, and some of them live in religious community settlements. Nearly all the Sab belong to the Qadiriyya or Ahmadiyya. They have more mosques and religious institutions than the nomadic Samaale and celebrate their festivals and ceremonies more regularly.

The years of chaos in Somalia in the 1990s were marked by bitter clan struggles, robbery, murder, looting, independence struggles in parts of the country (Somaliland, Puntland, and southwestern Somalia in 2002), UN operations, international aid campaigns, famine, and movements of refugees and displaced persons. The religious and social relations I have outlined were in chaos. Even today it is still difficult to get a clear picture. But in relation to Islam, there are four events of note:

1. After Barre's fall in 1991, the first interim president, 'Ali Mahdi Muhammad, introduced a shari'a court in north Mogadishu that attempted to stem the growth in crime with drastic sentences. Following this example, shari'a courts were soon set up in other cities as well.

2. In some parts of the country so-called court militias—mostly financed by private businessmen—imposed severe penalties. These militias operated similarly to the shari'a courts and were linked to them.

3. A whole series of Islamic parties and movements were active in the country; some were—or still are—connected to clans, while others operated

on a national or international level. Only one seems noteworthy: al-Ittihad al-islami, which campaigned for a strictly Islamic state for all Somalis, including those in neighboring countries. A militant organization with violent tactics, it has also been active in Ethiopia, where it carried out spectacular attacks. This caused the Ethiopian military to mount several punitive expeditions to Somalia, putting a constant strain on relations between the two countries.

4. Somalia has been one of the countries under particular scrutiny in the international fight against terrorism launched after the events of September 11, 2001, in the United States. The country stands accused of being a hiding place for terrorists and having contact with Osama bin Laden and his network via al-Ittihad al-islami. With military help from Ethiopia an interim government under President Abdullahi Yusuf Ahmed was established in the capital to combat Islamism. By the time he resigned from power in 2009 and was replaced by Sharif Shaykh Ahmed, it still remained to be seen whether these efforts and the projected assistance from the African Union peace corps (Amisom) would succeed in helping Somalia out of its chaos.

b. Ethiopia

In sharp contrast to Somalia, there is no unity among the population of Ethiopia in terms of religion, ethnicity, language, or culture. Even after Eritrea split off, Ethiopia still consisted of around ninety ethnic groups. The largest, the Oromo (formerly called the Galla), probably accounts for some 40 percent of the total population of over 50 million. The next largest groups are the Amhara and Tigre, with around 30 percent combined; notable minorities include the Guragie, Kafa, Sidama, Somali, and Nilotes. Around seventy languages are spoken in Ethiopia; they can be classified into Semitic and Cushitic (spoken by about 45 percent of the population each), Omotic, and Nilo-Saharan. The official language is Amharic (Amharigna), a Semitic tongue and the language of a largely Christian group that dominates the country's politics and culture despite being a minority. The two biggest religious communities are the Ethiopian (Monophysitic Coptic) Orthodox Church (around 40 percent of the population) and Sunni Islam (around 45 percent). (Contrary to official figures, the Islamic community overtook the church in size some years ago.) Around a tenth of the population follow natural religions. Protestants and Catholics combined probably account for nearly a million inhabitants. Ethiopia's Jews, known as the Falashas, used to be settled north of Lake Tana, but nearly all those remaining were evacuated to Israel in recent decades.

The majority of Amhara and Tigre belong to the Ethiopian Church. Islam dominates among the Somali, Harari, Afar, and Saho, as well as some Tigre-speaking groups in the north and larger Oromo groups in the country's central and southern provinces. In general, Islam dominates in the flatlands and hills of the eastern half of Ethiopia and forms large or small islands in the rest of the country. The Islamic areas in the north and northeast of the former state territory now belong to the new state of Eritrea. Around three times as many Muslims live in Ethiopia, which is more densely populated, as in Somalia, where the population is almost purely Muslim.

As indicated in the section of this volume titled "The Islamization of Sub-Saharan Africa," the history of Islamization in Ethiopia is marked by constant conflict with Christian groups. After temporary territorial successes won by the jihad led by Imam Ahmad ibn Ibrahim (1506–1543, known as Grañ, "the left-hander"), Christian invaders successively conquered many of the Muslim sultanates. Their inhabitants were killed, converted to Christianity, or expelled. In the first half of the nineteenth century, small new sultanates emerged in Sidamo province, set up by Oromo who had previously been heathens and were converted to Islam by Muslim traders. But in the second half of the century, the Ethiopian emperors Theodore II (1855–1868) and Yohannes IV (1872–1889) began strengthening the central power of the Christians in the highlands. Emperor Menelik II (1889–1913) subsequently managed not only to keep the European colonial powers away from the center of his empire but also to expand the territory he ruled to almost the size it is today. He did this by advancing southward into the region that comprises Ethiopia's present southern provinces and subjecting the non-Christian ethnic groups there to the military, economic, and cultural domination of the northern feudal aristocracy, Amhara settlers, and the Ethiopian Church. Not until the reign of Haile Selassie, who was crowned emperor in 1930, did the Muslims gain greater freedom and independence. In particular, the position of the Islamic shari'a courts, which had always existed alongside the state courts, was reinforced. They applied mainly Shafiite law, and their *kadhis* (from Arab. sing. *qadi*) were responsible for inheritance matters and questions of marriage, divorce, maintenance payments, parental powers, and family relationships among Muslims.

Ethiopia's socialist era began after the overthrow of the emperor in 1974. Immediate results were revolutionary changes and nationalization of land use, industries, banks, and insurance companies. But at the same time, resistance and liberation movements developed in Tigre, Eritrea, the Oromo regions, and Ogaden and threatened to split the country. From the religious viewpoint it was very important that the new rulers had abolished the privileged status of the Ethiopian Church and proclaimed equality of religion under a Marxist-Leninist regime.

The Muslims initially had high expectations for these apparently democratic precepts; but they soon had to recognize that the military government was increasingly obstructing their efforts to win greater influence in shaping the political, social, and cultural life of the country. The government imposed state control on Islamic schools—which were mostly attached to mosques and, like the mosques, maintained by trust funding—along with all the private schools. It confiscated part of the estates of Muslim religious trusts (Arab. *awqaf*), as well as those of Christian churches. To avoid losing popular support, however, the regime had to take account of the population's deep-rooted religious needs. In 1986, for example, when a commission was set up to draft a new socialist constitution, the archbishops of the Ethiopian and Catholic churches were involved alongside the leaders of the Muslims and Lutherans. The ban on polygamy included in the first draft of the constitution was dropped out of consideration for the Muslims. The overthrow of Mengistu Haile Mariam in 1991 was followed by the interim government of Meles Zenawi, which was regularized in 1995 and gave Muslims more scope in the country's development. They are nevertheless still generally underrepresented in the government and the public higher education system, and not represented at all in many key positions, although they are indispensable to economic life. In November 1994 Muslims gave vent to their frustration in a mass demonstration in Addis Ababa attended by several hundred thousand protestors. They called for Ethiopian society and the new constitution to take more account of their interests. This led to a split in the Supreme Council for Islamic Affairs, and conflicts with Muslim extremists in the capital in March 1995. Al-Ittihad al-islami admitted responsibility for several attacks in Ethiopia and was pursued by the military in southeastern Ethiopia, and occasionally in Somalia as well. Each country accused the other of supporting terrorism, but they were also fearful of Islamic infiltration from Sudan.

Muslims make up by far the largest number of the several million refugees who fled from Ethiopia to neighboring countries during the years of the revolution; many have still not returned. To date there has been no way of assessing statistically or qualitatively the extent to which Muslims in Ethiopia's interior were affected by the large-scale socialist resettlement and villagization operations. Mostly enforced by violence, they have been partly reversed. Although it is impossible to measure their effect on Muslim institutions and religious practice, they certainly created tangible and lasting damage.

The religious life of Ethiopian Muslims is basically similar to that in other countries: city dwellers fulfill ritual duties more fervently than villagers or nomads. The most important Muslim institutions in Ethiopia are the Sufi (*sufi*) orders, the places of pilgrimage, and other centers of Islamic teaching. The orders have hundreds of branches spread all over the country (except for some areas in the Amharic highlands). Qadiriyya branches are the most widespread. The Tijaniyya is mainly represented in the southwest, the Mirghaniyya in Tigre (and Eritrea), while the Salihiyya has followers in Ogaden and the Sammaniyya in the southwest provinces.

Many branches have become holy places where their founders are worshipped, and to which pilgrimages are made. Here, as in Somalia and elsewhere, many people use these pilgrimages as a substitute for the journey to Mecca. The holy places are frequently in remote areas far from cities. Young followers eager for knowledge often spend years there under instruction from savant shaykhs; sometimes they are drafted into field work. In some places there are regularly over a thousand students preparing for clerical professions. The best-known and most important Islamic shrine in Ethiopia is Shaykh Husayn, an old Oromo shrine around a hundred kilometers

northeast of Goba, near the Shebelli River in the province of Bale. Legend
has it that centuries ago Shaykh Husayn converted Oromo pilgrims visiting their shrine to Islam. Today—as far as possible in the confused political situation—thousands of pilgrims from all over northeast Africa visit his
grave every year (especially in February and August) to pray and seek healing, comfort, and counsel.

c. Eritrea

From around 1960, rebel and liberation movements developed successively
among the larger population groups in Ethiopia. They had varied aspirations for independence, drafted programs that were often fairly diffuse and
utopian, split into factions, and engendered rival movements. Some of them
quickly vanished again or were submerged in other organizations, which
makes it hard to distinguish among them. Broadly speaking, the Oromo
movements called for independence and even their own state, Oromia, while
the largest Tigrean movement, the Tigre People's Liberation Front (TPLF),
simply demanded regional autonomy for Tigre within Ethiopia. Meanwhile,
the most important Somali Muslim movement, the Western Somali Liberation Front (WSLF), was agitating for the unification of all Somalis through
annexation of the Ogaden region to Somalia—that is, transnational unification. Despite some temporary successes, none of these movements has
achieved its goals to date.

The oldest armed liberation movement in Ethiopia, the Eritrean Liberation Front (ELF), was founded in 1960. Largely but not exclusively Muslim,
the ELF fought for the independence of Eritrea with the backing of several
Islamic Arab countries. After increasing numbers of Eritrean Christians and
members of the urban intelligentsia joined its ranks, there were growing
internal problems and differences, and the party split into several groups. In
1970 the Eritrean People's Liberation Front (EPLF) emerged as the strongest
group politically and militarily; although Christian-dominated, it included
many Muslim activists. Its initial program was revolutionary socialism, but
in 1987 it turned away from Marxism-Leninism and promoted a multiparty
system. The EPLF was renamed the People's Front for Democracy and Justice (PFDJ) on February 16, 1994, and went on to become the main party
in Eritrea. Its general secretary, Issaias Afewerki, was made head of state
and government of Eritrea, which formally became an independent state on
May 24, 1993, after a plebiscite.

In terms of international law, the decades-long Eritrean liberation struggle cannot be described as a domestic Ethiopian conflict. Eritrea was basically created by Italy, and was an Italian colony from 1890 until 1941. After
a period under British military administration from 1941 to 1952, a UN
resolution in 1952 united Eritrea with Ethiopia in a federation with internal
autonomy. In 1962, in contravention of international law, Haile Selassie
integrated Eritrea into the Ethiopian state. This reinforced a process already

under way, in which Eritrea was increasingly influenced by the Amharic Christian tradition. The inevitable result was opposition from the country's Islamic and non-Amharic populations.

With only 3.5 million inhabitants, Eritrea may seem small on the map of Africa; but in ethno-cultural terms, as well as socially and economically, it is a heterogeneous multiethnic state. Put very simply, the population can be divided into two sections: the largely Muslim nomads who live in the low-lands, and the mainly Ethiopian Christian farmers and city dwellers in the highlands (whose spiritual leader is based in Addis Ababa). Both groups are numerically around the same size. The highland inhabitants largely speak Tigrinya or Tigre, whereas the lowland dwellers mostly speak dialect forms of Tigre or Afari and Arabic. Tigrinya and Arabic have become the two official languages, replacing the unpopular choice of Amharigna. To some extent Tigrinya symbolizes Christianity, and Arabic Islam, although very few of the Muslims actually speak Arabic.

The Muslim ethnic groups, particularly in the north, include the nomadic Banu 'Amir, some of whom speak Beja; they also move across the Sudan border. They belong to the Mirghaniyya, like most of the nomadic and semi-nomadic Tigrinya or Tigre-speaking groups. Farther to the south are the semi-nomadic Saho, and finally the Afar (also known as the Danakil). The Afar's traditional locus of movement reaches to Djibouti and the Ethiopian provinces of Tigre and Wollo. The Afar number several hundred thousand, and it is impossible to know exactly how many of them belong to each country. Given this fact, it is hardly surprising that an Afar liberation move-ment evolved, the Afar Liberation Front (ALF), which demanded its own (Muslim) Afar state including the key port of Assab. Both the Saho and Afar consist of a number of smallish ethnic groups and tribes that have not been individually researched in detail; some, who are partly sedentary, profess Ethiopian Christianity. The Muslim majority practices a form of Islam that varies quite considerably between the different groups. On the one hand, it is influenced by the Qadiriyya; on the other, it is still strongly imbued with elements of Cushite religion such as the sky god Zar/Wak (who has been downgraded to an evil spirit), sacrificial rites, magic, oracle dancing, and the killing of enemies for honor.

All four Sunnite schools of law are present in Eritrea's big cities, and re-ligious institutions such as mosques, schools, institutes, and cemeteries are mostly maintained by religious trusts (*awqaf*). The government is evidently trying to operate a national policy of equalization that respects the language and culture of individual ethnic groups. Tigrinya-speaking Christians domi-nate in the centers of power, but the Muslim share of the population seems to be increasing faster and growing in influence. In August 1992 a mufti was appointed as spokesman for the Muslim population; the previous mufti had died back in 1969.

One major remaining problem is the return and integration of over 500,000 refugees who fled to neighboring countries during the war; around

250,000 of them were housed in camps in Sudan, and only some of them have returned. In the current situation we cannot ignore the extent to which Sudanese Islamists are succeeding in winning support from people who want to return and using them to influence the future development of Eritrea. In any case, the Eritrean Islamic Jihad Movement (EIJM) has caused persistent and considerable problems for the government with its militant operations, which have spread into Eritrea itself. The EIJM, a radical opposition group founded in Sudan in 1988, split into a military and a political wing in August 1993. Its goal was to overthrow the Eritrean government and establish an Islamic state. The law on religion of July 15, 1995, prescribed strict separation of religion and politics, and allowed religious communities to engage only in charity work, religious services, and clerical social work. Measures like this law, and the ban of May 2002 on "missionary churches" holding services, were aimed primarily against missionizing Christian groups. But they have also been used to combat Islamist activities against the regime, which increased considerably after Eritrea's costly and futile border war with Ethiopia from 1998 to 2000.

d. Djibouti

Djibouti is by far the smallest country in the Horn of Africa, around five to six times smaller than Eritrea. Around 95 percent of the population is Muslim. The population consists mainly of Sunnite Somali (around 50 percent) and Afar (around 40 percent), with perhaps 6 percent European Christians (mostly French) and 4 percent Muslim Arabs. The Afar maintain close, though sometimes tense, relations with their kinfolk in neighboring Eritrea and Ethiopia. The great majority of the Somali population consists of the Issa clan and members of the Gadabuursi and Ishaq clans, who settle or live as nomads in northern Somalia as well. The colonial borders cut through Djibouti's two biggest population groups, which inevitably causes constant tension, domestically as well as abroad. There are potential threats from Somalia, where there are lively hopes of uniting all the Somalis, as well as from Ethiopia, which has had some difficulty coping without Djibouti's internationally important deep sea port. Ethiopia needs this port for the overseas transport that is vital for its existence. The port is linked to Addis Ababa by a 781 kilometer railroad line and a tarmac road.

Afar and Somali people were already settled and working their pastures on the territory of present-day Djibouti in the precolonial period. For strategic reasons related to the Suez Canal and the wish to create a counterforce to Aden, between 1862 and 1885 the French purchased lands from Afar and Issa sultans living in Djibouti, and by negotiating with the Ethiopian emperor, Menelik II. In 1896 these lands were united to create French Somaliland. In 1967 the colony was given the title Territoire Français des Afars et Issas. After gaining independence in 1977, the new state called itself the Republic of Djibouti. The French were skillful at constantly playing off the mutually hostile Afar and Somali against each other. Even today the two groups have trouble dealing with each other, although they are basically quite similar. In general, their religion, tribal organization, and egalitarian democratic structure, their largely nomadic lifestyle, and their material and intellectual culture have a great deal in common, and are congruent with those of their kinfolk across the border.

The differences between the nomadic tribes and urban population are much greater—a constellation familiar to the neighboring states as well. The nomads stick more firmly to their traditional customs (common law) and pre-Islamic religious concepts and practices. They pay scant attention to Islamic cultic duties and are more strongly influenced by the Muslim brotherhoods (especially the Qadiriyya). By contrast, the urban Afar and Issa have more mosques, Qur'an schools, and religious communities, and are more influenced by orthodoxy. But there is a wider problem in Djibouti: the blatant social contradiction within the urban population. On the one hand there are the prosperous Arab and other traders and the French military and civilian personnel with their purchasing power and their own institutions, and on the other the African part of the population, former nomads and refugees from neighboring countries, some of whom live in extremely impoverished conditions.

The first president of state, Hassan (Hasan) Gouled Aptidon, who came from the Somalian Issa clan, held office until April 1999. He tried to bring together the two largest population groups by inviting both to participate in the government, by creating a—provisional—single party, and by introducing other measures toward equalization. He also appealed to the people's common belief in Islam. This did not prevent either an armed revolt by the Afar at the end of 1991 or persistent rivalry between different population groups, particularly as the president adopted increasingly authoritarian methods, and the Afar never regarded him as neutral.

A new constitution, which came into force on September 15, 1992, restored the multiparty system and a more democratic order in Djibouti. The restriction that allowed only four political parties was eventually revoked in 2002. Article 6 of the 1992 constitution prohibited political parties from identifying with a particular race, ethnic group, sex, religion, sect, language, or region. It is worth noting that the languages of the two largest population groups, Afari and Somali (two related Cushite languages), were not transformed into written languages and were not given the status of official languages. Instead Article 1 of the constitution prescribed Arabic and French as the official languages. Djibouti has belonged to the Arab League since independence in 1977, and the language decision earned it a goodwill bonus from the world's Islamic Arab states. In the future its destiny will probably be determined more by the growing strategic importance it has acquired through its commitment to the international fight against terrorism.

Translated by Karen Margolis

14. Libya

(Hanspeter Mattes)

The history of Islam in Tripolitania, Cyrenaica (Arab. Barqa), and Fazzan, the three historical provinces that make up the present-day territory of Libya, is closely tied to the development of the Maghreb region as a whole.[1] Arab troops first invaded Cyrenaica in 642 CE. They advanced toward Tripolitania but succeeded in permanently occupying the coastal towns only after the second offensive in 645. In 663 Muslim Arab invaders made their first thrust into Fazzan; in 694 strong resistance by the Berbers drove them back into Cyrenaica. At the beginning of the eighth century, the Muslims were able to consolidate Islam by successful missionary work among the North African Berbers. From the mid-eighth century on, many of them converted, joining the Kharijite tradition of Islam in particular. Kharijism had its heyday in the ninth to tenth centuries but has survived up to the present only in its Ibadite form in a few geographically remote areas (in Wadi Mzab in Algeria, on the island of Djerba in Tunisia, and in Libya in Djebel Nafusa, Tripolitania).[2] Tripoli was captured in 910, and Tripolitania became part of the Shi'ite Fatimid Empire from the tenth century until the invasion of the Banu Hilal and Banu Sulaim Arab tribes in 1049. On the decline of Fatimid influence in the Maghreb, the region split into several autonomous Berber Arab emirates; in the twelfth century it was part of the Almohad Empire and in the thirteenth century it belonged to the Hafsid Empire. Barqa was mainly under Egyptian rule, while Fazzan, which was largely Arabized, was ruled until modern times by independent or semi-independent forms of state with economies based on trans-Saharan trade. Tripoli was recaptured by Muslim corsairs in the "reconquista" of 1551, and the Regency of Tripoli, including the administrative district of Barqa, came under Ottoman sovereignty. By then—aside from Djebel Nafusa—Libya was completely Sunnite (Malikite school of law), and its religious policy remained unchanged for the next three centuries. The first changes came in the mid-nineteenth century with the activities of the Sanusiyya Brotherhood and, from 1975, with Muammar el-Qaddafi's "religious revolution." What these changes affected, however, was not the character of Sunni Islam but rather the concept of religion—the relation between man and God—and the schism of the Sunnites into adherents of the four traditional schools of law. These schools were rejected both by the Sanusiyya Brotherhood and by Qaddafi.

a. The Sanusiyya Brotherhood and the Founding of the Kingdom

The founder of the Sanusiyya, the brotherhood later named after him, was Muhammad ibn 'Ali al-Sanusi al-Khattabi, who was born on December 22, 1787, near Mostaganem in Algeria. He studied in his birthplace until 1805, and from 1805 to 1820 in Fes, where he was accepted by the most important North African brotherhoods, the Shadhiliyya, Nasiriyya, Darqawiyya, and Tijaniyya. He traveled to Mecca via Tripoli, Benghazi, and Cairo in 1826, before the occupation of Algeria by French colonial troops. In Mecca he became a follower of the Moroccan Sufi Ahmad ibn 'Abdallah ibn Idris al-Fasi (ca. 1749–1837), the founder of the Ahmadiyya or Idrisiyya. Al-Sanusi was one of the three foremost disciples of Ahmad ibn Idris, along with Muhammad 'Uthman al-Mirghani, founder of the Sudanese Khatmiyya Brotherhood, and Ibrahim al-Rashid.[3] According to al-Sanusi Ibn Idris was the perfect Sufi master that he had always sought but never found before he met him. In al-Sanusi's teachings, the Idrisi tradition was especially notable in the areas of *fiqh, tasawwuf,* and prayer, but became prominent only after his death. Al-Sanusi recorded his thought in nine books, three of which can be described as theological works in the narrow sense.[4] In these writings al-Sanusi critically examined the existing brotherhoods and their religious practice, preaching an intellectual path to mystical union with the Prophet Muhammad instead of traditional dervish dancing and ecstatic singing. He said that each person should seek intellectual argument with himself. Al-Sanusi's version of Sufism (*tasawwuf*) was called Sufism of the "short way" because it used prayer exercises and special prayers to seek mystical union not with God but with the Prophet.[5] The second important aspect of the teaching al-Sanusi expounded in his writings refers to the rejection of the *taqlid* practiced by the orthodox *'ulama',* that is, the stereotyped adoption of long-existent (legal) decisions from one of the four recognized Sunnite schools of law. Al-Sanusi advocated the opinion that the "gate of *ijtihad*" was not shut forever, but that free decision on questions of religious law should be possible at any time on the basis of a reinterpretation of the Qur'an and sunna, because only this could prevent theological atrophy. Unlike Muhammad ibn 'Abd al-Wahhab, the founder of the Wahhabiyya, who advanced the same opinion but never departed from the framework of the Hanbalite school of law, al-Sanusi increasingly tried to pick out the best from all the schools of law (*madhhab;* pl. *madhahib*), to imbue this with his own knowledge and by doing so, to establish a unified new course. This was intended to form the quintessence of the existing *madhahib,* and to refer to the age of the Prophet's comrades, or to return to those times. Al-Sanusi's position on the schools of law earned him the enmity of the *'ulama'* in Cairo and Mecca; they went so far as to accuse him in a fatwa of "confusion, hallucinations, and the influence of the devil."

The institutional center for al-Sanusi's teaching was the first Sanusi *zawiya,* Abu Qubays, to the east of the Grand Mosque in Mecca. Founded in 1826 and upgraded in 1837, it was soon followed by other mosques to consolidate al-Sanusi's authority. The strong opposition from the *'ulama'* of Mecca to the Sanusi system of thought put a brake on these ambitions and was the main reason to search for a new working location. Al-Sanusi found it in Barqa in northern Libya, where he set up the first *zawiya* in al-Baida'.

Thanks to the vacuum left by diminishing Turkish influence in Libya—despite the intervention of 1835—al-Sanusi and his missionaries succeeded in winning followers; the most influential were 'Abdallah al-Tuati and Muhammad al-Sunni. Al-Sanusi also managed to set up a whole network of bases (*zawiyas*) reaching into the Sahel zone. This expansion southward was reflected in the removal of the main Sanusi base from al-Baida' to the oasis of Jaghbub in 1856, or after the death of the Grand Sanusi (September 7, 1859) and the takeover of the leadership by his son Muhammad al-Mahdi al-Sanusi (1844–1902) in the oasis of Kufra in southern Cyrenaica in 1895. The brotherhood's missionary success was originally due to the great respect for the Grand Sanusi as a religious teacher and mediator in conflicts between the tribes of Barqa. Under his son and successor, the brotherhood's modern outlook had an increasingly positive effect on membership development and the growth of influence. Based on the "pray and work" principle, the Sanusis' specific identity included key aspects such as acquiring land, promoting handicrafts and trade, building an infrastructure, and developing the education system.[6]

The activities of the Sanusiyya, which were motivated by religious policy, began to develop into growing state power in the interior of Barqa. The Ottoman state, which had legal sovereignty over the Wilayat Tarabulus, acknowledged this power in 1856 with a *firman* from the sultan, 'Abd al Majid I. The Ottoman sultan and caliph retained sovereign status. The development of a theocratic Sanusi state based on *zawiyas* reached its peak under Muhammad al-Mahdi al-Sanusi. Under his successors, Ahmad al-Sharif al-Sanusi (1902–1916, when he went into Egyptian exile) and Muhammad al-Idris al-Sanusi (1916, from 1922 also in Egyptian exile), the Sanusiyya's role as a factor in the political order was destroyed in the armed conflict with the Italian colonial power that began in 1911. Targeted destruction of the *zawiyas* robbed them of their religious infrastructure.[7] After the defeat of the Italians in the Second World War, however, and during the British military administration in Libya (1943–1951), the historical role of the Sanusiyya in Barqa, their entrenchment in the tribal system, and the lack of unity of Tripolitania's political leaders contributed to their revival as a political factor. This occurred first in Barqa, where the British, pursuing strategic interests, recognized Idris al-Sanusi as emir of a nominally independent Cyrenaica (in the Proclamation of Benghazi, June 1, 1949). From 1951 it extended to the whole of Libya after the Tripolitanian leaders accepted Idris al-Sanusi as ruler of a "united kingdom" because they saw this as the only possibility of creating an independent pan-Libyan state. Yet in the united kingdom proclaimed on December 24, 1951, Idris al-Sanusi officiated only as the temporal ruler on the basis of the constitution passed on October 7, 1951, although he had also initiated moves toward a religious revival of the Sanusiyya movement in his capacity as spiritual leader of the Sanusiyya Brotherhood. This involved setting up twelve religious schools in 1948–49 as a first step, and founding the al-Sayyid Muhammad ibn 'Ali al-Sanusi Institute of Religion, with headquarters in al-Baida' and branches in Tripoli and Benghazi. The institute was upgraded to an Islamic university by a law of October 29, 1961.

b. Muammar el-Qaddafi's Religious Revolution

On September 1, 1969 the Free Officers' Movement led by Qaddafi (*Muammar el-Qaddafi*) overthrew King Idris. The coup was a reaction to the corruption in the economy and domestic politics that had developed in Libya since the mid-1960s as a result of the oil boom, complemented and exacerbated by the country's foreign policy of open dependence on the United States and Britain. The Revolutionary Council became the new key decision-making body, introducing a policy of political, economic, and cultural self-emancipation strongly influenced by Nasserism. At first this involved only limited intervention in religious affairs. After the special troops loyal to the king (TRIDEF, CYDEF) had been disarmed, the new regime embarked on a process of consolidation in which the *zawiyas* were dissolved and the Sanusi University was integrated into the Libyan state university as a faculty. The Westernization begun under the Sanusi monarchy was reversed in favor of Islam, and appropriate measures were introduced such as prohibiting alcohol, shutting down late-night bars, proscribing the Latin alphabet, enforcing exclusive use of the *hijra* calendar, turning churches into mosques, and banning prostitution and gambling. The regime fostered the restoration of Islamic Arab identity.

But these measures did not indicate revaluation of Islam as a defining political factor.[8] The revolutionary leadership's ambition to present the "September Revolution" as an Islamic revolution (*thawrat al-fatih thawra islamiya*) took specific shape only after the death of Gamal Abdel Nasser (Jamal 'Abd al-Nasir) in 1970. In 1971 a special committee was set up to work on the revision of positive legislation "in the light of shari'a." To maintain political control, it consisted of just two members. Its work emerged as rather superficial, as illustrated by the obvious lack of coherence in the two draft laws on theft and adultery enacted on October 11, 1972, and October 20, 1973, but rejected by the populace. Aside from the *zakat* law and the implementation of the *waqf* law of September 16, 1972, which provided for extended state control in the area of religious trusts, these re-Islamification measures—unlike the formal re-Islamification of 1969–70—had no real effect. The codified penal (shari'a) regulations such as flogging and amputation were not applied owing to the complex legal situation, and were rendered obsolete by political events from 1975 on.[9]

Meanwhile, two elements of Sanusi thought that later became more clear-cut emerged in this early phase of Qaddafi's Islam policy, though it is impossible to establish that he was directly influenced by the Grand Sanusi's writings. The first element relates to Qaddafi's instruction to the committee for the revision of positive legislation to consider not only the Malikite but also the other three Sunnite schools of law as well as the Shiʿite Imami, the Zaydite, and the Ibadite school of law. The second element concerns Qaddafi's attitude toward *ijtihad,* which he emphasized because he saw it as a means of reinterpreting Islam in terms of revolutionary ambitions for political and social change. But Qaddafi's view on this had as yet no ideological structure. It took shape more clearly in the course of speeches he made as chairman of the Revolutionary Command Council in 1972, and finally on April 15, 1973, in the keynote Zuwara speech. The future political development and institutional reorganization of Libya required a new definition of the relationship between the state and religion. The "People's Revolution" (*thawra shaʿbiyya*) launched by the Zuwara speech signaled a move away from the previous Nasserite road to development which had led Libya to adopt the Egyptian constitutional model in 1969 and to introduce the one-party Arab Socialist Union model in June 1971. But the People's Revolution also resulted in a growing split between Anwar el-Sadat and Qaddafi in relation to economic and foreign policy, and to Libya's decision-making structures being personally centralized around Qaddafi, who simultaneously claimed ideological leadership.

At the end of 1974 Qaddafi temporarily withdrew from official duties. On April 27, 1975, he personally presented the Libyan public with the discourses he had formulated as interpretations of the "Third Universal Theory" (*al-nazariyya al-thalitha*) and concretized in guidelines for political action. He titled this "The *Jamahiriyya* Experiment: The Rule of the People" (*tajribat al-jamahiriyya—sultat al-shaʿb*). From December 1975 to January 1976 the concept was circulated in written form as the first part of the "Third Universal Theory" (TUT, *al-nazariyya al-ʿalamiyya al-thalitha*). Part two of the TUT ("The Solution of the Economic Problem: Socialism") and part three ("The Social Foundations of the TUT") appeared successively in November 1978 and June 1979. The three parts make up what is known as the *Green Book* (*Al-Kitab al-akhdar*). Significantly, this fundamental document contains no explicit reference to Islam, although there are texts related to religion in the Arabic version. For example, the section on the law of society is neutrally translated as "law of society" in the English version, whereas in the original it is defined in relation to Islamic law with the phrase "shariʿat al-mujtamaʿ." Qaddafi's Bedouin origin undoubtedly had a deep influence on his socialization, and this is shown in the way the TUT prioritizes the fulfillment of basic needs as well as political and economic egalitarianism. This also applies in practice to the structuring of policy relating to women, even if the relevant passages in the *Green Book* (part three) give a first impression of a conservative image of women.

Part one of the *Green Book* is significant in terms of religious policy. The political system for which it lays the groundwork was developed from 1973 to 1975 and is based on legislative grass-roots people's conferences (Muʾtamarat shaʿbiyya asasiyya) and executive people's committees (Lijan shaʿbiyya). It takes the form of direct democracy, which means it rejects mediatory bodies such as political parties, and therefore the system of parliamentary government. This rejection has been logically and consistently pursued in the military sector since 1976 by means of the plan to replace the traditional army with universal military training of men and women on the principle of "supremacy, wealth, and weapons in the hands of the people" (*al-sulta wa-l-tharwa wa-l-silah fi yad al-shaʿb*). The same applies to religion. The "religious revolution" (*thawra diniyya*) began on May 2, 1975, with a ban on religious scholars and imams making speeches about the country's political and economic development.[10] This came after the grand mufti of Tripoli criticized the conscription of female public servants for universal military service. Qaddafi also made several speeches advocating a direct relationship between man and God, a relationship without mediators and interpreters such as religious scholars. By this time the committee on the revision of positive legislation had long since been dissolved because of its inflexible attitude.

Qaddafi highlighted the Qur'an alone as the "law of society," and urged that the basic people's conferences should address all social needs by studying the Qur'an and using *ijtihad* to help develop a new order adapted to the present. This put him predictably to a confrontation course with religious scholars. In addition, three of the four postulations in the Proclamation of the Establishment of Popular Authority (Iʿlan sultat al-shaʿb), which had constitutional status, defined the Qur'an as the sole law of society. The proclamation was passed by the General People's Conference, the national assembly of all the representatives of basic conferences and people's committees, at a special session on March 2, 1977. It omitted reference to sunna and hadith (*hadith*) as sources for legislation. By describing the Qur'an as the "essence of Islam" (*jawhar al-islam*) but the Prophet as a mortal human being, Qaddafi relegated sunna and hadith to a secondary role as Prophet-related sources of Islam. Qaddafi regarded the enormous importance that some *ʿulama'* attribute to sunna and hadith as idol worship (*shirk*); he reproached the *ʿulama'* for placing the two interpretations almost on a level with the Qur'an and ascribing near-divine origin to them.

The conflict between Qaddafi and the religious scholars heated up in 1978. On February 19, in a sermon in the Mulay Muhammad mosque in Tripoli to mark the Prophet's birthday, and again on July 3 at a gathering of leading clerics in the same place, he attacked the imams personally, saying, "The Qur'an is written in the Arabic language, which means we can all understand it without needing an imam to explain it to us." Qaddafi also sharply attacked the whole edifice of Sunnite teaching and jurisprudence. He questioned the value of sunna and hadith and postulated that if the Qur'an were the only source of Islamic law, the system of Islamic law (*fiqh*)—as compiled in the classical compendia and split up into four schools—could not be seen definitively as Islamic. He argued that this was because it had developed from sunna and hadith and went back to *qiyas* and *ijma'*. He called it "positive law" (*qanun wad'i*) and said it was no more nor less religious than Roman law or the Code Napoléon. Only the Qur'an was not artificial law (Arab. *wad'i*)—that is, not created by human hands—and the religious schism among Muslims caused by the different schools of law could be overcome only by returning to the Qur'an.[11]

That was not the end of Qaddafi's reforms. In a speech in February 1978 he also derided the practice of saint worship and pilgrimages to Marabout graves as "pre-Islamic" customs. For the first time, he made an explicit link between the *jamahiriyya* state model and Islam by referring to the phrase "and whose affairs are a matter of counsel" ("wa-amruhum shura bayna-hum") in sura 42, verse 38, of the Qur'an, and stressed that part one of the *Green Book* showed the way to constitutional implementation of the Qur'an. Finally, in December 1978 he decreed that Libya should replace the *hijra* calendar normally used in Islamic countries with the calendar based on the date of the Prophet's death. This date, he argued, was incomparably more important than the *hijra* from Mecca to Medina.

The religious scholars' growing opposition to the religious revolution was countered by a sweeping campaign in May and June 1978, when many imams were arrested. This was followed by further campaigns ("to cleanse the House of God") lasting until the mid-1980s.[12] The repressive measures were accompanied by rapid training of so-called revolutionary imams—even though official Libyan discourse held imams to be superfluous. Qaddafi's reforms, described as "heresy" by the Saudis, even led to foreign policy controversies with Saudi Arabia and the World Islamic League.[13] But Qaddafi stuck firmly to his Islam policy.

c. The Conflict with Islamists

The Libyan revolutionary leadership's conflict with Islamists goes back further than the 1980s; in fact, it is as old as the revolution itself. At first the main issue was the Islamists' conspiratorial activities against the regime rather than specific questions of divergence. The Five-Point Program of the 1973 Zuwara speech included a point about "purging the land of the politically ill." Qaddafi described the followers of the Muslim Brotherhood and the Islamic Liberation Party by name as "a plague on the people." The conflict deepened with the beginning of the religious revolution, while the Libyan population's general sensitization to Islamic questions was discernible at the end of the 1970s (the time of the Iranian Revolution). Other Islamist groups such as the Holy War organization and the League of Da'wa were able to recruit supporters during this period.[14] But open conflict first broke out in the mid-1980s, when two Islamist students were hanged by members of the Revolutionary Committee on April 17, 1984, and security forces destroyed an infiltration squad from the Libyan opposition in exile. The infiltrators belonged to the National Front for the Salvation of

Libya (NFSL), an organization close to the Muslim Brotherhood. Six surviving squad members were publicly hanged in June during Ramadan. Events reached an initial climax on April 4, 1989, when Islamists fired on people attending mosques in Benghazi, Misurata, and Ajdabiya, condemning them as "heretics" for supporting the official version of Islam.

Events reached another climax from 1992 to 1996, when Libyan Islamists who had returned from fighting against the Soviets in Afghanistan campaigned, particularly in eastern Libya, for the establishment of a state based on shari'a. Three groups were especially noteworthy: the Islamic Martyrs' Movement (Harakat al-shuhada'al-islamiyya); the Militant Islamic Group (al-Jama'a al-islamiyya al-muqatila); and the Libyan Islamic Group (al-Jama'a al-islamiyya al-libiyya). The massive repression by the security forces, which had succeeded in liquidating all armed Islamists or driving them into exile by 1997, was accompanied by a parallel rhetorical conflict that started in March 1989. Qaddafi personally made dozens of speeches expounding his position on the problem of "political Islam" (*al-islam al-siyasi*), and describing the "tendency of religion to monopolize politics" as a dangerous development and a disaster. His criticism was aimed not just at the Muslim Brotherhood but at all Islamist groups, which he described as "devils," a "religious mafia," "charlatans," and "more dangerous than AIDS."[15] In fact, on July 19, 1990, Qaddafi explicitly called for the liquidation of Islamist groups because, he said, they were destroying Islam from within, posing as self-appointed "guardians of the religion," and characterizing Muslims as infidels. He added that the intermingling of politics and religion should be rejected. Another state strategy for stemming the tide of Islamist groups consisted of introducing shari'a regulations in seven laws to reduce the scope of possible criticism. This partial Islamification of penal law, which came into force on January 29, 1994, involved prohibition of alcohol, punishment of bloody deeds (introduction of the principle of talion), penalties for robbery and theft, and a law to combat corruption. There were also new ordinances in inheritance law and personal law. The first sentence under the newly introduced *hadd* penalties was carried out on July 3, 2002.

The status of Islam in Libya at the beginning of the twenty-first century is ambiguous because it is related both to Qaddafi's personal image and to the arduous process of defining the position of the state and Islam. On the one hand, Qaddafi is the ideologist of the TUT, the tireless propagandist of the *Green Book,* and the initiator of the *jamahiriyya* state model. On the other hand, as a missionary for his nondogmatic conception of Islam he has slipped into the role of an imam, a religious reformer. Since 1975 the revolutionary leadership in Libya has evidently tried to create a state legitimized by Islam but still secular, a state whose modernization and transformation should not be restricted by religious prescriptions, but which is simultaneously influenced in every area by Islamic Arab culture and civilization. This has been opposed by growing tendencies that operate on the maxim of *taqlid* rather than *ijtihad* by utilizing the introduction of shariʿa as the basic principle of the Islamic state. This schism inevitably results in the revolutionary leadership's irreconcilable attitude toward Islamists, and this attitude also defines the scope for liberalizing the political system.

Translated by Karen Margolis

15. Egypt

(Alexander Flores)

In Egypt, Islam provides orientation and gives meaning to life, regulates daily routine, and grants legitimacy to political and social action.[1] In this sense it hardly differs from other religions in comparable situations. Yet Islam fulfilled these functions unchalleneged only under premodern conditions. The modernization processes that started to have an influence in the nineteenth century threw into question Islam's impact in this regard. It is very apparent that the forms of Islamic consciousness and standards of behavior that have prevailed up to now no longer correspond to rapidly changing living conditions. By no means has this meant that they have stopped functioning entirely, however; they continue to exert an influence to an extent that is astounding considering the manifest gap. On the one hand, Islam offers legitimation for rejecting the status quo, according to a perception that is widespread here. But on the other, governments and social conditions in the Arab world also owe their stability largely to the—spontaneous or consciously exercised—Islamic legitimation they enjoy and the consoling and calming functions of religion.

In the mid-nineteenth century the traditional hegemony of Islamic regulations and institutions started being hollowed out by law and the state constitution. Egypt took a large step in this direction in its "liberal" phase from 1919 to 1952. European thought was accepted on a large scale; in the economic and social sectors, which were restructured or newly established along Western models (and largely under Western dominance), European thought proved to be a good fit, whereas old patterns of thought that identified with Islam were not. The corresponding processes gained widespread influence as modern concepts became accessible to larger segments of the population through the vast spread of schooling, especially as a more effective system of state influence and control gained a foothold.[2]

These processes ultimately led people to question the hegemony of Islamic ideas and institutions. Without doubt a certain secularization of state and society had taken place. This generally was not a problem for Muslims, especially since the governments and the religious authorities subject to them did all they could to make the development acceptable within Islam.

But it did become problematic for the social strata that were marginalized by the ensuing modernization. Furthermore, it was and is a problem when the state is obviously not in a position to control an intensifying social crisis. In such situations it becomes clear that the de facto secularization of Islamic societies has no adequate corresponding impact at the level of mass consciousness and that the state and politics ultimately have no alternative but to resort to Islamic legitimation.[3]

The assumption that the state must or should be religiously sanctioned remained alive within the consciousness of broad segments of society; and this assumption then became virulent when the "pragmatic" legitimation of the state and its policies (that is, through their success) no longer held true. This situation did arise occasionally, which is why the governments of the Islamic countries were reluctant to make an open break with the old Islamic legitimation. Here modernization was neither so profound or thorough nor, in particular, so successful that it could have completely replaced the traditional Islamic legitimation of the state. The results in present-day Egypt remain to be seen.

a. A Paradigm Change

Since the early 1970s an increased emphasis on Islam can be observed in Egypt and other Arab countries. This is apparently connected to the fact that there has been constant social upheaval since that time, and the state can no longer cope with the results, which are unfavorable for large segments of the population. The resulting insecurity brings forth nostalgia for the "good old days," which many see symbolized in Islam. Whatever the reason, however, the phenomenon itself cannot be disputed. The change that has thus ensued in the atmosphere of the country and in its political and intellectual discourse has been fittingly described as a "paradigm change."[4] The previous dominance of Arab nationalist ideas with objective Marxist leanings was gradually eclipsed in the first half of the 1970s by a new focus on Islam.[5] This development reached a peak (with a decidedly political emphasis) toward the end of the decade, catalyzed by the Islamic Revolution in Iran.[6] It also distinctly influenced secular intellectuals and political forces and can be very clearly recognized there.[7] This has by no means led to an Islamic homogeneity. Instead, extremely divergent projects are being pursued. But typically after the implied "turning point," a general feeling prevails that some reference to Islam is necessary in bringing forth one's concerns.

The stronger emphasis on Islam and the resulting change in the atmosphere in Egypt can be observed primarily in three areas:

1. A greater number of Muslims now practice their faith in public (increased participation in Friday prayers, "Islamic" beard styles and clothing customs).
2. References to Islam are articulated wherever possible in many areas. This is particularly evident in public debate.

3. There is a pronounced Islamic sociopolitical movement that ties into the phenomena named in points 1 and 2, which aims to strengthen and steer those developments as far as possible. This is the movement of political Islam, which is also referred to as an Islamist or fundamentalist movement. It is by no means uniform, but instead is made up of an "integrist" main current and many smaller, more radical cells that generally operate underground.[8]

All of this has influenced not only the intellectual and cultural atmosphere in Egypt but also the basic conditions for political development. The Islamist movement became the best-anchored oppositional force to the government. If prior to this change the main line of political debate was the contrast between conservative and progressive, between pro-Western and anti-imperialist, now the contrast is between a movement in state and society toward Islamism, on the one hand, and preservation of the status quo on the other. The main proponent of change is the Islamist opposition, though its members are not in agreement on how to go about making that change. The main force for preservation is the government. In view of this conflict, all other forces are compelled to take a stance. The conflict is practical and political, but it is also manifested in intensive intellectual debate. Characteristic of the course of the conflict is that is has changed far more in the general atmosphere and the cultural sphere than in the political and legal reality.

b. Legal Anchoring of Islam

Religious courts were abolished in Egypt in early 1956, and their remaining areas of jurisdiction were transferred to the secular courts. Since then Egypt's judicial system has been secular. The laws have a modern, Western character, even though they take their inspiration from shari'a rules, especially those related to personal status. This situation persists, but in the course of the accentuation of Islam, legal references to the shari'a that were never completely eliminated have been given greater emphasis and are in part legally grounded.

The Egyptian constitutions since 1923 have designated Islam as the state religion. Such a declaration is missing only in the 1958 constitution of the United Arab Republic. Article 2 of the Egyptian constitution of 1971 goes further than the previous provision, stating: "Islam is the religion of the state and Arabic is its official language. The principles of the shari'a are a main source of the legislation." A constitutional amendment went into force in May 1980 as a result of a referendum. Among other things, it intensified the wording of Article 2 to read, "The principles of the shari'a are *the* main source of the legislation." This article was not meant to prescribe that laws must in fact be derived from shari'a provisions. Instead it documents that the prevailing legal situation in Egypt did not arise through an open break with the shari'a and that valid law is viewed as conforming with

what was cautiously and tentatively referred to as the principles (*mabadi'*)
of the shari'a. One can understand that to mean either the "spirit" of the
shari'a—however that is interpreted—or the *usul al-fiqh,* that is, the sources
and methods of Islamic jurisprudence.[9]

This article of the constitution thus also expresses or takes into account
the peculiar legal situation in Egypt. Law and jurisprudence are secular in
nature, but to a certain extent in the public consciousness they receive their
legitimacy through Islam. Consequently it is imperative to include some reference to the shari'a in the general line of reasoning and in some specific
cases. This situation has existed for a long time, but since the recent emphasis
on Islam it has become the point of departure for demands by Islamists to
reinstate the shari'a. The aforementioned article of the constitution, for example, is understood not as a confirmation that valid law is compatible with
the shari'a but as a demand to replace existing law with a codification of the
shari'a. This demand has repeatedly been put forward since the early 1970s.

For some time the government also responded to this demand by promoting projects to codify the shari'a. Different bodies—from the government
and parliament to al-Azhar University—dealt with these projects, and in
early July 1982 they actually submitted drafts to the parliament for six legal
codes that conformed to the shari'a. These were transferred to the responsible committee but were never brought up again, since the government
was not really interested in reintroducing the shari'a. After having favored
Islamist organizations in the early 1970s in order to combat the influence
of the left and the Nasserists, the government came into conflict with the
Islamist movement toward the end of the decade and wanted to stop its
advance. One motive for advocating the introduction of the shari'a was
therefore eliminated. For other reasons as well (such as reservations of the
United States), the government showed reluctance to reinstate the shari'a.
It therefore tabled the corresponding draft bills and then abandoned them
entirely in 1985.[10]

Also in the 1970s Egyptian legal developments did not take a consistently
"Islamic" course. In 1979 the civil status law was amended, giving women
more rights and freedoms in the event of divorce.[11] This amendment, which
was initiated by Jehan Sadat, the wife of the president, Anwar el-Sadat,
and therefore called Lex Jehan, faced such intense resistance in the parliament that Sadat had to put it into force by means of a presidential decree.
Under the pretext of its having been approved through an unconstitutional
procedure, it was annulled by the Supreme Court in 1985. The true reason,
however, was the substance of the law, which conservative and Islamist
circles felt went too far in expanding the rights of women.

c. The Shari'a Debate

The added emphasis on Islam brought only minor changes to Egypt's legal
situation. The way it was presented in the public consciousness, however,

changed dramatically. Although the replacement of valid positive law with shariʿa law, no matter how it is codified, remains unlikely, demands for it frequently top the national agenda and are the subject of intense debate.

The demand to reinstate the shariʿa was introduced in the early 1970s by representatives of political Islam, who were soon joined by religious scholars close to the state. Only a few intellectuals spoke out against this demand in the 1970s, most of them only by calling for caution and moderation in implementing the reinstatement.[12] The arguments used by opponents of codifying the shariʿa became much more comprehensive and systematic in the 1980s, but those put forward by the supporters remained essentially the same.

From the perspective of those in favor of introducing the shariʿa, the main arguments are: (1) the nature of the shariʿa as God-given law, which makes it superior to any legal regulations created by human beings, so it therefore must be followed; (2) its inherent, close connection between statutory regulations and morality; (3) its emphasis on social values, which promotes justice and facilitates social reform; and (4) its "endemic" nature, which promotes the preservation or regaining of a sense of identity and independence. The arguments opposing an immediate introduction of the shariʿa are: (1) doubts that in its present form the shariʿa truly is God's pure commandment, all the more so as it has to be implemented by human beings, with all their weaknesses; (2) the limited actual application of shariʿa rules even in premodern times; (3) the incompatibility of the shariʿa with present-day circumstances and the difficulty in adapting it to them; and (4) the fact that shariʿa principles have already been taken into consideration in valid law, within the scope of what is reasonable.[13]

Although these arguments have often been asserted, the issue at hand for both advocates and opponents of introducing the shariʿa does not have to do solely with its validity as law. Instead the advocates are at least equally interested in the possibility of agitating against the status quo. They see this agitation as connected to their campaign, through which they wish to increase their power and influence, ultimately with the aim of changing conditions, a goal that goes far beyond merely replacing certain laws. And that is precisely what the opponents—or at least some of them—fear, which is one reason why they are fighting the demand to introduce the shariʿa. It is especially the *principle* of introducing the shariʿa that is open to debate, not so much the introduction itself. For the most part this is not a substantive legal question. Instead it is a struggle between opposing political forces over the nature of the state and the political culture in Egypt, and it is being fought with intellectual means on the basis of a legal issue.

It is very important to many advocates of a speedy introduction of the shariʿa to convey the impression that existing positive law is totally irreconcilable with the shariʿa, so it must be replaced by the shariʿa if the rule of the latter is desired. Against this background it was common in the 1980s for judges with Islamist leanings to rule according to existing law but simultaneously put on record that these statutory provisions contradicted the stipulations of the shariʿa and should therefore be replaced by it, according to Article 2 of the constitution. Some judges made their rulings in accordance with shariʿa regulations from the outset.[14] The intention was the same in both cases: to demonstrate the irreconcilability between existing laws and the shariʿa, thereby furthering the campaign to introduce the shariʿa. The great media attention paid to these rulings is evidence of this intention behind the actions. The rulings have generally been annulled by the higher court, but they continue to occur occasionally. A particularly blatant case was that of the Cairo linguistics professor Nasr Hamid Abu Zayd, who in June 1995 was ordered by the family court to divorce his wife because he was considered an apostate of Islam for applying modern methods of linguistic research to sacred texts.

Several rape cases that were very much in the public eye in Egypt in the mid-1980s provided further opportunities to shed light on the tension between existing law and the shariʿa, as well as on consideration of the shariʿa in the current legal system. In one of these cases the court wanted to give the defendant the death penalty, and it consulted the mufti of Egypt, as called for in this case by the code of criminal procedure. The mufti considered the rape to be *zinaʾ* (fornication) and declared that the crime could not be considered proved owing to the particularly strict shariʿa stipulations in such instances; therefore the designated *hadd* (the punishment prescribed by the Qurʾan) could not be imposed. The mufti thus refused to approve the court ruling. Consequently he was harshly castigated by the media for obstructing the severe punishment of rapists.[15] In a similar case that was tried only a short time later, the mufti heeded the criticism. This time he considered the offense not *zinaʾ* but *hiraba* (forcible assault) and declared the crime sufficiently proved.[16] This case highlights the strange legal situation in Egypt, caught between two systems: positive law is valid under the more or less fictitious guise of deliberations based on the shariʿa.

d. The Political Debate

The debate on introducing shariʿa was not only legal but ultimately also political in nature. Other debates here were even more closely related to the political sphere and the major conflict over the country's future direction. The Islamist movement has been able to join this controversy as an important player. Its presence has become firmly established. Even if its organizations are largely still officially illegal, they are generally recognized as an important force. The main force behind the Islamist movement in Egypt, the Muslim Brotherhood, uses legal means in pursuing its goals. Radical groups, by contrast, have resorted to violent methods of confrontation (robbing of Coptic jewelers, assaults on tourists, attacks on political adversaries).

This movement strives to change existing conditions in an Islamic direction, not well defined but in any case characterized by the hoped-for validation of shari'a law. Countering this demand for change are the political forces that seek to preserve the status quo in at least one respect, that is, political autonomy from institutionalized religious influence. This includes primarily the government and the National Democratic Party which supports it, but also the non-Islamist opposition (especially the Wafd Party and the Tajammu' Party). Some opposition parties are so strongly influenced by Islamism and tied to the Muslim Brotherhood through election alliances that they could be regarded as part of the Islamist movement. This applies especially to the Socialist Labor Party and the Liberal Party. Sympathies for Islamism and its influence have also worked their way into the government camp.

The Islamist movement's undisputed presence on the political stage in Egypt does not mean that its goals are also generally approved, however, as there is heated debate on these aims. The state attempts to keep the Islamist movement in check by means of a twofold strategy: partial co-optation of the Muslim Brothers and an increased "Islamic bias" of the state, on the one hand, and more severe repression of radical groups on the other.[17]

The conflict is taking place under a political regime that is still authoritarian, despite some opening in recent decades. This opening was not anchored in the legal system but (often for reasons of maintaining an image) enacted by presidential decree. The state of emergency that was imposed in 1981 is still in force, and the law governing political parties continues to ban the establishment of religious parties. Islamist organizations that are overtly political are therefore illegal, even if many of their activities—up to and including participation in elections—are tolerated. This is a benefit that was graciously granted and thus can ungraciously be taken back.[18] Most charitable organizations, by contrast, are legal. Those operating within a Muslim context even have more favorable legal status than those without such a reference point.[19] In the press as well, including the state-controlled press, the Islamist movement has broad options for expression; on radio and television, however, the government maintains its right to impose harsher controls. Under these circumstances the Islamists can bring their presence to bear on society and the public consciousness but not—at least not legally—in party politics.

The left-right, pro-West–anti-imperialist contrast that used to help shape political discourse in Egypt has not lost all meaning but has instead been eclipsed by the new opposition of critics versus defenders of the status quo. This has led to new options and challenges for many forces, including the question whether they should adapt to the new atmosphere for the sake of their own popularity, or if they should fight the change in order to defend the secular, civil foundations of state and society, even in alliance with the present government.[20]

e. Controversies

Some debates that took place in the 1980s cast a harsh light on the status of Islam in present-day Egypt and the conflict surrounding it. One of these debates concerned the question if and under what conditions Islam justifies or even demands rebellion against an existing government. After members of the radical Islamist Jihad group murdered Sadat in October 1981, they defended themselves in court with the argument that they were following a command of Islam, namely, to correct a situation recognized as wrong, using force if necessary. The group felt that through his behavior Sadat demonstrated that he had committed apostasy from Islam and he therefore had to be killed.[21] In a report refuting "Al-Farida al-gha'iba," the most important programmatic document of the Jihad group, the mufti of Egypt spoke out against such an interpretation.[22] He contradicted claims that a Muslim is apostasized from Islam through misconduct, that jihad is an individual obligation of all Muslims, that Egypt does not belong to the Islamic world so it must be won back through jihad, and other similar arguments.

It is noteworthy that both sides involved in the conflict accepted a traditional Islamic conception as a fitting criterion for evaluating a modern ruler such as Sadat. The mufti's statement was within the framework of the traditional Sunni consensus, while his adversaries argued along the traditional lines of the Kharijites.[23] Within the scope of the _fiqh_ (Islamic jurisprudence), the mufti was certainly right—and both sides argued at least officially within this framework. But this is problematic, since the traditional _fiqh_ is not an adequate instrument for judging the character of the Sadat regime or any regime in present-day Egypt, which is largely secularized, both politically and socially.

The mufti assumed that the Egyptian regime represented Islamic rule in a traditional sense, and he introduced arguments that would make this interpretation plausible in the eyes of the public—in the interest and on behalf of the government, for which such an image was important. The radical Islamists at least had a sense that Sadat was not a traditional ruler. But they assumed he could be, so they viewed his policies as apostasy from Islam, declared jihad, and assassinated him. They obviously knew how secularized the situation was, but they believed that they could return it to premodern conditions by violent means.

At the time there were many similar debates between the accused Islamists and legal scholars who supported the state over the issues dealt with in the trials. They were organized and widely publicized by the government, which was eager to use this opportunity to polish its "Islamic" image before the public. It generally did not succeed in doing so, because regardless of how theologically superior the scholars were to the young radicals, it was obvious that they were acting in consultation with and in the interests of the government, while the Islamists just as obviously spoke and acted from conviction.

Another debate had to do with the conception of "consultation" (_shura_) in Islam and its relevance in modern times. According to the traditional political conception of Islam, a ruler is obliged to "consult" with suitable people in making political decisions. Yet nowhere is it laid down definitively who these suitable people are and how binding their advice is. In contrast to what is often claimed apologetically, it can hardly be established that this principle actually hindered autocratic rule in the course of Islamic history. Today people like to mention it in order to point to democratic elements in the Islamic understanding of politics. It is often simply considered equivalent to democracy.

In the summer of 1985 the well-known author Yusuf Idris wrote an open letter to Khalid Muhammad Khalid, asking why, in such difficult times, when there are so many existential questions, he would bring up such a marginal issue as that of introducing shari'a law. Khalid Muhammad Khalid was a scholar educated at al-Azhar University who in 1950 spoke out decidedly as a secularist.[24] But in the course of the subsequent emphasis on Islam he adopted an integralist interpretation of Islam in 1981; after that he proposed the necessity for an Islamic state and the introduction of the shari'a.[25] In his open letter Idris also asked what kind of Islamic state Khalid was calling for and which shari'a laws were to be introduced.[26] Khalid's response was: "Why the shari'a? We must agree that Islam is both religion and state.... But if Islam is state, then it needs jurisprudence and laws that come forth from it as religion!...The system of rule in Islam is the *shura*. What is the *shura*? It is the democracy that we see today in the democratic countries." Then Khalid mentioned some characteristics of a modern Western understanding of democracy and simply claimed that these were also the essential characteristics of the *shura*.[27] Khalid thus wanted humane, tolerant, progressive conditions that corresponded politically to those in Western democracies, but he felt that it was necessary—for the sake of their acceptance and unassailability—to refer to these conditions as Islamic, even prescribing them in accordance with religious law, which in his interpretation corresponds to the "true" essence of Islam.

In response to Khalid's article, Faraj Fuda (Farag Foda), the most vehement Egyptian critic of the Islamist position and practice in the 1980s, found his aims to be good in principle but considered it wrong that he based his arguments on religious law. The modern concept of democracy, as Khalid viewed it, was developed outside the realm of Islam, said Foda. While this does not prevent Muslims from adopting it, since it certainly does not contradict the spirit of Islam, Foda felt that declaring it to be genuinely Islamic was contrary to historical fact. He went on to say that equating the Islamic state with democracy serves to endorse it. But once it has been endorsed, Foda argued, the majority of its proponents would have succeeded in achieving an Islamic state that is totally different from how it was conceived by Khalid—namely, a state that is backward, intolerant, and repressive.[28]

The influential *Ahram* journalist Fahmi Huwaydi took a very different position. Like Khalid he advocated placing concepts that one wanted to propagate into an Islamic context of justification, with the pragmatic reasoning that only such a procedure could ensure that such ideas would be heard by the profoundly religious Egyptian masses.[29]

The well-known philosopher Fu'ad Zakariyya, the most consistent Egyptian representative of fundamental secularism, often confronts the opinions of Islamists in his writings. Like Foda he doubted that Khalid's interpretations would gain much approval among proponents of an Islamic state and the immediate introduction of shari'a law. But he found it even more significant that Khalid was not able to develop these interpretations solely on his knowledge of the basic texts. Instead, according to Zakariyya, they were profoundly influenced by the conditions of present times. That underscores a thought that Zakariyya generally considers very important, namely, that the development of shari'a provisions from the basic texts is human-made and inconceivable in isolation from the conditions and influences of the respective times. Zakariyya thus concluded that a fundamental opposition between divine law and positive law does not exist.[30]

There was also no lack of voices that rejected Khalid's equating universalistic concepts with an Islamic state and the shari'a from an Islamist standpoint. Jamal Sultan, a prominent member of the Muslim Brotherhood, for instance, cited Khalid's equation of Islamic systems of rule with those of Western democracies, asking where, in the logical consequence of his argumentation, he would characterize the U.S. and British governments as Islamic.[31]

The different positions in the debate over Islam and politics become very clear here. The position of the "Islamic center," assumed by Khalid and Huwaydi, is very popular. The secularist position of Foda and Zakariyya is openly shared by only a few intellectuals, and even the radical Islamist stance of Sultan is encountered less frequently—openly expressed, that is—and is not typical of remarks by, for example, members of the Muslim Brotherhood.

When dealing with the significance of Islam for Egyptian society and politics, we find that one of the most important questions concerns the relationship of Muslims to non-Muslims. This issue was the subject of heated debate in the 1980s, and the same principal positions as in the aforementioned debate can be made out here as well. There is a radical Islamist position, though it is rarely expressed openly, which advocates officially reinstating legal discrimination against non-Muslims.[32] The "Islamic center" exists here too, supporting full civil rights for non-Muslims within the framework of an Islamic order but at the same time downplaying the de facto discrimination against non-Muslims in Islamic history as well as in present-day Egypt.[33] There is also a secularist position which emphatically champions the rights of non-Muslims *independently* of the Islamic understanding of this issue, indicating the dangers that are necessarily connected with any form of discrimination against religious minorities.[34]

f. A New Secularism

In the course of the recent emphasis on Islam, the secularist spiritual direction in Egypt, as in other Islamic countries, has been pushed into the background. Some prominent secularists have declared their support for political Islam. In view of the danger they saw in the offing in the form of the Islamist movement and its growing influence, a new generation of Egyptian secularists began speaking openly in the mid-1980s. Reservations against institutionalization of religious hegemony, which were raised in connection with the debate on shari'a law and some political controversies, became comprehensive and fundamental and were defended in sometimes widely followed controversies with proponents of an integralist understanding of Islam. Despite their differences, these controversies all revolved around one major question: Is secularism reconcilable with Islam, or must Islam necessarily be understood in such a way that it excludes all secularist ideas? In other words, does a commitment to Islam prescribe a certain political conduct that is then enforced institutionally, or does it leave Muslims free to shape this realm as they see fit?

Five authors have been especially connected with this new secularism in public discussion because of the related articles they have published, mostly in newspapers: Farag Foda, Husayn Ahmad Amin, Fouad Zakariyya, Muhammad Nur Farahat, and Muhammad Sa'id al-'Ashmawi.[35] Using different formulations and with different reasoning, all of them advocated for autonomy of human life as opposed to giving religion an institutionalized claim to hegemony.[36] They generally attempted to provide evidence of the danger of the integralist concept of Islam on the basis of practical examples or fundamental considerations. Their adversaries, by contrast, explained that the dangers either were nonexistent or else arose from a flawed application of Islam and could be avoided through proper application of the religion.

The debate was most heated from 1984 to 1987 and very quickly reached its limits. It turned out that neither side could convince the other. The two different interpretations of Islam remained irreconcilably juxtaposed. Debate at an intellectual level gave way, again leaving more room for the practical, political confrontation that had initiated it in the first place. This became more than clear from the assassination of Foda by a radical Islamist group on June 8, 1992.

g. Recent Developments

The major outlines of Egypt's political configuration are highly durable, in that an authoritarian government and an Islamist opposition continue to face off, leaving little room for the secular opposition and efforts supporting the structures of a civil society. In the early 1990s the government started a program for economic liberalization and privatization, but having been implemented under conditions of a continued—or even intensified—lack of political liberality, it is therefore halfhearted and halting, and favors its clientele. Of course that leads to widespread dissatisfaction, which Egyptian politics seems to be intent on isolating or neutralizing. At the same time, the same old approach is carried on vis-à-vis the Muslim Brothers. They are still banned, but are often given free rein, although sometimes the authorities crack down on them—in the form of a warning—and try at least to prevent any independent political movements. None of the various attempts from the ranks of the Muslim Brothers to establish a legal political party has been permitted.

The radical Islamists have made the most obvious progress. In the early 1990s they still engaged in actual armed struggle against the security forces in some places, and after being brutally repressed by the government, they committed a number of outright massacres of tourists (quite spectacularly in November 1997 in Luxor). Since then, however, there has been a process of reflection within their ranks, as a result of which many of their leaders decided to desist from armed actions. To all appearances this decision was made in good faith, and it was substantiated in a number of publications. The government reacted slowly to this process, but then publicized it prominently in June–July 2002. Many radicals were released after having spent decades in prison. The process seemed likely to lead to the reintegration of former radicals into the Muslim Brotherhood or its milieu.[37]

The government, for its part, has maintained a kind of modus vivendi with the Islamists, which serves to control them and keep them quiet. This situation may be jeopardized by the generally growing dissatisfaction with the government, which is being expressed loud and clear and, along with occasional U.S. demands for democratization, suggests continued instability.

Translated by Allison Brown

16. Sudan

(Hanspeter Mattes)

Sudan is the only country in the Arab League whose political structures and internal conflicts can be traced back to its particular course of Islamization starting in the sixteenth century. It is also the only Arab League country whose four main political currents are closely tied to specific religious groups, each with its own Islamic traditions and, correspondingly, its own political and social agenda for shaping the nation: the Mahdiyya movement, the Khatmiyya Brotherhood, the Muslim Brethren, and the Republican Brothers.

a. The Origins of the Ta'ifiyya in Sudan

Islamization in Sudan, introduced in the seventh century by nomads who migrated from the Arabian Peninsula, gained momentum in 1504 with the founding of the first Islamic state in the northern Sudanese region of

Sennar, the Funj sultanate. The Funj dynasties brought in many Islamic scholars (*'ulama'*) and Sufi leaders (*shuyukh*) from the Hejaz to instruct the nomadic clans and local inhabitants. The Sufis' method of closely integrating their efforts with the local social structures and culture made them very successful, not only putting a Sufi stamp on Islam such that Sufism and Islam became almost synonymous in Sudan, but also setting up an oppositional relationship between the Sufis and the *'ulama'* that came to shape the future of the nation.[1]

Up until the nineteenth century, two brotherhoods prevalent throughout the Arabic world predominantly influenced the Sudanese Nile Valley, particularly the Jazira region. The first was the Qadiriyya brotherhood, which spread starting in the mid-sixteenth century through the teachings of Shaykh Idris ibn Muhammad al-Arbab (b. 1507); and the second was the Shadhiliyya movement, which spread in the early eighteenth century via the teachings of Shaykh Khupali 'Abd al-Rahman (d. 1743). This political-religious structure did not change until the nineteenth century, with the introduction of reformist ideas and the modernization impulses of the Turkish-Egyptian administration installed in 1821 by the Egyptian ruler Muhammad 'Ali in the regions under his rule, affecting primarily northern Sudan.[2]

Reformist ideas were disseminated in Sudan in particular by the members of new brotherhoods that developed in the Hejaz, most prominently the Sammaniyya and branches of the Idrisiyya. The teachings of 'Abd al-Karim al-Samman (1718–1775), who positioned the Prophet Muhammad and the doctrine of the coming mahdi at the center of the Sufi universe, was spread in northern Sudan by his most important student, Ahmad al-Tayyib ibn al-Bashir, starting in 1800. Bashir gained influence over many clans and extended his power into West Kordofan (Kurdufan). Muhammad Ahmad ibn 'Abdallah (1844–1885), who later became mahdi, was a student of Nur al-Da'im (1841–1908), the grandson of Ahmad al-Tayyib.

The teachings of the Moroccan Sufi Shaykh Ahmad ibn Idris (1760–1837), who lived in Mecca for a long period, were disseminated by three of his students—though partly in versions differing from the original—in various regions of Sudan: in Darfur particularly by the Sanusiyya order, founded by Muhammad ibn 'Ali al-Sanusi (1787–1859), with its main seat in Cyrenaica, and in the Red Sea region and al-Damer by the brotherhood of Muhammad al-Majdbub al-Sughayir (1796–1833). The third brotherhood, the Mirghaniyya or Khatmiyya, became the most important in Sudan with the largest number of followers. It was founded by Saiyid Muhammad 'Uthman al-Mirghani (1793–1853), who hailed from a wealthy sharif family in Mecca.[3]

All three brotherhoods advocated renouncing blind acceptance of existing religious laws (*taqlid*), transcending the four existing Sunni schools of religious law, reopening the "gate of *ijtihad*," and making the Prophet Muhammad the singular reference point in their unitarian "Muhammadian" path (*tariqa muhammadiyya*).

The already existent dichotomy between the Sufi shaykhs and the ʿulamaʾ grew during the two periods when the Turkish-Egyptian influence was strong, that is, from 1821 to 1849 (the conquest of northern Sudan and the creation of a central administration) and from 1863 to 1879 (the extension of the administration into Darfur and Equatoria). The goal of the Turkish-Egyptian magistrates (the so-called Turkiyya) was not only to bind Sudan to Egypt but also to weaken the power of the clans. Because the clans represented the majority of followers of the Sufi shaykh, the Turkish-Egyptian administration intervened primarily in religious affairs in order to push through its own agenda. The urban orthodox ʿulamaʾ were to be bolstered by recruiting new graduates from al-Azhar University in Cairo, by the construction of mosques, and by sending Sudanese students to al-Azhar. Between 1860 and 1870 the lack of success of this strategy in combination with the Khatmiyya's communication efforts eventually led to closer ties—allegedly in the interest of the brotherhood and the Muslims—between the Turkiyya, who held power locally, and the Khatmiyya, who represented the most important brotherhood. This strategic political alliance between the Khatmiyya and the foreign rulers, which lasted until Sudan's independence and included the ʿulamaʾ, was rejected by much of the population and constituted one of the grounds for the Mahdist Revolt in 1881, carried out primarily by western Sudanese clans.

A further reason for the revolt was the expectation, at the end of the nineteenth century, also beyond the Sudan, of the coming of a mahdi, a religious leader who would restore purity and unity to Islam as well as revive equality and justice on earth. The turbulence of the Sudanese economy and the questioning of traditional clan structures and hierarchies effected by the administration's modernization policies mobilized the population under the Idrisi-inspired Sammaniyya Shaykh Muhammad Ahmad ibn ʿAbdallah from Dongola. In 1881, three years after he broke with his Sufi teacher Nur al-Daʾim, ʿAbdallah declared himself the mahdi. His political-religious agenda consisted of propagating a life of austerity, a return to the Islam of the Prophet Muhammad, and jihad against the infidels (first and foremost the Turkish-Egyptian administration). The Mahdist Revolt, which had a xenophobic current, represented the height of the confrontation between the ʿulamaʾ and the Sufi shaykhs.

The theocratic state established by the mahdi and continued after his death in 1885 by his successor (*khalifa*) ʿAbd Allahi ibn Muhammad al-Taʿaʾishi (executed in 1899) was wiped out by the British military expedition at the battle of Omdurman on September 2, 1898; but his followers (*ansar*) constituted and still constitute the second major political and ideological group responsible for shaping the political landscape in the Sudan. The Khatmiyya and the Mahdiyya *ansar* initially acted only as an interest group counter to the British colonial powers. The rise of a Sudanese nationalist movement, the secularization of the political sphere, and the formation of political parties beginning in the 1940s led the Khatmiyya and the Mahdiyya to create denominational parties. The *ansar* established the Umma Party in 1945, and in 1953 the Khatmiyya joined with the Ashiqqa', which had been legalized in 1943, to found the National Unity Party (NUP; starting in 1967 the Democratic Unity Party, DUP). The two new parties were rivals, particularly during the final phase of joint British-Egyptian rule, with the Khatmiyya-NUP oriented toward Egypt and even promoting annexation by Egypt, while the *ansar*–Umma Party opted for a monarchy and advocated an independent foreign policy. During the phases of civil rule following independence in 1956 (1956–1958, 1964–1969, 1985–1989), both parties—each representing a traditional religious camp—participated in government and/or the political shaping of the country. And during the phases of military rule (the 'Abbud regime, 1958–1964; the Numayri regime, 1969–1985; and the Bashir regime beginning in 1989, though the military element became formally less prominent in 1995) both parties have represented a strong factor that is not to be ignored. The political activities of both the Mahdiyya and the Khatmiyya have been characterized by opportunism, the lack of a clear program, and an ideological vacuum. Political sectarianism (*ta'ifiyya*) aimed at short-term power gains became an increasingly significant factor in Sudanese politics, ultimately rendering the country ungovernable.

b. The Third Political Factor: The Muslim Brotherhood

The modernization impulse of the Anglo-Sudanese administration in creating an efficient administration, introducing modern production methods for agriculture (cotton farming), and shaping the sectors of education, transportation, and communication led to the establishment of a local educated class concentrated in the towns of central Sudan beginning in the 1920s. Starting in the 1940s, this stratum undertook a few attempts at creating autonomous political groups outside the two established political-religious movements and with their own political and social agenda. One of these was the communist movement, founded in 1946, from which emerged the most influential communist party in the Arab world (the Sudanese Communist Party, SCP). To this day, however, the SCP has not recovered from the backlash against a failed attempt to overthrow Ja'far al-Numayri in 1971. Other religiously based political movements also developed in this context with the goal of breaking free from the political stalemate caused by *ta'ifiyya*. The two most important of these were the Muslim Brotherhood and the Republican Brothers.

The Sudanese cells of the Muslim Brotherhood, formed in 1945 as an offshoot of the original Egyptian organization, joined with cells of the autochthonous Harakat al-tahrir al-islami to form the Sudanese Brotherhood (al-Ikhwan al-muslimun).[4] Initially their agenda was strongly influenced by the ideology of Hasan al-Banna and aimed at creating an Islamic constitution. In 1955 they went public with this goal by founding the Islamic

Front for the Constitution. Following independence, in November 1964 the Muslim Brotherhood founded the Islamic Charter Front (Jabhat al-mithaq al-islami) and thereafter focused mainly on participating in parliamentary elections. But they could not successfully compete with Umma, the DUP, and the SCP. By the early 1960s two leaders had emerged in the Muslim Brotherhood who would determine its future course. In 1962 Sadiq 'Abdallah 'Abd al-Majid succeeded the imprisoned al-Rashid al-Tahir as leader (*al-murshid al-'amm*) of the Muslim Brotherhood, though the brotherhood had already become politically ineffectual since the rise of Hasan al-Turabi within the National Islamic Front (NIF, al-Jabha al-islamiyya al-qawmiyya) in April 1985.[5] Hasan al-Turabi (born in 1932, he married the sister of Sadiq al-Mahdi in 1961), who had played an active role in the Khartoum student organization at the end of the 1950s before going abroad to study law at the Sorbonne, returned to Sudan in 1962. His charisma, experience, and knowledge led initially to a post as secretary general of the newly founded Islamic Charter Front, which advocated the introduction of shari'a and a constitutional system based on the Qur'an, the sunna, and the *shura* of the *umma*, as well as measures in the economic sphere such as *zakat* and prohibitions on speculation, lending for interest, and the hoarding of commodities (*ihtikar*). A concession was made for the people ("minorities") of non-Islamic southern Sudan to create their own personnel statute.

The first sign of success in efforts to instate an Islamic constitution came with Turabi's appointment to the forty-four-member National Commission for the Constitution and to its fifteen-member technical committee, both called into existence by the government in January 1967. The process of Islamization thus begun was interrupted by the second military intervention into constitutional matters on May 25, 1969. The so-called Free Officers Movement, led by Ja'far al- Numayri, initially looked to Egyptian president Gamal Abdel Nasser (Jamal 'Abd al-Nasir)—and, starting in September of the same year, also to the Libyan president Muammar el-Qaddafi—and to the Egyptian constitutional model, orienting itself toward "Arab socialism" and entering into religious conflict in particular with the Muslim Brotherhood. In August 1973, and again in September 1975 and July 1976, the brotherhood was the target of repressive measures owing to its antigovernment activities. Likewise, the open opposition of the *ansar* to Numayri's regime was silenced in March 1970, when the leader of the Mahdiyya, Imam al-Hadi al-Mahdi, and many *ansar* were killed, and others (including Sadiq al-Mahdi) were exiled to Egypt. Growing internal conflicts within the Numayri regime—which sent its leaders in search of coalition partners in an effort to stabilize the government—in conjunction with Numayri's personal turn toward Islam beginning in the late 1970s,[6] led to a "national reconciliation" with the *ansar* (and the return of Sadiq al-Mahdi from exile) in 1976 and ultimately to reconciliation with segments of the Muslim Brotherhood. A tangible sign of this was Turabi's appointment as attorney general (1979).

This initiated a course that lent the Turabi faction of the Muslim Brotherhood political influence and furthered the process of Sudan's Islamization in the form of the September Laws of 1983. On September 8, 1983, Numayri issued a presidential decree abolishing the existing legal system and establishing the shari'a as the new foundation for an Islamic code of law, adopting in full the *hadd* punishments for theft, robbery, adultery, and other offenses as prescribed by the shari'a. Further steps followed, including the adoption of Islamic law for the economic sphere and the use of special courts for enforcing the new penal law code.[7] This process of Islamization cannot be directly attributed to the efforts of the Muslim Brotherhood but is due rather to the influence of Numayri's closest advisers (including al-Naiyil Abu Qurun and Ahmad al-Jid). Yet it was Turabi who praised the new Islamic policies as exemplary and attributed them to the efforts of the brotherhood.

The political result of this forced process of Islamization from above, however, was an erosion of power. Conflicts were reignited with both the southern Sudanese, who were fighting for a more secular state, as well as with the Muslim opposition led by the Republican Brothers, who objected to the widespread and inhumane enforcement of the shari'a. In conjunction with the effects of disastrous economic developments, these conflicts ultimately led to Numayri's deposition on April 6, 1985, by the Transitional Military Council and the suspension of the September Laws. But this did not bring an end to pressures toward Islamization. The Muslim Brotherhood consolidated around Turabi as the Transitional Military Council introduced democratization under the leadership of General Siwar al-Dhahab. In April 1985 the Muslim Brotherhood founded the NIF, which became the third-strongest party (with 51 of 301 parliamentary seats) alongside the Umma Party (99 seats) and the DUP (63 seats).

c. The Republican Brothers

The introduction of Islamic law in 1983 was not unanimously accepted. Sadiq al-Mahdi, as leader of the Mahdiyya, and Sayyid Muhammad 'Uthman al-Mirghani, as leader of the Khatmiyya, along with other important figures in traditional Islamic organizations came out against the introduction of Islamic law in such a rigorous form, given the religious heterogeneity of Sudan—and in particular given the economic and social situation in the country at the time. But the Republican Brothers were the only organization to object openly and vehemently to this move at a fundamental level, questioning its legitimacy according to Islam.[8]

The Republican Brothers (actually the Brothers of the Republican Party, Ikhwan al-hizb al-jumhuri) was founded by the organization's spiritual and political leader, Master (*ustadh*) Mahmud Muhammad Taha (1909–1985), in October 1945 alongside the Muslim Brotherhood and defined itself from the beginning as an Islamic movement. The party arose as a counter to the two dominant organizations in the nationalist movement, the Mahdiyya and the Khatmiyya, with Taha promoting neither annexation to Egypt nor a monarchy but instead the formation of an independent, democratic, and republican nation-state. Following independence and up until the early 1960s, the Republican Brothers' activities were centered on conflicts with the _ta'ifiyya_ forces and their ideological and platform deficits. Thereafter they focused on demands for an "Islamic system," as voiced by the Muslim Brotherhood. It is no coincidence that Taha's two main works, _Muhammad's Path_ (1966) and _The Second Message of Islam_ (1967), were written during this period. These texts served as the foundation for debates with the legalistically oriented forces of political Islam, first and foremost the Muslim Brotherhood, and as a reference point for a critique of the political measures taken by government decision makers. Mahmud Taha, who believed in "the propaganda of setting a practical example" in terms of both the brotherhood's individual and its social behavior, established the Republican Party as an organization that, on the one hand, fell within the tradition of a mystical brotherhood and yet, on the other hand, clearly remained connected with socioeconomic realities and acted accordingly—for example, in its insistence on women's equality and its objection to arranged marriages. This lent the Muslim Brothers an ideological foundation that distinguished them from traditional brotherhoods. In concrete terms, Taha espoused the historicity of the shari'a and the notion that it is inherently subject to development over time. He maintained that God's word reveals itself each day in a different form and that the individual tenets of the historical shari'a should yield to general principles that can lead the way to a "virtuous" society. These general principles relate to the three pillars of economic, political, and social equality and are complemented by the principle of a tolerant public opinion (_ra'y 'amm samh_). These ideas were vehemently rejected, as were Taha's new definition of the sunna and his notion of the Qur'an's containing an inherent principle of development.

The initial consequence of Taha's teachings was an irreconcilable rift with the Muslim Brotherhood, which in 1968 had accused him of apostasy (_ridda_) in the highest shari'a court in Khartoum and thereby procured a death sentence—which, however, it was not possible to carry out under federal law. When Numayri's September Laws of 1983 changed the political and legal parameters, Taha's message and his critique of the introduction of shari'a now represented a challenge to the state. The response was his arrest for sedition and subversion of the constitutional order on January 5, 1985. The court of appeals found Taha to be additionally guilty of apostasy, despite the lack of such an offense in the September Laws. On January 18, 1985, Taha was hanged in Khartoum's Kubar Prison—despite his advanced age of seventy-six. The execution of this "atheist heretic and enemy of God, Mahmud Taha, president of the Republican Brothers, who are delusive and far apart from Islam," was emphatically welcomed with these words by the highest Saudi religious scholar, Shaykh Ibn Baz, in a telegram he sent to Numayri. This position echoed the satisfaction of those who rejected Taha's critiques of the *'ulama'*, the institutions of a legalistic Islam, and the traditional form of shari'a. The reactions to Taha's execution, however, also reflected the fundamental conflict between Islamic mysticism and legalistic Islam.

d. Forced Islamization under al-Bashir

The third period of parliamentary rule in Sudan after independence, from April 1986 to the military intervention on June 30, 1989, can be character-ized as a time of political stalemate and strategizing—at both the domestic and foreign policy level. There was, on the one hand, the political opposition between Ahmad 'Ali al-Mirghani (DUP), head of the five-member Supreme Council, and Prime Minister Sadiq al-Mahdi (Umma) regarding a solution to the southern Sudan conflict and the constitutional assembly, while on the other hand, there was also the vacillation between finding a military versus a political end to the war. The domestic political situation became even more complicated when the Umma and the DUP allowed the NIF to join the governing coalition in April 1988 in an attempt to consolidate the government and move forward. With his rigid position on imposing the shari'a, however, Turabi—who was serving the new government as minister of justice in addition to his post as attorney general—blocked all attempts to find a peaceful solution to the southern Sudan conflict. This led the DUP to leave the governing coalition in December 1988, allowing Turabi to become foreign minister as well, which meant that he had an almost hegemonic position in the government.

In February 1989 the military leadership issued a memorandum with an ultimatum calling for improvements in both the foreign and domes-tic situations. This indirect threat was followed by a military intervention in March 1989 and the creation of a new government without the NIF. This new government, which rejected the introduction of the shari'a, was toppled on June 30, 1989, by the Revolutionary Command Council for Na-tional Salvation (RCCNS, Majlis qiyadat al-thawra li-l-inqadh al-watani) led by Brigadier 'Umar Hasan al-Bashir, who became president in 1993. The deposed government was accused of "adulterating democracy, abus-ing institutions, causing an economic demise, ruining public institutions, corruption, isolating the country, waging war in the south, and neglecting the armed forces" (in the words of Bashir). All constitutional bodies were dismissed, political parties were banned, and their leaders were either taken into custody or, like Turabi, put under house arrest. But alongside mea-sures to give Islam priority again, the fact that Turabi maintained a certain influence despite being under house arrest quickly made it clear that the RCCNS was not acting autonomously but was under the sway of the NIF. It is generally said that Turabi, who was set free on January 1, 1990, had been pulling the strings.

Bashir's usurpation of power (and, de facto, Turabi's as well) reinitiated and intensified the country's course of Islamization, which was completed in three main areas starting in the fall of 1989 and continued to dominate Sudanese politics.[9] The first area of Islamization included traditional measures such as those adopted in 1989: support for domestic missionary efforts, the mandatory closing of shops during Friday prayers, and the introduction of the *zakat;* followed by those in 1990, such as separate public transportation for men and women, the ban on men working in women's beauty salons, and a prohibition on interest in banking; and in 1991 came an Islamic dress code for women and schoolgirls, encroachments on the media based on the belief that they do not do justice to Islam, and in March of the same year the introduction of the Islamic penal code in all states but three in the south. Measures toward further Islamization followed (for example, a 2003 ban on fashion shows, which are considered a threat to Islamic morality). In addition, after a long planning phase the structure of the state was reorganized in 1992 on the basis of people's congresses, and in 1999 the National Congress Party was founded—both measures intended to help realize the Qur'anic *shura* principle.

The second area of Islamization concerned finding a solution to the conflict in southern Sudan, where, contrary to the official show of willingness to negotiate with the Sudanese People's Liberation Movement (SPLM), the direction of efforts was clearly toward imposing a military solution. But this campaign, openly apostrophized as a jihad, ultimately failed because the SPLM was able to mobilize sufficient foreign support (from Uganda, Israel, and the United States, among others) to lead several successful military operations. After the government abandoned its military strategy in 1997, peace negotiations were begun in Machakos, Kenya, in June 2002, resulting in a peace declaration signed in Nairobi in June 2004 and a treaty signed in January 2005. Although the government had to make considerable concessions to the SPLM, it was able to establish shari'a law for the capital city of Khartoum.

The third area, foreign policy, also started out in the direction of Islamization. This became apparent in Sudan's close relations with Iran, particularly following a visit by Iranian president 'Ali Akbar Hashemi Rafsanjani in December 1991, and in international cooperation concerning the military, the justice ministry, and crude oil, as well as the establishment of a cooperation network with other Islamic organizations in the Arab world (the Algerian Front Islamique du Salut or FIS, the Tunisian Nahda, and the Egyptian Muslim Brotherhood). Besides the government ministries, the body responsible for this cooperation was the Popular African and Islamic Conference, founded in April 1991 by Turabi, who was elected its secretary general. The task of the conference was, according to its charter, "to create a broad anti-imperialist front of Islamic organizations with the goal of preventing the return of colonialism in the Islamic world." In this context Turabi and the NIF set up recruitment activities in Arab and African countries, giving rise to the notion that Turabi was spearheading an emerging "Islamic International." In December 1999 Hasan al-Turabi, who had meanwhile risen to the position of parliamentary speaker, was deposed by President Bashir owing to political conflicts. Thereafter Islam played a lesser role in Sudan's foreign policy as the government took a more pragmatic approach, particularly under pressure from the United States (to negotiate with the SPLM) and in the wake of September 11, 2001. For example, Sudan began cooperating with the United States in fighting Islamic terrorism. But in terms of its domestic affairs, the country still has an Islamic state doctrine.

In February 2003, the Darfur conflict erupted. In contrast to the previous war in Southern Sudan with its strong religious component, this was and still is mainly a clash between ethnic groups: Almost the whole population of the Darfur provinces are Muslims, but of non-Arab origin. With the other ethnic communities in the south, east, and west of the Sudan—who taken together represent the majority of the population of the country—they are politically and economically marginalized by the Arab tribes of central Sudan and its leaders. Therefore it does not come as a surprise that the principal liberation movement in Darfur calls itself the "Justice and Equality Movement."[10]

Translated by Christina White

17. Israel and the Occupied Territories

(Thomas Philipp)

It is Jerusalem that gives the land of Palestine its special religious significance in Islam. Jerusalem was the location toward which the early Muslims turned in prayer; this was later changed to Mecca after the *hijra,* the Muslim emigration to Medina. In his famous ascension by night, the Prophet is supposed to have ridden to Jerusalem on his horse, al-Buraq, so as to rise up to heaven from there. The Dome of the Rock covers the rock from which, according to Muslim belief, the Prophet began his ascent to heaven. The complex of the Dome of the Rock and the Aqsa mosque form the site known as al-Haram al-sharif, making Jerusalem the third holiest city of Islam. It lies on the terrain of the former Jewish Temple. Even the Western Wall of this area, the Jewish Wailing Wall, has significance for Islam. Its Arabic name, al-Buraq, refers to the fact that Muhammad is said to have tethered his horse there.

In the Muslim reception of history, Palestine is assigned another kind of religious significance as the goal of the Christian Crusades. The enduring attack on this key Islamic country, and thus on Islam itself, was finally repelled after two hundred years of fighting, and the Muslims regained political and military control of the territory. The historical experience of the Crusades has kept its relevance for Muslims, particularly as an analogy to the present-day political situation.

After the Crusades the territory had no special status. Within the region it was simply part of Bilad al-Sham, that is, geographical Syria. In the Ottoman Empire it was divided administratively between the *wilayet* of Damascus and that of Sidon (later Beirut)—with the additional district of Jerusalem, which was occasionally under direct rule by the imperial government.

It was the British occupation and establishment of a military district of Palestine at the end of the First World War that first highlighted the region as a special territory. Eventually the mandate treaty defined it politically and administratively as the British Mandate for Palestine.

Since the First World War, political developments in the region have been wholly dominated by the activities of the Zionist movement, with its program for the establishment of a Jewish state in Palestine, and the Arab and Palestinian reaction against this project. The Great Powers—Britain up until the end of the Second World War, then increasingly the United States—have been actively involved in this conflict. They have primarily sought to maintain their own interests by playing off the two parties in the conflict against each other.

In so far as Islam has developed, or is developing, in a specific way for the Palestinian territory and the Palestinians—whether in its institutional manifestations, in its political forms of organization, or in concrete statements—this can be located in the reaction to Zionist ambitions and Great Power interventions on the one hand and the debate with the Palestinian Arab nationalist movement on the other.

The establishment of the British Mandate for Palestine and the separation of Transjordan from it created the political and legal framework: Great Britain claimed the administration of the territory for an unlimited period and pledged itself to fostering "the establishment of a national homeland for the Jewish people." At the same time, it promised to do this "without infringing on the civil and religious rights of the existing non-Jewish community in Palestine."[1] Both points of this program—British supremacy and the establishment of a Jewish national homeland—aroused resistance among the indigenous Palestinian Arab population from the very beginning.

Palestinian resistance during the Mandate period went through several phases and assumed various forms, which I shall not describe here in detail. It centered on leading figures from Palestinian society, ideologically oriented parties, and social and cultural associations. Although different frames of reference were established—the Arab nation, Greater Syria, or Palestine—the resistance took its forms of expression and legitimation largely from the symbols and terms of secular nationalism.[2]

Any discussion of the role of Islam in political developments during the Mandate is closely connected with the figure of the mufti of Jerusalem, Hajj Amin al-Husayni.[3] Descended from what was probably Jerusalem's most important Muslim family, Hajj Amin had risen to prominence after the First World War as a nationalist and anti-Zionist activist. He was appointed mufti in 1921 at the age of twenty-six without any special religious training. His appointment mainly expressed his family's claim to power, as well as Britain's hope of finding a pro-British figure for the post.

After the collapse of the Ottoman Empire, the mufti of Jerusalem became de facto mufti of Palestine and the highest religious authority in the territory. This position was reinforced by the Supreme Muslim Council set up in 1921, which was responsible for all questions of Islamic law, administration of mosques, religious trusts, and so on. As chairman of this council, Hajj Amin had control of a suitable instrument for building up his power. One of the first major projects was the restoration of the two mosques on the Haram al-sharif site. In 1923–24 Hajj Amin organized fund-raising among Muslims abroad to finance the project. This gave him the opportunity to make contact with Muslims in other countries, and to make Muslims aware of Jerusalem and Palestine.

In the 1920s the struggle against Zionism was mainly conducted by organizations such as the Muslim-Christian Association and the Arab Executive Committee. In some cases, however, they engaged in fierce rivalry with the Muslim Council under Hajj Amin's control. This was not an issue of the nationalist movement's religious orientation but primarily a question of securing various Palestinian families' claims to power.

The incidents at the Wailing Wall in 1928–29 boosted the importance of the Islamic aspect of the Palestinian nationalist movement to some extent. The dispute itself was extremely old and fairly typical of the different religious communities in Jerusalem. Like many other sacred sites, the Wailing Wall was claimed by groups from two different faiths. It was part of both the Muslim Haram al-sharif and the last remains of the Jewish Temple. Both religious communities tried to consolidate their respective claims and were joined in the attempt by increasing numbers of nationalistically minded politicians and their clientele. The subsequent unrest led to fierce riots in August 1929, leaving many dead on both sides. The politicization of religious conflicts had enabled the Palestinian national movement to mobilize broad sections of the population for its cause, while the Zionists gained sympathy abroad, even from Jews who were confirmed non-Zionists.

There are various different verdicts on the role of the mufti in the riots. What is clear is that he won decisive influence in the nationalist movement but simultaneously lost the cooperation and support of the British.[4] A prime example of the new relationship between Islam and the nationalist movement, and of the mufti's enlarged role, is his fatwa that prohibited the sale of land to Jews and threatened to excommunicate anyone contravening the ban.[5]

The mufti's efforts to compensate for the loss of British support and to mobilize the Muslim world for the struggle for Palestine culminated in the Islamic Congress he convened in Jerusalem in 1931. Palestine was the main topic of the resolutions passed by the congress, which condemned Jewish immigration and Jews' gaining possession of land. There were proposals for a boycott of Jewish goods, the establishment of a Muslim university (as a counterpart to the Hebrew University, founded in 1925), and an endowment fund for purchase of land.

The congress finally enabled the mufti to focus the eyes of the Muslim world on Palestine. His personal popularity and prestige increased as well. The specifically nationalist struggle of the Palestinians had received support from the Muslim religious community. The Zionists had already partly succeeded in forging this link between a secular nationalist movement and a religious community with the reorganization of the World Zionist Organization and the Jewish Agency in 1929.

While Hajj Amin al-Husayni succeeded in making use of organizations and institutions to support the Palestine nationalist movement, no concrete political successes could be notched up for the movement's goals. The mufti increasingly lost control of the ensuing radicalization of different social and political groupings. One religious group led by Shaykh 'Izz al-Din al-Qassam interpreted the struggle against Zionism and the British as a holy war, a jihad, which had to be launched immediately. In 1935 British troops liquidated the shaykh and his entourage before open rebellion could break out.

The shaykh's death (hailed as martyrdom) became the symbol of the resistance and certainly accelerated the outbreak of the major Arab revolt of 1936. With the collapse of this revolt, the old Palestinian leadership lost both the initiative and its cohesion. From the 1940s the neighboring Arab countries increasingly took responsibility for upholding Palestinian interests. It is hardly surprising that the specifically Islamic participation in the 1948 war to prevent the establishment of a Jewish state came from outside. Egypt's Muslim Brotherhood had inscribed in its program the liberation of Palestine from infidel rule. By 1946 the Muslim Brotherhood had set up branches in Jerusalem, Nablus, Tulkarem, Haifa, and Jaffa. In 1948 it dispatched volunteers to fight in the conflict in Palestine.

The division of Palestine between Egypt, Jordan, and the newly founded State of Israel simultaneously meant the complete dissolution of the Palestine nationalist movement. In this period there is no evidence of any particular political or cultural development of Islam among the Palestinians.

The Muslim Brotherhood remained active in the Gaza Strip until 1954, when it was suppressed in Egypt by Gamal Abdel Nasser (Jamal 'Abd al-Nasir). Arab protest in Israel was expressed mainly in the form of membership in the Communist Party. The Muslim Brotherhood organized groups in the West Bank, especially in Hebron and other cities. The Jordanian government licensed them as registered associations in 1953. They were careful to avoid political activity, and generally adopted a pro-Hashemite position. This, along with their suppression in Egypt and Syria, weakened their position in the West Bank. Another Islamic group, Hizb al-tahrir al-islami, was founded in 1951 by the Palestinian Ahmad Taqi al-Din al-Nabhani. It was immediately banned on account of its revolutionary program (armed overthrow of the existing government), and could only operate underground.

A general observation on the period 1948–1967 is that political conflicts in the Arab world mainly employed the terminology of secular ideologies, particularly nationalism and socialism. Islamic political approaches found little support and were rigorously suppressed by the majority of regimes. The conflict over Palestine was sustained by a pan-Arabic ideology and manipulated by the organizations and alliances based on it, such as the Arab League and the United Arab Republic (UAR), among others. It was not until the mid-1960s that the first signs of a specific Palestinian nationalism became identifiable again. There was no recognizable Islamic tendency devoted specifically to Palestine.

The 1967 war created a fundamentally new political situation. Since then, every part of the former Mandate territory of Palestine has been under Israeli rule. After the Arab defeat in 1967, pan-Arabism, which had been questionable since the disintegration of the UAR in 1961, completely lost its validity as an approach to solving the Palestine conflict. Other contributions in the present volume describe the thrust of tendencies toward Islamization in the social and political field since the 1960s. In the case of the Palestinians, this can be observed only later, and to only a limited extent.[6] The difference can be explained by the rise of the Palestine Liberation Organization (PLO), with its quest for a specifically Palestinian nationalist solution.[7] The PLO succeeded in staking its claim as the overall legitimate representative of Palestinian interests.

The development of Islamist tendencies among the Palestinians should therefore be seen partly as a process of demarcation from, and rivalry with, what were by far the most important political groups—the secular Palestinian nationalist groupings of the PLO. In considering the role of Islam in Palestinian society, we should also bear in mind that political and historical conditions in the three regions—the Gaza Strip, Israel, and the West Bank—demonstrate significant differences. This has led to highly differentiated developments and tendencies among the activists of political Islam.

The first Islamic reaction to the Israeli occupation of the Gaza Strip and the West Bank in 1967 came not from the existing Islamic organizations there but from a newcomer. In July 1967 the Islamic Council was set up in Jerusalem "to guide Islamic affairs in the West Bank and Jerusalem until the end of the occupation."[8] The East Jerusalem elite were represented on the council, and Jordan gave it official support. The council represented the interests of the Haram al-sharif district in Jerusalem together with other sites of religious importance, and shielded religious trusts from Israel's grasp, as well as dealing with taxation matters, application of Israeli law, and the like. From the end of the 1970s the council also increasingly tried to take on responsibility for Islamic affairs in Israel. As the official representative of Islamic interests, the council obtained enormous financial support from Saudi Arabia and political recognition from the PLO. For a long period it confined itself exclusively to Islamic religious affairs without giving them a specifically Palestinian coloration. But it remained the only political power center in the West Bank until the PLO developed its own infrastructure there at the end of the 1970s. After that the Islamic Council took on a more Palestinian orientation.[9]

Studies on the topic of Islamic activism agree that nothing of note occurred until the end of the 1970s. The Muslim Brotherhood and the Hizb al-tahrir al-islami were not involved in attacks on the occupying power, which consequently tolerated them. Subsequent conflicts with nationalist and Marxist groups made Islamic circles almost attractive to the occupying power. It was the nationalist and Marxist groupings that originated the accusations—which have never been conclusively proved—that Israel protected these circles for a long while and supported them financially.[10] At the same time, the Islamist groups implemented a program of Islamization of society that resulted in the spread of Islamic symbols, terms, and arguments and created a more positive atmosphere for political programs formulated in Islamic terminology.

Among the various reasons adduced for the visible growth in Islamic activity from the late 1970s on, the lack of political success of the nationalist program and the phenomenon of the Iranian Revolution are seen as the most important factors. Alongside these, the Palestinian author E. F. Sahliyeh mentions the parallel development of growing Islamist tendencies on the one hand and the rise of Likud, with its religiously tinted arguments for the incorporation of the occupied territories, on the other. He also refers to the 1982 Lebanon war, during which the Phalangist massacres in Sabra and Shatila— tolerated by the Israelis—roused the impression of a "Jewish-Christian conspiracy against Islam."[11] Ultimately, these groups were able to flourish better than the nationalist organizations because the occupying forces hesitated to attack religious sites such as mosques, or to take direct control of them.[12]

Inspired by developments in Egypt, radical groups such as al-Takfir wa-l-hijra or al-Taliʿa al-islamiyya were established in the Gaza Strip. They and other radical groupings concluded that the reconstitution of an Islamic society could be achieved only by liberating Palestine through violence. In this they were influenced by the Islamic Revolution in Iran and the activities of Hizbullah (Hizb Allah) in Lebanon. At the same time, the PLO, which had moved toward a political compromise in the 1980s, was sharply criticized. Only the Fatah (al-Fath) organization succeeded in drawing some of the groups into its own sphere of activity: the Islamic Vanguard; the Islamic Jihad, which had close relations with the PLO in terms of ideology and personnel;[13] and the Islamic Fatah, which was directly organized by Fatah.[14]

The militant groups also distinguished themselves clearly from the Muslim Brotherhood, which they criticized as too passive. Shaykh Ahmad Yasin took over the organization of the Muslim Brotherhood in the Gaza Strip and built up a network of schools and welfare organizations. The Islamic Center, al-Mujammaʿ al-islami, was set up in 1973. It was soon officially recognized by the occupying authority and became the center for the Muslim Brotherhood in Gaza. Whereas Ahmad Yasin enjoyed maximum independence in the Gaza Strip, the Muslim Brotherhood in the West Bank was directed and largely financed by the Jordan branch. The goal of the Muslim Brotherhood was to transform Palestinian society into an Islamic society through education. The idea was that only then could the long-term goal, the liberation of Palestine, be achieved. This strategy relieved the Muslim Brotherhood of the obligation to engage in concrete political action or struggle. At the same time, it could attack nationalist or Marxist ideologies for their lack of success. The Muslim Brotherhood clearly dissociated itself from the PLO and offered itself as the alternative, "the only real solution."[15]

The signing of the peace treaty between Egypt and Israel, on top of the continuing occupation of the West Bank and Gaza Strip, worsening economic and social conditions, especially in the Gaza Strip, and—probably the most important factor—the success of the Islamic Revolution in Iran led to the emergence of increasingly radical and militant Islamic groups calling for armed struggle. One example is the Jihad group, founded in Gaza in 1980 by Ahmad al-Shiqaqi. Following the model of Shaykh 'Izz al-Din al-Qassam, Sayyid Qutb, and Ayatollah Khomeini, it was one of the first groups to endorse suicide bombings.[16]

Before the outbreak of the first intifada at the end of 1987, the PLO and the secular nationalist liberation struggle had the greatest support and membership in the occupied territories. The Islamists presented a serious challenge to the PLO and its power. The Muslim Brotherhood advocated a long-term strategy for re-Islamizing society. At the same time, this made it vulnerable to the accusation that its attitude toward the occupying power was too passive and cooperative. This was precisely the criticism of the militant Islamic groups, whose activism originally brought them closer to the PLO. Nevertheless, the PLO's increasing openness to political compromise created tension here.

The Muslim Brotherhood and other groups that had previously confined themselves to educational work and cultural and social activity realized very quickly that in the new situation of revolt they either had to participate actively or run the risk of being marginalized. The Muslim Brotherhood already showed signs of recognizing this before the intifada but failed to act on it even after the revolt broke out. The rivalry among militant Islamist groups, the Muslim Brotherhood, and nationalistic elements, particularly in the Gaza Strip, intensified during the spring of 1987.[17] Shaykh Yasin was forced to yield to the pressure of the younger and more radical elements in the Gaza Strip. Renaming his organization Hamas was probably an attempt to dissociate himself from the Muslim Brotherhood, which was reluctant to identify with the new radicalization up to the point of armed struggle, in case it failed.[18] A leaflet from the Islamic Resistance Movement (Hamas) was distributed for the first time in March 1987, followed by a second leaflet in November. After the outbreak of the intifada, Hamas proclaimed itself in further leaflets "the strong hand of the Muslim Brotherhood."[19] Yet Hamas was not willing to agree to armed struggle against Israel until early 1988. The Muslim Brotherhood and Hamas were now prepared to add an activist, specifically Palestinian dimension to the general Islamic context. As the Islamic alternative, they became the main rival of the nationalist groups. But there were distinct regional differences: in the Gaza Strip the militant initiative originated from Hamas, whereas in the West Bank the Muslim Brotherhood was still unable to free itself completely from its organizational center in Jordan.[20]

A charter published by Hamas on August 18, 1988, clearly reflected the turn from a general Islamist solution to a specific Islamic-Palestinian context. It defined itself as a "specifically Palestinian movement," fighting "to hoist the banner of God over every foot of Palestine" (§ 6).[21] At the same time it is also a global movement, to the extent that it supports Muslims all around the world. Hamas developed out of the group led by 'Izz al-Din al-Qassam and the Muslim Brotherhood but sees itself as just one of several groups in the holy war against Zionism (§ 7).

Hamas's relationship to the PLO is complex but is described in detail in the charter: "Our father, our brother, our friend are in the PLO. Would a Muslim turn away from his mother, his brother, his relative or friend? We have the same fatherland[,] ... we have a common enemy" (§ 27). According to Hamas, the PLO has turned toward secularism only under the confusing influence of intellectual imperialism, western oriental studies, and missionary work. Hamas, however, cannot renounce the Islamic character of Palestine: "But on the day the PLO adopts Islam as its existential form, we [Hamas] will become its soldiers." Meanwhile the relationship is to remain like that of family members (§ 27).

The movement emphasizes its patriotism (*wataniyya*), which it regards as part of its faith. According to its program, beyond all human and material ties, Islamic patriotism has a view of the divine, which is actually what lends patriotism its spirit and life in the first place (§ 12).

To prove its credentials as an explicitly Palestinian Islamic movement, Hamas had to come to grips with the problem of a specific territoriality, which in fact has no place in Islam as a religion. Palestine is thus regarded as an Islamic *waqf,* that is, a land belonging to a pious foundation. Surrendering even a foot of it would therefore mean betraying the religion (§ §11, 13)—a clear warning to the PLO not to engage in any kind of political compromise.

The successful combination of nationalism and Islam gives Hamas's program great legitimacy, but precisely because this has been elevated to a metaphysical level—like all fundamentalist programs—its ability to compromise is reduced. Hamas's followers, however, scorn the stubborn insistence on doctrine at the expense of real, potential political gains just as much as they condemn opportunistic adaptation to every political change. In this respect Hamas has demonstrated very successfully how it can negotiate the fine line between metahistorical doctrine and rhetoric, on the one hand, and concrete, politically rational action on the other.[22]

It would be hard to overlook the parallels in terminology between radical Islamic and Israeli religious nationalist groups; they even emerged at around the same time. In both cases it is a question of the territory as a whole (in Hebrew, Yisrael ha-Shlema), and issues are discussed in terms of the religious importance of the country, the Islamic *waqf* (a religious foundation), or Eretz ha-Kodesh, the Holy Land. In both cases Jerusalem is invested with extreme religious significance.

The various manifestations of Arab nationalism differentiated carefully between Zionism and Judaism. Whereas Zionism was seen as something to be fought as part of European imperialism, there was explicit reference to the historically harmonious relationship between Muslim society and the Jewish minority. The relationship to non-Muslim monotheistic minorities, which was legally guaranteed by Islam, was used precisely as an argument against Zionism and the necessity for a Jewish state.

In this respect the Islamists' position differs clearly from that of the nationalists. The Islamists blur the difference between Zionists and Jews and focus much more on the latter, demonstrating the Jews' fundamental hostility to Islam with Qur'anic quotes. In the Islamists' view, the situation is as follows. The Jews control the destiny of the world through control of the media, by means of their wealth, and with the help of their secret organizations such as the Freemasons, the Rotarians, and the Lions Club, in order to achieve their Zionist goals. The Jews were behind the French Revolution, created Bolshevism, fanned the flames of the First and Second World Wars, and controlled the governments of imperialist powers (§ §17, 22, 28). It comes as no surprise that the "Protocols of the Elders of Zion" is cited as evidence for these claims (§ 32). According to the Islamists, Islam is challenging a worldwide Jewish conspiracy and fighting a global war between good and evil, truth and falsehood (§ 33). The struggle for Palestine is the decisive battle in this war, and the liberation of Palestine is therefore the primary task.[23]

The occupation of the Gaza Strip and the West Bank has made the borders between these territories more porous. Islamist tendencies originating in the occupied territories have become identifiable in Israel as well. The first organization that saw itself as a pan-Palestinian instrument was the Islamic Council. The initial step in this direction was financial support for Muslim institutions, buildings, and so on in Israel in the 1970s. Beginning in 1978 the council enabled Israeli Arab citizens to join the pilgrimage to Mecca. In October 1986 Israeli Arabs took part for the first time in a protest demonstration in Jerusalem initiated by the council.[24]

In the municipal elections in Israel in February 1989, Hamas and the Islamist groups close to the Muslim Brotherhood registered notable successes. These were greater, however, in the region known as the "triangle"—the area settled by Arabs west of the Green Line and north of Petah Tikva—than in Galilee. The successes were preceded by years of activity in the social sphere of local government. As with the Muslim Brotherhood in Egypt in the 1930s, this won them a political following among the population. Despite the successes, the Islamist movement in Israel was very different from similar groups in the occupied territories.[25]

The very fact of participation in elections signified acceptance of the existing political system and willingness to play a part in it. Armed struggle was not an issue. In its political goals the Islamist movement in Israel followed the ideas of the PLO much more closely. An Islamic state postulated by Hamas was not regarded here as a possible alternative to the national state. The movement engaged in grass-roots work to gain the widest possible support. Unlike in the occupied territories, its power base was not among students or intellectuals. This probably also explains why the movement neglected ideological articulation and deliberatively avoided taking a specific position. Its program of action was almost exclusively based on social and community work, and its ideological discourse was imprecise and limited to the general Islamic level. Among Arabs, its electoral successes were regarded less as an "Islamic threat" to the Israeli state than as a defeat for the old Communist Party. It remained to be seen how far the Islamic movement could convert its actual participation in local politics and government administration into its own political successes.

Hamas gained legitimacy with its uncompromising armed struggle against the Israeli occupying forces during the intifada and advanced to become the second-largest Palestinian organization after Fatah. Hamas's first reaction to the PLO's willingness to negotiate was the attempt to establish a "rejection front" with Syria's blessing. This "alliance of Palestinian forces" was intended to unify the Marxist groupings, the Popular Front for the Liberation of Palestine (PFLP) and the Democratic People's Liberation Front (DFLP), and the Islamist groups Jihad and Hamas. Hamas insisted on continuing the armed struggle and rejected any form of negotiation. But it failed to develop this alliance into an effective political instrument and programmatic alternative. Events during the Gulf War (1990–91) showed how precarious Hamas's position could be. While most Palestinians sympathized with Iraq, Hamas had to consider the position of its most important donor, Kuwait.[26] The banning of 415 Hamas members by the Israeli military authorities in December 1992 gave Hamas renewed legitimacy but weakened it organizationally.

After the Gulf War the PLO realized that it had lost almost all its support in the Arab world and that the cold war was finally over. It was forced to engage in serious proposals for negotiations with Israel. The Madrid Peace Conference in the fall of 1991 brought Israel and the Palestinians directly and officially to the negotiating table for the first time.

By 1993 the first arguments were already being aired in Hamas for acceptance of partial sovereignty in Gaza and the West Bank, but without renouncing armed struggle.[27] It was clear, at the latest by the Oslo Agreement between the PLO and Israel in September 1993, that once the parties to the conflict had embarked on the road to negotiations, this would remain the decisive political course despite all setbacks, and would eventually lead to Palestinian autonomy in the occupied territories. On the one hand, this insight strengthened extremist reaction on both sides, leading, for example, to the massacre of Palestinians by an Israeli settler in a mosque in Hebron, and repeated bomb attacks by Islamist death squads in Israel. On the other hand, Hamas was faced with the question whether it would marginalize itself by its complete refusal to compromise.

The establishment in 1994 of the Palestinian Authority for autonomy in Gaza and Jericho meant that persisting with armed struggle—at least from the standpoint of the PLO—could only endanger the new institutions of autonomy and would increasingly become a direct challenge to the authority of PLO chairman Yasir 'Arafat. The Palestinian Authority carried out mass arrests of Islamists. This situation led particularly to the younger generation, which had grown up during the intifada, moving away from rigid ideological models because they were afraid that excluding themselves from the political process could result in losing the strength they had won by armed struggle. In fact, Hamas's popularity declined at this time from 30 percent to 15 percent. During the summer of 1995 Hamas cautiously edged toward a redefinition of its own role.[28]

It began to see itself as a "loyal opposition" to the Palestinian National Authority, renounced armed struggle in September 1995, and founded its own political party, the Islamic Salvation Party, in December of that year. This programmatic change was accompanied by a fierce argument inside Hamas between members in Jordan and Lebanon on the one hand and those in the occupied territories on the other. Young pragmatists, especially in the Gaza Strip, could certainly envision the ultimate cessation of armed struggle—on condition that Israel withdraw to the 1967 borders. But the exiles did not want to accept giving up the greater part of Palestine. This revealed a conflict that had occurred once before during the first intifada between the PLO in exile in Tunisia and its followers in the West Bank and Gaza. After the Palestinian Authority had become an established political factor, the pragmatists gained influence and were able to win out with their policies.

Although Hamas and Jihad rejected the Authority and did not want to submit to the PLO, at the same time they did not want to start an internecine war among the Palestinians, nor did they wish to be marginalized. In October 1995 Fathi Shiqaqi, the leader of Jihad, was murdered in Malta, and in January 1996 an important member of Hamas, Yahya 'Ayyashi, known as "the Engineer," was also murdered. Both liquidations were attributed to the Israeli secret service—probably not without reason. Hamas counterattacked with suicide bombings that claimed fifty-six victims. But this did not yet signal the ultimate return to armed struggle. In 1996 the election of Benjamin Netanyahu as prime minister, whose victory was obviously influenced by the Palestinian attacks, and the blockade he imposed on any further implementation of the Oslo Treaty, led to renewed deliberations on armed struggle.

In April 2000, after the election of Ehud Barak as Israeli prime minister, Hamas proposed a limited treaty with Israel on the basis of a future Israeli withdrawal to the 1967 borders. For the first time, the Islamic Salvation Party, Hamas's political wing, sent delegates to the Palestinian Central Council. From the outbreak of the second intifada, and under the impact of the Israeli army's provocative and brutal methods, Hamas apparently returned to its original position, that is, the determination to wage armed struggle until "the destruction of Israel." It is important to note that Hamas has always been careful to remain within a minimal Palestinian consensus. All its programmatic political formulations—concerning armed resistance, the establishment of a political party, and so on—have been directly related to its interpretation of the Palestinian situation and not to abstract slogans about the essence of Islam.

This thesis seems to have been confirmed by events since the death of Arafat on November 11, 2004. Earlier, in the spring of 2004, two Hamas leaders, Ahmad Yasin and Abdel Aziz Rantisi, were killed within a short time of each other by targeted Israeli rocket attacks. A year later, when interim Palestinian leader Mahmoud Abbas (Mahmud 'Abbas) indicated that he was prepared to negotiate with the Israelis and announced regular elections for the Palestinian parliament, Hamas was also prepared to agree to a cease-fire with the Israelis; it was negotiated by Abbas in March 2005. Hamas participated in the local council elections in May 2005 and won a majority in twenty-four of the eighty-four local councils, while Fatah won fifty-two. In December 2005 Hamas won an overwhelming victory in the West Bank municipal elections, and in January 2006 it gained 76 of the 132 seats in the Palestinian parliament. The European Union and the United States refused to continue funding the Palestinian Authority as long as Hamas refused to recognize the peace agreements with Israel. An uneasy standoff developed between Hamas and Fatah when the latter refused to join a coalition government with the former, which would have given Hamas legitimacy. The tension between the rival groups increased, especially in the Gaza Strip, from which Israel had withdrawn in August 2005. (In 2009 Netanyahu and his more hard-line Likud Party returned to power in Israel.)

Repeated mutual attacks, kidnappings, and exchange of fire finally led to open confrontation and Hamas's takeover of power in Gaza in May 2007. With Hamas now claiming to constitute the legal government of both Gaza and the West Bank, and the Fatah movement under Abbas denying the legitimacy of this claim and retaining control of the West Bank, the rivalry between the two movements acquired an additional territorial dimension, and the question of the legality of any government remained in limbo.

Apparently Israeli military operations in the Gaza strip in January 2009 have not resulted in any softening of Hamas's attitude toward Israel and the Palestinian authority.

Translated by Karen Margolis

18. Syria

(Andreas Christmann)

a. Official Law and Shari'a

According to the constitution in force since 1973, Syria is a secular state. Article 1.1 of the constitution makes it clear that the Syrian Arab Republic is a "socialist and popular democratic state." Although it also says that "Islam must be the religion of the president" (Art. 3.1), Islam is cited neither as the state's official religion nor as the sole basis of state legislation. And even though Islamic jurisprudence (*al-fiqh al-islami*) is mentioned as "a source of law" (Art. 3.2), there is no reference at all to the shari'a, the divine law of Islam. Whereas the constitutions of 1950, 1953, and 1962 had still guaranteed both "protection of the freedom of religion" and "personal status law as prescribed by the religious communities" (Art. 3.3, 3.4), the constitution of 1973 no longer held any such provision. The main reason for this omission lies in the fact that the Arab nationalist ideology of the Ba'th Party, in power since 1963, which promotes the ideal of a national unity of all Arab people irrespective of religious creed, does not allow a privileged position for Islam or the shari'a. Hence legal practice in Syria is regulated by the General Legal Code (*qanun al-sulta al-qada'iyya*), introduced in 1965, which places most areas of state jurisdiction under (originally) European civil law (*al-qanun al-madani*). The only exceptions are the areas of personal status, family, and *waqf* law, which are, in spite of having no firm constitutional support, still governed by shari'a law.

Syria's Code of Personal Status (*qanun al-ahwal al-shakhsiyya*) groups the Syrian population (of approximately 17 million, according to a 2003 UN estimate) into three religious sects (*tawa'if*): (1) Muslims, (2) Druze, and (3) Christians and Jews. This corresponds demographically with the general composition of Syria's population. Sunni and Shi'a Muslims together account for about 82 percent of the total population, including the 'Alawi, Twelver, and Sevener Shi'ite Muslims. The Druze number only about 3 percent, and Jews less than 1 percent, while Christians (subdivided into eleven churches) make up around 14 percent.[1] What is surprising about legal practices in present-day Syria is that despite the official division into three different sects, Islamic personal status law applies indiscriminately to *all* Syrians (e.g., in cases of inheritance and questions of legal guardianship). The three religious communities exercise their own jurisdiction only in matters of family law (marriage, divorce, dowry, adoption, custody of children, and so on). It was for this area of law that shari'a courts were set up for Muslims, *madhhab* courts for the Druze, and *ruhi* courts for Christians and Jews.[2] In questions of personal status law, all Syrians are hence regarded as Muslims, whereas in family law they are treated according to their actual religious affiliation. The impression the constitution gives that Islamic jurisprudence is only "a" source of law is therefore somewhat misleading, because it does not apply to Syrian civil law, in which Islamic law plays no role at all, or to personal status law, where it is actually the sole source of legislation.

This rather ambiguous legal practice reveals the underlying tension between the official secular state doctrines on the one hand and, on the other, the social practices of the Syrian Muslim population, in which Islamic legal and moral norms still dominate. Since the establishment of Ba'th rule, two factors have therefore determined the development of Syria's legal system: first, increasingly tight state control over Islamic jurisprudence, and second, the establishment of a central system of administration for the regulation of religious *waqf* property, which historically has always been the financial backbone of Muslim governance.

b. The Ifta' System and Awqaf Administration

The process of centralising the *ifta'* system and *awqaf* administration began during the nineteenth century under Ottoman rule. The Tanzimat reforms resulted in the establishment of a central *awqaf* office in Istanbul (1840), which came in 1875 under the control of the finance ministry. From 1921 the Ottoman *awqaf* authority was de facto replaced by the Contrôle Général des Waqfs Musulmans, a legal authority established by the French Mandate government, which was based in Beirut. In 1930 an independent *awqaf* office for Syria was set up in Damascus, enabling better coordination of state measures to gain access to Syria's *waqf* estates. After the Second Word War, many trusts were brought under the treasury's fiscal laws, making them liable to state taxation from 1947 on. After independence in 1947, the governments of Shukri al-Quwatli (1947–1949) and Husni al-Za'im (April–August 1949) brought the entire *awqaf* and *ifta'* system under state control. By a directive of Adib al-Shishakli (whose government served from 1949–1954), the office of the mufti and the *awqaf* authority were even briefly assigned to the Ministry of Justice, but were later brought under the supervision of the Council of Ministers. In 1961, after the end of the union with Egypt (1958–1961), the Syrian government, headed by General 'Abd al-Karim al-Nahlawi, passed legislative orders 204 and 185, which created the basis for the future *awqaf* ministry. By law, this national ministry was now responsible for all activities resulting from the administration of endowed property (mosque buildings, charity donations, the running of welfare organizations, and the like). A similar bureaucratic apparatus was set up for the *ifta'* administration (responsible for the training of imams and preachers, the running of Qur'an schools, and the supervision of the office of Syria's muftis), for which a separate department was erected within the *awqaf* ministry. Right from the beginning these measures were introduced with the aim of gradually disempowering the old Sunni elite and also neutralizing the potentially disruptive force of sectarian animosities.

The Baʿth regime (from 1963) kept most of the administrative structures that its predecessors had introduced, but it appointed new personnel to key posts and put the entire administration under direct control of the party and its security services. The *Awqaf* High Council (*majlis al-awqaf al-aʿla*), which had been set up with considerable powers as the ministry's supervisory body, was put under the direct control of the Presidential Council in 1965 and, thus, de facto disempowered. The *Iftaʾ* High Council (*majlis al-iftaʾ al-aʿla*), the supervisory body for the mufti's office, suffered a similar fate: in 1971 its jurisdictional authority was transferred to the newly inaugurated *awqaf* minister. In 1964 Ahmad Kuftaro (Ahmad Muhammad Amin Kaftaru, 1915–2004) was controversially elected Syria's grand mufti. Kuftaro, the rulers' favored candidate, was elected in spite of the fact that he lacked the broad support of the Sunni establishment (which had backed Shaykh Muhammad Hasan Habannakah), a scandal unprecedented in Syria's political and religious history. Kuftaro's "appointment" as a member of parliament in 1971 further discredited the authority of the grand mufti and earned Kuftaro the reputation of being a puppet in the hands of Syria's authorities. The phase of nationalizing *waqf* property in the 1990s can be seen as the final step of the state's centralization efforts. *Waqf* property, which was then still in private hands, was either radically expropriated or transferred, by state decree, from shariʿa law to civil law, which made the property easy prey for the insatiable needs of the finance ministry.

In sum, Syria's legal system has seen over the last two hundred years a dramatic change of administrative structures; most decisively it oversaw the loss of *waqf* property and the administrative centralization of religious affairs. A brief outline of Baʿth religious politics is necessary to explain the place of Islam and the role of Islamic institutions in Syria.

c. The Place of Islam in Baʿth Ideology and Policy

Baʿth policy toward Islam has developed in several stages. The first—from the Baʿth takeover in 1963 until 1970—showed the efforts of the new regime to lay the legal foundations for a tighter grip on all issues related to religion. The overall aim was thereby to break the power of the Sunni middle class in the urban centers of the country, and at the same time to reduce the political influence of the Muslim Brotherhood, which was extremely popular in the 1960s. After the military coup in 1963, all independent newspapers were banned, repressive press censorship was introduced, and a general state of emergency was proclaimed (which is still in force today). The nationalization of *waqf* property, which had already started under previous governments, was utilized to the full as a convenient tool to undermine the economic autonomy of religious schools and charitable organizations. The forced replacement of teaching staff at the shariʿa faculty at Damascus University and Kuftaro's controversial election as grand mufti predictably led to a serious loss of moral credibility and political influence of these institutions.

But this did not occur without enormous resistance from the Islamic opposition, as it became evident in the numerous riots and revolts in this period: in Hama in 1964, in Damascus and Aleppo in 1965, and all over the country in 1967. A second, more moderate phase was introduced by an internal changeover of power in 1970 and the inauguration of President Hafiz al-Asad (1970–2000); this phase ended, however, in 1976 owing to the sudden turn to violence of the Syrian Muslim Brothers and the political instabilities caused by Asad's pro-Shi'ite policies in Lebanon. The third stage, between 1976 and 1984, was marked by the Islamists' militant attacks against government institutions and the brutal reprisals by state authorities and the security forces. The massacre of civilians by the Syrian army in 1982 in Hama, then a bastion of Islamist resistance, and the subsequent repression of any form of public display of Islamic religiosity (headscarves, long beards, public Qur'an recitations, and so on) marked the culmination of this violent stage and ended (if, perhaps, only temporarily) with a victory of the Ba'th regime.[3] Finally, from the mid-1980s, and more forcefully after the collapse of the Soviet Union in 1991, a process of re-Islamization began that has lasted up to the present. This renaissance of Islamic religiosity involved the building of new mosques and Qur'an schools; a public display of religious symbols; the population's turn to Islamic rituals, dress codes, and ways of speaking; and a completely new approach in the mass media, where religious programs were again broadcast. In line with this tendency, two amnesties (1995 and 2002) were issued to facilitate the rehabilitation of former members of the Muslim Brotherhood (which had been banned since 1980), allowing some of those who had been pardoned to take up their work again.

Two things can be discerned from this development. First, right from the start the most sensitive issue involving the religious policies of Syria's rulers was the problem of legitimizing minority rule (first that of the Ba'th Party, and after 1970 that of the 'Alawi elite as well) vis-à-vis a Sunni majority, in particular in Syria's urban areas. And second, beginning around the mid-1980s a shift in power strategy could be observed, from open confrontation with any Islamic opposition (including physical elimination, torture, and deportation of the Syrian Muslim Brothers) to a policy of controlled co-optation of Islam into public life and official discourse.[4] In order to achieve such a transition, however, it was necessary that state authorities carefully select politically suitable interpretations of Islam, for which the concept of an "official Islam" (*al-islam al-rasmi*) was absolutely vital.

d. Official "State Islam"

Ba'th ideology is secular and socialist—and yet it is neither antireligious nor anti-Islamic. It interprets religion, however, and in particular Islam, as primarily one portion of a much broader moral and cultural heritage of the Arab people. Michel 'Aflaq, the founder of the Ba'th Party, regarded Islam as primarily a vehicle for the intellectual and moral revival (*al-ba'th*) of

Arabism. The Prophet Muhammad was in this respect only the "embodiment of the true and noble Arab spirit."[5] Such interpretation, of course, reduces the divine aspects of Islam to a cultural and ethical dimension of Arabism. On the one hand, it denies the metaphysical roots of shari'a religiosity as it also ignores the ideal of an Islamic state. On the other hand, it also provides the possibility of harmonizing Islam with secular ideologies, so much so that public discourse can be Islamized without seriously contradicting the ideological parameters of Ba'th rule. The precondition, however, has always been that it must not threaten the "national consensus" about the marginalized status of Islamic law (limited to the realms of personal status, family, and *waqf* law), leaving the more sensitive areas of politics and Syria's economy entirely untouched.

The grand mufti of Syria, Ahmad Kuftaro, was crucial in achieving such harmony.[6] Under his leadership the Naqshbandiyya-Khalidiyya-Kuftariyya order became one of the largest Islamic movements in Syria, with networks throughout the Middle East. Founded in 1972, Kuftaro's Abu Nur Center (Majma' Abi al-Nur al-Islami), with branches in almost all the large cities in Syria, is regarded as one of the country's most active and influential Sunni orders. The Islam taught there is a slightly modified version of the official Islamic teachings that the *awqaf* ministry prescribes. It focuses on themes such as interreligious tolerance, harmony between faith and rationality, and the unity of Syria's Arab-Islamic *umma*. It certainly answers to the description of it by critics of the regime as politically opportunistic and conformist. Indeed most of Kuftaro's teachings are formulated so as always to accord with the dominant Ba'th state doctrines. In turn, the Kuftariyya enjoys many privileges (in the form of financial support and media concessions) that are otherwise a national rarity. It comes, therefore, as no surprise that the movement begun by Kuftaro is constantly growing, while membership in the traditionally established but largely quietist Sufi orders in Syria has been either stagnating (Shadhiliyya, Qadiriyya) or perilously declining (Mawlawiyya, Rifa'iyya). The Kuftaro movement has also benefited from the general trend toward Islamization noted earlier. The secular background of many "reborn" Muslims is relatively easy to reconcile with Kuftaro's ethically defined and politically tolerant Islamic teachings. Moreover, criticism of the government and the immense corruption in the state and party apparatus can be aired with impunity under the roof of the Abu Nur complex. Many Syrians have expressed their anger and frustration with the social and political stagnation by a decisive turn toward Islam, a quietist rebellion that the Kuftariyya is ideally suited to absorb. The expansion of Kuftaro's headquarters in Damascus in 1994 (which was actually state-funded), and the permission to establish a private Islamic university, headed by Shaykh Muhammad 'Abd al-Latif al-Farfur (b. 1945), shows that the government has clearly recognized the stabilizing effect of Islamic institutions that can channel government-friendly interpretations of Islam and harness dissent if frustrations come dangerously close to boiling over.

This policy of Islamic appeasement could not, however, prevent the establishment of a kind of "alternative or informal Islam" that develops independently from the officially propagated norms of religiosity. To date this has been articulated either in informal shari'a student circles attached to the publicly less visible Ma'had institutes, or as the "personal opinion" of so-called dissident *'ulama'*. Even though no direct criticism of leading national figures and state institutions can be heard, it is known that these circles discuss legal issues of trade law, taxation law, and even Islam's penal code which are elsewhere taboo topics. By skillfully circumventing prescribed norms in the interpretation and application of Islam, these groups manage to circulate Wahhabi polemics against Sufism, Sunni criticism of the Shi'ite faith, and independent definitions of jihad that are unheard of in Syria's "official Islam." It is of course difficult to establish how far this kind of alternative Islam has spread, but frequent arrests, long prison sentences, and even deportation of Islamic scholars who dared to criticize the regime indicate that the official top-down version of a "state Islam" is not capable of exercising sufficient control over public opinion.[7]

e. Liberal Islam of Muslim Intellectuals

Since the early 1990s, disturbing news from countries such as Algeria, Sudan, and Afghanistan (where a similar Islamic revival led either to civil war or to fundamentalist terror) activated a liberal response from the so-called Islamic Left, through which Muslim intellectuals raised a substantial critique of the Islamist movement. In 1990 the Sunni Muhammad Shahrur, a professor of civil engineering at Damascus University, published *The Book and the Qur'an: A Contemporary Reading,* in which he condemned the prevalent Qur'an interpretations as hopelessly out of date and highly unsuitable for advancing a modern understanding of Islam.[8] Shahrur's book became the subject of a debate that lasted more than ten years. In this debate the positions of liberal Islam were vehemently rejected as a potential threat to Muslim orthodoxy, and yet the controversy forced the Sunni religious establishment to distance itself from the extreme views of radical Islam. In the mid-1990s the journalist and freelance writer Nabil Fayyad published several books and articles in which he accused Syria's religious scholars of indirectly advancing the cause of Islamic fundamentalism by adhering to the same inflexible conceptions of Islamic law that the Islamists support. A number of replies followed, most prominently by Muhammad Sa'id Ramadan al-Buti, Syria's leading legal expert on Shafi'i law, in which the distance between militant, obscurantist Islam and a too literal interpretation of Islamic law was once again emphasized. Then in 1998 a controversy between the philosophy professor Tayyib Tizini and Shaykh al-Buti was published as a book and caused equally intense debate in the public media. It struck everyone as quite daring how openly Tizini attacked the dogmatic nature of the Islamic discourse and how directly he demanded from scholars such as al-Buti a decisive turn toward a more pluralistic understanding of the Qur'an, a more flexible interpretation of Islamic law, and the long-overdue acceptance of historical criticism in the study of Islam's sacred texts. Challenged in this way, al-Buti felt again the need to accentuate his critical and flexible methods of Qur'anic exegesis as well as the moderate and accommodating methods of Islamic jurisprudence. It was one of the major achievements of liberal Muslims in Syria that they were able to push mainstream conservative Muslim scholars such as al-Buti into issuing such a public denial of any involvement with the religious Right.

The death of Hafiz al-Asad in June 2000 did not result in a radical end of corruption and the long-overdue reform of state bureaucracy. The transition of power from father to son (Bashar al-Asad, b. 1965) instead guaranteed a smooth continuation of old and trusted models of domestic and religious policies. Official statements made it clear that, in the face of fears of a "second Algeria" and of too much popularity for the Muslim Brotherhood, gradual change was preferred over sudden disruptions whose outcomes were unpredictable and whose ramifications were uncontrollable. The short-lived "Damascus Spring" (between August 2000 and February 2001), when religious and secular intellectuals campaigned for reforms of the state and for a stronger civil society in Syria, proved to be a flash in the pan, with little or no effect on either the wider society or the status of public Islam.[9]

Translated by Karen Margolis

19. Iraq

(Henner Fürtig)

The territory of Iraq is one of the oldest and most important traditional centers of the two main branches of Islam. Baghdad was the capital of the Sunni 'Abbasid caliphate. Southern Iraq includes one of the regions where Shi'a originated and is the location of its most important shrines, the graves of 'Ali and Husayn in Najaf and Karbala, respectively, as well as those of four other imams in Samarra and Kazimiya.[1] For centuries Iraq belonged to the Sunnite-dominated Ottoman Empire, mostly on its neglected periphery. The Iraqi pilgrimage cities continued to be centers of religious life for the Shi'ites. By the nineteenth century, however, the tribes that had settled in the south of Iraq had increasingly converted to the Shi'ite tradition, partly as a way of expressing their opposition to the domineering attitude of the "Sublime Porte," the Ottoman government. Given the traditional rivalry between the Ottomans and the neighboring Shi'ite Persians, the Iraqi Shi'ites were often seen as a fifth column and largely excluded from senior positions in the Ottoman civil and military services.[2] Nevertheless, in the First

World War the Shi'ites only partially confirmed Ottoman prejudices. In 1915 and 1916 Shi'ite rebels staged anti-Ottoman riots, mainly in Najaf and Karbala. But they were of no benefit to the Persians (who were also victims of the war); nor did the rebels ally with the British expeditionary force. On the contrary, the majority of the Shi'ite clergy called for resistance against the "infidel invaders."[3] Their anti-British impulse lasted beyond the end of the First World War and the Ottoman Empire. In 1919 the renowned Ayatollah Muhammad Taqi al-Shirazi declared in a fatwa that "only Muslims have the right to rule over Muslims."[4] He was undoubtedly warning against indications that Ottoman domination of Iraq was being replaced by that of the British.

a. Islam as a Factor in the Birth of Modern Iraq

Anticipation became certainty in San Remo on April 20, 1920, when Great Britain received the League of Nations mandate over the state of Iraq, which had been created from the Ottoman provinces of Mossul, Baghdad, and Basra. The Sunnite and Shi'ite inhabitants of the mandate area were united in their rejection of foreign rule. Between July and November 1920 Muslims of both confessions rose up against the British occupying power. Nearly ten thousand rebels lost their lives in bloody battles, along with four hundred British soldiers. Defeating the rebellion cost London £40 million,[5] and the experience led the British government to opt for indirect rule over Iraq from then on. Britain's new strategy was personified by its ally from the First World War, Faysal Ibn Husain, a (Sunnite) Hashemite still in exile in Italy. On August 27, 1921, he ascended to the throne of the kingdom of Iraq, which had been established especially for him. In fact this British "trick" has determined the mutual relations of the different confessions and ethnic groups in Iraq right up to the present day.

There had been extremely little political, social, and economic solidarity or exchange between the provinces of Mossul, Baghdad, and Basra until they were unified in San Remo. The three provinces had all been oriented toward Istanbul rather than toward one another. Consequently, apart from British pressure, the new state of Iraq initially lacked any kind of major indigenous binding factor. The extremely heterogeneous nature of confessional and ethnic affiliations intensified the country's fragility. In 1932, the year of Iraq's formal independence, the population consisted of a Shi'i Arab majority (54 percent) and a Sunni Arab minority (21 percent), along with Sunni Kurds (14 percent), non-Muslim Arabs (5 percent), and other religious and linguistic groups (6 percent) comprising Sunni Turcomen, Syriac Christians, and others.[6] The British, pursuing their proven policy of divide and rule, pinned their hopes on the weaker faction, that is, the Sunnites. As the majority of Sunni Kurds were hoping for the independence promised in the Treaty of Sèvres and showed little affinity with Iraq, the Sunni Arabs remained the pillars of indirect British rule. Sunnite tribal leaders and urban notables had an interest in perpetuating British domination, yet at the same time their actual status as a minority left them (and above all the foreign king) dependent on British protection. As a result, for a long period the majority of the population—that is, the Shi'ites, especially as they were largely excluded from senior positions in the state and the military—viewed the Iraqi patriotism propagated by the royal court and the rapidly changing governments as a thin veneer over Sunni Arab ambitions for supremacy.[7] As most of the independence struggle took place under the banner of nationalist slogans, however, the confessional aspects of politics remained a background issue until the overthrow of the monarchy in 1958.

b. Political Islam under the Primacy of Nationalism

Given the experiences of 1920, senior Shi'ite clergy in particular abstained from making political statements. As opportunities within state education increased in a national climate of change, the attractions of religious education declined. Between 1918 and 1958 the number of students in Najaf fell from six thousand to two thousand.[8] Confessional and ethnic ties remained strong, but their effects were increasingly overlaid by the social and ideological positions of individuals and groups. Radical opponents of the regime, whether Kurds, Sunni, or Shi'i Arabs, expressed their attitudes by joining nationalist and/or left-wing parties. The proportional relations in the population were reflected in the membership of the different parties. Shi'ites formed the majority of members and leaders in both the Ba'th Party, which was active in Iraq from 1950, and the Iraqi Communist Party (IKP), founded in 1934. The head of the IKP, Husayn al-Radi, was a *sayyid* and the son of a Shi'ite law scholar from Najaf.[9]

Many Shi'ite clergymen saw the drifting away of considerable portions of their following as an elementary challenge. In 1958 the law scholar Muhammad Baqir al-Sadr founded Call to Islam (*al-da'wa al-islamiyya,* the Da'wa Party) as the Shi'ite political party. His two major works, *Falsafatuna* (Our Philosophy, 1959), and *Iqtisaduna* (Our Economy, 1961), gave the party's activities a theoretical basis aimed at establishing an Islamic state. The most famous Shi'ite clergyman of the time, Grand Ayatollah Muhsin al-Hakim, supported the party's goals, at least indirectly, without deviating from quietist principles. In a fatwa in 1960 he forbade believers to join the IKP and simultaneously urged them to support the Da'wa Party.[10] But in light of the political situation, the party went underground immediately after its establishment. It was joined in the mid-1960s by the Islamic Action Organization (Munazzamat al-'amal al-islami), founded in Karbala by the ayatollahs Hasan al-Shirazi and Muhammad al-Mudarrisi.[11]

The Sunnites were also troubled by secular and nationalist tendencies in the 1950s. In 1951 the Muslim Brotherhood (MB) was formally established in Iraq. The MB shared the Shi'ite clergy's rejection of communism and nationalism. In 1959 the head of the MB, Muhammad Mahmud al-Sawwaf, and Grand Ayatollah Muhsin al-Hakim agreed to offer their followers the possibility of mutual membership in the MB and the Da'wa Party.[12] In 1960 the MB was renamed the Iraqi Islamic Party (IIP). Like all Islamist parties, it was exposed to the scorn and persecution of the ruling Ba'th Party after 1968.[13]

The Ba'th Party's pan-Arab nationalism earned it the enmity of non-Arab Kurds and Islamists of all shades. But the persecution by the Ba'th primarily affected the Shi'ites. This may have been partly due to the fact that the Ba'th Party developed by degrees from a "Shi'ite" into a "Sunnite" party in the course of its transition from opposition to governing party. At the time of the first Ba'th coup in 1963, 54 percent of its leading members were Shi'ites; this figure fell to 6 percent between 1963 and 1968.[14] The new positioning of fronts led the Kurds to step up their struggle for self-determination while the Shi'ites became increasingly politicized. After Grand Ayatollah Muhsin al-Hakim died in 1970, his successor, Abu l-Qasim al-Khu'i, continued the quietist tradition. Islamist activism grew considerably, however, led by the al-Hakim faction in Najaf, the al-Sadr faction in Kufa and Baghdad, and the al-Mudarrisi faction in Karbala. In December 1974 and again in February 1977 there were spontaneous Shi'ite riots, connected both times with the celebration of the 'Ashura' festival. The riots were brutally suppressed.

c. Saddam Hussein's Dictatorship: The Carrot and the Stick

Some months before Saddam Hussein seized power in Baghdad in July 1979, the Islamic Revolution had triumphed in Iran, the neighboring Shi'ite state. It hardly needed encouragement from Tehran to motivate the Shi'ite opposition in Iraq to step up their activities vigorously. By the summer of 1980 there had been numerous attacks on symbols and persons associated with the hated Ba'th regime. After a failed assassination attempt on the foreign minister, Tariq 'Aziz, on April 1, 1980, Saddam Hussein's security machine launched heavy reprisals. Hundreds of Shi'ite activists were murdered, including the Da'wa Party founder, Muhammad Baqir al-Sadr, who was killed on April 13, 1980. Tens of thousands of Shi'ites "of Iranian origin" and Shi'i Kurds (so-called Faili Kurds) were deported. The punitive operation culminated in the attack on Iran on September 22, 1980, which Saddam Hussein declared to be a "preventive war."[15] In 1982 a third organization emerged in Iranian exile, the Supreme Council of the Islamic Revolution in Iraq (SCIRI). Conceived as an umbrella organization during the eight-year Iran-Iraq War, it actually developed into a power base for the al-Hakim family, in just the same way that the Da'wa Party had always been seen as the party of the al-Sadrs and the 'Amal organization as the caucus of the al-Mudarrisis.

While the majority of the Shi'ite service ranks in the army emerged as committed Iraqi patriots during the war, many (Sunni) Kurds allied with the Iranian opponents.[16] Toward the end of the war the Ba'th regime mounted a particularly cruel campaign of reprisals against the Kurds (Operation Anfal, which left tens of thousands of Kurds dead or missing). The Kurds' attempt to rid themselves of their torturer, the Ba'th Party, after its defeat in the Gulf War ended in a fiasco in March 1991—partly because of confusing promises of assistance from the U.S. government. The Shi'ite revolt in southern Iraq that same month met a similar fate. The slogan written on the Republican Guard's tanks, "As of today there will be no more Shi'ites" (*la shi'a ba'd al-yaum*), was practically a statement of intent.[17] Between thirty thousand and sixty thousand Shi'ites, including religious leaders, were murdered. Grand Ayatollah al-Khu'i was put under house arrest, where he remained until his death in 1992.[18]

After the stick, Saddam Hussein decided it was time for the carrot. In the summer of 1993 he initiated a "National Campaign for Faith" aimed at using Sunni Islam to legitimate his regime. By 1997 a theological university (Saddam University) and hundreds of mosques had been opened, along with other teaching institutions.[19] According to official statistics, 5 million pupils were studying in them.[20] The government printed the requisite number of copies of the Qur'an and set up a broadcast station, "Holy Qur'an Radio," in September 1997. Meanwhile, state television relayed (Sunnite) Friday sermons. The pledge of allegiance to the Islamic faith was integrated into the Iraqi national flag in 1994, twelve clergyman were admitted to parliament, and some legal norms grounded in secularization that deviated too far from shari'a were withdrawn.[21]

Backed by these measures, Saddam Hussein went on unyieldingly to attack the Shi'ites again. By systematically draining the marshlands in southern Iraq, he deprived thousands of Shi'ites of the basis of their existence. Their religious leaders were persecuted the moment they spoke out or took political action. In February 1999 in Najaf the secret service murdered the Da'wa leader Ayatollah Muhammad Sadiq al-Sadr, the cousin and successor of Muhammad Baqir al-Sadr, as well as two of the ayatollah's sons. Another of his sons, Muqtada, survived by going underground. By the time Saddam Hussein was overthrown in April 2003, he had almost completely eliminated Islam as a political force in Iraq. Even the religious aspects of Islam were very tightly restricted. The number of Shi'ite clergy fell to just three hundred (for 15 million worshippers). Their de facto leader, Grand Ayatollah 'Ali al-Sistani, refrained from any kind of political statement (like his deceased mentor, al-Khu'i), but was nonetheless banned from preaching. The authority of 'Abd al-Karim al-Mudarris, the *qadi* of Baghdad and nominally the most senior Sunnite religious leader, was limited to ceremonial questions such as fixing the starting and finishing date of the month of fasting.[22]

d. New Constellations after the Fall of the Ba'th Regime

The violent overthrow of Saddam Hussein and the *Ba'th* regime, which was engineered from abroad, meant a new beginning for Iraq and had effects similar to those that occurred when the state was founded in 1920. To demonstrate radical change, the new occupying power (the Coalition Provisional Authority, CPA) no longer backed the Sunni Arabs as a confessionial force, but both structurally and institutionally its plan for political reconstruction of the country followed a strict pattern of ethnic and religious divisions. Political life became increasingly dominated by confessional and ethnic distinctions, which gave renewed impetus (albeit unintended) to a potential new ethnic or confessional dictatorship or civil war rather than encouraging other possibilities such as the projected program for democracy. Given this background, in each of the possible models for a new order the Kurds were primarily interested in retaining at least the level of self-determination they had achieved under the conditions of the UN sanctions in force since 1991; the Sunni Arabs, for their part, did everything to avoid the decline from ruling minority to a minority subject to discrimination, while the Shi'ite Arabs finally wanted to make political capital out of their numerical superiority.

The Shi'ite Arabs, the majority of the population, hardly needed the legally prescribed proportional representation for religious groups to experience the new situation as a collective liberation. Only days after the fall of the regime, millions of them celebrated during the Arba'in festival. It was evident, however, that their newfound self-awareness as Shi'ites did not yet imply any kind of political statement. Politically, socially, and economically, Iraq's 15 million Shi'ites are extraordinarily heterogeneous. The then interim prime minister, 'Iyad 'Allawi, was just as much a Shi'ite as Hamid Majid Musa, the head of the Communist Party, and Tawfiq al-Yasiri, the leader of the multiconfessional Iraqi Patriotic Alliance, or Ghalib al-Rikabi, the spokesman for the Association of Shi'ite Tribal Leaders (formed on July 8, 2003), or 'Abd al-Karim Mahmud al-Muhammadawi, the leader of the self-defense group of marshlands inhabitants founded in 1991 and known as the Iraqi Hizbullah.[23] According to estimates, only around a third of the Shi'ites have primarily religious motives for their attitudes and actions.[24] Despite this, the religious teaching institutions in Karbala, and especially in Najaf (*hawza 'ilmiyya*), and the clergy that represented them, became very important politically after 2003. Grand Ayatollah 'Ali al-Sistani, operating in Najaf as *primus inter pares,* became the most important spokesman of "authentic Iraq" in dealings with the CPA and its head from May 2003 to June 2004, Paul Bremer. This can be explained not only by the proven integrity and impartiality of Sistani and other clergymen under the dictatorship but also by the fact that secular politicians were often referred to as quislings and—last but not least—by the CPA-initiated policy of promoting confessionalism.

After the official restoration of Iraqi sovereignty in June 2004, Sistani's role progressively declined because the formation of different camps undermined his pan-nationalist ambitions. The Shi'ite camp was now focused mainly on the naked ambition of the Mahdi Army and its leader, Muqtada al-Sadr. Muqtada's considerable prestige derived less from theological merit

than from the fact that he was the foremost surviving member of the famous al-Sadrs. But Sistani's relative loss of importance did not correspond
in any way to a decline in the importance of religion as a factor in political
and social life as a whole. Quite the opposite: Sunnites and Shi'ites, Kurds
and Arabs, as well as countless smaller ethnic and religious groups rarely
referred to programs or ideas to articulate, negotiate, or mutually situate
their interests. Instead they were almost exclusively occupied with religion
and family background. This inevitably created enormous tension in the
political situation because attacking or objecting to personal viewpoints was
nearly always interpreted as an attack on the religion involved. Things de-
generated as far as the ominous custom of specifically attacking opponents'
religious symbols and ceremonies. In the seemingly endless series of bloody
assaults, the attack on the Shi'ite holy mosque of Samarra on February 22,
2006, and the massacre of forty-four members of the Yezidi community
on August 14, 2007, stand out. The destruction of the Samarra mosque
brought Iraq to the brink of open civil war; the Yezidi victims demonstrated
how heterogeneous the confessional conflict had become. The struggle between the remaining occupation troops—who stayed in the country at the
request of the Iraqi government—and the militant underground influenced
by the activities of the terrorist group al-Qa'ida in Mesopotamia, was reflected abroad in particular. Ultimately it determined only part of the spectrum of conflict, especially because the transnational terrorists around Abu
Mus'ab al-Zarqawi and his successors intervened on the Sunnite side in the
confessional conflicts.

Under these conditions, the elections to the provisional national assembly
held on January 30, 2005, again showed quite clearly how the process of
political reconstruction was being influenced by the emphasis on confessional and ethnic issues. The great majority of Sunni Arabs obeyed their
religious leaders' calls to boycott the elections and did not vote. Among
the other losers in the election were the secularly oriented Arab parties.
The United Iraqi Alliance (UIA), the so-called Shi'ite slate, won the election
with 140 of the 275 seats. While this made them the undisputed victors,
they lacked the necessary two-thirds majority, for which they needed the
75 Kurdish votes. As the Kurds held the balance, they emerged as the real
winners of the election.

This balance of power also defined the work of the constitutional commission, which was given until the end of 2005 to create the legal preconditions for elections to a permanent assembly. There were vehement clashes
of interest between the different religious and ethnic groups over the crucial
questions about the future form of the state (political monopoly status for religion or a secular republic), and the state structure (federal versus centralized
state), and the related distribution of power. The Kurds and Shi'ites managed
to get their way on major questions, but to rescue the constitution as a document for the whole nation, they had to co-opt the Sunni Arabs and concede
substantial rights to them. The constitution was approved in a referendum

on October 15, 2005, with 78.59 percent voting yes. The relatively high level of acceptance had evidently been purchased by formulating the key provisions very vaguely and by making broad concessions to the Sunnites.

Articles 1–4 of the constitution described Iraq as multinational, multi-confessional, and multicultural. It belongs, the constitution specified, to the Muslim world, and its Arab inhabitants are part of the Arab nation. The constitution defined the form of state as republican, federal, democratic, and pluralist—although these adjectives were not explained in detail. It guaranteed religious freedom and freedom in religious practice. Islam was specified as the state religion and one of the main sources of the law, but not the only one. The constitution left open the question who should exercise authority and in what capacity and how the courts should be constituted. The two official languages, Kurdish and Arabic, received equal status. The federal state of the Republic of Iraq was said to be composed of a capital city, regions, decentralized provinces, and local bodies. Kurdistan was recognized as an autonomous region.[25]

Part of the agreement with the Sunnites was that the constitution would remain provisional for an indefinite period and that after the elections on December 15, 2005, parliament would set up a revisions commission for the constitution, which would make amendment proposals within a time limit of four months after the date of the formation of the government (May 21, 2006). This simply postponed dealing with the facts and circumstances of persistent controversies. Nevertheless, the creation of the legal preconditions for holding the December 2005 elections could be counted as a minimal level of success. For the first time, the goal was not the formation of a provisional body but the establishment of a regular parliament.

As anticipated, the UIA confirmed its position as the favorite in the second parliamentary elections as well, winning 128 seats; but this time the party failed to gain a majority. Even for that, it again needed the cooperation of the Kurds, who won fifty-three seats. For a two-thirds majority the UIA actually needed third-party votes. The election results did not engender a more stable situation. It took until May 21, 2006, for the formation of a government under Nuri al-Maliki, a Shi'ite, and even longer—until June 8, 2006—to fill the key ministerial posts of defense, home affairs, and national security.[26] The instability was due not least to the unfinished constitutional debate and the continuing violence in Iraq, which claimed 34,000 civilian victims in 2006. According to United Nations statistics, an additional 36,000 persons were wounded. The violence reached a climax in the months of November and December 2006, with 6,367 dead and 6,875 injured.[27]

Elected delegates and the government reacted with growing helplessness. The constitution remained incomplete, and important legal projects were postponed or watered down. A good example is the federalism law passed in October 2006, designed to create "super provinces" that would be largely autonomous. Sunnite politicians saw this as a threat to Iraqi unity and managed to defer the law for eight months.[28] A similar fate befell the law on the distribution of income from oil exports presented to parliament on February 26, 2007. The draft envisaged distribution to the provinces according to their respective population size, in conjunction with the right of provincial authorities to make their own agreements with international oil firms. This draft was also rejected because of vehement protests by Sunnite members of parliament.

On August 1, 2007, this rejectionist attitude also hit the government: all the Sunnite ministers resigned after accusing the Shi'ites of using their majority for their own ends and neglecting the security of their Sunnite fellow citizens. At the end of August 2007, in an attempt to head off the threat of a renewed state crisis, a supraconfessional and multiethnic commission led by the president of the state, Jalal Talabani, offered the prospect of largely reversing the de-Ba'thification of April 2003.[29] The process of political reconstruction remained stagnant and the situation uncertain, even as coalition forces began their scheduled withdrawal from Iraqi territory.

Translated by Karen Margolis

20. Jordan

(Renate Dieterich)

a. Religion

Islam is constitutionally established as the state religion in Jordan. The great majority of Jordan's population are Sunni Muslims, with Christians numbering less than 3 percent of the country's inhabitants.[1] Jordanian society is rather traditional; firmly based on tribal relations, it professes a conservative, but not fundamentalist, conception of Islam. Jordan's large Palestinian population, which is less tightly bound by tribal ties, is no exception.

The religious coexistence of the Muslim Arab majority and the Christian minority is marked by tolerance. The Christians occupy a stable position in the country and are entitled to minority quota seats in parliament. The same applies to the ethnic minority groups, the Circassians and Chechnyans (around 0.5 percent combined). They are groups of Sunni Muslims settled by the Ottoman sultan in the territory of present-day Jordan in the late nineteenth and early twentieth centuries. To date there is hardly any legal discrimination against the minorities, and no sign of interreligious tensions.

b. The Religious Legitimation of Hashemite Rule

The territory of present-day Jordan, which belonged to the Ottoman Empire until its collapse, was relatively sparsely populated for a long period and had no notable economic or political significance. No centers of Islamic scholarship emerged to create a religious tradition that the Transjordanian nation-state could have built on. Instead, from the time the emirate was established in 1921, new central state institutions were created and have assumed control of religious practice. As in other Arab countries, the Jordanian state tried to win over the population to its version of Islam and to prohibit the emergence of an independent form of political Islam that could enter into opposition with the governing system.

The status of Islam in Jordan is determined in a special way by the religious legitimation of the Hashemites. The royal family traces its descent back to the tribe of Banu Hashim, and thus to the family of the Prophet Muhammad. For centuries the Hashemites were guardians of the holy sites in Mecca and Medina, up until 1925, the date of the expulsion of 'Abdallah, the father of the first Transjordanian emir. The Jordanian monarchs have always harked back to their descent from the Prophet's family, and have used this to underpin their legitimacy to govern. This religious bond has considerably enhanced their prestige among the local population. In 1949 Jordan took control of Jerusalem by annexing the West Bank—an act not recognized by international law. While this reinforced the monarch's religious image, it also resulted in a variety of financial and administrative responsibilities. Even after the 1988 decision to disengage from the West Bank, Jordan has continued to acknowledge responsibility for the Islamic sites in Jerusalem.

King Hussein (Husayn), who ruled the country from 1953 until his death in 1999, invoked the Hashemite family's religious heritage and its consequent responsibility in various ways. He was skilled at making statements that continually appealed to the population's strong religious bonds, and at enforcing political concepts by invoking religious duties and commandments. It was only after the accession of the young King Abdullah ('Abdallah) II in 1999 that this constant recourse to the monarchy's religious roots gradually began to change. Abdullah (b. 1962) sees himself as an enlightened monarch with a Western outlook who wants to modernize his country and promote social and economic development. He faces considerable opposition from some traditional circles whose self-image is rooted in Islamic values, as well as from a cohort of technocratic Islamic politicians who vehemently demand participation in political decision making.

c. The Relationship among the State, Islamic Clergy, and Islamist Opposition

The ruling family, headed by the king, regards Islam as a part of the legitimation of its hegemony, and consequently has an interest in maintaining the prescribed Islamic order and observation of Islamic law. But it is not prepared to let Islamic legal scholars and theologians restrict its freedom to maneuver, so the regime keeps them under surveillance. The Ministry of

Religious Affairs is the key institution for supervising religious practice; it hires the imams in the mosques and keeps the content of sermons in check. The government pays the religious teachers and theologians, and finances the maintenance and repair of mosques and other Islamic buildings. A permit is required for Friday preachers to perform their offices. Undesirable preachers who criticize the royal family or make fundamental criticisms of the government are dismissed from their posts and even legally prosecuted on occasion if they argue in the mosques against basic precepts of the system.[2] Imams and other religious scholars are educated at state universities, where the curriculum is designed to suit the regime. As a result, the state-employed clergy, such as the Supreme Mufti of the country, conform to the system and—if necessary—even issue legal pronouncements (Arab. sing. *fatwa*) supporting the position of the government and royal family in critical situations.[3]

Nonetheless, Jordan, like other countries, has witnessed the emergence of an Islamic opposition that should not be underestimated, and that challenges the regime's exclusive power of decision making, not only in religious affairs but also on general political issues. The main forces in this opposition are, on the one hand, the Muslim Brotherhood and, on the other, the Salafiyya movement, which operates underground and has militant sections. Although both groupings call for an "Islamic state," they differ in the ways they actively pursue this goal and in their dealings with the government and royal family. The Muslim Brotherhood presents itself as much more pragmatic and moderate than the Salafiyya movement. Some sections of the Salafiyya are involved in militant operations, relying on a variety of transnational contacts.

The Muslim Brotherhood in Jordan was founded in 1945 with the explicit agreement of the emir, ʿAbdallah Ibn Husayn. It was particularly successful in the 1950s because, after the general ban on political parties, it was allowed to continue as a social welfare organization. The royal family gave the Muslim Brotherhood special support up until the 1980s as a counter to left-wing and nationalistic forces. The brotherhood responded with steadfast loyalty to the royal house. Relations between the Muslim Brotherhood and the regime first began to change gradually with the growth of revolutionary Islamic forces in the region. The brotherhood has a broad following owing to the long period of sponsorship by the royal family, as well as its commitment to welfare work; it has wide social influence in all strata of society and a strong presence in the education system. The Muslim Brotherhood has participated in most of the parliamentary elections since the restoration of democratic life in 1989 and even provided five ministers for a six-month period in 1991. The brotherhood attempted to use this brief phase to implement its concept of an Islamized society with the prohibition of alcohol and strict separation of the sexes in public. These plans contradicted the monarchy's efforts to project a modern, Westernized image; they never got beyond the early stages, and the Jordanian government barred the brotherhood from further government participation. In 1992 the Muslim Brotherhood founded its own party, the Islamic Action Front (IAF), to act as its political wing. While the movement gained a considerable number of seats in the parliamentary elections of 1989, 1993, and 2001, the elections in 2007 showed a sharp reduction in its influence.

Relations between the monarch and the Muslim Brotherhood have distinctly cooled since Jordan's peace treaty with Israel in 1994. For the Islamist movement, Jordan's agreement with its neighbor state not only is wrong as a political decision but also is a religious injustice, because the movement regards the entire territory of historical Palestine as eternal and inalienable Muslim property (*waqf*). The Muslim Brotherhood categorically rejects any attempt at normalizing relations with Israel, or even with individual Israeli citizens. Despite all its criticisms, however, it has remained within legal boundaries and refrained from participating in violent operations.

In contrast, the Salafiyya movement, which operates underground and faces heavy repression by the security forces, has not come to terms with prevailing relations and rejects the form of state in Jordan. A loose movement with a network structure, the Salafiyya regards the Hashemite monarchy and the democratic form of government as "un-Islamic" and illegitimate. As a result, the Salafiyya, unlike the Muslim Brotherhood, decisively rejects participation in the political process. In fact part of the Salafiyya has dedicated itself to armed struggle. It has grown considerably since the late 1980s, attracting militants who had been trained in anti-Soviet resistance camps and had fought in Afghanistan (*mujahidun*). After returning home to Jordan, they wanted to impose their fundamentalist interpretation of Islam by violence. A series of trials at the State Security Court beginning in the 1990s demonstrated the regime's determination to break this resistance, but it has not entirely succeeded. These militants have been joined by a younger generation who are committed to violent struggle against the Jordanian regime, and who received ideological and military training in Iraq.

d. The Status of Islamic Law

After the creation of the emirate of Transjordan, the Ottoman laws initially remained in force. They were first successively changed under the aegis of the British Mandate government. Large parts of the present-day legal system show notable European, especially British, influences. Islamic law—that is, law according to shari'a—is applied only in matters of personal law, and is still partly based on the Ottoman *mecelle;* but even in this area there have been a large number of changes. The family law of 1951 was rewritten in 1976 and carefully adapted to modern standards. The regulations on child custody, for example, stipulated that children should be allowed to stay with their mother until puberty—which goes significantly beyond the ruling of the Hanafite school of law followed in Jordan. In particular, elements of jurisprudence based on shari'a that discriminate against women in civil and penal law have come under fierce criticism in recent years. Women's rights supporters strongly advocate that women be granted their own independent right to divorce and the opportunity to pass on their (Jordanian) citizenship to their children. A very hotly debated topic is the considerable leniency of sentencing in cases of so-called "honor killings," murders of women who have contravened Jordan's strict moral codes and are held to have disgraced the "family honor." The murderers, usually male relatives of the victim, have received hardly any punishment. The Islamist movement, spearheaded by the Muslim Brotherhood, regards this kind of leniency as right and proper according to Islamic law, and claims that legal reform would pave the way for "moral decay" in the nation. The royal family, however, has strongly advocated a revision of the relevant laws.

Translated by Karen Margolis

21. Lebanon

(Axel Havemann)

We can discuss the status and importance of Islam in Lebanon only if we simultaneously consider the non-Islamic forces and recognize clearly that the two aspects cannot be mutually separated. No other country in the Middle East has been—and still is—comparably and as deeply affected by the coexistence of Muslims and non-Muslims; and nowhere else does development depend so much on the coexistence of different religious communities. I therefore refer here to the role of Christians whenever it seems relevant.

a. Population and Religious Communities

It is impossible to give exact statistics on the total population of Lebanon, and just as difficult to specify the size of the individual religious communities (*ta'ifa*, pl. *tawa'if*). The system of political and administrative confessionalism (*ta'ifiyya*) has been practiced since the mid-nineteenth century.[1] No census has been taken since 1932, to avoid demands to adapt the system to the numerical change in the proportion of Christian to Muslim communities. Factors such as differing birth and death rates within the communities, and the big increase in emigration since the beginning of the twentieth century, initially mostly among Lebanese Christians, have contributed significantly to the demographic shifts.[2] The main point of controversy which has blocked a new census has been the demand by the Christians, especially the Maronites, to include Lebanese citizens living abroad—a demand rejected by the country's Muslims. Some Muslims have gone so far as to stipulate that the Palestinians in Lebanon be included in a new census, and have also called for naturalization of Muslim Kurds and Bedouins living in the country. This explains why all the statistics on demographic development after 1932 are merely estimates, and sometimes vary greatly depending on their source.

The total population is probably around 4.35 million inhabitants, but there are also higher and lower estimates.[3] Figures on the size of the individual confessional groups should be treated even more cautiously. Lebanon has seventeen religious communities recognized by the state (eleven Christian, five Muslim or derived from Islam, and the small, dwindling Jewish community). The most important of the Christian groups are the Maronites, Greek Orthodox, and Greek Catholics; the most important Muslim groups are the Sunnites and Shi'ites, along with the Druzes, an esoteric sect. If we compare the results of the 1932 census with later registration data and estimates (1943, 1953, 1973, 1984, and 1988), the following picture emerges:

1. Before the civil war broke out in 1975, majorities appeared very narrow (1932: Christians 50 percent, Muslims 49 percent; 1973: Christians 49 percent, Muslims 51 percent); none of the Christian or Muslim groups had an absolute majority, and the larger in each case—whether Maronite or Shi'ite—accounted for less than a third of the total population.

2. During the civil war, the Christian-to-Muslim ratio reversed significantly in favor of the Muslims (1984: Christians 43 percent, Muslims 57 percent; 1988: Christians 40 percent, Muslims 60 percent, with the trend continually rising since then).

3. The Shi'ites have become the largest community (by 1988, if we assume a total of around 4 million inhabitants, there were already over 1.3 million Shi'ites, almost a third of the total population).[4]

While the individual figures should be treated with caution, it is possible to say generally that the size and significance of the most important religious communities has decisively changed. This definitely cannot be explained only in terms of the effects of the war; it actually goes further back to the different paths of development of the individual communities on the historical, political-ideological, social, cultural, and economic levels. This discussion focuses particularly on the Sunnites, Shi'ites, and Druzes.

b. The Sunnites

After the dissolution of the Ottoman Empire at the end of the First World War, Greater Lebanon was proclaimed in 1920 under the French Mandate. It was renamed the Lebanese Republic (al-Jumhuriyya al-lubnaniyya) in the 1926 constitution but remained under the French Mandate until independence in 1943. Up to that date the entire territory had been almost permanently under Muslim supremacy for nearly 1,300 years; during the final 400 years (from 1516 on) it was part of various provinces of the Ottoman

Empire. In other words, the region did not constitute an administrative entity. From 1861 on, however, there was a special district, Mount Lebanon (Jabal Lubnan, Mont Liban), confined to the central mountain region roughly between Tripoli in the north, Saida in the south, and Zahle in the east, but excluding the three port cities of Beirut, Saida, and Tripoli.[5]

Owing to natural factors (rugged mountainous country and geographic location) but partly also to the politics of the Muslim rulers, the territory attracted a wide variety of minorities—both Christian and heterodox Muslim—as a place where they could settle and hold their own politically in the context of limited autonomy. The main groups here were the Maronite Christians in the north and the Druzes in the south. But the question as to whether the Lebanese mountains can be described as a kind of "refuge" for victims of persecution is problematic and has been in dispute.[6]

What is clear is that the Sunni community—who belonged to the absolute majority of Muslims in the Ottoman Empire—lived not in the central mountain region but in the cities along the coast (and in parts of the far north). The Sunnites were the only group that backed the state, even in the areas inhabited by the minorities. The Ottoman rulers treated the minorities as not only religious but also "national" communities (Arab. *milla;* Turk. *millet*) that were allowed to regulate their own affairs of civil law as a matter of course; the various groups were awarded formal status at different times and were also legally recognized from then on.

The creation of Greater Lebanon in 1920 resulted in the Sunnites losing their function as the only ruling group in the state. After the coastal towns and the peripheral areas in the north, south, and east (especially the Biqaʿ Plateau) had been annexed to the core area of the Lebanese mountains, the Sunnites remained the second-largest community in the new state. But they were far from satisfied. In their view the loosening of ties with Syria and integration into the artificially created, French-dominated Maronite state meant permanent separation from the Muslim Arab world and the danger of being ruled by non-Muslims. The Shiʿites and Druzes felt similarly, though less strongly.

Whereas the Christian communities could rely on support from church institutions, the Sunnites first had to set up comparable authorities: in 1932 the office of mufti of the republic was established by law, with a Supreme Islamic Council of Law to back him up (al-Majlis al-sharʿi al-islami al-aʿla). For a long time the mufti was little more than the holder of an honorary title. It was not until 1955 that his main tasks were defined by law: he was the lifelong elected spiritual leader of the Sunnites and their state representative; he was the direct chief of the Sunnite religious functionaries; and he was responsible for supervising all religious issues such as endowments (*awqaf*), and for issuing expert legal opinions (*fatawa*).[7] The office of mufti became important politically during the time of Hasan Khalid, who held the post from 1968 until his assassination in 1989.[8] The mufti had wide authority, but this did not extend to the shariʿa courts. Their judges were appointed and controlled by the state, which angered the Sunnites. As in the case of the other religious communities, the judges' scope of jurisdiction was limited to personal law.[9]

The Muslims' fears of being forced to live in a Christian-dominated state were to be allayed primarily by continuing the system of confessionalism. Article 95 of the constitution specified that in the appointment of political and administrative officials, as "a provisional measure" adequate consideration should be given to the different religious communities (that is, according to their demographic size).[10] At first it seemed impossible to achieve any kind of national orientation; the various political ideologies relating to the identity and definition of Lebanon were too different.[11] But gradually even the Muslims, especially the large Sunnite bourgeoisie, were willing to accept the state; eventually they were prepared to work actively for its independence. When this was formally achieved in 1943, the country's leaders believed that they had found the recipe for harmonizing domestic and foreign policy or surmounting the divergent loyalties of the country's inhabitants. The protection of the Arab character of Lebanon as well as its openness toward the West was enshrined in an unwritten agreement between the Maronite president of the state and the Sunnite prime minister, known as the National Covenant (*al-mithaq al-watani*). There was also agreement on continued allegiance to the constitution, which included the principle of confessionalism.[12]

Both these programs turned out to have a boomerang effect. The principle of integrity and sovereignty in foreign policy was repeatedly shattered; and confessionalism—aside from the fact that it determined political power relations on the basis of unrealistic population figures—was largely responsible for hindering the country's inhabitants from developing any genuine national feeling of belonging.

In the long run, the results of independence in 1943 were unsatisfactory for the Sunnites—and not just for them. Although they had succeeded in securing the second most important office of state (that of prime minister) for their community, over time the Sunnites' equal status with all the other confessional groups and the limited room to maneuver in foreign policy (e.g., toward a clear-cut "Arab policy") meant that many Sunnites believed they could receive backing only within their own community. Added to this was a poorly developed political culture and other social, cultural, and economic disadvantages in relation to the Christians, as well as growing ideological radicalization.[13] After the collapse of Shihabism (the "reform period" under President Fu'ad Shihab from 1958 to 1964), and in view of the state's failure to function adequately in terms of public order and integration, many Sunnites had nowhere to turn for guidance except to their traditional leaders (*za'im*, pl. *zu'ama'*), who came from prominent families. The relationship between them was more like that of clients to their patrons than voters to party politicians.[14]

One example of this was the Maqasid Society in Beirut (Jam'iyyat al-maqasid al-khayriyya al-islamiyya fi Bayrut), the most important of several

Muslim associations that originated in the nineteenth century.[15] Founded in 1878 by Sunnite notables in Beirut, the Maqasid was a kind of welfare organization with its own cost-free schools, hospitals, and other charitable institutions. The society still plays an important role for the Sunnites in Lebanon as an expression of their own identity and ability to reach their goals. From the start, the direction and control of the Maqasid was in the hands of a few influential people, particularly from the Salam family. They frequently used the Maqasid to achieve their political ends and win the largest possible clientele.[16]

Despite the Sunnites' efforts to promote their role as a religious community, like the other groups they were repeatedly faced with the demand to dispense with confessionalism. But few Sunnites were prepared to support complete secularization, which was blocked by the resistance of religious dignitaries.[17] Agreement was finally reached on the formula of "political secularization," that is, abolition of proportional representation based solely on religion. This demonstrated clearly that the Muslims were mainly interested in redistributing powerful positions.[18] The New National Pact proposed in 1976 tried to accommodate to this by allocating parliamentary seats and top administrative posts between Christians and Muslims in a one-to-one ratio (instead of the previous six-to-five) and strengthening the position of the Sunnite prime minister.[19] But the plan failed; it was acceptable only to the traditional *zuʿama*'.

During the war, broad segments of the Muslim population (more Shiʿites than Sunnites, of course) increasingly dissociated themselves from the exclusive leadership of the *zuʿama*'. The major factor here was the rapidly worsening economic and political situation. Like other groups, the Sunnites sought new concepts and leadership groups. In the context of the civil war, this meant militias. But the only noteworthy Sunnite militia, the Murabitun, proved neither an adequate basis nor a substitute for the *zuʿama*'.[20] In 1985 it was destroyed by the Druzes and the Shiʿites, whose militias had already captured Sunnite West Beirut the previous year. Militant fundamentalist Sunnite groups (al-Jamaʿa al-islamiyya and Harakat al-tawhid, especially in Tripoli), attempted to restore the Sunnites' position in political and ideological terms but failed—not least because of tremendous competition from the Shiʿites.[21]

c. The Shiʿites

Unlike the Sunni Muslims, the Shiʿites—almost exclusively Twelver Shiʿites)—lived in rural areas to the south (Jabal ʿAmil) and east (Biqaʿ) of Mount Lebanon. The Shiʿites have always been (and still are) mainly peasant farmers in these regions, which are economically, culturally, and socially the most badly neglected areas of Lebanon. Moreover, after the outbreak of the war the south suffered particularly under the heavy political and military burden.[22] In recent decades these factors have led large numbers of inhabitants to flee the countryside and settle in the southern suburbs of Beirut, where large slum districts have grown up. Around 30 percent of the Shi'ites (or perhaps more) now live there.[23]

The Shi'ites were excluded from the country's overall progress for a long time. The great majority could survive only as debt-ridden tenant farmers or agricultural workers, dependent on a few big landowning families. No other part of the country had such a decrepit infrastructure, such a deficient health care and social services system, and such poorly developed educational facilities; the Shi'ite population had the highest illiteracy rate. It was almost impossible to develop any kind of social and political consciousness. The Shi'ites' ties to the *zu'ama'*, who simultaneously exercised political control as landowners, were more extensive than those of any other religious community. One instrument of this political patronage was the Shi'ite welfare organization 'Amiliyya (comparable to the Sunni Maqasid), whose leadership was in the hands of the Bayduns, a *za'im* family.[24] The first hesitant signs of change came in the reform period under President Shihab. The volatile demographic development, the opening of educational opportunities, and an increase in emigration abroad all contributed to the development of a new social stratum. These factors also required the Shi'ites to develop a greater degree of political consciousness and willingness to help shape the future in their own community.

At first the Shi'ites, like the Sunnites, resisted integration into the new state of Greater Lebanon; but they soon dropped their opposition when they realized that their status would be more secure as a large minority in Lebanon than a small minority in Sunnite-dominated Syria. Moreover, the Shi'ites had been officially recognized as a religious community of their own in 1926, which gave them the right to jurisdiction in personal law. But for a long period their legal autonomy remained very limited (e.g., in the appointment of judges, or the election of the Sunnite mufti of the republic, who was supposed to represent the Shi'ites as well). It was not until 1967 that the Shi'ites were legally granted the Supreme Islamic Shi'ite Council (al-Majlis al-islami al-shi'i al-a'la), which was constituted two years later. The council, the overall representative body for the Shi'ites, consists of a general assembly, a legal committee for shari'a judgments, and an executive committee for social, educational, and religious affairs. The executive committee automatically includes the Shi'ite parliamentary deputies as well as religious scholars. The council is headed by a chairman who is required to consult it on decision making. In this respect his authority seems more limited than that of the Sunnite mufti. The chairman, however, also presides over shari'a jurisdiction, whereas the mufti is not empowered to do this.[25]

The first elected chairman of the council was Musa al-Sadr, an Iranian religious scholar of Lebanese ancestry. He had been mufti of Tyre in Lebanon since 1959 and had tried explicitly to publicize the Shi'ites' desperate situation. Aside from his work on social reform, Musa al-Sadr held press conferences and lectures, and wrote essays on the Islamic image of man and on social teachings for the benefit of his religious community. He gradually distinguished himself as the representative of a new Lebanese Shi'a. By appearing as a social reformer, he found a natural ally in the Shi'ite bourgeoisie, and tried to keep the mass of his fellow believers away from ideologies he saw as extreme (such as pan-Arabism, Marxism, and communism). He pinned his main hopes on the Lebanese state.[26]

Musa al-Sadr used the chairmanship of the Shi'ite Council for political ends. Taking his cue from the council's declared goals, he repeatedly called for equal political, economic, and social opportunities for the Shi'ites, consolidation of national unity, cooperation with other religious communities, protection and defense of southern Lebanon against Israeli attacks, support for the Palestinians, and solidarity with the Arab states. In view of the specific political situation, he had considerable success with his appeals. Musa al-Sadr's relationship to the Shi'ite *zu'ama'*, which was extremely tense, especially in the case of Kamil al-As'ad, played a major role here; his political attitude contributed considerably to large segments of the Shi'ite population looking to throw off their underdog status, and they were attracted by his demands. This culminated in 1974 in Musa al-Sadr's founding the Movement of the Deprived (Harakat al-mahrumin), which mobilized the Shi'ite masses with language and symbols based on religion.[27]

In the summer of 1975 a militia emerged from this movement and started operating under the name Amal (Hope). Up until 1978—the year of Musa al-Sadr's disappearance during a trip to Libya under circumstances that remain unexplained—Amal presented itself more as reformist than as militant and revolutionary. Its statute (*mithaq harakat amal*) emphasizes the "great Lebanese heritage," national unity, social and economic justice as a state responsibility, and the nationalist, nonconfessional character of the movement; in other words, it is a profession of the national sovereignty and territorial integrity of Lebanon.[28] The program reflects Musa al-Sadr's convictions; he knew how to maneuver skillfully between the warring parties. He tried to encourage dialogue for the conservation of the nation with the other Lebanese communities, including Christian ones, and rejected "Arab" and "pan-Arab" ideas (particularly as propagated by the Sunnites and Druzes). He also rejected the demand for complete abolition of the confessional system and the establishment of a secular, laic order. His main concern was with improvements for the Shi'ites. This was also the motive of Amal's temporary alliance with the National Movement and the Palestinians.[29]

Influenced by subsequent events of the war, the Lebanese Shi'ites became more vocal in demanding radical change, especially after the Iranian Revolution of 1979. The then leader of Amal, Nabih Berri (Birri), was the son of Shi'ite emigrants to West Africa and did not represent either the *zu'ama'* or the clergy. On a number of occasions he felt impelled to declare sympathy for events in Iran in order to maintain his position against less moderate persons and forces within the Shi'a. Even so, in 1982 a group calling itself Islamic Amal split from the main movement. It was firmly based on Iranian Islamic concepts of religion, domination, and politics. Its leaders emphasized that sooner or later the Iranian Revolution would encompass Lebanon and transform it into an Islamic state; they firmly rejected the existing political system.[30]

Positions like this were propagated most fiercely by Hizbullah (Hizb Allah), the Party of God, a movement that provided cover for various militant organizations, while others claimed to operate in its name.[31] Hizbullah, Amal's major rival since 1982, has articulated the dissatisfaction of people no longer prepared to accept the politics of compromise. The movement's ideas are based directly on Ayatollah Khomeini's concepts, and can be gleaned from several works by its religious leaders, especially their main ideologist, Muhammad Husayn Fadlallah. Despite divergent views on points of detail, Hizbullah over many years advocated the establishment of an Islamic Republic of Lebanon based more or less on the Iranian model. A draft constitution for this was submitted.[32] An "Open Letter," a kind of party program published by Hizbullah in 1985, explicitly spoke of unconditionally following the "rightly guided imam" (i.e., Khomeini), instituting Islamic rule in Lebanon, and wiping out any opponents of these goals, both on the domestic front and abroad (particularly the United States and Israel).[33] In recent years, Hizbullah seems to have softened its position with regard to the establishment of an Islamic Republic in Lebanon. The fundamental ideological differences between Hizbullah and Amal, from which both derived their claim to sole supremacy, repeatedly led to fierce military clashes. As both sides were backed by Syria (often in collaboration with Iran), neither could gain the upper hand.

d. The Druzes

In the course of the Lebanon war—which was not caused primarily by religion—the conflicts developed ever sharper confessional contours from the 1980s on. The state had failed to show that its authority could supersede religious ties; the two major non-Lebanese actors, Syria and Iran, were also deeply marked by sectarianism. All the social and ethnic groups more or less withdrew to their religious communities, even those such as the Druzes, who had long advocated a secular order.

The Druzes, who emerged in the eleventh century from the Isma'ili Shi'a, practice a secret religion that developed far removed from Sunni and Shi'i Islam. For some decades the Druzes have produced intellectuals who have worked to open the community in terms of the principles of faith on the one hand and Druze allegiance to Islam and "Arabism" (*'uruba*) on the other. For political reasons the Druzes often regard themselves as Muslims, or are seen as such. Nonetheless, they hold strictly to the idea of not sacrificing the essential and special nature of their religious community for the sake of a greater unity.[34] The structure of the Druze community is marked by a tension between duality and unity that pervades its whole history. On the one hand, there are the religious, political, and socioeconomic dualities:

"the knowing men" (initiates) and "the ignorant men" (noninitiates) (Arab. *ʿuqqal* and *juhhal*); faction building (Jumblatiyya versus Yazbakiyya); the "landed aristocracy" (Arab. *muqataʿajiyya*) and the peasants. On the other hand, the Druzes live in a closed social and political environment and with a high degree of centralization based on a policy of shrewd alliances.[35]

The vast majority of Lebanese Druzes live in south-central Lebanon, mainly in the Shuf Mountains. They number around 10 percent of the total population. There are also much larger Druze communities in parts of Syria, as well as a group in Israel (the smallest numerically). Most of the Druzes in Lebanon are mountain farmers who lead a relatively modest and retiring life in villages, apart from a few who have achieved reputation and wealth during long periods abroad or through intellectual and political commitment in their home country.[36]

Up until the nineteenth century the Druzes, together with the Maronites, were the main actors in Lebanese history; they were jointly responsible for the autonomous Mount Lebanon region. Recognized de facto as a religious community on account of their historical importance, the Druzes—like the Shiʿites—were granted official status in the 1926 constitution. Laws of 1948, 1960, and 1962 regulated their personal law, their jurisdiction, and their communal institutions (particularly the election of the *shaykh al-ʿaql*, the Druzes' representative for state affairs).[37]

Despite this official recognition, during the French Mandate the Druzes lost the prominent role they had played from the sixteenth to the nineteenth century. In the enlarged territory of Lebanon they were relegated in size from their former second place to fifth place. But their great skill and flexibility in times of crisis enabled them to avoid the risk of political marginalization: the Jumblatiyya—the faction led by the old feudal Jumblat family—replaced their pro-British position with a pro-French one.[38] Yet this change of course proved of little help after independence in 1943, as politicians with more pro-British tendencies came to occupy leading state positions, and the National Pact confirmed the Sunnis as the second-strongest political group. By then the Druzes had been definitively edged out of their old position. This makes it all the more remarkable that the Druzes are still a political force to be reckoned with today. It is largely due to the fact that the community was led for over thirty years by Kamal Jumblat, one of the most interesting figures in recent Lebanese history.[39] Jumblat, who was politically active from independence onwards on many levels and in a wide variety of positions, combined two roles that were unusual under Lebanese conditions. On the one hand, he was a traditional leader (*zaʿim*) of his community (or at least of the Jumblatiyya faction), reinforced by his claim to be spiritual leader of the Druze; on the other, he was a Lebanese politician at the national level with a supraconfessional and secular program. He expressed his politics by his establishment of the Progressive Socialist Party, involvement in various opposition alliances—some outside Lebanon (such as the Nasserites, and later the Palestinians)—and his persistent, uncompromising demand for abolition of confessionalism and for establishment (or, in Jumblat's view, reestablishment) of a secular society in Lebanon. Jumblat was not just unusually active in day-to-day politics; he also developed a political and historical concept that he expounded in a large number of writings.[40] The most important aspects of this were the call to acknowledge Arabism and the Islamic Arab heritage as a unifying bond for all Lebanese; the presentation of the Druze community as a crucial factor for Lebanese unity and Arab independence; the importance of Druze religion and culture as a focal point of all religions; and, finally, a humane conception of an "Arab nationalism" that would foster harmony while preserving national sovereignty and the role of Lebanon as the avant-garde for other Arab states to follow.

Jumblat failed, both with his theories and with his practical politics, including the military option in 1975–76. He did not succeed in changing the country's political system and solving the "Lebanon crisis" by means of a secular order—which in his view had already proved its worth once in the "golden age" from the sixteenth to the nineteenth century. But he did succeed in gaining increased recognition for the Druzes as a political and military force within the existing confessional system.

After Kamal Jumblat's murder in 1977, his son Walid took over the leadership, and the Druzes again developed a degree of centralization and cohesion that helped them to win militarily. In 1983–84, for example, they drove the Christian militias out of the Shuf Mountains. With an astute policy of dependence on Syria as well as Israel, the old Druze principle of strategic alliances proved successful once again. After 1984 the Druzes settled into a "homogeneous corner" in the Shuf, the area they had mainly inhabited in the past, and took their first steps toward establishing their own local government administration, economy, and infrastructure.[41] Among the Druzes (as with other communities) this "retreat" fostered the increasing tendency to fall back on their own confession.

e. Future Prospects

In the fall of 1989 a majority of the surviving Lebanese deputies (a new parliament had not been elected since 1972) convened in the city of Ta'if, Saudi Arabia. They agreed on the text of a document of national accord.[42] The goal of this agreement, which was drawn up under pressure from the Arab League, was to initiate a process of pacification and reform in Lebanon.

The section in the accord on domestic policy represented something new in many respects. The National Pact of 1943 (i.e., the principle of confessionalism) was to hold for an indefinite period, but the formula that had been used for the distribution of power was changed. The parliamentary seats, previously allocated in a six-to-five ratio, were now shared equally between Christians and Muslims—a proposal that had been made previously in 1976. In addition, the number of seats was increased from 99 to 108.

The role of the Sunnite prime minister and the function of the Council of Ministers (cabinet) were strengthened considerably, and the Shi'ite president of the Chamber of Deputies was given extended powers. The main loser in this shift of authority was the Christian president of the state, who was no longer chief of the executive and had to be content with a largely symbolic role. In all, the decisions represented a major improvement in the political position of the Muslims, particularly the Sunnites. It took a year to implement the reform program: parliament did not vote on the necessary changes to the constitution until the fall of 1990.[43]

In relation to the pacification of Lebanon, the Ta'if Accord provided for the formation of a new government whose first task was to disband all militias and establish public security and order throughout the state. Implementation of this resolution started out only gradually. This was mainly due to the position of the Shi'ite organization Hizbullah, which insisted on remaining armed until the whole country was liberated from foreign troops.[44] At the end of 1990 a new government was constituted—de facto by Syria. It largely succeeded in disarming the militias and taking over their territory. The war in Lebanon has been officially over since then.

Meanwhile, the result of the Lebanese parliamentary elections in the fall of 1992 clearly showed that even over three years after Ta'if, there could be no talk of rapid national unity. Muslims of every religious and political shade were represented in the new parliament, including—for the first time—Shi'ite and Sunnite fundamentalists.[45] In any case, this meant that the old demands for increased political representation for Muslims, and especially those from socially weak strata, were at least partially satisfied. These developments basically continued in the subsequent elections in 1996 and 2000.[46] Nevertheless, it was impossible to ignore the general decline in the former influence of the Christians, especially the Maronites. This led many Christians to feel evident dissatisfaction with or a sense of alienation toward the "new Lebanon," this "state created by Ta'if."

The Ta'if Accord aroused a great variety of sustained criticism. There were fears that the changes in the constitution would eventually lead to confessional structures in the social and cultural area being reinforced and more deeply embedded. In fact the private confessional school system is flourishing more than ever today, the Lebanese University is still divided along confessional lines, and new, religiously oriented educational institutions have emerged. Even the project under discussion since the end of the war, which involves compiling uniform history textbooks on a national basis and generally updating the historical disciplines in terms of method and content, is still stuck in the early stages. The calls by prominent Lebanese historians to surmount or harmonize the divergent religious and political viewpoints are in blatant contradiction to the majority of existing historical accounts. With few exceptions, Lebanese historiography is a clear-cut mirror image of Lebanese reality—the dilemma of the still unresolved tension between confessional and national (i.e., secular) identity.[47]

There is no dispute about the considerable efforts by Lebanese governments since the 1990s to overcome the wartime destruction, mostly under the prime ministership (2000–2004) of Rafiq al-Hariri (whose murder in 2005, which Syria was suspected of instigating, resulted in the withdrawal of Syrian troops from Lebanon). These include administrative reforms, reconstruction and modernization of the physical infrastructure (gigantic building programs in the center of Beirut, a new airport, and so on), regaining international credit status, and the creation of a viable economy. Even in the political arena Lebanon has regained some importance both regionally and internationally. In 2009, full diplomatic relations between Syria and Lebanon were established for the first time. And there are still enormous unresolved problems in the social and economic field, especially the chronic deficit of state funds, neglect of the population's vital needs (particularly in the peripheral areas in the north and south of the country), and lack of efficiency in the social services and social security. The individual religious communities still provide these services for their members, as they did during the war. Old power structures based on patronage and clientism still persist, despite the adoption of some modern elements.[48]

Domestic policy, too, is still determined on the confessional pattern through the power constellation of the "troika" consisting of the Maronite president of state, Sunnite prime minister, and Shiʿite president of the Chamber of Deputies. Politically moderate Christians are trying to regain some of their influence, and the Muslims use every opportunity to establish themselves more firmly as a political and social force. The Shiʿites under the leadership of Hizbullah were particularly successful at this.

The most important and difficult problem confronting Lebanon remains unresolved: the question of political confessionalism and the secularization of the political and social system. The Taʾif Accord declared the solution to this question to be a key task, but without giving precise details and a specific timetable. Lebanese society still has some way to go toward achieving internal consensus, a deep-seated secular sense of national identity, and a clear, positive attitude toward the state.

Translated by Karen Margolis

22. Saudi Arabia

(Guido Steinberg)

a. The Wahhabiyya and the Creation of the Saudi State

The Saudi state emerged in 1744–45 when the ruler of the small city-state of Dirʿiyya in central Arabia, Muhammad ibn Saʿud (d. 1765), joined forces with the Muslim reform scholar Muhammad ibn ʿAbd al-Wahhab (ca. 1704–1792). According to their informal agreement, Muhammad ibn Sa'ud would support the spread of Ibn 'Abd al-Wahhab's doctrine. In return the scholar lent religious legitimacy to the ruler through the "Wahhabiyya," a purist-militant ideology named after its founder.[1] It provided the ideological basis for the expansion of the Saudi state through the conviction that there was a jihad to be fought against all non-Wahhabi Muslims.[2] Since that time the religious scholars have been in control of all aspects of religious life, the judiciary, and education within the Saudi state. The rulers of the Sa'ud family have made use of military and political means to propagate the Wahhabiyya while profiting from the religious legitimacy offered by that agreement. This alliance between the ruling family and the religious scholars has been maintained to this day and has had a significant impact on Saudi Arabian society.

The relationship between the ruling family and the scholars, however, was affected by several serious crises that led to the collapse of both the first (1744–45 to 1818) and the second Saudi state (1824–1891). Within only a few decades after 1744–45 the Saudi-Wahhabi alliance conquered large swaths of the Arabian Peninsula, including the holy cities of Mecca and Medina. This antagonized the Ottoman Empire, which was in control of the Hejaz region at the time, and it took action. The Ottoman Porte sent its viceroy in Egypt, Muhammad 'Ali Pasha, to reconquer the province. It did not take long for the Hejaz to fall. Then Egyptian troops razed Dir'iyya in 1818. The Sa'ud family managed to gain a foothold in the neighboring city of Riyadh as early as 1824, but it learned from the events that transpired: the Sa'ud family did not venture to attack Ottoman territory again during the nineteenth century, although the Wahhabi scholars called for a continuation of the jihad against the infidels in the neighboring Muslim territories. Henceforth issues of realpolitik were granted higher priority than the expansionist ideology of the Wahhabiyya.[3]

The second crisis surfaced in 1865. A civil war erupted as the sons of the deceased Imam Faysal ibn Turki competed for control. It ended in 1891 when troops from the rival emirate of the Rashid family from Ha'il occupied the Saudi capital of Riyadh and eradicated the remnants of the second Saudi state. The fraternal strife, however, was far more than just a political crisis. It put the very survival of the Wahhabiyya in question when major conflicts arose among its leaders. The conflicts were inflamed as scholars sided with the rival brothers, and in particular because one of them, 'Abdallah ibn Faysal (r. 1865–1871), turned to the Ottoman governor of Baghdad with a request for help. The scholars unleashed a fierce debate on the status of the Ottomans. If the predominant opinion indicated that they were infidels, then those who collaborated with them were also infidels. For the first time in the history of the Wahhabiyya its scholars pointed fingers at certain individuals within their ranks, accusing them of being "infidels," which in turn threatened to crush the entire reform movement. At the beginning of the twentieth century, cooperation with the founder of the third

Saudi state, ʿAbd al-ʿAziz ibn ʿAbd al-Rahman Al Saʿud, also known as Ibn
Saʿud (r. 1902–1953), finally helped to restore the former unity after years
of conflict. The scholars learned from their experiences in the civil wars that
they could retain their wide-reaching authority only in a stable state. For
this reason they agreed to accept a subordinate role to the ruling family.

b. Politics and Religion in the Infancy of the Third Saudi State

It took only a few years for Ibn Saʿud to reconquer central and eastern
Arabia. But for the lasting stability (and also the further expansion) of his
nascent state, he needed to bring the large Bedouin tribes under his control.
There was a discernible rivalry between these tribes and town dwellers in
the desert areas of central Arabia. Each group attempted to take control of
the other's political and economic domains. One reason for the failure of the
earlier Saudi states was that they could not wield lasting control over the
Bedouins, who were militarily unreliable. For this reason Ibn Saʿud, who
came from southern Najd (Arabic for central Arabia) himself, attempted to
mobilize the Bedouin tribes to channel their military strength for the benefit
of the state. Around 1911–12 the Ikhwan (literally "brethren") abandoned
their nomadic lifestyle for agriculture-based settlements that they called
hijar. They used the singular form of the term, *hijra,* to evoke the image of
the prophet Muhammad's flight from Mecca to Medina in 622. It symbolized the fact that their tribe had left the realm of (nomadic) infidelity and
now embraced true (sedentary) Muslim life. There is some evidence, however, that Ibn Saʿud's role is overemphasized in the official account.[4]

The Saudi government provided the Bedouin tribes with the necessary
means to settle down by giving them land and helping to build villages. The
scholars also supported this process by sending preachers to introduce the
Bedouins to the Wahhabi doctrine. They concentrated on the basics as laid
out in the short treatises (*mukhtasarat*) by Muhammad ibn ʿAbd al-Wahhab,
and they emphasized the importance of the jihad against non-Wahhabis.[5]
Those who perished in this holy war would enter paradise, which the
preachers portrayed in the most brilliant of colors. The Bedouins, who were
often indifferent in regard to their religious beliefs, were transformed into
fanatical religious warriors under the influence of the scholars. Together
with their teachers, they had now become a powerful community of interests that called for an even greater Wahhabization of Saudi politics.[6]

Over the next two decades Ibn Saʿud, aided by the Ikhwan, was able to
conquer nearly all the provinces that had been part of the first Saudi state.
Saudi troops captured the Ottoman province of al-Hasa in the eastern part
of the peninsula, the emirate of the Rashid family in the north, the Hejaz,
and the ʿAsir, a region in the southwest, between 1913 and 1932. The Wahhabi scholars together with the Ikhwan campaigned for the Wahhabization
of all areas of life in these provinces, that is, the adoption of the religious
and religious-political conditions of Najd. Yet Ibn Saʿud was mainly intent

on integrating these provinces into his emerging state as quickly and completely as possible. Measures conceived to be too drastic could incite unrest and unsettle the tenuous foundations of Saudi control there. Ibn Saʿud, however, was still dependent on the scholars and the Ikhwan. Therefore he made concessions that would placate them for a while yet would not too greatly alienate the people living in these provinces. Nevertheless, the policy of Wahhabization of these decades perpetuated the conflicts between the people of the regions and those from Najd.

The Shiʿites, who just barely constituted the majority in the eastern province, were particular hard hit by this policy. Because the Wahhabis regarded them as the epitome of infidelity, even a pragmatic ruler who did not want to endanger the legitimacy of his rule could not treat the Shiʿites as he did the Sunni Muslims. Shortly after its victory the Saudi state confiscated large estates, executed or exiled political leaders, and levied new, disastrous taxes on the Shiʿi population. In addition, the scholars and the Ikhwan implemented a particularly oppressive religious policy starting in 1915–16. A ban was placed on the religious ceremonies practiced by Shiʿites such as the ʿAshura' and celebrations marking the birthdays of the imams. There were numerous violent attacks. As the influence of the alliance between the scholars and the Ikhwan reached its pinnacle in 1926–27, they publicly called for all Shiʿites in the kingdom to be "converted" to Islam. Anyone who refused would be deported.[7]

In the Hejaz the conquerors acted in a similar fashion, albeit with significantly more consideration. The Ikhwan and the scholars immediately attempted to implement the Wahhabi code of conduct there. To this end they destroyed the houses where highly venerated persons such as the Prophet and several of his followers had been born, as well as graveyards and tombs at the sacred cemeteries in Mecca and Medina. Saudi authorities began to prevent anyone from worshipping there at the graves of the companions of the Prophet, the imams, and the saints by destroying them and, depending on the political mood, effecting rigid controls. Ibn Saʿud, however, avoided resorting to more widespread destruction and restrictive measures so as to minimize the imminent threat of a boycott by Muslim pilgrims from abroad. Because he relied on the revenues from the pilgrimage and feared potential unrest, he was forced to keep the Ikhwan and the scholars in check. Nevertheless, the measures that were eventually implemented posed substantial problems because they brought protests from around the world.

Ibn Saʿud ordered the contingents of Ikhwan to return to Najd when they began to incite hostilities during the pilgrimage of 1925. He also established the infamous religious police, officially called the Commission for the Promotion of Virtue and the Prevention of Vice (*hayʾat al-amr bi-l-maʿruf wa-l-nahy ʿan al-munkar*). There had already been a similar institution established in Najd in 1918–19 consisting of a commission headed by Wahhabi scholars who were in charge of groups of "religious policemen." Initially they served a dual purpose in the Hejaz. On the one hand, these units acted as moral watchdogs enforcing the Wahhabi code of conduct in the province. On the other hand, they helped keep the reins on the Ikhwan troops, because the situation was threatening to get out of hand in the towns of the Hejaz. The religious police have retained this dual religious and political function to this day.[8]

In the years that followed it gradually became evident to the Ikhwan that Ibn Saʿud would not shape the emerging Saudi state according to their plans. In fact he was actually attempting to consolidate his hold on the conquered territories and build a modern centralized state. Whereas Ibn Saʿud was concerned with maintaining stable relations with neighboring states, in particular British-controlled Iraq and Transjordan, the Ikhwan continued to conduct raids in these territories, a situation that risked upsetting the British. After several failed negotiation attempts, the Ikhwan initiated a rebellion that was quashed by troops loyal to Ibn Saʿud at the battle of Sibilla in 1929.

The defeat of the Ikhwan was a decisive factor in the relationship between the ruling family and the scholars within the third Saudi state. Although the scholars shared the Ikhwans' belief in the need for a strict domestic and foreign policy based on Wahhabi teachings, they had learned from the tumultuous situation at the end of the nineteenth century that their strong position was solely due to their alliance with the Saudi ruling family. For this reason they attempted to mediate the conflict between the Ikhwan and Ibn Saʿud. Only after the rebellion became apparent did they decide to side with the ruling family. A handful of younger scholars and students remained loyal to the Ikhwan. Over the course of the twentieth century, similar conflicts emerged in crises related to domestic policy. The Wahhabi scholars had a sympathetic ear for the demands of their more radically minded adherents; nevertheless, these scholars sided with the state in times of conflict, thus losing the support of Islamist circles. This happened, for example, in 1979, when militant Islamists stormed the Grand Mosque in Mecca and took visiting pilgrims hostage.[9]

c. Religion and the Political System

The Wahhabi scholars have still not created a comprehensive political theory. Initially they based their teachings on those of Ibn ʿAbd al-Wahhab, who had actually only adopted a handful of ideas from the medieval Damascene scholar Ibn Taymiyya (d. 1328) on the interaction of ruler, scholar, and people as well as their respective duties.[10] First and foremost was their conviction that only a tight-knit cooperation between rulers (*umaraʾ, aʾimma*) and scholars (*ʿulamaʾ*) could create an Islamic community. According to this concept the ruler was ascribed a very prominent role. His principal task was to implement the law of God (*al-sharʿ*) as defined by the Wahhabi scholars. Furthermore he was, and still is, responsible for political issues, in particular for establishing and guaranteeing security both domestically and abroad, monitoring the administration of finances and the judiciary, and leading the jihad.

According to this concept the scholars also had a strong position in line with that of the ruler. Their principal task was to ensure that all aspects of life in the Wahhabi community conformed to shari'a and that everyone followed in the footsteps of the pious ancestors (*al-salaf al-salih*). They were expected to offer assistance to the ruler in all issues that they deemed important by providing "good advice" (*nasiha*). In turn the ruler was duty-bound to seek their advice. This approach was intended to prevent the ruler from violating the shari'a, and if he did violate it, to allow him to rectify his commands. The scholars were bound by their duty to obey the imam. They were relieved of this duty only if he attempted to force his people to act in direct violation of shari'a.

After the civil wars, the need to preserve the community (*jama'a*) of Muslims was a prominent issue in Wahhabiyya political writings. And even in everyday politics the scholars tried to avoid arousing the ire of the ruler over the following decades. If a conflict were to arise, the fear of *fitna* (literally "trial," "temptation"), that is, schism in or secession from the Islamic community, would have kept them from confronting the power elite in any serious way because schism stands in diametrical opposition to the *jama'a*. The scholars still consider all things that threaten the cohesion of the community of (true) Muslims to be *fitna,* including the abundance of sins as well as discord among Muslims in general, and within the ruling family and scholars in particular. Therefore Ibn Sa'ud was able to advance a policy of increased centralization of political and judicative powers for the ruler after 1902 without encountering major resistance from the scholars.

The political theory of the Wahhabiyya also influenced the development of the Saudi Arabian constitution. To this day, officials continue to claim that the Qur'an is the constitution of Saudi Arabia, yet the twentieth century gave rise to several documents that smacked of constitutional law. On August 28, 1926, Ibn Sa'ud pronounced the creation of the Basic Regulations for the Kingdom of the Hejaz (*al-ta'limat al-asasiyya li-l-mamlaka al-hijaziyya*), which applied only to the Hejaz and remained valid only until the kingdom of Saudi Arabia was established in 1932. Even the decree for the creation of a council of ministers for Saudi Arabia in 1953 contained several elements reminiscent of a constitution. Notwithstanding this fact, the royal family showed no interest in formulating a comprehensive body of constitutional law. The pressure for a constitution mounted in the 1950s, when pan-Arab nationalist and leftist tendencies became more prevalent in Saudi Arabia under the influence of Nasserism. It was quite telling that liberal members of the royal family led by Prince Talal ibn 'Abd al-'Aziz (b. 1931) were among those demanding a constitution. They did not, however, have a lasting influence on political developments in the country.[11] It was actually King Faysal (r. 1964–1975) who encouraged the missionary work of the Wahhabiyya, in particular through the Muslim World League

(Rabitat al-ʿAlam al-Islami), founded in 1962, during his brother Saʿud's reign.[12] He emphasized the religious character of the kingdom during his own reign. In response to the occupation of the Grand Mosque and disturbances in the eastern part of the kingdom in 1979, his successor, Khalid (r. 1975–1982), introduced a more conservative religious policy to mollify the Wahhabi critics of the government's policy of modernization.

Since the beginning of the 1960s, the Saudi kings have promised a constitution numerous times. But only after the second Gulf War in 1991 did the pressure on domestic and foreign policy build up to a sufficient level to prompt the Saʿud family to make this move. King Fahd (r. 1982–2005) enacted the Basic Law of Governance (*al-nizam al-asasi li-l-hukm*) in a royal decree on March 1, 1992. The first article stipulates that the Qurʾan and the sunna are the "constitution" (*dustur*) of Saudi Arabia, indicating that the Basic Law does not have this status. Nevertheless, the text contains the fundamental elements of a constitution. For example, it establishes that Islam is the state religion (Article 1); the monarchy is the system of government; and only sons and grandsons of the ruling founder of the kingdom, Ibn Saʿud, are permitted to ascend the throne (Article 5). In accordance with traditional Wahhabi doctrine, governance in Saudi Arabia is based on Islamic law (*al-shariʿa al-islamiyya*).[13]

At the same time, King Fahd announced the establishment of a Consultative Council (Majlis al-Shura) and enshrined it in Article 8 of the Basic Law by proclaiming consultation (*shura*) to be an integral aspect of legitimate rule. This Consultative Council, which is akin to a parliamentary body, was at the heart of his reform program. In order to lend legitimacy to this move, the monarch in his official speech announcing the establishment of the Basic Law also alluded to the institution of similar councils in the early years of the kingdom, which had been transformed into the Saudi Council of Ministers in 1953–54. These councils had been the self-government bodies of the Hejaz, whose names were changed at various times. They had been designed to acknowledge the socioeconomic position of the respective notables without having any political consequences. In effect the allusion to these institutions was somewhat fictitous.[14]

All members of the council continue to be appointed by the king, and even Shiʿites are represented on it. The Islamist opposition, however, has no representation. The majority of council members come from the "new middle class," a term referring to people who were mostly educated in the West, including businessmen, technocrats, diplomats, and high-ranking retired officers. The Consultative Council is strictly an advisory body, and its influence on the political system of Saudi Arabia is limited. Saudi Arabia continues to be an absolute monarchy. Since the death of Ibn Saʿud in 1953, however, all major political decisions are no longer made by the king himself; they are reached by consensus among the most influential members of the royal family. Since the discovery of oil, the substantial export revenues from oil production are funneled directly into the state and thus to the royal family.

In this manner the royal family receives revenues that are independent of fiscal policy, which has led to a considerable increase in the influence of the power elite and a loss of influence among all other politically relevant social groups. Therefore Saudi Arabia is considered the prototype of a "rentier state," that is, a state in which the power elite derive their income through a "pension" and are not dependent on taxation of their own citizens.[15]

The most important role of the scholars has been and remains lending legitimacy to the rule of the Sa'ud family in general and to individual decisions in particular. The key figures are represented in two institutions. The most prominent Wahhabi scholars belong to the Council of Leading Scholars (Hay'at Kibar al-'Ulama'), the most influential body for religious policy in the country, which was founded in 1971.[16] The Presidency for Scientific Research and Religious Edicts (Dar al-Ifta' wa-l-Ishraf 'ala l-Shu'un al-Diniyya), which was founded in 1953, is primarily responsible for the monitoring of religious opinions (*ifta'*) in the kingdom. Today both institutions are presided over by the state-appointed grand mufti, who is the most influential scholar in all of Saudi Arabia.

d. The Legal and Justice Systems

The ruler has always held a pivotal position in Saudi Arabia's legal system, which is based on the doctrine of *siyasa shar'iyya*, Ibn Taymiyya's model of "politics in accordance with shari'a." This model dictates that the ruler has the right to take any action as long as it does not contradict a regulation or principle of shari'a and it serves the good of the community (*maslahat al-'umum*) in the opinion of the ruler. The foundation of his prerogative to administer punishments (*ta'zir*), including the death penalty, is built on this model. When put into practice it often led to overlapping spheres of authority between rulers and scholars because both sides claimed to have prevailing jurisdiction. The development of the legal system in Saudi Arabia reflects the strong position of the ruler to this day.[17]

Over the course of the twentieth century, the strength of the ruler's position became apparent in the establishment of a parallel nonreligious justice sector, which for the first time was not under the scholars' control and was more likely to respond to political influence than the jurisdiction of the religious scholars. This development took root after the conquest of the Hejaz, when it became apparent that Ibn Sa'ud could not transfer the Wahhabi judicial system from Najd to the Hejaz if he wanted to guarantee the smooth functioning of trade in the province, which was crucial for all of Saudi Arabia. He retained Ottoman laws, chiefly involving trade, despite major resistance from the Wahhabi scholars, who continued to call for the sole use of the shari'a. In 1926 a commercial council (Majlis al-Tujjar) was founded in Jidda—a tribunal with legal authority, which had already existed during the Ottoman era. In August 1931 the Hejaz government introduced a revised trade law that sanctioned the establishment of this institution.

Over the following decades the Saudi rulers set up nonreligious legal institutions whenever it was deemed necessary to do so. It had become a necessity primarily because legislation was expanded by means of new regulations. Yet these regulations were not called laws (*qawanin,* sing. *qanun*) by the Saudi rulers because the Wahhabis believe that only God is entitled to make laws for mankind. The rulers were merely issuing royal decrees (Arab. sing. *nizam* or *marsum*), which did not contradict the shari'a, or at least not in theory. In practical terms they were a compromise between religious teachings and the practical need to develop new laws.

It was the beginning of oil production in commercial quantities in 1945 that forced the government to establish new legal institutions that chiefly dealt with commercial and administrative law. In general a legal institution was set up after each new regulation was issued. For example, in 1954 a board was created to control the application of a new law on foreign investments and thus received sweeping judicial authority within this framework. A commission to mediate disputes between businesses was set up in 1965. Later another relevant institution was established in 1969 to interpret the new labor law.[18] These institutions kept the scope of Islamic law in check in everyday Saudi life.

Even in the religious justice sector the government has attempted to gain more influence since the first half of the twentieth century and harmonize and centralize legislation. This process began after the victory in the Hejaz. In central Arabia the Hanbaliyya school of law is predominant, even though the Wahhabi scholars have routinely pointed out that they do not follow any specific school and orient themselves strictly toward the principles of the Qur'an and sunna. In the Hejaz, however, all canonical Sunni schools of law are present, although the Hanafiyya, the official school of law in the Ottoman Empire, reigns alongside the popular Shafi'iyya. In June 1928 Ibn Sa'ud ordered all judges in the Hejaz to base their rulings on the positions approved by the Hanbaliyya. From that time onward, judges were required to abide by the Hanbali legal compendia, which also formed the basis of jurisprudence in Najd. Only under special circumstances could they refer to the doctrines from one of the other three schools. The Hanbaliyya still shapes legal practice in all of Saudi Arabia.[19]

Since the beginning of the twentieth century the Saudi rulers have also increasingly exercised influence over the judiciary. The conquest of the Hejaz was a pivotal factor as well, giving rise to sweeping changes. There the organizational work processes in the courts were considerably more developed than they were in Najd. A Hanafi chief judge (*ra'is al-qudat*) had always ruled over a rudimentary hierarchy even before the Saudi conquest. For the most part, Ibn Sa'ud did not reform the Hejaz court system, which had been established by the Judiciary Act of August 12, 1927. The summary courts (Mahakim musta'jila) heard cases in which the amount involved did not exceed a certain sum and the punishment would not include amputation or the death penalty. Cases that did not fall under the jurisdiction of summary courts—severe crimes, civil law cases exceeding a specific amount, property matters, wills and inheritance, and marriage law—were heard in the general courts (al-Mahakim al-kubra). In the end Ibn Saʿud created a judicial review commission (Hayʾat al-Muraqaba al-Qadaʾiyya) to monitor the entire judicial system and deal with appeals. The Wahhabi supreme judge for the Hejaz presided over it and in turn oversaw the judiciary.

The reorganization of the court system in the Hejaz also had an impact on Najd, where courts with bureaucratic structures had been set up in stages since the 1930s. The process of harmonization in terms of roles and hierarchy did not begin until 1949–50, however, when a court was set up in Riyadh that could hear only cases involving small claims. It was intended to ease the caseload of the regular courts. In the 1950s and 1960s the reforms, such as courts composed of several judges, verdicts by majority decision, and an appellate court system, were gradually implemented in Najd too. The judiciaries of the Hejaz and Najd were gradually brought more into line with each other. Nevertheless, it was only after the death of the powerful grand mufti and supreme judge of the kingdom, Muhammad ibn Ibrahim Al al-Shaykh, in 1969 that the government could complete the reforms of the judiciary. When in 1970 the Ministry of Justice was established, the minister of justice, who also had to be a senior scholar, in effect replaced the supreme judge. Today he oversees the more than three hundred courts in Saudi Arabia. Under the Judiciary Act of 1975 the Supreme Judicial Council (Majlis al-qadaʾ al-aʿla) was founded as a part of the Ministry of Justice. It enjoys a supervisory role over all lower courts, issues statements on questions of principles and details related to Islamic law, and reviews court decisions involving the death penalty, stoning, and amputation. The appellate court (Mahkamat al-tamyiz) is the next tier after the Supreme Judicial Council in this hierarchical structure. It has one seat in Mecca and another in Riyadh. The next tier includes the general courts (al-Mahakim al-ʿamma) and the summary courts (al-Mahakim al-juzʾiyya). Their jurisdiction is comparable to that of the general courts and small claims courts that had previously been established in the Hejaz.

e. Islamism in an Islamist State?

The close relations between the scholars and the ruling family have created several problems over the course of Saudi Arabia's history. Radical Wahhabis have accused the scholars in "official" positions of betraying true Islam whenever they lent legitimacy to controversial political decisions at the government's behest. This is what happened after August 1990, when Iraq occupied the emirate of Kuwait and threatened to invade Saudi Arabia too. After initial hesitation the Council of Leading Scholars published a legal opinion (*fatwa,* pl. *fatawa*) supporting the ruling family's decision to summon U.S. troops to the country. A large majority of the population rejected this move, and the contradiction between a pro-Western security policy and a conservative domestic policy led to the emergence of an Islamist opposition movement.

During the Gulf crisis, young scholars and preachers attempted to fill the ideological vacuum that was served up to them by the political pragmatism of the establishment scholars. The religious opposition formulated their demands in the famous "memorandum of good advice" (*mudhakkirat al-nasiha*) of July 1992, in which the signatories addressed the chairman of the Council of Leading Scholars, ʿAbd al-ʿAziz ibn Baz (1912–1999), who would later become grand mufti. The opposition argued for a comprehensive Islamization of Saudi Arabia that would have the religious scholars, whose position was to be strengthened greatly, overseeing all political and religious affairs of the country. Other demands of the opposition included the remobilization of a Saudi army strong enough to defend the country as well as a ban on any military cooperation with non-Muslim powers.[20] Over the years that followed, the memorandum became transformed into a document enshrining the principles of the Islamists in the opposition. The extremely tense situation in Saudi Arabia eased up only after the government arrested many dissidents in 1994, including the popular young scholars Safar al-Hawali and Salman al-ʿAwda. Some members of the opposition began disseminating anti-Saudi propaganda from their base in London, while militant groups affiliated with Osama bin Laden resorted to acts of terrorism aimed at toppling the ruling family. Yet the internal situation did calm down eventually.

The majority of dissidents who were arrested in 1994 were released again in 1999, apparently having come to terms with Saudi Arabia. But a new group of scholars and intellectuals who criticized the regime's pro-Western policy in the "war on terror" appeared on the scene after the attacks of September 11, 2001. Several of them openly backed Osama bin Laden and the Taliban. Thus the close ties between the Wahhabi scholars and the Saudi Arabian state regularly give rise to new Wahhabi opposition groups.

Translated by David Fenske

23. The Small Gulf States

(Katja Niethammer)

The complexity of the small Gulf states has yet to receive sufficient attention. Given the limited empirical research available on these countries, Western decision makers, journalists, and scholars have tended to apply observations and analyses about Saudi Arabia to the smaller neighboring monarchies of the Persian Gulf. As a result these states are often perceived as a homogeneous group.

In fact a number of striking similarities are apparent at first glance. The political systems of the small Gulf states—Bahrain, Kuwait, Qatar, Oman, and the United Arab Emirates (UAE)—greatly resemble one other. All of these countries are ruled by monarchs with extensive participation by the respective ruling families, which have largely monopolized leading government posts.[1] Thus members of ruling families hold the most important ministerial offices, and both high-ranking military and judicial positions are often in their hands as well.

The ruling elites of these countries understand themselves as sharing a common bond, at least in the face of external threats. One indication of this is the Gulf Cooperation Council (GCC), established by the five small Gulf states and Saudi Arabia in 1981. While the GCC was unable to fulfill adequately its originally intended function as a defense alliance against Iran and Iraq,[2] the council does serve as a platform for closer regional economic integration.[3] The GCC has not only intensified the contacts between ruling families, which in many cases were already intimate, but also contributed to the emergence of an embryonic identity, "Gulf state citizens" (sing. *khaliji*, from Arabic *khalij*, "gulf"), among the populations of these countries.[4]

Another apparent commonality of the small Gulf states is their economic and social development. Financed by oil and gas rents,[5] these states have been able to establish systems of education and public health comparable to those of OECD nations.[6] In all of the Gulf monarchies, economic development is dependent on the recruitment of cheap foreign labor.[7] This is accompanied by massive unemployment among the very young local populations; at the same time, the massive presence of foreign workers has resulted in an increased diversity of religious institutions of the different Christian and Muslim communities.[8]

Despite these similarities, however, a closer look at the small Gulf states also reveals important differences. First of all, the social structures of the populations of Bahrain, Qatar, Kuwait, Oman, and the seven emirates that constitute the UAE differ significantly. This is true of both the confessional and ethnic homogeneity of these societies as well as the tribal forms of organization. Along the Gulf littoral, starkly fragmented states such as Bahrain and Oman are located right next to quite homogeneous communities such as the smaller emirates of the UAE. The degree of politicization of Gulf Shi'ites is also quite varied. While Bahrain's history is marked by recurring conflicts between Shi'ites and Sunnis, the Shi'a minorities in Qatar and Kuwait have largely supported the ruling dynasties of the their respective countries. Furthermore, the ruling families of the various states use different institutions and strategies to generate legitimacy for their rule. For example, rulers in Bahrain and Kuwait have established parliaments with some supervisory and legislative authority, while other states have merely created symbolic parliament-like bodies. There is, however, no linear relation between the extent to which the populations are allowed to participate in the political process and the degree to which different segments of the populace ascribe legitimacy to the ruling dynasties. On the contrary, ruling families such as those of the UAE (apparently) face only minor problems of legitimacy, although they allow only very limited participation. In contrast, Bahrain's ruling elite is regarded by a portion of its citizens as illegitimate because of historically evolved and unresolved distribution conflicts between Shiʿi and Sunni communities. Unlike in Saudi Arabia, religious support for the political leadership plays little if any role in the small Gulf states, with the partial exception of Qatar, where the propagation of Wahhabi doctrine has been used to bolster the ruling dynasty's legitimacy.

This section presents an overview of the similarities and differences in the religious sphere of the small Gulf monarchies. In doing so, it also highlights the confessional orientation of the societies and ruling families, the justice system, and the role of political Islam.

a. Legal Schools and Confessional Affiliations of the Ruling Families and the Societies

Given their small geographical size, small Gulf states possess a surprising heterogeneity of religious affiliations. This is in part the result of their history in the pearl trade and the related migrational movements. All four Sunni schools of law are represented, although the Malikiyya predominates with the tribal Sunnis. The Hanbaliyya and the Shafiʿiyya are also present, however, as is to a lesser extent the Hanafiyya. In Oman the rulers (the Al Bu Saʿid dynasty) and presumably the majority of the population belong to the ʿIbadiyya, a school of thought in Islam that in the countries of the Arab Gulf appears only in Oman.[9] While all Shiʿites of the Gulf states are Twelver Shiʿites, they follow different "sources of emulation" (*marajiʿ al-taqlid*).[10]

With the exception of the special case of Oman, the ruling families of the small Gulf states—Bahrain, Qatar, Kuwait, and the seven principalities of the UAE (Abu Dhabi, Ajman, Dubai, Fujaira, Ras al Khaimah, Sharja, and Umm al Qaiwain)—are tribal Sunnis, though they adhere to different schools of law and theological currents. Along with the Al Saʿud, the Al Thani of Qatar are the only Hanbali ruling family in the Gulf region. The Al Thani adopted the Wahhabi doctrine in the late eighteenth century. This doctrine also found fertile ground with the Al Qasimi rulers in Ras al Khaimah and Sharja. Even today these Wahhabi-influenced emirates are regarded as more socially conservative, as is evident, for example, in their more rigid restrictions (in comparison to Dubai) regarding the sale of alcohol. In contrast, the ruling tribal families in Abu Dhabi and Dubai, the Bani Yas (the Al Bu Falasa in Dubai and the Al Bu Falah in Abu Dhabi), follow the Malikiyya school of law, as do the ruling Al Khalifa and Al Sabah in Bahrain and Kuwait, and exhibit little Wahhabi influence, except in isolated cases.

None of these states collects official figures for religious and confessional affiliation, owing both to efforts of the small Gulf states to promote a national consciousness and to their fear of confessional conflicts. Even estimates of the percentages represented by the different migrant workers' communities diverge. If we take only Gulf state nationals into account, these states have almost exclusively Muslim populations, although the precise distribution of legal schools and confessions is often disputed.[11] The populations of the coastal cities and states, however, in particular Ajman, Bahrain, Dubai, and Ras al Khaimah, are clearly more heterogeneous in terms of ethnicity and confession than the people of the desert regions in the hinterland, as the coastal inhabitants have been involved in trade for centuries.[12] In particular, emigrants from Iran settled in the coastal trade cities during the past centuries. These Iranian emigrants were ethnically and confessionally diverse and included Shi'ites (called 'Ajam), who have retained their Persian mother tongue, as well as Sunnis. This latter group consists of ethnic Baluchis, who primarily occupy a lower social status, and the so-called Huwala. These nontribal Sunnis, who emigrated primarily in the early twentieth century, regard themselves as Arabs. During the British colonial era, many Huwala families rose socially by working for the colonial administration, securing privileged positions in the economy. Huwala families follow the Shafi'iyya school of law.

Gulf Arab Shi'ites are also a heterogeneous group. There are the Persian-speaking 'Ajam already mentioned and more recent Iranian immigrants, as well as Arab Shi'ites from Bahrain (Baharna) and the Hasawis from the eastern province of Saudi Arabia. Insofar as the meager sources available allow for any conclusions, it appears that the current Shi'a populations in Abu Dhabi, Dubai, Qatar, and Sharja include members from all of the above-mentioned groups. In contrast, more than one-third of Kuwaiti citizens are Shi'ites and are almost exclusively 'Ajam. Bahrain is the exception here, as Shi'ites constitute a solid majority, approximately 70 percent, of the population. Among the Bahraini Shi'ites, the largest group is the Arab-speaking Baharna people, who view themselves as autochthonous.

All Gulf Arab Shi'ites are Twelver Shi'ites who follow different *maraji' al-taqlid*.[13] The two main *maraji'* in recent years have been al-Sayyid 'Ali al-Sistani in Iraq and the Iranian spiritual leader 'Ali Khamene'i. A minority followed Muhammad al-Shirazi.

b. Judiciary

With the exception of Oman, the small Gulf monarchies obtained their independence as nation-states at a late date, Bahrain, Qatar, and the UAE in 1971 and Kuwait in 1961. As a result, they were forced to engage in rapid state building, including the establishment of a justice system and the issuing of legal texts in various domains of law, a task that could hardly be

completed prior to independence. While there is little scholarly literature
about the justice systems of the small Gulf states before the arrival of the
British, it appears that these countries were not limited exclusively to shariʿa
courts during the nineteenth century.[14] Their most important legal authorities were their respective rulers. They resolved a wide variety of conflicts, including those involving penal law. In doing so, they followed tradition (ʿurf),
which participants seem to have understood as more or less consistent with
the shariʿa, although this was not necessarily the case. The legal authority
of rulers and their family members varied greatly in the different emirates.
The ruling families in Kuwait and Bahrain exercised the most extensive legal
authority.[15] The dominance of the ruling family in the legal system was particularly pronounced in Bahrain, where not only the ruler but also all male
members of the Al Khalifa could potentially administer justice. In their dealings with Sunni tribes, traditional norms of consultation were applied; in
contrast, the Al Khalifa were not bound to such norms in regard to the Shiʿi
population. It was not until British reforms in the 1920s that this enormous
legal uncertainty was rectified; only thereafter was legal authority limited to
the ruler himself.[16] Qatar is located at the other end of the spectrum. Here
rulers delegated legal authority in most conflicts to shariʿa judges, including
those involving penal law.[17] The exceptional position of Qatar is presumably the result of Wahhabi influence, through which the status of shariʿa
courts surpassed that of the ruling family court as well as tribal mechanisms
for conflict resolution.[18]

In addition to courts of the ruling families and shariʿa courts, different
clans almost certainly employed their own mechanisms of mediation. Furthermore, traders had their own arbitrating committees at trade locations.
With the exception of Qatar, issues of civil status law were probably adjudi-
cated at this time primarily by shariʿa courts.

Over the course of the twentieth century, judicature in the Gulf states
changed significantly. Initially the British revoked the legal authority of Gulf
rulers over foreign non-Muslims.[19] Parallel to this, the legal system was
progressively formalized—which meant the introduction of several penal
codes and rules for legal proceedings as well as formal courts with permanent staffs—and was made hierarchical. These procedures signaled the
end of trade committees and tribal mediation processes. Simultaneously the
jurisdiction of shariʿa courts was increasingly restricted, even in Qatar. In
Kuwait separate shariʿa courts were abolished, and even familial status law
was assigned to so-called civil courts, which issued judgments on the basis
of codified, shariʿa-based law.

When these countries gained independence, they were compelled to expand the legislative basis of their states rapidly. After independence in 1961
Kuwait adopted Egyptian legal texts in particular. The other small Gulf
states followed the Kuwaiti example a decade later. This was not surprising, as Egyptian legal texts were written in Arabic and the judges active
in the emirates were primarily Egyptian. Furthermore, the ruling autocrats

regarded the hierarchical and centralized Egyptian model as compatible with state building—despite the tense political relations between the Gulf monarchies and Egypt under Nasser at the time. Apparently the calculus of the rulers was that the development of a judicature oriented more strongly toward the British model would have placed fewer restrictions on the influence of religious scholars.

Today the small Gulf monarchies employ a mixture of shari'a-based family status law and British law, as well as French law (mediated through Egypt)[20] The structure of the judicature largely follows the Egyptian model.[21] With the exception of Kuwait, all of the small states have a dual system, with shari'a courts for adjudicating cases of civil status law and other courts (for penal law, commercial law, and so on) that issue decisions on the basis of codified legal texts. In the meantime, the legal domain has become largely textualized.[22] State leaders dominate their respective judiciaries in both realms insofar as they either appoint judges themselves or approve the appointment of judges, even for shari'a courts.

None of the small Gulf States has abolished the death penalty. Political demands for the introduction or implementation of *hadd* punishments vary from country to country. The UAE is the only small Gulf state to issue physical punishments (such as flogging and stoning), although these are not necessarily *hadd* punishments.[23]

c. Currents of Political Islam

The possibilities for political participation by citizens in the small Gulf states vary from country to country. This is true in terms of formal institutions such as parliaments as well as in terms of civil rights such as freedom of opinion, freedom of assembly, and freedom of association. These differences also affect the organization and the strategic options of groups whose political goals are determined by a religious frame of reference.

Roughly speaking, two groups can be distinguished among the small Gulf states: those states that allow few political rights, such as Oman and the UAE; and those that allow—in comparison to Arab countries in general— rather extensive political rights, such as Bahrain and Kuwait. Qatar lies somewhere in between these two groups. Judged by its constitution, which was approved in a referendum in 2003 and came into force formally in 2005, Qatar belongs to the latter group; de facto, however, it remains part of the former group.

In Qatar, Oman, and the UAE, civil society is very restricted; demonstrations are prohibited and political parties—regardless of their orientation— are illegal. In recent years these states have instituted largely symbolic policies in order to provide the appearance of reform. In Oman and in the UAE, for example, women have been appointed to ministerial positions, and the governments have held elections for parliamentary-like bodies, although in Qatar this occurred only on the local level. In the UAE the government appointed an election committee made up of fewer than 1 percent of the country's citizens.[24] The responsibilities of these bodies are very limited. Elected officeholders in the UAE and Oman do not exercise legislative functions, nor do they have any say in the configuration of the executive branch. These bodies are charged solely with discussing government proposals as well as supervising governance, if only to a very limited extent. Representatives in Oman can in principle question their ministers, though not about issues of foreign policy or security. In addition, representatives campaign solely as individuals. While they can rely on familial and tribal support, political platforms do not exist.

Consequently there are no official political parties that pursue the aims of political Islam in these three countries. Literature on unofficial Islamic committees with a more or less pronounced political agenda is scarce. In the northern UAE (Ajman, Fujaira, and Sharja), the Muslim Brothers are active in the philanthropic realm. In the UAE the government generally monitors mosques, while government offices must approve the orientation of preachers. The emirates have not become a site for "radical" preachers. The situation is somewhat different in Qatar. Here as well information is scarce about existing political Islamic groups. In the spring of 2005 an Egyptian residing in Qatar detonated a bomb in a theater.[25] There was no indication that this attack was carried out with the support of a group of Qatari citizens. Qatar attained prominence, however, as the home of Yusuf al-Qaradawi, a globally influential legal scholar of Egyptian descent who took up residence in the emirate in 1961 and was later granted Qatari citizenship. Al-Qaradawi maintained intimate personal ties to the emir who ruled Qatar until he was deposed in 1995 by Shaykh Hamad bin Khalifa Al Thani and was also a central figure in the construction of various religious educational institutions in the emirate.[26] Al-Qaradawi's presence in Qatar turned the small state into an important reference point for Muslim activists and scholars from other Arab countries, who do not appear, however, to have formed much of an alliance with the local population. Al-Qaradawi became globally influential in particular through his program *Shari'a and Life* (*Al-Shari'a wa-l-Hayat*), broadcast by al-Jazeera, the television satellite station established in Qatar in 1996.[27] In Oman as well there has been little recognizable activity by organized Islamic political groups. Although the government did arrest over one hundred people in early 2005 and accused them of intending to carry out Islamist attacks, the subsequent clemency issued several months later suggests that these accusations were not justified.[28]

In Bahrain and Kuwait, in contrast, political activists are able to work openly and legally. This is also the case for representatives of political organizations whose programs are in part established and derived from religion. While political parties are prohibited, partylike organizations are permitted de facto as so-called political societies, which also participate in parliamentary elections.[29] In both states women enjoy active as well as passive voting rights, although this has been the case in Kuwait only since 2005. Members of parliament in both states do not determine the composition of the executive. Thus they never assume governmental responsibility; they possess blockade power but not formative power. Political associations with both Shi'a and Sunni religious programs exist in Bahrain and Kuwait. There is close interaction between Kuwaiti and Bahraini activists.[30] Two Shi'a groups are active in Kuwait: the Justice and Peace Alliance (*tajammu' al-'adala wa-l-salam*), in which Shi'ites who follow Muhammad al-Shirazi as *marja'* (model of religious emulation) in particular are active; and the National Islamic Alliance (*al-tahaluf al-watani al-islami*). Similarly, there are two Shi'a political associations in Bahrain. The supporters of al-Shirazi have established the Islamic Action Society (*al-'amal al-islami*); Shi'ites who follow different religious exemplars (e.g., al-Sistani and Khamene'i) are more likely to participate in the National Islamic Society (*al-wifaq al-watani al-islami*). In both countries Sunni groups with various orientations are also active, from the Muslim Brothers to the Salafis. The Kuwaiti Muslim Brothers are active under the name Muslim Brotherhood as well as the name Islamic Constitution Movement (*al-haraka al-islamiyya al-dusturiyya*). In contrast, the political branch of the Bahraini Muslim Brothers operates under the designation Islamic Platform (*al-minbar al-islami*), while the Bahraini Salafi group calls itself Purity, or Authenticity (*al-asala*). Since political associations in Kuwait are tied de jure to their presence in parliament—and thus do not exist de facto as political parties—these unions are less consolidated than in Bahrain. For this reason there are several Salafi associations in Kuwait: the Islamic Salafi Alliance (*al-tajammu' al-islami al-salafi*), the Salafi Movement (*al-haraka al-salafiyya*), and simply the Salafis (al-Salaf). All of the political Islamic groups identified here have developed from active social and philanthropic associations that continue to exist in the respective societies.[31] The open organization of these groups, however, has had several rather ambiguous effects. One significant problem is that an abrupt political opening has led to a restrengthening of primordial, primarily confessional ties. In ethnically and/or religiously fragmented societies, political associations are organized primarily along precisely such dividing lines. It has become apparent in Bahrain that the open presence of different groups with religiously based political programs has triggered a competition leading to increasingly radicalized demands. Islamist members of parliament in Bahrain, for example, have called for the introduction of a religion police along the lines of the Saudi model, the segregation of colleges, and the introduction of corporal punishment. Furthermore, fragmented societies are highly susceptible to external influences. The conflict in Iraq has contributed enormously to an increase in the confessional agendas in the Gulf littoral states.

Translated by Tom Lampert

24. Yemen

(Iris Glosemeyer)

The legendary Queen of Sheba and her famous visit to King Solomon, related in the Old Testament, have inspired generations of researchers and
artists. Today numerous ruins and archaeological sites in Yemen bear testimony to the existence of great empires such as the Sabaean and Himyarite
kingdoms, some of which date back to the first millennium BCE. The economies of these civilizations relied heavily on the frankincense trade and on
elaborate irrigation systems.[1] In the past two millennia many of the great
powers in the Middle East have also left their mark in Yemen, including the
Abyssinian and Sassanid empires in the first millennium CE, and the Ottoman Empire from 1538 to 1635 and 1872 to 1918.

More than most other Arab states, the Republic of Yemen is distinguished by a diversity of climate zones and landscapes. In the west the
Tihama, a hot and humid coastal region, runs along the Rea Sea from
Saudi Arabia in the north to beyond Mocha (al-Mukha'), the former port
of export for coffee in the south. Farther to the east, the face of the Yemeni
highlands, which shelter Yemen's capital, Sanaa (San'a'), is still greatly
influenced by terraced farming. Between the highlands and the border
of Oman in the east, the fringes of the central Arabian desert, al-Rub'
al-Khali, or the "Empty Quarter," and the wadis, in particular the Wadi
Hadhramaut, dominate Yemen's landscape. Situated in the south on the
Arabian Sea (Indian Ocean) is Aden, the capital of the former People's
Democratic Republic of Yemen and the official economic capital of today's
Yemen. These regions have developed specific economic systems based on
the range of options permitted by their respective geographical location
and climate, including terraced farming, cattle breeding, oasis farming,
fishing, and trade, and have been exposed to external influences in different
ways. This variety has been mirrored in the dissemination and persistence
of various Islamic denominations.

The Yemenis were among the first followers of the Prophet Muhammad,
and several Islamic denominations gained roots relatively early in Yemen's
history. The longest-lasting religious and political force was the Zaydi imamate, which al-Hadi ila al-Haqq Yahya ibn al-Husayn established in 897. He
was a *sayyid* (pl. *sada*), or descendant of the Prophet, from Medina.[2] In the
following centuries nearly sixty Zaydi *sayyid* families and the families of
learned *qudat* (sing. *qadi*, lit. "judge") produced high-ranking administrative officials, military commanders, and scholars. Tribal leaders (*masha'ikh*,
sing. *shaykh*), were excluded from leading administrative positions. Many
tribes, however, had close ties to the *sada*, whose settlements (*hijar*, sing.
hijra), often Zaydi learning centers, were situated on tribal land and offered
protection by the host tribe.

The many attempts to replace the customary law practiced by the tribes (*'urf,* pl. *a'raf*) with Zaydi law and to place the tribes under lasting control were of limited success. To date tribal structures play a crucial role in the social and political life of many Yemenis, especially in the northern regions of the highlands and the bordering areas to the east.[3] At various times the imams, initially based in the present-day province of Sa'da in the north, were able to expand their borders to include regions inhabited by Shafi'is, Isma'ilis, and Jews. The imams did not interfere in the religious lives of conquered groups but retained the right to appoint the judges.[4]

In 1635 Zaydi imams succeeded once again in extending their dominion into southern Yemeni territory, but the sultanate of Lahej (Lahj), which also included Aden and the Hadhramaut (the Qu'ayti and the Kathiri sultanates) broke with Zaydi rule in the 1730s. The British occupied Aden in 1839 and developed it into a supply station for steamships headed to India. Several decades later the Ottoman Empire conquered parts of North Yemen for a second time. Starting with the coastal region, the Ottomans expanded their rule until eventually conquering Sanaa in 1872. Resisting this rule were imams from the Hamid al-Din family.[5]

a. North Yemen

The Imamate in the Twentieth Century

With the Da'an agreement in 1911, Imam Yahya Hamid al-Din (r. 1904–1948) succeeded in bringing the Zaydi community under his jurisdiction, thus replacing Ottoman (Hanafi) with Zaydi law.[6] By the end of Ottoman rule in 1918, Imam Yahya had gained control over a territory that comprised the territory of the later Yemen Arab Republic but also included areas that belong to modern-day Saudi Arabia. Furthermore he laid claim to South Yemen, which had come under British colonial rule, and by 1926 he proclaimed himself king (regnal name al-Mutawakkil 'ala Allah). His attempts to annex the territory from the short-lived Idrisi dynasty led to a war with Saudi Arabia in 1933.[7] The following year Imam Yahya lost not only the areas that he had recently seized but also parts of Yemeni territory. This military defeat and the border treaty negotiated with the British that same year further weakened his position in internal affairs.

Without any attempt at developing the country, the Hamid al-Din dynasty tried to adapt to a new era by legitimating their rule with nationalist ideals, emphasizing the unity of Yemen, and introducing hereditary rule. They also began building a modern army to protect the dynasty and territory from European colonialism and new political currents such as the Islamic reform movement and Arab nationalism. In the 1930s this gave a boost to an opposition that was no longer limited to members of rival *sayyid* families.

Much as in other Arab societies at the beginning of the twentieth century such as Egypt and Syria, the Yemeni military began to offer a chance at upward mobility, even for less privileged groups. Following the defeat by Saudi Arabia in 1934, Imam Yahya sent young men to Baghdad for military training. They not only learned about modern warfare while in Baghdad, however, but also came into contact with new political views, forcing the imam to suspend the program shortly thereafter.[8]

At about the same time, the activities of reform-minded intellectuals, which later became known as the Free Yemeni Movement, signaled the advent of a new era. They tried to persuade the imam to modernize the country, which had hardly any schools, roads, or hospitals. Yet these young reformers neglected to seek the support of the rural population. And in spite of the Muslim Brotherhood's backing, they were not capable of advancing the plans for political reform that they laid down in a draft constitution at the end of the 1940s. Their Holy National Charter called for a constitutional imamate in line with shari'a. The Free Yemeni Movement also claimed to represent the different social groups within the nation, for whom it demanded a greater say in political matters. A strategic coalition with members of the al-Wazir *sayyid* family proceeded to enmesh the Free Yemenis in power struggles that they could not control. This precipitated a coup attempt in 1948. It failed, but not without claiming the life of Imam Yahya. His son, Imam Ahmad, quelled the revolt and maintained the course of his father's domestic policies. Resistance to the imamate, however, had spread by then to prominent shaykh families.

The Yemen Arab Republic

Muhammad al-Badr succeeded his father, Ahmad, in September 1962. One week later, on September 26, 1962, a group within the military, calling itself the Yemeni Free Officers in the style of their Egyptian role models, staged a coup. Assuming that Muhammad al-Badr had been killed, these officers proclaimed the Yemen Arab Republic (YAR). But the young imam had in fact escaped to Saudi Arabia, and the first eight years of the existence of the YAR were marred by a civil war waged between republicans and supporters of the imamate. Attempts at negotiations, undertaken by tribal leaders and eminent scholars, failed.

The different constitutions that were passed in the 1960s are a reflection of the conflicts between the various political forces, even within the republican camp, which was strongly influenced by the Egyptian government. It was only after Egypt and Saudi Arabia ceased their support of both civil war parties in 1967 that a republican council, led by Qadi 'Abd al-Rahman al-Iryani, finally achieved reconciliation in 1970. In the same year a republican constitution was passed. Remaining essentially unchanged until 1990, it granted the parliament a strong position and declared shari'a the source of all laws. Thus the domestic policy of the YAR was heading in the opposite direction from that of the People's Democratic Republic of Yemen (PDRY), which had been created in South Yemen in the meantime. In 1972 the first war between the YAR and the PDRY was waged, ending with both sides declaring their intent to unify the two states.

In 1974 Ibrahim al-Hamdi, leader of the YAR's military command council, took over the executive branch of the government with the initial consent of tribal leaders. He suspended the constitution and dissolved the elected parliament in 1975. This move placed full control of the legislative branch in the hands of the executive. Although the laws passed during al-Hamdi's term were labeled a codification of shari'a, in several areas these laws were adopted from other Arab countries and originated in Europe.[9] Al-Hamdi aimed at equal representation of Zaydis and Shafi'is in high-ranking positions, diminished the influence of officers with tribal allegiances, and showed lenience toward leftist parties, which were organized in the National Democratic Front (NDF) and supported by the PDRY. This political agenda threatened the interests of conservative forces within the YAR. There is still speculation as to whether this fact played into al-Hamdi's assassination in October 1977.

The reins of government control were handed over to Ahmad al-Ghashmi, another member of the military command council. Instead of reinstating the parliament, he set up a People's Constituent Council which was officially in charge of legislation. The chairman of this council temporarily assumed the presidency in June 1978 after al-Ghashmi's assassination in the first year of his term. In July 1978 the council declared 'Ali 'Abdallah Salih president. A Zaydi officer from Sanaa province like both of his predecessors, and a member of the Sanhan tribe, he was considered eligible thanks to his military career under al-Hamdi, although he did not hail from a family belonging to the traditional elite. Al-Hamdi's ideas were characteristic of an Arab republic in the 1970s, and 'Ali 'Abdallah Salih to some extent crafted his agenda on the basis of those ideas, though he avoided confronting tribal shaykhs.

Salih managed to remain in power without being dependent on external military support. Ministerial positions were increasingly given to civilian professionals, and the governors were initially recruited from the ranks of tribal shaykhs, and later from the military; often they were officers with tribal allegiances. Members of the judiciary, however, continued to be selected primarily from *sayyid* and *qadi* families. Although other groups in society now had access to these posts, in particular since the founding of the University of Sanaa in 1970, their training in *fiqh* and their interest in serving as a judge were limited. In addition, as the traditional learning centers in the *hijar* began to lose their importance in the 1960s, Sunni-Salafi "scientific institutes" (*madaris 'ilmiyya*) started to appear alongside the emerging public education system.[10]

The Political Role of Islam

With backing from Saudi Arabia, a new religious and political movement established itself in the 1970s. In both the northern part of the YAR and the NDF strongholds bordering the PDRY an Islamist movement emerged that was increasingly influenced by Wahhabism. This new movement competed with the influence of the Muslim Brotherhood, represented in Yemen since the 1940s. On the one hand, this movement was intended to prevent PDRY-backed socialism from advancing. On the other, it was supposed to undermine the significance of Zaydi teachings, which some politicians still considered a threat to the nascent republic.[11]

The NDF was defeated in 1982, and many of its followers who had not fled to the PDRY were co-opted into the General People's Congress (al-mu'tamar al-sha'bi al-'amm, or GPC). From 1982 until unification in 1990 this political organization allowed President Salih to control formal political participation. The National Charter which the GPC passed in 1983 paid tribute to the role of the *'ulama'* in the fight against the imamate. The *'ulama'* were also to determine the interpretation of shari'a. Rule by religious scholars, however, was explicitly dismissed because it was seen as contradicting the Islamic faith. On the one hand, this stance was likely based on experiences under imamate rule. On the other hand, the model of the Islamic Republic of Iran, established in 1979, was also rejected. Nevertheless, the content of the GPC's National Charter can be regarded as a synthesis of Islamic teachings and Yemeni nationalism. Nearly all political movements of the Middle East from the Muslim Brotherhood to the Nasserists were represented in the GPC—as long as they did not challenge President Salih. Political parties, however, remained banned.

b. South Yemen

Although developments in North and South Yemen were intertwined, the history of South Yemen was shaped by entirely different structural conditions, especially colonialism, regional fragmentation, and internal migration.

In Aden, immigration, in particular from India, Pakistan, and East Africa, as well as from the protectorates and North Yemen, had given rise to an urban population. In the 1950s Aden began to experience an economic upswing that affected the social structure of the city. The expansion of Aden's port facilities (Aden became one of the most important ports worldwide until the Suez Canal was closed in 1967) and the opening of an oil refinery in 1954 accelerated the development of urban cultural and political organizations such as labor unions.

British colonial rule achieved a limited amount of control over the adjacent Aden Protectorates. Subsidy payments and protectorate treaties meant involvement in the internal affairs of the shaykhdoms and sultanates only insofar as they propped up the ruling families. Yet these measures upheld the regional fragmentation and promoted a stagnation of political, economic, and social development. British attempts to consolidate Aden and the protectorates into one state resulted in the creation of the Federation of South Arabia in 1959. The local leaders, however, appeared more concerned with the British subsidies than with forming an alliance.[12]

The regional fragmentation of South Yemen could also be felt in the legal system: Shafi'i law or customary law was applied in the protectorates, and British law was used in Aden. When the British withdrew in November 1967, control of the government was passed not to the British-backed Federation of South Arabia but to the socialist-inspired National Liberation Front (NLF), a group that had defeated rival organizations in sometimes violent confrontations. The leadership of the NLF proclaimed the People's Republic of South Yemen, which was renamed the People's Democratic Republic of Yemen in 1970 to demonstrate its claim to represent all of Yemen.

From the early 1970s on, financial aid, primarily from the Eastern bloc, and even from some Gulf states, not only helped the country build up its military and security apparatus but also facilitated social welfare and educational services far beyond the PDRY's own economic resources. The NLF made a concerted effort to destroy the existing social structures, fend off the influence of the religious elite, and (with a certain amount of success) replace local law with laws that were in part inspired by those from the socialist Eastern bloc.[13]

As the NLF was transforming itself into a Marxist party, the Yemeni Socialist Party (YSP), the 1970s and 1980s set the stage for internal power struggles. Eventually, on January 13, 1986, President 'Ali Nasir Muhammad tried to murder his opponents and triggered a civil war in the process. Within a few days the fighting ended when thousands of military officers and civilians, including the president, fled to North Yemen.

A new government, quickly responding to the loss of legitimacy caused by internal strife and civil war, held elections for the People's Supreme Assembly (the PDRY's quasi-parliament) in the fall of 1986. If the Soviet Union had not collapsed, the PDRY might have withstood even this crisis. In 1989, however, the decline of economic aid from the Eastern bloc forced the YSP leadership to plot a new course. The end of the cold war, the wave of democratization worldwide, and the discovery of oil in shared border areas provided a strong motivation for both Yemeni states to unite and seek a political and economic opening.

c. The Republic of Yemen

Shari'a as a Political Symbol

YAR president 'Ali 'Abdallah Salih and the secretary general of the Yemeni Socialist Party, 'Ali Salim al-Bayd, signed an agreement in Aden in November 1989 that contained a roadmap for the unification of the YAR and the PDRY. As they had done in the 1970s, conservative forces within the YAR, with Saudi Arabia's support, attempted once again to prevent unification with what they perceived as the "atheist" or "communist" south. This resistance only accelerated unification. On May 22, 1990, the Republic of Yemen was proclaimed, enjoying an unusual magnitude of political freedoms compared to the other states of the Arabian Peninsula. The two former single-party states divided power equally between them, even though the population of the YAR was several times larger than that of the PDRY. Initially the laws of both countries remained in force.

Against the backdrop of the expected oil revenues, the liberalization of domestic policy appeared to signal the dawn of a new era in a prosperous, unified, and democratic Yemen. All political players grasped the chance to organize in political parties, including the opponents of unification, from leftist and liberal groups to conservative groups, members of the Muslim Brotherhood, and other Islamist currents. A party dominated by Zaydi *sayyids* even emerged, although it distanced itself from reestablishing the imamate.

Nevertheless, opposition to the domestic policy pursued by the new republic remained strong. This opposition attached great significance to the role of shari'a in legislation. The Yemeni Congregation for Reform (al-Tajammu' al-Yamani li-l-Islah), a conservative Islamist party founded in the summer of 1990 by the YAR's most influential tribal leader, Shaykh 'Abdallah Husayn al-Ahmar, opposed the referendum on the constitution held in April 1991, but to no avail.[14] In contrast to the constitution of the YAR, this constitution declared that shari'a was the main source of laws but no longer the only source. As in the controversy surrounding unification, the call for a boycott represented a power struggle between conservative pro-Saudi and liberal-leftist forces. Furthermore, since the end of the 1980s, several thousand Yemenis who had fought against the Soviet occupation in Afghanistan had returned. Once back in Yemen, many of them hoped to implement the political ideas they had garnered in Afghanistan. Others, however, left the country again in the early 1990s.

Meanwhile, the economy of the new republic suffered a series of setbacks. In 1990 and 1991 the Gulf states interpreted the Yemeni government's refusal to support the liberation of Kuwait by an international military coalition as support for Iraq. Consequently, they expelled nearly 800,000 Yemeni migrant workers and drastically cut back their financial support for Yemen. While efforts at implementation of the unity agreements were still in their early stages, workers' remittances dried up, the already high unemployment level rose dramatically, and the value of the Yemeni currency fell sharply. Oil production and the new tourism industry could not compensate for these developments.[15]

The parliamentary elections on April 27, 1993, entirely changed the balance of power. The Yemeni Socialist Party captured no more than approximately one-fifth of the seats, while the Yemeni Congregation for Reform entered parliament with equal political backing. The election results demonstrated how successful Islamist ideologies had been in combating socialism, in particular in the border region between the two countries. The Yemeni Socialist Party had to enter a coalition with the General People's Congress and the Yemeni Congregation for Reform to avoid having its administrative and political apparatus fall into the hands of a government dominated by North Yemenis. The North Yemen alliance consisting of tribal shaykhs, military officers, and technocrats was now colliding head-on with South Yemeni party cadres. The following year was witness to serious conflicts, and not just verbal ones. After the power struggle had escalated into a war in early May 1994, a group of South Yemenis, mostly leading members of the Yemeni Socialist Party, proclaimed the Democratic Republic of Yemen (DRY) in South Yemen on May 21, 1994. The DRY, however, failed to receive international recognition, even from Saudi Arabia, which had allegedly supported the secession.

A coalition of North Yemeni troops, tribal militias, some units of the South Yemeni army, and former Afghanistan fighters ousted the self-proclaimed heads of the southern state in early July 1994. The Yemeni Socialist Party lost the rest of its political clout, and in the fall of 1994 parliament amended the constitution, officially returning to shariʿa as the source of all laws. Simultaneously, the long-planned criminal law code was finally adopted. It was now applicable to all of Yemen and included corporal punishment for alcohol consumption, extramarital affairs, and theft. In terms of procedural law, however, it became clear that substantial evidence was necessary for this punishment to be exerted.

The kidnapping of foreigners, the war in 1994, and conflicts between the government and individual tribes damaged the tourism industry. In the mid-1990s the government adopted a structural reform program that improved macroeconomic data yet reduced even larger segments of the population to poverty. Nevertheless, the GPC captured a two-thirds majority in the parliamentary elections in April 1997, which were boycotted by the Yemeni Socialist Party and several smaller parties. The Yemeni Congregation for Reform left the government coalition and became the biggest opposition party in the parliament. It was compensated by having its leader, Shaykh ʿAbdallah Husayn al-Ahmar, elected speaker of the parliament with the support of the GPC. Thus it retained some control over the legislature until Shaykh al-Ahmar's death in December 2007. The Yemeni Congregation for Reform returned the favor in the fall of 1999, supporting President Salih when he ran in the first direct presidential elections in a unified Yemen—without a single competitor from another party. The local elections of 2001 and 2006, the parliamentary elections of 2003, and even the presidential election of 2006, in which President Salih was actually confronted for the first time with an opponent of any consequence, did little to change the balance of power. By this point the political enthusiasm that marked the early 1990s had long since dissipated. The constitution was amended in 2001 but continued to espouse shariʿa as the source of all laws.

Islam as a Means of Modern Political Expression

Relations with Kuwait and Saudi Arabia remained tense until the end of the 1990s. Saudi Arabia had allegedly supported the secessionists in 1994, a situation that made rapprochement more difficult. Moreover, Saudi Arabia's

support for the proliferation of Salafi teachings incited unrest in several locations,[16] and there were repeated allegations that Saudi Arabia was in part
responsible for terrorist attacks in the border region. After difficult negotiations and skirmishes, a border agreement was finally signed on June 12,
2000, and relations with Saudi Arabia and even with Kuwait improved
noticeably.[17]

Nevertheless, developments in domestic policy were influenced by external events. The attacks of September 11, 2001, in the United States and the
wars in Afghanistan and Iraq also affected Yemen. Even though none of the
perpetrators of the September 11 attacks was a Yemeni citizen, there had
been numerous terrorist attacks directed at Western targets in Yemen since
the early 1990s. The Yemeni government cooperated with the United States
in the area of security in order not to be accused of supporting international
terrorism. This move was criticized, however, and not just by Sunni Salafis
and nationalists. In the summer of 2004, and for the first time since the end
of the civil war in the 1960s, Sa'da province saw massive clashes between
security forces and followers of a Zaydi scholar. Several hundred lives were
lost. The *sayyid* Husayn Badr al-Din al-Huthi is purported to have acted initially with the government's approval in his attempt to repress the mounting
influence of Salafi-Wahhabi teachings in the Zaydi heartland by (re)estab-
lishing Zaydi learning institutions. It appears, however, that both he and
the Sunni Islamists finally arrived at the same conclusion: that the Islamic
world is threatened by a U.S.-Israeli coalition. Accordingly, he and his followers began to voice their protest publicly. The heavy-handed government
response triggered a violent confrontation. Although the military standoff
at the beginning of September 2004 appeared to have ended when al-Huthi
was killed, other family members assumed the leadership of the rebellion,
and the government was unable to settle the affair for several years. It is not
clear whether the majority of al-Huthi's followers actually believed in his
teachings. They may simply have been tribesmen who felt threatened by the
massive deployment of security forces or who followed the local traditions
of protecting a *sayyid* family from the security forces whom they perceived
as intruders—or a mixture of all of these factors. As this example elucidates,
Islam and its many interpretations are as much a means of political expression as they are a basis for legislation in Yemen today.

d. Conclusion

Even though Yemen is situated at the periphery of the Arab world, regional
and international events nevertheless have an impact on economic and political developments there. Not all foreign influences have left their mark on
legislation and the judiciary. For instance, the Ottoman era in North Yemen
and the decades-long socialist rule in South Yemen are barely evidenced
in present-day legislation. Despite the adoption of shari'a in the constitution as the source of all laws, there is in fact a coexistence of state law from

various sources, religious law, and customary law. The little-known tribal customary law has prevailed over the many manifestations of Islamic and non-Islamic laws in some regions, even though various rulers over the centuries attempted to use legislation as a means of extending their control over these regions.

The diverse characteristics of the different parts of the country and the social and religious pluralism of Yemen are reflected not only in the plurality of the law but also in the political system. The Yemeni Socialist Party may have lost a great deal of its influence and political support since 1994, yet different political movements, most of which are represented among the political parties, continue to compete with one another. Several parties, including the Yemeni Congregation for Reform and the Yemeni Socialist Party, have attempted to set aside their ideological differences in recent years in order to build an alliance against the dominant GPC. Yet it is the autonomy of the tribes that has prevented Yemen from developing into a full-blown authoritarian political system, similar to other Arab republics that served as models for the Yemeni presidents.

Translated by David Fenske

V

The Islamic Diaspora: Europe and America

1. Western Europe

(Nico Landman)

a. Introduction

The status of Muslim communities in western Europe has changed rapidly in the first few years of the twenty-first century. They consist of a growing number of individuals who were born in Europe and are able to speak English, French, and German better than Turkish or Arabic. Yet as diaspora communities, they continue to maintain close ties with their coreligionists outside Europe. The Islamic diaspora has created new challenges for Muslims and western European countries alike. Muslims must decide how they want to practice their religion and how they wish to pass it on to younger generations who are living in a strongly secularized society. Meanwhile western European countries must come up with strategies to integrate Islam into their religious infrastructure. They also face growing social tensions since the increased visibility of Islam has provoked hostile responses among some groups in society. For reasons that require no further elaboration here, these tensions have worsened since the terrorist attacks in New York City on September 11, 2001, and those in Madrid on March 11, 2004, and in London on July 7, 2005.

With regard to these developments, each of the countries in western Europe looks back on a specific history. There are important differences among them concerning the ethnic makeup of the Muslim population, the history of migration, the legal status of immigrants, integration policy, and the role of religion in public life. It is therefore risky to make generalizations about *the* Muslims of western Europe. Nevertheless, the Muslims in the different regions of western Europe have a great deal in common. There are numerous connections among them and a wealth of mutual influences. A disproportionately large number of Muslims can be found in socially and economically disadvantaged population groups in all countries. Their relationship with the non-Islamic environment is partially shaped by international events that have the same impact everywhere. European integration is also contributing to the exchange of information and the convergence of the status of Islam. For instance, the headscarf ban passed by France in early 2004 immediately sparked debates on the same issue in other regions of Europe. Muslims, for their part, are discussing forms of cooperation that transcend national borders.

This chapter describes the status of Islam in western Europe as a whole without blurring the differences between individual countries. Subsequent chapters examine a number of these countries in greater detail.

b. Demographics: The Muslim Population in Western Europe

In the first half of the twentieth century, the Muslim presence in western Europe was largely confined to two groups: students from Islamic countries, and Europeans who had converted to Islam—mostly after trips to the Islamic world—and were often at the center of an Islamic congregation or study group. This changed in the 1960s.[1]

The emergence of independent states in former colonies caused profound political upheaval that prompted some population groups to settle in western Europe. Pakistanis and Indians emigrated to Great Britain, Algerians and Tunisians to France, and Surinamese to the Netherlands. Labor immigration was also destined to play an increasingly important role: recruitment efforts in North Africa and Turkey brought growing numbers of workers with an Islamic background to western Europe. In the 1980s the Muslim population expanded, primarily owing to the influx of asylum seekers. The number of countries from which the different groups of Muslim immigrants came also increased.

Estimates of the number of Muslims in western Europe are generally based on statistical data concerning residents with a foreign nationality or a foreign birthplace. While such statistics provide information on the cultural and religious background of the individuals in question, they reveal nothing about their attitude toward religion. There are hardly any reliable data on conversions to Islam, and naturally no data on Muslims who do not hold residence permits, the so-called illegal aliens. With these qualifications, the following discussion presents an estimate of the number of Muslims in each country and specifies their origins (see Table 4).

For all of western Europe the number of Muslims is estimated to be between 11 and 12 million, or roughly 3 percent of the population. Most come from North African states (33.6 percent) and Turkey (28.3 percent), but migration from the Indian subcontinent (12.0 percent) is also a significant factor. Migration from the Middle East plays a much less important role statistically.

Table 4. Muslims in Western Europe (Estimated Numbers, 2000–2001, in Thousands)

	Turkey	Balkan States	Indian Subcontinent and Afghanistan	Arab States in the Middle East	North African States	Other African States	Iran	Other/Unknown	Muslims (Estimated)	Population (in Millions)	Percent of the Population
France	350		125	100	2,900	350		175	4,000	59	6.8
Germany	2,300	167	100	110	100		116	107	3,000	82.11	3.7
Great Britain			1,100	220		115		165	1,600	59.8	2.7
Netherlands	299		35	60	264	35	24	127	844	16	5.3
Italy		120	35	30	230	50		135	600	57.8	1.0
Belgium	154	2	2	2	221		1	18	400	10.3	3.9
Spain			15	5	270	20	2	38	350	39.5	0.9
Switzerland	59	164				5		82	310	7.4	4.2
Austria	134	120		8		2	7	29	300	8.1	3.7
Sweden	30	69	8	52	8	21	48	14	250	8.8	2.8
Denmark	38	26	10	27	6	15	5	23	150	5.3	2.8
Norway	21	16	5	8	5	7	9	3	74	4.2	1.8
Portugal						35		0	35	10	0.4
Finland						6		14	20	5.1	0.4
Ireland								7	7	3.8	0.2
Luxemburg								5	5	0.4	1.3
Total	3,385	684	1,435	622	4,011	654	212	942	11,945	377.6	3.2
Percentage of Muslims in Western Europe	28.3	5.7	12.0	5.2	33.6	5.5	1.8	7.9	100		

Sources: The studies of individual countries in S. T. Hunter, ed., *Islam, Europe's Second Religion* (London, 2002); the studies of individual countries in B. Maréchal, ed., *L'islam et les musulmans dans l'Europe élargie: radioscopie* (Louvain-la-Neuve, 2002); and F. Dassetto, "The Muslim Populations of Europe," in *Muslims in the Enlarged Europe: Religion and Society,* ed. B. Maréchal, S. Allievi, F. Dassetto, and J. S. Nielsen (Leiden, 2003).

In terms of geography, Muslims are not distributed equally across all the countries of western Europe. The greatest concentrations can be found in France (6.8 percent) and the Netherlands (5.3 percent). Also noteworthy is the fact that the great majority of Muslims in western Europe live not just in large cities but in specific neighborhoods within these cities. As a result of this uneven geographic distribution, the Islamic diaspora is a key factor in many cities and urban neighborhoods while being marginal or nonexistent in others.

c. Creating an Islamic Infrastructure

The Founding of Mosques

Running parallel to immigration from the Islamic world was a drastic increase in the number of Islamic houses of worship in the 1970s and 1980s, particularly after immigrants were joined by family from their countries of origin. Many saw this as evidence that the immigrants had accepted that they would be living in western Europe for a lengthy period of time. Because of their new future prospects and the awareness that their children would be growing up in Europe, they wanted institutions that would guarantee continuity of religious tradition. This need was met by different authorities: the unofficial heads of local immigrant groups, national and international Islamic organizations, and Islamic states.

The dominant pattern of mosque openings in the 1970s and 1980s reflected the marginal social status of most Muslim immigrants. The success of mosque initiatives depended on the organizational skills of their leaders, the financial resources of the members they were able to mobilize, and, finally, the cooperation of the authorities. Generally speaking, the process of raising funds and founding mosques was extremely difficult and the results modest. Many Islamic centers were and continue to be highly provisional. They are often located in the urban neighborhoods where most of the immigrants live, and the buildings are in poor condition. Sometimes the congregations have bought or rented a vacant school building, an old factory space, an abandoned shop, or an unused church. Smaller congregations often use converted residential buildings for religious gatherings. In 2000 there were between 3,500 and 4,000 of these mostly provisional mosques.[2]

In the 1990s the temporary houses of worship were gradually replaced in many European countries by new buildings, often with minarets.[3] Because of their architectural styles, some are instantly recognizable as Turkish or North African mosques, while others feature newer architectural designs. For example, the Süleymaniye mosque in Tilburg (Holland) has a floor plan shaped like a star and crescent moon.

As a rule, the money needed to establish these mosques is raised by the members of the local organization responsible for building them. Sometimes collections are taken in existing mosques, in nearby congregations, or even in other countries. Gifts from oil-producing nations and from wealthy organizations and individuals in the Islamic world have also contributed to the construction of a number of mosques in western Europe. The Islamic World League in Jidda and the Jami'at al-da'wa al-islamiyya in Libya are among the organizations that have supported mosque projects in European countries. In the 1980s Turkish mosque initiatives were also financed by Diyanet, the Turkish office for religious affairs.

Organizations Affiliated with Mosques

Despite the often modest spatial arrangements, most mosques have become centers of religious life and educational activity in their neighborhoods. They

have also become local centers around which other organizations have crystallized. Many constitute a local branch of national or international Muslim
associations.

Their core activities include ritual prayers and Qur'an lessons for children. In most mosques the pupils—mostly boys and girls aged twelve or
younger—memorize passages from the Qur'an and are taught the proper
way to read the texts. Daily and weekly meetings in the mosques are attended
primarily by adult men. This reproduces practices in the Muslims' countries
of origin with the main exception that women have an even more restricted
role owing to the lack of space. There are often no special prayer rooms for
women, and their religious life unfolds largely within the family.[4]

Beyond these core activities, a growing number of mosques are evolving
into multifunctional Islamic centers that offer myriad educational and social
activities. Such activities often have little or nothing to do with Islam as a religion, yet they contribute to building a religious community. Some mosques
provide language and computer courses or even teach participants how to
write a proper job application. These side activities have become so important
in many areas that the authors of one Rotterdam study felt compelled to distinguish between "religious" and "social" mosques.[5] The broader interests
often give rise to new activities offered for and by women.[6]

Social, Economic, and Cultural Activities
In addition to the establishment of mosques and Islamic centers, the 1980s
and 1990s saw a large number of initiatives designed to promote Islamic
instruction, the Islamic press, halal food (from Arab. *halal,* permitted), Islamic burials, and other services compliant with Islamic law. Many of these
initiatives originated in the mosque organizations, while others emerged independently. Naturally, when immigrants from Pakistan, Algeria, and Turkey
sell products from their home countries in the European city neighborhoods
where a large number of their countrymen live, this has little to do with Islam.
But Islamic dietary laws, especially those requiring the ritual slaughter of animals, have given rise to an extensive network of Islamic butcher's shops that
are supplied by Islamic wholesalers and slaughterhouses. The advertising slogan "100 percent halal!" has added diversity to the western European retail
trade. Institutions have been established in various western European countries to inspect the halal quality of meat and to award a halal hallmark.[7]

The ban on interest payments is another Islamic law that has created a
special economic infrastructure. Although it is a matter of dispute whether
the Qur'anic term *riba* has anything to do with the moderate interest rates
paid in modern banking transactions, many Muslims, including those in
western Europe, feel that mortgages and interest payments on savings accounts are problematic. This has led to a rise in "Islamic banking" in western Europe.[8]

Special Islamic cemeteries are a line of business that is still in its infancy.
Most Islamic immigrants continue to have the remains of their loved ones

returned to and buried in their countries of origin. But as the desire grows among Muslims to have their family members buried near them in western Europe, there seems to be a greater need for special Islamic cemeteries. The first Muslim undertakers have also opened for business.

Islamic instruction has evolved differently in the various countries of western Europe, depending on the different legal conditions.[9] In a number of countries—including Holland, Denmark, and England—it is relatively easy to open special Islamic schools and secure full or partial funding from the state. In other countries (Germany, England, Austria, and Belgium), religious instruction for Muslim pupils has become, or is becoming, part of the curriculum in public schools. In still others, Islamic instruction is developing entirely outside the purview of the state. The spread of Islamic instruction has been accompanied by an array of supporting activities. Educational material is created in the respective national language and incorporates national didactic concepts, and training programs are offered for teachers.

Finally, the Islamic media have come to play an increasingly important role in western Europe. In addition to the importation of religious literature—common in the 1970s and 1980s—an Islamic press has emerged in many countries over the past few decades. Whereas many Islamic publishing houses began by publishing translations from the Arabic or Turkish, a growing number are now putting out books written by Muslims living in Europe. Newspapers such as *Q-news* and *Islam de France* serve as discussion forums for Muslims in England and France.[10] Increasingly, Muslim organizations in western Europe have access to the airwaves or cable and broadcast religious programs. A subsequent chapter investigates whether the emergence of the Islamic media in Europe has produced a "European Islam."

Heterogeneity and Affiliation

Creating the infrastructure just described was possible only because resources were pooled and like-minded Muslim organizations worked together. This cooperation at national and international levels has taken on various forms in the different Muslim communities. Turkish Muslim organizations, in particular, have created hierarchical structures in which local member groups are uniformly constructed and are subordinate to national umbrella associations. Alternatively, Muslims have set up informal Islamic networks that the British anthropologist Pnina Werbner calls "chaordic."[11] In combining the words "chaotic" and "orderly," Werbner emphasizes that, while like-minded local organizations work autonomously, they have a shared culture which enables them to cooperate even without a formal structure.

Ethnic background is an important unifying element in the umbrella associations, but it also creates obstacles to broader cooperation among ethnic groups. Intra-European borders are of little importance in this regard since the process by which certain ethnic groups form religious organizations in different western European countries is characterized by the same developmental patterns and is influenced by the same religious and political conflicts. For example, all the major Turkish Islamic movements can be found in Germany, the Netherlands, Belgium, France, Switzerland, Austria, and Denmark. Among Moroccans in France, Belgium, and the Netherlands, organizational forms are determined by, among other things, the Moroccan state's efforts to exercise control over mosques. Teachers of mysticism from Pakistan and India travel back and forth between their students' congregations in Great Britain, the Netherlands, and Denmark. These students almost always come from southern and southeastern Asia.[12]

Critics have repeatedly pointed out that the divisions between the various Muslim networks in western Europe are inconsistent with the idea of Islamic unity. This criticism is particularly popular among western European converts to Islam but is also shared by second-generation Muslims, primarily those attracted to Islamist movements. It therefore comes as no surprise that the organizations established by followers of the Muslim Brotherhood and Jama'at-i Islami have created associations that work together across the boundaries of European countries and different ethnic groups.

In nearly all western European countries, the great ethnic and politico-religious heterogeneity of the Muslim communities has caused difficulties with respect to the public representation of these communities and the promotion of their interests. There is no shortage of self-proclaimed spokesmen claiming to represent *the* Muslims, but there is a distinct dearth of representative Muslim bodies. A hierarchy that might provide a basis for such representation—like that of the Roman Catholic Church—does not exist in Sunni Islam. A state-decreed religious infrastructure for the Islamic communities of western Europe is hardly conceivable. There has been only slow progress toward setting up Islamic councils on which Muslim organizations work together at a national level.

Even so, attempts are under way in most western European countries to launch such councils—partly as a response to state ideas, partly with the active participation of state agencies. State bodies need representative partners from religious communities, but they are unable to work effectively with the combination of heterogeneous and "chaordic" groups in western Europe, especially since these groups hold very different opinions. The Islamische Religiöse Gemeinschaft (Islamic Religious Community) has served as a representative umbrella association for diverse Muslim organizations in Austria since 1979.[13] The Comisión Islamica de España (Islamic Commission of Spain), a union of two Muslim associations, holds a similar position in Spain, although many question whether it reflects the heterogeneity of the Muslim community.[14] Belgium has had an Islamic body for the various ethnic Muslim communities since 1999: the Exécutif des Musulmans de Belgique (Muslim Executive of Belgium). Although this body is recognized by the state, it seems to function as an institution devoted to a few special tasks, such as Islamic instruction in schools, and not as an umbrella association representing the various Muslim groups in the country.[15] The scene in most western European countries is dominated by several at times competing Islamic councils whose representative function is doubtful.

Although the importance of both the umbrella organizations and the unity of various forms of Islam is repeatedly emphasized in societal debates and specialist literature, it has been challenged by the British researcher Dilwar Hussain, who points out that British Muslims have been much more successful at promoting their interests through informal lobbying than, say, the state-recognized Islamic organization in Belgium.[16] Hussain argues that the demand for unity should not be seen as an absolute but must be subordinated to concrete goals that can often be achieved—and achieved exceedingly well—by ad hoc cooperation. In view of the great heterogeneity of Muslims in western Europe and their diverse ethnic and religious backgrounds, one may indeed question how realistic it is to expect a single body to act legitimately on behalf of all Muslims.

d. Integration and Assimilation: The Response of the Majority Society

Over the past few decades the establishment of Islamic organizations has given Islam greater public visibility in a large number of regions. In western Europe this visibility has resulted in a social and cultural transformation process that has created tensions and political conflicts. The question is how western European countries can integrate the newly arrived Muslims into society as a whole and to what extent they can, or want to, meet the Muslims' special demands. In answering this question, we must take a closer look at both the status of religion in public life and the state policies governing the individual and collective integration of immigrants.

State and Religion

Religious freedom is a basic right in all western European states, but these states differ in terms of how and to what extent they make public funds available to religious organizations.[17] While a few countries pay the salaries of religious officeholders, others view religious activity as the sole responsibility of the religious organizations themselves. According to François Messner, European states can best be categorized into three groups on the basis of historical differences among them.[18]

The first group consists of countries such as Great Britain, Denmark, and Portugal that grant special privileges to a single church. This is not necessarily unfavorable for the recognition and possible support of Islamic organizations in society. The Church of England, for instance, has repeatedly used its special status in British society to further the interests of Muslim congregations vis-à-vis the state.

In the second category we find countries that have a formal procedure for recognizing religious communities: Germany, Austria, Switzerland, Italy, Spain, and Belgium. Recognition brings privileges to which unrecognized religions are not privy, such as religious instruction at public schools. The recognition procedure has had a great impact on the development of Islamic infrastructures. If Islamic organizations do not fulfill the legal conditions for recognition—which has been the case in Germany and Italy—they will not get certain forms of material support that other religious communities receive. On an immaterial level, the awareness of their subordinate role is perpetuated and reinforced. By contrast, the formal recognition of Islam in Austria, Spain, and Belgium has substantially influenced the Islamic infrastructure. In each of these countries a state-recognized Islamic body has assumed a dominant position in the heterogeneous Muslim communities. This model leads to the formalization of religious structures and, to a certain degree, fosters a hierarchical organization.

A third group of western European countries—France, the Netherlands, Ireland, and Sweden—has no special recognition procedure but acts on the principle that all religious communities are to be treated equally. If the state supports religious facilities (in the Netherlands more than 50 percent of the state-funded educational system is in the hands of religious organizations), this support must be based on general rules that apply to each worldview. Islamic organizations naturally seize the opportunities offered them. For instance, Islamic elementary schools have become an integral part of the educational landscape in large Dutch cities. Since there is no formal recognition of religion in these countries, however, this model offers no incentive for establishing representative bodies for Muslims.

Acceptance and Rejection of the Islamic Minority

In western Europe the social position of Islamic organizations and the fulfillment of their needs are not determined only by the status of religion in public life. It is also significant that, as a religion of immigrants, Islam is a relative newcomer to the social and religious arena.

As a result, the social acceptance or rejection of the Islamic presence in western Europe largely reflects the patterns governing the acceptance and rejection of immigrants in general. In many places the local population initially accepts a limited number of foreign nationals. Once these newcomers start demanding their place in society, however, tensions increase. Later on, society adapts to the changed makeup of the population and to its different religious composition. In a few British cities where large Muslim populations have lived for longer than one generation, the presence and visibility of Muslims as a religious community go unquestioned. Muslims have a status that is inconceivable in other towns with smaller Muslim populations or with Muslims who have arrived later. Local schools have learned to accommodate the Muslim students' special dietary requests, and Muslims are a recognized interest group and take part either individually or collectively in politics.[19]

But the non-Muslims' acceptance of this situation is far from certain. Even if the permanent presence of immigrants from Islamic countries is an undeniable fact, many non-Muslims still see (and increasingly so, it must perhaps be added) the immigrants' cultural background and, in particular, their religion as a foreign element that can undermine their role as citizens of a western European state.

This widespread opinion is primarily the result of negative perceptions of Islam among the western European public, who above all associate this faith with fanaticism and intolerance toward others. Although this perception has very old roots,[20] it has been reinforced by recent international political developments: first the breakup of the Soviet Union, then the growing influence of revolutionary Islamic movements (in Iran and the Arab world), and finally international Islamist terrorism.

In their agitation against Islam, right-wing extremist groups and parties in western Europe, such as the Front National in France and the Vlaams Blok in Belgium, have repeatedly pointed to the presence of radical Islamist and anti-Western tendencies, even though the great majority of Muslims in western Europe do not support them. In recent decades it has become increasingly acceptable to see this Islamic minority as a "fifth column" and a threat to the West. The anti-Islamic discourse has become more strident as a result of events in the West rather than in the Islamic world. The dispute over Salman Rushdie's *Satanic Verses,* published in the fall of 1988, is an early example. Radical anti-Western preachers in many European countries appear to supply recurrent proof of the "fifth column" theory. And, naturally, the attacks of September 11, 2001, had a devastating influence on public opinion. The anti-Islamic discourse is no longer the obsession of extreme right-wing obscurantists. Populist politicians have pulled it into the mainstream debate.

In this social climate, groups of young Muslims who already suffer from a lack of social and economic opportunities feel so marginalized that they have begun to hate the society in which they live. They become easy prey for recruiters for the international Islamist struggle.[21] The anti-Islamic agitation against Islamist radicalism in western Europe runs the grave risk of becoming a self-fulfilling prophecy.

e. From Foreign Element to European Religion?

Despite the polarization of the social debate on Islam, it is becoming ever more problematic to view the Muslim communities in western Europe as a community of foreign nationals. The Muslim population is increasingly made up of individuals who are not immigrants but French, British, or Dutch by birth. Their religious and political decisions are influenced by their experiences in these countries. Even the contempt that many younger Muslims feel for western European society cannot be dismissed as an import from a foreign culture. It is the dark underside of life in modern Western cities.[22]

Numerous studies on the religious and ethnic identities of second-generation immigrants address the cultural and religious changes that are affecting the generation of Islamic immigrants growing up in western Europe. The situation in the diaspora differs markedly from the situation in the Muslims' countries of origin, since Islam is not an inherent part of the ruling culture in western Europe but something that distinguishes Muslims from this dominant, strongly secularized culture.[23] Muslim religiosity is part of a subculture. The diaspora forces faithful Muslims to redefine the relationship between their religion and the dominant culture. New forms of religiosity are emerging, particularly among second- and third-generation immigrants, forms that are fashioned by conscious decisions about religious practice rather than by efforts to conform to the norms and values of one's family and ethnic group. The experience of Islam is becoming individualized.[24]

One aspect of this change is the relationship between ethnic and religious loyalties. For the first generation these loyalties were intertwined. The religious organizations they founded often reflected the politico-religious conflicts in their countries of origin. Their religious practice was strongly colored, say, by Turkish, southern Asian, or Arab versions of Islam. The religious leaders who were imported from their home countries often reinforced these regional styles of religious practice. Although ties with home, primarily family ties, may remain intact for generations, many young Muslims in western Europe are searching for an Islam that transcends the ethnic bonds of their parents.[25]

Another aspect of this change is the role Islamic prescriptions play in daily life. A small yet growing minority of young Muslims in western Europe are taking them a great deal more seriously than their parents' generation ever did. They are deliberately studying the sources of Islam in order to find out what "true Islam" is. It is easy to understand why Islamist movements appeal to these young Muslims. The religious leaders of these movements refuse to reduce Islam to a personal religious practice and instead emphasize the fact that Islam represents a social system and has political implications.[26] A lively debate is taking place over what exactly these social and political implications are in the context of western Europe. This debate is primarily centered on the content and form of a *fiqh al-aqalliyyat,* an Islamic law for Muslim minorities.[27] Some of the young Muslims who are searching for religious guidance turn to authoritative legal scholars from the Middle East. In satellite TV shows and on "fatwa" websites these scholars are frequently consulted by Muslims living in Europe. In addition, young Muslim leaders in Europe are increasingly raising their voices, including the Swiss philosophy professor Tariq Ramadan, whose writings examine the differences between the universal dimensions and the temporal, local aspects of Islamic sources.[28]

Nevertheless, fewer western European Muslims than is often assumed have embarked on this search for the "true Islam" with the intention of actually practicing it. In many more cases the young Muslims may identify with Islam and the Islamic community, but they lead lives that are barely, if at all, in accordance with Islamic prescriptions. At times this symbolic identification with Islam can be interpreted as a defiant response to experiences of discrimination.[29]

These tendencies toward individualization and positional definitions in a non-Islamic environment provide the backdrop to discussions on the emergence of a European Islam—also known as "Euro-Islam." There is a great deal of wishful thinking embodied in this term. While Euro-Islam is often used to signify a modern, liberal version of Islam that is adapting to the basic norms of western European society, it can also be applied analytically, that is, as a description of forms of Islam that are sculpted by interaction with western European society. Because of the intricate nature of this interaction, European Islam is anything but uniform; it takes on very different shapes and guises.[30] Of crucial importance are the conditions in the diaspora and the influence exerted by the respective surrounding cultures, as well as the hostility shown Islam, which is latent in some cases but which has become much more visible since September 11, 2001. Life in the diaspora leads to more conscious religious decisions, to selective ways of dealing with the elements of religious teachings and laws, and to influences from the non-Islamic environment. Muslim preachers must deliver truly convincing arguments to their followers, who are confronted with many different views on morality in their daily lives. It remains to be seen how the increased fear of Islamic terrorism and the hostility toward Islam in western Europe will affect, over the long term, the identity of the Muslims who live there.

Translated by Adam Blauhut

2. France, Great Britain, the Netherlands, and Germany

(Nico Landman)

The foregoing discussion described the emergence of Muslim communities in different European countries in conjunction with twentieth-century migration movements. In what follows we take a closer look at the situation in European countries that have large Muslim minorities: France, Great Britain, the Netherlands, and Germany.

In many studies of Islam in Europe, France and England are portrayed as opposites in terms of the way they respond to the Muslim presence.[1] Their responses can be explained by the different relationship between religious organizations and the state in public life. While the state plays a prominent role in France and attempts to restrict that of religion as much as possible, Great Britain grants religious organizations a greater presence in the public sphere. The Netherlands and Germany take the middle ground.

This section moves from country to country, outlining typical developments in recent debates on Islam, showing the heterogeneity of the Muslim community, and describing the institutionalization and representation of Islam in various sectors of society.

a. France

Reconfirming the Principle of Laïcité

The year 2004 was a highly eventful one for French Muslims. It started with a series of recommendations by the Stasi Commission—named after its chairman, Bernard Stasi—regarding "the application of secularist principles in the republic." Of these the proposal to ban prominent religious symbols (primarily Islamic headscarves) attracted the greatest international attention, especially when President Jacques Chirac came out in support of it. Among the more conservative Muslims in and outside France, this attempt to restrict what they saw as Muslim girls' freedom of expression caused great indignation. The often heated debate took a near-tragic turn when two French journalists were kidnapped by Islamist groups in Iraq demanding that the headscarf ban be abolished.[2] While the ban itself appeared to have a polarizing effect on the relationship between Muslims and non-Muslims, the hostage drama resulted in feverish and unified efforts by French Muslim authorities and organizations to bring about the release of the hostages in cooperation with the government. This prompted the French Arabist Gilles Kepel to remark that the Muslims had shown themselves to be "good republicans."[3]

The hostage-taking incident once again illustrated that we live in a global village: the connection between the act itself and the discussion in France is evident. But the French ban on headscarves, as proposed by the Stasi Commission, had primarily a domestic background. It must be seen in relation to the central role played the concept of *laïcité* (loosely: secularism) in French state ideology. The Stasi Commission report begins with an extensive discussion of *laïcité*.[4] Stasi argues that this concept, which was defined in the December 9, 1905, law on the separation of church and state, implies full freedom of conscience for every individual as well as state neutrality. This means that the state is expected to guarantee equal treatment of all residents without regard to religion. Furthermore, the state must not recognize or subsidize any single religion. The ban on conspicuous expressions of religious identity (such as the wearing of headscarves) in public schools is based on the assumption that *laïcité* is threatened by religious "communitarism"— that is, the formation of religious subgroups in society that impose their will on others, thereby restricting citizens' individual freedoms. According to the Stasi Commission, Muslim girls need to be protected from the pressure to conform to an Islamic code of conduct, as exerted by a religious community.

The headscarf ban is the concrete expression of a dominant trend in French attitudes toward Islam. The formation of Islamic organizations is a matter of growing concern to the country's intellectual and political elite, as they see such organizations as a threat to the principle of *laïcité*, which they prize above all else.

Muslims and Their Religious Organizations

Muslim history in France is closely linked to the country's colonial past. The organized migration of labor from Algeria and Morocco dates to the First World War and the period of reconstruction in the 1920s. In the 1950s and 1960s workers were also recruited from Algeria to compensate for the labor shortage in France's expanding industries. Most of these Algerian immigrants were unmarried men who came to France for a limited time only. The most important exception was the group of Harkis—Algerians who had fought alongside the colonial rulers in the war of independence and now sought refuge in France because they were seen as traitors by the new Algerian regime. Even though organized labor migration came to an end in the 1970s, the number of Muslims continued to grow, and there were also changes in the social structure of the Muslim population, which now included families with children who were growing up in France. Ethnic diversity increased as a result of the new waves of immigration from former French colonies and from Turkey (see Table 4). Most of these immigrants have become naturalized French citizens, and any children born to them in France were able to acquire French nationality according to *ius solis*. In terms of their social and economic position, these groups are characterized by poor education, high levels of unemployment, and ghettoization in the outlying districts of large cities.

Many have correctly pointed out that the newcomers' lifestyle cannot be understood in terms of religion alone. Rai music (traditional Algerian music fused with rock, reggae, funk, and soul) is only one highly popular, non-Islamic expression of North African culture. Nevertheless, the presence of these immigrants has resulted in the founding of approximately 1,500 prayer rooms and local Islamic centers as well as the emergence of national Islamic organizations.

A prominent role is played by the Mosquée de Paris, which the colonialist French state helped found in 1926 as a token of appreciation to its Muslim subjects. In the postcolonial era it attempted to secure a leading role for itself among Muslims in France and was able to attain a position of power thanks to the recognition and support of the French authorities. (For a time, Interior Minister Charles Pasqua granted the mosque a monopoly over the certification of halal butchers.) The director of the mosque continues to appoint the imams of some one hundred mosques in France,[5] but its strong ties to the leaders of the Algerian state have aroused suspicion among Algerian opposition groups, including sympathizers of the Front Islamique de Salut (Islamic Salvation Front).

The largest and best-organized rival of the Mosquée de Paris is the Union des Organisations Islamiques de France (UOIF, Union of Islamic Organizations of France), which was founded in 1983. Around two hundred mosques are members of this union, which has close ties with the Syrian and Egyptian Muslim Brothers.[6] Working together with like-minded organizations in western Europe and supported by well-known international theologians such as the Egyptian Yusuf al-Qaradawi, the UOIF became involved in creating a *fiqh al-aqalliyyat*—a special form of Islamic law addressing the position of Muslims under non-Muslim governments. More generally, it has been concerned with forms of coexistence between Islam and the secularist French state. A number of other associations have emerged from the ranks of the UOIF, including the Jeunes Musulmans de France (JMF, Young Muslims of France) and the Union de la Jeunesse Musulmane (UJM, Union of Muslim Youth, 1987), in which the ideas of Tariq Ramadan are popular.

The Fédération Nationale des Musulmans de France (FNMF, National Federation of French Muslims) is yet another institution that was established in response to the powerful position of the Mosquée de Paris. Initially, in 1985 it united Muslim groups of a heterogeneous nature—Moroccans, Turks, and French converts to Islam—but it now primarily consists of Moroccan organizations. Turkish Muslims, most of whom live in northeastern France, have founded their own national associations, of which Milli Görüş (Tendance Nationale Union Islamique de France) has been the largest. Muslims from regions south of the Sahara also have their own national organization: the Fédération d'Associations Islamiques d'Afrique, des Comores et des Antilles (FAICA, Federation of Islamic Associations of Africa, the Comoros, and the Antilles).

In addition to these federated associations, diverse Islamic movements exist in France that in many cases control their own network of Islamic centers. They include the Muridiyya order, which has many Senegalese members; the order of Les Amis de l'Islam, made up of followers of the Algerian shaykh Ahmad ibn Mustafa al-ʿAlawi (1869–1934); and other mystical orders.

A final organization that exerts substantial influence over French mosques is Foi et Pratique (Faith and Practice), the French arm of the Tabligh movement founded by Muhammed Ilyas (1885–1944, from northern India). In the early 1970s Tunisian followers of this movement began using itinerant preachers to spread their message among French Muslims, urging them to follow the Prophet's example even in the smallest details of everyday life. This message provided moral and emotional support for thousands of first-generation immigrants. The movement has also been involved in bringing Islam to North African youth, but often the young people who find Islam through Tabligh later criticize its pietistic, apolitical stance and join more radical groups.[7]

Institutionalization and Representation

Reflecting the spirit of *laïcité*, these religious institutions were founded without the financial or organizational support of the French state. For the most part they are private Muslim associations that have little or no affiliation with state authorities. There is no Islamic instruction in public schools, and the few Islamic schools that do exist receive no funding from the state.

But despite the formal separation between church and state, French government authorities must deal with Islamic organizations and Muslim religious identity on many different levels. A study by the Haut Conseil à l'Intégration (High Council for Integration) discusses the obstacles to institutionalizing Islam and proposes possible solutions.[8] One of the council's findings is that, in terms of numbers, physical condition, and capacity, Islamic houses of worship lag far behind those of other religious groups in France. Minarets are rare in French cities, and communal prayers are mostly held in unused department stores or industrial buildings. The legal status of many mosque organizations is weak, and in around four hundred cases the organization managing the mosque is not legally recognized by the state. The council also found that local authorities often resist attempts to set up Islamic prayer rooms and that Muslims are powerless against them. The council made a series of recommendations to local authorities on how they could help Muslims set up proper prayer rooms without violating the principle of a church-state separation. With regard to the employment of imams, the state plays only a limited role, but the council noted with concern that only 4 percent of the imams active in France hold French citizenship. It also found that prisons, the army, and the health system employ only a very small number of Muslim social workers. One of the reasons given is that there is no official authority to propose suitable candidates.

France permits the ritual slaughter of animals based on Islamic custom, but animals may be slaughtered only by certified butchers. The state cooperates with the mosques in Paris, Lyon, and Evry in awarding certification, but—according to the council—problems arise in connection with the Feast of Sacrifice, since the certified slaughterhouses have insufficient capacity and are inadequately organized.

The council also found a few practical problems and insufficient capacity in the area of Muslim burials, but none of these was deemed to be of a fundamental nature.

The council requested that public schools offering lunch programs to their students serve halal meals. It found no legal difficulties in this area that might stand in the way of pragmatic solutions.

The recommendations made by the Haut Conseil in 2000 as a pragmatic response to Islamic demands reflect the reserve that the local and national authorities, citing the 1905 law on church-state separation, had previously shown toward the Muslim community. This reserved response to Muslim organizational efforts, together with the weak socioeconomic position of large Muslim groups, seems to restrict the public visibility of Islam in France.

Nevertheless, in response to social problems in the suburbs and the radicalization of Muslim youth, the French state is looking for ways to cooperate with Islamic organizations. As in other western European countries, these efforts have raised the question, at a national level, as to which Islamic organization can be seen as representative of the Muslim community. For a time the Mosquée de Paris was treated as this representative, but in 1999 Interior Minister J.-P. Chevènement began consulting with additional Islamic groups active on both a national and local level. The result of these talks was the agreement in 2001 to hold elections to a Conseil Français du Culte Musulman (CFCM, French Council of the Muslim Faith). The elections finally took place in April 2003. Since then the CFCM has been recognized as the government's official partner. The largest French Muslim organizations are represented on the board of the CFCM. One year after the CFCM was founded, it became clear that the organization needed to extend its activities beyond religious practice alone. Subsequent developments such as the headscarf ban and the hostage drama in Iraq are forcing it to become involved in sensitive political issues, which is inevitably leading to tensions within the CFCM. It remains to be seen whether it will be able to cope with the increasing problems.

The institutionalization of Islam in France has revived the debate on the status of religion in public life. In 1905 this discussion was ended by a law that emphasized the separation of church and state and relegated the church to the clearly demarcated area of religious life. The ban on headscarves in public schools, passed in 2004, once again emphasized this secularist understanding of the public sphere as a realm in which religion is not permitted greater visibility. Yet the debate on the status of Islam in the secular French Republic is far from over.

b. Great Britain

Secular Multiculturalism and Islam

At a time when the French political elite were discussing headscarves worn by Muslim girls as a problematic form of expression by a religious group and as an assault on national unity, British politicians were discovering Islamic voters. In the London electoral district of Brent East, Labour candidate Robert Evans praised the work of local mosques in a letter sent to Muslim residents. He promised: "I will work for a solution to the issue of parking during Friday prayers. I am a strong supporter of the Islamic Primary School, set up thanks to Labour legislation, which for the first time puts Islam on an equal footing with every other religion in Britain." Two years earlier, in 2001, Labour had lost the electoral district to the Liberal Democrats, partly because of the voting behavior of Muslims, who account for 12 percent of the electorate. In France this sort of sensitivity to religious feelings in an election would have been seen as a betrayal of republican principles, but it fits in well with the British tradition of multiculturalism, which accepts the existence of different ethnic groups and welcomes the display of a minority's identity in public. Still, Labour's appeal to Muslim voters marked the transition to a more explicit recognition of Muslim political influence.

In the 1960s, when Great Britain saw a large influx of immigrants from former colonies, the Labour politician Roy Jenkins defined multiculturalism as "cultural diversity coupled with equal opportunity in an atmosphere of mutual tolerance."[9] The concept has gained popularity ever since, despite reservations among many sectors of the Conservative Party. The active and passive voting rights Great Britain grants to immigrants from Commonwealth countries has also helped give these immigrants greater visibility in public life.

In the 1980s multiculturalism was mainly associated with a struggle against racism. In this context ethnic background was emphasized more strongly than religious identity, and Muslims were seen primarily as part of a population group that originated in Asia. This changed after the Rushdie affair in 1989, which shifted the focus to the religious identity of this group. The failed efforts by Muslim activists to ban *The Satanic Verses,* together with public book burnings, provoked a crisis in British multiculturalism. In debates on cultural difference the categories "black" and "Asian" were increasingly replaced by the term "Muslim." According to Tariq Modood, Islam became a prominent minority identity that was recognized by the left and the right, by both intolerant and open-minded people, by the media and the state.[10]

The Muslims and Their Religious Organizations

In the seventeenth century, the Muslim population of Britain was apparently limited to a few British converts to Islam. This is reflected in the work *Islam in Britain, 1558–1685,* whose title suggests an in-depth discussion of the Muslim presence in the country, but which devotes greater attention to British relations with the Islamic world and British scholarly studies of Islam.[11] With the rise of the British colonial empire, however, a growing number of Muslims—including sailors and students from countries such as Yemen—immigrated to British cities. Cardiff had its own mosque by 1860, and diverse Islamic associations were founded in the course of the nineteenth century. A large number of immigrants arrived in the 1950s and 1960s, first from Cyprus, then from India, Pakistan, and Bangladesh, and finally from East African countries. Until 1962 Great Britain did not impose immigration restrictions on residents of Commonwealth states, and afterward it allowed them to join family members who were already in the country. In the final decades of the twentieth century, there was a small influx of Muslims from other regions of the Islamic world, including Malaysia, a number of Arab countries, and Iran. According to the 2001 census, 1.6 million Muslims were living in Great Britain at the turn of the twenty-first century.[12] The majority (69 percent) were immigrants, or their descendants, from India, Pakistan, and Bangladesh. Like immigrants from other Commonwealth states, almost all had British citizenship.

British Muslims are not distributed equally across the country. Roughly half live in Greater London, with the largest concentration in the district of

Tower Hamlets in the eastern city center, where 36.4 percent of the population are Muslim. Birmingham also has a large Muslim population, as does Bradford (West Yorkshire), which attained international fame as the city that saw the fiercest agitation against *The Satanic Verses*. In his book *Islamic Britain*, Philip Lewis nicknamed the city "Britain's Islamabad."

With regard to the social and economic status of immigrants from Islamic countries, the same pattern can be observed as in other regions of western Europe. Unemployment is high and educational levels are below national averages, particularly among Pakistanis and Bangladeshis. That said, the international city of London is home to many immigrants who come from the political, economic, and intellectual elites of their respective countries of origin.

From an ethnic, socioeconomic, and religious point of view, the Muslims in Great Britain are a highly disparate group, which is mirrored in the religious organizations they have founded. The Muslims from Pakistan, Iran, Iraq, and East Africa include a large number of Shi'ites. One of the larger Twelver Shi'a organizations is the Iraqi Imam al-Khoei Foundation, which publishes the journal *Dialogue*.

The majority of British Muslims, however, are Sunnites, and many are followers of the various movements that have their origins in the Indian subcontinent. Special mention must be made of the Brelwi movement, which venerates and accepts the spiritual power of the *pirs* (Islamic holy men). European Brelwis continue to visit the shrines on the Indian subcontinent that have great spiritual importance for them, which clearly shows the diasporic nature of this form of Islam. In 1994 Coventry became the first British city to contain the grave of an Islamic saint—that of Pir 'Abd al-Wahhab al-Siddiqi. The *mazar* of 'Abd al-Wahhab is now a pilgrimage site that tries to attract new visitors with stories of miraculous healing. The Brelwi movement is bonded together by personal relationships and a common religious ethos that is expressed in verses praising and commemorating deceased saints. It has no hierarchical organization, however.

Another large group is the Deobandi movement, which is not only more puritanical than the Brelwis but also critical of the practice of venerating saints. Conflicts in British mosques are often portrayed as conflicts between the Deobandis and Brelwis, when they are in fact feuds between clans. In Great Britain the network of the pietistic Jama'at-i Tabligh movement with its itinerant preachers—already mentioned in connection with France—is closely interwoven with that of the Deobandis. Its most important centers are the Islamic schools in Dewsbury (Yorkshire) and Bury (Lancashire), which train teachers to carry out missionary work in the movement's mosques. Other movements of Indian origin are the Ahl-i Hadith and the Ahmadiyya. Deserving special attention is the UK Islamic Mission. This organization was founded in 1962 by followers of Jama'at-i Islami, which was itself established by Abu l-A'la al-Maududi, one of the most important ideologues of political Islam. In 1972 the UK Islamic Mission opened its own research and publishing institute, the Islamic Foundation in Leicestershire, which has published several hundred English books on Islam, including translations of Maududi's works, and is also responsible for magazines such as the *Muslim World Book Review, Review of Islamic Economics,* and *Encounters*.[13] Through its activism and publishing projects the organization has had a large impact on British Sunnites.

After 1984 two organizations made attempts to unite British mosque organizations and to transcend the boundaries of the different movements. The first was the Imams and Mosques Council of Great Britain, which was connected to the Libyan Islamic Call Society, and the second was the Council of Mosques in the UK and Eire, a branch of the Muslim World League. The Rushdie affair promoted several other initiatives that sought to improve cooperation among Muslims. The UK Action Committee on Islamic Affairs (UKACIA) brought together many organizations in the fight against *The Satanic Verses*. After the Muslim Parliament was founded in 1992, its initiator, Kalim Siddiqi, regularly made headlines with his Islamic radicalism and confrontational rhetoric—though it must be noted that his radicalism marginalized him in the eyes of the moderate majority. The Muslim Council of Britain (MCB), established in 1997, has had greater success: with 250 member organizations, it soon became the largest umbrella group for Muslims in Great Britain.

Institutionalization and Representation
Owing to both the length of time that has passed since the last major waves of immigration and the widespread acceptance of cultural difference in Great Britain, Muslim religious life in the country is marked by a degree of institutionalization significantly higher than in most other western European countries. The same is true of integration into the major institutions of society. Many of the conflicts that have flared up in other countries over the acceptance of Islam in public life are a thing of the past in Great Britain. Forms of recognition that are commonplace here are out of the question in these other countries. While France, Germany, and the Netherlands heatedly debate whether to allow headscarves in schools or the civil service, London's Metropolitan Police approved a hijab uniform for Muslim policewomen. Islamic models of interest-free economic activity have been tested not only by the branch offices of Saudi banks but also by the Bank of England. The Ministry of Defence has changed its rules on beards to accommodate Muslim staff. There are now Islamic clergy in prisons and hospitals, and the British ministries of defense and health provide medical care for British Muslim pilgrims through the British consulate in Mecca.

Muslims have scored successes in the educational system, too. British schools do not offer confessional religious instruction for the different denominations of their pupils, but they have taught "multi-faith" lessons for several decades. Local school authorities cooperate with religious organizations—even with mosques—to develop methods and materials for these lessons. There are around fifty Islamic secondary schools and Islamic centers for advanced training in Britain, a few of which are supported by the state. In higher education there are several institutes for Islamic studies, some of which offer bachelor's and master's programs recognized by the state.

Muslims, most from the Labour Party, serve on parish councils in London, Bradford, Birmingham, and other cities, and they wield great influence in local politics, though by 2004 there had been only two Muslim MPs in the House of Commons and one in the House of Lords.

This high level of institutionalization in public life is not the result of formal central recognition of Islam. There are not only regional differences between England, Scotland, Wales, and Northern Ireland but also local particularities. Progress in institutionalization is therefore the result of negotiations between Islamic lobbyists and different local authorities rather than the product of national policies. The MCB is not a formally recognized partner that speaks to the government on behalf of the entire Muslim community. Nevertheless, the progress made on the local level shows that the absence of a single representative body has not been a serious obstacle to meeting Muslim demands.

Although the institutionalization of Islam can be called successful, there is no denying that it has created tensions in Great Britain. The Rushdie affair was the first internationally visible sign of these tensions. Since then, radical preachers such as 'Umar al-Bakri have shaped the face of British Islam as seen on television. Intelligence agencies have for years expressed concerns about young British Muslims fighting in the wars in Palestine, Afghanistan, Chechnya, and other conflict regions. September 11, 2001, and British involvement in the 2003 invasion of Iraq worsened fears of Islamic radicalism—fears that came true in the London transit bombings of July 7, 2005.

For their part, Muslims have enough reason to worry about the increased anti-Islamic sentiment and the mobilization of this sentiment by the right-wing British National Party. Despite these tensions, it must be noted that British Muslims, both individually and collectively, have become an important factor in social and political life in Great Britain.

c. The Netherlands

An End to Dutch Tolerance?

Until recently, Europeans regarded the Netherlands as a country that was highly tolerant of foreign nationals and that boasted a friendly climate for Muslims and other groups. It seemed that cosmopolitan cities such as Amsterdam and Rotterdam could easily absorb large numbers of migrants from the Islamic world and were happy to give them a great deal of freedom to set up their own religious institutions. In 2002 this image received its first blemishes when the populist politician Pim Fortuyn scored a landslide victory in local elections in Rotterdam with his anti-Islamic rhetoric ("Islam is a backward religion"; "If it were up to me, we wouldn't allow any more Muslims into the country"). Just when it seemed that he and his party (Lijst Pim Fortuyn) might win the parliamentary elections, Fortuyn was murdered by a radical animal rights activist. Despite his assassination and the rapid disintegration of his party, Fortuyn's success caused a shift in the Dutch political landscape and changed the tone in the debate over Islam. The main liberal party (Volkspartij Voor Democratie, VVD), in particular, took up Fortuyn's criticism that Muslims were treated too leniently. The party not only began focusing on the fight against Islamic radicalism but also put integration at the top of the political agenda as an important social issue, arguing that integration was undermined by Islam.

Most other Dutch politicians and opinion leaders felt compelled to take a stronger stand on multicultural coexistence in general and political Islam in particular. The sharper tones of the debate over Islam, which could be heard all across Europe after September 11, 2001, were particularly striking in the Netherlands because in the past, both the "decent" center parties and the media had stifled or marginalized the anti-Islamic attacks coming from right-wing extremist splinter groups. But now, for the first time, this sentiment was becoming socially acceptable. The idea that integration had failed because of unwillingness among Muslims to accept "our Western norms and values" increased in popularity.

A new source of tension over Islam was the murder of film director Theo van Gogh by an Islamic extremist on November 2, 2004. Van Gogh's killer, a young man of Moroccan descent who had grown up in the Netherlands, left a letter on his body threatening the MP Ayaan Hirsi Ali. For some years Hirsi Ali had been the most prominent critic of Islam in the VVD party, and in 2004 she produced the film *Submission* about the abuse of women in Islam in cooperation with van Gogh. Although Theo van Gogh was highly controversial because of his extremely offensive remarks about Muslims and his provocative style, his assassination turned him into a "martyr of the free word," and a group of sympathizers pledged to continue his incisive attacks on Islam in the interests of freedom of opinion. In the weeks following the murder, mosques and Islamic schools in many Dutch cities became the targets of arson attacks and vandalism. The increasingly hostile climate has in turn influenced the attitudes of young Muslims, and their radicalization is a growing concern. Dutch society is in a state of confusion about the future place of Islam in the country.

Muslims and Their Religious Organizations

In early 2004 immigration statistics put the number of Muslims in the Netherlands at 944,000, or 5.8 percent of the Dutch population.[14] Whereas immigrants from former colonies dominate the scene in Great Britain and France, the largest groups of Muslims in the Netherlands are labor immigrants and their descendants from Turkey and Morocco. Labor migration from these countries began in the 1960s and continued into the 1970s, when family members joined Muslims already in the country. In 2004 these two groups made up around 75 percent of the Muslim population in the Netherlands. More than half of them have become naturalized Dutch citizens, but many have also kept their original nationality. Among Moroccans this double nationality can hardly be avoided, since there is no official procedure for renouncing Moroccan nationality.

When Dutch colonial rule came to an end in Indonesia in 1949, only a few hundred Muslims left this primarily Islamic region for Holland. The decolonization of Surinam in 1975 took a different course and spurred mass migration to the Netherlands. Surinamese society, which is marked by great ethnic and religious heterogeneity, is characterized by two Muslim groups: the Hindustani Muslims, who migrated from India to Surinam as contract workers starting in the late nineteenth century, and the Javanese Muslims, who began settling in Surinam in the early twentieth century.

Finally, since the 1980s and 1990s the ethnic makeup of the Muslim population in the Netherlands has been increasingly influenced by asylum seekers from various parts of the Islamic world, including Iraq, Afghanistan, and Somalia. As a result, the Muslim population is becoming ever more heterogeneous.

While the two separate networks established by Turks and Moroccans dominate the Islamic infrastructure of the Netherlands,[15] the Hindustani Muslims from Surinam have also founded their own local and national organizations. These are affiliated with international movements originating in India and Pakistan. Many other Muslim ethnic groups have their own associations, but in only a few cases do they have their own mosques. Of the approximately 436 registered mosques, more than half (225) are run by Turkish organizations, 139 by Moroccans, and 47 by Surinamese and Pakistanis.[16]

One finds the same politico-religious currents among Turkish organizations in the Netherlands as in Germany.[17] The largest federation of Muslim organizations is the Diyanet network, which boasts 140 mosques, 30 of which have been built recently. The Islamitische Stichting Nederland (Islamic Foundation of the Netherlands, Hollanda Diyanet Vakfı) is the body in this network that is nationally responsible for imams and mosques, while the Turks-Islamitische Culturele Federatie (Turkish Islamic Cultural Federation) promotes the social and cultural interests of its members. The Dutch arm of the Milli Görüş movement controls about thirty-five Islamic centers, which attract a large number of young people. Owing to their liberal views, the Dutch leaders of Milli Görüş have earned a respected and valued place in the public debate, even if their own conservative followers find their outlook too extreme. The Stichting Islamitisch Centrum (Islamic Center Foundation), a Dutch Süleymanlı organization, also has an extensive network of about forty centers. This movement is mainly attempting to set up new educational centers to take in and look after older school students.

In recent years the Nurcu movement, and in particular the Nurcu branch led by Fethullah Gülen, has gained some influence over young Turks in the Netherlands and established its own organizations.

Turkish Islamic networks show a relatively great cohesiveness, which results partly from the hierarchical organizational structure and partly from a shared ideology. In contrast, the Moroccan Islamic networks are much more loosely organized. Their main representative at the national level is the Unie van Marokkaanse Moslim Organisaties in Nederland (UMMON, Union of Moroccan Muslim Organizations). Although it claims to have ninety member mosques, the real number is probably smaller, owing to the autonomous nature of the local Moroccan houses of worship. In the 1990s opponents of King Hasan II's regime harshly criticized the organization for its loyalty to the Moroccan government, but this form of criticism died down once King Mohammed VI ascended the throne. Today the UMMON is accepted and respected as part of the Muslim establishment in the Netherlands, though doubts about its influence remain, and its position is sometimes challenged by regional Moroccan councils.

A number of international organizations and movements are also active in the Moroccan mosque network. The Jama'at-i Tabligh (see the sections on France and Great Britain) controls the ar-Rahman mosque in Amsterdam and uses it as a base to send out its itinerant preachers. A much more visible network of mosques is the one close to Saudi Wahhabism comprising the Tawheed mosque in Amsterdam, the as-Soenna mosque in The Hague, and the Faroek mosque in Eindhoven. In recent years it has usually been labeled Salafi, a term referring to the Prophet's companions and connoting a strict adherence to Islamic prescriptions and an uncompromising attitude toward non-Muslim culture. Because of the close scrutiny with which its activities are followed by the intelligence agencies, its members have moderated their tone and advocated a nonviolent, nonconfrontational approach to Dutch society. While some observers see the preachers of these mosques as a means of safely channeling the frustrations of Muslim youth, others fear that they may contribute to segregating and polarizing society.

The Surinamese Islamic network is dominated by the Brelwi movement (see the section on Great Britain) and thus by a few internationally active leaders (*pirs*). The most important Brelwi organization is the World Islamic Mission (WIM), which oversees more than ten mosques in the Netherlands. The spiritual leader of the WIM used to be the Pakistani politician Shah Ahmad Noorani, but he died in 2003 and was succeeded by his son. In the Netherlands, Noorani was criticized for his bitter polemics against the Ahmadiyya movement, which is particularly widespread among Surinamese Muslims and maintains over half a dozen mosques in the Netherlands.

Institutionalization and Representation
The development of Islam in the institutions of Dutch society must be seen in conjunction with the institutionalized pluralism (*verzuiling,* or

"pillarization"),[18] which was a main feature of the Netherlands in the 1960s but has since lost much of its influence because of secularization.[19] The pillarization system provided religious communities with many opportunities to create and receive state funding for a separate social infrastructure consisting of schools, hospitals, and welfare institutions. Muslim immigrants were able to use the remnants of this system to increase their public visibility, particularly in the field of education. By 2004 there were forty-one Islamic elementary schools and two Islamic secondary schools in the Netherlands. These developments were supported, in particular, by Christian confessional politicians who regarded the establishment of a Muslim religious infrastructure as an instrument for collective emancipation.

Many, however, consider pillarization an obsolete model that causes antagonism between social groups and prevents individuals from emancipating themselves from the oppressive bonds of tradition. From this perspective the foundation of Islamic schools was a step backward. The Dutch debate on the institutionalization of Islam has been dominated by opposing currents, including those who want to deconstruct the remnants of the old pillars and those who want to establish a new Islamic pillar.

Since the early 1970s Islam has gained considerable ground in the Dutch public arena. There are now about 436 mosques, 60 of which have been recently built. Broadcasting the Islamic call for prayer over loudspeakers on minarets is protected by law (within certain limitations), and there are state-subsidized Islamic channels on publicly owned radio and television networks. I have already discussed the establishment of Islamic schools. In this respect it is interesting to note that most Muslim parents send their children to state or Christian schools, mostly for practical reasons: these are usually the ones that are closest to their homes. Islamic religious instruction is only rarely on the curriculum in state schools. Although these schools are legally required to offer instruction if parents ask them to do so, it is up to the parents to arrange to have a teacher come in and to pay his or her salary. In these circumstances Muslim parents usually prefer their children to have religious instruction in local mosques. State and denominational universities offer a growing number of Islamic studies programs that target mainly Muslim students. Moreover, two Islamic institutes of higher education, the Islamitische Universiteit in Rotterdam and Islamitische Universiteit Europa in Schiedam, have applied for state accreditation. Muslim chaplaincies in prisons and hospitals are also on the rise.

In the 1980s Holland encouraged participation in politics by granting voting rights for town councils to foreign nationals who had been living legally in the country for three years. As a result, Turkish and Moroccan Muslims were elected to municipal councils in nearly all large cities, and they have gradually risen to responsible positions in local politics. Furthermore, Turkish and Moroccan Muslims have become MPs and, in recent years, even cabinet ministers.

These forms of institutionalization demonstrate that Muslims have become an important religious minority in the Netherlands. Nevertheless, their institutions are too small and too fragmented to be compared to the Protestant or Catholic pillars of the 1950s and 1960s. The Muslim politicians have carved out careers for themselves *within* the established parties and merely disseminate party ideas instead of acting as representatives of Islam in Dutch politics. There have been attempts to launch an Islamic political party, but it is doubtful that such a party would be able to win over the very heterogeneous Islamic population in Holland.

As is the case in most other European countries, this heterogeneity has been an obstacle to establishing a representative body for all Muslims. Two Islamic councils existed in the 1990s, the Islamitische Raad Nederland (Islamic Council of the Netherlands) and the Nederlandse Moslimraad (Dutch Muslim Council), but their rivalry only emphasized their lack of unity. After two years of internal diplomatic efforts, Muslims founded the Contactorgaan Moslims en Overheid (CMO, Council for Communication between Muslims and the Government), which includes all the major Turkish, Moroccan, and Surinamese mosque associations and is officially recognized by the state as a dialogue partner. This body must still prove itself in practice, but it is in a position to play a central role in the dialogue between Muslim groups and the state.[20]

One subject of this dialogue will doubtless be the necessity to counter the radicalization of younger Muslims, which is of great concern to the Dutch state. The CMO can also be expected to criticize the declining social tolerance toward Muslims and their religion. In today's polarized social climate the difficult challenge for a council like the CMO is to act as a serious and respected partner in its relations with the authorities without alienating parts of its rather heterogeneous rank and file.

d. Germany

Foreign Nationals, Mixed Feelings

In his analysis of studies about Muslims in Germany, the sociologist Levent Tezcan argues that the political and academic debates in the country revolve around such questions as "Can Muslims be integrated?" and "To what extent is Islam reconcilable with our modern lifestyle?"[21] This link between the debates on Islam and the problems of both immigration and integration can be observed throughout western Europe and is surely not confined to Germany alone. The German debate, however, has been framed in terms of a clash of cultures for a longer period of time and to a greater extent than in the countries discussed to this point. Many opinion leaders have suggested that there is a fundamental opposition between the Qur'an and the German constitution. German studies of the Muslim presence routinely refer to the concept of *taqiyya* (the concealment of a true intention), claiming that the outward adaptation of Muslims to the norms of Germany society must be seen as a tactical move not based on principle.[22] This distrust is partly due to secularist Turkish journalists who attack Turkish Muslim organizations for speaking with forked tongues: while emphasizing the Turks' commitment to German society in their German-language publications, these organizations triumphantly portray Islam as superior to a corrupt, godless Western society in their Turkish sermons and writings.

The distrust of multiculturalism is reflected in the concept of *Leitkultur*— a "guiding" culture whose norms and values have been shaped by German Christian history and must be accepted by newcomers. Friedrich Merz, the former floor leader of the Christian Democratic Union, introduced this term in 2000 when demanding that foreign nationals adapt to German culture, but soon afterward it became clear that a precise definition was highly problematic. Skeptics had a field day: Does *Leitkultur* mean beer and bratwurst? Does it refer to love of the German Fatherland? Of Christian values? The debate has revealed the deep divisions in German society caused by the Muslim presence. On the one hand, there have been rather protective reactions to the increasingly visible Muslim community. On the other, the intense responses to the *Leitkultur* concept demonstrate that multicultural ideals are strongly anchored in German society.

Muslim Immigration to Germany

In contrast to that in France and Great Britain, the development of the German Muslim community is not shaped by the country's colonial past. The Muslims have no pre-migration knowledge of the German language, they are not acquainted with German culture, and they do not have a special legal status based on former colonial ties. Most of the 3 million Muslims in Germany come from Turkey (2.3 million, or 76 percent), and immigration patterns resemble those in other European countries: temporary residence of male workers in the 1960s, family reunifications and long-term residence in the 1970s, and finally chain migration as a result of marriages with spouses from their countries of origin. The influx of "first-generation" labor migrants, however, continued until 1993. Half a century after the first major wave of immigration, many Germans still refer to members of this community as *Ausländer* (foreigners), even though this description is increasingly perceived as unfair. Since only 340,000 Turks have taken on German citizenship, 2 million do indeed have the legal status of foreign nationals. Citizenship in Germany is traditionally based on *ius sanguinis,* and it was not until 2000 that regulations changed; now children born to foreigners living in Germany are automatically granted German citizenship if one parent has been living in the country for eight years.[23]

The scholar Muhammad Salim Abdullah has challenged the dominant idea that the Islamic presence in Germany is a relatively recent phenomenon and the result of immigration (primarily of Turks). In his work he attempts to anchor Islam more strongly in German history.[24] To make this point, he refers to twenty Turks who served the Prussian king Friedrich Wilhelm I and were given their own prayer room near Potsdam in 1732. He also mentions the mosque in Wünsdorf, which was built for Muslim prisoners of war by order of Kaiser Wilhelm II.[25] Furthermore, he describes the Muslim organization in Berlin that published the *Moslemische Revue* during the Weimar Republic.

Turkish migrants are not the only group worthy of attention in the period following the Second World War. A fairly large contingent of Iranian businessmen settled Hamburg in 1950. In the 1960s labor immigrants came not only from Turkey but also from Morocco and Tunisia. Large numbers of asylum seekers from Iran, Afghanistan, and Iraq followed in the 1980s. Civil war brought many Bosnians to Germany in the 1990s, and for a time they formed the largest Muslim group after the Turks. When the war came to an end, however, their numbers declined as a result of remigration to their country of origin. Finally, an estimated fifty thousand Germans have converted to Islam, most of them women married to Muslim men.

Until the collapse of communism in 1989, this Muslim population was a purely West German phenomenon, concentrated in the country's centers of industry. After 1990 the states of the former German Democratic Republic, now part of a unified Germany, also saw the number of Muslim inhabitants grow, primarily because asylum seekers are distributed across all the federal states of Germany. Nonetheless, their numbers are small in the East, and their public visibility is low.[26]

The weak social and economic status of labor migrants, who suffer from relatively poor educational levels, overrepresentation in unskilled jobs, and high unemployment rates, is changing only gradually, but a growing number of immigrants have opened small or medium-sized businesses. There are currently more than 55,000 Turkish-owned small businesses in the Federal Republic.[27]

Religious Movements and Organizations

In terms of numbers, Turks dominate the Muslim community in Germany, which can be seen in the country's Islamic movements and organizations. The largest Muslim organizations not only have Turkish majorities but also reflect the religious and political landscape in Turkey.

Turkish Muslim Organizations

As a result of the Turkish immigration to Germany, long-standing struggles in Turkey between secularism and Islamization, and between Diyanet (the agency for religious affairs) and opposition Islamic groups, were transferred to European soil. Yet power relations in Europe differ from those in Turkey. The Islamic groups that worked illegally or enjoyed only limited freedom of movement in their home country benefit from much more favorable conditions in Europe. They have been able to set up European branches of their organizations, raise funds, and boost their membership without restrictions being placed on their activities by Turkish authorities.

In the 1970s, for instance, students of Süleyman Hilmi Tunahan, a Naqsh-bandi shaykh who died in 1960, set up a broad network of Islamic centers in Germany and other western European countries. Called the Verband der Islamischen Kulturzentren (VIKZ, Association of Islamic Cultural Centers), this network was structured hierarchically, with headquarters in Cologne and branches in the German states and neighboring countries. Each branch is led by a senior imam and controls local organizations. By its own account the VIKZ has some three hundred member congregations in Germany.[28] Among other activities, it runs Qur'an schools which offer Arabic and basic religious lessons to elementary and middle school students, particularly during school vacations and on weekends. In addition, it offers homework help to secondary school students. In some places these activities have been criticized as an obstacle to integration, but Turkish parents regard them as a useful contribution to their children's school careers. In a comprehensive study Gerdien Jonker has shown that the spirituality of the movement is rooted in the mystic tradition of the Naqshbandiyya, though its members no longer have a personal relationship (*rabita*) with a living shaykh because Tunahan did not name a successor. In Süleymanli doctrine, Kemal Kacar, who led the movement from 1959 until his death in 2000, was regarded not as a mystical teacher but only as a "worldly" leader. Nevertheless, his authority was nearly unassailable, even in theological matters. Jonker's study also makes clear that for the European branch of the movement, dialogue with the non-Islamic environment assumed increasing importance in the late 1990s as a result of the opening of the Islamic Islah academy and involvement in inter-religious forums. But then in 2000 this outward orientation was rejected by a new leader in Turkey, Arif Ahmet Denizolgun, who shifted the focus back to deepening the religiosity of the congregations.[29]

Milli Görüş is the other highly successful Islamic movement among Turks in Germany. It brings together the sympathizers of Necmettin Erbakan, who, beginning in the late 1960s, tried to Islamize Turkish society using the instruments of party politics. After the coup d'état in 1980, which temporarily ended Erbakan's political career and sidelined his National Salvation Party, his followers created a broad-based organization in western Europe—first called Avrupa Milli Görüş Teşkilatları (Milli Görüş Organizations in Europe) and then renamed the Islamische Gemeinschaft Milli Görüş in 1995 (IGMG, Islamic Community of Milli Görüş).[30] Around five hundred mosque congregations throughout Europe are members of the IGMG, including three hundred in Germany. These local congregations are organized into associations at a regional level. In 2004 there were fifteen regional branches in Germany (Hamburg, Bremen, Berlin, Hanover, the Northern Ruhr Region, the Ruhr Region, Düsseldorf, Cologne, Hesse, Rhine-Saar, Stuttgart, Freiburg, Northern Bavaria, Southern Bavaria, and Swabia), and fourteen branches in Europe (Denmark, Sweden, Northern Holland, Southern Holland, Belgium, Paris, Strasbourg, Lyon, Annecy, Switzerland, two in Austria, Norway, and England). The European association is headquartered in Germany.[31] Although the Milli Görüş movement clearly originated in political Islam, opinions differ as to the extent to which its European branches have adapted to secularized and pluralistic societies. In the 1990s in particular, members of the Turkish immigrant generation that grew up in Germany attempted to distance themselves from political conditions in Turkey and to concentrate on Europe instead. One aspect of this European orientation was the acceptance of religious pluralism and the pursuit of amicable relations with the non-Islamic environment. Even so, at mass meetings in soccer stadiums, members reaffirmed their support for Erbakan and other party leaders as part of a collective identity, and proselytizing rhetoric was an integral part of the speeches.[32] Insofar as developments in Turkey continue to influence the course taken by the European branch of Milli Görüş, it is of central importance that the last party led by Erbakan (Saadet Partisi, or Felicity Party) has been marginalized by the Adalet ve Kalkınma Partisi (Party of Justice and Progress), headed by Recep Tayyip Erdoğan. The Felicity Party also has its origins in the Milli Görüş movement but takes a stronger pro-European position.

In 1983 a radical wing of Milli Görüş, which looked to revolutionary Iran for inspiration, split from the movement under the leadership of Cemaleddin Kaplan (d. 1995). Known as Islami Cemaat ve Cemiyetler Birliği (ICCB, Federation of Islamic Associations and Congregations), this organization is working to establish an Islamic state in Turkey as the first step toward unifying the Islamic world under a caliph. It rejects participation in the system of political parties as a way to reach this goal. In 1994 Kaplan proclaimed a "caliphate state" and appointed himself caliph; the ICCB disseminated his ideas via a dozen Islamic centers, the newspaper *Ümmet-i Muhammad,* and the private broadcaster Hakk TV. A case study undertaken by the anthropologist Werner Schiffauer traces how the ICCB evolved from a revolutionary movement of political Islam into a sect that is increasingly focused on the figure of the leader, whose position is similar to that of a shaykh in a Sufi order. As a result of the dispute over leadership after Kaplan's death in 1995, support dwindled, and the Kaplan movement became a marginal group with fewer than a thousand members. Nevertheless, its radicalism continued to attract attention. Kaplan's son Metin served a prison sentence in Germany after he was found guilty of soliciting the murder of one of his rivals. He was extradited to Turkey in late 2004 and sentenced to life imprisonment in June 2005. Earlier, in December 2001, Kaplan's caliphate state and affiliated organizations were banned by the German minister of the interior.

The Nurcu movement was founded by Said Nursi (d. 1960), who resisted the secularization of Turkey under Kemal Atatürk by publishing the *Risale-i Nur,* a series of meditative commentaries on the Qur'an. In this work Nursi attempted to prove the rationality of Islamic doctrine and the irrational character of atheist ideologies that gained influence in Turkey. Despite staunch opposition from the Kemalist elite, who regarded Nursi and his movement as reactionary, Nursi attracted several million followers, primarily organized into study groups around the *Risale-i Nur*. In the last few decades of the twentieth century, one branch of the movement, led by Fethullah Gülen, established an international network of educational institutes and private universities. In Germany there are 120 Nurcu congregations with a few thousand members.[33]

Another movement that has gained a foothold among Turks in Germany is the Türkisch-islamische Synthese (Turkish-Islamic Synthesis). Originating in the 1970s along the extreme right fringe of the Turkish political spectrum, it seeks to reconcile Turkish nationalism with Islamic teachings by assigning Turks a leading role in the Islamic *umma*, or world community. The movement attracted attention in Germany when in 1978 its supporters founded the Avrupa Demokratik-Ülkücü Federasyonu (ADÜTDF, Federation of Associations of Turkish Democratic Idealists in Europe). Like other Turkish umbrella organizations in Germany, it works across national borders and boasts around two hundred member organizations throughout Europe. In 1987 a group broke off that wanted to put greater emphasis on religious identity as opposed to Turkish national identity. In 1993 this new organization became known as Avrupa Türk-Islam Birliği (ATIB, Turkish Islamic Union of Europe); it too is thought to include some two hundred member organizations.

In response to these developments, Diyanet, the Turkish state's agency for religious affairs, launched a counteroffensive in the 1980s in an effort to build its own infrastructure of Turkish mosques in western Europe. It sent salaried imams as "religious functionaries" to the region and had their activities coordinated by religious attachés at the Turkish embassies and consulates. Moreover, mosque organizations were encouraged to give up their local autonomy, become part of a hierarchically organization controlled by Diyanet, and transfer ownership of their mosques to this authority. In the Netherlands this policy was so successful that the Dutch Diyanet organization Islamitische Stichting Nederland gained control of roughly 70 percent of Turkish mosque organizations and was able to marginalize rival Turkish Islamic organizations. Competing organizations put up greater resistance in Germany, but Diyanet Işleri Türk-Islam Birliği (DITIB, Turkish Islamic Union for Religious Affairs) was undeniably the largest such organization in the Federal Republic, with 870 member associations.[34]

This development can be explained by a variety of factors: the pressure that Turkish civil servants apply to their compatriots in foreign countries, the financial and organizational advantages of using an imam sent by the Turkish authorities rather than having to find suitable candidates and pay their salaries; and, finally, persuasive propaganda depicting rival organizations as extremist and hostile to the beloved Turkish fatherland. Unlike the aforementioned Islamic movements, the DITIB does not represent specific ideologies or a specific religious school of thought. Its publications focus on a Sunni orthodoxy based on the Hanafi school of Islamic law and generally support friendly relations with the non-Islamic environment and loyalty to the non-Islamic state. At the same time, they emphasize the bonds shared by the Turkish Islamic community in Germany in such a way as to stress both a Turkish national and an Islamic identity.[35]

An important recent development among Turks is the revival and institutionalization of Alevi Islam. This religious movement, whose followers make up around 20 percent of the Turkish population, is often considered part of Shi'ite Islam because of the central role played by 'Ali ibn Abi Talib in its system of beliefs. The movement, however, is characterized by independent liturgical and social traditions, including both the *cem*—a liturgical commemoration of a mythical meal with forty men and women in the early age of Islam—and the *musahiplik,* a spiritual bond between two men and their wives that commits them to lifelong solidarity and shared property. The revival of Alevi Islam among Turks in western Europe parallels developments in Turkey in the 1980s. These developments were themselves a response to the right-wing extremist violence against this group in the late 1970s, and they were also spurred by the suppression of the leftist organizations in which Alevis were active. Various Alevi organizations that were founded in the 1980s came together in 1990 to form the Alevi Cemaatleri Federasyonu (Federation of Alevi Communities). In order to draw attention to cooperation with other organizations in Europe, this federation changed its name in 1993 to Avrupa Alevi Birlikleri Federasyonu (AABF, Federation of Alevi Associations in Europe). By its own account the AABF has some 140 member organizations, including 90 in Germany.[36]

Two schools of thought can be distinguished in the revived Alevi form of Islam: the first regards Alevism as a mystical teaching rooted in Islam; the second seeks to separate Alevi doctrine from Islam and treat it as a humanist philosophy. The European branches of the Alevi network are strongly oriented toward Turkey and regard the emancipation and recognition of their fellow Alevis in Turkey as a major goal.

Other Muslim Organizations

Compared with these broad-based Turkish Islamic organizations—nearly all of which have several hundred local centers—the Muslim organizations founded by other ethnic groups in Germany may at first glance seem marginal. Nevertheless, some of the non-Turkish Muslim networks have also shaped the face of Islam in Germany and should be discussed here, particularly those run by Arab Muslims. One example is the Islamische Gemeinschaft in Deutschland (IGD, Islamic Community in Germany), which maintains centers in Munich, Stuttgart, Frankfurt, Münster, Nuremberg, Marburg, Braunschweig, and Cologne. By its own account the IGD works together with twenty-eight local Muslim associations,[37] the oldest of which, the Islamische Zentrum München (Islamic Center of Munich), was set up between 1967 and 1973 and for years has published the quarterly *Al-Islam.* In the 1960s the IGD—or to be more precise its predecessor—was directed by Saʿid Ramadan, the brother-in-law of Hasan al-Banna, who founded the Muslim Brothers in Egypt. This family tie is a reason why the IGD is often associated with the Muslim Brothers,[38] although many doubt that such a connection really exists.[39]

A second network of Arab Muslims in Germany has emerged around the Islamisches Zentrum in Aachen (IZA, including the Bilal mosque), which was founded in 1970 and was led for many years by the Syrian Muslim brother ʿIsam al-Din al-ʿAttar. Since it was founded in 1966, the Islamisches Zentrum in Hamburg, which publishes the journal *Al-Fadschr,* has played a leading role among Shiʿite Muslims in Germany. It represents Twelver Shiʿism and maintains close ties to the leaders of the Islamic Republic of Iran.[40] Bosnian Muslim organizations have also established their own national umbrella association: the Vereinigung Islamischer Gemeinden der Bosniaken in Deutschland (Federation of Bosnian Islamic Communities in Germany), with fifty-five member congregations. Finally, there are a variety of small yet active organizations for Muslims of German descent.[41]

This overview shows the heterogeneity and complexity of organized Islam in Germany. The diversity becomes even more apparent if we consider the many smaller groups listed in the reports by the German Federal Office for the Protection of the Constitution—groups ranging from Sufi congregations to radical Islamist splinter groups. Such diversity raises the question as to how Islam is represented in the public arena and to what extent Muslim organizations are recognized by the German state.

Institutionalization and Representation
Of all western European countries Germany has the largest number of mosques (approximately 2,200, or one mosque for every 1,300 or so Muslims). These mosques are not merely religious centers but hubs for a wide variety of religious, educational, economic, and publishing activities. Many of the umbrella organizations discussed so far publish their own journals: aside from the quarterlies *Al-Islam* and *Al-Fadschr,* the publications include the IGMG's *Milli Görüş: Perspektive,* and DITIB's newsletter *Haber Bülteni.* The Zentralinstitut Islam Archiv Deutschland (Central Islamic Institute and Archive in Germany), which is based in Soest, puts out the quarterly *Moslemische Revue,* having revived the similarly named magazine published between 1924 and 1942. The women's magazine *Huda* offers female-friendly interpretations of Islamic works. A variety of Sufi groups publish German-language magazines, including the weekly *Lichtblicke* and the quarterly *Morgenstern,* both supported by followers of Shaykh Nazim al-Kubrusi. Muslims have also been publishing a growing number of books, either translated from the Arabic or Turkish or written in German. Finally, the Internet has become an ever more important medium used by like-minded Muslims to exchange ideas.[42]

Apart from the widespread Qurʾan schools and several dozen boarding facilities for students attending nearby schools, there are only a handful of

Islamic educational institutes in the country: an accredited, state-supported Islamic elementary school in Berlin, an Islamic high school in Munich, and several institutes of Islamic higher education. The last include the Institut für Internationale Pädagogik und Didaktik (Institute of International Pedagogy and Didactics), which offers a two-year program, and the Islamisches Zentrum Hamburg, which provides Shiʿite theological training.[43] A chair was established in 2004 at the Westfälische Wilhelms-Universität in Münster to train teachers to give Islamic religious instruction in German schools.[44]

In the economic sphere, one must point to the branch offices set up by banks from the Islamic world, including the Islam Tekaful Kurumu. Furthermore, all the larger Islamic umbrella organizations have their own businesses, ranging from grocery stores to real estate companies.[45]

The scale of these religious, educational, and economic activities has led some observers to complain that "a parallel, independent Muslim society has evolved in nearly all areas of life."[46] Although the Muslim presence seems vibrant, the integration of Islam into the institutions of German society is notably weak. Unlike Germany's established religions, Islam has yet to be formally recognized. Like Belgium, Austria, and several other western European countries, Germany has a procedure for recognizing religious communities as public bodies. This recognition gives them important privileges, including access to the so-called church tax, which the state collects from members of a religious community and transfers to their church. Moreover, formally recognized religious communities are entitled to state-funded broadcasting opportunities and subsidies for youth activities. They are also granted the so-called parochial right, by which any adherent of their religion is automatically considered a member of their community.[47] In addition to these concrete privileges, recognition under public law has a symbolic value in that it enhances the religious community's status. By contrast, the absence of recognition is seen by many Muslims as an indication of the second-class status of their faith.[48] Muslim organizations have been trying since 1977 to secure recognition as public bodies, but they have failed because none of the organizations applying could be seen as representative of the heterogeneous Muslim community. Moreover, they do not yet meet the legal requirement of being a stable organization that is firmly rooted in German society.

The requirement of representativeness has provided an important stimulus for Muslim organizations to form coalitions in Germany. One example is the Islamrat für die Bundesrepublik Deutschland (Islamic Council of the Federal Republic of Germany), founded in 1986. In this council Milli Görüş, the Suleymanlis, and the Nurcus have worked together with a number of smaller Muslim organizations from different ethnic communities, including both Sunnis and Shiʿites. The Islamrat has applied for recognition as a public body, but so far without success. After the Suleymanlis left the council in 1988, it was dominated by organizations affiliated with Milli Görüş, and in 1994 a rival body was founded, the Zentralrat der Muslime in Deutschland (Central Council of Muslims in Germany). Although this second council also unites Islamic organizations of various ethnic groups and religious currents, it does not include the major Turkish associations; the Suleymanlis were among the cofounders, but they left in 2000. The previously Islamic centers in Munich, Aachen, and Hamburg are members of the Zentralrat.

Although both councils contribute to both the cooperation within and the internal cohesion of the fragmented, heterogeneous Islamic community in Germany, it is clear that they represent only a fraction of Muslim organizations in the country. The Islamic umbrella organization DITIB with its 870 member organizations did not join them, and the VIKZ of the Suleymanlis participated for only a short time on both councils. The establishment of a single representative body for the Muslims in Germany seems unlikely in the near future. In addition to the problem of diversity and rivalry, it is hard for Islamic organizations to determine the exact number of their followers since only a small number of Muslims in Germany are registered as members.[49]

In debates about legal recognition of Muslim organizations, it is not just the size of their rank and file that is being questioned but also their loyalty to German society. The organizations are accused of abusing Western democracy, freedom of religion, and tolerance in order to disseminate an undemocratic and intolerant model of society. In response to this criticism, Muslim organizations never tire of emphasizing their loyalty to Germany's "Basic Law" and energetically condemning terrorist attacks carried out in the name of Islam. This stance is exemplified by the Islamische Charta (Islamic Charter), which the Zentralrat released in early 2002. Among other things, it embraces the principles on which the Federal Republic of Germany is based and which are guaranteed by the German constitution: separation of powers, rule of law, democracy, a multiparty system, active and passive suffrage for women, as well as freedom of religion. The charter also recognizes the "right to change religions, to have a different religion, or to have no religion at all." Such declarations of loyalty do little, however, to dissipate the distrust many harbor toward the Islamic organizations' intentions.

In recent years the debate over state recognition of Islam has changed as different federal states have attempted to resolve the issue of Islamic instruction at public schools by making arrangements with regional rather than national Islamic umbrella organizations. For this religious instruction they need to cooperate with an Islamic organization, but this Muslim partner does not necessarily have to be a public body.[50] In 2000the Islamische Föderation Berlin (IFB, Islamic Federation of Berlin)—an organization associated with Milli Görüş—was recognized by Berlin as an authority entitled to provide religious instruction. The IFB offered instruction at thirty-seven schools in 2004–5, and lessons were given in German.[51] State recognition of the IFB was primarily a blow for the DITIB, which wanted courses to be held in Turkish.[52]

The Islamische Religionsgemeinschaft Hessen (IRH, Islamic Religious Community of Hesse) has been granted the right to offer Islamic religious instruction in Hesse, and state authorities and Islamic organizations in various other federal states are negotiating similar arrangements. As Islamic religious instruction has become more popular at German public schools, the need for qualified religion teachers has grown, and the next logical step in institutionalizing Islam in Germany has been the establishment of academies to train teachers for Islamic religious instruction.

The area of religious instruction reveals the willingness on the part of state agencies to incorporate Islam into German social structures and to work together with the major Muslim organizations to achieve this goal. In other areas, though, the problem of integrating Islam into society is proving thorny. Islamic ritual slaughter without first stunning the animal is not yet permitted, even though an exemption is in place for Jewish ritual slaughter. Nor have issues such as the right to take a day off on Islamic holidays been resolved. The course of the headscarf debate, in which policymakers have tended to favor a general ban on a hijab for women in the civil service, is a sign of the limited acceptance of Islam in Germany.

Translated by Adam Blauhut

3. Eastern and Southeastern Europe

(Hermann Kandler)

Since the first reports in 1981 of conflicts between Muslim Albanians and Christian Serbs in Kosovo, Islam has grown stronger in eastern and southeastern Europe. Ongoing unrest and struggles between Muslims and Christians, particularly after the end of communist rule and the collapse of the multiethnic states of Yugoslavia and the Soviet Union, represent the "fault line wars" characterizing Samuel Huntington's "clash of civilizations."[1] The Balkans[2] are the core region in the geopolitical boundary zone between the Islamic and the Western worlds—"between Vienna and Mecca."[3] Islamic-Christian antagonism is rooted in the idea of static religious bodies, yet regional processes show that the pursuit of national and ethnic uniformity is assuming greater importance and can jarringly intersect with a sense of religious community. Religious antagonism does indeed exist, but it is not the prime mover. Nation building makes greater use of historical-religious components.[4] After all, one can observe an extensive overlap of Islam and national sentiment primarily in Islamic border areas.[5] As a result, there is no longer talk in southeastern Europe of a clash between religious communities but rather talk of conflicts between ethnic groups.

The history of Islam, which has influenced eastern and southeastern Europe in interaction with Christianity, is linked to the expansion of the Ottoman Empire on the European continent. Islam did not spread across entire territories; rather, from the fifteenth century onward it was concentrated in the basins (*ova*) controlled by the cities and in the peripheries of mountainous regions (*yaka*).[6] Only rarely was Islam able to assert itself in the mountains (the Rhodope range) or the border areas of the Ottoman Empire.[7] The withdrawal of the Ottoman Empire from Europe, which started in the seventeenth century, was the result of one of its state organizational principles, the concept of *millet*,[8] which many regard today as an early example of a tolerant policy toward minorities. By recognizing the Muslim or non-Turkish population groups as *millet*, the Ottomans conferred upon them the right to govern their internal affairs, which included religious and legal matters. These *millets* often became incubators for the nationalism that first appeared in the sixteenth century and from which emerged the ethnic particularism whose barbaric consequences can be seen in present-day ethnicism. Or they became the breeding grounds of the ethnic particularism on which, for instance, the autocephaly of the Eastern Orthodox Church was founded. From the seventeenth century on, European powers supported national forces in the *sanjaks* in their struggle against the Ottoman Empire.[9] The coexistence of different power structures gave rise to the concept of Balkanization as a synonym for the tribal, the backward, the primitive, and the barbaric.[10]

As a result of the strong political and regional shifts and the lack of uniform guidelines in the censuses after 1990, population figures are not entirely dependable, especially those pertaining to the Muslim groups. These censuses recorded 2.28 million Muslims living in Albania (1982), at least 1.2 million in Bulgaria (1992), 1.8 million in Bosnia-Herzegovina, 1.9 million in the autonomous region of Kosovo (2000), around 200,000 in Sandžak,[11] 480,000 in Macedonia (1995), 150,000 in Greece (1993), 50,000 in the federated state of Montenegro (2000), 3,000 in Poland (1992), 50,000 in Romania (1993), and a few thousand in the Czech Republic, Slovakia, and Hungary. Muslims make up the majority population in Albania (70 percent of the total population) and Kosovo (about 85 percent), and a plurality in Bosnia-Herzegovina (43.7 percent).

Together with political restructuring programs, the wars and unrest in eastern and southeastern Europe from the 1980s onward gave rise to four groups of states in the area between the Baltic Sea, the Czech Republic, Cyprus, and Ukraine. These states underwent different national territorial developments, and their emergence was accompanied by corresponding bi- and multicommunal interactions.[12] Deviating from contributions to earlier editions of this volume, the present discussion is based on a classification of these states growing out of these differences. Currently Kosovo is characterized by the greatest internal conflict, since a large part of the population is struggling for state autonomy. In Cyprus and Montenegro the scope and form of social participation granted Muslims is not yet clear. Macedonia and Bosnia-Herzegovina have set off down the path of nation building and are breathing new life into the multiethnic state on the basis of existing constitutions. Albania, Greece, and Bulgaria are stable nation-states that are developing policies toward minorities that meet international standards. In other eastern European states, Muslim groups are integrated into the overall population or have adapted to it.

a. Mixed Religious Spatial Entities

Owing to the expulsions and escapes during the wars in Bosnia (1992–1995) and Kosovo (1998–1999), Muslims are now concentrated in Serbia and the autonomous region of Sandžak in Montenegro.

The basic problem confronting Kosovo is its bi-communal structure, made up of Serbs and Albanians who have never been able to cooperate and who were exploited as the hegemonic representatives of an external power.[13] The Serbs base their territorial claims to Kosovo on its existence as a former region of the Serbian empire of Rascia, which was the cradle of the Serbian national church. The Serbs, however, were vanquished by the Ottomans in the battle of Amselfeld (Kosovo polje) in 1389, around which many myths have sprung up. The defeat has been felt as a nationally unifying stigma, especially after the rise of Serbian nationalism in the nineteenth century. This nationalism stands in opposition to the claims of Kosovar Albanians, who proclaim the region to be their traditional land of origin. In contrast to the surrounding territories, though, they were never able to take responsibility for governing it alone or as part of a Greater Albania.

When Serbs took control of the province from the Ottoman Empire in 1912, half of the Kosovar population were Serbs and half Albanians. Except for approximately fifty thousand Catholics, the Albanians are Muslims. The Serbs are chiefly Orthodox Christians, and only a small percentage, the Gorani, profess Islam. Over the years, population ratios have changed dramatically. Around 2000, nearly 90 percent of the population were Muslim Albanians. This shift can be attributed to both the Albanians' natural growth rate (owing to high fertility) and their influx during the Second World War, when Kosovo was part of Albania. During this period many Serbs left the territory. In the interbellum period there were attempts to cope with the increasing numbers of Albanians through assimilation campaigns and the suppression of both the Albanian language and Islamic culture. In 1937 the Serb historian Vaso Čubrilović developed a program to resettle Albanians in Turkey, and this was used as an ideological tool by Serb nationalists until 1997. To be sure, in the communist era Albanian minority rights—including the rights to territorial self-government and to school and university instruction in Albanian—were restored; but Yugoslavia never granted Kosovo the status of a republic because the Yugoslavians believed that, on the one hand, the Kosovar Albanians were not south Slavs and, on the other, that a nation-state—Albania—existed as their external representative. In the early 1980s the conflict over the language used at schools unleashed the first wave of unrest between Albanians and Serbs. Since nonviolent resistance brought no success, the Ushtria Clirimtare e Kosovës (UCK)[14] organized in 1986 and began armed resistance in the form of an intifada. In 1989 autonomy was re-voked for Kosovar Albanians, and Slobodan Milosevic dissolved parliament in 1990—moves that were accompanied by despotic police actions, human rights violations, and the dismissal of Albanian teachers and professors. A kind of "apartheid" prevailed.[15] In 1990 the moderate Lidhja Demokratike Kosovës (LDK)[16] organized a referendum on the secession of the region from Serbia, which in 1992 led to the establishment of a parallel educational and administrative system. Although pro-national efforts rather than Islamic fundamentalism were the engine behind the internal Kosovar division, reli-gious differences have remained a major source of the collective hatred.[17] The massacre of eighty Muslim Albanians in Drenica in September 1998 marked the start of Serb attacks on Muslim towns that were intended to create a cordon sanitaire against Albania. After destroying the UCK, Serbs contin-ued to terrorize the civilian population. The number of internally displaced persons from other war zones, including 400,000 Kosovars, increased in the period up to October 1998, radically shifting the ratio of Muslim to Christian towns. Afterward, through February 1999, Kosovo underwent systematic "ethnic cleansing" despite concurrent negotiations in Rambouillet. The Serb advance was stopped only by NATO air strikes beginning in March 1999.[18] It is noteworthy that the Kosovar Albanians have always defined their national identity more in terms of language than of religion, which was demonstrated by the lack of fundamentalist activity during the eight-year period of non-violent resistance against the Serbs, and also during the occupation between 1998 and 1999. In this phase neither Islamic leaders nor a turn to radical Islam—as provoked by the repression—had a determinant influence on the Kosovars' lives.[19]

The pursuit of national independence for the Kosovar Albanians holds out the prospect of unification with the neighboring Albanian state, yet the international community—the actual protective power for Kosovo—has re-jected this goal. In fall 2000 internationally monitored local elections were held for the first time since the war. The winner was Ibrahim Rugova, the leader of the LDK. In 2003 Serb and Kosovar representatives, meeting in Vienna, entered into the first negotiations on the province's future. They did not address questions of public law, which was perhaps a sign that disputes were being resolved. But even the slightest provocations have managed to disrupt the peace, as in spring 2004, when Albanians attacked Serbs (and NATO-led KFOR, or Kosovo Force, troops) in the divided city of Mitrovica. Serbian arson attacks on mosques in Belgrade and Niš seemed a nearly logi-cal consequence.

The future status of Muslims in Montenegro remains unclear. Even under the Ottoman Empire the principality enjoyed a degree of autonomy, and after the First World War it was incorporated into the kingdom of Yugoslavia because of linguistic affiliations. The approximately 200,000 Muslims cur-rently living in the Republic of Montenegro include Albanians (6.6 percent) in the border area with Albania, and Bosnian Muslim Slavs (14.6 percent), who mostly inhabit the *Sandžak* of Novi Pazar (divided between Serbia and Montenegro). Since late 1990 massive pressure has been applied to stop attempts by Slavic Muslims to gain autonomy. Like the Muslim Albanians in Kosovo, the Slavic Muslims in the *Sandžak* define themselves in national terms—that is, primarily through their common language rather than their religion. Here, too, Islamic leaders played no major role during the conflicts between 1989 and 1999. Even in times of war, Islamic political and social fundamentalism attracted little interest.

The same is true of Cyprus. Its northern part was occupied by the Turks in 1974. When independence was declared in 1960, Cyprus had 393 "Greek" and 120 "Turkish" villages, as well as 106 towns with a mixed population. From 1974 on, the ethnic structure of Northern Cyprus, in particular, changed substantially. Fifty thousand Turkish Cypriots fled the south, and eighty thousand Turks from Anatolia were settled in the north, which later, in 1983, was proclaimed the Kuzey Kıbrıs Türk Cumhuriyeti (KKTC),[20] recognized only by Turkey. Some thirty thousand Turkish soldiers were stationed there, and only a few Greeks remained. The border, guarded by UN troops,[21] which had previously been closed to Cypriots, was reopened in 2003. With the failed referendum on April 26, 2004, the divided country threw away the chance to reunify the mainly Christian Greek Republic of Southern Cyprus with the primarily Muslim northern part occupied by Turkey (home to 200,000, or 26 percent of the entire Cypriot population). As a result, only Southern Cyprus became a member of the European Union. While 64.9 percent of Turkish Cypriots voted for unification, 75.8 percent of the Southern Cypriot population rejected it, ruining the chances for a "double yes" vote. There were several reasons for this outcome: the lack of a guarantee for the withdrawal of Turkish occupation troops from Northern Cyprus; the UN plan by Secretary-General Kofi Annan, which provided only for limited resettlement of Greeks to the north; and the fear of losing acquired rights and the expense of supporting Northern Cyprus. The Northern Cypriots, for their part, were uneasy about the expected relocation of Greeks and about Greek economic dominance. Nevertheless, it is remarkable that religious reservations did not influence reunification discussions. In the end, the EU was unable to apply greater pressure to Southern Cyprus as it held the same view as the UN, which had recognized the successor governments in the south as the legitimate representatives of Cyprus ever since 1964. In this position it was unable to maintain official contacts with representatives of the north. In the future Brussels can be expected to accommodate Northern Cyprus (e.g., by abolishing the trade embargo) because of its positive stance toward the EU. On April 28, 2004, the EU resolved to retain the liberal border traffic regulations between Northern and Southern Cyprus despite the general mandate to protect the island's outer borders. This brings hope that exchanges can take place on all levels.[22] In the future, attention will be paid to intensifying the kind of cross-group contacts that have so far been actively pursued by only two towns, Potamia and Pyla.[23]

In Potamia, in particular, efforts are under way to bring together Turkish and Greek Cypriots. A double town board has been established from the ranks of Greek and Turkish Cypriots, and a joint radio station has been set up.

b. States in the Process of Nation Building

Common to Bosnia-Herzegovina and Macedonia are a valid constitution and territories situated within internationally recognized borders. Nonetheless, it is impossible to speak in either country of a *Staatsvolk*—a national people who accept a common administration and are prepared to participate actively in it.

Bosnia-Herzegovina (Bosna i Hercegovina; 4.55 million inhabitants in 2005) is the actual heir to the former multiethnic state of Yugoslavia. It is marked by a constitutionally based, tripartite division of ethnic groups between Bosnians (mainly Muslim: 48 percent), Serbs (mainly Orthodox: 37 percent), and Croats (primarily Catholic: 14 percent; 1 percent other). The first free elections in Bosnia and Herzegovina were held on November 18 and December 2, 1990. Of the 240 seats, one-third went to the Bosnian Muslim Stranka Demokratske Akcije (SDA),[24] which formed a coalition with the Croatian Hrvatska Demokratska Zajednica (HDZ),[25] and thus posed a threat to the Srpska Demokratska Stranka (SDS)[26] and the Serbs. In a 1992 referendum on Bosnian independence, 67 percent of the population, primarily Croats and Bosnians, supported independence, while Bosnian Serbs were eager to remain part of Yugoslavia. The resulting declaration of independence from Yugoslavia sparked the war fought between 1992 and 1995, the worst seen in Europe since 1945. The roots of that war are documented, inter alia, by a pamphlet (*Islamci deklarasyon*) by the subsequent president Alija Izetbegovich, who was compared in the 1990s with Muhammad 'Ali Jinnah, the founder of the Pakistani state.[27] In this publication Izetbegovich praises the superiority of Islamic culture and describes Bosnia-Herzegovina—then still a Yugoslavian republic—as part of the Islamic world. He and his supporters were subsequently arrested for counterrevolutionary activities.[28] Greater Serbian propaganda presented this as an attempt to set up an Islamic theocracy with the help of religious fighters from Arab countries.

Between 2.5 and 4.1 million people fled the war zones, and 250,000 were killed. A large number were the victims of mass killings such as the Srebrenica massacre of some seven thousand Muslim Bosnians by Serbs in 1995.[29]

After the involvement in the Balkan wars between 1912 and 1923 and World War II, the 1990s war was the third on Bosnian-Herzegovinian territory in the twentieth century. The Dayton Peace Accords, negotiated on November 21, 1995, and signed three weeks later in Paris, resolved the conflict with a compromise. The peace treaty guaranteed the continued existence of the state of Bosnia-Herzegovina, which was divided into two entities: the Bosnian-Croatian federation and the autonomous territory of Srpska.[30]

Progress was made in the ensuing period. There was rapid economic recovery after 1996 thanks to $600 million in reconstruction aid. The NATO-led SFOR[31] began supporting civilian programs in 1997, and the first war criminals were arrested. The inflammatory Bosnian-Serbian broadcaster Srpska was seized, and Bosnian reform forces were promoted. Citizenship law came into effect in 1998 along with additional public laws previously voted down by the Serbs. The country got its own flag, coat of arms, national anthem, and license plates.

The political system generally grew more stable. The media abandoned the nationalist rhetoric, and the country's own legal system gained more clout. Occupied property was returned to its rightful owners under the threat of punishment, and by 2000, around sixty thousand members of minority groups had returned. These successes were the result of giving Bosnia-Herzegovina responsibility for national and international tasks.

But the elections in 2000 showed that political structures continued to have an ethnic orientation—despite the fact that the old bosses Franjo Tudjman (d. 1999), Slobodan Milosevic (b. 1941), and Alija Izetbegovich (d. 2003) no longer wielded power. This was shown by the nationalist Croatian and Serb parties[32] and the Bosnian Muslim leadership, which to some extent allowed itself to be exploited as an advance guard by Middle Eastern organizations.

The de facto goal associated with the "Bosnian question" is to establish Bosnia-Herzegovina as an independent state. But this is just the Bosnian goal. Despite the provisions of the Dayton Agreement, both Bosnian Croat and Bosnian Serb organizations lay claim to special relations with their respective titular state, thereby keeping alive the parallel structure of independent entities in Bosnia in breach of the agreement. Consequently, the desire for a formal division of the country has not died out. Owing to distrust on all sides, there continue to be calls for a "soft partition" into three parts that would unite the Croatian-dominated section of the federation with Croatia and the Republika Srpska with Serbia while leaving a rump Bosnian state.[33]

The Republic of Macedonia, established in 1991, emerged from the Yugoslavian republic of Makedonija. The country has been a strategically important area between the Mediterranean and the Danube states ever since antiquity. The current state constitutes only a part of historical Macedonia, whose territory falls within the state boundaries of Greece, Bulgaria, Serbia, and Albania. As a result, since its independence Macedonia has repeatedly become embroiled in territorial conflicts with neighboring states, especially with Greece. The majority of its 2.1 million residents (2002) are Slav Orthodox (66 percent), while 400,000 (23 percent) are ethnic Albanians, most of Muslim faith. Between seventy and eighty thousand (4 percent) are ethnic Turks, and around half of these are Slavic-speaking Muslims (Torbeši, Pomaks, and Poturs), and ethnic Roma and Vlachs.

As the largest Muslim group, ethnic Albanians inhabit the Macedonian regions around Tetovo on the border to Albania. They differ from the Slavic- and Turkish-speaking Muslims in terms of their language, history, and tradition. In contrast to ethnic Turks, the Albanians do not consider themselves part of a national people tied to the Macedonian state.

The Torbeši are closely aligned with the Turkish-speaking Muslims of Macedonia but are subject to the political influence of Albanian Muslims, above all in the form of the Albanian *hocas*. The number of Torbeši increased from 1,591 in 1953 to 39,555 in 1981, and they included many Muslims who formerly spoke Turkish. This development was probably related to the first Slavic Muslim conference, held in the St. John Bigorski monastery in 1970, at which participants once again openly professed their Muslim Slav identity. A large percentage of the estimated seventy thousand Torbeši who had mixed with other ethnic groups after the Second World War, particularly with Albanian Muslims, followed suit.[34]

Macedonia is an example of a region in which the manipulation of an ethnic national consciousness has repeatedly thwarted nation building. The conflicts of the civil war in 1998–99 are only the endpoint of a historical development that many southeastern European states underwent after 1912–13, namely, the reinterpretation of the state as a mono-ethnic nation-state despite its conflicting ethnic makeup. The 1988 draft constitution spoke of the "state of the Macedonian people and the Albanian and Turkish minority," but then, owing to pressure fromMilosevic, this was changed on November 21, 1991, to the "nation-state of the Macedonian people, in which Albanians, Turks, Vlachs, Roma, and other nationalities shall receive equal rights." The Albanian minority was deliberately ignored in what has been labeled Macedonian "constitutional egotism."[35] The 1990s were marked by an oscillation between tense relations and rapprochement, and between 1995 and 1997 the latent tensions boiled over into an ethnic conflict between Slav Macedonians and ethnic Albanians. The first riots resulting in deaths took place in Tetovo, which is predominantly Albanian, even though the Albanian Muslim Partia Demokratike Shqiptare (PDSh),[36] led by Arben Xhaferi, was integrated into the government of Ljubčo Georgievski's Vnatresna makedonska revolucionerna organizacija, Demokratska partija za makedonsko nacionalno edinstvo (VMRO-DPMNE)[37] in 1998. The flows of refugees from Kosovo after spring 1999 considerably impeded the building of the state. They not only endangered the fragile Albanian-Macedonian balance but also in spring 2001 led to warlike conflicts in Tanuševci and Tetovo between Orthodox Slavs—represented by the Macedonian security forces—and Muslim Albanians, led by Macedonian Ushtria Clirimtare Kombetare (UCK)[38] troops.[39] Under the supervision of the EU and the United States, this conflict was settled by means of the Ohrid Framework Agreement of August 13, 2001, with representatives of the Slavic and Albanian Macedonian parties participating in negotiations. The key points were equal treatment of the Albanian language in territories where Albanians account for more than 20 percent of the population, the awarding of public office on the basis of stipulated proportional representation, and the strengthening of local self-government.[40] The Ohrid Agreement, however, can hardly be seen as a guarantee of successful nation building. In spring 2003 Georgievski, the chairman of the Slavic Macedonian VMRO-DPMNE, once again provoked a discussion of the territorial division of the state along ethnic lines. Among other things, he suggested that Macedonian and Albanian population groups be exchanged in order to create mono-ethnic settlement areas.[41] These separatist efforts are contrasted by cooperative projects such as the joint use of Albanian University in Tetovo by Albanian and Macedonian students.[42]

c. Established States with Ethnic Religious Minorities

Greece, Bulgaria, Ukraine, and Albania are states founded by the early twentieth century that, because of historical conditions, are home to constitutionally recognized minorities that have yet to receive equal status as citizens. While Muslim minorities live in Greece and Bulgaria, Christian Orthodox and Catholic groups are the minorities in the primarily Muslim country of Albania.

Up to the late twentieth century, the fate of the Turkish Muslim minority in Greece was dictated by the rivalry between Greece and Turkey. From 1920 on, Muslims in the Greek section of Thrace were the pawns in a controversial foreign policy. In the 1923 Treaty of Lausanne, Muslims in the Greek part of Thrace were granted residence rights, as were Greek Orthodox Christians both in Istanbul and on the Aegean islands of Tenedos (Bozcaada) and Imbros (Gökçeada). All the other minorities in Greece and the Turkey were subject to the population exchanges regulated by the treaty.[43] For years the Muslim population was the target of repressive measures by Christians who had resettled in Thrace and who still felt the defeat by the Turks in 1922 as a humiliation. But around 1930 the situation eased as a result of the reconciliation between Atatürk and Eleftherios Venizelos, who viewed their minorities as a bridge between nations. Rather than supporting the Islamic tradition of its Thracian minority, Greece did much more to promote the development of a Turkish identity, which was fully in Atatürk's interests. In the Greek civil war (1949), Muslims sided with the government despite communist recruitment efforts, and when the war ended, their loyalty was rewarded with far-reaching freedoms (the establishment of the Celal Bayar High School in Komotini and other secondary schools for minorities, the full spectrum of minority rights guaranteed in the Treaty of Lausanne). As a result, the Muslim minority remembers this period as the "Golden Fifties." The unrest in Cyprus and the expulsion of a large part of the Greek minority from Istanbul in the mid-1950s caused these freedoms to be revoked in the period after 1955.[44]

After the Greek military junta took power in 1967, minority rights were radically restricted, specifically its members' right to describe themselves as a Turkish minority. Testifying to the violations of the treaty was the implementation of a battery of repressive laws under the military government, including the annulment of Greek citizenship in the event of leaving Thrace, the repeal of the right to buy or sell real estate, the withdrawal of the control and management of religious foundations (*vakıflar*), and the elimination of the free election by the minority of muftis in Komotini and Xanthi.

The preservation and toughening of these laws despite the post-1974 democratization process must be seen as a response to the Turkish occupation of Northern Cyprus that same year. The incidents of this period are linked to the ascendancy of the minority politician Sadık Ahmet (1947–1995), who called upon the minority to resist repressive Greek measures. Ahmet made the international public aware of the minority's problems, particularly after Greece joined the then European Community. At the peak of his career he was cheered as "Batı Trakya Türklerinin lideri" (leader of the Turks in Western Thrace).[45] Ahmet was known for his great devotion to the Turkish minority while serving as a representative in the Greek parliament. His career was hampered not only by the partially dubious proceedings instituted against both him and his supporters, but also by the mistake he made in allowing himself to be used as a pawn by external political powers. The commemoration day of the Turkish Muslim memorial community and the prelude to grave conflicts between the Turkish minority on the one hand and the Greek state and the Christian population of Thrace on the other was January 29, 1988, when thousands of Thracian Muslims attended a protest rally in Komotini.[46] Greek nationalist groups responded to this demonstration with attacks on Turkish businesses and individuals. There were similar confrontations in both early 1990, when Ahmet was the target of a court case, and in 1991, when the Turkish minority protested against the removal of the mufti in Xanthi, whom they had elected. After 1981 efforts were made to revoke the tough restrictions, partly because of pressure from the EU, but these efforts were always relative to the changing moods in Athens and Ankara. Reconciliation between the groups started, and since that time, at least on the state level, there has been work toward restoring and implementing minority rights. In Thrace itself, though, Athens has only slowly implemented its new measures. One "victim" of the political rapprochement between Greece and Turkey was ultimately Ahmet himself, which became keenly apparent after his death in a car accident: most Turkish politicians rejected the "conspiracy theory" that the accident was a political assassination. In a public speech in Thrace in 1997, state president Kostis Stefanopoulos accorded all members of the Turkish minority the right to describe themselves publicly as Turks, using whatever form of expression they wished.[47] This right had earlier been denied them under the threat of punishment. Ever since the earthquake in Turkey and Greece in 1999 and the resulting "earthquake diplomacy"—successfully pursued by the Greek foreign minister Giorgos Papandreou and his Turkish counterpart Ismail Cem—the hot topic of Thrace has no longer been on the agenda in bilateral contacts.[48] Political progress, however, has not necessarily been followed by a quick normalization of relations in the Greek Christian and Turkish Muslim region of Thrace, where deep-seated ideas about the self and the other disrupt daily existence.

The identity of the 150,000 members of the Turkish minority (50 percent of the population in Greek Thrace) is essentially based on a Turkish rather than a Muslim historical consciousness. This consciousness extends back to the founding of the first of four western Thracian republics in the summer of 1913. Although this state existed for only fifty-five days, it was also the first Turkish republic. Until the late 1980s the Muslim population saw itself as a unified Turkish minority with a clear allegiance to Turkey—partially in response to repressive measures on the part of the Greeks. It was not until the policy of détente in the 1990s that there was an interest in the wide variety of ethnic roots that do not necessarily fit in with the Turkishness defined by Ankara. According to Greek sources, 45 percent of the 114,000 Muslims living in Thrace in 1993 were Turkish-speaking Muslims, also known as Osmanlı. Thirty-six percent were Pomaks (Slavophone Muslims), and 18 percent were Athinganoi, Turkish-speaking Roma. On the basis of self-perceptions and external views, each of these groups is assigned a specific environment that is congruent with reality primarily in terms of its spatial component. For instance, the Osmanlı are described as tobacco and cherry farmers who live in the mono-ethnic towns along the edge of the Rhodope Mountains (*yaka*). Their way of life and their attitudes most strongly recall the Ottoman Turk tradition, which was preserved in Thrace without Kemalist reforms. The daily life of the Turkish Muslims in the midlands (*orta kôpla*) takes a different form. Chiefly cotton farmers, these Muslims live in bi-communal towns together with Christian Greeks. The Athinganoi, who reside in communities near the provincial cities, are merchants, musicians, and traveling entertainers. The Pomak centers are located in the Rhodopes, which for a long time were inaccessible to the outside world. Ever since the border to Bulgaria was opened in the 1990s, the Greek state has helped improve the infrastructure of this backward area. While it can be assumed that the Greek politicians' increased interest in—and documentation of—Pomak culture and language aims at strengthening Pomak identity at the expense of a common Turkish culture, this development has signaled the first step toward guaranteed minority rights. Nevertheless, this process is far from being completed—as cases of individual discrimination have shown, especially in property purchases.

In places where both the majority and minority populations live side by side, the two sides are usually willing to try to come to grips with the challenges of daily coexistence. Acceptance of the other and a willingness to coexist on good terms are shown, for instance, by the use of the other group's language. Most Christians are able to speak, or at least understand, Turkish, and most Turks have a working knowledge of Greek.

An examination of age distribution reveals trends that are typical of Thracian society. At first glance, the larger percentage of young Muslims appears to confirm Christian fears of an Islamization of Thrace—fears that have been fueled by right-wing nationalist groups and religious leaders. The relative decline of the Christian population aged twenty and older in many areas of Thrace can be explained by the fact that better-educated Christians have moved to the more affluent, mainly Christian residential areas of cities or to other parts of Greece. Even so, young members of the Muslim population have also left the region, moving to other European countries (mainly to Germany) and to Turkey. Around twenty-five communities have been established in Germany alone.

Nationalist positions on both sides repeatedly arouse distrust. The relationship between Greece and Turkey provides the latent foundation for this sentiment. Greek and Turkish newspapers often speak of Muslims and Christians, but what they really mean are Turks and Greeks. In contrast, the religious sphere produces the least resentment. It is only natural for a Christian widow to invite her female Muslim neighbors to commemorate the anniversary of her husband's death and, conversely, for Muslims to give Christians cake on Islamic holidays, as if they were members of the Muslim community. There are also close business ties between the groups.

But the social differences between Christians and Muslims remain a source of friction. The Christians include a disproportionately large number of better-skilled workers, mainly because of the Turks' inadequate Greek language skills. This has had a special impact on the rural Turkish population because of the previous absence of educational programs offering minority members the chance to make up for the handicaps they have experienced since kindergarten in comparison to native speakers of Greek.

It is obvious that this disadvantage carries over to the occupational world. The lack of proportional representation in public service is particularly oppressive. Political reasons naturally play an additional role in this regard in connection with Greece's relationship to Turkey. Only recently have there been attempts to create positions at all levels of the public sector, especially in the administration, to remedy the underrepresentation of the Turkish minority.[49]

In Bulgaria the structure of the Muslim population resembles its composition in Greece. Here one also encounters a tripartite division between ethnic Turks (700,000 in 1996), Muslim Roma (300,000), and Pomaks, who are "Bulgarian" (Slavic-speaking) Muslims (200,000).[50] All told, Muslims make up about 14 percent of the entire population and are dispersed across certain districts of the country. Ninety-nine percent of the Muslims in Bulgaria are Sunnites, and 1 percent are Shi'ites (mostly Pomaks). Ethnic Turks form the majority population in the districts of Razgrad (northeastern Bulgaria) and Kardžali (southeastern Bulgaria). Large groups also exist in the districts of Shumen, Burgaz, and Silistra. The ethnic Turks in these regions mainly reside in urban areas. Most of the Pomaks live as tobacco farmers in the mountainous regions of the Balkans and Rhodopes and in the district of Lovech. They are descended from the Bulgars who converted to Islam between the seventeenth and nineteenth centuries.

The Roma, who can be found chiefly in rural areas, represent the socially weakest group of Muslims. They have high birth and mortality rates and suffer from poor living conditions, high unemployment, and a lack of public representation.

After 1913 and, in particular, 1984, Muslims were targeted by the repressive Bulgarian assimilation campaign that accompanied the state's national revitalization movement. The more rapid growth of the Muslim population relative to that of the Slavic Bulgarians—as determined by a national census—provided the backdrop to this campaign and aroused fears among the Bulgarian Christian majority of infiltration by Islamic fundamentalism.[51] A entire catalogue of restrictive measures was implemented: Turkish literature was banned from school curricula, Turkish clothing was prohibited, the celebration of Turkish holidays was outlawed, and Muslims were forced to adopt Bulgarian surnames. These rules were aimed at the ethnic homogenization of Bulgaria. After violent demonstrations in northeastern Bulgaria, the repression led to the exodus of around 350,000 Turks to Turkey. The tragedy culminated in the sealing of the borders to Turkey owing to the large numbers of refugees.

By 2004, between 120,000 and 180,000 Turks had returned to Bulgaria, and since the end of the communist regime in 1990, the religious ethnic consciousness of Muslims has burgeoned, manifesting itself in the establishment of the Dvisenie za prava i svobodi (DPS)[52] by ethnic Turks. The party also succeeded in integrating Pomaks, which in turn exacerbated fears among the Christian majority. The fact that a large percentage of the Pomaks living in the Rila community of Jakoruda stated that Turkish was their mother tongue, although it was not widespread there, once again fueled suspicions that fundamentalism was gaining a foothold in Bulgaria. The DPS managed to gain political power, primarily in the chiefly Turkish-speaking district of Kardžali, which was especially hard hit by unemployment after the collapse of the state-run tobacco trade. In 1991 unrest broke out in both Kardžali and Razgrad when Bulgarian nationalists erected barricades on the paths taken by Turkish-speaking children walking to school.[53] Between 1990 and 1992, a total of 653 mayors and 1,114 councilors came from the ranks of the DPS, and Güner Taher became its first deputy governor in the district of Ruse. The DPS secured 10 percent of the seats during the 1992 national elections, and beginning in 1993, under the leadership of Ahmed Doğan, it increasingly developed into an ethnic national party. Although this violated the national constitution, it was tolerated out of consideration for Turkey. The population gradually lost trust in the DPS because of changing coalitions, corruption, and scandals. From the mid-1990s, the close relations between Bulgaria and Turkey ultimately eliminated the minority issue from the bilateral agenda. In the period that followed, Turkey did not attempt to influence Bulgaria's policy toward minorities.[54] The report released in 2003 by the Bulgarian Helsinki Committee shows that the state continues to demonstrate little interest in providing economic support for the structurally weak regions inhabited by Muslims, although it is precisely this support that would prove it is treating religions equally.[55]

In 2004 there were around 250,000 Sunnite Muslims living in 391 communities in Ukraine. Islamic culture in this country was mainly influenced and passed down by Crimean Tatars, whose roots extend back to the khanate of Crimea, established in the fifteenth century. The khanate was initially a vassal state of the Ottoman Empire before it was annexed by Russia in 1783. In the late nineteenth century, 161,000 Muslims lived in Crimea; in 1917 they made up 11 percent of the peninsula's entire population. The Soviets accused the Crimean Tatars of collaborating with the Third Reich and deported around 190,000 to the Asian regions of the Soviet Union. Although an official decree allowed them to return in 1967, they received no real support, and it was not until Ukrainian independence that greater numbers of Crimean Tatars made their way home and large Muslim communities emerged in Crimea and Kiev. The majority of Muslims are organized into regional associations in Crimea, Kiev, and the Donets Basin. Additional pillars of the Muslim community are charitable institutions such as Life after Chernobyl.[56] Nevertheless, as can be seen in Ukraine and in other states mainly inhabited by Christians, the Muslim community's fight for equality and recognition is met with distrust and resistance. In February 2004, on the sidelines of ceremonies commemorating the sixtieth anniversary of the deportations, Crimean Tatars demonstrated against the anti-Islamic campaigns of Russian Cossacks. The patriarch of the Ukrainian Orthodox Church in Simferopol and the mufti of Crimea unanimously condemned the agitation by Russian politicians and the one-sided representation of interethnic conflicts in the mass media.[57]

In contrast to countries with a Christian majority, Albania is the only state in southeastern Europe where a Christian minority coexists with a Muslim majority. The self-conception of Albanians, however, is more strongly characterized by national rather than Muslim religious aspects. This ultimately found expression in the deeds of Skanderbeg, who, as the leader of the League of Lezhe, advanced against the Ottomans and successfully withstood the siege of Kruja by Mehmet II (1450–1457).

It was not until 1913 that Albania gained independence, becoming the last state in southeastern Europe to do so. Enver Hoxha became the leader of the country in 1946, and he created a Stalinist state that opposed all forms of religion. In 1967 he declared Albania the "first atheist state in the world."[58] He shut down over two thousand churches and mosques and banned all religious practices. An estimated 700,000 Albanians, both Muslims and Christians, were imprisoned or executed for religious reasons. When the communist bloc disintegrated in December 1989, students demonstrated in Tirana for political change and a lifting of the ban on religion.

These demonstrations marked the start of the mass exodus of thousands of Albanians to other countries.[59]

After the collapse of the communist regime in 1991, 70 percent of the 3.3 million inhabitants once again professed the Islamic faith. Nevertheless, religious denomination in Albania is subordinate to national identity. The remark once made by the Albanian poet Pashko Vasa apparently still holds true today: "The religion of the Albanian is his Albanianism!"[60] Broad segments of the Albanian population have no strict religious affiliation, which is encouraged by Section 7 of the constitution: "The right to freedom of religion...includes the freedom to change religions." The 1990s saw mass conversions of Muslim youth to both Catholicism and the Bahai religion—in many incidences for personal gain. Family tradition, however, continues to play the dominant role in determining creed today. Public institutions have also been affected by the increase in religious activity. For example, religious practices have been introduced in state institutions, Islamic courses are being offered in secular schools, and religious niche channels have emerged in the media. In addition, religious affiliation has become a criterion for employment, and Muslim and Christian teams compete at sporting events. Many see this as the start of a fundamentalization of Albanian society.[61]

On a political level, Albania is drawing closer to the Islamic world. At the instigation of former state president Sali Berisha, Albania in late 1992 became a member of the Organization of the Islamic Conference. Seventeen Islamic aid organizations were active in Albania in 1993. Qur'an schools were opened and scholarships were awarded for study in Islamic countries. While socialists regarded this development as a turn toward the East, and the Albanian author Ismail Kadare wanted to see greater emphasis placed on Albanian's Christian heritage, the country's political leaders regarded it as a benefit. The country maintains economic ties with the Islamic Development Bank and has found a political partner in Turkey. A number of factors paved the way for these occurrences: Turkish food aid in 1991–92, the scheduling of regular flights between Tirana and Istanbul, and the awarding of scholarships to civilians and military personnel for study in Turkey. That said, Albania's political leaders reject all forms of fundamentalism and are seeking to establish closer ties with all religious leaders—as shown, for example, by Berisha's reception of Pope John Paul II on April 25, 1993.[62] Indeed, recommendations issued to Albania in 2003[63] include no direct warning to ensure religious freedom. The domestic reform process, however, has been undermined by socioeconomic problems, corruption, and inefficient public administration, as well as by additional factors such as organized crime, weak law enforcement, high unemployment, and low production levels.[64] Because of the protective function it performs for the Albanians living in the neighboring states of Kosovo (1.9 million), Macedonia (443,000), Montenegro (50,000), Serbia (80,000), and Greece (50,000), Albania's foreign policy remains enmeshed in the problem-ridden domestic policies of these countries, creating the potential for conflict. Pan-Albananism, whose goal is the autonomy of all Albanian groups in adjacent countries, is currently seen as the greatest threat to stability in the Balkans.[65]

d. States with an Assimilated or Hardly Visible Muslim Culture

Only small groups of Muslims can be found in the other states of eastern and southeastern Europe. They include Romania (ca. 50,000 in 1993), Hungary (3,000 in 1993), Slovakia (ca. 5,000 in 2003), Moldova (3,000 in 2002), and Poland (3,000 in 1992). These Muslims either are members of newly emerging communities such as the ones in Slovakia[66] and Moldova, where they must fight for recognition,[67] or else they represent the last vestiges of historical communities that for the most part are Islamic only in terms of culture and tradition. In this context the Tatars in Poland deserve special attention. They descend from the Tatars of the Volga region who were deported to Poland as prisoners of war by the Lithuanian prince Witold (1397) and who for three hundred years promoted the relocation of additional Tatars to the area, particularly to the regions of Vilnius, Lublin, and the Tatra Mountains. One hundred thousand Tatars are thought to have lived in Poland in 1631, and after the third division of the country, Muslims fought in the ranks of Polish armies. Of the nineteen Muslim communities still existent in 1936, only those in Bohoniki and Kruszyniany in the Voivodeship of Białystok managed to survive the Second World War. A congress of Polish Muslims has met every five years since 1969, and today there are also Muslim communities in Gdańsk-Oliwa, Szczecin, and Warsaw. Religious practice is based on Qur'an texts in Polish and White Russian with Turkish elements, partially in modified Ottoman script. As the lack of Qur'an schools and the regular marriages with non-Muslims show, Islam exerts hardly any active influence on public, let alone political, life in Poland, even if it lives on in the traditions of the Muslim communities and in its members' private lives.[68]

Translated by Adam Blauhut

4. The Americas

(Monika Wohlrab-Sahr)

Because of the specific migration and missionary history of the Americas, the Muslims living there are usually small migrant minorities, while the great majority of the population are members of Christian denominations. The tiny countries of Surinam, Guyana, and Trinidad, which have ethnically and religiously mixed populations, are exceptions. In Surinam, for instance, Muslims account for 20 percent of the population (in addition to

Christians and Hindus, the other large population groups). These Muslims are descendants of the Indian and Indonesian laborers who were brought to the country under Dutch colonial rule. Small Muslim communities exist in Argentina, Venezuela, and Mexico, but they have no great cultural influence. The same is true of Brazil.[1]

There is no precise information on the number of Muslims living in the United States.[2] The country's statistics on religion are based on data from religious communities and primarily cover church-organized groups that are able to provide precise figures on membership. It has been quite some time since the authorities last conducted a representative population survey that included questions on religious affiliation, and the results of the telephone surveys in different areas vary widely. Estimates put the total number of Muslims in the United States between 3 and 6 million.[3] In 2007 the Pluralism Project at Harvard University listed 1,621 Muslim mosques and centers in the country.[4]

This indicates that, in contrast to many European countries, the United States has a relatively small Muslim population. Even so, this population includes a relatively large percentage of American converts to Islam. In 1986 Yvonne Haddad assumed that one-third of what she estimated to be 3 million American Muslims were African American converts to Islam.[5] In 1992 the American Muslim Council released its own figures, according to which 42 percent of the Muslims in the United States were African Americans, 24.4 percent South Asians, 12.4 percent Arabs, and 2 percent white Americans.[6] Naturally these estimates cannot be considered precise, but they do give an impression of the great importance of African American conversion to Islam in the United States. They also show that conversion is not primarily an expression of intercultural contact, as is the case in other countries, but is a phenomenon that mainly takes place within the black community. White converts, whose numbers are much smaller, are largely focused on Sufism.

A specific American version of Islam has emerged among African Americans, one that is closely linked to the nationalist and messianic movements of black America. Despite their seeming foreignness, these groups must be seen as a genuine expression of American culture.[7]

The fact that conversion to Islam is concentrated in the largest minority group in the United States (and the one facing the most severe problems) suggests that there is a close link between these two issues. Muslim groups in the United States directly address the issues affecting the country's African Americans, especially those facing young men in the urban centers. They also adapt their missionary strategies to this population (for example, in prisons). It is this circumstance that, not least, lends conversion a collective character in the United States. One consequence is that, in recent American history, prominent converts such as Malcolm X (al-Hajj Malik Shabazz) and famous athletes such as Muhammad Ali have served as important role models both in Muslim circles and beyond.

The collective character of Islamic conversion in the United States is also reflected in the long history of blacks who have converted to Islam, often supported by nationalist ideas. While it is true that, as Muslim groups like to emphasize, the history of Muslims in the United States can be traced to the African slaves brought to America,[8] these slaves played no role in establishing Islam in the New World. Rather, the emphasis placed on these "African" origins of American Islam must be seen as part of a collective myth among blacks in the country,[9] a myth in which the question of this group's independent roots and forms of expression plays a critical role. While this discourse on the genuine roots of African American culture reached a peak in the Black Power movement of the 1960s and the subsequent cultural movements of the 1970s and 1980s, it goes back much further—namely, to the numerous separatist and nationalist efforts among American blacks, who pursued a program of collective emigration in response to the racism they experienced in the country. "Back to Africa" was often the aim, but some groups had other places in mind as well. One primary reason why Islam took on such significance in this discourse on authentic African American culture is that it could be set in opposition to "Euro-American" Christianity as the independent African heritage of blacks. In addition, it later created an ideological link to anticolonial and anti-imperialist struggles in the Third World.

Islam first became important in the United States in the late nineteenth century as the result of several waves of immigration. The largest group of Muslim immigrants arriving in the country were Indo-Pakistanis, Albanians, Yugoslavians, Egyptians, Syrians, and Palestinians. After the Iranian Revolution, a growing number of Iranians also immigrated.

Not only did the twentieth century see an influx of Muslim immigrants into the United States, but also, owing to the need for labor in America's expanding industry, there was a major migration of black workers from the agrarian South to the industrialized cities of the North. This migration had massive psychosocial consequences for the migrants, and a large number of organizations were founded in response. Some were religious in nature, and an independent American Islam also developed in this context.[10] It is mainly associated with the Nation of Islam, which Wallace Fard Muhammad founded in Detroit in 1930. Elijah Muhammad took over leadership in 1934, at which time its headquarters moved to Chicago.

The founding of the Nation of Islam cannot be considered separately from two early-twentieth-century nationalist movements: the Moorish Science Temple, a group founded by the American citizen Noble Drew Ali in Newark, New Jersey;[11] and the Universal Negro Improvement Association (UNIA), led by Marcus Garvey, who came to the United States from Jamaica in 1916 and made Harlem the center of UNIA activities in the space of a year.[12] Black nationalism, which stretches back to the eighteenth century, reached a preliminary peak in Garvey's movement. Both of these movements can be considered nationalist insofar as they fought to establish an autonomous state on African soil. The parallels to other nationalist movements in the first half of the twentieth century, such as Zionism, are obvious. The bond with the nation was grounded in the shared experience of being repressed by whites, a common history, and, above all, by racial affiliation. Social rules such as strict endogamy were used to ensure racial purity.

In contrast to Garvey, who was active in the African Orthodox Church and made abundant use of Christian symbolism, Noble Drew Ali regarded himself as a "prophet" of Islam and was convinced that Islam was the only instrument capable of bringing unity to blacks and improving their living conditions. He taught his followers that they were not "Negroes" but "Moors" whose ancestors had come from Morocco before they were brought to North America as slaves. Through this mythological link to the ancient Moroccan empire of Mauritania, he ideologically reinvented a past (and future), thereby providing a substitute for a history truncated by slavery. Following struggles over leadership and the murder of an opponent, Noble died under mysterious circumstances, leading to the final schism in the movement in 1930. One of the new factions was headed by W. D. Fard, who described himself as the reincarnation of Noble Drew Ali. The Nation of Islam, which set up headquarters in Chicago in 1934, emerged from this splinter group. It was led by Elijah Muhammad, who called himself "Allah's apostle."

The Nation of Islam profited from the division and the weakening of both Garvey's movement and the Moorish Science Temple, but at the same time it took up some of their central issues. After a period of decline in the war years—during which Elijah Muhammad and other members served prison sentences for desertion—it experienced steady growth.

During the 1950s and 1960s the Nation of Islam, with its separatist and nationalist politics, was a significant rival to the civil rights movement of Martin Luther King Jr. King's most important personal opponent was Malcolm X, who had just as much charisma and played an increasingly prominent role as an agitator in the Nation of Islam.

Characteristic of the Nation of Islam was a rhetorical radicalism that vilified members of the civil rights movement as "Uncle Toms" and verbally toyed with the possibility of armed resistance. On a symbolic level, the idea of founding an autonomous African American state on U.S. soil (or elsewhere)—to which the movement still subscribes today—represented a radical rejection of American society. At the same time, the followers of the Nation of Islam were never involved in the concrete conflicts with the state that characterized the civil rights movement, and they continue to present themselves today as emphatically middle class.

Their separatist ideology is founded on an undisguised racism. In the writings of Elijah Muhammad, the white race is portrayed as the race of the devil, and marriages to whites and the adoption of black children by whites are considered illegitimate. The movement has its own mythology to justify this concept of black superiority: originally the black race existed alone, but then a crazy black scientist named Yakub invented whites (or Caucasians) as the race of devil. According to this doctrine, whites were destined to rule blacks for six thousand years until a black man emerged to destroy Yakub's world.[13] The reverence shown Elijah Muhammad and the terminology used to describe him suggests seeing him as this "savior." Herein lies a characteristic shift in the transcendental dimension: the Nation of Islam pared back the transcendental references in Islam, including the idea of an afterlife, and replaced the idea of transcendence with the utopian goal of a separate nation, which functioned as an antithesis to the "immanence" of reality in the United States. This utopian nationalism was linked to apocalyptic ideas of an imminent divine war in which the "world of evil," embodied by white America, would be annihilated with the help of a divine spaceship.

After a long-smoldering conflict, there was an open break between Malcolm X and the Nation of Islam in 1964. Malcolm X set up an alternative organization, embraced political action more strongly, and turned to orthodox Islam on several longer trips to the Middle East. After these journeys he also distanced himself from his earlier racist positions. Together with Alex Haley he wrote an autobiography that was released posthumously in the year of his death. His assassination by gunmen at a public event on February 21, 1965, turned him into a martyr, and by "anticipating" the killing in the final chapter of his autobiography, he left the book as a kind of legacy. While it was assumed that his murderers came from the ranks of the Nation of Islam, this suspicion was never verified. Even so, one man who had leveled repeated verbal attacks against Malcolm X in public before his assassination and even declared him worthy of death was Louis Farrakhan, who subsequently became the leader of the Nation of Islam.

After Elijah Muhammad's death in 1965 there was a struggle over the future course of the Nation of Islam, and it ultimately divided the movement. Warith Deen Mohammed, one of Elijah Muhammad's sons, aligned his branch of the former Nation with orthodox Islam, eliminating its former heretical elements and nationalist focus. All that remained of the old platform, in fact, was the strong emphasis on black autonomy and economic self-help.[14] Louis Farrakhan continued to represent the Nation of Islam's old line[15] and to distribute the writings of Elijah Muhammad, but the mere symbolism of the nationalist position became evident in even clearer ways. Whereas the followers of the Nation of Islam once refused military service and regarded elections as a farce, Farrakhan made a public appeal in 1996 to "register to vote," and in 1995 he organized a highly effective public protest, the Million Man March on Washington, D.C., which drew 100,000 black men and transcended the organization's boundaries in terms of both the participants and the public attention it attracted.

From the outset the issue of gender has played an important role in the doctrine and practice of the Nation of Islam, as in many other nationalist movements. The group believed that the poor condition of the "black race" was expressed symbolically by the inability of black men to protect and control black women. As a result, black women were constantly subject to sexual harassment, including sexual relations with white men. In the eyes of the Nation of Islam, this commingling was destroying the black race. According to this logic, the protection and control of women was equated with racial preservation. The utopian goal of establishing a separate nation was thus directly linked to a gender order: "The woman is man's field to produce his nation."[16] Consistent with this thinking, an emphasis was placed on men's roles as providers and guardians, and women were urged to be modest and reserved and were given responsibility for the household and family. Men and women sat separately in meetings, and both sexes had their own uniform: women wore a kind of chasuble with long headscarves, and men dark suits and ties.

Although the nationalist theme continues to have a symbolic function, it has more recently receded into the background, while the gender issue has assumed greater importance. This was demonstrated at the Million Man March, which emphasized solidarity, male responsibility for the family, and hard work. This picture contrasted with public perceptions of black men as promiscuous and violent, as criminals and addicts. By inviting only black men to assemble at the protest, the group was also able to link the concept of separation to a more general issue, that is, to the widely discussed topic of "family values," a favorite among diverse religious and political movements. Nevertheless, with the march, the movement for all practical purposes shelved the idea of national separation.

One characteristic of the Nation of Islam and a reason for the public attention it attracts is its ability to link the foreignness of Islam in the American context with typical forms of expression in American culture. By making this connection, the Nation of Islam is able to create an amalgam that expresses both radical difference and affiliation. Expressed in socio-religious terms, the Nation of Islam is a black nationalist sect that has been able to forge a link to civil religion.

Many black Muslims currently profess a religion that they describe as "orthodox" Islam, and they reject the Nation of Islam as heretical. Nonetheless, the Nation has had relevance for many Muslims in the course of their lives; or at the very least, these Muslims regard it as an important mouthpiece for black interests. Malcolm X, whose autobiography sold more than 1 million copies, continues to be a central figure for many blacks. His autobiography is a kind of politico-religious bildungsroman, a work that touches upon a wide range of relevant topics: a poor childhood in a large family that continued to be traumatized by slavery, the racist violence of the Ku Klux Klan, the resistance mounted by the Garvey movement in 1920s America, the experience of migration, life in the large cities of the North, the descent into crime, and the confrontation with a racist legal system. His development undergoes a fundamental change with his political and religious awakening in prison, the civil rights battles of the 1960s, and finally his repudiation of the Nation of Islam and conversion to the "true Islam."

The last chapter anticipates his political martyrdom, which ultimately became reality in a highly dramatic turn of events. The story itself is a collective myth that offers the potential for identification even if the readers' lives have taken them far from the black ghetto, far from the hustler's existence and the political activism of the 1960s.

In quantitative terms—that is, in terms of the percentage of Muslims in the entire population—Islam plays only a small role in the United States. Yet it has attracted considerable public attention owing to its specific African American manifestation. Its importance can be understood only by considering the background of black nationalism, the opposing tensions between nationalist Islam and the Christian-influenced civil rights movement, as well as the conflict between separation and integration articulated within these struggles. African American Islam has gained significance not only because of this particular constellation but also because it allows its followers to assume the legacy of specific themes and myths of American culture and, at the same time, to demarcate themselves from American society. It seems to continue to do so today, even if the nationalist ideology has been reduced to a purely symbolic function, and gender and family issues have come to the fore. The old function of nationalist Islam has been transferred to "orthodox" Muslim groups in African American society. On this new level, it permits a symbolism of distance at the heart of the system. African American Islam fills a niche that has gone unoccupied since the struggles of the civil rights movement in public space.

While nationalist forms of expression were obviously an adequate channel for articulating collective identity in the 1950s and 1960s—particularly in opposition to the civil rights movement—the situation has changed. An identity discourse that is increasingly focused on ethnic definitions and a link to "African" origins is replacing nationalist forms of articulation. Yet Islam can also be integrated into this discourse since it can be connected to the idea of African ancestry through myths of origin. It also offers a universal framework above and beyond this ethnic particularism.

The Islamist suicide attacks on the World Trade Center in New York City and other targets on September 11, 2001, caused thousands of deaths and severely strained relations between the country's Muslims and non-Muslims. Actual and suspected Muslims were arrested and attacked in its wake. Even so, the large ceremony held at Yankee Stadium in New York City a short time afterward impressively demonstrated the typical American mixture of interreligious diversity and patriotism. This made the event into a documentation of an American civil religion in which Muslims also participate.

Translated by Adam Blauhut

VI

THE DISCUSSION WITHIN ISLAM ON SECULARISM, DEMOCRACY, AND HUMAN RIGHTS

(Alexander Flores)

The relationship to modernity is one of the key themes—if not *the* central theme—for politicians and intellectuals in the Muslim world who are concerned with their societies' social and political issues and perspectives. In general they have few problems with aspects of modernity such as material and technical modernization or the use of rational methods of thought. It is the aspects that imply acceptance of a catalogue of "Western" values that tend to be more problematic and arouse fierce controversy. There are frequently disputes within Islam about the nexus of topics around democracy, human rights (not least women's rights), and secularism. The complex of issues related to secularism is particularly controversial because it involves a powerful clash of different value concepts. On one side is the anthropocentric catalogue of values that has long been accepted in the West, which culminates by affirming human autonomy in relation to religious dominance, that is, a secular attitude. On the other, many Muslims attach great importance to the role of religion as an all-embracing regulative system.

1. The Context

The context of the dispute is the European—or Western—superiority that large parts of the Muslim world have been aware of since the nineteenth century, and which has fundamentally reshaped that world by penetration, direct rule, and continuing dependency. As a result, Muslim countries were affected by processes of secularization. Traditional acceptance of the hegemony of Islam was shaken by a number of changes, including restructuring of some sectors of society and consequent mobility, use of positive law to replace traditional law (which usually operates in the name of the shariʿa), introduction of an education system on the European model, the spread of scientific knowledge, and the emergence of a modernist version of Islam that joined debate with other Islamic schools.[1] In the process, modern achievements seem to have taken on a twofold character. In many ways Muslims recognized and appreciated the positive opportunities (material and technological progress, regulated political relations and legal security, extension of personal freedom); yet all this came from Europeans, who were hated by Muslims for their hard-nosed, superior attitude, and for what many saw as the negative effects of incomplete modernization.

The debate on secularism among Muslim intellectuals should be seen against the backdrop of this ambiguous relationship to modernity. Some regard secularization as a necessary precondition for progress and humanitarian social relations, while others see it as a deliberate attack by the West on the hegemony of Islam in Muslim societies, the last bastion of their own identity and strength. This appears especially threatening in a situation of weakness in relation to the West. Many Muslims who feel marginalized in the modern world regard attachment to their religion as a mainstay, and the more they see their situation as precarious, the more vehemently they emphasize the religious aspect. The secularization of Muslim societies is not actually an attack on Islam as a religion; but it certainly challenges its function as the overall regulative force in society. This is why many Muslims take particular offense at secularism as an attitude that affirms secularization and aims to pursue it consistently.[2] The two main opposing fronts here are the Muslim secularists (Muslims who advocate that life in the Islamic world, as in the West, should be free from institutionally guaranteed religious hegemony) and their integralist opponents (taking integralism to mean support for the function of religion as a social regulator). The conflict between them is an important part of the dispute over the right orientation for Muslim societies.

From the start of this dispute in the nineteenth century, the various positions have hardly ever been clearly and explicitly formulated. Modern Muslims usually present secularism implicitly, that is, as an attitude that leads in practice to autonomy from religious hegemony in large parts of life, without questioning this openly and explicitly. This position is sharply delineated and made explicit by only some of its advocates and only in specific circumstances. The counter position also started off as implicit. It was based on the conviction that Islam was an essential regulator for society; this was symbolized mainly by the nominal validity of the shari'a, however fictitious this may have been even under premodern circumstances. It was only when the influence of European penetration changed these circumstances quite officially that Muslims started explicitly formulating the demand for religious dominance and advocating it with growing aggressiveness. "Islam is religion and state," the catchphrase that was usually used, is far from being the ancient formula that representatives of this position would have us believe: it actually dates back only to the late nineteenth century.[3] The emergence of an Islamist movement trying to enforce this concept against the reality of secularization, and the spread of this concept in the course of the twentieth century, resulted in the integralist position gaining strength and becoming clearly identifiable. It developed an intensely antisecularist polemic. Meanwhile, the secularist literature—whether implicit or explicit—honed itself on the integralist position and the dispute with it.

2. Important Stages in the Debate

During the nineteenth century, Islam's institutionally guaranteed hegemony was questioned in practically every Muslim country. This arose because of the modernization of society through European penetration, the displacement of traditional institutions and regulations, and, on the intellectual plane, the adoption of Western-inspired models and ways of thinking. These processes of secularization were usually not consciously understood but rather ignored, or their meaning was downplayed. They—and their intellectual counterpart, secularism—only occasionally developed into subjects of controversy.[4]

One of the first cases was the controversy between the Lebanese Christian intellectual Farah Antun (1874–1922) and the great Islamic reformer Muhammad 'Abduh (1849–1905). Antun rigorously propagated the tradition of enlightened and rational thought in his magazine, *Al-Jami'a*. In an essay on Averroës he made a passing comment tracing back what he saw as the greater freedom of thought in Europe in comparison to the Islamic world to the separation of civil and religious authority in Christendom. By contrast, he argued, in Islam they were unified "because of religious legal prescription."[5] Muhammad 'Abduh contradicted this sharply. First, he questioned Antun's rationale. If free thought had been established in Europe, 'Abduh argued, then it was not *because of* the specific qualities of the Christian religion but *in spite of* the dominance enforced by the church. Second, 'Abduh claimed emphatically, Islam was essentially a religion of rationality and advocacy of civil (that is, not theocratic) government in the political sphere, which meant that it did not restrict intellectual and political freedom. And third, 'Abduh decisively opposed separation of the two authorities. He argued that human nature made this quite impossible, but he rejected it in any case because it could constrain the beneficial effect of Islam as he understood it.[6] After reading this criticism, Antun reconsidered his position and published an open call for universally formulated secularism based on natural law—probably the first time this was so uncompromisingly and explicitly expressed in the Muslim world.[7]

Two fundamental positions emerged clearly in this controversy and have since been repeatedly taken up in the debate: explicit secularism, which advocates the autonomy of human life from religious dominance, and implicit secularism, which also aims at wide-ranging autonomy, but is religiously based and explicitly refuses to abandon the claim to religious hegemony. Nevertheless, the argument goes, this claim should be achieved not by rigid prescription but through permeation of life with the "spirit" of Islam or the shari'a. As I mentioned earlier, this was the position of Muhammad 'Abduh, whose influence as an Islamic reformist in the Arab realm was similar to that of Sir Sayyid Ahmad Khan in Indian Islam. The 'Abduh school went on to develop itself and work on various possibilities. On one side, Qasim Amin, 'Ali 'Abd al-Raziq, and others explored the secular implications, and on the other, 'Abduh's Salafi followers, the Muslim Brotherhood, and other Islamists buttressed the claim to religious hegemony.

In 1925 in Cairo, 'Ali 'Abd al-Raziq, a pupil of 'Abduh and a graduate of al-Azhar University, published his book *Islam and the Foundations of Power*, in which he emphatically claimed that Islam does not prescribe any specific organizational form of state and society; instead it is a message of essential inner religiosity. 'Abd al-Raziq regarded any other convictions as a retrospective falsification of the original Islamic mission. He therefore made the case for secularism, but with an explicitly religious rationale. This made him dangerous—unlike Farah Antun, who had deliberately not argued from a religious standpoint. The al-Azhar authorities, along with several writers, vehemently opposed 'Abd al-Raziq. He was expelled from the circle of al-Azhar scholars and lost his post as a judge at a shari'a court.

> When Shaykh 'Ali 'Abd al-Raziq...published his book *Islam and the Foundations of Power* in 1925, the book was important and dangerous not because it was a plea for secularism and the separation of religion from the state..., but because it was the first attempt at "the Islamization of secularism," with the claim that Islam is secular because its foundations—Qur'an, sunna, and consensus—do not say that it is "religion and the state." Instead, he argued that Islam is a religion, not a state, and is a spiritual mission that is not concerned with politics, does not call for any particular regime, and has nothing to do with organization of society and specification of a particular form of communal life.[8]

The author of this assertion, Muhammad 'Amara, not only reproached 'Abd al-Raziq for his "Islamic secularist" position but also criticized the position of the al-Azhar committee which condemned him, accusing it of claiming that religious government was an integral part of the shari'a. He argued that if this opinion were right, or if it spread, it would justify a Western-influenced type of secularism that saw theocracy in the Islamic world like that in medieval Europe—a theocracy that had to be defeated through secularism.[9] In any event, 'Abd al-Raziq's open expression of secularism was refuted and banned from public discourse; even many people who evidently supported secular conditions in practice did not want to have this clearly spelled out theoretically.

In 1950 another exponent of secular opinions within Islam, Khalid Muhammad Khalid, published his book *From Here We Start* in Cairo. From a social-critical position, Khalid described the real situation of the Muslim "priesthood," by which he obviously meant the deployment of religion and religious personnel in the interests of the state and its ruling classes. He argued that religion in its basically humanitarian essence had to be distinguished from this and liberated again. He wrote that the state did not need any particular religious quality; the sole rationale for such a thing—to guarantee that Qur'anic punishments were carried out—was questionable anyway, because such punishments had stopped long since.

This was, at least implicitly, a secular program. It was accordingly banned by the al-Azhar authorities (as well as the Egyptian public prosecutor), but a court revoked the ruling. The book was allowed to remain on sale (there were nine editions up to 1959), and, like Khalid's other writings, it played an important role during the Nasser era.[10] Its content was explicitly placed in the context of Islamic rationale, and therefore in the tradition of 'Abd al-Raziq. Neither the latter nor Khalid discussed secularism as a comprehensive concept, and other secularists did not deal with it explicitly either. Secularist concepts were followed in practice but generally were not championed openly. It was antisecularist polemics that first discussed secularism explicitly and comprehensively; this occurred in the Arab countries, for example, in the writings of Anwar al-Jundi, Muhammad al-Bahiy, Yusuf al-Qaradawi, and Muhammad Mahdi Shamsaddin. Relevant contributions began appearing in the late 1950s, and there has been an unbroken series of publications on the topic ever since. In this polemical literature, secularism is awarded a larger dimension and more important status than usual. Here it does not simply represent support for the autonomy of life from institutionalized religious hegemony but becomes a general term for everything the authors want to condemn in Western civilization. A single aspect, a specific idea of Western thought, has become an all-embracing program; secularist developments in the Muslim world are traced back to the West's intention of weakening Muslims and Islam. I shall return later to the various strands of argument in these antisecularist polemics.

What should be noted here is that secularism in the Islamic world first took on definable contours in the polemics against it. This is hardly surprising: secularist developments were an almost inevitable outcome of modernization, which large Muslim circles welcomed and actively pursued. The supporters of modernization, however, avoided highlighting its secularizing byproducts, precisely because they were what seemed to attack Muslim religion or its privileged status, which meant a great deal to many people, particularly in a situation of weakness. This was the most obviously "Western" aspect of modernization and, in the light of Western dominance, a highly problematic one. It was therefore downplayed by its supporters and stressed all the more by its opponents.

The more insistent call for Islamization raised by the growing Islamist movement often led to the arguments being adapted to the changed atmosphere,[11] and even, in some cases, to secularist positions being formulated clearly and openly. Egypt in the 1980s was the scene of particularly acrimonious debates on this topic. The Islamist movement there succeeded in loading public discourse with Islamic concepts so heavily that there were widespread calls for reintroduction of shariʿa law, and hardly anyone dared speak out against it. In 1985, when the government made it clear that there was no hope of these demands being satisfied, the Islamists protested so vehemently that some of their opponents were provoked into publicly stating their opinions. Among them were secularists, both explicit and implicit, that is, on the one hand, people who appeared openly as secularists and explained their position in universal terms, and on the other, those who avoided the term "secularism" and generally explained their viewpoint in Islamic terms.[12] The authors involved oscillated fairly often between different positions and methods of argument.

The intellectual atmosphere was so highly charged, and there were such strong reservations against the idea and concept of secularism, that large parts of the debate were focused not on the advantages or dangers of secularism but on the attempt to establish the right in principle to make secularist statements at all, or to dispute them. This was shown very typically in a roundtable discussion held in Cairo in the spring of 1989, which brought together several representatives of Islamist positions with some "moderate" secularists. ("Extreme," that is, explicit secularists were deliberately not invited to begin with.) There was practically no discussion on the basic problem of secularism in an Islamic context; instead, considerable time was taken up with the demand of the secularists at the roundtable not to be addressed as such, but to be called representatives of the "worldly tendency," and with the arguments over this demand. This shows how discredited the concept of secularism appeared to be. "It is a historical fact," noted one observer, "that nobody describes himself with the word 'secularist.' Instead, it is the Islamic tendencies that use it. When they want to deride their opponents, they label them as secularists.... The others call themselves something else: nationalists, liberals, democrats, socialists, or Nasserists.... I don't know of a single political tendency that calls itself secularist."[13]

The opposing side was also not concerned with fundamental and substantive questions; its supporters were engaged in the almost convulsive effort to argue that, given the urgent social and political problems to be solved, everybody should be committed to a common definitive Islamic point of reference (*marjaʿiyya*), however symbolic that might be. In other words, they justified their theoretical position by pointing to practical imperatives.

On the whole, more recent disputes on secularism in Islamic milieus have not been calm, sober discussions but acrimonious battles with the corresponding tone and method of argument. This is because secular positions are hampered by their association with Western hegemony over the Islamic world, and most of the opponents of secularism today have ties to the Islamist movement, which is heavily engaged in conflict with other forces. This makes the tone of the arguments almost necessarily polemical.

3. Arguments

In their contributions on the secularism issue, Muslim integralists like to refer to the conditions of the secularization processes in Europe during which secularism emerged as a position. In their view this is largely determined by the existence of the Christian Church. The church embodied religion's claim to hegemony over human life, often claimed authority over temporal rulers, and strictly prescribed not only the attitude of believers but also their worldview. According to the integralists, this was why every intellectual and social advance was forced up against the narrow limits that had been set; it had to assert itself against the church's and religion's claim to hegemony. This, in fact, was secularization. In the Christian sphere it could be established without much difficulty because there was a predetermined breaking point in the separation of the spiritual and profane spheres, which was already part of the content of faith. This made it possible to edge religiosity and the church out of public life without threatening their existence.[14]

The proponents of the integralist argument assert that things are different in the Muslim world. State and religion form a unity here; there is no religious organization separate from the state. God makes the laws, and the state and individuals are equally under his authority. Religious hegemony over life is guaranteed not by the church but by the shari'a. Religious compliance and enforcement is the most important guarantee of the Islamic quality of life; achieving this is consequently the noblest task of the Islamic state, and its most important characteristic. In the Islamic sphere there is no constellation of the kind that demanded and rationalized secularization in medieval Europe, because Islam calls for common sense, and its nature is such that it opposes neither scientific nor social progress. According to the proponents of this position, this means that in the Muslim world secularism is not only unnecessary but also impermissible, because in Islam, unlike in Christianity, there is no dogma that prescribes or allows a position of retreat for religious life. An Islam confined to the inner life and severed from application of the shari'a would no longer be Islam.[15]

Independently of whether such claims are factually correct, the integralists advance two main arguments against the secularists: first, that the different conditions of origin and different character of the two religions mean that secularism is appropriate for Christian Europe but not for the Muslim world; and second, its "importation" into the latter is contrary to Islam's claim to all-embracing validity.

Another motif that repeatedly occurs in this context is Islam's historical greatness. The argument runs that in the age of its unchallenged hegemony (often taken as identical with the validity of the shariʿa), Islam secured the superiority of Muslim societies along with the flowering of their civilization and their prosperity. It was precisely because of this that Western colonizers attacked it—with the unhappy results we all know about. Muhammad ʿAmara, in his capacity as a spokesman for the integralist viewpoint, formulated it this way:

> Under the auspices of Islamic civilization, the call for the reign of secularism is far more strange and abnormal than just being an imitation of the West...and borrowing from it a solution for a problem we don't actually have!...
>
> If the European renaissance was linked to secularism, or even based on it, after its decline had been tied to the hegemony of religion and church over state and society[,]...then the march of our Arab-Islamic civilization was exactly the opposite. For the Arab-Islamic renaissance was intimately linked to the hegemony of the Islamic shariʿa over a state that was civilian and Islamic at the same time, while the deviation from the Islamic character of the law was the beginning of the path of our nation into inertia and decline.[16]

Moreover, ʿAmara says, secularism should be rejected because of its negative effect on society and the individual, in both Western and oriental Muslim civilization. Because secularism destroys, or at least undermines, the religious orientation of society, and because it centers on man and his needs, it leads to cultural disorientation, destruction of values and the family, unfettered dominance of the pleasure principle, premarital sex, pornography, homosexuality, alcohol and drug abuse, unchecked materialism, and a host of other detrimental phenomena. ʿAmara argues that this applies primarily to the West, but as the Muslim Orient imitates the West, it applies there as well.[17] He sees this as irreconcilable with Islam and its values: Islam teaches the necessity of the unity of religion and state, and religious guidance for people.[18] ʿAmara says that scientific and scholarly achievements, including those taken from the West, are certainly compatible with Islam, but he firmly rejects the materialistic philosophy that often accompanies them and is a facet of secularism.[19]

On the whole, Muslim secularists, whether or not they describe themselves as such, have entirely different opinions on the complex of issues I have outlined. In relation to the allegedly specific European conditions of the origins of secularism, many of them think not only that the Islamic world had similar problems to those in medieval Europe but also that these problems still exist today. They include objectionable rulers who can cloak themselves in the mantle of religion all the more easily because they can point to the widely held Muslim conception of a close relationship between state and religion. The lack of a church and a hieratic caste in the Muslim world is more an aspiration and an ideal than a reality.

The secularists cite many instances from contemporary Islamic history and Muslim life to show the detrimental effects of a close relationship between religion and state.[20] Fouad Zakaria even declares the background to the emergence of secularism a latent threat, ubiquitous and ever-present:

> The conditions of medieval Christianity were not fundamentally different from the conditions prevailing in Islam. Of course, the two beliefs differ in many details[,]...but they shared the general feature of comprehensiveness, and thus one of the reasons justifying the emergence of secularism in Europe can also be advanced under the conditions prevailing in the Islamic world....
>
> The Middle Ages are not only a period in time but they are also a state of mind, capable of re-emerging in many societies and at different times....Many characteristics of this state of mind are present in our contemporary Islamic societies....This means that the reasons that pushed Europe in the direction of secularism are cropping up in our present Islamic world, and it means too that the widespread idea that secularism is the result of specifically European conditions in a certain stage of its development is baseless.[21]

The main argument of earlier "implicit" secularists was the claim that the Islamic mission is essentially ethical and spiritual, and this gives rise to the vehement objection, based on fundamental principles, against the integralist conception of Islam. The same argument has recurred in the debate more recently. Muhammad Sayyid al-ʿAshmawi, a prominent Muslim secularist (although he avoids this label) expressed it this way:

> God wanted Islam to be a religion, but people wanted it as politics. Religion is general, human and all-pervasive—as for politics, it is narrow, limited, tribal, regional and ephemeral. If you force religion into the limitations of politics[,] you nail it down to a certain scope, a special region, a given group of people and a certain time....Muhammad's...mission is not a legislative one, like that of Moses, but is basically a mission of clemency and ethics, in the sense that its legislative character has to be considered as subsequent, secondary and non-essential.[22]

Al-ʿAshmawi's argumentation is similar to ʿAbd al-Raziq's: it recognizes that neither the Qurʾan nor the hadith contain precise statements about the relation between state and religion, and declares the conception of the religious function of the state derived from the early history of the caliphate as secondary, and thus dispensable; indeed, the argument goes, given the experiences of that era, it could actually be harmful. In view of the basic texts and Islamic history, this is one possible position, but it does not alter the fact that many people take a completely different view. This certainly applies to the large majority of scholars and intellectuals who voice their opinions publicly. As I mentioned earlier, some representatives of this group have also strongly objected to "implicit" secularists.[23] After intense skirmishes, on the whole these positions seem mutually irreconcilable at present.

The secularists usually refuse to respond to the integralists' accusations that secularism leads to the destruction of values and promotes every possible form of reprehensible behavior and cultural decadence—accusations that amount to a caricature of Western civilization. As Zakaria once commented mockingly: "Everybody believes that Europeans live in a state of constant moral turpitude, think of nothing but free sexuality, and have no room in their lives for any kind of moral values; that the law in European states is designed to protect perverts and defend incest; and that crazy ideas and distortions like that make up the entire intellectual baggage of millions of people."[24]

The arguments on both sides basically involve three levels of debate. The first involves a very fundamental issue of religion and the question whether it should play a special social role, enforced in some circumstances by coercion, or whether it should be restricted to the personal sphere. The second level concerns Islam in particular, and the question how far secular attitudes within its scope are practically meaningful and religiously permissible. Third, it is becoming increasingly clear that the vehemence of the dispute over secularism is partly due to the fact that it is a bone of contention in the Muslim Orient's relations with the West.

There have been repeated calls or proposals for both sides in this controversy to meet on common ground. These calls can be based in principle as well as in pragmatic considerations. In so far as the contradictions are simply about differences in theoretical options, it certainly makes sense to talk about common issues; but when they are intensified by acrimonious political debate, probably not much can be achieved by dialogue. There is no sign of lasting reconciliation in the West's relationship to the Muslim Orient. It is likely that certain aspects of the existing controversy will continue for some time to come.

4. Democracy

Most Muslims today have a very positive view of democracy in the Western sense, in common with other modern concepts; in many ways it is the benchmark by which they judge their own societies. Western critics often claim that democracy and Islam are incompatible, while many Muslims, especially if they want to tie into Islamic tradition, are concerned with the issue of compatibility as well.

In fact, traditional Islamic theory and practice of governance are not compatible with modern concepts of democracy. This is a statement that obviously applies to the premodern non-Islamic world as well, and it has to be particularly stated because some Islamic apologists claim otherwise. Traditional Islamic governance is autocracy, which was legitimated by the fiction of theocracy or theonomy. According to this theory, the sovereign, originally the caliph, is chosen from an authorized circle by a kind of election, and invested in office in a homage ceremony (*bay'a*), which is like the conclusion of a contract between him and his "subjects." In performing his office he is obliged to "consult" with appropriate people according to the principle of *shura*. He is answerable to God, and the community of believers can more or less remind him of this obligation. He is subject to divine law just like any other believer; if he offends against the law or neglects his duties, he can be called to account and ultimately even removed from office. Some people have always been keen to posit this "obligation of resistance" of Muslim subjects as a mechanism of democratic control, but it has very rarely been used in practice. On the level of theory, such points of contact with democratic ideas are guarded and vaguely formulated; in practice they have usually yielded to autocratic governance, which was then legitimated by a quietist concept developed by law scholars.[25]

Most Muslim authors would not agree unambiguously with this statement of the case. To the extent that they perceive the situation, they explain the unfortunate course of Islamic history as a departure from the true Islamic conception, according to the saying, "It is not Muslims that are an argument against Islam, but Islam that is an argument against Muslims." Attitudes differ toward the modern concept of democracy. Some authors acknowledge the conflict between democracy and the traditional conception of Islam, and regard the latter as so superior that they think Muslims should dispense altogether with "Western" democracy. According to one of these authors, introducing concepts of foreign origin and nonreligious character such as Western democracy into questions of the political order is a "political illness," because it "makes the people into the origin of powers and thus into the legislator and sovereign."[26] This position openly rejects the democratic conception of governance by the people because it contradicts the Islamic view of the role of God as the unique lawgiver and sovereign.

The opposing view is that given the conflict between democracy and conventional Islamic political conceptions, Muslims should adopt democracy and confidently push aside the traditional conception. Proponents of this approach argue that it might contradict the letter of the traditional conception but not the spirit of Islam, because it promotes the common welfare, and that calls for the introduction of democracy. This implies renunciation of any specific Islamic rationale for democracy. Given the marked accentuation of Islam we have seen in the past decades, we can hardly expect this approach to gain general acceptance, and it is seldom put forward.[27]

Much more common is the attempt to propagate democracy as it is generally understood today, but to tie it to specific elements of the Islamic tradition, or sometimes to rename it entirely using these elements. In this context some people like to recall the "election" of the caliph as laid down in the original concept, the "contract" associated with the *bay'a,* and the community's obligation to warn and, if necessary, depose the sovereign. Some authors refer particularly to the term *shura* and the concept it embodies. The term is Qur'anic (42:38), and generally means consultative decision.

It is often interpreted as the duty of those in government to seek advice, although in practice and in jurisprudence—which reflects actual practice—no kind of precise agreement has been reached on the character of the advisers and the extent to which their advice should be binding. As critics of this approach have sometimes pointed out, the drawback is that in Islamic history this concept was hardly able to ensure an even remotely democratic form of government. The advantage of the concept's vagueness, however, is precisely what makes it suitable for investing with new content. There are certainly authors who define *shura* in such a way that it corresponds to the Western concept of democracy. Others emphasize that differences should be acknowledged to avoid the odium of adopting anything from the West. There are many individual variations here, and the motives for such an approach are also varied. Some people want to retain an Islamic identity while participating in positive modern achievements; others, who acknowledge the concept of democracy to be beneficial, want to make it attractive to the common people because they do not trust them to accept it in "foreign" packaging; still others want to formulate traditional concepts in the best possible humanitarian way, to prevent Islamists from utilizing them. And yet the movement I have outlined certainly includes Islamists who do not want to relinquish issues of democracy to their opponents along with the revaluation they see associated with it—not to mention the wholly pragmatic attempt by Islamists to make use of democratic possibilities and demands in their confrontations with autocratic regimes. Other Islamists bitterly accuse the whole movement, even its Islamist segments, of flirting with Western concepts.

In any case, the effort to propagate or introduce democratic concepts under Islamic auspices—including those that correspond to Western perceptions of democracy—as well as the whole spectrum of such positions and the objections to them, show that in this area, as elsewhere, there is nothing in the content of Islamic belief, and no laws or regulations, that would hinder Muslims a priori from positively accepting democracy.[28]

5. Human Rights

The debate around the Muslim position on human rights is also part of the conflict between the challenge of the West and the response to it from different tendencies within modern Islam. The challenge is that the central concept of human rights today, as embodied in the Universal Declaration of Human Rights adopted by the UN in 1948, and the subsequent pacts of 1966, envisions human rights as universal—yet at times it is heavily emphasized that this concept was first developed in the West. In terms of its claim to universality, the concept of human rights is still relatively young and has not been part of the Muslim discussion for very long either. It should be mentioned that Farah Antun justified some human rights in terms of natural law in 1981 in his extended plea for a secularist conception: "In their unique nature as humans, i.e.[,] leaving aside their religion or faith, human beings have the right to all good deeds and goods, as well as small and great offices right up to the presidency of the nation."[29] In this case, as with other conceptions, Western ideas have deeply influenced Muslims' horizons of judgment, even among those who strongly reject Western influence. This applies all the more to the issue under discussion here, because the concept of universal human rights, which is founded on natural law and therefore not based on religion, is often greatly emphasized in relation to non-Western societies, including Islamic ones—which react with corresponding defensiveness.[30]

The various "Islamic declarations of human rights" offer a good illustration of the situation. They were undoubtedly formulated under pressure of the 1948 Universal Declaration and the resulting focus on human rights issues. Muslims felt obliged to react if they wanted to remain part of the discussion. Yet given the declaration's claim to universality and its foundation in natural law, many Muslims had great difficulty accepting it wholesale. Some concerned groups and institutions, such as the Islamic Council of Europe and the Organization of the Islamic Conference, responded with catalogues of human rights. Absolutely parallel to the Universal Declaration, these basically called for the same human rights—but with the fundamental difference that the Islamic versions contained long preambles setting out the rationale in an Islamic context, and some rights were made less absolute by the stipulation "within the framework of the shari'a."[31] The Islamic rationale contradicts the universality of human rights. Its evident presupposition of the validity of the shari'a, and the constant emphasis on this, also contradicts several clearly defined demands such as freedom of religion and the equality of religions and of the sexes. For example, the question of the apostasy prohibition—part of the traditional conception of the shari'a—is not mentioned in the Islamic Council declaration because it is obviously an extremely critical point. The question of minorities is resolved in a Solomonic way: on a religious level the *Qur'anic* principle "There should be no compulsion in religion" is applied, and in civil and personal matters, questions of minorities are dealt with according to the shari'a or according to the minorities' own religious law.[32] The result is that this declaration—like other similar ones—presupposes conditions that do not actually exist, which clearly indicates that such declarations are less about orienting themselves to reality than about intervening in a controversial dialogue with the West in which some Muslim representatives oppose the Western claim to hegemony over questions of values and insist instead on their own identity.

The whole complex issue of the universality of human rights versus cultural relativism is a frequent topic of discussion, especially at meetings on intercultural dialogue between the West and Islam;[33] but it is also the subject of acrimonious disputes among Muslims. On one side are the hardliners who stick to the traditional Islamic view or want to give it renewed validity, defying present-day reality. They generally see no cause for apology, and often do not even refer to human rights as a concept; they prioritize the shariʿa one-sidedly as divine law that may not be relativized by taking account of human needs.[34] A fairly wide "mid-range" of Muslim intellectuals try to show that Islam is compatible with a modern perception of human rights, if only it is properly understood; most of these writers are apologists. Another frequent claim is that Islam is superior to other conceptions in terms of protecting human rights. The sensitive questions of Islam's compatibility with what are universally understood as human rights, especially with respect to discrimination against women, treatment of religious minorities, and achieving complete religious freedom, are usually evaded, or presented as largely unproblematic. This field of opinion includes a wide range of positions from moderate Islamists to authors who argue quite openly. Yet they never question the fundamental commitment to an Islamic framework for social organization. Representatives of the third basic position recognize that this commitment must inevitably come into conflict with a consistent universalist position, to which they see themselves pledged. They question the Islamic framework, but not Islam as a religion. For example, Faraj Foda points out that the equality principle in the Egyptian constitution contradicts the constitution's stipulation of Islam as the state religion, in the same way that discrimination against non-Muslims contradicts the Universal Declaration of Human Rights, to which Egypt is actually a signatory.[35] The Sudanese author ʿAbdullahi Ahmed An-Naʿim and the Tunisian commentator Mohamed-Chérif Ferjani have been similarly open in pointing out the contradictions between the shariʿa and the universal conception of human rights—which is why they have vehemently opposed the demand for implementation of shariʿa law.[36]

The discussion on human rights and their foundation involves a broad spectrum of opinion, not only between advocates of Islamic and "Western" positions but also in the related debate among Muslims themselves, although only a few examples could be discussed in this chapter. In any event, it appears as if the current disputes on this issue, which are often very acrimonious, are only at first glance about an intellectual "clash of civilizations." On the whole, the opposing positions have a global range. The putative "clash of civilizations" often turns out to be a "clash *within* civilizations."[37]

Translated by Karen Margolis

VII

The Situation of Women in Islamic Countries

(Wiebke Walther)

1. Introduction

The status of women in Islam has been an issue for over two hundred years and is currently one of the world's most controversial subjects both inter- and intraculturally, which means also for Muslims of different regions and orientations. In fact the situation of the world's almost 600 million Muslim women varies so greatly today that it will be possible to address only some of the more essential aspects. My focus here is on the Middle East, that is, the Arab world from North Africa to Iraq, as well as Turkey and Iran. These countries have different languages and historical developments, and diverse economic, political, and social conditions, yet Islam has shaped them all in various distinct ways.[1]

To begin with, in contrast to ratios in more economically developed re- gions, the percentage of women in several Middle Eastern countries—as in other developing countries—is somewhat lower than the percentage of men.[2] This is a result of frequent childbirth and inadequate medical care for women in these regions, especially in rural areas, and many women's inad- equate knowledge of hygienic measures, as well as the strenuousness of the physical tasks they have to perform.

In the 1960s, the first debates took place on the acceptability and ne- cessity of family planning from the perspective of religious, political, eco- nomic, and social concerns in Tunisia and Egypt.[3] Today all Middle Eastern countries—even those that rejected the idea until fairly reecently, such as Iran until 1990, Saudi Arabia, and the Gulf countries that have tried to get by without guest workers—now promote family planning in view of rapid, and thus economically and socially destabilizing, population growth. Contraceptives are distributed, and abortion is permitted for eugenic and medical reasons, as long as the husband gives his consent. Fatwas back this policy, since contraception, as is often pointed out, had already been permitted under Islam in the Middle Ages. Moreover, Islam claims to have always been family- and child-oriented, maintaining that smaller families could improve the situation of women and children, for example, by raising their standard of living. Statistics in these countries show a steady decline of births and a rise in the percentage of women receiving medical care during childbirth, though it should be taken into account that such improvements apply more to the urban middle and upper classes than to rural and nomadic populations (e.g., on the Arabian Peninsula). One should also bear in mind, however, that statistics from developing nations and dictatorial regimes have to be treated with some reservations, as they may be incomplete or doctored to create a positive image.

In all societies there are differences in the status of women depending on their family and social, regional, communal, and ethnic backgrounds, as well as, of course, individual factors such as aptitude, education, age, and experience. For some time now, modern technologies such as the transistor radio and (satellite) television have helped improve access to information about other countries and cultures, even for illiterates, and this is also true under governments where state censorship tries to control content. Nevertheless, reforms and/or state decrees are not able to overcome age-old customs, traditions, and ways of thinking overnight, and this is particularly true in rural communities and among the urban poor.

The Internet offers the young and educated many ways to access information and communication, and this enables them to network globally, beyond regional and other boundaries. Email, cell phones, and text messages free women and girls, who according to conventional Muslim notions of honor should be largely segregated and confined to their homes, from their isolation. All the same, the percentage of individuals who can access the Internet in the Arab world is reportedly low: Tunisia was the first to go online in 1991 (the World Bank did so in 1992); Saudi Arabia was last, in 1997, because—as the responsible royal institution has admitted—it had wanted to wait until surveillance technologies were more advanced. Yet despite censorship, Saudi Arabia soon became the Arab country with the most Internet connections and a large number of bloggers expressing criticism of the system, including many women. Censorship of pornographic material and politically "objectionable" statements, which may even lead to a blogger's imprisonment, is also common in other countries, including Egypt and Turkey—though supraregional acts of solidarity between bloggers are also quickly organized. Nowadays foreign ministries, ruling houses, and women's organizations in these countries have their own websites for self-presentation as well as disseminating information. More than ever, policies toward women and various forms of state feminism have become a means of demonstrating a country's progressiveness. These are used as a kind of trump card for power systems, helping them win women's votes, where women are entitled to vote, though in the long run this works only if preelection promises are kept. At the same time, internal and external criticism of some countries' policies toward women has become common on the Internet. And although the situation varies from country to country, the relationship between self-presentation or apologia for the system and critique from within is revealing. Saudi Arabia, for example, extols polygyny not only as conducive to the birth of sons but also as socially superior to monogyny, claiming that the latter is what destroyed Western societies. In contrast, prominent Saudi women have called for family planning and monogyny on behalf of their country.

Large sections of the Muslim population and their orthodox religious leaders continue to see women as the embodiment of Islamic morals and ethics in light of a steadily degenerating Western world. Men should protect women's morality, yet their own morals are never at issue. Hence policies toward women are also a balancing act between secularization along so-called Western, often leftist lines of thought and orthodox tendencies within each country, whereby an Islamic feminism has existed for years alongside a secularized, more leftist feminism. In turn, the two are represented by a number of different groups. In other words, feminism takes a wide range of forms.[4]

I would also point out that not everything currently formative or decisive for the existence of Muslim women is rooted in Islam, even if Islam often strives to determine the lives of its adherents in all ways. The Qur'an—which religious Muslims view as the divine revelation of God and the sole basis of their faith—offers believers guidance and direction, as well as concrete advice in many spheres of life. It is primarily addressed to men, but several verses acknowledge the equality of man and woman (e.g., 33:35–36, 2:187, 4:1, 4:32). Other verses clearly proclaim woman's subordination or inferiority (e.g., 4:34, 2:228). The hadiths—large collections of narratives documenting what Muhammad as "*the* fine example" is believed to have said, done, or just silently tolerated—augment and elaborate the Qur'an. Since first being systematically collected and recorded in the ninth century, they have grown in number, and they reflect the diversity of regional circumstances and developments over time. Right up to the present, many followers of diverse movements cite hadith literature to justify their views, also and especially with regard to women's issues.[5] There are, however, other Muslims who emphasize the significance of the Qur'an (in its "contemporary" interpretation) as the sole legitimate source of orientation.

And although "the second sex" has been subject time and again to stronger social constraints than "the first," there have always been women in Islamic countries who—thanks to their social or individual circumstances—have risen above the demands of daily life. These women, who have lived within or even sometimes beyond the sociocultural limits imposed by Islam or, as many Muslim women call attention to today, limits imposed by male theologians and/or their surroundings, became personalities recognized by historians and biographers.[6] In fact the rise of Islam itself is inconceivable without women such as Khadija and 'A'isha, Muhammad's two most distinguished wives.

As modernization set in, and the very religious and highly educated were confronted with an overwhelming and, for them, strange—that is, Western—culture, they began to reflect on their own golden era in history. In Egypt, from about 1870 on (and later in other countries), intellectuals started incorporating their pre-Islamic heritage, so highly esteemed abroad, into their culture. Reformers resourcefully focused on what might be viewed in their own, Islamic history as exemplary, stabilizing, or pioneering for, or even superior to, Western ways of life and thought. Beginning in the 1850s, evidence of Islam's plurality manifested itself increasingly in an awareness heightened by mounting social conflicts on the one hand and the lucid insights of a growing range of controversial voices on the other.

2. Reevaluation: The Revival of Traditions and Modernization since the Nineteenth Century

As the Egyptian historian al-Jabarti (1753–1825/6) revealed in the third and fourth volumes of his chronicle on the French occupation of Cairo from 1798 to 1801, with its—for the times—typically ornate title, *'Aja'ib al-athar fi l-tarajim wa-l-akhbar* (Miraculous Monuments: On Biographies and Novelties), Egyptian women from the upper and lower classes alike were not so constrained in their mobility, decisions, and influence at the outset of the era of modernization as a number of European travelers in the nineteenth century would somewhat later portray them.[7]

Women, especially from upper-class families, had fortunes of their own, as according to Qur'an 4:11–12 they were entitled to half the amount inherited by males of the same degree of kinship. In addition, the shari'a did not stipulate community property or profits between husbands and wives in Islamic marriages. This meant that women could manage their own wealth and exert influence despite the tradition of gender segregation and the exclusion of women, in particular of high rank, from public life. Women were required, at least when they were young, to engage middlemen for many transactions—something that is still true today for Saudi Arabian businesswomen, for example, to obtain a state license. In the nineteenth century, upper-class Turkish women shopped at the bazaar escorted by servants, who were an indication of their social prestige (and served to protect them, not unlike harem walls).[8] This custom can also be found in the tales of different towns and regions in *The Thousand and One Nights*. For excursions women used coaches, brought to the country in the seventeenth century. In Istanbul, from about 1870 on, transport in trams with special curtained compartments gave women greater mobility. In the late 1920s, when upper-class women took to riding through Istanbul in open carriages, they were pelted with stones. The response was similar when the first individuals donned hats after Kemal Atatürk banned traditional head coverings for men and women.[9]

In the Middle East, as in Europe and the United States, the upper classes initiated both the women's movement and the so-called renaissance movement (*nahda* or *nahzet*) for social and cultural change. And since these women not only had contact, for example, through their fathers and/or husbands with Europeans and Americans in their own country but also traveled (accompanied by male relatives) to Europe and America, they cannot be seen as isolated from the women's movement on these continents. They must also be considered within the context of the process of political, administrative, economic, and cultural modernization that began as a power-driven "top-down" reform movement in the nineteenth century after encounters with representatives of the European colonial powers, for example, in Turkey, then Egypt, and later Iran.

Members of a variety of Christian missions were also very active as socio-cultural mediators, especially in the Syro-Lebanese region. Of course, they first forged links to upper-class Christian families and founded schools, including some for girls, modeled on western European schools. As early as 1849, Butrus al-Bustani (1819–83), a leading advocate of the *nahda* in Beirut, held a lecture on the need for women's education at the Syrian Society for the Sciences and Arts, which Eli Smith, an American missionary, had established a year earlier.[10] Indeed, the first Arab woman to speak publicly on women's issues was an Aleppine Christian woman, Maryana Marrash (1848–1919), who came from a literary family.[11] In 1879, in an article in *Al-Jinan* (The Gardens), a magazine published by her compatriot Salim al-Bustani (1848–1884), a son of Butrus al-Bustani, she followed the example of western European and American upper-class women and called on her fellow (wealthy Christian and Muslim) female citizens to adorn themselves with knowledge instead of gold, jewels, and sumptuous garments.

In Turkey, not long after 1850, the question of allowing formal education for girls or of replacing Islamic dress with European clothing, which involved the issue of women's veils, sparked debate in the country's newly established newspapers and in special monographs.[12] There was also criticism of some of the rules and principles in the shari‘a, especially the right of men to practice polygyny and divorce their wives at will (*talaq*).[13]

In Egypt in the year of his death Rifa‘a Rafi‘ al-Tahtawi (1801–1873) published his comprehensive guide, *Al-Murshid al-amin li-l-banat wa-l-banin* (A Reliable Guide for Rearing Girls and Boys), on the occasion of the opening of the first state girls' school in Cairo. Al-Tahtawi, a graduate of al-Azhar in Cairo, one of the world's oldest religious universities, was from 1826 to 1831 the religious tutor for the first large Egyptian delegation of students to Paris. There he began translating books on geography, history, and ethnography from French into Arabic. In doing so he also took care to explain and coin terms for what was unknown or not commonly known to his compatriots. Later he became the director of the first school for translation in Cairo, and then Khedive Ismail's adviser on reform and educational policies. Citing many passages, even controversial ones, from classical Arabic literature and undoubtedly inspired by (unspecified) French works—most likely including Fénelon's *De l'éducation des filles* (1687), Rousseau's *Émile, où l'éducation,* and other later works—al-Tahtawi called attention, in dialectical discussions with opponents of women's education, to women's abilities and talents. He argued that to educate girls (in primary schools) was to lay the foundation for partnership in a harmonious Muslim marriage, which constituted the nucleus of the state and was a prerequisite for raising children properly. He also advocated that women be allowed to participate in public life as well as hold a job; in other words, he demanded even more than Fénelon had.[14]

Beginning in 1892, the Egyptian poet Aysha Taymuriyya ('A'isha 'Ismat Taimur, 1840–1902), who came from the distinguished Kurdish-Arab Taymur Pasha family in Cairo, was the first Muslim woman to write in elegant prose in the newly founded Egyptian newspapers and magazines. She demanded more education for women and the reform or rather elimination of all rules and regulations confining women to "domestic prisons." She stressed women's pedagogical and psychological skills, and insisted that they should be entitled to determine their own lives and choose their future partners.[15]

Also inspired by Western models and the spirit of early Arab nationalism, Zaynab Fawwaz (ca. 1860–1914) was more comprehensive in her approach to the struggle of women for emancipation. Born into a Shi'i family in South Lebanon, she moved as a very young women—apparently after dissolving an early, arranged marriage—to Cairo with her brother, a lawyer.[16] Her biographical dictionary on 456 famous women from the Middle East and Europe, decoratively titled *Al-Durr al-manthur fi tabaqat rabbat al-khudur* (Scattered Prose Pearls: On Generations of Noble Women) and published in 1893–94,[17] continued an unfinished work by the Syro-Lebanese Christian Maryam al-Nahhas Nawfal (1856–1888). The latter had begun writing the dictionary in 1873 but only succeeded in publishing the first volume in 1879 by selling her jewels. Zaynab Fawwaz also portrays Maryam al-Nahhas in an essay.[18] Her objective was to show that Arab and oriental women had achieved positions in society and culture earlier than European women. In the foreword she mentions the difficulties she had, as a veiled woman forced to live in segregation, in compiling the work from an array of Arab sources;[19] at the time these works existed largely in manuscript form, and many of them were obtainable only from private libraries (the Egyptian National Library, modeled on the Bibliothèque Nationale in Paris, was founded in 1873). She does not mention any European sources, but she must have used some. It is noteworthy, though, that she lists more Arab and oriental women from pre-Islamic and Islamic times than European women, and prefaces the dictionary with excerpts from articles and speeches by the Lebanese immigrants Hana Kurani (1870–1898), Sara Nawfal (n.d.),[20] Maryam Khalid (n.d.), and Esther Azhari Moyal (1873–1948); the first three were Christians, the fourth

Jewish. Sara Nawfal, a daughter of Maryam al-Nahhas, worked for the first Egyptian women's magazine, *Al-Fatat* (The Young Woman), founded by her sister Hind and her father, Nasim Nawfal, in Alexandria in 1892. After working at *Al-Fatat,* Esther Moyal founded her own women's journal, *Al-'A'ilah* (The Family), in Cairo in 1898.[21] She was also a teacher, first at two Christian girls' schools, and then at a Jewish and a Muslim school. She wrote articles for the newspapers *Al-Ahram* and *Al-Hilal* and later translated French novels into Arabic. Originally she and Hana Kurani had hoped to present the manuscript of Zaynab Fawwaz's women's dictionary in the women's section of the Chicago World's Fair in 1893.[22] As an unmarried Muslim, Fawwaz could not, however, make the trip, which—as she wrote in a letter to the initiator and patron of the fair, Bertha Honoré Palmer, wife of a famous industrialist—she deeply regretted.[23] When her husband divorced her because she had borne him no children, she first earned her living by giving a lecture tour through large North American cities for three years. After returning to Lebanon, she worked as a teacher, book author, and translator of English literature until her untimely death.[24]

Zaynab Fawwaz published a closet drama, *Riwayat al-hawa wa-l-wafa* (The Story of Passion and Fidelity), in verse and rhymed prose under a pseudonym in 1892–93. In it she narrates the story of a pure, chaste, and self-sacrificing oriental love and—probably motivated by educational objectives—presents a counterimage of gender relations then undergoing change owing to influences from Europe. She also explored other genres that were new for Arabic literature: in 1899 she wrote a family novel set in South Lebanon, titled *Husn al-'awaqib au ghadat al-Zahira* (Good Consequences, or The Girl from al-Zahira),[25] and in 1905 a historical novel titled *Al-Malik Kurush awwal muluk al-Furs* (Cyrus the Great, the First King of Persia), in which she lauded monotheism. Both works are interspersed with verse and have turbulent plots reminiscent of Arabic folk novels. In *Al-Rasa'il al Zaynabiyya* (The Zaynab Epistles) from 1905—a collection of letters and essays on contemporary issues that she published in Egyptian newspapers from 1892 on—she strongly advocates women's education, equal rights, and equal opportunities, as well as women's participation in political life.[26]

Confrontation with European colonial powers also inspired the reinterpretation of the Qur'anic verses related to women's social situation. Muhammad 'Abduh (1849–1905), who was the grand mufti of Egypt from 1899 until his death, divided the Qur'an into passages that were eternally valid and those that were valid only during a specific period. In doing so he set an example for later reformers. He interpreted Qur'an 4:34, "Men are in charge of women," and Qur'an 2:228, "and men are a degree above them," as confirming man's role as the head of the family and protector of women in society. Women are, however, endowed with equal intellectual powers. It is only because of their emotionality that they are weaker than men, and this is what makes man better suited to head a family. In this role man is as indispensable as the (male) head of state—also a popular stereotype in Europe and the United States since the seventeenth century.[27] 'Abduh explained Qur'an 4:3, the verse quoted even today to justify polygyny, by referring to the situation of the early Muslim community after the battle of Uhud, in which many Muslim men had died, and as a consequence their wives and children required support. He also justified the verse by men's potency and the need to provide for sick, older, or infertile women, who, contrary to what occurred so often "in the West," were not abandoned for a younger woman, though in Qur'an 4:129, which denies that men are capable of treating multiple wives justly, he saw a religious commitment to monogyny. Moreover, he believed that it was historical constraints and necessities that had led to centuries of polygyny.[28] Today this controversy is still raging between conservatives and proponents of largely secular-minded women's organizations which are demanding that polygyny be banned in the countries where it is still legal.

After completing his law studies in Cairo, Qasim Amin (1863–1908) studied law in Montpellier from 1881 to 1885. During this period he was in close contact with Muhammad 'Abduh and experienced the gender debate in France. In his work *Les Égyptiens* (1894) he defended the social conditions in Egypt against the negative picture presented by a Frenchman, the duc d'Harcourt, in his book *L'Égypte et les Égyptiens* (1893). A few years later, in 1899, Qasim Amin himself criticized Egyptian living conditions and gender relations in his book *Tahrir al-mar'a* (The Liberation of Women).[29] Following fierce attacks by orthodox Muslim circles, he published a revised edition in 1902, *Al-Mar'a al-jadida* (The New Woman). He based his proposals for reform on 'Abduh's interpretations of the Qur'an and the shari'a. He explained how political despotism in the Middle East had caused women to be suppressed over the centuries. He deduced that men, as the socially stronger sex, passed the tyranny of which they were also victims on to their wives, as the socially weaker sex. He criticized the education of (upper-class) girls in Cairo during this period as being based on the education of upper-class girls in Europe (it included instruction in reading and writing, in Arabic and a foreign language, as well as sewing, embroidery, and European music). He advocated an education oriented more toward practical life and its responsibilities—for man and woman had been created equal. A nation could develop along progressive lines only if women were no longer denied opportunities for education and participation in public life. Segregation of the sexes and the veiling of women were the main causes of backwardness in the Islamic world. His Muslim adversaries accused him of having been swayed by the social-critical drama *Al-Mar'a fi l-Sharq* (Woman in the Orient), written by the Coptic lawyer Marqus Fahmi (1870–1955), who, like Amin, was a graduate of Cairo's khedivial law school and the law school in Aix-en-Provence.[30]

Amin also spoke out on other issues, including the practice of veiling. As he saw it prescribed in Qur'an 24:31, veiling should involve the "covering of the neckline." And a better education in ethics for both women and men would lead to the establishment of monogyny, with loving relationships between men and women as defined in Qur'an 30:21, as well as the necessary social reforms. He goes on to describe the rivalry between wives and their children in polygynous marriages as socially destructive.

Orthodox Muslims (in Iran as well, where the entire book was published in Persian translation in 1911) reacted strongly to Qasim Amin's writings, while generations of Western orientalists saw him as *the* champion of women's emancipation in the Arab world, as he argued his case with extraordinary clarity, astuteness, and logic. Only later did Western scholars realize that Arab and Iranian women had already been fighting for emancipation for some time before him. Because of Amin's harsh critique of Egyptian-Islamic conditions, some Egyptian-Arab male and female nationalists even started seeing him in the early 1990s as a proponent of colonialist thought, for they had begun to blame the conditions prevalent in those days directly on the policies of the khedives under the influence of colonial rule.[31]

Amin's compatriot Malak Hifni Nasif (1886–1918) was more conservative in her writings,[32] especially in matters related to the veil. Undoubtedly this was the case because as a woman she was familiar with the sense of shame a woman felt if her face was unveiled after having been covered since puberty. She demanded that women be permitted to decide for themselves if they wanted to wear a veil or not. In this she anticipated the stance taken later by modern feminists, including Shirin Ebadi, an Iranian lawyer and the first Muslim woman to receive the Nobel Peace Prize (on October 10, 2003).[33] In articles and speeches Nasif called on her fellow citizens to follow the example of prominent and self-confident Arab women from the early days of Islam while emulating the social activities and dynamism of contemporary Western women.

After they had been confined to the domestic sphere for centuries, it was new for Arab and/or Muslim women to turn to the public in their writings. Like European and American women some generations before them, they first did so anonymously or under a pseudonym, and of course initially from their homes. Yet it was not long before newspapers and magazines began printing articles by renowned women who addressed women's issues. These articles included, for example, a debate between the Syro-Lebanese Christian immigrant Mayy Ziyada (1886–1941), author and founder of a well-known "salon" for both men and women in her father's house in Cairo in 1914, and Malak Hifni Nasif. Hence even in its early years the press was not reserved exclusively to men and was also successful in overcoming confessional barriers.[34]

3. Educational Opportunities

For centuries, daughters of upper-class families primarily received religious instruction at home. In Qur'an schools, similar to the ones for boys, girls from the poorer classes were occasionally taught to recite the Qur'an and the rudiments of reading, writing, and arithmetic. Beginning in the mid-nineteenth century, representatives of Christian missions established girls' schools in the Syro-Lebanese region. The first state school for girls opened in Cairo in 1873 and was initially met—as would also later be the case in other Islamic countries—with strong opposition from orthodox groups, which wanted to continue limiting girls' movements to their homes. The first girls to attend this newly opened state school in Cairo were slaves of upper-class families (this remained the case until slavery was abolished in 1877) and daughters of upper- and upper-middle-class families (especially those with ties to the state), who—as was often the case also in Europe—were more or less ordered to attend.

In Iran in 1835, American Presbyterian missionaries established a girls' school for Armenians in Reza'iyeh and in 1875 another school in Tehran. As of about 1895, Muslim girls were also allowed to attend.[35] In Iraq the girls' schools established after 1860 by French missionaries in Mosul and Baghdad first admitted only Christian students. The various speeds at which regional developments unfolded can be documented by the following dates: In Turkey, the first two-year state school for girls opened in 1858–59, that is, before the law on secularizing education was ratified in 1869.[36] The first training college for women teachers opened in Istanbul in 1863, so that upper-class families would no longer need to hire European women to tutor their daughters in their homes. In the course of an emerging nationalism, teachers from Turkey (who were to have a knowledge of both cultures) educated girls in autochthonous values and their mother tongue.

In preparation for eventual EU membership, Turkey has launched a number of measures to improve the situation of women. To increase literacy, it aims at providing support for children, especially girls, from financially disadvantaged families.[37] Despite general compulsory education since the 1920s, lower-class families still require more nonmaterial as well as material incentives to educate their daughters than they do to educate their sons.

The opening of the first state girls' school in Cairo in 1873 was followed by others, for example, in Baghdad in 1898 (a Turkish girls' school focusing on needlework),[38] in Tehran in 1918,[39] and in Bahrain in 1928. After coming to power in Oman, Sultan Qaboos opened the first state boys' school in 1970 and the first state girls' school in 1971, both of which were in Muscat, the capital.

In Riyadh, the capital of Saudi Arabia, the Ministry of Education was established in 1953 and opened the first state boys' school the same year. With the discovery of oil in 1935 and the resulting prosperity, rich Saudis were able to send their sons to other Arab or European countries to study and their daughters to boarding schools in Cairo or Beirut. After completing their studies, many Saudi men returned with foreign wives, explaining that it would not have been possible to find a woman in Saudi Arabia who met their educational standards. As a result, young Saudi women were becoming less likely to marry. This led to criticism in the press. Hence Queen

'Iffat, King Faisal's distant cousin and wife, who had grown up in Istanbul, decided to establish a private girls' school in Jidda in 1956. The first pupils were slaves and the daughters of palace servants. Today it is an elite private school for girls, which also has a department for women's education. The first state girls' school with a strong emphasis on religious instruction and home economics opened in Riyadh in 1960 after a royal decree authorized its establishment for religious reasons. All the same, protest from orthodox groups was so strong that military protection was required at its opening.[40]

On the European continent prior to 1900, women had been permitted to study at universities only in Austria and Switzerland; as of 1900 they were also able to do so in Germany.[41] Universities in the Middle East were founded later and did not admit women until after 1920, though Istanbul constituted an exception: women were allowed to audit lectures at the medical faculty of the university as of 1893, and from 1899 on they could pursue a regular course of studies. This had become possible because Turkish women were so accustomed to segregation that they demanded female, rather than male, doctors to examine and treat them.[42] In October 1913 a women's university was founded in Istanbul; in February 1914 regular courses for women were offered at Istanbul University; and from 1921 on women and men in Istanbul were allowed to attend class in the same lecture halls.

In Egypt the first state secondary school for girls opened in 1925, thirty-seven years after the first one for boys. The first state grants for women were awarded in the same year. They went to six students, two of whom were Christian, who studied medicine in London. Backed by the British, however, Cairo University (founded in 1908) continued to forbid the enrollment of women, as it would have meant introducing coeducation.[43]

The Egyptian Nobel Prize winner Naguib Mahfouz (Nagib Mahfuz) (1911–2006) recounts with some irony how he, as a man, experienced the initial difficulties both genders faced in studying together. Permitted to attend such courses in Egypt for the first time in 1929, only a few upper-class women did so.[44] The Iranian feminist and educationist Badr ol-Moluk Bamdad (1905–1987)—who was not only among the first students of the newly founded Women's Teachers' Training College in 1918 but also one of the first twelve women admitted in September 1936 to the University of Tehran (founded in 1935) following a decree by the shah—also gave a rather sarcastic account of the situation.[45] This same decree had also given women access to certain professions and government posts. Nonetheless, the first women to attend the University of Tehran were subject to death threats, just as the women founders and teachers of the first private girls' school in Iran had been two generations before them.[46] Rifaʿa Rafiʿ al-Tahtawi, who had most certainly been influenced by French essays on the subject, had pointed out in his *Murshid* that not only male competitiveness but also potential rivalries among women could hinder women's education, the purpose of which was to prepare for a profession (and not just a good marriage and motherhood).[47]

Ever since four women set the stage by attending evening courses in 1960–61, women in Saudi Arabia have been allowed to study, albeit in strict segregation, at the country's more than fifteen academic institutions, universities, and colleges, of which Riyadh University, established in 1959, was the first. According to official statistics, the number of women students today is (and has been since about 1990) larger than that of men, and this is also the case at the new universities in other Gulf countries. Unlike men, who may also study abroad, which means leaving their families for long periods, women are rarely allowed to do so, though upper-class women from Bahrain had no choice but to study abroad until a university was founded there in 1982.[48] In Iran, where about 65 percent of the students are women, married women under twenty-eight are now allowed—as the outcome of fierce public debates from 1995 on—to receive funds to study abroad along with their husbands. In Yemen this has been possible since the 1990s.

Since gender segregation and the ever-growing number of women students have caused a great demand for women teachers, there is a relatively large percentage of female professors in Saudi Arabia. Women students follow courses instructed by male professors on monitors and may interact with them only virtually. In 1989 the King ʿAbd al-ʿAziz Library in Riyadh opened a women's department, and since 1995 it has had a separate women's library and a children's library, both of which have all-woman staffs. Prior to this arrangement, women were forced to ask male relatives to bring them the materials they needed.[49] Many university libraries have now followed suit. For some subjects, such as architecture and pharmaceutics, women may still not attend, though this is most likely because there are— as was also the case during the period when universities shut down in Iran (1979–1983)—too few applications to make a separate study program for women practicable.

It is not just at the traditional Islamic al-Azhar University in Cairo, which was restricted to men until Nasser's socialist reforms in 1960, that women may attend only the women's college. (A dress code was established in 1978, even though it has not always been strictly observed.) In Iran, coeducation existed at state schools until 1979, especially in villages with a single school. After 1979 only boys were allowed to attend these schools, for gender segregation had become mandatory in the Islamic Republic. Beginning in the mid-1980s, as the population grew, more girls' schools were founded. They required female instructors, and this meant more job opportunities for women. At state schools in Tunisia, Turkey, and more recently Morocco, coeducation is now possible or even common; in other Middle Eastern countries coeducation usually exists through the fourth grade at most, that is, until the beginning of puberty. In Kuwait, gender segregation was reintroduced at the university in 2003 despite a wave of student protests.

As early as 1873 Rifaʿa Rafiʿ al-Tahtawi had demanded coeducation in his *Murshid;* he saw it as the best preparation for a good marriage and a harmonious family life, both of which were, in his eyes, fundamental to a healthy state.[50] In American schools, coeducation has been the norm since the early nineteenth century; in Europe, after extensive debate the Scandinavian countries were the first to introduce coeducation in 1876.

Statistics on the Internet document (albeit with fluctuations) a steady increase in girls' enrollment in Middle Eastern countries since 1975, though of course it varies from country to country. In addition, there is a significant difference between urban and rural populations, a difference usually not recorded by statisticians. Saudi Arabia and a number of other Gulf nations report a growth rate of almost 100 percent; in Dubai and Bahrain girls' enrollment is even higher than boys'. The rate of growth at secondary schools and institutions of higher education, as well as the number of female teachers, especially at primary schools, is very high. The average literacy rate in Arab countries between 2000 and 2004 was 56 percent—67 percent for men and 44 percent for women. Jordan leads with 89.7 percent (up from 80 percent in 1990) and Bahrain with 87 percent (there are no data for 1990). Morocco reports 52.6 percent (1990: 50 percent), Egypt 58.5 percent (1990: 48 percent), with the male-to-female ratio at 64.9 to 40.5 percent (1990: 61 to 38 percent), and 68.9 to 47.9 percent (1990: 63 to 34 percent) respectively. Yemen, as the poorest country, has the lowest literacy rate: 49 percent (1990: 36 percent). Although at 69 percent (1990: 53 percent) the rate among men is not unusually low, at 28 percent for women (1990: 26 percent) it is extremely so.[51] Saddam Hussein's government attempted to promote literacy in Iraq by issuing a decree in 1978 and was relatively successful among the urban population. If illiteracy has sharply risen again over recent decades, it is the outcome of the country's continuous destruction since the Iran-Iraq War began in 1980.

Because of their social needs and the desire to maintain traditional roles for women, lower-class urban and rural families are more hesitant about educating girls. Moreover, the nomadic lifestyle of Bedouins is hardly compatible with formal education. Yet such attitudes have no more to do with Islam than does the existence of child labor among boys (and, albeit less common, among girls), who are also unable to attend school. Owing to poverty, child labor exists throughout the Middle East, though depending on a country's economic and political situation to varying degrees, and—according to official statistics—decreasingly. Often such labor degenerates into the shameless exploitation of children by adults in begging rings and other forms of organized crime, including child prostitution (predominantly boys), even though almost all of the Middle Eastern countries have signed the United Nations' Convention on the Rights of the Child. Among girls, child labor usually occurs in the home, often at carpet looms.[52]

Child abuse, including sexual abuse, has been a topic in sociocritical Middle Eastern literature since the 1950s.[53] For a number of years it has also been an issue in critical women's journals and newspapers, such as Iran's *Zanan* (Women) and *Zan-e ruz* (The Contemporary Woman), and at public conferences. Female lawyers—such as the Iranian Mahrangiz Kar, who was imprisoned in 1999 after a dreadful media campaign against her,[54] and the aforementioned Shirin Ebadi—provide legal assistance to those fighting this long-taboo crime. Jordan made child abuse the subject of a pan-Arab conference in 2003. Turkey revised its laws against it in 2002 to include longer terms of punishment. These laws also apply to forced marriages involving very young girls, which have, in fact, been illegal for decades. Regarding child abuse in such marriages in Iran, Shirin Ebadi, who has gained even more enemies since receiving the Nobel Peace Prize (and, by association, others along with her) succeeded in getting the marriage age raised from nine to thirteen for girls and from fourteen to fifteen for boys—that is, closer to the age of physical maturity but still below the legal age allowing young men, among other things, to provide for their families and assume legal responsibility. These revisions were preceded by a heated discussion on the age of consent for marriage, and whether a partnership should require not only an individual's physical maturity (*bulugh* in Islamic law) but also his or her mental maturity. Arranged marriages at a younger age are still possible in Iran today with the consent of a court and are more common in rural areas. A number of authors report that judges and courts—in addition to differing in their decisions depending on local and/or regional circumstances, and deciding more traditionally in small towns and slums than in the urban centers—are sometimes bribed or at least pressured.[55] In other words, although the practice is legally restricted, very young girls in Iran are sometimes still forced to marry in accordance with age-old customs, and this is true even when it violates the law regulating compulsory education for boys and girls age seven and older. For centuries, young girls, predominantly from poor families, have wed older—even elderly—men, making pederasty acceptable where society sees the need, a topic that has repeatedly been scrutinized in sociocritical Middle Eastern literature since the 1950s.

In Iran the average age of both men and women at marriage has been higher in big cities for years. Economic uncertainty and high unemployment rates make starting a family—often an expensive enterprise—more difficult. Many young women choose to learn a profession rather than enter into an arranged marriage, or any other kind of marriage, with its domestic constraints, and they know which tactics to use to assert themselves in their (urban, middle-class) families.[56]

4. Working Women

When Muhammad 'Ali founded a school of midwifery in Egypt in 1832, he created the first educational institution for a women's profession in the Middle East. Yet it was not until 1836 that eight female slaves and orphans, all of whom had been forced to enroll, actually crossed its threshold. To maintain a semblance of tradition, each of them was promised a husband, a place to live, and a donkey as a means of transport.[57] For centuries women had been able to work as vendors (they were often middle-aged or older Christians or Jews who supplied harems with articles such as perfume and toilet water or fabric) or as agricultural laborers. There was a long tradition of women producing crafts that they marketed or assisting at childbirth. It was also acceptable for them to be attendants at women's baths or to wash women's corpses. Owing to gender segregation, female marriage brokers were indispensable as well. And of course prostitution existed in urban areas.[58]

Modernization made new professions with new work conditions inevitable, though gender segregation was maintained. For instance, women teachers were required for newly opened girls' schools. At first they came from Europe. As of 1903 a study program for teachers was offered in Cairo. Nabawiyya Musa (1890–1951)[59] was the first (and until independence from the British, the only) woman in Egypt to complete, by special permission, college preparatory school, in 1907. She had excellent grades but was still not allowed to enroll at Cairo University, which was founded the following year. Nevertheless, only a short time later, in 1909, she was asked to join its staff as an instructor for women's classes. The large and semiofficial Egyptian daily paper *Al-Ahram* printed her lectures in 1912. In 1920 Musa published *Al-Mar'a wa-l-'Amal* (Woman and Work),[60] the first Arabic book on the topic, a terse, combative feminist analysis influenced by the author's nationalism and social origins. In it she calls for increased educational opportunities for Egyptian women from the middle and upper classes, and especially for colleges where women could study to become doctors, lawyers, secretaries, and dressmakers (for their own gender). This was crucial, as a woman without a husband and/or financial support had to be able to make a living and support other women while still abiding by the ethics of Islam.

Around 1890, in an article cited by Zaynab Fawwaz in the preface to her women's dictionary, the Arabic term "al-Anisa" (the friendly and sociable person) was proposed—instead of the English term "Miss"—for a new social phenomenon: the unmarried, independent woman. Fawwaz also suggested using "'Aqila" (the intelligent one) to replace "Mrs." Both terms are still in use today, though at present, depending on the job market, women still often give up their profession when they marry. According to Nabawiyya Musa, an educated woman was to be her husband's equal, as this would eventually lead to eliminating such socially adverse developments as polygyny, and would improve national self-esteem as a whole. Musa became the first Egyptian woman director of a girl's school, in Faiyum, and in 1924 the first Egyptian female inspector for girls' schools, though by 1926 she had already been fired for criticizing the curriculum. She then founded a private school with branches in Cairo and Alexandria.

In Turkey, workingwomen became crucial during World War I (as they did in many other countries, and to an even greater degree during World War II). In 1916 the Islamic Association for the Employment of Ottoman Women was established with the goal of enabling Turkish Muslim women to join the workforce. At about the same time, the Society for the Protection of Women's Rights, which strongly advocated paying women for their work, forced Turkish state post offices to hire women by organizing public protest actions. A prerequisite for these developments was the emergence of a middle class whose daughters had received an education and were able to contribute to the family income. Women from these families were often trained, for instance, as nurses by the Ottoman Red Crescent Society, or they worked for charities, or in post offices, banks, and other offices.[61]

In 1910 the secretary of the Association for Ottoman Women caused an unpleasant stir by allowing herself to be photographed.[62] Until recently, in Saudi Arabia and other Gulf countries a woman could receive an ID card—required, for example, in court, at banks, and to travel abroad—only if a male relative verified her identity (and even this was not possible until 2001), since she was not to be photographed. Saudi women had long protested against this policy, which failed to acknowledge that women had identities of their own. Since autumn 2007 Saudi women have been permitted to have photos in their passports. All the same, some Saudis feel that these photos dishonor both genders so greatly that one man even invented a "shame veil" to attach over them. These "veils" are now on sale, though they have, of course, caused an outcry among emancipated and educated Saudi women, who also fear they may damage their country's reputation. Conversely, in other Arab countries visual media, including the Internet, actually make use of the attractiveness of influential women in their presentations, as Yemen, for instance, has done with its pretty minister for human rights, appointed in 2003 (and whose predecessor in 2001 was also a woman). Moreover, women can be seen making public appearances dressed and coiffed as befitting the country and the occasion (whether with headscarves in different colors and styles or without a headscarf) not only in the women's pages of magazines but also, of course, on television and in the cinema. On March 17, 2005, *Al-Qabas,* one of the largest papers in Kuwait, printed a photo in conjunction with an article on the debate within the Writers' Association on the right of women to vote. The photo reveals how differentiated women's appearances have become: three female university professors, whose hair is uncovered, and a pretty young graduate with a headscarf are shown sitting on a panel with two male colleagues.[63] Even today, however, Iranian and Saudi newspapers tend not to publish pictures of women.

Despite years of protest, Saudi Arabia still forbids women to drive. In comparison, the shaykhdom of Dubai—which of all the Gulf countries has made the most headway toward becoming an open and progressive society—launched "pink taxis" for women and their families in 2007. Special driving courses, which are also attended by local Muslim women, are offered to train female taxi drivers. First introduced at the airport, this safe service has become so popular it is spreading rapidly.

In most Middle Eastern countries factory work has always been segregated. This has been true under both secular and Islamic governments, for example, in Egypt under Nasser, Iraq under Saddam Hussein, Iran under the shah, and in the Saudi textile industry. Women from lower-class families who require additional income are thus able to receive permission from their male relatives to work in a factory. And yet according to popular views on marriage, a man who allows a female relative to work under the supervision of a male foreman is not much better than a pimp. This is true even if the foreman is separated from the women workers by a glass partition. Moreover, a married nonworking woman often has higher status, and not just among the lower classes, than a single workingwoman. Nevertheless, in Riyadh, for example, residents have become accustomed to seeing female factory workers without male escorts on their way to work.[64]

In Turkey, Atatürk's reforms opened up educational opportunities for women, opportunities hardly available, if at all, to women in other Middle Eastern countries. In Istanbul the first Turkish female physician opened her office in 1922, the first female lawyer in 1927; the first woman judge was appointed in 1930, the first public prosecutor in 1932. After Turkey adopted the Swiss civil code in 1926, women in Turkey were granted the right to pursue a profession or a career as a civil servant, though in 1932 a decree had to be issued forcing state institutions to hire women. Female academics were employed at Turkish universities soon after 1930. And although the tendency toward Islamization has increased in Turkey since 1949, and the number of women in the workforce in 1978 was only 10 percent of the total urban working population, every fifth practicing lawyer and every sixth practicing doctor was a woman. It was gender segregation that had made female academics a necessity.[65] Meanwhile their number has increased substantially. Nevertheless, since many women are still forced to give up their jobs after marriage, Turkey plans to improve child care for working mothers.[66]

Opportunities existed in a few other countries as well. In 1937 the first Iraqi woman graduated from the American University of Beirut as a doctor of medicine.

The current average employment rate for women in Arab countries is around 29 percent. For the Gulf countries the rate is less than 25 percent. These numbers do not include unpaid work by family members in agriculture or at home. Since 1995 a number of women lawyers in Iran have championed paid housework, though more educated women prefer teaching and/or state jobs. And yet at universities, for instance (and this was also true in Iraq under Saddam Hussein), "segregated" offices and staffrooms are still quite common even in rather secularized countries.

Service jobs (e.g., saleswoman, secretary, bookkeeper, waitress) that evolved into women's professions in Western countries during and after World War I or, at the very latest, after World War II are even today—owing to prevailing role stereotypes in Islamic countries—reserved mostly for men, and in rich countries for guest workers as well. In countries currently interested in acquiring a more progressive image, state institutions are now demonstratively joining forces with representatives of women's organizations to effect change in this sphere.

Employment in occupations traditionally off-limits for Muslim women has increasingly become a yardstick of a society's progressiveness. Employment in these fields was first introduced in countries where some form of socialism was propagated. Thus in the late 1970s there were traffic policewomen in Tunis and female gas station employees in Iraq. Today there are also traffic policewomen in Iran, in Muscat in Oman, as well as in Al-Ain in the UAE, where they have specially designed uniforms with long skirts.[67] Since 1998 in Iran, policewomen have been assigned to female criminals and also as guards, though it is rather surprising that this did not occur earlier in all Muslim countries, given the gender segregation and worldwide notions of decency. Iraq, Syria, and Libya introduced (segregated) military service for women in around 1980; in Oman it was introduced more recently. Iraq deployed women's regiments in the Iran-Iraq War and the First Gulf War; Kuwait followed suit in the latter. This war also led to an alliance of different national forces, especially among women, though it was not long until it fell apart.[68] For some time now Libyan president Muammar el-Qaddafi's escort has consisted of attractive women guards—though this has by no means met with general approval, as for many, even in the Western world, this still violates traditional gender roles.

Nowadays, other than in Yemen, there are very few Islamic countries where women are not permitted to become judges. Originally defined by religious law, this profession for centuries was reserved for men. Governments wanting to display their progressiveness appointed female judges to hear family law cases, as in Syria from about 1985 on. In Iraq in 1979 three female lawyers were appointed judges in family courts. In Iran—after the Islamic Revolution of 1979 had relegated women to traditional roles and triggered a wave of emigration—women shrewdly reclaimed many positions when the Iran-Iraq War (1980–1988) altered the situation economically and socially. By the late 1990s the number of women journalists was considerably larger than had been the case in the late 1970s, prior to the shah's fall, and today the women's press critically debates contemporary gender issues—with the support of male theologians—as well as successfully puts forward important demands. In 2000 the Iranian Businesswomen's Association convened for the first time.[69] When the shah's regime fell in 1979, sixty family judges—including Shirin Ebadi—lost their positions nationwide and were allowed to work only as lawyers. Since 1992, after loud demands were voiced in the women's media, female advisers may be called in on court cases concerning women.

In Egypt the first woman judge was appointed in 1995 despite considerable opposition from orthodox groups; in 2007, thirty-one new female judges were appointed. In 2005, ten years after the World Conference on Women in Beijing, Algeria reported thirty-four female chief judges, two female ambassadors, and a new position for a woman, not just in the Arab world but internationally: the first female president of a central bank.

The ability of state-prescribed segregation to promote jobs for women can be observed in Saudi Arabia, where some banks and enterprises have all-female personnel and clients, and there is also a (rather small) businesswomen's association. Yet women still object that they are forced to send male relatives to interact with male colleagues in public, where life continues to be dominated by men. Since 1981 Saudi women journalists who cover specific women's and social themes have been able to work out of a segregated "women's office" at the daily *Al-Riyadh*.[70] For Saudi women who are university graduates, however, it has become increasingly difficult to find a job, a development sure to reach other Gulf countries soon, if it has not done so already. Moreover, many believe that a college education prepares a woman better for marriage to a well-to-do man than for a profession. A similar trend has recently been observed in Turkey.[71]

In Saudi Arabia and in Iran, gender segregation has led to the profession of the female theologian. The Iranian Martyrs Foundation funded a theological institution of advanced education for women in the holy city of Qom, mainly for students from underprivileged families. It trains them as prayer leaders, religious instructors, and theologians for female congregants. A woman may become a *mujtahid* and so voice her opinions on religious matters, though whether she may also pronounce judgments that are generally binding and assume the position of a *marja'*—in the hierarchy, a high authority on religious laws—is very controversial.[72] Since 2005 Morocco has educated over four hundred *wa'izat*, young women who work, for example, as assistants in mosques, religious instructors, and leaders of pilgrimages for pious women. They convey an understanding of Moroccan Islam in its present-day official form to their compatriots. Mostly autodidactic in their knowledge, leaders of religious women's circles in Iran started meeting in the 1970s to oppose the secularization policies of the shah's government. Varying in their demands and political leanings, these circles met in specially designated private rooms called *husayniyyes* (named after Husayn, the Prophet's grandson and first Shi'i martyr).[73]

In Libya under Qaddafi, whose *Green Book* guarantees equality between men and women (though equal pay for the same job has still not been achieved everywhere), there are departments in banks with entirely female staffs. Women administrative employees at Libyan universities and other government agencies may also work for male superiors; in other words, gender segregation is not strictly observed. Kuwaiti women, by contrast, have criticized the fact that in an attempt to demonstrate (so-called) modernization, they are hired only for specific (so-called) leading positions, in which, however, they have no decision-making powers.[74] Of course, here as elsewhere, women from elite families are the first to be hired for such top positions.[75]

5. Women's Organizations and Magazines: Voting Rights and Politics

As a rule, a certain degree of democratization has to have been reached for a country to develop a plurality of women's organizations, including NGOs.[76] Authoritarian governments—not only in the Middle East—have often created *one* official women's organization to propagate and implement its policies toward women. These organizations have frequently been headed by a member of the ruling family, such as Ashraf Pahlavi, twin sister of Muhammad Reza Pahlavi, shah of Iran until 1979; or in Egypt, Jehan Sadat, until President Anwar el- Sadat's assassination in 1980. Suzanne Mubarak has served as president of the Egyptian National Council for Women's Rights, under President Hosni Mubarak's jurisdiction, which organizes events such as pan-Arab women's conferences. Like her predecessor, Queen Rania of Jordan, who studied in England, holds a similar position as the king's wife. According to Internet sources, in 2005 Egypt, Turkey, Morocco, and Jordan were the countries with the greatest diversity of women's organizations. (Included on this list are also two associations for lesbians and gay men in Turkey—quite an astonishing phenomenon for a country shaped for centuries by Islam—as well as an AIDS support network in Morocco.)

Starting in the 1880s in Egypt, upper-class women founded societies for women based on European and American models, whose goals were primarily charitable in nature. The struggle of women's organizations for social and political rights began later. When Malak Hifni Nasif addressed the Egyptian parliament in 1911 and outlined her demands for the legislature to protect women, especially in the family, her efforts were rejected. In 1914, on the initiative of Huda Sha'rawi (1879–1947) and with the aid of the khedivial princesses, an association was founded to organize educational events for upper-class women in Cairo.[77]

After World War I it became increasingly important to involve women interested in party work in political causes. In March 1919 Huda Sha'rawi headed a series of demonstrations throughout Cairo that were staged by veiled women carrying banners declaring their demands.[78] In 1923 Sha'rawi became president of the Feminist Union (Jam'iyyat al-ittihad al-nisa'i) of the nationalist Wafd Party and began collaborating on the French-language magazine *L'Égyptienne,* which was published from 1925 to 1940.

In 1932, following long battles with the government, the Egyptian Feminist Union opened its large, self-financed headquarters in central Cairo. Soon known as the House of Woman, the organization decided to hang a sign bearing that name on its façade. Awhile later Sa'iza Nabarawi (1897–1984), who had been brought up in Paris and was at the time secretary of the Feminist Union, sarcastically depicted in an interview the uproar that followed: "To affix the secret name 'woman' on a building in public view! To announce openly that this creature has a social existence, has an integrity, a personality, and has ceased to be the chrysalis of collective anonymity, oh!"[79]

Zaynab al-Ghazali (1917–2005), daughter of an al-Azhar University graduate who was also her teacher, founded the Muslim Women's Association (Jama'at al-Sayyidat al-Muslimat) in 1937 and became its first president. According to her almost hagiographic autobiography, it was only six months later that she met Hasan al-Banna. He had founded the Muslim Brotherhood in 1928 and, a few years later, a women's section called the Muslim Sisterhood, as well as educational institutions for men and women. Although she was invited to merge her organization with his, she did not do so—though eventually, shortly before his assassination in 1949, she declared her loyalty to him. In sermons at mosques and in many journal articles and books, including her very emotional memoir about her imprisonment from 1965 to 1971 under Nasser, and her extensive commentary on the Qur'an (the first volume appeared in 1994), she propagated the principles of the Muslim Brotherhood for orthodox Muslim women.[80]

In Turkey during the second constitutional era, from 1908 to 1916, there were twelve women's organizations, and a number of them had legal and social gender equality on their agenda.[81] In Iran women's groups had begun meeting in 1906, before proposals for the country's first constitution; yet it was not until after World War I that an organized women's movement emerged.[82] In 1998, after President Muhammad Khatami came to power, Iran had twenty-four women's organizations with a variety of goals, including those advocated by Zoroastrian, Jewish, and Christian women.[83] But the number of organizations soon declined. By 2006 only two women's centers were still listed online: the Center for Women's Studies in Tehran and the Office for Women's Research Studies in the holy city of Qom; in 2004 the latter invited women to a small conference for Muslim women from Africa and Asia.

The first women's magazines were launched around 1890, following the establishment of the first periodicals of any kind in Turkey in the 1860s, and in Egypt a short time later, in the 1870s. Initially these magazines focused on demanding more social rights for women: the right to education, to a husband of their own choice and not that of their parents, to a paid job outside the home, and equal rights to divorce. Only later did women demand political rights such as the right to vote and to run for office.

The first Arab women's magazine was *Al-Fatat* (The Young Woman), founded in Alexandria in 1892 by Hind Nawfal, a Lebanese Christian, in collaboration with her father, Nasim, and her sister Sara (discussed earlier). They wanted to disseminate literary, sociohistorical, and pedagogical knowledge as well as information on topics such as housekeeping, hygiene, painting, and needlework. According to the foreword of the first issue, they intended, however, to steer clear of politics and religion (as did other journals published by Christian Lebanese immigrants in Egypt). Outwardly Nasim Nawfal was the magazine's spokesman. *Al-Fatat* folded in January 1894, after Hind Nawfal married. *Majallat tarqiyat al-mar'a* (Journal of Woman's Progress), published in Egypt in 1908 by Fatima Rashid, was the first journal for Muslim women in Arabic.[84] The editorial staff of the Egyptian bimonthly *Al-'Afaf* (Virtue), founded in 1910, strictly observed gender segregation in its journalistic work—not unlike *Payam-e Zan* (Women's Message), a women's journal published by Iranian male theologians in Qom since 1990, though it also prints contributions by female journalists. Unlike the first women's journals founded after 1892, whose titles focused entirely on women's issues, Arabic magazines established later, such as Balsam 'Abd al-Malik's *Al-Mar'a al-misriyya* (The Egyptian Woman, 1920–1939), had a nationalist component. The first Egyptian magazine (1925–1940), the aforementioned *L'Égyptienne,* with its explicit feminist and national objectives, was printed in French, and so clearly addressed upper-class women readers who, unlike the generation before them, had been educated by French governesses, at French schools, or in France. Its publishers, Sa'iza Nabarawi and Huda Sha'rawi, were in any event not proficient enough in Arabic to contribute otherwise. Sha'rawi mentions in her memoirs how she tried to learn to write Arabic secretly, studying it more or less on her own.[85]

The first Iranian women's journal, *Danesh* (Knowledge), founded in 1910, sought to educate women for successful marriage and motherhood, but because of the poor reading skills of women (or of the men who might read the journal to them), it was published for only a year.[86] In Turkey a number of women's magazines launched between 1908 and 1918 had the same goal, even if from different perspectives. They included *Mahasin* (Good Moral Qualities, 1908), *Kadın* (The Woman, 1909), and *Kadınlar Dünyası* (Women's World, 1913).[87] In both countries, nationalist tendencies did not play a role until after World War I.

At the outset, male and female members of the upper class were primarily concerned with improving the position of women of their class, though they were also interested in spreading knowledge of history and literature, as well as in improving educational, modern medical, and hygienic skills. State women's organizations still train women, in particular from the urban lower classes, in hygiene and child care, housekeeping, and needlework. And where these organizations once offered typing courses, they now offer computer and Internet courses, provided computers are available. Saudi women also teach management courses online to university graduates to increase their chances of finding a job.

A parliamentary democracy or a constitutional monarchy—or, at the very least, the existence of a parliament—is a prerequisite for elections and the voting process. Authoritarian regimes are prone to postponing and canceling elections without reason, or strongly influencing them.

In comparison to the Middle Eastern countries, in Germany and Austria women were granted the right to vote and run for office in 1919; in Switzerland, which was the last country in Europe to grant them the vote, women gained these rights in 1971. Consequently, (a few) female parliamentarians were elected and confirmed. In the autumn of 1949 there were four women members of the Parliamentary Council of the Federal Republic of Germany.

In 1987 women held just under 10 percent of the seats in the Bundestag. By 2008, six of sixteen cabinet members were women, including as of 2006 the first female chancellor of Germany. In Austria the 10 percent hurdle was cleared in 1983. At the ministerial level, 31.5 percent were women in 2001.[88]

In Turkey, which has been a laicist state since the constitution of 1924, women were granted the right to vote in 1930. They have been able to run for the municipal councils of elders since 1933 and for the Grand National Assembly since 1934. The first eighteen female representatives (thirteen of whom were teachers) were elected to the National Assembly in 1935. In 1950 only three women were still members of parliament. Between 1954 and 1983 the number of women in the four hundred–seat National Assembly fluctuated between four and twelve.[89] After the elections on July 22, 2007, the number of women in the Assembly rose from 4.1 percent to 9.1 percent, that is, from twenty-four women to fifty. Both Istanbul and Izmir have had female deputy parliamentary speakers, though Turkey has not had any female ministers.

Since being politically active involves making public appearances, female politicians often meet with the disapproval of conservatives, who, because of their ideas about role distribution, continue to see women solely as housewives and mothers. Nowadays, however, even orthodox groups are adept at using women to promote their political goals. Hence, to enhance their image, most governments consciously include a certain percentage of women. In Egypt women gained the right to vote in 1956, four years after the Egyptian Revolution. In 1957 the first two women were elected to the Egyptian parliament, which had 360 members at the time.[90] For many years the percentage of women remained very low and fluctuated little. In the People's Assembly from 1977 to 1984 the figure was 0.9 percent; from 1984 to 1987, 8.3 percent; from 1987 to 1990, 3.9 percent; from 1990 to 1995, 2.2 percent; from 1995 to 2000, 1.6 percent; and from 2000 to 2005, 2.4 percent. As the women's movement never tires of pointing out, the proportion of women at the ministerial level rose only from 6.1 percent to 9 percent between 2004 and March 2008. All the same, in 2008 the vice president of the People's Assembly was a woman.

In most Middle Eastern countries women have enjoyed the right to vote since the 1960s, for instance, in Iran since 1963. Depending on the stability or instability of their individual governments, however, elections in a number of these countries have been held only at great intervals and often under repressive conditions.

Contrary to expectations, in winter 2004–5 women in Saudi Arabia were not allowed to vote in the first series of communal elections since the introduction of their right to vote in 1965. The government—that is, the country's large ruling family, with its often conflicting standpoints—appeased women when elections were held in 2009 with the explanation that rigorous gender segregation had made it complicated for women to vote, and even more so to hold political office. The positive precedents set by other Islamic countries were dismissed with reference to the lack of success of female candidates in the 2003 elections in Oman and Bahrain. In Kuwait, which is a constitutional monarchy, the women's movement emerged in 1963 and began demanding the right to vote and to hold office in 1965. Only after decades of public dispute did women gain these rights by parliamentary decree on May 16, 2005. People immediately took to the streets to celebrate the event. Nevertheless, no woman won a parliamentary seat in the 2006 election. Despite public protest, Maʿsuma al-Mubarak, a professor of political science and a liberal of Shiʿi origin (who always wore a headscarf in public), was appointed minister of planning and then of health in 2006. Nevertheless, it was only a short time later, in August 2007, that she stepped down from office.[91]

Women have held seats in the Iranian parliament since 1990, even if their numbers are still not as high as desired. Women were allowed to vote (albeit at segregated polling places) and run for office in the parliamentary elections held in April 2005 and April 2008.

In the Iraqi parliament elected in April 2005, women held one-third of the seats. They have also been appointed to head over thirty ministries—the highest percentage in a Middle Eastern country to date. Nevertheless, women of different political and religious persuasions continue to demand more social and political rights.[92] Under Saddam Hussein it was government policy to promote women rather extensively. Moreover, in recent years many exiled Iraqis have returned to their country with modern ideas on many issues, including gender, though these are probably alien to certain segments of the population.

Women were granted the right to vote in Algeria in 1964, following independence in 1962, a struggle in which they had played a significant role. At the time the country had a one-party government. In 1997 and 2002 the number of female candidates for the two chambers was ten to twenty times higher than the number of female representatives actually elected. In 2005 there were thirty-one female representatives in the Algerian parliament.

Today, in almost every country in the Middle East, polling places remain segregated by gender to accommodate citizens who still wish to adhere to tradition.

In the aftermath of World War I, Palestinian women participated in a range of charitable organizations. After 1948 they became more political, especially if they were members of the Palestinian Women's Organization. A woman was elected to the Central Committee of the PLO for the first time in 1980. The number of women in the Palestinian National Council and diverse Palestinian organizations at home and abroad has risen continuously since the late 1980s.[93] In recent years Palestine's ambassador to Paris has been a woman.

In 1959 the first female Arab cabinet minister, the leading Iraqi feminist and first female gynecologist, Dr. Naziha al-Dulaymi (1924–2007), who was also the author of a booklet titled "Al-Mar'a al-'Iraqiyya" (The Iraqi Woman; Baghdad, 1952),[94] as well as a member of the Iraqi Communist Party, was appointed minister of municipalities in Iraq. She had to leave this post in September 1960 because "sole leader" General Abd al-Karim Qasim was seeking reconciliation with the Ba'thists.

Since the 1970s, and especially since the beginning of the twenty-first century, the number of female ministers has increased. Initially, women were appointed to cabinet positions considered compatible with their roles in society, in other words, as head of the Ministry of Social Affairs (in Egypt since 1962)[95] or of the Ministry of Education. In December 1979 in Iran, Farrokhru Parsa, the minister of education under the shah from 1968 to 1974, was executed on the charge of fostering "prostitution and corruption on earth" (by having abolished gender segregation) and of "warring against God."[96] In 1997 two positions in the Iranian cabinet were originally reserved for women, but owing to the strong opposition of orthodox groups toward women in politics, President Khatami appointed just one. Ma'sumeh Ebtekar became one of Iran's seven vice presidents and head of the environmental protection department. Another woman, Zahra Shoja'i, was appointed one of Khatami's advisers and head of the Center for Women's Participation.[97] The ratio of one female to six male vice presidents persisted, and the number of female parliamentarians has remained extremely low. In the women's magazine *Payam-e Hajar* (Message of Hajar), which was banned from 1996 to 1999,[98] the daughters of famous theologians, including Shahla Habibi (daughter of Ayatollah Habibi) and A'zam Taleghani (daughter of Ayatollah Taleghani), have called for the reinterpretation of all Qur'an verses related to women, as well as for better opportunities for women in business, politics, and law. Fatima and Fa'ezeh Hashemi, daughters of former president 'Ali Akbar Hashemi Rafsanjani, have voiced similar concerns.[99] In the contentious presidential election of 2009, Zahra Rahnavard, a former adviser to Khatami, campaigned publicly for her husband, Mir-Hossein Mousavi, enhancing his popularity with young voters eager for reform.

In Syria, Najah al-'Attar, a professor of English literature, who comes from an old and famous family, held the position of minister of culture from 1980 to 2000. She was appointed vice president of the republic in March 2006. A second female minister, Buthayna Sha'ban, also a professor of literature and a well-known author, held positions in a number of fields and headed the Ministry for Emigrant Affairs, which is concerned with Syrians abroad. Since 2005 other Arab countries, including Morocco and Yemen, have also established such ministries and, in accord with modern public relations strategies, appointed women to head them. Jordan, Morocco, and Oman have had female ministers of tourism—a clever way to promote relations with non-Islamic countries.

In 2004 two female ministers in Lebanon were appointed to ministries "atypical" for women for the first time. Morocco had four women ministers between 2004 and 2008; Jordan had three from 2003 to 2009. In Algeria, which signed the United Nations' Convention on the Rights of Women in 2004, four women were chosen in that same year to head the ministries of culture, of family and women's affairs, of emigrant affairs, and of agricultural development. Other important political positions have since been held by women, including, as of 2009, three female governors (two of whom were deputy governors), each with a female secretary general, seven female county heads, and two female party leaders.[100]

In Afghanistan a woman was appointed minister for women's and family affairs. In Pakistan conservative groups strongly opposed Benazir Bhutto's election to prime minister in 1989; all the same, she remained in office until 1996. After years in exile in London and many fierce attacks, including accusations of corruption, she returned to Pakistan in spring 2007 to run for prime minister again.[101] Only months later, on December 27, 2007, she was assassinated.

From June 1993 to October 1995, Tansu Çiller was Turkey's first female prime minister, though she too attracted much criticism. And although Atatürk had granted women the right to vote and supported their running for office early on, women are less common in Turkish politics today than they were in the past.

To express their dissent, women activists also nominated themselves for the office of president in Iran in 1997, and in Egypt in 2002—an act that caused religious authorities in both countries to issue fatwas, few of which were supportive.[102] In fact in Iran, nominations of this kind were later banned. In some Gulf countries emirs who were previously considered conservative took to backing women who were running for parliament, such efforts failed owing to the disapproval of both male and female voters.

Two Iranian women, who were elected to parliament for the first time in March 2000, attempted to show that female parliamentarians could also have an impact on living conditions and attitudes. Belonging to the generation of the revolution, they announced that they would appear in parliament wearing overcoats and headscarves—that is, permissible street attire—instead of the black chador. Yet the other female parliamentarians protested adamantly, stressing the significance of the latter. In contrast, a woman elected to parliament in Turkey in 2002 was not allowed to assume office when she defiantly wore a headscarf.[103]

6. A Headscarf or Veil: Clothing as an Indication of an Individual's Attitude

Many non-Muslims regard headscarves and other "Islamic garments" worn by Muslim women (and men) as a sign of backwardness. Often they are considered *the* symbol of a political-ideological standpoint or of (Islamic) "cultural identity." This issue is also very controversial in the Islamic countries of the Middle East. The Qur'an (33:33) urges Muhammad's wives to stay in their homes and not to dress with "the bedizenment of the Time of Ignorance," and admonishes "women to lower their gaze and be modest, and to display of their adornment only that which is apparent, and to draw their veils over their bosoms [*bi-khumurihinna 'ala juyubihinna*] and not to reveal their adornments" (24:31) except to their husbands and close male relatives—though neither verse mentions a face veil or headscarf.

Yet as women's rights activist Shirin Ebadi—who must wear both a headscarf and an overcoat in Iran but appears without them abroad—underscores, these garments are not necessarily an expression of backwardness. Muslim feminists from Turkey take a similar stance.[104] Depending on a country's policies, both veiling and unveiling can symbolize resistance; that is, both headscarves and veils have become political issues. In Turkey, for instance, which declared itself a laicist state in its constitution of 1924, since 1929 women as well as men have been forbidden to wear head coverings that have a symbolic religious meaning or to cover the entire body with a *charshaf*, a black cloak, in state institutions. Demonstrations held in the early 1980s protested in vain against the fact that female students who wore headscarves were not admitted to the university. Years of dissent—indirectly supported by leading advocates of the ruling conservative Islamic government, and by the conduct of their wives and daughters—led in late February 2008 to a law abolishing the ban on headscarves for students at state universities (though not for instructors and administrative staff or employees at other state institutions). The law was, however, almost immediately repealed, as both male and female supporters of secularism in Turkey, in particular the military, fiercely opposed it. Consequently, the daughters of Prime Minister Recep Tayyip Erdoğan, leader of the (religious) Justice and Development Party (AKP), decided to study in the United States, where they might wear headscarves. When his wife accompanied him abroad, she always covered her hair.

First Lady Hairünnisa Gül, wife of President Abdallah Gül, also wore a headscarf. Married at fifteen, she was supported by her husband in her efforts to finish college preparatory school. There was even talk of her desire to take legal action to enforce her right to study at a university with a headscarf. Younger pious Turkish women call their headscarves, which often have colorful patterns and reveal their hairlines, *türben* (turbans), for centuries the name of an exclusively male accessory and thus a symbol of male power. The trend has also been influenced by male religious instructors who aspire to change Turkish society to fit their ideals.

Saudi Arabia is the only country in which it is still mandatory for women to veil their faces in public, though under the Taliban it was also obligatory in Afghanistan. In Saudi television programs, women wear face veils even when they are at home, for after all, the camera crews are mostly male.

In Western discourse on the veiling of Muslim girls and women, what is often referred to as a veil is actually a wide outer garment or cloak that covers both the body and hair but not the face or any part of it. Commonly black—though it may come in other colors and patterns—it has different names depending on the region. Traditional male clothing is often quite similar in appearance and may consist of a long shirt that loosely covers the whole body, as well as a kind of headscarf, called a kufiya *(kufiyya),* which also serves as protection against the sun.

In contrast, what is known in ordinary usage as a veil often just conceals the face and has for centuries varied regionally in form, color, and name.[105] The burqa *(burqa')*, which women in Afghanistan were casting off as some women in Bahrain were putting it back on, is one of its most rigid forms. Like the black face veil imposed on Saudi women, it completely conceals women's faces and allows the wearer a very limited view of the world. In the history of Islam, men have also occasionally worn face veils. Unlike their women, Tuareg-Berber men from the oasis of Ghadames in Libya conceal their faces up to their eyes even today. In Turkish miniatures from the late sixteenth century on, Muhammad and his family are portrayed as holy figures whose faces are completely covered by a white cloth.[106]

In modern times, clothing modeled on European dress has become acceptable across the entire Middle East. This trend was first observed among men of the urban elite, but it later spread in cities to the wives and especially the daughters of the upper-middle class, above all when they were traveling in Europe.[107]

During World War I, when a growing number of Turkish women took jobs, they often adopted European fashion, including shorter skirts, as it was considered more becoming and practical. In 1917 the police issued a decree ordering Muslim women to wear longer skirts and thicker *charshafs* (black cloaks), and forbidding (figure-accentuating) corsets—though it was not long before the decree was annulled. By 1915 a decree had already gone into effect that allowed workingwomen to remove their veils inside offices.[108] When the first state girls' school opened in Cairo in 1873, Khedive Isma'il also insisted that girls attending it, even those already past puberty, should do so without veils. Yet his order turned out to be untimely, since feelings were already running high: orthodox religious groups were enraged by the very existence of the school.

The first women to unveil their faces were Christians from elite families. Nabawiyya Musa recounts in her memoirs that she was sitting unveiled in a Cairo tram in 1909 when a woman asked her, presumably reproachfully, whether she was Christian. Musa responded by commenting that while she was revealing her face, the other woman was revealing her arms and upper body more than was proper. Moreover, women's face veils covered little more than their timidity, for along with tight-fitting street clothes, soft, transparent face veils had become popular.[109] It was only after World War I that upper-class women in Islamic countries actually made a point of removing their face veils. Huda Sha'rawi and the younger Sa'iza Nabarawi emphatically cast off their face veils (though not their cloaks) when they arrived at the main train station in Cairo in May 1923 after returning from an international women's conference in Rome.[110] They were immediately joined by a number of enthusiastic like-minded women. In the 1920s and 1930s there was an ongoing debate on veiling versus unveiling, and in Iraqi—as well as Iranian—newspapers it was often conducted in neoclassical verse. Advocates of the veil emphasized that it did not, or at least should not, hinder women from acquiring an education.[111] The young Druse Nazira Zayn al-Din (1908–1976), daughter of the man who would later preside over the first court of appeals in Beirut, published her courageous book *Al-sufur wa-l-hijab* (Unveiling and Veiling: Lessons and Views on Women's Liberation and Social Renewal in the Islamic World) in 1928. After severe critique from conservative authors, who attributed the book to her father, she wrote *Al-Fatat wa-l-shuyukh* (The Girl and the Sheikhs: Ideas and Disputes on Unveiling and Veiling, Liberation of the Mind, Liberation of Woman and Social Renewal in the Islamic World).[112] The fatwas issued by al-Azhar scholars ultimately supported and sanctioned the movement to unveil women. Nevertheless, in Egypt the face veil remained a part of court ceremony until the dynasty of Muhammad 'Ali fell in 1952.[113]

The shah of Iran imposed a ban on veiling on January 7, 1936, though as early as 1934 women teachers and pupils had been encouraged not to wear veils in public. Accompanied by his wife and two eldest daughters—the latter unveiled and in European attire—, the shah visited the newly established University of Tehran in 1936.[114] After his abdication in 1941, the ban on veiling was lifted as a result of the continuing extreme resistance to it. Many middle-aged and older women had stopped leaving their homes, and even men were said to have gone out hardly at all during these years for fear of encountering an unveiled woman.[115]

In Algeria, which had for decades belonged to France administratively, though it was a France populated by a majority of second-class citizens,[116] women in black cloaks played a major role in the success of the revolution of 1962. "Camouflaged" in this manner, they were able to carry weapons and leaflets. That middle-class Palestinian women—be they religious or more secular in their beliefs—have increasingly taken to wearing so-called "shari'a clothing" (long, fitted dark coats) over the past several decades can also be seen as an act of defiance against prevailing circumstances and a demonstration of their commitment to a (more or less contrived) tradition.

In the early 1970s the miniskirt sparked still another heated debate on "Western immorality." In Baghdad and Mosul, the conflict peaked when the police ruthlessly pursued young women who had adopted the fashion.

Since the 1980s, workingwomen in a number of countries have justified their decision to wear different forms and colors of the "Islamic" clothing, or hijab, that covers their hair and body, with the argument that it increases their freedom of movement and enables them to work in male-dominated fields without their being reduced to sexual objects.[117]

A similar trend can be observed among upper-class women and girls as a result of growing "re-Islamization." These women wear relatively long, loose-fitting, single-colored, often dark garments that cover the entire body. This form of dress is nowhere to be seen in the brightly colored miniatures of (courtly) Islamic illustrated books from the thirteenth to the nineteenth centuries.[118] In the 1920s and 1930s Arab, Turkish, and Persian writers, both male and female, even rejected the veil as a sign of hypocrisy, since outward anonymity could also "cover up" all kinds of behavior that did not conform to the rules of society, including immorality. For centuries, men who were on the run, including swindlers and rogues, used cloaks and face veils to disguise themselves.[119] All the same, in many Islamic countries of the Middle East today, when a woman veils herself in a long cloak, it is regarded as an affirmation of her moral integrity and cultural identity. In 1970 wives of parliament members in Syria, a relatively secular country, began wearing "Islamic clothing" before elections, even though it was not their usual attire. Today, during the fasting month of Ramadan, young actresses are often seen wearing hijabs in television series.

On March 4, 1979, shortly after Ayatollah Khomeini became the leader (Pers. *rahbar*) of the newly founded Islamic Republic, and four days before International Women's Day, he declared it mandatory for workingwomen to wear "Islamic clothing," meaning the black chador (though, interestingly, not a face veil). At first many women refused to obey his decree. As of March 1980, despite protest marches, the regime began enforcing the regulation more strictly, which meant that not just female employees and visitors at public institutions had to wear the black chador but all women whenever they left their homes. Beginning in April 1983 the decree was even extended to female tourists.[120] In 1989 it was tightened further, undoubtedly because those in power felt a need to do so in the aftermath of the Iran-Iraq War (1988) and the death of Khomeini (1989).[121] Even today there are laws criminalizing women who are inadequately covered, as well as those who wear excessively heavy makeup. Disobedience can lead to imprisonment, though since about 1990 women's rights advocates have achieved a certain liberalization with regard to this issue and others.[122] And since the late 1990s women, especially tourists, have been permitted to wear coats over fashionable modern clothes. Many girls and young women now wear knee-length coats over skin-tight pants. Iranian women within Iran, and Saudi women abroad, often display a more playful and relaxed style of veiling, and a subtle use of decorative cosmetics as a form of rebellion against official constraints. A woman's decision whether to wear a coat or a chador is frequently ideological and/or social in nature. Nowadays, most likely for psychological reasons, schoolgirls are often allowed to wear colorful clothes under their chadors.

Iranian sportswomen feel that it is almost impossible to compete internationally in "Islamic sports clothes," even if they have been free since 1990 to train and participate in (at least segregated) sports events again.[123] Fa'ezeh

Hashemi, daughter of President Rafsanjani and a sportswoman herself, initiated the first Muslim Women's Olympics in Tehran in 1993 for an entirely female audience, and so enabled women to participate in "normal" sports clothes.[124] The event has grown steadily ever since. For some years now there has been an Iranian Women's Sports Association as well as leagues for women. In 2007 Iran's national women's soccer team even staged a match against a multicultural women's soccer club from Berlin before an all-female audience in Tehran. Iranian women are permitted to swim, row, cycle, jog, or climb mountains only in regions where segregation is possible, since the clothes worn for these sports are viewed as accentuating their figures too much.[125] All in all, a beginning has been made, and it may also inspire Saudi Arabian authorities to do more for women's health and fitness.

In Turkey since about 1980, the tendency toward re-Islamization has also become visible. A growing number of women wear headscarves and/or black outer garments in certain districts of the larger cities. The gap has grown between the generations, that is, between women who once welcomed Atatürk's secularization measures and benefited from them, and younger women who believe that the movement has failed. In fact modern and fashionable young Turkish women do not want to sit next to women in Islamic clothing for fear of being associated with them. All the same, it is not unusual for women who wear Islamic clothing to consider themselves the more emancipated Muslims or to feel that the ban on headscarves in state institutions limits their freedom.[126]

For Saudi women, the face veil is compulsory within their own country but not when traveling abroad. In some Gulf countries, the wearing of cloaks is widespread among female nationals. In Bahrain women first cast off their veils in the 1950s; many others followed after independence was achieved in 1971. And yet since about 1980 large numbers of women have started wearing veils again. Particularly among students, it has come to be viewed as a sign of cultural identity. This was especially the case for the first women who studied at universities in other Arab countries after 1971 and returned home disappointed. In the interim, there are even a few women who wear the burqa to protest against "decadent" Western attitudes.[127]

Conversely, young women in the modern districts of Cairo, in particular Heliopolis, are keen on showing that individual, fanciful, and elegant veiling or "aesthetic coverings" are possible. Here boutiques for fashion-minded Muslim women have opened. These shops also market stylish, colorful "Muslim" garments, along with decorative cosmetics, on the Internet. Headscarves "designed" in Paris are, for instance, the latest rage and are worn with the same coquetry as once were the small, colorful kerchiefs seen in Persian miniatures from the sixteenth century.[128] As is true of Iraqi fashion designers in the past, Turkish designers are fond of drawing inspiration from historical, even pre-Islamic models, which they then adapt along Islamic lines so as to underscore their independence. Because of gender segregation, designers in most Middle Eastern countries still have to be female.

Women from the upper classes in Iran and Saudi Arabia often wear high fashion under their cloaks, while lower-class women tend to use them to conceal their poverty. For centuries these outer garments have been an instrument of imposing (outward) social discipline.

7. Islamic Family Law: Preservation, Abolition, Reinstatement, Reform

Since their inception, women's organizations in the Middle East have been fighting to change Islamic family law to conform to the proposals made by reformers such as Muhammad ʿAbduh and Qasim Amin at the turn of the twentieth century.[129] Each country has proceeded differently, either codifying the rulings of Islamic law within the state or integrating them in a more modified, modern interpretation into their national code of law. On October 25, 1917, the first Islamic family law code came into effect, in Turkey. It selected the rulings most favorable for women from the four Sunni schools of law and declared them binding—without actually infringing in any way on what was laid out as "God's revelations" in the Qur'an.[130]

In Saudi Arabia the shariʿa is still in effect, although it has reincorporated the old principle of *ijtihad* that the Sunnis had suspended for centuries and Muhammad ʿAbduh advocated reintroducing at the end of the nineteenth century. *Ijtihad* involves the search for independent judgment in both legal and theological questions. It may run contrary to tradition but must draw on approved sources and, in exceptionally controversial cases, requires a consensus opinion from religious leaders.[131] In Libya, Qaddafi reinstated the shariʿa after assuming power in 1969, though here, too, modifications soon followed, including a provision on a minimum marriage age for both genders, a matter not regulated in the shariʿa. Women's rights to divorce were also strengthened. Later—in line with the basic tenet of gender equality (though to date it has still not been sufficiently implemented)—polygyny was outlawed, even if exceptions are still made today.

In 1980 the Iranian government restored the shariʿa—the basis of Islamic social justice—as interpreted by Khomeini and the Twelver Shiʿa. By doing so it nullified the Pahlavi family's secular legal system—modeled on the French code of law—with its 1969 and 1975 family protection acts. A 1988 addition to the preamble of the 1979 constitution of the Islamic Republic of Iran defines the Islamic family as the fundamental social institution promoting development and progress. It also sets forth the importance and naturalness of a woman's role as mother, for which she has been chosen by God, as well as her responsibility for the family's well-being. Article 21 of the constitution asserts that the government must in all ways ensure women's rights in accordance with Islamic principles. Consequently it must "create a favorable environment for the growth of woman's personality and the restoration of her rights, both material and intellectual," as well as protect "mothers, particularly during pregnancy," and provide "special insurance for widows."[132] And yet with the reinstating of the shari'a, men's almost absolute right to divorce was back in effect, as was also a minimum marriage age of nine for females and thirteen for males (calculated according to the lunar calendar), as well as the Islamic penal code, with its *hadd* punishment for theft, premarital and extramarital sex, and the consumption of alcoholic beverages.[133] Khomeini's understanding of the shari'a had medieval dimensions.[134] Ayatollah Murtaza Mutahhari (born in 1920 and killed by radicals in 1979), a spiritual pioneer of the revolution, took a more liberal view of the shari'a when it came to gender issues.[135] Over the past decades his writings have been reprinted more than twenty times. Following the Iran-Iraq War and Khomeini's death, social conditions changed, and a younger generation came to power. Since 1992, with the support of women's rights advocates the Iranian parliament has gradually passed several reforms related to family law. Each amendment to a law had first to be presented for review to the Guardian Council, which checked its compatibility with the shari'a. If vetoed, it was passed on to the Expediency Council, which often meant it faced even greater opposition from conservatives. Nevertheless, it is now legal for a woman to be the head of a family. Iranian war widows may also petition for independence from their husband's family, and for state support for themselves and their children. In fact, in the interim, state support for widows is obligatory.

According to the gender conceptions prevailing when the Qur'an was conceived, *two* female witnesses may replace *one* male witness in cases of debt if a second male witness cannot be found (Qur'an 2:282).[136] In cases of homicide, regulations on "blood money" have come to replace the previous custom of "blood revenge." The Iranian government has reintroduced the law requiring that if a murderer is executed, the murder victim's family must pay "blood money" as compensation to the murderer's family. The amount paid for a female murderer who is executed is only half as much as for a male murderer (whose victim is most commonly a woman); in any case the sum is often so high that it is ruinous for the victim's family. Generally speaking, since 1980 the crime rate for women has risen with their increased poverty, and this correlates directly with the fact that women have fewer job opportunities than men, who are also able to get a divorce more easily. And though prohibited by law, prostitution and drug trafficking have increased among women. *Hadd* punishment is still enforced for premarital and extramarital sex. According to Qur'an 24:2, it consists of one hundred strokes of the lash in front of witnesses—that is, if four trustworthy males are able to testify to having witnessed the act. (Qur'an 24:4 prescribes eighty strokes for anyone unable to substantiate their allegations with the obligatory witnesses.) As a rule, two (or four) female witnesses may now replace the one (or two) male witnesses. Often based on forced confessions from suspects who have no access to legal assistance, punishment today is imposed, and implemented at public stonings, according to instructions specified for each gender (e.g., women are placed in pits to protect their lower bodies). After extracting a confession, the judge must throw the first stone; the crowd hurls the rest. An exiled Iranian author recorded fifty cases of stoning between 1980 and 1997: nine involved men and forty-one involved women. The charges included prostitution, "immoral conduct," rape, and murder.[137] In June 2008 eleven people, nine of them women, were awaiting punishment by stoning for adultery and/or other acts of immorality. Over a recent twelve-month period at least eight people had their fingers or hands amputated for theft or robbery.

Virtually no Islamic country has ever completely disregarded the rules and principles laid out in the Qur'an. According to verses 2:221 and 60:10 it is forbidden to wed either a "polytheist or a "nonbeliever." Nevertheless, verse 5:5 states that a Muslim man may marry a Christian or a Jew, while a Muslim woman may not. Under Saddam, Iraq altered this law in 1978 so that it was henceforth permissible for a Muslim woman to marry someone of another faith. All the same, such couples often felt isolated, and this was true even in academic circles. It took the Iran-Iraq War and the First Gulf War for people to become more tolerant. It is nevertheless difficult to predict how things will evolve. In Islamic countries the ban on interconfessional marriages for women is usually rationalized by arguing that as the weaker and more impressionable gender, they are more susceptible to persuasion and thus may convert to Christianity. Moreover, children from such marriages will not grow up to be Muslims, since tradition demands that they be raised according to their father's religion.[138] Women activists from Islamic countries recurrently protest against this policy, as it violates the 1985 UN resolution condemning discrimination against women. Most Islamic countries signed the resolution, though some did so without endorsing all its articles.

As of 2009 Turkey was the only country in the Middle East that had abolished the shari'a. In 1926 Turkey adopted—almost without modification—the complete Swiss civil code, which at the time was Europe's most conservative legal system. In 1928 it incorporated the Italian penal code, with its commentary in French. The implementation of these divergent legal systems was not unproblematic. Moreover, between 1935 and 1981 eight "amnesties" had to be declared to legalize children from "imam marriages," that is, marriages in which a man and a woman wed without a civil ceremony but with the "blessing" of an imam; in most cases these wives were additional wives, alongside a man's official, first wife. A ruling by the Turkish constitutional court from September 11, 1987, led to the annulment of a paragraph that had discriminated against children from an imam marriage, who had not been entitled to inherit as much as children from a marriage registered by the state. This ruling made further amnesties unnecessary.[139] Today such marriages still exist in the countryside, though their numbers are decreasing. In light of Turkey's candidature for the EU, and the growing number of women with positions in the Turkish legal system, additional reforms have been enacted since 1998. Most important, they stipulate the equality of man and woman as head of family and require financial support for women after divorce with reference to marriage as a community of profit, as well as providing equal rights and obligations with regard to their children after divorce. Moreover, men and women are entitled to equal shares of an inheritance and separate property (as prescribed in the shari'a). Women have also been successful in opposing the reintroduction of punishment for premarital and extramarital sex (*zina* as described in the shari'a) by arguing that it would affect them more severely than men owing to the social dominance of the latter, who may move about more freely in any event.

Tunisia and South Yemen (until the coup in 1990) enacted laws limiting the *mahr*, the gift to the bride from the groom (consisting of money, animals, and/or other rather costly items), the amount of which, according to Qur'an 4:4, had to be set down in the marriage contract. In Tunisia in the 1970s this gift was even further reduced to one (symbolic) dinar. The idea was to prevent parents from demanding a large *mahr* so as to hinder their daughter's marriage to someone of her liking, but whom they felt was unsuitable. Not long after Muhammad's death the *mahr* had already become an indication of a bride's social status and thus an important factor in negotiating a marriage contract. The (often much greater) sum a man had to pay his wife after dissolving their marriage—the so-called deferred gift or payment (*mahr mu'ajjal*)—was also defined in the contract. After the *mahr* had been limited in Tunisia, other kinds of traditional gifts from the groom became a factor in marriage negotiations.

Following independence from the early 1950s on, many countries established a minimum age for marriage. For the most part this had to do with demographic developments. Often the age was set at eighteen for males and sixteen for females. Countries with rising birthrates and stunted economic growth, such as Tunisia in 1959 and Iran in 1974, fixed the minimum age for men at twenty; in Algeria in 1984 it was even raised to twenty-one. For women in all three countries the minimum age was eighteen.

The *jabr*, the right of a father or guardian to force his will on a minor and make her wed ("forced marriage" such as has recently become controversial in Germany, for instance), has been illegal in most Middle Eastern countries since the 1960s or 1970s. Nevertheless, some poor lower-class urban families, and an even greater number of rural ones, as well as less affluent Turkish and Croatian immigrant families in Germany and elsewhere, still practice this custom. They want to ensure that their daughters of marriageable age will be provided for and that they adhere to autochthonous traditions.[140]

As of 2009 Tunisia was the only Arab country to have imposed a ban on polygyny, which it did in 1956, after gaining independence. Yet the fact that a clause had to be added in 1959 threatening severe punishment of anyone involved in such a marriage indicates that the practice persisted.

In other countries, as in Morocco with its 2004 Mudawwana, a husband has to notify his first wife and receive her consent if he wants to marry a second woman. He must provide proof to a judge that he can afford to support an additional household. The shariʿa also sets out that a husband must provide a home for each wife, and while at one time this might have meant separate rooms or floors in the same house, today it usually means completely separate dwellings. Modern literature frequently documents why women, as the socially weaker partners, agree to a husband's second marriage, especially if they have remained childless, for a man's desire to have children is considered natural. There are others who, because of physical and/or psychological abuse, have little choice but to give their consent.

The shariʿa makes no allowances for community property or profits in marriage. A woman is entitled to property of her own and need not, at least in theory, contribute to the family's livelihood. It is the responsibility of the husband (*nafaqa*) to provide for his wife, as long as she performs her duties, and this includes, most significantly, absolute obedience to her husband. Nevertheless, in almost all schools of Islamic law, one of the basic tenets is social suitability and compatibility in marriage (*kafaʾa*). This means, for example, that the husband has to provide domestic help for his wife if this is what she is used to. The personal status codes of a number of countries—for example, Tunisia and South Yemen until 1990 and Algeria since 1984—also specify that a woman must contribute to the livelihood of the family if required and feasible. Such reforms were justified by a woman's joint financial (and thus general) responsibility for her family, a responsibility postulated for the first time in this form.

Despite sharp protest, even the shah's family protection acts, ratified in 1967 and 1975, did not ban a practice known as *mutʿa*, that is, "temporary marriage" or "marriage for pleasure." It was a form officially permitted only among the Twelver Shiʿa and had for centuries been called *sigheh* (contract). These acts, however, made confirmation in court as well as the official registration of such marriages mandatory.[141] *Mutʿa* marriages permit sexual relations between a man and a woman for a specific period agreed upon in a contract, a period that may range from twenty-four hours to ninety-nine years, without the man's having to present a gift to the bride or support her, although, according to Iranian law, provision may be made for either of these in the contract, as well as for the number of sexual contacts and the amount of "compensation" to be received by the woman. A man may contract as many *mutʿa* marriages as he likes alongside his "regular" marriage or marriages, even with women of other confessions.

Ideologues of the Iranian Revolution have come to idealize these marriages since the Iran-Iraq War, seeing them as a solution for the sexual problems of the younger generation and as a form of emotional and sexual "support" for single women. They also believe that such arrangements are proof of the social tolerance of Islam's matrimonial laws, which others have often regarded as too rigorous. Directly following the 1979 Islamic

Revolution, the large red-light district in Tehran was set on fire. The women who survived were forced to agree to *mut'a* marriages. In London in 1989 the Iranian anthropologist Shahla Haeri, who is from a well-known Shi'i family, published the findings of her field research on the *mut'a* in Iran: after the founding of the Islamic Republic and during the ruthless retaliation of the regime against its opponents, the legality of *mut'as* made it possible for prison guards to force young women from dissenting families to marry before their execution. Having lost their virginity, they would not, according to Islamic belief, be automatically admitted into paradise.[142] On the basis of case studies, Haeri also shows that by legalizing shorter relationships, "temporary marriage" may become a means of evading the morality usually applied to marriage and sex in Islam, as well as harsh punishment for premarital or extramarital sex. At the same time, women often do not benefit from the *mut'a*. They are frequently unaware of their rights, or are unable to assert themselves against the constraints imposed on them by men. Nevertheless, divorced women often see the *mut'a* as a way to avoid social stigma when they want to have a relationship with a man, even if such women still feel socially inferior to "conventional" wives. In 1990, after the war and in light of stricter *hadd* punishment for premarital and extramarital sex, President Rafsanjani endorsed a law that reformed *mut'a* marriages with the argument that they took the sexuality of both genders into account. The law was hotly disputed in the media and labeled the legalization of prostitution, since it did away with the need for a contract, an imam, and witnesses, all of which were required to make a conventional marriage legal. Henceforth a man and a woman had only to recite the proper lines; they could even be in Persian if the parties did not speak Arabic. Today women are actually encouraged to initiate *mut'as*, since a guardian is not required unless they are under age. Nevertheless, because a virgin entering into such a marriage usually jeopardizes her chance for a "normal" marriage, the government advises her to draft a contract which guarantees that the relationship will not affect her virginity; in other words, it authorizes a form what may be viewed as premarital friendship in a country where it is still taboo for a couple to hold hands when they are out for a walk.

At the turn of the twentieth century, temporary marriages were popular during pilgrimages to (Sunni) Mecca. In 1947 the Egyptian (Sunni) writer 'Abbas Mahmud al-'Aqqad (1889–1964) stated that he saw the *mut'a* as a legitimate means for Arab students in Europe and the United States to enjoy their sexuality.[143] I have heard, for instance, of German women who have occasionally been willing to accept these foreign-language marriage contracts. For several years now, "unofficial marriages" (*zawaj 'urfi*) have also become popular, especially among students in large Egyptian cities, since marriage is expensive and open relationships are taboo. These "marriages" also involve contracts, though they are drawn up between the man and the woman and not her *wali* (guardian), and have only to be confirmed by one religious representative in the presence of two witnesses. In addition, the man has no material obligation toward the woman. He may end the relationship at any time by tearing up the contract and is then free to contract a new marriage. In contrast, until recently, women who wanted to remarry were charged with polyandry. Since 2002, however, women also have the right to dissolve these marriages and remarry afterwards.[144] In Wahhabi Saudi Arabia (a strict Sunni school of Islam), the Mecca-based Islamic Jurisprudence Assembly issued a fatwa on April 12, 2006, approving *misyar* (travel) marriages for men when they are away from home. This fatwa authorizes marriage contracts in which the woman relinquishes her rights to housing and support and accepts that her husband may visit her in her home whenever he likes. The estimated divorce rate (currently for largely arranged marriages) is about 20 percent nationwide and about 39 percent in the capital, Riyadh. Nowadays both *'urfi* and *misyar* marriages are hotly disputed on the Internet, and Muslim theologians and ideologists, such as the Egyptian Amr Khalid, warn young women to be careful about renouncing their rights and not obtaining their father's consent.[145] A few countries—for instance, Lebanon, with its relatively large number of Shi'is, as well as Libya—have banned the *mut'a* in their personal status codes.

Since the 1930s both male and female writers of modern Middle Eastern literature have addressed the issue of "honor killings" in short stories, novels, and poems. This practice cannot be traced back to Islam alone but derives from ancient principles of chastity. Women must adhere to them, though their close male relatives are the ones held responsible for their observance (often by women of the older generation). If these principles are violated, punishment of the woman is required. Even today, friends and family are willing to cover up for these male "guardians of the family honor." Many lawyers and women activists, in Iran and Lebanon, sharply criticize the laws enabling judges to pronounce lenient sentences for killings of this kind—that is, for those exercising their unwritten "right"—for ultimately the legal system is still strongly male-dominated.[146] In a new penal code ratified on June 1, 2005, Turkey threatened to impose "life sentences under aggravating circumstances" for murderers who commit honor killings; in addition, rape in marriage has been defined as a crime.[147] At the same time, life in the diaspora—for example, in Europe—has sometimes exacerbated cultural identity complexes among conservative (lower-class) Muslim families and so led to an increase in honor killings. The same is true for others threatened in their identity, such as Palestinians living in Israel and/or in refugee camps since the early 1980s.[148]

Neither the Qur'an nor early hadith literature—the two main sources of Islamic law—recommends female circumcision. Yet despite its illegality, it is still practiced, in particular among the lower classes in Egypt and Sudan. These Islamic works also do not have anything to say about the "virginity cult," which still exists in the southern parts of several Christian Mediterranean countries.

Egypt banned female genital cutting (removal of the clitoris by a doctor) by ministerial decree in 1959, which became law in 1979. After controversial debates the law—which still indirectly authorizes "women folk healers" to perform the operation—was upheld in 1997, and in 2005, after the death of a twelve-year-old girl in a private hospital in Minya, was tightened even further.[149] According to UNICEF, 95 percent of married women between the ages of fifteen and forty-nine and about 50 percent of girls between ten and eighteen are circumcised in Egypt. Also in the Sudan, where "pharaonic circumcision," that is, the removal of all the external female sexual organs, is still customary in some regions, conservative Islamic groups and members of the lower classes cite later hadiths to justify the practice as beneficial both to marriage and to a woman's appearance and fertility. Lower-class Christian and Jewish women in Egypt and the Sudan are also circumcised. Encouraged by their families, young women believe that circumcision will improve their chances for marriage, as it is said to raise the (moral) status of a woman without harming her fertility and maternal instinct. In other words, it is a question not of religious issues but of regional traditions for which religious explanations were found, or rather invented, later. This is also the case in Iraqi Kurdistan, where, according to recent information, approximately 20 percent of the women are circumcised secretly. Women's organizations, teachers, and physicians have joined forces to combat the practice.

Evidence of the importance of virginity for Muhammad can be found in the Qur'anic idea of lovely black-eyed young women (*huris*) awaiting Muslim men in paradise, maidens "of modest gaze, which neither man nor jinn will have touched before them, in beauty like the jacinth and the coral stone" (55:70ff.). Male fantasies of the never-ending virginity of *huris* originated later. Islamic mystics and modern exegetes interpret *huris* esoterically, viewing their very existence as propitious for both genders.[150]

Even today the bride's virginity must be recorded in the marriage contract.[151] Only a widow or a divorced woman may be *thayyib* (deflowered). If on the wedding night a man discovers that his bride is not a virgin although the contract stated she was, he may divorce her, disgracing both her and her family. Shortly after the Iranian Revolution it became compulsory for all unmarried female officials to be checked for virginity. If a women's hymen was not intact, she was fired. Popular Arab literature on "prophetic medicine" has provided recipes for restoring the hymen. Stories from the *Thousand and One Nights* at the time of the Mamluks in Egypt also depict some tricks. And since the 1930s, urban doctors have offered surgical assistance. Today "hymen repair"—a surgical practice in which the remains of an allegedly once intact hymen are stitched together—is recommended on Arab websites and performed even on young women from conservative Christian families, who have come to place increased value on a bride's virginity.[152] Another method involves inserting a blood-filled leather ball into the vagina before the wedding night, a practice that has replaced the deceptive blood-soaked wads of cloth recommended in earlier works of folk medicine.

The more modern law reforms have restricted the almost unlimited rights of a man to divorce his wife without reasonable grounds or without consulting a judge, a practice called *talaq* and often mentioned in (reformed) Qur'anic verses. The Qur'an does advise the couple to call in members of their families to arbitrate first. Early hadith literature characterizes *talaq* as the practice most hated by God. Moreover, the fact that a husband is required to pay the remaining portion of the (often large) sum agreed upon in the marriage contract to his ex-wife is seen as a deterrent, one that should make him refrain from acting too hastily. In marriage contracts negotiated by their *walis,* women could and may still lay down conditions that entitle them to file for divorce, for example, if their husband beats them or marries a second wife (though it must be noted that the Qur'an permits both). In addition there are factors such as mental illness, long absences, impotence, or the husband's inability to earn a living, all of which a woman must substantiate in court. In one chapter of the *Maqamat,* the sardonic masterpiece of Arabic literature by the famous writer and scholar al-Hariri of Basra (d. 1122), the (aging) author self-mockingly depicts in rhyming prose the grievances of an Arab woman who files for divorce before a judge on the grounds of her aging husband's impotence. This scene is often portrayed on the Arab miniatures illustrating manuscripts of the *Maqamat* from the thirteenth century on.[153] Evidently such options disappeared after Arab countries encountered the legal systems of the colonial powers. This might explain why Muslim feminists—such as Amira El-Azhary Sonbol, professor of Islamic history at the Center for Muslim-Christian Understanding at Georgetown University in Washington, D.C.—claim that modern law reforms (developed under colonial influence) often put women in a worse position than the shari'a.[154]

Whether a woman asserts her right to divorce depends on her social situation and position, not to mention her self-confidence. Middle-aged and older Muslim women in the Middle East often say that family life is so important to them they would rather remain in an unhappy marriage than file for divorce. Of course this may also be the case because even today reformed family law codes seldom force a man to pay alimony. They also give the father custody of boys over seven (and sometimes even younger) and of girls after puberty. Hence if a woman has no profession or is unable to pursue one, she and her children may have no choice but to move in with her father or brother, who will then have to support her. Egypt's personal status code stipulates in Article 100/1985 that in the event of a divorce after several years of a marriage that is to the disadvantage of the woman, she is to receive custody of the children and exclusive rights to the marital home. Otherwise the husband must provide alternative accommodation (the difficulty of which should not be underestimated, considering the widespread housing shortage) and pay alimony for two years. And yet if a man marries a second wife (by law, the registrar's office, not the husband, has to notify the first wife of his intentions), it is no longer considered an "injury" of a magnitude that would automatically entitle the first wife to divorce. Instead the first wife must wait a year and then prove that she has in fact suffered "injury." Jealousy alone is not sufficient grounds.[155]

Since 1992 Iranian women may incorporate a clause in their marriage contract that quotes the "marriage code" and so prevents the husband from marrying a second wife. In addition, men have to submit their petitions for divorce to a family court and substantiate their claims. If these are proved "unjust," they are required to pay their wife an adequate amount for having done the housework and raised the children during their marriage (*ujrat al-mithl*). The "deferred *mahr,*" which has been set in the marriage contract, must also be adjusted for inflation. During the summer of 2000 and again in 2002, more (mostly young) Muslim women than men petitioned the Tehran family court for divorce. This has become the case because most men prefer to wait until their wives cannot stand living with them any longer, and file for divorce themselves, since by doing so they forfeit all rights to a "deferred *mahr.*" But let there be no mistake: some young women do so voluntarily, as they are well educated and self-confident. In addition, among young couples who have been married for only a short time, "amicable divorce" is becoming more common.[156]

Ignoring strong opposition in parliament, Anwar el-Sadat issued a presidential decree in 1979 that not only allowed a woman to leave her husband if he married a second wife but also awarded the first wife their mutual home. This decree was declared invalid on procedural grounds in 1985 but was essentially reinstituted—despite renewed opposition from orthodox groups which invoked the Qur'an. An amendment to Egypt's personal status code (1/2000) stunned conservatives in the Islamic world by modifying the pre-Islamic right of women—adopted in the shari'a (but not mentioned in the Qur'an)—to dissolve a marriage by reimbursing the *mahr* received upon marriage or a sum not exceeding it, known as *khul'*—divorce for compensation, in which a woman, so to speak, buys back her freedom. Now a woman no longer had to have her husband's consent or provide any reason for discontinuing her marriage other than personal aversion. In Egypt, as in many other Islamic countries, it has become common practice to encourage marriage by keeping the compulsory *mahr* low, whereas the "deferred *mahr*" is often kept high so as to prevent the couple from divorcing on impulse. In *khul',* by contrast, women forfeit their right to a (relatively low) *mahr* payment, as well as to the set "contract penalty," the deferred *mahr,* upon divorce.[157] According to this amendment, if the husband files for divorce but then refuses to pay alimony, payments can be deducted from his income. If he has no income or his address is unknown, a state bank must bear the costs of supporting his ex-wife and children.

As a rule, mothers retain custody of their sons until they are seven years old; in Algeria the age was raised to ten in 1984. Mothers have custody of their daughters until they are of age, unless the mother remarries or conducts herself immorally, though the latter is certainly open to interpretation.

8. The Algerian Family Law Code of June 9, 1984, and Later Reforms: Some Information on the Moroccan Mudawwana of January 2004

The Algerian Family Law Code (CFA) of June 9, 1984,[158] which reformulated the CFA from September 1981 after protest from the powerful women's movement in Algeria, triggered a battle for further reforms. Women's organizations criticized the symbiosis between these overly cautious reforms and their adherence to the shari'a in line with Maliki principles. Yet it was not until President Abdelaziz Bouteflika was campaigning for reelection in June 2004 and promised to reform the CFA radically that changes became possible. On International Women's Day (March 8, 2005), Bouteflika newly reelected president, announced a number of amendments, all of which the Algerian parliament had approved only a few days earlier. Nevertheless, critics called them a mere "reformette," since they were not viewed as having introduced true reform nor as having significantly modified the 1984 CFA.

For example, even though the age requirement for marriage has been raised and set at nineteen for both sexes, a judge may still, according to Article 7, "waive" the age requirement and declare a minor marriageable "if it is in the interest of the parties or otherwise advisable." Specific grounds and a minimum age are not specified.

Civil marriage now must precede any form of religious ceremony. In addition, Article 8 sets forth that a man has the right to contract marriage with more than one woman within the bounds of the shari'a, if there are "just legal grounds" (*mubarrir shari'a*) and he can guarantee his wives fairness in their circumstances. He must also notify his current and future wives of his plans. A clause added in December 23, 1984, defines the illness or sterility of a man's first wife (certified by a doctor) as legitimate grounds. In the case of a second marriage, both women have to provide written consent to a judge, who must then decide whether the man will be able to afford two wives plus their children and households. (The number of men who have two wives is small: only about 1 percent.) The marriage ceremony has to be attended by the "bride's guardian" (*wali*)—usually her father or a close male relative—as well as two witnesses in whose presence the bride and groom must give their consent. The gift or payment to the bride is also due immediately, though the amount is not defined by law. A woman may do as she pleases with the payment (Qur'an 4:4), and separation of property is now guaranteed by law. According to Hanafi law a woman may be wed without a guardian present if she has been married before. According to North African Maliki law, by contrast, a guardian is indispensable, which is why he has been retained in the current CFA despite much protest from the women's movement. Another amendment adopted in spring 2005 declares that a young woman has the right to choose her guardian; all the same, pressure from her family often affects her choice.

Article 12 states that the father has the right to prevent the marriage of his virgin daughter (no matter her age) "for her own good," without stating any grounds. She can, however, attempt to disprove his allegations in court. If she is successful, the judge is authorized to approve the marriage against her guardian's will.

Article 36 of the CFA formulates the mutual obligations of husband and wife in marriage. They must maintain conjugal relations and fulfill the obligations of living together, safeguard the interests of the family, protect and educate the children, and cultivate contact with their relatives—a detail criticized by conservatives. According to Article 37, upon marriage a husband must provide for his wife and all their children within the scope of his ability (food, clothes, medical care, living quarters, and whatever else is conventionally supplied), independently of his wife's property and income. (If, however, a man is unable to provide for his family, the woman must take over, if she can.) In return a wife has to fulfill her marital duties: obey her husband as head of family and raise his children, whom she must breastfeed if possible—that is, unless her social position exempts her. If a man is married to several women, he must treat them equally and justly, as set forth in Qur'an 4:3. According to Article 38 the woman has the right to visit her parents (even at a distant location) and to receive them in her home. And yet her husband can determine the frequency and duration of these visits; he also has the right to be present. The wife's obedience to her husband as head of the family, as prescribed in Article 39, is somewhat relativized in Article 38 but is still required today. The wife has a right to sexual intercourse once a month and may withhold herself from her husband only under certain conditions. She must keep house, provide for the children, and respect her husband's parents and relatives. If they all live in the same house (as is traditional in a patrilocal marriage), it may mean that the wife also has to obey her husband's parents or at least his mother. A 2005 amendment determines that both parents are responsible for their children; nevertheless, the father has sole custody.

The male's right to flog his wife for "disobedience, [or] (sexual) rebellion" (*nushuz*), as formulated in Qur'an 4:34, is not mentioned in the CFA. Commentators have confirmed that this right still exists, but husbands are asked to proceed in the order set out in the Qur'an (admonishment, sexual abstinence, then flogging), for (physical) violence is to be avoided if possible. Today such violence is grounds for divorce.

According to Article 48 a marriage can still be dissolved on the request of the husband without his providing any grounds, by mutual consent (according to Article 54), or on the petition of the wife. Yet a woman may be granted a divorce only on grounds established by law. In recent times divorce may be finalized in court only after the judge has tried to reconcile the couple over a period of three months. A man may remarry his ex-wife, but only if she married to another man afterwards (a *muhallil*, "he who renders lawful") who has divorced her in the interim (Qur'an 2:230). According to Article 52 the court may judge in favor of the woman and her petition for "proper" compensation (though the amount is not defined) if it makes a finding of the husband's "arbitrariness" and/or "unwarranted harshness" (*ta'assuf*). According to this same article, a woman forfeits this right upon remarriage and/or if there is proof that she has "continually behaved immorally" (for example, if she has had extramarital sex).

According to Article 53 a wife may petition for divorce on the following grounds: (1) Her husband has failed to provide for her, that is, unless she knew he was penniless prior to marriage. (2) The husband has an infirmity and/or mental disorder of which the wife was unaware upon marriage, especially impotence. (3) Her husband has refused to have sexual intercourse with her for more than four months. (4) Her husband has been condemned to prison for more than a year for a crime "dishonoring the family." (5) Her husband has been absent for more than a year without adequate reason and has not provided support. (6) She has suffered injury or been dishonored as defined by law, in particular in violation of Articles 8 and 37, specifying that a woman must be notified if her husband wants to marry another woman and that he must continue to provide for her and the children. (7) Her husband has conducted himself in a morally reprehensible manner. The 2005 reform defines three further reasons: the husband has not fulfilled the clauses laid down in the marriage contract; there is radical disagreement between the parties; and/or there is violence. This makes it somewhat easier for women to file for divorce, and a judge may give the wife custody of the children. In such cases the man has to provide her with housing either by moving out of their joint home or by renting or buying a new home for her. Nevertheless, some divorced women and their children, having trusted that the authorities would enforce the reform, have found themselves destitute. The husband continues to live in the conjugal home, while they are forced to lodge in remote neighborhoods, even slums. Sometimes the ex-husband even stops paying the rent, so the woman has no choice but to live on the streets. The severe housing crisis in Algiers has aggravated the situation and indirectly promoted male chauvinism.[159]

"Divorce by mutual consent" as laid out in Article 54 specifies that a woman may obtain a divorce by the aforementioned *khul'*. Since March 2005 she can do so even without her husband's consent, though a "waiting period" of three months (*'idda*), as prescribed in the Qur'an, following a divorce or the death of a husband, is still in effect. During this period a woman may not remarry (this is to ensure that she will be provided for if it turns out she was pregnant at separation) but has a right to alimony, though the amount is not specified. Clauses may be added to the marriage contract and expand regulations as they are defined by law.

The inheritance rights outlined in the Qur'an (4:4–12)—and by which female descendants are entitled to half the amount inherited by males of the same degree of kinship—have been essentially preserved. The testator, however, may specify a person who will inherit up to one-third of the estate, including someone of a different faith (for example, his Christian wife), who, according to the shari'a, would previously have received nothing. The 2005 reform also determines that the child of an Algerian mother automatically receives Algerian citizenship.

Hence on several counts the CFA is at odds with the Algerian constitution with regard to the equality of all citizens (Article 29), in other words, the equality of men and women before the law. With regard to the legality of polygyny, this is true for all countries of the Middle East except Tunisia and Turkey. With respect to inheritance rights and the right of Muslim women to marry a non-Muslim, this applies to the entire Middle East. And although in Algeria women are allowed to hold almost any position, from judge or high judicial official to minister, they are in many ways still regarded as second-class citizens by the family law code.

After years of criticism by women's organizations, Morocco substantially reformed its Mudawwana (personal status code) in January 2004. These reforms were more radical than the Algerian ones, but the Sharifian king, Muhammed IV, declared that Qur'anic regulations were still to be respected. Two of the most important revisions determined that both husband and wife could be head of the family, and a wife no longer had to display complete obedience to her husband. A woman's right to travel and work without her husband's consent was also established by law. Her right to divorce was expanded, and now more women file for divorce than ever before because they are no longer as worried about whether they will receive alimony or housing. Men may, however, still practice polygyny, though there are more restrictions. Nevertheless, until May 2005, 80 percent of the petitions submitted to court by men asking to marry a second wife were decided positively, even if the absolute number of these requests was very small.[160] Guardians are no longer required; adult women may now marry without having to obtain the consent of a man.

9. Extended and Nuclear Families: Gender Segregation

Like Christianity and Judaism, Islam has always been family-oriented. Marriage is based on a civil contract, whose details are normally negotiated by the groom and a male relative, and the father or another close relative of the bride. Although these contracts have long resembled sales contracts, marriage has strong religious connotations—even if it is not a sacrament as in the Catholic Church. Hadiths, some of which have become proverbs, refer to marriage as "one half of religion." The Qur'an commands, "And marry such of you that are solitary and the pious of your slaves and maid servants!" (24:32), calling it a sign from God that "he created for you [i.e., men] helpmeets from yourselves that ye might find rest in them," and goes on to speak of the love and mercy that God ordained between spouses (30:21). Qur'an 25:74–75 promises paradise to all those who ask the Lord to provide comfort for their wives and offspring. Hadiths demand that children respect their parents (*birr al-walidain*); they praise mothers and promise paradise to fathers if they love their daughters, raise and educate them well, and find husbands for them to marry.[161] Admittedly, a relatively large number of misogynic hadiths also exist.

For centuries, especially in Sunni regions, families lived in larger groups.[162] In public they were represented by the father, who also had the final say in the home. Mothers, especially of sons, were respected and honored by all social classes. Within the home they had positions of power, and for the younger generations a mother's word was their command. Especially for women from more humble circumstances, a mother's pride in her sons still has great significance. If the father dies before the mother, the eldest son usually becomes responsible for his younger siblings and for marrying off his sisters. He must also provide for his aging mother and unmarried sisters. Since men are often much older than their wives, this occurs relatively frequently. In early Arabic literature there are verses in which men revile women who have given birth only to daughters. In other verses, proud mothers defiantly reproach fathers for their responsibility for the situation. In still other verses, both fathers and mothers extol their daughters.[163]

Across the Middle East, contact with Europe and other modes of living, as well as subsequent economic upheaval, led to changes in family and social life, especially among the urban middle and upper classes. Social structures in rural and Bedouin populations, especially in the Gulf countries, tended to survive longer. In the constitutions of many of these nations, the family is defined as the nucleus or basic component of the state, and man is defined as its head. Only recently have amendments in Turkey and Morocco defined both man *and* woman as the head of the family. Nevertheless, these changes will take time to put into practice, as even in other cultures man—especially in his role as provider—claims leadership.

In today's large and medium-sized cities the nuclear family dominates. As a consequence women are sometimes more strongly controlled by authoritarian husbands than they were in the extended family, where there was a "network of women" protecting them. Such networks were and still are particularly important for internal communication and relations—as well as for negotiating marriages—in urban working- and lower-middle-class districts.[164] Centuries of gender segregation have created social networks that continue to exist in the lower and middle classes of many regions.

According to the French anthropologist Camille Lacoste-Dujardin's observations in North Africa, up through the 1980s mothers of sons became "high priests of male supremacy," even oppressing younger women, specifically their daughters and daughters-in-law. Mothers often raised their daughters according to patriarchal traditions and manipulated their sons in the choice of their wives and in their sexual behavior with them.[165] During comparative field studies in Morocco and Iran in the early 1990s, the Iranian scholar Ziba Mir-Hosseini observed that in Morocco, despite patriarchal Maliki family law, lower-class families have become more matriarchal because the women—owing to the husbands' more frequent unemployment—often have jobs as washerwomen, maids, vendors, or the like. Hence women are able to earn their own income, while the husband is no longer the family's only wage earner and provider. Divorce is now more common, as custody of the children does not automatically go to the father, as was previously the case, but may now go to the mother or sister of the divorcé.[166] In other words, the social impact of a universal patriarchal system of law such as the shari'a on the family and its members varies depending on the economic conditions. Modern literature has made it clear that young women who are eager to obtain an education and enjoy a more cosmopolitan lifestyle have felt held back in the past fifty or sixty years by patriarchal family life, with its social controls and constraints. In her gripping autobiography *My Home, My Prison* (1986), the Christian Palestinian writer Raymonda Tawil describes how her father, brothers, and considerably older husband, who was also of Christian origin—and ultimately the Jordanian authorities—all exerted pressure on her, and how she found this confining in comparison to the liberal mentality of her Israeli schoolmates. In her autobiographical novel *Habbat al-naftalin* (*Mothballs*), the exiled Iraqi author Alia Mamduh (b. 1944) gives a complex picture of the tense relationships between the generations and among women in a large and conventional middle-class family during her childhood and youth in Baghdad.[167]

It was common for families to arrange marriages, a custom still practiced today in the more impoverished urban districts. Women's networks play a major role in such negotiations.[168] In a middle-class district in Cairo in 1983 and again in 1992, Homa Hoodfar, an anthropologist of Iranian origin, observed how parents searched, with their daughter's consent, for a socially acceptable and amicable husband, a husband who would make her happy. Even young women believed (despite an abundance of romantic love stories in films and on television) that love matches usually ended more unhappily for women than marriages of convenience based on mutual sympathy. Nevertheless, the fact that this might not be true for especially pretty, well-educated, and high-earning women from well-to-do backgrounds is documented in modern Arab literature, such as in *Chicago*, a 2007 novel by the Egyptian author Ala'a al-Aswani (b. 1957). Marriage contracts—which might even include clauses covering a time frame for taking birth control pills, veiling versus no veiling, or even the weekly meat rations a husband must provide—were drafted after long negotiations between the groom and often one of his friends, on the one hand, and the male relatives of the bride, on the other. The mother of the bride operated in the background. Since ample means were required to marry (that is, for the payment or gift to the bride, the often costly wedding, and new lodgings with furnishings), the couple frequently waited several years while, for example, the groom took a better-paying position in one of the oil nations. Usually the "right" suitor was in fact ten or fifteen years older than the bride and had a secure job. Consequently the common age at marriage rose, even though a woman's chances for marriage declined as she approached twenty. Often poorer women, or childless divorcées who still wanted children, were willing to be the second wife of a (wealthy) married man—and this step usually met with approval in their surroundings. Otherwise women did not think highly of the position of second wife.[169]

As more women study and achieve greater social mobility, love and friendship between the sexes has become more probable. In fact such relationships are what the younger generation desires, especially educated young people in the cities, though this too varies regionally. And yet, since starting a family is expensive, "unofficial marriages" are on the rise; according to the website of the Egyptian ideologist Amr Khalid from February 5, 2008, 17 percent of Egyptian students nationwide (with a very high percentage at Cairo University) are living in "unofficial marriages." This trend may soon serve as a model for other Sunni countries.

All the same, few women live alone and independently in these regions, and the majority of those who do are middle-aged or older divorcées, or widows in prestigious professions. Younger unmarried women, even in metropolises like Cairo and Tehran, usually share lodgings if their families do not live in the same town.

Among middle-aged or elderly Arab married couples, the educated and self-assured woman holds considerable sway over her family, that is, over the attitudes and views of her husband and children (whether sons or daughters). In her role as colleague and employee, the clever and skilled woman often exerts great influence on her male superiors.

Yet men still tend to dominate the streets; this is true even in regions where one might have thought tourists (especially women tourists) would have had an impact on the cityscape. This is evidently a consequence of the age-old tradition of excluding women from public life. Then again, there are regional and local differences, even in the urban centers, as well as differences related to class. Saudi Arabia is the only country in the Middle East where women hardly ever leave their homes without a male escort (usually a close male relative), and they are not permitted to drive a car, despite years of protest and debate, even within the large royal family. So far the many demonstrations by educated women from elite families driving cars through the center of Riyadh have not been successful, and in fact they have on occasion even led to the women being arrested by the police. Since male family members were willing to vouch for them, everyone detained was released; nevertheless, a number of women who had jobs were fired. The country's first female pilot, who worked for Prince al-Walid bin Talal's private line, appeared in a photo in the *Arab News* (in a press release for readers abroad) wearing tight-fitting pilot's gear, and—also an affront to Islamic conceptions of morality—shaking the prince's hand. Nonetheless, she still had to have someone drive her to the airport.[170] In Libya, a rich nation thanks to its oil exports since 1959, Muammar el-Qaddafi has propagated and promised Islamic socialism since 1972 in his *Green Book* (*Green Charter*), yet women in white or colorful cloaks (though almost always without face veils) are still part of the streetscape in small towns. In the large cities such as Tripoli and Benghazi the situation is different. Here it is possible to see women alone at the wheel of a large car. Neither veiling nor gender segregation is strictly enforced.

Of course, modern public transport systems throughout the Middle East were originally conceived with separate compartments for men and women. Iran actually reintroduced segregation in trams and busses in 1980–81. Other countries followed suit, in part to protect women against harassment by men when public transport was overcrowded (of course, those who can afford them prefer their own cars). Yet since a large number of women have to use these smaller rear compartments, for example, when they take their children to school or day care centers, gender segregation often turns out to be impracticable. Moreover, many young women today try to avoid using them. In trains, women may choose their seats; in airplanes, flight attendants usually regulate matters by not seating a woman who is alone (even a European woman) next to a man.

The shari'a states that if a woman travels at all she must be escorted by a male relative or another woman, and in some countries this is still the custom, even for women in prominent positions. As recently as 1988 a female Egyptian minister had to provide proof that she had permission from her husband for an official trip abroad. In 2004 Morocco reformed this regulation in the Mudawwana. Iran has also become more tolerant since the mid-1990s. In recent years Gulf countries such as Bahrain and Yemen have occasionally sent women without male escorts (though in the company of other female students) to study at universities in other Arab countries or in Europe and the United States. A number of these same women went on to hold prestigious jobs.

For the most part, women are still socially defined by their relationships with men, be they husbands, fathers, or brothers—a situation that is also still prevalent in some parts of Europe and the United States. In recent years young women in, for example, Iran, have insisted on learning a vocation before getting married, and their incomes are often now indispensable to their families. Just the same, after marriage they often suppress their desire to pursue a career (as is also true in other cultures) and devote themselves, as expected, to the well-being of their husband and children. Moreover, child care services are rare, and household help in cities such as Tehran has become expensive.[171]

In 1999 Suad Joseph, a Lebanese sociologist of Christian origin, published a volume titled *Intimate Selving in Arab Families*.[172] Written by different authors, the essays suggest that there is hardly any difference between

Arab Christians and Muslims, or with the situation in central Europe, with respect to the hostilities and/or sympathies among female family members. All the same, the authority that fathers and brothers have over their daughters and sisters—patriarchy within the family—still tends to be strong, and this is true even in upper-class families.

In Egypt nearly a dozen organizations are engaged in offering family planning services. Their advertisements address women and are primarily successful among the urban middle and upper classes. In countries such as Libya, Tunisia, Egypt, and Algeria, termination of pregnancy is permitted for eugenic and medical indications, if the husband gives his consent. The religious justification is usually sought in early hadiths that recommend coitus interruptus ('azl) as a means of contraception, at least for female slaves, who were regarded as objects of pleasure; the free woman who desired sons or was expected to give birth to them could reject this method.[173] In Turkey since 1983 there has been a provision permitting abortion within the first ten weeks of pregnancy provided the husband agrees or, if the woman is under age, her parents.[174] In Iran and, of course, Saudi Arabia the shari'a prescribes a fine for abortion—similar to the one for battery or assault—that is, "blood money" for murder. The amount the mother has to pay depends on the stage of development of the fetus; if it is regarded as already having "a soul," then—in line with old gender conceptions—only half the amount must be paid for a girl.[175] Not long after the end of the Iran-Iraq War in 1988 and Khomeini's death in 1989, the new government began to promote family planning in the media. This was necessary because, despite the war, the population of Iran had increased from over 39 million in 1980 to almost 60 million in 1990.[176] Contraceptives for men and women were free, but there were still many illegal abortions. Since the late 1990s, termination of pregnancy has been permitted for medical reasons, and more recently also for eugenic indications, if three doctors and an examining magistrate confirm that the fetus is abnormal and both parents give their consent. The sentence for illegal abortions is anywhere between three and ten years; nevertheless, they are not uncommon in impoverished families.

The Middle Eastern countries are now registering a much lower fertility rate than they were a few years ago: 1.87 percent for Turkey compared with an average of 2.5 percent in general. According to the *Middle East Times* from June 19, 2008, only Yemen and Palestine show higher rates; in Yemen, the poorest of all the Arab countries, the rate is an estimated 6.4 percent. Lower-class parents still find it desirable to have many children, especially sons, who are then to provide for them in old age. Evidently in Palestinian families, having a large number of children is seen as indispensable for survival; there also seems to be the hope that population growth might contribute to defeating Israel, with its rather low birthrate.

Shi'i theologians like 'Ali Shari'ati, Muhammad Husayn Tabataba'i, and Murtaza Mutahhari, all architects of the Iranian Revolution, view Muhammad's daughter Fatima, with her ascetic, diligent, and family-oriented approach to life, as a role model for all women. Muhammad's granddaughter Zaynab became another and different kind of model in the years of the Iran-Iraq War: the female religious warrior. Since the early 1990s female journalists in the more female-oriented media have also extolled Fatima for her exemplary political and social engagement. Her (presumed) date of birth, calculated according to the lunar calendar (on 22 Jumada II), was already a folk festival at the time of the Fatimid dynasty in Egypt. Since 1977 it has been celebrated as "Muslim Women's Day" in Iran and other Islamic countries, as well as by pious Muslims in Turkey.[177] Fatima and Zaynab both came to be considered women worthy of identifying with in the face of a superficial Westernization (with a tendency toward consumerism) and the pseudo-image of the Muslim woman in her material and social enslavement first by her father and then by her husband. Fatima symbolizes the loving, self-sacrificing daughter, wife, and mother, but also freedom, gender equality, and moral integrity. She is the most important link in a line that has progressed from Abraham to Noah, Moses, and Jesus, to Muhammad and Husayn, with their outstanding qualities as religious-political leaders and fighters for social justice.[178]

10. Women Artists, Writers, and Theologians

Despite the tradition of defining the female voice in medieval Islam as something that had to be hidden like genitalia (*sawt al-mar'a 'awra*), a few gifted women—singers, musicians, calligraphers, and poets—succeeded in becoming quite influential. For the most part they were slaves of the court and of non-Arab descent.[179] In the 1890s talented women writers, as mentioned earlier, began playing a significant role in the women's emancipation movement. They started making their presence felt in public, a right previously denied women. At first they did so anonymously or under a pseudonym, not unlike women in Europe and the United States in the early stages of the women's movement in the eighteenth century.

As late as 1920 the Turkish actress Afife Jale Hanim was arrested for performing onstage. At the time, a Muslim Turkish woman could at most accompany her husband to the cinema or theater dressed as a man or a Christian woman.[180] Throughout the Middle East, female roles in the theater were initially played by male actors and later by Christian or Jewish actresses. It was not until 1923 that Afife Jale Hanim succeeded in becoming Turkey's first celebrated actress.[181] The first Egyptian actress of renown was the Coptic performer Mary Ibrahim. In 1869 the first opera house in the Arab world opened in Cairo. In the beginning, only European artists, both male and female, performed in front of what was most likely a largely male, European, and/or non-Muslim audience.

From the start, the Egyptian state conservatory, founded in 1925, did not accept women, even though it had in the interim become acceptable for daughters of upper-class families to learn how to play the piano from European governesses. Oriental music was rediscovered, initially by men, and underwent a revival. The famous Egyptian female singer Umm Kulthum (1898 or 1904–1975) was the daughter of a village imam and Qur'an reciter from the Nile Delta, who also sang at weddings. Her father encouraged her talents by teaching her religious songs. Initially she performed at weddings in the provinces dressed as a boy. After the family moved to Cairo in 1923, she received invitations to sing at events put on by the Egyptian Feminist Union and performed at the House of Woman, founded in 1932. She was at her zenith during World War II and in the aftermath of national independence in the 1950s. Her repertoire included religious, national, and love songs. When she died, Egyptian radio broadcast Qur'anic verses, an honor previously reserved for heads of state.[182] Women singers such as 'Asmahan (of Druze origin, born Amal al-Atrash, 1912–1944) and the Lebanese Fayruz (born Nuhad Haddad in 1935) are well known throughout the Arab world. There is also a younger generation of singers who lived through the Lebanese civil war as children. They try to overcome their traumatic experiences in song. As their names reveal, many, though of course not all of them, are of Christian origin. Fayruz, for instance, is also famous for incorporating Christian musical traditions into both her patriotic hymns and her love songs.

Egypt's first Muslim actress, Fatima al-Yusuf (ca. 1895–1958), lost her mother at birth, and her father, who was a merchant, was often away on business. She grew up with a Christian family in what is now the Lebanese town of Tripoli, and then moved to Alexandria as an adolescent. There she made friends with the Christian actor Iskandar Farah—who had started a theater group—and his family. Appearing first as an extra, she was soon performing under the name Ruz al Yusuf, or Rose al-Youssef, in a vaudeville theater. As of 1918 she also played dramatic roles. In 1923 she began forging a new career and became the first Arab woman to start a publishing company and a periodical (both under her stage name). She received financial support from prominent Egyptian cultural figures. She soon turned the periodical into a satirical magazine, and a while later into a daily paper. Some issues were so severely criticized that they were confiscated. Her *Dhikrayati* (My Memories), first published in Cairo in 1953, portrays her as a strong woman who played a major role in the turbulence affecting Egyptian cultural and educational policies until 1945.[183]

The actresses who starred in Egyptian silent films from 1923 on were self-taught (as was also true in Europe), and of either Jewish or Christian descent. It was not until 1974 that the first female Arab filmmaker screened a work at the Cannes film festival: *Sa'at el Tahrir Dakkat, Barra ya Isti'ma*r (The Bell of Liberation Has Tolled: Away with Colonialism!). The film was a documentary by the Jewish Lebanese filmmaker Heiny Srour on Oman's war of liberation. Twenty years later the Tunisian director Moufida Tlatli received the Golden Camera award in Germany for her 1994 directorial debut, a period film titled *Samt el qusur* (The Silence of the Palace). It focused on the sexual exploitation of slaves in the palaces of the beys before national liberation, though it also showed how a country's liberation did not necessarily mean the end of sexual exploitation. Today, actresses in the Middle East have a similar status as in the rest of the world. Moreover, since the 1970s, especially in Tunisia, Egypt and Lebanon/Palestine, a growing number of women have made names for themselves as directors, also of auteur cinema. Since the 1980s these directors include famous writers such as Assia Djebar from Algeria and Fatima Mernissi from Morocco. Arab women, living in exile or as emigrants, whether of Christian or Muslim descent, have made films that reveal women's experiences and female perspectives on diverse cultures and gender behaviors. The film *Bab al-Sama' Maftuh* (A Door to the Sky), made by the Moroccan filmmaker Farida Ben Lyazid in 1989, for example, baffled many of its French viewers. In it a woman returns to Morocco after several years in Paris to see her father on his deathbed. While there she finds the meaning of life in a traditional form of mystical Islam, a form often popular with Moroccan women. She takes up the veil and establishes a *zawiya,* a kind of convent for women, in her father's house. Norma Marcos, a Palestinian of Christian descent who studied in Paris, showed in *L'espoir voilé* (The Veiled Hope, 1994) how suspicion alone could keep women from becoming active in the struggle for independence: it was said that young Palestinian women who were imprisoned by the Israelis for their political activities were sometimes sexually abused and then, upon their release, ostracized by Arab society.

Female filmmakers in the Middle East have a more difficult time raising funds than their male colleagues. Yet since the 1990s a growing number of women directors have shown their works at international film festivals and series in Europe and the United States.[184] Many of their films focus on criticizing conventional notions of honor that tend to blame women for infringements, and on the social and familial restrictions that follow. They often direct attention to honor killings and female genital mutilation. Above all, they feature women's emancipation as a goal in and of itself, and not merely in the context of the struggle for national liberation—for experience has shown that women tend to be relegated back to traditional roles afterwards.

In Saudi Arabia, movie theaters were shut down in the early 1980s, though it was not long before shops began offering videos (albeit "cleansed" of all love scenes). In spring 2006 the first private Saudi festival of short films was held in Jidda for a mixed-gender audience. In contrast, the first official Saudi festival of short films, in Riyadh in May 2008, was gender-segregated, with one room for men and a smaller one for women. Cineastes in Saudi Arabia looked forward to screening their country's first feature film, the family comedy *Keif al-hal?* (How's It Going?), which was made in Dubai by the young self-taught Saudi filmmaker Haifaa al-Mansur in 2006 and shown at the Cannes film festival that same year.

The leadership of the Islamic Republic of Iran and the Ministry of Culture endorse a cinematic and pictorial art that, on the one hand, presents the traditions of the revolution and, on the other, depicts "proper" morals for society, for gender relations, and—in particular—for women. Shortly after coming to power, Khomeini condemned the cinema of the Pahlavi era for the way it had presented women and open relationships with the other sex; it had fostered immorality and been anti-Islamic. It was, however, not long before the ideologues of the Islamic Revolution also began using the cinema as a means to reach the masses and assert new forms of social relationships in accord with "the norms of hijab [modesty]." Whereas in the early 1980s scenes depicting unveiled women were deleted on principle, women could later be seen on the screen, initially as housewives and then in other supporting roles. In 1990 director Rajab Mohammadin devoted an entire film, *Be khatere hame chiz* (For Everything), to the hardships of women working in the textile industry. The film also counteracted the image of women as sexual objects prevalent in Western cinema. In the same year, Iran's ninth annual International Fajr Film Festival (*fajr* means "dawn"), the most important of its kind in the country, sponsored a so-called women's series of films, all involving women either in front of or behind the camera. Many censorship regulations were relaxed—including those limiting entertaining scenes, physical contact, and/or eye contact between men and women (an "averted gaze" had been mandatory), as well as those restricting close-ups of women and erotic and/or attractive images, and those making veils compulsory even during scenes in homes because of all-male camera crews and anticipated mixed-gender audiences. Today there are several internationally renowned Iranian women directors,[185] and in 1995 an audacious young theater troupe was founded with female members. Moreover, since 2000 a number of films have addressed the cruel repression endured by girls and women of the lower classes. The animated film *Persepolis* (2007), written and co-directed by the exiled Iranian Marjane Satrapi (b. 1969) about her childhood and youth in Iran, was highly applauded in Europe and the United States, though it was only after the film had become available on the Internet that it was screened, in abridged form, at a few Iranian movie theaters in the larger cities. Yet observers have reported that the young middle-class audience seems to prefer entertaining, colorful "Bollywood" films, and to crave works about "Tehrangeles" and its community of former Iranian nationals.

Orthodox Muslim groups began acknowledging the importance of cinema and television in the 1960s. They funded works (for example, the so-called "white cinema" in Turkey) that countered Western or secular films with the Islamic image of woman. Today, religious and rhetorically skilled young women who wear headscarves take part in Arab TV debates. Mothers across the Middle East can even buy their little girls Muslim Barbie dolls, cloaked in black but adorned with handsome and colorful needlework.[186]

In recent decades female painters and graphic artists have developed modern versions of traditional art forms such as calligraphy. Here they reinterpret typical messages allegorically, including verses from the Qur'an.

Of course, many artists are also skilled in other genres—everything from realistic art to more surrealistic representation. Some women art photographers, a number of whom live in exile, focus on exposing women's roles and suppression. They often do so in collages laden with symbolism. Depending on a country's political system and the critical content of individual works, modern art museums in the Middle East are now purchasing and exhibiting art by women.[187]

Since the early 1950s the number of women writers in the Muslim world has risen steadily, as has also the quality of their work in almost all literary genres. Hence it is impossible to mention more than a few.[188] From 1948 on, the Iraqi poet and scholar Nazik al-Mala'ika (1923–2007), who taught at various universities, played a pioneering role, along with her compatriot Badr Shakir al-Sayyab (1926–1963), in what was seen as a revolutionary movement in Arabic: free verse poetry. Moreover, she addressed unusual themes in her poems; for example, she pleaded passionately against the rigidity of pseudo-religious traditions in "To Wash Disgrace" (i.e., with blood: *ghusl al-'ar*), a poem against "honor killings." She also dealt subtly with the topic of love from a sensitive, female point of view.[189] In the early 1970s she wrote tender mystical poems. She moved to Kuwait in 1970, where she lived until she settled in Cairo in 1990. On behalf of the Egyptian Highest Council of Culture, her son and grandson edited a volume of some of her earlier stories in 1997. It was symbolically titled *Al-shams allati wara'a l-qimma* (The Sun behind the Peak).

In recent years the works of women prose writers have become more autobiographical. Depicting the world of women and their families, they expose the injuries inflicted on women inside and outside the family under patriarchy. What is more, they reveal strategies for coping and surviving, ways to live with and assert themselves against overprotective men and family structures—for protection often escalates into control, surveillance, and the authoritarian attempt to dictate women's lives.

One of the first such authors was Latifa al-Zayyat (1925–1996), professor of English studies at the Ain Shams University in Cairo. In 1959 she wrote her sociocritical novel *Al-Bab al-Maftuh* (The Open Door) and later, in 1992, her modern memoir *Hamlat taftish: Awraq shakhsiyya* (literally "The Attack of Control: Personal Papers").[190]

It was only after terminating two unhappy marriages that Egyptian writer Alifa Rifaat (1931–1996) found the space to write her sensitive tales. In one she tells about a little girl's traumatic memories of her circumcision, in another about the torments and dreams of a woman wed to a man who was chosen by her family and whom she does not love.[191]

In 1971 the Egyptian doctor Nawal El Saadawi (b. 1931) caused a stir with her monograph *Al-Mar'a wa-l-jins* (Woman and Sexuality). In it she compares findings from Freudian psychoanalysis, neopsychoanalysis, the Kinsey Report, works by the American sexologists Masters and Johnson, and the anthropologist Margaret Mead on sexual conduct and norms in

Egypt. Despite her often critical analysis, she repeatedly attempts to relativize the conduct of her compatriots. Nevertheless, she lost her position as director of the Cairo department of health after the book was published. The entire topic was taboo in this form, for instance, her explanations of the physiological requirements for the female orgasm. El Saadawi's next books were published in Lebanon. After 1977 everything she wrote was published in Cairo. This included a book on male sexuality, another on the psychological consequences of sexual repression in women and female genital mutilation, and one on the suppression of the Arab woman in family and society across the centuries. This last, *Al-Wajh al-'ari li-l-mar'a al-'arabiyya* (1977; literally "The Naked Face of the Arab Woman"), was published in English as *The Hidden Face of Eve* (1980), a title that correlates with how Westerners stereotype Islamic women. Over the years El Saadawi wrote a large number of books, most of which her husband, Sherif Hetata, revised and translated into English with her approval. She also published many short stories and novels after 1961, for the most part subtle but stern social and religious critiques. They also explore how the thoughts of Egyptian Christians, or more specifically Copts (one of her grandmothers was a Copt), have been shaped by their beliefs and superstitions. These works—such as *Firdaus: Imra'a 'inda nuqtat sifr* (Women at Point Zero, 1977) and *Suqut al-Imam* (The Fall of the Imam, 1987)—are rather intellectual and difficult. In her satirical allegorical novel *Jannat wa-Iblis* (The Innocence of the Devil, 1992), an insane asylum turns into a distorting mirror of the world with its patriarchal, destructive power structures that have been shaped by representatives of the monotheistic world religions and authoritarian states and institutions. In her 1995 autobiography, *Awraqi—Hayati* (literally "My Writings—My Life," published in 2002 under the title *Walking Through Fire*),[192] which she wrote while a visiting professor in the United States—a time when a death warrant had been issued for her in Egypt—she depicts scenes from her lifelong struggle against authoritarian, patriarchal power structures in the family, school, state, and society. Often she also tells—with love and understanding for simple folk—of the fate of previous generations, of women like her mother and grandmother.[193]

Similarly critical is the Moroccan sociologist Fatima Mernissi (b. 1940). She has written several works of nonfiction for a wider audience in French. In them she draws on Arabic historical literature to illustrate the confidence and independence of Arab women over the centuries, and then calls on contemporary women to follow in their footsteps. She critically reflects on and analyzes Islam's understanding of democracy and its concept of modernism while examining negative Western stereotypes of Islam.[194] In *Harem Within* (1994), her light and ironic recollection of her childhood in Fez, she gives an intimate look at women's fate and familial relationships of the period.[195] Mernissi has also ironically explored traditional gender roles in short films.

The women and young girls in a number of eventful tales by the Kuwaiti writer Layla (al-)'Uthman (b. 1945) take deadly revenge on males who have violated them.[196] And while such stories are certainly no more than a psychological outlet, for modern Arab literature they constitute a new and remarkable attempt to address reality. In 2000 the author's metaphorical, sensual description of ocean waves churning into one another in the 1999 novel *Al-Khuruj* (The Departure) led to her being sentenced to two months in prison for "offending public decency and fundamental values of society"; the sentence was reduced on appeal to a fine of 1,000 dinars. The title of her next work, *Yawmiyyat al-sabr wa-l-murr: Maqta' min sirat al-waqi'* (Diaries of Patience and Bitterness: A Slice of Real Life), which came out in 2003, says it all.

In 1964, nine months after the Lebanese writer Layla Ba'labakki (b. 1936) had published the story "Safinat al-hanan ila l-qamar" (Spaceship of Tenderness to the Moon) depicting a couple's passion for each other, the author was charged with "offending public decency" and threatened with six months in jail. She was accused of arousing sexual feelings in readers through her explicit description of a love scene.[197] The author was acquitted, but her book was confiscated. Her 1958 debut novel, *Ana ahya* (I Am Alive), which had been influenced by existentialism, also caused a stir. Its protagonist, the daughter of a well-to-do family, rejects the role being forced on her by her parents and her surroundings and seeks—albeit in vain—her own definition of happiness.

Like Layla Ba'labakki, Hanan al-Shaykh (b. 1945) is from southern Lebanon and of Shi'i descent. She has lived in London since 1982 and first attracted international attention in 1980 with the publication of *Hikayat Zahra* (The Story of Zahra).[198] Operating on several levels and using different voices, this work tells the tragic story of a young woman from Beirut in a world ridden with male violence. The book is set against the Lebanese civil war but also follows the protagonist during an interlude with other Lebanese emigrants in Africa. In 1988 she again drew attention, this time with *Misk al-ghazal* (literally "Gazelle's Musk"; published in English as *Women of Sand and Myrrh* in 1992).[199] She wrote this novel from 1977 to 1982, during a stay in Saudi Arabia. Revolving around four female figures in an unspecified town in the Gulf region, it depicts the frustration and double moral standards in a country with strict gender segregation, where women are banned from public life. Since she also describes a lesbian relationship, the book was prohibited in a number of Arab countries. In her novel *Barid Bayrut* (1993), literally "Beirut Post" but translated as *Beirut Blues*,[200] the main character, a Lebanese woman who lives in exile in London, takes a trip home. After years of absence during the civil war, she experiences the social conditions, her family, and gender relations against the backdrop of her memories of her previous life there. Her novel *Innaha Lundun, ya habibi* (2001), literally "It's London, My Darling," but published under the title *Only in London*,[201] presents the world of Lebanese immigrants in multicultural London from a slightly ironic female perspective.

The very prolific and creative Ghada al-Samman (b. 1942 in Damascus) moved to Beirut in 1969 and founded a publishing house to print her works, before moving to Paris. In her novels *Bayrut 75* (1975)[202] and *Kawabis Bayrut* (1977),[203] she documents the inhumanity of the war and its repercussions. Her short stories, novels, and, more recently, prose poetry—her later works include *Sahra tanakkuriyya li-l-mawta* (Costume Ball for the Dead, 2003) and *Al-Abadiyya—lahzat hubb* (Eternity: The Moment of Love, 2004)—often address the problems of educated Arab workingwomen in a male chauvinistic society, and deal with love, resignation, and self-discovery at jobs of their choice. In interviews, al-Samman has explained that she has no desire to see the world split into men and women, but rather divides it into those who work and those who do not.

Algerian writer and filmmaker Assia Djebar (b. 1936) has won many awards, including the Peace Prize of the German Book Trade in 2000 for her literary oeuvre. Her first novel was *La soif* (Thirst), which came out in French in 1956 in Paris, where she moved after teaching for a time at Tunisian and Algerian universities.[204] Published in 1987, *Ombre Sultane* is another impressive work. It reflects the plight of a man's two wives—one an intellectual, the other a simple woman.[205] Beginning in 1978 Assia Djebar also made documentary films in Algerian dialect. Set against the colonial and postcolonial history of her native land, they portray the diverse fates of women in her country.

Following two earlier novels, Ahlam Mosteghanemi (b. 1953) received widespread acclaim in 1993 for her brilliant work *Dhakirat al-jasad* (Memory in the Flesh). It was the first novel by an Algerian woman in Modern Standard Arabic. (In 1963 the first Algerian constitution had declared Arabic the country's official language, but owing to its long occupation by France, French remained the language of many educated citizens, including writers. A number of attempts were made to alter matters, including educational reforms. On July 5, 1998, Arabic was made Algeria's sole national language. After strong protest from the Berbers, an amendment was adopted recognizing Tamazight as an official language.) Criticism notwithstanding, the book has sold more than 130,000 copies in the Arabic-speaking world, an extraordinary number for a modern Arabic novel; it has also been translated into French and English.[206] In a stream of consciousness, Muteghanemi interlaces memories of her country's colonial era and its disappointing postcolonial days with real and dream sequences of a love affair between an aging exiled man and a young Algerian woman, whom literary scholars see as a symbol for Algeria. The protagonist's double first name—Ahlam ("dreams") and Hayat ("life")—symbolizes how things oscillate between reality and fiction, while demonstrating a proximity to the author, who lived in Paris for many years before residing with her Lebanese husband in Beirut. While living there she published two more novels revolving around a passionate love as seen from the perspective of a young woman writer who expresses her views and reflections in interior monologues.

Since World War I it has become common in Arabic and Persian literature for female characters to embody the hopes of a nation. To a certain
degree this is reminiscent of the allegorical female figures that have existed
in European art since the baroque era. In the Muslim world sculpture first
evolved as a genre, often with nationalistic symbolism, in Egypt around
1900 under the influence of European artists. Since the 1930s, sculptors in
both Egypt and Iraq have created figures of women as symbols of national
strength and hope.[207]

The young Saudi Rajaa Alsanea (Raja' al-Sani'), a student of dentistry at
the University of Chicago, caused an uproar when her debut novel, *Banat
Riyad,* published in Beirut in 2006 (published in English as *The Girls of
Riyadh* in 2007), triggered fierce debates which led to its being prohibited
in her own country before a minister came out unequivocally in favor of
its publication. In the interim, it had been published in Saudi Arabia and
translated into many languages. It received coverage throughout the Arab
world as well as in Europe and the United States. In the book the hopes and
dreams of four young Saudi women from upper-class families are revealed
in the email they exchange. In both their words and actions, her protagonists rebel against fundamentalist constraints. The author cites the Qur'an
and early and modern Arab writings, as well as famous works of world
literature. In doing so she broadens her readers' horizons and provides them
with food for thought.

It was not until the late 1970s that female writers in Saudi Arabia were
allowed—initially anonymously or under a pseudonym—to intervene critically into male discourses on power. They did so in newspapers and magazines, with their poetry, short stories and essays, dramas and novels.[208]
Today their works are displayed at Saudi book fairs, where they are then
debated at gender-segregated events. Nevertheless, some of these writers
have encountered such great opposition from conservative critics (including a few female literary critics) that there have been attempts to prosecute
them and/or to prohibit bookshops from carrying their works. In February
2008, at the Riyadh International Book Fair, which has grown in prestige in
the Arab world in recent decades, a female publisher of Arab descent from
Paris became the first woman ever allowed to be an exhibitor.

Modern Turkish and Iranian authors often address similar problems as
Arab writers.[209] Since the early 1980s the realism of the early years has
given way to more allegorical, reflective, and often strongly introspective
and/or self-conscious depictions of female emotions in male-dominated social networks. This has been particularly the case in Iran since the revolution, with its harsh restrictions for women. Immediately after ascending to
power, Khomeini called on writers to propagate the Islamic Revolution in
their works on the grounds that it had always been an Islamic tradition to
view the pen as superior to the sword. Simin Daneshvar (who was born in
Shiraz in 1921 the daughter of a physician and was an associate professor
at the University of Tehran from 1955 to 1975) was the first Iranian female

writer to publish a volume of short stories in Persian, *Atesh-e khamush* (Fire Quenched), in 1948. Strongly inspired by O'Henry, it soon became popular despite a number of shortcomings. In 1969 her work *Savushun* (*Savush's Mourning,* 1990) was the first novel in Persian by a female writer to be published in Iran. In this and in her later novels and short stories she deals brilliantly with women's issues. She depicts the harsh social and political circumstances and constraints prevailing at the time from a female point of view. In two later essays, published as *Ghoroub-e Jalal* ("Jalal's Sunset" or "The Loss of Jalal") in 1981, she emotionally portrays her beloved but somewhat difficult husband, the famous writer Jalal Al-e Ahmad (1923–1969), and his sudden death.[210] In 1992 Shahin Hannaneh, who was considerably younger than Daneshvar, offered insights previously unknown for Iranian literature into the personal relationships and intimate feelings of more educated, Western-oriented, and rather frustrated women in *Pusht-e derecheha: Guftegu be-hamsaran-e hunarmandan* (Behind the Windows: A Conversation with Artists' Wives). No matter how unusual the presentation of these topics may have been, the fact that women were resorting to more private and intimate spheres can also be seen as a form of escape from the prevailing political circumstances. In novels and short stories, Fattaneh Hajj Seyyed Javadi (b. 1945), Shahrnush Parsipur (b. 1946), Monira Ravanipur (b. 1954), and others portray from a variety of perspectives the problems of women and their families through the generations in a society facing major upheaval. Since the 1950s, poets such as Forugh Farrokhzad (1935–1967), Simin Behbahani (b. 1927), and Tahereh Saffarzadeh (b. 1939) have resisted centuries of "social imprisonment" by males in their poetic depictions of emotions.[211] Over the years their audiences have grown, which has led to larger first editions and to reprints of their works.[212]

Since the mid-1970s a number of Iranian women, some of them well-known historical personalities, have published memoirs. They include the Qajar princess Taj al-Saltanah (1884–1936), who completed her memoirs in 1924, though it was not until 1982 that they were published under the title *Khatirat-e Taj al-Satanah* (published in English in 1993 as *Crowning Anguish: Memoirs of a Persian Princess from the Harem to Modernity,* with a comprehensive introduction by Abbas Amanat); the second wife of Shah Muhammad Reza Pahlavi, Soraya Bakhtiyar (*The Autobiography of H.I.H. Princess Soraya,* 1963); his third wife, Farah Diba, also called Farah Pahlavi (*My Thousand and One Days: An Autobiography,* 1978);[213] and his twin sister, Ashraf Pahlavi (*Faces in a Mirror: Memoirs from Exile,* 1980; and *Never Resigned,* 1984); as well as the Marxist activist Marziye Osku'i (*Khaterati az yek rafiq,* n.d.; Memoirs of a Comrade); the confirmed Muslim Parvin Noubakht (*Sa'at-i Shish: Deryache-ye Marivan,* 1981; Marivan Lake: At Six o'Clock); and the singer and journalist Shusha Guppy (*The Blindfold Horse: Memories of a Persian Childhood,* 1988; and *A Girl in Paris,* 1991). Whereas the memoirs of the three Pahlavis focused more on presenting themselves and justifying their political positions to readers around the world, Osku'i and Noubakht, who as their husbands' good companions conformed to them ideologically, wrote as their propagandists for a domestic audience. In contrast, al-Saltanah and Guppy describe—each from the perspective of her own period and social position—their experiences in a country undergoing radical change, including gradual Westernization and secularization. And while the princesses all tend to give their readers insight into their thoughts and feelings, Guppy—who after studying in Paris never returned to Iran (perhaps because she married a non-Muslim)—takes an informative, almost folkloric approach.

Among the memoirs written since the turn of the twenty-first century by Iranian women living in exile, *Reading Lolita in Tehran* (2003) by literature professor Azar Nafisi (b. 1955) was a sensation, and not just in the United States. The author—who is the daughter of a former mayor of Tehran and one of the first women to be elected to the Iranian parliament—interweaves her own memories of the Iranian Revolution, the Iran-Iraq War (1980–1988), and the impact of these events on the country's inhabitants, especially on intellectuals, both male and female, with her own and her students' responses to a large number of Western works of literature. Focusing primarily on American literature, they read everything from Vladimir Nabokov to Henry James, F. Scott Fitzgerald, and Jane Austen. After ten years of schooling and university in England and the United States, Nafisi began teaching at the University of Tehran in 1978 but was then dismissed for refusing to wear the chador in 1982. With the support of a colleague, she took a position in 1984 at another university in Tehran. Yet in 1995 she decided to resign and to teach a small circle of students in her home. In 1997 she emigrated to the United States with her family because she was no longer allowed to teach English literature as she saw fit. Here literature has become a means of survival or, at the very least, the intellectual counter-world to an almost incomprehensible reality. The author mentions personal matters—for instance, her childhood, marriage, and family—only in passing.

A number of other recent memoirs provide interesting and even suspenseful insights into the experiences of educated women of Iranian origin living in exile. There is, for example, the aforementioned *Persepolis* (2006), Marjane Satrapi's recollections in comic book form, which was quickly turned into an animated film; and the vivid and stirring memoir of the Iranian Jew Roya Hakakian, *Journey from a Land of No: A Girlhood Caught in Revolutionary Iran* (2004). In contrast, the personal account of the illustrious Shirin Ebadi, *Iran Awakening: A Memory of Revolution and Hope* (2006), tells of her painful struggle as a lawyer against religious conservatives and political and social injustice. She also reveals a number of appalling human rights violations in Iran over a period of thirty years. The preliminary manuscript was revised by the journalist Azadeh Moaveni, who, born in exile and socialized in California, also penned her own autobiographical book, *Lipstick Jihad: A Memoir of Growing Up Iranian in America and American in Iran* (2005). To what degree such works—which in both language and

content address interculturally informed or interested readers outside Iran—
are acknowledged in Iran also depends on the thoroughness of airport security controls and/or Internet censorship. One Iranian critic, certainly a loyal
supporter of the regime, has even gone so far as to compare Nafisi's work to
the atrocities committed by American soldiers in Iraq.

Alongside literature criticizing traditional patriarchal conditions, there
is also a strongly emotional, largely devotional body of work by women
in Arabic, Persian, and Turkish. Formulated in rather simple language,
these writings are often nonfictional in nature, and present, for example,
the women of the Prophet's family as role models. Of course a number of
short stories and novels have also been written along these lines. Worth
mentioning here is the Iraqi writer Amina al-Sadr (b. 1938), who wrote
from 1966 on under the pseudonym Bint al-Huda, "Daughter of Guidance."[214] She came from a famous Shi'i family in Iraq and was executed,
along with her brother Musa al-Sadr, for religious dissidence in 1981 under
Saddam Hussein's regime. Another such author was the Egyptian 'A'isha
'Abd al-Rahman (1913–1998), who was born in Damietta, the daughter
of a conservative theologian. She wrote her first sociocritical articles under
the name Bint al-Shati', "Daughter of the Shore," for the semiofficial daily
paper *Al-Ahram*. While a professor at the Ain-Shams University in Cairo
and at several other Arab universities, she wrote a two-volume "rhetorical"
Qur'an commentary (1962 and 1969), which has been reprinted several
times. She also edited numerous classical texts, gave lectures, and wrote
many books on different aspects of classical and modern Arabic literature,
as well as several on the women in Prophet Muhammad's family. In *'Ala al-
jisr: Bayna al-hayat wa-l-mawt* (On the Bridge: Between Life and Death),[215]
published in 1968, the year her husband, the linguist and literary scholar
Amin al-Khuli (1895–1966), died, she describes her education between her
more secular mother and her more theological father, and her ability to assert herself, as the path, predestined by God, leading to "him," the man to
whom she was married for twenty years.

For centuries male theologians had little objection to women passing on
the traditions of the Prophet, for it involved only memory work. By contrast, Qur'an commentary, which entails understanding and interpretation,
remained the privilege of men, and as such an instrument of social power.
After studying theology, Qur'an commentator Hajiyeh Sayyedeh Nosrat
Begom Amin (1886–1983) from Isfahan, who was better known under the
modern pseudonym Banoo-ye Iran or Banoo-ye Isfahan (Daughter of Iran
or Daughter of Isfahan), wrote a number of theological works in Arabic
and Persian. She became the first woman to receive the title of *mujtahid*. In
retrospect, she is highly regarded and serves as a role model for young theologians. This is especially the case because she was also married and gave
birth to eight children, though only one survived to adulthood. Today she
exemplifies correct social norms for pious Iranian women. She also wrote a

fifteen-volume Qur'an commentary, though it has received little attention to date; her interpretation is said to take mystical factors into account.[216]

Presumably inspired by Christian and Jewish feminists, Muslim women in the United States (mostly Black Muslims, but also Muslims of Pakistani descent) began in the mid-1980s to reinterpret those Qur'an verses that deal with the situation of woman in society. Amina Wadud Muhsin, a black Muslim and mother of five children, demanded in *Quran and Woman* (1992) that the sacred book be reinterpreted to suit the times—as this was a prerequisite for "female empowerment." Indeed she claimed it was the misinterpretations of male theologians that had led to the suppression of women in Islamic countries. According to Muhsin, women are men's equals in the Qur'an, and mutual respect and affection are indispensable. The Qur'an merely acknowledges social differences among people of the same sex, that is, between one man and the next, and one woman and the next. Hence Qur'an 4:34, which is usually translated along the lines of "Men are in charge of women, because Allah hath made the one of them to excel over the other, and because they spend of their property (for the support of women)," is to be understood not as a reference to the preordained subordination of woman to man by God, also based on men's financial superiority, but as a command to take responsibility for each other.

Riffat Hassan (Rif'at Hasan), of Pakistani descent and a professor in the Department of Religious Studies at the University of Louisville in Kentucky, drafted a paper, in cooperation with other Muslim feminists in the United States, titled "Religious Human Rights in the Quran." It includes the right to a "good life."[217] Such activities have drawn attention in the Middle East, as evident in Iran, where daughters of famous ayatollahs, so-called "chador feminists," now fight for increased political, social, and economic rights by reinterpreting the verses of the Qur'an. Similar to Muslim women in other countries, and those around the world for generations before them, they are putting into practice a tactic that the leftist Turkish feminist Deniz Kandiyoti called "bargaining with patriarchy" a generation ago. In contrast, Muslim feminists today speak of "gender jihad," the (resolute and verbal) "feminist religious battle" for more women's rights.[218]

Translated by Catherine Kerkhoff-Saxon

VIII

Islamist Groups and Movements

(Guido Steinberg and Jan-Peter Hartung)

1. Islamism

Islamist groups and movements have left their mark on the history of the Muslim world since the first half of the twentieth century. Since the 1980s and 1990s they have even become important actors on the world stage. They can be found everywhere Muslims live, including the large diasporas in Europe, North and South America, and Australia. There are currently so many different groups that even specialists have difficulty keeping track of them, so this chapter can make no claim to completeness. Its objective is to introduce the most important groups, discuss their characteristics, and show trends in the development of Islamism as a whole.

In this context the term "Islamism" will be used synonymously with the widely used expressions "political Islam" and "fundamentalism," as well as with the term "integrism," which is common in the French-speaking world. Islamists demand that Islam govern all aspects of private and public life. They even claim to offer a religiously based solution to every problem cropping up in society. This attitude is reflected most clearly in their call for the introduction of the shariʿa, which they see as an all-encompassing system of laws and values founded directly on the texts of revelation (the Qurʾan and sunna). As a rule, Islamists differ from other Muslims in that they offer their interpretation of Islam as a political program and equate others' positions with infidelity—at least implicitly.[1]

Islamist movements have a strong affinity with the idealized early age of Islam, the period of the "pious elders" (*al-salaf al-salih*). They are thus linked to the classical Salafiyya, which emerged in the Middle East in the late nineteenth century. At the time, European expansion provoked a debate on the causes of Muslim weakness, one that continues to the present day. Many Muslims felt there was a need to explain and overcome the discrepancy between foreign Christian rule and the conviction that they were themselves in possession of God's true and final revelations. While secular Muslims called for full-scale modernization along the lines of Western states, the Salafiyya emerged as a major counter-movement. Its leaders, including Jamal al-Din al-Afghani (1839–1897), Muhammad 'Abduh (1849–1905), and 'Abd al-Rahman Kawakibi 1849–1902), argued that Muslims could regain their former power only by returning to the purity of early Islam.[2] To this end they formulated the vision of a highly idealized seventh-century society in Medina whose ethical model Muslims needed to emulate in order to restore Islam to its former status in the world. They thus lived out a slogan espoused by many revivalist movements in Muslim history.[3]

The primary goal of the Salafis was a peaceful renewal of society using the forces of their own revived tradition. There was, however, another movement closely connected with the classical Salafiyya—one that in many cases could be distinguished only analytically—which propagated a political rather than a spiritual and moral understanding of reform. This movement had its roots in several religious currents that had evolved in the eighteenth and nineteenth centuries in central Arabia, northwest India, Yemen, northern Nigeria, and the northern Sahara. Prominent representatives are the Deoband school in India and the central Arabian Wahhabiyya. While the Deobandis—along with other scholarly reform movements— provided the intellectual weaponry for many Islamists in South Asia, the Wahhabiyya exerted an influence on a large number of twentieth-century Islamists in the Arab world. One of these was the scholar and intellectual Rashid Rida (1865–1935), who was born in Ottoman Syria and is often mentioned in the same breath as the representatives of the classical Salafiyya noted earlier, but who can more accurately be described as synthesizing Salafiyya and Wahhabiyya. Rida was a pupil of Muhammad 'Abduh but, in contrast to his teacher, was more of an "ideology entrepreneur" who ran a transnational network of various reformist and Islamist groups out of Cairo. As such Rida became the most important intellectual father figure of Hasan al-Banna (1906–1949), the founder of the Egyptian Muslim Brotherhood.

Despite its strong fixation on the past, Islamism was primarily a response to the challenges of modernity and a protest against the Muslims' own governments, which were perceived as tyrannical and blamed for the Muslim world's socioeconomic problems, cultural alienation, and political weakness. That Islamism is a modern phenomenon can also be seen in the Islamists' critical engagement with modern ideas such as the concept of revolution,[4] as well as with modern organizational forms and techniques. Furthermore, these groups grappled intensely with the West, which they perceived as all-powerful and which they blamed for a large share of the problems in the Muslim world. This criticism remained largely rhetorical until the 1990s, since before that time Islamists were bent on assuming power in their own states and defending themselves against nonreligious indigenous interpretive models.

In the last two decades of the twentieth century there was a trend toward transnational communication and organization among Islamist groups. This trend reflected the increased interaction known as "globalization" observable throughout the world. As a result of international networking, Islamist groups that had previously been unable to play any major political role at home now had an easier time gaining support and refuges. This could be seen on a large scale among militant groups, the best-known example being al-Qaʿida, founded by Osama bin Laden (b. 1957). But nonviolent Islamist organizations, including both the Hizb al-tahrir (Islamic Liberation Party)— which was originally a Palestinian group—and the South Asian Tablighi Jamaʿat (Missionary Society), seized the opportunities for expanded international networking. Above all this meant communicating via the Internet, which had become accessible to broader groups in most Muslim countries in the 1990s.[5]

2. The Muslim Brotherhood

The first Islamist movements emerged in the 1920s. In 1928 the elementary school teacher Hasan al-Banna founded the Egyptian Muslim Brotherhood (al-Ikhwan al-muslimun) and, together with Abu l-Aʿla al-Maududi (1903– 1979), became the most important pioneer of political Islam in the twentieth century.[6] Al-Banna and his followers worked to renew, unify, and strengthen Egyptian society and the Muslim *umma,* primarily in defense against Western cultural influences. They based their efforts on a political interpretation of Islam, one centered on the shariʿa.[7] In his missives (*rasaʾil*), al-Banna elaborated the group's ideological principles, though it must be noted that he wielded more influence as the charismatic leader (*al-murshid al-ʿamm*) of the strictly hierarchical organization than as a systematic thinker.[8] The organization had a mass base as early as the mid-1940s. Its members came from all strata of society, though the majority were members of the newly emerging urban middle classes as well as farmers. Scholars from al-Azhar University in Cairo, such as Muhammad al-Ghazali (1917–1996) and Yusuf al-Qaradawi (b. 1921), were also among the first Muslim Brothers.

In the period up to the late 1930s the Muslim Brothers aimed for gradual change, which they wanted to effect chiefly through primary education, public relations work, and charity services. Al-Banna did not reject the Egyptian state as such but took action to transform it gradually. In addition to the annulment of all laws violating shariʿa, he demanded that the party system be abolished, since he believed it did more to divide than to unify the nation. While the Muslim Brothers did not call for armed revolution, they did not reject the use of force in principle. Their relations with other political groups changed with the overall political situation. Whenever they came under pressure, as in their fight against Gamal Abdel Nasser (Jamal ʿAbd al-Nasir, 1918–1970), they attempted to cooperate with other groups, but

their relations with non-Islamist—and especially with left-wing elements—
were otherwise characterized by great friction. In this early phase they were
highly intolerant of Muslims who did not share their ideas about the inter-
relatedness of religion and the state. At the Fifth General Conference of the
Muslim Brotherhood in Cairo in 1939, al-Banna formulated a multistage
model, saying that the phase of gradual spiritual and ethical preparations
had ended, and he would now intensify efforts to spread the Muslim Brotherhood's message. He continued to regard the use of force as a last resort,
but henceforward other parts of the organization increasingly turned to
militancy. In the early 1940s the Muslim Brotherhood set up the "secret apparatus" (*al-jihaz al-sirri*), and in the years that followed its members were
blamed for many acts of violence against Egyptian politicians and foreign
institutions.[9] When a Muslim Brother murdered the Egyptian prime minister in 1948, the state struck back for the first time: al-Banna was murdered
in February 1949, allegedly by the Egyptian secret service.

Starting in the late 1930s, the Muslim Brotherhood also gained a foothold
in neighboring states. In addition to Sudan, Jordan, Lebanon, Palestine, and
Iraq, it played an important political role in Syria under the leadership of
Mustafa al-Siba'i (1915–1964). At times prominent members of the organization even held government positions there. It was not until the start of
Ba'th Party rule in 1963 that a period of repression began, which reached a
preliminary peak in the Hama revolt in 1964. Between 1979 and 1982 Islamist groups waged a guerrilla war against the state. The shelling of Hama
by government troops in February 1982 marked the Islamists' defeat. A
key figure in internationalizing the Muslim Brotherhood was the Palestinian
mufti Muhammad Amin al-Husayni (1895–1974), who tried to make the
"liberation" of Palestine a central concern of Islamist groups.[10]

The decisive turning point in the history of the Egyptian Muslim Brotherhood was the suppression of its activities by the Free Officers Regime, following a failed attempt by a Muslim Brother to assassinate President Nasser
in 1954. From this point on its relationship with the state was marked by
repression. A second wave of arrests followed in 1965, culminating in the
execution of Sayyid Qutb (1906–1966), the most important intellectual driving force behind the militant Muslim Brothers. The Egyptian government's
decision to execute Qutb, who had been imprisoned on and off starting in
1954, testifies to just how dangerous it considered his ideology. His experience behind bars seems to have contributed significantly to a process of
radicalization that can be reconstructed in his prison writings. His book
Ma'alim fi l-tariq (*Milestones*) became the manifesto of militant Islamism
in the second half of the twentieth century.[11] In this work Qutb offers a
concise description of a revolutionary ideology that largely abandoned the
course taken by Hasan al-Banna. Qutb declared the Egyptian government
to be faithless and appealed for armed resistance (*jihad bi-s-sayf*) against
Nasser. A large number of Egyptian militants cited these ideas in the 1970s,
and Qutb's works continue to shape the ideology of violent Islamists today.

Radical groups emerged within the Muslim Brotherhood at the same time that the core organization was becoming more moderate. The latter made its peace with the Egyptian state and was offered the opportunity to reorganize under President Anwar el-Sadat (1918–1981). Yet it continues to be officially banned even if it is allowed to operate in a narrowly defined political framework and a few of its members run for parliamentary elections.

Because of the repressive state measures against the Muslim Brothers in Egypt and Syria, the organization shifted many of its activities to Europe. The Islamic Center in Geneva, which the Egyptian Muslim Brother Sa'id Ramadan (1926–1994) founded after escaping from exile in Syria in 1958, became the center of a network that connects Islamist figures and groups from the Middle East and South Asia with those in Europe and North America. Western converts such as Muhammad Asad (born Leopold Weiss, 1900–1992) and the American Maryam Jamila (born Margret Marcus, 1934) have played an important role in this regard.[12]

Ever since, branches of the Muslim Brotherhood have shaped political developments in other Arab countries as well. Worth mentioning is Hasan al-Turabi (b. 1932), the chairman of the Sudanese National Islamic Front (al-Jabha al-islamiyya al-qaumiyya), one of the world's leading Islamist thinkers. Together with the military, al-Turabi managed to seize power in Khartoum in the 1989 coup d'état, but it became clear in the 1990s that the Muslims Brothers were mere junior partners to the military. Thus their accession to power in Sudan turned out to be only a brief episode that ended with al-Turabi's arrest in 2001. In contrast, many Muslim Brothers—such as those in Kuwait and especially Jordan—were integrated into their home countries' political systems and attempted to give their demands added weight by participating in elections. One example is the Muslim Brotherhood in Jordan, or rather the organization it founded, the Islamic Action Front (Jabhat al-'amal al-islami), which regularly takes part in elections and supports the rule of the Hashemite royal family.[13] Academics and analysts continue to dispute whether this is a tactical maneuver or a sign of actual moderation.

3. Groups in South Asia

After the Mughal Empire collapsed in the eighteenth century, many Muslim thinkers saw the situation of the Muslims living there as critical. The dramatic suppression of the 1857 revolt by the troops of the British East India Company heightened this impression. Various scholarly movements emerged in this period, and all of them saw it as their mission both to guide the Muslim communities of the subcontinent back to true piety by reforming religious education and to restore the preeminent cultural and political status once enjoyed by Muslims, especially during the Mughal period. The first important movement was the purist Ahl-i hadith, which was closely associated with the central Arabian Wahhabiyya. The key items on its agenda were a strict rejection of all existing schools of law and popular religious practices, above all the pious visitation of graves and the related cult of saints. One of its main adversaries was a movement of Hanafi scholars that founded a seminary in the northern Indian town of Deoband in 1867 (dar al-ʿulum) and that was able to quickly set up a network of religious schools throughout the subcontinent. Over time, the conflicts over legal theory between these two movements led to the radicalization of subgroups in both camps as they attempted to recruit as large a following as possible.[14]

Deserving special attention are three of the subgroups in the Deoband movement that were founded directly after the collapse of the caliphate movement in 1924. The first is the Jamʿiyyat-i ʿulamaʾ-i Hind (JUH, Society of Indian Scholars), an organization that supported the Indian National Congress under Gandhi and Nehru and that opposed the separatist plans of Muslim spokesmen. The most prominent representative of these separatist tendencies was the All-India Muslim League, headed by Muhammad ʿAli Jinnah (1876–1947).[15] The second subgroup that emerged from the Deobandi movement is the Tablighi Jamaʿat (TJ), founded by Muhammad Ilyas Kandhalawi (1885–1944) in the early 1920s. Its intellectual center is Mazahir al-ʿulum, the Deobandi seminary in Saharanpur in northern India. This emphatically apolitical movement is widely regarded as one of the most successful transnational Muslim movements worldwide. Islamist groups are particularly attracted to its effective, network-like organizational structure and its missionary goal of guiding Muslims back to their original piety.[16]

It was also this very movement that made a great impression on Abu l-Aʿla al-Maududi on a 1939 visit to its headquarters in Delhi two years before he founded the Jamaʿat-i islami (JiI, Islamic Society). Maududi, who had been educated at both modern educational institutes and a Deobandi college, was the first systematic thinker of Islamism. His conception of Islam as an all-encompassing "life system" (*nizam-i zindagi*), developed in the 1930s, is founded on an idiosyncratic interpretation of four Qurʾanic terms which he regarded as axioms of an Islamic worldview. In deductive fashion he formulated the concept of "Islamic rule" (*hukumat-i islami*) as a "theo-democracy" (*jumhuriyyat-i ilahi*), which in his view was a necessary precondition for a norm-based religious lifestyle. It was in this point that he differed greatly from the grassroots approach of the Tablighi Jamaʿat. According to Maududi, the theo-democracy had to be established through an "Islamic revolution" (*inqilab-i islami*). The JiI, which Maududi greatly inspired and led for nearly four decades, served as a paradigm for this understanding of society. Most of its members came from the educated lower middle classes that were emerging in cities. The JiI was meant to provide a counterweight to the Muslim League's nationalist ideology, which had been put into practice in the foundation of the Islamic Republic of Pakistan in 1947. Nationalisms of various hues continue to be seen as bogeymen by the JiI in Pakistan and Bangladesh, and it was only during the military dictatorship of General Zia ul-Haq (Ziya' al-Haqq) between 1977 and 1988 that the state supported JiI. Its organizational structure is strictly hierarchical and resembles that of the Muslim Brotherhood.

The JiI's strategy in Pakistan was mainly directed at organizing mass campaigns, but these often resulted in violent clashes with other groups and the government's security forces. JiI began taking part in elections as a political party in 1970, but with only moderate success. During the rule of Zia ul-Haq, JiI increasingly focused its activities on education, founding a nationwide network of schools that combined religious curricula and the use of modern communications technologies.[17]

It was again the TJ, however, that played an instrumental role in spreading Maududi's ideology, above all in Arabic-speaking regions. After a short time, a number of the JiI's early supporters from the scholarly milieu—particularly Sayyid Abu l-Hasan 'Ali Nadwi (1914–1999), later chairman of the Nadwat al-'ulama' ([National] Council of Scholars)—turned away from the politically focused JiI and embraced the more ethically oriented TJ. In efforts to internationalize this missionary movement, these figures not only used their diverse contacts with the Arabic-speaking world but also introduced their new colleagues to Maududi's ideas. In the 1950s, for example, Sayyid Qutb was exposed to elements of Maududi's thinking in this way, and there is evidence that he integrated them into his own thoughts as well.[18]

The third subgroup to emerge from the Deobandis during the Indian independence movement was Jam'iyyat-i 'ulama'-i Islam (JUI, Society of Scholars of Islam). In contrast to the majority of Deobandis organized in the JUH, the JUI consisted of a small group of Deobandi scholars who supported the separatism of Jinnah's Muslim League. Nevertheless, in the ensuing constitutional debate in Pakistan the JUI held radical positions similar to those of the JiI. In the final phase of the civil protests against the regime of General Muhammad Ayub Khan (in power 1958–1969), there was a schism in the JUI that produced a political party strongly rooted in the Pashtun environment of Baluchistan and the Northwest Frontier Province. After the 1970 elections this party headed the governments of two provinces. It was not until 1993, however, that changing political alliances secured the JUI—headed by Maulana Fazl al-Rahman (b. 1953)—a brief role in the central government. Even so, the ultraconservative JUI is considered the most influential force in the Pashtun tribal regions; it controls the majority of mosques and religious educational centers in Pakistan.[19]

4. Militant Groups in the 1970s and 1980s

The first trends toward radicalization in the Arab world were observable among young Egyptian Islamists in the 1960s and 1970s. Although they followed the teachings of Sayyid Qutb, they went one step further than their mentor by declaring those Muslims who lived in the allegedly un-Islamic

Egyptian society to be infidels. Sayyid Qutb, for his part, insisted on making a sharp distinction between Islam and *jahiliyya*, literally ignorance, whereby the term, in its traditional use, refers mostly to the conditions in pre-Islamic Arabia. In Qutb's view, Egyptian Muslims lived in a "new *jahiliyya*." Although he thereby implied that the Egyptian state was faithless, he evaded the question as to whether individuals could be declared infidels and therefore outside the protection of the law. His pupils, however, were more radical. Many believed that an armed jihad against the state, its rulers, and the population was a fundamental religious duty.[20] Their radical positions were mainly the result of the brutal repression and long prison terms they had endured. While the mainstream of the Muslim Brotherhood swore off violence, militant groups broke off from it. This reveals the influence of the Wahhabi ideology, in which the excommunication of Muslims (*takfir*) has played a central role since the eighteenth century. With the support of the Saudi Arabian state, the Wahhabiyya managed to disseminate this ideology starting in the 1960s.[21]

In the early 1970s militant Islamists in Egypt began carrying out attacks on state institutions and members of government. The best-known organization was the Jama'at al-takfir wa-l-hijra (Excommunication and Migration Group), which was led by former Muslim Brother Shukri Ahmad Mustafa (1942–1978), and was responsible for the 1977 kidnapping and killing of the Egyptian minister of religious affairs. The leading members of this group, including Mustafa himself, were arrested in 1978 and subsequently executed.[22] Although they called themselves Jama'at al-muslimin (Group of Muslims) and were referred to as al-Takfir wa-l-hijra only by the Egyptian public, militant Islamists have increasingly begun to adopt this name, because the two words in it clearly describe their intellectual attitude: they accuse the Muslims who oppose them of unbelief (*takfir*) and withdraw from their company (*hijra*). Finally, they wage an armed jihad against them. Today *takfiri* has become a common Arab designation for the most militant followers of a worldwide jihad against the West.[23]

In the course of the 1970s additional militant groups formed and carried out violent attacks on their governments. The Egyptian organizations included the Jama'a islamiyya (Islamic Group), but it was above all the so-called Jihad Group that caused an international stir when it assassinated President Anwar el-Sadat in October 1981. Its mastermind was Muhammad 'Abd al-Salam Faraj (1952–1982). In his work *Al-Farida al-gha'iba* (The Neglected Duty) he calls it a religious obligation to lead an armed jihad against a government that does not rule in accordance with Islamic principles.[24]

In 1979 militant Islamism swept over Saudi Arabia as well. On the first day of the fifteenth Islamic century (1 Muharram 1400, coinciding with November 21, 1979), a group of several hundred Islamists, mainly Saudis, occupied the Grand Mosque in Mecca (*al-haram al-sharif*) and took a large number of pilgrims hostage.[25] The Islamists demanded that Saudi society return to the lifestyle of the "pious elders," and they sharply criticized the ruling dynasty's alliance with the United States. Their action had a strong millenarian dimension, since their leader, Juhayman al-'Utaybi, claimed that one of his companions, Muhammad ibn 'Abdallah al-Qahtani, was the anticipated mahdi, or "the Rightly Guided One." It took two weeks for Saudi troops, assisted by French special forces, to subdue the occupiers. Al-Qahtani was killed during the fighting, and al-'Utaibi and sixty-three of his followers were subsequently executed in January 1980.

5. Shi'ite Islamism

Since Shi'a Islam was originally a politico-religious movement, its adherents would seem predestined for state-oriented activism. The topos of the struggle for the social justice promised in the Qur'an—the fight to overcome real conditions—crops up very early among Shi'ites. For instance, this topos can be found among both the ninth-century Qarmatiyya sect in southern Iraq and later among the Isma'iliyya. The violent activism of the "assassins" made one branch of this latter group infamous in the Middle Ages.

In the 1960s in Iran these radical and often militant protest traditions were carried on by a number of groups that were united against the rule of Mohammed Reza Shah Pahlavi (r. 1944–1979) and organized in the Liberation Movement of Iran (Nahzat-i azadi-yi Iran). Influenced by Marxist-Leninist ideologies that can be found, not least, in the writings of 'Ali Shari'ati (1933–1977), groups split off from this movement between 1963 and 1977 to pursue militant activism, including the Iranian People's Mujahidin (Sazman-i mujahidin-i khalq-i Iran).[26]

But even the Shi'ite clergy, who had previously supported the state, began rebelling against the Pahlavi regime. As early as the 1940s Ayatollah Ruhollah Musavi Khomeini (1902–1989) sharply criticized the shah's anticlerical policies in his writings. In his influential work *Hukumat-i islami ya vilayat-i faqih* (The Islamic State, or The Trusteeship of the Jurist), Khomeini drew on a series of lectures given to students of theology in 1970 during his long exile in the Iraqi city of Najaf. Following the 1979 revolution this work served as a blueprint for the political system of the Islamic Republic of Iran. Nevertheless, the euphoria that the victory of the Islamic Revolution unleashed among Islamist groups worldwide quickly faded, as the rift between the two large Muslim denominations was simply too large. As a result, the revolution had a sustained impact only on Shi'ite minorities in the Middle East.[27]

Shi'ite protest movements emerged in Lebanon roughly at the same time as in Iran. In a period of increasingly rapid social change, they aimed to improve the Shi'ites' underprivileged social status, which had been exacerbated by the civil war (1975–1990). The best known among them was initially the Movement of the Deprived (Harakat al-mahrumin), with an armed wing called Battalion of Lebanese Resistance (Afwaj al-muqawama al-lubnaniyya), which became better known by its acronym AMAL (Hope). This movement was founded in 1974 under Ayatollah Musa al-Sadr (b. 1925), who went missing in Libya in 1978. It was above all the Israeli invasion of southern Lebanon and the victorious revolution in Iran that inspired a group of Shi'ite clergymen to found the Hizbullah (Hizb Allah, or Party of God in Arabic) in the Bekaa Valley. Their stated objective was an Islamic revolution based on the Iranian model, which was to result from the "just defensive war" (*al-jihad al-difa'i*) declared on Israel in 1985.[28] The Hizbullah has meanwhile come to terms with the Syrian-dominated political system in postwar Lebanon. It has taken part in elections, and MPs have come from its ranks. While the extermination of Israel continues to be high on the Hizbullah's agenda, it is a matter of dispute whether it still aims to set up an Islamic state in Lebanon.

The widespread trend toward politicization in the 1970s also affected the Shi'ites in Iraq, but the limited ability of Shi'ite Islamism to mobilize support in the country was shown during the First Gulf War (1980–1988), when the majority of the Shi'ites fought against Iran on the side of the regime of Saddam Hussein (1937–2006). That was possible not least because Saddam was able to keep the Shi'ites under control after he had Muhammad Baqir al-Sadr (1935–1980) executed, the most important Islamist scholar among the Shi'ites in Iraq at the time and a staunch opponent of the ruling Ba'th Party. Together with several like-minded companions, Sadr co-founded the Da'wa Party in the late 1950s and rose to become its leading thinker in Najaf in the 1960s and 1970s.[29] After its bloody suppression by Saddam's regime, the party did not play an important role again until the 1991 revolt, when Shi'ite groups in southern Iraq rebelled during the Second Gulf War. They were quickly put down, however. It is impossible to say what long-term consequences the "liberation" of Iraqi Shi'ites during the U.S. war against Iraq beginning in 2003 will bring. The Da'wa Party has been working in the government in close collaboration with local representatives of the United States, but it must compete with other Shi'ite groups. It is also difficult to say how the events in Iraq will influence the plight of the Shi'ites' brethren in Saudi Arabia and Bahrain. Starting in the 1970s, the Islamist movements in these countries were also affected by the trend toward mobilization. They turned toward "Khomeinism" but took moderate positions in the 1990s and became reconciled with their respective regimes.[30] Even so, since the Shi'ites in these countries are discriminated against both socioeconomically and culturally, tensions continue to exist with their Sunni rulers.

6. Kashmir, Afghanistan, and the Taliban

Current Islamic-motivated militancy in Kashmir began in 1989, when the Jammu and Kashmir Liberation Front (JKLF) called for armed resistance against the massive presence of Indian troops. Its roots extend back to the late nineteenth century, however, when the first Ahl-i hadith arrived in the Kashmir Valley, which had previously been heavily influenced by folk religious traditions. Their radical agitation for a form of Islam cleansed of these traditions not only set in train a process of cultural self-affirmation among the Kashmiri Muslims but also resulted in competition over religious leadership in the valley. This competition revolved around the office of the chief preacher (*mir wa'iz*), domiciled in Srinagar. Around 1910 two men lay claim to this office: the Hanafi Mir Wa'iz-i Hamadani, who represented indigenous religious traditions, and the Mir Wa'iz-i Kashmir, who was associated with reform movements originating outside the region. To the present day, all struggles in and around Kashmir reflect these religious tensions.[31]

The military conflict between India and Pakistan over Kashmir, which goes back to 1947, also led to the political polarization of the Kashmiris. While the choice of remaining in the Republic of India was hardly considered an option by residents of the region, they were of different opinions as to whether self-government or integration into Pakistan was preferable. The internal conflicts over the future of Kashmir Valley intensified owing to a number of factors: the integration of both the northern valley and Pashtun tribal territories (the "Northern Areas") into the Pakistani state after 1947, the emergence of further groups such as the Jama'at-i islami (JiI), and the support that Zia ul-Haq's government provided Afghan mujahidin in their struggle against Soviet troops. The withdrawal of the Soviet military from Afghanistan in 1988–89 and the outbreak of civil war also impacted Kashmir: the fight against the ongoing presence of Indian troops, which had long been supported by the JKLF and which culminated in the aforementioned 1989 call for armed resistance, increasingly gave way to activities by militant groups operating out of Pakistan. In many cases these groups had formed during the jihad against the Soviet occupation of Afghanistan, and their members were often recruited during the annual mass gatherings of the TJ (Tablighi Jama'at) in Raiwind near Lahore.[32] Since 1993 the most important of these militant groups has been Lashkar-i tayyiba (the Pure Army), the armed wing of the Markaz-i da'wat wa irshad (Center for Preaching and Guidance), which was founded in 1986 in the Pakistani province of Punjab by Ahl-i hadith.[33] A rival is the All Parties Hurriyat Conference, which was also launched in 1993 and was run for a time by the Mir Wa'iz-i Kashmir. The conference unites indigenous groups such as the JKLF and JiI (Jammu wa Kashmir), and it has been working with the Indian government to achieve a nonviolent solution to the conflict.

Whereas the armed struggle in Kashmir was strongly influenced by Pakistani Ahl-i hadith, a prominent Islamist force emerged in Pakistan in the schools of the JUI (Jam'iyyat-i 'ulama'-i islam), which were rooted in the Deoband tradition. This force ended the Afghan civil war in 1994 and established the Islamic Emirate of Afghanistan in the period between 1995 and 2002: the Taliban.

As discussed earlier, the JUI wields great influence, especially in the Pashtun tribal areas. Most of its schools are situated in the northwestern border provinces, and among them the Dar al-ʿulum al-haqqaniyya seminary in Akora Khattak has achieved special prominence.[34] After 1979 these schools became increasingly popular among Afghan refugees, and during the civil war in Afghanistan (1989–1994) they became training grounds for the Taliban. Nevertheless, the Dar al-ifta' wa-l-irshad (House for Expertise and Guidance) in Karachi was their ideological center, and it was there that Deobandi doctrine was adapted to the specific situation in Afghanistan. Its head, Mufti Rashid Ahmad (b. 1922), is also thought to have been the teacher of the enigmatic Taliban leader Mulla Muhammad ʿUmar (b. ca. 1959).

But only a part of the Taliban's military success in Afghanistan is attributable to its purist doctrine. Its great initial popularity can be explained by two factors: first, it was seen as a force that was able to end the anarchic conditions in the country, and second, it was a relatively homogeneous ethnic Pashtun movement that could count on tribal solidarity, especially in southern Afghanistan. Even so, following the conquest of Kabul in September 1996 and the alliance with bin Laden's al-Qaʿida network, the repressive Taliban regime encountered increased opposition at home and abroad, which ultimately led to its removal in December 2001 by U.S. troops and their allies.[35]

7. Al-Qaʿida and International Arab Networks

Arab volunteers had taken part in military operations against Soviet troops in Afghanistan, and in Peshawar in northwestern Pakistan a large community of exiles emerged that brought together Islamist activists from the entire Arab world. Their most important leader, the Palestinian ʿAbdallah ʿAzzam (1941–1989), formulated the theoretical foundations for an armed jihad against Soviet occupation troops in his work *Al-Difaʿ ʿan aradi l-muslimin ahamm furud al-aʿyan* (The Defense of the Muslim Lands Is the First Individual Obligation). According to ʿAzzam, when enemy forces invade Muslim territories, jihad is an obligation for every Muslim (*fard ʿain*). ʿAzzam brought this view to bear on Palestine and other occupied Muslim countries. The first international Islamist networks formed in Afghanistan—initially under the leadership of ʿAzzam, then under bin Laden—and they later provided a foundation for the emergence of al-Qaʿida. For the "Islamist International," current conflicts became increasingly important and replaced the transnational symbols that had previously guided Islamist actions. These conflicts included the wars in Kashmir, Afghanistan, Bosnia, Chechnya, and Iraq (from 2003), as well as the Israeli-Palestinian conflict. The Soviet invasion of Afghanistan, in particular, mobilized Islamists worldwide to participate actively in the armed resistance.

After the Soviet withdrawal, many "Arab Afghans" returned to their homes, most going to Saudi Arabia, Egypt, Yemen, and Algeria. Many took part in the revolts that broke out in 1992 against the governments in Egypt and Algeria. Others served as mercenaries or volunteers in the wars in Bosnia, Kosovo, Chechnya, Tajikistan, the Philippines, and Kashmir.

In the early 1990s the Saudi citizen Osama bin Laden began molding the dispersed Afghanistan veterans into an international organization. Bin Laden had spent most of the 1980s in Pakistan and Afghanistan, and in close cooperation with ʿAzzam he had provided logistical aid for the insurgents there. As the son of a prominent Saudi construction magnate with a Yemenite background, bin Laden had excellent ties to wealthy businessmen in the Gulf states, who made a large financial contribution to the struggle. After his return to Saudi Arabia, bin Laden clashed with the ruling family. Following the Iraqi occupation of Kuwait in August 1990, the government called in American troops to protect the kingdom against a possible Iraqi invasion, which bin Laden considered a sacrilege. Because of his protest, he was forced to leave Saudi Arabia for Sudan, then ruled by Hassan al-Turabi. Under mounting pressure from the United States he was also expelled from this country in spring 1996. He made his way to Afghanistan, where an unprecedented string of victories had put the Taliban in control of nearly the entire country. Under its protection he succeeded in setting up al-Qaʿida and in transforming it into an international organization. In the programmatic jihad declaration issued on August 23, 1996, bin Laden stated that his principal goal was to overthrow the Saudi ruling family, and he also declared war on the United States for occupying the "land of the two holy sites."[36]

Finally, in 1997–98, al-Qaʿida took on the form that it was to keep until late 2001. At the time, the Egyptian Ayman al-Zawahiri (b. 1951) joined bin Laden's Saudi-dominated organization with parts of the Egyptian Jihad Group and the Jamaʿa islamiyya. Al-Qaʿida now devoted itself increasingly to the international struggle against the West. The declaration of the Islamic World Front for the Jihad against Jews and Crusaders (al-Jabha al-islamiyya al-ʿalamiyya li-jihad al-yahud wa-l-salibiyyin) in February 1998 provided a programmatic foundation for the revised strategy.[37] Beginning in 1997–98, the new group concentrated on American targets and agreed on an anti-American strategy, which was first put into action through the attacks on the U.S. embassies in Dar es Salaam and Nairobi in August 1998. The attacks on the World Trade Center and the Pentagon on September 11, 2001, were a logical consequence of this new strategy, which was aimed at forcing the United States to withdraw from the Muslim world as the first step toward overthrowing the governments there, primarily those in Egypt and Saudi Arabia. Since the mid-1990s a large number of Egyptians have assumed leading positions in al-Qaʿida, partly because of the end of the revolt in Egypt in 1997.[38] The United States struck back immediately, and by winter 2001–2 al-Qaʿida had lost its base in Afghanistan. The ensuing period saw the emergence of two lines of development.

First, in 1996 al-Qaʿida began attempting to bring various militant organizations and figures under its control and to integrate them into the existing transnational organization. The most prominent example was Khalid Shaykh Muhammad (b. 1965), a Kuwaiti of Baluchi descent who was the chief architect of the attacks on September 11 and who had been involved in the first bombing of the World Trade Center in 1993. In 1994–95 Khalid Shaykh Muhammad also laid plans in the Philippines to blow up American planes over the Pacific after they had taken off from airports in Southeast and East Asia. Al-Qaʿida had only limited success integrating these groups into its organization, and after 2002 it lost control over them when their followers fled and some returned to their homelands. Lacking central coordination, it was unable to organize major attacks on the scale of September 11. Instead it increasingly turned to regional targets, as demonstrated by attacks in Saudi Arabia, Morocco, and Turkey in 2003. The result of this decentralization was that militant Islamism once again became a mainly regional problem—as in the period before 1997.

Second, the leaders' diminishing control gave individual groups the opportunity to establish rival networks that drew on al-Qaʿida's ideology. The most important figure in this context was the Jordanian Abu Musʿab al-Zarqawi (1966–2006). With his Jamaʿat al-tawhid wa-l-jihad (Group of the Oneness [of God] and the Just War) based in Iraq, he became the most dangerous Islamist militant worldwide beginning in the latter half of 2003. While he shared the same general goals as al-Qaʿida, he placed emphasis on the struggle against the ruling family in Jordan as well as the fight against Israelis in particular and Jews in general. In an audio message released on April 30, 2004, he claimed responsibility for a failed attack on the headquarters of the Jordanian secret service. At the same time, though, he rejected the accusation that he had attempted to deploy chemical weapons, although "God knows that we would not hesitate to use such a bomb against Elat, Tel Aviv, and other cities if we possessed it."[39]

8. Islamism on the Wane?

Since the mid-1990s a growing number of moderate voices have been heard in Islamist circles, prompted by the Islamists' failure to assume political power in the period after 1989. This failure was most obvious in Egypt and Algeria, where Islamist rebels were unable to score victories over state security forces and increasingly turned to random, brutal violence, which undermined their support in the majority population. As a result, after 1996–97 they no longer represented a serious military threat. The election of reform-minded Mohammed Khatami (b. 1943) to the Iranian presidency in 1997 first highlighted the fact that the majority of the Iranian people no longer fully believed in the Islamic Revolution or its protagonists. On the basis of these trends, Gilles Kepel states in his popular book *Jihad: Expansion et déclin de l'islamisme* that Islamism is nearing its end. This, however, is a thesis that Olivier Roy had already put forward in a work published in 1992.

Even after the attacks on September 11, Kepel continued to defend his thesis, arguing that these acts could only be understood against the backdrop of Islamism's shrinking ability to mobilize followers. He interpreted the killings as a desperate, senseless attempt to reverse the decline. By contrast, Roy's argument is more subtly nuanced: it does not address "Islamism" as we defined the term at the beginning of this chapter but instead distinguishes between two forms of political Islam, "Islamism" and "neo-fundamentalism." Islamism, according to Roy, is a version of political activism that aspires to political power and the establishment of an Islamic state. The Islamism of the Islamic Republic of Iran is a case in point—and the only successful example so far. Neo-fundamentalism (or Salafism), by contrast, endeavors to create an ideal Islamic society modeled on the early age of Islam in seventh-century Mecca and Medina. Its followers do not necessarily attempt to assume political power but rather prefer to change other areas of life. Roy writes that neo-fundamentalism does not create any new "political forms" but confines itself to executing shari'a. One highly important example is the Tablighi Jama'at. The growing appeal of neo-fundamentalism therefore weakens Islamism, which has forfeited a great deal of its influence. According to Roy, Islamism has failed to achieve the important goal of establishing Islamic states and is increasingly being replaced by neo-fundamentalism. Still, in our view, the sociocultural success of today's Islamists, which potentially could again be translated into political programs, calls into question Roy's and Kepel's thesis that Islamism is on the wane.

Translated by Adam Blauhut

IX

MYSTICAL BROTHERHOODS
AND POPULAR ISLAM

(Frederick De Jong)

1. Mystical Brotherhoods

Islamic mystical brotherhoods (dervish or *sufi* orders, Arab. *tariqa*, pl. *turuq*) can be defined as hierarchically organized initiatory associations rooted in a mystical conception of Islam.[1] Fundamental to this concept is the implicit or explicit axiomatic stance that human beings can attain a state of direct knowledge of God or oneness with God. This mystical conception of Islam is evident in numerous brotherhoods, structuring their doctrines and religious practices.

The mystical teacher (*shaykh, murshid, pir*) stands at the top of the hierarchy of a brotherhood. He generally justifies his claims as teacher and head of the brotherhood through the fact that he has been initiated into a particular mystical tradition by a mystical teacher, has been instructed by that teacher, and has ultimately received permission to become a teacher himself. A mystical teacher must be able to prove that he stands in an unbroken succession of mystical teachers. This chain of mystical succession should lead back, if possible, to the Prophet, whose way of life and whose statements—in addition to the Qur'an—provide the different currents in Islamic mysticism with the ultimate justification for the bulk of their doctrines and practices.

The degree of formal organization of a mystical brotherhood appears to depend on the scope of its membership. This can vary from a single mystical teacher with a small group of local followers who not infrequently live together in a kind of monastic community (*khanaqah, tekke, zawiya, dargah*) without formalized functions up to a supranational hierarchical structure with all the characteristics of a bureaucratic organization. That brotherhoods share the same name (often referring to more or less fictive founders) does not necessarily mean that their theological system, their rituals, and their mystical methods are identical.[2] A number of mystical groups using the same name are known to practice different mystical methods. This can occur even when such groups are located close to one another in spatiotemporal terms. The basic elements are the same for almost all brotherhoods and include the recitation or reading of prayer formulae and texts (*awrad, ahzab*), liturgical assemblies with singing and dance (*hadra*), general life rules—with an emphasis on the ethics of social interaction (*adab*)—and sometimes precepts about periodic fasting and retreats (*khalwa*).

In Western literature on Islam, mystical brotherhoods have often been and continue to be regarded as organizational forms whose primary function is to satisfy certain spiritual needs not accommodated by the central tradition within Islam. Such an interpretation of mystical brotherhoods, however, appears to be derived from a particular philosophical-anthropological approach to the existence of basic religious needs in human beings. More recent studies bear out the existence of a variety of functions of brotherhoods. In addition to purely religious functions, brotherhoods of the past and present have also had social and political functions. The sociopolitical relationships of these groups and their leaders, who have occasionally competed for worldly power, prestige, and wealth, often appear to have had a decisive influence on their historical development.

At different locations and at different times, leaders of mystical brotherhoods have occupied positions of great power and influence. In several cases the territories controlled by mystical brotherhoods have developed into political entities and even into independent states. Examples from recent history include the Idrisid state in 'Asir (1909–1928) and the kingdom of Libya (1951–1969), which arose from the Sanusiyya.

Only in a single case, that of the Mevleviyye[3] do we have access to documents indicating that a mystical brotherhood with more than local significance had a form of centralized authority for a century or longer. The Bektashiyye is another mystical grouping that appears at first glance to have had a centralized authority structure.[4] Through its organizational relations with the janissary corps, the Bektashiyye was able to become quite influential in the Ottoman Empire before it was dissolved together with the corps in 1826. Prior to 1826 and then again beginning in the mid-nineteenth century, the Bektashis were a centrally led organization, which developed a supranational character after the end of the Ottoman Empire. Within this group, however, there are specific theological conceptions related to the dogma of the divine nature of 'Ali ibn Abi Talib (the son-in-law of the Prophet and the fourth caliph, according to Sunni doctrine). In light of these conceptions as well as the group's liturgical practices and its conception of Islamic ritual duties, which deviates sharply from that of both Sunni and Shi'a Islam, it would appear more correct to classify Bektashism as a special mystical sect or even as an independent religion. For this reason it is incorrect to view this group as a mystical brotherhood comparable to the Mevleviyye.

In general, the different Islamic mystical brotherhoods exhibit very little internal cohesion. One significant factor was certainly the absence of authority structures—which has its origins in the inevitable conflict between the charisma necessary for effective mystical leadership and the institutionalization necessary for the continuity of this leadership. There is also the paradoxical phenomenon that schismatic groupings within a mystical brotherhood have often emerged in the region where the spiritual center of that brotherhood was located, while branches of the same brotherhood in peripheral territories of the Islamic world remained untouched by these divisions and frequently continued to cultivate intense contacts with that center. The reason for this phenomenon appears to be that a brotherhood often has its largest following in the region where its center is located and that the increase of membership renders more difficult the establishment of personal authority; it becomes necessary to delegate (leadership) functions, which make possible (semi)autonomous positions of power that can lead to a schismatic movement.

One example of this is the Sa'diyya, a brotherhood with its center in Damascus, where the spiritual leader resided. In Syria itself this brotherhood split into numerous independent groupings over the course of the nineteenth century, while branches of the brotherhood in Macedonia and Albania continued to regard themselves as subject to the authority of the original center in Damascus. Documents from these branches in the periphery authorizing a member to become a mystical teacher or delegating certain leadership functions were occasionally sent to Damascus for editing or ratification.[5]

2. Popular Islam

The term "popular Islam" is problematic as a sociological category, as is demonstrated by the fact that the term has different meanings in both popular scientific literature and scholarly literature—which also points to the still rather underdeveloped state of Islam scholarship informed by the sociology of religion. In this literature the term "popular Islam" is used to cover at least five different meanings, which are frequently juxtaposed to one another in an undifferentiated manner or used in an incorrect context. These meanings are:

1. regional variations of Islam
2. the way in which the broad, largely illiterate masses understand Islam
3. the forms of piety manifest in the cult of saints and in mystical brotherhoods
4. ideas and practices that are identical with Islamic mysticism
5. superstition and heresy

In all of these cases the term "popular Islam" is used as an expression for noncanonic Islam—that is, a form of Islam that stands more or less in opposition to "official Islam"—and also has the corresponding negative connotations.

The term "popular Islam" is not as a rule used in the Islamic world. Rather, those phenomena designated as such in European literature are classified as *ʿadat* and *taqalid* (customs and traditions) or *bidʿa* and *kufr* (unlawful reforms and polytheism). The first two categories are relatively free of normative value judgments and can be understood as more or less equivalent to the term "popular Islam." This is not the case for the latter two categories, which imply a direct condemnation of the phenomena designated as such.

The distinction between "popular Islam" and "high Islam" is further complicated by the fact that within Islam only a limited degree of consensus exists about which phenomena should be classified as *bidʿa* and *kufr*. When outsiders attempt to make such classifications, almost invariably they argue implicitly for or against a particular conception of Islam: that is, they inevitably place themselves on the side of either the apologists for or the critics of the respective phenomena.

Furthermore, the category of "popular Islam" is problematic because religious institutions such as the *zar* and the cult of saints (which in Western literature is usually—and in general correctly—regarded as a manifestation of popular religion) also find patronage and active involvement among the educated population. This is also true for formally trained religious specialists (*ʿulamaʾ*), who are usually regarded as the carriers of the central tradition of Sunni Islam, but who often participate in the veneration of saints and adhere to magical practices, thereby contributing to the continued existence of both.[6]

Nevertheless, the relevant ideas and practices—regardless of how they are designated—are generally viewed by educated Muslims as manifestations of backwardness and underdevelopment, which for this reason should not be investigated, and certainly not by Western researchers, whose publications on these issues, they argue, only contribute to the spread of "incorrect" notions of Islam. On the basis of these and similar considerations, authorities in the respective countries often make it difficult or impossible for scholars, even local researchers, to investigate aspects of "popular Islam."

My discussion of ideas and practices falling under one of the five meanings of "popular Islam" will be restricted primarily to those connected to Islamic mysticism, with an emphasis on such practices as are manifest in mystical brotherhoods. Regional variants of Islam will not be investigated here. These are discussed elsewhere in the present volume. Furthermore, the complexity and variety of the ideas and practices examined here necessitate that certain simplifications and generalizations be made in this chapter.

The influence of mystical Islam is clearly recognizable in common notions about the essence and rank of Muhammad, who is attributed a status beyond that of the prophet of God identified in the official religion. At times he is referred to as *asl al-wujud*, "the root of all existence." This corresponds to the idea that all existence was created in a gradual process from the light of the Prophet (*al-nur al-muhammadi*), which God himself had separated from his own light as the first act of creation. This widespread belief in the preexistence of Muhammad[7] is evident in innumerable *mawlids,* poetic reports about occurrences before, during, and after the Prophet's birth that are recited at various festive occasions (in particular, at the *mawlid al-nabi* and the *mi'raj*) as well as at liturgical assemblies.[8] Furthermore, there is a widespread understanding of Muhammad as the redeemer and mediator of all grace, who intercedes with God in heaven for his community and whose spirit is miraculously present during the liturgical ritual of the brotherhoods (*hadra*) as well as at the reading of certain passages of *mawlids.*[9]

For the broad masses, however, saints appear to be more important than the Prophet in everyday life, particularly local saints, around whom a significant part of regional religious life is concentrated and who are chosen—alongside Muhammad—as ethical models.[10] More or less explicitly monist or pantheist conceptions of God are evident in widespread practices aimed at discerning divine manifestations in the world through the interpretation of the forms of the letters of the Arabic alphabet or through calculations based on the numerical value of these letters.[11] The letters of the Arabic-Persian alphabet, individually or in combination, are also attributed special powers. This explains to some extent the use of written texts in magic, including on or as part of amulets and talismans. These are two widespread complexes of ideas and practices that are supported by or tied to mysticism and that are more or less connected to a system of cosmological conceptions.[12]

These two complexes, saint veneration and magic, constitute the central focus of critiques of mysticism by those who adhere to a nonmystical conception of Islam.

3. Magic and Related Issues

The problem of drawing an adequate distinction between religion and magic has been discussed numerous times in anthropological and ethnographic literature. This distinction is also problematic for Islam. It is not possible within the scope of the present chapter to contribute to a solution of this problem. Following the example of Rudolf Kriss and Hubert Kriss-Heinrich,[13] we will limit ourselves here to the statement that religion and magic partially overlap in Islam: magic is encountered as a part of religion, and parts of religion are intertwined with magic. The focus of the present chapter will be those phenomena that can generally be classified as magic.

In Islam a distinction is made between licit forms of magic (*ruqya*) and illicit ones (*sihr*). The latter is practiced (and presumed to be known) by a number of specialists, although there are implicit and explicit prohibitions on this kind of magic in the Qur'an and the prophetic traditions. Illicit magic is supposed to make it possible to injure other people and to give power over life and death. Knowledge of this kind of magic is said to have been passed on uninterrupted since (and by) Salomo up to magicians of the present day, although according to another version it came from Harut and Marut and from the devil, who are said to have instructed magicians in this secret science.[14] Writing on amulets (*hijab,* plural *ahjiba*) is a form of licit magic, as long as there is no *shirk* (attributing a partner to God or idolatry) and no *da'wa* (here the invocation for protection and/or exorcism through recited or written texts or prayers). Muhammad himself is supposed to have recommended the use of certain formulae against the evil eye.[15] Nevertheless, many Muslims reject this because they regard it as *shirk* or believe that it contradicts the call to trust in God (*tawakkul*).

Many amulets are used primarily for protection against the evil eye (*al-'ain, al-nazra, al-hasad*), the jinn, and the *'afarit.* The widespread belief in the existence of the mysterious power of evil is justified by passages in the Qur'an and the prophetic traditions (hadith).[16] This is also true of jinn, which are usually described as aerial beings with transparent bodies who can assume different shapes, are created from fire, and are a kind of being between humans and angels.[17] In contrast, the belief in the existence of *'afarits*[18] is difficult to justify through the Qur'an and the hadith and is not compatible with most established notions about the fate of spirits of the deceased situated between death and resurrection. *'Afarits* are believed to be evil spirits created from the blood of someone who died a violent death.

There is also a widespread belief, especially in the Nile Valley, that from the moment of birth everyone has a duplicate in the invisible world (*'alam al-ghayb*). This twin brother (*qarin*) or twin sister (*qarina*) can, for example, cause problems for its sibling in this world because of jealousy.[19] One of the ways to protect oneself against all of these threatening, potentially evil, and dangerous powers is to wear an amulet inscribed with particular verses of the Qur'an, portions of prophetic traditions, certain prayers, or magic formulae and symbols—sometimes in particular patterns or written in substances other than normal ink. These magical formulae and signs include the "seven seals of Salomo," the so-called "ring letters," as well as combinations of the seven letters of the Arabic alphabet that do not appear in the first chapter of the Qur'an.[20] These seven letters refer to the seven kings of the jinn as well as to a cosmological system that does not need to be examined here because it is largely unknown to the general population and is in fact reserved for a small number of specialists.[21]

These specialists are in part members and leaders of mystical brotherhoods, who are regarded generally as particularly knowledgeable about writing amulets, especially given the widespread belief that they have been initiated into the secrets of the jinn and that they can see jinn and can even have jinn as servants. Occasionally such a specialist claims that he has had a jinn as a shaykh, who has initiated him into a mystical brotherhood.[22] These specialists also engage in fortunetelling and divination. Depending on the techniques employed, a distinction is usually made here between *istikhara, darb ar-raml, fath al-kitab,* and *darb al-mandal;*[23] given the intertwinement of magical practices and popular medical knowledge, such specialists may employ practices involving a medium. One reason for this is the belief that many forms of illness and suffering are caused by jinn, which can be identified only by this medium. Moreover, there is a widespread belief that the sacredness of Qur'anic Arabic is transferred to the ink (or other substances) in which Qur'anic texts or formulae are written in Arabic letters. Dissolved in water, the ink is then consumed as medicine in the belief that it leads or contributes to healing.

Employing such specialists in magic and popular medicine (who are often connected to brotherhoods) is not the only way to protect against the evil powers of jinn or similar spirits. One can also attempt to help oneself, which is what most people initially try to do through the use of amulets (including the "hand of Fatima" and blue glass pearls in the form of an eye), which can be purchased readymade of various materials (including salt, iron, and steel). These amulets are supposed to break the spell and scare away the jinn. One attempts to do the same thing through blood sacrifice. An animal is slaughtered (usually as part of a lengthy ritual), and some of the animal's blood is smeared on the object or site (for example, a house, grave, or grain silo) that one wishes to protect from jinn (or 'afarit) or from which jinn are supposed to be exorcised.[24] In both past and present, these blood sacrifices—which are widespread especially in rural areas—have usually been condemned as potential sources of *shirk* by those who claim to be defenders of true Islam because such practices can be understood as sacrifices to jinn.[25]

Ernst Zbinden has accurately characterized the central position of jinn belief as the "via regia through which the entire essence of oriental magic and divination, in association with all the popular superstition in the Mohammedan religion, has found a homestead."[26] The many folktales in which jinn play a role, the many published treatises on jinn, as well as the many pages of popular handbooks on magic dedicated to the identification, classification, neutralization, and other ways of influencing jinn all confirm Zbinden's thesis.[27]

A special form of this jinn invocation occurs in the *zar* cult, which is widespread in Ethiopia, Eritrea, Djibouti, Somalia, the Arabian Peninsula, south and southwestern Persia, Egypt, and Sudan. In this cult, which has been described in detail in various publications,[28] one or more jinn, the *zar* spirits, are believed to reside in the body of a person, making him or her ill. The objective is to mollify these jinn and get them to stop tormenting the person in whom they reside. The type and number of jinn involved is determined by a person who is presumed to have the requisite knowledge as well as the ability to establish contact to the corresponding jinn.

This person is usually a woman who is also the leader (*kudiya*) of a *zar* group consisting of singers, musicians, and occasionally other participants. Details of the ritual—in particular the clothing that the "patient" is to wear and the kinds and numbers of animals that are to be sacrificed—are determined in accord with the jinn's demands and instructions. The most important part of the ritual is an ecstatic, usually collective dance centering on the patient. These *zar* sessions can take place at the patient's residence or in rooms in private houses where the particular *zar* group regularly holds sessions. The participants at these *zar* sessions are often exclusively women, although men are sometimes present as well; frequently local leaders of mystical brotherhoods take part in the organization of the sessions, playing a regulating, coordinating, and/or general organizing role.

Despite repeated critique since the 1880s that the *zar* is a form of *shirk* and thus an un-Islamic practice, its significance has not decreased. For example, in Egypt after the Arab-Israeli War of 1967 there appears to have been an increase in *zar* sessions, which were carried out at established times and in rooms specially prepared for such sessions. It was necessary to obtain permission from government authorities, who probably intended in this way to maintain control over this development and, if possible, to contain it. Particularly in rural areas, *zar* sessions are frequently performed at the graves of saints, although this is officially forbidden. This can occur, for example, as part of the instructions of the particular jinn who is supposed to be appeased. Frequently, however, this seems to happen in the hope and expectation that the mysterious healing power (*baraka*) of the saint will be transferred to the patient, simultaneously mollifying the jinn.

Saints' graves exist everywhere in the Islamic world, and a number of them possess a transregional or even supranational significance as pilgrimage centers. Performing several pilgrimages (*ziyara*, pl. *ziyarat*) to one of these graves is sometimes regarded as the equivalent of performing a pilgrimage (*hajj*) to Mecca.[29] There is also some similarity between the *ziyara* ritual and the hajj.[30] Furthermore, there are living saints—usually (local) leaders of mystical brotherhoods—whose reputations are based on the performance of miracles (*karamat*), which is the basis for their canonization. There is no preestablished formal procedure for this, nor are there generally accepted criteria for recognition as a saint. This status of sainthood can also be lost if the person in question fails to perform subsequent miracles.[31] The *baraka* of a saint—who can also be a woman, though this is less common—can to a certain extent be inherited, that is, transferred to one's biological or spiritual progeny. Furthermore, it is believed that a part of this *baraka* can be transferred more or less constantly to other people or objects.[32] An important motive in visiting the grave of a saint is the desire or expectation of obtaining part of this *baraka*. This is also a motivation for traveling to locations (mountaintops, grottos, trees, or wells) connected to saints. Saints' graves can also be visited to ask for protection from particular saints or to request mediation in resolving various kinds of problems.

Baraka is also attributed to anything located for either a short or a longer period of time at the grave, for example, the cloth covering (*kiswa*) of a grave. In many cases the *kiswa* is annually replaced by a new one during the celebration of the saint's birthday (*mawlid, mawsim, 'urs, hawliyya*). Pieces of the old *kiswa* are then frequently distributed among those present at the celebration, who use them as amulets. This is sometimes also done with dust that has been collected at the grave or with soil from around the grave.[33] The dust and soil, as well as other articles (for example, olive oil that has been placed at the grave for some time), are also attributed with *baraka;* for this reason such articles are frequently used in magic and folk medicine. Saints and saints' graves also play a role in folk medicine because it is believed that contact with the *baraka* provides protection from diseases or contributes to the healing of diseases. Some saints' graves are visited because they have a reputation for healing in general; other are visited because of their reputation for healing particular diseases or ailments (including infertility).[34]

The brotherhoods play an important role in *mawlids* and in the administration of saints' graves. This may be due to the fact that a saint founded a particular brotherhood—as has often been the case—or belonged to one, or to the fact that the grave is administered by someone who is a member of a brotherhood. It is known that a number of saints' graves do not actually contain the remains of the saint. In such cases graves have been established either at locations where the saint appeared in a miraculous way at some point, or after someone was told in a dream or by an apparition of the saint to establish a gravesite.[35] At both of these kinds of saints' graves, there is often a wide array of items donated as alms (*sadaqat*) or presented as votive offerings (*nadhr,* pl. *nudhur*), ranging from food to decorative objects for the grave.[36] In a number of cases the type of gift—for example, model ships found at graves in Egypt—indicates a continuation of elements from pre-Islamic religious customs. Of sociological interest is the fact that the entire complex of the veneration of saints creates a number of social contexts in which men and women are allowed to participate in the same way and at the same time.[37]

Orthodox Muslims condemn the veneration of saints as *shirk* insofar as the saints' miracles are understood not as the result of divine grace but rather as the manifestation of the saint's own miraculous powers, insofar as contact with the saint's *baraka* is not sought as a means of indirect communication with God but as an aim in itself, or insofar as the votive offerings and almsgiving, including the sacrifice of animals, is intended for the saint or as veneration of the saint and not intended for God.

In conjunction with the idea that saints are capable of miraculously intervening with God for the benefit of a believer or of acting independently in the world, the belief in a hierarchy of saints in the hidden world also exists. At the top of this hierarchy is the *qutb,* around whom the universe evolves. These saints are said to form an inner council (*diwan batini*) in the world of the unseen, through which God is supposed to act in the world. These conceptions are presented in detail in a series of mystical treatises.[38]

In addition to the celebration of *mawlids,* the brotherhoods in a number of countries (including Egypt, Sudan, and Syria) also appear in public at different general Muslim holidays and commemorations as well as at night during the month of Ramadan. On these occasions a procession (*mawkib*) of the brotherhoods and sometimes also public liturgical assemblies (*hadra* or *dhikr*) are organized.

Traditionally in the Arab world brotherhoods have also made public appearances in processions on the occasion of circumcisions and burials. At circumcision processions members of the brotherhood are paid to march with flags and musical instruments to add to the celebratory atmosphere. At burial processions they appear only with flags. Through the recitation of prayers during the procession and the performance of a *dhikr* at the grave of the deceased, they attempt to mitigate the agony of being buried and the definitive separation of body and soul. In rural areas in Egypt it is also customary to place a copy of the Qur'an and at times other objects in the grave next to the deceased, as well as to inscribe the cloth in which the corpse has been wrapped with Qur'anic verses, in particular with *surat al-kahf* and *surat yasin*,[39] although these customs are condemned by the orthodox tradition. At the request of surviving family members, a *dhikr* is occasionally held at the grave at the end of the mourning period, forty days after the death.

4. Mystical Brotherhoods in Contemporary Islam

In recent decades the public presence of mystical brotherhoods has increasingly disappeared throughout the Islamic world. Their participation in rites of passage has become rare. A number of mystical brotherhoods have completely ceased to exist, and although new brotherhoods have also arisen, a notable decline of organized Islamic mysticism has occurred since the period between the two world wars. It appears justifiable to attribute this decline primarily to secularization, in particular to the results of—and connected to—processes of social and economic development that have occurred in part through Western influence. Such development is evident in the growing autonomy of the different spheres of life—art and science, politics and the economy, morality and religion—whereby the religious sphere has also undergone a transition from "religiousness" to "religious-mindedness."[40] Furthermore, the criticism and activities of nonmystical or antimystical adherents of Islam may also have had a significant effect on the decline of organized mysticism.

Since the end of the nineteenth century, Islamic mysticism has been subject to attacks, especially by reform-minded nonmystical individuals and organizations with both modernist and traditionalist orientations. By depicting Sunni nonmystical Islam as corresponding optimally to human nature and by placing particular emphasis on the logical character of the religion, these critics present their rejection of mystical conceptions of Islam and their own opposition to it as necessary correlates.

In addition to Islamic antimystical activism, several laical currents have also opposed Islamic mysticism, claiming a causal connection between underdevelopment and mystical conceptions of Islam—in particular those conceptions involving the complexes of magic and the veneration of saints discussed in the preceding section. Because these conceptions are most evident in the mystical brotherhoods, the latter are regarded as an impediment to socioeconomic development. Under the communist regimes in Albania and the former Yugoslavia,[41] as well as in Tunisia and Turkey, these and similar ideas—combined with the respective political ideologies of these countries—led to a general prohibition of mystical brotherhoods, which was not always or not uniformly enforced. In some Islamic countries, including Syria and South Yemen, the brotherhoods have indirectly and perhaps not even intentionally been driven to extinction or robbed of their important social role through the restructuring or dissolution of religious endowments (*awqaf*), resulting in a significant reduction of revenue for the brotherhoods and the loss of the financial basis for positions of authority within these organizations. Nevertheless, there are only a few regions in the Islamic world,[42] and in non-Islamic countries with an Islamic minority,[43] where no adherents of mystical conceptions of Islam are active in connection with mystical brotherhoods. Even in those countries where mystical liturgical assemblies are expressly forbidden and where mystical brotherhoods are not permitted to operate as formal organizations, mystical Islam persists in the form of such brotherhoods, practiced in more or less secret assemblies.

The vitality of mystical brotherhoods, even in the face of persecution and suppression, is evident, for example, in recent information about the continuity of the brotherhoods during communist rule in Central Asia, in the Caucasus, and in the Kazan region. Here large orders such as the Naqshbandiyya and the Qadiriyya were able to survive, despite atheist propaganda and numerous measures aimed at eliminating mystical brotherhoods.[44] There now appears to be a revival of mystical Islam in connection with the re-Islamization movements in these territories. In several countries, including Sudan, authorities have also attempted in individual cases—in addition to direct and less systematic interventions—to establish a centralized organizational form for mystical brotherhoods, through which these authorities can control the brotherhoods either directly or indirectly. These attempts appear to be motivated by the desire and the necessity to secure popular support through the promotion and privileging of those organizations that are based on widely accepted conceptions of Islam and have significant popular followings.

5. The Special Case of Egypt

One of the earliest attempts by the authorities of an Islamic country to gain centralized control of mystical brotherhoods occurred in Ottoman Egypt at the beginning of the nineteenth century. Over the following decades an organizational framework developed that is unique in the Islamic world. Its most important structural characteristic was the distinction between

brotherhoods officially recognized by the state and those not officially recognized. Two ordinances, which were in force from 1903 and 1905 respectively until 1975, further defined this framework and have determined the
more recent reforms of the administration and administrative practices of
mystical brotherhoods in Egypt.

These reforms provided the legal framework for a law that was passed
by the Egyptian parliament in September 1976. A supplementary "administrative ordinance" was issued as a presidential decree in January 1978.
These texts emphasized the significance of mystical Islam within the organizational framework of the officially recognized brotherhoods. Already in
the 1950s organized mysticism in Egypt had been revived to a significant
extent. Under the auspices of the *sufi* council, colloquia on mysticism were
organized, a journal was founded (*Al-Islam wa-l-tasawwuf*), and a number
of new brotherhoods were officially recognized. Membership in the brotherhoods generally increased. This *sufi* council, which functioned as a central coordinating authority, consisted of a permanent chair and four active
members, each of whom served for four years. Council members were chosen from among the leaders of the recognized brotherhoods, and the council
itself possessed decision-making authority for most affairs concerning the
brotherhoods.

Furthermore, organized mysticism was given a prominent role in various
religious celebrations. More *mawlids* were held, and the scope of these festivities was even greater than in the decades before the revolution. The Arab
Socialist Union almost always participated in the organization of these
mawlids, and the government used these events for propaganda purposes
through pamphlets, banners, and political addresses. The brotherhoods and
their umbrella organizations served increasingly as channels for spreading
political and ideological propaganda. The Arab Socialist Union also assumed a prominent role in another respect: appointees for offices within the
hierarchy of officially recognized brotherhoods had to present a certificate
of good conduct signed by a member of the local committee of the Arab
Socialist Union. The brotherhoods were also obligated to submit a proposal
for recognition to the Ministry for Religious Affairs (Wizarat al-awqaf), and
in some cases authorities intervened in the appointment procedure for leaders of the brotherhoods.[45] This active intervention by the government was
clearly aimed at preventing the emergence or continuation of uncontrolled
concentrations of power as well as at tying the widespread mystical brotherhoods to the government. According to an official estimate in the early
1970s, these mystical brotherhoods had a membership of approximately
3 million.[46] The popularity of the brotherhoods is rooted in the traditional
and unique experience of Islam they provide, and the Egyptian government
had a great interest in controlling the institutions that allow for this experience. This increased intervention by government authorities, however,
including the Arab Socialist Union, into the affairs of the brotherhoods
has also had a—presumably unexpected—side effect: the growth of those

brotherhoods not officially recognized by the government and the emergence of several new nonrecognized brotherhoods.

Recent Legislation

One conspicuous element of the aforementioned law of 1976 is that the *sufi* council, which had consisted of four members and a council chair, was replaced by a committee of fifteen members. This council now consists of four representatives of different ministries (including a representative of the Ministry for Religious Affairs) and a representative appointed by the rector of al-Azhar University.

The committee also includes ten members who are the leaders of officially recognized brotherhoods. This expansion of the *sufi* council may have been a consequence of the recent increase in the number of officially recognized brotherhoods, which had reached sixty-seven in 1994.[47] The inclusion of five "external" members with virtually the same authority as the leaders of the brotherhoods in fact implies a reduction in the autonomy of officially recognized organized mysticism. At the same time, however, the new composition of the council also represents a step toward the integration of the organization of the brotherhoods and al-Azhar University in connection with the organization of the Ministry for Religious Affairs. Because the organizational aspects of Islam are largely determined in Egypt either directly or indirectly by organizations that are part of these latter two institutions, the *sufi* council in its new form may be able to increase the significance of the brotherhoods for the ways in which Islam in Egypt manifests itself. The law and the administrative ordinance of 1978 also contain articles that reduce the autonomy of leaders of the brotherhoods. They are, for example, supposed to report all of their revenues, both money and goods, to the *sufi* council and are required to submit annual reports about the activities of the brotherhoods they lead. The *sufi* council also performs an annual inspection of all of the administrative records of the brotherhoods.

These measures appear to be aimed at providing greater governmental access to the activities of the brotherhoods and thereby increasing governmental control over them. This objective is also reflected in the many formulations of the law and the administrative ordinance about elevating the quality and maintaining the continuity of organized mysticism. These enable a certain monitoring of the leader cadre and the activities of the brotherhoods. The administrative ordinance prescribes, for example, that local leaders of the brotherhoods must hold a ritual assembly on a weekly basis. The leader of the brotherhood is then supposed to submit a written report about this assembly to the inspection authorities. In addition to articles stipulating certain qualifications for the different cadre positions in the brotherhoods, the law and the administrative ordinance contain the legal basis for the establishment of institutes of mystical studies. According to the administrative ordinance, candidates for positions within the administrative hierarchy of the brotherhoods who have been awarded a diploma from one of these institutes are to be treated preferentially over candidates who do not have such a diploma. The *sufi* council began its activities in a quite modest institute in 1981. Courses lasting for several weeks with twenty to forty participants are offered on a regular basis.

The Revival of Islamic Mysticism: Aims and Implications

The establishment of institutes for mystical studies is still on the agenda of the Egyptian *sufi* council. The regulations concerning formal and specialized training in Islamic mysticism—with a diploma from one of these institutes offering career prospects in the brotherhoods—remain the most remarkable part of the new law and the administrative ordinance. It is likely that these planned institutes will contribute to the revival, cultivation, and spread of Islamic mysticism in general and to the consolidation of the position of the brotherhoods in Egypt in particular. This improved position of adherents of the mystical conception of Islam will probably lead to an intensification of antagonisms between mystical currents and those groups that reject and oppose the mystical conception because they regard it as a corrupted form of Islam or even as disbelief (*kufr*) and polytheism (*shirk*).

The groups in Egypt opposed to mysticism are largely identical with those circles in which religious opposition to the government of Hosni Mubarak has been concentrated (and should continue to be concentrated in the future). The legal framework for mysticism that has existed in Egypt since 1978 has created an institutional context in which mystical Islam can develop in loyalty to the regime that has made this possible. It has allowed the government to strengthen its position among the adherents of the *sufi* orders, since their mysticism is based on widely accepted elements of popular Islam and is in part identical with them. The fact that no special rules about mystical practices and rituals or about the *mawlids* were included in either the law or the administrative ordinance suggests that the consolidation of a front of adherents of mystical Islam and popular Islam against the Salafi-inspired opposition to the government was indeed one of the regime's aims. There is only a single passage addressing such practices; it prescribes that everything that occurs during *mawlids* must comply with the Islamic code of conduct, without providing any more detailed specifications. Nevertheless, the ordinance does contain a reference to a future review of possibilities for correcting and punishing conduct not sanctioned by Islam, which suggests that authorities attempted at the time to spare the largely ecstatic and widespread mystical brotherhoods (al-Rifaʿiyya and al-Ahmadiyya).

These more recent reforms can thus be seen as a continuation of the policies implemented by the government of Gamal Abdel Nasser (Jamal ʿAbd al-Nasir), which aimed at controlling the mystical brotherhoods and thereby rendering them useful to the regime in the sense of establishing a maximum of legitimacy for the government through privileging mystical brotherhoods rooted in popular Islam.

The revival of mystical Islam in Egypt began during the Nasser era in the late 1950s and was continued a quarter of a century later in Egypt under Anwar el-Sadat, when the government attempted to arm itself, apparently with the assistance of mystical Islam, against the religiously inspired political opposition. The Mubarak government continued and intensified these policies. In response to Islamic groups opposed to the government, there have been conferences on correcting and combating deviant religious positions as prescribed by the ordinance of 1978. The leaders and members of the brotherhoods have been mobilized ideologically against the radical Islamic opposition. This in turn provides the opposition, which is found primarily among nonmystical or antimystical Muslims, with additional reasons to oppose the Egyptian government. Thus the continuation of a policy aimed at the continued revival, consolidation, and stimulation of mysticism will also contribute to an intensification of the conflict between the Egyptian government and the Islamic opposition. Even if the government alters this policy and reduces its support of mystical brotherhoods, the brotherhoods should continue to be an important constitutive element of Egyptian politics, if only on the basis of their large membership and their roots in Egyptian society.

Translated by Tom Lampert

X

Sects and Special Groups

(Werner Schmucker)

In an apocryphal story about the Prophet related in collections of traditions (hadith) and heresiographies, Muhammad predicts that his own community will split into seventy-one sects. While this figure may have been merely a literary approximation, the historical reality proved to be even more diverse. Nevertheless, Muslim contemporaries can now affirm with satisfaction that the immense spectrum of classical sects has been reduced to a mere handful and that only a few new sects such as the Bahai and the Ahmadis have emerged in the modern era. In light of other divisions within the *umma,* this advance in the idea of unity may offer contemporary Muslims some consolation and perhaps even lead them to the conclusion that it is the Sunna to which the final words of the aforementioned prophecy—that "only a single community will partake of salvation"—refers. They may also interpret this as the defeat of Islamic competitors for this title.

Almost all sects in fact claim to be this elect group. Their belief in having been chosen, their claim to embody *the* Islamic homestead, and their inclination to declare other Muslims infidels and engage in a holy war against them all point to this. These sects, however, have long since abandoned their militancy and their zealotry toward the outside world. They have returned to quietism and to concealing their doctrines and rituals and now live in quiet introspection.

Developments in recent decades have been determined almost exclusively by the two "great" forms of Islam, Sunna and Twelver Shi'a, which repolarize Muslims today. The surviving smaller forms with in part renowned (or infamous) pasts, the Ibadis, the Isma'ilis, the 'Alawites, and the Druzes, as well as the rather ancient syncretists—for instance, the Ahl-i haqq and the Yazidis—have been spoken of less frequently than the more recent Islamic secessions of the Bahai and Ahmadis. Occasionally newspaper headlines still cast light on their existence, for example, the Druzes in the Middle East wars or the Lebanese civil war (Kamal Jumblatt was a prominent representative).

The Isma'ili Aga Khan is mentioned from time to time in the media. The Ahmadiyya movement is talked about in Europe because of its missionary work. Literary products of the unobtrusively missionizing Bahai universal religion (which emanated from the Shi'a world of thought) have enriched book markets in the West as well for some time now. The domestic crisis in Syria called attention to the 'Alawites or Nusayris, the ostensible co-conspirators of the Ba'th, while the tirades of intolerant Muslim Brothers have resulted in additional public attention.

One reason why the Bahai and the Ahmadis have been so active is that, in comparison to the six other groups, they are young and contemporary movements carried by the momentum of their message and still rather unspent forces. These two movements are grounded in Islamic modernism, or in the case of the Bahai, they seek to overcome the frictions and frustrations of Shi'ism in order to attain universal horizons alongside and beyond Islam. Both missions have made them activist, rebellious, and reformist conquerors from the start.

This is no longer the case with the other sects. For the former sworn enemies of the established Islam—or those declared to be such by others—who have already failed historically to establish their religious-political ideals and who have retreated underground either voluntarily or in response to persecution or have been pushed to seclusion, secret religions with *disciplina arcani* (with the exception of the Ibadis), their mission and their recruitment of new members have become illusory, if not been expressly forbidden. If these sects are now forced into the public spotlight, it is not so much polemics that they require but rather apologetics, self-justification, and an extremely delicate self-defense (again, this is less the case for the Ibadis). These sects continue to constitute a hopeless and ostracized minority dismissively smiled upon by a majority that maintains its historical prejudices (which, from the latter's standpoint, were in part justified at the time). Owing to its genuine proximity to Islam and its adaptability, the Ibadiyya has been far less affected by this and has successfully maintained its special position in Islam. The others—the extremists of history—seem less to influence the zeitgeist themselves than to motivate the majority to action, that is, to a contemporary self-portrayal or even to reform and revival. The Druzes, the Isma'ilis, and the 'Alawites are at most subject to the pressures of modernity. Otherwise their tendency toward self-perpetuation and secrecy has proved so powerful that an internal movement would have had great difficulty arising if an external polemic had not flushed out a group of intellectuals within these sects. A tendency toward self-perpetuation, if not to ossification, can also be found among the Ahl-i haqq and the Yazidis. Neither tensions with contemporary reality nor declines in membership have induced counterreactions from them.

Both of these alternatives—self-awakening and being awoken by external forces—are extremely problematic. These sects, according to their critics, "keepers of the Grail of secrets," of rigid, antiquated notions and structures, confront this situation almost defenseless. The example of the disconcerted

'Alawites, who have had their secret teachings and rituals exposed by the Muslim Brotherhood, is instructive. Their sudden confrontation with modernity, the careless revealing of their inner religious and social world, their social self, and the loss of identity can result in irreparable damage. Efforts to come to terms with the present, when they exist at all, vary from group to group.

This is a relatively simple task for the oldest sect, the Ibadiyya (or Abadiyya), a branch of the intransigent, extremist Kharijiyya of early Islam. In its relative moderation, the Ibadiyya has even succeeded in establishing relations with Sunni Islam and of appearing to be Sunni, apart from a few remarkable signs of a new self-confidence. For several decades now a number of Ibadi authors from Libya and the Maghreb have even tried to demonstrate that the Ibadiyya has nothing to do with the early Islamic Kharijites—whom both Sunnis and Shi'is regard as anarchist fanatics—insisting that this connection (usually made by other Muslims) is a misunderstanding that can be traced back to defamatory statements in ancient Sunni heresiologies.

Smaller islands of historically significant Ibadis were located in Tripolitania, southern Algeria, the island of Djerba, Zanzibar, and Oman. Their activist phase began in the Umayyad era (661–750 CE) in North Africa and lasted until approximately 960. As warriors, missionaries, and merchants, they spread their doctrine of Islam as well as Islam itself to sub-Saharan Africa and, in their wake, sacral Islamic architecture as well. Their Kharijite egalitarian recruitment, which resulted in social repercussions all the way up to southern Spain, and their preaching of an unadorned popular Islam were very successful among local (Berber) tribes.

A religious-spiritual unity of Ibadism arose briefly from east to west during the Rustamid's impressive rule in Tahert (777–909 CE). The establishment of the Fatimids in North Africa (909 CE) and internal divisions—sub-sects still exist today—gradually depoliticized the Rustamids, without at the same time robbing them of their internal dynamic at their oasis retreats (Wargla, Mzab). There are even indications today of a revived communal life based on newly available religious sect writings, intensified Kharijite-Ibadi Qur'an instruction, and a revival of the rigorous deontology.

The religious communal life of the Ibadis, at least in Mzab, continues to be oriented around the *halqa*, which survived political disempowerment by the French in 1882 as an "ecclesiastical council" and continues to be *the* religious and moral authority even today; it is still headed by the historical council of twelve with apparently social functions as well. It is quite conceivable that the impulse for an Ibadi revival could come from these former centers of a religious renaissance (during the fourteenth century at the latest). It would not be difficult to establish them on variants of the council collectives, those simultaneously theocratic and democratic governing bodies that personified the Ibadi community: the community as a self-administering community of salvation constituted on the power of its divine consecration, which did not necessarily require an imamate for this. There was even a supervisory representative body—the council of the (twelve) shaykhs—in case a leader (*shaykh* or imam) became too powerful. This provided a democratic dimension, offering the community certain codetermination rights.

The Mzabis have also been portrayed in modern literature, which ascribes to them at times unambiguous and at times transparently Ibadi traits as well as legendary and novelesque characteristics: Mzabi men, tied to their homeland while laboring in foreign countries, apparently petty-minded misers from the five cities, puritanical executors of a heretical, ascetic Islam, who lead a "reduced life" full of hardship but nevertheless strive for higher objectives and seek "to support this creation of the spirit and the spirit alone" (Albert Camus, *The First Man*); female Mzabis, who received their long-awaited husbands or lovers from the north with dreamy Berber love songs and who are portrayed as representatives of a half-archaic matriarchal society headed by charismatic priestesses (actually female corpse washers), empowered with the capacity to punish and curse, who enforce their fearful authority through expulsion of dissenters and who—like the protagonist Mamma Sliman—at the same time serve with knowledge, justice, and moderation, granting exemption from punishment (Assia Djebar, *The Tongue's Blood Does Not Run Dry*). Here, too, there is a mixture of Ibadi "otherness," perhaps freer, lived spirituality, and strict observance.

There has also been a reorientation among the eastern Ibadis in Oman. There the Ibadiyya represents, so to speak, Islam itself, recruiting its supporters first and foremost from the most influential Hinawi and Ghafiri tribes. It is perhaps the oldest southern Arabian bastion of the Ibadiyya, which was established from the educational and missionary center of Basra. The historical significance of the Ibadiyya in Oman appears to persist despite the country's transition from imamate to worldly sultanate. The imam was completely disempowered in 1959. Nevertheless, the absent spiritual head of the Ibadis still enjoys significant support among the tribes settled in the interior of the country, who challenge the sultan on an almost daily basis. Improvements in the infrastructure have mollified the tribal people but have not reconciled them to state power.

It appears that in response the sultan and his entourage have developed more extensive plans. They not only recruit supporters of the rival imam but also attempt to appropriate that imam's authority, perhaps even to inaugurate a quasi-imamate sultanate. The direction that this is supposed to take can be deduced from the still semi-opaque developments. Omani media have revived the Ibadi heritage, although in doing so they emphasize its moderation and its proximity to Sunni Islam. It is claimed that a "time-honored Islamic community" is being revived; Omanis are said to feel connected to fellow North African believers, while the indissoluble ties of the Ibadis to Islam are emphasized. Implicitly—and in Libya even explicitly—it is argued that the historical Ibadiyya is a moderate offshoot of the Kharijiyya, the flag-bearer of the Sunna, the prophet tradition, concerned with an *occasional* balance with the Umayyads; the Ibadiyya is also said to have been

close to the Muʿtazila without the intransigent concept of the enemy present
in other branches of the Kharijiyya. The Ibadiyya is supposed to be capable
of dialogue and respectful of the established rights of others, although its
own rights should not get short shrift in the process.

Concessions to the ruling religious majority are necessary; local tradition also requires this. The traditional opponents of the sultanate connected
to the Ibadiyya should receive their due without the sultanate ending up
empty-handed. A wave of Ibadi revival overwhelms the country. With unusual earnestness and a scrupulousness bordering on pedanticism, Islamic
deontology is encouraged, in particular the social "pillar" of almsgiving,
which is consciously presented in antiquated terms; apparently outmoded
rules of almost primal Islamic spirit (division of plunder, blood money, *lex
talionis,* and so on) are inculcated, while martial and social-ethical values
(jihad, self-sacrifice) are preached. The Kharijite sensibility regarding minor
as opposed to major sins is omnipresent. Editions of Ibadi source texts accompany the campaign. This rewriting of history warns of the fateful, re-
silient discord with tribal feuds and disputes about imamate successions and
also presents "malicious" imamate pretenders, while appealing at the same
time to the pride and national sentiment of Omanis.

The semiofficial analysis of the country's history, however, is even more
cryptic. The monarchic glorification of Ahmad ibn Saʿid, the founder of
the Bu Saʿid dynasty, involves more than ancestral pride: he is supposed
to have established a historical precedent that allows his dynastic successors to justify their own usurpation of power. Ahmad ibn Saʿid based his
rule on the Ibadi principle of the deposibility of a "sinful" imam. This is
ostensibly what occurred in 1741. There are many indications that a connection is supposed to be established between this first ancestor and Qaboos (Qabus); both are celebrated as the preservers of Muslim rule—that
is, they are the loyal Ibadis—who broke the power of the "sanctimonious";
they are pure reformers and warriors of the faith. This is apparently an attempt to make credible Qaboos's claims to the succession of the spiritual
imamate. Like his ancestor, Qaboos is supposed to go down in history as a
political-religious unifier, the overcomer of tribal thinking, and the cultiva-
tor of religion. The Ibadiyya plays in this way a central religious, social,
integrative, and political role in contemporary Oman and should not be
underestimated in the future. It serves as a weapon for the government as
well as the opposition, one that either side could use to destroy the other.
It is unlikely that the Ibadiyya, with its "intermediate standpoint" on the
theological spectrum, will be subject to an Islamic condemnation.

1. Ismaʿilis, ʿAlawites, Druzes

For the Ismaʿilis, the ʿAlawites, and the Druzes, the transition from an intact
internal world to an external world always regarded as "unholy" has proved

more difficult. Their Islamic-ness remains suspect even today, although the religious-political radicalism (particularly of the Isma'ilis, Ismaili assassins, and Qarmatians) that characterized their relationship to Islam and to one another has been abandoned. Their secret teachings and rites are still viewed with mistrust, as is the religious-social isolation—particularly in the Arab environment—that they either chose themselves (as elitist separation) or were forced to adopt (through persecution). This gave them a certain popular character or at least looked like eccentricity and anti-Arabism. While the Twelver Shi'a proudly claims to be and is recognized as a power equal to the Sunna and as a genuine part of Islam, these three more extreme factions of the Shi'a, which battled against institutionalized Islam in the form of the caliphate overtly and covertly, dogmatically and politically-militarily (Isma'ilis), bear the stigma of traitors, mortal enemies, and destroyers of the Sunna.

The current settlement areas of these three sects are not the regions in which each originated, with the exception of the Isma'ilis in Syrian Salamiya and in Yemen. The movements of the proto-Isma'iliyya and the Qarmatians began in Iraq, western Iran, and eastern Syria at the end of the eighth century; the ancestors of the 'Alawites also emerged at this time, although their doctrine was provisionally established in stages and layers from Kufic extreme Shi'a positions only in the middle of the eleventh century. The Druzes arose as dissidents of the Isma'ili Fatimids in Egypt in 1018. Most impressive was the Isma'ili expansion beginning in the ninth century, which was promoted by a hierarchically differentiated, adept, and universal recruitment. Isma'ilis continue to exist today, in part as a number sub-sects, in eastern and western Syria, in Yemen, in Najran (Saudi Arabia), dispersed throughout India, and in East Africa, Iran, Afghanistan, and Central Asia. The 'Alawites are found primarily in the so-called Ansari Mountains between the Orontes and the Mediterranean coast in western Syria, in the coastal area of Antakya and Iskenderun through Adana and Tarsus up to Mersin in Turkey, and in and around Hama as well as in Aleppo. The Druzes are located in Lebanon, Syria, Israel, and Jordan. All three groups have a lively diaspora in the New World.

The three sects have recently sought to present themselves in an up-to-date form to the Islamic and/or Arab world. Almost without exception, the leading interpreters here are Syrian and Lebanese.

Within the Isma'iliyya, which split in 1096 into the Musta'lis and the Nizaris (and later divided again), it is less the theologically conservative or antiscientific Musta'lis than the broad-minded Nizaris (followers of Aga Khan) in Syria—previously religious and political radicals (assassins) inclined to imam apotheosis, abrogation of the shari'a, and (particularly in India) syncretism—who, represented by several literati, have attempted to reinterpret the movement's historical mission. As with the Druzes and the 'Alawites, these are local "orientalists" or critical lay believers. These neo-Isma'ili intellectuals understand themselves first and foremost as taskmasters of their backward community. Their views are not necessarily identical with those of the conservative shaykhs. In any case, they are more aware of existing problems, and their engagement is broader. They concede that certain social and educational programs promoted in Syria with funds from wealthy Indian communities on the initiative of Aga Khan have already begun to yield initial fruits. Nevertheless, they criticize the predominance of Nizari notions of economic, administrative, and charitable reform, according to which businesspeople primarily held sway. This ostensibly delayed the elimination of inadequacies at the institutional level and even more so in the educational sector. Disoriented young people are said to be the primary sufferers, and the goal is now to reawaken them and to fortify them with the Isma'ili heritage. The cohesion of society in general, it is claimed, has fared no better. Tribal-familial instincts predominate instead of the reconciliatory-fraternal ethos of the old Isma'ilis, as does antisocial acquisitiveness rather than the traditional Isma'ili exchange of goods and the readiness to make financial sacrifices.

This criticism of "economists" is not of course aimed at the highly esteemed Imam Aga Khan, who continues to be regarded as the inspired infallible leader, who in his "incomprehensible wisdom" has already outlined a reform worthy of the Isma'ilis and is fully supported in this by the aforementioned intellectuals. Accordingly his progressive and humanitarian strivings are also directed at the economic domain, the essence of Isma'ili existence; his socioeconomic stimulus measures are expressions of idealistic sacrifice, an appeal to fellow members to do as he does, to tie the weal and woe of the community not to tax revenue but to engaged voluntary charity and solidarity in order to imitate the almsgiving and love feasts of the past. As the imam himself says, he does not want mere recipients of charity. Pragmatist that he is, albeit with a religious undercurrent, he invokes the initiative, creative spirit and self-responsibility of the Syrian followers, who, like their forefathers, regard inactive parasitism as the most inappropriate behavior. He also calls on them to take the fate of their group into their own hands, again as their own fathers did; and in doing so they should not act in a sectarian way and condemn others but rather should interact in a fraternal and humanitarian spirit with people of different faiths. As pacesetter for the League for Islamic Unity, the Aga Khan of course places great emphasis on service to the whole of Islam, or to a "partial whole," the fatherland (Syria) and the Arabs, in order to counter accusations of an Isma'ili isolationism.

As with the Druzes and the 'Alawites, however, the unity of Islam is understood here in a way that does not blur the special character of the sect and thus does not become the diktat of a majority religion over all others; every group is supposed be independent, respected, and active. Philanthropist that he is, the Aga Khan likes to combine his antidiscriminatory ideals regarding race, skin color, and wealth with references to the fraternal influence of the historical Isma'iliyya. He is as proud of this universalist dimension as he is of the essential spirituality of the movement, whose historical vitality he and other interpreters—true to the central trait of Isma'iliyya—attribute to trans-temporal substance rather than superficial, rigid tradition. He derives the Isma'ilis' capacity for revival from this and their self-confidence as well from their solidarity and their unconditional loyalty to their leader(s).

Through their rewriting of the history of the Isma'iliyya and a commentary of Isma'ili text editions, Isma'ili intellectuals flesh out the plan outlined by the Aga Khan. It is an unprecedented idealizing, suggestive-doctrinaire historiography intended to convey ideal norms in modern terms to a contemporary world. Moreover, it reveals a total Shi'a understanding of history, portraying its own movement as at best a genuine striving of the Shi'a for the realization of what they believe is their legitimate rule over Islam and for the reform of an Islam distorted by a reactionary power cartel.

In the face of a joint Shi'a reform project, inter-Shi'a factionalism fades retrospectively. Non-Isma'ilis are recruited by supporting but not overemphasizing the successor rights of Isma'il, the son of the sixth imam, Ja'far al-Sadiq (d. 765), and celebrating Ja'far—who is sacred for all tendencies—as the spiritual forebear and father of esoteric movements in Islam (the so-called Batiniyya). Neo-Isma'ili are effusive in their praise of this "incomprehensible, suprahuman personality," who is said to be responsible for the essential impulse of the Batiniyya. What the followers of his spiritual school teach is ostensibly nothing other than his systematized "progressive ideology," which they paraphrase in "-isms," such as idealism, humanism, rationalism, applied socialism, and revolutionary radicalism.

The once superb and admittedly very speculative attempt by their best thinkers to provide a coherent and authoritative salvific-historical declaration of being—as a provocative counterpart to the existing spiritual culture as well as to the political and social order that is at the same time adapted to every intellectual level—seduces neo-Isma'ilis to unbounded exaggeration and one-sidedness toward themselves and to a devaluation and even defamation of the equally momentous and serious strivings of the Sunni opposition. The community of Syrian Isma'ilis, necessarily concerned with Islamic integration as well as a balance between such integration and the preservation of their own special existence, will have difficulty in asserting their delicate standpoint to the majority in this way if, drawing upon the scholarly upswing for their rehabilitation, they now lapse into unrestrained polemics. The reviving powers that have initially benefited their own society could boomerang with regard to the still suspicious outside world. Adequately presenting this orientation will require the sense of proportion of a sovereign Aga Khan.

While the Isma'ilis, particularly in the theology of the Fatimids (909–1171), are generally restrained in their exaltation of the imamate, the 'Alawites or the Nusayris deal with this issue quite differently. Through a conflux of extreme Shi'a teachings, the 'Alawites, who were originally Twelver Shi'is, came to exalt or even idolize the imams. As with the Isma'ilis and the Druzes, the 'Alawites believe that imams are preexistent in terms of ideas and, as a Gnostic-speculative cosmogenesis teaches, descend incrementally into the physical world, which is actually the work of these demiurgic incarnations; here they perform their repeated salvation mission in several cycles and periods. In this sense a unified manifestation, they appear individually or in groups (for example, pentads) under various names, followed by further embodiments of cosmic-spiritual subprinciples, which also include numerous figures from the early history of the ʿAlawites.

The appearance of the divine in ʿAli, or under the name ʿAli, predominated early in overpowering (re)incarnation ideas, which became as a matter of course the most important literary topos. What trickled through to the public about the ʿAlawites' secret beliefs concerning the idolatry of Shiʿa saints and imams angered other believers, as did rumors about their rites, for example, the symbolically rich three-level initiation of neophytes or the ritual dimension in their ultra-Shiʿa allegorical interpretation of the canonic rites of Islam, as well as their syncretistic calendar of celebrations, their bizarre religious-social customs, and their strange notions of reincarnation, to say nothing of a Nusayri "Qurʾan" in their liturgy.

Not only Sunnis but also the spiritually related Druzes and *Nizari*-Ismaʿilis have opposed these "arch-heretics," as they call them, up to the present-day. Following a brief pause, the ʿAlawites are now surrounded by a new wave of agitation, initiated by the Muslim Brothers, who distort the complex background of the Baʿthist patronage of the ʿAlawites and the interaction of a religious community and a secular party. They speak only of an "unholy alliance" and carry out a campaign with educational pamphlets that indiscriminately mixes truth and fabrication, through which they have created a dangerous pogrom attitude. The secret sect was completely unprepared for the divulging of its mysteries.

The state of consciousness of the ʿAlawites—in contrast to the Ismaʿilis or the Druzes—is not yet mature enough, not yet sovereign enough, to present the sect's precarious dogmatic positions in abstract philosophical garb or in a demythologized form. A Sufi allegorical interpretation similar to that of the Druzes exists at best in incipient form, and even this is attacked by the Muslim Brothers—not entirely correctly—as hermeneutic finesse. Otherwise they limit themselves to the naïve rejection of that which is essentially Nusayri, an approach that amounts to an objective "self-denial." Disputing the facts only reinforces the explosiveness of the conflict, while the Muslim Brothers have in the meantime presented scholarly evidence about the nature of the ʿAlawite faith. The justification of the ʿAlawites, designated as naïve, includes, for example, the portrayal of their historical Arab-ness, their affiliation to the Twelver-Shiʿa ʿAlids, their belief in the Qurʾan, and their understanding of the prophethood and imamate. They explain both the "natural differences on a few points" (as they say) and their suspected secrecy through the inherent inwardness of their Batini religiosity and their historically compelled introversion. An underground mentality that arose from the trauma of persecution led to Sufi-meditative and passive attitudes, while internal and external subjugation led to a mindset of suffering, submission, and humility coupled with expectations of religious-social salvation.

This motive, which is less profound with the 'Alawites than with the Druzes, nevertheless continues to contain a real explosive force up to the present day, namely in the remarkable commingling of 'Alawite expectations of the imam and mahdi (that is, religious expectations of a second coming), on the one hand, and yearnings for social liberation on the other. Recent interpretations of 'Alawite dogma combine the appeal of Sufi-mahdi salvation with the idea of a divine actualization in order to revive the minority. It is no coincidence that the great figure of the poet-prince Hasan al-Makzun (d. ca. 1240) with his mystic symbolic poetry has again become a focus of attention. This is supposed to be more than merely a camouflaging gesture behind a Sufi smokescreen.

Finally, the Druzes also find themselves in the embarrassing dilemma of having to embellish their own historical mission when questioned about their affiliation to Islam and their "Arab-ness." They reject for the most part irreproachable scholarly research with the justification that only "the knowers," that is, the initiated, can actually understand what the Druze faith is. Certainly much has been fabricated and slanderously asserted about the Druzes. The fact remains, however, that early and medieval Druze doctrine was directed against the religious and political foundations of Islam, as is evident, for instance, in the self-declaration of the initiators of the movement in Cairo in 1018. This signified a break in their religious-political loyalty to Sunna and Shi'a, the renunciation of the laws of both, and the establishment of an independent "spiritual legislation." Their own self-designation as the "third path" also points in this direction, with their exclusive claim to be the one true community of salvation led by a "spiritual imamate" that demands absolute subordination to its laws. Where this was headed is also evident in the catchphrases used by the Druzes in dissociating themselves from the old order, in the contractual obligation to a new order, and in the self-isolation that occurred after the discontinuation of missionizing in 1043. The impossibility of conversion and the limitation of the possibility of obtaining salvation to those who had already converted as well as the restriction of "true affiliation" to the innermost circles of the sect—with the (fifteenth-century) division between "knowers" and "the ignorant"—all point in the same direction.

Islam—that is, the Sunna—assumes that this fundamental stance is one that the Druzes have not yet abandoned and is indeed eternal to the movement. From the Crusades to the Middle East wars, the Druzes have been accused of disintegrative tendencies, sectarian egoism, and national treason with regard to Islam and Arabs. The Druze response, which repeats in almost legalistic fashion elements of the modern Shi'a apologetic, is extremely complex and the most mature answer offered by any of these three sects. It is in principle more than a mere justification; it is a reorientation, an attempted revival that has progressed farthest in Lebanon and in the American Druze diaspora.

Several new directions have even emerged from the passionate debates, although orthodox Druzes remain hesitant and very skeptical. The most important question is whether the sect should retain or abandon its arcane character. The adherents of the Gnostic way and orthodox members support preserving this secret dimension, while diaspora Druzes and socially engaged pragmatists are opposed. The two sides touch on crucial issues: a religion within the religion is inconceivable; this would exclude the masses, who would be left to nourish themselves on the "refuse" of the faith; this would discriminate against the majority ("the ignorant"), promote inequality, and completely alienate the vacillating youth. The complaints about inequality and injustice frequently lead to a critique of the system. These critics call upon the Supreme Spiritual Leadership, which likes to designate itself as the successor to the imamate, to rule in a more democratic, less absolutist manner.

All of this as well as the complacency of the "knowledgeable initiates," who are drawn to the "celestial" out of fear of earthly maculation, results in numerous blows to the very heart of Druze doctrine, which consists of the dogma of the joint divine-human nature of the Fatimid imam-caliph al-Hakim (r. 996–1021), the other nine manifestations before him, the divine principles cyclically rendered incarnate, and the celestial primal images in the propaganda hierarchy, with its irreplaceable creative-redemptive mediating function in the cosmology and the salvific history.

It is not only devout members but also "liberals" in the service of orthodoxy who want to rescue the essence of Druze dogma. The latter attempt to mitigate the scandal of the apotheosis through philosophical and Gnostic-mystic overinterpretations, objectivizing the playful, esoteric allegorical interpretation of the holy scriptures, declaring the meditative immersion of the "knowers" to be a Gnostic path of purification (catharsis), self-realization in isolation with the sacred, and identifying the inauguration of new members and an oath of secrecy as postulates of Gnostics in all eras. The ethical dimension of the "knowers" is a central issue for all revival tendencies. Since the reforms of the medieval Druze faith at the latest (from the fifteenth to the seventeenth centuries), individual self-realization has been regarded as a step toward knowledge of the divine.

For a number of critics, however, the adamant self-sanctification of the "knowers" merely demonstrates their self-serving and undemocratic nature. These critics demand instead collective social reform through edification of the masses. They, too, derive their basic values from classical Druze doctrinal and ethical norms, a seven- to tenfold catalogue of commandments and prohibitions derived from an allegorical interpretation of the "Pillars of Islam" (*arkan al-islam*), which are supposed to be introduced in order to attain intrasocietal peace (disrupted for centuries by familial disputes).

These values, which can also be found in the Isma'iliyya, are now supposed to be propagated in unrestricted form as Druze forces of integration and discipline. That which was practiced from the Middle Ages up to the present day exclusively within the innermost circle of the "knowers" should now become communal norms for contemporary society as a whole. In the circles that recommend this externalization of the Druze mission, we find a certain distancing from a literal interpretation of their holy scriptures of the founding era, a profanation of the imamate and thereby the rehabilitation of the Isma'ili Fatimids, and a certain valorization of the Qur'an. The Supreme Spiritual Leadership in Beirut, which has been controversial in modern times, is rather conservative and not necessarily the mouthpiece of the diverse reform currents, although it does function as a coordinating body on the basis of the council's composition. It is—or it likes to see itself as—the spokesman of Druzes, even in Syria and Israel, and thus also represents the political dimension.

The Druzes in Lebanon, who are politically experienced and active on a national level through the participation of Druze representatives in the Lebanese confessional system, have found a platform to promulgate from the top down the historical, religious, and political role of the Druzes as understood by their representatives. Contrary to all rumors, they are powerfully eloquent emissaries of a national-Arab, Islamic, and pro-Palestinian Druze faith, referring skeptics to the Druze entanglement in Syria's and Lebanon's often bloody history in order to refute accusations of being unpatriotic.

Nevertheless, like Isma'ilis and 'Alawites, Druze spokesmen also seek to ensure that this claimed engagement for the larger whole does not come at the cost of their sect's own special character. They call for the preservation of the special rights they have traditionally enjoyed and an appreciation of their historically developed particularities. This leads to a difficult balancing act between self-assertion and an exchange with larger entities (regional states, the Arab world, and Islam).

This process, unparalleled for Islamic minorities, is, however, threatened today. Given the religious and political overstimulation in the Islamic and Arab worlds, the large number of reform leaders who have been lost in the civil war, as well as the power of traditions, it is doubtful that this unique and elevated experiment—which presents the central monistic ideas of Druze spirituality in ever newer variations, weaving them philosophically and sociopolitically into present-day realities—can persist and identify a spiritual-moral and political-religious niche in modernity. The fact that a substantial portion of Druzes living in Israel are loyal to the Jewish state and even perform military service there complicates the situation for Druzes living in Arab countries.

2. Ahl-i haqq

Like the other three sects just discussesd, the Ahl-i haqq (people of the truth) asserts a priori the soteriological exclusivity of its own faith. The Ahl-i haqq is a not entirely uniform secret religion possessing no canonic holy scriptures; it shares with the other sects the acculturation of extreme Shiʿa ideas: it recognizes seven successive divine manifestations, each with five epiphanies of divine hypostases called angels or ministers, which emanate from the divine and each of which constitutes a single essence. While Islamic figures preponderate in the second cycle—albeit with an extreme Shiʿa emphasis (ʿAli, companion of the prophet Salman al-Farisi, and Muhammad)—this is not decisive for the overall system since the inclusion of Muslim names is accommodated only in the "Islamic era" typical in these types of religion. In fact this era represents merely a preliminary stage on the path to perfect knowledge, since such knowledge is potentially present in pre-eternity through the divinity and then gradually approaches maturity—again part of the intellectual cosmos of extreme Shiʿa. Nor does the existence of figures from Islamic, Jewish, Christian, and Muslim-Arabic popular or religious history in earlier cycles mean that these names hold sway through all of the manifestation forms. (The belief in the transmigration of souls allows for any and every arbitrary transposition and multiplication of the hypostases.) Rather the center of focus is the fourth cycle, in which the manifestation of Sultan Suhak, the actual founder of the religion, predominates.

This means, however, that it is precisely in the Ahl-i haqq's historical environment that this faith—the one truth—attains maturity. Numerous myths of the origins of the world already reflect this fact; the legends surrounding the manifestations beginning in the third cycle appear to be quite regionally defined and primeval. Indeed beginning in the third cycle, when the manifestations of the divine and the accompanying manifestations begin to "wander," this very displacement appears to mark the development and the spread of the Ahl-i haqq faith: from Luristan through Guran (the fourth cycle: sacred language of Gurani) to Azerbaijan (at the latest in the early eighteenth century). This corresponds approximately to the current distribution of the sect in western Iran (Luristan, Kurdistan, in particular Guran, Azerbaijan) and northern Iraq.

The conspicuous local complexion of the Ahl-i haqq pantheon, its opalescent Shiʿa religiosity, the earthy syncretism of its rites, and its eschatology (the longed-for messiah holds his judgment day in their homeland) all point to the development of this faith in the milieu of Turcoman Shiʿa heterodoxy, in proximity to the Safawid and Kizilbash and in the direction of the Kara Koyunlu. Its religious-social gatherings include original practices such as the *dhikr* of the Sufis, ecstatic dervish practices, obligatory alms and sacrificial offerings, expressive initiation rituals with "spiritual marriages," and the like. The traditions of this religion, whose members are drawn largely from the lower social classes, have a rather demotic character, as is evident in the proliferation of elements drawn from miracle stories and folklore.

The Ahl-i haqq community appears to have assimilated religiously and socially almost everything it has encountered in its popular history, in a number of cases without having altered the symbols. As in extreme Shiʿa, the first three Islamic caliphs as well as Muʿawiya and ʿAʾisha remain negative, bound to devilish darkness; they possess "black earth natures," that is, negative primal qualities. Muhammad, though otherwise by no means preeminent, possesses a "golden earth nature," that is, a positive primal quality.

There is yet another conspicuous phenomenon associated with evil (one that is even more predominant with the Yazidis). Evil seems to lose its "sting," which means that eternal hell perhaps disappears, while paradise may also be of an immaterial nature.

The long history of this religion, which has endured and absorbed so much from Islam and yet is ultimately so distant from it, suggests that it may continue to be able to adapt in the future. A modern theology by a member of the Khamushi group (d. 1920) permits no prognosis on this issue. At the same time, phenomenological similarities to other communities, such as millennial expectations of the Manifestation (or further Manifestations), have established connections to groups completely outside the Ahl-i haqq milieu. Members of the Ahl-i haqq, for example, have converted to the Bahai religion, in which they have sought and found the fulfillment of their expectations and then called upon their former religious brethren to recognize "the sign of the times."

3. Yazidi

The Yazidis are even less marked by Islam. They have settled from Jabal Sinjar in the west, from Mosul to Aleppo, northeast through Armenia to the South Caucasus, and in eastern Turkey, though most densely north of Mosul in the Shaikhan territory, where their cultic center is located along with the tomb of their national saint, Shaykh ʿAdi. Strictly organized according to clan and tribe, the Yazidis are also divided into five dioceses. Although they prefer to speak a Kurdish idiom, their racial and social background is by no means unambiguously Kurdish. They practice an exclusive secret religion that prohibits, solely on the basis of their myth of ancestry, commingling with non-Yazidis under punishment of excommunication. This exclusivity with regard to the outside world also corresponds to an internal form of exclusivity: it is impossible for a layperson to become a member of the clergy. The latter constitute noninterchangeable castes, each of which is exclusively endogamous.

The Yazidis have a strict secret order with the usual Shiʿa consistency: external adaptation to the neighboring religions as a cover. The Yazidis have also been anathematized by the Sunna, if only for their reverence for Yazid, the otherwise most hated Umayyad. (Whether the name of their religion was derived from this caliph remains an open question.) Up to the time of the Ottomans, Sunnis employed every means to justify their measures to convert or exterminate the Yazidis. Not coincidentally, the Yazidis have a (counter-) jihad that their supreme cleric, Shaykh Nasir, is authorized to issue.

Their wild mixture of cultural and religious elements, even more extreme than that of the Ahl-i haqq, virtually induces slander. In truth the Yazidis are neither "devil worshippers" nor "sex fiends," nor do they deify luminaries. For all its substantive mixing, theirs is a luminous-optimistic religion, in which goodness and decency mean everything. Significantly, evil powers or their incarnations, which in extreme Shi'a are preexistent and are reproduced in the cycles as opponents of the good powers, hardly exist here. The imposing peacock-rooster symbol ("peacock angel," *malak ta'us*) has become entirely positive.

This reversal of the satanic symbol of Caliph Yazid to something nondemonic is shocking not only for extreme Shi'a. Behind the preeminent peacock symbol, the fallen angel—who is temporarily "satanized" for the purpose—is hidden; his penitence and God's grace break the sovereignty of evil, fundamentally overcoming evil, hell, and eternal punishment. Accordingly, reincarnation, understood as a path of purification, is supposed to include only the nobility of souls and lead to paradise. The extermination of evil in *malak ta'us* is so complete that he becomes the actual executioner of divine will, the creator and sustainer of the universe.

The elaborate cosmic pearl egg-bird myths provide details about the origins of the world. The work of creation was actually performed by the seven divine angels in alliance with the demiurge-like *malak ta'us* substituting for God, so that the Supreme Being ultimately stands over the entire cult, while all thoughts and liturgical action are directed at *malak ta'us* and the angels. Similar to the hypostases with extreme Shi'a and the Ahl-i haqq, the seven divine angels give birth to themselves in the spatiotemporal domain, or certain personalities sacrosanct to the Yazidis purify themselves through rebirth as divinities, represented in the cult through the seven peacock-rooster figures (*sanjaqs*), the most sacrosanct symbols and objects of general devotion. These include a colorful mixture of Jewish (David), Islamic-Arabic (Yazid ibn Mu'awiya, Hasan al-Basri, the mystic Mansur al-Hallaj), and regional figures (Shaykh 'Adi), the namebearer from their own milieu. (Behind Shaykh 'Adi stands the historical Sufi Shaykh 'Adi bin Musafir from the twelfth century.) The mediating position of these figures between the divine and the human is essential for salvation, whereby their divine-human nature is only vaguely defined, even that of Shaykh 'Adi.

Finally, the Yazidis also have secondary guarantors of salvation, for example, "prophets" such as Muhammad and Jesus (an Islamic conception of Jesus predominates) in the wake of the cyclical manifestations. Whether involving Islamic or Christian figures, this dualism is again resolved with light clearly predominating. As mentioned earlier, even Yazid loses his un-angelic dimension in "Sufyani" (from Sufyani, an Umayyad mahdi figure) transfiguration and revaluation parallel to the *malak ta'us*. Evil has been merely a phase on the path to good; the latter returns to its ancestral place, the sole factual ruler. Something similar occurs with minor figures as well.

This proliferation drawn from the ideas and customs of diverse cultures is also evident in Yazidi religious festivities, which—contrary to claims—involve no derogatory statements about other religions and their rituals. A solemn dignity predominates in the main prayers, angel invocations, and the celebratory *sanjaq* processions, as well as in the pilgrimage to Shaykh 'Adi's grave, the New Year's festival, and the initiation rites marked by an elevated social ethos. Ancient Middle Eastern, Iranian mythical notions as well as Muslim and Christian traditions are powerful, even more so where Muslims or Christians have lived close together. The multilayered oral tradition often overshadows the two Yazidi holy books, the contents of which can deviate significantly from these traditions.

Yazidi belief and ritual extend to the details of conducting one's life. The reason for this is that the Yazidis constitute a single people of God, in which laypersons, though separated from the clergy in a castelike manner, are individually tied as neophytes to the *pirs* or shaykhs of the clergy in a mystic form. In addition to the actual clergy and pastors, who not infrequently lead celibate-ascetic lives, there are also certain clerics who function in dervish form or even as shamans, in particular the *faqirs, qawwals,* and *koçaks,* serving in part voluntarily in brotherhoods. Some, such as the *koçaks,* suggest—even in their altered functions—their uncanny shamanist past or at least recall the mahdis' socioreligious and political power that their (now extinct) namesakes "possessed" in the primarily nomadic milieu.

Despite countless Islamic details, the Yazidis are the greatest outsiders among the special groups described in this chapter. Their unique religious status, reinforced by their specific type of social entity, offers few possibilities for dialogue, though the tolerance of this religion would be capable of promoting dialogue. Given the fusion of the religious and the social domains, any internal social change will affect the overall substance of this minority and disrupt the unique harmony of its elements.

4. Bahai

The globally missionizing universal religion of the Bahai is closer to the Shi'a intellectually than many of its publications would suggest in terms of primary notions of the universalist tendencies or the overall system. A Bahai religion is almost inconceivable without two predecessor movements of entirely Shi'a-mahdi and reformist character that were certainly not predestined to merge and culminate in the Bahai faith. A nonconformist intra-Shi'a group, the Shaykhis, sought to gain access to the promised mahdi through a search for the Bab (Gate), the secret intermediary to the hidden twelfth imam. In 1843 Saiyid 'Ali Muhammad was identified as the Bab, and Babism, the second predecessor movement, was born.

The self-conception of this Bab, however, was not as clear as the Babis themselves and their successor movement, the Bahai, claimed. Saiyid 'Ali

Muhammad did designate himself as Bab, that is, the harbinger of another, in Shiraz in 1844, though he may also later have played with the idea of being an apocalyptic imam, a mahdi, himself. It would not be the first time in the history of the Shi'a that a "mediator" (*bab*) or a "witness" (*hujja*) rose to become an imam. However that may be, the Bab's vague allusion to something greater "still to be revealed by God" that would usher in a new era worldwide and initiate a new main cycle of world history—this prophecy, to whomever it might have applied, did hang provocatively in the air. As if the Bab himself wanted in mahdi fashion forcibly to usher in a new age, Saiyid 'Ali Muhammad broke with Islam at the Conference of Badasht (1848) and abrogated the shari'a, the law, a gesture of total revocation as had long occurred in extreme Shi'a without yet having a universalist orientation in the later sense of the Bahai.

The Bab was serious about his mahdi-reformist program. He relentlessly denounced real abuses in the spiritual and worldly realms and simultaneously proclaimed shockingly progressive plans for a comprehensive reform. Between 1849 and 1852 Iranian authorities instituted brutal suppression measures against the still militant minority. In their subsequent banishment (to Baghdad, Constantinople, Edirne, and Haifa), exile Babis established the pacifist and clearly universalist Bahai community.

The transition was not without friction and appeared somewhat arbitrary owing to tensions regarding the Bab succession (1863–1864). The Babis' Baha'Allah and his half-brother Subh-i Azal competed for the title promised by the Bab of "He whom God shall make manifest." The majority supported Baha'Allah; the so-called Azalis remained a minority. The issue of legitimacy inherited from the Shi'a emerged again following Baha'Allah's death. Testament disputes, incitement, and backbiting persisted until 'Abd al-Baha, Baha'Allah's eldest son, was able to establish himself and, through his towering achievements in theology, administration, and missionary work, proved himself worthy of the highest spiritual office. This was also the case for his successor Shogi Efendi (Shawqi), who evidently assumed the leadership unchallenged.

The Bahai faith adopted the theology of Babism in modified form. The central focus was, of course, the Manifestation, the prophet of the new era; the universalist dimension was emphasized, while Shi'a terminology and symbolism continue to exert an influence. The organization and administration of the Bahai system developed rapidly.

In the religious sphere, the Bab is recognized as the true and independent, if temporally limited, Manifestation—as if this were a confirmation of Saiyid 'Ali Muhammad's later claims. Baha'Allah has become the preeminent figure of salvation. The completely transcendental God externalizes himself through continual acts of creation, revealed or "reflected" most purely in the prophets, who are indeed mortal but also elevated to the supernatural level reserved in the Shi'a for prophets and imams. Baha'Allah's predecessors are the prophets of Judaism and Christianity recognized in Islam, as well as Muhammad. Zoroaster is also included. This means that the earlier religions are recognized as essentially true but no longer timely. The Bahai faith is regarded as the currently adequate religion. After its millennium, it could be followed by quite different, more adequate manifestations.

The irruption of the eternal into the temporal realm through physical manifestation promotes spirituality. The spirit of this faith becomes the actual current of life, filling all of existence with light. As in the Shiʿa, however, this requires being existentially touched by the Manifestation, the sole guarantee of happiness and salvation. The eschatological world in itself is devalued; the future spiritual fate begins to be formed under the influence of the appearance of the divine. Thus there is no physical resurrection (and also no rebirth), no paradise, and no hell; there is only a moving toward perfection in spirit that is continued after death through divine grace.

Despite this emphasis on the spiritual, the Bahai correctly pride themselves on the "horizontal dimension" of their faith and its relation to the here and now and to society. They share with their predecessors the Babis an elevated and rigorous ethos in their deontology, although they have universalized the Bab's Shiʿa intrasocial reformism and abandoned the pettiness of many of the Bab's rules. ʿAbd al-Baha' and Shogi Efendi pushed for the unity of humanity and the true unity of all religions, the abandonment of national, religious, racial, and political prejudices, the cultivation of world peace, the improvement of universal education, and the like. It is certainly a consequence of the predecessor movement, Babism, when Bahai emphasize the lay apostolate by means of self-sanctification, reject clericalism (after the Bab's experiences with Shiʿa theologians) and public ceremonies, and regard and perform their assemblies as a kind of divine service. Their well-ordered and complex supervisory and administrative bodies, endowed by God, so to speak, have been conceived as anticipations of a future ideal world order or government.

The affiliation to this "ideal state" in miniature also excludes membership in political parties. Bahai do missionary work for their cause, or rather recruit for it by exemplifying their ideals in their own lives. Owing to their religious tolerance toward people of other faiths, their temples are open to all confessions; since their mission is to a great extent educational, their chapels are supposed to be surrounded by educational and social institutions. Their holy sites, in particular Mount Carmel in Haifa, where their World Centre and the graves of their founders are located, occupy a central position. This is in itself symbolic for the universalist movement, which was unable to flourish within the religious and national constrictions of its Iranian homeland and which is regarded as apostate by Muslims and in particular by Shiʿis. Up to the late 1950s Bahai were not permitted to publish their texts in Iran, and after the Islamic Revolution there they were again subject to reprisals. Their unparalleled idealism and dedication, however, appear to be unbroken everywhere.

5. Ahmadis

Millennial movements, repeatedly initiated by Shi'is, can be traced throughout the entire history of Islam up to the present day. The nineteenth century represented a new highpoint for Mahdism, even among Sunnis. The Ahmadis are an Eastern example of this, or more precisely of an Indian Islam, in which Hinduist *avatara* ideas and late Indian Sufi notions provided additional stimuli.

The founder of this intra-Islam revival movement was Ghulam Ahmad (ca. 1839–1908) from Qadian in Punjab. In 1889 Ahmad—a religious and introspective man who had visions and heard voices—announced that he had received divine revelations. Two years later he claimed to be the messiah or mahdi, to be prescient and capable of performing miracles, and to be an avatar of Krisna, Jesus Christ returned to Earth, and a reincarnation of Muhammad. Following this, he and his students encountered increased opposition.

After the death of Ahmad's successor (called "caliph") in 1914, a dispute that had almost certainly been latent under this "caliph" became an open conflict, ultimately causing the movement to split. A minority subsequently became active in Lahore. The withdrawal of these dissidents initially robbed the movement of its administrative elite, who—despite their Western education—had also functioned as a moderating force with a pan-Islamic and anti-imperialist orientation. The central theological objection of this minority was that it did not consider Ghulam Ahmad a prophet but thought of him merely as a reformer. They strove, it appears, more for Islam itself and, according to their intellectualist conception, also recruited more for it than for themselves. They have remained active to the present day with worldwide publications and missionary work, particularly in English-speaking Islam.

After the schism in 1914, the majority initially remained in Qadian, perhaps to demonstrate their devotion to the prophet's family and to the successor principle of the "caliphate." In 1914 this majority included Ghulam Ahmad's twenty-five-year-old son as "second caliph of the promised messiah," the "leader of the Ahmadiyya movement of Islam." Discussions of the Ahmadiyya movement usually refer to this majority. In addition to India and Pakistan, the movement has spread to West Africa, Southeast Asia, and in fact throughout all of the Islamic world—although it is prohibited or very controversial in several Arab countries—as well as to Europe and America. Since 1947 its headquarters have been located in Rabwah, Pakistan.

A membership of more than 1 million and an elaborate recruiting network suggest substantial financial power and a strict, centralized organization. The latter serves, so to speak, as the cement of the community, whereby the activities of Ahmadi corporative life—educational and training programs in institutions created especially for these purposes—and its exercise of legal sovereignty emphasize the movement's profile. As it presents itself today, the Ahmadi faith remains virtually the creation of the founder's son Hazrat Mirza Bashir al-Din Mahmud Ahmad and the founder's grandson Mirza Nasir Ahmad (1909–1982).

Thus the figure of the founder and the first "caliphs" continue to live on in the Ahmadi educational and congregational legacy; the "caliphs" function as the supreme authority and as the interpreters of the scriptures. The heirs' claims are almost as lofty as those of the founder, whose community— as is the case for the previous six groups discussed here—is sustained by his daring pretensions. The Ahmadis regard themselves as the sole true embodiment of Islam, which "Ahmad" (almost certainly a synonym for Muhammad) revived and revealed and which the "caliphs" have continued in the spirit of "God's envoys."

The self-conception of such a "caliph," who cannot be entirely oblivious to the political implications of the term "caliphate," speaks for itself. While this "caliphate" is supposed to be a reflection of the so-called "Holy Prophet" (Muhammad), only with significant effort can the boundaries between the two be maintained so that the former does not approach the latter too closely. The Qur'an is regarded as everything, as ultimate revelation. Certain Qur'an passages, however, are used to derive the possibility or even the necessity that, in order to correct a forgetful, confused, and stubborn humanity, enlightened holy men must emerge who have received their spiritual light from the Holy Prophet (Muhammad): reformers or prophets who, however, proceed according to the strict instructions of that Holy Prophet. Furthermore, the appearance of a kind of "super prophet," the spiritual image of the Holy Prophet, to whom he is almost equal in value, has also been derived from the Qur'an and other holy scriptures. This image is sometimes the messiah, sometimes the mahdi of the canonic traditional collections of Islam, and sometimes another figure "descended from the heavens." He is supposed to be living proof of the truth of the Qur'an, called upon by God to reestablish the rule of Islam.

According to the majority, God has bestowed precisely this prophet status on Ghulam Ahmad, admittedly—they concede—on the condition that he, as perfect successor to the Holy Prophet, follow the Qur'an. (As we saw earlier, the minority regard him merely as a "reformer.") He issued no new laws. Nevertheless, he stood above everything human. Like the Holy Prophet, he demonstrated his unique dignity through powerful authentication miracles and demonstrated his "knowledge" through examples of his prescience and his divinations. Even the fact that he was persecuted everywhere—the heritage of all prophets—is a sign of his election. Just as the divine-human youth al-Hakim triumphed over the sophistic world of evil and intrigue in the writings of the Druze founders, the "caliphs" of the prophet Ahmad are presented as divinely guided and intrepid heroes. The Lahore group, influenced by Western ideas, ostensibly demanded the abolition of the "caliphate." The executive organs of the community, it was claimed, were controlled by precisely these "caliphate opponents." The descendants of the prophet

Ahmad consider it almost miraculous that this group, robbed of its intellectual, executive, and administrative elite and headed by an inexperienced youth—that is, the son (the second caliph) of the "promised messiah"—rose up and triumphed. This son, the second caliph, claimed to have received further revelations. He enhanced his own status, calling himself the "promised son" because his father, Ahmad, the (visionary) promised messiah, had proclaimed him five years before his birth (in 1884). He called himself "the authorized interpretive source of the eternally correct Qur'an," the coherence of which he demonstrated with new scientific theories.

The second caliph championed an authentically mahdi program but focused it completely on the Qur'an; he sought to "establish the absolute rule of the Qur'an," thereby bringing about the paradisiacal order and the intramundane ideal condition, "initiating God's kingdom." This assertion was also a vision, presented in the garb of a prophecy and repeating the claims of the Shi'a or general-mahdistic (i.e., Sunni) bringer of salvation and justice. All of this was supposed to occur in the service of and through the Qur'an.

In fact a new theory of the uniqueness of the Qur'an, which employs the classic theological notion (*i'jaz* in Arabic) but leads to a grotesque exaggeration, is defended almost fanatically by the Ahmadis. It is therefore only consistent that they expend enormous energy demonstrating the inferiority, errors, and contradictions of other holy scriptures such as the Old and New Testaments or the Vedas. The deficiencies of these texts, however, cannot be all that serious since it is precisely these other holy scriptures that provide the Ahmadiyya with "true prophecies" about Islam as *the* truth and the Qur'an as the Book of Books.

Their exaggerated Qur'anic scripturalism and their irrepressible missionary zeal emanating from the extravagant prophetic mahdism of their founder and the "caliphs" not only explain the successes of Ahmadiyya missionary work but also suggest how uncanny their overzealousness is for other Muslims, who are designated as "infidels" by the Ahmadis. The association with Shi'a enthusiasts, including—according to the terminology of the old heresiologies—several of the sects discussed in this section, is not too far removed.

Translated by Tom Lampert

XI

ISLAM AND NON-ISLAMIC MINORITIES

(Johanna Pink)

The status of religious minorities in the Islamic world is a potentially explosive issue in numerous respects. Even the use of the term "minorities" is not unproblematic. In many countries of the Islamic world, part of the political rhetoric of both Muslims and non-Muslims is the claim that classifying the population into majority and minorities violates the fundamental unity of the nation. The adherents of this position tend to regard any attempt to explore the situation of minorities as a threat to national unity and as fostering sectarianism and division. In Egypt, for example, the existence of minorities is regularly denied with the assertion that members of all religious groups are simply Egyptians, among whom no distinctions can be made.[1] This defensive stance can be traced back in part to historical sensibilities. During the colonial era religious minorities in the Islamic world enjoyed special protection from Western powers, and even today calls to elevate the status of these minorities conjure up fear of Western influence. Another apologetic line of defense is the repeated reference to the remarkable tolerance of Islam historically toward other religions—for instance, in medieval Andalusia—as a means of countering accusations regarding deficiencies in the contemporary observance of human rights.[2]

The term "minority" is unpopular not only in political discourse but also in Muslim religious discourse. For example, one contemporary Muslim theologian argues that the term is "foreign to Islam and the spirit of this faith" because Islam does not recognize "in principle this Western opposition between 'majority' and 'minority,'" but rather presumes the unity of the *umma,* the Islamic nation, which also includes non-hostilely disposed non-Muslims.[3] A more sober approach regards the issue as simply insignificant in numerical terms. Islamic law is concerned not with the relation of majority to minority but rather with the relation of Islam to the non-Muslim population in a Muslim-ruled state, even if non-Muslims constitute the majority of the population—as was the case after the Islamic conquests for an extended period of time. In the debate about the status of non-Muslims, Jews and Christians constitute the center of focus. The status of other religions is discussed relatively infrequently.[4]

Classical Islamic law distinguishes in principle between polytheists and "people of the book" (*ahl al-kitab*). According to the Qur'an, the *ahl al-kitab* include Jews, Christians, and Sabaeans. In the course of the Islamic conquests, this category was expanded to include other religions such as Zoroastrianism, Buddhism, and Hinduism. While Muslims were supposed to fight polytheists until they converted to Islam or were killed or enslaved, the *ahl al-kitab* could claim protection from Muslim rulers within the scope of a contractual relationship (*dhimma*) that obligated them to pay a poll tax (*jizya*). Furthermore, Islamic legal theory placed various restrictions on them. A number of these injunctions aimed at demarcating and establishing an order of rank between Muslims and non-Muslims, for instance, the prohibitions on riding horses, wearing silk, and carrying a weapon. Religious processions or cultic acts that were potentially offensive to Muslims were also prohibited. Furthermore, there was a ban on building new churches or renovating existing ones. In reality, however, many of these restrictions were frequently not enforced, although they did remain the normative standard of legal practice.

Dhimmis could claim protection from the ruler and enjoyed extensive autonomy in the realm of family and estate law, in communal administration, and in religious affairs—a principle that found its clearest expression in the late Ottoman Empire, where there were a number of officially recognized religious groups (*millet*) that were represented by their spiritual leaders in dealing with the state.[5]

In the nineteenth century, the increasing dominance of Western countries, modernization efforts within the Islamic world, and emerging national movements greatly influenced the status of religious minorities. During the Tanzimat era in the mid-nineteenth century, the Ottoman Empire proclaimed the equality of Muslims and non-Muslims and abolished the poll tax in favor of compulsory military service or, alternatively, payment of a levy. Civil status law, however, continued to be dependent on a person's religious affiliation.

Western states attempted to use the protection of religious minorities as means of gaining influence in the Middle East. Russia declared itself responsible for the Orthodox Christians and France for the Catholics. Given the small number of Protestants, England assumed responsibility for the Jews. The protection non-Muslims were able to obtain included improved access to Western-style educational institutions; the close contact with Western countries also led to new economic possibilities for non-Muslims. Consequently there emerged within these religious minorities an educated middle and upper class, which frequently clashed with their own traditional clergy. These developments, as positive as they were for the non-Muslim populations, also led to interreligious conflicts. Many Muslims reacted with fear and hostility to Western dominance, which was often expressed in animus toward the *dhimmis* protected by Western states.[6]

In this chapter I briefly outline the demographic situation of Christians and Jews in the core countries of the Islamic world before turning in more detail to their legal status and their political role, as well as to current debates in contemporary Muslim societies.

The end of the Ottoman Empire had varying effects on the demographic development of non-Muslims in its successor states. Turkish nationalism, which ultimately became the basis of the Turkish nation-state, virtually excluded non-Muslims, in particular Greeks, Armenians, and Jews. With the end of the Ottoman Empire and the establishment of the Republic of Turkey, the Christian and Jewish populations in Turkey were decimated through massacres, expulsions, population exchanges, and emigration. Between 1914 and 1927 the proportion of the non-Muslim population sank from 19.1 percent to 2.5 percent. Turkish nationalism and laicism also led to measures that increased emigration tendencies in the Turkish republic over the following decades, for instance, the suppression of Greek-language cultural and educational activities and the closing of theological training centers. In 1942 a capital tax was introduced that was more onerous for non-Muslims than for Muslims. In the following decades the remaining Greek population, primarily in Istanbul, again decreased significantly as a result of public animosities, particularly during the Cyprus crisis. In 1991 Turkey had only 145,000 non-Muslim citizens, approximately 0.2 percent of the population.[7]

Within the countries of the Arab world, Christians represented significant population groups in the Levant (Syria, Palestine, and Lebanon) and in Egypt during the late Ottoman Empire. With the demise of the caliphate and the *dhimma* system, new freedoms and opportunities arose for them. Christians had a comparatively high social status and relatively low death rates, contributing in the era prior to the First World War to an increase in the Christian portion of the population, which grew to more than 25 percent in the Levant and around 8 percent and possibly higher in Egypt. Over the course of the twentieth century, however, the life conditions and death rates among the Muslim population achieved similar levels, while birthrates in Christian families sank disproportionately, owing to their high educational level. The divergence in birthrates between Christians and Muslims was particularly stark in Palestine, especially in the occupied territories. Finally, emigration—above all from Syria, Jordan, and Palestine to Lebanon as well as from Lebanon to non-Arab countries—contributed to a marked decline in the Christian population, which now accounts for only about 10 percent of the overall population in the Levant. The civil war in Lebanon provided a particularly strong stimulus for the predominantly well-educated and wealthy Christians to leave the region. According to the 1986 census in Egypt, approximately 5.9 percent of the population is Christian, a figure that Copts regard as too low.[8]

In Iran, Armenians make up the majority of the Christian population. Their relation to the Muslim majority used to be largely unproblematic. But then in the 1930s the nationalist policies of Reza Shah led to closing down Armenian schools and giving Iranian names to Armenian towns and cities. The internal autonomy of Armenian communities was reestablished during Muhammad Reza Shah's rule (1941–1979). In the 1970s approximately 250,000 Armenians were living in Iran. After the Islamic Revolution, this figure dropped to between 150,000 and 200,000. The smaller groups of Assyrian and Chaldean Christians suffered from internal divisions triggered by the activities of foreign missionaries during the second half of the nineteenth and the early twentieth centuries. Moreover, the decision of Iranian Nestorians to affiliate themselves with the Russian Orthodox Church and the Russian protection resulting from this affiliation led to Christian-Muslim tensions, which culminated in acts of violence when Russian protection ceased in the wake of the October Revolution in 1917–18. A significant portion of the Assyrian and Chaldean population left the country at this time. Approximately 30,000 members of these Christian communities still lived in Iran in the 1970s. Their numbers also declined significantly after the Islamic Revolution.[9]

For the most part, the social status and educational level of Jews in the Ottoman Empire and Iran clearly lagged behind those of Christians. From the late eighteenth century on the Jewish population was increasingly subject to hostilities motivated by Western-style anti-Jewish stereotypes. Accusations of ritual murders, which were often made during this era, can be traced back primarily to local Christians. In a number of cases diplomatic representatives of Western states provided support, and frequently the result was outbreaks of violence against Jews. Ottoman authorities usually sought to prevent this type of violence. In Iran, on the contrary, this was not the case; in Iran, Anatolia, and the European part of Turkey, Jews were rarely able to obtain a Western-style education and to advance economically. The situation was different in the Arab world, where a Jewish elite emerged in several countries, for instance, in Iraq and in Egypt. Nevertheless, the participation of this Jewish elite in the political life of their homeland was significantly more limited than that of local Christians.

The Jewish settlement of Palestine and the establishment of the State of Israel marked the decisive turning point for Jewish communities in the Islamic world. Beginning in the late nineteenth century, anti-Semitic hostility stemming from European anti-Jewish propaganda spread increasingly among Middle Eastern Christians and Muslims. Under the influence of Arab nationalism there were riots against the Jewish population, which intensified after the establishment of the State of Israel and led to a relatively rapid emigration of the majority of Middle Eastern Jews to Israel, although the ideology of Zionism was hardly familiar to most of them, much less a motive for emigration.[10] When the possibility existed, Jewish emigrants chose other countries as well; only a relatively small portion of Algerian, Tunisian,

Syrian, and Lebanese Jews went to Israel.[11] The majority of Algerian Jews, for example, had French passports and chose to emigrate to France rather than Israel, which they perceived as culturally more distant. Approximately half of Egyptian Jews also emigrated to countries other than Israel; wealthy Egyptian Jews in particular preferred European nations and the United States.[12] Iraqi and Libyan Jews, in contrast, emigrated almost entirely to Israel within several years of its establishment, and almost all the 55,000 Yemeni Jews were brought to Israel in a large-scale transfer operation by the Jewish Agency. Most of the 250,000 Moroccan Jews emigrated to Israel as well, although there are still several thousand Jews living in Morocco today, primarily in Casablanca.[13] In Iran, approximately one-third of the Jewish population emigrated to Israel in the years after its establishment. The economic status and the educational level of the remaining 80,000 Iranian Jews improved markedly during the rule of Muhammad Reza Shah, with the result that the next wave of Jewish emigration from Iran did not occur until after the Islamic Revolution, when approximately two-thirds of the Jews left the country, the earlier support from the shah and contemporary animus against the State of Israel having greatly aggravated their situation.[14]

The situation of religious minorities living in Muslim countries today is determined by a number of factors: their legal status, their political integration, and their perceived or actual ethnic affiliation to the "nation," as well as controversies about the introduction of an Islamic state, the observance of human rights, and "Western intervention." Only a few central aspects of this complex issue can be outlined here.

While in every state in the Islamic world religious affiliation does have at least some legal relevance, nationalist ideas are equally widespread. According to the latter, non-Muslims are, at least on a rhetorical level, first and foremost citizens of an undivided nation and only secondarily members of a different religious community. Non-Muslims have readily adopted these nationalist ideas since their emergence in the nineteenth century as a means of replacing their *dhimma* status with full legal equality and political participation.

In the Arab world, Western-educated non-Muslim elites—in particular Christian elites—were strongly influenced by the ideas of nationalism and began to call into question their status as *dhimmis* and to propagate the idea of an equal community of the citizens of a nation. In many countries Christians were leading protagonists of the national movement, which was initially pan-Arab. Pan-Arabism was based on the Arabic language as a common bond. Its non-Muslim representatives, however, were also confronted with currents of pan-Arabism that emphasized a connection between Arab-ness and Islam or that propagated pan-Islamic ideals as part of the new caliphate movement.[15] The recourse to pre-Islamic elements that were regarded as constitutive for national history and that were supposed to anchor non-Muslims historically within their own country was widespread among many members of non-Muslim minorities. For Copts, for example, the guiding element was old Egypt, and in Lebanon it was the Phoenicians. Following the failure of pan-Arabism and the rise of political Islam, these pre-Islamic contributions were increasingly emphasized. In Iran this was the case in particular for Zoroastrians, who, prior to the Islamic Revolution, had profited from the shah's efforts to shore up national consciousness by recourse to the pre-Islamic history of Persia. Although this policy was reversed after the Islamic Revolution and the Islamic history was now portrayed as the sole basis for national awareness, the approximately 55,000 Zoroastrians living in Iran today belong to one of the state-recognized religious minorities.[16]

As widespread as nationalist ideas were, they never displaced the significance of religious affiliation in the Islamic world. Although in no Muslim state today is the legal status of non-Muslims determined by the rules of classical Islamic law, this does not necessarily mean that there is complete equality between Muslims and non-Muslims. The religious affiliation of the inhabitants of Muslim states—even in laical Turkey—is registered by the state and has more or less significant legal consequences. A poll tax (*jizya*) for people of the book is no longer levied today in the Islamic world. Most constitutions guarantee religious freedom and prescribe the equality of Muslims, Jews, and Christians. In reality, however, there are real distinctions. In most Muslim countries only Muslims are eligible to become head of state; frequently this is true for judges as well, as Islamic law is applied in certain legal domains. Several states—including Jordan and the Islamic Republic of Iran—have established a set number of parliamentary representatives for every recognized religious community. The precept of classical Islamic law that prohibits the building of new non-Muslim places of worship and the renovation of existing places is usually not implemented—except in Saudi Arabia, which does not recognize any non-Muslim minorities. Nevertheless, many states do have restrictions or require special approval for building churches and synagogues.

Religious and confessional affiliation has particularly great practical significance in regard to family law. In most Muslim states (with the exception of Turkey), family law is subject to religious law. In cases concerning members of the same state-recognized religious confession, the law of this confession applies; in other cases Islamic law usually applies. Thus the marital impediments of Islamic law that prohibit a non-Muslim man from marrying a Muslim woman do apply, while the reverse is permitted—at least where a Jewish or Christian woman is concerned.

Irrespective of these legal issues, relations between the Muslim majority and non-Muslim minorities are not always free of tension in everyday life, however much the age-old tradition of peaceful coexistence is emphasized in public rhetoric. In Upper Egypt, for instance, there have been repeated violent conflicts between Muslims and Christians. The reaction to such occurrences usually unfolds according to a similar pattern: organizations of expatriate Copts, particularly in the United States, level serious accusations at the Egyptian government; Egyptian Muslims point to Islam's traditional tolerance; the government warns that the emergence of a debate over minorities would undermine national unity and sow division between religious groups; part of the Coptic population in Egypt supports the government, while another part protests against the actions of the security forces and the courts, although hardly any of them want to risk being associated with expatriate Coptic organizations, which are regarded as a mouthpiece of the United States.

As such debates illustrate, one of the difficulties in clarifying the role and status of non-Muslim minorities in the countries of the Islamic world lies in the ambivalent relation that most governments have to the question of applying the shariʿa. No country actually applies the precepts of classical law concerning the status of *dhimmis,* nor do governments have an interest in implementing them. Nevertheless, they also show no inclination to admit publicly the lack of relevance of the shariʿa in determining the treatment of religious minorities. Such an open confession seems too risky, given the influence of political Islam and the widespread sentiment regarding the earlier power politics of Western countries, which had relied in part on religious minorities. Instead the political rhetoric is characterized by vague professions of Islam's tolerance without addressing in greater detail the theological and religious-legal problems, to say nothing of the actual conflicts between religious groups.

The theorists of political Islam have adopted a similarly evasive stance about the contemporary status of non-Muslims. The issue does not play an important role in most Islamic conceptions of the state and is often not even addressed or is outlined only vaguely. An apologetic stance is frequently evident when such spokesmen are confronted with the discriminatory precepts of classical Islamic law.

The Universal Islamic Declaration of Human Rights adopted in Paris in 1981 states in its preamble that no human being should enjoy privilege or suffer disadvantage or discrimination by reason of race, color, sex, origin, or language. Religion is conspicuously absent from this list. Paragraph 13 of the declaration guarantees the right to freedom of conscience and worship in accordance with religious beliefs; paragraph 10 states that the religious rights of non-Muslim minorities shall be governed by the Qurʾanic principle "There is no compulsion in religion" (2:256) and grants minorities the right to apply their own law in civil and personal matters. No mention is made here of an equal treatment of religions. The Cairo Declaration of Human Rights in Islam of 1990 does not even address the status of minorities, and the prohibition on discrimination it contains refers only to "basic human dignity" and "basic obligations and responsibilities" without defining the scope of these more precisely.

A number of conservative Islamist authors incorporate the institution of the *dhimma* as part of an Islamic conception of the state, emphasizing, however, that this does not mean subordinating non-Muslims. The *jizya,* for example, is said to allow non-Muslims to contribute to paying for the costs of defending the state in lieu of participating in military service, since they cannot be expected to provide active support for the Islamic jihad. These authors also emphasize that *dhimmis* would not have to pay alms tax (*zakat*). It is evident in their writings, however, that this model of the state does not aim at the complete equality of Muslims and non-Muslims. For example, non-Muslims would not be permitted to hold any office related to religious matters, including that of the head of the state, the army, and the judiciary. Non-Muslims would be subject to Islamic law in issues not affecting the legal autonomy of their communities and would be obligated in the practice of their religion to be considerate of Muslim sensibilities, whereas similar considerations would not be explicitly expected of Muslims. The details of such legal regulations remain vague. Instead these authors usually devote a lot of space to refuting Western accusations concerning discrimination against minorities. In doing so they contrast the tolerance of historical Islamic societies to the intolerance of Europe during the Crusades and its persecution of Jews, emphasizing the Qur'anic principle "There is no compulsion in religion," although they usually avoid discussing the more problematic Qur'anic verses.[17]

Moderate Islamic authors, in contrast, tend to rule out the application of the institution of the *dhimma* in the present day. They argue that the *dhimma* is a body of laws that was appropriate to a particular historical situation rather than an inalterable, fundamental principle of Islamic law. Today, they continue, the focus has shifted from contractual relations among different communities to a constitutional state and from the concept of the *dhimmi* to that of the citizen (*muwatin*). Several modernist Islamic theorists derive from this the full political and legal equality of Muslims and non-Muslims. Nevertheless, modernist authors often neglect to apply this fundamental reorientation to concrete individual issues. A few of the questions that need to be answered include whether an Islamic state as conceived by these theorists would maintain the prohibition on marriage between a non-Muslim man and a Muslim woman, whether it would apply Islamic law to marriages of mixed confessions between non-Muslims, and whether a non-Muslim head of state is conceivable.[18] The Islamic mainstream, which moves between these conservative and modernist positions, simply avoids discussing the issue of equality of Muslims and non-Muslims. While the mainstream does regard non-Muslims as citizens (*muwatinun*), it does so in the sense of the Arabic term, namely, those people who share a common homeland and thus have claim to protection of the law and to just treatment. This understanding of justice, however, aims not at equal treatment but rather at treating every individual in an appropriate manner.[19] This means, for example, that non-Muslims are allowed to practice their religion but are not allowed to proselytize among Muslims; at the same time, proselytizing for Islam and conversion to Islam are supported.

If the status of non-Muslims in general is a problem in human rights discourse with Muslims and the representatives of Muslim states, the status of people without religious affiliation, apostates,[20] and followers of post-Qur'anic religions is even more problematic. While Christians and Jews—and in Asian countries Hindus and Buddhists as well—have a clearly defined legal status, people not belonging to one of the religious communities recognized by the state do not. This problem is particularly evident for followers of the Bahai religion.[21]

There are probably several hundred thousand Bahai currently living in Iran, where their presence has led to a series of conflicts, as it has in the Arab world as well, although their numerical significance is considerably lower there. Nevertheless, the legal status of Bahai has hardly ever been discussed systematically, in terms of either religious law or substantive law. In public perception in the Muslim world, the issue overlaps with the problem of apostasy: Bahai are simply regarded as apostate Muslims. This position, however, fails to take into account the existence in the Islamic world of Bahai who are of Christian and Jewish descent and who for this reason cannot be accused of apostasy by Muslims. The well-known Egyptian-born Islamist Yusuf al-Qaradawi has been the only theologian to address the issue of the classification of Bahai of non-Muslim descent. In his fatwa, al-Qaradawi comes to the conclusion that they are polytheists since they worship a prophet who is not recognized by Islam and believe in a scripture that, from the Muslim perspective, is not of divine origin.[22]

In the intra-Islamic public discussion, the argument is often made that the Bahai faith is not a religion but rather a heresy that lures Muslims away from their religion or that pursues political objectives. The Bahai religion is regularly accused of having close ties to Zionism. Both arguments serve to exclude the Bahai religion from debates about religious freedom. In 1975 the Egyptian Supreme Court—a precursor of the Supreme Constitutional Court of Egypt—argued that the law that had been used to dissolve the Bahai community fifteen years earlier did not violate freedom of worship because the authors of the constitution had intended that this freedom be granted only to Jews, Christians, and Muslims. The court also argued that the issue of religious freedom had not been affected since all people have the freedom to believe inwardly what they think is right as long as they do not display this belief outwardly. Furthermore, the court argued that the antidiscrimination clause had not been violated because this law merely prohibits discrimination between persons with comparable legal status but does not mandate the equal treatment of persons with different legal status.[23] When the Human Rights Committee of the International Covenant on Civil and Political Rights criticized the situation with respect to religious freedom in Egypt in 1993 and explicitly mentioned that of Egyptian Bahai, the Egyptian government responded with a statement that avoided addressing this issue, emphasizing instead its tolerance toward revealed religions as well as the fact that its constitution guaranteed freedom of belief.[24] Since 2006 Egyptian Bahai have been involved in an ongoing legal struggle and face enormous difficulties owing to the government's refusal to issue ID cards—the possession of which is mandatory and a necessary prerequisite in the performance of all vital functions of everyday life—that list any religious affiliation other than "Muslim," "Christian," or "Jew."

Following the Islamic Revolution, the persecution of the Bahai in Iran occurred on a much more open and massive scale than in Egypt. In the initial years after Ayatollah Khomeini's assumption of power, numerous Bahai were killed or "disappeared" after being arrested. Dismissals, plundering, and violence against Bahai were commonplace. This persecution was often justified by the claim that the Bahai were foreign agents. In its response to the Human Rights Commission of the United Nations on the situation of the Bahai, the Iranian government argued that the Bahai were a political organization founded by colonial powers and supported by Israel with anti-Islamic objectives and that the Bahai had also been an important pillar of the shah's regime and as a consequence bore co-responsibility for human rights violations committed under the shah. Although the situation improved somewhat in the 1990s, and there have been no more mass executions since Khomeini's death, the Bahai have still been subject to numerous restrictions—from the nullification of their marriages to their exclusion from universities—and have continually been threatened with arbitrary arrest on the basis of their religious affiliation. There have also been occasional death sentences and even executions.[25] Since 2005 the situation appears to have deteriorated drastically.

The post-Qur'anic religious communities in the Islamic world—the largest of which is the Bahai religion—are much less significant numerically than the Christian minorities. Nevertheless, any examination of the situation of religious minorities that accepts the conventional restrictions within Muslim discourse to exclusively Christian and Jewish minorities would uncritically appropriate an Islamic-influenced understanding of religion and omit a particularly important dimension of the minorities question. The frequently repeated apologetic invocation of a tolerant Islam and of the ideal of a unified nation masks this and a number of other serious issues and is thus poorly suited for clarifying the status of minorities in the Islamic world.

Translated by Tom Lampert

XII

INTERNATIONAL ISLAMIC ORGANIZATIONS

(Johannes Reissner)

The idea of an all-Islamic congress marked the beginning of developments that led to the establishment of contemporary international Islamic organizations. Already in the second half of the nineteenth century, representatives of reform Islam such as Muhammad 'Abduh and Jamal al-Din al-Afghani envisaged such a congress. The Ottoman sultan—whose position as caliph and thus "protector of Islam" had been affirmed in the Ottoman constitution of 1876—then exploited the idea politically in an attempt to preserve the unity of the Ottoman Empire against emerging national movements, in particular the Arab national movement. The ideology of pan-Islamism also influenced anti-Ottoman pan-Arabism. For example, 'Abd al-Rahman al-Kawakibi included in his book *Umm al-qura* (another name for Mecca) the protocol of a fictive pan-Arab conference, which envisaged the creation of a purely "spiritual" caliphate under the leadership of an Arab member of the Quraysh tribe. Because pan-Islamism was divided politically into pro-Ottoman and anti-Ottoman tendencies, initial efforts to convene an all-Islamic congress—especially those by Isma'il Gaspirali at the beginning of the twentieth century—failed to materialize.[1] The path for Islamic conferences opened only after the collapse of the Ottoman Empire in 1920 and in particular after the abolition of the caliphate by Kemal Atatürk in 1924, through which Muslims lost the institution that could at least have symbolized the idea of the fundamental unity of Muslims. In principle Muslims have overcome the elimination of the caliphate rather easily; today only the Hizb al-Tahrir, active in Central Asia, call for its reestablishment. None of the contemporary international Islamic organizations has been able to gain real recognition as a contemporary symbol of the unity of the Muslim community, the *umma*.

1. The First International Islamic Conferences

In the same year as the abolition of the caliphate, King Husayn of Hejaz convened a pilgrimage conference (Mu'tamar al-hajj). Husayn's objective in calling for the conference was to garner support for his claim to the caliphate as the successor to the Prophet and ruler of the holy cities of Mecca and Medina. Several months later, however, the Wahhabis, led by Ibn Saud ('Abd al-'Aziz Al Sa'ud), founder of the contemporary kingdom of Saudi Arabia, conquered Mecca and (in 1925) Medina.

A caliphate congress was held in Cairo in May 1926. The initiators of the congress had originally intended to declare King Fu'ad of Egypt caliph. In the course of the congress, however, the participants were forced to clarify the general question of the constitutional character of the caliphate, and even addressing this question had to be postponed owing to differences of opinion.

The Islamic World Congress (Mu'tamar al-'alam al-islami) took place in Mecca (now under Saudi rule) in June and July 1926. This congress focused on the organization of the pilgrimage and the administration of the holy cities following the Wahhabi conquest. Significant conflicts had arisen between the Wahhabis and the other Islamic tendencies, in particular the Shi'a in Iran.[2]

Questions regarding the pilgrimage were settled during and after this congress. Since the congress in Cairo in May 1926, the caliphate has no longer been a serious object of the international policies of the young nation-states of the Islamic world. Nevertheless, discussions at the General Islamic Congress (al-Mu'tamar al-islami al-'amm), convened in Jerusalem in 1931 by the mufti of Jerusalem, al-Hajj Amin al-Husayni, focused on an issue that continues to function as a catalyst for international Islamic congresses and organizations even today, namely, the Palestine problem.

This congress in Jerusalem in 1931 was able to achieve one of the objectives of the congresses in 1926, that is, the creation of a permanent organization, the Executive Committee. In 1932 a Central Office was also established.[3] Even if this office was active for only three or four years, it was nevertheless an expression of the desire to have a central institution that addressed the concerns of Muslims all over the world beyond the borders of nation-states. A further novelty of the Jerusalem congress was that representatives of new, middle-class Muslim associations such as the Young Men's Muslim Association in Egypt had been invited to participate, that is, members of those groups—such as the Muslim Brothers—that would be essential participants in the development of international Islamic organizations.

Martin Kramer, author of the first coherent overview of the recent history of international Islamic organizations, regards these organizations as a substitute field of action for *'ulama'* and "Muslim activists" of Salafi Islam such as Rashid Rida, since the traditional domain of the *'ulama'*—that of education and law—had been significantly restricted by reforms in the Ottoman

Empire in the nineteenth century and the development of secular nation-states. In general it is certainly correct, as Kramer details in his book, that these congresses tended to highlight the disunity of Muslims rather than the unity invoked at the meetings. Nevertheless, despite this new division of the Islamic world into nation-states, the desire to establish new forms of Muslim unity continued to exist.

The rise of nationalist ideas in the 1930s and 1940s triggered by colonialism pushed pan-Islamic notions into the background. With the exception of Shakib Arslan's congress in Geneva in 1937, there were no international Islamic conferences between 1931 and 1947. The founding of the Islamic state of Pakistan in 1947 provided new initiative for efforts to establish international Islamic organizations. An international congress, at which the Muslim Brothers from Arab countries played a central role, was held in Karachi in 1949. It was here that the Islamic World Congress was founded, which subsequently sponsored a national congress in Karachi in 1951 and a regional congress in Kuala Lumpur in 1962. The Islamic World Congress is the oldest international Islamic organization in existence today. Its driving force was longtime Secretary General In'amullah Khan. In 1962 al-Hajj Amin al-Husayni was elected president of the congress; he was succeeded by Ma'ruf al-Dawalibi, who had been an important politician in Syria and was a former member of the Syrian Muslim Brothers.

The significance of the Islamic World Congress, however, became secondary after the establishment of the Muslim World League in 1962 and the Organization of the Islamic Conference in 1969.

2. The Muslim World League

The Muslim World League (Rabitat al-'alam al-islami) was founded at an international Islamic conference in Mecca during the pilgrimage month in 1962. The founding committee was composed of twenty-six prominent Muslim scholars from twenty-two countries, including *'ulama'* from Ceylon and China. Although several of the founding members held official positions, including the Grand Mufti of Saudi Arabia, Muhammad ibn Ibrahim Al al-Shaykh, and then minister-president of Northern Nigeria al Hajj Ahmadu Bello, the Muslim World League is not a state-level organization but rather is operated by individuals and Islamic associations. While it has the status of a nongovernmental organization in Saudi Arabia, it functions de facto as a kind of religious-political organization of the Saudi state.

The league's statutes define its objective as follows:

> In fulfillment of the duty placed upon us by God to spread the message [*da 'wa*] of Islam, to elucidate its principles and teachings, to dispel misgivings about it, and to combat the dangerous conspiracy through which the enemies of Islam seek to lure Muslims away from their religion and to destroy the unity and

fraternal ties [*ukhuwa*]; furthermore to attend to the affairs of Muslims in a way that protects their interests [*masalih*] and their hopes and contributes to the resolution of their problems.

The statutes identify the annual pilgrimage to Mecca, which is regarded as a kind of natural international Islamic conference, as the means for attaining this objective through holding seminars and instructing pilgrims. Also envisaged was the establishment of an Islamic broadcasting station, the publication of books, and the establishment of a permanent office (which exists today in Mecca).

The founding committee headed by a secretary general determines the league's general policies. According to the league's statutes, the secretary general is elected for five years and should also belong to the "sons of the country," that is, should come from Saudi Arabia.

Both this prerequisite and the ideological orientation of several of the league's founding members, including Abu l-A'la al-Maududi from Pakistan and former leading Muslim Brothers Sa'id Ramadan (Egypt) and Mahmud al-Sawwaf (Iraq), reveal that the organization was conceived by Saudi Arabia as a pan-Islamic counterweight to the "revolutionary" Arabism of Gamal Abdel Nasser (Jamal 'Abd al-Nasir). Nasser attempted to establish the Academy for Islamic Research (Majma' al-buhuth al-islamiyya), which had existed in Cairo since 1961, as an opposite pole to the league. In 1964 the academy held its own international Islamic conference. According to the semiofficial Egyptian newspaper *Al-Ahram,* the Muslim World League was at the time merely a means for using religion for "reactionary, imperialist, and capitalist forces," while the conference of the Academy for Islamic Research had been convened solely for the purpose of "serving God and science."[4]

The battle between "progressive" and "reactionary" Arab states, however, began to lose its sharpness after the Six Day War in 1967. As a consequence of the defeat, Nasser found himself dependent on money from Saudi Arabia, while King Faysal was able to introduce his notion of Islamic solidarity increasingly into the realm of politics.

Today the league is the most important international Islamic organization operating on a nongovernmental level. It has observer status at the United Nations. Its longtime secretary general was Shaykh Muhammad 'Ali al-Harakan (d. 1983). The league is affiliated with the World Supreme Council of Mosques (al-Majlis al-a'la al-'alami li-l-masajid). The league's monthly journal, *Majallat rabitat al-'alam al-islami,* is also published in English. The political activities of the league focus first and foremost on the Palestine problem and on supporting Muslim minorities and resistance groups, for instance, in the Philippines. Missionary activities in Europe and the United States also play a significant role.

There is no institution in Islam that can proclaim ex cathedra what the correct doctrine is. As a consequence, the league's role—which has grown over time—of expressing positions on questions of Islamic doctrine (primarily in the sense of Islamic integralism) deserves our attention. For example, in February 1979 an international delegation of *'ulama'* that included leading members of the league called upon Muammar el-Qaddafi—who denies the validity of the sunna as it is recorded in the hadith collections—to make a public declaration of remorse.

The league's statutory commitment to spreading the word of Islam has also led to political conflicts, for example, as a result of its significant financial support for Islamic groups in Turkey opposed to the country's laical constitution. Considered as a whole, the league should continue to be seen as an organ of conservative, Saudi-influenced Islamism. The league has demonstrated little interest to date in reducing the tensions between Sunnites and Shi'ites that have played a significant subliminal role in the political-ideological conflict between Iran and Saudi Arabia, in particular following the Islamic Revolution in Iran.[5]

After the terrorist attack on the World Trade Center and the Pentagon on September 11, 2001, the league was strongly suspected of participating in the financing of terrorist groups. In order to improve the league's reputation, Secretary General 'Abdullah al-Turki visited the United States and Europe in the summer of 2002.

3. The Organization of the Islamic Conference

The ideological predominance of Arab nationalism over claims for a principled Muslim unity has existed since the 1930s and is evident in the fact that while the Arab League was established in 1945, a comparable Islamic organization on the governmental level arose only in the early 1970s: the Organization of the Islamic Conference (Munazzamat al-mu'tamar al-islami), often identified by its English designation and abbreviated OIC.[6]

The decisive catalyst for the establishment of this organization was the burning of the al-Aqsa Mosque in Jerusalem on August 21, 1969. Following the attack on the mosque, Saudi Arabia and Morocco convened the First Islamic Summit Meeting in Rabat in the fall of that year (September 22–25). During this conference plans were made for an Islamic conference of foreign ministers the following year, at which the establishment of a permanent secretariat was to be discussed. It was only at the Third Islamic Conference of Foreign Ministers in Jidda (February 29–March 4, 1972), however, that participants were able to agree to a resolution on the issue. Syria and Iraq in particular had objected to the creation of a permanent institution, arguing that the Islamic Conference would not be able to accomplish anything for either Jerusalem or the Arab cause and would ultimately serve only to increase the power of conservative Arab states.

The Organization of the Islamic Conference was able to attain a crucial breakthrough at the Second Summit Meeting in Lahore on February 22–24,

1974. The Arabs' partial victory in the October War of 1973 and the subsequent oil boycott contributed to an easing of tensions between "progressive" and "conservative" Arab states. While Syria and Iraq were present in Lahore only as observers, thirty-six nations participated in the summit conference, which proved to be a success, particularly for Saudi Arabia. Anwar el-Sadat, Qaddafi, and the president of North Yemen, Abdul Rahman al-Iryani, even proposed that King Faysal of Saudi Arabia be given the title of a caliph, "Commander of the Faithful" (*amir al-mu'minin*), which, however, he wisely refused. According to a report by the newspaper *Berliner Tagesspiegel* on January 27, 1981, there were again rumors at the Third Islamic Summit Conference in al-Ta'if (Saudi Arabia) on January 26–28, 1981, that the Saudi monarch, King Khalid, was supposed to be proclaimed caliph, an indication that the fascination with the caliphate as a symbol of Muslim unity could also be exploited diplomatically.

In addition to spectacular Islamic summit conferences, the permanent secretariat of the conference established in Jidda and the annual Islamic conference of foreign ministers have proved to be the most important bodies for implementing the ambitious aim of moving a step closer to the unity of the Islamic world.

According to Article 3 of the charter of the OIC adopted by thirty states at the Third Conference of Islamic Foreign Ministers in Jidda (February 29–March 4, 1972), the organization is composed of three elements: the conference of kings and heads of state and government of Islamic countries; the conference of foreign ministers, which according to Article 4 is to be held annually; and the general secretariat and subsidiary organs. The conferences of kings and heads of state and government have supreme authority in the organization and are to be convened whenever it is deemed necessary or warranted (Article 4). The responsibilities of the conference of foreign ministers are: to consider the means of implementing the general policy of the conference; to review progress in the implementation of resolutions adopted at previous sessions; and to adopt resolutions on matters of common interest. The most important organizational responsibilities of the conference of foreign ministers are to discuss the report of the financial committee and to appoint the secretary general (Article 5). The secretary general is appointed for a period of four years, renewable only once (Article 6). The main responsibility of the secretary general is to organize the summit conference and the conference of foreign ministers and to coordinate the work of the political, cultural, social, and economic committees. All expenses of the OIC are borne by the member states proportionate to their national incomes (Article 7), through which the Arab oil states wield significant power. According to Article 8, every Muslim state is eligible to join the conference. Nevertheless, the fact that Lebanon, where Christians are officially in the majority, and Senegal, whose head of state until January 1981 was Léopold Senghor, a Christian, are both members of the OIC suggests that the term "Muslim state" is interpreted rather broadly.

The most important institutions of the Organization of the Islamic Conference are the Islamic Solidarity Fund and the Islamic Development Bank. The creation of the Islamic Solidarity Fund (Sanduq al-tadamun al-islami) was adopted at the Fifth Islamic Conference of Foreign Ministers in Kuala Lumpur in 1974. The objective of the fund is to provide financial assistance in case of disasters and natural catastrophes; to support Islamic countries and Muslim minorities and communities in building mosques, hospitals, and schools; and to promote Islamic universities and youth groups and the Islamic call (*da'wa*). Saudi Arabia was to provide one-third of the total budget of the fund.

The Islamic Development Bank (al-Bank al-islami li-l-tanmiya) was opened in Jidda on October 20, 1975. It was the most important of the existing Islamic banks, which in accord with the shari'a do not charge interest on loans. According to the bank's statutes, its capital at the time was 6 billion Islamic dinars, whereby one dinar was equivalent to one Special Drawing Right of the International Monetary Fund (in 1977, $1.92). Saudi Arabia was the most important shareholder with 21.88 percent, followed by Libya (13.87 percent), the UAE (12.27 percent), and Kuwait (11.20 percent). Loans to poor Islamic countries in Asia and Africa, not least to cover increased oil prices, constituted the lion's share of the bank's projects.

The Jerusalem Fund, created in Jidda in 1975, is also part of the OIC. Its mission is to preserve the Islamic character of the third-holiest city of Islam. The fund's deposits with the Islamic Development Bank amounted to almost 4 million Islamic dinars in 1976–77.

In addition to its monetary organs, the OIC also operates the International Islamic News Agency (IINA). The agency was called into being at the Conference of Foreign Ministers in Jidda in 1972 and endowed with $2.5 million. According to a Saudi press release, initial trial programs of an Islamic radio station were broadcast on May 11, 1979.

It is extraordinarily difficult to achieve political consensus among the fifty-seven member states of the OIC. The conference has been able to demonstrate the greatest unity regarding the Palestine question. This is the sole political issue that is expressly addressed in the OIC charter. Article 2.5 of the charter names as an objective the coordination of efforts for the safeguarding of the holy places and support of the struggle of the people of Palestine. The PLO has observer status at the conference. But as demonstrated indirectly by appeals from the OIC and the Muslim World League that Palestine is an important issue for all Muslims because of the city of Jerusalem, the Palestine problem is less urgent for states such as Senegal and Malaysia, for example, than for those countries sharing a border with Israel. The fact that Turkey long maintained diplomatic relations with Israel—as did Iran before the fall of the shah—was an important point of conflict at the Third Islamic Summit Conference in Taif in early 1981.

The most difficult problem within the OIC has been the dominance of Arab states over Asian and sub-Saharan African member states. This was already evident in the initial years after the establishment of the OIC in regard to what was certainly the organization's most important decision at that point, namely the suspension of Egypt's membership, which was resolved at the Conference of Foreign Ministers in Fez on May 8–12, 1979. At the Conference of Foreign and Economic Ministers of the Arab League in Baghdad on March 27–31, 1979, participants had recommended that the OIC and OAU (Organization of African Unity) suspend Egypt if it agreed to a peace settlement with Israel. After the peace treaty on March 26, the OIC in fact voted to suspend Egypt, although Oman, Sudan, Somalia, and North Yemen abstained from the debate. Prior to this, Indonesia and Malaysia had publicly welcomed the peace treaty, but then agreed to the suspension. Senegal, Gabon, Gambia, Niger, Upper Volta (today Burkina Faso), and Guinea-Bissau abstained from the vote, which—according the journal *The Middle East* of May 11, 1979—was taken as a sign that they were dissatisfied with the assistance provided by the Organization of the Islamic Conference.

Arab predominance again became an issue during the election of the new secretary general in the same year. The Asian member states demanded that the secretary generalship rotate among candidates from Asian, Arab, and sub-Saharan countries. Adopting this proposal would have meant recognizing regionally defined special interests. The proposal was defeated by Libya and Kuwait, which insisted that the unity of the Islamic *umma* recognized no geographic divisions.

Over the course of its official existence, the OIC has in fact successfully avoided the establishment of blocs, despite the in part substantial ideological and political differences among its member states, which became especially apparent during the Iran-Iraq War. Nevertheless, certain coalitions can be identified. Roughly speaking, there is a Saudi Arabian faction and a sub-Saharan African faction. After the collapse of the Soviet Union, six former Soviet republics with Muslim majorities were admitted to the OIC in 1992.[7]

The OIC has not been able to establish itself as a bloc in international politics. Its concrete significance lies more in the promotion of intra-South cooperation, in particular through the organizations affiliated with it. The OIC has proved to be a status quo organization in terms of the political influence it exerts on its member states. The opposition between pro-Western Sunni Saudi Arabia and anti-Western revolutionary Shi'a Iran formed the backdrop of the conference's failed mediation efforts at the beginning of the Iran-Iraq War. Only the OIC summit in Teheran in December 1997, half a year after Muhammad Khatami's election as president of Iran, demonstrated that Islamic revolutionary Iran had been accepted again among the ranks of "established" Islamic states. It was a first sign of the rapprochement between Iran and Saudi Arabia; the official reconciliation of the two states occurred in April 1999.

Political agreement in the OIC occurs most readily when the Islamic *umma* is threatened externally. The Palestine problem remains the top priority. The conference also demonstrated solidarity with the Muslims of Bosnia-Herzegovina, and an official OIC delegation attempted to intervene in Moscow in response to the Chechnya question.

The OIC does not, as a rule, concern itself with questions of Islamic doctrine. This made all the more remarkable the resolution at the summit meeting of January 1981, which declared the jihad to rescue Jerusalem, to support the Palestinian people, and to obtain the withdrawal from the occupied Arab territories to be the duty of all Muslims.[8] In doing so, the state leaders of the OIC gave themselves the authority to determine the obligations of Muslims—a noteworthy step in light of the jihad discussion that arose in the Islamic world as well after the terror attacks of September 11, 2001.

Overall the OIC has had little success in its attempts to mediate within the Islamic camp. The definitive mediation of the Yemen conflict in 1991 and the mediation efforts in the Moro Conflict in the Philippines in the 1970s are more the exception than the rule. Political conflicts on the scale of the Kuwait crisis of 1990 and the first Gulf War or even the war led by the United States against Iraq beginning in 2003 completely exceeded the capacities of the organization. Its efforts in recent years to contain the growing conflict between Sunnis and Shi'is have remained rhetorical.

One accusation that has been leveled at the Organization of the Islamic Conference (as well as at the Arab League) is that it has been less successful at establishing unity and Islamic solidarity than its rhetoric would suggest. Considered in historical terms, the OIC remains important as an all-Islamic body that recognizes the principle of the territorial nation-state (which for Muslims continues to be a principle of only limited self-evidence) and functions at the highest governmental level. It is the sole intergovernmental international organization that is committed to a particular religion, operating according to the overarching premise that religion must not be damaged by one-sided political positioning.

Translated by Tom Lampert

Part Three

Present-Day Islamic Culture and Civilization

I

"Orientalistics" and Orientalism

(Reinhard Schulze)

Although the "Oriental" was already seen in the seventeenth and eighteenth centuries as a cultural tradition distinct from that of the Occident, and was also considered separately in academic research and teaching, only in the nineteenth century did the view emerge that research on the "Orient" represented a separate academic discipline. The German name for this discipline, "Orientalistics" (*Orientalistik*), is more recent, while the English term "Orientalism" is older. The latter did not so much refer to academic dealings with the Orient itself as actually describe those types of thinking and lifestyles that made explicit reference to the Orient. Accordingly, the substance of the concept originally described the attitude and activities of a person who would then become an "Orientalist." The usage is first found around 1779 in English and 1799 in French.[1] The concepts "Orientalist" and "Semitic studies" were used to express academic treatment of texts from the Orientalist tradition; until the early nineteenth century, "Orientalist" was almost exclusively linked with the languages of the Near East (for example, Arabic, Persian, Ottoman Turkish, Ethiopian, and Syrian-Aramaic). Language, however, was already used early on to gain access to historical and cultural traditions. In the famed *Bibliothèque Orientale,* an encyclopedia collected by Barthélemy d'Herbelot (1625–1695) and completed by Antoine Galland (1646–1715) in 1697, there are a large number of such references.[2]

In addition to this tradition, starting in the fifteenth century an additional context existed for the use of the phrase "Orientalist": it referred to those who, in contrast to the "classicists," saw an equivalent to the Latin and Greek textual traditions to which the humanists had returned. Through this a certain antagonism arose between "classicists" and "Orientalists," an antagonism that, on the one hand, perpetuated the ancient split between the late Scholastic "Arabists," who explicitly reached back to the Arabic text traditions in the fields of philosophy and medicine, and the "Hellenists," who started with the original Greek tradition (especially that of Aristotle).[3]

On the other hand, this antagonism was newly identified and continued into the nineteenth century through a reinterpretation of the "classical" as "Occidental."[4] The establishment of the "Orient" upon the cultural traditions of the "Near East" was only abandoned in the course of the nineteenth century. Now traditions oriented toward China, India, and Japan were added.

In the nineteenth century the earliest studies on the history of Orientalistics were already being written,[5] and they continued to be written, especially from the mid-twentieth century on.[6] In these studies Orientalistics was mainly viewed as a biographically determined body of work.[7] In this view the study of Oriental languages was first of all a science ancillary to theology that was to have been established at the universities, among others those of Paris and Oxford, after the Council of Vienne in 1311–12. Around 1600 an academic discourse began to unfold that also included Oriental languages; a chair for Arabic was established in 1599 in Leiden, the stronghold of the Arabists; in 1631 in Cambridge; and in 1635 in Oxford. But the tie to theology continued to exist. Johann Fück closely linked the emancipation of Orientalist disciplines from theology, which began around 1730, with the "European Enlightenment." In fact, in the eighteenth century a "new image of the Orient" gradually asserted itself; it was, first of all, based on a general desire for the exotic on the part of the bourgeoisie and the royal courts, and second, determined by fundamental theological debates, primarily on deism, which were accompanied by a specific preoccupation with the Qur'an and the person of Muhammad.[8] The Islamic Orient became not only an exotic idyll, created in part by Antoine Galland, with his highly idiosyncratic paraphrase of the stories from the *Thousand and One Nights*, compiled shortly before in the *Bibliothèque Orientale*, but also the site of an ambiguous culture. On the one hand, it was seen as a perfect, rational society; some, like the French novelist Henry De Boulainvilliers (1658–1722), celebrated the Prophet Muhammad as the harbinger of a rational religion superior to Christianity and as the prototype of the philosopher-prophet.[9] On the other hand, however, it was condemned: Voltaire could not keep from characterizing the Prophet as the embodiment of a dictator in his poetic tragedy *Mahomet*, which premiered on April 10, 1741, in Lille.[10] Dramatist James Miller (1706–1744), too, staged his version of Voltaire's *Mahomet* the same year he died.[11]

Around 1740 a change of heart set in at German-speaking universities that would do justice to this ambiguous Oriental imagery.[12] At the University of Göttingen, founded in 1738, Arabic studies were assigned to the philosophy department. This established a completely different framework for the credibility of scholarly treatment of the Orient. Johann Jacob Reiske (1716–1774) tried to encapsulate this in "didactic prefaces" on "Muhammedan" history:

> In brief, in studying Muhammedan history, enough and plenty can be found to occupy and captivate whoever wishes to become acquainted with the various

articles of faith of the nations on God and divine things and the history of religion, or the mores, laws, and legal systems of the races and states and the forms of government; anyone, too, whom the history of physical objects, sicknesses, and remedies captivates, or who loves to observe the shape of the globe through the ages and the rise and fall of cities.[13]

Observing the world through the Orient was Reiske's brash program: this universalism was also clearly noted in other writers and scholars of the eighteenth century. The traditions on which this Orientalistics was based were multifaceted and contradictory. In the eighteenth century, knowledge of the Islamic-Oriental world was based mainly on the following traditions:

1. perpetuation of the Spanish reception of Islam from the thirteenth century (especially Jimenez)
2. the reception of the Qur'an in the thirteenth century, passed down in printed Qur'an editions in the sixteenth century (Ketenensis, Bibliander)
3. the "Arabistics" of the late Scholastics (medicine, philosophy, and so on)
4. the works of the Renaissance philologists (philosophy, language, sciences)
5. the flood of texts surrounding the Turkish wars, including the corresponding polemical literature (seventeenth century, Abraham a Santa Clara)
6. the tradition of philological theology and the Sacra Philologia in England (Pococke, Ockley) and Germany (seventeenth and eighteenth centuries)
7. the new "scientific" Anglican, Catholic, and Protestant apologetics (late seventeenth and eighteenth centuries, including Prideaux, Marracci, Reelant)
8. reference to Islam in the early Enlightenment period (Pascal, Spinoza) and in the deism and miracle debates (eighteenth century, Locke, Hume, Stubbe, *de tribus impostoribus*)
9. French encyclopedism and Orientalism (seventeenth century, Bayle, d'Herbelot, Galland)
10. inclusion of Islamic history in French post-deist Enlightenment writings (eighteenth century, Boulainvilliers, Montesquieu, Voltaire)
11. academic Orientalistics and historicism after around 1730 (Gagnier, Sale, Reiske, Reimarus, Niebuhr)[14]

Academic treatment of the Islamic Orient in the eighteenth century meant, first of all, criticism of traditional views and judgments; the new Orientalistics received its methodological polish, however, in the early nineteenth century, when the philological basis of Orientalistics was established. Now that Orientalistics had installed itself at the universities as an independent discipline, the academic worldview, and the teacher-student relationship with which it was closely linked, increasingly determined the development of the subject. There were mentors such as Josef von Hammer-Purgstall (1774–1856) and Antoine Silvestre de Sacy (1758–1838), who blazed a path for nineteenth-century scholars. Philologist Georg Wilhelm Freytag (1788–1861) came to the University of Bonn, and Romanticist Friedrich Rückert

(1788–1866) was appointed to the University of Erlangen. Another student of de Sacy's, Heinrich Leberecht Fleischer (1801–1888), ultimately broke with the Romantic tradition and introduced critical methods in philology, highly modern at the time, to Orientalistics. Historicism, too, mastered by Leopold von Ranke, became a model in the second half of the nineteenth century for Orientalist historians in the German-speaking countries.[15] The Orientalist became a critic of the Orient: as a philologist and historian, he drafted a sober, in comparison to the Romantics even a dry, picture of early Islamic history, always with the goal in mind of highlighting the uniqueness of the one and the other, in accordance with historical dogmatics. Researchers worked, in fact dug, themselves ever deeper into the history of the text; there they imagined themselves safe from the all-encompassing grasp of the historians around von Ranke, who gave opinions on contemporary issues in accordance with the political order, and in the process viewed the Orient as "their" terrain. Orientalist studies were to lead away from "the history of nations" (*Völkergeschehen*) and to an "essentialist" reflection on the Orient.[16]

While various advocates made a case for considering the contemporary Orient, and this was even adopted into the mandate of the Deutsche Morgenländische Gesellschaft (German Oriental Society), founded in 1845, the retreat into early Oriental history and critical review of textual and linguistic materials had become the main task of Orientalistics, which thus separated itself from the study of *Realienkunde,* Oriental culture and everyday life.[17] As philologists and historicists, the Orientalists had meanwhile committed themselves entirely to the relativism of the times: Oriental societies were not viewed with the help of a dynamic concept of development expressing a universal civilization, but were frozen in their historical individuality. The scholarly terrain of Orientalistics thus seemed secure, for few historians of the time could compete with the philological knowledge of the Orientalists. As critics, the late-nineteenth-century Orientalists were thus able to distinguish between the "blossoming of Islam" (the subject of their research) and its "decay" (the reason for not researching). August Dillmann (1823–1894), professor in Kiel and later rector of the Friedrich Wilhelm University of Berlin, said in 1876, "Historical criticism, the chemistry of the humanities, the art of distinguishing truth from fiction, never known in the Orient, least of all in the Islamic world, is one of the fruits of the new spirit of our age."[18]

Thus the Orientalists had split once and for all from the Romantic tradition and the universalism of the Enlightenment; the Orient, and Islam, had been reduced to objects, finding the "true facts" of which would now be the task of the discipline. Dillmann also made no secret of the actual purpose of historical criticism: "Only a Christianity purified by it will entirely preserve its world-conquering power, also preserve it in the world that until now gave it the toughest opposition, the people of Islam.[19]

Historical criticism acted censorially. The "truth" of the Orient was determined by Orientalistics; early Islam was seen as a totality, which—following fully in the footsteps of Wilhelm Dilthey (1833–1911)—was to be understood as the "centering significance" of Islamic history.[20]

When, at the beginning of the twentieth century, historicism was critically examined by Ernst Troeltsch (1865–1923)[21] and the brothers Max and Alfred Weber, among others, and was expanded through a specific concept of culture, Orientalists such as Carl Heinrich Becker (1876–1933) and his student Hans-Heinrich Schaeder (1896–1957) adapted to this trend and gradually separated Islamic studies from the field of Oriental philology, now generally termed "Semitic philology," which had been dominated by the scholarly consideration of the Orient.[22] At the same time, at over twenty German-speaking universities, new scholarly institutes emerged that were generally termed "Oriental seminars." "Islamic studies" was not yet the term typically used in such seminars in the business of scholarship. It appeared for the first time in 1929, in the Seminar for Semitistics and Islamic Studies founded under the leadership of Becker at the University of Berlin.[23] Historicism now had two pillars in Orientalistics: one was represented by critical philology, the other by religious or cultural history. Philology had highlighted the "objective peculiarity" of Oriental history and language; now scholars of Islam worked on establishing the individuality of Islamic culture. They saw this to be firmly anchored in the "facts" of early history that had been painstakingly elaborated by the philologists, from which there was no escape.

Through the adoption of Islamic studies into the canon of Orientalist subjects, Oriental philology hardly sacrificed its self-confidence; for the philologists, the Qur'an itself presented an extraordinary challenge. In the nineteenth century, various well-known Orientalists had already approached the Qur'an from a philological perspective, but they did not yet consider themselves able to produce a "critical edition of the Qur'an." Not until 1930 did the philologist Gotthelf Bergsträsser (1886–1933) venture an attempt to offer a plan for a critical edition of the Qur'an. After his premature death, his student Otto Pretzl (1893–1941) pursued this plan, though unsuccessfully.[24] A "critical edition" of the Qur'an would have meant the victory of philology over religion.

With Theodor Nöldeke (1836–1930) and Julius Wellhausen (1844–1918), critical philology and critical assessment of sources reached a peak and triggered early reflections on the subject; in Islamic studies the same is true of Ignaz Goldziher (1850–1921), the aforementioned C. H. Becker, Christiaan Snouck Hurgronje (1857–1936), and Martin Hartmann (1951–1918).[25] In the West, however, the breadth of publication on the Islamic Orient was hardly dominated by the research of these Orientalists, based in the classic areas of Orientalistics. Over three-quarters of all publications in the nineteenth century dealt with research—understood as *Realienkunde,* the study of culture and everyday life—on individual countries or with language and literature. Barely 7 percent of all publications were devoted to the Islamic religion in the narrower sense, only 1.5 percent to Islamic law, and around 1 percent to early Islamic history. In the twentieth century this profile did not change fundamentally: aside from a constantly growing interest in Islamic law and Islamic art, this distribution continued. Only a decrease in publications on Turkey is apparent; after 1924 Turkey threatened to disappear more and more from the focus of Orientalists, while interest in countries of the Fertile Crescent grew. This profile, however, was not reflected in research at German-speaking universities. There those subjects at the center of academic research were precisely those receiving less attention worldwide, namely the Islamic religion itself, Islamic law, Islamic philosophy, and Islamic history before 1258. This philologically oriented development of concentration would characterize German-language Orientalistics until the 1970s. Thus, until then, publications on Islamic religion made up around 12 percent of all Orientalist publications, and those on Islamic history until 1258 around 15 percent. This specificity in German-language Orientalistics was also connected with the fact that, in contrast with France, the Netherlands, and Great Britain, points of contact with colonial studies interests were relatively weakly developed and concerned, at most, the Ottoman Empire.[26]

Until the early 1970s the works of scholars such as Nöldeke, Wellhausen, and Goldziher formed the working model for most Orientalists. They remained mired much longer than other historians or scholars of religious studies in philologically based historicism; the critique of historicism, and subsequently philology, that began with Nietzsche was not reproduced by the Orientalists, so that a deep gulf slowly developed between the systematic sciences and the Orientalists.[27] The "hermeneutic reflection" that could be observed in the 1920s in history and philosophy, and led gradually to the displacement of historicism, left Orientalistics untouched,[28] as did the positivism debate that marked German social sciences after 1961. In 1966 the Tübingen-based Orientalist Rudi Paret wrote, "The goal and purpose of our scholarly work is to break through the intellectual horizon set by our own environment and to cast an eye on the world of the Orient, in order to learn to better understand, through a foreign entity, the possibilities of human existence and thus, ultimately, ourselves."[29]

On the one hand, the period of National Socialist rule meant a major break with the research tradition of Orientalistics.[30] Nine of the seventeen Orientalist full professors were fired for racial or political reasons, or emigrated;[31] five assistant professors had to leave the university, and the number of completed Orientalistics dissertations shrank by almost half.[32] On the other hand, the remaining professors strove to maintain continuity; thematically they remained loyal to their tradition, although a clear decrease in interest in Islamic theology and Islamic law could be observed. The restoration of Orientalistics after 1945 brought no appreciable reorientation of the discipline.[33] In East Germany, Orientalistics retained its philological profile; at the same time, it was greatly impaired by the development of a politically controlled field of "Middle East Studies."[34]

In the early 1960s the first change of heart began to emerge. In Egypt in 1961 Muhammad al-Bahiy (1905–1982), who had been educated at Hamburg, published a short paper in which he directly linked the scholarly interests of the Orientalists with the colonial ambitions of Christian missionaries.[35] Linking colonialism with the Christian mission had long been a leitmotif of Islamic intellectuals, but now Orientalistics itself was identified as the handmaiden of missionary work, and therefore of colonialism. In the same year the Egyptian scholar Muhammad al-Ghazali (1917–1996), who had close ties to the Muslim Brotherhood, vehemently rejected the results of the historian Goldziher's critique of Islamic religious history.[36] Paret wrote that the Orientalists "took this calmly."[37] But when in 1963 two Arab scholars, Egyptian sociologist Anouar Abdel-Malek (Anwar ʿAbd al-Malik, b. 1924) and Palestinian historian ʿAbd al-Latif al-Tibawi (1910–1981), critically examined the results of Orientalist research, uneasiness arose;[38] both, after all, wrote for a Western public and sought direct contact with the Orientalists. Tibawi's thesis that Islam, like every other religion, could ultimately be understood only by its believers touched directly on the Orientalist monopoly of Islamic studies; Abdel-Malek placed Orientalistics in direct proximity to imperialism, which saw the "Orient" as an object of study, and polemicized strongly against the spirit of critical historicism in Orientalistics, which he said had prevented awareness of the lines of development of Oriental societies. Criticism of Orientalistics was also raised in related disciplines. Norman Daniel had meanwhile carefully examined the image of Islam in medieval and modern Europe and showed that it was closely linked to European cultural history and had also influenced the Orientalists' scholarly discourse.[39] Religious scholar Jacques Waardenburg took up the idea of the reflection of European identity in Orientalist scholarship and dedicated himself intensively to five exponents of European Orientalistics.[40]

These critical views can be concentrated around three theses: first, Orientalistics had not recognized its political dependency on the age of colonialism; second, it had justified its own, fundamentalist discourse on Islam by declaring the early Islamic period to be the center of understanding, and thus disregarding all developmental ideas, and especially any consideration of the present as the result of historical continuity or discontinuity; and third, it had not ultimately recognized that its own image of Islam was thoroughly reflective of the exotic desires of the European bourgeoisie.

In the early 1970s at least one point of criticism was taken up by many Orientalists: people were now calling, as a matter of course, for the adoption of issues related to the present into the scope of Orientalistics.[41] This did not, however, mean a split with the basic theses of historicism; the present situation of Oriental countries was seen as one of tension between Islam, which supplied meaning and upon which the Orientalists had elaborated for their early history, and European modernism.[42] An opposing thesis, which assumed that the development of Oriental societies up to the present day had followed the laws of history, was attempted mainly by Marxist historians; but since they could not do without research from the classical period of Orientalistics, the view of early Islam that had been established persisted, now supplemented by a clear emphasis on the present.[43]

The more contemporarily oriented research therefore could not be seen as a logical continuation of classical Orientalistics, even though, as mentioned earlier, questions regarding the present day could be found sporadically among the Orientalists. Rather, the opening of the systematic sciences to non-European countries played a decisive role, with geography, political science, and social anthropology having an important function.[44] Initial surveys in 1972 and 1974 showed, however, that it was still not possible to speak of research on the Orient that was truly focused on the present day.[45]

Orientalistics and the study of the Orient differ, in the common view, according to the sources or texts on which they focus. Orientalistics, as a philological science based on written texts, would always emphasize questions of history, literature and linguistics, and religious and scientific history. But because the methods of critical philology, in the view of many Orientalists, could not sufficiently comprehend a culture's developmental processes, Orientalistics always depended on an expansion of its methodological bases.[46] In the late 1960s it received a decisive push in this direction from the social sciences. Max Weber's ideal-typical models had an effect on Islamic societies, though to a quite limited extent,[47] and were positively received by C. H. Becker, among others.[48] In the 1980s Orientalist statements on the applicability of Weber's categories to Islamic societies grew in number.[49] The result was thoroughly negative; in connection with the Eurocentrism discussion, it was repeatedly pointed out that Orientalistics could not transfer European ideal types to "other" cultures if it wished to avoid imposing European interpretive models on "foreign" cultures. Nevertheless, the desire to embed Orientalistics in a broader social science discourse remained; it especially influenced present-oriented Orientalistics, which was by nature in a difficult position in relation to research on the Orient in systematic disciplines such as geography, sociology, and political science.

Internal scholarly critiques of Orientalistics proceeded cautiously: Maxime Rodinson pointed to the historical deficiency in theory and demanded an end to the primacy of philology and the "cultural essentialism" applied to "classical" Islam.[50] Others attempted to scrutinize the image of Islam among some Orientalists, taking on, in particular, the Austrian American scholar Gustav von Grunebaum, whose works were long the target of criticism.[51]

In 1978 the Palestinian American literary critic Edward Said (1920–2003) intensified the debate on Orientalistics with his famous book *Orientalism*.[52] Said attempted to prove that what called itself Orientalistics could be incorporated into a broad European discourse that he called "Orientalism." Said's critique was based on Michel Foucault's discourse analysis, elaborated mainly between 1966 and 1975.[53] Like him, Said sees Orientalism as a culturally specific system of power that is represented by the creation of a European Orient; this is proved through science and art to such a degree that it can be used to coerce the "Orientals" (the "Orientalization of the Orient"). The deconstruction of the Orient threatened to turn into deconstruction of Orientalistics. For the first time, Orientalists were directly confronted with a new critical view from an external perspective; in the numerous responses to Said the attempt was made to keep Orientalist studies out of the discourse on Orientalism.[54] But the years of neglected theoretical and methodological discussion within Orientalistics took their toll: it was mainly representatives of related disciplines interested in the Orient who opposed overgeneralizing Said's theses. Their critique accused Said of reductionist tendencies and charged him with a tendency to confirm his own preconceived opinions with his choice of evidence.[55] The Damascene philosopher Sadiq al-'Azm (b. 1934) referred to Said's "reverse" Orientalism, in which he had, in reaction, created the character of an anti-Oriental Westerner.[56]

The theme was widely taken up and initiated a very belated critique within Orientalistics of the epistemological and methodological bases of the subject. The critique, however, was not much affected by Said's theses; the concept of deconstruction, based heavily on Foucault, lacked a constructive element. Foucault's early death had prevented him from elaborating his philosophy, which would have made possible a search for "different rules" in dealing with the Orient.

Because of Edward Said, Orientalistics, now itself an object of scholarly discourse, was forced to take a look at the contemporary philosophical discussion. What it discovered seemed problematic to some Orientalists, for once they accepted the rules of discourse theories, little room was left for unprejudiced Oriental studies. The philosophical-sociological discourse based on Foucault demanded more than Orientalistics as a whole was prepared to offer. The rediscovery of Nietzsche and Heidegger,[57] the reinterpretation of the concept of truth as part of a redefined hermeneutics, and the criticism of "going native"—an anthropological counterpart to Orientalism within the social sciences—had little effect on Orientalistics.[58] There were exceptions. The Parisian scholar of Islam Mohammed Arkoun (b. 1928) attempted to incorporate hermeneutics into Orientalistics;[59] the Turkish-American historian Şerif Mardin pointed out similar paths. But the "new understanding of Islam," for example, through a "rereading [*relecture*] of the Qur'an" called for by Arkoun, was difficult to convey to Orientalists, as "the expectations connected with it could hardly be fulfilled."[60]

To a certain degree the debate surrounding Said's theses reanimated the old cultural pluralism of Ernst Troeltsch, as received above all by the Orientalist Jörg Kraemer.[61] The theoretical debate was reduced to the question of whether the interpretive categories elaborated or confirmed by Orientalistics were universal or reflected Eurocentrism. In 1980 Jean-Paul Charnay, the French sociologist and scholar of Islam, published a detailed study in which he traced the development of Eurocentrism in Orientalistics.[62] "We have become more careful," said Jacques Waardenburg in 1980, referring to the theretofore common attempt to determine the meaning of Islam and to compare Islamic societies on that basis. He called for a semiotic interpretation of Islam "as a network of symbols."[63] This caution also applied to dealing with the "Other" in order to avoid the suspicion of Eurocentrism or Orientalism. But Rodinson once again pointed to the dangers of ethnocentrism ("xenocentrism") in Orientalistics, which represented the converse of Eurocentrism and essentially ran parallel to it.[64]

The problem of Eurocentrism has preoccupied Orientalistics more in recent years than the accusation of being part of a Western discourse on the Orient. Once the European scholarly discourse had been revealed as power over the studied object, the question immediately arose of how one could speak about the Other without exerting this power. Islamic political groups soon recognized this dilemma and rubbed salt in the wounds. The contemporary demand that Orientalists "convey respect for the historically developed character of their partners in the Orient and at the same time create awareness of the close ties of common intellectual premises and historical experience between the Islamic world and Europe" nourished their hopes of finally bringing to bear their own, "Islamic" categories and their own lived significance.[65]

Some Orientalists and ethnologists now turned the tables and constructed a "counter-Orient" on the basis of what they assumed to be the "Other's" perceptions. The relativism that historians had already espoused in extreme cases gained a new lease on life as cultural relativism. Whether Euro- or ethnocentrism, the Other remained the Other, the "foreign entity."

Despite all its theoretical demands, Orientalistics remained a textual science. That a source had to be interpreted philologically was not up for debate; thus the critique of Orientalism never targeted philological Orientalistics as such. The main issue instead was the interpretation of a historical event, into the center of which had stepped an Orient constructed alongside scholarship that had fascinated Montesquieu but at times disgusted Voltaire; an Orient that gave the fantasies of the non-Oriental the space to metamorphose, to become a disguised, but "true" and "better," Oriental; an Orient that could at the same time become a place that was the exact, forbidding opposite of the Occident—that is, the East. The historical critique could not prevent this classification; it is striking that the older Orientalists developed a certain fondness for the "last representative" of rational Islamic philosophy, Ibn Rushd (Averroës, d. 1198), the historian Ibn Khaldun (d. 1406), and the mystical rebel al-Hallaj (executed 922) and made them into features of a different Orient, whose legacy they administered themselves, in contrast to the Muslims. Their preference for the philosopher Ibn Sina (Avicenna, d. 1037), the moralist al-Ghazali (d. 1111), and the mystic Ibn ʿArabi (d. 1240) was shared at first by only a few Western Orientalists.[66] The Orientalistic reading of the Orient surely corresponded to a large extent to the self-perception of the European researchers, who saw a reflection of their own identities in their objects of study; this only rarely coincided with the Islamic reception of history, which seemed to pass on exactly the opposite of what the Orientalists had created. Ultimately this critically developed Orient was made the center of understanding. The Orientalist discourse thus possessed precisely the "procedures" that Foucault had highlighted for all discourses.[67]

In 1973, as present-oriented questions increasingly pushed their way into Orientalist research, Rodinson noted that for some observers, Orientalistics was "at an end."[68] They seemed to be convinced that social science discourse would lead to an "Americanization" of the subject—that is, to a breakdown of Orientalistics into systematic disciplines. In fact, in part under pressure from UNESCO, the term "Orientalistics" was now erased from the title of the world congress of all Orientalist disciplines. Nevertheless, the subject was able to preserve its academic independence, and in return to integrate social-science models increasingly into its own research. The connection striven for here between philological tradition and the social sciences in the broadest sense required new questions, which presented a growing criticism of Orientalistics' old image of the Orient. It became ever clearer that "early Islam" could no longer be viewed as the focus for understanding the Islamic world; research also departed more and more from essentialist interpretations, in which the essence of a "foreign," all-defining Islam was taken as a constant. In this way, room was made for an understanding of Islamic culture as a dynamic historical process.

In the early 1980s the Orientalism debate once again raised doubts about the justification for independent academic Orientalistics.[69] It was indisputable that European Orientalism had also influenced scholarly treatment of Oriental societies. This time, unlike in the debate over social sciences in the 1970s, the philological methods and their research outcomes were not criticized.[70] Now the issue involved the general interpretive horizons to which research results were "adapted." Bryan Turner was probably one of the first to point to Orientalistics' disastrous "deficit thesis." According to this thesis, the Islamic Orient, because of its "Islamic essence," did not possess the characteristics of European identity. Turner referred above all to the concept of "civil society," which was seen as a feature of European modernity and which, like many other phenomena of modernity, the Islamic Orient lacked.[71] In fact it now appeared that in Orientalistics generally, precisely those epochs and themes were omitted that characterized the nature, indeed the singularity, of European modernity: historical research was rarely taken up on the early modern era in Islamic societies, on developments in intellectual history in the seventeenth and eighteenth centuries, and on issues of social history in the transition to the period of European colonialism.[72] Even today, the comparison between the dynamic West based on individualism, on the one hand, and the static Islamic East oriented around the collective, on the other, is a very popular one. It became increasingly clear, however, that the West was trying to prove its own advanced identity compared with the "Other," "backward" Orient by means of classical Orientalistics. The moment the functionality of Orientalism to Europe's self-definition was recognized, say many critics, following Said, "the end of Orientalistics" had been reached. The Arabist and scholar of Islamic studies ʿAziz al-ʿAzmeh summed it up: "The contribution of Orientalistics to [general] scholarly knowledge [was] very small."[73]

In determining the position of Orientalistics after Orientalism, two tendencies clearly emerged at the end of the twentieth century: for one, the independence of Orientalistics—now generally known as Islamic studies—as a discipline was highlighted by an emphasis on its philological bases. Philology was for many the basis of research, and in fact the actual task through which an objective critique of the Islamic textual tradition, and thus Islamic intellectual history, was made possible in the first place.[74] Others emphasized that philology might be indispensable as an ancillary discipline for analyzing Islamic text traditions, but that the historicity of Islamic traditions could be recognized only if other humanities and social science methods and questions were used.[75] In contrast to the early decades, the issue now was not a comparison between philological Orientalistics and research on the Orient focused on the present, but rather the purposes and subjects of Orientalist research and the significance that should be attributed to the methodology and theory formation of a discipline of Islamic studies newly understood as a branch of cultural studies. The scientification of the reading and interpretation of texts continues to be the main task of philology; establishing this as the task of Orientalistics is the goal of those critics who oppose, sometimes vehemently, a repositioning of Islamic studies from a cultural theory perspective. Thus Orientalistics shares with all scholarly disciplines stemming from the classic philological tradition of the nineteenth century a debate on principles regarding the question of the autonomy of philology within the humanities and social sciences.

Translated by Belinda Cooper

II

ISLAM AND CULTURAL SELF-ASSERTION

(Rotraud Wielandt)

Cultural self-assertion is not a basic human need felt everywhere and in every period. The wish for it is, rather, the symptom of a crisis: it is perceived only when people find the basic values of their native culture threatened by an alien culture that is novel to them. Such a threat arises, in the perception of Muslims today, from the technical, industrialized civilization of modern Europe. An awareness that this endangers their own cultural existence has spread widely in the Islamic world since traditional ways of life began to be Westernized under the influence of the political and economic superiority of European countries. At present it also animates many Muslims in the central and western European diaspora, such as Turkish guest workers in Germany, who are discomfited by the thought of having to make a broad adaptation to their new environment.

Muslims—similarly, for example, to Christians—have a complex cultural tradition, the development of which was affected not solely by religion but also by a multitude of historical forces. Thus, viewed objectively, their cultural group characteristics arise not only from their religious affiliation but also from sharing in a bundle of varied factors that influence culture. In the self-assessment of most Muslims, Islam holds a special place among these factors. The exact relationship between Islam and culture, however, is understood quite variously. Some consider the civilization in which they live or would like to live in all important points a fruit of the Islamic faith and the human creativity that it inspires. Others, while convinced that important cultural impulses came from Islam, or even that it is the integrative heart of the spiritual life of their society, also recognize in the civilization they belong to quite different components that they believe contribute significantly. Opinions vary on the character and origins of these components, as well as on the value ascribed to them within the overall civilization.

It is no surprise that Muslims have such differing views of the bases of their civilization. First of all, the historical conditions out of which people in, for example, Indonesia, Turkey, Saudi Arabia, Egypt, Morocco, and Nigeria accepted the Prophet's message are so varied that the residents of all these countries are confronted with highly divergent cultural contexts of Islam; therefore they cannot perceive Islam as having exactly the same significance everywhere that it has for their own identities. That individuals or groups assess the achievements of Islam for their civilization in different ways results, further, from the fact that people may at times orient themselves more toward the timeless ideals of the religion, and at other times more toward its historical manifestations; many Muslim statements about the power of Islam to generate civilization are based on religious enthusiasm, not empirical evidence. Furthermore, in the course of the last century and a half, among Muslims the concept of what civilization is and what constitutes the unity of those who transport it has in some respects changed considerably through European influences, overall becoming very varied. This has resulted, in turn, in differing interpretations of the relationship between Islam and culture.

In the 1860s and 1870s, as the transfer of European educational concepts to the Islamic world progressed along a broad front, the primary cultural reference group for Muslims in general was, quite understandably, their own religious community and its most valuable cultural component, Islamic revelation. Under such premises, the value and future of their culture was still unquestioned, even if they clearly perceived that in certain areas of great practical relevance this culture found itself, for the moment, in an alarming state of developmental backwardness in comparison to European culture. The only question was how this backwardness had come about and how it could most quickly be overcome. It was raised with even greater urgency, given that the actual power relationships under the God-given historical division of roles seemed to be turning into their converse. According to Islamic law of the state, and in the pious popular view established through centuries of its cultural heyday, the domain of the faithful was meant to spread ever farther over the occupied earth. Instead, the infidel Europeans, with their superior knowledge and abilities, were now pushing ever farther into the "house of Islam." The Ottoman Empire, Islam's supreme power, was forced under pressure from Europeans to abandon one position after another, and in many parts of the Islamic world they were already in charge politically and economically; in some places they were even the colonial power, whose expansion was to be feared. How had this become possible?

Faithful Muslims could not seek the causes of the backwardness and external weakness of their religious community in the essence of the Islamic religion. Often they would not even seek them among its adherents. Therefore since the late nineteenth century an explanatory model that spares them this embarrassing task has been very popular: the ascription of the downfall of Islamic civilization to the pernicious influence of outside forces. Jewish efforts at division, infiltration by Iranian religious doctrine or Greek philosophy, destructive behavior by Mongols or Turks who had not really converted, the barbaric ravages of the Crusaders, and ultimately even European colonialism—which in reality could not have succeeded without the prior emergence of a difference in cultural level—were held responsible for the fact that the Islamic religious community had lost its cultural vitality and its powerful political position. In addition to this scheme of comfortable self-justification, however, self-critical diagnoses were and are also found. One of them, already formulated by Rifaʿa Rafiʿ al-Tahtawi of Egypt (1801–1873), is that Muslims brought about their own inferiority through centuries of neglecting certain useful areas of knowledge, which would have been perfectly available to them and whose cultivation would in fact have been required by their religion. A different diagnosis, popularized by the agitator Jamal al-Din al-Afghani of Persia (1839–1897) and the Egyptian reformist theologian Muhammad ʿAbduh (1849–1905), placed responsibility for the backwardness of the Muslim world on the fact that Muslim scholars had, as early as the ninth century, arbitrarily declared "the gates of *ijtihad*"—that is, the possibility for independent norm creation through analogies with statements in the Qurʾan and hadith—"to be closed," thus blocking development of the law. A generation after Muhammad ʿAbduh, Egypt's Salafi movement, which influenced today's numerous fundamentalist groups as far as West Africa and the Malay archipelago, located the fall from grace even earlier and more comprehensively: they declared the ways of life and thought of the "righteous forefathers," that is, the first four caliphs and their contemporaries, to be the complete historical realization of Islam and any later deviation from this model to be a degeneration.

The less Muslims could base their self-confidence on more recent history, given Europe's superiority, the more eagerly many of them looked back to medieval times. This gave proof, they believed, that Islam and supreme civilizing achievements not only were compatible but actually very much belonged together. The memory of the splendid civilization of medieval Islam provides effective protection against feelings of inferiority. For this very reason it took up a great deal of space in Muslim writings in the nineteenth and twentieth centuries. Back then, one could tell oneself, the Islamic world was far ahead of Europe; back then Europeans took lessons from Muslims, for example, in philosophy and medicine. Because of the fact that such a cultural connection undoubtedly does exist in some areas, people frequently feel justified in drawing the much farther-reaching conclusion that all the positive aspects of modern European civilization came out of medieval Islamic culture. This thesis was first developed in detail in 1867 in a work by Khayr al-Din al-Tunisi, and has since been repeated in many places. The theory that the rise of European civilization in the modern era was based entirely on stimuli from medieval Islam, as erroneous as it is, has the positive function of lowering psychological inhibitions in Muslims who would like to learn from Europe in some respects. It removes the opprobrium of something alien and potentially threatening from the methods of working and the cultural assets that some would like to adopt, for by borrowing from Europe, they are merely taking back what originally was theirs. In this way they are adding nothing to their own cultural tradition that could go against its nature and perhaps even destroy it.

The assimilation of European cultural elements in general is relatively unproblematic, as long as people believe that they affect only marginal areas of their own lives but not the core of their understanding of the world or their behavioral norms. This view was shared in the nineteenth century by still prominent Muslim advocates of modernization on the European model, such as Egypt's Rifaʿa Rafiʿ al-Tahtawi and ʿAli Mubarak (1823–1892) and Khayr al-Din al-Tunisi (1810–1890) in Tunisia. In their judgment, the center of their native cultural tradition, Islamic doctrine, and the branches of knowledge and modes of behavior that build upon it, were not at all affected by attempts to adapt to the Europeans; they were only externally expanded, through knowledge and skills that aimed for worldly utility. Thus cultural change appears to be a purely additive process, which does not change the content and scope of the essence of the existing culture.

This view, however, assumed that the Muslims involved were capable on their own of limiting European cultural influences to areas of thought and action not regulated by religion. As would soon be seen, this was precisely what they could not do. Simply to deal successfully with modern natural sciences, for the sake of practical utility one had to adapt one's worldview to that of contemporary Europeans to such an extent that conflicts with Islamic doctrine were to be expected. Furthermore, efforts at modernization, European colonial policies, and the increasing economic interdependence of the continents brought a growing number of people into contact with European ways of life; many did not first reflect on their compatibility with traditional values but simply imitated them, especially as the power and prosperity of European civilization was impressive. In addition, the Westernization process developed its own dynamic, which could not be slowed. Certainly people may at first have sought knowledge of European languages, attendance at educational institutions organized along European lines, or studies abroad in Europe merely for the purpose of attaining useful skills, for example, in medicine or engineering; but their interests or talents would naturally go beyond these fields, so that they inevitably gained access to very different areas of European culture, such as philosophy, literature, art, and political thought. And here opportunities arose to discover ways of interpreting and evaluating reality that sometimes clearly contradicted traditional Islamic ideas and principles but nevertheless directly fascinated even many faithful Muslims. Under these conditions the principle of hermetically sealing a religiously based worldview and value system against European ideas could not be sustained.

With the awareness of this fact, which can already be found among Egyptian authors at the turn of the twentieth century, the process of rapprochement with European civilization entered a critical stage. From then on, ambivalence toward European-oriented progress was clearly felt. If no firm boundaries were set to Western cultural influence, was there not a risk, despite all the political strength and material prosperity that might be gained through the process of modernization, of losing something crucial—one's religion, one's entire historical heritage, and therefore one's cultural identity? Since becoming aware of this danger, Muslims have not ceased to be concerned with the problem of cultural self-assertion. The problem is manifested most clearly among intellectuals; they deal with it explicitly and can plumb it most deeply, as they are better informed about both Islamic traditions and their possible European alternatives than the majority of their coreligionists, and therefore have a better knowledge of what is at stake. But it is not only a problem for intellectuals; the mass of less-educated believers may not express concern about their own cultural identity in subtle trains of thought, but may instead do so through fear of innovation and sometimes through general anti-Western resentment, as has flared up in the recent past in Iran.

The dilemma of being caught between their own traditions and modern Western civilization is rarely as easily resolved for most Muslims as it was for the Egyptian author and scholar Taha Husayn (1889–1973), who declared in a highly regarded programmatic article on education policy in the 1930s that his fatherland was not separated from Europe at all by cultural differences, and had even in a certain sense always been culturally part of Europe, to the extent that it, like Europe, had always belonged to a single "Mediterranean" civilization.[1] Usually Europe's civilization, as much as one might appreciate certain characteristics of it, is the alien civilization against which one must recall the uniqueness of one's own. Fundamentalist-oriented individuals and groups have at times attempted to escape the dilemma of civilizations by going to the other extreme, that is, the simple denial of any cultural commonality between their own group and modern Europeans. But this solution, too, is not viable in the eyes of most Muslims today, since it substitutes a romantic utopia for a reality that is obvious to everyone. No matter how much members of the Muslim Brotherhood or adherents of Ayatollah Khomeini may wish to live in a "pure" Islamic culture, in reality their society too is already in many respects irreversibly Westernized; if they wish to survive under decent conditions, they cannot avoid, for the time being, learning even more from the West. Muslims, and especially the intellectuals among them, as a rule are well aware that their present culture—like all other cultures with a broad range—has, to a certain degree, a syncretistic character. What most of them do not want is a syncretism that destroys all the Islamic properties of their civilization through an ill-considered break with the past and mushrooms out of control. For this reason, in the twentieth century great efforts were made to find a structural formula for a modern civilization that did not renounce its connection to Islamic history but was, at the same time, capable of creatively accomplishing all the tasks of the present day, especially the task of seeking access to the civilizational standard of modern Europe.

Such a formula, in order to achieve what is desired of it, must be designed so as to leave room for the interplay of heterogeneous cultural factors
while always seeing something distinctive and incapable of obliteration at
work in it. Both can be especially well achieved by use of the concept of the
nation, which was adopted from Europe by the Islamic world in the mid-
nineteenth century. A nation can be defined quite variously: it may be seen
as an ethnic unit, or not; a common language or religion may be declared to
be constitutive, but need not be; one can postulate for it a clearly defined,
constant geographic area, but can also dispense with this. What is indispensable, however, is the acceptance of a specific historical heritage, of whatever
kind, common to all its members, that can be sustained through time in all
its essential components. Precisely because the concept of such a national
heritage can be filled with very different substantive components while at
the same time assuming something constant in all its variables, it has often
and gladly been used throughout the Islamic world in the attempt to comprehend analytically the problem of asserting one's historically achieved self
within the cultural transformation occurring through Westernization.

Since the late nineteenth century, many Muslims have accepted as a matter of course the axiom that their culture is a national culture. This does not
necessarily mean that they consider a differently defined unit, other than
the religious community, to be the bearer of culture. Pan-Islamism, whether,
for example, in the guise of the Turkish poet Namık Kemal (1840–1888) or
that of Jamal al-Din al-Afghani, equated the community of the faithful as
a whole with the nation; the national culture was thus still identical with
Islamic culture. Starting at the turn of the twentieth century, however, different concepts of the nation, which were no longer one-sidedly based on the
Islamic component of historical heritage, predominated. Until World War II,
nationalism in the Islamic world, to the extent it existed, was above all a
territorially determined nationalism. The nation was seen as the population
of a fatherland clearly defined in geographical terms, which had long made
up a historical unit and differed from the neighboring countries through the
specific constitution of its traditions. This understanding of the nation was
dominant at the time, for example, in Egypt, in Iraq, and, since the establishment of the republic, in Turkey. In view of this background, cultural self-
assertion meant the preservation of all traditions that had coalesced in the
territory and were considered especially relevant. Islam was overwhelmingly
counted as one of these traditions. But for intellectuals it was not in every
case the cornerstone of their national cultural consciousness. They were
frequently interested above all in what distinguished their fatherland from
other countries, and this was not in fact Islam but primarily the more distant
past. Thus Egyptian nationalism of that epoch was "Pharaonic"; that is, it
emphasized a permanent core of the national culture that came from ancient Egypt, upon which many other cultural elements had accumulated—
the country's Islamic tradition as well as, more recently, characteristics of
modern European civilization. Asserting its cultural identity against Europe

meant, on this premise, primarily remaining conscious of the "Pharaonic" heritage, and only secondarily preserving the Islamic heritage.

From World War II on, a more comprehensive concept of nationality, which continues to be influential today, came largely to prevail in the Arab countries: that of pan-Arabism. Smaller, territorially defined nations were replaced by the larger "Arab nation," constituted through common language, history, and in the opinion of many, race. Belief in this nation once again lent Islam a higher status in the effort to achieve cultural self-assertion. The Islamic religion, and the cultural achievements that emerged in its wake, unquestionably have a prominent place in Arab history, and therefore those wishing to base their cultural identity primarily on this history must make it their business to give it enduring recognition. Incidentally, pan-Arab nationalism made Islam a first-order object of cultural self-awareness not only for Arab Muslims but sometimes also for Arab Christians. Even if it is not their religion, it is a central piece of their historical heritage, to the extent that they see themselves as part of a single Arab nation. At the beginning of the twentieth century, in awareness of this fact the Lebanese Christian Jurji Zaydan, one of the intellectual pioneers of pan-Arabism, had already authored a five-volume "History of Islamic Civilization." In 1943 Michel ʿAflaq, founder of the Baʿth Party and also a Christian, made a speech on the birthday of the Prophet Muhammad that would become famous, in which he celebrated Islam as the manifestation of a worldwide Arab humanism and its founders as the embodiment of Arab genius.[2]

Since the late 1960s, admittedly, the concept of the nation has increasingly been called into question by Arab authors as an instrument for understanding the problem of self-assertion. There are several reasons for this. For one, the tension between pan-Arabism and territorially limited nationalisms in various countries of the Arab world proved difficult to resolve; both tendencies continued to exist irreconcilably side by side, and sometimes side against side. Under these circumstances, it was and remains difficult to agree on the extent and constituent elements of one's own national culture. For another, it was often easier than it had been at the turn of the twentieth century to see that national consciousness was not simply a fixed historical reality with universal effect, but rather a historically determined mode of thought of European origin. Both of these, along with a more recent result of the Westernization process—namely the progressive adoption of descriptive categories from cultural psychology—led to a situation in which, in discussions of the difficulty of cultural self-assertion, the identity to be preserved was frequently no longer defined as national identity but as a collective "personality" (*shakhsiyya*). In the early twentieth century, Ahmad Lutfi al-Sayyid had already spoken of an Egyptian cultural "personality," which set the stage for the concept of national identity that would become known in his country as "Pharaonism"; after him, in the thirties, Taha Husayn did the same in his theory of Egyptian culture, ascribing to it a historical affinity with European culture. Now the category of collective cultural "personality" gained momentum on a larger scale, in connection with the attributes "Islamic," "Arab," and "Islamic-Arab."

Above all, however, under the influence of the movement commonly known as "re-Islamization," which has quite perceptibly defined the public climate in Arab countries as well as other parts of the Islamic world in recent decades, the tendency once again to define oneself culturally primarily through membership in the Islamic religion has increasingly challenged national identification patterns. Under these changed conditions, in the debate over cultural theory among Arab intellectuals, two conceptual pairs that had not previously been common took a prominent position: first, cultural "heritage" (*turath*) and "renewal" (*tajdid*), in the sense of modernization; second, authenticity (*asala*) and contemporaneousness (*mu'asara*), in the sense of creative participation in modernity through timely ways of life and forms of thought. These two conceptual pairs were particularly well suited for the type of discussion that now began to dominate the discourse on cultural theory: the debate between Islamists, who propagated a return to a genuine Islamic culture, in addition to the ideal of an "Islamic" state; and their opponents, who continued to adhere to a secular conception of the state and—despite a weighing of religious and secular components of culture that differed in details—held to the concept of a national culture accessible to Muslims and non-Muslims alike. The concepts of tradition and authenticity could be filled, depending on the speaker's standpoint, with either primarily religiously determined or overwhelmingly secular and national content; the concepts of renewal or modernization and contemporaneousness raised the question of which precise method of cultural interpretation and relationship to one's own history, in the view of the various participants in the discussion, could best master the present and win the future.

During the last few decades a flood of books and articles has appeared in the Arabic Middle East on the relationship between the concepts just mentioned: cultural "heritage" (*turath*) and "renewal" or "modernization" (*tajdid*), cultural authenticity (*asala*), and contemporaneousness (*mu'asara*). In many cases these concepts are even found in the titles themselves. Their authors represent very varied facets of the current intra-Islamic spectrum of opinion; among them are intellectuals with decidedly secular points of view as well as avowed Islamists. Since the 1970s, cultural heritage and its significance for the future has also been the subject of numerous conventions and symposia, in some cases with a pan-Arabic character. At one of them, early warnings were sounded against the misunderstanding that authenticity was identical with a one-sided fixation on a statically understood heritage of ages long past, which was simultaneously viewed as timelessly normative.[3] Such objections were raised primarily against backward-looking religious currents of the Wahhabi and extreme Islamist type, whose representatives pursued a program aimed, in the field of culture as well as elsewhere, at a consistent orientation toward the model of the first Muslims. Critics also pointed out the widespread tendency to use the demand for authenticity mainly to prevent thinking and publicly speaking about necessary political and societal change.[4]

In contrast to such tendencies toward perpetuating the old at the expense of the new, many prominent intellectuals, some of whom had been involved for decades in the debate on tradition and modernization, authenticity and contemporaneousness, developed the idea that no unbridgeable contradiction exists between cultural tradition and modernity, authenticity and contemporaneousness; instead they can and must be brought together into a synthesis. In the view of these thinkers, cultural heritage is not a self-contained, complete cultural pattern of unlimited normative applicability to which one must be tied imitatively. Instead, despite some variations in emphasis, they agreed on the necessity of creatively adopting the values and intellectual challenges contained in this heritage and using them productively in the search for sustainable solutions to current problems. Thus they came down firmly on the side of a dynamic interpretation of what cultural self-assertion can mean. Unlike the Islamists, who are primarily interested in a way back—reversion to the principles of "pure" primordial Islam, return to their application, and rediscovery of those phases of one's own past in which, it is believed, these principles were once fully put into practice—they manifested their conviction that cultural assertion was possible only by going forward with the heritage of one's forefathers and constantly reinvestigating and testing its significance for the respective present. They started from the assumption that cultural communities, like individuals, are not "themselves" from the start and for all time, but that they develop their nature by constantly developing their inherent potential, which is in essence also established quite essentially by cultural tradition, through interaction with new situations and ideas. Such a concept of Arab-Islamic culture was formulated by, among others, the Tunisian educator Mahjub ibn Milad[5] and his compatriot, historian Hisham Ju'aiyit (Hichem Djait),[6] both also known for writings on cultural theory, as well as the Moroccan historian and cultural philosopher 'Abdallah al-'Arwi (Abdallah Laroui).[7]

The program of a synthesis of cultural tradition and modernity, authenticity and contemporaneousness, was championed with particular emphasis during the last few decades by some thinkers from the ranks of philosophy professors at Arab universities. Thus the Egyptian Zaki Najib Mahmud (1905–1993), once a professor at the University of Cairo, made a name for himself as a passionate advocate of such a synthesis. He called for common efforts by those involved in the creation of Arab culture to achieve a new "formula for life" (*sigha hayatiyya*) that would adopt scientific knowledge and methods, industrial skills and modes of artistic expression, as well as certain political institutions and the social order from Western civilization, and tie them organically to the constituent ethical principles and a range of other cultural elements from Islamic tradition.[8] His younger colleague Fouad Zakaria (Fu'ad Zakariyya, b. 1928), who taught first at the same university and then later in Kuwait and is known as a shrewd critic of the

Islamist trend in politics and culture, judged the idea that authenticity and contemporaneousness are alternatives between which one can choose as a false approach, since no one is able to escape the present and its contemporary demands. In reality, he explained, the issue is one of maintaining the necessary intellectual independence from both one's own cultural heritage and Western-influenced modernity, and taking from each, depending on current problems, whatever makes the best solution possible. In many cases, he said, concepts of cultural independence and dependence are employed that are no longer tenable. In an age of ever closer global communications and a developing world culture, from whose potential everyone benefits, one can no longer yearn nostalgically for an idea of the purity of one's own traditions, even though the danger of complete loss of meaning for native regional cultures outside Europe and North America that currently accompanies this development must be opposed as far as possible, for the sake of maintaining the richness of a plurality of cultures.[9]

Muhammad 'Abid al-Jabiri (b. 1936) of Morocco, who taught in Rabat, on the one hand rejects the universal claims of one-sidedly European-influenced modernity, but on the other accepts Arab participation in what he calls "worldwide modernity" (*hadatha 'alamiyya*). Such participation is, in his view, possible and legitimate simply because the Arabs created important conditions for this "worldwide modernity" through elements of their own cultural tradition, and thus contributed as much as the Europeans to its development. In his opinion, participation in it, within the framework of various regional cultural traditions, would need in each case to be implemented in such a way that it would start with historically developed local conditions. This means that both the current state of Arab culture and the Arab heritage would need to be understood historically, and that elements would have to betaken, especially from the latter, that correspond to current needs. These would include, for example, the tradition of Arab-Islamic philosophy, to the extent that it encourages the necessary rationality of efforts to diagnose and overcome social problems, and elements of earlier Islamic political theory that spoke out against despotic forms of government and could aid democratization. Through such use and development of one's own cultural traditions, one not only keeps them alive but also at the same time creates one's own variant of modern world culture. This corresponds to its structure, which is pluralist from the start; one can become a permanent part of it only through regionally based forms.[10]

Hasan Hanafi (b. 1935), who, like Zaki Najib Mahmud and Fouad Zakaria, held a chair in philosophy at the University of Cairo, describes himself as a pioneer of the Islamic left and a fundamentalist; nevertheless, as can be clearly enough inferred, despite many inconsistencies in his thought processes, from his strongly selective and often arbitrarily interpretive treatment of ideas from both the Islamic cultural tradition and European modernity, he still advocates, in his books and articles on cultural theory, the idea of a synthesis of Islamic tradition and modernity. Particularly to non-Muslim audiences he sometimes reveals that for him the Islamic heritage is nothing more than a cultural code in which he consciously clothes his actual intention, the revolutionary transformation of Arab thought and social relationships, in order to achieve the desired mobilization of a domestic population that is at home in the Islamic tradition. He sees cultural authenticity as the constant reinterpretation of cultural traditions in the service of a restructuring of contemporary Arab-Islamic reality for the better. In the process, he affirms the basic monotheistic order of Islamic-Arab culture as an immutable principle, from which, through the ages, it has drawn and continues to draw its developmental potential; but he refuses to view the religious and cultural tradition as a place of permanent, binding truths and norms. Instead he considers it justified to undertake new interpretations in each period, based on its spirit and needs, and believes that there are no limits to its permissibility. He expands on this understanding of a historical perspective on native cultural traditions with the demand that Europe's cultural tradition should also be placed in historical perspective. For him this means reducing it to its actual historical format by making its errors apparent, and thus toppling its claim to universality. In his book *Muqaddima fi 'ilm al-istighrab* (Introduction to a Science of Occidentalism, 1991), he goes a step further: he not only objects to the worldwide dominance of, in his description, morally degenerate Western culture but also declares that its downfall has arrived and calls openly on Muslims to make this culture an object of study, in order to subject it ultimately to the dominance of their own Islamic culture. In this way he factually turns the tables on the West after accusing it of cultural colonialism.[11] This anti-Western turn does not, however, change the fact that, in the substance of his view of the changes desirable today in Arab culture and society, he borrows largely from ideas of European origin.

Hanafi shares his rejection of Western culture's unjustified claims to universality with al-Jabiri, but especially with the Islamist camp. Some of its more moderate representatives do see the adoption of the fruits of Western cultural developments, to a limited extent, as possible and desirable—as shown by the example of Shaykh Yusuf al-Qaradawi of Egypt, who has long worked in Qatar and is widely known for his television programs.[12] But Islamists without exception reject the idea of the general and universal normativity of Western standards of modernity. Many of them, often supported by organs of Saudi Arabia's Wahhabi Islam and the Saudi-sponsored World Muslim League, explicitly promote a program of cultural re-Islamization, in which all sciences and the entire field of cultural production would be systematically liberated from the damaging effects of the "cultural invasion" (*ghazw thaqafi*) instigated by the West.

Nevertheless, the numerous efforts, in theoretical writings and at congresses, to determine more precisely the distinguishing features of the methods of, for example, Islamic biology, chemistry, literature, sociology, or pedagogy, or even Islamic fiction and fine arts, have not yet brought many concrete results. They generally do not go beyond a claim of the a priori

compatibility of modern natural sciences with the Qur'an, correctly understood; advocacy of traditional societal and family models; emphasis on the
binding nature of traditional Islamic values, especially traditional standards
of female modesty, for present-day arts and sciences; and above all, the
collective conviction that a particular Islamic model, independent of the
Western model and undoubtedly superior to it, exists not only for the ordering of political relations but also for cultural matters. The primary issue
for them is, apparently, emphasizing cultural differences from the West. Detailed explanations of how a cultural life influenced by Islam actually differs, or does not differ, from the many types of cultural activity that occur
in Europe or North America seem neither to exist nor to be of interest. This
is shown, for example, by the very vague ideas propagated in this regard by
Muhammad Qutb in two books on the supposed special characteristics of
"Islamic" education and "Islamic" aesthetics,[13] as well as in the writings of
Najib al-Kilani, who also made a name as a novelist, on a theory of Islamic
literature,[14] and in the stereotypical assertion, found repeatedly in numerous
publications by the moderate Egyptian Islamist Muhammad 'Amara, that
Islam has a specific method of its own for everything, be it political, social,
or cultural. What is exclusively Islamic about the principles he presents in
each case is often unclear.

   All the basic patterns of cultural identification and self-assertion discussed
in this chapter coexist today in the Islamic world. Muslims, especially those
from populations and regions that have experienced little Westernization or
who have, in the recent past, again become more strongly rooted in their
own religious traditions, see themselves primarily from the perspective of
Islam and view its guidelines as the most secure bulwark against foreign
cultural influence from the West. Others, who have participated more extensively in the development of ideas inspired by Europe, see themselves as
bearers of one or another form of national culture, or are seeking a cultural
"personality," for which the Islamic tradition can in turn have varying significance. Which of these benchmarks will, over the long term, become the
focus of the self-concept of a majority of Muslims, and thus of their search
for self-assertion, remains to be seen. At the moment, the impulses that keep
the cultural theory debate going are coming largely from advocates of a
decidedly Islamic civilization that sharply distinguishes itself from Western
patterns. In large parts of the Islamic world, the population of larger cities, in particular, must at the same time face the intellectual and practical
challenges of dealing with a plurality of often strongly diverging cultural
orientations.

Translated by Belinda Cooper

III

ISLAM AND LOCAL TRADITIONS

Syncretic Ideas and Practices

(Olaf Schumann and Lode Frank Brakel)

1. The Concept of Syncretism

(Olaf Schumann)

The term "syncretism" originated in antiquity, but there are only a few examples of its use. One can be found in the essay "On Brotherly Love," in which Plutarch cites the example of the Cretans. Though quarreling frequently, the Cretans quickly overcame their differences and joined in an alliance when faced with a common enemy. According to Plutarch, they called this *synkretismos*. Erasmus of Rotterdam took up the term in a generalized way in 1519, when he exhorted Melanchthon to behave peacefully toward the humanists. He derived the word from the Greek *synkeránnymi*, meaning "to mix together." He intended the term to have a positive connotation, but this turned negative in the age of Lutheran and Calvinist Orthodoxy, in which all attempts to reconcile the feuding Protestant denominations were disqualified as "syncretic." This was also the case with efforts to overcome the different schools of thought in Catholic theology.

In religious studies, the concept of syncretism was initially, and mainly, applied to the religious phenomena of late antiquity. With the rise of Alexander the Great, there was a tendency to mix together, or even to see as identical, gods, cults, and other phenomena that had developed separately in difficult cultures.

Beginning in the second half of the nineteenth century, the more intense study of non-ancient religions, some of which still existed, led to the discovery, in such religions, of the syncretic phenomena and processes that were known from the history of religion in late antiquity. Scholars now demanded, however, that the concept of syncretism be defined more clearly and that, if necessary, different forms be distinguished and described by means of narrower concepts such as assimilation, symbiosis, parallelism, relational processes, and so on.

In recent years, Collaborative Research Center 13, based in Göttingen, has led the efforts to analyze and systematize syncretic phenomena. In a preliminary report, Ulrich Berner writes that syncretism always refers to a process that emerges either out of an encounter between different religions or through competition arising between different religions in the same region. In the case of an encounter between two religions, this process can unfold on two levels: on that of the two religious systems, dissolving their shared boundaries, or on that of the individual elements or religious ideas that are combined. The process can have a variety of outcomes: a new system may emerge that differs from that of its surroundings but does not contain any new elements; or a creative process may be triggered that ultimately produces a synthesis made up of new elements. Finally—and regardless of whether the goal is to reconcile, establish distance to, or distinguish among elements— there are a variety of ways in which the different systems or their elements may be set in relation to one another (e.g., old/new or temporary/final).

Berner's primary aim is to create a heuristic model. The following examples of syncretic forms from Indonesia show the variety of processes that emerge in real-life religious practice, ranging from reconciliation to renunciation.

Translated by Adam Blauhut

2. Indonesia as a Case Study

(Lode Frank Brakel)

When Islam became a world religion, Indonesia had been part of the international trade network for a long time. Since an ever-growing number of Muslim traders participated in this trade network, it is only natural to suppose that they would also have landed on the coasts of Indonesia. And indeed a long list of travel reports from Arab and Persian sea captains confirms that this supposition is correct.[1] Yet several centuries had to pass until, near the end of the thirteenth century, an Islamic kingdom was first mentioned in the region.[2]

Two conclusions may be drawn from this apparent paradox. First, in Indonesia we are dealing with a slow and extremely gradual process of individual, peaceful penetration of Islam. Only after a very long time did the Muslims succeed in establishing themselves as a political majority, though they were not an absolute numerical majority. Second, there is apparently a connection—which has not yet been sufficiently investigated—between developments in Indonesia and in India, the country of origin of both Hinduism and Buddhism, until that time the predominant religions in the Indonesian region.[3] This is indicated by the fact that in Indonesia—especially in the former Buddhist centers on the north coast of Sumatra—the road to political victory was cleared for Islam only after the supremacy of Islam had been established in Gujarat and Bengal, and after the destruction of the great Buddhist university of Nalanda (in present-day Bihar), with which the important Sumatran state of Sriwijaya had for a long time been closely connected.

Three hundred years of active Islamization followed until in approximately 1600, when the states of South Celebes had also embraced the "new" religion,[4] an important part of the archipelago had at least nominally come under Islamic rule. There are two points that have to be taken into special consideration. First, the increasing intensity of the international spice trade during this period attracted more and more foreigners, among them a growing number of Europeans, who created a power base in the area through the Portuguese conquest of Malacca in 1511. There is a theory that the "competition" with the Portuguese even played an essential role in the further spread of Islam over large parts of the archipelago during the sixteenth century. Once again the developments in India, this time in South India, from where the islands of Java and Bali received their Shivaite type of Hinduism, seem to have been equally important for developments in the archipelago. The fall of the last great Hindu kingdom of Vijayanagaram anticipated, as it were, the end of the Hinduized states in Java. In the fourteenth century, Islam first established itself in the capital of the Hindu-Javanese realm of Majapahit in the form of a small religious community, which did not receive much attention from official poets and chroniclers.[5] When in the following period some important seaports on the north coast succumbed to Islam, this finally became the state religion of the newly founded realm of Mataram in Central Java.

No matter how sketchy this historical survey may be, it is nevertheless important in helping to explain the divergences and problems that are still prevalent in Indonesian Islam today. Generally speaking we are facing a religion that had to conquer a territory which had long been accustomed to syncretistic tendencies. On the one hand, the two great Indian religions had been obliged to come to terms with the ancient indigenous religions, but on the other hand, these two great religions themselves had merged to a great extent, or rather, they had formed a coalition, mainly in Java and Bali, and perhaps also in Minangkabau (west-central Sumatra).[6] What had been maintained was not so much the belief system(s) of the ancient religions but rather the traditional systems of formalized social conduct and patterns of behavior, usually called *adat* (a derivation from Arabic), considered to have been prescribed by semi-divine ancestors.

On the basis of what has been said to this point, the development of Indonesian Islam may be divided into three types:

1. Islam has been able to assert itself most intensively in the ancient trade centers along the coast, where the ground had already been prepared by Mahayana Buddhist concepts.[7]

2. In the ancient Shivaite centers of Central and East Java its reception has been only partially successful, while in Bali it failed almost completely.
3. In the inaccessible regions of the interior, where the population lived in primitive conditions and remained largely out of contact with the great Indian religions, Islam was initially even less successful. It was not until the Dutch had expanded their authority into these regions in the course of the nineteenth and the beginning of the twentieth centuries that Islam could make real progress there, albeit in strong competition with Christianity.

The discussion that follows is limited to the first two types.

Another point that is important for understanding Indonesian Islam needs to be stressed here: Islam came mainly via a region (India) where it had already acquired syncretistic characteristics, not only through its relation with the Indian religions but also internally, since in India more than anywhere else, Sunnite and Shi'ite elements had merged. Early Indonesian Islamic literature as well as some remaining customs indicate that there was a time when the situation was not so different in Indonesia. Moreover in the religious vocabulary some isolated expressions have been maintained which definitely point to a Persian-Indian origin, such as *abdas* (Pers. *ab-dast*), meaning ritual cleansing (Arab. *wudu'*); *bang* (Pers. *idem*), or summons to the divine service (Arab. *adhan*); and *kanduri* (Pers. *kanduri*), a ceremonial meal for well-being (Arab. *walima*). This Indo-Persian influence, however, has been gradually replaced by an Arabic one (mainly from Mecca, Medina, Cairo, and Hadramaut), in which, just as in southern India, the Shafi'ite school of interpretation was authoritative. One should also keep in mind that by the time Islam was able to establish itself in Indonesia, it already possessed a largely fixed doctrinal structure, so that it was received in a fairly closed state. Therefore Abu Hamid al-Ghazali (1058–1111) was generally recognized as the foremost and most authoritative teacher.

Finally, it is necessary to point to the difference between Javanese and non-Javanese Islam. This difference is so decisive that it would be a considerable error to speak of a uniform "Indonesian" Islam (which should also include present-day Malaysia and the southern part of the Philippines). While, as explained earlier, outside East and Central Java Islam mainly had to deal with indigenous ancestral customs, in Java it was subjected to extensive reinterpretation in a speculative-mystical sense.

a. Islam outside Java

First, let us consider briefly how Islam developed in the main centers outside Java, including the coastal districts of Sumatra and Kalimantan (Indonesian Borneo) as well as Madura and South Celebes. Essentially the situation does not differ too much from that in most other places where Islam covered an older, partly ancestral culture, as there is a continuous battle between Islamic rules (shari'a) and hereditary customs. While the latter usually win in practice, the shariʿa, having an idealistic, theoretical orientation, does not give up its generally acknowledged superiority. Accordingly the Islamic scholars (*ʿulamaʾ*) frequently disapprove of and attack the continuation of ancient cultural elements (including music, dance, and so on). There are important cases among these, such as the well-known matrilegal system of the Minangkabau, according to which both inheritance and descent are matrilineal. This is in sharp contrast with the patrilineal Islamic system. Moreover the system has matrilocal characteristics.[8] Another case is the group of *bissu* priests among the Buginese inhabitants of South Celebes, a term that must be derived from the Buddhist *bhikshu/bhikku,* a mendicant friar.[9]

Remarkably, in all these cases one attempts to achieve harmony, which leads to the annihilation of differences, or rather these are brought into balance with one another. This endeavor is also expressed in the language. The foreign Arabic words *musawarat* (*mushawara*) and *mupakat* (*muwafaqa*), meaning, respectively, deliberation and agreement, are among the most common expressions in Indonesian languages. The Arabic word *rukn* (support, pillar) has been changed into *rukun* and now means harmony. Only in some isolated cases, which mostly had (at least partially) a political cause, some violent developments have taken place. For example in West Sumatra an effort was made to erase the ancient customs completely and consequently to help Islamic law to victory during the so-called Padri War (in the first half of the nineteenth century). And in Aceh, North Sumatra, the long war against the Dutch (starting in 1873 and lasting, with interruptions, until the invasion by the Japanese in 1941) led to a discussion between Islamic scholars and traditional chieftains. Finally, during the turbulent period after the Second World War there were frequent clashes between Muslim zealots and their adversaries.[10]

This struggle against ancestral customs also resounds in the writings of Islamic scholars. In an interesting article G. W. J. Drewes (1976) pointed out that the writings of the important eighteenth-century South Sumatran scholar ʿAbd al-Samad al-Palimbani contain polemic expressions against certain pre- and non-Islamic practices, among others the institution of transvestites, the practice of making small offerings in order to placate dangerous forces, and the construction of dolls used as representations of people who are threatened by disaster. The great mystical poet Hamza Fansuri, who lived in North Sumatra at the end of the sixteenth century, also fiercely attacked surviving Hindu yoga practices.[11] In a magnificent poem he contrasts the jungles of the interior, where such practices frequently occur, with the seashore and the Islamized coasts, which are open to the world. This division corresponds almost exactly with the geographic expansion of Islam in Indonesia.[12] He writes:

> The seekers in the forest
> Live in seclusion for months on end
> Yet from an early age till their hairs are gray
> They will never meet the Lord.

Their bodies are worn out through ascetic practices
When one looks at them they are like slaves
They draw their breath into the brain
Lest their fluids get into a commotion....

Knowledge of the Reality is not difficult to obtain
It is not in rolling the eyes
Nor in twisting the abdominal muscles
By such practices your Beloved is roused to anger....

Know yourself, o son of a merchant
Turn into a vessel for your return
Then steer a settled course without wavering
So that you can [soon] return.[13]

In spite of these practices it is beyond question that Islam has taken possession of the minds of non-Javanese Islamized peoples both in an ethnic and in an ethical sense. Being a Minangkabau, Acehnese, Madurese, or Makassarese implies being a Muslim. People have Islamic names, the mosque marks the village square—be it often in a form that clearly betrays its pre-Islamic origin—and traditional literature is mainly written in Arabic script. Yet to a non-Indonesian Muslim some of the traditional customs may seem rather foreign to the nature of Islam, such as the abovementioned *kanduri,* religious meals organized on every festive occasion with the purpose of sharing the blessing inherent in the food, which is summoned by prayers. It is remarkable that time and again attempts are made to incorporate these customs into Islam by approximating them to rituals mentioned in Islamic law books (in this case the *walima*). In fact the good wishes, sayings, and blessings (called *mantera*) which are uttered on these occasions demonstrate the peculiar mixture that is so characteristic of syncretism.[14] The medicine man, who is still a highly respected person among many Islamized peoples, obtains his knowledge from indigenous as well as from Hindu sources, invoking ghosts and gods from three different cultures and religions in perfect harmony.

b. Islam in Java

The situation in Java differs considerably from that in the non-Javanese areas. To a large extent the Javanese population has been practicing Islam for several centuries, and, as Christiaan Snouck Hurgronje rightly pointed out, there is in principle no reason to question this confession. But if one views Javanese Islam in the context of Islam at large, it is impossible to disregard a number of rather profound differences that are typical of the special character of this faith. The strongest indication of this is the fact that major segments of the Javanese population do not wish to identify themselves completely as part of the Islamic community. In contrast, they profess a religious variant named *agama Jawa,* which contains a large amount of Shivaite ideas. This has led some sociologists to assume that the dichotomy between a strictly Islamic minority called *putihan,* "of a white color," and a majority called *abangan,* "red- or brown-colored" (i.e., the real Javanese), as experienced by the Javanese themselves, would be an empirical reality. These *putihan,* however, are in fact also Javanese, and most *abangan* profess Islam, although their particular basic attitude can be understood only from their ancient Javanese and Shivaite heritage. What we are dealing with here is more a continuum, the question being merely whether one gives priority to "Javanese" or to "Islamic" values in the conflicts that keep arising time and again. Clifford Geertz's attempt to divide Javanese society into three classes, in which besides the nobility, the *santri* represents the middle class and the *abangan* the lower class, must therefore be considered wrong.[15] Consequently the best way to do justice to the very complex state of affairs may be to make a distinction between, on the one hand, customs and literature, and on the other hand between purely Islamic, syncretistic, and anti-Islamic elements in literature.

Customs

As early as the reign of Sultan Agung (r. 1613–1646), the greatest Muslim ruler of Java and king of the realm of Mataram, examples are found of the incomplete manner in which Islamic cultural values were absorbed. When introducing the Islamic lunar calendar, this ruler also maintained the Hindu Shaka era. As for Arabic script (called *pégon*), this could never really replace a variant of Hindu script, and is now mainly used in communities of religious students (*pasantrèn*).

The ancient heritage is also clearly expressed in the terminology of Javanese Islam. Thus the fasting month of Ramadan is usually called *wulan puasa* (or *pasa*), recalling the Hindu fasting rites, *upawasa.* The eighth month, Sha'ban, which precedes this month, is called *ruah* (Arab. *arwah,* souls [of the dead]), as during this month the Javanese, in accordance with the ancient Indonesian ancestor cult, visit the graves of the dead in order to pray and sprinkle them with flowers. This last custom is called *nyadran,* an expression deriving from the Sanskrit *shraddha,* which in ancient Java designated the ceremonies of the great festival of the dead.[16] Students at an Islamic boarding school for advanced religious studies are called *santri* (which probably derives from Sanskrit *shastri,* doctor of the holy doctrine); their institute is generally called *pasantrèn* (place of the *santri*).

The following customs with a syncretistic flavor deserve to be especially mentioned.

Many of the ancient gods continue to live on, particularly in the countryside, where in many places the cycle of the year is still marked by agricultural customs that reach far back into history. We mention in particular Devi Sri (Sanskrit Shri, the *shakti* or wife of the Hindu God Vishnu), who is especially worshipped as the rice goddess; the goddess of the Southern Ocean, Nyai Lara Kidul;[17] and the mysterious "great hunter" Bau Reksa, who is implored for protection and help. Moreover, the goddess Uma or Durga is still venerated in the forest of Krendhawahana, not far from the ancient capital city of Surakarta.[18] Furthermore, the traditional shadow puppet play (*wayang kulit*), the gamelan orchestra, and classical dance (*beksa*) have been maintained despite misgivings in orthodox Muslim circles. To a large extent the shadow puppet play is still devoted to the ancient myths created from the Indian Mahabharata and Ramayana epics, in which the typical Javanese element finds expression through the servants accompanying the main hero. These are the old Semar, who is sexless (i.e., having male and female characteristics) and may in fact personify the Javanese progenitor, with his two sons, Petruk (from Sanskrit *pitara,* perhaps meaning ancestral spirit) and Nalagarèng. The traditionally religious character of the *wayang* is especially clearly expressed in the exorcistic performances named *ngruwat,* the aim of which is to pacify the destructive demon Kala, a son of the Hindu God Shiva.

At the village level these pre-Islamic customs are most apparent in the annual *mbersih desa* (cleansing of the village) ritual, which is primarily intended to honor the spirit of the deceased village founder (*cakal bakal*), and at the same time has the character of a purification. In addition to a number of rituals such as *wayang kulit,* masked dances, trance performances, and the like, it also features the usual beneficial meals (*slametan*). The counterpart of these village rituals at the royal courts are the *grebeg,* held three times a year.[19] These processions, which in spite of all the political changes still take place in old residential towns such as Cirebon, Surakarta, Ngayogyakarta, and Demak, are in conformity with the Muslim calendar and mark the most important festivals: (1) *muludan* (Arab. *mawlid*), that is, the day of the birth and death of the Prophet Muhammad on 12 Rabiʿ al-awwal; (2) the "small festival" at the end of the month of fasting, on the first of Shawwal; and (3) the "great festival" on the occasion of the pilgrimage to Mecca on 10 Dhu l-hijja. The Islamic element, however, is limited mainly to the fact that the large "male" and "female" rice mountains (*gunungan*) are carried from the palace to the mosque before being distributed among the waiting crowd, who expect to receive blessings from this, just as from the *slametan*. Otherwise the ritual consists mainly of two parts: first the annual fair, Sekatèn, which starts a week before the second, the festival for the Prophet. Characteristically, throughout the duration of Sekatèn the sound of a special set of royal gamelan is heard. This custom is attributed to Sunan Kalijaga, apostle of Islam in the interior of Java and one of the nine Islamic saints (*wali sanga*) who are believed to have spread Islam in Java. It is said that it was his intention to win the Javanese over gradually to the new religion in this manner.

On the actual festival day there is a procession in which the rice mountains are carried around in a festive manner, escorted by royal soldiers in battle dress. Before the revolution in 1945 the rulers themselves used to take part in these processions, and became as it were immersed in the deity.

Théodore Pigeaud made an attempt to identify the *grebeg* with the great court festivals of the Hindu era, Caitra-Phalguna and Shrawana-Bhadra.[20] One is also reminded of the main annual festival, celebrated by the tribal peoples of Indonesia, when the entire tribe is united in a ceremony enacting the ritual (self-)renewal of the world.

Pigeaud also draws attention to the fact that many characteristics of the Shivaite settlements called *ashrama* or *mandala* are still found in the *pasant-rèn*.[21] It is remarkable, too, that the five taboos of Indian Tantrism, the *pan-camakara*, starting with the letter *M*, are still known in present-day Java; these are *minum* (to drink), *madon* (to mix with women), *main* (to play), *madat* (to smoke opium), and *maling* (to steal).

To summarize, one may say that Islam has been only partly integrated into the spiritual life of the Javanese and has also been modified to some extent. It is therefore not surprising that many Javanese still have a Hindu rather than a Muslim name, or a combination of the two. Moreover, conversion to another religion, though infrequent, is not considered as despicable as in other Islamic countries, and when a Javanese Muslim woman marries someone who belongs to a different religion, it is not always an absolute condition that the non-Islamic partner must convert to Islam. For the average Javanese, Islam represents only one of many possible ways to achieve the (ultimate) goal, that is, to become absorbed into the divine and to annihilate the difference between Lord and servant. The Javanese thus profess a religious tolerance that is rather exceptional not merely in the rest of the Islamic world but also in Indonesia. Relatively few religious rules and obligations are kept, of which admittedly the pilgrimage to Mecca and the paying of religious taxes are considered more important than the fast of Ramadan or saying the prescribed prayers five times a day.

Escape from frequent admonitions to keep the commandments more strictly is sought in mystical-theosophical religious movements called *keba-tinan*, where "purification of the heart" is given preference over the observance of ritual laws. Recently these movements have even managed to gain recognition as a special religion alongside Islam.[22] It is not without reason that Indonesia, in terms of population the largest Islamic state in the world, has until now declined to proclaim Islam its state religion. In this respect the state occupies an exceptional position within the Islamic world. This refusal should be attributed not so much to its respect for the Christian and Hindu minorities as to the influence of the syncretistic Javanese majority, to which two recent presidents, Sukarno and Suharto, also belonged. There are strong indications that the role of Islam in present-day Java may be compared to that of Buddhism in the pre-Islamic era. In both cases a "foreign" religion with a strongly doctrinal structure is opposed by a syncretistic folk religion, and at the same time blends with it.

Literature

The strictly Islamic literature that developed in the *pasantrèn* does not differ significantly from that found outside Java, and has above all been strongly influenced by the Malay language and literature. Islamic Javanese literature is of similar interest because of the polemical passages criticizing doctrines and customs that are not in accordance with "pure" Islam. As an example we mention two fragments published by Drewes which probably date from the sixteenth century.[23] These say among other things that it is disbelief to maintain that "there are no commandments or prohibitions in this world, because God gives, and I eat and drink, without making a distinction between what is forbidden and what is allowed." Moreover, a Muslim who refuses to shave his head, to wear a turban, or to cut his nails and thus to follow the example of the Prophet would be a *kafir*. It is also considered disbelief to raise the question, for example, whether the Javanese or the Islamic faith is better, and so on.

Meanwhile, the literature that we consider syncretistic Islamic is of greater significance for the Javanese ethos. It concerns a rather elaborate literature in metrical poetry which must be recited or sung and is often in the form of a dialogue. There are two themes that attract attention. First, it is emphasized that a Javanese should not assimilate too much to Islamic-Arabic manners. He must remain Javanese above all. Second, there are writings that attempt to bridge the gap between the old and the new faiths through mysticism. One should follow the four stages of the mystic path: *shari'a, tariqa, haqiqa,* and *ma'rifa,* which are also known from Sumatran mysticism, and strive to arrive at a state in which the dualistic distinction between God and worshipper is extinguished. Then, in a condition of unconsciousness, there is no longer Master and servant:

> There is no difference
> between worshipper and worshipped
> both are only He
> because the Being of the universe
> is indivisible.
> Now and in all eternity
> it is as [it has] always [been].[24]

The concept of *suksma* plays a prominent role in this context. According to P. J. Zoetmulder this term refers to the Divine Immaterial. The idea has been taken from Shivaism (Sanskrit *suksma*). It signifies both the highest divinity (Hyang Suksma) and "the part of the human being which is connected with the divinity and has an identical nature."[25] The divine immanence in human beings, the unity and merging of a human being with the divine, is possible because of the *suksma*. It is perceived by means of *rasa* (intuitive perception).

A text from the second half of the nineteenth century, the *Serat Wéd-hatama* (Writing on the Highest Knowledge), is particularly informative on these two matters. This text, which—probably incorrectly—has been attributed to Prince Mangkunagara IV of Surakarta, is meant to serve as a guidebook for the path through life of a young Javanese nobleman.[26] The Javanese themselves regard it as a kind of creed. In the text,[27] the following admonition occurs (2.7):

> If you insist on imitating
> the example of the Prophet
> then, young man, you overreach yourself
> as a rule you will not hold out long
> as you are indeed a Javanese!
> and further (2.10,11)[28]:

> By and by I realized
> that as I was the son of an official[29]
> if I should strive to be a *kaum* I would degrade myself...
> It would probably be preferable to adhere to
> the rule that in life it is one's duty
> to follow the course
> traced out by the forefathers,
> from the earliest times
> right down to the present day,
> which amounts to no more than merely earning a living.

And in the final, fourth canto the poet tries to show the way to the mystical experience, which culminates in the following (4.19)[30]:

> Now I shall teach you
> in its turn the fourth kind of worship,
> the worship of the essence, which is felt to be the core of creation
> how it happens cannot be pointed out,
> only that it is achieved by inner firmness.

The *Serat Centhini,* which originated in similar surroundings, also contains many examples of this Islamic-Javanese mentality.[31] Kyai Amongraga,[32] son of the saint of Giri (North Java, not far from Surabaya), wanders all over Java and eventually marries Tambangraras, daughter of a local Muslim leader. He gives her religious instruction, which forms the core of the long text. When his teachings lead many of his followers to practice an explicit antinomianism, Sultan Agung has him cast into the sea. His widow continues to practice asceticism until she too dies. Both of them still appear to those faithful followers who have been able to annihilate the consciousness through mystical practices (*dhikr*) and ecstasy. Then they receive the highest instruction, and in this all differences are abolished. A comparison is made with somebody watching a *wayang* performance, when the figures are no longer seen as (mere) forms but are experienced through merging with their essence.[33] Yet one should not go so far as to regard oneself as God. God's essential being can be comprehended only in a state of nonconsciousness, in quiet and emptiness.[34] Although the law does not need to be despised and keeps its validity for the masses, the true mystic will turn away from it "because if there is no servant, there can be no service of God."

So far we have been dealing with relatively moderate forms of discussion between traditional Javanese concepts and newly imported Islamic ways of thinking. Yet the borderline is crossed when in an anti-Islamic sphere Islam is actually attacked in the name of the indigenous religion. Characteristic of this direction are two related writings that probably both date from the 1870s: the *Serat Dermagandhul*[35] and the *Serat Gatholoco*.[36] In the first book the teacher Kalamwadi explains to his student Dermagandhul (most names in this work have a sexual connotation) how in 1478 the *wali* from the north put an end to the Hindu-Buddhist realm of Majapahit and imposed their religion upon the population. After four hundred years, however, the Javanese should turn away from Arabia and return to the faith of their ancestors with the help of Dutch scholarship (an educational institution for the sons of Indonesian leaders was established in the East Javanese town of Probolinggo in 1879). The author makes quite a few nasty remarks about Muslims. The Javanese, not being suited for Arabic studies anyway, should above all turn toward their ancestral wisdom, as they will never develop into true Muslims. The soil of Arabia, where people kept slaves and cohabited with female slaves without marrying them, should be cursed. Muslims should be despised because of their ridiculous prayer postures and their disgusting dietary laws. Their priests are hypocrites. They prove better at performing *salat* and *dhikr* than at fighting in battle, their highest aim being the cooking pot. Expressions of a sexual nature are attributed to the *wali* Sunan Kalijaga; thus the *shahada* should be understood as the sexual act. The *santri* are compared to frogs, and the pilgrims going to Mecca are said to look like crickets. Arab Muslims are like rats which have undermined the Javanese kingdom, while Muslims in general are likened to bees because of their sting (greed). Both *santri* as well as Chinese are compared to herons because of their cupidity.

In the second work the monster Gatholoco unites in a cave with the female hermit Perjiwati, after having been victorious in a debate with several *santri*. He does not hesitate to associate the name of God, Allah, with the Javanese word *ala* (bad, ugly), to accuse the *santri* of being disbelievers because they have betrayed the religion of their ancestors, and to give a new interpretation of Islam (*sarak Rasul*) as *larasan unsul* (following a false doctrine).

On the one hand, both writings are certainly exceptional phenomena, which may also have been affected by political-economic factors. On the other hand, the fact that, following the events of 1965, millions of Javanese opted for Christianity or even for Hinduism instead of Islam—as they had to chose to which of the officially recognized religions they belonged—may be explained only by an aversion to Islam among large sections of the Javanese population.

When the Indian poet Tagore visited the island of Bali in the 1920s he remarked that, although he noticed India everywhere, he could not recognize it anywhere. About ten years later the French specialist on Islam Georges Henri Bousquet traveled through Java. He was astonished to find that the Javanese ruler Mangkunagara VII was unable to answer his question when he asked in whose name the *khutba* (Friday sermon) was read in his realm. Both cases may serve to illustrate the special character that, under the influence of extant syncretism, the great religions acquired in the Indonesian region.

Translated by Clara Brakel-Papenhuijzen

IV

Is There an Islamic Linguistic Sphere?

Islamic Idiom in the Languages of Muslim Peoples

(Otto Jastrow)

For Muslims, the Qur'an represents a linguistic miracle. They believe that its unique character prohibits translation of any kind into other languages, and actually makes the idea of translation seem meaningless. The Qur'an can, however, be elucidated and explained in other languages—just as Arabic-speaking Muslims rely entirely on explanation for understanding many passages—but only the original Arabic text of the Qur'an is allowed to be read aloud and publicly recited. The same applies to ritual prayer (*salat*), from the muezzin's call to prayer chanted in Arabic, and the Qur'an verses recited during prayers, to the concluding words "Al-salamu ʿalaykum wa-rahmatu llah" (God's blessing and peace be upon you!). This means that being a Muslim results in constant contact with the Arabic language, if only in the form of reciting the Qur'an without necessarily understanding it.

Medieval Arab Islamic culture developed an enormous attractive force that was not just confined to the religious sphere but also deeply affected the languages of Islamized peoples. In any event, many of the territories won for Islam were completely Arabicized in linguistic terms as well. We should note that until Islam emerged, the Arabic language was confined to the Arabian Peninsula and the neighboring territories of Syria and Iraq, that is, the periphery of the region known as the Fertile Crescent; the remainder of Syria and Mesopotamia, as well as Egypt and North Africa, first became Arabic language areas in the course of Islamization. Although the other areas of Islamic culture—the Iranian, Indian, Indonesian, Turkish, and sub-Saharan African regions—have not been fully immersed in the Arabic language, Arabic has deeply influenced these linguistic groups as well.

This is clear from the fact that the most important languages in all these Islamic cultural regions adopted the Arabic script system, regardless of factors such as their own existing script traditions, and ignoring the fact that the Arabic alphabet was not really suited to transmitting Turkish, Urdu, or Hausa. The Arabic script often had to be painstakingly adapted to the phonology of the respective language through the use of additional symbols. The deficient writing of vowels in Arabic was a particularly serious obstacle in all these languages. Despite these problems, it was not until the twentieth century that most Muslim languages, such as Turkish, Swahili, and Indonesian (Malayan), abolished the Arabic alphabet and replaced it with the Latin alphabet. In the Soviet Union a modified Cyrillic alphabet was introduced into the Turkic languages (Azerbaijani, Uzbek, Turkmen, Tatar, and so on); after the collapse of the Soviet Union, Uzbekistan and Azerbaijan decided to change to the Latin alphabet. In addition to Arabic itself, Persian, Urdu, and Pashto (one of Afghanistan's national languages) have retained Arabic script up to the present. Along with purely functional reasons for replacing the Arabic alphabet, nationalist tendencies and, in cases such as that of Turkey, secularism as well usually played a role. Consequently the introduction of Latin script in Turkey met with hostile rejection by broad groups of Muslims, and this hostility is still maintained by individual groups today, over seventy-five years after the writing reform.

Along with Arabic script, it was primarily Arabic vocabulary that made a huge impact on the languages of Muslim peoples. Innumerable Arabic expressions found their way into other Muslim languages, starting with formulas from religious life, going on to Islamic law and the language of philology, medicine, and natural sciences, and beyond this, right into everyday speech. In the process, Persian acted as a transmitter for the languages of the Turkish and Indian regions in the sense that these languages did not draw directly on Arabic but adopted expressions from Persian, which was the dominant cultural language in the Turkish and Indian world for centuries. This is evident from the Persian phonetic structure still discernible in many of the loan words. For instance, the Arabic feminine ending *-ah* is often pronounced *-at* in Persian, and this form is also found in loan words in Turkish, Urdu, Pashto, and so on. Examples of this include Arabic *haqiqa* (truth): Persian, Pashto *haqiqat,* Turkish *hakikat;* Arabic *darurah* (necessity): Persian, Urdu, Pashto, *zarurat,* Turkish *zaruret;* Arabic *baraka* (blessing): Persian *barakat,* Turkish *bereket,* Urdu *barkat;* Arabic *hukuma* (government): Persian, Pashto, *hukumat,* Turkish *hükümet.* In words loaned into Persian, the complex consonant system of Arabic was adapted to the simpler Persian one; the Arabic *s, ṣ,* and *th,* for instance, were combined into the Persian *s,* the Arabic *z, dh, ḍ,* and *ẓ* into the Persian *z,* and the Arabic *h* and *ḥ* into the Persian *h.* As we can see from these examples, this simplified pronunciation was adopted by Indian and Turkic languages.

The Muslim world in Africa lacks a transmission language analogous to Persian in the Middle East and Asia; instead, African languages have generally borrowed their Arabic elements directly from Arabic itself. Some of the more important African Muslim languages, however, have operated as transmitters within a smaller geographical radius; these include Hausa and Swahili, as well as Tamasheq, the most southerly Berber language. An example of how Arabic words are loaned into Islamic languages is demonstrated

Table 5. Names of the Weekdays in Some Important Islamic Languages

	Arabic	Persian	Urdu	Turkish	Hausa	Bahasa Indonesia
Sunday	al-ahad	yak shambe	itwar	pazar	láhadi:	minggu
Monday	al-ithnain	do shambe	somwar	pazartesi	littinin	senin
Tuesday	al-thalatha'	seshambe	mangal(war)	salı	talá:ta	selasa
Wednesday	al-arba'a'	chahar shambe	budh(war)	çarşamba	lá:rabá:	rebu
Thursday	al-khamis	panj shambe	jum'a rat	perşembe	alhamis	kemis
Friday	al-jum'a	jom'e	jum'a	cuma	Júmmá'a:	Djuma'at
Saturday	al-sabt	shambe	sanichar	cumartesi	asábat	sabtu

by a small vocabulary sample—the days of the week—displayed in the table. It shows the Arabic names and their counterparts in the most important Islamic languages (Persian, Urdu, Turkish, Hausa, and Indonesian). As we can see, this word series has been adopted to different extents, but all these Islamic languages have introduced the Arabic term for Friday, the Muslim weekly holiday. The Hausa language has adopted the whole series, as has Indonesian, but in the latter case Sunday, the Christian holiday, has kept the name *domingo* (*minggu*) from a European language, Portuguese. Persian uses indigenous names for all the days except Friday, as does Urdu. (An interesting, if somewhat divergent, observation is that in Persian the weekdays are expressed by a simple numerical system: *yak* to *panj* are the numbers from one to five; a similar case in the European context is Portuguese, with *segunda feira, terça feira,* and so on.) Turkish undoubtedly has the most interesting terms for the days of the week: this is a really fine example of the hybrid character of this once global cosmopolitan language, because it combines indigenous terms with loans from Arabic and Persian. The word *salı* (Tuesday) is indigenous; likewise *ertesi* (the day after), which is used to form the term *cumartesi* (the day after Friday), that is, Saturday; and *pazartesi* (Monday). In Turkish the name for Friday also comes from the Arabic *cuma* (with "c" pronounced as "j"), while the remaining names derive from Persian.

The permeation of Arabic loan words into Muslim languages cannot be seen as a single event limited to a specific time period but rather appears as an extended process of progressive enrichment. Arabic was consistently practiced, and not only by religious scholars; it was also part of the educational tradition of Muslims with academic training. Similar to the role of Latin in European languages, Arabic represented a fund from which new foreign words could continually be drawn, not only for academic but also for administrative use. In the process, as with medieval Latin, Arabic was developed further by non-Arab users, with the result that it is not unusual to find Arabic neologisms in Persian and Turkish that do not exist in Arabic itself. Likewise, Arabic terms can be endowed with new meanings they have never had in Arabic. One noteworthy example is the very popular derivational ending *-iyyat* in Persian and Ottoman Turkish, which actually signifies a plural but is often used in the singular, for example, the Persian *nashriyyat* and Turkish *neşriyat,* meaning publication(s), derived from the Arabic word *nashr* (publishing); or the Persian word *naqliyyat* and the Turkish *nakliyat,* meaning transportation(s), from the Arabic *naql,* which means (to) transport. An example from the state and administrative language of the Ottomans is the term for the Grand Vizier, *sadr-ı aʿzam.* This is made up of two Arabic words, *sadr,* meaning breast, frontpiece, or leader, and *aʿzam* (most important, most powerful)—but the resulting term is a purely Ottoman coinage. In turn, *sadr-ı aʿzam* is used to form the abstract term *sadaret* (the Grand Viziership), a derivation that is also possible in Arabic but does not have the same meaning. Meanwhile, neologistic formulas, or ones with new meaning, have been loaned back into the written Arabic language, for example, *qadaʾ,* which means the office of judge (*qadi*) in classical Arabic; in Ottoman Turkish the word was given the additional meaning of a territorial administrative unit such as a jurisdictional area, rural district, or department, and this is the meaning it has today in Arabic usage in Syria and Iraq.

The official language of the Ottoman Empire, Ottoman Turkish, consequently drew from a number of sources (making it eminently comparable to English, the language of another global empire), and achieved a high degree of complexity and linguistic differentiation that enabled expression of the finest nuances. The Persian-Arabic vocabulary, with its constant stock of loans, made possible the formation of new specialist terms whenever necessary; this is comparable to the Greek and Latin vocabulary still used today in European languages as a source of specialist terms. In recent decades, however, the language reform initiated by Atatürk has resulted in Persian-Arabic words being largely eliminated, and as Persian and Arabic language teaching was abolished at the same time, the following generation grew up completely cut off from the cultural heritage of their forefathers. Attempts were made to fill the ensuing lexical vacuum with Turkish neologisms; but the Turkish language has lost much of its cultural complexity and rich capacity for nuances. Paradoxically, this so-called language purification—that is, the suppression of the Persian-Arabic elements—resulted in a huge influx of loan words from French to fill the terminological vacuum. For instance, the expression for healthy common sense is no longer *aklıselim* (Arabic) but *bonsans* (from the French *bon sens*), while the Sphinx of Giza is no longer *ebülhevil* (Arabic) but *sfenks* (from the French *sphinx*). As these examples show, the borrowed French words are reproduced with Turkish phonetic values, which can result in very different written forms, such as *mayo* (bathing suit) from the French *maillot.* These European loan words in French guise are far more damaging to the Turkish language than its Persian-Arabic components because they are more difficult to integrate into the consonant and syllable structure of Turkish.

As is often rightly said, Islam is not only a religion but also a way of life, which means that the religion permeates the whole of life. In linguistic terms this is shown by the use of religious expressions in many typical everyday situations. Believers often call out the name of God—Allah—or formulas like *ya Allah* (Oh God!) and *ya rabb* (Oh Lord!); depending on the tone of voice, they can express a wide variety of emotions, from ecstasy, joy, and surprise to shock and anger. *Bi-smillah* (In the name of God) is the formula for starting an activity, setting off on a journey, beginning a speech, or similar situations. When a Muslim voices an intention, he never forgets to add *in sha'a-llah* (If God wills); a statement such as "I'll be in the capital tomorrow" would sound almost like heresy without the obligatory *in sha'a-llah*. The phrase *ma sha'a-llah*, literally "What God wills," expresses admiration. Joy, gratitude, and amazement are expressed by the formula *al-hamdu li-llah* (God be praised), and the words *astaghfiru-llah* are used to beg God for forgiveness. Gratitude to others is expressed by formulas such as *baraka-llahu fik* (God bless you). Muslims ask for God's protection with the words *a'udhu bi-llahi (min al-shaytani l-rajim):* "I seek God's protection (against the accursed Satan)."

These formulas date back to the dawn of Islam and belong to the basic stock of Muslim expression; they are used throughout the Islamic world in their (classical) Arabic form—though adapted to indigenous pronunciation, of course. There is also a large stock of formulas and more or less standard sayings with religious connotations, used on specific occasions or habitually in conversation, for example, as greetings and farewells, good wishes, and forms of regret. There are fixed expressions used in a variety of situations, as when somebody goes on a journey, returns from a pilgrimage, has just taken a bath, or comes from the barber, or for announcing a death, meeting somebody at work, and so on. This second, much larger stock of formulas is phrased not in classical Arabic but in the respective languages of the Muslim countries; in the Arabic-speaking world, too, these sayings are not in classical Arabic but derive from local dialects. The formulas are very similar in form and content, however, and can usually be transposed word for word from one language into the other. Greetings, for example, belong to the second group. Aside from the classical Arabic phrase *al-salamu 'alaykum* (Peace be with you!), answered by *(wa-) 'alaykum al-salam* ("[And] with you be peace!"), indigenous sayings are found everywhere, and are often more widespread than the classical formulations. In Turkey the popular form *merhaba* is generally used (the word also comes from Arabic), or the more formal phrase *günaydın* (Good day), based on the European model. Aside from *al-salamu 'alaykum*, in modern written Arabic and in Arabic dialects there is a nonreligious expression not infrequently used for greetings related to the time of day: *sabah al-khayr* (Good morning), *masa'al-khayr* (Good evening). In Persia the most common greeting formula is *salam 'alaykom*, but the reply is identical, and not, as in Arabic, a reversal of the two clauses of the expression. Words of farewell are rather more complicated. The departing person says something like "At God's command," while the person staying behind responds, "God be with you." In Turkish both these phrases are expressed by *Allaha ısmarladık,* "I commend (you) to God," with the response *güle güle,* "With laughter" (that is, "May all be well with you"). Persian has a very similar expression, *khoda hafez* (May God protect you), or *be-khoda sepordamat* (I have commended you to God), with the reply *be-amane khoda* (Under God's protection). There are different regional forms for farewells in the Arabic world. In Iraq, "good-bye" is *fi amani-llah,* usually pronounced *fimalla* (Under God's protection), with the response *alla wiyyak* (God be with you). In Syria the common formula is *khatrak* (roughly translated as "Stay well disposed to me"), and the response *maʿis-salame* (Come back safely). In Egypt and Morocco people say farewell to a departing person with the words *maʿis-salama* or *be-s-slama,* and are answered with the phrase *alla ysallimak,* or *llah isellmek* (God keep you well).

These examples show how politeness formulas are often exchanged in the form of a dialogue that flows fairly automatically as soon as the relevant social situation arises. The phrase chosen by the first speaker automatically engenders a uniform phrase in response. In a fine essay on politeness formulas in Syrian Arabic, Charles A. Ferguson has shown how the verbal and nominal roots (the three significant consonants that form the basis of the noun or verb) that are used in the first part of a formulaic dialogue have to recur in the accompanying response. For example, if a person greets somebody at work with the formula *alla yaʿtik ilʿafye* (God give you strength), the response is not simply "Thank you"; the obligatory reply is *alla yʿafik* (God strengthen you). The noun *ʿafye* (strength) and the verb *yʿafik,* "he strengthens you" (*-k* = you), clearly have the same root. In Syria, happy events such as births and weddings, as well as other occasions such as buying new clothes, are greeted with the word *mabruk* (blessed). The obligatory response is *alla ybarek fik* (God bless you); here, too, the root *brk,* meaning "to bless," is repeated in both formulas. The expression *naʿiman* is more difficult to translate: it is used to greet somebody who has just come from the barber or taken a bath. It means something like "May you feel good," and the response is *alla yinʿam ʿalek* (May God make you feel good). Similar formulas occur outside the realm of the Arabic language, but they lack the kind of echo referring to the word's root, which is possible only in Arabic. In other Muslim languages the various kinds of good wishes are usually followed by an invariable "Thank you" formula. In Turkey, for instance, a person at work is greeted with the words *kolay gelsin* (May it be easy for you), or *allah kuvvet versin* (May God give you strength), while the equivalent phrase in Persia is *khoda qovvet dehad,* which also means "God give you strength." Congratulations in Persia are expressed by the formula *mobarak-ast,* and in Turkey by *tebrik ederim;* while in Turkey a freshly shaven man or someone who has just come from the bath is greeted with *sıhhatlar olsun* (May it bring you health). Good wishes like these are reciprocated in Persia with the formula *motashakker-am and* in Turkey with *teşekkür ederim* (I thank you), *sağ olunuz* (Good health to you), or *eksik olmayınız* (May you lack nothing).

Converts to Islam usually adopt a Muslim name, that is, a name that generally comes from classical Arabic. As a result, typical Arabic men's names such as 'Umar, 'Ali, and 'Uthman, or women's names such as Zaynab, Fatima, and 'A'isha have spread with Islam from South Africa to Indonesia. Probably the most popular and common name is that of the Prophet himself, Muhammad, literally "The Praised One." Through the ages, parents' firm belief in the blessed power of this name has led them to give it to their sons, particularly the firstborn. This custom has not been affected by the equally widespread view that the name of the Prophet has to remain taboo for later generations in order to prevent blasphemy against him (for example, if somebody called Muhammad turns out to be a criminal). Muslims, however, often tend to pronounce the name of the Prophet Muhammad differently from the profane version of his name, with the pronunciation of the Prophet's name based more closely on the classical Arabic norm than that of the ordinary name. This practice is expressed most typically in Turkey, where there is evidence of it since the Middle Ages. While the Prophet's name was pronounced as Muhammed, the profane name had the form Mehemmed, which gave rise to the popular form Mehmed; only this form of the name has survived up to the present day in Turkey as Mehmet or Memet.

The theophoric names—that is, first names using the name Allah—constitute an important group of Muslim names. The original version of the name is 'Abdallah or 'Abdullah, which comes from *'abd Allah* (Servant of God). Replacing Allah with one of the other ninety-nine names of God (the "beautiful names"), for example, al-Ghafur (the Forgiving), al-'Aziz (the Strong), al-Qadir (the Mighty), or al-Karim (the Noble), gave rise to other common names such as 'Abdurrahman, 'Abdulghafur, 'Abdul'aziz, 'Abdulqadir, 'Abdulkarim, and so on. Rulers not infrequently adopted names formed with the word *din* (religion), or *dawla* (state), such as Sayfaddin (Sword of Religion) or Sayfaddawlah (Sword of State). One should also mention names with *nur* or *diya* as their first component—both words mean light, or glory—such as Nuraddin (Turk. Nurettin), which means Light of Religion, or Ziya'al-Haqq (Zia ul-Haq), meaning the Glory of God. The Western media have a fondness for abbreviating compound names like these but sometimes use the wrong breaks: there are no such names, for instance, as Abdul or Abdur, because -*l*- and -*r*- are abbreviated forms of the article and really belong to the following word; for example, 'Abdur-Rahman is actually 'Abd al-Rahman.

Although the most important names occur in all Muslim countries, there are certain regional peculiarities. In Shi'ite regions, for example, the name of 'Ali and the names of his two sons, Hasan and Husain, are very popular. Typical Iranian names include Reza and Mirza. In the Ottoman regions it is common to find men's first names with the feminine ending -*at* or -*et* (the

Arabic feminine ending, pronounced *ah* in the original Arabic, as explained earlier); Ismet, Şevket, Behcet, and Saffet are examples here. This type of name has also been loaned back into Arabic and is still found today, mainly in Egypt, for instance, 'Ismat, Shawkat, Bahjat, Safwat, and so on. Men's names with the ending *-i,* such as Fawzi or Ramzi, are also very popular in Egypt.

Translated by Karen Margolis

V

ISLAM REFLECTED IN THE CONTEMPORARY LITERATURE OF MUSLIM PEOPLES

(Johann Christoph Bürgel)

1. Introduction

Whereas Islamic expansion once encompassed large areas of Asia and considerable peripheral regions of Africa and Europe, changing them forever, in the modern era European civilization has practically overrun and changed the whole world. A similar process has occurred in literature. Literary forms and means of expression originating in Europe have become the model for literature in the so-called developing countries, although autochthonous literary traditions have endured and merged with Western influence to create new forms of expression. The process of literary renewal in non-European countries generally exhibits some important common features. These include the introduction of printing and newspapers (which changed the social basis for writers, enabling them to shake off dependence on their patrons and become the voice of the people); translations of European literature, and initial indigenous literary efforts based on the European model; growing critical self-reflection in relation to the past and present; and critical commitment to national independence and social and intellectual renewal.

In the Muslim world, the phenomenal early successes of Islam, which lasted under various regimes for nearly a millennium, had created a triumphal sense of superiority. The sudden confrontation with the Occident, with its advanced progress in technology and, in some respects, in civilization as well, came as an enormous shock. At first the Muslim world reacted by greatly admiring the ideals of freedom and equality that Europe seemed to have achieved, the constitutional guarantee of fundamental human rights in European states, and European science and technology. Before long, of course, skeptical opinions emerged alongside the advocacy of radical Westernization, and those who had believed in Western ideals were often bitterly disappointed by imperialist practice. The following three testimonies give an indication of this.

Sadullah (Sa'd Allah) Pasha (1838–1891), an influential Turkish intellectual, wrote an ode to the nineteenth century which included a passage that read:

> The rights of person and possession are protected from attack,
> A new order has been given to the world of civilization.
>
> Amr is not Zeyd's slave, nor is Zeyd Amr's master,
> A clear and indubitable rule establishes the basis of equality.
>
> The spread of science has enlightened the minds of men,
> The printing press has completed what was lacking.
>
> Alas, the Western lands have become the daysprings of knowledge,
> Nothing remains of the fame of Rum and Arab, of Egypt and Herat.
>
> The time is a time of progress, the world is a world of science,
> Is the survival of societies compatible with ignorance?[1]

Ziya (Diya') Pasha (1825–1880) was one of the pioneers of literary renewal, and by no means a conservative obscurantist. Yet he warned against slavish imitations of the West:

> To impute fanaticism to men of zeal
> To ascribe wisdom to men without religion is now the fashion.
>
> Islam, they say, is a stumbling-block to the progress of the state
> This story was not known before, and now it is the fashion.
>
> Forgetting our religious loyalty in all our affairs
> Following Frankish ideas is now the fashion.[2]

Our third example consists of three bitter lines by Egypt's "prince of poets," Ahmad Shawqi, from his reply to the farewell speech of British consul-general Lord Cromer in 1907:

> Today a government has broken its promises, a government whose
>   pledges we took as the Gospel.
> It entered Egypt, in the name of friendship and its obligations, as a
>   penetrating illness.
> It destroyed her lineaments and demolished her foundation and
>   caused the loss of her expected independence.[3]

This gives some idea of the conflict into which the Islamic world was plunged by its encounter with Europe. It led to a deep identity crisis that caused Islam to develop a new kind of self-confidence based on its own glorious—and often glorified—past, and on belief in the values of its own tradition. Mindful of their responsibility, writers throughout the Islamic world have participated in this development with praise and criticism, remembrance and appeals. This is evident in their work.

It is possible to mention only a few examples from the huge stock of Islamic literature. Some large areas of the Muslim world, such as Indonesia and Malaysia, are not dealt with here because this is beyond the author's scope. What follows is an overview that aims to give a balanced and representative picture of a variety of aspects of the literature under review. I begin with a survey of the past, including Qur'anic stories, works about Muhammad, and Islamic history. I then move on to the present, discussing criticism of literary works related to Islam, affirmations of the living tradition, and fundamentalist fiction.

2. Qur'anic Themes

I begin with a play, *Solomon the Wise,* by Tawfiq al-Hakim (1898–1987). Drama as a genre was adopted from Europe, and al-Hakim was one of its leading representatives in Arab countries, and probably the Muslim world as a whole. The play shows how a story in the Islamic tradition can be very freely adapted without losing sight of typical Muslim concerns. Al-Hakim explained that the play was based on three sources: the Qur'an (27:17–44), the Bible, and the *Arabian Nights.* (The work centers on motifs from two fairy tales, "The Fisherman and the Jinn" and "The Bronze City.")

The cast of the play includes King Solomon, his vizier Asif, and his priest Saduq; a fisherman and a jinn; Bilqis, the Queen of Sheba, her vizier and generals, her handmaid Shahba', and her prisoner Mundhir. Love and power dominate the complex web of relationships that develops among the characters. While Solomon loves Bilqis, she loves Mundhir, who loves the handmaid. The connection between Solomon and the story of the fisherman and the demon goes back to the Jewish-Islamic legend—which also features in "The Bronze City"—according to which Solomon is supposed to have imprisoned insubordinate spirits in bottles. At the beginning of the play one of these bottles ends up in the fisherman's net. At first the jinn threatens his captor, but sighting Solomon's boat on the horizon, he lets himself be imprisoned again in the bottle and asks the fisherman to plead with Solomon on his behalf. Solomon agrees to the jinn's request on condition that the fisherman take the consequences—just as the body has to take the consequences of the spirit that inhabits it. This reveals an explicit symbolic function of the play: the demon stands for human intellect, reason, and invention. Later on in the play he is used to force Bilqis to submit to Solomon. When Bilqis resists the king, who is used to easy female conquests, Solomon turns to the demon, who advises him to attain his goal by action and struggle. "Do you really believe that a woman's heart can be won by action and struggle?" Solomon asks doubtfully. The fisherman echoes, "Does the shari'a of the heart and of love allow that?" But Solomon eventually follows the demon's suggestion: Mundhir is turned into a statue and placed in a marble basin. To release him, Bilqis has to weep until the basin is full and her tears reach the statue's heart. Every evening the king arrives and laughs mockingly at the weeping woman. When only a few more tears are needed, he tricks her into coming away from the basin; her maid then weeps the final tears. Mundhir is released, and the lovers sink into each other's arms. When Solomon and Bilqis return, the king laughs once again, but Bilqis is shocked and collapses. Remorse follows quickly: "How could I have done this?" Solomon asks. Saduq tries to convince him that he has not sinned because he is a prophet, and therefore infallible. (Qur'anic teaching identifies Solomon as a prophet.) But the king sees things differently. This is the moment when al-Hakim embarks on a key dialogue about the essence of religion, and prophets in particular. Rejecting the priest's theory of infallibility and his fear of the masses' reaction to an admission of fallibility, al-Hakim has Solomon confess vehemently to his sinfulness before his people and emphasize "that I am no better than them, except for the pain that tortures me whenever I think of what I have done wrong!" For the priest, religion is an art whose principles have to be mastered; for Solomon, however, it is "the true core [*haqiqa*] of the human heart with its good and bad traits; it is the conviction of our inability as humans to reach perfection, and of our unceasing efforts to do good, while we sometimes trip over the train of our bad qualities.... Religion is hope and comfort."

The author ends the play with a few concluding scenes. The spirit is imprisoned in the bottle again and thrown into the sea. Solomon and Bilqis are reconciled, while the human heart is lauded as "the great miracle." Solomon realizes that the heart is superior to every earthly power and that only God is capable of opening it; and Bilqis comments, "Solomon, I'm shocked you didn't know that!" The final scene depicts the death of the title figure, Solomon, according to Qur'anic legend (Qur'an 24:14).

At least two aspects of the play are eminently Islamic. The first is the emphasis on the fallibility of the Prophet, represented by Solomon. As we know from the Qur'an (18:110), Muhammad was wont to admit, "I am a man just like you." Since he had already been transformed into a luminous, transcendent figure in the Middle Ages, it is obvious that the issue of fallibility relates to an internal Muslim polemic. The second aspect is the meaning of the heart, which has been at the core of Islamic mysticism for centuries.

Tawfiq al-Hakim also wrote another play based on a legend from the Qur'an, "The People of the Cave" (18:9–22), which explored the theme of man's futile struggle against time.[4] Finally, I should mention his Muham-mad play—which brings us to the next section: the treatment of the Islamic Prophet in contemporary literature.[5]

3. Muhammad

Reverence for Muhammad, a key element of Muslim religiosity, is still as important as ever today, and has inspired significant works by some of the best-known Muslim writers. It suffices to mention the traditional poems of praise that were written by Mahmud Sami al-Barudi (1839–1904), and the "prince of poets," Ahmad Shawqi (1868–1932), in the style of Sharaf al-Din al-Busiri's famous "Ode to the Mantle."[6] They paint the traditional picture of a transcendent human being who is perfect in every respect. In Shawqi's poem "Burda" there is an additional new element: the attempt to portray Muhammad as a peace-loving prophet who resorted to the sword only in an emergency—a polemical reaction probably inspired by ideological at-tacks by Christian missionaries or objective portrayals by Western schol-ars. In contrast, a 450-page epic poem by Ahmad Muharram (1877–1945), "Divan of Islamic Fame, or the Islamic Iliad," blithely glorifies the warlike spirit of Muhammad and early Islam.[7] The following overview indicates the strong effect the Prophet's personality has persistently exercised on en-lightened writers, even those with a critical view of Islam or some of its institutions.

Mahmud Taymur (1894–1973) was one of the most prolific twentieth-century Egyptian writers. As we shall see, his critique of Islam-related works ranged from bitter to sarcastic. He devoted a series of writings to the Mes-senger of God, published under the title *The Human Prophet and Other Essays*. The book contains an autobiographical sketch showing the author's spiritual development from blind faith through tortuous doubt to an en-lightened and confirmed form of belief. The image of the Prophet played an important role in this conversion process. Taymur wrote:

> The key to my understanding the message of Islam was granted to me when I pursued the life of the Prophet, in all its aspects: herein I found clearly a personality teeming with all the great virtues necessary for building a nation, and for the moral discipline of the individual, for a proper course of life for all manner of human beings.
>
> This outstanding personality took me by the hand and led me to the way of Truth and Faith, with the result that I found myself loving this Religion and loving in it the message it has brought to provide guidance and compassion to mankind. The personality of Muhammad is a living translation of the Book of God....It seems that God intended that the way of religion set forth in His Book should receive its practical application in the life of Muhammad and that Muhammad should be the model for all human beings.[8]

Taymur was impressed that Muhammad was both a man of faith and a man of this world. Muhammad, he writes,

> loved what is good in the pleasures of life, which he sought after like a good man, pursuing good means, for he saw God in all he did, setting up his conscience as a watchful censor.... [T]his is pure essence of religion.... This is Islam. For Islam urges you to enjoy your life here to the full and to your heart's desire,... to enjoy what you will in the way of food, drink, clothes and to pursue every pleasure in its lawful aspect... as long as in doing so you do not go to an excess or cause harm to others.... Muhammad loved and hated, rewarded and punished, treated people as they ought to be treated, being neither unduly merciful nor cruel except when wisdom necessitated cruelty.... Thus Muhammad lived in this world, a part of it; he neither divorced himself from it nor did he behave as an exception to the rest of mankind.... [L]ike Muhammad, Muhammad's religion is human. Whoever understands its secrets... will find in it the roots of human nature, with all its impulses and stages of development and at the same time a sublimation of it to the highest level.[9]

Like Taymur, another well-known Egyptian author, ʿAbbas Mahmud al-ʿAqqad (1889–1964), also devoted a book to the Prophet by the title *The Genius of Muhammad*. (Unlike Taymur, al-ʿAqqad was mainly an essayist.) The book includes chapters on two of the most strongly criticized attributes of the Prophet: his warlike proclivities and his relationship to women. The author tries to prove that although Muhammad was a warrior, he did not spread faith by the sword, and the purpose of his nine wives was not to serve the desires of the flesh. Al-ʿAqqad endeavors to show Muhammad's greatness as a preacher, statesman, administrator, military leader, man, husband, and father. In all these fields he achieved the limits of human perfection; he was "a man peerless among men."[10]

In contrast to Taymur's and al-ʿAqqad's essay collections on Muhammad, the four works I now turn to have a more pronounced literary character.

The distinguished critic of Arabic literature M. M. Badawi, who can be quoted as a reliable authority, describes al-Hakim's play *Solomon the Wise* as Brechtian in the bad sense. It consists of a loose sequence of nearly two hundred scenes tracing the Prophet's life story. The playwright sticks close to his sources, even using the occasional verbatim quotation. The main emphasis is on Muhammad's relationship to people, not to God. Al-Hakim also shows us the Prophet's human—all too human—features, not excepting his domestic problems with willful women, which led to a strict reproof in the Qur'an (sura 66:3–5). Al-Hakim does not even cover up or excuse the massacre of the Banu Qurayza, which claimed several hundred Jews as victims, while Muhammad picked out one of the surviving widows, Rayhana, for his harem. The play also depicts how one of the Jews went to his death with courage and dignity. The short dialogue between Muhammad and the Jewish woman who had tried to poison him seems remarkably objective as well.

> Muhammad (*to the woman*): What made you do what you did?
> The Jewess: You have inflicted not a little upon my kinsfolk. You have killed my father, my uncle and my husband. So I said: If he is a prophet it will do him no harm, and if he is a liar I shall have rid the people of him.
> Muhammad (*to those around him*): Kill this woman.[11]

The atmosphere of the dawn of Islam has rarely been more authentically and openly depicted from a Muslim perspective in modern times.

Another great Egyptian writer, Taha Husayn (1889–1973), deals more freely with Muhammad's life than al-Hakim's play about the Prophet, as indicated by the title of his collection of fictional sketches and stories, *On the Margin of the Life of the Prophet*, a biography of Muhammad.

"These pages," Taha Husayn writes in the introduction, "were not written for scholars or historians.... [T]hey constitute a picture that emerged in my mind in the course of my reading about the life of the Prophet, so I hastened to record it and I saw no harm in publishing it.... I was driven to write this book by an inner compulsion. As I read about the life of the Prophet I found my soul swelling with it, my heart overflowing and my tongue set free."[12]

Like al-Hakim, Husayn quite intentionally incorporates miraculous and transcendental elements, because this appeals to the heart and emotions. Husayn's stories can be divided into two main categories—those in which the heroes are simple, submissive believers, and those in which restless spirits plagued with doubts, such as "the errant philosopher," seek the truth. In this context the Prophet appears as a person of deep spiritual experience who establishes a new relationship between God and man. His warlike proclivities are barely mentioned. Two other works, which bear the stamp of modern political ideology, portrayed Muhammad as a social revolutionary, as some Western scholars had already done. In *The Great Rebel* by Fathi Radwan, this aspect is less obvious than the title suggests. Another issue is worth noting here: the author is concerned with highlighting the youthfulness of most of the Prophet's disciples. Many of the men who later became Muslim leaders were still very young at the time of their conversion: for example, 'Umar was twenty-six years old, 'Ali fourteen, and Sa'd ibn Abi Waqqas, one of the greatest military leaders of early Islam, was seventeen. To quote Radwan: "The Prophet blessed youth when he was on his deathbed, and God chose for his soldiers young men to defend his faith. May people then make way for the young everywhere." Radwan is obviously using the medium of history as a topical lesson for people who criticized the officers of the Egyptian Revolution for their youth and inexperience.[13]

Our final example is the novel *Muhammad, Apostle of Freedom*, by the Marxist author 'A.-R. al-Sharqawi (b. 1920). His aim was to write "the story of a man with considerable heroism, who fought against brutal powers of oppression for the sake of universal brotherhood, justice, freedom, and the dignity of those with troubled hearts, for the sake of love, compassion and a better future for all without exception, those who believed in his Prophecy and those who did not alike."[14]

Al-Sharqawi paints a picture of a secular Muhammad, a humane revolutionary. Even the Prophet's revelations merely seem like dreams, while other miracles and mystical events are entirely absent. The author sees the struggle of emergent Islam as a class struggle, a battle between the capitalist merchants and moneylenders of Mecca, supported by the Meccan gods' priesthood, and the have-nots robbed of their rights, with the men largely slaves and the women forced into prostitution (which is actually an ideological distortion). Al-Sharqawi's Muhammad not only fights for the poor but also stands for freedom from slavery, free scientific research, and "Arab nationalism"; he glorifies craftsmanship and attacks monasticism because it implies support of the exploiting class. All this has very little in common with historical reality. We need only remind ourselves that Islam did not abolish slavery at all; in fact it gave a new boost to slavery through the Holy War, whose prisoners were slaves under Muslim law. (Male prisoners could even be killed if circumstances required.)

4. Islamic History

In studies by Muslims of their own history, the story of Muhammad and the early period of Islam up until around the time of Harun al-Rashid, or sometimes only until the death of ʿAli, the last of the four "righteous" caliphs, represents the final taboo, the last bastion, unquestionably beyond any criticism. Later Islamic history, however, may seem strongly idealized in the work of certain authors such as Altaf Husayn Hali and Muhammad Iqbal, but it was already being subjected to critical examination in the nineteenth century.

The novels of Jurji Zaydan (1861–1914) are the main works to mention here. Although they reflect the viewpoint of a Christian author, this did not prevent them from being highly appreciated in Muslim circles for many years. Zaydan's novel *Al-ʿAbbasa, the Sister of Harun ar-Rashid*, is a good example of the author's "enlightenment" tendencies. The story is based on the legend of Harun and his constant companion, adviser, and vizier, Jaʿfar the Barmakid, and al-ʿAbbasa, Harun's favorite sister. Wanting to keep them both at his side, Harun forced Jaʿfar and his sister to enter into a sham marriage; but it turned into a genuine union, and a son was born to them. This compelled Harun to save his family honor by executing Jaʿfar (which also consolidated his power by wiping out the Barmakid family).

Some historians questioned the truth of the story, while others thought Harun himself had fabricated it to justify the murder, which would otherwise have created a scandal; but it was considered pardonable to avenge an insult to the family honor. Zaydan shows the events in a completely new perspective, using the story to attack despotism, which he personifies in the figure of the caliph and condemns through the mouth of al-ʿAbbasa. Zaydan is less concerned with Harun's personal qualities than with the despotic order itself, which distorts human nature, for Harun's human qualities are repressed and eventually superseded by his role as caliph. As a man, Harun would have been prepared to show compassion to his old friend and forgive his sister. In his role as caliph he is unable to do this. Zaydan explains why: "Since his youth, he had seen his orders obeyed, and thus despotism had become second nature to him, subduing his reason and commonsense, particularly in moments of wrath."[15]

Zaydan's interpretation is all the more daring because it contradicts the opinion of the great historian and philosopher of history Ibn Khaldun (1332–1406). Khaldun regarded the story of the illegal relationship between the Abbasid princess and the scion of a Persian freeman as incompatible with the nobility and piety of the early caliph. He rejected the legend on the principle that what must not exist cannot exist, or ever have existed.[16]

a. The Glory of the Past

Attacking despotism through the medium of the historical novel—and Zaydan undoubtedly did this with a sidelong glance at the Ottoman sultanate, which still existed in his lifetime—is just one way of using history to illuminate the present. Modern Arabic theater has also frequently drawn on historical sources for indirect criticism of the present, especially when there was fear of intervention or prohibition by the censors. Yet criticizing the present can also be linked to glorifying the past; in this case it has the twin functions of lightening the gloomy depiction of present deficiencies while replacing the resulting sense of unease (the feeling of inferiority, in fact) with a new, historically based self-confidence.[17]

A typical example can be found in the work of two Hindustani poets, Hali (1837–1914) and Muhammad Iqbal (1877–1938). In his famous long didactic poem "The Ebb and Flow of Islam," written in six-line strophes (*musaddas*), Hali confronts the condition of Islam in his time, which he saw as entirely negative, with its self-glorified past on the one hand and the glorious present of the West on the other; he presents the latter to his Muslim contemporaries as a lost ideal and a worthy model for imitation. Islam, and specifically the Arabs, appear here as saviors of errant peoples and decayed cultures, a blessing for all of humanity:

> Christians took from them sciences and arts,
> Clerics acquired their ethics,
> The Persians learned from them behavior and belles-lettres
> Monotheists assembled to declare, "Lord, at your service!"
> The root of ignorance was torn from every heart.
> No house around the world was left in darkness.[18]

European science thus owes its flowering to the Arabs:

> Historians who carry out research today
> with marvelous methods of scholarship
> sifting the archives of the world
> exploring all the strata of the earth,
> it is the Arabs who inspired them,
> it's from the Arabs that they learned their speedy progress
> ...
>
> In short, those arts on which state and religion rest
> whether it be natural science, theology,
> mathematics or philosophy or medicine,
> geometry, chemistry or astronomy,
> architecture or agriculture, statesmanship or trading,
> Wherever you look, you'll find the Arabs' traces.
>
> The garden of the Arabs has been trampled down,
> and yet the world strikes up the ghazals of the Arabs,
> the Arabs' rain gave everything its verdure,
> their noble care encompassed black and white,
> Those nations who are nowadays creation's crown,
> will always be the bashful heirs of Arab favors.[19]

The poet goes on relentlessly to develop the motif of the trampled garden. He allows the reader to look down on the world from the heights of an imaginary mountain with a view of flourishing fields and gardens. But one garden is in ruins: the Islamic world, "where indecision has turned everything to rubble."[20] Hali's criticism of his own Indian Muslim society achieves an almost inconceivably forceful, truly scathing intensity in verses such as the following:

> They are despised by other nations, worthless their assemblies,
> There is no confidence, no mutual solidarity
> There's langour in their veins, arrogance in their brains,
> meanness in their fantasy, horror of virtues,
> There's hidden enmity showing the face of friendship,
> humbleness for a purpose, calculated adulation.
>
> We do not count as trustworthy with governments,
> we have no pride in dealing with civil servants.
> In scholarship we merit no great esteem,
> nor do we shine in arts and handicrafts.
> Even as servants we're devoid of merit.
> As merchants we're deprived of any profit.[21]

It is good to recall lines like these, because they illustrate the degree of shock caused by the sudden encounter with Western civilization (which was superior at the time), and—even more important—they show how far Muslims have been able to catch up since. Hali preached his sermon with stirring pathos. His unsparing depiction of contemporary misery and his invocation of the glorious past, linked with the call for a new self-awareness and dynamic renewal, were a major early contribution. It is important to note Hali's achievement, even if it is largely overshadowed today by that of Iqbal. What Hali developed in several hundred *musaddas* strophes, Iqbal unfolded in two extended poems in the same form, each only thirty strophes long.[22] These poems, "The Complaint" and "The Response to the Complaint," helped to establish his early fame. The two poems were provocative in the way they linked self-glorification with the reproach addressed to God, asking why Muslims, despite all their efforts to spread the true faith, were so much worse off in the present than infidels. Iqbal was also provocative in attributing criticism of contemporary Islam, as well as the call for renewal, to God himself. To quote "The Complaint":

> Tell us Thou, by whom was uprooted the gate of Khaibar
> By whom was conquered the city which was Qaisar's?
>
> By whom were the images of created gods destroyed?
> By whom were the armies of infidels slaughtered?
>
> By whom was the fire temple of Iran extinguished?
> By whom was the story of Yazdan restored to life?
>
> Which nation did become Thy seeker exclusively?
> And became embroiled in wars' calamities for Thee?
>
> Whose world-conquering sword did world-ruler become?
> By whose *Takbir* did Thy world enlightened become?
>
> Through whose fear idols did perpetually alarmed remain?
> Falling on their faces saying "Huwa Allah al Ahad."
>
> If the time of prayer right during the battle fell
> Hijaz' nation in prostration facing the Ka'ba fell
>
> Both Mahmud and Ayaz in the same row stood
> None as the slave and none as the master stood
>
> The slave and the master, the poor and the rich all became one!
> On arrival in Thy Audience all were reduced to one!
> . . .

We effaced falsehood from the earth's surface
We freed the human race from bonds of slavery

We filled Thy Ka'ba with our foreheads
We put Thy Qur'an to our hearts

Still Thou complaineth that we are lacking fealty
If we are lacking fealty Thou also are not generous

There are other *ummas,* among them are sinners also
There are modest people and arrogant ones also

Among them are slothful, indolent as well as clever people
There are also hundreds who are disgusted with Thy name

Thy Graces descend on the other people's abodes
Lightning strikes only the poor Muslims' abodes

The idols in temples say, "The Muslims are gone"
They are glad that the Ka'ba's sentinels are gone

From the world's stage the *hudi* singers are gone
They, with the Qur'an in their armpits, are gone

Infidelity is mocking, hast Thou some feeling or not?
Dost Thou have any regard for Thy own *Tawhid* or not?[23]

Further on in the poem Iqbal laments that it is "Outrageous that infidels are rewarded with *Houris* and palaces / And the poor Muslims are placated with only promise of *Houris.*"[24] He continues:

Why is the material wealth rare among Muslims?
Thy omnipotence is boundless and inestimable

With Thy Will the desert's bosom would produce bubbles
The desert's rambler can be facing food of mirage's waves

Others' sarcasm, disgrace and poverty is our lot
Is abjection the reward for Loving Thee?

Now, this world is the lover of others
For us it is only an imaginary world

We have departed, others have taken over the world.[25]

This sounds rather like an Old Testament psalm. But in God's reply in "The Response to the Complaint," we read:

> Who effaced false worship from the face of the world?
> Who rescued the human race from slavery?
>
> Who adorned my Ka'ba with their foreheads in Love?
> Who put my Qur'an to their breasts in reverence?
>
> They were surely your ancestors, but what are you?
> Sitting in idleness, waiting for tomorrow are you![26]

Hali's "Ebb and Flow" concludes in a rather pessimistic tone, with a prayer whose last strophe reads:

> Save them, oh Lord, from misery and evil,
> the straits, where guides and guided lose their way, where
>   help from friends and comrades is not hoped for,
> and no support in sight from any hand or staff,
> where darknesses invade from every side,
> and hearts are ruled by grief instead of hope.[27]

In contrast, Iqbal's poem "The Response to the Complaint" ends with an apotheosis of Muhammad and a call to spread his light throughout the entire world. Here is one more strophe as an example of the adjuratory, prophetic tone that Iqbal often adopts in his verse:

> Like fragrance you are contained in the flower bud, become
>   scattered
> Become the chattel traveling on the wings of the breeze of
>   the rose garden.
>
> If you are poor, changed from an atom to a steppe be!
> From the melody of the wave changed to tumult of the
>   storm be!
>
> With Love's power elevate every low to elegance
> With Muhammad's name illuminate the whole world![28]

In Iqbal's work we find a new form of Islamic triumphalism that belongs to the character of the religion just as pacifism, with its acceptance of suffering, is part of the character of Christianity. Basically what we find here is one of the key differences between the two religions, although history has blurred this all too often. Iqbal's entire concern as a poet and thinker aims at deriving the ideal type of faithful Muslim from the past, positing him as the anthropological precondition for Islamic greatness, and repeatedly evoking him as the true content of the Islamic message. Iqbal frequently interpreted Islamic tradition and Qur'anic revelation boldly and freely. He merged them ingeniously with elements of Islamic mysticism and the influence of European thought—above all, Goethe's idea of "personality" and the Faustian zest for action, Nietzsche's superman, and Bergson's *élan vital*. His vision was a perfect man with cosmic dimensions, and he saw him personified in the great figures of Islamic history—Muhammad, 'Ali, and the mystic al-Hallaj. Iqbal worked from a dynamic concept of love derived from Neoplatonism: love is aroused by beauty, and beauty is the manifestation of the divine in Creation and history. Iqbal can thus assert that the Islamic armies that conquered the world were driven by love. Love is zest for action born of faith, and the duty of the believer is to help divine beauty achieve its full manifestation as a contribution to the perfection of Creation, which is still imperfect. Running through Iqbal's poetry is the call to build a new world, and he sees himself as a prophet of the new world to be built in the spirit of Islam. The precondition for this is renunciation of the mystical tradition based on self-denial, asceticism, and mystical transport, and the development of the self, the ego, the personality—indeed, of the ideal Islamic type who is poor but proud, who makes kings tremble, and who has an effect on the heavenly bodies instead of letting the stars decide his fate. The supreme prototype of this cosmic man is, of course, Muhammad, by virtue of his ascension (*mi'raj*); although this is not mentioned in the Qur'an, it is deeply rooted in tradition. This is shown, for example, in the following poem by Iqbal, "Mi'raj":

> That mote which, thanks to its turbulent longing,
> enjoys the delight of flying—
> it wields the power to exploit both sun and moon.
> Companions of the meadows! To defeat the falcon
> is easy for the partridge, if in its breast it has a glowing soul.
> The Muslim is a lance whose target is the Pleiades
> The secret of the soul's seraglio is the miracle of the Ascension.
> If you do not conceive the meaning of "By the star"[29]—no wonder!
> Your ebb and flow is now in need of the moon [i.e., Iqbal].[30]

b. Iqbal's Book of Eternity

Iqbal's poetry is intoxicating and adjuratory, yet it suffers from a weakness that has earned him criticism from Muslim quarters, among others: it is utopian and idealistically abstract, avoiding concrete historical detail and realistic proposals for the present. In Iqbal's poetry, historical figures appear as types, as symbols of ideas or modes of behavior. Figures like Farabi (d. 950) and Ibn Sina (d. 1037), great philosophers whose thought was concerned with the attempt to reconcile religion and philosophy, reason and revelation (a tenet of early Islamic philosophy as a whole, with a few exceptions), are mere ciphers in Iqbal's poetry for the reason that is counterposed to love, the cold *ratio* incapable of the "folly" of intoxication and enthusiasm. Similarly, the figures in Iqbal's much-praised major work, the brilliant *Book of Eternity,* are typecast representatives of ideas. The book is based on medieval descriptions of Muhammad's ascension and other journeys of the soul; it recalls the epic poem "Journey of the Servants of God to the Place of Return" by the Persian mystical poet Sana'i (d. 1141), the parodic vision of the netherworld by the Arab skeptic Abu l-ʿAlaʾ al-Maʿarri (d. 1057), and of course Dante's *Divine Comedy.* The *Book of Eternity* describes a visionary journey through the planetary heavens inhabited by the spirits of the dead.[31] What is remarkable is that this poetic interpretation and treatment of history not only reaches into the recent past, with the appearance of figures such as the Mahdi of Sudan, or reformers like Jamal al-Din al-Afghani and Saʿid Halim Pasha, but also breaks out of its Islamic boundaries to incorporate figures such as Nietzsche and Lord Kitchener, Indian sages, and the Bahai poetess Tahira Qurrat al-ʿAyn. Tahira inhabits the sphere of Jupiter together with Iblis, the Qurʾanic Satan; the mystic al-Hallaj, who was executed as a heretic by the authorities in Baghdad in 922; and the Hindustani poet Ghalib (1797–1869), a minnesinger of morbid sweetness. Tahira and the other poets represent the category of great lovers. It is clear that in this book Iqbal's concept of love, elsewhere frequently equated with Islam, is given much wider scope and infused with an odor of heresy. In fact, love in Islamic mysticism, and the Persian *ghazal* poetry influenced by it, began early on to break away from orthodoxy as a kind of heresy, and prided itself on bearing the "girdle" (Arab. *zunnar,* from Gr. *zonarion*), the prescribed distinction of monotheist non-Muslims.[32] This is not the place to discuss this complex of issues in detail. It should be noted, however, that Iqbal is not concerned with al-Hallaj's social-revolutionary commitment, or Tahira's advocacy of the emancipation of Iranian women, or Ghalib's epicurean egoism.[33] Iqbal's poetry constantly glides over the concrete details with a rhetorical sweep, even when he castigates modern education, capitalism, and women's liberation.

c. The Tragedy of al-Hallaj

We now consider a more recent work whose main protagonist is a figure that also appears in Iqbal's book, the mystic al-Hallaj, and which clearly expresses the latter's interests: the play *The Tragedy of al-Hallaj* by the Egyptian poet Salah ʿAbd al-Sabur (d. 1981).[34] As already mentioned, al-Hallaj was executed as a heretic. He had provoked the government and the orthodoxy on several occasions, once when he called out in mystical ecstasy, "I am the truth!" which seemed to invoke identification between God and man, although in mystical teaching this was simply seen as expressing a state of complete abandonment. Al-Hallaj's provocation continued with criticism of the Abbasid government's tax decrees, advocacy for the poor, miracles, and finally his proposal to substitute for the pilgrimage to Mecca a simple ceremony at home, and to use the money thus saved to feed orphans. This last transgression played an important role in the trial that led to his conviction.[35] Leaving aside this last point, which is still a sensitive issue, it is clear that 'Abd al-Sabur explores the social commitment and charismatic character of the great mystic, whose spiritual kinship with Jesus has long been recognized, within the tradition sympathetic to him, whereas the orthodoxy has tended to regard him as a heretic, a rebel, and a swindler.

The style of *The Tragedy of al-Hallaj* is decidedly modern. The playwright uses just five scenes to develop the dramatic action, with the first scene anticipating the ending, in which the audience sees al-Hallaj in the background, hanging from a tree in a public square. A farmer, a merchant, and a priest talk about him and ask the reason for his execution. A group of artisans representing "the masses" tell them. The four subsequent scenes show flashbacks to the most important episodes of the story: al-Hallaj speaking to the mystic Shibli (a historical figure), vainly trying to convince him of the need for concrete struggle against poverty; al-Hallaj being arrested during a public sermon against poverty as the root of all crimes; and al-Hallaj in prison, talking to fellow prisoners, a scene built around the theme of Jesus and the just ruler. Unlike Jesus, who was the only man capable of raising people from the dead, al-Hallaj merely claims to be able to awaken dead souls with his words. The last scene shows the hero before his judge and the crowd, which is consulted just as it was once in the case of Jesus; and it is the crowd that calls out, "Heretic, heretic!"—"Death, death!" and "Let his blood come upon us!" The play attacks the combination of religion and power, the corruptibility of judges, the fearful attitude of the pious—Shibli refuses to testify before the court—and the susceptibility of the masses.[36]

5. Criticism of Issues Related to Islam

a. Basic Remarks

'Abd al-Sabur's play, which enjoyed great success, has brought us to another aspect of our theme: the concrete criticism by contemporary authors of Islamic institutions and the traditions of their society. While general criticism of Islam as a religion is rare, and is probably more a subject for philosophical discussion, certain social phenomena related to Islamic law or Islamic tradition are popular narrative themes that are frequently tackled—notably subjects that today's enlightened observer is inclined to interpret negatively. In this context, two aspects persist as a driving impetus. On the one hand, these themes are fruitful in literary terms—whether based on emotions and sentiments, such as subjects related to women; whether because of a criminological angle, such as in stories of vendettas; or whether because of picaresque details such as the description of folk beliefs, holy cults, or mystical ceremonies. On the other hand, there is the sociocritical commitment I mentioned at the outset. Not all the themes treated in contemporary sociocritical literature can be dealt with here; I concentrate only on those with a clearly discernible relationship to Islam.

Admittedly, fundamental criticism of Islam is rare because it is a sensitive issue and is likely to be risky for the author. Where criticism of this kind is ventured, it tends to be cloaked in symbolism, to appear in coded form, to bring in other religions, or to leave open the question whether the criticism is about Islam or another religion.[37] Let us now now briefly consider two well-known and important examples.

In 1955 Mahmud al-Mis‘adi (later Tunisia's minister of culture) published a play, *The Dam,* which inspired a lively, indeed passionate, discussion immediately after its publication. No less a figure than Taha Husayn himself joined in the debate. The play was unanimously praised by Arab critics as a masterpiece of modern Arabic prose, and celebrated by some as the cornerstone of a new literary school. (Labels like "Islamic existentialism" were suggested.) The story centers on a loner, Ghaylan, a religiously emancipated intellectual full of the passionate will to do great deeds. Ghaylan has started building a dam to end the drought and barrenness in a desert valley. The wadi inhabitants are worshippers of Sahabba, the goddess of heat and drought; her priests curse the dam construction, and the voices of her prophets warn the people not to rebel against the goddess and fate. Ghaylan's wife, Maymuna, is increasingly influenced by these warnings. She is not willing to risk secure reality for a potentially dangerous gamble. But Ghaylan refuses to let anything shake his faith in what he is doing. "It is a matter of denying laws, boundaries and obstacles, not accepting weakness and resignation, not giving credit to nothingness—in short, believing in the deed!" This is his credo. Maymuna, however, speaks of the prophets, saying: "They tell every living person what his destiny is in life, and warn and set limits for him." Maymuna turns away from Ghaylan— at the same time a symbolic process, because she embodies his doubt. She is replaced by a beautiful fairy-like woman, who personifies his wishful dream. The fairy figure encourages Ghaylan to continue working on the dam, and both of them enthuse about creating storms, and even making the gods serve human ends. But when the dam is finished, an apocalyptic storm blows up, destroys the construction, and sweeps the bold utopians away into the air.[38]

The play is not suited to theatrical production, but it was broadcast as a radio drama in several languages. We can see that the author does not take a one-sided position but seems to present the reader with an aporia: traditional religion hampers progress, even though the latter may be desperately needed for the well-being of society; but the protagonists of progress succumb to hubris and finally destroy nature as if it were implementing the revenge of the insulted religion. This interpretation is not sufficient either, however, because the hero and his enthusiastic companion experience the fall as completion, as the departure to new realms remote from earthly afflictions. Al-Misʿadi is obviously on their side here. What makes the play relevant to our theme, and what makes it offensive to the traditional Muslim reader, is the fact that when Ghaylan attacks the submissive attitude toward fate that is hampering construction of the dam, the author uses the word "Islam" several times; he has Sahabba's priests conduct a ceremony that clearly recalls the meditation sessions of mystical Islamic orders; and he generally presents the Sahabba cult in a way that at least hints to the reader that it is on a par with backward forms of Islam. Taha Husayn conjectured that the miserable inadequacy and crippling lack of freedom of this barren religion symbolized the French colonial era, but al-Misʿadi himself denied this interpretation.

Leaving these arguments aside, let us turn to a symbolic novel whose codification is so transparent that there can be no doubt as to its meaning. It is not merely about Islam; the three great monotheistic religions are all brought into question. This is a novel by Naguib Mahfouz (Najib Mahfuz, 1911–2006), indisputably the best-known Egyptian fiction writer of the twentieth century, and Nobel Prize laureate for literature in 1988. *Children of the Alley* was published as a serial in the magazine *Al-Ahram* in 1959 and caused quite a sensation. Conservative forces, particularly at al-Azhar, an old established religious university, indignantly criticized the "irreverent questioning of holy things," and the novel was rejected so fiercely that the Egyptian government felt obliged not only to ban its publication in book form but also to prohibit any further public discussion about it. The idea of the book is brilliant: it projects the history of monotheism with its three great founding figures into the daily life of an urban quarter in Cairo. In other words it is an appreciation and critical examination of the history of religion in conceptual terms, particularly as social history.

In the "empty space" between old Cairo and the mountainous desert of Muqattam, an old man of obscure origins named al-Jabalawi (= God) has accumulated a large estate that he wants to leave to his family as *waqf*, an endowment based on Islamic law. But his sons give him little joy. Idris (= Iblis, Satan) cannot accept that his father has conferred the administration of the *waqf* on his younger brother, Adham (= Adam). Adham tries to read the foundation charter, which the father has kept a close secret. This results in the father's casting out both sons. He tries to persuade a son of Adham's, Humam (= Abel), to return home, but the plan collapses when Humam is killed by his jealous brother Qadri (= Cain). After these grim experiences, al-Jabalawi retreats completely to isolation in his big house, leaving the administration of his property to a custodian, who symbolizes the temporal ruler. Before long a city district has grown up on the estate, and the custodian tries to swindle the inhabitants out of the foundation's income without the old man's intervening.

Gangs of hooligans disturb the peace; the custodian tolerates and even uses them. But when the situation becomes unbearable, a man named Jabal (= Moses) stands up and fights along with his followers for their share of the foundation property. Soon afterwards, Rifaʿa (= Jesus) arrives; he is not interested in the *waqf* income but wants only to release the good people from the evil spirits of their desires. When he gathers followers, however, and claims to speak in the name of al-Jabalawi, the custodians and the hooligan gangs see him as a danger and kill him. The situation worsens again; then the figure of a new leader appears, Qasim (= Muhammad), who puts a stops to the teenage terrorist gangs, sometimes using violence. For the first time, Qasim arranges for all the inhabitants of the quarter to receive their share of the foundation income, regardless of clan or family origins. But after his death it is not long before the bad old situation breaks out again, because the inhabitants have forgotten their leader's teaching. Now, however, the story takes a twist typical of Mahfouz. A magician called ʿArafa (the name derives from the Arabic root *ʿrf*, meaning knowledge) follows the epoch of the prophets; it is clear that he symbolizes science. Although ʿArafa does not belong to any of the three groups, he settles in the subdistrict of the Rifaʿiyya (= Christians), and takes up the struggle against urban terrorist gangs and for fair distribution of the *waqf*. But to get a clear picture of what the charter contains, he forces his way into the old man's house, unsure whether the man is still alive. After accidentally killing the servant guarding the charter, ʿArafa escapes and enters the service of the custodian, providing him with a dangerous weapon that the latter uses to defeat the hooligan gangs. When the custodian plans, with the help of the magician, to subjugate the inhabitants of the quarter, the magician comes to his senses and escapes; but the custodian's henchman catches and kills him. The inhabitants now focus their hopes on Hanash, ʿArafa's brother, who has escaped with the magic book. Having initially accused ʿArafa of murdering al-Jabalawi, they soon accept that the old man has died, probably from shock at the murder of his servant. "We don't care about the past," they say. "We are putting all our hopes in ʿArafa's magic. If we have to choose between al-Jabalawi and magic, then we'll choose magic."[39]

In this novel, Mahfouz's faith in science, muted in later works by skepticism and mystical leanings, still seems almost intact. The religions are depicted as very human but hardly effective attempts to achieve a just distribution of the social product. Marxist thought is evident in the notion that Jabal and Qasim, as well as Rifaʿa's father, are avid smokers of hashish—though Rifaʿa himself cannot tolerate it—while the magician rejects the drug because his work demands wakefulness and attention to detail. In the novel the differences in character of the religious founders are carefully and fairly nuanced, and the role of science is relativized in the sense that the magician enters the custodian's service (a tendency, one has to add, that can apply almost equally to religion).

b. Criticism of Specific Deficiencies

Using a few selected examples, I now look at criticism of specific aspects of Muslim society.

The clergy. It is hardly surprising that the profession of mullah, imam, or mosque preacher is a frequent target of criticism in Muslim literature. The main accusations are obscurantism and support for the ruling or property-owning classes. In the great peasant novel *The Soil*, by the Egyptian author al-Sharqawi, the mosque preacher is on the side of the ruling class.[40] Al-Sharqawi is a socially committed novelist; even a short story such as "Scorpions" shows his great concern with social problems and his relentless exposure of the interweaving of religion and social structure. "Scorpions" takes place in a little village during the Second World War. After several fruitless attempts to find work, the hero of the story, a young man named Hasan, is doing an odd job for a mosque preacher as a scorpion catcher. This same imam had recently chased him away because, after working as a water carrier for five piasters a month, Hasan complained to the mayor about the starvation wages and demanded double payment. The imam is on good terms with the "effendi," the farm owner, who unscrupulously takes advantage of inflation to sell maize and fertilizer at exorbitant prices. The preacher, however, spits at Hasan. Meanwhile the mosque becomes overrun with scorpions, and Hasan dies from a lethal sting.[41] This is a story of pointedly exaggerated social criticism and symbolic intensity that accentuates the religious authorities' failure to support the just distribution of *waqf* income.

Naguib Mahfouz, who portrayed Moses and Muhammad as hashish smokers in *Children of the Alley*, did not hesitate to develop this theme in topical form in his novel *Adrift on the Nile*, which deals with the problem of escape into drugs. A group of men and women, artists, journalists, and civil servants, meets every evening for a gossip on a houseboat. The boat's watchman, who is also the imam of the nearby house of prayer, provides them with hashish, and even supplies prostitutes on request for a member of the group.[42]

In Persian literature, Sadeq Hedayat is the main author to have portrayed the figure of the hypocritical, perfidious *akhund*. The examples already discussed, however, must suffice as a brief introduction to this topic.

Criticism of the clergy is closely linked to criticism of specific aspects of popular religiosity and mysticism. Like imams and mosque preachers, mystics are often accused of abusing their influence. The Persian writer S. A. Gilani (1871–1934) wrote these lines at the turn of the twentieth century:

> When I was an orphan, the sheikh robbed me of my house,
> Snatched away my property and devoured my fortune.
> The so-called ascetics have already engulfed many houses
> depriving helpless people of their livelihood.[43]

In 1950 the Turkish writer Mahmut Makal published a documentary report about an East Anatolian village, written in the form of a literary journal. Here it is a mystical movement that exploits both the religiosity and simplemindedness of the farmers.[44] Another example, from Persian literature, is based on the saying "The world wants to be deceived." An intellectual, disillusioned and emotionally distraught after bitter political experiences, manages to get a lucrative job as custodian at a Persian saint's tomb by pretending to perform a healing miracle that gives him the aura of holiness. Significantly, it was Hedayat, an author critical of Islam, who thought up the theme of this story, which is titled "Conversion"; but he never developed it further, and it was left to Muhammad 'Ali Jamalzadah to write it.[45] In another short story, Mahfouz portrays a despotic leader of an order who enjoys a life of luxury, untouched by the poverty around him. But in this case a group of young people rises up in revolt, and when it emerges that their leader is an illegitimate son of the mystic, the latter is forced to give in, and the story ends with insight and reconciliation.[46]

While hypocrisy, lust for power, and misleading and exploiting the masses are the targets in these examples, other authors take obscurantism to task. Iqbal, for instance, criticized contemporary Sufism (Arab. *tasawwuf*) as one of the decadent forms of the old true spirit of mysticism:

> In Sufi circles the ardor of longing is extinguished.
> Only legends of miracles are left over.
> In ruins are the sultan's palace and the dervishes' cloisters.
> Alas, that throne and oratory have turned into perfect hypocrisy.
> The Judge of the Last Day will be ashamed
> of the books of the Sufis and the stupidity of the mullahs.[47]

Once again, the disturbing thing about these lines is the basic feature of Iqbal's poetry that I have already examined critically: the generalization and clichéd nature of many of his statements. Mysticism and popular religiosity continue to exist today, and social commitment and the impulse toward charitable and political activity are often found in mystical circles in particular, while there are not infrequent examples in Islamic history of revolts of socially disadvantaged groups led by mystics.

'Abd al-Hakim Qasim, an important Egyptian author, has courageously criticized the Muslim Brotherhood in his stories. He points out that whatever the reason may be, membership in this organization always amounts to schooling in fanaticism.[48]

Blood revenge. A theme often tackled in Islamic literature, blood revenge is based on the Qur'an (2:179) and is part of Islamic law, though Muslims today stress that the Qur'an advocates peaceful resolution. Blood revenge originated as an instrument of vigilante justice in a nomadic society. In the Qur'an, the institution of *talio* was supposed to be an isolated act of revenge for murder to reinstate justice, but it tended to be used as a form of collective punishment of families for the crimes of one of their members, often persisting over generations. This is precisely the situation described in two novels with the title *Blood Revenge,* the first by the Syrian writer Habib Jamati,[49] the other by the well-known Egyptian novelist Ihsan 'Abd al-Quddus (b. 1922). Jamati describes the extermination of a whole family except for one last surviving member, who escapes the same fate only because he joins up with Palestinian guerrillas and is killed in a skirmish. 'Abd al-Quddus describes the attempt by a young, enlightened Egyptian who refuses to carry out the duty of blood revenge when his turn comes; but his family despises him for this.[50] *Taxi to Beirut,* a realistic novel by the Syrian author Ghada al-Samman, shows that blood revenge can still play a role in Beirut today.

Women's rights. The issue of women is one of the most sensitive problems not only in the debate between Muslims and critics of Islam but also in the internal discussion between Islamic conservatives and modernists. Apologists for Islam have long taken the position that Islam has done more for the liberation and dignity of women than any other religion, and modern exegesis has succeeded in reinterpreting nearly all of the offensive passages in the Qur'an, as well as justifying Muhammad's polygamy by arguing that there were other motives for it than sensuality.[51]

In fact, modernizing tendencies have been largely successful, partly in practice and partly in the constitutions and legislation of individual Muslim states; but traditional Islamic law still has considerable influence on the situation of women in society (or is regaining influence). Practices not laid down in the Qur'an and by law are often based on traditional sayings of the Prophet, which have had an almost equally powerful effect, even if some of them were invented later. The socially committed critical fiction on this theme demonstrates one thing: there are issues related to women that are rooted in Islamic law and tradition, even if Muslim apologists refuse to acknowledge this.

Leaving aside stories that deal with the subject of so-called disgrace (i.e., premarital sex), I focus directly on the specifically Islamic theme of polygamy. There are a large number of novels and stories that examine the problems and disastrous consequences, particularly for women. This is shown, for example, in a short story, "Shaykh Mursi Marries the Field," by Mahmud Kamil, a widely respected international law expert.[52] It tells of a young, happily married man whose father forces him to marry his aunt and sister-in-law as well, so as to keep the lands of deceased relatives in the family. The young man obeys his father's command but does so reluctantly, and against his Muslim conscience. Like modern Qur'an interpreters generally, he understands the passage "Marry of the women, who seem good to you, two or three or four; and if ye fear that ye cannot do justice [to so many] then one [only]" (Qur'an 4:3) as a call to monogamy.[53]

Social criticism of an even harsher variety is found in the story "The Second Wife" by another Egyptian author, Ahmad Rushdi Salih (b. 1920). 'Uthman, a rich, childless miser, feels compelled to take a second wife in order to keep his property. But since she is merely supposed to have the status of a maid in relation to the first wife and be capable of childbearing, and not to cost anything, the only available woman is the wife of a poor man in the village who has already borne children. The victims are a happy couple with three children. When the husband becomes aware of 'Uthman's plan, he is desperate but dares not refuse, while his pride will not allow him to talk openly about the problem with his wife, Fatima. Instead he starts a quarrel that causes him to reject Fatima. She becomes 'Uthman's second wife and bears him the desired son; but her happiness and that of her family is destroyed.

The lack of children, or more precisely of sons, was a frequent reason for taking a second wife. In "In Quest of Absolution" the great Persian writer Sadeq Hedayat (1903–1951), whom I have already mentioned, describes a similar case. His story focuses on the first wife and her feelings rather than on the husband. The more her husband turns away from her and toward his new bride, the more the first wife's jealousy grows, until it finally drives her to murder. She kills the couple's first child, and then the second and third, without falling under suspicion; but then, seized with remorse, she sets off on the "pilgrimage of atonement" to Mashhad. There she confesses her shameful deeds to a fellow pilgrim. This woman also has murder on her conscience: she killed her husband's first wife. Both women now feel cleansed, however, because, as one of them says, "Surely you've heard from the pulpit that as soon as a pilgrim makes up his mind and sets off, even if his sins equal the number of leaves on a tree, becomes good and pure."[54] Hedayat's story seems rather exaggerated but is definitely a realistic portrayal of the destiny of innumerable women in his country.

We shall now look at literary figures related to an aspect of Islamic divorce law that can scarcely appear to the modern observer as anything but bizarre, grotesque, and contrary to human dignity. It is easy to understand why two famous Muslim writers have explored this theme satirically, while another equally well-known author has tried to show it from a human angle, even lending it an idyllic, romantic perspective. The theme is the practice of *tahlil,* a type of temporary marriage. As is widely known, under Islamic divorce law the husband can reject his wife by uttering a simple phrase, but if he has regrets he can take her back again without difficulty. The Qur'an (2:229–230) set a limit on this process continuing endlessly; yet it also left a loophole via a clause stipulating that a man who has divorced his wife three times (or pronounced the triple rejection formula) is not permitted to take her back unless she has married another man in the interim and then been divorced by him. This has led to the institution of the "interim spouse" or "legalizer" (*muhallil*).

Mahmud Taymur's story about this, "Shaykh Na'im, or the Marriage Master," describes how an aging, pious village clergyman, Shaykh Na'im, is visited one day by a troubled fellah who asks him to act as an interim husband. After some hesitation, the shaykh is persuaded to agree to this request because he sees it as a religious duty he cannot avoid. Not long after, another petitioner arrives with a similar request—and the shaykh soon turns into a temporary husband for every occasion. For a while all goes well, until the interim husband falls so deeply in love with one of the women entrusted to him that he does not want to renounce her again. When his client insists on his rights, the shaykh even defends his action from the pulpit and incites his loyal congregation to drive his rival from the village in disgrace and ignominy. Meanwhile the hero, "puffed up like a turkey cock, [leaves] the mosque and [walks] towards his house, wreathed in an aura of awe and dignity, and surrounded by a large crowd of faithful disciples."[55]

In Hedayat's short story "The Legalizer" two old men meet in a coffee-house; they strike up a conversation and one of them starts telling his life story. After two brief marriages for pleasure (Twelver Shi'ites are permitted short-term marriages), he married a nine-year-old girl and lived with her happily for three years. But after he got the idea of taking a rich widow as his second wife, he started destroying his first wife's love, and then, provoked by her tantrums, he rejected her three times. Regret soon followed; looking for an intermediate husband, he lighted on a stupid grocer who seemed to fit the part. They agreed to a fee, and the grocer married the divorcee; but the next day, when the ex-husband came to collect his ex-wife, the grocer laughingly told him that he wouldn't give her back even for a thousand *tuman*. Since then the man has lived a restless, joyless life. He thinks it was probably the revenge of the two wives he had enjoyed beforehand. Meanwhile, the storyteller in the café is so absorbed in his confession that he doesn't notice his conversation partner growing more and more uneasy. The man turns out to be none other than the "stupid grocer," who has long since been deserted by the wife he had once obtained.[56]

The third story on the theme of interim husbands comes from Jamalza-dah's late works. Here he obviously intended to paint a more positive picture of the Muslim tradition than he had done in his early works, particularly his first book, the well-known novella collection *Once Upon a Time*.[57] In this later story, a young man from a noble family is confronted with the problem of temporary marriage. His quick temper has led him to reject his wife, whom he actually loves and admires, and to divorce her by the triple formula for the sake of a minor quarrel. He looks for a harmless temporary husband, and chooses the old family shoemaker, a wonderful soul who takes on the duty reverently and goes through the wedding ceremony with the young noblewoman as if in a dream of paradise.[58]

This brings us to the next section, which looks at stories that affirm the Islamic tradition without utopian self-glorification and that express a clearly different position from the Western, occidental tradition, but without hostility.

6. Affirmation of the Living Tradition

In characterizations of the Orient and Occident, there is a widespread cliché that spiritualism resides in the East and materialism in the West. Taha Husayn has demonstrated the falsity of this quite clearly in his programmatic essay *The Future of Culture in Egypt.* "There is certainly quite a lot of materialism in European civilization, but it would be absurd to deny that it has spiritual content," he writes, emphasizing that the Middle East was "actually the source of the revelationary religions adopted by Europeans as well as Arabs, Christians, Jews and Muslims. Is it possible for these religions to be about the spirit in the East, yet about material things in the West?"[59]

This criticism also applies to another cliché, Iqbal's classification of Orient and Occident as the opposite poles of love and reason, a notion that has been emphasized in Islamic mysticism for centuries. We should recall that Iqbal also saw the conquests of Islamic armies as an act of love. But if we look at the Christian concept of love, it is hard to avoid criticizing Iqbal for denying to the Christian West precisely the historical dimension he uses to rescue the honor of his own religion, and which is the basis for Islam's newfound self-confidence. If we look at the present, however, his statement seems to hold some truth. Anybody who has visited the Muslim East has experienced the special warmth and heartiness to be encountered there, and which people from the Middle East often sadly miss in Europe. The stories by Muslims that affirm their own tradition without indulging, like Iqbal, in visions of a utopian future place value on the force of the heart that Jörg Krämer once saw as the special, real essence of Islam.[60] Yet the issue here is primarily a legacy of mysticism, and in these circles the mulla and *faqih,* the representatives of law and theology, have always been regarded as part of the faction of cold reason.

Mysticism and popular religiosity as positive Islamic power is the main theme of the three stories I shall now discuss briefly. The first is a novel by the Persian writer Jalal Al-e Ahmad (1924–1970). Like Jamalzadah and Hedayat, Al-e Ahmad ranks among the great Persian prose writers of the twentieth century. His manifesto-like essay on the "Western disease" or "occidentitis" (*gharbzadegi*) played a major role in Muslims' return to the values of their own tradition. After renouncing Marxism, Al-e Ahmad intentionally wrote works to serve this return; in a fictional "Epistle from St. Paul to the Writers and Poets" he called for writers to be aware of their responsibility for truth and humanity as a holy duty.[61] The title of his novel, *Nun wa-l-qalam,* refers to this duty: it is from the beginning of sura 68 of the Qur'an, whose first verse contains the call not to exaggerate things, and not to obey the slanderer who obstructs good and is guilty of sins and transgressions. Al-e Ahmad was a staunch opponent of the shah's regime, and his premature death, officially explained as the result of a heart attack, is widely regarded in Iran as a covert murder by agents of SAVAK. *Nun wa-l-qalam* was first published in 1952; today its contents seem prophetic. It describes the revolt by a group of Qalandar dervishes against the shah's regime in an unspecified period in the past. The revolt succeeds, the shah is forced to flee, and the dervishes set up a form of self-administration, a communal system in which each person contributes according to his own abilities, for example, women by doing housework. Yet the military remains loyal to the shah, and when it counterattacks, the dream of the dervishes is over.[62]

The well-known Sudanese author al-Taiyib Salih (b. 1929) also tries to show that popular religiosity is an enduring force that protects humanist values. His stories are nearly all set in Wad Hamid, a village on the banks of the Nile in northern Sudan named after a Muslim saint. The symbol of this saint and his village is a *doum* palm, which is also the symbol of endurance (*doum* means endurance). Remembrance of a dead saint is not the only feature of this village: there is also a living saint, al-Hanin, attributed with magical powers such as bilocation, the ability to be in two places at the same time. The villagers live simply, like their saint: "We are people who live on what God sees fit to give us!" They are happy and contented. Al-Zayn, the hero of the story "Al-Zayn's Wedding," enjoys playing tricks. He is a friend and special protégé of al-Hanin's, and is popular in the village because he takes care of the sick and crippled. The only person who dislikes al-Zayn is the arrogant, bad-tempered imam, a graduate of al-Azhar University, who cares little about the villagers' problems. The main issue, however, is not the contradiction between popular religiosity and orthodoxy—although the author makes no secret of where he expects future salvation to come from—but that between town and country, tradition and modernity. The conflict erupts when plans are made to build a steamer docking station, which means the palm has to be felled. On this occasion the whole country responds to the saint's appeal, and the opposition leads to the fall of the government. Al-Taiyib Salih's narrator says: "There will be no need to fell the palm, and there is also no reason to remove the saint's tomb. What all these people have overlooked is that there is plenty of room for all things: the doum tree, the tomb, the water-pump and the steamer's stopping place."[63]

"The Lamp of Umm Hashim" by the Egyptian writer Yahya Haqqi (1905–1993) is undoubtedly one of the most successful Arabic stories on the theme of tradition and modernity. Passionate commitment, human warmth, and mature experience, coupled with masterly description, combine to make this work a jewel of modern Arabic prose.[64]

Isma'il, the son of a small grocer in a quarter in Cairo's old city, returns home after studying medicine in England, fully convinced of the superiority of Western civilization in general and medicine in particular. On his arrival he is immediately shocked by the local poverty and backwardness, and even more horrified when he hears that his mother has treated his sick cousin Fatima, who lives in their house, with oil from the lamp of the nearby mosque of Umm Hashim. This leads to an agitated dialogue in which he accuses his mother of superstition, until his father appears and accuses him in turn of unbelief. Isma'il finally throws the oil canister out the window, rushes out of the house, and goes to the mosque of Umm Hashim. There he spends time watching the faithful milling around the lamp—a scene that disgusts him. He ends by smashing the lamp in a fit of rage. Nearly lynched by the crowd, he is recognized just in time and carried home soaked with blood. After his recovery he puts great effort into trying to cure his cousin, but to no avail. Although the professors at the eye clinic agree with his treatment methods, the ailment worsens, and one morning Fatima appears blinded. Isma'il's failure plunges him into an emotional crisis. For weeks he wanders around aimlessly, asking why he has failed. He finds the answer, at the same time discovering the solution to his personal conflict. He begins to see Egypt with new eyes, and Europe from a greater distance. At the next festival of Umm Hashim the light of the lamp shines once again, for Isma'il as well, and he realizes that there can be no science without faith. Armed with this new attitude, he is able to heal his cousin. He marries her and opens a doctor's office in a poor quarter of Cairo.[65]

This brief description cannot convey the appeal of Haqqi's highly atmospheric story, but at least it may suggest to the reader how an event based entirely on reality can become poetically transformed into a symbol. We hardly need point out that the lamp and its oil do not stand for the maintenance of superstitious practices; at most they may suggest the ambivalence of religious forces. Above all, they are familiar symbols of holiness in the tradition of all the Abrahamic religions. What concerns Haqqi is the preservation of the spiritual values that are needed to complement rational thinking if humanity is to avoid degeneration and atrophy.

7. Fundamentalist Fiction

Undoubtedly the most important and certainly the most remarkable phenomenon in the fiction of Muslim countries since 1980 is the development of so-called "Islamic" fiction (which could be labeled "Islamist"). By now this runs to several hundred titles. Within this literary trend these works are described as *adab islami*, a reference to the medical tendency that developed in the Middle Ages and dubbed itself "Islamic" or "prophetic" medicine (*tibb islami, tibb nabawi*). Its declared aim was to oust the Greek system based on Galen, which the fundamentalists of the time regarded as pagan.[66] This process seems logical and fits in easily with the conception of Islamic cultural history as a never-ending story of the Islamization of cultural phenomena whose (pagan) power has to be subjugated to the almighty power of God.[67] The authors of these works regard Western literature—and Western-oriented literature in their own countries—as morally corrupt and corrosive,[68] and believe it is high time that Islamic works are counterposed to them. This movement is clearly backed by fundamentalist groups, societies, and mystical orders such as the Naqshbandiyya, and runs numerous publishing houses and magazines; in fact a World League of Islamic Fiction has been founded and has held several congresses.[69] According to one of its leading protagonists, the Egyptian author Najib al-Kilani, "The main goal of this kind of Islamic fiction is to propagate the Islamic worldview and promote the establishment of Islamic society."[70] In al-Kilani's view, this kind of literature is aiming toward an Islamized form of *littérature engagée*. Aside from a large number of theoretical essays, al-Kilani has published over two dozen novels whose heroes' lives follow the pattern of Muhammad and other Qur'anic prophets.[71]

Also indicative is an allegory by Ali Nar, the secretary of the Turkish office of the World League of Islamic Fiction, titled "The Land of the Bees" ("Arılar ülkesi"). Its structure faintly recalls the legendary story "Man and Beast before the King of the Jinn" by the Brethren of Purity, a tenth-century intellectual circle concerned with religious philosophy. Ali Nar's version, however, lacks the wit, irony, and complexity of the original. His allegory is a simple, blatantly transparent parable. The bees and ants live peacefully together on an island without human inhabitants in the Persian Gulf, until the snakes on a neighboring island grow jealous of this paradise. Using the ruse of sticking dead bees to their bodies, the snakes conquer the paradisical island and subjugate and exploit the insects there. In the end, the bees awake from their stupor and manage secretly to muster a huge bee army, with each soldier bee ready to lay down its life in battle. They destroy the snakes and reinstate *nizam*, the divine order, which religious Muslims see as a synonym for Islam and the guarantee of living in peace and justice. As we can see, the parable lacks even the slightest touch of an independent critical perspective: it portrays only good guys, and bad guys who want to disturb the peace of the good, are guilty of every evil, and thus have to be destroyed.[72]

Two less militant works come from the genre of science fiction: "The Space Farmers" ("Uzay çiftliklileri"), also by Ali Nar, is a Turkish story, while *The Fifth Dimension*, a utopian play, is by Ahmad Ra'if, a member of the Muslim Brotherhood, who wrote it in Arabic in a Cairo prison. Both tales are about the spread of an idealized kind of Islam in space. The heroes of *The Fifth Dimension* find it already in existence on Mars; the "Space Farmers" bring it to a planet they have discovered. Although their plots are more imaginative, both stories suffer from unrealistic clichés similar to those in "The Land of the Bees."[73]

For some time now, increasing numbers of committed women have been joining the ranks of fundamentalist authors. Their goal is to describe a life under the strict prescriptions of shari'a as the only true fulfillment for a Muslim woman. The authors portray young women who somehow realize that they have departed from Islamic norms, turn away from their secularized family with its corrupt morals, and—as the inevitable first step toward religiosity—take up wearing Muslim dress, and above all the headscarf. They give up work or studying, avoid social contact with men, and return to the woman's role prescribed by Islam, confined to the household; there they find happiness and, if need be, survive by doing "clean work," that is, paid work done at home. Some of these novels even disinter the Islamic prohibition on images, using the example of statues and arguing that it is a sin to erect them. In one story the heroine removes the European furniture that "suffocates" her, hangs up pictures of the Ka'ba and Islamic calligraphy, and gets rid of the television set, which "spreads poison with Christian films." These exemplary women finally want to rear great Muslim scholars and a new generation of great Muslim warriors; they are ready and determined to become religious warriors (*mücahide*), and even to do military service (*askerlik*) for their religion.[74]

Priska Furrer has written a study of a Turkish novel that actually recommended to its readers the names of preachers and authors living at the time the book was written, including militant fundamentalists such as Sayyid Qutb and Abu l-A'la Maududi.[75] The novel also praised the autobiography of the Muslim woman activist Zaynab al-Ghazali, *Days of My Life,* which was written in prison. Furrer remarks that it combines religious and feminist features.[76]

To date, official Turkish literary criticism has largely ignored these novels, which in terms of literary quality are little better than cheap propaganda. Yet they are widely read and obviously meet a demand from readers whom the official literature, which is wholly oriented toward Western models, is not capable of satisfying.[77]

To round off this brief survey of fundamentalist fiction, let us look at a contemporary theatrical play, *The Chain (Al-Ganzir),* which deals with the problem of "terrorism," or more specifically militant Islamist fundamentalism. The author, Mohamed Salmawy (Muhammad al-Salmawi), is a chief editor of the Egyptian daily *Al-Ahram.* His plays in English translation include *Come Back Tomorrow* and *Two Down the Drain (Ithnayn fi l-balla'a),* a poignant satire on contemporary life in Cairo. *The Chain* was published in Cairo in 1995 and, like Salmawy's previous plays, is written in Egyptian dialect. Salmawy showed considerable courage in writing it. Egyptian theaters initially refused to stage the play, and he almost gave up hope of a production in an Arabic theater. When it was eventually produced in a Cairo theater, however, it enjoyed great success and ran for more than a year. The main plot can be summarized as follows.

A middle-class housewife in Cairo is running errands in town when she meets a young veiled woman on the street. As the young woman seems in need of help, the housewife invites her home and tries to talk to her but gets no response. When the housewife's son arrives, however, the "girl" takes off her veil—to reveal a young male "terrorist" in disguise. Brandishing a revolver, he commands the woman and her son to keep absolutely still. He tells them that he has been ordered to take hostages as a way to force the government to free imprisoned comrades of his. He is awaiting further orders and may even be told to kill the woman and her son. Gradually the hostages manage to suppress their shock and panic and start communicating with their captor. They offer him tea, and a familial atmosphere begins to develop. The woman talks to him in a motherly way, arguing that his actions and intentions are absurd and inhuman. The young man remains intransigent at first; but as time goes on he starts showing signs of human feelings. Then the phone rings. The caller tells him the government has rejected the terrorists' demands, and his orders are to kill the family at once. He refuses to obey—fully aware that this will surely cost him his life.

Soon afterward there are sounds of shooting outside the house; then police officers break in. Simultaneously a terrorist squad bursts into the room and shoots the repentant hostage taker. *The Chain* is a realistic, moving play and well worth staging in Western as well as Arabic theaters.

8. Conclusion

This brings us to the end of our brief tour of the contemporary literature of Muslim countries. Our survey has revealed a wide variety of refractions and evaluations of Islam, from an outdated system that hampers progress and contravenes the requirements of human dignity, to an ideal model for the whole of human society, whether proven in the past or promising for the future. Committed writers tend to focus on one particular failing without really considering to what extent the Muslim tradition as a whole is responsible for it. In general these writers support renewal, and—like apologists for Islam—see themselves as spokesmen for interests that people in Western countries generally regard as humanist Christian ideals, while among Muslims these ideals have come to be seen as a component and mission of their own tradition. It has been noticeable for some time that a growing number of influential Muslim authors have an attitude of respect, even reverence, toward the spiritual and emotional values of their own legacy. The face of Islam has been changed by the upheaval of our epoch. Islam's capacity for renewal and its conservative strength are reflected in its literature, which is involved not only in recording but also, to a large extent, in influencing trends.

Translated by Karen Margolis

VI

CONTEMPORARY PAINTING AND GRAPHIC ART IN THE ISLAMIC WORLD

(Peter Heine)

1. Historical Background of Modern Islamic Visual Art

There are two fields of art with a limited tradition in today's Islamic world, namely, the visual arts and the different forms of musical and straight theater. The medieval Islamic world was familiar with different rudimentary forms of drama, but in the case of Greek comedy and tragedy it did not adopt the forms of antiquity as extensively as it did in the natural sciences and medicine. The visual arts were no exception. Ancient sculptures in temple and palace complexes were familiar from representations, but they did not find their way into works by Islamic artists. A comparable development can also be seen in those regions of the Islamic world that came into contact with the advanced civilizations of the Indian subcontinent and the Indonesian islands, where there are also ancient traditions of visual representation. While the respective Hellenistic, Indian, and Javanese traditions and techniques in painting and graphic art were indeed copied and refined, the artistic activities took place on a very limited scale, particularly if we consider how broad both the timeframe and the geographic area are. Lacking a larger audience for fruitful debate, visual artists and their works did not attain broader social relevance. It was only the Islamic elites who took notice of the products of visual art. As a rule, such artworks were confined to miniature painting and book illustrations that provided the makers with the opportunity for artistic expression. They are very intimate forms, conceived for a very small audience. Consequently, from the start, artists were unable to explore many forms of visual expression that were associated with larger formats. Monumental works were nearly impossible, and it was difficult to carry out formal experimentation. The texts to be illustrated placed additional restraints on the motifs selected by artists.

These restrictions on artistic expression are attributable to the "image ban" in Islam. While there was no general prohibition of visual representation, depictions of living creatures, above all human beings, had a forbidden and dubious quality for quite some time. In contrast to the Old Testament (Exodus 20:4), the Qur'an makes no reference to such a ban, but the numerous traditions of the Prophet (Arab. *hadith*)—in which, out of a fear of idolatry, the creation of images was attacked—led to a stunted development of visual art in the Islamic world.[1] Artistically gifted Muslims responded to this situation in various ways over the centuries. On the one hand, they turned to the book and miniature forms of painting just mentioned. On the other, they devoted themselves to calligraphy as a special form of abstract expression.[2] Arabic script, which is used to write Persian, Turkish, and the other languages of Islamic peoples, not only offered artists many opportunities for artistic development but also had the aura of a religious deed: the texts that the artists embellished were mostly centered on confessions of faith, the name of God, and quotations from the Qur'an. Moreover, writing the word "God" is an act that is supposedly pleasing to Allah.[3] From calligraphy it is only a short step to the interlaced, meandering abstractions that entered the European art of various epochs as arabesques.[4] This form of expression had the advantage of social recognition. It was incorporated into public art at mosques and state buildings and did not have to be hidden away from visitors in private homes. In several Islamic countries the use and refinement of calligraphy lives on in the guise of impressive handicraft traditions, thanks in part to state support.

A form of visual expression that can currently be described as independent Islamic art evolved from these two medieval traditions—from figurative art on the one hand and abstract art based on calligraphy on the other. Despite the size of the geographic region and the myriad social and economic conditions in modern Islamic states, this art is remarkably homogeneous, though one must note that many different factors affect the artists themselves.[5] The basic line of distinction that can be drawn in modern Islamic art reflects the degree to which the artworks follow a figurative or abstract tradition. In the present situation, differences can be discerned between countries where Sunni or Shi'ite Islam predominates. Particularly in its popular religious forms, Shi'ite Islam exhibits more image-friendly tendencies,[6] just as it offers, with the passion plays of the mourning month of Muharram, one of the few pieces of evidence for a dramatic tradition in Islamic literature. Cheap prints depicting the martyrdom of the various saints of the Shi'ite religious community have been available for quite some time. They serve as illustrations of this story and are comparable to the medieval Biblia Pauperum in the Western Christian world. On the one hand, the forms of artistic expression stemming from popular religion live on, embodied by the artifacts of Iranian, Afghani, and Pakistani folk art. This is demonstrated by "lorry art"—the decoration of trucks with popular religious, or nonreligious, motifs.[7] On the other hand, national schools of painting, such as that in the Qajar period (1779–1924), have come into being, producing their own distinctive artistic style.[8]

As a result of the Islamic world's direct confrontation with the modern West in the early nineteenth century, Muslims also came into contact with different types of artistic expression and ways of organizing artistic life. Rifaʿa al-Tahtawi, a member of one of the first Egyptian study missions to France, adopts a neutral tone in describing the various art academies in Paris. He lists the five departments of the Académie des Beaux-Arts and then notes that students learn graphic art, painting, and architecture at the affiliated École des Beaux-Arts.[9] While this rather laconic cataloging exercise shows his distanced stance toward the visual arts, it also demonstrates that the Muslim visitor had indeed taken note of the phenomenon. In this period, however, works by Muslim artists continued to be confined to traditional areas, above all calligraphy, despite the emergence of a broader public with an interest in figurative art. This was a result of the illustrated books that were published in the Islamic world, primarily in the eighteenth century and later. The various popular novels and fairy tale collections contained illustrations that clearly drew on the tradition of miniature painting. The public also saw pictures of the stories' protagonists on the book covers—an encounter with the expressive forms of the visual art that was largely accepted in Islamic countries. Here a field of applied art asserted itself that confronted the public with vivid promotional art that often had little to do with a book's contents. The developmental line from medieval miniature painting to modern book illustrations was thus a consistent one, even if it did not always lead "upward" in terms of quality. Even so, it is important to note that this was the first time the Muslim world was introduced to promotional art, which was destined to play an important role in Muslim viewing habits in the period that followed.

2. The Development of Modern Art

In the nineteenth and twentieth centuries, the history of most of the Islamic world was characterized by two trends.[10] On the one hand, there was a clear rejection of the West in political and religious matters, which one still encounters in the present. On the other, there was admiration for the technical and social accomplishments of the West as compared to the Islamic world. This fascination resulted in a largely uncritical adoption of Western technologies, business practices, and ideological systems. It is no surprise that various Western visual art forms also made a great impression on many Muslims. In the second half of the nineteenth century a few political groups began building opera houses and museums as a sign of openness to both the West and Western modernity. The museums then mainly exhibited the works of European artists. In the 1920s and 1930s art academies opened in several Islamic capitals, too, with teaching staff who either came from Europe or were nationals trained at European art schools. Between this period and the late 1950s, one encounters an academic painting tradition in the Islamic world that has decidedly European influences—even if pre-Islamic painting traditions in the eastern regions, such as India and Indonesia, were never neglected. In addition, the young generation of artists was confronted with the technical problems of artistic representation. One must always bear in mind that the artists were young people who had to come to terms with the hostile view of images in their cultures. Depicting people and other living creatures was an act of emancipation from religiously determined aesthetic norms.[11] The public support the visual artists received in Muslim countries with secular state ideologies was in part a result of the distance between these ideologies and Islam.[12]

3. "State Art"

In the nineteenth and mid-twentieth centuries, role models from the European art scene exerted a thematic and formal influence on the art of the Islamic world. The importance of Orientalism in Western art initially played a key role, particularly in the nineteenth and early twentieth centuries. Artists embodying different styles, from Jean-Auguste-Dominique Ingres, Emil Orlik, and Pierre-Auguste Renoir to August Macke and Paul Klee, made use of Eastern motifs and drew inspiration from trips to North Africa and the Levantine countries. Their works of art met with great interest—still observable today—especially among the new elites in the Muslim world. In terms of style, Muslim artists adapted Western models with a marked time lag. For example, in the 1950s, Syrian and Lebanese artists were still painting in a style reminiscent of European fin-de-siècle impressionism, while others were engaged in a dialogue with the works of artists such as Pablo Picasso, Georges Braque, and Juan Gris from the first few decades of the century.

With improved communication channels in the 1960s, artists in the Islamic world became increasingly aware of artistic developments in Europe and America. The greater formal liberties taken by Western artists made a strong impression on them. Nevertheless, in some Islamic countries both the broader knowledge of the art scene in the West (including the Eastern bloc) and the growing importance of European ideologies such as nationalism and socialism caused artists to adopt ideologically tainted styles such as socialist realism. This development was an outcome not only of the close political and economic cooperation between Islamic countries and socialist states but also of the large number of Islamic artists who had trained in Moscow, Prague, and Warsaw as a result of this cooperation. This ideologically influenced school of art enjoyed a popularity that can still be seen in the present, especially in state and propaganda art. While the combination of naïve motifs and a lack of technical proficiency often produced inferior works that are trying on the eyes, there also exist impressive monumental works of "state art" of an international stature. One example is the 1960s relief by Jawad Salim on the Bab Sharqi in Baghdad. The favorite subjects of this artistic style are not only workers and peasants but also soldiers and freedom fighters. In addition it shows a clear trend toward history painting that makes use of pre-Islamic themes and representational forms and contributes to legitimizing current power relations.

In much the same way, promotional art rose to an international standard in the Muslim world, primarily in the area of political agitation and propaganda. As in former socialist states, formal and thematic experimentation in this field was limited. The work of caricaturists in many Muslim countries is especially popular and often of high quality. As a form of applied art, it offers graphic artists a variety of possibilities for formal experimentation and is a way to express subtle or open criticism of the prevailing social, economic, and political conditions. This explains its continued popularity today.[13] The portraits of state leaders seen everywhere in authoritarian Muslim countries also had an impact on the national art scenes. On the one hand, the portraits provided the artists with a means to earn a living. On the other, showing an interest in the visual arts, political leaders served as role models for political, economic, and intellectual elites. When influential figures of political life opened art exhibitions or attended "vernissages," members of such social groups began to take interest in their country's contemporary art, from which they had previously remained aloof. A country typical in this regard is Iraq, where an especially lively art scene sprang up under the rule of the socialist Baʿth Party.[14] This was mainly the result of the special situation in Iraq, which is home to a large number of different ethnicities and religious communities. By encouraging artists to explore the cultures of the ancient Near East, the state attempted to build a cross-ethnic Iraqi national identity.[15] Artists had a much more difficult time in countries where state art funding had no priority.[16]

In the various applied arts forms mentioned earlier—painting, graphic art, and caricature—representation is the first requirement for the artist, even if symbols such as the dove, the Kalashnikov, and the tulip can have a highly abstract appearance. The symbols chosen must be recognizable if the work is to have the desired effect on the viewer. But aside from this requirement, which applies to all "state art," the political leadership in many Islamic countries refrained from imposing nonartistic norms on artists. It is important to emphasize that even in those Islamic states that take a more rigid view of their citizens' personal freedoms, visual artists were never restricted in the sense that they could not—and cannot—follow a style that diverges from the official line. Furthermore, the state did not attempt to prevent artists from establishing their own associations. As a result, painters, graphic artists, and sculptors were able to collaborate and benefit from joint stimulus.

4. Abstract Islamic Artists

It was precisely these artists' associations that played a pivotal role in the artistic engagement with the increasingly rapid developments in the art scenes in western Europe and North America. The various abstract movements in these countries had a particularly strong influence on Muslim artists, while pop art and photorealism provoked little interest. The adaptation of such influences to Muslims' visual and formal vocabularies and expressive forms exhibits surprising overlaps in states such as Saudi Arabia and Senegal, which are otherwise marked by great differences. Forms of action painting and highly expressionist abstract art were not well received in either state or in the diverse art scenes in the Muslim world. The exaltation of the individual and the nonconformist attitudes that are expressed by these art movements are elements of a lifestyle that is probably too foreign to Islamic society to be espoused by its artists. Instead one finds works that in formal-expressive terms are comparable to those by Paul Klee or Eduard Bargheer—works, that is, in which artists create increasingly abstract representations of landscapes or architectural scenes in a playful yet deliberate, disciplined manner. Some are so abstract that the visual impression of the artwork has liberated itself from the original. Even with the dependence on Western role models, a special, entirely distinct formal vocabulary emerged, one that reflects the particularities of Islamic landscapes and architecture yet is surprisingly homogeneous despite the diverse art scenes in individual states. The color palettes, especially the preference for green and blue, are also typical of this school. At the same time, the avoidance of living creatures as motifs reflects—even in this abstract art—compliance with the Islamic ban on images. To judge by the number of exhibition openings and responses in magazines and newspapers in Muslim countries, the products of this art movement appear to enjoy a degree of popularity among the public.

5. Arabic Calligraphy and Modern Art

In terms of art production, Islamic artists have gained a degree of independence from European and American role models since the 1970s, yet these artists have continued to follow developments in the West closely. They have experimented with new methods, including spray and brushing techniques, and tried out new materials such as acrylic. Yet they present viewers with a series of special thematic features that result from the cultural tradition of the Islamic world and that are increasingly shaping Islamic art. Treatment of the line plays a central role, and in this area one repeatedly encounters the influence of Paul Klee. Artists primarily favor Arabic script, which is revered throughout the Islamic world as a graphic expression of the Qur'an and which seems to possess a nearly magical power in many cultural contexts. This shared perception of Arabic script in Muslim countries (and, to a degree, even in secular Turkey) has led to a generally accepted form of artistic expression that contributes to the impression of homogeneity in contemporary Islamic art. This art ranges from playful representation to the use of calligraphic signals that oscillate between the traditional art of Islamic writing and experimental graphemes. For instance, it offers views of cities that are built of Arabic letters such as *qāf, lām, bā,* and *alif.* Living creatures are also assembled out of these letters. The letters do not form any meaningful words but have been reduced entirely to their graphic value. Incidentally, this use of Arabic script can be found not only in graphic art and painting but also in the field of ceramic art, which has recently experienced a gratifying revival in many Muslim states. Artists not only incorporate individual letters into their art but also examine the visual impressions of Arabic words that have concrete meanings, such as "Allah," experimenting with different font sizes and graphic intensities.[17] From this technique of depicting objects or persons with Arabic letters and individual words, it is then just a short step to a form of abstraction that is confined to the visual impression of the script. The artists apparently do not wish to convey concrete information through the alphabet or its semantic content. Rather their focus is on experiencing the graphic value of the individual letter. This can be seen, for instance, when the letter *wāw* is varied and modified through different font sizes, densities, and colors. Here there is reason to speak of a trend toward minimalism in Islamic art. A more extensive study is required to determine whether there are links—at least on a theoretical level—to Western uses of script in graphics, as was common in the 1960s. At any rate, this is a form of expression whose Islamic character cannot easily be called into question owing to the use of Arabic script. There is significant public acceptance of this art form, especially since a number of artists are well-known calligraphists. The clear insistence on script as a recognizable graphic system is typical of this phase of artistic development in the Muslim world.

In the 1990s artists began removing dots from the Arabic alphabet (which consists of lines and dots), moving to an even higher level of abstraction. In such work all that remains of the letters is the *rasm,* or line. This development enabled the artists to use script as graphic material in a much freer and more expressive way. Using the script style as a basis, artists developed a floral and vegetative formal language that resembles traditional calligraphy. Even so, one also encounters styles reminiscent of architectural forms, which appear to be draw on the ancient Arabic Kufic script. This focus on the *rasm* has had complex repercussions for artistic forms of expression. Highly emotive works have been possible for the first time, while an identity-building link to traditional forms has remained intact. It has been possible to combine traditional calligraphy and modern minimalist creations of Arabic script, often resulting in quite impressive works of art.

6. Modern Islamic Art in Response to Ideological Developments

Modern art—particularly art that has a limited tradition in society—evolves out of a difficult interplay with the social, political, and cultural transitions in society. Since the visual arts, with the exception of calligraphy, can be described as more or less un-Islamic, painters and graphic artists were initially marginalized when the West began exerting an influence on the Muslim world. Their marginalization was much more pronounced than that of the Muslim writers who drew inspiration from Western role models, or the musicians who primarily stuck to traditional forms and hardly took notice of modern schools of music. Visual artists have often been the avant-garde of the cultural scene throughout the Muslim world. With some exceptions, painting, graphic art, and sculpture have had a more important secular character than other artistic forms of expression. To a greater extent than other art genres, painting and graphic art have also taken their cue from Western art movements. The social acceptance of these works has depended on the ruling classes' attitudes toward the West. As a result, there are parallels between artistic developments and the ideological trends shaping society.

Although the early history of modern Islamic art is characterized by emulation of Western art movements, it must be noted that there was a time lag of up to five generations in the adaptation of styles. This mirrored the often unsuccessful attempts by politicians and ideologues to modernize societies through a process of Westernization. The efforts by states to shift religion from the public domain into the private sphere (epitomized by Kemalism in Turkey) gave figurative art freedoms that it managed to take advantage of. Yet its acceptance was limited to the new elites, or it was not accepted at all. The relatively unsuccessful modernization attempts, however, as well as the process of "re-Islamization" that has taken place since the mid-1960s, have not been able to marginalize painting and graphic art completely. It is impossible to imagine society today without these art forms, in part because of their manifestations in the applied arts. The start of re-Islamization also coincided with the search for an Islamic identity in the visual arts. The parallels between artistic and sociopolitical developments are perfectly clear in this field. Critical engagement with traditions of Islamic calligraphy has led to an autonomous art that is not dependent on Western role models. At the same time, this art has a universal character since it has developed a formal vocabulary and artistic expressiveness that are accessible to viewers schooled in modern Western art.

Translated by Adam Blauhut

VII

CONTEMPORARY "ISLAMIC" ARCHITECTURE AND REPRESENTATIONAL ART

(Mohamed Scharabi)

Asking whether it is possible to talk about contemporary "Islamic" architecture and representational art raises another question: Did "Islamic" architecture and representational art ever really exist? Before we look at the present-day situation, we should therefore consider the art and architectural history of Islamic culture in the period before European or Western forms of life and economy permeated Islam; In other words, we have to address the intrinsic local tradition.

1. The Tradition

Early Islamic urban construction, and the related architecture and representational art, were mainly concerned with preexisting cultures. The newly founded residential cities, for instance, were based on typical models such as the Roman *castrum* (e.g., 'Anjar) or the circular cities of Mesopotamia and Iran.

Although Islamic culture was partly based on ancient Greek and Roman principles, the nature of the city in the traditional Muslim world generally excluded public open spaces such as the agora, forum, and theater. As public space had already lost its importance during the Byzantine era, the street increasingly became the basic structural element for the city center. This change occurred not only because churches, and later mosques, were introduced as places for both worship and public meetings—unlike the temples of antiquity—but also because of the climate. The ancient structural forms of the agora and forum are clearly better suited to the northern Mediterranean, while the inner courtyards, arcades, columned halls, and covered streets of the suq or bazaar in Oriental Muslim cities are better for the climate of the eastern and southern Mediterranean and neighboring regions. Nevertheless, climatic conditions alone could not have been decisive. We know from tradition, and from the fabric of some buildings today, that the urban markets in Spain during the Islamic era were conceived similarly to Moroccan and Arabic suq complexes. By contrast, the present-day *mercados* and *zoccos* in cities that were once strongholds of the Islamic West, such as Córdoba, Málaga, and Toledo, no longer have any parallels in the Orient; nowadays markets of this type are found in France and Italy instead. The decline of the traditional form of bazaar construction in Spain is evidence of the bazaar form's dependence on specific ethical, social, economic, and legal factors—those of the ancient Orient and Islam. The moment these factors changed, the structural form changed as well.

The persistence of a certain degree of cultural continuity in urban development in the Islamic world meant that fully developed, independent architectural achievements could emerge only gradually. We can see this by looking at urban elements such as housing and palace construction, places of worship, trade complexes, and other central institutions, as well as the development of representational art.[1] The innumerable agglutinates in the Middle East, with their courtyard houses that avoid any kind of opening to the outside world, aspiring to an architecture with almost no decoration and a closed, massive appearance, have direct precursors, especially in the Syrian-Mesopotamian region. The so-called desert castles in this region, such as Qasr al-Khayr al-Gharbi, built in 727 CE, and Mshatta Palace, built in 744 CE, are quadrangular palaces surrounded by circular towers with living quarters arranged around a courtyard on the model of the Roman *limes* fort.

The Dome of the Rock in Jerusalem was completed in 691 CE. With an octagonal central building ringed by concentric circular and eight-sided arcades, it was evidently based on old local Christian buildings. The Christian *xenodochia* or *pandocheia* built from the fourth century in the Greek eastern and Latin western territories can be seen as precursors of the *khan* complexes; they were sometimes based on similar types of plans.

The cultural continuity was demonstrated not only in terms of structural types but also stylistically. The architectural forms of the Umayyad Empire in Syria and the Abbasid Empire in Mesopotamia were expressed in the local residences, which were independent of the power centers. In Spain, Umayyad design vocabulary persisted independently of the contemporaneous Abbasid architecture. A local style had developed with the Great Mosque in Córdoba (built in 785) and the palatine city Madinat al-zahra' (built in 936), influenced by both Umayyad and local building traditions (e.g., the horseshoe form). In contrast, the close contact with Iraq was evident in Kairuan (the Great Mosque) and Cairo (the Ibn Tulun mosque). In the Fatimid era, Abbasid architectural forms (e.g., the Great Mosque in Mahdia in Tunisia and the Azhar mosque in Cairo) continued as the model, with some local variations. The increasing expansion and establishment of the Fatimid Empire under Caliph Mustansir (1036–1094) enabled interchangeability between local building forms. Linked with local traditions, this opportunity for interchangeability encouraged the development of independent forms, though they were still reminiscent of pre-Islamic times. The development in the Ottoman Empire was generally similar, particularly after the conquest of Constantinople in 1453.

The antagonism of the Muslim religion toward portrayal of humans and animals has hampered figurative art. In general, plant and object themes without the "breath of life" are permissible. Occasionally there was greater acceptance for a liberal interpretation of the Qur'an and hadith, allowing pictorial reproduction of persons and animals in some places and specific periods. In time, however, the dogmatic attitude hardened, allowing ever fewer opportunities for figurative painting to develop. Artistic aspirations concentrated on vegetative and geometric ornamental forms, as well as a special kind of scriptorial design (calligraphy) found throughout the Islamic world. The tendency toward abstraction, rhythmic structuring, and completely filling out the space is an inherent element of all the ornaments and calligraphic works, while the ornamental tendrils or writing can branch out in any chosen direction. The ornamentation and calligraphy are not always directly related to the object: they obey their own independent laws.

Originally there were no holy images in Islamic culture because the divine message itself was transmitted in verbal form by an ordinary person, the Prophet. In place of holy pictures, Islam used writing and ornamentation to decorate buildings and objects. The nature of this kind of art meant that it had no religious function and could not be used for epic or dramatic poetry as in the Byzantine world. This kind of art was not intended to illustrate historical accounts, legends, or allegories, or to express lyrical or visionary feelings. The portrait was outside its scope; and the human body, the basis of classical art, was usually ignored. There were exceptions in some Islamic cultural regions, especially Iran and India, where painting with clear religious themes, such as portrayals of Muhammad and the Shi'ite imams, can be found from the Middle Ages up to the present.[2]

One can sum up by saying that Islam preserves more than a few elements of older African and Asian cultures, and that its teaching has had only a limited influence on urban planning, architecture, and visual art. But it would be wrong to say that this has led to uniform urban planning or a unified kind of architecture and representational art. The cultural preconditions and later influences in the individual regions of the Muslim world in the course of history were too varied for that. The last important epoch in the history of Islamic art and architecture was the Ottoman period, which had widespread influence. Yet even in this phase one cannot talk of unified development; that is, in no way can Ottoman works be equated with Islamic art and architecture as a whole in this epoch.

Perhaps we should conclude by asking: What is "Islamic" and what is "oriental"? Is there an oriental architecture in which geometry, and above all decoration, developed in a typical way? Consider the glazed bricks in Babylon with whole walls of murals, the ancient Egyptian buildings covered with narratives, and the characteristic design of ceramic-tiled walls from the thirteenth to the nineteenth centuries throughout the Islamic Orient. Was this tradition actually ruptured? (By contrast, in the Greek-occidental world, decoration has always been something that emphasized tectonics, although in the modern era, art nouveau is obviously an exception to this.) The sense of time in the Orient, and therefore in Islam, has played an important role here. There is no "development" in the art of ancient Egypt, ancient Iran, and Mesopotamia in the Western, modernist sense. This created a different kind of historical consciousness in which the past was perceived as part of the present. Is this still true of the Islamic Orient today? Or has something changed?

2. Westernization, Classicism, Neo-Baroque, Art Nouveau, and Neoclassicism

The great rupture, the clear departure from the experience, skills, knowledge, and insights of previous generations, occurred in the age of baroque and rococo. Maydan-i Shah grew up as a new city center in the Safavid city of Isfahan. It was a large area measuring around 500 by 150 meters, containing nearly all the key institutions of a traditional Islamic city. The square's huge size and clear, unified structure recall European urban planning concepts. The murals of the 'Ali Qapu Palace at Maydan-i Shah show distinct features of the contemporaneous Dutch school. The artist, Muhammad Zaman from Persia, studied in Italy in the late seventeenth century; his works helped to spread the existing European influence on painting in the Muslim world.

In 1744 the Ottoman Empire signed a peace treaty with Russia, with the loss of large territories on the Black Sea and in Europe. This was the beginning of the end of Turkey's role as a great power and of the last cosmopolitan Muslim state; independent nation-states then emerged on its territory. The Islamic realm experienced further political and cultural divisions during the nineteenth and twentieth centuries. In the east, Afghanistan, the Sikh Empire, and Persia fell under British influence; in the west, France took control of the North African countries of Algeria (1830) and Tunisia (1881), and Morocco came under joint French-Spanish control in 1912. Libya became an Italian colony in 1911. After the First World War, Syria-Lebanon, Palestine, and Iraq came under French or British mandate. From 1882 Egypt was under British occupation for several decades.[3]

These political developments were decisive for the development of urban planning, architecture, and art—in the sense of a profound Westernization. This was already evident in Egypt after the French conquest of the country in 1798, and after Egypt split off from the Ottoman Empire under Muhammad 'Ali (1805–1848). By the time the British occupied Egypt in 1882, the country had been subject to foreign influence for decades, and its cultural landscape was already greatly altered. In Cairo, the home of al-Azhar

University, which was renowned throughout the Islamic world, the French army had built broad straight streets for housing and business, and open squares on the Parisian pattern. Muhammad ʿAli set out to complete the work of the French: he had several bazaar complexes demolished and "modernized." Some quarters of Cairo, such as al-Azbakiyya, show the influence of French urban planning. Even Muhammad ʿAliʾs mosque, built in 1830 and still conceived in Ottoman terms, contains details that clearly reveal the baroque tradition of forms. New, imported types of buildings such as hotels changed the functional lines of the traditional city. The old *khan* complexes rapidly lost importance as trading centers with overnight accommodation, giving way to the new hotels built in the freshly created urban quarters, such as Shepheardʾs Hotel, built in 1845. Parallel to the decline of the *khan* complexes was a more gradual decline of traditional housing as residents moved to the newly built apartment houses in the modern quarters of town. The Westernization process intensified during the era of Khedive Ismaʿil, who ruled from 1863 to 1879. He tried to bring the development of his country and its cities into line with western European culture, which he saw as more important and richer in technical experience. For the state opening of the Suez Canal, Ismaʿil had a classicist-style opera house built in Cairo on the model of La Scala in Milan. He commissioned a German architect to design his palace and a French architect to design the park.[4]

The structural form of other new types of buildings introduced in cities such as Cairo and Aleppo in the second half of the nineteenth and first half of the twentieth centuries was also classicist (or neoclassicist after around 1915). The neoclassicist Mediterranean look of the house built in 1933 in Aleppo on Shariʿ al-Mutanabbi (Mutanabbi Street) has nothing in common with the traditional formal vocabulary of Syrian architecture (fig. 1).

The Egyptian Museum in Cairo, which dates back to 1911 in its present form but was originally planned in 1858, bears not the slightest resemblance to ancient Egyptian or Islamic construction forms. With its distinctly classicist style, it could be a building in Italy, France, or Germany (fig. 2). Department stores (e.g., Sednaoui and Omer Efendi) and banks (e.g., Bank Misr) built around the turn of the twentieth century or later are identical to Parisian stores and bank buildings in both interior structure and exterior design; they clearly display the influence of Parisʾs École des Beaux-Arts, which is also familiar in central Europe.[5] The architecture of the new market hall at Maydan al-ʿAtaba has an affinity to the Parisian market halls of the mid-nineteenth century. Also at Maydan al-ʿAtaba, the British influence creates a contrast, with buildings such as the headquarters of the postal service and fire brigade, examples of English-type fortress architecture. Innumerable residential, business, and administration buildings, not only in the new urban districts but also in the old city of Cairo (e.g., no. 4 Darb Qirmiz), followed the style of nineteenth-century European architectural trends, changing the constructed environment of a society in which new economic and education systems were moving away from their own tradition.[6]

1. *Apartment house in Aleppo on Shariʿ al-Mutanabbi (1933), architect Subhi Kababa.*

The development in Cairo should be seen as just one example. In the Ottoman metropolis of Istanbul, the process of change in urban planning and architecture was essentially similar but occurred after a time lapse. Here, as in Cairo, long straight boulevards and open squares were created inside and beyond the traditional city, increasingly altering the ground plan and appearance of the city. Fine examples of neo-baroque style include the Ortaköy mosque (built in 1854) and Beylerbey Sarayı (built in 1865). In Baghdad a residential and shopping street, Shariʿ al-Rashid, based on the European colonnade style, was constructed in 1916 (fig. 3). In Damascus the Suq al-Hamidiyya was restructured in the 1870s with a two-story wing—in defiance of the traditional norm of one-story shop buildings in the suq district; the details have a classicist touch. The Suq al-Hamidiyya was given steel girder roofing in 1878, at exactly the same time as the Galleria Vittorio Emanuele II in Milan was covered with a similar construction.[7]

Examples of how the form of cities and buildings became Westernized are too numerous to discuss in detail and can be referred to only briefly here. It is worth noting, however, that European classicism became widespread not only in Egypt, Turkey, the Syrian region, and neighboring areas but also in the eastern Islamic world (e.g., the royal palace in Kabul) and in western Islamic countries (e.g., the opera house in Algiers). As in Europe, it was

2. *Egyptian Museum, Cairo, 1911, a classicist building that might well be found in Italy, France, or Germany.*

3. *Baghdad. The left-hand side of the photo shows part of Shariʿ al-Rashid (1916), a residential and commercial street. The buildings on the cross-street are from the same period; they also illustrate, though less clearly, how architecture expressed the tendency toward Westernization.*

gradually replaced by art nouveau. Typical examples of art nouveau can be found in Cairo (the synagogue on Shari' 'Abd al-Khaliq Tharwat), in many buildings in Alexandria's Garden City district (e.g., Pastroudi's Cake Shop), and in Istanbul (e.g., the Egyptian consulate in Bebek, once used as a summerhouse by the Egyptian khedives).

In the field of representational art, the portrait painting trend was spreading. Nearly all rulers and members of the grand bourgeoisie commissioned portraits of themselves—and sometimes their wives as well (e.g., Isma'il Pasha in Egypt). While traditional arts and crafts continued to flourish, Europe was increasingly providing the models. All the European styles of the nineteenth century were copied, and an observer in Egypt today would find it hard to detect whether surviving handicraft objects from that period were imported or home-produced.

3. Nationalism, Supranationalism (Islamism), and Internationalism

Meanwhile, many people were becoming aware of the risk of losing their cultural roots. Nationalism was unmistakably spreading, affecting both politics and culture. Once again Egypt is a case in point: the movement led by Ahmad 'Urabi offers an instructive, and in some respects pathbreaking, example.[8]

The rise of nationalism changed the historical horizon and shifted the focus of a number of people working in the arts. Some deliberately turned toward presentation of pre-Islamic stylistic methods. The representatives of this tendency saw the glorification of ancient Egyptian culture (and beyond Egypt the achievements of the Persians, Phoenicians, and Turks) as the remedy for helplessness and confusion in the face of what they perceived as overwhelming foreign influence. Others saw nationalism as a racial idea imported from Europe and tried to protect against foreign encroachment and rupturing of cultural continuity by employing the "Islamic" forms they regarded as still valid.

The representatives of the "national" style who built the roadhouse for King Farouk at the foot of the pyramids in Giza based their design on ancient Egyptian forms of building and decoration. In the 1920s the Egyptian sculptor and painter Mahmud Mukhtar created *Nahdat Misr* (Egypt's Awakening), a freestanding sculpture of a woman protecting a rising sphinx with her headscarf; the work's meaning and formal repertoire were influenced by ancient Egypt. Artworks like this embody the break with Islamic tradition, which does not include sculpture in the round; they also indicate the politicization of art—a phenomenon as yet unknown to traditional Islamic culture in such a direct form. Mahmud Mukhtar made reliefs in which ancient Egypt can be discerned in the content as well as technique and type of design, such as his work *Small Traders* (fig. 4). Meanwhile, representatives of supranationalism (Islamism) were occupied during the first half of

4. *Mahmud Mukhtar,* Small Traders, *relief. The content and design recall ancient Egyptian reliefs.*

the twentieth century with reworking traditional Islamic forms of art and architecture for the modern era. In Cairo, for example, entire housing and office blocks in districts such as Heliopolis-Roxy and Zamalek were designed in pseudo-Islamic style (fig. 5); the same forms were naturally used in the design of the Islamic Museum. In Istanbul the Vakıf Hanı, built in 1918, is a six-story residential and office building whose arrangement and construction owe more to central European housing and office blocks of the second half of the nineteenth century than to the *khan* style; its exterior, however, is based on Islamic models. Again in Istanbul, the street Fuat Paşa Caddesi was built up at the beginning of the twentieth century. Its exterior form reveals the intention of building in "Islamic" style, despite the undeniable touch of classicism. The development of Abu Khusaisat Street in Fes al-Jedid (New Fez) took place almost contemporaneously; its form shows the attempt to revive the local Muslim or Moorish tradition. Parallel to this, in almost all Islamic countries, especially from the 1930s on, there was continued orientation to the development of European and American architecture. Architectural trends such as "Objectivity," the "International style," and Bauhaus grew in influence. Frank Lloyd Wright's "organic" architecture began to spread; disciples who had studied directly with Wright worked

5. *Cairo, Heliopolis-Roxy, residential and office buildings. The pseudo-Islamic architecture is unmistakable.*

6. *Corm House on Shari' al-Mathaf (Museum Street), Beirut, an example of an imported expressionist architectural form (badly damaged by the civil war).*

in the Middle East, especially in Egypt. Examples of these forms and styles of building can easily be found in every Islamic city. Expressionist building forms familiar in central Europe also have their counterparts here, such as Corm House (fig. 6) on Shariʿ al-Mathaf (Museum Street) in Beirut.[9]

Representational art, too, was—and still is—influenced primarily by European tendencies and trends.[10] The work of the new artists concentrated on framed pictures and no longer on the familiar tradition of structuring walls, ceilings, and floors. The Egyptian painter Ahmad Sabri painted expressionist pictures such as *After Reading* (1926), while the cubist movement was represented by Gadibiya (Jadhibiyya) Sirri (*Nile Panorama,* 1950?) and Salah ʿAbd al-Karim (*Colonialism,* 1962); meanwhile, Mahmud Saʿid (*Nude Model,* 1943) followed the formal canon of New Objectivity. In this context, can we still talk of Islamic art?

4. Industrial Development

It is clear that the change in Islamic society, urban structures, and architecture affected not only form but content as well. There were great efforts to introduce an industrial economy, mainly in Egypt (but also elsewhere in the Middle East, such as in Syria). Muhammad ʿAli, who ruled Egypt in the first half of the nineteenth century, hired large numbers of Europeans as consultants to help his regime with its plans to industrialize Egypt. He encouraged cultivation of specific agricultural products to provide raw materials for the textile industry. New factories and workshops were set up, not only in Cairo and its environs but also in many locations in Upper and Lower Egypt, especially for producing textiles from wool, cotton, and silk, and for chemicals, weapons, munitions, and many other products. The substance of these buildings has largely been destroyed, partly because most of Muhammad ʿAli's industrial enterprises collapsed after the defeat of his army in 1841, and partly because it is in the nature of industrial architecture to react to rapid changes in economic relations with equally fast changes in its basic structure. Yet there are still some surviving complexes today; they bear impressive witness to the importance of bygone industrial enterprises, for example, the paper factory in Bulaq, built in Muhammad ʿAli's era (fig. 7). By the second half of the nineteenth century, hardly any industrial enterprises of that size were being built because the British colonial power opposed industrialization in Egypt.

Egypt's industry began to grow on a broader basis from the 1920s (primarily after the establishment of the Bank Misr), but only really took off in 1936, when the country gained a degree of fiscal autonomy. In this respect one could even say that the Second World War had a stimulatory effect. The military coup in 1952 signified a major break in Egypt's economic and industrial history; later, industrialization made great progress in the country, particularly after 1970 in conjunction with the economic liberalization under Anwar el-Sadat. Egypt's built-up areas and construction barely differ

7. *Cairo-Bulaq. Foreground: paper factory, first half of the nineteenth century. In the background are modern administration buildings that have replaced old industrial plants, and the technical college from the same period.*

8. *Al-Isma'iliyya, Schweppes soft drink factory, 1985. The architectural form is no different from that in Europe or North America.*

from those in Europe and North America (fig. 8). The architecture is anonymous, and the construction workers have likewise become anonymous. Since 1899 they have been organized into the *niqaba* (labor union), and are no longer represented by the traditional *hirfa* (craftsmen's guild).[11]

5. Site-Specific Architecture and Urban Planning

Particularly since the 1960s, some urban planners and architects based in the "Muslim" world—and some foreigners, too—have begun to feel that they are in a transitional phase and have achieved works of only limited validity. They have realized that the nation-state has triumphed, but not the nation. They are unsure as to whether Islam as a single nation, the Islamic supranation (*umma*), or the linguistic allegiance of individual states should constitute their future framework. They see the real task as planning and building on a local basis, in line with the present geographical, social, and economic situation, as a way to preserve cultural continuity and prevent people from becoming alienated from their constructed environment.

The Egyptian architect Hassan Fathy (Hasan Fathi) criticized the narrowness and monotony of imported ground plans and advocated adopting traditional building techniques and using local building materials. His project at Gourna village from the end of the 1940s was an attempt to put his theoretical approach into practice.[12] Another Egyptian architect, Omar Azzam ('Umar Azzam), argued that the perceptions and lifestyles of the indigenous population had to be the starting point for any new development. He questioned whether introducing new technologies and imitating Western industrialization in concentrated form would really be a solution to the problems.[13]

The Iraqi architect Rif'at al-Jadarji took up the meaning of the term "style." To avoid formal chaos, he thought it was necessary to repeat forms that have stood the test of centuries, or even millennia (without falling into formalism). His designs and buildings show a fondness for brick, the play of light and shadow, detailed but unified construction, and the interplay of interior and exterior (fig. 9).[14]

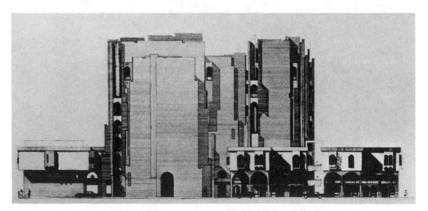

9. *Rif'at al-Jadarji, Baghdad, 'Imarat al-Awqaf, 1960s. Deliberate repetition of forms and techniques that have endured for centuries in the Mesopotamian region.*

The German architect Rolf Gutbrod was among the foreign architects working in Muslim countries who took local tradition seriously. Gutbrod and Partners built a hotel and conference center in Mecca from 1969 to 1974. Although commissioned to design a modern, not a traditional complex, they came up with a solution based on local conditions (fig. 10). The proximity of the site to the Kaʿba and the beautiful Wadi Mountains required a restrained building that would blend harmoniously with the landscape. The building's architects were evidently able to envisage the heat, the desert, and the great value of oases with their water, vegetation, and shade. They were aware that Western architectural styles such as Bauhaus, Brutalism, or Rationalism should not simply be transplanted there. In their construction in Mecca, kafesses (from the Arabic *qafas*) on spider web–type cable structures provided shade to artificial "oases." The window walls have vertical kafesses; these are wooden lattices of the type found on traditional houses in the Hejaz (in Mecca, Medina, Jidda, and Taif). Borrowing from traditional tent construction, the architects created hanging roofs made of steel cable and heat-insulating materials as the main feature of the conference center. Local wood carvers produced inscribed wooden tablets. The architects also developed aluminum tablets inscribed with Arabic that were used to construct areas such as large stairwells.[15]

This chapter concludes with a description of two further projects: the Civic Center in Jidda and the Jubail New City development. Both projects were conceived from 1972 to 1978 by a team of architects including

10. *Rolf Gutbrod et al., Mecca, Hotel and Conference Center, 1969–1974. Site-specific architecture with the contribution of local artists.*

Omar Azzam, David and Hiram Corm, Mohamed Scharabi (Muhammad Sharabi), and others. After in-depth research on the project requirements, the architects of the Civic Center developed a differentiated spatial and building program involving a cultural and business center based on the bazaar, the true center of the traditional city in the Islamic world. The bazaar's trading institutions are the continuous shopping street, the hall as a separable extension, and the courtyard complex as a secluded private space or storehouse. The changing assortment and arrangement of goods on offer has not affected the developmental character of these three elements—the shopping street, hall, and courtyard. Rather, the utilization of the bazaar and its institutions is typified by a high degree of anonymity; this allows for interchangeability in the various sectors and in the overall utilization. Moreover, given its place in the urban structure and the opportunity for additional construction, the bazaar is a flexible form that easily permits expansion or reduction.[16] These were some of the decisive aspects in the planning of the Civic Center in Jidda. The concept was designed to create a kind of continuity with the old suq, the old Jidda bazaar. It envisaged a covered shopping street interlinking different buildings for culture and commerce. Most of the buildings are courtyard complexes designed for multifunctional use. The complex can be extended in phases, and can be almost arbitrarily expanded (fig. 11).[17]

The second project is virtually a small town for around sixteen thousand inhabitants, near Jubail on the Persian Gulf. The planners' goal was to develop a concept appropriate to the site's natural qualities, the climate, and a new "Islamic society." To understand what is meant here by the term "Islamic society," we have to go back to nineteenth-century urban society in central Europe, to the emergence of a relatively broad layer of academics and quasi-academics who felt privileged, and actually were. The members of this social group aspired to the ideals and lifestyle of the nobility and grand bourgeoisie. They were aware of the new industrial age but simultaneously bound to tradition. Unwilling or unable to abandon the old ways of thinking and living, they compromised with the new era by nurturing the basic traditional order of the family, preserving the traditional social structure, and developing a sense of the nation. They did this by using modern technological advances. Intentionally or not, this group submitted to the laws of the rapidly developing division of time and labor. A new rhythm of life emerged, determined by the conditions of industrial production. A similar development is taking place in Muslim society today. Jubail New City was planned for this new kind of society.

It is common knowledge that the traditional city in the Middle East is usually densely built up, with its structure largely characterized by courtyard-type buildings. In contrast to the streets outside, which are mostly irregular, the inner courtyard with its regular quadratic form is peaceful. On the whole, the basic ground plan of the buildings does not vary greatly; it

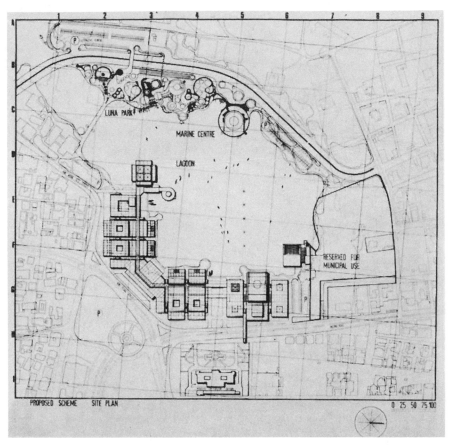

11. Architects' team Omar Azzam, David and Hiram Corm, Mohamed Scharabi et al., Jidda, Civic Center, 1973. Based on the bazaar concept, the plans involve a covered shopping street interlinking various cultural and commercial buildings.

repeats a specific number of variations with minor alterations. The basic climatic and social reasons for building inner courtyards are fairly obvious. What is striking in the traditional housing is the richness in design of the inner courtyard and interior rooms as a whole. In contrast, the exterior design of the houses is usually simple. It is difficult for observers looking at these houses from outside to tell whether the residents are rich or poor; it is the interior construction that reveals poverty or wealth. Alongside this design canon, there are a large number of design methods for protection against external elements. The question of providing shade, as well as that of ventilation, plays a major role here. The interior layout of the house is as clear and simple as possible. Usually it involves two or three areas that have to be spatially separated: the private or family quarters, the public or

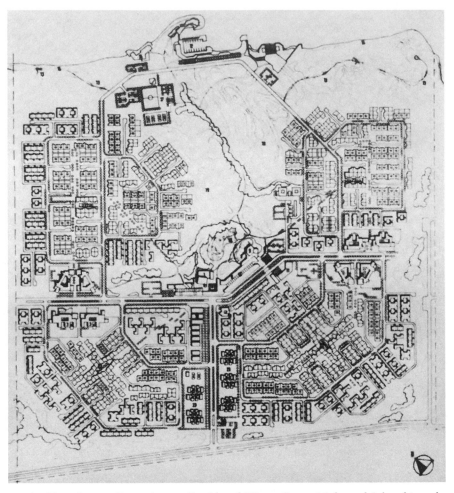

12. Architects' team Omar Azzam, David and Hiram Corm, Mohamed Scharabi et al., Jubail New City, overall complex. Creating inner courtyards was the primary planning goal for both the urban planning concept and the individual buildings.

13a (facing page, above) and 13b (facing page, below). Architects' team Omar Azzam, David and Hiram Corm, Mohamed Scharabi et al., Jubail New City, detached houses and apartment buildings. The issue in site-specific architecture is to draw inspiration from traditional forms but without copying them.

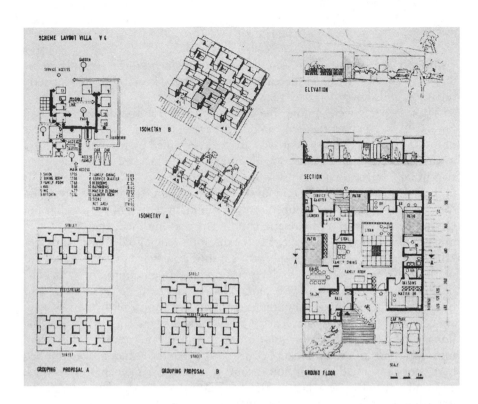

SCHEME LAYOUT VILLA V 4

ISOMETRY B

ISOMETRY A

ELEVATION

SECTION

GROUPING PROPOSAL A

GROUPING PROPOSAL B

GROUND FLOOR

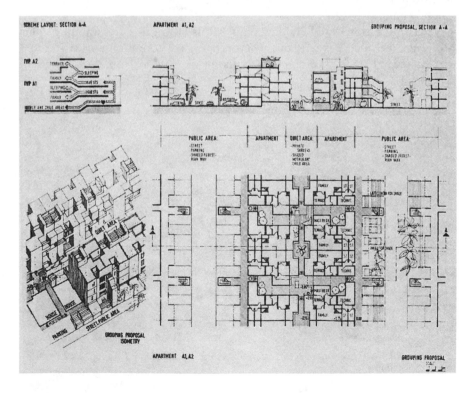

SCHEME LAYOUT: SECTION A-A

APARTMENT A1, A2

GROUPING PROPOSAL, SECTION A-A

TYP A2

TYP A1

| PUBLIC AREA | APARTMENT | QUIET AREA | APARTMENT | PUBLIC AREA |

GROUPING PROPOSAL ISOMETRY

APARTMENT A1, A2

GROUPING PROPOSAL

visitors' quarters, and finally—for prosperous residents—the servants' quarters. In the past it was considered very important to keep these areas strictly separate, and this still applies today.

These aspects were among the guiding motifs for the design of Jubail New City (fig. 12). At the same time, the planners were guided by principles of modern urban development, which are determined by present and future infrastructural requirements. The planning was influenced by the need for two main factors: a constant flow of sea air in the city—the climate here is humid—and a smoothly functioning transport structure. The plan envisaged four residential quarters grouped around the main center, the suq or bazaar. Owing to the social and climatic conditions just outlined, the creation of inner courtyards was highlighted as the main planning goal. The four neighborhoods are loosely grouped to form a public courtyard that takes account of the existing sand dunes and vegetation and opens onto the gulf. The neighborhoods themselves were planned so as to create an inner courtyard by means of high boundary buildings; and naturally most of the houses were conceived as courtyard complexes. On the model of the traditional city, the houses were given an almost uniform appearance. The traditional division into *haramlik* and *salamlik*, the private and public domains, was applied here, not only for detached houses but also for apartment buildings (figs. 13a and 13b). The detached houses are mainly one story, while the apartment buildings have four stories, obviating the need for elevators in any of the housing.

The application of old building regulations meant that freestanding villas were not included in the plans. The need for air conditioning was almost eliminated by the use of abutting walls as well as horizontal and vertical

14. Jubail New City, 1989, architects' team Omar Azzam, David and Hiram Corm, Mohamed Scharabi et al.

15. Aleppo, villa in al-Shahba' development area, 1992.

recesses and juts, and by the creation of small courtyards and spatial orientation to the courtyard. The use of brick as the main building material was also important in this respect. The few openings on the exterior façades were kept so small that there was no need for extra sunshades. All the houses were whitewashed to reflect the sun rather than absorbing it (fig. 14).

The aim of the foregoing descriptions is to show that in site-specific urban planning, architecture, and representational art in the Islamic context, the point is to draw inspiration from the nature of traditional architectural forms but certainly not to copy them. What is decisive here is the attempt at meaningful links with traditional forms of art and architecture, without sweeping claims about designing in an "Islamic" way.

Nevertheless, some architects are still greatly tempted by the possibility of creating constructions in the "Islamic" way. Postmodernist culture—which is not properly understood in the Middle East—offers numerous opportunities for this. One example can be seen in Aleppo, where a variety of different types of buildings were designed with reference to the architecture of long-ago epochs (fig. 15). This illustrates the reemergence of a kind of historicism that lacks content and force.

Translated by Karen Margolis

NOTES

Part One
Historical Expansion, Political and Religious History

III. Shiʿi Islam *(Werner Ende)*

1. See M. G. S. Hodgson, "Ghulāt", in *The Encyclopedia of Islam,* vol. 2 (Leiden, 1965), 1093–95; and H. Halm, *Shiʾism.* See also Part Two, Chapter X, "Sects and Special Groups" by Werner Schmucker, in this volume.
2. M. G. S. Hodgson, "How Did the Early Shiʾa Become Sectarian?" *Journal of the American Oriental Society* 75 (1955): 1–13.
3. E. Kohlberg, "Some Shiʾi Views of the Antediluvian World," *Studia Islamica* 52 (1980): 41–66.
4. R. Brunner, *Islamic Ecumenism in the 20th Century* (Leiden, 2004) (with an excellent bibliography). On a particularly controversial point of contention, see R. Brunner, *Die Schia und die Koranfälschung* (Würzburg, 2001).
5. M. M. Ayoub, *Redemptive Suffering in Islam: A Study of the Devotional Aspects of Ashura in Twelver Shiʾism* (The Hague, 1978).
6. On the early development of the imamate theory of the Twelver Shiʿa, see H. Modarresi, *Crisis and Consolidation in the Formative Period of Shiʾite Islam* (Princeton, 1993).
7. On classical Shiʿi *tafsir,* see the relevant chapter in H. Gätje, *The Qurʾan and Its Exegesis: Selected Texts with Classical and Modern Muslim Interpretations,* trans. and ed. A. T. Welch (Berkeley, 1976).
8. See P. Chelkowski, ed., *Taʾziyeh: Ritual and Drama in Iran* (New York, 1979), and "Taʾziya" (also by P. Chelkowski), in *The Encyclopaedia of Islam,* 2nd ed., vol. 10 (Leiden, 2000), 406–408.
9. W. Ende, "The Flagellations of Muharram and the Shiʿite ʿUlamaʾ," *Der Islam* 55 (1978): 19–36.
10. See W. Ende, "Musa al-Sadr", in *The Encyclopaedia of Islam,* 2nd ed., vol. 12 (supplement) (Leiden, 2004), 641–42; and C. Mallat, *The Renewal of Islamic Law:*

Muhammad Baqer al-Sadr (...) (Cambridge, 1993). The Iranian president Abu l-Hasan Bani Sadr, who was deposed in 1981, did not belong to this family.

11. R. Strothmann, *Die Zwölfer-Schi'a* (Leipzig: O. Harrassowitz, 1926), 6.
12. On this subject, see several articles in S. A. Arjomand, ed., *Authority and Political Culture in Shi'ism* (Albany, N.Y., 1988).
13. Ayatollah Chomeini, *Der islamische Staat* (Berlin, 1983), 102–106 and passim; see also S. A. Arjomand, "Khumaynī", in *The Encyclopaedia of Islam,* 2nd ed., vol. 12 (Leiden, 2004), 530–31.
14. From the wealth of literature on this subject, see, for example, D. Menashri, ed., *The Iranian Revolution and the Muslim World* (Boulder, Colo., 1990).
15. See *On the Sociology of Islam: Lectures by Ali Shari'ati,* trans. H. Algar (Berkeley, 1979); on the author, see "Shari'ati," in *The Encyclopaedia of Islam,* vol. 9 (Leiden, 1997), 328–29.
16. R. Strothmann, *Das Staatsrecht der Zaiditen,* Strassburg 1912, 38, 61.
17. See M. W. Wenner, *The Yemen Arab Republic: Development and Change in an Ancient Land* (Boulder, Colo., 1991); and R. Leveau et al., eds., *Le Yemen contemporain* (Paris, 1999), which contains chapters in English. On more recent developments, see the chapter on Yemen by Iris Glosemeyer in this volume.
18. On the role of tribes in the past and present, see P. Dresch, *Tribes, Government, and History in Yemen* (Oxford, 1989).
19. G. vom Bruck, "Being a Zaydi in the Absence of an Imam," in Leveau et al., *Le Yemen contemporain,* 169–192; B. Haykel, "Rebellion, Migration or Consultative Democracy? The Zaydis and Their Detractors in Yemen," ibid., 193–201.

V. The Distribution of Muslims throughout the World
(Peter Heine and Riem Spielhaus)

1. Baer, *Population and Society in the Arab East,* 36; see also Population and Housing Census Commission, *Population and Housing Census.*
2. See Roy, *Globalized Islam,* 124.
3. Adrian, *Ethnologische Fragen der Entwicklungsplanung,* 25; see also Brenner, "Constructing Muslim Identities in Mali."
4. Ibn Battuta, *Voyages d'Ibn Battuta,* 422.
5. Heine, "I am not the Mahdi, but..."
6. This term is derived from the Arabic *umma,* the community of believers.
7. Panjwani, "Muslims in Malawi," 167.
8. Wilks, "The Position of Muslims in Metropolitan Ashanti in the Early Nineteenth Century," 328; see also Launay and Soares, "The Formation of 'Islamic Sphere' in Colonial West Africa."
9. 'Umari, *L'Afrique moins l'Égypte,* 60; Bakri, *Description de l'Afrique Septentrionale par el-Bekri,* 178–79.
10. Heine and Stipek, *Ethnizität und Islam,* 21–22.
11. Lewis, *Islam in Tropical Africa,* 60–61.
12. Adams, *Islam and Modernism in Egypt,* 195–96.
13. See Part Two, XII.3, "The Organization of the Islamic Conference," by Johannes Reissner in this volume.
14. A. Alkazaz, "Regionalorganisationen," in *Nahost Jahrbuch* (1994), 177–186, esp. 181f.; and http://www.oic-oci.org.
15. Islamic Secretariat, *The Muslim World: Basic Information about the Member Countries of the Islamic Secretariat* (Karachi: Islamic Secretariat, 1974).

16. Senghor, a Christian, was president of Senegal from 1960 to 1981; see also Part Two, IV.11, "The Independent States of Sub-Saharan Africa," by Jamil M. Abun-Nasr and Roman Loimeier in this volume.
17. Tariq Ramadan is only one of the most prominent advocates of the concept of *dar al-'ahd*. See Ramadan, *To Be a European Muslim.*
18. See Part Two, chapter V, "The Islamic Diaspora," sections 1–2, "Western Europe" and "France, Great Britain, the Netherlands, and Germany," by Nico Landman in this volume.
19. Estimates are based on the 1999 census.
20. Census of Population in Singapore, 2000. Published by the Department of Statistics, Ministry of Trade and Industry, Republic of Singapore.
21. For a comprehensive discussion, see Spielhaus, "Religion and Identity."
22. See, for example, Dassetto, Ferrari, and Maréchal, *Islam in the European Union.*
23. For a discussion of available estimates on Muslims in France, see Laurence and Vaisse, *Integrating Islam,* 19.
24. *Bundestag Printed Paper 16/5033* (2007).
25. "More than 850 thousand Muslims in the Netherlands," cited from CBS *Webmagazine,* October 25, 2007, http://www.cbs.nl/en-GB/menu/themas/vrije-tijd-cultuur/ publicaties/artikelen/archief/2007/2007-2278-wm.htm?Languageswitch=on (accessed September 5, 2008).
26. For a discussion of various estimates of the size of the Muslim American community, see the Pew Research Center report "Muslim Americans: Middle Class and Mostly Mainstream," in particular chap. 1, "How Many Muslims Are There in the United States?" 9–14.

Part Two
The Political Role of Islam in the Present

I. The Intra-Islamic Discussion on a Modern Economic and Social System *(Johannes Reissner)*

1. P. Pawelka 2003, 86.
2. See W. Ende, "Sozialismus," in *Lexikon der islamischen Welt,* ed. K. Kreiser et al., vol. 3 (Stuttgart, 1974), 115–117.
3. For an English translation, see S. A. Hanna and G. H. Gardner 1969, 275–289.
4. For extracts in English translation, see ibid., 205–216.
5. For an English translation, see ibid., 266–274. On Abu Dharr, see U. Haarmann, "Abu Dharr: Muhammad's Revolutionary Companion," *Muslim World* (Hartford, Conn.) 68 (1978): 285–289.
6. On India and Pakistan, see the chapter "Three Theories of Islamic Socialism" in A. Ahmad 1967, 195–207.
7. See J. Reissner 1980, 316–321.
8. On these two groups, see also chapters AII and III in W. Ule 1969, 58–103. On the Marxist view, see N. Balluz, "Nichtkapitalistische Entwicklung und Islam," *Mitteilungen des Instituts für Orientforschung* 16 (1970): 521–540.
9. On the Islamic Development Bank and the Islamic Conference, see "International Islamic Organizations" by Johannes Reissner in this volume.

10. See A. Rieck, *Unsere Wirtschaft: Eine gekürzte kommentierte Übersetzung des Buches "Iqtiṣādunā" von Muḥammad Bāqir aṣ-Ṣadr* (Berlin, 1984).

11. Of Bani Sadr's books, two have been translated from Arabic into Persian: the more general, "standard" title, *The Economy According to Islam* (*Eqtesad dar maktab-e eslam*), translated by Ali Hojjati-Kermani (Tehran, 1350 [1971]), and a book on the working class written after the revolution, *Work and Workers in Islam* (*Kar wa kargar dar eslam*) (Tehran, 1359 [1980]). On the People's Mujahidin and social unity resulting from ontological unity, see K. Rajavi, *La Révolution iranienne et les Moudjahedines* (Paris, 1983), 111.

12. Apart from the works of Sayyid Qutb and Mustafa al-Sibaʿi previously mentioned in the text, Muhammad al-Mubarak also refers to *Islam and the Present Economic Systems* (*Al-Islam wa-l-nuzum al-iqtisadiyya al-muʿasira*) by Abu l-Aʿlaʾ al-Maududi and *Iqtisaduna* by Muhammad Baqir al-Sadr; see Rieck, *Unsere Wirtschaft*.

13. Important, more recent summaries of the basic principles of Islamic economic theory are contained in H. Müller 2002, 43–45; V. Nienhaus 2002, 131–134.

14. An English translation of the relevant chapter is contained in S. A. Hanna and G. H. Gardner 1969, 149–179.

15. On the prohibition of interest, see "Islamic Economics in Practice" by Volker Nienhaus in this volume.

16. "Großbritannien testet den Markt für 'Islamic Banking,'" *Frankfurter Allgemeine Zeitung,* August 17, 2004, 16.

17. V. Perthes, "Die Fiktion des Fundamentalismus: Von der Normalität islamistischer Bewegungen," *Blätter für deutsche und internationale Politik* 2 (February 1993): 188–200.

18. P. Pawelka 2003, 94.

19. See H. Müller 2002, 50–53.

II. Islamic Economics in Practice *(Volker Nienhaus)*

1. See M. Ahmad, *Business Ethics in Islam* (New Delhi, 1999); N. M. A. B. N. Yusoff, *Islam and Business* (Subang Jaya, 2002).

2. See M. A. Haneef, *Contemporary Islamic Economic Thought* (Kuala Lumpur, 1995).

3. See N. Saleh, *Unlawful Gain and Legitimate Profit in Islamic Law* (Cambridge, 1986); S. Haron and B. Shanmugam, *Islamic Banking System: Concepts and Applications* (Subang Jaya, 1997); T. Usmani, *Islamic Finance,* www.darululoomkhi. edu.pk/fiqh/islamicfinance/islamicfinance.html; M. M. Billah, *Applied Islamic Law of Trade and Finance: A Selection of Contemporary Practical Issues,* 3rd ed. (Petaling Jaya, 2007).

4. For a description of the financing instruments with sample contracts, see State Bank of Pakistan, *Essentials and Model Agreements for Islamic Modes of Financing* (Karachi, April 16, 2004), http://www.sbp.org.pk/press/Essentials/Essentials-ModAgreement. htm; see also M. Iqbal, ed., *Islamic Banking and Finance: Current Developments in Theory and Practice* (Leicester, 2001); S. Archer and R. A. A. Karim, eds., *Islamic Finance: Innovation and Growth* (London, 2002); M. Ayub, *Understanding Islamic Finance* (Chichester, 2007).

5. In addition to profit-and-loss-sharing deposits into "investment accounts," there are also deposits that primarily serve for payment transactions—analogous to current accounts with conventional banks. The customers receive no return for their funds,

but they also have no share in risks, and the bank guarantees access to their deposits at any time as well as full repayment.

6. The price may be higher if it is paid at a later date than on immediate cash payment. Although this difference is equivalent to interest in economic terms, it is legally interpreted as a markup on the price of the goods and not as a remuneration for the capital tied by this transaction.

7. See M. A. M. Al-Amine, *Istisna' (Manufacturing Contract) in Islamic Banking and Finance: Law and Practice* (Kuala Lumpur, 2001).

8. Similar contracts are used in Malaysia under the name of *bay' al-inah* for money market transactions by the central bank and for the construction of shari'a-compliant credit cards. The website of the International Shariah Research Academy for Islamic Finance (ISRA), www.isra.my, contains a continually updated list of relevant and pioneering fatwas (in Arabic and English), including those of the International Fiqh Academy of the Muslim World League, on the conditions for the permissibility of *tawarruq* from 1998, and those of the Shari'a Advisory Council of the Malaysian Central Bank on deposit and financing products on the basis of *tawarruq* from 2005, as well as a report on a symposium in September 2007 at which leading Islamic legal scholars came out in favor of banning *tawarruq* in general because of the great risk of misuse. There is no indication, however, that the practice of Islamic banks has changed since then.

9. See M. A. M. Al-Amine, "The Islamic Bonds Market: Possibilities and Challenges," *International Journal of Islamic Financial Services* 3, no. 1 (2001).

10. Income-yielding assets may also be trade goods, which are sold at a fixed markup and for which the purchaser and the sales price are already fixed—for example, by long-term supply contracts.

11. *Tawarruq* loans also allow the financial sector to separate itself off from the real economy to a great extent. The transactions on the metal market have no real function and only satisfy formal needs. The same unit of metal can form the "real" basis for any number of financial transactions within a very short period, which can prompt the formation of shari'a-compliant "credit pyramids."

12. See www.aaoifi.com/aaoifi_sb_sukuk_Feb2008_Eng.pdf.

13. Sudan is an exception here. That country does have better legal foundations for *takaful* undertakings organized on a cooperative basis, which differ fundamentally in structure from *takaful* undertakings in all other Islamic countries.

14. The TOs' business models differ as to how this fee is calculated. There are two basic types, with numerous variants in practice. First, in the *wakala* model, a fee is calculated as a percentage of the individual *takaful* contributions, to which the TO is entitled as payment for its risk and asset management. This fee is intended to cover all management and sales costs on the part of the TO and to generate a return on investment for the TO or its shareholders. The costs of dealing with claims are covered not out of the fee but from the risk pool itself. It is seen as permissible that the fee contains a profit-related component based on the level of the surplus in the risk pool (but not comprising a direct share of this excess). Second, in the *mudaraba* model, the TO does not receive a fee but has a share in the profit from the asset management and a direct share of the risk pool surplus. This model is particularly widespread in Malaysia, and is very controversial, partly because a surplus in the risk pool is not profit generated by business activities but merely indicates that the total contribution payments exceed the costs of covering claims. This may be due to efficient risk management, but it may also result from excessively high contributions. The members of the mutual benefit association can collect no interest from the latter situation, even if the excess contributions are (partly) paid back at the end of the

year. A share in the surplus for the TO, however, creates an incentive to calculate contribution levels in this way.

15. In a small town in the Nile Delta (Mit Ghamr), an attempt was made to set up interest-free savings banks in order to alter the rural population's savings habits. Instead of hoarding cash or purchasing tangible assets (such as jewelry and real estate) and later selling them, the rural population was encouraged to open savings accounts. This is the prerequisite for passing on those portions of current income that are set aside for later consumption through the banking system, for intermediate use as productive loans for business investments. These interest-free financial institutions, however, which were intended to prompt a local economic cycle, were an alien element in Gamal Abdel Nasser's centralized economic system; economic difficulties within the savings banks (overliquidity and insufficiently profitable financing projects) were used as an opportunity to close them down in the late 1960s. There are occasional references to be found in the literature to an even earlier short-lived experiment in Pakistan in the late 1950s; see R. Wilson, "The Evolution of the Islamic Financial System," in *Islamic Finance: Innovation and Growth,* ed. S. Archer and R. A. A. Karim (London, 2002), 29ff.

16. Case studies on Islamic financial institutions in Australia, Britain, Bangladesh, Indonesia, Palestine, South Africa, Thailand, and Turkey are contained in B. Shanmugam, V. Perumal, and A. H. Ridzwa, eds., *Islamic Banking: An International Perspective* (Serdang, 2004); see also S. Ahmed, *Islamic Banking, Finance and Insurance: A Global Overview* (Kuala Lumpur, 2006).

17. Islamic Research and Training Institute and Islamic Financial Services Board, *Islamic Financial Services Industry Development: Ten-Year Framework and Strategy* (Jidda and Kuala Lumpur, 2007), www.ifsb.org.

18. Further estimates on the quantitative dimension of the Islamic financial sector—not all of them with comprehensible databases and with partially diverging findings—can be found in Standard & Poor's, *Islamic Finance Outlook 2008,* www.standardandpoors.com; Ernst & Young, *The World Takaful Report, 2008,* www.ey.com; Ernst & Young, *The Islamic Funds and Investments Report, 2008,* www.ey.com; A. Hassoune and K. Howaladar, *Islamic Banks and Sukuk: Growing Fast, but Still Fragmented,* Moody's Global Banking, Special Comment (April 2008); F. Hijazi and D. Gribot-Carroz, *2007 Review and 2008 Outlook: Islamic Finance,* Moody's Investors Service, Special Report (February 2008); KPMG, *Growth and Diversification in Islamic Finance,* KPMG International (March 2007), www.kpmg.com; S. Timewell and J. DiVanna, "Top 500 Islamic Financial Institutions," *The Banker,* November 3, 2008, 2–8.

19. For example in Britain, the Philippines, Singapore, South Africa, and Thailand.

20. See M. D. Baker, "The Shari'a Supervisory Board and Issues of Shari'a Rulings and Their Harmonisation in Islamic Banking and Finance," in Archer and Karim, *Islamic Finance,* 74ff.

21. The terms "profit-sharing account" (PSA) and "profit-sharing investment account" (PSIA) are also commonly used.

22. In this respect Islamic banks do not differ significantly from the conventional banks in Islamic countries, which also prefer short-term and low-risk trade financing. To mobilize resources for medium- to long-term financing, Islamic banks offer their customers subscriptions to funds, which use the customers' money for specific individual projects or for specific types of projects (e.g., real estate deals).

23. Malaysia and Bahrain are exceptions; see the individual country sections later in this chapter.

24. See http://www.aaoifi.com.

25. See http://www.ifsb.org.
26. See www.iifm.net.
27. In its early years the IIFM concentrated on developing and offering a type of shariʿa certification for security flotations. According to its website, however, only six *sukuk* issues were certified between 2002 and 2004, and no further issues since then.
28. See www.lmcbahrain.com.
29. Bahrain Islamic Bank, Dubai Islamic Bank, and Kuwait Finance House.
30. The financial quality or risk-yield balance of securities depends on the credit status of the (state or private) issuers and on the value and yield potential of the commodity values on which they are based; the quality in terms of Islamic law is determined by the structure of the contract used.
31. Amounting to $24.7 billion as of October 24, 2007. Data from the LMC website, not including the monthly issues of Al Salam Sukuk by the central bank of Bahrain, which were designed with a three-month term as special liquidity papers for the local Bahrain market.
32. Amounting to $61 million in 2005, $113 million in 2006, and $55.5 million in 2007.
33. See www.iirating.com.
34. See www.difc.ae; also Dubai International Financial Centre, *A Guide to Islamic Finance in or from the DIFC* (Dubai, 2007), www.praesidium.ae/press/Guide-to-Islamic-Finance-in-or-from-the-DIFC.pdf; Norton Rose, *The Dubai International Financial Center* (September 2005), www.nortonrose.com/knowledge/publications/2005/pub10999.aspx?page=all&lang=en-gb.
35. Additional regulations apply to institutions in the Islamic sector, which are summarized in Dubai Financial Services Authority, *The DFSA Rulebook, Islamic Financial Business Module (ISF)*, Ver 2/07–08, www.complinet.com/net_file_store/new_rulebooks/d/f/DFSA_4598.pdf.
36. Dubai International Financial Centre, *Guide to Islamic Finance*, 7.
37. See http://www.djindexes.com.
38. For example, Dow Jones offers a global Islamic market index as well as regional Islamic indexes for Europe and the Pacific, plus national indexes for the United States, Canada, Britain, Japan, and Turkey. There are, for example, industry-based Islamic indexes for raw materials, consumer goods, the energy industry, and telecommunications.
39. See *Guide to the Dow Jones Islamic Market Indexes,* status May 2008, www.djindexes.com/mdsidx/ downloads/rulebooks/imi_rulebook.pdf.
40. See http://www.ftse.com. Along with a global shariʿa index, there are regional Islamic indexes for the United States, Europe, the Pacific region, and South Africa. In addition, FTSE has also developed several Islamic indexes in conjunction with the Singapore Exchange, Bursa Malaysia, and Dubai International Financial Exchange.
41. According to information on the Yasaar website (www.yasaar.org/FTSE-Yasaar_criteria%5B1%5D.pdf), the following criteria apply to the FTSE entities: ratio of debts to balance sheet total less than 33 percent, cash balance and interest-bearing items less than 33 percent, receivables and cash less than 50 percent, shariʿa-noncompliant income types (not including income from interest) less than 5 percent, total income from interest less than 5 percent, and impermissible income less than 5 percent of the dividend. For an overview of further filter methods, see S. Nisar, "Islamic Norms for Stocks Screening," *Finance in Islam,* February 15, 2007, www.financeinislam.com/article/10/1/551.
42. See www.mscibarra.com, www.globalinv.net, and www.difxhsbcindices.com.

43. For a typical example of the range of services offered by these firms, see www.sim mons-simmons.com/docs/islamic_finance.pdf or www.nortonrose.com/knowledge/ publications/2005/pub11126.aspx?page=all&lang=en-gb.
44. Publisher of the highly respected Islamic Funds and Investments Reports, www. ey.com/Global/assets.nsf/UK/Islamic_funds_and_investment_report_2008/$file/EY_ Islamic_funds_investment_report_2008.pdf); and World Takaful Reports (most recently 2008), www.ey.com/Global/assets.nsf/UK/ World_Takaful_Report_2008/$file/ World_Takaful_Report_2008.pdf).
45. Publisher of a 2007 study, "Growth and Diversification in Islamic Finance," www. kpmg.com/Site CollectionDocuments/Growth%20and%20Diversification.pdf.
46. See www.moodys.com, www.standardandpoors.com, and www.fitchratings.com.
47. This is also emphasized in the perspectives paper published by IsDB/IRTI and IFSB (*Islamic Financial Services Industry Development: Ten-Year Framework and Strategies*); with this in mind, IFSB formed a task force in 2007, with the aim of highlighting possible solutions.
48. See www.inceif.org; on the endowment capital, see the press release dated December 10, 2005, www.bnm.gov.my/index.php?ch=8&pg=14&ac=1145.
49. See press release from the central bank of Bahrain dated July 2, 2007 (www.cbb.gov. bh/cmsrule/index.jsp?action=article&ID=2587) and its 2007 annual report, www. cbb.gov.bh/cmsrule/media/2008/ AR%2007%20e.pdf, 19.
50. For an overview of memberships of the leading shari'a experts on the various shari'a boards, see Failaka, *The Shariah Report, 2008: Profiles of the World's Leading Scholars* (Dubai, 2008).
51. See www.isra.my.
52. See N. A. Zaidi, *Eliminating Interest from Banks in Pakistan* (Karachi, 1987); A. Mehmood, "Islamisation of the Economy in Pakistan: Past, Present and Future," *Islamic Studies* 41, no. 4 (2002): 675–704; State Bank of Pakistan, *Annual Report, 2001–2002* (Karachi, 2002),chap. 10, "Islamization of Financial System in Pakistan," 189–198 (www.sbp.org.pk).
53. See C. Gieraths, "Pakistan: Main Participants and Final Financial Products of the Islamization Process," in *Islamic Financial Markets,* ed. R. Wilson (London, 1990), 171ff.
54. See Pakistan Federal Shariat Court, "Judgement on Interest (Riba)," in *The All Pakistan Legal Decisions,* vol. 44 (1992), reprinted with translation of text passages into Arabic and Urdu as no. 8 of the Islamic Economics Translation Series of the Islamic Research and Training Institute of the Islamic Development Bank (Jidda, 1995).
55. The formulation in the standard agreement for financing was: "The Customer has agreed to sell the Bank raw materials/finished goods/spare products/machinery, etc.... [and] to purchase the same from the Bank on the basis of mark-up and terms and conditions hereinafter appearing." A. R. Akhtar, *The Law and Practice of Interest-Free Banking with Banking Tribunals Ordinance* (Lahore, 1988), 185.
56. See the section written by Maulana Justice Muhammad Taqi Usmani in *The Text of the Historic Judgement on Riba (Interest), Given by The Supreme Court of Pakistan, 23rd December 1999* (Petaling Jaya, 2001).
57. See Shaukat Aziz, budget speech, *Federal Budget, 2001–2002,* http://www.cbr.gov. pk/budg2002/speech.htm.
58. See State Bank of Pakistan, *Frequently Asked Questions (FAQs) on Islamic Banking,* http://www.sbp.org.pk/ibd/faqs.pdf.
59. Published on the Supreme Court website, www.supremecourt.gov.pk.
60. See State Bank of Pakistan, *Strategic Plan, 2005–10,* www.sbp.org.pk.
61. State Bank of Pakistan, "Instructions and Guidelines for Shari'ah Compliance in Islamic Banking Institutions," in *Islamic Banking Department Circular No. 02 of*

March 25, 2008, www.sbp.org.pk. The new list replaces the old catalog of permissible financing techniques dating from 1984.

62. *Mudaraba, musharaka,* diminishing *musharaka,* and equity participation in the form of shares in a corporate entity.

63. *Ijara* or *ijara wa iqtina', murabaha, musawama, salam,* and *istithna'.*

64. *Wakala,* assignment of debt, and *kafala.*

65. See State Bank of Pakistan, *Islamic Banking Bulletin* (September–December 2007): 2 (www.sbp.org.pk).

66. See S. Akhtar, governor's speech, in *Financial Sector: Ten-Year Vision and Strategy,* July 1, 2008, 5 (www.sbp.org.pk).

67. These speeches are published on the central bank's website, www.sbp.prg.pk.

68. See J. Kooroshy, *Wirtschaftsordnung der Islamischen Republik Iran* (Hamburg, 1990); I. Hetsch, *Islam und Unterentwicklung: Konzeptionelle Ansätze zur Überwindung der Unterentwicklung in islamischen Wirtschaftstheorien; Das Beispiel Iran* (Berlin, 1992); W. Buchta: "Ein Vierteljahrhundert Islamische Republik Iran," *Aus Politik und Zeitgeschichte* 9 (2004): 6ff.

69. See A. Jbili, V. Kramarenko, and J. M. Bailén, *Islamic Republic of Iran: Managing the Transition to a Market Economy* (Washington, D.C., 2007).

70. See S. Ilias, *CRS Report for Congress: Iran's Economy* (Washington, D.C., 2008), updated June 12.

71. See IMF Staff, *Islamic Republic of Iran: Staff Report for the 2006 Article IV Consultation,* IMF Country Report no. 07/100 (Washington, D.C., 2007), 11f. For further details, see the website of the Iranian Privatization Organization, www.en.ipo.ir.

72. See S. Timewell, "Change Is Coming," *The Banker,* December, 2003, 104; A. Jbili, V. Kramarenko, and J. Bailén, *Islamic Republic of Iran: Selected Issues,* IMF Country Report no. 04/308 (Washington, D.C., September 2004).

73. Figures for the end of year 1386 (= March 2008) from Central Bank of the Islamic Republic of Iran, *Selected Economic Indicators: Monetary and Credit Aggregates,* Esfand 1386, Table 7 (Tehran, 2008), www.cbi.ir.

74. See Central Bank of the Islamic Republic of Iran, *Annual Review, 1385* (2006–7) (Tehran, 2007), 16.

75. See Ilias, *CRS Report for Congress: Iran's Economy,* 9.

76. See H. Aryan, "Iran: The Impact of Islamization on the Financial System," in Wilson, *Islamic Financial Markets,* 155ff.; M. R. Taheri: "A Comparison of Islamic Banking in Iran with Other Islamic Countries." in: Shanmungan, Perumal, and Ridzwa, *Islamic Banking,* 63ff.

77. See Central Bank of the Islamic Republic of Iran, *Selected Economic Indicators: Monetary and Credit Aggregates,* Esfand 1386, Table 8 (Tehran, 2008), www.cbi.ir.

78. An interesting point is that the International Monetary Fund has made proposals for the further development of CBPPs into shari'a-compliant instruments of liquidity management and on Iran's indirect monetary policy. The fund based these proposals on ideas and constructions from Sudan, Malaysia, and Bahrain. Among other things, it suggested extending the pool of objects on which the CBPPs are based in quantitative terms; with regard to the type of objects contained in the pool, improving transparency concerning the value and yield capacity of the objects in the pool; and actively supporting the development of a secondary market for CBPPs. See Jbili, Kramarenko, and Bailén: *Islamic Republic of Iran,* 66ff.

79. See G. Shabsigh, *Sudan: Final Review under the 2002 Staff-Monitored Program and the 2003 Program,* IMF Country Report no. 03/273 (Washington, D.C., September 2003); IMF Staff, *Sudan: Staff Report for the 2007 Article IV Consultation and Staff-Monitored Program,* IMF Country Report no. 07/343 (Washington, D.C.,

October 2007); IMF Staff, *First Review of Performance under the 2007–8 Staff-Monitored Program,* IMF Country Report no. 08/174 (Washington, D.D., June 2008).

80. See A. Kireyev, *Financial Reforms in Sudan: Streamlining Bank Intermediation,* IMF Working Paper WP/01/53 (Washington, D.C., 2001); Bank of Sudan, *Annual Report, 2003,* http://www.bankofsudan.org.

81. See E. Stiansen, "Interest Politics: Islamic Finance in the Sudan, 1977–2001," in *The Politics of Islamic Finance,* ed. C. Henry and R. Wilson (Edinburgh, 2004), 155ff.

82. The central bank includes information on these regulations in its annual reports; see www.cbos.gov.sd.

83. See G. Shabsigh et al., *Sudan: Staff Report for the 2003 Article IV Consultation and First Review of the 2003 Staff-Monitored Program,* IMF Country Report no. 03/390 (Washington, D.C., December 2003).

84. See IMF Staff, *Sudan—Staff Report for 2007,* 16.

85. See Kireyev: *Financial Reforms in Sudan,* 48ff.

86. The central bank offers the commercial banks these funds by auction, at which the bank offering the highest percentage of the profit resulting from the funds wins.

87. As of July 31, 2008; see www.cbb.gov.bh/cmsrule/media/2008/IslBL-July08.pdf, and www.cbb.gov.bh/cmsrule/media/ 2008/CBL-July08.pdf.

88. As of June 30, 2008; see www.cbb.gov.bh/cmsrule/media/2008/SB%20June%2008.pdf.

89. See Central Bank of Bahrain, *Financial Sector Factsheet,* August 10, 2008, www.cbb.gov.bh/cmsrule/index.jsp?action=article&ID=1256.

90. Interestingly, conventional banks were also involved in such consortium loans.

91. In 2006 the Bahrain Monetary Agency became the Central Bank of Bahrain (CBB); see www.cbb.gov.bh.

92. See Bahrain Monetary Agency, *Islamic Banking and Finance in the Kingdom of Bahrain* (Manama, 2002), 72ff., with updates from the website of the Central Bank of Bahrain.

93. See www.cbb.gov.bh/cmsrule/media/2008/SB%20June%2008.pdf.

94. Bahrain is also the location of the General Council for Islamic Banks and Financial Institutions (CIBAFI), which was set up to provide information on the Islamic financial system, promote cooperation among Islamic financial institutions, and establish quality standards for Islamic financial products; see www.cibafi.org.

95. Bahrain was competing in this field with Malaysia (see the discussion later in this chapter). Following an expansion of the Malaysian Islamic financial sector in quantitative and qualitative terms through innovative financial techniques in the mid-1990s, the spread of the Islamic financial system to Indonesia and Brunei in particular could lead to the development of a regional Southeast Asian market. The local products, however, are not widely accepted in other parts of the Islamic world, which are opposed to further-reaching globalization.

96. See www.dfm.ae. Borse Dubai was founded in 2007 as a holding company for DFM and DIFX.

97. See the fatwa on the conversion of DFM into an Islamic institution, www.dfm.ae/documents/News%20Files/5d62cb8b-c749–47cd-92cb-cede21d37843.pdf.

98. Comparative statistics from the Zawya Industry Benchmarks: for Bahrain, www.zawya.com/cm/profile.cfm/cid631039/; for Dubai, www.zawya.com/cm/profile.cfm/cid1000015/ricDFM.DFM.

99. Noor Islamic Bank's vision is "to be the world's ultimate Islamic bank," and its aim is "to be the most recognized Islamic banking brand, by being the largest global financial institution in its field"; www.noorbank.com.

100. Other Islamic banks have achieved a similar level of equity—for example, the Dubai Islamic Bank, with called-up capital of 2.8 billion AED (approximately

$800 billion)—but only after (in most cases several) increases in equity at greater intervals.

101. J. Irish, "Noor Islamic Eyes Europe, Asia Banks for 2008," *Arabian Business.com*, November 19, 2007, www.arabianbusiness.com/504328-noor-islamic-eyes-europe-asia-banks-for-2008?ln=en.

102. See www.arabianbusiness.com/508515-al-hilal-bank-to-launch-in-june-?ln=en.

103. See www.bnm.gov.my/index.php?ch=20.

104. The government supported the foundation, participating in the bank's capital; shares have been traded on the Kuala Lumpur stock exchange since 1992.

105. See www.mifc.com/index.php?tpt=&tpl=th008_viewpdf.tsl&filelink=/index.php?ch=38%3Epg=104%3Eac= 28%3Ebb=268.

106. See www.mifc.com/repository/0014key.IB.indicator.2007.pdf. The number of conventional banks participating in the Islamic Banking Scheme (IBS) with their own Islamic windows, branches, and subsidiaries was fourteen in 2007; this figure is not suitable for comparison with 2001 owing to various fusions in the banking sector. A Malaysia International Islamic Financial Centre (MIFC) list dating from early November 2008 includes seventeen Islamic banks, six commercial banks, seven investment banks, and six development financial institutions with Islamic financial services as participating in the IBS; see www.mifc.com/index.php?ch=con_dir&pg=con_dir_fin.

107. One must bear in mind for these financial statistics that the assets, financing, and deposits all include a percentage of state institutions, transactions based less on commercial decisions than on political motivations, so the figures do not express only the market acceptance of the Islamic banking system.

108. See Securities Commission, Capital Market Masterplan Malaysia, Kuala Lumpur, 2001, http://www.sc.com.my/eng/html/cmp/cmpmainpage.html.

109. Formerly Government Investment Certificates (GICs).

110. Up to 2001 GIIs were legally designed as interest-free loans from the banks to the state, with a right to repayment but no right to remuneration (*qard hasan*). The state could, however, pay the lending bank a "voluntary" remuneration, which was de facto oriented toward the monetary market interest rate. From 2001 on the legal character was altered such that GIIs represent a package of state assets with a fixed nominal value, which the government offers for sale to the banks on the primary market at auction, accepting a purchase price below the nominal value. The government buys this package (i.e., the GIIs) back at the nominal value, paying the repurchase price on a fixed future date. The greater the difference between the GIIs' purchase price and the later due nominal value, the more profitable the purchase is for the banks. Depending on the liquidity situation or investment opportunities, banks can sell their GIIs to other banks on the secondary market at a price determined by supply and demand, creating liquidity or financial means for other investments.

111. For a characterization of these instruments, see http:/iimm.bnm.gov.my/index.php?ch=4&pg=4&ac=22.

112. See www.bursamalaysia.com/website/bm/products_and_services/islamic_capital_market/ICM_Derivatives.html.

113. For more detail, see www.sc.com.my/eng/html/icm/sas/sc_syariahcompliant.pdf.

114. See www.sc.com.my/eng/html/icm/0807_msianicm.pdf, 18.

115. The lists of shares adopted into the indexes differ from one another and from the SEC list in some details, primarily owing to differing cut-off levels for tolerable profits from banned or undesirable business operations.

116. The first stockbrokerage companies were formed in 1993–94; see OICV-IOSCO, *Islamic Capital Market Fact Finding Report*, July 2004, www.iosco.org/library/

pubdocs/pdf/IOSCOPD170.pdf. In the course of the gradual international opening of the financial sector from 2004 on, foreign stockbrokers and fund managers were granted licenses, and restrictions on capital transactions were reduced.

117. See www.sc.com.my/eng/html/icm/0807_msianicm.pdf, 18.

118. Ibid.

119. The offshore financial industry on the island of Labuan, not discussed in this chapter, is regulated by the Labuan Offshore Financial Services Authority (LOFSA); see www.lofsa.gov.my.

120. See www.iclif.org.

121. See www.inceif.org.

122. See www.bnm.gov.my/index.php?ch=200&pg=618.

123. See www.bnm.gov.my/index.php?ch=8&pg=14&ac=1594.

124. See www.mifc.com.

125. That is, as we have seen, a business owner sells his or her stock to a bank in return for a cash payment of $100 and immediately buys it back at a price of $110, paying the repurchase sum at a later date or in installments. Many critics regard a contract for sale and repurchase as a classic legal trick to evade the ban on interest.

126. The discussion at this point follows S. A. Rosly and M. M. Sanusi, "The Application of *bayʿ al-ʿinah* and *bayʿ al-dain* in Malaysian Islamic Bonds: An Islamic Analysis," *International Journal of Islamic Financial Services* 1, no. 2 (1999), http://islamicfinance. net/journals/journal2/art1.pdf.

127. If the issue rate were not lower than the nominal value, there would be no incentive to buy otherwise return-free securities. Technically this can also be structured in such a way that subscribers of the interest-free bonds receive a return not only on the due date of the nominal value but during the financing term itself as well. For example, a company could create, instead of a security with a nominal value of 1,000 and a term of four years, which is issued today at a price of 800 (resulting in a return of 200), a package of securities, consisting of one paper with a nominal value of 800 and a term of four years, and four additional papers with a nominal value of 50 each and terms of one, two, three, and four years. By repurchasing the papers with the nominal value of 50, the company distributes the return of $4 \times 50 = 200$ across the term rather than repaying the whole nominal value at the end of the term.

128. In principle, financial transactions are regarded as impermissible if they are linked with payments depending on a time factor. Nevertheless, such a dependent relationship can often be assumed, as the nearer one gets to the due date, the more the market price will approach the nominal value under "normal conditions." Moreover, the sale of a security below its nominal value constitutes a purely financial transaction, the advantages of which can hardly be presented as a legitimate profit from trading.

129. We saw earlier how state *sukuk* issues can have a very artificial yield potential.

III. Developments in Law *(Hans-Georg Ebert)*

1. The discussion in this chapter takes account of the conclusions of Konrad Dilger in previous editions. I am grateful to my colleague Professor Dilger.

2. See H. Bobzin, *Der Koran: Eine Einführung* (Munich, 1999), 102–109.

3. H. Motzki, *Die Anfänge der islamischen Jurisprudenz bis zur Mitte des 2./8. Jahrhunderts, Abhandlungen für die Kunde des Morgenlandes*, vol. 50.2 (Stuttgart,

1991), 1–49; in contrast, see J. Schacht, *An Introduction to Islamic Law* (Oxford, 1964), 15–22.

4. T. Nagel, *Das islamische Recht: Eine Einführung* (Westhofen, 2001), 8.

5. A clearly arranged compilation of important *fiqh* works and collections of legal statements (Arab. sing. *fatwa*) is found in O. Spies and E. Pritsch, "Klassisches Islamisches Recht," in *Handbuch der Orientalistik,* supp. vol. 3, *Orientalisches Recht* (Leiden and Cologne, 1964), 237–270.

6. O. Elwan, "Gesetzgebung und Rechtsprechung," in *Grundlagen, Strukturen und Problemfelder,* vol. 1 of *Der Nahe und Mittlere Osten: Politik, Gesellschaft, Wirtschaft, Kultur,* ed. U. Steinbach and R. Robert, with editorial assistance by M. Schmidt-Dumont (Opladen, 1988), 227–228.

7. M. S. W. Hoyle, *Mixed Courts of Egypt* (London, 1991), 12–30.

8. See A. A. A. Fyzee, *Outlines of Muhammadan Law* (Delhi, 1974), 48–64.

9. Schacht, *Introduction,* 2.

10. For details, see *The Encyclopaedia of Islam,* CD-ROM edition version 1.0, vol. 1 (Leiden, 1999), 170a ('ADA).

11. See B. Krawietz, *Hierarchie der Rechtsquellen im tradierten sunnitischen Islam* (Berlin, 2002).

12. See section 4 of this chapter. And see H.-G. Ebert, "Wider die Schließung des 'Tores des ijtihād': Zur Reform der Šarī'a am Beispiel des Familien- und Erbrechts," *Orient* 43 (2002): 367–370.

13. K. Dilger, "Das Schweigen des Gesetzgebers als Mittel der Rechtsfortbildung im Bereich des islamischen Rechts," in *Die islamische Welt zwischen Mittelalter und Neuzeit: Festschrift für H. R. Roemer zum 65. Geburtstag,* ed. U. Haarmann and P. Bachmann (Beirut and Wiesbaden, 1979), 81–93.

14. This epistle is found in the so-called *nahj al-balagha,* a work valued by Sunnis as well, with speeches, letters, and words of wisdom by 'Ali that were recorded later.

15. On the phases of constitutional development in the Arab world, see M. Tworuschka, *Die Rolle des Islams in den arabischen Staatsverfassungen* (Walldorf, 1976), 18–32.

16. Effective in the version of July 28, 1989; see *Kayhan* (Tehran), November 17, 1979, 1–4; *Tehran Times,* August 3, 1989. On the constitution, see A. Schirazi, *The Constitution of Iran: Politics and the State in the Islamic Republic* (London and New York, 1997).

17. H. Baumann and M. Ebert, eds., *Die Verfassungen der Mitgliedsländer der Liga der Arabischen Staaten* (Berlin, 1995); this source does not take into account constitutional amendments or new texts in Algeria (November 28, 1996), Bahrain (February 14, 2002), Yemen (February 20, 2001), Lebanon (October 13, 1998), Qatar (April 29, 2003), Sudan (July 1, 1998, and July 6, 2005), Syria (June 11, 2000), Iraq (October 15, 2005), and Egypt (March 26, 2007). See also H.-G. Ebert, *Die Interdependenz von Staat, Verfassung und Islam im Nahen und Mittleren Osten in der Gegenwart* (Frankfurt am Main, 1991), 97–108. The constitutional texts may be found on the Internet through the link catalogue http://www.islamkatalog.uni-leipzig. de/ (accessed March 26, 2008). On constitutional history, see E. A. von Renesse, W. Krawietz, and C. Bierkämper, *Unvollendete Demokratien: Organisationsformen und Herrschaftsstrukturen in nichtkommunistischen Entwicklungsländern in Asien, Afrika und im Nahen Osten* (Cologne, 1965).

18. One of the five pillars of Pancasila, the Indonesian state ideology, is belief in one God. This can include various monotheistic religions. See Th. Hanstein, *Islamisches Recht und Nationales Recht: Eine Untersuchung zum Einfluß des Islamischen Rechts auf die Entwicklung des modernen Familienrechts am Beispiel Indonesiens,* pt. 1 (Frankfurt am Main, 2002), 86.

19. Under Article 1 of the Sudanese constitution of July 1, 1998, Islam is "the religion of the majority of the population; Christianity and traditional religions enjoy a large following." This wording largely follows prior constitutional documents. The Interim National Constitution of the Republic of the Sudan of July 6, 2005, prescribes in Article 38 that "every person shall have the right to the freedom of religious creed and worship." See M. Böckenförde, "The Sudanese Interim Constitution of 2005: A Model to Establish Coexistence between an Islamic and a Secular Legal Regime," in *Islam and the Rule of Law: Between Sharia and Secularization,* ed. B. Krawietz and H. Reifeld (St. Augustin and Berlin, 2008), 81–90.

20. According to Article 3(1) of the Syrian constitution, Islam is the president's religion.

21. K. Bälz, "Islamisches Recht, Staatliche Rechtsetzung und verfassungsgerichtliche Kontrolle," *Zeitschrift für ausländisches und öffentliches Recht und Völkerrecht* 57 (1997): 233–234.

22. For more, see R. Badry, "Die zeitgenössische Diskussion um den islamischen Beratungsgedanken (*Šūrā*) unter dem besonderen Aspekt ideengeschichtlicher Kontinuitäten und Diskontinuitäten," in *Freiburger Islamstudien,* ed. H. R. Roemer and W. Ende, vol. 19 (Stuttgart, 1998).

23. For details of punishments and crimes, see A. El Baradie, *Gottes-Recht und Menschenrecht: Grundlagenprobleme der islamischen Strafrechtslehre* (Baden-Baden, 1983).

24. See B. Johansen, "Der *'iṣma*-Begriff im hanafitischen Recht," in *Contingency in a Sacred Law: Legal and Ethical Norms in the Muslim Fiqh,* vol. 7 of *Studies in Islamic Law and Society* (Leiden, 1998), 238–262.

25. See B. Johansen, "Eigentum, Familie und Obrigkeit im hanafitischen Strafrecht: Das Verhältnis der privaten Rechte zu den Forderungen der Allgemeinheit in hanafitischen Rechtskommentaren," ibid., 360–367, according to which the starting point for the assessment is the establishment of values for a free person.

26. On this and other Islamic legal concepts, see the concise legal dictionary by S. Abu Jaib, *Al-qamus al-fiqhi: Lughatan wa-l-tilahan* (Damascus, 1988), 250.

27. El Baradie, *Gottes-Recht,* 162.

28. I thank Thoralf Hanstein of Leipzig for this information.

29. N. Gürelli, *The Turkish Criminal Code* (South Hackensack, N.J., 1976).

30. At first with a safeguarding clause favoring Islamic law; see S. Tellenbach, "Strafgesetze der Islamischen Republik Iran," in *Sammlung außerdeutscher Strafgesetzbücher in deutscher Übersetzung,* no. 106 (Berlin and New York, 1996), 3.

31. Published in *Legal Bulletin (Al-waqa'i' al-misriyya),* no. 71, August 5, 1937.

32. For more comprehensive discussion, see Dilger, "Das Schweigen."

33. See Fr. E. Vogel, *Islamic Law and Legal System: Studies in Saudi Arabia* (Leiden, Boston, and Cologne, 2000).

34. B. Botiveau, "Islamiser le droit? L'exemple Égyptien," *Maghreb-Machrek* 126 (1989): 13–14.

35. H.-G., Ebert, "Zur Anwendung der šari'a in Libyen," *Zeitschrift der Deutschen Morgenländischen Gesellschaft* 143 (1993): 366–367; H. Mattes, "Libyen 2002," in *Nahost Jahrbuch 2002: Politik, Wirtschaft und Gesellschaft in Nordafrika und dem Nahen und Mittleren Osten* (Opladen, 2004), 125–126.

36. "The Criminal Act of 1991," *Arab Law Quarterly* 9 (1994): 32–80. See P. Scholz, "Die koranischen Delikte (ḥudūd) im sudanesischen Strafrecht," *Zeitschrift für die gesamte Strafrechtswissenschaft* 112 (2000): 431–460.

37. Tellenbach, "Strafgesetze"; A. Tellenbach, "Neues zum iranischen Strafrecht," *Zeitschrift für Ausländerrecht und Ausländerpolitik* 1 (1998): 38–42.

38. See F. Faqir, "Intrafamily Femicide in Defence of Honour: The Case of Jordan," *Third World Quarterly* 22 (2001): 65–82; S. Tellenbach, "Ehrenmorde an Frauen in der arabischen Welt," *Wuqûf* 13 (2003): 74–89.

39. Comparative statements on the Internet are found at http://gaystation.de/law/asien. html (accessed April 2, 2008).

40. See R. Badry, "Zur 'Mädchenbeschneidung' in islamischen Ländern: Religiös-rechtliche Aspekte und feministische Kritik," *Freiburger Frauen Studien* 2 (1999): 211–232.

41. On conflict of laws in Islamic countries, which is not the subject of this discussion, see the extensive collection of documents in J. Kropholler et al., eds., *Außereuropäische IPR-Gesetze* (Hamburg and Würzburg, 1999).

42. H. Odendahl and C. Rumpf, trans., "Türkei: Das neue Zivilgesetzbuch—Personen-und familienrechtliche Bestimmungen—mit Einführungsgesetz," *Das Standesamt* 4 (2002): 100–122. See http://www.byegm.gov.tr/on-sayfa/new-civil-code.htm (accessed March 26, 2008).

43. A German translation of the Qadri Pasha Codification was made in 1883. Excerpts are found in a revised reprint of the first volume, *Das Eherecht nach der hanafitischen Rechtsschule* (Trebbus, 1997); and A. Bergmann and M. Ferid, *Internationales Ehe-und Kindschaftsrecht,* 19th ed., loose-leaf collection, *Vereinigte Arabische Republik* (VAR)-I, *Egypt* (Frankfurt am Main, 1960), 32–74.

44. On the textual sources of these codes, see H.-G. Ebert, *Das Personalstatut arabi-scher Länder: Problemfelder, Methoden, Perspektiven* (Frankfurt am Main, 1996), 59–88; H.-G. Ebert, *Das Erbrecht arabischer Länder* (Frankfurt am Main, 2004), 29–72. Changes in the "original laws" are also included. A new Moroccan personal status law went into force through Royal Decree No. 1.04.22 of February 3, 2004. Under Decree No. 05-02 of February 27, 2005, the 1984 Algerian family code was reformed. The new personal status law of the UAE is published in *Legal Bulletin* (*Al-jarida al-rasmiyya*) no. 439, November 30, 2005.

45. M. A. R. Taleghany, trans., *The Civil Code of Iran* (London, 1995). On the family law provisions in effect in Iran, see N. Yassari, "Die Brautgabe nach iranischem Recht," *Das Standesamt* 7 (2003): 199.

46. See Fyzee, *Outlines of Muhammadan Law,* 468–484; Th. Koszinowski, and H. Mattes, eds., *Nahost Jahrbuch 1991: Politik, Wirtschaft und Gesellschaft in Nordafrika und dem Nahen und Mittleren Osten* (Opladen, 1992), 129; A. Bergmann and M. Ferid *Internationales Ehe- und Kindschaftsrecht,* 153rd ed., loose-leaf collection, *Pakistan,* ed. A. Weishaupt (Frankfurt am Main, 2003), 1–116.

47. Hanstein, *Islamisches Recht,* pt. 1, 269–327, 365–431, 581–594, 616–683.

48. See Ebert, *Das Personalstatut,* 94–95.

49. For details, see Th. Rauscher *Sharīʿa: Islamisches Familienrecht der Sunna und Shīʿa* (Frankfurt am Main, 1987), 34–39.

50. Y. Courbage, "Péninsule arabique: Les surprises de la démographie," *Maghreb-Machrek* 144 (1994): 9.

51. See *The Encyclopaedia of Islam,* CD-ROM edition, version 1.0, vol. 7, ed. W. Heffening (Leiden, 1999), 757a–759a (MUTʿA).

52. See N. Yassari, "Überblick über das iranische Scheidungsrecht," *Zeitschrift für das gesamte Familienrecht* 16 (2002): 1092–93.

53. To minimize conflicts from the start, the law was included under the rules of proce-dure, although its substantive legal effects are clear. See M. Rohe, "Das neue ägyp-tische Familienrecht: Auf dem Weg zu einem zeitgemäßen Islamischen Recht," *Das Standesamt* 7 (2001): 193–207; H. Denker, "Die Wiedereinführung des *khulʿ* und die Stärkung der Frauenrechte: Eine Studie zur Reform des Personalstatusrechts im islamischen Rechtskreis am Beispiel des ägyptischen Gesetzes Nr. 1 von 2000," in *Beiträge zum Islamischen Recht,* vol. 4, ed. S. Tellenbach and Th. Hanstein, Leipziger Beiträge zur Orientforschung 15 (Frankfurt am Main, 2004), 125–209. The rules in this regard in Jordan and Morocco are based on the Egyptian laws.

54. S. Tellenbach, "Übersichtsbericht Arabische Staaten," in *Schwangerschaftsabbruch im internationalen Vergleich: Rechtliche Regelungen—Soziale Rahmenbedingungen—Empirische Grunddaten,* pt. 2, *Außereuropa,* ed. A. Eser and H.-G. Koch (Baden-Baden, 1989), 125. On the shariʿa law rules in regard to abortion, see A. R. Omran, *Family Planning in the Legacy of Islam* (London and New York, 1992).

55. H. Krüger correctly classified acknowledgment as a "legal concept of a peculiar type" that "not only [has] evidentiary functions…but also [serves] as a basis for legal relationships." H. Krüger,"Anerkenntnis der Vaterschaft im tunesischen Recht," *Das Standesamt* 9 (1977): 247.

56. See A. Rieck, "Die Rolle des Islam bei Eheverträgen mit einem nichtmoslemischen Ehepartner," in *Beiträge zum Islamischen Recht,* ed. H.-G. Ebert, Leipziger Beiträge zur Orientforschung 9 (Frankfurt am Main, 2000), 80–85.

57. Ebert, *Erbrecht arabischer Länder,* 137.

58. On the rules regarding inheritance law, see N. J. Coulson, *Succession in the Muslim Family* (Cambridge, 1971); Ebert, *Erbrecht arabischer Länder;* A. Cilardo, *Dritto ereditario islamico delle scuole giuridiche sunnite* (Rome and Naples, 1994); A. Cilardo, *Diritto ereditario islamico delle scuole giuridiche ismailita e imamita* (Rome and Naples, 1993); P. Scholz, *Internationales Erbrecht: Quellensammlung mit systematischen Darstellungen des materiellen Erbrechts sowie des Kollisionsrechts der wichtigsten Staaten,* loose-leaf collection, ed. H. Dörner and R. Hausmann (Munich), Egypt (as of January 1, 2003), Morocco (as of January 1, 2001), Tunisia (as of January 1, 2002).

59. See N. Barham, "Landfragmentation in Jordanien: Ursachen und Konsequenzen," *Orient* 35 (1994): 273–277.

60. See J. Chr. Wichard, "Zwischen Markt und Moschee. Wirtschaftliche Bedürfnisse und religiöse Anforderungen im frühen islamischen Vertragsrecht," in *Rechts- und Staatswissenschaftliche Veröffentlichungen der Görres-Gesellschaft,* vol. 75 (Paderborn, 1995).

61. For the text in English, see C. R. Tyser, trans., *The Mejelle: Being an English Translation of Majallah el-Ahkam-i-Adliya and a Complete Code on Islamic Civil Law* (Kuala Lumpur, 2001).

62. H. Krüger has presented this theme comprehensively; H. Krüger, "Zum Geltungsbereich der osmanischen Mejelle," in *Liber amicorum Gerhard Kegel* (Munich, 2002), 43–63.

63. See H. Krüger, "Überblick über das Zivilrecht der Staaten des ägyptischen Rechtskreises," *Recht van de Islam* 14 (1997): 67–131.

64. For a list of civil and commercial codes currently in force, see H. Krüger, *Arabische Staaten: Gesetzesübersichten; Internationales und ausländisches Wirtschafts- und Steuerrecht* (Cologne, 1999).

65. Here I follow the views of Dilger in the earlier edition of *Der Islam in der Gegenwart* (1996), 197–200.

66. See H. Krüger, "Vermögensrechtliches Privatrecht und Shariʾa am Beispiel der Vereinigten Arabischen Emirate," *Zeitschrift für Vergleichende Rechtswissenschaft* 97 (1998): 370–380.

67. For more information, see Bälz, "Islamisches Recht"; R. Lohlker, "Schariʾa und Moderne: Diskussionen über Schwangerschaftsabbruch, Versicherung und Zinsen," in *Abhandlungen für die Kunde des Morgenlandes,* vol. 51, no. 3 (Stuttgart, 1996), 47–105.

68. Dilger, *Islam in der Gegenwart,* 199.

69. Krüger, "Vermögensrechtliches Privatrecht," 364–365, 382. On the Islamic prohibition on interest, see H. Krüger *Zum islamischen Zinsverbot in Vergangenheit und*

Gegenwart: Festschrift Rudolf Welser zum 65. Geburtstag, ed. Constanze Fischer-Czernak et al. (Vienna, 2004), 579–595.

70. See the chapters by Johannes Reissner and Volker Nienhaus in this volume.

71. For more information, see Fl. Amereller, *Hintergründe des "Islamic Banking"* (Berlin, 1995); I. N. Dalkusu, *Grundlagen des zinslosen Wirtschaftens: Eigentum, Geld, Riba und Unternehmungsformen nach den Lehren des Islam* (Saint Gall, 1999); C. Mallat, ed., *Islamic Law and Finance* (London, Dordrecht, and Boston, 1988).

72. See K. Bälz, "Islamic Banking," in *Projekte und Projektfinanzierung: Handbuch der Vertragsgestaltung und Risikoabsicherung bei deutschen und internationalen Projekten,* ed. U. R. Siebel (Munich, 2001), 242–250.

73. Ibid.; see also Fr.-R. Grabau, "Der Gesellschaftsvertrag im klassischen Islamrecht und das geltende Gesellschaftsrecht der islamischen Staaten," *Zeitschrift für vergleichende Rechtswissenschaft* 89 (1990): 330–357.

74. S. Hamadeh, "Urheberrecht in Ägypten," in *Beiträge zum Islamischen Recht,* vol. 2, ed. H.-G. Ebert and Th. Hanstein, Leipziger Beiträge zur Orientforschung 12 (Frankfurt am Main, 2003), 137–164; K. Al-Ahmar, "Recent Development in Intellectual Property Laws in Syria," in *Beiträge zum Islamischen Recht,* 2:165–174; Abu-Ghazalah Intellectual Property (TMP Agents), *Intellectual Property Laws of the Arab Countries* (The Hague, London, and Boston, 2000).

75. See M. H. Loutfi, "The Protection of Intellectual Property Rights," in *Beiträge zum Islamischen Recht,* vol. 3, ed. H.-G. Ebert and Th. Hanstein, Leipziger Beiträge zur Orientforschung 13 (Frankfurt am Main, 2003), 205–223.

76. H. Krüger, in particular, has described this problem in numerous publications; see, e.g., H. Krüger, "Rechtliche Aspekte im Geschäftsverkehr mit Partnern im Nahen und Mittleren Osten," in *Recht und Steuern international: Internationales und ausländisches Wirtschafts- und Steuerrecht,* vol. 3 (Cologne, 2001), 47–64; H. Krüger 2003, 52–66; H. Krüger, "Neues Handelsrecht in Ägypten," in *Beiträge zum Islamischen Recht,* ed. H.-G. Ebert, Leipziger Beiträge zur Orientforschung 9 (Frankfurt am Main, 2000), 29–33; S. Saleh, "Commercial Agency and Distributatorship in the Arab Middle East," in *A Study in Shari'a and Statute Law,* vol. 1 (London, Dordrecht, and Boston, 1989).

IV. The Status of Islam and Islamic Law in Selected Countries

1. Turkey *(Ursula Spuler-Stegemann)*

1. Statistical data are not available, but estimates put the number between 15 and 20 percent. For their part, the Alevis cite exaggerated figures of up to 25 million (35 percent).

2. The Anatolian Alevis must be distinguished from the Syrian Alawites, or Nusayris, who also live in the province of Hatay (capital city, Antakya), often under difficult conditions. Hatay was ceded to Turkey in 1939.

3. The German state of Bavaria owns the rights to Hitler's inflammatory work, which is outlawed in Germany. It was able to stop the pirated editions through the Turkish courts.

4. See, for example, J. Keetman, "Appell an den Sozialneid," in the Swiss weekly *Wochenzeitung,* April 14, 2005.

5. J. H. Schoeps, "Der verdrängte Genozid," http://www.d-armenier.de/cms/html/index.php?module=pagesetter&tid=4 (homepage of the Central Council of Armenians in

Germany); the essay by O. Luchterhandt, which is also relevant to the issue of religious freedom for other Christian minorities, "Der türkisch-armenische Konflikt, die Deutschen und Europa," Institut für Friedensforschung und Sicherheitspolitik (*IFSH*) 132 (May 2003), is out of print but available at http://www.ifsh.de/pdf/pub likationen/hb/hb132.pdf (accessed August 2008); R. Hosfeld, *Operation Nemesis: Die Türkei, Deutschland und der Völkermord an den Armeniern* (Cologne, 2005); W. Gust, *Der Völkermord an den Armeniern: Die Tragödie des ältesten Christenvolkes der Welt* (Munich, 1993).

6. See, for example, Ö. Erzeren, "Buchverbrennung in der Türkei: Die Stunde der Nationalisten," *Qantara,* http://www.qantara.de/webcom/show_article.php/_c-468/_nr-317/i.html (accessed August 2008).

7. For instance, when the UN condemned Iran on December 20, 2004, for its human rights violations—including torture, discrimination, and floggings (of children as well as adults)—the Turkish representative left the room before the motion was put to a vote. A large number of concrete examples of human rights violations in Turkey can be cited: the beating of both men and women at an unauthorized women's demonstration on International Women's Day in 2005; the court proceedings initiated afterward; attempts to introduce adultery as a crime, which were thwarted by the EU; virginity tests that must now be applied for at court, with doctors requiring no approval. Many court proceedings continue to be delayed, such as those against the assassin of Hrant Dink and the murderers of Alevis in Sivas and Christians in Malatya. See Amnesty International's 2006 Annual Report.

8. Under the law to reform the penal code, which went into effect in modified form on June 1, 2005, the government still has the power to prohibit unwanted commentary and condemn offenders to long prison sentences.

9. A situation unlikely to be changed by the "Garden of Religions" in Urfa or the presence of the prime minister at the ceremony to lay the foundation stone. See *Milliyet,* May 15, 2005.

10. See also O. Oehring, *Die Türkei im Spannungsfeld extremer Ideologie,* and http:www.missio-aachen.de. On the plight of Christians, see G. Duncker, "Zwischen Konstantinopel und Istanbul," in *Feindbild Christentum im Islam,* ed. U. Spuler-Stegemann (Freiburg, 2004), 75–86.

11. See R. C. Repp, *The Müftü of Istanbul: A Study in the Development of the Ottoman Learned Hierarchy* (Oxford, 1986), xix; also 115f., 120f.

12. Law 3716, which went into effect on May 16, 1991, legalized marriage-like relationships that had produced at least one child (almost exclusively imam marriages). Between that date and December 30, 1993, 67,074 marriages and 239,979 children were registered in civil registry offices. The children's birthdates were recorded as January 1 of the corresponding year. The number of imam marriages that are still unregistered is unknown, but experts assumed that 1 million Turkish women and at most half a million Turkish men were living in polygamous relationships in 2004. Since 1933 the government has regularly passed "amnesty laws" at intervals of about five years.

13. The other state principles set forth in Article 2 of the 1937 constitution are republicanism (*cumhuriyetçilik*), nationalism (*milliyetçilik*), populism (*halkçılık*), statism (*devletçilik*), and "revolutionary reformism" (*inkilapçilik*). They were modified in Article 2 of the 1982 constitution. For a discussion of revolutionary reformism, see E. Hirsch, "Die Verfassung der Türkischen Republik vom 9. November 1982," *Jahrbuch des Öffentlichen Rechts der Gegenwart,* new series 32 (1983): 507–623.

14. See K. Kreiser, "Die Religionspolitik der Türkei im Jahre 1985: Re-Islamisierung—Osmanismus—Özalismus; Beiträge zu einer Begriffsbestimmung," in *Erziehung zur*

Kulturbegegnung: Pädagogische Beiträge zur Kulturbegegnung, vol. 3, ed. J. Lähnemann (Hamburg, 1986), 216–229.

15. The party has had a varied history under the chairmanship of Necmettin Erbakan: the Milli Nizam Partisi (MNP) was banned in 1971, and the MSP was abolished in connection with the military coup on September 12, 1980.

16. Günter Seufert describes the AKP as a "conservative party, but not Islamic" in his article "Das aufgeklärte Antlitz," *ZEITonline,* May 1, 2007.

17. See "Drama mit vertauschten Rollen," *Der Spiegel,* May 7, 2007.

18. David L. Edgerly offers a valuable analysis of the political situation in "Demokraten ohne Volk," *Frankfurter Allgemeine Zeitung,* May 29, 2007.

19. By mid-2009 the case had not yet been ruled on.

20. For a comprehensive discussion of Article 163 and the more moderate Articles 141 and 142, see C. Rumpf, *Laizismus und Religionsfreiheit in der Türkei* (Ebenhausen, 1987), 61. According to leading legal scholars, Turkey still lacks a legal foundation to defend the constitution against Islamists. Turkish branches of terrorist organizations such as Hizbullah, Islamic Jihad, Hizb al-tahrir, and IBDA-C (Islami Büyük Doğu Akincilar Cephesi) recruit members through their own publications (e.g., *Tahkim, Taraf, Selam*) and other Islamist newspapers.

21. See M. Emin Değer, *Bir Cumhurizet Düšmaninin Portresi ya da Fethullah Gülen Hocaefendi'nin Derin Misyonu* (Istanbul, 2000).

22. O. Oehring, *Die Türkei im Spannungsfeld extremer Ideologien* (1984), 13; B. Agai, *Zwischen Netzwerk und Diskurs: Das Bildungsnetzwerk um Fethullah Gülen (geb. 1938); Die flexible Umsetzung modernen islamischen Gedankenguts,* vol. 2 of *Bonner Islamstudien* (Schenefeld, 2000), 246–254. Agai's study is informative, but it ignores central aspects, and the author's sympathy for his subject is all too apparent. He does warn, however, that "instead of searching for Gülen's 'ideology' and 'hidden intentions,' researchers should focus on the way expectations are fulfilled for the individual participants in the different parts of the network with its various types of discourse" (363f.).

23. In April 2005 the German public broadcaster ZDF even signed a cooperation agreement with the Fethullahcı station Samanyolu.

24. Precise information can be found in the 201-page report *Imam-Hatip Liseleri: Efsaneler ve Gercekler* (The İmam-Hatip Secondary Schools: Truth and Myth) by Ruşen Çakır, Irfan Bozan, and Balkan Talu, published June 14, 2004, by TESEV (Turkish Economic and Social Studies Foundation).

25. The graduates of the theological faculties find positions in libraries and the media or work for the religious administration (e.g., as muftis and *vaizes,* that is, preachers at large mosques). With further pedagogical training, they also serve as religion teachers in schools.

26. In *Revisionist Koran Hermeneutics in Contemporary Turkish University Theology* (Würzburg, 2005), F. Körner analyzes the writings of four reform theologians: Mehmet Paçaci, Adil Çiftçi, Ömer Özsoy, and Ilhami Güler.

27. For an assessment of the YÖK by the Islamist Milli Görüş movement, see *Milli Gazete,* May 5, 2005.

28. Books and newspaper articles on the threat posed by Christian missionaries to Turkey are legion. See, for example, the collection of titles by Osman Kılıç, "Sanal Alemden Misyonerlik Bibliografyası," in the thirty-six-page dossier of *Hisar Gazetesi,* February 1, 2005; also Sinasi Gunduz, *Misyonerlik* (Ankara, 2005).

29. Concerning this point, see U. Spuler-Stegemann, "Der Islam in der Türkei," in *Türkei, Südosteuropa-Handbuch* (Göttingen, 1985), 594f.

30. See www.diyanet.gov.tr/turkish/tanitimistatistik.asp, January 27, 2005 (accessed March 15, 2008).

31. As of January 1, 2005.
32. An estimated two years are needed to obtain the Hafiz diploma, which certifies that the bearer has learned the entire Qur'an by heart.
33. See *Birgün,* July 11, 2004. Bardakoğlu justified his stance as follows: "The message of religion never differs for the sexes or for social classes." He referred to the Qur'an, which, he said, first emphasized the "equality" of the sexes fourteen centuries ago. The High Council has even issued a few fatwas on female imams (called "legal opinions" in English);see http://www.diyanet.gov.tr/english/default.asp.
34. Between 1982 and 1984 the Muslim World League paid a monthly sum of $1,100 to the DİB's staff in foreign countries. This was known to the then president of Turkey, Kenan Evren, who played a key role in the 1980 coup d'état that had been staged as a reaction to fundamentalist activities. Uğur Mumcu, editor in chief of *Cumhuriyet,* documented this scandal in *Rabita* (Istanbul, 1994) and paid for this work with his life. See also Hansjörg Schmid, "Auf dem Weg zum Integrationslotsen? Das Rollenverständnis der Imame in Deutschland ändert sich," *Herder-Korrespondenz* 1 (2007); see http://www.schattenblick.de/infopool/religion/islam/risbe059.html (accessed March 15, 2008).
35. Cf. Spuler-Stegemann, "Der Islam in der Türkei," 602f.
36. One example is the Saudi Arabian company Al-Baraka Türk Özel Finans Kurumu, which founded the Bereket Vakfı. With its various goals—building mosques, offering Qur'an courses, and the like—this foundation's basic aim is to Islamify Turkey. Faisal Finans also maintains close business ties with Vakıf Bank. The government has repeatedly used bank secrecy as a pretext for blocking parliamentary inquiries into the capital of non-interest-paying banks. In fact this opens the way for uncontrolled transactions and ties in the business community and for tax-advantaged money laundering.
37. E. Aydın, "Diyanet'i ne yapmalı?" (What Next for the Religious Authority?), *Radikaliki,* March 23, 2003, cited in G. Seufert, "Die AKP—eine islamisch-konservative oder islamistische Partei," http://www.konrad.org.tr/index.php?id=625 (accessed May 8, 2005).
38. See K. Kehl-Bodrogi, "Die 'Wiederfindung' des Alevitentums in der Türkei: Geschichtsmythos und kollektive Identität," *Orient* 34 (1993): 267–282, with bibliography; and G. Väth, "Zur Diskussion über das Alevitentum," *Zeitschrift für Türkeistudien* 6, no. 2 (1993): 213–222.
39. For instance, the 1978 pogroms in Kahramanmaraş, Çorum, and Sivas; the attempted assassination of poet Aziz Nesin in Sivas in 1993, an attack that killed thirty-seven Alevi poets and singers; and the bloody rioting in March 1995, primarily in Istanbul and Ankara.
40. In book form, M. F. Bozkurt, *Das Gebot: Mystischer Weg mit einem Freund* (Hamburg, 1988).
41. There is a great variety of literature available, including Ismail Engin and Havva Engin, eds., *Alevilik* (Istanbul, 2004); and I. Kaplan, *Das Alevitentum: Eine Glaubens- und Lebensgemeinschaft in Deutschland* (Cologne, 2004).
42. For example, in Mersin, where on March 20, 2005, 35,000 Alevis enthusiastically celebrated the opening of the first religious center.
43. K. Yeşilgül, "Laik Cumhuriyet'te zorunlu din derslerinin rolü Eğitim dinselleştirmek" (The Role of Obligatory Religious Instruction in the Secular Republic Is to 'Religionize' Education), *Alevilerin sesi/Die Stimme der Aleviten in Europa* (April 2005): 5–7.
44. See Ismail Kaplan, "Bardakoğlu, der Präsident des Religionsamts in der Türkei behauptet: 'Cem-Haus trennt Aleviten vom Islam,'" April 4, 2008, http://www.alevi.com/pressemeldung+M563594fc76d.html.

2. Iran *(Udo Steinbach)*

1. See the contribution in this book by Werner Ende, "Shiʿi Islam."
2. See also H. R. Roemer, *Persien auf dem Weg in die Neuzeit: Iranische Geschichte von 1350–1750* (Beirut and Stuttgart, 1989).
3. H. Algar, *Religion and State in Iran, 1785–1906* (Berkeley, 1969); H. Busse, "Der persische Staatsgedanke im Wandel der Geschichte," *Saeculum* 28 (1977): 53–74; N. R. Keddie, "Iran: Islam and Revolution," in *Iran in der Krise: Weichenstellungen für die Zukunft* (Bonn, 1980), 37–50.
4. For more on the many factors involved in the Iranian Revolution, see the essays in *Iran in der Krise.*
5. For a short biography of Khomeini, see K.-H. Göbel, *Orient* 19, no. 4 (1978): 10–13; for more extensive depictions, see A. Taheri, *The Spirit of Allah: Khomeini and the Islamic Revolution* (London, 1985); and B. Moin, *Khomeini: Life of the Ayatollah* (London, 1999).
6. For more on these events, see P. Avery, *Modern Iran* (London, 1965), 95–105; N. R. Keddie, *Religion and Rebellion in Iran: The Tobacco Protest of 1891–1892* (London, 1966); A. K. S. Lambton, "The Tobacco Regie: Prelude to Revolution," *Studia Islamica* 22 (1965): 119–157, and 23 (1965): 71–91. See also M. Gronke, *Iran: A Short History* (Princeton, 2007); and H. Halm, *The Shiites: A Short History* (Princeton, 2007).
7. P. Avery, *Modern Iran* (New York, 1965), 106–139; for another great read, see E. G. Browne, *The Persian Revolution of 1905–1909* (Cambridge, 1910).
8. See S. Akhavi, *Religion and Politics in Contemporary Iran: Clergy-State Relations in the Pahlavi Period* (Albany, N.Y., 1980), 15–16.
9. Ibid., 25–32.
10. Y. Richard, "Ayatollah Kashani: Ein Wegbereiter der Islamischen Republik?" in *Religion und Politik im Iran: mardom nameh; Jahrbuch zur Geschichte und Gesellschaft des Mittleren Orients* (Frankfurt am Main, 1981), 277–305; W. Floor, "Iranische Geistliche als Revolutionäre: Wunschdenken oder Wirklichkeit?" ibid., 306–336.
11. A. K. S. Lambton, *The Persian Land Reform, 1962–1966* (Oxford, 1969); H. Algar, "The Oppositional Role of the Ulama in Twentieth-Century Iran," in *Scholars, Saints, and Sufis,* ed. N. R. Keddie (Berkeley, 1972), 231–55.
12. Akhavi, *Religion),* 91–116.
13. Ibid., 117–29; see also D. Brumberg, *Reinventing Khomeini: The Struggle for Reform in Iran* (Chicago, 2001), 55–97.
14. R. Khomeini, *Islam and Revolution,* trans. Hamid Algar (Berkeley, 1981). For more background information, see also Werner Ende's chapter "Shiʿi Islam" in this volume; for more on Khomeini's ideas in the context of the time, see K.-H. Göbel, *Moderne schiitische Politik und Staatsidee* (Opladen, 1984); see also N. Calder, "Accommodation and Revolution in Imami Shiʿi Jurisprudence: Khumayni and the Classical Tradition," *Middle Eastern Studies* 18, no. 1 (1982): 3–20.
15. For a very knowledgeable and lively description of instruction at a madrasa in contemporary Iran, see M. M. J. Fischer, *Iran: From Religious Dispute to Revolution* (Cambridge, Mass., 1980), 61–103; R. Mottahedeh, *The Mantle of the Prophet: Religion and Politics in Iran* (New York, 1985).
16. N. R. Keddie, "The Roots of the Ulama's Power in Modern Iran," *Studia Islamica* 29 (1963): 31–53; see also M. Naficy, *Klerus, Basar und die iranische Revolution* (Hamburg, 1993).
17. Fischer, *Iran,* 104–135.
18. Akhavi, *Religion,* 23.

19. For books by the shah, see Mohammad Reza Pahlavi, *Mission for My Country* (London, 1961), and *Answer to History* (New York, 1980).

20. For more on the developments of the Iranian Revolution with regard to this, see Fischer, *Iran,* 181–231.

21. For a typical critique of Westernization from a religious standpoint, see A. Falaturi, "Die iranische Gesellschaft unter dem Einfluss der westlichen Kultur," in *Iran in der Krise,* 51–75.

22. For more details, see Fischer, *Iran,* 213ff. For an in-depth study of these developments, see S. Bakhash, *The Reign of the Ayatollahs: Iran and the Islamic Revolution* (New York, 1984). Also informative is S. Zabih, *Iran Since the Revolution* (London, 1982).

23. U. Steinbach, "Die Entwicklung des politischen Systems in Iran seit der Revolution," in *Iran in der Krise,* 105–118; idem, "Iran: Halbzeit der islamischen Revolution?" *Außenpolitik* 31, no. 1 (1980): 52–69; S. Bakhash, *Reign* (1984), 52–70; G. Thoß and H.-H. Richter, *Ayatollah Khomeini: Zur Biographie und Hagiographie eines islamischen Revolutionsführers* (Münster, 1991); see also D. Brumberg, *Reinventing Khomeini* (2001), 98ff.

24. S. Bakhash, *Reign* (1984), 71–91; for a very extensive work, see S. Tellenbach, *Untersuchungen zur Verfassung der Islamischen Republik Iran vom 15. November 1979* (Berlin, 1985); for a more critical analysis, see A. Schirazi, *The Constitution of Iran: Politics and the State in the Islamic Republic* (London and New York, 1997).

25. M. Milani, "Shi'ism and the State in the Constitution of the Islamic Republic of Iran," in *Iran: Political Culture in the Islamic Republic,* ed. S. K. Farsoun (London, 1992), 133–59.

26. For more recent developments, see A. K. Moussavi, "A New Interpretation of the Theory of 'vilayat-i faqih,'" *Middle Eastern Studies* 28, no. 1 (January 1992): 101–107.

27. See S. Tellenbach, "Zur Änderung der Verfassung der Islamischen Republik Iran vom 28. Juli 1989," *Orient* 31, no. 1 (1990): 45–66; and A. Schirazi, "Die neuere Entwicklung der Verfassung in der Islamischen Republik Iran," *Verfassung und Recht in Übersee* 24, no. 2 (1991): 105–122.

28. For more about these events, see *Iran Press Digest* 7 nos. 48, 50, 80, and 81 (1994); and W. Buchta, "Die Islamische Republik Iran und die religiös-politische Kontroverse um die *marja'iyyat, Orient* 36, no. 3 (1995): 449–474.

29. On the politicization of the pilgrimage, see M. Glünz, "Das Manifest der Islamischen Revolution: Ayatollah Khomeinis Botschaft an die Mekkapilger des Jahres 1407/1987," *Die Welt des Islams* 33 (1993): 235–255.

30. See *Yearbook Iran* (Bonn, 1988), 116–119. This work also contains very useful information on the geography, politics, society, and economy of the Islamic Republic.

31. S. Tellenbach, "Zur Re-Islamisierung des Strafrechts in Iran," *Zeitschrift für die gesamte Strafrechtswissenschaft* 101, no. 1 (1989): 188–205; and see *Yearbook Iran,* 92–107. I thank Nadjma Yassari from the Max Planck Institute for Comparative and International Private Law in Hamburg for her assistance in formulating a number of the passages on the legal system.

32. N. Ramazani, "Women in Iran: The Revolutionary Ebb and Flow," *Middle East Journal* 47, no. 3 (Summer 1993): 409–428.

33. See the contributions in this book by J. Reissner, "The Intra-Islamic Discussion on a Modern Economic and Social System," and V. Nienhaus, "Islamic Economics in Practice: Interest-Free Financial Management." See also A.-H. Banisadr and P. Vieille, *Quelle révolution pour l'Iran?* (Paris, 1980); V. Nienhaus, "Islamische Ökonomik: Entwicklungen, Inhalte und Probleme," *Zeitschrift für Wirtschaftspolitik* 30, no. 3

(1981): 245–300; as well as V. Nienhaus, *Literature on Islamic Economics in English and German* (Cologne, 1982); and A. Rieck, *Unsere Wirtschaft: Eine gekürzte, kommentierte Übersetzung des Buches Iqtisaduna by Muhammad Baqir as-Sadr* (Berlin, 1984).

34. A. Schirazi, *The Problem of Land Reform in the Islamic Republic of Iran: Complications and Consequences of an Islamic Reform Policy* (Berlin, 1987); and idem, *Texte zur Agrargesetzgebung in der Islamischen Republik Iran* (Berlin, 1988). See also S. Bakhash, "The Politics of Land, Law, and Social Justice in Iran," *Middle East Journal* 43, no. 2 (Spring 1989): 186–201; A. A. Kiafar, "Urban Land Policies in Post-Revolutionary Iran," in *Modern Absolutism and Islamic Ideology in Iran,* ed. C. Bina (London, 1992).

35. D. Menashri, *The Iranian Revolution and the Muslim World* (Boulder, Colo., 1992).

36. For an in-depth analysis, see A. Rieck, *Die Schiiten und der Kampf um den Libanon: Politische Chronik 1958–1988* (Hamburg, 1989); for more on the ideological dimensions, see C. Mallat, *Shi'i Thought from the South of Lebanon* (Oxford, 1988); A. A. Khalil, "Ideology and Practice of Hizballah in Lebanon," *Middle Eastern Studies* 27, no. 3 (1991); A. R. Norton, *Amal and the Shi'a: Struggle for the Soul of Lebanon* (Austin, Tex., 1987).

37. Summary of World Broadcasts (SWB)/Middle East/0210/A/2ff. (July 22, 1988).

38. For more on the edict, see SWB/ME/0385/A/2 (February 15, 1989); see also H. Busse, "Salman Rushdie und der Islam," *Geschichte in Wissenschaft und Unterricht* 4 (1990): 193–215. For more on the political backdrop in Iran and the international response to it, see R. Schulze, "The Forgotten Honor of Islam," and M. Kramer, "The Invasion of Islam," in *Middle East Contemporary Survey,* ed. A. Ayalon, vol. 13 (Boulder, Colo., 1989), 173–180, and vol. 14 (1990), 177–180, respectively.

39. See also N. R. Keddie and E. Hooglund, eds., *The Iranian Revolution and the Islamic Republic* (Syracuse, N.Y., 1986), 67–90.

40. U. Steinbach, "Die 'zweite Islamische Revolution': Der Gottesstaat auf dem Weg in die Normalität," *Außenpolitik* 41, no. 1 (1990): 73–90; M. Kamrava, "The Civil Society Discourse in Iran," *British Journal of Middle Eastern Studies* 28, no. 2 (2001): 165–185; A. Gheissari, "Iran's Democracy Debate," *Middle East Policy* 11 (2004): 94–106; W. Buchta, "Fundamentalkritik von Radikalreformern in Iran," in *Politische und gesellschaftliche Debatten in Nordafrika, Nah- und Mittelost,* ed. S. Faath (Hamburg, 2004), 241–244.

41. For more comprehensive information, see W. Buchta, *Who Rules Iran? The Structure of Power in the Islamic Republic* (Washington, D.C., 2000). I owe many of the details discussed here to this source as well as to an essay by the same author, "Ideologische Fraktionen in Irans Machtelite: Reformer vs. Konservative," *Orient-Journal* 5, no. 1 (Spring 2004): 10–11.

42. See the chapter "Iran," in *Nahost Jahrbuch: Politik, Wirtschaft und Gesellschaft in Nordafrika und dem Nahen und Mittleren Osten,* ed. T. Koszinowski and H. Mattes (Opladen, 1996–2004); and M. P. Amineh, "Demokratisierung und ihre Feinde im Iran," *Aus Politik und Zeitgeschichte* 9 (February 2004): 25–28; as well K. Amirpur, "Gibt es in Iran noch einen Reformprozess?" 18–24 in the same issue of *Aus Politik und Zeitgeschichte.*

43. For a concise evaluation, see W. Buchta, "Ein Vierteljahrhundert Islamische Republik Iran: Eine vorläufige Bilanz," *Aus Politik und Zeitgeschichte* 9 (February 2004): 6–17.

44. See also N. Kermani, *Die Revolution der Kinder* (Munich, 2001).

3. Afghanistan *(Abbas Poya)*

1. Sistan included large parts of the modern Afghan provinces of Nimruz, Helmand, and Farah, along with the east Iranian area of the same name.

2. Khurasan covered various territories, including the modern Afghan regions of Herat, Badghis, Faryab, and Balkh.

3. See H. Brechna, *Die Geschichte Afghanistans: Das historische Umfeld Afghanistans über 1500 Jahre* (Zurich, 2005), 33–35.

4. See C. Schetter, *Kleine Geschichte Afghanistans* (Munich, 2004), 29–36.

5. This Kharijite movement contributed to unrest in the region and ultimately to Abu Muslim's uprising (747), which then led to the victory of the Abbasid dynasty. See W. Kraus, ed., *Afghanistan: Natur, Geschichte und Kultur, Staat, Gesellschaft und Wirtschaft* (Tübingen and Basel, 1972), 113.

6. On the history of Afghanistan from Islamization to the Durrani dynasty, see L. Dupree, *Afghanistan* (Princeton, 1980), 312–334.

7. Whereas Western scholars are skeptical about tracing the history of modern Afghanistan back to ancient Aryana, Afghan authors assume a continuity of Afghan history from ancient Aryana to Khorasan to the present state of Afghanistan. There is also controversy over the question of when to date the beginnings of the Afghan nation-state. See C. Schetter, *Ethnizität und ethnische Konflikte in Afghanistan* (Berlin, 2003), 163ff.

8. The term *baba* applied to Ahmad Shah Durrani was not an official title. He is still referred to—at least by Pashtuns—as Ahmad Shah Baba out of respect for his achievements as the founder of the Afghan state. The title *baba-i millat* was officially bestowed on Zahir Shah, however, in return for renouncing the throne.

9. See M. Gh. Ghubar, *Afghanistan dar masir-i tarikh* (Qom, 1980), 647.

10. As in all other historically significant situations in Afghanistan, the Pashtuns played a key role in this rebellion and in King Amanullah's downfall. Amanullah's reform plans promoted the interests of other religious and ethnic minorities. It was Pashtun Sunni *'ulama'* who first called for the population to rise up against Amanullah's anti-Islamic modernization. The other ethnic groups were then drawn into the rebellion. See M. N. Shahrani, "State Building and Social Fragmentation in Afghanistan: A Historical Perspective," in *The State, Religion, and Ethnic Politics: Afghanistan, Iran, and Pakistan*, ed. A. Banuazizi and M. Weiner (Syracuse, N.Y., 1986), 45–50.

11. The differences not only were ideological in nature but also were due to ethnic and social divides. Whereas the Khalq wing mainly recruited its members from among the Pashtun migrants coming to study in Kabul from the rural interior areas of south and east Afghanistan, the majority of members of the Parčam wing were originally from Kabul and the other cities, and had good connections to the traditional establishment for family and professional reasons. The social and ethnic differences had led to a divide within the PDPA on a previous occasion. Tahir Badakhshi, a Shi'i Tajik and member of the PDPA central committee, finding that the power structure was dominated by Pashtuns, left the party in 1978 and formed his own party under the provocative name National Oppression *(sitam-i milli)*. The party's membership consisted almost exclusively of Tajiks and Uzbeks and a small number of Hazaras. Badakhshi founded the party on a platform of equal rights for all ethnic groups. The PDPA government had him executed in prison on December 6, 1979. See M. H. Kakar, *Afghanistan: The Soviet Invasion and the Afghan Response, 1979–1982* (Berkeley, 1997), 56ff.; Sh. N. Haqshinas, *Dasayis wa jinayat-i rus dar afghanistan* (Tehran, 1984), 314.

12. For some time there were groups within the resistance movements that did not have Islamist goals. In the initial phase of the resistance, the left-wing Sitam-i milli group fought the central government in Panjshir. The group, however, was quickly crushed between the state troops and the Jam'iyyat-i islami mujahidin. Among the Shi'a resistance groups was the organization Mujahidin-i khalq, which had Islamic-socialist motivations. Similarly to its namesake in Iran, it had strictly organized cadres and recruited its membership among school and university students. When the Mujahidin-i khalq was persecuted and declared anti-Islamic in the Islamic Republic of Iran, the Afghan group of the same name and convictions had to change its name to Mujahidin-i mustaz'afin. It was particularly active in Bamiyan, in the center of the Shi'a Hazara region, later joining the *Hizb-i wahdat,* in which it no longer played a significant role.

13. This Islamist movement was Sunni influenced, although it had a small number of Shi'a members. Shi'a Islamism did not emerge until 1979, with the formation of autonomous Shi'a resistance parties, which had strong ideological and financial links to the Islamic state in Iran. The charismatic Shi'a preacher Saiyid Isma'il Balkhi had called for his followers to build an Islamic society as early as the 1950s, undertaking initiatives in this direction. His efforts were, however, more traditionally religious in character than Islamist. He was accused of planning a coup with his accomplices and was imprisoned from 1950 to 1964. He later died, allegedly owing to the consequences of his imprisonment, but Balkhi's charismatic aura outlived him. He remains an important figure for the Shi'a population to the present day, referred to as the founder of the Shi'a Islamist movement in Afghanistan. See Mu'assisa-i farhangi-yi thaqalain, ed., *Afghanistan dar sih daha-i akhir* (Qom, 2002), 92–96.

14. The term "fratricidal war" is particularly used in conjunction with the events of the nineteenth century. At that time, not only were decade-long wars over the throne waged between the two Pashtun clans of the Saduzai and Muhammadzai, but also the country was confronted by the Sikh uprisings taking place under Randjit Singh (1801–1839). In this period the Afghans had to defend themselves against invasions by British India on two occasions (1839–1842 and 1878–1880). See C. Schetter, *Ethnizität und ethnische Konflikte in Afghanistan* (Berlin, 2003), 452ff.

15. See P. Heine, *Terror in Allahs Namen: Extremistische Kräfte im Islam* (Freiburg, 2004), 115.

16. The Indian Islamic reform movement Deobandi, which arose in the second half of the nineteenth century, represents a strict form of Islam based on the text of the Qur'an and the tradition of the Prophet, and rejecting any form of folk Islam.

17. Pashtunwali is an oral tradition of norms and values to which the Pashtuns are required to adhere. The individual content therefore varies among the clans. These tribal codes of honor and morals include values such as *nang/namus* (honor), *nanawat* (protection of the weaker), and *turah* (bravery). See Schetter, *Ethnizität und ethnische Konflikte in Afghanistan* 137–143.

18. In Persian, the term *atba'* means both citizens and subjects. This term has been used in all previous Afghan constitutional texts, including the constitution of the Islamic Republic of Afghanistan, to refer to Afghan citizens. There has been a general refusal to use the accepted term for citizens in modern Iranian Persian, *shahrwand* (pl. *shahrwandan*). The use of this old and certainly ambiguous term led to controversial discussions in the debate on the 2004 constitution.

19. The constitution stipulated that a law regarding political parties was to be prepared and sent to parliament for approval. This important step toward parliamentary democracy was undertaken only very haltingly, however. The act in question was not passed and presented to the king until 1968. The king failed to ratify the act before

he was finally toppled in 1973. See G. Moltmann, "Staats- und Verfassungsentwicklung Afghanistans," in *Afghanistan seit dem Sturz der Monarchie: Dokumentation
zur Politik, Wirtschaft und Bevölkerung,* ed. M. D. Ahmad, E. Franz, and M. Weidenhiller (Hamburg, 1981), 12.

20. For a detailed study of the constitution of the Islamic Republic of Afghanistan, see
A. Poya, "Perspektiven zivilgesellschaftlicher Strukturen in Afghanistan: Ethische
Neutralität, ethnische Parität und Frauenrechte in der Verfassung der Islamischen
Republik Afghanistan," *Orient* 44 (2003): 367–384; and G. Gerber, *Die neue Verfas-
sung Afghanistans: Verfassungstradition und politischer Prozess* (Berlin, 2007).

4. Russia, the Islamic Republics of the Caucasus, and Central Asia
(Rainer Freitag-Wirmingshaus)

1. See B. Fragner, "Der Islam in Zentralasien: Viel mehr als eine Religion," in *Zentralasien und Islam, Mitteilungen,* vol. 63, ed. A. Strasser et al. (Hamburg: Deutsches
Orient-Institut, 2003), 21–29.
2. The approximately 300,000 to 400,000 Ismailites of the Pamir are viewed as heretics
and are considered relatively secular.
3. In 1922 they were occasionally reintroduced under Soviet leadership.
4. O. Roy, *The New Central Asia: The Creation of Nations* (New York, 2000), 150.
5. A. Rashid, *Jihad: The Rise of Militant Islam in Central Asia* (New York, 2003), 40.
6. Y. Ro'i, "The Secularization of Islam and the USSR's Muslim Areas," in *Muslim
Eurasia: Conflicting Legacies,* ed. Y. Ro'i (London, 1995), 13.
7. On Sufism in the Soviet Union, see A. Bennigsen and S. E. Wimbush, *Muslims of the
Soviet Empire: A Guide* (Bloomington, 1986), 157f.
8. Originally from the Turkish word for "oppressor." The rebellions of the *basmachi*
began at the time of World War I and were not finally suppressed until the 1930s. On
the history of the Naqshbandiyya in Central Asia, see E. Özdalga, ed., *Naqshbandis
in Western and Central Asia: Change and Continuity* (Istanbul, 1997).
9. *Yeni Şafak,* October 10, 1995. See also U. Halbach, *Islam im nachsowjetischen
Zentralasien: Eine Wiedergeburt?* in Strasser et al., *Zentralasien und Islam,* 9–20.
10. International Crisis Group (ICG), *Is Radical Islam Inevitable in Central Asia? Priorities for Engagement,* Asia Report no. 72 (Osh and Brussels, 2003), 4.
11. S. Akiner, "Islam in Post-Soviet Central Asia: Contested Territory," in Strasser et al.,
Zentralasien und Islam, 78.
12. Rashid, *Jihad,* 129.
13. This is not true of all regions. In the Fergana Valley the number of mosque attendees
continued to rise, especially among young men. See the section of this chapter titled
"Islamist Organizations in Central Asia."
14. T. Faradov, "Religiosity in Post-Soviet Azerbaijan: A Sociological Survey," International
Institute for the Study of Islam in the Modern World (ISIM), *Newsletter* (2001): 28.
15. T. Swietochowski, "Azerbaijan: The Hidden Faces of Islam," *World Policy Journal*
19 (Fall 2002).
16. I. Husseinova, "Azerbaijani Muslims Lose Faith," Institute for War and Peace Reporting, *Caucasus Reporting Service* 27 (1999).
17. R. Motika, "Islam in Post-Soviet Azerbaijan," *Archives de Sciences Sociales des Religions* (2001): 115 (July–September, 2001): 111–124.
18. As always, figures vary.
19. The authorities also see a danger in so-called Wahhabism, which has adherents especially in the north, among the Lezgins. The adherents of Wahhabism are estimated

to number approximately seven thousand. In connection with September 11, 2001, there was considerable speculation about connections between Islamic organizations and al-Qaʻida.

20. See Motika, "Islam in Post-Soviet Azerbaijan"; R. Motika, "Das Religionsrecht in Aserbaidschan," in *Das Recht der Religionsgemeinschaften in Mittel-, Ost- und Südosteuropa,* ed. W. Lienemann and H. R. Reuter (Baden-Baden, 2005), 75–103. On Fethullahçı's influence in Central Asia, see Bayram Balci, "Fethullah Gülen's Missionary Schools in Central Asia and Their Role in the Spreading of Turkism and Islam," *Religion, State, and Society* 31, no. 2 (2003).

21. See Halbach, *Islam im nachsowjetischen Zentralasien,* 29.

22. In Dagestan the number of mosques rose at the dissolution of the Soviet Union from 18 to some 1,500; in Tatarstan, it rose from 18 to around 1,000. Ibid., 31, 42.

23. In connection with the increasing Islamization of the Chechnya conflict, Uwe Halbach speaks of a Chechenization of Russian perceptions of Islam. Ibid., 6.

24. See M. Atkin, "The Rhetoric of Islamophobia," *Central Asia and the Caucasus* 1 (2000): 123–132.

25. A. Malashenko, "Islam and Politics in Russia in the 1990s," in *Islam in Politics in Russia and Central Asia,* ed. S. A. Dudoignon and H. Komatsu (London, 2001), 308. On Islam in Russia, see also A. Malashenko, "Does Islamic Fundamentalism Exist in Russia?" in Roʼi, *Muslim Eurasia;* A. Malashenko, *Islamkoe vozrozdenie v sovremennoj Rossii* (Moscow: Moskovskiy Tsentr Karnegi, 1998); U. Halbach, "Rußlands muslimische Ethnien und Nachbarn," *Aus Politik und Zeitgeschichte* B 16–17 (2003): 39–46.

26. See B. Mirkasymov, "Salafism in Central Asia and the Northern Caucasus," *Central Asia and the Caucasus* 3, no. 21 (2003): 35–43.

27. S. Akiner, *The Formation of Kazakh Identity* (London: Royal Institute of International Affairs, 1995), 90.

28. See Mirkasymov, "Salafism in Central Asia and the Northern Caucasus." On the Salafi reform movement of the early twentieth century, see *Encyclopedia of Islam,* 2nd ed., vol. 8 (Leiden, 1995), 900–909.

29. See V. Naumkin, "Militant Islam in Central Asia: The Case of the Islamic Movement of Uzbekistan," paper for Berkeley Program in Soviet and Post-Soviet Studies, 2003; Rashid, *Jihad,* 97.

30. A fifth of the population is said to advocate this. See ICG, *Is Radical Islam Inevitable?* 14.

31. On the problem of the use of the term "Wahhabism" as an analytical and rhetorical concept in Russian media and literature, see A. Knysh, "A Clear and Present Danger: 'Wahhabism' as Rhetorical Foil," *Die Welt des Islams* 44 (2004): 3–26.

32. See Naumkin, "Militant Islam."

33. In Dagestan, too, a number of communities organized their court systems on the basis of shariʻa after 1997. They explained this by referring to the corruption of the local authorities.

34. According to a study by the Carnegie Institute in Moscow in 2002, the proportion of Islamists or Wahhabists in the Muslim population of the region is only between 5 and 20 percent. A. Malashenko and D. Trenin, *Vremja Juga: Rossija v Čečne. Čečnja v Rossii* (Moscow: Gendalʼf, 2002), 87. See Halbach, "Russlands muslimische Ethnien," 35.

35. See A. Seifert, *Der islamische Faktor und die Stabilitätsstrategie der OSZE in ihrer euro-asiatischen Region,* Zentrum für OSZE-Forschung (CORE), Institut für Friedensforschung und Sicherheitspolitik, Working Paper 4 (Hamburg, 2001).

36. This support came from Uzbeks who had emigrated to Saudi Arabia after the *bas-machi* rebellion. Rashid, *Jihad,* 141.
37. Naumkin, *Militant Islam.*
38. According to Uzbek government officials, the movement was brought to Uzbekistan by a Jordanian in 1995. Rashid, *Jihad,* 120.
39. It was established by Sheykh Taqi al-Din al-Nabhani (1909–1977) in the part of Je-rusalem controlled at the time by Jordan. See *Encyclopedia of Islam,* 2nd ed., vol. 10 (Leiden, 1965), 133. The organization had some influence in Jordan, the West Bank, and Beirut. See International Crisis Group, *Radical Islam in Central Asia: Respond-ing to Hizb ut-Tahrir,* ICG Asia Report no. 58 (Osh and Brussels: International Crisis Group, 2003), 17.
40. The party was banned in Germany in January 2003 because of anti-Israeli propa-ganda, not because of terrorist connections.
41. International Crisis Group, *Radical Islam in Central Asia,* 10.
42. After September 11, 2001, it was claimed that the United States had declared war on the entire *umma* and was reaching for Central Asia.
43. The Uzbek leadership attempted to hold HT responsible for bloody attacks in Tash-kent and Bukhara in spring and summer 2004. It was said to have contacts with al-Qaʿida. In the opinion of human rights organizations, this is propaganda. Olivier Roy believes the attacks were carried out by family networks. O. Roy, "Eurasia In-sight: Expert: U.S. Failure to Comprehend Islamic Radical Motivations Undermines Democratization Hopes for Middle East," *Central Asia,* May 13, 2004.
44. O. Roy, "Changing Patterns among Radical Islamic Movements," *Brown Journal of World Affairs* (Winter–Spring 1999). See also Roy, *The New Central Asia.*
45. In 2003 there were approximately six thousand religious prisoners. International Crisis Group, *Central Asia: Islam and the State,* ICG Asia Report no. 59 (Osh and Brussels: International Crisis Group, 2003), i.
46. All mosques are now subordinate to the Spiritual Leadership. According to the committee, only 410 of 2,000 religious organizations in the country were regis-tered, including subversive organizations that were financed by Iran or Arab coun-tries. Some five thousand to six thousand people have converted to Christianity (Protestant denominations, Adventists, Jehovah's Witnesses), Hinduism, or Bahai, which is apparently interpreted as subversive. Twenty-two religious schools fi-nanced by Iran have been closed in the meantime. Activities of foreign missionaries have been forbidden since 1996. See "Azerbaijan Moves to Impose Tighter Con-trol over Religious Organizations," *Radio Free Europe/Radio Liberty Caucasus Report,* August 16, 2001. Madrasas are also subject to compulsory registration. On the committee and state religious policy, see Motika, "Das Religionsrecht in Aserbaidschan."
47. In 1992, 1993, and after 1997, President Karimov had hundreds of ordinary Mus-lims arrested for supposed connections to Islamists and prosecuted as Wahhabis, closed mosques, and drove mullas into exile or "disappeared" them. Bombings in Tashkent in February 1999 aimed at Karimov were used by the government as a pre-text to eliminate not only thousands of oppositional Muslims but also the opposition as a whole.
48. On the Islam policies of Central Asian countries, see ICG, *Central Asia.*

5. The People's Republic of China *(Thomas Heberer)*

1. See D. C. Gladney (1996). A more complete overview of the ethnic groups in Xin-jiang can be found in T. Hoppe (1995).

2. H. Y. Chang (1981), 31. Some sources claim that an uncle of Muhammad, Sa'd Ibn Abi Waqqas, carried out this mission. As is the case with many other stories about Sa'd, this is a legend.
3. J. N. Lipman (1997), 107ff.; F. Aubin (2003), 351f.
4. R. Israeli (1984), 275f.
5. M. Hartmann (1913), 183.
6. J. N. Lipman (1984), 251ff.
7. L. J. Newby (1988), 927.
8. Compare ibid., 934.
9. Compare D. C. Gladney (1987), 502.
10. Compare R. Israeli (1984), 298f.
11. Here the term *"qubba* cult" refers to honoring dead leaders of Sufi orders with folkloric practices. The name is derived from the Arabic word for "dome," *qubba*.
12. R. Israeli (1984), 257f.
13. J. M. H. Lindbeck (1950), 480.
14. For more on the different sects and sub-sects, see D. C. Gladney (1987), 502ff.; S. Iwamura (1948), 42ff.; and J. N. Lipman (1984), 257ff.
15. Also compare D. C. Gladney (1987), 502f.
16. A reference to this effect is also made in T. Hoppe (1995), 362.
17. A dance performed by the dervishes in which the dancer sways his torso back and forth and recites short verses from the Qur'an until he goes into a trance.
18. Also compare J. Wang (2003), 230.
19. Compare H. Ziemann (1984) and L. Benson (1990).
20. *Xinjiang Ribao* (Xinjiang daily newspaper), January 16, 1998, and January 22, 1999.
21. L. Wang, "Zai dang de minzu quyu zizhi zhengce yinxia jianshe jinrong, fuyu, wenming de Xinjiang" (Building for the Nationalities a Blossoming, Prosperous, Civilized Xinjiang under the Direction of the Party's Policy for Territorial Autonomy), *Qiushi* (Truth) 19 (1995): 31. The causes for the separatist movements in Xinjiang are analyzed by C. Mackerras (2001).
22. Also compare M. Winchester (1997). T. Razak, "Gaoju minzu tuanjie he zuguo tongyi de qizhi shenru chijiude kaizhan fan fenlie douzheng" (Flying and Deepening the Banner of Ethnic Solidarity and the Unity of the Fatherland, Unfurl the Long-Term Fight against Separatism), *Xinjiang Shehui Kexue* 2 (2002): 51–59, reports more than two hundred "violent acts of terrorism by East Turkistan terrorists" between 1990 and 2001, with 162 deaths and 440 people injured.
23. For more detailed information, see *China aktuell* 12 (2003): 1442–1444.
24. Compare *China aktuell* (March 2003): 287f.
25. S. Dongsheng, "Yao qieshi zhongshi dui qing shaonian fandui minzu fenliezhuyi de jiaoyu" (One Must Pay Diligent Attention to the Education of Young People to Fight Ethnic Separatism), *Xinjiang Shehui Jingji* (Society and Economy of Xinjiang) 4 (1992): 94.
26. There is a corresponding development taking place in the Hui territories; compare D. C. Gladney (1996), 160ff.
27. X. Xu, "Guanyu Xinjiang minzu fenliezhuyi wenti de shehuixue sikao" (Sociological Contemplations on the Problem of Separatism in Xinjiang), *Xinjiang Daxue Xuebao* 2 (1992): 15ff.
28. Also compare J. Wang (2003), 228.
29. Further examples can be found in E. Allès (2003).
30. Compare the translation by B. Staiger (1991), 12f.
31. Ibid., 13 and 14.

32. D. E. MacInnis (1989), 256.
33. Q. Long, "Lun zongjiao dui Xinjiang jingji fazhan de yingxiang" (The Influence of Religion on the Economic Development of Xinjiang), *Xinjiang Shehui Kexue* (Social Sciences of Xinjiang) 7 (2003): 74ff.
34. B. L. K. Pillsbury (1981b), 51.
35. Ibid., 50.
36. Compare D. C. Gladney (1994).
37. R. C. Bush (1970), 294.
38. L. Wang (1995), 31.
39. Compare the report by the State Council on the ties between "terrorists" from Xinjiang and Osama bin Laden in *China aktuell* (January 2002): 12–13.

6. India *(Munir D. Ahmed)*

1. See K. S. Lal, *Growth of Muslim Population in Medieval India: A.D. 1000–1800* (Delhi, 1973); idem, *Indian Muslims: Who Are They?* (New Delhi, 1993); Kh. Z. Amani and L. Siddiqui, "Trend of Growth of Muslim Population in India, 1951, 1991," *Asian Profile* 27, no. 5 (Hong Kong, October 1999): 409–426.
2. I. Ahmad, *Caste and Social Stratification among the Muslims* (New Delhi, 1973); S. P. Jain, *The Social Structure of Hindu-Muslim Community* (Delhi, 1975).
3. Y. Friedmann, "The Attitude of the Jamʿiyyat al-ʿulamāʾ-i Hind to the Indian National Movement and the Establishment of Pakistan," *Asian and African Studies* 7 (Jerusalem, 1971): 157–180; idem, "The Jamʿiyyat al-ʿulamāʾ-i Hind in the Wake of Partition," *Asian and African Studies* 11 (Jerusalem, 1976): 181–211.
4. For a detailed study, see P. Hardy, *Partners in Freedom—and True Muslims: The Political Thought of Some Muslim Scholars in British India, 1912–1947* (Lund, 1971); Z. ul-H. Faruqi, *The Deoband School and the Demand for Pakistan* (Bombay, 1963).
5. Abu l-Kalam Azad was a celebrated Qurʾan exegete and author. See H. Kabir, *Maulana Abul Kalam Azad: A Memorial Volume* (London, 1959); see also "Azad," in *The Encyclopaedia of Islam,* supplement, fasc. 1–2, vol. 12 (Leiden, 2004), 106f.
6. Its retreat from politics continues. Following the destruction of the Babri mosque in December 1992, the Jamaʿat-e Islami was designated a radical group by the authorities and prohibited by law from engaging in political activity.
7. See K. R. Malkani, *The Politics of Ayodhya and Hindu-Muslim Relations* (New Delhi, 1993); U. Rao, *Kommunalismus in Indien: Eine Darstellung der wissenschaftlichen Diskussion über Hindu-Muslim-Konflikte* (Halle a. d. Saale, 2003); R. Zakaria, *Communal Rage in Secular India: With Reference to Gujarat 2002* (Mumbai, 2002); Ch. Wagner, "Kommunalismus in Indien: Die Entstehung und innenpolitische Bedeutung des Hindu-Muslim-Gegensatzes," *Asien* 44 (Hamburg, July 1993): 59–74.
8. Discussion of secularism has subsided somewhat. For a comprehensive account, see H. Dalwai, *Muslim Politics in Secular India* (New Delhi, 1972); Mushirul Hasan, ed., *Living with Secularism: The Destiny of India's Muslims* (New Delhi, 2007).
9. See T. Mahmood, *Muslim Personal Law: The Role of the State in the Subcontinent* (New Delhi, 1977); I. A. Ansari, "Muslim Personal Law in India," *Journal of the Institute of Muslim Minority Affairs* (hereafter *JIMMA*) 1, no. 2 (London, 1979–80): 86–96; P. Risso, "Indian Muslim Legal Status (1964–1986)," *Journal of South Asian and Middle Eastern Studies* 16 (1992): 55–74; A. A. Engineer, ed., *Islam, Women and Gender Justice* (New Delhi, 2001).
10. The case involving Shah Bano's right to maintenance launched a debate on the necessity of reforming shariʿa law. See S. J. Hussain, "Shariʾah, Shah Bano and the

Supreme Court of India," *Islamic and Comparative Law Review* 12 (New Delhi, 1992): I:13–24; K. Zaromba-Radziwill, "L'affaire Shah Bano: ses implications juridiques, politiques et sociales," *Hemispheres Studies on Cultures and Societies* 7 (Semper, 1990): 53–64.

11. A decision in this regard by the Allahabad High Court (Lucknow Bench) in April 1994 led to countrywide protests.

12. The survival of Urdu has become a major problem for Indian Muslims. See O. Khalidi, "Urdu Language and the Future of Muslim Identity in India," *JIMMA* 7 (London, 1986): 395–403; K. Schwerin, *Die indischen Muslime und die Hindi-Urdu-Kontroverse in den United Provinces* (Wiesbaden, 1972).

13. See I. Ahmad, "The Problem of Muslim Educational Backwardness in Contemporary India: An Inferential analysis," *JIMMA* 2, no. 3 (London, 1980–81): 55–71.

14. See O. Fahad, "The Role of India's Madrasa System in Islamic Revival," *Muslim World League Journal* 21, no. 11 (Jidda, 1994): 47–54.

15. Attacks against Muslims have become a major problem for the Congress (I). See Riyad al-Rahman Shirwani, *Musalmanān-i hind se waqt ke mutālabāt* (Demands of the Time by India's Muslims) (New Delhi, 1987).

16. See J. G. Tiwari, "R.S.S. Policy toward Indian Muslims: Origins and Development," *JIMMA* 8 (London, 1987): I:79–87.

17. M. R. A. Baig, *The Muslim Dilemma in India* (New Delhi, 1974); I. A. Ansari, ed., *The Muslim Situation in India* (New Delhi, 1990); M. K. A. Siddiqui, *Hindu-Muslim Relations* (Calcutta, 1993).

18. For a comprehensive account of this conflict, see M. S. Chaudhry, *Der Kaschmirkonflikt: Seine Ursachen, sein Wesen sowie Rolle und Bemühungen der Vereinten Nationen* (Munich, 1976).

19. The headquarters of the Indian Tablighi Jama'at are located in Delhi. The renowned author and cleric Abu l-Hasan 'Ali Nadwi is said to have been a member. For its impact in France, see G. Kepel, *The Revenge of God: The Resurgence of Islam, Christianity and Judaism in the Modern World* (Cambridge, 1994); E. Faust, "Islam on Tour: Die indo-pakistanische Bewegung Tablighi Jama'at," *Orient* 39 (Opladen, June 1998): 219–234; D. Reetz, "Keeping Busy on the Path of Allah: The Self-Organisation (*intizam*) of the Tablighi Jama'at," *Oriente Moderno,* n.s. 23 (Rome, 2004): 295–305.

20. See M. A. Kalam, "Religious Conversion in Tamil Nadu (India)," *JIMMA* 10 (London, 1989): 343–350.

7. Pakistan *(Khálid Durán and Munir D. Ahmed)*

1. Iqbal's life and work have been documented in numerous publications. See, e.g., Masud-ul-Hasan, *Life of Iqbal: General Account of his Life* (Lahore, 1978); W. Köhler, ed., *Muhammad Iqbal und die drei Reiche des Geistes/Muhammad Iqbal and the Three Realms of the Spirit* (Hamburg, 1977). A good introduction to his religious ideas is found in Annemarie Schimmel, *Gabriel's Wing: A Study into the Religious Ideas of Sir Muhammad Iqbal* (Leiden, 1963); she also translated some of his poetic works into German: *Muhammad Ikbal: Das Buch der Ewigkeit (Jawid-nama)* (Munich, 1957); *Muhammad Iqbal: Botschaft des Ostens; als Antwort auf Goethes West-Östlichen Diwan* (Wiesbaden, 1963).

2. Iqbal's idea of a separate Muslim state in northern India was later reinforced by Jinnah's "two nations theory." See Sh. A. Khan, *Two Nations Theory—as a Concept, Strategy and Ideology* (Karachi, 1985); M. Ahmed, "Iqbal and Jinnah and the 'Two-Nations-Theory,'" in *Pakistan: 35 Jahre nach der Staatsgründung/Pakistan: 35*

Years after Independence, ed. K. J. Newman (Hamburg, 1983), 83–113; A. Salim, *Pakistan of Jinnah: The Hidden Face* (Lahore, 1993). For Jinnah's life and work, see A. Jalal, *The Sole Spokesman: Jinnah, the Muslim League and the Demand for Pakistan* (Cambridge, 1985); M. H. Saiyid, *Muhammad Ali Jinnah: A Political Study* (Chicago, 1978); H. Bolitho, *Jinnah: Creator of Pakistan* (London, 1964); G. Allana, *Quaid-e-Azam Jinnah: The Story of a Nation* (Lahore, 1967); S. Wolpert, *Jinnah of Pakistan* (New York, 1984).

3. For Deoband, see B. D. Metcalf, *Islamic Revival in British India: Deoband, 1860–1900* (Princeton, 1982); idem, *"Traditionalist" Islamic Activism: Deoband, Tablighis and Talibs* (Leiden, 2002).

4. Jamal al-Din al-Afghani is said to have used the formulation "Islamic social democracy" as long ago as 1890 in Istanbul. See F. Rahman, "Sources and Meaning of Islamic Socialism," in *Religion and Political Modernization,* ed. D. E. Smith (Princeton, 1974); for Bhutto's life and work, see K. Niazi, *Dīdawar* (The Seeing One) (Lahore, 1977); S. Wolpert, *Zulfi of Pakistan: His Life and Times* (New York, 1993); A. H. Syed, *The Discourse and Politics of Zulfikar Ali Bhutto* (New York, 1992).

5. See the section on India in this volume.

6. See the section on India in this volume.

7. See the section on India in this volume.

8. I. H. Douglas, *Abul Kalam Azad: An Intellectual and Religious Biography,* ed. G. Minault and C. W. Troll (Delhi, 1993).

9. For more on this topic, see M. D. Ahmed, "The Shi'is of Pakistan," in *Shiism, Resistance, and Revolution,* ed. M. Kramer (Boulder, Colo., 1987), 275–287; M. K. Jalalzai, *The Sunni-Shia Conflict in Pakistan* (Lahore, 1998); A. Rieck, "Sectarianism as a Political Problem in Pakistan: The Case of the Northern Areas," *Orient* 36, no. 3 (Opladen, 1995): 429–448; A. Rieck, "A Stronghold of Shi'a Orthodoxy in Northern Pakistan," in *Islamstudien ohne Ende,* ed. R. Brunner (Würzburg, 2002), 383–408.

10. See his autobiography, *The Memoirs of the Aga Khan: World Enough and Time* (London, 1954).

11. Abu l-A'la Maududi (1903–1979), founder of the Jama'at-i Islami and author of many works on Islam, is considered the most influential theoretician on the "Islamic state." See S. R. Ahmad, *Maulana Maududi and the Islamic State* (Lahore, 1976); idem, *Maududi's Concept of the Islamic State* (Lahore, 1976); C. Adams, "The Ideology of Maulana Mawdudi," in *South Asian Politics and Religion,* ed. D. E. Smith (Princeton, 1966), 371–397; E. Lerman, "Mawdudi's Concept of Islam," *Middle Eastern Studies* 17 (1981): 492–509; S. A. Araghchi, "Islamic Theo-Democracy: The Political Ideas of Abul A'la Mawdudi," *Iranian Journal of International Affairs* 8 (1996–97): 772–797.

12. Josh Malihabadi came to be called "Poet of the Revolution" on account of his anti-imperialist verse. His autobiography, *Yadun ki baraat* (Marriage Procession of Memories) (New Delhi, 1988), caused quite a public stir.

13. See Ziya al-Islam Ansari, *Janaral Muhammad Ziya al-Haqq: Shakhsiyat aur karname* (General Muhammad Zia ul-Haq: Personality and Heroic Acts) (Lahore, 1990).

14. See M. A. Khan, *Friends Not Masters: A Political Autobiography* (London, 1967).

15. Literature on the Jama'at-i Islami is available in many languages. See S. A. Gailani, *Jama'at-i Islami: 1941 ta 1947* (Jama'at-i Islami: From 1941 to 1947) (Lahore, 1992); K. Bahadur, *The Jama'at-i Islami of Pakistan: Political Thought and Political Action* (Lahore, 1978); S. V. R. Nasr, *The Vanguard of the Islamic Revolution: The Jama'at-i Islami of Pakistan* (Berkeley, 1994); S. V. R. Nasr, "Islamic Opposition to the Islamic State: The Jama'at-i Islami," *International Journal of Middle East Studies* 25 (1993): 261–283; S. V. R. Nasr, "Students, Islam and Politics: Islami Jami'at-i

Tulaba in Pakistan," *Middle East Journal* 46 (1992): 59–76; F. Grare, *Political Islam in the Indian Subcontinent: The Jamaat-i Islami* (New Delhi, 2001).

16. Dhikris, originally known as *mahdawiyya,* are followers of Muhammad Jaunpuri (1443–1505), who proclaimed himself the mahdi. He and later his disciples were persecuted by the state. By keeping their teachings secret, by passing them on orally, and by withdrawing to remote areas, they managed with considerable effort to survive as a group. The loss of their writings means that they have reverted to the level of nature worshippers. Only in Deccan (India) are there said to be educated Dhikris, one of whom became the prime minister of the Hyderabad-Deccan principality under British rule. For more on their history and teachings, see S. A. A. Rizvi, *Muslim Revivalist Movements in Northern India in the Sixteenth and Seventeenth Centuries* (Agra, 1965), 68–134.

17. Recommended works include M. B. M. Ahmad, *Ahmadiyya or the True Islam* (Rabwah, 1959); M. Z. Khan, *Ahmadiyyat: The Renaissance of Islam* (London, 1978); L. Spencer, *The Ahmadiyya Movement: A History and Perspective* (Delhi, 1974); Y. Friedmann, *Prophecy Continuous: Aspects of Ahmadiyya Religious Thought and Its Medieval Background* (Berkeley, 1988); M. D. Ahmed, "Ahmadiyya: Geschichte und Lehre," in *Der Islam,* pt. 3, ed. A. Schimmel et al., 415–422, series, Die Religionen der Menschheit, vol. 25, 3 (Stuttgart, 1990).

18. See S. J. Malik, "Legitimizing Islamization: The Case of the 'Council of Islamic Ideology' in Pakistan, 1962–1981," *Orient* 30 (1989): 251–268.

19. See M. D. Ahmed, "The Permanent Constitution of Pakistan," *Orient* 14 (1973): 118–126.

20. See M. D. Ahmed, "Ausschluß der Ahmadiyya aus dem Islam: Eine umstrittene Entscheidung des pakistanischen Parlaments," *Orient* 16 (1975): 112–143.

21. See M. D. Ahmed, "Die Wahlen in Pakistan im März 1977: Eine erste Bilanz," *Orient* 18 (1977): 102–127.

22. See Khálid Durán, "The Final Replacement of Parliamentary Democracy by the 'Islamic System' in Pakistan," in *Pakistan in Its Fourth Decade,* ed. W.-P. Zingel (Hamburg, 1983), 147–174.

23. See C. Gieraths and J. Malik, *Die Islamisierung der Wirtschaft unter Zia-ul-Haq* (Bad Honnef, 1986); I. D. Pal, "Pakistan and the Question of *Riba,"* *Middle Eastern Studies* 30 (1994): 64–78; C. Gieraths, "Pakistan: Main Participants and Final Financial Products of the Islamization Process," in *Islamic Financial Markets,* ed. R. Wilson (London, 1990), 171–195.

24. For more detailed accounts, see M. D. Ahmed, "Islamisierung in Pakistan," in *Pakistan,* ed. D. Conrad and W.-P. Zingel (Wiesbaden, 1992), 69–76 (Zweite Heidelberger Südasiengespräche); S. S. Bindra, *Politics of Islamisation: With Special Reference to Pakistan* (New Delhi, 1990); L. A. Delvoie, *The Islamization of Pakistan's Foreign Policy* (Kingston, Ontario, 1994); C. H. Kennedy, "Islamization and Legal Reform in Pakistan, 1979–1989," *Pacific Affairs* 63 (1990): 62–77.

8. Bangladesh *(Hans Harder)*

1. Compare R. M. Eaton (1993), particularly chap. 5.
2. Compare A. Roy (1983); and D. Cashin (1995).
3. Compare R. Ahmed (1981), particularly chap. 2; and J. Maitra (1984), 9ff.
4. K. Gardner (1995).
5. There is a comprehensive compilation of secondary literature available on the Bauls, who can be considered the best-investigated, and most difficult to define, folk religion group in Bengal.

6. Compare, for example, E. Rahim, "Bengali Muslims and Islamic Fundamentalism: The Jama'at-i-Islami in Bangladesh," in *Understanding the Bengal Muslims: Interpretative Essays,* ed. R. Ahmed (Delhi, 2001), 236–261.

7. Compare U. A. B. Razia Akter Banu (1991), 63.

9. Southeast Asia *(Olaf Schumann)*

1. I. Wandelt, *Der Weg zum Pancasila-Menschen: Die Pancasila-Lehre unter dem P4-Beschluß des Jahres 1978* (Frankfurt am Main, 1989).

2. O. Schumann, "Herausgefordert durch die Pancasila: Die Religionen in Indonesien," in *Gottes ist der Orient—Gottes ist der Okzident,* ed. U. Tworuschka (Cologne, 1991), 322–343.

3. These irregularities were mentioned in the Indonesian press in early 1981.

4. The Muslim and non-Muslim politicians who have been backing Pancasila since 1945 are referred to here as Pancasila supporters in an effort to avoid using the imprecise term "secular nationalists," which is common elsewhere. The latter term is usually used in juxtaposition with "Islamic nationalists" to underline that both groups were and are still "nationalists."

5. *Adat* is the set of customary laws and religious traditions passed down from one generation to another.

6. The Serikat Islam was founded in 1911 as the successor to the Union of Islamic Batik Traders in Solo. It finally became a party in 1929. Haji Oemar Sa'id Tjokroaminoto, who came from a Javanese *adat* family, was its most prominent chairman (from 1912 to 1934). He was closely connected to Islam for reasons of politics and ideology (i.e. its anti-Western attitude) as opposed to religious reasons. He was very receptive to socialist thought. Sukarno, who later became Indonesia's president, spent several years as a youth at Tjokroaminoto's home in Surabaya.

7. This confrontation was naturally nothing new; it has been present throughout Indonesia's history since the arrival of Islam. The Dutch generally backed the *adat* groups in the clashes, which occasionally turned bloody.

8. See C. van Vollenhoven, *Het Adatrecht van Nederlandsch-Indië,* 3 vols. (Leiden, 1918–1933).

9. Also see the contribution by F. L. Brakel in this volume, "Islam and Local Traditions: Syncretic Ideas and Practices."

10. Since the seventeenth century the Javanese have held the Ratu Adil (the Just King) to be the messianic ruler who will establish a new world order from the present chaos.
    The movements developing based on this expectation combine Shi'ite, Hindu, and Buddhist elements that concentrate on the arrival of the mahdi, the tenth avatara of Vishnu, or the Buddhist Maitreya. Tjokroaminoto occasionally made use of this expectation. His name contains the element *cokro* (San. *chakra*), the spinning disc of Vishnu that serves justice. See A. P. E. Korver, *Sarekat Islam 1912–16* (Amsterdam, 1982). Bernhard Dahm has to be credited with having uncovered the connection between the central importance of Javanese mythology and the Ratu Adil expectations for Sukarno's sociopolitical ideology. B. Dahm (1966), passim.

11. See B. J. Boland (1971), 17–27; B. Dahm (1966), 255–261; and W. Wawer (1974), 100–111. The abstract term *ketuhanan* is derived from *tuhan,* which is the Malay equivalent of the Arabic *rabb.*

12. B. Dahm (1966), 256.

13. These are the famous "seven words" in Indonesian: "Dengan kewajiban menjalankan syari'at Islam bagi pemeluk-pemeluk-nya."

14. The Indonesian text is in B. J. Boland (1971), 243. Compare E. S. Anshari, *Piagam Jakarta 22 Juni 1945* (Bandung, 1981).

15. The final version of the preamble of the constitution from 1945 can be found in the undated official translation of the constitution of the Republic of Indonesia, first adopted August 18, 1945, available from the Ministry of Information of the Republic of Indonesia (n.d.).

16. C. van Dijk (1981); K. D. Jackson, *Traditional Authority, Islam, and Rebellion* (Berkeley, 1980); H. H. Dengel (1986); B. Sillars Harvey, *Tradition, Islam, and Rebellion: South Sulawesi, 1950–1965* (1987) (Indonesian translation: *Pemberontakan Kahar Muzakkar, Dari Tradisi ke DI/TII* [Jakarta, 1989]).

17. K. E. Ward, *The Foundation of the Partai Muslimin in Indonesia* (Ithaca, 1970).

18. Alfian, *Muhammadiyah: The Political Behavior of a Muslim Modernist Organization under Dutch Colonialism* (Yogyakarta, 1989). The founder of Muhammadiyah, K. H. Ahmad Dahlan, was greatly influenced by the Salafiyya movement established by Muhammad 'Abduh in Egypt.

19. This provision was suspended by the law on religious courts passed in 1989.

20. "Soal 'Negara Islam,'" *Tempo* (Jakarta), May 2, 1981, 12–17.

21. H. E. S. Anshary, *Tempo* (Jakarta), May 2, 1981, 16.

22. See E. Sitompul, *NU dan Pancasila* (Yakarta, 1989).

23. A. G. Abdullah, ed., *Himpunan Perundang-undangan dan Peraturan Peradilan Agama* (Yakarta, 1991).

24. For the wording of the law including the implementation rules, see the text published by the Ministry of National Education of Indonesia (Sistem Pendidikan Nasional, UU RI Nomor 2 tahun 1989, beserta Peraturan Pelaksanaannya 1990) (Jakarta, 1990).

25. A. Muhammad, ed., *ICMI dan harapan umat* (Jakarta, 1991).

26. This special right was revoked in 1993 by Prime Minister Mahathir ibn Muhammad and replaced by a new law.

27. A. Ibrahim, "The Position of Islam in the Constitution of Malaysia," in T. M. Suffian et al. (1979), 41–68, 53.

28. Ibid., 59.

29. V. Venturini, *Politik und Verfassungsrecht in Malaysia*, in B. Grossman (1966), 19–64, in particular 52ff.; V. Sinnadurai, "The Citizenship Laws of Malaysia," in T. M. Suffian et al. (1979), 69–100. For more on the MCA, see Heng Pek Koon, *Chinese Politics in Malaysia: A History of the Malaysian Chinese Association* (Singapore, 1988).

30. See Mahathir bin Muhammad (1979). Muhammad was the prime minister of Malaysia from the summer of 1981 to the fall of 2003.

31. P. G. Gowing (1978), 56; Ibrahim, "Position of Islam," 41–68, in particular 51–52.

32. P. G. Gowing (1978).

33. Raja Y. A. M. Azlan Shah, "The Role of Constitutional Rulers in Malaysia," in F. A. Trinidade and H. P. Lee (1986), 76–91.

34. J. P. Ongkili (1972), 102; H. Luping, "The Formation of Malaysia Revisited," in J. G. Kitingan and M. J. Ongkili (1989), 1–59, in particular 31ff.

35. T. Abdul Rahman (1978), 142–145; P. Means (1991), 40ff.

36. The PBS won the election for regional parliament in 1994 as well. Several of its parliamentarians, however, switched over to parties belonging to the National Front with rather enticing financial kickbacks, cheating the PBS of a victory.

37. J. Ahmad, *Konflik UMNO-PAS dalam isu islamisasi* (Petaling Jaya, 1989), in particular 51ff.; Ch. Muzaffar (1987), 55–97.

38. See also Ch. Muzaffar (1987), passim; idem (1989); and Patricia Martinez, "Islam, Constitutional Democracy, and the Islamic State in Malaysia," in *Civil Society in Southeast Asia,* ed. Lee Hock Guan (Singapore, 2004), 27–53.

39. T. Abdul Rahman (1978), 157.

40. H. Mutalib (1993) offers a critical analysis of the discussion.

41. See W. Larousse (2001), 182–186, for more on the "Moro Wars" during the colonial period as a model for mutual relations; R. Werning, "Regulierte Anarchie in Basilanistan. Abu Sayyaf: Antikoloniale Revolte oder organisierter Terror?" *Südostasien* 17, no. 4 (2001): 72–75.

42. P. G. Gowing (1979), 173.

43. Ibid., 191–198.

44. For more on education, see the contributions of A. G. Macawaris and A. T. Madale, "Muslim Society: Higher Education and Development: The Case of the Philippines (1) and (2)," in Sh. Ahmat and Sh. Siddique (1987), 78–127.

45. N. Mandale, "Kebangkitan Kembali Islam dan Nasionalisme di Filipina," in *Tradisi dan Kebangkitan Islam di Asia Tenggara,* ed. T. Abdullah and Sh. Siddique (Jakarta, 1989), 341–384, in particular 342ff.

46. W. Larousse (2001), 186.

47. Johor had been a vassal of Malacca and only gained greater significance when Malacca fell to the Portuguese in 1511; see C. M. Turnbull (1989), 53. Although the story of a princess from Johor is told in the official lore of Brunei, a tie to Malacca is more probable; in addition, see the entry on Brunei in *The Encyclopedia of Islam,* 2nd ed., supplement (Leiden, 2004), 151–152.

48. See D. S. Ranjit Singh (1991), 130ff., for more details on the role of Azahari and the PRB.

49. Liaw Yock Fang, *Undang-undang Melaka: The Laws of Malacca* (The Hague, 1976), 62ff.

50. See T. Li (1989), e.g., 130.

51. See also Sh. Siddique, "Administration of Islam in Singapore," in T. Abdullah and Sh. Siddique (1986), 315–331, in particular 317ff.

52. Sh. Siddique and Y. R. Kassim, "Muslim Society, Higher Education and Development: The Case of Singapore," in Sh. Ahmat and Sh. Siddique (1987), 128–176, in particular 128; see also Sh. Siddique, "Der Einfluß von Politik, Wirtschaft und Gesellschaft auf den Islam in Singapur," in W. Draguhn (1983), 141–153.

53. Quoted in Siddique and Kassim, "Muslim Society, Higher Education and Development," 128.

54. See the detailed work by J. Djamour (1966).

55. Siddique and Kassim, "Muslim Society, Higher Education and Development," 141.

56. Siddique, "Administration of Islam in Singapore," 326f.

57. See also Siddique, "Der Einfluß von Politik," 149f.

58. "Pattani" is the spelling in Thai and "Patani" is the spelling in Malay.

59. For sources, see P. Wheatly, *The Golden Khersonese* (Kuala Lumpur, 1980), 252–267; A. Teeuw and D. K. Wyatt (1970), 1:1–3.

60. For more information, see S. Pitsuwan (1989), 49ff.

61. Ibid., 59; see also ibid., 64, for more on the problem of parliamentary representation.

62. See D. K. Wyatt, *Thailand: A Short History* (London and Bangkok, 1981), 252ff.

63. S. Pitsuwan (1989), 69; D. K. Wyatt (1981), 253f.; and D. G. E. Hall (1968), 813.

64. See *Sejarah Kerajaan Melayu Patani,* published in the 1950s in Kelantan under the pseudonym Ibrahim Syukri, for accounts from Malay eyewitnesses on how they viewed Phibun's politics. Shortly after its publication a ban was placed on disseminating it in Thailand and the Federation of Malaya. An English translation

of the text by Ibrahim Syukri, including a preface, can be found in *History of the Malay Kingdom of Patani*, trans. C. Bailey and J. N. Miksic (Athens, Ohio, 1985), in particular 63–77. See also A. Teeuw and D. K. Wyatt (1970), 1:46–49, for more on Syukri's work.

65. See S. Pitsuwan (1989), 117f.; *History of the Malay Kingdom of Patani*, 71f.; O. Farouk, "Malay Muslim Nationalism, Southern Thailand," in T. Abdullah and S. Siddique (1986), 250–281, in particular 262–263.

66. S. Pitsuwan (1989), 127.

67. Ibid., 133.

68. P. Thim Kham, D. Baka, and P. Petkla, "Muslim Society, Higher Education and Development: The Case of Thailand," in Sh. Ahmat and Sh. Siddique (1987), 177–219.

69. U. Dulyakasem, "Emergence and Escalation of Ethnic Nationalism: Southern Siam," in Sh. Ahmat and Sh. Siddique (1987), 208–249, in particular 229; see also A. D. W. Forbes, "Thailand's Muslim Minorities: Assimilation, Secession or Co-existence?" in A. D. W. Forbes (1988–), 2:167–182, in particular 173–174.

70. Roland Platz, "Aufruhr im Königreich: Die islamische Minderheit im Süden von Thailand," *Südostasien* 20, no. 2 (June 2004): 35–38.

10. Maghreb *(Franz Kogelmann)*

1. General introductions to the history of the Maghreb can be found in J. M. Abun-Nasr, *A History of the Maghreb in the Islamic Period* (Cambridge, 1987); and A. Laroui, *The History of the Maghrib: An Interpretive Essay* (Princeton, 1977); on the Western Sahara conflict, see E. Jensen, *Western Sahara: Anatomy of a Stalemate* (Boulder, Colo., 2006); on the history of Mauritania, see G. Désiré-Vuillemin, *Histoire de la Mauritanie: Des origins à l'indépendance* (Paris, 1997).

2. On the political development of the Maghreb, see the relevant reports on the specific countries in *The Middle East and North Africa*, published annually since 1948 by Europa Publications (London).

3. J. Damis, "The Free School Phenomenon: The Cases of Tunisia and Algeria," *International Journal of Middle East Studies* 5 (1975): 434–449; idem, "The Origins and Significance of the Free School Movement in Morocco, 1919–1931," *Revue de l'Occident musulman et de la Méditerranée* 19 (1975): 75–99.

4. On the early development of the Salafiyya movement in Tunisia, see A. H. Green, *The Tunisian Ulama, 1873–1915: Social Structure and Response to Ideological Currents* (Leiden, 1978), 175–177; on the national movement, see K. J. Perkins, *A History of Modern Tunisia* (Cambridge, 2004), 73–129.

5. On the Salafiyya movement in Algeria, see A. Merad, *Le réformisme musulman en Algérie de 1925 á 1940: Essai d'histoire religieuse et sociale* (Paris, 1967); J. Ruedy, *Modern Algeria: The Origins and Development of a Nation* (Bloomington, 1992), 133–136; M. Willis, *The Islamist Challenge in Algeria: A Political History* (New York, 1996), 8–22.

6. On the Salafiyya movement in Morocco, see H. Munson Jr., *Religion and Power in Morocco* (New Haven, 1993).

7. See F. Kogelmann, "Muhammad al-Makki an-Nasiri alias Sindbad der Seefahrer: Networking eines marokkanischen Nationalisten in den dreißiger Jahren des 20. Jahrhunderts," in *Die islamische Welt als Netzwerk: Möglichkeiten und Grenzen des Netzwerkansatzes im islamischen Kontext*, ed. R. Loimeier (Würzburg, 2000), 257–286.

8. See 'A. al-Fasi, *The Independence Movements in Arab North Africa*, trans. H. Z. Nuseibeh (New York, 1970); originally published in Arabic as *Al-Harakat al-istiqlaliyya fi'l-Maghrib al-'arabi* (Cairo, 1948).

9. See R. Loimeier, *Säkularer Staat und islamische Gesellschaft: Die Beziehungen zwischen Staat, Sufi-Bruderschaften und islamischer Reformbewegung in Senegal im 20. Jahrhundert* (Münster, 2001), 104, 177; on Islam in Mauritania, see C. C. Stewart, *Islam and Social Order in Mauritania: A Case Study from the Nineteenth Century* (Oxford, 1973).

10. Loimeier, 2001, 176–177.

11. 276–278; M. M. Kane, "La vie et l'œuvre d'Al-Hajj Mahmoud Ba Diowol (1905–1978): Du pâtre au patron de la 'Révolution Al-Fatah,'" in *Le temps des marabouts: Itinéraires et stratégies islamiques en Afrique occidentale française, 1880–1960,* ed. D. Robinson and J.-L. Triaud, (Paris, 1997), 431–465.

12. For English translations of the constitutions, see the University of Richmond online constitution finder, http://confinder.richmond.edu.

13. A. Bouslama, "La réforme du régime des Habous en Tunisie," *Revue juridique et politique* 24, no. 4 (1970): 1113–18.

14. On the Algerian Ministry of Endowments, see F. Kogelmann, "Islamische Stiftungen und 'religiöse Angelegenheiten' im Algerien des 20. Jahrhunderts," *Orient* 42, no. 4 (2001): 639–658; idem, "Islamische Stiftungen und andere wohltätige Einrichtungen in Nordafrika: Algerien," in *Islamische Stiftungen und wohltätige Einrichtungen mit entwicklungspolitischen Zielsetzungen in arabischen Staaten,* ed. S. Faath (Hamburg, 2003), 121–133.

15. Décret no. 80–30, 09.02.1980, *Journal Officiel de la République Algérienne* (hereafter *JORA*), February 12, 1980; www.joradp.dz/JO6283/1980/007/F_Pag.htm.

16. See M. al-Ahnaf, B. Botiveau, and F. Frégosi, *L'Algérie par ses islamistes* (Paris, 1991), 186.

17. *JORA* 21 (1991); Arabic ed., 23 Shawwal 1411, 690–693; www.joradp.dz/JO8499/1991/021/A_Pag.htm.

18. *JORA* 16 (1991); Arabic ed., 25 Ramadan 1411, 535–543; www.joradp.dz/JO8499/1991/016/A_Pag.htm.

19. *JORA* 38 (2000); Arabic ed., 29 Rabiʿ al-Awwal 1421, 13–17; www.joradp.dz/JO2000/2000/038/A_Pag.htm.

20. See F. Kogelmann, *Islamische Stiftungen und Staat: Der Wandel in den Beziehungen zwischen einer religiösen Institution und dem marokkanischen Staat seit dem 19. Jahrhundert bis 1937* (Würzburg, 1999).

21. On the practice of contemporary Islam in Mauritania, see U. Clausen, *Islam und nationale Religionspolitik: Das Fallbeispiel Mauretanien; Sonderforschungsprogramm "menavision 2010"* (Hamburg, January 2005), www.giga-Hamburg.de/dl/download.php?d=/content/imes/menastabilisierung/pdf/mena_tp3_aspekte_1.pdf.

11. The Independent States of Sub-Saharan Africa
(Jamil M. Abun-Nasr and Roman Loimeier)

1. The figures given here for sub-Saharan Africa are based on critical comparison of estimates and censuses but are only approximations. This is because national statistics are frequently manipulated for political reasons, with the number of Muslims cited as sometimes more and sometimes less. There is agreement that the number of Muslims in sub-Saharan Africa is steadily growing: the figure quoted for Muslims in the second German edition of this book, based on statistical information from the 1960s and 1970s, was almost 99 million. See the earlier editions of the present volume, and R. Loimeier, "Gibt es einen afrikanischen Islam? Die Muslime in Afrika zwischen

lokalen Lehrtraditionen und translokalen Rechtleitungsansprüchen," *Afrika Spectrum* 37, no. 2 (2002): 175–188.

2. The development of the Republic of Sudan will not be considered in this section.

3. A term coined by Terence Ranger; see T. Ranger, "The Invention of Tradition in Colonial Africa," in *The Invention of Tradition,* ed. E. Hobsbawm and T. Ranger (Cambridge, 1983), 211–262.

4. See C. Rivière, *Guinea: The Mobilization of a People* (Ithaca, 1977), 235.

5. For the Maitatsine movement, see the first German edition of the present volume (1984), 393f.

6. See R. Loimeier, "Patterns and Peculiarities of Islamic Reform in Africa," *Journal of Religion in Africa* 33, no. 3 (2003): 237–262.

7. See J. Lacunza Balda, "Translations of the Quran into Kiswahili, and Contemporary Islamic Revival in East Africa," in *African Islam and Islam in Africa,* ed. D. Westerlund and E. Evers-Rosander (London, 1997), 95–126.

8. L. Kaba, *The Wahhabiya: Islamic Reform and Politics in French West Africa* (Evanston, 1974), 64–72, 135–154.

9. For the more recent development of the Subbanu groups and the Islamic schools movement in Mali, see particularly L. Brenner, *Controlling Knowledge: Religion, Power, and Schooling in a West African Muslim Society* (Bloomington, 2001).

10. See R. Loimeier, *Säkularer Staat und islamische Gesellschaft: Die Beziehungen zwischen Staat, Sufi-Bruderschaften und islamischer Reformbewegung in Senegal im 20. Jahrhundert* (Hamburg, 2001), 175ff.

11. V. Monteil, *L'Islam noir: Une religion à la conquête de l'Afrique* (Paris, 1980), 272–275.

12. Kaba, 1974, 234–243.

13. See Loimeier, 2001, 257ff.

14. On the general history of the 'Yan Izala, see R. Loimeier, *Islamic Reform and Political Change in Northern Nigeria* (Evanston, 1997).

15. See specifically K. Hock, *Der Islam-Komplex: Zur Wahrnehmung des Islams und der christlich-islamischen Beziehungen in Nordnigeria während der Militärherrschaft Babangidas* (Hamburg, 1996).

16. On the general historical development of the shari'a debate, see J. M. Abun-Nasr, ed., *Muslime in Nigeria: Religion und Gesellschaft im Wandel seit den 50er Jahren* (Hamburg, 1993); on the more recent debate, see R. Peters *Islamic Criminal Law in Nigeria* (Ibadan, 2003).

17. See the interviews with Ibrahim al-Zakzaki in *Thisday,* March 14, 2000; and *Africa Today* (December 1999).

18. See, e.g., M. Klein, *Islam and Imperialism in Senegal: Sine-Saloum, 1847–1914* (Stanford, 1968); and P. M. Holt, *The Mahdist State in the Sudan, 1881–1898* (Oxford, 1958).

19. See I. M. Lewis, *A Modern History of Somalia* (Boulder, Colo., 1988), 63–91.

20. M. Bates, "Social Engineering, Multi-racialism and the Rise of TANU: The Trust Territory of Tanganyika," in *History of East Africa,* ed. D. A. Low and A. Smith, vol. 3 (Oxford, 1976), 168–169.

21. Kaba, 1974, 184–194.

22. J. N. D. Anderson, *Islamic Law in Africa* (London, 1978), 3–7 and passim.

23. L. Behrman, *Muslim Brotherhoods and Politics in Senegal* (Cambridge, Mass., 1970), 48–54; Monteil, 1980, 163–183.

24. J. C. Froelich, *Les Musulmans d'Afrique Noire* (Paris, 1962), 292; Monteil, 1980, 404–408.

25. Ayi Kwei Armah, *Two Thousand Seasons* (London, 1973), esp. chaps. 2 and 3.

26. See, e.g., B. F. Mrina and W. T. Matoke, *Mapambano ya ukombozi Zanzibar* (Dar es-Salam, 1980); and R. Wegemund, "Die Rassenunruhen in Senegal und Mauretanien 1989, *Afrika Spectrum* 89 (1989): 255–274.

27. On the concept of "Islam noir," see C. Harrison, *France and Islam in West Africa, 1860–1960* (Cambridge, 1988).

28. For an analysis of this attitude toward the history of Africa, see J. D. Fage, *A History of Africa* (New York, 1979), 61ff.

29. On Senegal in general, see Loimeier, 2001; and L. A., Villalon, *Islamic Society and State Power in Senegal: Disciples and Citizens in Fatick* (Cambridge, 1995).

30. See D. B. Cruise O'Brien, *The Mourides of Senegal* (Oxford, 1971), esp. chaps. 8 and 9.

31. Loimeier, 2001, 311.

32. 329.

33. 309.

34. R. A. Adeleye, "The Sokoto Caliphate in the Nineteenth Century," in *History of West Africa,* vol. 2, ed. J. F. A. Ajayi and M. Crowder (London, 1974), 57–92.

35. See generally Abun-Nasr, 1993, esp. chaps. 1 and 2.

36. On the political and economic development of Zanzibar in the colonial period, see esp. A. Sheriff and E. Ferguson, eds., *Zanzibar under Colonial Rule* (London, 1991).

37. Only defense and foreign policy, along with currency questions, were defined as union affairs in 1964.

38. See A. Clayton, *The Zanzibar Revolution and Its Aftermath* (Hamden, Conn., 1981).

39. See F. Ludwig, *Church and State in Tanzania: Aspects of a Changing Relationship, 1961–1994* (Leiden, 1996).

40. See the debate on this subject in the Tanzanian newspapers the *Guardian, An-Nuur, Dira,* and *Maarifa.*

41. On the development of this issue in Algeria, see S. Faath, *Algerien: Gesellschaftliche Strukturen und politische Reformen zu Beginn der neunziger Jahre* (Hamburg, 1990); and H. Mattes, ed., *Wuqûf,* vol. 6 (Hamburg, 1992).

42. This analysis of the establishment of Islam in sub-Saharan Africa draws on the work of many scholars. We refer here only to the comprehensive account in R. Pouwels and N. Levtzion, eds., *The History of Islam in Africa* (Oxford, 2000).

43. See the translation of the travel report by Ibn Battuta (d. 1368) in J. F. P. Hopkins and N. Levtzion *Corpus of Early Arabic Sources for West African History* (Cambridge, 1981), 281–304.

44. Cf. Loimeier, 2003, 256.

45. E. P. Skinner, *African Urban Life: The Transformation of Ouagadougou* (Princeton, 1974), 302.

46. R. Delval, *Les Musulmans au Togo* (Paris, 1980), 207–228.

47. See Abun-Nasr, 1993; A. Bosaller and R. Loimeier, "Radical Muslim Women and Male Politics in Nigeria," in *Gender and Identity in Africa,* ed. M. Reh and G. Ludwar-Ene (Münster, 1995), 61–70.

48. Cf. Ludwig, 1996.

49. Cf. U. Günther, "Lesarten des Islam in Südafrika: Herausforderungen im Kontext des sozio-politischen Umbruchprozesses von Apartheid zur Demokratie," *Afrika Spectrum* 37, no. 2 (2002): 159–174.

50. On Ahmed Deedat, see esp. D. Westerlund, "Ahmed Deedat's Theology of Religion: Apologetics through Polemics," *Journal of Religion in Africa* 33, no. 3 (2003): 263–279; on Reinhard Bonnke and the confrontation with Ahmed Deedat, see

R. Loimeier, "Die Dynamik religiöser Unruhen in Nordnigeria," *Afrika Spektrum* 27 (1992): 59–80; and O. Kane, *Muslim Modernity in Postcolonial Nigeria: A Study of the Society for the Removal of Innovation and Reinstatement of Tradition* (Leiden, 2003).

14. Libya *(Hanspeter Mattes)*

1. See the old standard work by E. F. Gautier, *L'Islamisation de l'Afrique du Nord: Les siècles obscurs du Maghreb* (Paris, 1927); and J. Abun-Nasr, *A History of the Maghrib* (Cambridge, 1975).
2. See the contribution by Guido Steinberg on Saudi Arabia in the present volume.
3. On Ahmad ibn Idris's influence on his disciples, see R. S. O'Fahey, *Enigmatic Saint: Ahmad Ibn Idris and the Idrisi Tradition* (London, 1990).
4. The three works in question are *Al-Salsabil al-ma'in fi l-tara'iq al-arba'in, Bughyat al-maqasid fi khulasat al-marasid,* and *Iqaz al-washnan fi l-'amal bi-l-hadith wa-l-qur'an.* On the content of these three works, see N. A. Ziadeh, *Sanusiyah: A Study of a Revivalist Movement in Islam* (Leiden, 1968), 73–98.
5. For example, the "Al-Salah al-'azimiyya" by Ibn Idris, said to be the "best prayer for the Prophet," which was completely integrated into the Sanusi "Al-Wird al-kabir."
6. For details on the functioning of the *zawiyas,* see H. Klopfer, *Aspekte der Bewegung des Muhammad Ben 'Ali as-Sanusi* (Wiesbaden, 1967), 40–53.
7. On the development of the Sanusiyya as a factor in the political order, see the standard work by E. E. Evans-Pritchard, *The Sanusi of Cyrenaica* (Oxford, 1949).
8. On these early measures, see H. Mattes, *Die innere und äußere Mission Libyens: Historisch-politischer Kontext, innere Struktur, regionale Ausprägung am Beispiel Afrikas* (Mainz and Munich, 1986), 24–28.
9. On Islamification from above, see ibid., 28–52; and A. E. Mayer, "A Survey of Islamifying Trends in Libyan Law since 1969," in *Society for Libyan Studies: Seventh Annual Report* (London, 1975–76), 53–55. The fundamental work from the Libyan viewpoint is 'A. 'A. Mansur, *Khutwa ra'ida nahwa tatbiq ahkam al-shari'a al-islami yya fi l-jumhuriyya al-'arabiyya al-libiyya* (Beirut, 1972).
10. On the content of the religious revolution, see H. Mattes, *Islam und Staatsaufbau: Das theoretische Konzept und das Beispiel der Sozialistischen Libyschen Arabischen Volksgamahiriyya* (Heidelberg, 1982).
11. Cf. Y. M. 'Uraybi, *Al-Islam biduni madhahib* (Tripoli, 1981).
12. See "Da'wa li-tathir buyut allah," in the May 21, 1984, edition of the Revolutionary Committee newspaper, *Al-Zahf al-akhdar.*
13. On the Saudi accusations, see Mattes, 1986, 78ff.; and the Saudi pamphlet *The Decisive Answer to the Lies of Qaddafi (Al-Radd al-shafi 'ala muftarayat al-Qaddafi)* (Jidda, 1980). For a Libyan response, see K. Jawad, *Al-Radd al-wafi 'ala al-radd al-shafi* (Tripoli, 1983).
14. For an overview, see G. Joffé, "Islamic Opposition in Libya," *Third World Quarterly* 2 (1988): 615–631; H. Mattes, "Qaddafi und die islamistische Opposition in Libyen: Zum Verlauf eines Konflikts," *Deutsches Orient-Institut,* Mitteilung 51 (Hamburg, 1995).
15. See "The Statement on Islam's Judgement and the Heresy of Al-Takfir wa Al-Hijra Delivered by Muslim Imam Muammar Qaddafi," published in the monthly journal of the Libyan Missionary Society, *Risalat al-Jihad* 75 (La Valletta, Malta, 1991): 90–100; "Qadhafi Criticises Islamic Extremist Groups," *Summary of World Broadcasts,* ME/1670, A9–13 (BBC London, April 23, 1993).

15. Egypt *(Alexander Flores)*

1. See also the chapter on Egypt by Miklos Muranyi in the first three (German) editions of *Islam in der Gegenwart,* including the sources listed there.
2. A. Schölch, "Säkularistische Traditionen im Vorderen Orient," in *Jahrbuch 1985–86* of the Berlin Institute for Advanced Study (WiKo) (Berlin, 1987), 191–201; D. Crecelius, "The Course of Secularization in Modern Egypt."
3. Ibid., 198–200.
4. Such as in G. Krämer, "The Change of Paradigm: Political Pluralism in Contemporary Egypt," *Peuples méditerranéens* 41–42 (October 1987–March 1988): 283–302.
5. The phrase "Arab nationalist ideas" refers to elements of a Marxist analysis and aims that are said to be irrefutably imposed on the Third World; see A. Laroui, *L'idéologie arabe contemporaine* (Paris, 1973), 139–155.
6. M. Arkoun, *La pensée arabe,* 3rd ed. (Paris, 1985), 4.
7. See, e.g., S. J. al-ʿAzm, "Orientalism and Orientalism in Reverse," *Khamsin* 8 (1981): 22–25; and E. Sivan, *Radical Islam,* 153–190.
8. For a summary of presentations of the Islamic movement in Egypt, see R. P. Mitchell, *The Society of the Muslim Brothers;* G. Kepel, *Prophet and Pharaoh;* and E. Sivan, *Radical Islam.*
9. M. Saʿid al-ʿAshmawi, *Usul al-shariʿa* (Beirut, n.d.), 183–195.
10. M. Martin and R. M. Masʿad, "Return to Islamic Legislation in Egypt," in *CEMAM Reports, 1976* (Beirut, 1978), 47–78; R. Peters, "Divine Law or Man-Made Law? Egypt and the Application of the Shariʿa," *Arab Law Quarterly* 3, no. 3 (August 1988): 231–253.
11. For the exact wording of the amendment and a commentary on it, see *CEMAM Reports, 1978–79* (Beirut, 1981), 203–219.
12. E. S. Sabanegh, "Débats autour de l'application de la loi islamique (shariʿa) en Égypte," *MIDEO* 14 (1980): 329–384.
13. On the debate, see ibid.; Peters, "Divine Law or Man-Made Law?"; and A. Flores, "Secularism, Integralism, and Political Islam: The Egyptian Debate," in *Political Islam: Essays from Middle East Report,* ed. Joel Beinin and Joe Stork (Berkeley, 1996), 83–93, esp. 86–88.
14. Peters, "Divine Law or Man-Made Law?" 240–243.
15. *Revue de la presse égyptienne* 19 (1985): 81–91, 98–100.
16. Ibid., 102–104.
17. G. Krämer, "The Integration of the Integrists: A Comparative Study of Egypt, Jordan and Tunisia," in *Democracy without Democrats? The Renewal of Politics in the Muslim World,* ed. G. Salamé (London and New York, 1994), 200–226.
18. I have borrowed this wording from W. Grab, *Der deutsche Weg der Judenemanzipation 1789–1938* (Munich, 1991), 8.
19. S. Zubaida, "Islam, the State and Democracy: Contrasting Conceptions of Society in Egypt," *Middle East Report* 179 (November–December 1992): 2–10.
20. Flores, "Secularism, Integralism and Political Islam," 90–92.
21. For testimony by the defendants in the trial and the text of their programmatic document "Al-Farida al-ghaʾiba," see the appendix in N. Jinina, *Tanzim al-jihad: Hal huwa al-badil al-islami fi Misr?* (Cairo, 1988), 147–273. For an English translation, see J. J. G. Jansen, *The Neglected Duty,* 159–230.
22. See Jinina, *Tanzim al-jihad,* 275–311; and for an English translation, *CEMAM Reports, 1981* (Beirut, 1985), 55–86.
23. See the chapter by Heribert Busse in this volume.
24. K. M. Khalid, *Min huna nabdaʾ* (Cairo, 1950); in English, K. M. Khalid, *From Here We Start* (Washington, D.C., 1953).

25. K. M. Khalid, *Al-Dawla fi l-islam* (Cairo, 1981). On his "transformation," see R. Wielandt, "Zeitgenössische ägyptische Stimmen zur Säkularisierungsproblematik," *Die Welt des Islams* 22 (1982 [published 1984]): 129f.

26. *Al-Ahram*, June 17, 1985.

27. *Al-Ahram*, June 24, 1985.

28. *Al-Ahram*, July 1, 1985. On Foda, see A. Flores, "Egypt: A New Secularism?" *Middle East Report* 153 (July–August 1988): 27–30.

29. *Al-Ahram*, November 25, 1986.

30. *Al-Ahram*, August 12, 1985. On Zakariyya's positions, see F. Zakariya, *Laïcité ou islamisme;* idem, "Das kulturelle Erbe historisch sehen," in *Kopfbahnhof, Almanach 4: Orient-Express; Ansichten zum Islam* (Leipzig, 1991), 167–179; idem, "Säkularisierung: Eine historische Notwendigkeit," in *Der Islam im Aufbruch?* ed. M. Lüders (Munich, 1992), 228–245. It should be noted, however, that throughout the very significant last-named article the word for "secularism" is translated into German as "secularization."

31. J. Sultan, *Ghazw min al-dakhil* (Cairo, 1988), 38f.

32. For example, ʿAbdaljawad Yasin, *Muqaddima fi fiqh al-jahiliyya al-muʿasira* (Cairo, 1986), 53–64, 97–102.

33. In this respect Fahmi Huwaydi is an astute representative of an "Islamic center" position; see F. Huwaydi, *Muwatinun la dhimmiyyun* (Beirut and Cairo, 1985). On debate on this problem in general, see T. Philipp, "Nation-State and Religious Community in Egypt: The Continuing Debate," *Die Welt des Islams* 28 (1988): 379–391; and F. Rasoul, "Die Gemeinschaft der Kopten in ihrer Beziehung zu Staat und Gesellschaft," in *Kultureller Dialog und Gewalt: Aufsätze zu Ethnizität, Religion und Staat im Orient* (Vienna, 1991), 67–104.

34. For a typical publication, see F. Foda, Y. Labib, and K. ʿAbd al-Karim, *Al-Taʾifiyya...ila ayna?* (Cairo, 1987).

35. Al-ʿAshmawi was a judge of the Egyptian Supreme Court for State Security and dealt especially critically with the call for the immediate introduction of the shariʿa; on his views, see M. S. al-Ashmawy, *L'islamisme contre l'islam* (Paris, 1989); R. Wielandt, "Zeitgenössische ägyptische Stimmen zur Säkularisierungsproblematik," 125–133; and D. Sagiv, "Judge Ashmawi and Militant Islam in Egypt," *Middle Eastern Studies* 28, no. 3 (July 1992): 531–546.

36. On the secularism debate in Egypt, see A. Flores, "Egypt: A New Secularism?" 32–38; A. Roussillon, "Islam, islamisme et démocratie: recomposition du champ politique," *Peuples méditerranéens* 41–42 (October 1987–March 1988): 320–329. Important contributions to the debate can be found in "Islam, islamisme et politique," *Revue de la presse égyptienne* 23 (1986): 6–105. For the text of a debate on Islam and secularism that took place in spring 1989 in Cairo, in which generally moderate voices spoke out in favor of secularism, see F. Rasoul, *Kultureller Dialog und Gewalt*, 139–201.

37. See also L. Rogler, "Al-Jamaʿa al-islamiyya: Reuevoll in eine ungewisse Zukunft," *inamo* 31 (Fall 2002): 14–17.

16. Sudan *(Hanspeter Mattes)*

1. On the emergence of brotherhoods in Sudan, see A. S. Karrar, 1992.

2. These religious developments are comprehensively analyzed in N. Grandin, "Traditions religieuses et politiques au Soudan contemporain," in *Le Soudan contemporain,* ed. M. Lavergne (Paris, 1989), 227–270; see also J. S. Trimingham, 1965.

3. See R. S. O'Fahey, *Enigmatic Saint: Ahmad Ibn Idris and the Idrisi Tradition* (London, 1990), in particular 130ff. (concerning al-Sanusi and al-Mirghani).
4. On the Muslim Brotherhood in Sudan, see H. M. M. Ahmad, *Harakat al-ikhwan al-muslimin fi l-Sudan 1944–1969* (Khartoum, 1982); idem, *Al-Haraka al-islamiya fi l-Sudan* (Khartoum, 1988); G. Prunier, "Les frères musulmans au Soudan: un islamisme tacticien," in *Le Soudan contemporain,* ed. M. Lavergne (Paris, 1989), 359–380.
5. On al-Turabi and the NIF, see A. el-Affendi, 1991; P. N. Kok, "Hasan Abdallah at-Turabi (Kurzbiographie)," *Orient* 2 (1992): 185–192; H. at-Turabi, *Al-Haraka al-islamiya fi l-Sudan: Al-Tatawwur, al-kasb, al-minhaj* (Khartoum, 1989).
6. See Numayri's two publications, *The Islamic Way: Why?* (Khartoum, 1978), and *The Islamic Way: How?* (Khartoum, 1982).
7. On Numayri's Islamic politics, see G. R. Warburg, "The Shari'a in Sudan: Implementation and Repercussions, 1983–1989," *Middle East Journal* 4 (1990): 624–637; C. Fluehr-Lobban, 1992; H. Bleuchot, "Kadhafi, Nimeiri et l'Islam," *Annuaire de l'Afrique du Nord 1987* (Paris 1989): 477–490.
8. On the Republican Brothers, see M. M. Taha, 1987; M. Khayati, "Introduction à la pensée de Mahmud Muhammad Taha," in *Sudan: History, Identity, Ideology,* ed. H. Bleuchot et al. (London, 1991), 287–298.
9. On Islamization policies under Bashir, see R. Marchal, "Le Soudan entre islamisme et dictature militaire," *Monde Arabe: Maghreb-Machrek* 137 (1992): 56–79; G. Prunier, "Soudan: Les 'frères' et l'armeé," *Cahiers de l'Orient* 27 (1992): 53–70.
10. Abdullahi Osman El-Tom and M. A. Muhammad Salih, *Black Book of Sudan: Imbalance of Power and Wealth in Sudan* (http://www.sudanjem.com/2004/sudan-alt/english/books/blackbook_part1/20040422_bbone.htm); Robert O. Collins, *A History of Modern Sudan* (Cambridge, 2008), 287–299.

17. Israel and the Occupied Territories *(Thomas Philipp)*

1. See the Balfour Declaration (1917).
2. See Y. Porath, *The Emergence of the Palestinian-Arab National Movement, 1918–1929* (London, 1974); idem, *The Palestinian Arab National Movement, 1929–1939* (London, 1977); A. Moseley Lesch, *Arab Politics in Palestine, 1917–1939* (Ithaca, 1979); M. I. Darwaza, *Al-Qadiyya al-filastiniyya fi mukhtalif marahiliha,* 2 vols. (Sidon, 1951); J. S. Migdal, *Palestinian Society and Politics* (Princeton, 1980); C. D. Smith, *Palestine and the Arab-Israeli Conflict* (New York, 1988).
3. S. P. Mattar, *The Mufti of Jerusalem* (New York, 1988).
4. Ibid., 49; Smith, 1988, 90.
5. Porath, 1974, 205.
6. Y. 'Abd al-Qadir, *Hamas-Harakat al-muqawama al-islamiyya fi Filastin* (Cairo, 1990); I. Barghouti, "Religion and Politics among the Students of the Najah National University," *Middle Eastern Studies* 27, no. 2 (April 1991): 203–218; J. F. Legrain, "Islamistes et lutte nationale palestinienne dans les territoires occupés par Israël," *Revue française de Science Politique* 36 (April 1986): 227–247; idem, "Les islamistes palestiniens à l'épreuve du soulèvement," *Maghreb-Machrek* 121 (July–September 1988): 5–42; T. Mayer, "Pro-Iranian Fundamentalism in Gaza," in *Religious Radicalism and Politics in the Middle East,* ed. E. Sivan and M. Friedman, (Albany, N.Y., 1990), 143–155; A. Navarro, "Palestiniens: L'expansion islamiste," *Cahiers de l'Orient* 7 (1987): 51–65; E. F. Sahliyeh, "The West Bank and the Gaza Strip," in *The Politics of Islamic Revivalism,* ed. S. T. Hunter (Bloomington, Ind., 1988), 88–100; M. K. Shadid, "The Muslim Brotherhood Movement in the West Bank and Gaza," *Third World Quarterly* 10, no. 2 (April 1988): 658–682.

7. Sahliyeh, 1988, 90.

8. Quoted in R. Paz, "Islamic Radicalism in the Westbank and Gaza," unpublished paper (1987).

9. Ibid.

10. Sahliyeh, 1988, 91; Z. Schiff and E. Ya'ari, *The Intifada* (New York, 1990), 223ff.; Legrain, 1986, 246; Shadid, 1988, 648.

11. Sahliyeh, 1988, 90; Shadid, 1988, 662; Paz, "Islamic Radicalism."

12. Legrain, 1986, 242.

13. For a detailed discussion of these relations, see H. Mustafa, "Al-Tayyar al-islami fi l-ard al-muhtalla," *Al-Mustaqbal al-'Arabi* (July 1988): 75–90.

14. Paz, "Islamic Radicalism"; Shadid, 1988, 667.

15. Legrain, 1986, 229; Shadid, 1988, 679.

16. Ziad Abu Amr, "Hamas: A Historical and Political Background," *Journal of Palestine Studies* 22 (Summer 1993): 5–19, 122–134; idem, *Islamic Fundamentalism in the West Bank and Gaza* (Bloomington, Ind., 1994), 103.

17. On the intifada, see J. R. Nasser and R. Heacock, eds., *Intifada: Palestine at the Crossroads* (New York, 1990).

18. Hamas is an acronym for *harakat al-muqawama al-islamiyya,* which means roughly "zeal, eagerness, enthusiasm."

19. R. Paz, "Hagorem ha-islami be-intifada," in *Be'ayin ha-sikh sukh: ha intifada,* ed. G. Gilbar (Tel Aviv, 1992), 11.

20. Ibid., 84–87.

21. Document published by Hamas, "Mithaq harakat al-muqawama al-islamiyya: Filastin" (Muharram 1409 [August 18, 1988]). Section references are given in the text.

22. S. Mishal and A. Sela *The Palestinian Hamas* (New York, 2000), 44–48.

23. Document cited in note 21.

24. Paz, "Islamic Radicalism," 15.

25. For this discussion, see particularly R. Paz, "The Islamic Movement in Israel and the Municipal Elections of 1989," *Jerusalem Quarterly* 53 (Winter 1990): 1–26; see also E. Zureik and A. Haider, "The Impact of the Intifada on the Palestinians in Israel," *International Journal of the Sociology of Law* 19 (1991): 475–495.

26. On these problems, see J.-F. Legrain, "A Defining Moment: Palestinian Islamic Fundamentalism," in *Islamic Fundamentalism and the Gulf Crisis,* ed. J. Piscatori (Boston, 1991), 70–87. In 1989 Kuwait apparently funded Hamas with the sum of $60 million; ibid., 75.

27. W. Kristianasen Levitt, "De l'islamisme radical à la logique nationaliste," *Le Monde Diplomatique* (May 1993);idem, "Hamas se prépare à la nouvelle donne," *Le Monde Diplomatique* (February 1994).

28. W. Kristianasen Levitt, "Islamistes palestiniens, la nouvelle génération," *Le Monde Diplomatique* (June 1995).

18. Syria *(Andreas Christmann)*

1. Figures taken from N. van Dam, *The Struggle for Power in Syria: Politics and Society under Assad and the Ba'th Party* (London, 1996), 1, 167. Reliable figures are notoriously difficult to obtain because in official surveys questions about religious adherence are omitted entirely.

2. On legal practices in Syria's family law courts, see M. S. Berger, "The Legal System of Family Law in Syria," *Bulletin d'Études Orientales* 44 (1997): 115–127.

3. Cf. U. F. Abd-Allah, *The Islamic Struggle* (Berkeley, 1983); and R. Hinnebush, "The Islamic Movement in Syria," in *Islamic Resurgence in the Arab World,* ed. A. Dessouki (New York, 1982), 138–169.

4. On the Ba'th government's policy toward religion and minorities, see H. G. Lob-meyer, "Islamic Ideology and Secular Discourse: The Islamists in Syria," *Orient* 32 (1991): 395–418.

5. K. A. Jaber, *The Arab Ba'th Socialist Party: History, Ideology, and Organization* (Syracuse, N.Y., 1966), 129.

6. On this, see esp. A. Böttcher, *Syrische Religionspolitik unter Asad* (Freiburg, 1998), 147–224; also L. Steinberg, "Naqshbandiya in Damascus: Strategies to Establish and Strengthen the Order in a Changing Society," in *Naqshbandis in Western and Central Asia: Change and Continuity,* ed. E. Özdalga (Istanbul, 1999), 101–116.

7. A prominent example was the expulsion in the 1990s of the hadith scholar Nasir al-Din al-Albani (1914–1999), who died in Jordanian exile. His uncompromising hostility to both Islamic Sufism and the traditional Sunni schools of law had already caused several scandals in the 1960s and 1970s.

8. On Shahrur's work, see A. Christmann, "The Form Is Permanent, but the Content Moves: the Qur'anic Text and Its Interpretation(s) in Mohamad Shahrour's *Al-Kitab wa-l Qur'an,"* *Die Welt des Islams* 43, no. 2 (2003): 143–172.

9. A summary of the key events is given in E. Zisser, "A False Spring in Damascus," *Orient* 44, no. 1 (2003): 39–61; idem, *Commanding Syria: Bashar al-Asad and the First Years in Power* (London, 2007).

19. Iraq *(Henner Fürtig)*

1. See the chapter by Werner Ende, "Shi'i Islam," in this volume.

2. Cf. Y. Nakash, *The Shi'is of Iraq* (Princeton, 1994), 6–7, 13–48; R. Soeterik, *The Islamic Movement of Iraq (1958–1980)* (Amsterdam, 1991), 4–5. For details, see S. Deringil, S., "The Struggle against Shiism in Hamidian Iraq," *Die Welt des Islams* 30 (1990): 45–62.

3. Cf. A. Baram, "The Radical Shiite Opposition Movements in Iraq," in *Religious Radicalism and Politics in the Middle East,* ed. E. Sivan and M. Friedman (New York, 1990), 110.

4. Quoted in F. Ajami, *The Vanished Imam: Musa Sadr and the Shia of Lebanon* (Ithaca, 1986), 38.

5. Cf. S. Longrigg, *Iraq, 1900–1950* (London, 1950), 123.

6. Cf. K. Makiya, *Republic of Fear: The Politics of Modern Iraq* (Berkeley, 1998), 215. Ethnic and confessional relationships have not basically changed since 1932; but in terms of population trends the Shi'ite Arabs have increased most. By the early years of the twenty-first century they made up 60–65 percent of Iraq's total population and 80 percent of the Arab population; see W. A. Terrill, *Nationalism, Sectarianism, and the Future of the U.S. Presence in Post-Saddam Iraq* (Carlisle, Pa., 2003), 17. Partly enforced internal migration means that the Shi'ites are no longer confined to the south of the country. Some experts estimated the Shi'ite share of Baghdad's population at 50 percent; see Y. Nakash, "The Shi'ites and the Future of Iraq," *Foreign Affairs* 58, no. 7–8 (2003): 18.

7. During this period only four of the twenty-three prime ministers who had been in office since the war were Shi'ites; see H. Batatu, *The Old Social Classes and the Revolutionary Movements of Iraq: A Study of Iraq's Old Landed and Commercial Classes and of Its Communists, Ba'thists, and Free Officers* (Princeton, 1978), 176, 186. In 1936, a year after the introduction of universal conscription, only two of the sixty most senior officers were Shi'ites; see Makiya, *Republic of Fear,* 215.

8. See F. Jamali, "The Theological Colleges of Najaf," *The Muslim World* 50 (1960): 15–22.

9. Batatu, 1978, 999.

10. See B. Moin, *Khomeini: Life of the Ayatollah* (New York, 1999), 144; German translation of the fatwa text by O. Spies in *Die Welt des Islams* 6 (1959–1961): 264–265.

11. See A. Baram, "The Impact of Khomeini's Revolution on the Radical Shii Movement of Iraq," in *The Iranian Revolution and the Muslim World*, ed. D. Menashri, (Boulder, Colo., 1990), 132.

12. The Shiʿites and Sunnites were supposed to join each other's parties when their fellow supporters were in the majority in their own; see J. N. Wiley, "The Position of the Iraqi Clergy," in *Iran, Iraq, and the Arab Gulf States*, ed. J. A. Kechichian (New York, 2001), 57–58.

13. The religious leader of the Sunni Islamists, Shaykh ʿAbd al-ʿAziz al-Badri, was murdered in prison in 1969, and independent houses of prayer and mosques were shut down. Most of the IIP leaders went into exile; the remaining Sunnite clergy in Iraq lived under strict control by the Baʿth regimes; ibid., 58.

14. See Batatu, 1978, 1080.

15. See L. Kubba, "Domestic Politics in a Post-Saddam Iraq," in Kechichian, *Iran, Iraq, and the Arab Gulf States,* 79.

16. One of the best-known Kurdish Islamists, Mulla ʿUthman ʿAbd al-ʿAziz, defected to the Iranian side with five thousand men in 1983; see Wiley, "Position of the Iraqi Clergy," 59.

17. See A. Baram, "Broken Promises," *Wilson Quarterly* (Spring 2003): 48.

18. Saddam Hussein made it a custom to open a new mosque every year on his birthday, April 28. He also banned restaurants from serving alcohol. See W. A. Terrill, *The United States and Iraq's Shiʿite Clergy: Partners or Adversaries?* (Carlisle, Pa., 2004), 10.

19. See *Al-Thawra,* September 25, 1997.

20. See G. E. Fuller, *Islamist Politics in Iraq after Saddam Hussein* (Washington, D.C., 2003), 10.

21. See Wiley, "Position of the Iraqi Clergy," 60.

22. See J. Cole, "The United States and Shi'ite Religious Factions in Post-Ba'thist Iraq," *Middle East Journal* 57, no. 4 (2003): 548.

23. Ibid., 544.

24. For the full text of the Iraqi constitution, see *Washington Post,* October 12, 2005.

25. H. Fürtig, "Irak: Ein Modell externer Demokratisierung auf dem Prüfstand," *Internationale Politik und Gesellschaft* 3 (2006): 58.

26. CNN, January 17, 2007.

27. "Irak: Parlament verabschiedet Föderalismusgesetz," *Die Zeit,* October 11, 2006.

28. C. Snow, "An Agreement in Baghdad," *Middle East Economic Survey* 50, no. 36 (2007): 26.

20. Jordan *(Renate Dieterich)*

1. G. Chatelard, "Jordanie: entre appartenance communautaire et identité nationale," *Cahiers de l'Orient* 4 (1997): 117–122.

2. One example is the Muslim Brother Munʿim Abu Zant, who was banned from preaching Friday sermons because of his harsh criticism of the Jordanian-Israeli peace treaty.

3. For example, in the 2003 parliamentary elections, on the question whether women should lift their veils to prove their identity at the polling stations. The Supreme Mufti agreed to this, drawing protests from radical forces.

21. Lebanon *(Axel Havemann)*

1. The system was the basis of politics and administration from 1861 on; its beginnings were already discernible in the 1840s. J. P. Spagnolo, *France and Ottoman Lebanon, 1861–1914* (London, 1977); E. D. Akarli, *The Long Peace: Ottoman Lebanon, 1861–1920* (Berkeley, 1993).

2. Cf. the contributions in the first part of A. Hourani and N. Shehadi, eds., *The Lebanese in the World: A Century of Emigration* (London, 1992).

3. For an estimate of 4.04 million as long ago as 1988, see M. Halawi, *A Lebanon Defied: Musa al-Sadr and the Shi'a Community* (Boulder, Colo., 1992), 50; contrast M. Jansen's figure of 2.9 million for 1991 in *Middle East Review* (1992): 73.

4. T. Hanf, *Coexistence in Wartime Lebanon: Decline of a State and Rise of a Nation* (London, 1993), 86–90; M. Johnson, *Class and Client in Beirut: The Sunni Muslim Community and the Lebanese State, 1840–1985* (London, 1986), 24, 226; Halawi, 1992, 50. Other authors cite earlier figures showing much stronger Muslim dominance, e.g., *Maghreb-Machrek* 73 (1976): 69.

5. K. S. Salibi, *The Modern History of Lebanon* (London, 1965); T. Touma, *Paysans et institutions féodales chez les druses et les maronites du Liban du XVIIe siècle à 1914*, 2 vols. (Beirut, 1971–72); Spagnolo, *France and Ottoman Lebanon;* Akarli, *The Long Peace.*

6. K. S. Salibi, *A House of Many Mansions: The History of Lebanon Reconsidered* (London, 1988), 130–150.

7. H. Bartels, *Das Waqfrecht und seine Entwicklung in der libanesischen Republik* (Berlin, 1967), 110; *Al-Fikr al-islami,* special issue (July–August 1974): 46f.; L.-H. de Bar, *Les communautés confessionelles du Liban* (Paris, 1983), 28f.

8. For the position of the mufti in the "al-'Azm affair," see S. Wild, "Gott und Mensch im Libanon," *Der Islam* 48 (1972): 206–253, esp. 229ff.; for cooperation after 1970 between the Lebanese-Arab nationalist forces and the Palestinians (known after Khalid as "the Army of Islam"), see Hanf, 1993, 331; for the conflict with Sa'ib Salam, the head of the Maqasid, see note 16.

9. *Al-Fikr al-islami* (1974): 93f.

10. Text reprinted in H. Miller Davis, *Constitutions, Electoral Laws, Treaties of States in the Near and Middle East* (New York, 1970), 291–305.

11. For details on the attitude of the Sunnis, see R. El-Solh, *Lebanon and Arabism: National Identity and State Formation* (London, 2004); idem, "The Attitude of the Arab Nationalists towards Greater Lebanon during the 1930s," in *Lebanon: A History of Conflict and Consensus,* ed. N. Shehadi and D. H. Mills (London, 1988), 149–165; on the attitude of the Maronite Christians, see F. Kiwan, "La perception du Grand-Liban chez les maronites dans la période du mandat," in Shehadi and Mills, 1988, 124–148.

12. F. el-Khazen, *The Communal Pact of National Identities: The Making and Politics of the 1943 National Pact* (Oxford, 1991).

13. On the economy, see de Bar, 1983, 34–36; on culture and education, see T. Hanf, *Erziehungswesen in Gesellschaft und Politik des Libanon* (Bielefeld, 1969); for subsequent developments, see B. Labaki, *Education et mobilité sociale dans la société multicommunautaire du Liban* (Frankfurt am Main, 1988).

14. M. Johnson, *Class and Client in Beirut: The Sunni Muslim Community and the Lebanese State, 1840–1985* (London, 1986), esp. 45ff., 82ff.; A. Hottinger, "Zu'ama' in Historical Perspective," in *Politics in Lebanon,* ed. L. Binder (New York, 1966), 85–105.

15. L. Schatkowski, "The Islamic Maqased of Beirut: A Case Study of Modernization in Lebanon" (M.A. thesis, American University of Beirut, 1969).

16. Sa'ib Salam was president of the Maqasid for over twenty years; his position was unsuccessfully challenged several times, with explosive political implications; see M. Johnson, "Factional Politics in Lebanon: The Case of the 'Islamic Society of Benevolent Institutions' (Al-Maqasid) in Beirut," *Middle Eastern Studies* 14 (1978): 56–75; de Bar, 1983, 30f.

17. J. Reissner, "Säkularisierung des Libanon? Äußerungen von Muslimen zum neuen Schlagwort 'Almana," *Orient* 17 (1976): 13–37.

18. Hanf, 1993, 130ff.

19. Text in *Maghreb-Machrek* 72 (1976): 81–83.

20. P. Sluglett and M. Farouk-Sluglett, "Aspects of the Changing Nature of Lebanese Confessional Politics: Al-Murabitun, 1958–1979," in *Islamic Dilemmas: Reformers, Nationalists, and Industrialization,* ed. E. Gellner (Berlin, 1985), 267–283.

21. M. Humphrey, *Islam, Sect, and State: The Lebanese Case* (Oxford, 1989); M. Deeb, *Militant Islamic Movements in Lebanon: Origins, Social Basis, and Ideology* (Washington, D.C., 1986).

22. F. Nasrallah, *The Questions of South Lebanon* (Oxford, 1992).

23. F. Khuri, *From Village to Suburb: Order and Change in Greater Beirut* (Chicago, 1975); A. R. Norton, *Amal and the Shi'a: Struggle for the Soul of Lebanon* (Austin, 1987), 13ff.; M. Pohl-Schöberlein, *Die schiitische Gemeinschaft des Südlibanon (Gabal 'Amil) innerhalb des libanesischen konfessionellen Systems* (Berlin, 1986), 86ff.

24. E. A. Early, "The Amiliyya Society of Beirut: A Case Study of an Emerging Urban Za'im" (M.A. thesis, American University of Beirut, 1971); Hanf, 1969, 212–214.

25. F. Ajami, *The Vanished Imam: Musa al Sadr and the Shia of Lebanon* (Ithaca, 1986), 113ff.; Norton, 1987, 44.

26. See the accounts in Norton, 1987; Ajami, 1986; and Halawi, 1992.

27. Halawi, 1992, 163–199.

28. For an English translation of the statute, see Norton, 1987, 144–166.

29. Norton, 1987, 42–44; Ajami, 1986, 161–164.

30. Deeb, *Militant Islamic Movements in Lebanon,* 12f.

31. For details, see S. Rosiny, *Islamismus bei den Schiiten im Libanon: Religion im Übergang von Tradition zur Moderne* (Berlin, 1996).

32. Deeb, *Militant Islamic Movements in Lebanon,* 13–17; C. Mallat, *Shi'i Thought from the South of Lebanon* (Oxford, 1988), esp. 37ff.; A. Hottinger, "Verfassungsentwurf Teherans für Libanon—über die Ausbreitung der iranischen Revolution," *Neue Zürcher Zeitung,* May 6, 1987.

33. English translation in Norton, 1987, 167–187. In the summer of 2001 it was decided to rework this letter and adapt it to the changed conditions: an expression of a pragmatic realpolitik attitude.

34. The most comprehensive modern study on the Druzes is B. Schenk, *Kamal Gunbulat: Das arabisch-islamische Erbe und die Rolle der Drusen in seiner Konzeption der libanesischen Geschichte* (Berlin, 1994); see also K. M. Firro, *A History of the Druzes* (Leiden, New York, and Cologne, 1992), *Handbuch der Orientalistik,* sec. 1, *Der Nahe und der Mittlere Osten,* supplementary vol. 9.

35. A. Havemann, *Rurale Bewegungen im Libanongebirge des 19. Jahrhunderts* (Berlin, 1983), 38–41, 48–65; Abu-Izzeddin, 1984, 223–226; Touma, *Paysans et institutions féodales,* 78ff.

36. R. B. Betts, *The Druze* (New Haven, 1988), 37f., 52–54, 57ff.

37. Ibid., 91, 96f.; de Bar, *Les communautés confessionelles du Liban*, 131; W. Schmucker, *Krise und Erneuerung im libanesischen Drusentum* (Bonn, 1979), 117ff.
38. W. R. Goria, *Sovereignty and Leadership in Lebanon, 1943–1976* (London, 1985), 30.
39. F. al-Khazen, "Kamal Jumblatt, the Uncrowned Druze Prince of the Left," *Middle Eastern Studies* 24 (1988): 178–205; Goria, 1985, 30ff. and passim; cf. Jumblat's autobiography, K. Joumblatt, *I Speak for Lebanon* (London, 1982).
40. For details, see Schenk, 1994.
41. J. P. Harik, "Change and Continuity among the Lebanese Druze Community: The Civil Administration of the Mountains, 1983–90," *Middle Eastern Studies* 29 (1993): 377–398; Schenk, 2002, 240ff.
42. Text in *Les Cahiers de l'Orient* 16–17 (1990): 115–128; see also a detailed commentary by J. Maila, ibid., 135–217 (English translation in *Prospects for Lebanon* 4 [Oxford, 1992]); on the political context, see Perthes, 1994; A. R. Norton, "Lebanon after Ta'if: Is the Civil War Over?" *Middle East Journal* 45 (1991): 457–473; Hanf, 1990, 567ff., esp. 583–590.
43. For the text of the new constitution, see *Al-Safir* (Beirut), August 22, 1990; English translation in *Beirut Review* 1 (1991): 119–160.
44. Even after the Israeli withdrawal from southern Lebanon (2000), Syrian troops still remained on Lebanese territory. The Ta'if Accord explicitly legalized the Syrian presence "for an indefinite period." They were withdrawn in 2005 after the assassination of Rafiq al-Hariri.
45. For election reports and analysis, see "New Parliament, New Policies?" *Lebanon Report* 3 (October 1992); V. Perthes, "Problems with Peace: Post-war Politics and Parliamentary Elections in Lebanon," *Orient* 33, no. 3 (1992): 409–432, esp. 419ff.; F. el-Khazen, *Lebanon's First Postwar Parliamentary Election, 1992: An Imposed Choice* (Oxford, 1998).
46. V. Perthes, *Die libanesischen Parlamentswahlen von 1996: Akzeptanz des Faktischen* (Ebenhausen, 1996); T. Scheffler, "Abschied vom Konfessionalismus? Die Parlamentswahlen im Libanon," *Informationsprojekt Naher und Mittlerer Osten* (hereafter *INAMO*) 8 (1996): 31–34; idem, "1989–1999: Zehn Jahre Ta'if-Abkommen," *INAMO* 20 (1999): 4–8.
47. Havemann, 2002, 188ff., 216ff., 248ff.; see also K. M. Firro, *Inventing Lebanon: Nationalism and the State under the Mandate* (London and New York, 2003), 42–67.
48. B. Rieger, *Rentiers, Patrone und Gemeinschaft: Soziale Sicherung im Libanon* (Frankfurt, 2003).

22. Saudi Arabia *(Guido Steinberg)*

1. Many of its followers reject this name. They call themselves the "People of Monotheism" (*al-muwahhidun, ahl al-tawhid*), followers of the pious ancestors, *salaf salih* (*al-salafiyyun*), that is, the early Muslims in Mecca and Medina, or simply "the Muslims" (*al-muslimun*). The movement is generally referred to as *al-da'wa ila l-tawhid,* or "a call to the belief in monotheism."
2. See E. Peskes, *Muhammad ibn 'Abdalwahhab (1703–92) im Widerstreit* (Beirut and Stuttgart, 1993), for the early history of the Wahhabiyya.
3. The source book on this period is R. B. Winder, *Saudi Arabia*.
4. G. Steinberg, *Religion und Staat,* 433–436.
5. See ibid., 87f., for the six basic treatises.
6. J. S. Habib, *Ibn Sa'ud's Warriors of Islam*.

7. They made these demands public in a legal opinion on February 11, 1927. See the annotated text of the document in C. M. Amin, B. C. Fortna, and E. B. Frierson, eds., *The Modern Middle East: A Sourcebook* (New York, 2005).

8. See Michael Cook, *Commanding Right and Forbidding Wrong in Islamic Thought* (New York, 2000), for more on the concept of *amr bi-l-maʿruf.*

9. For more information, see the chapter by G. Steinberg and J.-P. Hartung in this edition.

10. See also G. Steinberg, *Religion und Staat,* 423–431, for further discussion.

11. See S. Yizraeli, *The Remaking of Saudi Arabia: The Struggle between King Saud and Crown Prince Faysal, 1953–1962* (Tel Aviv, 1997), for more on the "Free Princes."

12. See the chapter by J. Reissner on Islamic internationalism in this volume.

13. F. Ibrahim, "Die neue saudische 'Verfassung': Eine kontrollierte 'Öffnung' des saudischen Systems?" *Verfassung und Recht in Übersee* 25, no. 4 (1992): 446–454.

14. See I. Glosemeyer, "Saudi-Arabien," for more information on the Consultative Council.

15. See P. Pawelka, *Der Vordere Orient und die Internationale Politik* (Stuttgart, 1993); and C. Schmid, *Das Konzept des Rentier-Staates: Ein sozialwissenschaftliches Paradigma zur Analyse von Entwicklungsgesellschaften und seine Bedeutung für den Vorderen Orient* (Hamburg, 1991), for more information on the concept of a "rentier state."

16. See R. Schulze, *Islamischer Internationalismus,* 296f., for more information on Hayʾat Kibar al-ʿUlamaʾ.

17. See also G. Steinberg, *Religion und Staat,* 356–395, for further discussion.

18. J. Reissner, "Saudi-Arabien," 539.

19. F. E. Vogel, *Islamic Law and Legal System: Studies of Saudi Arabia* (Ann Arbor, 2000), 256ff.

20. R. H. Dekmejian, "Political Islamism in Saudi Arabia," *Middle East Journal* 48, no. 4 (Autumn 1994): 627–643, esp. 633–635.

23. The Small Gulf States *(Katja Niethammer)*

1. On this "dynastic" form of government, see Herb, *All in the Family.*

2. For this reason all GCC states have bilateral defense treaties with the United States; the UAE also has a bilateral treaty with France.

3. Although the original goal of establishing a common currency and market modeled on the European Union could not realistically be achieved by 2010, the GCC has contributed to regional integration through common external tariffs and the facilitation of freedom of travel, investment, and settlement.

4. The emergence of such an identity is evident, for example, in discussions on blogs and Internet forums based in the Gulf.

5. While resources are unequally distributed among the small Gulf states, even the poorest Gulf monarchies use oil revenues to finance almost 70 percent of their government budgets, according to 2005 figures.

6. On the basis of the Human Development Indexes (HDI), all of the small Gulf states have been included in the category of highly developed countries. Kuwait and Qatar, for example, have approximately the same standard of development as the Czech Republic and Hungary. With the exception of Libya, the other Arab states are ranked as countries with a medium level of development.

7. Workers from India and Pakistan as well as domestic workers from Indonesia and the Philippines constitute the largest contingents.

8. Christians and Hindus in Oman, the UAE, Bahrain, and Kuwait are permitted to hold religious services openly in churches and temples. Recently, the situation for Christian residents changed dramatically in Qatar; while previously all outward non-Muslim religious symbols were prohibited, the state has since 2008 shown its willingness to

accomodate its Christian inhabitants. State authorities designated a compound area for them outside Doha. At Easter 2008, a Catholic cathedral was opened there. A Lutheran and an Anglican church are said to be under construction. See U.S. Department of State, Report on International Religious Freedom, www.state.gov.

9. The Ibadiyya is often traced back to the Kharijite movement of the early centuries, although it is not clear that this is correct. See T. Lewicki, "Ibāḍiyya," in *Encyclopaedia of Islam*, vol. 3 (Leiden 1971), 648a. There are no exact figures. Estimates of the share of Ibadis within the total *native* population of Oman range between 50 and 75 percent.

10. See J. Calmard, "Mardjaʿ-i taḳlīd," ibid., 6:548b.2001. For more details, see Badry, "Marjaʿiyya and Shūrā," 188–206; Nasr, *Shia Revival;* and Walbridge, *The Most Learned of the Shiʿa.*

11. The few Christian citizens come from the Levant and Iraq and have been naturalized. The small community of Bahraini Jews also fled there from Iraq in the 1940s.

12. Anthony, *Arab States of the Lower Gulf,* 10ff.

13. In addition, Zaidi Yemenis work in the small Gulf states; as a rule they do not possess the citizenship of the host country.

14. See Brown, *Rule of Law,* 130ff.

15. Ibid., 146–149.

16. Khuri, *Tribe and State,* 35–84.

17. Brown, *Rule of Law,* 150.

18. Hamzeh, "Qatar," 79–90.

19. Here the British applied the laws of their colonial administration in India of the nineteenth century; see Brown, *Rule of Law,* 135.

20. Ibid., 132ff.

21. Ibid., 154.

22. There is the least amount of written law in Qatar, the most in Kuwait and Bahrain. United Nations Development Programme, Programme on Governance in the Arab Region, www.undp-pogar.org.

23. See Amnesty International, human rights by country, www.amnesty.org.

24. BBC News, December 15, 2006, http://news.bbc.co.uk/. Migrant workers, who constitute an estimated 90 percent of the population in Dubai, were not permitted to vote.

25. BBC News, March 20, 2006, http://news.bbc.co.uk/.

26. B. Gräf, "Sheikh Yūsuf al-Qaraḍāwī in Cyberspace," *Die Welt des Islams* 47 (2007): 403–421.

27. Ibid.

28. BBC News, January, 26, 2005, http://news.bbc.co.uk/.

29. The parliaments also exercise legislative and budgetary functions.

30. On the Muslim Brotherhood, see Brown, *Pushing Toward Party Politics?* On Bahraini Islamists, see K. Niethammer, "The Paradox of Bahrain."

31. This relativizes the distinction proposed by Oliver Roy between Islamists and "neo-fundamentalists" or "neo-Salafis"; see O. Roy, *L'échec de l'Islam politique* (Paris, 1992), n. 52.

24. Yemen *(Iris Glosemeyer)*

1. See also the various articles in W. Daum, *Yemen.*

2. Within the Zaydiyya (also called Hadawiyya after al-Hadi ila al-Haqq, primarily by its opponents) there was consensus until 1990 that their religious and worldly leader, the imam, had to be a *sayyid.*

3. Yemeni tribes, often organized in informal federations such as the tribes of the Hashid and the Bakil federations, are almost exclusively sedentary. There are few academic

publications available on the tribes, in particular those in the east and south. See P. Dresch, *Tribes, Government, and History*; and S. Weir, *A Tribal Order*, for information on tribes in the north of Yemen.

4. The Shafi'i *fiqh* differentiates itself from the Zaydi *fiqh* primarily in terms of ritual affairs and to a lesser extent in matters of civil law. Nevertheless, in some aspects the Zaydiyya is closer to the Sunni denominations than the other Shi'a denominations. This does not mean that relations between Zaydis and other groups have been without tensions. See also the essays by Werner Ende and Bernd Radtke in this volume; and W. Madelung, "Zaydiyya," in *The Encyclopedia of Islam*, 2nd ed., vol. 11, 477–481. It also provides an overview of the different currents within the Zaydiyya.

5. Unless otherwise indicated, refer to I. Glosemeyer, *Politische Akteure*, for the discussion that follows. Further bibliographical references can also be found there.

6. See M. W. Wenner, *Modern Yemen*, 47–48.

7. See also J. Reissner, "Die Idrisiden in 'Asir," *Die Welt des Islams* 21, nos. 1–4 (1981): 164–192.

8. A. K. al-Saidi, *Die Oppositionsbewegung im Jemen zur Zeit Imam Yahyas und der Putsch von 1948* (Berlin, 1981); J. E. Peterson, *Yemen*; and L. Douglas, *The Free Yemeni Movement*.

9. A. Würth, *Ash-Sharī'a fī Bāb al-Yaman*, 44–46.

10. Ibid., 62–63; B. Haykel, "Rebellion, Migration or Consultative Democracy? Zaydis and Their Detractors in Yemen," in R. Leveau, F. Mermier, and U. Steinbach, *Le Yémen contemporain*, 193–201.

11. G. vom Bruck, "Being a Zaydi in the Absence of an Imam: Doctrinal Revisions, Religious Instruction, and the (Re-)Intervention of Rituals," ibid., 169–192.

12. For information on the political developments in South Yemen, see also H. Lackner, *P.D.R. Yemen*; F. Halliday, *Arabia without Sultans*; and C. Scheider, *Der südliche Jemen und die Sowjetunion: Großmachtengagement und politische Radikalisierung in der Dritten Welt* (Hamburg, 1989).

13. A. Würth, "Stalled Reform: Family Law in Post-Unification Yemen," *Islamic Law and Society* 10, no. 1 (2003): 12–33.

14. See also L. Stiftl's dissertation, "Politischer Islam und Pluralismus" (Free University of Berlin, 1998); and J. Schwedler, "The Islah Party in Yemen," in *Islamist Activism: A Social Movement Theory Approach*, ed. Q. Wiktorowicz (Bloomington, Ind., 2004), 205–228.

15. Yemen is a poor country in spite of its oil revenues, which have financed up to two-thirds of the national budget. Oil production in Yemen is only one-twentieth the level of that in Saudi Arabia, a country with nearly the same number of inhabitants. Many Yemenis still work abroad, and the government relies on foreign aid.

16. S. Weir, "A Clash of Fundamentalisms: Wahhabism in Yemen," *Middle East Research and Information Project* 204, no. 27.3 (1997): 22–23, 26; and vom Bruck, "Being a Zaydi," 169–192.

17. See I. Glosemeyer, "Der Vertrag von Jidda," *Jemen-Report* 32, no. 1 (2001): 5–11.

V. The Islamic Diaspora

1. Western Europe *(Nico Landman)*

1. The studies of Islam in western Europe that discuss the period before 1900 usually treat it in introductions. For a comprehensive discussion, see H. Ansari 2004; for more information on Germany, see M. S. Abdullah 1981.

2. According to one source (B. Maréchal 2002), Germany had the largest number of Islamic houses of worship by far (2,200), followed by Great Britain (1,200), France (1,150), the Netherlands (450), Spain (320), and Belgium (310). The remaining European countries had only 100 or fewer mosques.

3. This is especially true of the Netherlands (55), Germany (66), and Great Britain (100). France lagged with only eight new mosques; ibid. For Great Britain, see P. Clark 2001.

4. S. Andézian 1988.

5. K. Canatan, C. H. Oudijk et al. 2003. Most of the Moroccan mosques in Rotterdam appear to be "religious mosques," while the Turkish mosques in particular tend to be "social mosques."

6. Cf. A. S. Roald 2001; G. Jonker 1999.

7. B. Maréchal 2003b.

8. Ibid.; cf. the essay by Volker Nienhaus in the present volume.

9. B. Maréchal 2003c.

10. See in particular the report on Islamic periodicals by S. Allievi 2003.

11. P. Werbner 2002.

12. S. Allievi and J. S. Nielsen 2003.

13. S. Kroissenbrunner 2002.

14. B. Lopez Garcia 2002.

15. U. Manço and M. Renaerts 2000.

16. D. Hussain 2003.

17. Ibid.; and B. Maréchal 2003a.

18. F. Messner, "L'organisation du culte musulman dans certains pays de l'Union européenne," *Revue de Droit Canonique* 46, no. 2 (1996): 195–213.

19. Muslim political activism has gained greater public visibility since the violent protests among Muslims over Salman Rushdie's novel *The Satanic Verses* in 1988; see S. P. Werbner 1996.

20. N. Daniel, *Islam and the West: The Making of an Image,* rev. ed. (Oxford, 1993).

21. F. Khosrokhavar 2004.

22. See M. Khedimellah 2002, who shows that militant young Muslims often come from the hip-hop subculture.

23. W. Schiffauer 1991.

24. O. Roy 1999 and 2002; J. Cesari 2003.

25. T. Sunier 1995; S. Vertovec and R. Alisdair, 1998.

26. J. Cesari 2003, 264.

27. M. K. Masud 2002.

28. See T. Ramadan, *Être Musulman européen: Étude des sources islamique à la lumière du contexte européen* (Lyon, 1999). In English: *To Be a European Muslim: A Study of Islamic Sources in the European Context* (Leicester, 2000).

29. Cesari 2003, 261.

30. F. Dasseto 1996 distinguishes nine ways in which European Islam interacts with its environment, ranging from assimilation to protest (325–329).

2. France, Great Britain, the Netherlands, and Germany *(Nico Landman)*

1. G. Kepel 1994.

2. In late December 2004 word came that the hostages had been released.

3. Interview at www.algerie-dz.com/article1082.html (conducted on September 7, 2004).

4. "Le rapport de la commission Stasi sur la laïcité," *Le Monde* (Paris), December 12, 2003.

5. A. Boyer 1998, 284.
6. Ibid., 289.
7. M. Khedimellah 2002.
8. Haut Conseil à l'Intégration, *L'Islam dans la République* (2000), 1, (http://islamlaic ite.org/IMG/pdf/isl_repu_Ht_conseil.pdf).
9. J. Rex 2002, 72.
10. T. Modood 2001, 64.
11. N. Matar 1998.
12. This was the first census to include questions on religious affiliation. Prior to 2001, estimates of the number of Muslims in Great Britain were based on immigration statistics.
13. See http://www.islamic-foundation.org.uk/.
14. See www.cbs.nl (accessed December 2004).
15. A detailed overview of the Islamic infrastructure in the Netherlands can be found in N. Landman 1992. For information on more recent developments, see K. Canatan, M. Popovic et al. 2005.
16. At the time of writing there was no official national registry of mosques. These numbers are based on the author's collection of data on Islamic organizations.
17. For Germany, see the next section of this chapter.
18. *Verzuiling* comes from the Dutch word *zuil,* meaning pillar, and is often translated as "pillarization." It refers to the social segregation of Dutch society along religious denominational lines.
19. See J. Rath, R. Penninx et al. 1996 for a detailed study on the integration of Islam into the Dutch infrastructure.
20. It already has a rival organization, the Contactgroep Islam en Overheid (Contact Group between Islam and the Government). Its members include both the Ahmadiyya, who are unwelcome in the CMO, and the Turkish Alevis, who have few common interests with the CMO's other member organizations. The reach of this rival organization is limited.
21. L. Tezcan 2003.
22. See, for instance, U. Spuler-Stegemann 1998. Referring to the principle of *taqiyya,* Spuler-Stegemann asks, "Can one trust statements by Muslims?"; ibid., 65. See also K. Binswanger and F. Sipahioglu 1988, which emphasizes the anti-Western rhetoric of conquest in the Turkish-language publications of Turkish Islamic associations. A study by B. Johansen (1987) presents Islam and Western democracy as antithetical yet comes to the conclusion that individual Muslims apparently have no difficulty living under a non-Islamic government and granting it religious legitimacy.
23. A. Goldberg 2002.
24. M. S. Abdullah 1995.
25. Cf. G. Höpp, "Die Wünsdorfer Moschee: Eine Episode islamischen Lebens in Deutschland, 1915–1930," *Die Welt des Islams* 36 (1996): 204–218.
26. A. Goldberg 2002.
27. Ibid.
28. See http://www.vikz.de/, December 2004. According to T. Lemmen 2000, in 1997 there were an additional 125 affiliated communities in other countries.
29. G. Jonker 2002.
30. An additional group, active in real estate, is the Europäische Moscheebau- und Unterstützungsgesellschaft e.V. (European Mosque Construction and Support Society). Cf. T. Lemmen 2000.
31. See www.igmg.de (accessed December 2004). U. Spuler-Stegemann (2001) estimates the number of affiliated organizations to be 1,094, twice the number given by the

IGMG. This figure, however, probably includes other groups besides mosque organizations. On a local level there is often an overlap between Milli Görüş organizations and the "Islamic federations" in which some non-Milli Görüş organizations participate. These Islamic federations usually deny their strong ties to Milli Görüş and respond with irritation to press reports asserting their existence. The Islamische Föderation Berlin e.V. has even challenged such reports in court. This attitude is perhaps attributable to the negative portrayal of Milli Görüş in the German debate, which harms the federations' public respectability.

32. L. Tezcan 2002.
33. T. Lemmen 2000, 52.
34. See http://www.diyanet.org/de/ (accessed December 2004). The website's claim that the DITIB represents 70 percent of German Muslims was not substantiated and should be taken with a grain of salt.
35. G. Seufert 1999.
36. See www.alevi.com (accessed December 2004).
37. See http://www.i-g-d.com/ (accessed December 2004).
38. See, e.g. N. Feindt-Riggers and U. Steinbach 1997, 46.
39. T. Lemmen 2000, 61.
40. Ibid., 64–65.
41. For an overview, see ibid., 69.
42. S. A. Azimi and M. Brückner, "Muslim Communities in German Webspace," paper presented at the conference "The Impact of Information and Communication Technologies on Religious, Ethnic, and Cultural Diaspora Communities in the West," held at the University of Göteborg, Sweden, 2003.
43. U. Spuler-Stegemann 1998, 245–249.
44. *Das Parlament* 52–53 (December 20, 2004).
45. See E. Seidel, C. Dantschke et al. 2001.
46. U. Spuler-Stegemann 2001, 1.
47. M. Rohe 2001.
48. This symbolic meaning becomes clear on the Islamic Council's website, http://www.islamrat.de (accessed December 2004). The organization explains that it is trying to gain recognition as a public body in order to achieve equal status with the two major Christian churches and the Greek Orthodox Church.
49. U. Spuler-Stegemann (2001) estimates this figure to be between 10 and 15 percent.
50. M. Rohe 2001.
51. See http://www.islamische-foederation.de (accessed December 2004).
52. E. Seidel, C. Dantschke et al. 2001, 103.

3. Eastern and Southeastern Europe *(Hermann Kandler)*

1. S. Huntington, *The Clash of Civilizations and the Remaking of the World Order* (New York, 1998), 252.
2. The terms "the Balkans" and "southeastern Europe" are used synonymously in this discussion.
3. M. Apostolov, *The Christian-Muslim Frontier* (London, 2003), 94.
4. Ibid., 42.
5. B. Szajkowski, T. Niblock, and G. Nonneman, *Muslim Communities in the New Europe* (Ithaca, 1997), 16.
6. The Turkish words *ova* and *yaka* are technical geographical terms used to describe these spatial units.

7. X. de Planhol, *Kulturgeographische Grundlagen der islamischen Geschichte* (Zurich and Munich, 1975), 332.

8. The term *millet* was used to describe religious communities in the Ottoman Empire. It refers to the minority groups (mostly non-Muslim) to which the Sublime Porte granted a degree of self-government.

9. E. C. Suttner 1997, 8–9.

10. M. Todorova 1999, 17.

11. An autonomous region in southern Yugoslavia called Metohija in Serbian.

12. Communal in the sense of the Latin *communis*, meaning community.

13. Z. Lutovac, "Serbisch-albanische Beziehungen in Kosovo-Metohija," in *Minderheiten als Konfliktpotential in Ostmittel- und Südosteuropa*, ed. G. Seewann (Munich, 1995), 140.

14. Kosovo Liberation Army.

15. L. Steindorff 1997, 194–196.

16. Democratic League of Kosovo.

17. Apostolov, *The Christian-Muslim Frontier*, 75.

18. L. Steindorff 1997, 198–200.

19. See http://www.crisisweb.org/home/index.cfm?id=1591&1=1.

20. Turkish Republic of Northern Cyprus.

21. United Nations Peacekeeping Force in Cyprus (UNFICYP).

22. H.-J. Axt 2004, 65–66.

23. J. Asmussen 2003, 407–408.

24. Party of Democratic Action.

25. Croat Democratic Union.

26. Serb Democratic Party.

27. C. Wieland. "Izzetbegovic und Jinnah: Die selektive Vereinnahmung zweier 'Muslim-Führer,'" *Südosteuropa-Mitteilungen* 39 (1999): 351–368.

28. A. Lopasic, "The Muslims in Bosnia," in G. Nonneman et al 1997, 107.

29. M.-J. Calic, "Ethnische Konflikte in Bosnien-Hercegovina: Eine strukturelle Analyse," in G. Seewann 1995, 166.

30. W. Petritsch, "Bosnien und Herzegowina fünf Jahre nach Dayton," *Südosteuropa-Mitteilungen* 40 (2000): 299–312.

31. Stabilization Force in Bosnia and Herzegovina.

32. W. Petritsch, "Bosnien und Herzegowina fünf Jahre nach Dayton," *Südosteuropa-Mitteilungen* 40 (2000): 305.

33. M. Ignatieff, *The Warrior's Honour: Ethnic War and Modern Conscience* (London, 1998), 174–175.

34. H. Poulton 1994, 54.

35. C. Voss 2001, 277.

36. Democratic Party of Albanians.

37. Intra-Macedonian Revolutionary Organization, Democratic Party for Macedonian National Unity.

38. The Macedonian Ushtria Clirimtare Kombetare (UCK, National Liberation Army) expresses its proximity to the Kosovar model through its similar name.

39. C. Voss 2001, 279.

40. "Säen und Ernten: NATO moderiert die ethnische Spaltung Mazedoniens," *ak—analyse + kritik: Zeitung für linke Debatte und Praxis*, no. 453, August 30, 2001.

41. "Mazedonien: Opposition stellt Ohrid-Abkommen in Frage, "*Länderberichte der Konrad-Adenauer-Stiftung*, April 28, 2003.

42. St. Troebst 1999, 228.

43. According to Section 2 of Appendix A in the Convention, which was signed on January 30, 1923, by both the Grand National Assembly of Turkey and the Greek government, the "mandatory exchange of Turkish citizens of Greek Orthodox faith living in Turkish territory and of Greek citizens of Muslim faith living in Greek territory" (Section 1) does not include "the Greek inhabitants of Constantinople...and the Muslim residents of Western Thrace."

44. R. Meinardus, "Die türkisch-griechische Minderheitenfrage," *Orient* 26 (1985): 58.

45. H. Kandler 1998, 285–307.

46. The West Thracian journalist Haki described this event in verse: "Lion, my people's friend, who came out from the mountains between Meriç and Karasu, where he resides[,]...who wishes, on behalf of his Turkishness, to tear down the barricades and to be the first to enter the city, to oppose those who want to deny and destroy Turkishness in Western Thrace on Friday, January 29, 1988. Aged seven to seventy, they taught a historical lesson." Excerpt from Haki, "Güller dererek," *Ileri* 829 (1996): 2.

47. "A few...believe I am not honest if I fail to distinguish between Greek Muslims and Greek Christians....But I know very well: beside this...difference, there is also an ethnic [*milli*] difference, and I recognize it....Every person has the right to describe himself as he pleases. I describe myself as a Greek. Another person may describe himself as a Turk." Stefanopoulos quoted in A. Dede, *Trakya'nôn Sesi* (1997), 1.

48. H. Kandler 2000, 65–82.

49. H. Kandler, "Muslime in Griechisch-Thrakien: Zur heutigen Situation einer muslimischen Minderheit in Südosteuropa und ihre Beziehungen zu ihrer_christlichen Mitbevölkerung" (postdoctoral thesis).

50. B. Szajkowski et al., "Islam and Ethnicity in Eastern Europe: Concepts, Statistics, and a Note on the Polish Case," in G. Nonneman, T. Niblock, and B. Szajkowski 1997, 27–42.

51. R. Dimitrov, "Sicherheitspolitik und ethnische Konflikte aus bulgarischer Sicht," in G. Seewann 1995, 176.

52. Movement for Rights and Freedom.

53. R. Dimitrov, *Sicherheitspolitik und ethnische Konflikte aus bulgarischer Sicht* (1995), 181–183.

54. I. Ilchev and D. Perry, "The Muslims of Bulgaria," in G. Nonneman, T. Niblock, and B. Szajkowski 1997, 115–137.

55. Bulgarian Helsinki Committee, *The Human Rights of Muslims in Bulgaria in Law and Politics since 1878* (Sofia, Bulgaria, 2003), 138.

56. Religious Information Service of Ukraine: Muslims, www.risu.org.ua/content.php?page_id=64&l=en (accessed 2004).

57. "Two Religious Leaders Condemn Fomenting of Inter-Religious Conflicts in Crimea," February 2, 2004, http://www.risu.org.ua/eng/news/article;2567/.

58. See de.wikipedia.org/wiki/Geschichte_Albaniens.

59. C. Kohl, www.toms-place.de/albanien-geschichte.htm (accessed 2004).

60. St. Troebst 2000, 124.

61. E. Cela, "Albanian Muslims, Human Rights, and Relations with the Islamic World," in G. Nonneman, T. Niblock, and B. Szajkowski 1997, 140–144.

62. Ibid., 144.

63. By the International Crisis Group (ICG).

64. ICG, *Albania: State of the Nation, 2003; Executive Summary and Recommendations* (Brussels, 2003).

65. ICG, *Pan-Albanianism: How Big a Threat to Balkan Stability?* Europe Report 153, February 25, 2004.

66. Human Rights without Frontiers, "Why Can't Smaller Protestant Churches or Muslims Gain Legal Status?" July 3, 2003, http://www.hrwf.net/religiousfreedom/news/slovakia_2003.html.

67. Religioscope, "Moldova: Problems of Registration for Various Groups," 2002, www.religioscope.com/notes/2002/012_moldova.htm.

68. G. Nonneman, T. Niblock, and B. Szajkowski 1997, 34–39.

4. The Americas *(Monika Wohlrab-Sahr)*

1. See in the present volume "The Distribution of Muslims throughout the World: Figures and Information on the Present Situation" *by Peter Heine* and *Riem Spielhaus*. Cf. the essay "Amerika" by Durán Khalid in the fourth (German) edition.

2. For further information, see M. Wohlrab-Sahr 1999, 23–45.

3. See M. Siddiqi, preface to *Islam in North America: A Sourcebook*, ed. M. A. Köszegi and G. Melton (New York and London, 1992), vii–viii; I. Bagby et al., "The Mosque in America: A National Portrait; A Report from the Mosque Study Project" (Washington, D.C., 2001); G. Schmidt 2004, 1–15.

4. See http://www.pluralism.org/resources/tradition/index.php?trad=9 (accessed December 20, 2007).

5. Y. Y. Haddad 1986.

6. G. Schmidt 2004, 2.

7. W. J. Moses 1993.

8. L. Kaba, "Americans Discover Islam through the Black Muslim Experience," in *Islam in North America: A Sourcebook*, ed. M. A. Köszegi and G. Melton (New York and London, 1992), 25.

9. Alex Haley's book *Roots* (New York, 1976) and the TV series adaptation played an important role in reactivating this myth. Both were extremely popular in the United States in the 1970s. The slave brought to America at the start of the story is a Muslim. Alex Haley also collaborated with Malcolm X on his autobiography (*The Autobiography of Malcolm X*, 1965).

10. H. Baer, The Black Spiritual Movement: A Religious Response to Racism (Knoxville, 1984).

11. S. E. U. Essien-Udom 1962, 9–40.

12. W. L. Van Deburg, introduction to *Modern Black Nationalism: From Marcus Garvey to Louis Farrakhan,* ed. W. L. Van Deburg (New York, 1977), 1–20; W. J. Moses 1993, 124–141.

13. E. Muhammad 1965.

14. W. D. Mohammed, *Islam's Climate for Business Success* (Chicago, 1995).

15. L. Farrakhan, *A Torchlight for America* (Chicago, 1993).

16. E. Muhammad 1965, 58.

VI. The Discussion within Islam on Secularism, Democracy, and Human Rights *(Alexander Flores)*

1. See Schölch 1987.

2. See Flores 1987, 44–47.

3. See Schulze 1987, 7–11.

4. See Flores 1987.

5. F. Antun, *Ibn Rushd wa-falsafatuhu* (Beirut, 1981), 215f.

6. M. ʿAbduh, *Al-islam wa-l-nasraniyya maʿa l-ʿilm wa-l-madaniyya*, 2nd ed. (Beirut, 1983), 184–192, 65–133, 59–61.
7. Antun, *Ibn Rushd wa-falsafatuhu*, 137–184.
8. M. ʿAmara, *Maʿrakat al-islam wa-usul al-hukm* (Cairo and Beirut, 1989), 8.
9. Ibid., 8f.
10. On this incident, see the reprint of the book as a special edition of the Cairo weekly newspaper *Al-Ahali*, May 4, 1996, with documents on the case and its aftermath.
11. See Flores 2003.
12. See Flores 1997.
13. "Nadwat al-hiwar haula l-islamiyya wa-l-ʿalmaniyya," *Minbar al-Hiwar* 15 (Fall 1989): 32; in German, "Islam und Säkularismus: Protokoll einer Diskussion," in F. Rasoul, *Kultureller Dialog und Gewalt* (Vienna, 1991), 159.
14. For examples of integralist authors' argumentation on this, see Khoury 1998, 77–82.
15. Cf. M. ʿAmara, *Al-ʿalmaniyya wa-nahdatuna al-haditha* (Cairo and Beirut 1986), 19–31.
16. Ibid., cited (with slight alterations) from the English translation in Flores 1997, 85.
17. For relevant quotations and summaries, see Khoury 1998, 83–88.
18. Ibid., 88–93.
19. Ibid., 93–99.
20. Probably the most detailed discussion on this theme is in F. Foda, *Al-haqiqa al-ghaʾiba* (Cairo and Paris, 1986).
21. F. Zakariyya, *Al-sahwa al-islamiyya fi mizan al-ʿaql* (Cairo, 1989); English translation quoted from Flores 1997, 85.
22. M. S. Al-ʿAshmawi, *Al-islam al-siyasi* (Cairo, 1987), 7, 35; English translation quoted (with slight alterations) from M. Al-Ashmawy, *Islam and the Political Order* (Washington, D.C.: Council for Research in Values and Philosophy, 1994).
23. See, e.g., Fahmi Huwaidi versus al-ʿAshmawi, discussed in Flores 1994. Several articles Huwaidi published in this context are reprinted in F. Huwaidi, *Al-muftarun: Khitab al-tatarruf al-ʿalmani fi l-mizan* (Cairo and Beirut, 1996), 132–169.
24. Zakariyya, *Al-sahwa*, 79; French trans., F. Zakariya, *Laïcité ou islamisme: Les Arabes à l'heure du choix* (Paris and Cairo, 1991), 45.
25. See Steppat 2001.
26. ʿA. Hasanayn, *Hatta la tazalla al-shariʿa nassan shakliyyan fi l-dustur* (Cairo, 1985), 27.
27. See the "Controversies" section in my contribution on Egypt in the present volume.
28. For a more detailed presentation of the debate, see Krämer 1999, passim. See also R. Badry, *Die zeitgenössische Diskussion um den islamischen Beratungsgedanken...* (Stuttgart, 1998).
29. Antun, *Ibn Rushd*, 142.
30. See Krämer 1999, 147.
31. See also Schulze 1991.
32. The Arabic text of the declaration is reproduced in *Minbar al-Hiwar* 9 (Spring 1988): 92–106. On the question of religious minorities, see the contribution by Johanna Pink in the present volume.
33. See Bielefeldt 1997.
34. For example, without a hint of apology the Egyptian jurist ʿAbdaljawad Yasin posits the desirability of a return to the traditional treatment of religious minorities in Muslim states and the death penalty for apostasy from Islam; see ʿA. Yasin, *Muqaddima fi fiqh al-jahiliyya al-muʿasira* (Cairo, 1986), 97–102, 130–132.
35. F. Foda, Y. L. Rizq, and K. ʿAbdalkarim, *Al-taʾifiyya...ila ayna?* (Cairo, 1987), 40, 44.
36. An-Naʿim 1992, 161–187; Ferjani 1991, 227–251.
37. I owe the formulation related to this line of thought to Bernhard Trautner; see Trautner 1999.

VII. The Situation of Women in Islamic Countries
(Wiebke Walther)

1. For a comprehensive regional and largely chronological reference work with a good bibliography, see S. Joseph, A. Najmabadi, and J. Peteet, eds., *The Encyclopedia of Women and Islamic Cultures,* 6 vols. (Leiden, 2003–2007). It covers South and Southeast Asia, Europe, Canada, and the United States, even if with the inevitable gaps due to a shortage of more detailed studies. For a compact overview of the Middle East, see also W. Walther, "Die Frau im Islam," in *Der Islam: Religion, Ethik, Politik,* ed. P. Antes, K. Duran, T. Nagel et al. (Stuttgart and Berlin, 1991). For both oral and written information on recent developments, I thank several embassies in Berlin, in particular the Moroccan embassy, for providing me with the 2004 Arabic version of the Mudawwana; the Turkish embassy for an update on Turkey's personal status codes from 1998 to 2005; as well as the Iranian, Yemeni, Kuwaiti, and Algerian embassies for other details, suggestions, and material.

2. See V. M. Moghadam, "Human Development Indicators for the Arab Region," in *Gender and Development in the Arab World,* ed. N. F. Khoury and V. M. Moghadam (London, 1996), 182, data for 1990; 2005 data for Afghanistan from www.orientale.de.

3. See R. Badry, "Ausweg aus der 'demographischen Falle' oder 'Verschwörung gegen den Islam'? Zur zeitgenössischen innerislamischen Debatte über Geburtenkontrolle und Familienplanung," in *Mitteilungen/Deutsches Orient-Institut* 56 (Hamburg, 1999).

4. See, e.g., B. A. M. Karam, *Women, Islamisms and the State: Contemporary Feminisms in Egypt* (Houndmills, 1998); and H. Afshar, *Islam and Feminisms: An Iranian Case-Study* (Houndmills, 1998).

5. For basic religious texts, see N. Awde, ed. and trans., *Women in Islam: An Anthology from the Quran and Hadiths* (Richmond, 2000).

6. See W. Walther, *Women in Islam,* intro. G. Nashat (Princeton, 1993), 103–153; N. R. Keddie and B. Baron, eds., *Women in Middle Eastern History: Shifting Boundaries in Sex and Gender* (New Haven, 1999); G. R. G. Hambly, ed., *Women in the Medieval Islamic World* (Basingstoke, 1998); G. Nashat and J. Tucker, eds., *Women in the Middle East and North Africa: Restoring Women to History* (Bloomington, 1999); S. Guthrie, *Arab Women in the Middle Ages: Private Lives and Public Roles* (London, 2001), 162ff. See also R. Roded, *Women in Islamic Biographical Collections: From Ibn Sa'd to Who Is Who* (Boulder, Colo., 1994), 135ff; this work also addresses how women were increasingly excluded from biographical literature from the sixteenth to the nineteenth century. In contrast, during the sixteenth and seventeenth centuries in Turkey, for about 150 years during the Ottoman Empire the concubines of several rulers were extraordinarily influential in politics. Affluent women were very committed to charitable activities. These facts found their way into the historical but not the biographical literature of the era. In general, historical works have regarded periods in which women were politically powerful and influential as decadent.

7. 'A. al-Jabarti, *Al-Mukhtar min ta'rikh al-Jabarti, Ikhtiyar Muhammad Qindil al-Bakali,* vol. 2 (n.p., n.d. [1957]), 300, March 8, 1799, and July 28, 1798. See also T. Philipp and M. Perlmann, eds. and trans., *'Abd al-Rahman al-Jabarti's History of Egypt,* 4 vols. (Stuttgart, 1994). See also, e.g., J. Mabro, ed., *Veiled Half-Truths: Western Travellers' Perceptions of Middle Eastern Women* (London and New York, 1991).

8. For this interpretation, see L. P. Peirce, *The Imperial Harem* (New York and Oxford, 1993).

9. See also F. Davis, *The Ottoman Lady* (New York, 1986), 131ff. In my opinion, A. L. al-Sayyid Marsot, *Women and Men in Late Eighteenth-Century Egypt* (Austin, 1995), idealizes a number of matters; for example, she stresses the basic equality of man and woman in the Qur'an. Nevertheless, she gives an accurate description of women's financial situations and activities differentiated by class. See also B. Sagaster, *Im Harem von Istanbul: Osmanisch-türkische Frauenkultur im 19. Jahrhundert* (Hamburg, 1989), specifically 103ff.; M. Z. Zilfi, ed., *Women in the Ottoman Empire* (Leiden, New York, and Cologne, 1997), especially the introduction and contributions by M. A. Fay, C. Imber, and M. L. Meriwether.

10. B. al-Bustani, "Khitab fi ta'lim al-nisa'," in *Al-Jam'iyya al-suriyya li-l-'ulum wa-l-funun 1847–1852* (Beirut, n.d. [1990]), 45–53.

11. See F. de Tarrazi, *Ta'rikh al-sahafa al-'arabiyya*, vol. 2 (Beirut, 1913), 241; for a short biography and literature about her, see J. Zaydan, *Masadir al-adab al-nisa'i fi l-'alam al-'arabi al-hadith* (Beirut, 1999), 630–631. After studying medicine in France, her brother Faransis Marrash published novels certainly influenced by works and ideas of the French Enlightenment; see the entry by N. Tomiche, *Encyclopaedia of Islam*, 2nd ed. (hereafter *EI-2*), vol. 6 (Leiden, 1991).

12. See N. Seni, "Fashion and Women's Clothing in the Satirical Press of Istanbul at the End of the 19th Century," in *Women in Modern Turkish Society: A Reader*, ed. S. Tekeli (London, 1995), 25–45.

13. See N. Göle, *The Forbidden Modern: Civilization and Veiling* (Ann Arbor, 1996).

14. For more about the author, see the entry by K. Öhrnberg in *EI-2*, vol. 8 (Leiden, 1995), 523–524; for more on the *Murshid*, see W. Walther, "Ein Wegbereiter der Frauenbildung im 19. Jahrhundert: Rifa'a Rafi' al-Tahtawi," in *Schuld sind die Männer—nicht der Koran: Zur Situation der muslimischen Frau*, ed. M.-E. Enay (Saanenmöser-Gstaad, 2000), 29–42.

15. For an excerpt from one of her very contrived articles in a style typical of the times, see U. R. Kahhala, *A'lam al-nisa'*, vol. 3 (Damascus, 1959), 170ff.; for an English translation, see M. Badran and M. Cooke, eds., *Opening the Gates* (London, 1990), 125ff.; for more about her life, see J. Zaydan, *Tarikh adab al-lugha al-'arabiyya*, ed. S. Dayf, vol. 4 (Cairo, n.d.), 224; and Zaydan, *Masadir*.

16. See also S. Bräckelmann, *"Wir sind die Hälfte der Welt!" Zaynab Fawwaz (1860–1914) und Malak Hifni Nasif (1886–1918), zwei Publizistinnen der frühen ägyptischen Frauenbewegung* (Beirut and Würzburg, 2004). For a short biography, her works, and literature, see Zaydan, *Masadir*, 571ff.; for an English translation of an article in which she contradicts Hanna Kurani by demanding the universal right of women to work outside the home, see Badran and Cooke, *Opening*, 220–21.

17. The title page states that it was published in the Islamic year 1312; see also B. Baron, *The Women's Awakening in Egypt: Culture, Society, and the Press* (New Haven, 1994); and M. Badran, *Feminists, Islam, and Nation: Gender and the Making of Modern Egypt* (Princeton, 1995), index entries for Fawwaz, Zaynab.

18. Z. Fawwaz, *Al-Durr al-manthur fi tabaqat rabbat al-khudur* (Bulaq and Cairo, 1312), 515–516.

19. Ibid., 6–7.

20. According to Khayr al-Din Zirikli, *Al-A'lam*, vol. 8 (Beirut, 1987), 19, Nasim Nawfal, an emigrant from Tripoli in Lebanon, founded the journal *Al-Fatat* in Alexandria under the name of his daughter Hind in November 1892. In fact they published it together until March 1894, that is, until a few months after Hind married. See also Baron, *Women's Awakening* (1994), index entry for Nawfal. For Hind Nawfal's biography and opening article, which are both written in the ornate style of the period, see Badran, *Opening*, 215–219. For women's issues from the period, see

U. R. Kahhala, *A'lam al-nisa'*, vol. 5 (Damascus, 1959), 265; U. R. Kahhala, *A'lam al-nisa'*, vol. 5 (Damascus, 1959); and Bräckelmann, *"Wir,"* 215–267.

21. See the entries for Moyal in both the *Encyclopedia Judaica* (Jerusalem, 1977) and Zaydan, *Masadir;* see also the index entry for Moyal in Baron, *Women's Awakening* (1994); and Bräckelmann, *"Wir,"* 51–52.

22. According to Bräckelmann, *"Wir,"* 51, the dictionary was probably not presented as Zaynab Fawwaz had planned, as she seems not to have finished it in time for the fair's opening.

23. See F. Fawwaz, ed., *Zaynab Fawwaz: Husn al-'awaqib aw ghadat al-Zahira* (Beirut, 1984), 15; some sentences from Zaynab's letter are quoted in the editor's preface.

24. See Kahhala, *A'lam,* 5:213ff.; and Badran, *Feminists,* index.

25. See Bräckelmann, *"Wir,"* 55; she cites Sha'ban's opinion that this was the very first Arabic novel, which would mean that a woman introduced this genre into Arabic literature; B. Sha'ban, *Mi'at 'am min al-riwaya al-nisa'iyya al-'arabiyya* (Beirut, 1999), 37. The first Arabic novels, however, were in fact written by the Syrian Christians Faransis Marrash (*Ghabat al-Haqq* [Beirut, 1865]) and Salim al-Bustani. Their works were certainly influenced by contemporary and earlier French novels, and to a certain extent by Arabic folk novels; for more about Marrash, see the entry in *EI-2*.

26. Z. Fawwaz, *Al Rasa'il al-Zaynabiyya,* pt. 1 (Cairo, 1322 [1904–5]); a second part was never published, probably because—according to Bräckelmann, *"Wir,"* 66—her eyesight severely deteriorated after 1905; a second edition appeared in 1910. For quotations, see U. R. Kahhala, *A'lam al-nisa'*, vol. 2 (Damascus, 1959), 82ff.; and Fawwaz, *Husn,* 16ff.; for her central themes, see Bräckelmann, *"Wir,"* 215–267.

27. See also U. Weckel, *Zwischen Häuslichkeit und Öffentlichkeit: Die ersten deutschen Frauenzeitschriften im späten 18. Jahrhundert und ihr Publikum* (Tübingen, 1998).

28. Muhammad 'Imara, ed., *Al-Mu'allafat al-kamila li-Muhammad 'Abduh,* vol. 2 (Cairo, 1972), 78–95. See also H. Gätje, *Koran und Koranexegese* (Zurich and Stuttgart, 1971), 324 ff.

29. S. S. Peterson, ed. and trans., *Qasim Amin: The Liberation of Women, and the New Woman; Two Documents in the History of Egyptian Feminism* (Cairo, 2000).

30. See Badran, *Feminists,* 17ff., in which the khedivial law school is also mentioned; the school in Aix is mentioned only in Kayr al-Din Zirikli, *Al-A'lam,* vol. 7 (Beirut, 1987).

31. See M. J. Kishk, *Jahalat 'asr al-tanwir: Qira'a fi fikr Qasim Amin wa-'Ali 'Abd al-Raziq* (Cairo, 1990); and, for instance, A. L. al-Sayyid Marsot, "Women and Modernization: A Revaluation," in *Women, the Family, and Divorce Laws in Islamic History,* ed. A. E. Azhary Sonbol (Syracuse, 1996), 39ff. and intro., 1ff.

32. Majd al-Din Hifni Nasif, ed., *Bahithat al-Badiya: Malak Hifni* (Cairo, 1962). For her biography and her article, see Badran, *Opening,* 134–136; Bräckelmann, *"Wir,"* 69–83.

33. See also K. Amirpur, *Gott ist mit den Furchtlosen: Shirin Ebadi und der Kampf um die Zukunft Irans* (Freiburg, Basel, and Vienna, 2003).

34. See Badran, *Feminists;* and D. Glaß, *Der Muqtataf und seine Öffentlichkeit,* vols. 1 and 2 (Würzburg, 2004), index; see also the entries "Frauen" (Women) and "Frauenpresse" (Women's Press), vol. 1, 173–180; Bräckelmann, *"Wir,"* 85–214.

35. G. Nashat, *Women and Revolution in Iran* (Boulder, Colo., 1983), 23.

36. R. Haerkötter, *Mahasin: Ein Beispiel für die osmanische Frauenpresse in der zweiten konstitutionellen Periode* (Wiesbaden, 1992), 31.

37. This material came from the Turkish embassy in March 2005. I thank T. Bacinoghlu, Tübingen, for providing it to me.

38. 'Abd al-Razzaq al-Hilali, *Ta'rikh al-ta'lim fi l-'Iraq fi l-'ahd al-'uthmani 1638–1917* (Baghdad, 1959), 158ff.; see also W. Ende, "Sollen Frauen schreiben lernen? Eine

innerislamische Debatte und ihre Widerspiegelung in al-Manar," in *Gedenkschrift Wolfgang Reuschel,* ed. D. Bellmann (Stuttgart, 1994), 49–58.

39. E. Sanasarian, *The Women's Rights Movement in Iran* (New York, 1982), 39.
40. Al-Munajjed, *Women in Saudi Arabia Today* (London, 1997), 59ff.; see also M. Al-Rasheed, *A History of Saudi Arabia* (Cambridge, 2002), 153–154.
41. See M. Böhmer, "Wissenschaft," in *Frauenlexikon,* ed. A. Lissner, R. Süssmuth, and K. Walter (Freiburg, Basel, and Vienna, 1988), 1175ff.
42. For more on the inadequate medical treatment of women by doctors and/or healers in the court harems of Istanbul before 1900, see Sagaster, *Harem,* 60–64.
43. Badran, *Feminists,* 148–149.
44. See also N. Mahfuz, "Al-Maraya" (The Mirrors), quoted in Walther, *Women,* 225–226.
45. Badr ol-Moluk Bamdad, *From Darkness into Light: Women's Emancipation in Iran,* ed. and trans. F. R. C. Bagley (Hicksville, N.Y., 1977), 98–99.
46. See Sanasarian, *Women's Rights,* 39; and for more detailed information, see F. Milani, *Veils and Words: The Emerging Voices of Iranian Women Writers* (New York, 1992), 55ff., 26.
47. See Walther, "Wegbereiter."
48. M. Seikaly, "Women and Religion in Bahrain," in *Islam, Gender, and Social Change,* ed. Y. Haddad and J. L. Esposito (New York and Oxford, 1998), 169–189.
49. Al-Munajjed, *Women,* 68ff.; see also S. Arebi, *Women and Words in Saudi Arabia: The Politics of Literary Discourse* (New York and Chichester, 1994), 50–51.
50. See Walther, "Wegbereiter."
51. World Bank, "Human Development Report," *CIA World Factbook,* United Nations Development Programme. For data from 1990, see Moghadam, *Human Development,* 178ff.
52. E. Warnock Fernea, ed., *Children in the Muslim Middle East* (Austin, 1995), 227ff.
53. See F. al-Takarli "The Dying Lamp" (Al-Qindil al-muntafiʾ), in *Modern Arabic Short Stories,* trans. D. Johnson-Davies (London, 1967), 51–55. As a judge, this Iraqi writer (who was born in 1927 and lived in exile from 1980 until his death in Damascus in February 2008) had great insight into such problems in his country. See also N. Mahfuz, "Al-Jabbar" (The Almighty), in *Dunya Allah* (Cairo, 1963).
54. See H. Shahidian, *Women in Iran: Emerging Voices in the Women's Movement* (Westport, Conn., 2002), 28 and its index; see also the interview Kar gave while undergoing treatment for cancer in Paris to the Iranian journalist Haleh Esfandiari for "Iran.Dokht TV" (www.irandokht.com/TV/) on May 28, 2004; see also her concise demands in *Huquq-e siyasiyy-e zanan-e Iran* (Political Rights of Iranian Women) (Tehran, 1376 [1956–57]).
55. A. Würth, *Ash-Shariʿa fi Bab al-Yaman: Recht, Richter und Rechtspraxis an der familienrechtlichen Kammer des Gerichts Süd-Sanaa (Republik Jemen), 1983–1995* (Berlin, 2000); for Iran, see Shahidian, *Women.*
56. M. Poya, *Women, Work and Islamism: Ideology and Resistance in Islam* (London and New York, 1999), 107. The average age at marriage for women in both rural and urban areas was twenty-two, according to the *Iran Statistical Yearbook* (1996–97), 62.
57. S. Galal, *Emanzipationsversuche der ägyptischen Frau* (n.p., 1977), 22.
58. See Walther, *Women.*
59. See Badran, *Opening,* 238–246 and index.
60. Published in Alexandria. According to the title page, Musa was director of the Amiriyya Girls' School in Alexandria at the time; her biography and two excerpts from the book are also available in Badran, *Opening,* 257–69.

61. See S. Küper-Bašgöl, *Frauen in der Türkei zwischen Feminismus und Reislamisierung* (Münster and Hamburg, 1992), 108, 110.

62. Ibid., 110.

63. *Al-Qabas,* March 18, 2005, 4. I thank my colleague Dieter Blohm from the Kuwaiti embassy in Berlin for bringing this issue to my attention.

64. See also S. Shukri, *Social Changes and Women in the Middle East* (Aldershot, 1999), 93–104; the author goes into why women take such jobs but does not examine the working conditions.

65. See contributions by A. Öncü in *Women in Turkish Society,* ed. N. Abadan-Unat (Leiden, 1981); and by F. Yildiz Ecevit and F. Özbay in Tekeli, *Women.*

66. According to material provided to me by the Turkish embassy in Berlin, March 2005.

67. See the cover of *Al-istratijiyya al-wataniyya li-taqaddum al-mar'a fi dawlat al-imarat al-'arabiyya al-muttahida* (n.p., n.d. [Dubai, 2004]), distributed as material for the Frankfurt Book Fair, 2004.

68. M. Badran, "Gender, Islam and the State: Kuwaiti Women in Struggle," in Haddad, *Islam,* 190–208.

69. S. Aawani, "Musliminnen zwischen Tradition und Moderne," *Spektrum Iran* 14 (2001): 4, 105ff. I thank Ali Tareqhat, who was the cultural attaché at the Iranian embassy in Berlin, for providing me with this magazine and others.

70. See Arebi, *Women,* 35.

71. See A. Saktanber, *Living Islam: Women, Religion, and the Politicization of Culture in Turkey* (London and New York, 2002); the author contradicts Göle, *Forbidden.*

72. K. Amirpur, *Reformen an theologischen Hochschulen? Tendenzen der heutigen Diskussion im Iran* (Cologne, 2002), 58ff; for more information on terminology, see H. Halm, *Shiism* (Edinburgh, 1991), index.

73. See A. Torab, "The Politicization of Women's Religious Circles in Post-Revolutionary Iran," in *Women, Religion and Culture in Iran,* ed. S. Ansari and V. Martin (Richmond, 2002), 139–164.

74. K. Nath, "Education and Employment among Kuwaiti Women," in *Women in the Muslim World,* ed. L. Beck and N. R. Keddie (Cambridge, 1978), 172ff.

75. See Badran, "Gender," 190–208.

76. For more on the political role of women in the Middle East, see G. Nashat, "Women in the Middle East, 8000 B.C.—A.D. 1800," in *Restoring Women to History,* ed. M. Strobel and C. O. Johnson (Bloomington, 1988); and for more about their role in Iran, see G. Nashat and L. Beck, eds., *Women in Iran from the Rise of Islam to 1800* (Urbana, 2003), chaps. 1 and 2.

77. E. L. Sullivan, *Women in Egyptian Public Life* (Cairo, 1986), 171; see also H. Shaarawi, *Harem Years: The Memoirs of an Egyptian Feminist,* ed., trans., and intro. M. Badran (London, 1986), 98–99.

78. Ibid., 112–113.

79. Badran, *Feminists,* 102, 100. For more on Nabarawi's life, see Badran, *Opening,* 279–281, which includes an article by her.

80. See W. Walther, "Islamischer Fundamentalismus und Frauenglück: Die Ägypterin Sainab al-Ghasali als Propagandistin fundamentalistischer Sozialethik," in *Blickwechsel: Frauen in Religion und Wissenschaft,* ed. D. Pahnke (Marburg, 1993), 273–298; M. Cooke, "Zaynab al-Ghazali: Saint or Subversive?" *Die Welt des Islams* (hereafter *WI*) 34 (1994): 1–20; Z. al-Ghazali, *Return of the Pharaoh: Memoir in Nasir's Prison,* trans. M. Guezzou (Leicester, 1994).

81. See Küper-Bašgöl, *Frauen,* 108ff.

82. Sanasarian, *Women's Rights,* 15ff.; see also Bamdad, *Darkness,* 28ff.

83. Poya, *Women,* 40–43, 146.
84. Sullivan, *Women,* 171.
85. Shaarawi, *Harem Years,* 39ff.
86. Sanasarian, *Women's Rights,* 32; H. Shahidian, "Women and Journalism in Iran," in Ansari and Martin, *Women,* 70–87.
87. See Haerkötter, *Mahasin,* 2; and Baron, *Women's Awakening,* 66.
88. See M. E. Wolsky, "Parteien," in Lissner, *Frauenlexikon,* 876–877. *Human Development Report 2004* (statistics for 2002 and 2004), http://hdr.undp.org/en/reports.
89. M. Ileri, "Türkei," in *Der Nahe und Mittlere Osten,* ed. U. Steinbach and R. Robert, vol. 2 (Opladen, 1988), 442.
90. Sullivan, *Women,* 39.
91. See the report by A. Nüsse, *Tagesspiegel,* August 27, 2007. I thank Werner Ende for calling my attention to this article.
92. R. F. Worth, "In Jeans or Veils, Iraqi Women are Split on New Political Power," *New York Times,* April 13, 2005.
93. See A. Kawar, *Daughters of Palestine: Leading Women of the Palestinian National Movement* (New York, 1996).
94. Republished as *Namudhaj min mashakil al-mar'a al-'arabiyya* (An Example for the Problems of the Arab Woman) (Baghdad, 1958), in the series *Kitab al-Ba'th* (The Ba'th Book) with a foreword by its editor and Salwa Nafwat. The author's name is misspelled in it (al-Daylami). As a leftist al-Dulaymi saw Iraqi women's difficult lives rooted entirely in the economic backwardness of the country and began her analysis with the wretched situation of the exploited rural woman. Immediately after resigning from her post she went to Moscow to study political science, and then later to Prague, where she lived until her death in Potsdam, Germany, in 2007. This information was supplied by her nephew Saad al-Dulaymi, Aachen. As to the politics of 'Abd al-Karim Qasim and the role of the Iraqi Communist Party at the time, see C. Tripp, *A History of Iraq* (Cambridge, 2000), 149–163.
95. See Sullivan, *Women,* 49.
96. See Milani, *Veils,* 57.
97. Poya, *Women,* 146.
98. Hagar is the (second) Arab wife of the biblical Abraham, who is worshipped in Islam as the Prophet Ibrahim, precursor of Muhammad and founder of the monotheistic cult of Ka'ba. She is the mother of Ibrahim's son Isma'il, who is regarded as the forefather of all Arabs. She exemplifies *taqwa*—"trust in God" or "knowledge of God"—for Muslim feminists, especially in the United States. In the Qur'an she is not mentioned by name; see H. Abughideiri, "Hagar: A Historical Model for 'Gender Jihad,'" in *Daughters of Abraham: Feminist Thought in Judaism, Christianity, and Islam,* ed. Y. Haddad, J. L. Esposito, and K. Armstrong (Gainesville, 2002), 81–107.
99. Poya, *Women,* 147; for diverse standpoints and controversial debates, see also Afshar, *Islam,* 43ff.
100. Risalat al-Usra, *Milaff al-'adad* (Algiers, 2005), 26.
101. As to intrigues involving her in the "political rape" of one of her supporters and the wives of two other supporters, see S. Haeri, "The Politics of Dishonor: Rape and Power in Pakistan," in *Faith and Freedom: Women's Human Rights in the Muslim World,* ed. M. Afkhami (London and New York, 1995), 161–174.
102. See the almost psychotic fatwa issued by the Iranian theologian Najafabadi, in L. Abed, *Journalistinnen im Tschador* (Frankfurt am Main, 2001), 88.
103. Amirpur, *Gott,* 98–99; see Saktanber, *Living Islam.*

104. Amirpur, *Gott,* 58; see also Göle, *Forbidden,* 195; and for more on the basics, see apologetics by F. El Guindi, *Veil: Modesty, Privacy, and Resistance* (Oxford and New York, 1998).

105. See the Arab, Persian, and Turkish miniatures in Walther, *Woman in Islam* (London, 1981).

106. See, e.g., ibid., plate 51; and Walther, *Kleine Geschichte der arabischen Literatur* (Munich, 2004), 257.

107. For more on this topic, see N. Lindisfarne-Tapper and B. Ingrams, eds., *Languages of Dress in the Middle East* (Richmond, 1997).

108. See Küper-Bašgöl, *Frauen,* 112.

109. The photos in Shaarawi, *Harem Years,* show Huda (also as a child) and other Egyptians from elite families in elegant French attire around 1885.

110. Ibid., 131.

111. See W. Walther, "From Women's Problems to Images of Women in Modern Iraqi Poetry," *WI* 36 (1996): 2, 219–241; for Iran, see Bamdad, *Darkness,* 72–75.

112. See the sharp critique by Shaykh Mustafa al-Ghalayini, professor of Qur'an Commentary and Arab Literature at the Islamic Faculty in Beirut, *Nazarat fi kitab al-sufur wa l-hijab al-mansub ila l-anisa Nazira Zayn al-Din* (Beirut, 1928). It was published by Matabi' Quzma, which also published the book criticized. Al-Ghalayini begins by saying that he has exposed the erroneous ideas in the book at three Friday sermons as well as its true authors, to wit, Sunnis, Shi'is, and Christians; he also rants against men shaving off their beards. A photo at the beginning shows him in a suit and tie, fez, and mustache. For more details on Zayn al-Din's books, see B. Saaban, "Muted Voices of Women Interpreters," in Afkhami, *Faith,* 66–77.

113. Badran, *Feminists,* index entry for "veiling."

114. P. Avery, *Modern Iran* (London, 1965), 292; see also Milani, *Veils,* 33.

115. For more details and their sociocultural implications, see Milani, *Veils,* 38ff.

116. See also F. El Guindi, *Veil,* 169ff.

117. N. Hijab, *Womanpower: The Arab Debate on Women at Work* (New York, 1988), 52–53.

118. Many examples can be found in Walther, *Woman.*

119. See W. Walther, "Komik als Kontrast: Schwänke, Ränke und Rollenspiele in der schiitisch-irakischen Stadtkultur zwischen 1890 und 1950," in *Alltagsleben und materielle Kultur in der arabischen Sprache und Literatur: Festschrift für Heinz Grotzfeld,* ed. T. Bauer and U. Stehli-Werbeck (Wiesbaden, 2005), 357–380.

120. See also H. Afshar, "Khomeini's Teachings and Their Implications for Iranian Women," in *In the Shadow of Islam,* ed. A. Tabari and N. Yeganeh (London, 1982), 75–90, and the insights on Khomeini and other ideologists of the Islamic Revolution in "Documents on the Question of Women," 90–140.

121. H. Kusha, *The Sacred Law of Islam: A Case Study of Women's Treatment in the Islamic Republic of Iran's Criminal Justice System* (Aldershot, 2002), 246ff.

122. Amirpur, *Gott,* 98–99.

123. See Abed, *Journalistinnen,* 147–148.

124. Amirpur, *Gott,* 69; see also the illustration of "Islamic" sports clothing in Abed, *Journalistinnen,* 144.

125. Amirpur, *Gott,* 90.

126. See essays by S. Eraslan, F. Berktay, Y. Ramazanoglu, B. Pusch, and N. Šišman, in *Die neue muslimische Frau,* ed. B. Pusch (Istanbul and Würzburg, 2001).

127. M. Seikaly, "Women and Religion in Bahrain," in Haddad, *Islam,* 169–198.

128. See also Walther, *Women,* e.g., plates 19, 27, and 38; and in the 1993 edition, figures 14 and 19.

129. For a more extensive discussion, see C. Schirrmacher and U. Spuler-Stegemann, *Frauen und die Scharia: Die Menschenrechte im Islam* (Munich, 2004).
130. For background information, see S. Tellenbach, *Einführung in das türkische Strafrecht* (Freiburg im Breisgau, 2003), intro.; see also H.-G. Ebert, *Das Personalstatut arabischer Länder: Problemfelder, Methoden, Perspektiven* (Frankfurt am Main and Berlin, 1996); D. S. El Alami and D. Hinchcliffe, *Islamic Marriage and Divorce Laws of the Arab World* (London, 1996); for the opinion of a Muslim theologian, see Shaykh M. R. Uthman, *The Laws of Marriage in Islam* (London, 1995).
131. This was the case until 1987. See F. E. Vogel, *Islamic Law and Legal System: Studies of Saudi Arabia* (Leiden, Boston, and Cologne, 2000).
132. See also Kusha, *Sacred Law*, 251–252.
133. See S. Mahdevi, "Women and Shii Ulama in Iran," *Middle Eastern Studies* 3 (1983): 26ff.; for more recent information, see Poya, *Women*; Shahidian, *Women*; Amirpur, *Gott*. For more about Afghanistan, see I. Schneider, "The Position of Women in the Islamic and Afghan Judiciary," in *The Sharia in the Constitutions of Afghanistan, Iran and Egypt: Implications for Private Law*, ed. N. Yassari (Tübingen, 2005), 83–102.
134. See Ayatollah S. Ruhollah Mousavi Khomeini, *A Clarification of Questions: An Unabridged Translation of Resaleh towzih al-Masael*, trans. J. Borujerdi (Boulder, Colo., and London, 1984), 315ff. and 331; for further clarifications by Khomeini and other ideologues, see Tabari, *Shadow*, 168ff.
135. See M. Mutahhari, *The Rights of Women in Islam* (Tehran, 1401 [1981]), 147ff.; see also H. Algar, *Mutahhari*, in *EI-2*, vol. 7 (Leiden, 1993), 762–763.
136. For special cases and regional differences, see Schneider, "Position."
137. See Kusha, *Sacred Law*; see also S. Tellenbach, trans. and intro., *Strafgesetze der Islamischen Republik Iran* (Berlin and New York, 1996), intro.
138. S. Kuske, *Reislamisierung und Familienrecht in Algerien* (Berlin, 1996), 76.
139. See the review of A. Zevkliler, *Nichteheliche Lebensgemeinschaften nach deutschem und nach türkischem Recht* (Würzburg, 1989) by S. Tellenbach, *Orient* 33 (1992), 147.
140. For examples from southern Sanaa between 1983 and 1995, see Würth, *Ash-Sharia*.
141. D. von Denffer, "*Mut'a*: Ehe oder Prostitution?" in *ZDMG* 128 (1978): 299–325, in particular 317.
142. S. Haeri, *Law of Desire: Temporary Marriage in Iran* (London, 1989), 100.
143. W. Ende, "Ehe auf Zeit (*Mut'a*) in der innerislamischen Diskussion der Gegenwart," *WI* 20 (1980): 1ff., in particular 24.
144. See blog from March 13, 2005, www.discardedlies.com. See also the Egyptian writer S. al-Wardani, *Zawaj al-mut'a halal 'inda ahl al-sunna* (Cairo, 1997), and his religious justification of the *mut'a* for Sunnis, as well as the introductory sayings from Qur'an 4:24 and 5:87, and his opening words to "the Muslims of the oil era": "Islam is the religion of alleviation, not of affliction" (al-Islam din al-yusr, la din al-'usr'). According to him, the Sunnis banned the *mut'a* for centuries because of what is now an outdated ideological battle against Shi'i Islam. Al-Wardani formulates how marriage contracts need to include clauses on a woman's right to receive a *mahr* and to extend the term, as well as a man's right to terminate such a marriage before it expires. The *mut'a* is a "path of experience" for widows and divorced women, one that prevents their "deviation"; it is a way for a man and a woman who are unable to marry normally to be together. *Mut'as* are not for virgins. His many polemic works include *Al-Khud'a: Rihlati min al-Sunna ila l-Shi'a* (The Delusion: My Journey from the Sunna to the Shi'a) (n.p., n.d.).

145. *Al-Bawwaba,* April 19, 2007. For more on *zawaj 'urfi,* see www.amrkhaled.net/articles 2988.ltul.

146. See N. Hamadeh, "Islamic Family Legislation: The Authoritarian Discourse of Silence," in *Feminism and Islam: Legal and Literary Perspectives,* ed. M. Yamani (London, 1996), 331–349.

147. C. Schlötzer, "Türkei stärkt die Rechte von Frauen," *Süddeutsche Zeitung* 124, June 2, 2005, 7.

148. See N. Abdo, "Nationalism and Feminism: Palestinian Women and the Intifada. No Going Back?" in *Gender and National Identity,* ed. V. M. Moghadam (London, 1994), 148–170; R. Sayegh, "Researching Gender in a Palestinian Group," in *Gendering the Middle East,* ed. D. Kandiyoti (London and New York, 1996), 145–168.

149. See E. W. Fernea, *Children,* 168–175; and also idem, ed., *In Search of Islamic Feminism: One Woman's Global Journey* (New York, 1998).

150. See E. J. Wensinck and C. Pellat, "Hur," in *EI-2,* vol. 3 (Leiden, 1986), 581–582.

151. For more on the psychological and physical problems of young, especially academic women whose socialization included such notions, see A. Kayir, "Women and Their Sexual Problems in Turkey," in Tekeli, *Women,* 299–305.

152. T. Eich, "Was ist eigentlich eine Jungfrau? Arabische Debatten über Hymen-Rekonstruktionen," www.heceas.org/publications.

153. The fortieth "Maqama," trans. T. Chenery and F. Steingass (London, 1867–1898; reprinted 1969). See, e.g., Walther, *Women,* 25, fig. 10. For more on Hariri, see Walther, *Kleine Geschichte,* index.

154. See Azhary Sonbol, *Women,* intro. For more about her as a leading figure who issued a fatwa in the course of the "gender jihad," see Abughideiri, "Hagar," 93ff.

155. Hijab, *Womanpower,* 30; H. Denker, "Die Wiedereinführung des Hul' und die Stärkung der Frauenrechte," in *Beiträge zum Islamischen Recht IV,* ed. S. Tellenbach and T. Hanstein, *Leipziger Beiträge zur Orientforschung,* vol. 15 (Frankfurt am Main, 2004), 125–209.

156. N. Yassari, "Das iranische Familienrecht und seine Anwendung im Teheraner Familiengericht," in Tellenbach, *Beiträge,* 59–76.

157. Schirrmacher, *Frauen,* 152–153.

158. See Kuske, *Reislamisierung;* and B. Dennerlein, "Islamisches Recht und sozialer Wandel in Algerien: Zur Entwicklung des Personalstatuts seit 1962," in *Islamkundliche Untersuchungen,* vol. 221 (Berlin, 1998), which provides good explanations of historical and familial contexts and compares the legal status of women before and after 1984, including cases filed with the court of cassation and judicial decisions up through 1993. For passages from the CFA, see: http://www.equalitynow.org/english/campaigns/un/unhrc_reports/unhrc_algeria_en.pdf and http://asia pacific.amnesty.org/library/Index/ENGMDE280172007?open&of=ENG-2MD.

159. Ilham Rachedi, "New Law Leaves Divorced Algerian Women Homeless," Women's eNews, April 7, 2007, http://www.womensenews.org/ (accessed July 1, 2008).

160. I thank Dr. Qindil, cultural attaché at the Moroccan embassy in Berlin, for the Arabic version of the Mudawwana. See also "La femme et le code de la famille au Maghreb: De L'infamie au *paradis," http://www.afrik.com/article8433.html,* May 25, 2005 (accessed July 6, 2008).

161. See Walther, "Frau"; and idem, *Women.*

162. See Z. Mir-Hosseini, *Marriage on Trial* (London and New York, 1993), 195ff.; during field studies in Morocco and Iran, Mir-Hosseini confirmed N. J. Coulson's theory that the nuclear family forms the basis for testamentary dispositions in Shi'i family law.

163. See Walther, *Women,* 74–75.
164. See S. el-Messiri, "Self-Images of Traditional Urban Women in Cairo," in Beck, *Women,* 522–540; S. Joseph, "Women and the Neighbourhood Street in Borj Hammoud, Lebanon," ibid., 541–557.
165. See C. Lacoste-Dujardin, *Des mères contre les femmes: maternité et patriarcat au Maghreb* (Paris, 1996).
166. See Mir-Hosseini, *Marriage,* 191ff.
167. A. Mamdouh, *Mothballs,* trans. P. Theroux (London, 1996); published in the United States as *Naphtalene: A Novel of Baghdad* (New York, 2005).
168. See, e.g., Saktanber, *Living Islam,* 99–100.
169. H. Hoodfar, *Between Marriage and the Market* (Berkeley, 1998), 51–79.
170. See also the dpa news release *Schwäbisches Tagblatt,* June 20, 2005.
171. See Afshar, *Islam,* 150ff.
172. S. Joseph, ed., *Intimate Selving in Arab Families: Gender, Self, and Identity* (Syracuse, N.Y., 1999).
173. See Walther, *Women;* B. F. Musallam, *Sex and Society in Islam* (Cambridge, 1986). For more on the religious debate of the 1980s, see R. Lohlker, "Scharia und Moderne," in *AKM* 51, no. 3 (Stuttgart, 1996): 13–38.
174. See Tellenbach, *Einführung,* 219–220.
175. See Tellenbach, *Strafgesetze,* 136–137.
176. Shahidian, *Women,* 189.
177. See Küper-Bašgöl, *Frauen,* 243ff; B. Beinhauer-Köhler, *Fatima Bint Muhammad: Metamorphosen einer frühislamischen Frauengestalt* (Wiesbaden, 2002), 298–304. See also A. Shariati, *Fatima Is Fatima,* trans. H. Bakhtiar (Tehran, 1980).
178. A. Firdaus, "Women and the Islamic Revolution," *IJMES* 15 (1983): 283–298; for a good historical overview from the perspective of religious studies, see Beinhauer-Köhler, *Fatima,* 238–264.
179. See Walther, *Women,* 143–153; and Guthrie, *Arab Women,* index entry for "singing girls at court."
180. G. Dönmez-Colin, *Women, Islam, and Cinema* (London, 2004), 9.
181. See Küper-Bašgöl, *Frauen,* 112.
182. Badran, *Feminists,* 189, 191, index entry misspelled "Umm Kalthum"; and the V. Danielson essay in *EI-2,* vol. 10 (Leiden, 2000), 855–856.
183. This book has a long foreword by her son, the writer and journalist Ihsan 'Abd al-Quddus; see also Ibrahim 'Abduh, *Ruz al-Yusuf: Sira wa-sahifa* (Cairo, 1961).
184. See R. Hillauer, *The Encyclopedia of Arab Women Filmmakers* (Cairo and New York, 2005), in particular 9–34.
185. See also H. Naficy, "Veiled Vision/Powerful Presences: Women in Post-Revolutionary Iranian Cinema," in *In the Eye of the Storm: Women in Post-Revolutionary Iran,* ed. M. Afkhami and E. Friedl (London and New York, 1994), 131–150; and idem, "Women Heroes of the New Iranian Cinema," in Dönmez-Colin, *Women,* 155–186.
186. S. Naef, *Bild und Bilderverbot im Islam* (Munich, 2007), in particular 128ff.; photo of Muslim Barbie doll, 124.
187. For some examples of the modern art of Islamic countries, also by women, see Walther, *Women,* 177ff.
188. See also Badran, *Opening;* F. Faqir, ed., *In the House of Silence: Autobiographical Essays by Arab Women Writers* (Reading, 1998); for Iran, see Milani, *Veils;* A. Najmabadi, ed., *Women's Autobiography in Contemporary Iran* (Cambridge 1990); as well as F. Goldin, "Iranian Women and Contemporary Memoirs," in *Persian Heritage* (2004), http://www.iranchamber.com/culture/articles/iranian_women_contemporary_memoirs.php (accessed July 20, 2008).

189. For translations of some of these poets' works, see K. Boullata, *Women of the Fertile Crescent* (Washington, D.C., 1978), 13–22; for more general information and many examples, see N. Handal, ed., *The Poetry of Arab Women* (New York, 2001).

190. L. Zayyat, *The Search: Personal Papers,* trans. S. Bennet (London, 1996). For more on her life, see H. D. Taieb, "The Girl Who Found Refuge in the People: The Autobiography of Latifa Zayyat," *Journal of Arabic Literature* 29 (1998): 202–217. For more on her life and writings, see J. Donohue and L. Tramontini, eds., *Crosshatching in Global Culture: A Dictionary of Modern Arab Writers,* vol. 2 (Beirut, 2004), 1204–7.

191. See the anthology A. Rifaat, *Distant View of a Minaret,* trans. D. Johnson-Davies (London, 1983); for a list of her works and details about her life as of the mid-1980s, see Donohue, *Crosshatching,* 2:937–940, index entry Fatima Rifaat.

192. N. El Saadawi, *A Daughter of Isis* (London, 1999); and idem, *Walking Through Fire: The Life of N. El Saadawi* (London, 2002).

193. Other works by N. El Saadawi in English include *God Dies by the Nile* (London, 1985); *Two Women in One* (London, 1985); *Memoirs from the Women's Prison* (London, 1986); *She Has No Place in Paradise* (London, 1987); *Death of an Ex-Minister* (London, 1987); *Memoirs of a Woman Doctor* (London, 1988); *The Circling Song* (London, 1989); and *The Nawal El Saadawi Reader* (London, 1997).

194. See F. Mernissi's article "Arab Women Rights and the Muslim State in the 21st Century: Reflections on Islam as Religion and State," in *Faith and Freedom,* ed. M. Afkhami (London and New York, 1995), 33–50.

195. Also published under the title *Dreams of Trespass: Tales of a Harem Girlhood* (Cambridge, 1994); other works by F. Mernissi in English include *Beyond the Veil: Male-Female Dynamics in Muslim Society* (London, 1985) (based on her dissertation at the University of Michigan, 1974); *Women and Islam: A Historical and Theological Enquiry* (Oxford, 1991); and *The Forgotten Queens of Islam* (Cambridge, 1993). She uses Arab sources but tends to generalize, as in *Women's Rebellion and Islamic Memory* (London, 1996); for example, not all slaves were more subservient than women living in freedom and hence preferred by men, nor is it true that Arab women as a whole had no access to education until recent decades. Women from elite families have received an education for centuries. See Walther, *Woman, Women,* and *Frau,* also for anecdotes about insubordinate slaves. For more on the popular topic of "the wiles of women" (*kayd al-nisa'*), see the following works by W. Walther: *Tausendundeine Nacht: Eine Einführung* (Munich and Zurich, 1987); and "'Eure List ist sehr groß!' Weibliche List, Klugheit und Weisheit im Islam," in *Ein Hauch der Kraft Gottes: Weibliche Weisheit in den Weltreligionen,* ed. S. H. Lee-Linke (Frankfurt am Main, 1999), 73–92. See also Awde, *Women.*

196. See W. Walther, "Weibliche Verhaltensweisen, Geschlechter- und Familienbeziehungen im Werk der Kuwaiterin Layla al-'Uthman," in *Darstellung der Probleme der Frau in der Literatur des 20. Jahrhunderts,* ed. M. Übelhör et al. (Marburg, 1991), 133ff. For more about her life and writings, see Donohue, *Crosshatching,* 2:1147–50.

197. See U. Stehli-Werbeck, "Rebellion und Relativität der Maßstäbe: Zwei libanesische Autorinnen zur Situation der Frau," in Übelhör, *Darstellung,* 131ff. For more about her trial, see E. Warnock Fernea and B. Q. Bezirgan, *Middle Eastern Muslim Women Speak* (Austin, 1977), 280ff.

198. H. al-Shaykh, *The Story of Zahra,* trans. P. Ford (London, 1986).

199. H. al-Shaykh, *Women of Sand and Myrrh,* trans. C. Cobham (London, 1989); see also Stehli-Werbeck, "Rebellion," 119ff. Gazelle's musk is a very sweet (almost too sweet) perfume traditionally used by brides on their wedding day.

200. H. al-Shaykh, *Beirut Blues,* trans. C. Cobham (New York, 1995).

201. H. al-Shaykh, *Only in London,* trans. C. Cobham (New York, 2001).

202. See also Donohue, *Crosshatching,* 2:1005–10; and G. al-Samman, *Beirut '75,* trans. N. N. Roberts (Fayetteville, 1995).

203. G. al-Samman, *Beirut Nightmares,* trans. N. N. Roberts (London, 1997).

204. See B. Winckler, "Assia Djebar," in *Lexikon arabischer Autoren des 19. und 20. Jahrhunderts,* ed. M. Naggar and K. al-Maaly (Heidelberg, 2004); for more about women's literature from North Africa in French until around 1991, see N. al-Baghdadi, "Schreibende Töchter: Autobiographie und Familie in arabischer Frauenliteratur," in *Fatimas Töchter: Frauen im Islam,* ed. E. Laudowicz (Cologne, 1992), 181–197.

205. A. Djebar, *A Sister to Scheherezade,* trans. D. Blair (London, 1987).

206. A. al-Mostaghanemi, *Memory in the Flesh* (Cairo, 2003). The author completed the novel in Paris in 1988. For a good analysis, see F. J. Ghazul, "Dhakirat al-adab fi Dhakirat al-jasad," *Alif: Journal of Comparative Poetics* 24 (2004): 166–181.

207. See illustration in Walther, *Woman;* medieval Arab geographers and historians call ancient statues *asnam* (idols).

208. See Arebi, *Women.*

209. See, e.g., S. Paker, "Unmuffled Voices in the Shade and Beyond: Women's Writing in Turkish," in *Textual Liberation: European Feminist Writing in the Twentieth Century,* ed. H. Forsas-Scott (London and New York, 1991), 270ff. I thank Karin Schweißgut, from the Freie Universität Berlin, for calling my attention to this essay. See also, e.g., the anthology edited by N. M. Reddy, *Short Stories by Turkish Women Writers* (Bloomington, 1994).

210. According to Milani, *Veils,* 47–48, it was published in Tehran in 1981 in response to her husband's highly contested autobiographical essay "Sangi bar guri" (A Stone on a Grave), published posthumously in 1980, in which he complained about remaining childless despite many affairs. The 1996 Qom edition of *Ghoroub-e Jalal* does not name an editor and consists of two essays of forty pages each, "Shouharam Jalal" (My Husband, Jalal, 1345 [1975]) and "Ghoroub-Jalal" (1341 [1971]). The latter has been published in English as "The Loss of Jalal," in *Daneshvar's Playhouse,* trans. Maryam Mafi (Washington, D.C., 1989), 133–155. For more about Daneshvar's literary career, see her "Letter to the Reader," in *Daneshvar's Playhouse,* 155–170; and Milani, *Veils,* index entry.

211. For an excellent discussion, see Milani, *Veils,* 1–176.

212. For more on women's images in literature, see works by both male and female authors in a number of anthologies, including H. Moayyad, ed., *Stories from Iran: A Chicago Anthology* (Washington, D.C., 1991); N. Rachlin, *Veils* (San Francisco, 1992); J. Green and F. Yazdanfar, eds., *A Walnut Sapling on Masih's Grave and Other Stories by Iranian Women* (Portsmouth, 1993). For a sensitive description informed by the author's own biography, see Milani, *Veils;* and K. Talattof, *The Politics of Writing in Iran: A History of Modern Persian Literature* (Syracuse, N.Y., 2000), in particular 135ff. Other works by Shahrnush Parsipur include *Women without Men,* trans. H. Houshmand and K. Talattof (New York, 2003); and *Touba and the Meaning of Night,* trans. H. Houshmand and K. Talattof (New York, 2006).

213. The original title was *Les mille et un jour;* Farah Diba no doubt wrote this work in French because she had attended French schools in Iran and studied in France. For more on other autobiographies and a number of original titles, see Milani, *Veils,* 220–227 and the bibliography, 271–283.

214. Bint al-Huda, *Al-Majmu'a al-qisasiyya al-kamila,* 3 vols. (Beirut, n.d.).

215. According to the 1986 edition; the first edition was titled *'Ala l-jisr: Usturat al-zaman* (On the Bridge: The Myth of Time).

216. See R. Badry, "Zum Profil weiblicher 'Ulama' in Iran: Neue Rollenmodelle für 'iranische Feministen'?" *Die Welt des Islams* 40 (2000): 7–40.

217. In G. Webb, ed., *Windows of Faith: Muslim Women Scholar-Activists in North America* (Syracuse, N.Y., 2000), 241–248; see also R. Hassan's essay "Members. One of Another: Gender Equality and Justice in Islam," http://www.religiouscon sultation.org/hassan.htm.

218. D. Kandiyoti, "Patterns of Patriarchy: Notes for an Analysis of Male Dominance in Turkish Society," in Tekeli, *Women*, 306; according to her essay "Bargaining with Patriarchy," *Gender and Society* 2–3 (1988): 274–290; for more on "gender jihad," see Abughideiri, "Hagar," 81–107.

VIII. Islamist Groups and Movements
(Guido Steinberg and Jan-Peter Hartung)

1. See G. Krämer, *Politischer Islam, Fernuniversität Hagen, 1994,* 44.

2. On the Salafis, see also P. Shinar and W. Ende, "Salafiyya," in *Encyclopaedia of Islam*, new edition, vol. 8 (Leiden, 1995), 900–909.

3. See G. Krämer, *Politischer Islam,* 48.

4. See J.-P. Hartung, "Reinterpretation von Tradition und der Paradigmenwechsel der Moderne," 112–115.

5. See R. Lohlker, "Cybermuslim: Islamisches und Arabisches im Internet," *Orient* 38, no. 2 (1997): 236–244.

6. *The Society of the Muslim Brothers* by R. P. Mitchell is still considered the standard work on the Muslim Brotherhood today. See also B. Lia, *The Society of the Muslim Brothers in Egypt.*

7. The concept of shari'a is problematic insofar as Islamists repeatedly cite it without agreeing on what it actually means. But nearly all Islamists share the demand that the shari'a be fully implemented without compromise.

8. Structurally and terminologically the Muslim Brotherhood is organized like a Sufi brotherhood. In this it resembles the South Asian Jama'at-i islami: both are led by a commander (*amir*), to whom an advisory council (*majlis-i shura*) is assigned. The greater majority of the Jama'at-i islami are not its formal members (*arkan*) but its many activists (*karkun*) and sympathizers (*muttafiqan*), who may outnumber formal members by up to fortyfold.

9. See G. Krämer, *Gottes Staat als Republik,* 190.

10. See R. Schulze, *Islamischer Internationalismus im 20. Jahrhundert,* 93–122.

11. The work has been translated into English as S. Qutb, *Milestones* (Chicago, 1993).

12. An important figure in this connection is Ahmad Huber as-Swisri (b. 1927), who for years tried to unite Islamist figures with the "New Right" in Europe. See K. Coogan, "Achmed Huber, the Avalon Gemeinschaft, and the Swiss 'New Right,'" http://ftrsupplemental.wordpress.com/2002/05/01/achmed-huber-the-avalon-gemein schaft-and-the-swiss-new-right/ (accessed July 30, 2008).

13. See G. E. Robinson, "Can Islamists Be Democrats? The Case of Jordan," *Middle East Journal* 51 (1997): 373–378.

14. See B. D. Metcalf, *Islamic Revivalism in British India,* 268–296.

15. See, among others, Y. Friedmann, "The Attitude of the Jam'iyyat-i 'Ulama'-i Hind to the Indian National Movement and the Establishment of Pakistan," *Asian and African Studies* 7 (1971): 157–180.

16. See M. K. Masud, ed., *Travellers in Faith: Studies of the Tablighi Jama'at as a Transnational Islamic Movement for Faith Renewal* (Leiden, 2000).

17. See S. V. R. Nasr, *The Vanguard of the Islamic Revolution;* idem, *Mawdudi and the Making of Islamic Revivalism;* and J.-P. Hartung, "Reinterpretation von Tradition."

18. See J.-P. Hartung, "'*Ulama*'of Contemporary South Asia: Globalizing the Local by Localizing the Global," *Oriente Moderno* 23, n.s. 83, no. 1 (2004): 83–101.

19. See S. A. S. Pirzada, *The Politics of the Jamiat Ulema-i-Islam Pakistan;* B. D. Metcalf, "'Traditionalist' Islamic Activism: Deoband, Tablighis, and Talibs," *ISIM Papers* 4 (2002): 12–17.

20. See G. Krämer, *Politischer Islam,* 18.

21. The Muslim World League (Rabitat al-'alam al-islami, RAI), which was founded in 1962 in Mecca, became the most important instrument of such policies. See R. Schulze, *Islamischer Internationalismus im 20. Jahrhundert,* 181–456.

22. See G. Kepel, *Muslim Extremism in Egypt: The Prophet and Pharaoh,* 70–102.

23. See, for example, "Plusieurs personnes interpellées seraient membres du Takfir," *Le Monde,* September 26, 2001.

24. See E. Sivan, *Radical Islam,* 103f.

25. See J. Reissner, "Die Besetzung der Großen Moschee in Mekka," *Orient* 21 (1980): 193–203.

26. See E. Abrahamian, "Die Guerilla-Bewegung im Iran von 1963 bis 1977," in *Religion und Politik im Iran,* ed. K. Greussing and J.-H. Grevemeyer (Frankfurt am Main, 1981), 337–360.

27. See S. A. Arjomand, *The Turban for the Crown,* 91–174.

28. See S. Rosiny, *Islamismus bei den Schiiten im Libanon.*

29. See H. Batatu. "Shi'i Organizations in Iraq: Al-Da'wah al-Islamiyah and al-Mujahidin," in *Shi'ism and Social Protest,* ed. R. I. Cole and N. R. Keddie (New Haven, 1986), 179–200.

30. Concerning Saudi Arabian Shi'ites, see G. Steinberg, "Die innenpolitische Lage Saudi-Arabiens nach dem 11. September 2001," *DOI Focus* 8 (Hamburg, 2003), 20f.

31. See C. Zutshi, "Religion, State, and Community: Contested Identities in the Kashmir Valley, c. 1880–1920," *South Asia* 23, no. 1 (2000): 109–128; B. A. Khan, "The Ahl-i-Hadith: A Socio-Religious Reform Movement in Kashmir," *Muslim World* 90 (2000): 133–157.

32. See N. Chadha-Behera, *State, Identity and Violence: Jammu, Kashmir and Ladakh* (New Delhi, 2000).

33. See Y. Sikand, "Islamist Militancy: The Lashkar-i-Tayyeba," *ISIM Newsletter* 9 (2002): 14.

34. For an extensive discussion of this school, see S. J. Malik, *Islamisierung in Pakistan 1977–84: Untersuchungen zur Auflösung autochthoner Strukturen* (Stuttgart, 1989), 290–301.

35. See B. Glatzer, "Zum politischen Islam der afghanischen Taliban," in *Sendungsbewußtsein und Eigennutz: Zu Motivation und Selbstverständnis islamischer Mobilisierung,* ed. D. Reetz (Berlin, 2001), 173–182; A. Rashid, *Taliban: Islam, Oil and the New Great Game in Central Asia.*

36. The well-known English translation is titled "The Ladenese Epistle" and can be found on numerous websites. The title of the original Arab text is "Declaration of War against the Americans Occupying the Land of the Holy Sites," subtitled "Expel the Infidels from the Arabian Peninsula."

37. It was signed by the two leaders, as well as by Rifa'i Ahmad Taha (Jama'a islamiyya, Egypt), Mir Hamza (Jam'iyyat al-'ulama', Pakistan), and Fazl al-Rahman (Harakat al-jihad, Bangladesh). See also *The 9/11 Commission Report* (Washington, D.C., 2003).

38. For further discussion of al-Qaʿida, see R. Gunaratna, *Inside Al Qaeda: Global Network of Terror,* expanded new edition (London, 2003).
39. "New Tape Is Attributed to Wanted Qaeda Figure," *New York Times,* May 1, 2004.

IX. Mystical Brotherhoods and Popular Islam
(Frederick De Jong)

1. In most mystical brotherhoods women are not allowed to participate or to be initiated. There are cases, however, in which women can be initiated. This usually occurs according to a ritual that deviates from the male initiation ritual. Brotherhoods with mixed liturgical assemblies are a great exception. If a brotherhood accepts female members, it usually organizes separate assemblies that are open to women only. Deviating from the *hadra* of male members, these assemblies normally consist of Qurʾanic recitation, prayers, an instructional sermon, and occasionally a *dhikr* (always held while sitting). Since there are *tariqas* that also accept women as members, and many *tariqas* allow women and children who cannot officially become members to be initiated because of the *baraka,* it would appear incorrect to classify *tariqas* as part of the sociological complex of the male societies. See H. J. Kissling, "Die soziologische und pädagogische Rolle der Derwischorden im Osmanischen Reich," *Zeitschrift der Deutschen Morgenländischen Gesellschaft* 103 (1953): 18–28.
2. Names of the best-known and most widely distributed brotherhoods and their (presumed) founders include al-Ahmadiyya (Ahmad al-Badawi, d. 1276); al-Burhaniyya or al-Disuqiyya (Ibrahim al-Disuqi, d. 1288); al-Chishtiyya (Muʿin al-Din al-Chishti, d. 1236); al-Khalwatiyya (ʿUmar al-Khalwati, d. 1397); al-Naqshbandiyya (Muhammad Bahaʾ al-Din Naqshband, d. 1389); al-Qadiriyya (ʿAbd al-Qadir al-Jilani, d. 1166); al-Rifaʿiyya (Ahmad al-Rifaʿi, d. 1182); al-Shadhiliyya (Abu l-Hasan ʿAli al-Shadhili, d. 1258); al-Suhrawardiyya (Diyaʾ al-Din Abu Najib al-Suhrawardi, d. 1168); and al-Tijaniyya (Ahmad al-Tijani, d. 1815). Almost all mystical brotherhoods have a *silsila* that goes back to one of the mystics mentioned here.
3. Founded by Jalal al-Din al-Rumi (d. 1273), known as Mevlana (our Lord). The annual Mevlana celebrations in December in Konya—the location of the former center, which is now a museum—are primarily a tourist attraction. See H. Ritter, "Die Mevlanafeier in Konya vom 11.–17. Dezember 1960," *Oriens* 15 (1962): 249–270.
4. Named after Hajji Bektash Veli (d. 1335). The center of this sect is located in the town of Hacıbektaş (also named after him) in central Anatolia (Cappadocia). This center, where his grave is located, has remained a pilgrimage center for the many followers of Bektashism in Turkey and in the Balkans, despite the prohibition on mystical brotherhoods in Turkey in 1925 and the transformation of the center into a museum. The classic study on the history and doctrine of the Bektashis is J. K. Birge, *The Bektashi Order of Dervishes,* 2nd ed. (London, 1965).
5. On the Saʿdiyya in Syria, see F. De Jong, "Les confréries mystiques musulmanes du Machreq arabe: centres de gravité, signes de déclin et de renaissance," in *Les ordres mystiques dans l'Islam: Cheminements et situation actuelle,* ed. A. Popovic and G. Veinstein (Paris, 1986), 212–213.
6. See De Jong, "Cairene Ziyara-Days," 41–42.
7. Horten, *Die religiöse Gedankenwelt,* 1:6ff.
8. Probably the best known and most widely read *mawlid* today was written by Jaʿfar ibn Hasan al-Barzanji (d. 1764).

9. On the emergence of the cult of the Prophet, see the seminal work by T. Andrae, *Die Person Muhammeds in Lehre und Glauben seiner Gemeinde* (Stockholm, 1918), 290–390. See also Schimmel, *And Muhammad Is His Messenger.*

10. Horten, *Die religiöse Gedankenwelt,* 2:268.

11. See F. Dornseiff, *Das Alphabet in Mystik und Magie* (Leipzig and Berlin, 1925), 142–145; J. K. Birge, *The Bektashi Order of Dervishes* (London, 1937), 148–158.

12. For several concrete cases of criticism and bibliographical references, see De Jong, "Turuq and Turuq-Opposition."

13. Kriss, *Volksglaube im Bereich des Islam,* X.

14. See Horten, *Die religiöse Gedankenwelt,* 1:81; E. Diez, *Glaube und Welt des Islams* (Stuttgart, 1941), 68; see also Qur'an 2:96.

15. Zbinden, *Die Djinn des Islam,* 95.

16. Winkler, *Bauern zwischen Wasser und Wüste,* 150ff.; Donaldson, *The Wild Rue,* 13; and Loeffler, *Islam in Practice,* passim.

17. Zbinden, *Die Djinn des Islam,* 95.

18. In everyday usage, the terms *jinn* and *'ifrit* (pl. *'afarit*) are used synonymously; see Zbinden, *Die Djinn des Islam,* 60.

19. Blackman, *The Fellahin of Upper Egypt,* 69ff. For prophetic traditions on *qarina* and *qarin,* see Zbinden, *Die Djinn des Islam,* 144, 41.

20. For the Qur'anic verses used, see Zbinden, *Die Djinn des Islam,* 97; Seligmann, *Der böse Blick,* 1:340; Donaldson, *The Wild Rue,* 14. For other texts, substances, materials, forms of amulets, and further details, see Winkler, *Siegel und Charaktere,* passim; Kriss, *Volksglaube im Bereich des Islam,* 1:1–57; Seligmann, *Der böse Blick,* 2:342; and Horten, *Die religiöse Gedankenwelt des Volkes,* 1:109. On amulets in the Shi'a domain, see Fodor, "Types of Shi'ite Amulets from Iraq," 118–143.

21. See F. Dornseiff, *Das Alphabet Mystik und Magie* (Leipzig, 1922), 142; Winkler, *Siegel und Charaktere,* 96–97.

22. See Seligmann, *Der böse Blick,* 2:341; Krawietz, "Islamic Conceptions"; Zbinden, *Die Djinn des Islam,* 42, 147; Trimingham, *Islam in the Sudan* (1949), 172; H. Granqvist, *Muslim Death and Burial: Arab Customs and Traditions Studied in a Village in Jordan* (Helsinki, 1965), 1, 28 (Societas Scientiarum Fennica Commentationes Humanorum Litterarum 34).

23. See Trimingham, *Islam in the Sudan* (1949), 177–178; Donaldson, *The Wild Rue,* 194ff.

24. Blackman, *The Fellahin of Upper Egypt,* 236.

25. On blood sacrifice and other forms of sacrifice, see Curtiss, *Ursemitische Religion im Volksleben,* 206–260; see also Dermenghem, *Le culte des saints,* 152–161.

26. Zbinden, *Die Djinn des Islam,* 135.

27. Ibid., 70, 152–153. For the names and categories of jinn, see ibid., 64–65; see also Trimingham, *Islam in the Sudan* (1965), 171–174.

28. Cited in Kriss, *Volksglaube im Bereich des Islam,* 2:140ff. Some researchers have argued that the *zar* has Ethiopian origins. On this, see ibid. and R. Natvig, "Oromos, Slaves, and the Zar Spirits: A Contribution to the History of the Zar Cult," *International Journal of African Historical Studies* 20 (1987): 243–256. For further literature on the subject, see R. Khouri, "Contribution à une bibliographie du 'zar,'" *Annales Islamologiques* (Cairo) 16 (1980): 359–374 (and two illustrations); and the entry "Zar," in *Encyclopaedia of Islam,* vol. 11 (Leiden, 2002), 455–457.

29. For examples, see Einzmann, *Religiöses Volksbrauchtum in Afghanistan,* 103; Donaldson, *The Wild Rue,* 61.

30. See Bannerth, *Islamische Wallfahrtsstätten Kairos,* 5; R. Paret, *Symbolik des Islam: Symbolik der Religionen* vol. 2, ed. F. Hermann (Stuttgart, 1958), 61; De Jong "Cairene Ziyara-Days," 27.

31. For a classification of miracles, see Trimingham, *Islam in the Sudan* (1965), 136ff.
32. Ibid., 128; Kriss, *Volksglaube im Bereich des Islam,* 1:4–5.
33. Donaldson, *The Wild Rue,* 33.
34. Curtiss, *Ursemitische Religion im Volksleben,* 179; Einzmann, *Religiöses Volksbrauchtum in Afghanistan,* 94.
35. There are also graves in which only a part of the corpse has been buried. For example, according to tradition the grave of Abu Madyan Shu'ayb in Jerusalem contains only his hands, while the grave of Husayn ibn 'Ali in Cairo is said to contain only his head.
36. The custom of lighting candles at the graves of saints is widespread. For a specification of the categories *sadaqat* and *nudhur,* see Winkler, *Die reitenden Geister der Toten,* 119–120; Kriss, *Volksglaube im Bereich des Islam,* 1:32–43.
37. This appears to be much less the case for the most important saints' graves of the Islamic world (including a number of graves of the relatives and progeny of the Prophet) and for the graves of the founders of the largest mystical traditions and brotherhoods. Women are allowed to visit these graves only on certain days and/or at certain times, unless there are two separate sections at the grave, one of which is reserved for female visitors.
38. On this, see my article "Kutb," in the *Encyclopaedia of Islam,* vol. 5 (87–88).
39. Winkler, *Bauern zwischen Wasser und Wüste,* 130–131.
40. These concepts have been taken from C. Geertz, *Islam Observed: Religious Development in Morocco and Indonesia* (New Haven, 1968), 61.
41. With the exception of Macedonia and Kosovo. See A. Popovic, *L'Islam balkanique: Les musulmans du sud-est européen dans la période post-ottomane* (Berlin, 1986), 217f. (Balkanologische Veröffentlichungen 11).
42. The Shafi'i regions of Yemen constitute one such territory.
43. One example of this is western Thrace, where there are no brotherhoods active among the Muslim minority (approximately 120,000 people).
44. See A. Bennigsen and C. Lemercier-Quelquejay, *Le soufi et le commissaire: Les confréries musulmanes en URSS* (Paris, 1986), passim.
45. See F. De Jong, "Turuq and Turuq-Opposition," 91.
46. For names, details, and further bibliographical references, see ibid., passim.
47. Between 1976 and 1981 the number of the officially recognized brotherhoods rose from sixty-seven to seventy. Several brotherhoods were no longer active, however, and thus lost their official status, whereas others gained official recognition. In this way the number of officially recognized brotherhoods remained constant between 1981 and 1993.

XI. Islam and Non-Islamic Minorities *(Johanna Pink)*

1. On the debates in Egypt, see T. Philipp, "National State and Religious Community in Egypt: The Continuing Debate," *Die Welt des Islams* 28 (1988): 379–391. An interesting dimension is illuminated in V. Shafik, "Variety or Unity? Minorities in Egyptian Cinema," *Orient* 39 (1998): 627–648. See also A. Ayalon, "Egypt's Coptic Pandora's Box," in *Minorities and the State in the Arab World,* ed. O. Bengio and G. Ben-Dor (Boulder, Colo., 1998), 53–71.
2. Neither the concept of tolerance nor the question whether this concept applies to Islamic law or the historical reality of the Islamic world is examined here. For these issues, see A. Noth, "Möglichkeiten und Grenzen islamischer Toleranz," *Saeculum*

29 (1978): 190–204; and B. Radtke, "Auserwähltheitsbewußtsein und Toleranz im Islam," *Saeculum* 49 (1989): 70–79.

3. See N. El-Assad, "Minderheiten im Islam," in *Menschenbilder—Menschenrechte*, ed. S. Batzli, F. Kissling, and R. Zihlmann (Zurich, 1994), 154.

4. See U. Furman, "Minorities in Contemporary Islamist Discourse," *Middle Eastern Studies* 36 (2000): 1–20.

5. On the early Islamic era, see W. Kallfelz, *Nichtmuslimische Untertanen im Islam: Grundlage, Ideologie und Praxis der Politik frühislamischer Herrscher gegenüber ihren nichtmuslimischen Untertanen mit besonderem Blick auf die Dynastie der Abbasiden (749–1248)* (Wiesbaden, 1995). See also Krämer, "Minorities in Muslim Societies."

6. See Lewis, *The Jews of Islam*, 158–178; Krämer, "Minorities in Muslim Societies," 110; Courbage, *Christians and Jews under Islam*, 72–80.

7. See Courbage, *Christians and Jews under Islam*, 109–115.

8. Ibid., 174–209.

9. See Sanasarian, *Religious Minorities in Iran*, 34–43.

10. See Lewis, *The Jews of Islam*, 154–191.

11. See Courbage, *Christians and Jews under Islam*, 171.

12. See Krämer, *The Jews in Modern Egypt, 1914–1952*, 425.

13. See Lewis, *The Jews of Islam*, 191.

14. See Sanasarian, *Religious Minorities in Iran*, 44–48.

15. E. Dawn, "The Origins of Arab Nationalism," in *The Origins of Arab Nationalism*, ed. R. Khalidi (New York, 1991), 3–30.

16. See Sanasarian, *Religious Minorities in Iran*, 50.

17. See Furman, "Minorities in Contemporary Islamist Discourse," 4–13.

18. See J. S. Nielsen, "Contemporary Discussions on Religious Minorities in Muslim Countries," *Islam and Christian-Muslim Relations* 14 (2003): 325–333.

19. See Krämer, "Minorities in Muslim Societies," 111.

20. On the apostasy discussion, see R. Peters and G. J. J. de Vries, "Apostasy in Islam," *Die Welt des Islams* 17 (1977): 1–25; A. Hasemann, "Zur Apostasiediskussion im modernen Ägypten," *Die Welt des Islams* 42 (2002): 72–121.

21. On the origins and the doctrine of this religion, see the section on the Bahai in "Sects and Special Groups" in this volume as well as P. Smith, *The Babi and Baha'i Religions: From Messianic Shi'ism to World Religion* (Cambridge, 1987).

22. See, "Zawaj al-Muslim bi-ghayr al-Muslima," in *Huda l-Islam: Fatawa Mu'asira*, ed. Y. al-Qaradawi, vol. 1 (Cairo, 1981), 405–406.

23. J. Pink, "A Post-Qur'anic Religion between Apostasy and Public Order: Egyptian Muftis and Courts on the Legal Status of the Bahâ'î Faith," *Islamic Law and Society* 10 (1995): 430–432.

24. See K. Boyle, "Human Rights in Egypt: International Commitments," in *Human Rights and Democracy: The Role of the Supreme Constitutional Court of Egypt*, ed. K. Boyle and A. O. Sharif (London, 1996), 103.

25. See Sanasarian, *Religious Minorities in Iran*, 114–123.

XII. International Islamic Organizations *(Johannes Reissner)*

1. See Kramer, *An Introduction to World Islamic Conferences*, 11.

2. For a detailed presentation of the two congresses, see Sékaly, "Les deux Congrès généraux de 1926"; see also Kramer, *An Introduction to World Islamic Conferences*, 12–15; and Hartmann, "Zum Gedanken des 'Kongresses,'" 128–131.

3. See Gibb, "The Islamic Congress at Jerusalem in December 1931," 105.
4. See Kramer, *An Introduction to World Islamic Conferences*, 23.
5. See Schulze, *Islamischer Internationalismus im 20. Jahrhundert*, 356–362.
6. See the organization's official website, www.oic-oci.org. The designation Islamic Conference Organization (ICO) was also used earlier. In addition to Arabic, English is the official working language of the organization.
7. On the continuing development of the OIC and its political activities, see the annual *Nahost Jahrbuch*, beginning in 1987.
8. Schöne, *Islamische Solidarität*, 267–269.

Part Three
Present-Day Islamic Culture and Civilization

I. "Orientalistics" and Orientalism *(Reinhard Schulze)*

1. The first evidence of the word "Orientalism" is found in Edward Holdsworth (d. 1746), *Remarks and Dissertations on Virgil; with some other classical observations* (London, 1768), 265 ("There are frequent instances of the very same orientalism in Homer"). The first use of "Orientalist" in the sense of an expert on Oriental languages is found in Henry Rowlands, *Mona Antiqua Restaurata. An Archaeological Discourse on the Antiquities, Natural and Historical, of the Isle of Anglesey, the Ancient Seat of the British Druids, Redesmere*, reprint (1st Dublin ed., 1723), 318. In his biography of Edmund Smith (1672–1710), Samuel Johnson (1709–1784) wrote: "At Oxford, as we all know, much will be forgiven to literary merit; and of that he had exhibited sufficient evidence by his excellent ode on the death of the great orientalist, Dr. Pocock, who died in 1691, and whose praise must have been written by Smith when he had been yet but two years in the university." Samuel Johnson, *The Lives of the English Poets, 1779–81* (London, 1795), 515. G. Endress, *Der Islam: Eine Einführung in seine Geschichte* (Munich 1991), 20, notes that in the course of the restoration of Orientalist research in the French Republic in 1791–1794, the "orientaliste" was spoken of. In 1870 Johann Jakob Bachofen (1815–1887) first spoke of Orientalism (in relation to the Tanaquil saga).
2. The Zurich theologian Johann Heinrich Hottinger (1620–1667) still thought of a "Bibliotheca Orientalis" as a manuscript catalogue. In 1660, however, he titled his compilation of sources on Islamic history "Historia Orientalis."
3. H. Schipperges, *Ideologie und Historiographie des Arabismus* (Wiesbaden, 1961).
4. See the excellent portrayal of Orientalistics by J. D. J. Waardenburg, "Mustashriḳun," in *The Encyclopaedia of Islam*, new ed., vol. 7 (Leiden, 1993), 735–753, 739.
5. Earlier treatises include G. Dugat, *Histoire des orientalistes de l'Europe du XIIe au XIXe siècle précédée d'une esquisse historique des études orientales*, vols. 1–2 (Paris, 1868–1870); J. Darmesteter, "De la part de la France dans les grandes découvertes de l'orientalisme moderne" (1879), in *Essais orientaux* (Paris, 1883), 1–103; T. Benfey, *Geschichte der Sprachwissenschaft und orientalischen Philologie in Deutschland seit dem Anfang des 19. Jahrhunderts mit einem Rückblick auf die früheren Zeiten* (Munich, 1896); G. Behrmann, *Hamburgs Orientalisten* (Hamburg, 1901).

6. See, for example, A. J. Arberry, *British Orientalists* (London, 1943); J. Fück, "Die arabischen Studien in Europa vom 12. bis in den Anfang des 19. Jahrhunderts," in *Beiträge zur Arabistik, Semitistik und Islamwissenschaft,* ed. R. Hartmann and H. Scheel (Leipzig, 1944), 85–253; I. J. Kračkovskij, *Die russische Arabistik: Umrisse ihrer Entwicklung* (Leipzig, 1957); J. Fück, *Die arabischen Studien in Europa bis in den Anfang des 20. Jahrhunderts* (Leipzig, 1955), chaps. 2–29; see also V. V. Bartol'd, *La découverte de l'Asie: Histoire de l'orientalisme en Europe et en Russie* (Paris, 1947).

7. See also the substantive portrayal in H. Bobzin, "Geschichte der arabischen Philologie in Europa bis zum Ausgang des achtzehnten Jahrhunderts," in *Grundriß der arabischen Philologie,* vol. III, Supplement (Wiesbaden, 1992), 155–187.

8. R. Schulze, "Gibbons Muhammad," in Edward Gibbon, *Der Sieg des Islam* (Frankfurt am Main, 2003), 336f.

9. Henry De Boulainvilliers, *La vie de Mahomet; avec des réflections sur la religion des Musulmans* (London, 1730); Fück, *Studien,* 103, following S. Hurgronje, *Verspreide Geschriften,* vol. 1 (Bonn, 1923), 324. J. Waardenburg, in *Encyclopaedia of Islam,* vol. 7 (Leiden, 1993), 741, refers to the anonymous publication *Mahomet no imposter or a defence of Mahomet* from 1720.

10. In English, *Mahomet the Prophet or Fanaticism: A Tragedy in Five Acts,* trans. Robert L. Myers (New York, 1964). See also J. W. von Goethe's 1799 adaptation, *Mahomet. Ein Trauerspiel in fünf Aufzügen nach Voltaire* (Tübingen, 1802).

11. J. Miller (thought to be written with J. Hoadly), *Mahomet the imposter: a tragedy as it is acted at the Theatre-Royal in Drury Lane* (Dublin, 1745; rev. ed. London, 1778). There is substantial literature on Orientalist *imagery* in Europe. A fine introduction is provided in K. U. Syndram, "Der erfundene Orient in der europäischen Literatur vom 18. bis zum Beginn des 20. Jahrhunderts," in *Europa und der Orient, 800–1900,* ed. G. Sievernich and H. Budde (Gütersloh and Munich, 1989), 324–341. On the image of Muhammad, see M. Reeves, *Muhammad in Europe: A Thousand Years of Myth Making, with a Biographical Contribution by P. J. Stewart* (Reading, 2000).

12. D. Bourel, "Die deutsche Orientalistik im 18. Jahrhundert: Von der Mission zur Wissenschaft," in *Historische Kritik und biblischer Kanon in der deutschen Aufklärung,* ed. H. Reventlow, W. Sparn, and J. Woodbridge (Wiesbaden, 1988), 113–126.

13. J. J. Reiske, "Prodidagmata ad Hagji Chalifae librum memorialem rerum a Muhammedanis gestarium exhibentia introductionem generalem in historiam sie dictam orientalem," in J. B. Koehler, *Abulfedae tabulae Syriae,* vol. 2 (Leipzig, 1766), 239–240, quoted in Endress, *Der Islam,* 13; see also Fück, *Studien,* 112.

14. Schulze, "Gibbons Muhammad," 344f.

15. The total number of academic Orientalists in 1845 was small: a total of around twenty Orientalists taught at the time at German-language universities (twenty-six in 1856). See H. Preissler, "Deutsche Orientalisten und die Öffentlichkeit um die Mitte des 19. Jahrhunderts," in *Norm und Abweichung: Akten des 27. Deutschen Orientalistentages, (Bonn, Sept. 28–Oct. 2, 1998),* ed. S. Wild and H. Schild (Würzburg, 2001), 777–784. On the German image of the Orient in the first half of the nineteenth century, see L. Ammann, *Östliche Spiegel: Ansichten vom Orient im Zeitalter seiner Entdeckung durch den deutschen Leser 1800–1850* (Hildesheim, 1989).

16. See B. Johansen, "Politics and Scholarship: The Development of Islamic Studies in the Federal Republic of Germany," in *Middle East Studies: International Perspectives on the State of the Art,* ed. T. Y. Ismael (New York, 1990), esp. 79ff.

17. Here Alfred von Kremer (1828–1889) must receive particular mention; along with others, he elaborated the significance of this *Realienkunde,* corroborated through study trips.

18. A. Dillmann, *Der Verfall des Islam: Rede zur Gedächtnisfeier der Friedrich-Wilhelms-Universität zu Berlin am 3. August 1876* (Berlin, 1876), 16. On the founder of Ethiopian philology, see E. Littmann, *Ein Jahrhundert Orientalistik: Lebensbilder aus der Feder von Enno Littmann und Verzeichnis seiner Schriften,* comp. R. Paret and A. Schall (Wiesbaden, 1955), 1–10.

19. Dillmann, *Der Verfall des Islam,* 17.

20. H. G. Gadamer, "Das Problem der Geschichte" (1943), in *Wahrheit und Methode,* vol. 2 (Tübingen, 1986), 27–36, 29.

21. E. Troeltsch, *Der Historismus und seine Probleme,* vol. 1, *Das logische Problem der Geschichtsphilosophie* (Tübingen, 1992), and *Der Historismus und seine Überwindung,* 5 lectures (Berlin, 1924).

22. Johansen, "Politics and Scholarship," 86f.

23. L. Hanisch, *Die Nachfolge der Exegeten: Deutschsprachige Erforschung des Vorderen Orients in der ersten Hälfte des 20. Jahrhunderts* (Wiesbaden, 2003), 46–58. Over a hundred years after the original founding of "Orientalist seminars," today only four such institutions still maintain the specific term "Islamic studies" in their names. Nineteen institute names out of a total of twenty-nine scholarly institutions refer to the Orient or Orientalistics.

24. R. Paret, *Arabistik und Islamkunde an deutschen Universitäten: Deutsche Orientalisten seit Theodor Nöldeke* (Wiesbaden, 1966), 25f.

25. M. Horten, "Die Probleme der Orientalistik," *Beiträge zur Kenntnis des Orients* 13 (1916): 143–161.

26. Preissler, "Deutsche Orientalisten," 777–784.

27. The critique of philology had already begun with the establishment of philology as an independent academic discipline in the eighteenth century, and was expressed mainly through a large number of scholarly satires.

28. See H. G. Gadamer, "Hermeneutik und Historismus" (1965), in *Wahrheit und Methode,* vol. 2 (Tübingen, 1986), 387–424, 391. Johansen, "Politics and Scholarship," 92, names above all the "anti-historicist" Berlin Orientalist Walther Braune as an exception. See U. Haarmann, "Die islamische Moderne bei den deutschen Orientalisten," in *Araber und Deutsche: Begegnungen in einem Jahrtausend,* ed. F. H. Kochwasser and H. R. Roemer (Tübingen and Basel, 1974), 56–61, reprinted in *Zeitschrift für Kulturaustausch* 24 (1974): 5–18.

29. Paret, *Arabistik und Islamkunde,* 5.

30. Hanisch, *Die Nachfolge,* 114–173.

31. Albrecht Goetze (Marburg, 1933), Julius Lewy (Giessen, 1933), Eugen Mittwoch (Berlin, 1933–35), Gotthold Weil (Frankfurt, 1934), Anton Baumstark (Münster, 1935), Benno Landsberger (Leipzig, 1935), Theodor Menzel (Kiel, 1937), Paul Kahle (Bonn, emigrated 1939), and Josef Schacht (Königsberg, emigrated 1939).

32. Little is known about the fate of the Orientalist students. Among others, Heinz Kucharski, a student of philosophy and Orientalistics, helped Traute Lafrenz distribute pamphlets for the "White Rose" in 1943. After being convicted by the People's Court in Hamburg on April 17, 1945, Kucharski managed to escape on the way to his execution.

33. A. Mahrad, "Wiederbelebung der Orientalistik an deutschen Hochschulen nach dem Zweiten Weltkrieg," *Hannoversche Studien über den Mittleren Osten* 4 (1987): 227–279.

34. Kai Hafez, *Orientwissenschaft in der DDR: Zwischen Dogma und Anpassung, 1969–1989* (Hamburg, 1995).

35. Muhammad al-Bahiy, *Al-Mubashshirun wa-l-mustashriqun fi mawqifihim min al-Islam* (Cairo, 1961).

36. Muhammad al-Ghazali, *Ad-Difaʿ ʿan al-ʿaqida wa-l-shariʿa didda mataʿin al-mustashriqin* (Cairo, 1961); for a detailed discussion, see E. Rudolph, *Westliche Islamwissenschaft im Spiegel muslimischer Kritik: Grundzüge und aktuelle Merkmale einer innerislamischen Kritik* (Berlin, 1991), 29ff., and also for earlier Muslim critiques of Orientalist researchers (al-Afghani versus Renan, ʿAbduh versus Hanotaux, Rida versus Dermenghem, Mustafa al-Sibaʿi and Muhammad al-Ghazali versus Goldziher, and so on).

37. Paret, *Arabistik und Islamkunde*, 3.

38. A. Abdel-Malek, "L'orientalisme en crise," *Diogène* 44 (1963): 109–142; idem, *La dialectique sociale* (Paris, 1972), 79–113; and A.-L. Tibawi, "English-Speaking Orientalists: A Critique of Their Approach to Islam and Arab Nationalism," *Muslim World* 53 (1963): 185–204, 298–313 (separately printed in Germany by the Islamisches Zentrum, [Geneva, 1384/1965]). Among other responses to Abdel-Malek, see F. Gabrieli, "Apologie de l'orientalisme," *Diogène* 50 (1965): 128–136.

39. N. Daniel, *Islam and the West: the Making of an Image* (Edinburgh, 1960); and idem, *Islam, Europe and the Empire* (Edinburgh, 1966).

40. J. Waardenburg, *L'Islam dans le miroir de l'Occident; Comment quelques orientalistes se sont penchés sur l'Islam et se sont fermés une image de cette religion: I. Goldziher, C. S. Hurgronje, C. H. Becker, D. B. Macdonald, L. Massignon* (Paris, 1962; 3rd ed. 1970).

41. F. Steppat, ed., "Der moderne Vordere Orient als Aufgabe an deutschen Universitäten," *Zeitschrift der Deutschen Morgenländischen Gesellschaft* (hereafter *ZDMG*) 126 (1976): 1–34.

42. Ironically, the concept of modernity emerged from a critique of historicism; see R. Koselleck, *Vergangene Zukunft: Zur Semantik geschichtlicher Zeichen* (Frankfurt am Main, 1979); idem, "Neuzeit: Zur Semantik moderner Bewegungsbegriffe," in *Studien zum Beginn der modernen Welt*, ed. R. Koselleck (Stuttgart, 1977), 266; J. Habermas, *Der philosophische Diskurs zur Moderne: Zwölf Vorlesungen* (Frankfurt am Main, 1988), 9–33; W. Welsch, *Unsere postmoderne Moderne*, 2nd ed. (Weinheim, 1988), 66–77.

43. An illuminating example is *Geschichte der Araber*, published by an authors' collective at the University of Leipzig, vols. 1–7 (Berlin, 1971–1983). Volumes 1–2 contain the history from 600 to 1918; volumes 3–7 cover the period from 1918 to around 1980.

44. E. Wirth, "Orientalistik und Orientforschung: Aufgaben und Probleme aus der Sicht der Nachbarwissenschatten," *Deutscher Orientalistentag 1975 in Freiburg im Breisgau: Vorträge*, ed. W. Voigt (Wiesbaden, 1977): 55–82 (*ZDMG*, Suppl. 3); and F. Büttner et al., "Die Entdeckung des Nahen Ostens durch die deutsche Politikwissenschaft," in *Dritte Welt-Forschung: Entwicklungstheorie und Entwicklungspolitik*, ed. F. Nuscheler (Opladen, 1985), 416–435.

45. H. R. Roemer, ed., *Deutsche Orientalistik der siebziger Jahre: Thesen, Zustandsanalyse, Perspektiven* (Wiesbaden, n.d.; ms. printing by German Oriental Society, 1972); R. Büren, *Gegenwartsbezogene Orientwissenschaft in der Bundesrepublik Deutschland* (Göttingen, 1974).

46. J. Waardenburg, "Islamforschung aus religionswissenschaftlicher Sicht," *XXI. Deutscher Orientalistentag vom 24. bis 29. März 1980 in Berlin*, ed. F. Steppat (Wiesbaden, 1983): 197–211 (*ZDMG*, Suppl. 5).

47. B. S. Turner, *Weber and Islam* (London, 1974).

48. A. Salvatore, "Beyond Orientalism? Max Weber and the Displacements of 'Essentialism' in the Study of Islam," *Arabica* 43 (1996): 457–485.

49. W. Schluchter, ed., *Max Weber's Sicht des Islams* (Frankfurt am Main, 1987).

50. M. Rodinson, "Das Bild im Westen und westliche Islamstudien," *Das Vermächtnis des Islam,* ed. J. Schacht and C. E. Bosworth, vols. 1–2 (Munich and Zurich, 1980), 1, 24–81, esp. 80f. Rodinson had already turned against ethnocentrism regarding Muslims, which he said represented the other side of Eurocentrism; to him, such ethnocentrism ran through even the otherwise rich work of Norman Daniel; see Daniel, *Islam and the West,* 73ff.

51. See M. Arkoun, "L'Islam moderne vu par le professeur G. E. von Grunebaum," *Arabica* 11 (1964): 113–124; see also A. Laroui, "For a Methodology of Islamic Studies: Islam as Seen by G. von Grunebaum," *Diogenes* 81–84 (1973): 12–39.

52. E. Said, *Orientalism* (New York, 1978; paperback ed., New York, 1979).

53. Said refers primarily to M. Foucault, *L'archéologie du savoir* (Paris, 1969) and *Surveiller et punir: Naissances de la prison* (Paris, 1975).

54. See, for example, R. A. Kapp, M. Dalby, and D. Kopf, "Review Symposium: Edward Said's Orientalism," *Journal of Asian Studies* 39 (1989): 481–506; see also Rudolph, *Westliche Islamwissenschaft,* 61, n. 2; J. Osterhammel, "Edward W. Said und die 'Orientalismus'-Debatte: ein Rückblick," *Asien, Afrika, Lateinamerika* 25 (1997): 596–607; U. Freitag, "The Critique of Orientalism," in *Companion to Historiography,* ed. M. Bentley (London 1997), 620–638.

55. See, for example, H. Fähndrich, "Orientalismus und Orientalismus: Überlegungen zu Edward Said, Michel Foucault und westlichen 'Islamstudien,'" *Die Welt des Islams* 28 (1988): 178–186. Leonard Binder discusses this at length in the chapter "Deconstructing Orientalism" in his book *Islamic Liberalism: A Critique of Development Ideologies* (Chicago, 1988), 85–127. He also refers to the sometimes insufficient reception of Foucault by Said.

56. S. J. al-'Azm, "Al-Istishraq wa-l-istishraq ma'kusan," *Al-Hayat al-jadida* 1 (Beirut, 1981): 3, 7–51. A shorter English version is found in *Khamsin* 8 (1981): 5–26.

57. For our context, see G. Stauth and B. Turner, "Nietzsche's Dance: Resentment, Reciprocity and Resistance," in *Nietzsche's Dance: Resentment, Reciprocity and Resistance in Social Life* (Oxford, 1988).

58. See M. Abaza and G. Stauth, "Occidental Reason, Orientalism, Islamic Fundamentalism: A Critique," *International Sociology* 3 (1988): 4, 343–364.

59. M. Arkoun, *Pour une critique de la raison islamique,* vols. 1–2 (Paris, 1984). The title, of course, is reminiscent of Wilhelm Dilthey's "Kritik der historischen Vernunft." More than elsewhere, French Orientalistics tended to discuss and adopt theoretical models "foreign to the discipline" (especially Jean Sauvaget and Claude Cahen, among others).

60. J. C. Bürgel, *Allmacht und Mächtigkeit: Religion und Welt im Islam* (Munich, 1991), 19.

61. J. Kraemer, *Das Problem der islamischen Kulturgeschichte* (Tübingen, 1959).

62. J.-P. Charnay, *Les Contre-Orients ou Comment penser l'Autrui selon soi* (Paris, 1980).

63. Waardenburg, "Islamforschung," 204.

64. M. Rodinson, "Orientalisme et ethnocentrisme," *XXI. Deutscher Orientalistentag,* 77–86 (*ZDMG,* Suppl. 5).

65. Endress, *Der Islam,* 31.

66. See Charnay, *Les Contre-Orients,* 250.

67. M. Foucault, *L'ordre du discours: Leçon inaugurale au Collège de France prononcée le 2 décembre 1970* (Paris, 1986).

68. Rodinson, "Orientalisme," 81.

69. F. Rosenthal, "Die Krise der Orientalistik," *XXI. Deutscher Orientalistentag,* 10–21.

70. A different strand of criticism was described by H. R. Roemer, "Spezialisierung, Integration und Innovation in der deutschen Orientalistik," *Die Welt des Islams* 28 (1988): 475–495.

71. B. S. Turner, "Orientalism and the Problem of Civil Society in Islam," in *Orientalism, Islam, and Islamists,* ed. A. Hussein et al. (Brattleboro, Vt., 1984), 23–42.

72. An initial review of European works on the Islamic world indicates that treatments of diplomatic and economic history, especially on the Ottoman Empire, the Persian Safavid Empire, and the Indian Mughal Empire dominated scholarly interest.

73. A. al-Azmeh, "The Articulation of Orientalism," in Hussain et al., *Orientalism,* 89–124 (addressed in *Arab Studies Quarterly* 3 [1981]: 384–402, esp. 115ff.).

74. Formulated in the extreme by T. Nagel, "Die Ebenbürtigkeit des Fremden: Über die Aufgaben arabistischer Lehre und Forschung in der Gegenwart," *ZDMG* 148 (1998): 367–378.

75. An attempt at a preliminary reckoning is found in M. Schöller, *Methode und Wahrheit in der Islamwissenschaft,* Prolegomena (Wiesbaden, 2000); L. Ammann, "Islamwissenschaften," in *Phänomen Kultur: Perspektiven und Aufgaben der Kulturwissenschaften,* ed. E. Klaus (Bielefeld, 2003), 71–96.

II. Islam and Cultural Self-Assertion *(Rotraud Wielandt)*

1. On Taha Husayn's theory and its place within the contemporary discussion on Egyptian cultural identity, see R. Wielandt, *Das Bild der Europäer in der modernen arabischen Erzähl- und Theaterliteratur,* Beiruter Texte und Studien 23 (Beirut and Wiesbaden, 1980), 273f. and 380–382, in each case with context.

2. On the significance of Islam for the national cultural awareness of Christian Arabs, see in particular W. Ende, *Arabische Nation und islamische Geschichte: Die Umayyaden im Urteil arabischer Autoren des 20. Jahrhunderts,* Beiruter Texte und Studien 20 (Beirut and Wiesbaden, 1977), 171–189.

3. M. Scheffold, *Authentisch arabisch und dennoch modern? Zaki Najib Mahmud's kulturtheoretische Essayistik als Beitrag zum euro-arabischen Dialog* (Berlin, 1996), 63f.

4. See, e.g., I. J. Boullata, "Challenges to Arab Cultural Authenticity," in *The Next Arab Decade: Alternative Futures,* ed. H. Sharabi (Boulder, Colo.; London, 1988), 148.

5. On this author's individual views, see R. Wielandt, *Offenbarung und Geschichte im Denken moderner Muslime* (Wiesbaden, 1971), 163f.

6. Works by the two last-named authors can be found in the bibliography. For details of their views on cultural theory, see T. Nagel, "Identitätskrise und Selbstfindung," *Die Welt des Islams,* n.s. 19 (1979): 84–97.

7. See the author's two books listed in the bibliography.

8. In-depth analysis of his writings can be found in M. Scheffold, *Authentisch arabisch und dennoch modern?* On the summary of his concept given here, see esp. 213–216.

9. For a concise overview of his contribution to the cultural history debate, see ibid., 77–84.

10. See M. Gaebel, *Von der Kritik des arabischen Denkens zum panarabischen Aufbruch: Das philosophische und politische Denken Muhammad 'Abid al-Jabiris* (Berlin, 1995), 45–50.

11. See Hasan Hanafi, *Muqaddima fi 'ilm al-istighrab* (Cairo: Al-Dar al-fanniyya, 1990), esp. 768–773.

12. See, inter alia, Yusuf al-Qaradawi's book *Al-Thaqafa al-'arabiyya al-islamiyya bayna l-asala wa-l-mu'asara* (Arab-Islamic Culture between Authenticity and Contemporaneousness) (Beirut: Mu'assasat al-Risala, 1998), 92–94.

13. Muhammad Qutb, *Manhaj al-tarbiya al-islamiyya* (Methods of Islamic Education), 14th ed. (Cairo: Dar al-Shuruq, 1414 [1993]); idem, *Manhaj al-fann al-islami* (Methods of Islamic Art), 6th ed. (Beirut and Cairo: Dar al-Shuruq, 1983).

14. Najib al-Kilani, *Al-Islamiyya wa-l-madhahib al-adabiyya* (Islamism and Literary Schools), 4th ed. (Beirut: Mu'assasat al-Risala, 1985); idem, Afaq al-adab al-islami (Horizons of Islamic Literature) (Beirut: Mu'assasat al-Risala, 1985).

III. Islam and Local Traditions
(Olaf Schumann and Lode Frank Brakel)

2. Indonesia as a Case Study *(Lode Frank Brakel)*

1. S. G. Ferrand, *Relation de voyages et textes géographiques arabes* (1913).

2. See M. C. Ricklefs, *History of Modern Indonesia* (1990), stating that the first clear evidence of the existence of a Muslim Malay dynasty in the Indonesian-Malay area is the gravestone of the first Muslim ruler of Samudra, Sultan Malik al-Salih, dated 1297 CE.

3. M. B. Hooker, *Islam in Southeast Asia* (1983).

4. S. J. Noorduyn, "De islamisering van Makassar" (1956).

5. L.-C. Damais, "Études Javanaises" (1956); G. W. J. Drewes, "New Light on the Coming of Islam to Indonesia?" (1968).

6. See J. Ensink, "*Siva*-Buddhism in Java and Bali" (1978).

7. N. Levtzion, "Islamisierungsmuster" (1992), points to a similar situation on the Indian subcontinent.

8. Useful information about Indonesian Islam and its particular manners and customs is found in C. Snouck Hurgronje, *The Achehnese* (1906); Th. W. Juynboll, *Handleiding tot de kennis van de Mohammedaansche wet* (1935); and P. Zoetmulder, in W. Stöhr and P. Zoetmulder, *Die Religionen Indonesiens* (1965). See also Bowen, *Muslims through Discourse* (1993).

9. G. Hamonic, "Travestissement et bisexualité chez les bissu des Pays Bugis" (1975).

10. On the history of Indonesian Islam during the twentieth century, see D. Noer, *The Modernist Muslim Movement in Indonesia, 1900–1942* (1973); H. J. Benda, *The Crescent and the Rising Sun* (1958); and B. J. Boland, *The Struggle of Islam in Modern Indonesia* (1971).

11. S. M. Naguib al-Attas, *The Mysticism of Hamzah Fansuri* (1972). Also see L. F. Brakel, "Hamza Pansuri: Notes on Yoga Practices" (1979).

12. J. Doorenbos, *De Geschriften van Hamzah Pansoeri* (1933), 42–43.

13. Verses 1, 2, 6, and 8 of poem 23 in G. W. J. Drewes and L F. Brakel, *Poems of Hamzah Fansuri* (1986), 110–115 (with a few minor adaptations in the translation).

14. W. W. Skeat, *Malay Magic* (1967); R. O. Winstedt, *The Malay Magician* (1961).

15. C. Geertz, *The Religion of Java* (1960).

16. A detailed description is given in the Nagarakertagama, cantos 63–90. See Th. Pigeaud, *Java in the 14th Century,* 5 vols. (1960–1963); and S. O. Robson's translation, titled *Desawarnana* (1995), 69–90.

17. On the worship of the goddess of the Southern Ocean by the rulers of Surakarta and Yogyakarta, see C. Brakel-Papenhuyzen, *The Bedhaya Court Dances of Central Java* (1992).

18. C. Brakel-Papenhuyzen, "Sandhang Pangan for the Goddess" (1997).
19. M. Bonneff, "Le renouveau d'un rituel royal, les Garebeg à Yogyakarta" (1974).
20. Pigeaud, *Java in the 14th Century* 4:267.
21. Ibid., 95.
22. See N. Mulder, "The Rise of Contemporary Kebatinan Mysticism," in *Mysticism and Everyday Life in Contemporary Java* (1978), 1–13.
23. G. W. J. Drewes, *An Early Javanese Code of Muslim Ethics* (1978).
24. M. C. Ricklefs, "Islamization in Java" (1984), 16. The quotation follows Drewes's translation of the *Suluk Kadresan;* G. W. J. Drewes, "Javanese Poems Dealing with or Attributed to the Saint of Bonan" (1968), 225.
25. See P. J. Zoetmulder, *Pantheïsme en monisme in de Javaansche soeloekliteratuur* (1935), chap. 8.
26. See S. O. Robson's introduction to *The Wédhatama* (1990).
27. The verse quoted is canto 2.7 according to the text published in *Djawa* 21 (1941). The same verse is canto 2.10 in the text edited and translated by Robson in 1990. On the variant versions of the text, see Robson's introduction. The English translation follows Robson's.
28. Canto 2.13–14 in Robson's text.
29. The word *priyayi* may also be translated as "nobleman," as in the original German text.
30. Canto 4.23 in Robson's text.
31. See P. J. Zoetmulder, "Iets omtrent de naam 'Serat Tjentini'" (1939), and "Een merkwaardige passage in de onuitgegeven Tjentini" (1941).
32. His childhood name is Jayèngresmi.
33. See the passage from *Serat Centhini* 2.199–201, in P. Zoetmulder, *Pantheïsme en Monisme in de Javaansche soeloekliteratuur* (1935), 299–301.
34. This concept has its origin in Shivaite and Buddhist ideas of *shunyata* and *nirvana;* see K. A. H. Hidding's review of Zoetmulder (1936a).
35. See G. W. J. Drewes, "The Struggle between Javanism and Islam as Illustrated by the *Serat Dermagandul*" (1966).
36. See Ph. van Akkeren, *Een gedrocht en toch de volmaakte mens* (1951).

V. Islam Reflected in the Contemporary Literature of Muslim Peoples *(Johann Christoph Bürgel)*

1. Lewis, 1968, 133f.
2. Ibid., 139.
3. Khouri, 1971, 68–69.
4. Cf. Starkey, 1977, 136–52. The important Turkish poet Nazim Hikmet (1902–1963) used the Qur'anic story of Joseph to convey atheist ideas; see Spuler, 1968, 127.
5. The discussion on literature about Muhammad is based on Badawi, 1971, 154–177.
6. A poem of praise composed by al-Busiri after the Prophet had thrown his mantle (*burda*) over his shoulders, healing his lameness.
7. R. B. Campbell, ed., *Contemporary Arab Writers*, vols. 1–2 (Beirut, 1996).
8. Taymur, n.d., 11–13; Badawi, 1971, 162.
9. Taymur, n.d., 13–15; Badawi, 1971, 162.
10. 'Al-Aqqad, 1943, 313; Badawi, 1971, 166.
11. Cachia, 1971, 179–194, esp. 187.

12. ʿAla Hamish al-sira, 1958; Badawi, 1971, 169.
13. T. Radwan, *Al-Thaʾir al-aʿzam* (Cairo, 1954), 185–186; Badawi, 1971, 171–172.
14. Al-Sharqawi, 1962; Badawi, 1971, 172.
15. From Dolinina 1973, 147.
16. Ibn Khaldun, 1967.
17. On fictionalization of the past, see von Grunebaum, 1969, 229–272.
18. Translated from the Urdu "Madd-o-jazr-i Islam," in Siddiqi, 1978, 78, strophe 72.
19. Ibid., strophes 92, 103, 104.
20. Ibid., strophe 112, line 3.
21. Ibid., strophes 122, 123.
22. See also Bürgel, 1980, and Bürgel's German anthology of Iqbal's poetry written in Urdu, 1982.
23. "Shikwa" and "Jawab-i Shikwa," in the Urdu cycle "Bangi-i Dara"; English translation by M. A. K. Khalil, *Call of the Marching Bell* (Lahore, 1997), nos. 88 and 103; complete German translation in Bürgel, 1982, 46–60.
24. "Shikwa," strophe 16.
25. Ibid., strophes 17 and 18.
26. "Jawab-i Shikwa," strophe 11.
27. Translator's note: This is in fact the last but one (151st) strophe of the appendix (*zamima*); "Ebb and Flow" itself ends on a similarly optimistic note.
28. "Jawab-i Shikwa,", strophe 32.
29. Translator's note: The Qurʾan, beginning of sura 53, describes a vision of Muhammad's of a celestial being believed to have been the archangel Gabriel or God himself.
30. In the cycle "Zarb-i Kalim," in *Kulliyat-i Iqbal*; in Urdu, Siddiqi, 1968, 49.
31. The original (1957) German translation by Annemarie Schimmel is reprinted, slightly revised, in Schimmel, 1977, 199–327.
32. Cf. Bürgel, 1975.
33. Cf. Sadiq, 1964, 193.
34. Cf. Semaan, 1979, 517–531. For al-Hallaj, see Schimmel, 1975, 162–177.
35. Massignon, 1975, 594ff. For content, see the English translation by Semaan, "Murder in Baghdad," 1972.
36. This account of the plot is based on Semaan's translation, 1972.
37. See, e.g., Sadeq Hedayat's blasphemous satire *The Myth of Creation*, 1998.
38. German translation from Bürgel, 1983, 30–79. See also Bürgel, 1996, 165–185.
39. Content based on Steppat, 1975; Wessels, 1974, 105–120; Somekh,1973, 137–155. See also El-Enany, 1993.
40. See the summary by N. Baladi, *Mélanges de l'Institut Dominicain d'Études Orientales du Caire* 2 (1955): 307–310.
41. In Simon, 1971, 87–99; Manzalaoui, 1968, 180–192.
42. This summary is based on Walther, 1974b, 239–258, esp. 251; and idem, 1974a, 199–213, esp. 209. In English, Naguib Mahfouz, *Adrift on the Nile* (New York, 1983).
43. Alavi, 1964, 52.
44. M. Makal, *Bizim Köy*, 6th ed. (Istanbul, 1957) (*Varlık cep kitapları* 12), and the sequel, *Hayal ve Gerçek* (Istanbul, 1957) (*Varlık cep kitapları* 37). The first part was published in German under the title *Unser Dorf in Anatolien* (Frankfurt am Main, 1971).
45. "Qalb-i mahiyat"; in German, "Gesinnungswandel" (trans. Bürgel), in Behzad et al., *Moderne Erzähler der Welt: Iran, Tübingen 1978*, 40–44.
46. Summary based on Mikhail, 1974, 147–57.

47. M. Iqbal, "Kulliyat-i Urdu," *Bal-i Jibril,* 65, ghazal no. 45.
48. See "The Quest for Freedom in Modern Arabic Literature: Essays in Honour of Mustafa Badawi," ed. R. Ostle, *Journal of Arabic Literature* 26, nos. 1–2 (1995): 214ff.
49. Text and brief notes on the author in Bellamy et. al., 1963–64.
50. German translation in Ziock, 1963. A vendetta and the failed attempt to end it through a marriage between the hostile clans is also the focus of the successful Turkish film *Sürü* (The Herd), screenplay by Yılmaz Güney (Hamburg, 1980).
51. See Paret, 1934; see also the chapter by Wiebke Walther in this volume.
52. M. Kamil "Sheikh Mursi marries the land", Cairo 1984.
53. See Baljon, 1961, 115.
54. S. Hedayat, "The Search for Mercy" trans. B. Spooner, in *Sadeq Hedayat, An Anthology,* ed. E. Yarshater (Boulder, Colo.: Westview Press, 1979), 62.
55. M. Taymur, German translation in M. Taymur, *Der gute Scheich (Erzählungen,* Berlin 1961), 5–17.
56. Sadeq Hedayat, "Muhallil," in the anthology *Sih Qatreh khun, Majmu'e-i dastan* (Tehran, 1933). German translation by T. Rahnema and W. Bönzli, *die horen* 122 (1981): 61–67.
57. Jamalzadeh, 1985. See also the touching story "Molla Qorban 'Ali Pours Out His Heart"; German translation in Behzad et al., 24–39; and "Persian Is Sugar" (Farsi shakar ast), German translation in *Orient,* vol. 6 (1965): 54–56.
58. M. A. Jamalzadeh, "Pine-duz-i Shiraz," summarized from the Persian text in *Djamalzadeh, Qisseha-i kutah bara-i bachcheha-i rishdar* (Tehran, 1975), 177–200.
59. Hussein, 1954, section 12.
60. Kraemer, 1959.
61. Jalal Al-e Ahmad, *Risalat-i Pul,*in *Zan-i ziyadi,* 2nd ed. (Tehran, 1975).
62. Al-e Ahmad, *By the Pen,* trans. M. R. Ghanounparvar (Austin, Texas, 1988).
63. See Nasr, 1980, 88–104.
64. See Badawi, 1970, 145–161.
65. Yahya Haqqi, "Qindil Umm Hashim"; English version in Badawi, *The Saint's Lamp and Other Stories* (Leiden 1973). On the same theme, cf. Bürgel, 1977, 1042–48.
66. Cf. J. C. Bürgel, "Secular and Religious Features of Medieval Arabic Medicine, in *Asian Medical Systems: A Comparative Study,* ed. C. Leslie (Berkeley, 1976), 44–62.
67. J. C. Bürgel, "Omnipotence and the Powers: How to Deal with 'Mightiness' in a System of Religious Control," in *Islam i chrzescijanstwo* (Krakow, 1995).
68. Translator's note: Cf. J. C. Bürgel, "Language on Trial, Religion at Stake? Trial Scenes in Some Classical Arabic Texts and the Hermeneutic Problems Involved," in *Historical Archetypes and Symbolic Figures in Arabic Literature: Towards a New Hermeneutic Approach,* ed. A. Neuwirth et al., Proceedings of the International Symposium in Beirut, June 25–30, 1996 (Beirut, 1999), 189–204.
69. S. Guth and C. Szyska, "Das 'geordnete System' der Fleißigen Bienen: Belletristik im Geiste des Islam," *Neue Zürcher Zeitung* 35, nos. 11–12 (February 1998): 70.
70. Szyska, 1999, 221–235, esp. 222.
71. Ibid., 234.
72. Guth and Szyska, "Das 'geordnete System,'" 1998.
73. Szyska, 1995, 95–125.
74. Furrer, 1997, 88–111.
75. Ibid., 108.
76. Ibid. See Cooke, 1997.
77. Guth and Szyska, "Das 'geordnete System.'"

VI. Contemporary Painting and Graphic Art
in the Islamic World *(Peter Heine)*

1. See M. S. İpşiroğlu, *Das Bild im Islam: Ein Verbot und seine Folgen* (Vienna, 1971); S. Naef, *Y a-t-il une question de l'image en islam?* (Geneva, 2004); A. M. Issa, *Painting in Islam: Between Prohibition and Aversion* (Istanbul, 1996).

2. For a history of the various regional forms of calligraphy in the Muslim world, see "Khaṭṭ," in *Encyclopaedia of Islam,* 2nd ed., vol. 4 (Leiden, 1978), 1113–28; also A. Khatibi and M. Sijelmassi, *The Splendor of Islamic Calligraphy* (London, 1996).

3. For a discussion of the religious significance of writing holy texts, see J. Goody, intro. to *Literacy in Traditional Societies,* ed. J. Goody (Cambridge, 1968).

4. E. Kuehnel, *The Arabesque* (Graz, 1976).

5. See the works by the Pakistani painters Ismail and Amin Gulgee (father and son), the Algerian Rachid Korachi, and the Palestinian Kamal Boullata.

6. See Naef, *Y a-t-il une question de l'image en islam?*

7. See also M. Centlivres-Demont, *Popular Art in Afghanistan: Paintings on Trucks, Mosques, and Tea-Houses* (Graz, 1976).

8. See also S. J. Falk, *Qajar Paintings: Persian Oil Paintings of the 18th and 19th Centuries* (London, 1972).

9. Al-Tahtawi, *An Imam in Paris: Al-Tahtawi's Visit to France* (London, 2004).

10. In view of the large number of artists involved in developing painting throughout the Muslim world, I seldom refer to them by name in this discussion.

11. See also the various articles in B. Heyberger and S. Naef, eds., *La multiplication des images en pays de l'Islam* (Würzburg and Istanbul, 2003).

12. One example is the Ba'th regime's official support of artists in Iraq, which produced a lively and significant art scene in Baghdad in the early 1990s.

13. See for example, S. Faath, H. Mattes, and Gh. Al-Warfalı, *Muhammad al-Zawawi: A Libyan Caricaturist* (Hamburg, 1984).

14. Personal research in 1990.

15. This does not come from the realm of Islamic art but is related to the efforts by nationalistic regimes in the Muslim world to stress a secular national identity by using pre-Islamic art in official modern art production. Examples can be found in Egypt, Lebanon, Syria, and even Saudi Arabia. For Iraq, see A. Baram, *Culture, History, and Ideology in the Formation of Bathist Iraq, 1968–1989* (New York, 1991).

16. See also S. Faath, "Khalid Aloulou: 'La mémoire félée' oder: Die Suche nach Identität," *Wuqûf* 2 (1987): 111–140, particularly 125f.

17. These experiments are based on old Muslim traditions since declarations of faith such as the Basmala and the Shahada have always given artists the opportunity to invent new forms and use forms of script to create objects such as ships or animals. See also D. al-Azzawi, *The Influence of Calligraphy on Contemporary Arab Arts* (London, 1980).

VII. Contemporary "Islamic" Architecture
and Representational Art *(Mohamed Scharabi)*

1. See M. Scharabi, 1985. For the wider context, see Wirth, 2002.

2. There is no direct basis in the Qur'an for the prohibition on representation of humans and animals. It is targeted at certain kinds of "pagan" customs that allow

pictorial works to be used as idols. For the development of the "picture prohibition" up to the present day, see Naef, 2004, 2007.

3. See the essays by A. Schölch and H. Mejcher in Haarmann, 2001, 365ff.
4. See Scharabi, 1989.
5. See Scharabi, 1968; Myntti, 2003.
6. Cf. Scharabi, 1989; Raafat, 2003.
7. See Scharabi, 1985.
8. Cf. Schölch, 1981.
9. On expressionist architecture, see Scharabi, 1981, 66–82.
10. See Naguib, 1980; for further details on modern Arabic art in Egypt, Lebanon, and Iraq, see Naef, 1996; see also Peter Heine's chapter on painting and graphic art in the present volume.
11. See Scharabi, 1992.
12. See Fathy, 1973.
13. Cf. Azzam, 1960, 108.
14. See Jadarji, 1966, 1, 88–100.
15. See the brochure by the architects' team Rolf Gutbrod, Frei Otto, Ove Arup & Partners, London, Conference Center and Hotel in Mecca, n.d.
16. See Scharabi, 1985.
17. See Scharabi, 1974, 653–656.

BIBLIOGRAPHY

Part One
Historical Expansion, Political and Religious History

I. The World of Islam *(Heribert Busse)*

Bat Ye'or. *The Decline of Eastern Christianity under Islam: From Jihad to Dhimmitude, Seventh–Twentieth Century.* With a foreword by Jacques Ellul. Translated from French by M. Kochan and D. Littman. Madison, N.J.: Fairleigh Dickinson University Press, 1996.

Bosworth, C. E. *The Islamic Dynasties: A Chronological and Genealogical Handbook.* Edinburgh: Edinburgh University Press, 1967.

Brockelmann, C. *Geschichte der arabischen Litteratur.* Leiden: E. J. Brill, 1898–1902. Supplement vols. 1–3. Leiden: E. J. Brill, 1937–1942. 2nd ed. adapted to the supplementary vols. Leiden: E. J. Brill, 1943–1949.

The Cambridge History of Islam. Edited by P. M. Holt, A. K. S. Lambton, and B. Lewis. Vol. 1A, *The Central Islamic Lands from Pre-Islamic Times to the First World War.* Vol. 1B, *The Central Islamic Lands since 1918.* Vol. 2A, *The Indian Sub-Continent, South East Asia, Africa and the Muslim West.* Vol. 2B, *Islamic Society and Civilisation.* Cambridge: Cambridge University Press, 1970.

Cleveland, W. L. *A History of the Modern Middle East.* Boulder, Colo.: Westview Press, 1994.

Donner, F. M. *The Early Islamic Conquests.* Princeton: Princeton University Press, 1981.

Endress, G. *Der Islam: Eine Einführung in seine Geschichte.* 3rd ed. Munich: C. H. Beck, 1997.

Endress, G., and C. Hillenbrand. *Islam: An Historical Introduction.* New York: Columbia University Press, 2003.

The Encyclopaedia of Islam. 2nd ed. Prepared by a number of leading Orientalists; edited by an Editorial Committee consisting of H. A. R. Gibb et al. 12 vols. Leiden: E. J. Brill, 1960–2004. Index vol., compiled by E. van Donzel et al. Leiden: E. J. Brill, 2009. CD ROM edition. Leiden: E. J. Brill, 1999–2003.

The Encyclopaedia of Islam Three. Edited by Marc Gaborieau, Gudrun Krämer, John Nawas, and Everett Rowson. Leiden: E. J. Brill, 2007– (fasc. 1–3, 2007; fasc. 1, 2008).

Fischer Weltgeschichte. Vol. 14, *Der Islam, Part 1, Vom Ursprung bis zu den Anfängen des Osmanenreiches,* compiled and edited by C. Cahen. Frankfurt am Main: Fischer Taschenbuch Verlag, 1968. Vol. 15, *Der Islam, Part 2, Die islamischen Reiche nach dem Fall von Konstantinopel,* edited by G. E. von Grunebaum. Frankfurt am Main: Fischer Taschenbuch, 1971. Vol. 16, *Zentralasien,* edited by G. Hambly. Frankfurt am Main: Fischer Taschenbuch, 1966.

Haarmann, U., ed. *Geschichte der arabischen Welt.* 4th ed. Munich: C. H. Beck, 2001.

Handbuch der Orientalistik. Edited by B. Spuler. Part 1: *Der Nahe und der Mittlere Osten,* edited by B. Spuler. Vol. 6: *Geschichte der Islamischen Länder.* 1: B. Spuler: *Die Chalifenzeit* (1952); 2: B. Spuler: *Die Mongolenzeit* (1953); 3: *Neuzeit,* with contributions by H. J. Kissling et al. (1959). Vol. 8: *Religion.* 2: *Religionsgeschichte des Orients in der Zeit der Weltreligionen,* with contributions by J. Leipoldt et. al. (1961). Supplementary vol. 3: *Orientalisches Recht,* with contributions by E. Seidl et al. (1964). Vol. 7: I. Gomaa. *A Historical Chart of the Muslim World* (1972). Vol. 8: H.-J. Kornrumpf. *Osmanische Bibliographie mit besonderer Berücksichtigung der Türkei in Europa* (1973). Leiden: E. J. Brill, 1973.

Hawting, G. R. *The First Dynasty of Islam: The Umayyad Caliphate, AD 661–750.* Carbondale: Southern Illinois University Press, 1986.

Hourani, A. H. *A History of the Arab Peoples.* With a new afterword by M. Ruthven. Cambridge: Belknap Press of Harvard University Press, 2002.

Index Islamicus, 1665–1905. Bibliography of articles on Islamic subjects in periodicals and other collective publications compiled by W. H. Behn. Millersville, Pa.: Adiyok, 1989. *1906–2002,* compiled by D. J. Pearson, W. H. Behn, G. J. Roper, and C. H. Bleaney. Leiden: E. J. Brill, 1958–2007. *Quarterly Index Islamicus 1–17,* edited by J. D. Pearson, compiled by G. J. Roper, London: Mansell/Bowker Saur, 1977–1998. *Osmanistische Nachträge zum Index Islamicus (1906–1965),* compiled by H. G. Majer, *Südost–Forschungen* 27 (1968): 242–291.

Kennedy, H. *The Prophet and the Age of the Caliphates: Islamic Near East from the Sixth to the Eleventh Century.* London: Longman, 1986.

———. *An Historical Atlas of Islam.* 2nd ed. Leiden: E. J. Brill, 2002.

Kreiser, K., W. Diem, and H. G. Majer, eds. *Lexikon der Islamischen Welt.* 3 vols. Stuttgart: Kohlhammer, 1974.

Lapidus, Ira M. *A History of Islamic Societies.* 2nd ed. Cambridge: Cambridge University Press, 2002.

Lewis, B. *The Arabs in History.* Oxford: Cambridge University Press, 1993.

Matuz, J. *Das Osmanische Reich: Grundlinien seiner Geschichte.* 3rd ed. Darmstadt: Wissenschaftliche Buchgesellschaft, 1994.

Morony, M. G. *Iraq after the Muslim Conquest.* Princeton: Princeton University Press, 1984.

Schulze, R. *A Modern History of the Islamic World.* London: I. B. Tauris, 2002.

Serauky, E. *Geschichte des Islam: Entstehung, Entwicklung und Wirkung von den Anfängen bis zur Mitte des XX. Jahrhunderts.* Berlin: Deutscher Verlag der Wissenschaften, 2003.

Sezgin, F. *Geschichte des arabischen Schrifttums.* Leiden: E. J. Brill, 1967– (11 vols. and 1 volume of maps have been published; 20 vols. are planned).

Shaw, S. *History of the Ottoman Empire and Modern Turkey.* 2 vols. Cambridge: Cambridge University Press, 1976.

Spuler, B. *The Mongols in History.* Translated by G. Wheeler. New York: Pall Mall Press, 1971.

——. *A History of the Muslim World.* With a new introduction by J. Hathaway. Princeton: Princeton University Press, 1994.

Steinbach, U., and R. Robert, eds. *Der Nahe und der Mittlere Osten: Politik, Gesellschaft, Wirtschaft, Geschichte, Kultur.* 2 vols. Opladen: Leske & Budrich, 1988.

Trimingham, J. S. *The Sufi Orders in Islam.* Oxford: Clarendon Press, 1971.

Watt, W. M. et al., eds. *Der Islam.* Vol. 1, *Mohammed und die Frühzeit: Islamisches Recht; Religiöses Leben,* by W. M. Watt and A. T. Welch. Vol. 2, *Political Developments and Theological Concepts,* by W. M. Watt and M. Marmura. Vol. 3, *Islamische Kultur—zeitgenössische Strömungen—Volksfrömmigkeit,* by M. D. Ahmed, J. C. Bürgel, K. Dilger, K. Durán, P. Heine, T. Nagel, B. S. Amoretti, A. Schimmel, and W. Walther. Stuttgart: Kohlhammer, 1980–1990.

Weeks, R. V., ed. *Muslim Peoples: A World Ethnographic Survey.* Westport, Conn.: Greenwood Press, 1978.

Wellhausen, J. *The Arab Kingdom and Its Fall.* London: Routledge, 2000.

II. Sunni Islam *(Bernd Radtke)*

Coulson, N. J. *A History of Islamic Law.* Edinburgh: Edinburgh University Press, 1964.

De Jong, F. and B. Radtke. *Islamic Mysticism Contested.* Leiden: Brill, 1999.

Ess, J. van. *Theologie und Gesellschaft im 2. und 3. Jahrhundert Hidschra: Eine Geschichte des religiösen Denkens im frühen Islam.* 6 vols. Berlin: Walter de Gruyter, 1991–1997.

Fück, J. "Die Religion des sunnitischen Islams." In *Handbuch der Orientalistik/Handbook of Oriental Studies.* Section 1, vol. 8/2, *Religionsgeschichte des Orient in der Zeit der Weltreligionen,* 404–448. Leiden: Brill, 1961.

Gramlich, R. *Die schiitischen Derwischorden Persiens.* 3 vols. Part 2, *Glaube und Lehre.* Abhandlungen für die Kunde des Morgenlandes (AKM) 36, parts 2–4. Wiesbaden: Franz Steiner, 1976.

Massignon, L. *Essay on the Origins of the Technical Language of Islamic Mysticism.* Translated from the French with an introduction by Benjamin Clark. Notre Dame: University of Notre Dame Press, 1997.

Meier, F. "The Cleanest about Predestination: A Bit of Ibn Taymiyya." In *Essays on Islamic Piety and Mysticism,* edited by F. Meier, translated by J. O'Kane, 309–334. Leiden: Brill, 1999.

——. "The Mystic Path: The Sufi Tradition." In *The World of Islam: Faith, People and Culture,* edited by B. Lewis, 117–140. London: Thames and Hudson, 1976.

——. "A Resurrection of Muhammad in Suyuti." In *Essays on Islamic Piety and Mysticism,* edited by F. Meier, translated by J. O'Kane, 506–548. Leiden: Brill, 1999.

Motzki, H. *Die Anfänge der islamischen Jurisprudenz.* AKM 50, 2. Stuttgart: Franz Steiner, 1991.

Popovic, A., and G. Veinstein, eds. *Les voies d'Allah.* Paris: Fayard, 1996.

Schacht, J. *The Origins of Muhammadan Jurisprudence.* Oxford: Clarendon Press, 1967.

Spies, O., and E. Pritsch "Klassisches islamisches Recht." In *Handbuch der Orientalistik/Handbook of Oriental Studies,* section 1, supplement. Vol. 3, *Orientalisches Recht,* 220–. Leiden: Brill, 1964.

Trimingham, J. S. *The Sufi Orders in Islam*. London: Oxford University Press, 1971.
Watt, W. M. *Islamic Philosophy and Theology.* Edinburgh: Edinburgh University Press, 1973.
——. *Islamic Political Thought*. Edinburgh: Edinburgh University Press, 1968.
——. *The Formative Period of Islamic Thought*. Edinburgh: Edinburgh University Press, 1973.

III. Shiʿi Islam *(Werner Ende)*

1. Twelver Shiʿa

Brunner, R., and W. Ende, eds. *The Twelver Shia in Modern Times: Religious Culture and Political History*. Leiden: Brill, 2001. (With an extensive bibliography, 365–382.)
Gramlich, R. *Die schiitischen Derwischorden Persiens*. 3 vols. Wiesbaden: Franz Steiner, 1965–1981.
Halm, H. *Shiʿism*. Translated by Janet Watson and Marian Hill. New York: Columbia University Press, 2004.
Madelung, W. "Shiʿa." In *The Encyclopaedia of Islam*, vol. 9, 420–424. Leiden: Brill, 1997.
Mervin, S. *Un réformisme chiite*. Paris: Karthala, 2000.
——, ed. *Les mondes chiites et l'Iran*. Paris: Karthala, 2007.
Momen, M. *An Introduction to Shiʿi Islam*. New Haven: Yale University Press, 1985.
Monsutti, A., S. Naef, and F. Sabahi, eds. *The Other Shiites: From the Mediterranean to Central Asia*. Bern: Peter Lang, 2007.
Nakash, Y. *The Shiʿis of Iraq*. Princeton: Princeton University Press, 1994.
——. *Reaching for Power: The Shiʿa in the Modern Arab World*. Princeton: Princeton University Press, 2006.
Pinault, D. *The Shiites: Ritual and Popular Piety in a Muslim Community*. New York: St. Martin's Press, 1992.

2. Zaydis

Haykel, B. *Revival and Reform in Islam: The Legacy of Muhammad al-Shawkani*. Cambridge: Cambridge University Press, 2003.
Jarrar, M. "Some Aspects of Imami Influence on Early Zaydite Theology." In *Islamstudien ohne Ende*, edited by R. Brunner et al., 201–223. Würzburg: Ergon Verlag, 2002.
Madelung, W. *Der Imam al-Qāsim ibn Ibrāhīm und die Glaubenslehre der Zaiditen*. Berlin: Walter de Gruyter, 1965.
——. "Zaydi Attitudes to Sufism." In *Islamic Mysticism Contested*, edited by F. de Jong and B. Radtke, 124–144. Leiden: Brill, 1999.
——. "Zaydiyya." In *The Encyclopaedia of Islam*, vol. 11, 477–481. Leiden: Brill, 2002.
Mortel, R. T. "Zaydi Shiism and the Hasanid Sharifs of Mecca." *International Journal of Middle East Studies* 19 (1987): 455–472.

IV. Revivalist Movements in Islam from the Eighteenth to the Twentieth Century and the Role of Islam in Modern History *(Rudolph Peters)*

Adams, C. C. *Islam and Modernism in Egypt: A Study of the Modern Reform Movement Inaugurated by Muhammad ʿAbduh*. 1st ed. 1933. London: Routledge, 2000.
Ahmad, A. *Islamic Modernism in India and Pakistan, 1857–1964*. London: Oxford University Press, 1967.

'Amri, H. b. A., al-. *The Yemen in the Eighteenth and Nineteenth Centuries: A Political and Intellectual History.* London: Ithaca Press, 1985.

Badawi, Z. *The Reformers of Egypt: A Critique of Al-Afghani, 'Abduh and Rida.* Muslim Institute Papers 2. Slough, Berkshire: Open Press, 1976.

Bahadur, K. *The Jama'at-i Islami of Pakistan: Political Thought and Political Action.* Lahore: Progressive Books, 1977.

Baljon, J. M. S. *Modern Muslim Koran Interpretation, 1880–1960.* Leiden: Brill, 1961.

——. *The Reforms and Religious Ideas of Sir Sayyid Ahmad Khan.* Leiden: Brill, 1949.

——. *Religion and Thought of Shah Wali Allah Dihlawi, 1703–1762.* Leiden: Brill, 1986.

Berkes, N. *The Development of Secularism in Turkey.* Montreal: McGill University Press, 1964.

Binder, L. "'Ali 'Abd al-Raziq and Islamic Liberalism." *Asian and African Studies* 16 (1982): 31–57.

Commins, D. D. *Islamic Reform: Politics and Social Change in Late Ottoman Syria.* New York: Oxford University Press, 1990.

Dallal, A. "The Origins and Objectives of Islamic Revivalist Thought, 1750–1850." *Journal of the American Oriental Society (JAOS)* 113 (1993): 341–360.

Delanoue, G. *Moralistes et politiques musulmans dans l'Égypte du XIXme siècle (1789–1882).* 2 vols. Cairo: Institut français d'archéologie orientale du Caire, 1982.

Enayat, H. *Modern Islamic Political Thought.* Austin: University of Texas Press, 1982.

Ghazi, M. A. *Islamic Renaissance in South Asia, 1707–1867: The Role of Shah Wali Allah and His Successors.* Islamabad: Islamic Research Institute, International Islamic University, 2002.

Haddad, M. "Arab Religious Nationalism in the Colonial Era: Rereading Rashid Rida's Ideas on the Caliphate." *Journal of the American Oriental Society* 117 (1997): 253–277.

Haddad, Y. Y. "Muhammad Abduh: Pioneer of Islamic Reform." In *Pioneers of Islamic Revival,* edited by A. Rahnema, 30–63. London: Zed Books, 1994.

Haykel, B. *Revival and Reform in Islam: the Legacy of Muhammad al-Shawkani.* Cambridge: Cambridge University Press, 2003.

Hourani, A. *Arabic Thought in the Liberal Age, 1798–1939.* London: Oxford University Press, 1962. (Reprinted 1967, 1983, 1993, with revisions and corrections.)

Jansen, J. J. G. *The Interpretation of the Koran in Modern Egypt.* Leiden: Brill, 1974.

Keddie, N. R. *An Islamic Response to Imperialism: Political and Religious Writings of Sayyid Jamal al-Din "al-Afghani."* Berkeley: University of California, 1968.

——. *Sayyid Jamal al-Din "al-Afghani": A Political Biography.* Berkeley: University of California Press, 1972.

Kerr, M. Islamic Reform: *The Political and Legal Theories of Muhammad 'Abduh and Rashid Rida.* Berkeley: University of California Press, 1966.

Khan, S. A. *The Causes of the Indian Revolt.* Translated by F. Robinson. Oxford: Oxford University Press, 2000. (Originally published in Urdu, Benares: Medical Hall Press, 1873.)

Martin, B. G. *Muslim Brotherhoods in Nineteenth-Century Africa.* Cambridge: Cambridge University Press, 1976.

May, L. S. *The Evolution of Indo-Muslim Thought after 1857.* Lahore: Sh. Muhammad Ashraf, 1970.

Mitchell, R. P. *The Society of Muslim Brothers.* London: Oxford University Press, 1969. (Reprint, New York: Oxford University Press, 1993.)

Nagel, T. *Staat und Glaubensgemeinschaft im Islam: Geschichte der politischen Ordnungsvorstellungen der Muslime.* Vol. 2, *Vom Spätmittelalter bis zur Neuzeit.* Bibliothek des Morgenlandes. Zurich: Artemis, 1981.

O'Fahey, R. S. *Enigmatic Saint: Ahmad ibn Idris and the Idrisi Tradition.* Evanston: Northwestern University Press, 1990.

O'Fahey, R. S., and B. Radtke. "Neo-Sufism Reconsidered." *Der Islam* 70 (1993): 52–87.

Peskes, E. *Muhammad B. 'Abdalwahhab (1703–92) im Widerstreit: Untersuchungen zur Rekonstruktion der Frühgeschichte der Wahhabiya.* Beirut: Franz Steiner, 1993.

Peters, R. "Idjtihad and taqlid in 18th and 19th Century Islam." *Die Welt des Islams* 20 (1980): 132–145.

——. *Islam and Colonialism: The Doctrine of Jihad in Modern History.* The Hague: Mouton, 1979.

Ramadan, T. *Aux sources du renouveau musulman d'al-Afghani à Hassan al-Banna: un siècle de réformisme islamique.* Paris: Bayard/Centurion, 1998.

Smith, W. C. *Islam in Modern History.* Princeton: Princeton University Press, 1957.

——. *Modern Islam in India: A Social Analysis.* 3rd ed. Lahore: Sh. Muhammad Ashraf, 1969.

Troll, C. W. *Sayyid Ahmad Khan: A Reinterpretation of Muslim Theology.* New Delhi: Vikas Publishing House, 1978.

Vikør, K. *Sufi and Scholar on the Desert Edge: Muhammad b. 'Ali al-Sanusi (1787–1859).* London: Hurst, 1995.

Voll, J. O. *Islam: Continuity and Change in the Modern World.* 2nd ed. Syracuse: Syracuse University Press, 1994.

Wielandt, R. *Das Bild der Europäer in der modernen arabischen Erzähl- und Theaterliteratur.* Beiruter Texte und Studien 23. Beirut: Franz Steiner, 1980.

——. *Offenbarung und Geschichte im Denken moderner Muslime.* Wiesbaden: Franz Steiner, 1971.

V. The Distribution of Muslims throughout the World
(Peter Heine and Riem Spielhaus)

Abedin, S. M. "Demographic Consequences of Minority Consciousness: An Analysis." *Journal Institute of Muslim Minority Affairs* 1–2 (1979–80): 97–114.

Adams, C. C. *Islam and Modernism in Egypt.* London: Milford, 1933. (Reprint, New York: Russell & Russell, 1968.)

Adrian, H. *Ethnologische Fragen der Entwicklungsplanung: Gbeniki—Die ethnologische Erforschung eines Bariba-Dorfes.* Meisenheim: Hain, 1975.

Baer, G. *Population and Society in the Arab East.* London: Routledge, 1964.

Bakri. *Description de l'Afrique Septentrionale par el-Bekri.* Translated by M. de Slane. Algiers: A. Jourdan, and Paris: P. Geuthner, 1913.

Brenner, L. "Constructing Muslim Identities in Mali." In *Muslim Identity and Social Change in Subsaharan Africa,* edited by L. Brenner, 59–78. London: Hurst, 1993.

Bundestag Printed Paper 14/4530. Antwort der Bundesregierung auf die Große Anfrage der Abgeordneten Dr. Jürgen Rüttgers, Erwin Marschewski (Recklinghausen), Wolfgang Zeitlmann, weiterer Abgeordneter und der Fraktion der CDU/CSU. *Islam in Deutschland.* Berlin: Bundesdruckerei, 2000.

Bundestag Printed Paper 16/5033. Antwort der Bundesregierung auf die Große Anfrage der Abgeordneten der Abgeordneten Josef Philip Winkler, Volker Beck (Cologne), Renate Künast, Monika Lazar und der Fraktion BÜNDNIS 90/DIE GRÜNEN. *Stand der rechtlichen Gleichstellung des Islam in Deutschland.* Berlin: Bundestagsdruckerei, 2007.

Chishti, S. K. "Muslim Population of Mainland China: An Estimate." *Journal Institute of Muslim Minority Affairs* 2 (1979–80): 75–85.

Dassetto, Felice, Silvio Ferrari, and Brigitte Maréchal. *Islam in the European Union: What's at Stake in the Future?* Brussels: European Parliament, 2007.

Geertz, C. *Islam Observed: Religious Development in Morocco and Indonesia.* New Haven: Yale University Press, 1968.

Heine, Peter. "I am not the Mahdi, but…" In *Apocalyptic Time,* edited by Albert I. Baumgarten, 69–78. Leiden: Brill, 2000.

Heine, Peter, and Reinhold Stipek. *Ethnizität und Islam: Differenzierung und Integration muslimischer Bevölkerungsgruppen.* Gelsenkirchen: Müller, 1984.

Houben, Vincent J. H. "Southeast Asia and Islam." In *Islam: Enduring Myths and Changing Realities,* edited by Aslam Syed, 149–170. Annals of the American Academy of Political and Social Science vol. 588. Thousand Oaks, Calif.: Sage, July 2003.

Ibn Battuta. *Voyages d'Ibn Battuta.* Arabic with a translation by C. Defrémery and B. R. Sanguinetti. 4th ed. Paris: Imprimerie Nationale, 1922.

Launay, R., and B. F. Soares. "The Formation of an 'Islamic Sphere' in Colonial West Africa." *Economy and Society* 28 (1999): 497–519.

Laurence, Jonathan, and Justin Vaisse. *Integrating Islam: Political and Religious Challenges in Contemporary France.* Washington, D.C.: Brookings Institution Press, 2006.

Lewis, I. M., ed. *Islam in Tropical Africa.* London: Oxford University Press, 1966.

Martin, B. G. *Muslim Brotherhoods in Nineteenth-Century Africa.* Cambridge: Cambridge University Press, 1976.

Nahost Jahrbuch. Edited by Deutsches Orient-Institut (T. Koszinowski and H. Mattes). Opladen: Leske & Budrich, 1987–.

Panjwani, I. A. G. "Muslims in Malawi." *Journal of Muslim Minority Affairs* 1, no. 2–2, no. 2 (1979–80): 158–168.

Pew Research Center. *Muslim Americans: Middle Class and Mostly Mainstream.* Washington, D.C. May 22, 2007. http://pewresearch.org/assets/pdf/muslim-americans. pdf.

Population and Housing Census Commission. *Population and Housing Census: Preliminary Report.* Addis Ababa: Government Printer, 1984.

Ramadan, T. *To Be a European Muslim.* Leicester: Islamic Foundation, 1999.

Roy, Olivier. *Globalized Islam: The Search for a New Ummah.* New York: Columbia University Press, 2006.

Smajlovic, A. "Muslims in Yugoslavia." *Journal Institute of Muslim Minority Affairs* 2 (1979–80): 132–144.

Spielhaus, Riem. "Religion and Identity: How Germany's Foreigners Have Become Muslims." *Internationale Politik* (Spring 2006): 17–23.

Trimingham, J. S. *Islam in West Africa.* Oxford: Clarendon Press, 1959.

'Umari. *L'Afrique moins l'Égypte.* Translated by M. Gaudefroy-Demombynes. Paris: P. Geuthner, 1927.

Weekes, R. *Muslim Peoples: A World Ethnographic Survey.* 2nd ed. 2 vols. Westport, Conn.: Greenwood Press, 1984 (1st ed. 1978).

Wilks, I. "The Position of Muslims in Metropolitan Ashanti in the Early 19th Century." In *Islam in Tropical Africa,* edited by I. M. Lewis, 318–341. London: Oxford University Press, 1966.

Yegar, M. *The Muslims of Burma.* Wiesbaden: Harrassowitz, 1972.

Part Two
The Political Role of Islam in the Present

I. The Intra-Islamic Discussion on a Modern Economic
and Social System *(Johannes Reissner)*

Ahmad, A. *Islamic Modernism in India and Pakistan, 1857–1964.* London: Oxford University Press, 1967.
Ghaussy, A. G. *Das Wirtschaftsdenken im Islam.* Beiträge zur Wirtschaftspolitik 42. Bern: Paul Haupt, 1986.
Hanna, S. A., and G. H. Gardner. *Arab Socialism: A Documentary Survey.* Leiden: Brill, 1969.
Kotb, S. *Social Justice in Islam.* Translated from Arabic by J. D. Hardie. New York: Octagon Press, 1970.
Müller, H. *Marktwirtschaft und Islam: Ökonomische Entwicklungskonzepte in der islamischen Welt unter besonderer Berücksichtigung Algeriens und Ägyptens.* Leipziger Schriften zur Gesellschaftswissenschaft 9. Baden-Baden: Nomos, 2002.
Nienhaus, V. *Islam und moderne Wirtschaft: Positionen, Probleme und Perspektiven.* Graz: Styria, 1982.
———. "Kulturelle Prägungen und wirtschaftspolitisches Handeln im Nahen Osten." In *Kulturelle Prägungen wirtschaftlicher Institutionen und wirtschaftspolitischer Reformen,* edited by Th. Eger, 125–146. Berlin: Duncker & Humblot, 2002.
Pawelka, P. "Entwicklung und Globalisierung: Der Imperialismus des 21. Jahrhunderts." In Landeszentrale für politische Bildung Baden-Württemberg, ed., *Der Bürger im Staat* 53, 84–95. Stuttgart: Landeszentrale für Politische Bildung Baden-Württemberg, 2003.
Reissner, J. *Ideologie und Politik der Muslimbrüder Syriens, 1947–1952.* Islamkundliche Untersuchungen 55. Freiburg: Klaus Schwarz, 1980.
Siddiqi, M. N. *Contemporary Literature on Islamic Economics.* Research Report 1. Leicester: Islamic Foundation, 1978.
Ule, W. *Der arabische Sozialismus und der zeitgenössische Islam.* Schriften des Deutschen Orient-Instituts. Opladen: Leske, 1969.

III. Developments in Law *(Hans-Georg Ebert)*

Bälz, Kilian. *Versicherungsvertragsrecht in den arabischen Staaten.* Karlsruhe: VVW, 1997.
Coulson, Noel J. *A History of Islamic Law.* Edinburgh: Edinburgh University Press, 1964.
———. *Succession in the Muslim Family.* Cambridge: Cambridge University Press, 1971.
Dilger, Konrad. *Quellen und Schrifttum des Strafrechts.* Edited by Hans-Heinrich Jescheck and Klaus H. A. Löffler. Vol. 2. *Außereuropäische Staaten.* Part 2. *Asien/Nordafrika.* Munich: C. H. Beck, 1976.
———. "Das Schweigen des Gesetzgebers als Mittel der Rechtsfortbildung im Bereich des islamischen Rechts." In *Die islamische Welt zwischen Mittelalter und Neuzeit: Festschrift für H. R. Roemer zum 65. Geburtstag,* edited by Ulrich Haarmann and Peter Bachmann, 81–93. Beirut: Steiner, 1979.

Ebert, Hans-Georg. *Das Erbrecht arabischer Länder.* Frankfurt am Main: Lang, 2004.

——. *Die Interdependenz von Staat, Verfassung und Islam im Nahen und Mittleren Osten in der Gegenwart.* Frankfurt am Main: Lang, 1991.

——. *Das Personalstatut arabischer Länder: Problemfelder, Methoden, Perspektiven.* Frankfurt am Main: Lang, 1996.

El-Ashker, Ahmed, and Rodney Wilson. *Islamic Economics: A Short History.* Leiden: Brill, 2006.

El Baradie, Adel. *Gottes-Recht und Menschenrecht: Grundlagenprobleme der islamischen Strafrechtslehre.* Baden-Baden: Nomos, 1983.

Elwan, Omaia. "Gesetzgebung und Rechtsprechung." In *Der Nahe und Mittlere Osten. Politik, Gesellschaft, Wirtschaft, Kultur,* edited by Udo Steinbach and Rüdiger Robert, with editorial assistance by Marianne Schmidt-Dumont, 221–254. Vol. 1. *Grundlagen, Strukturen und Problemfelder.* Opladen: Leske & Budrich, 1988.

Fyzee, Asaf. A. A. *Outlines of Muhammadan Law.* Delhi: Oxford University Press, 1974.

Grabau, Fritz-René. "Der Gesellschaftsvertrag im klassischen Islamrecht und das geltende Gesellschaftsrecht der islamischen Staaten." *Zeitschrift für vergleichende Rechtswissenschaft* 89 (1990): 330–357.

Johansen, Baber. *Contingency in a Sacred Law: Legal and Ethical Norms in the Muslim Fiqh.* Vol. 7 of *Studies in Islamic Law and Society.* Leiden: Brill, 1998.

Juynboll, Theodor Willem. *Handbuch des islamischen Gesetzes.* Leiden: Brill, 1910.

Kemper, Michael, and Maurus Reinkowski, eds. *Rechtspluralismus in der Islamischen Welt: Gewohnheitsrecht zwischen Staat und Gesellschaft.* Berlin: Walter de Gruyter, 2005.

Krawietz, Birgit. *Hierarchie der Rechtsquellen im tradierten sunnitischen Islam.* Berlin: Duncker & Humblot, 2002.

Krüger, Hilmar. *Arabische Staaten: Gesetzesübersichten. Internationales und ausländisches Wirtschafts- und Steuerrecht.* Cologne: Bundesstelle für Außenhandelsinformation, 1999.

——. "An Introduction to Commercial Law in the States of the Arab Peninsula." In *Recht und Steuern International,* 52–66. Cologne: Bundesagentur für Außenwirtschaft, 2003.

——. "Überblick über das Zivilrecht der Staaten des ägyptischen Rechtskreises." *Recht von de Islam* 14 (1997): 67–131.

——. "Zum Geltungsbereich der osmanischen Mejelle." In *Liber amicorum Gerhard Kegel,* 43–63. Munich: C. H. Beck, 2002.

Liebesny, Herbert J. *The Law of the Near and Middle East: Readings, Cases, and Materials.* Albany: State University of New York Press, 1975.

Motzki, Harald. *Die Anfänge der islamischen Jurisprudenz bis zur Mitte des 2./8. Jahrhunderts: Abhandlungen für die Kunde des Morgenlandes.* Vol. 50.2. Stuttgart: Steiner, 1991.

Nagel, Tilman. *Das islamische Recht: Eine Einführung.* Westhofen: WVA-Verlag Skulima, 2001.

Rohe, Mathias. *Der Islam: Alltagskonflikte und Lösungen; Rechtliche Perspektiven.* Freiburg: Herder, 2001.

Schacht, Joseph. *An Introduction to Islamic Law.* Oxford: Oxford University Press, 1964.

Spies, Otto, and Erwin Pritsch. "Klassisches Islamisches Recht." In *Handbuch der Orientalistik.* Supplementary vol. 3, 224–343. *Orientalisches Recht.* Leiden: Brill, 1964.

Tellenbach, Silvia. Strafgesetze der Islamischen Republik Iran. *Sammlung außerdeutscher Strafgesetzbücher in deutscher Übersetzung,* no. 106. Berlin: Walter de Gruyter, 1995.

——. "Übersichtsbericht Arabische Staaten." In *Schwangerschaftsabbruch im internationalen Vergleich: Rechtliche Regelungen—Soziale Rahmenbedingungen—Empirische Grunddaten.* Part 2. *Außereuropa,* edited by Albin Eser and Hans-Georg Koch, 1119–86. Baden-Baden: Nomos, 1989.

Tworuschka, Monika. *Die Rolle des Islams in den arabischen Staatsverfassungen.* Walldorf: Verlag für Orientkunde, 1976.

Vikør, Knut S. *Between God and the Sultan: A History of Islamic Law.* London: Hurst & Company, 2005.

Yassari, Nadjma. "Überblick über das iranische Scheidungsrecht." *Zeitschrift für das gesamte Familienrecht* 16 (2002): 1088–94.

IV. The Status of Islam and Islamic Law in Selected Countries

1. Turkey *(Ursula Spuler-Stegemann)*

Andrews, P., ed. *Ethnic Groups in the Republic of Turkey.* Wiesbaden: Reichert, 2002.

Berkes, N. *The Development of Secularism in Turkey.* Montreal: McGill University Press, 1964.

Binswanger, K. "Türkei." In *Der Islam in der Gegenwart,* edited by W. Ende and U. Steinbach, 212–220. Munich: Beck, 1991.

Bruinessen, M. van. *Agha, Scheich und Staat: Politik und Gesellschaft Kurdistans; Beiträge zur Vergleichenden Sozialforschung.* Berlin: Edition Parabolis, 1989.

Dağı, İ. "Transformation of Islamic Political Identity in Turkey: Rethinking the West and Westernization." *Turkish Studies* 6, no. 1 (2005): 21–37.

Engin, Ismail, and Erhard Franz. *Aleviler/Alewiten.* Vol. 3. Hamburg: Deutsches Orientinstitut, 2000–2001.

Gottschlich, Jürgen. *Die Türkei auf dem Weg nach Europa: Ein Land im Aufbruch.* Berlin: Links, 2004.

Göle, N. *Rethinking Modernity and National Identity in Turkey.* Seattle: University of Washington Press, 1997.

Heper, M. "The State, Religion, and Pluralism: The Turkish Case in Comparative Perspective." *British Journal of Middle Eastern Studies* 8, no. 1 (1991): 38–51.

Hoffmann, J. *Aufstieg und Wandel des politischen Islam in der Türkei.* Vol. 5 of *Nahoststudien.* Berlin: Hans Schiler, 2004.

Howe, M. *Turkey Today: A Nation Divided over Islam's Revival.* Boulder, Colo.: Westwood, 2000.

Kalaycıoğlu, Ersin. "The Mystery of the Türban: Participation or Revolt?" *Turkish Studies* 6, no. 2 (2005): 233–251.

Körner, Felix. *Revisionist Koran Hermeneutics in Contemporary Turkish University Theology: Rethinking Islam.* Vol. 15 of *MISK—Mitteilungen zur Sozial- und Kulturgeschichte der islamischen Welt.* Würzburg: Ergon, 2005.

Kreiser, Klaus. "Notes sur le présent et le passé des ordres mystiques en Turquie." In *Les ordres mystiques dans l'Islam,* edited by A. Popovic and G. Veinstein, 49–61. Paris: Éditions de l'École des Hautes Études en Sciences Sociales, 1986.

——. Kleines Türkei-Lexikon. Munich: C. H. Beck, 1991.

Lewis, B. *The Emergence of Modern Turkey.* London: Oxford University Press, 2001.

Mardin, Ş. "Turkey, Islam and Westernization." In *Religion and Societies: Asia and the Middle East,* edited by C. Caldarola, 171–198. Berlin: Mouton, 1982.

——. "Religion and Politics in Modern Turkey." In *Islam in the Political Process,* edited by J. P. Piscatori, 138–159. Cambridge: Cambridge University Press, 1984.

Oehring, Otmar. *Die Türkei im Spannungsfeld extremer Ideologien (1973–1980): Eine Untersuchung der politischen Verhältnisse.* Vol. 102 of *Islamkundliche Untersuchungen.* Berlin: Klaus Schwarz Verlag, 1984.

———. "Zur Lage der Menschenrechte in der Türkei—Laizismus = Menschenrechte?" *mission,* 2nd expanded ed. 2002. http://www.missioaachen.de/Images/MR%20T%C3%BCrkei%20deutsch%202%2EAuflage_tcm14-11236.pdf.

Rumpf, C. *Laizismus und Religionsfreiheit in der Türkei: Rechtliche Grundlagen und gesellschaftliche Praxis.* Ebenhausen: Stiftung Wissenschaft und Politik, 1987.

Rumpf, C., and U. Steinbach. "Das politische System der Türkei." In *Die politischen Systeme Osteuropas,* edited by W. Ismayr, 2nd ed., 847–886. Wiesbaden: VS Verlag für Sozialwissenschaft, 2004.

Schüler, H. "Re-Islamisierung: Der Fall Türkei." *Zeitschrift für Türkeistudien* 2 (1989): 63–93.

Seufert, Günter. *Die Türkei: Politik, Geschichte, Kultur.* Munich: C. H. Beck, 2004.

Shaw, S. J. *Empire of the Gazis: The Rise and Decline of the Ottoman Empire, 1280–1808.* Cambridge: Cambridge University Press, 1988.

Shaw, S. J., and E. K. Shaw. *History of the Ottoman Empire and Modern Turkey.* Vol. 2. *Reform, Revolution, and Republic: The Rise of Modern Turkey, 1808–1975.* Cambridge: Cambridge University Press, 1977.

Spuler-Stegemann, U. "Der Islam in der Türkei." In *Türkei.* Vol. 4 of *Südosteuropa-Handbuch,* edited by K. D. Grothusen, 591–612. Göttingen: Vandenhoeck and Ruprecht, 1985.

Stefanos, Yerasimos, Günter Seufert, and Karin Vorhoff. *Civil Society in the Grip of Nationalism: Studies on Political Culture in Contemporary Turkey.* Istanbul: Orient-Institut der Deutschen Morgenländischen Gesellschaft and Institut Français d'Études Anatoliennes, 2000.

Steinbach, Udo. *Die Türkei im 20. Jahrhundert: Schwieriger Partner Europas.* Bergisch-Gladbach: Lübbe, 1996.

Tapper, R. *Islam in Modern Turkey: Religion, Politics and Literature in a Secular State.* London: British Academic Press, 1991.

Toprak, B. "The State, Politics, and Religion in Turkey." In *State, Democracy, and the Military: Turkey in the 1980s,* edited by M. Heper and A. Evin, 119–136. Berlin: Walter de Gruyter, 1988.

Ucar, Bülent. *Recht als Mittel zur Reform von Religion und Gesellschaft: Die türkische Debatte um die Scharia und die Rechtsschulen im 20. Jahrhundert.* Würzburg: Ergon, 2005.

Vorhoff K. *Zwischen Glaube, Nation und neuer Gemeinschaft: Alevitische Identität in der Türkei der Gegenwart.* Vol. 184 of *Islamkundliche Untersuchungen.* Berlin: Klaus Schwarz, 1995.

Wedel, H. *Der türkische Weg zwischen Laizismus und Islam.* Vol. 6 of *Studien und Arbeiten des Zentrums für Türkeistudien.* Opladen: Leske, 1991.

Yavuz, Hakan M. "Die Renaissance des religiösen Bewusstseins in der Türkei: Nur-Studienzirkel." In *Islam in Sicht: Der Auftritt von Muslimen im öffentlichen Raum,* edited by Nilüfer Göle and Ludwig Ammann, 121–146. Bielefeld: Transcript, 2004.

Zürcher, E. J. *Turkey: A Modern History.* London: I. B. Tauris, 1993.

2. Iran *(Udo Steinbach)*

Abrahamian, E. *Iran between Two Revolutions.* Princeton: Princeton University Press, 1982.

———. *Khomeinism: Politics and Ideology in Contemporary Iran.* Princeton: Princeton University Press, 1994.

Akhavi, S. *Religion and Politics in Contemporary Iran: Clergy-State Relations in the Pahlavi Period.* Albany: State University of New York Press, 1980.

Avery, P., G. Hambly, and C. Melville, eds. *The Cambridge History of Iran.* Vol. 7: *From Nader Shah to the Islamic Republic.* Cambridge: Cambridge University Press, 1991.

Bakhash, S. *The Reign of the Ayatollahs: Iran and the Islamic Revolution.* New York: Basic Books, 1984.

Berliner Institut für Vergleichende Sozialforschung, ed. *Religion und Politik in Iran: Mardom Nameh.* Frankfurt am Main: Syndikat Autoren- u. Verlags-Gesellschaft, 1981.

Boroujerdi, M. *Iranian Intellectuals and the West: The Tormented Triumph of Nativism.* Syracuse: Syracuse University Press, 1996.

Brumberg, D. *Reinventing Khomeini: The Struggle for Reforms in Iran.* Chicago: University of Chicago Press, 2001.

Buchta, W. *Die iranische Schia und die islamische Einheit, 1979–1998.* Hamburg: Deutsches Orient-Institut, 1997.

——. *Who Rules Iran? The Structure of Power in the Islamic Republic.* Washington, D.C.: Washington Institute for Near East Policy, 2000.

Chomeini, Ajatollah. *Der islamische Staat.* Translated and edited by N. Hassan and I. Itscherenska. Berlin: Schwarz, 1983.

Clawson, P., M. Eisenstadt, E. Kanovsky, and D. Menashri, eds. *Iran under Khatami: A Political, Economic, and Military Assessment.* Washington, D.C.: Washington Institute for Near East Policy, 1998.

Ehteshami, A., and M. Varasteh, eds. *Iran and the International Community.* London: Routledge, 1991.

Encyclopaedia Iranica, ed. E. Yarshater. Vols. 1–. London: Routledge, 1985–.

Farsoun, S. K., and M. Mashayekhi, eds. *Iran: Political Culture in the Islamic Republic.* London: Routledge, 1992.

Fischer, M. M. J. *Iran: From Religious Dispute to Revolution.* Cambridge: Harvard University Press, 1980.

Göbel, K.-H. *Moderne schiitische Politik und Staatsidee.* Opladen: Leske & Budrich, 1984.

Gronke, M. *Iran: A Short History.* Princeton: Wiener, 2007.

Hairi, A. H. *Shiism and Constitutionalism in Iran.* Leiden: Brill, 1977.

Halm, H. *Shi'a Islam: From Religion to Revolution.* Princeton: Wiener, 1996.

Hourcade, B. *Iran: nouvelles identités d'une république.* Paris: La Documentation Française, 2002.

Hunter, S. T. *Iran after Khomeini.* New York: Praeger, 1992.

Katzman, K. *The Warriors of Islam: Iran's Revolutionary Guard.* Boulder, Colo.: Westview, 1993.

Khomeini, R. *Islam and Revolution: Writings and Declarations of Imam Khomeini.* Translated by H. Algar. Berkeley: Mizan Press, 1981.

Kramer, M., ed. *Shi'ism, Resistance, and Revolution.* Boulder, Colo. and London: Westview and Mansell, 1987.

Mackey, S. *The Iranians: Persia, Islam, and the Soul of a Nation.* New York: Dutton, 1996.

Menashri, D. *Iran: A Decade of War and Revolution.* New York: Holmes & Meier, 1990.

——, ed. *The Iranian Revolution and the Muslim World.* Boulder, Colo.: Westview, 1992.

——. *Revolution at the Crossroads: Iran's Domestic Politics and Regional Ambitions.* Washington, D.C.: Washington Institute for Near East Policy, 1997.

Moin, B. *Khomeini: Life of the Ayatollah.* London: Tauris, 1999.

Mottahedeh, R. *The Mantle of the Prophet: Religion and Politics in Iran.* New York: Simon and Schuster, 1985.

Naficy, M. *Klerus, Basar und die iranische Revolution.* Hamburg: Deutsches Orient-Institut, 1993.

Rahnema, A., and F. Nomani. *The Secular Miracle: Religion, Politics and Economic Policy in Iran.* London: Zed Books, 1990.

Roy, O. *The Failure of Political Islam.* Cambridge: Tauris, 1992.

Schirazi, A. *The Constitution of Iran: Politics and the State in the Islamic Republic.* London: Tauris, 1997.

Tellenbach, S. *Untersuchungen zur Verfassung der Islamischen Republik Iran vom 15. November 1979.* Berlin: Schwarz, 1985.

Thurfjell, D. *Living Shiism: Instances of Ritualisation among Islamist Men in Contemporary Iran.* Leiden: Brill, 2006.

3. Afghanistan *(Abbas Poya)*

Adamec, L. W. *Historical Dictionary of Afghanistan.* Lanham, Md.: Scarecrow Press, 2003.

Brechna, H. *Die Geschichte Afghanistans: Das historische Umfeld Afghanistans über 1500 Jahre.* Zurich: vdf Hochschulverlag, 2005.

Clements, F. A. *Conflict in Afghanistan: A Historical Encyclopedia.* Santa Barbara, Calif.: ABC-Clio, 2003.

Dupree, L. *Afghanistan.* Princeton: Princeton University Press, 1980.

Edwards, D. B. *Before Taliban: Genealogies of the Afghan Jihad.* Berkeley: University of California Press, 2002.

Ewans, M. *Conflict in Afghanistan: Studies in Asymmetric Warfare.* London: Routledge, 2005.

Gerber, G. *Die neue Verfassung Afghanistans: Verfassungstradition und politischer Prozess.* Berlin: Schiler, 2007.

Glatzer, B. "War and Boundaries in Afghanistan: Significance and Relativity of Local and Social Boundaries." *Die Welt des Islams,* vol. 41 (2001): 379–399.

——. *Afghanistan.* London: Routledge, 2008.

Heine, P. *Terror in Allahs Namen: Extremistische Kräfte im Islam.* Freiburg: Herder, 2004.

Johanson, C., and Leslie, J. *Afghanistan: The Mirage of Peace.* New York: Zed Books, 2004.

Kraus, W., ed. *Afghanistan: Natur, Geschichte und Kultur, Staat, Gesellschaft und Wirtschaft,* Tübingen: Erdmann, 1974.

Löwenstein, W., ed. *Beiträge zur zeitgenössischen Afghanistanforschung.* Bochum: Institut für Entwicklungsforschung und Entwicklungspolitik, 1997.

Moltmann, G. "Staats- und Verfassungsentwicklung Afghanistans." In *Afghanistan seit dem Sturz der Monarchie: Dokumentation zur Politik, Wirtschaft und Bevölkerung,* edited by M. D. Ahmad, E. Franz, and M. Weidenhiller, 9–34. Hamburg: Deutsches Orient-Institut, 1981.

Mousavi, S. A. *The Hazaras of Afghanistan: An Historical, Cultural, Economical, and Political Study.* New York: Routledge, 1997.

Olesen, A. *Islam and Politics in Afghanistan.* Richmond: Curzon, 1995.

Pohly, M. *Krieg und Widerstand in Afghanistan: Ursachen, Verlauf und Folgen seit 1978.* Berlin: Das Arabische Buch, 1992.

Pohly, M., Durán, Kh., and Gleissner, B. *Nach den Taliban: Afghanistan zwischen internationalen Machtinteressen und demokratischer Erneuerung.* Munich: Ullstein, 2002.

Poya, A. "Perspektiven zivilgesellschaftlicher Strukturen in Afghanistan: Ethische Neutralität, ethnische Parität und Frauenrechte in der Verfassung der Islamischen Republik Afghanistan." *Orient* vol. 44 (2003): 367–384.

Rasanayagam, A. *Afghanistan: A Modern History; Monarchy, Despotism or Democracy? The Problems of Governance in the Muslim Tradition.* London: Tauris, 2003.

Rashid, A. *Taliban: The Story of the Afghan Warlords.* Including a new foreword following the terrorist attacks of 11 September. London: Pan, 2001.

Schetter, C. *Ethnizität und ethnische Konflikte in Afghanistan.* Berlin: Reimer, 2003.

——. *Kleine Geschichte Afghanistans.* Munich: Beck, 2004.

Spuler, B. "Afghanistans Geschichte und Verwaltung in früh-islamischer Zeit." In *Gesammelte Aufsätze,* 305–313. Leiden: Brill, 1980.

Tanner, S. *Afghanistan: A Military History from Alexander the Great to the Fall of the Taliban.* New York: Da Capo Press, 2002.

Upasak, Ch. S. *History of Buddhism in Afghanistan.* Sarnath: Central Institute of Higher Tibetan Studies, 1990.

Yarshater, E., ed. "Afghanistan." In *Encyclopaedia Iranica,* vol. 1, 486–566. London: Routledge, 1985.

4. Russia, the Islamic Republics of the Caucasus, and Central Asia
(Rainer Freitag-Wirmingshaus)

Akiner, Shirin. *The Formation of Kazakh Identity.* London: Royal Institute of International Affairs, 1995.

——. *Islamic Peoples of the Soviet Union.* London: Routledge, 1983.

——. *Tajikistan: Disintegration or Reconciliation?* London: Royal Institute of International Affairs, 2001.

Allworth, Edward, ed. *Central Asia: A Century of Russian Rule.* New York: Columbia University Press, 1967.

——. *The Modern Uzbeks.* Stanford: Hoover Institution Press, 1990.

Baldauf, Ingeborg. *Schriftreform und Schriftwechsel bei den muslimischen Rußland- und Sowjettürken (1850–1937): Ein Symptom ideengeschichtlicher und kulturpolitischer Entwicklungen,* edited by G. Hazai. Bibliotheca Orientalis Hungarica. Budapest: Akad. Kiadó, 1993.

Barthold, Wilhelm. *Turkestan Down to the Mongol Invasion.* London: Luzac & Company, London 1977.

——. *Zwölf Vorlesungen über die Geschichte der Türken in Mittelasien.* Darmstadt: Wissenschaftl. Buchgesellschaft, 1996.

Bennigsen, Alexandre, and Chantal Lemercier-Quelquejay. *L'Islam en union soviétique.* Paris: Payot, 1968.

Bennigsen, Alexandre, and S. E. Wimbush. *Muslims of the Soviet Empire: A Guide.* London: Hurst, 1985.

——. *Mystics and Commissars: Sufism in the Soviet Union.* Berkeley: University of California Press, 1985.

Carlisle, Donald. *Uzbekistan under Russian Rule: Communism, Nationalism and Islam in Central Asia.* London: Routledge, 2004.

Central Asia and the Caucasus: Journal of Social and Political Studies. Institute for Central Asian and Caucasian Studies, Lulea, Sweden, 2000.

Central Asian Survey. Abingdon: Society for Central Asian Studies, 1982/83.

Dudoignon, Stéphane, and Hisao Komatsu, eds. *Islam in Politics in Russia and Central Asia.* London: Kegan Paul International, 2001.

Halbach, Uwe. "Islam und islamistische Bewegungen in Zentralasien." *Aus Politik und Zeitgeschichte* B, nos. 3–4 (2002).

——. "Russlands muslimische Ethnien und Nachbarn." *Aus Politik und Zeitgeschichte* B, nos. 16–17 (2003): 39–46.

——. "Rußlands Welten des Islam." *SWP-Studie*. S15 Berlin: Stiftung Wissenschaft und Politik, 2003.

Hayit, Baymirza. *Basmatschi: Nationaler Kampf Turkestans in den Jahren 1917 bis 1934.* Cologne: Dreisam-Verlag, 1992.

——. *Sowjetrussische Orientpolitik am Beispiel Turkestans.* Cologne: Kiepenheuer & Witsch, 1992.

International Crisis Group. *Central Asia: Islam and the State.* ICG Asia Report no. 59. Osh: International Crisis Group, 2003.

——. *Is Radical Islam Inevitable in Central Asia? Priorities for Engagement.* Asia Report no. 72. Osh: International Crisis Group, 2003.

——. *Radical Islam in Central Asia: Responding to Hizb ut-Tahrir.* ICG Asia Report no. 58. Osh: International Crisis Group, 2003.

Kappeler, Andreas et al., eds. *Die Muslime in der Sowjetunion und in Jugoslawien: Identität, Politik, Widerstand.* Cologne: Markus, 1989.

Kemper, Michael. *Herrschaft, Recht und Islam in Daghestan: Von den Khanaten und Gemeindebünden zum Gihad-Staat.* Wiesbaden: Reichert, 2005.

——. *Sufis und Gelehrte in Tatarien und Baschkirien, 1789–1889: Der islamische Diskurs unter russischer Herrschaft.* Berlin: Klaus Schwarz Verlag, 1998.

Krämer, Anette. "Islam in Zentralasien: Blüte, Unterdrückung, Instrumentalisierung." *Osteuropa* 8–9 (August–September 2007): 53–76.

Malashenko, Alexey, and Martha Brill Olcott, eds. *Islam na postsovetskom prostranstve: vzglyad iz vnutri.* Moscow: Carnegie Endowment for International Peace, 2001.

Motika, Raoul. "Entwicklungstendenzen des Islams in Tatarstan." *Pera-Blätter* 18 (2004).

——. "Das Religionsrecht in Aserbaidschan." In *Das Recht der Religionsgemeinschaften in Mittel-, Ost- und Südosteuropa,* edited by W. Lienemann and H. R. Reuter, 75–103. Baden-Baden: Nomos, 2005.

Motika, Raoul, Michael Kemper, and Stefan Reichmuth, eds. *Islamic Education in the Soviet Union and Its Successor States.* London: Routledge-Taylor and Francis Books, 2005.

Naumkin, Vitaly. *Militant Islam in Central Asia: The Case of the Islamic Movement of Uzbekistan.* Berkeley: Program in Soviet and Post-Soviet Studies, 2003.

——, ed. *State, Religion and Society in Central Asia.* Reading: Ithaca Press, 1995.

Noack, Christian. *Muslimischer Nationalismus im Russischen Reich: Nationsbildung und Nationalbewegung bei Tataren und Baschkiren, 1861–1917.* Vol. 56 of *Quellen und Studien zur Geschichte des östlichen Europa.* Stuttgart: Franz Steiner Verlag, 2000.

Olcott, Martha B. *Sufism in Central Asia: A Force for Moderation or a Cause of Politicization?* Washington, D.C.: Carnegie Endowment, 2007.

Poliakov, Sergei P. *Everyday Islam: Religion and Tradition in Rural Central Asia.* New York: M. E. Sharpe, 1992.

Rashid, Ahmed. *Jihad: The Rise of Militant Islam in Central Asia.* New York: Penguin Books, 2003.

Ro'i, Yaacov. *Islam in the Soviet Union: From the Second World War to Gorbachev.* London: Columbia University Press, 2000.

——, ed. *Muslim Eurasia: Conflicting Legacies.* London: Frank Cass Publishers, 1995.

Roy, Olivier. *The New Central Asia: The Creation of Nations.* New York: NYU Press, 2000.

Rumer, Boris. *Soviet Central Asia: "A Tragic Experiment."* Winchester, Mass.: Unwin Hyman, 1990.

Strasser, Andrea, Siegfried Haas, Gerhard Mangott, and Valeria Heuberger, eds. *Zentral-asien und Islam:* Vol. 63 of *Mitteilungen.* Hamburg: Deutsches Orient-Institut Hamburg, 2003.

Swietochowski, Tadeusz. "Azerbaijan: The Hidden Faces of Islam." *World Policy Journal* 19, no. 3 (Fall 2002): 69–76.

5. The People's Republic of China *(Thomas Heberer)*

Allès, E. "Muslim Religious Education in China." *China Perspectives* 45 (2003): 21–29.

Aubin, F. "Islam." In *Das Große China-Lexikon,* edited by B. Staiger, S. Friedrich, and H.-W. Schütte, 349–352. Darmstadt: Wissenschaftliche Buchgesellschaft, 2003.

Benson, L. *The Ili Rebellion: The Moslem Challenge to Chinese Authority in Xinjiang, 1944–1949,* Armonk, N.Y.: M. E. Sharpe, 1990.

Bovingdon, G. "Heteronomy and Its Discontents: 'Minzu Regional Autonomy' in Xinjiang." In *Governing China's Multiethnic Frontiers,* edited by M. Rossabi, 117–154. Seattle: University of Washington Press, 2004.

Bush, R. C. *Religion in Communist China.* Nashville: Abingdon Press, 1970.

Castets, R. "The Uyghurs in Xinjiang: The Malaise Grows." *China Perspectives* 49 (2003): 34–48.

Chang, H. Y. "Muslim Minorities in China: A Historical Note." *Minority Affairs* 3, no. 2 (1981): 30–34.

Dillon, M. *China's Muslim Hui Community.* London: Curzon, 1999.

——. *Xinjiang—: China's Muslim Far Northwest.* London: RoutledgeCurzon, 2004.

Fogden, S. "Writing Insecurity: The PRC's Push to Modernize China and the Politics of Uyghur Identity." *Issues and Studies* 3 (2003): 33–74.

Gillette, M. B. *Urban Chinese Muslims.* Stanford: Stanford University Press, 2000.

Gladney, D. C. "Muslim Tombs and Ethnic Folklore: Charters for Hui Identity." *Journal of Asian Studies* 3 (1987): 495–532.

——. "The Hui, Islam, and the State: A Sufi Community in China's Northwest Corner." In *Muslims in Central Asia. Expression of Identity and Change,* edited by J. Gross, 89–111. Durham: Duke University Press, 1992.

——. "Salman Rushdie in China: Religion, Ethnicity, and State Definition in the People's Republic." In *Asian Visions of Authority: Religion and the Modern States of East and Southeast Asia,* edited by C. F. Keyes, L. Kendall, and H. Hardacre, 255–278. Honolulu: University of Hawaii Press, 1994.

——. *Muslim Chinese.* Cambridge: Harvard University Press, 1996.

——. "Islam in China: Accommodation or Separatism." *China Quarterly* (June 2003): 451–467.

Hartmann, M. "Vom chinesischen Islam." *Die Welt des Islams* 1, nos. 3–4 (1913): 178–210.

Heberer, T. *Some Considerations on China's Minorities in the 21st Century: Conflict or Conciliation,* Duisburg Working Papers on East Asian Studies 31 (2000). Duisburg: Mercator University.

——. "Die Nationalitätenfrage am Beginn des 21. Jhdts.: Konfliktursachen, ethnische Reaktionen, Lösungsansätze und Konfliktprävention." In *China: Konturen einer Übergangsgesellschaft auf dem Weg in das 21. Jahrhundert,* edited by G. Schubert, 81–134. Hamburg: Institut für Asienkunde, 2001.

Heuer-Vogel, Daniela. *Die Politisierung ethnischer Identitäten im internationalen Staatensystem: Muslime unter chinesischer Herrschaft.* Frankfurt am Main: Europäischer Verlag der Wissenschaften, 2000.

Hoppe, T. *Die ethnischen Gruppen Xinjiangs: Kulturunterschiede und interethnische Beziehungen.* Hamburg: Institut für Asienkunde, 1995.

Israeli, R. "Muslims in China: Islam's Incompatibility with the Chinese Order." In *Islam in Asia*, vol. 2, edited by R. Israeli and A. Johns, 275–304. Boulder, Colo.: Westview, 1984.

——. "A New Wave of Muslim Revivalism in Mainland China." *Issues and Studies* 3 (March 1997): 21–41.

Iwamura, S. "The Structure of Moslem Society in Inner Mongolia." *Far Eastern Quarterly* 1 (1948): 34–44.

Kim, Hodong. *Holy War in China: The Muslim Rebellion and State in Chinese Central Asia, 1864–1877.* Stanford: Stanford University Press, 2004.

Lindbeck, J. M. H. "Communism, Islam, and Nationalism in China." *Review of Politics* (October 1950): 473–488.

Lipman, J. N. "Patchwork Society, Network Society: A Study of Sino-Muslim Communities." In *Islam in Asia*, vol. 2, edited by R. Israeli and A. Johns, 246–274. Boulder, Colo.: Westview, 1984.

——. *Familiar Strangers: A History of Muslims in Northwest China.* Seattle: University of Washington Press, 1997.

MacInnis, D. E. *Religion in China Today: Policy and Practice.* Maryknoll, N.Y.: Orbis Books, 1989.

Mackerras, C. "Xinjiang and the Causes of Separatism." *Central Asian Survey* 3 (2001): 289–304.

Mees, I. *Die Hui: Eine moslemische Minderheit in China. Assimilationsprozesse und politische Rolle vor 1949.* Munich: Minerva Publikation Saur, 1984.

Newby, L. J. "'The Pure and True Religion' in China." *Third World Quarterly* 2 (1988): 923–947.

Pillsbury, B. L. K. "Muslim History in China: A 1,300-Year Chronology." *Minority Affairs* 3, no. 2 (1981a): 10–29.

——. "The Muslim Population of China: Clarifying the Questions of Size and Ethnicity." *Minority Affairs* 3, no. 2 (1981b): 35–58.

Rudelson, J. J. *Oasis Identities: Uyghur Nationalism along China's Silk Road.* New York: Columbia University Press, 1997.

Song, Q. "Islamische Kultur und China." *China Heute* 6 (1992): 168–171.

Staiger, B. "Xinjiang erläßt Bestimmungen über religiöse Aktivitäten und religiöses Personal." *China Heute* 1 (1991): 12–14.

Starr, F. S., ed. *Xinjiang: China's Muslim Borderland.* Armonk, N.Y.: M. E. Sharpe, 2004.

Wacker, G. "Xinjiang und die VR China: Zentrifugale und zentripetale Tendenzen in Chinas Nordwest-Region." *Berichte des Bundesinstituts für ostwissenschaftliche und internationale Studien,* Cologne 3 (1995).

Wang, J. "Einheit in Vielfalt: Wiederaufleben des Islam im heutigen China." *China Heute* 7 (2003): 227–234.

Winchester, M. "Inside Story China. Beijing vs. Islam." 1997. http://www.pathfinder.com/@@V=a=R...Y/Asiaweek/current/issue/is1.html.

Yee, H. S. "Ethnic Relations in Xinjiang: A Survey of Uyghur-Han Relations." *China Perspectives* 36 (2003): 431–452.

Zhao, Y. *Pivot or Periphery: Xinjiang's Regional Development and Chinese Central Asian Relations at the Century's End.* Ann Arbor: UMI, 1997.

Ziemann, H. *Die Beziehungen Sinkiangs (Ostturkestan) zu China und der UdSSR 1917–45.* Bochum: Brockmeyer, 1984.

6. India *(Munir D. Ahmed)*

Ahmad, A. *An Intellectual History of Islam in India.* Edinburgh: Edinburgh University Press, 1969.

——. *Studies in Islamic Culture in the Indian Environment.* Oxford: Clarendon Press, 1964.

Ahmad, I., ed. *Ritual and Religion among Muslims in India.* Delhi: Manohar, 1981.

Ahmad, I., and H. Reifeld, eds. *Lived Islam in South Asia: Adaptation, Accommodation, and Conflict.* New Delhi: Social Science Press, 2004.

Ali, A. A. *The Emergence of Feminism among Indian Muslim Women, 1920–1947.* Oxford: Oxford University Press, 2000.

Douglas, I. H. *Abul Kalam Azad: An Intellectual and Religious Biography.* Edited by C. Minault and C. Troll. Delhi: Oxford University Press, 1988.

Engineer, A. A. *Communalism and Communal Violence in India: An Analytical Approach to Hindu-Muslim Conflict.* Delhi: Ajanta, 1989.

Jaffrelot, C., ed. *L'Inde contemporaine de 1950 à nos jours.* 2nd rev. ed. Paris: Fayard, 2006.

Lal, K. S. *Return to Roots: Emancipation of Indian Muslims.* New Delhi: Radha Publications, 2002.

Metcalf, B. *Islamic Revival in British India: Deoband, 1860–1900,* Princeton: Princeton University Press, 1982.

Minault, G. *The Khilafat Movement: Religious Symbolism and Political Mobilization in India.* New York: Columbia University Press, 1982.

Narain, H. *The Ayodhya Temple-Mosque Dispute: Focus on Muslim Sources.* Delhi: Penman Publishers, 1993.

Troll, C. W., ed. *Muslim Shrines in India.* New Delhi: Oxford University Press, 2003.

——. *Sayyid Ahmad Khan: A Reinterpretation of Muslim Theology.* New Delhi: Vikas, 1978.

Van der Veer, P. *Religious Nationalism: Hindus and Muslims in India.* Berkeley: University of California Press, 1994.

7. Pakistan *(Khálid Durán and Munir D. Ahmed)*

Abdulla, A. *The Historical Background of Pakistan and Its People.* Karachi: Tanzeem Publishers, 1973.

Abou-Zahab, M., and O. Roy. *Islamic Networks: The Afghan-Pakistan Connection.* London: Hurst, 2003.

Ahmad, I. *The Concept of an Islamic State: An Analysis of the Ideological Controversy in Pakistan.* London: Pinter, 1987.

Ansari, S. "Pakistan." In *The Encyclopaedia of Islam,* 2nd ed., vol. 8, 240–244. Leiden: Brill, 1995.

Hussain, A. *Elite Politics in an Ideological State: The Case of Pakistan.* Folkestone: Dawson, 1979.

Iqbal, A. *Islamisation of Pakistan.* Lahore: Vanguard Books, 1986.

Jaffrelot, C., ed. *A History of Pakistan and Its Origins.* London: Anthem Press, 2002.

Malik, H. *Sir Sayyid Ahmad Khan and Muslim Modernization in India and Pakistan.* New York: Columbia University Press, 1980.

Malik, S. J. *Colonization of Islam: Dissolution of Traditional Institutions in Pakistan.* New Delhi: Manohar, 1996.

Masud, M. K. *Travellers in Faith: Studies of the Tablighi Jama'at.* Leiden: Brill, 2000.

Nasr, S. V. R. *Islamic Leviathan: Islam and the Making of State Power.* Oxford: Oxford University Press, 2001.

Salim, A. *Pakistan of Jinnah: The Hidden Face.* Lahore: Brothers, 1993.

Shah, N. M., ed. *Pakistani Women: A Socio-Economic and Demographic Profile.* Islamabad: Pakistan Institute of Development Economics, 1986.

Weiss, A. M. *Islamic Reassertion in Pakistan: The Application of Islamic Law in a Modern State.* Syracuse: Syracuse University Press, 1986.

8. Bangladesh *(Hans Harder)*

Ahmed, M. D. "Bangladesh." In *Der Islam in der Gegenwart,* edited by W. Ende and U. Steinbach, 359–366. 4th rev. and expanded ed. Munich: Beck, 1996.

Ahmed, R. *The Bengal Muslims, 1871–1906: A Quest for Identity.* Delhi: Oxford University Press, 1981.

——, ed. *Understanding the Bengal Muslims: Interpretative Essays.* Delhi: Oxford University Press, 2001.

Cashin, D. *The Ocean of Love: Middle Bengali Sufi Literature and the Fakirs of Bengal.* Stockholm: Association of Oriental Studies, Stockholm University, 1995.

Das, R. P. "Das Verhältnis zwischen Islam und Bangladesh." In *Bangladesh,* edited by D. Conrad and W.-P. Zingel, 7–14. Stuttgart: Steiner Verlag, 1994.

Eaton, R. M. *The Rise of Islam and the Bengal Frontier, 1204–1760.* Berkeley: University of California Press, 1993.

Gardner, K. *Global Migrants, Local Lives: Travel and Transformation in Rural Bangladesh.* Oxford: Clarendon Press, 1995.

Harder, H. *Der verrückte Gofur spricht: Mystische Lieder aus Ostbengalen von Abdul Gofur Hali.* Heidelberg: Draupadi Verlag, 2004.

Jahangir, B. K. *Problematics of Nationalism in Bangladesh.* Dacca: Centre of Social Studies, 1992.

Maitra, J. *Muslim Politics in Bengal, 1855–1906: Collaboration and Confrontation.* Kolkatta: K. P. Bagchi, 1984.

Maniruzzaman, T. *The Bangladesh Revolution and Its Aftermath.* Dacca: University Press, 1980.

O'Donell, C. P. *Bangladesh: Biography of a Muslim Nation.* Boulder, Colo.: Westview, 1984.

Roy, A. *The Islamic Syncretistic Tradition in Bengal.* Princeton: Princeton University Press, 1983.

——. *Islam in South Asia: A Regional Perspective.* New Delhi: South Asian Publishers, 1996.

Razia Akter Banu, U. A. B. *Islam in Bangladesh.* Leiden: Brill, 1991.

Siegfried, R. *Bengalens Elfter Kalif: Untersuchungen zur Naqšbandiyya Muǧaddidiyya in Bangladesch.* Würzburg: Ergon, 2001.

Stewart, Tony. "In Search of Equivalence: Conceiving Muslim-Hindu Encounter through Translation Theory." *History of Religions* 40, no. 3 (February 2001): 260–287.

Trottier, A.-H. *Fakir: la quète d'un Bâul musulman.* Paris: L'Harmattan, 2000.

Weiß, C. "Islam und Gesellschaft in Bangladesh." In *Islam in Asien,* edited by K. H. Schreiner, 70–85. Bad Honnef: Horlemann, 2001.

9. Southeast Asia *(Olaf Schumann)*

Abdullah, T., and Sh. Siddique, eds. *Islam and Society in Southeast Asia.* Singapore: Institute of Southeast Asian Studies, 1986.

Abdul Rahman, T. *Viewpoints.* Kuala Lumpur: Heinemann, 1978.

Abdul Rahman, T., et al., eds. *Contemporary Issues on Malaysian Religions.* Petaling Jaya: Pelanduk Publications, 1984.

Ahmat, Sh., and Sh. Siddique, eds. *Muslim Society, Higher Education, and Development in Southeast Asia.* Singapore: Institute of Southeast Asian Studies, 1987.

Anwar, Z. *Islamic Revivalism in Malaysia: Dakwah among the Students.* Petaling Jaya: Pelanduk Publications, 1987.

al-Attas, S. N. *Some Aspects of Sufism as Understood and Practised among the Malays.* Singapore: Malaysian Sociological Research Institute, 1963.

Benda, H. J. *The Crescent and the Rising Sun.* The Hague: W. van Hoeve, 1958.

Bianco, L., ed. *Das moderne Asien.* Fischer Weltgeschichte 33. Frankfurt am Main: S. Fischer, 1969.

Boland, B. J. *The Struggle of Islam in Modern Indonesia.* Verh. van het Koninklijke Instituut voor Taal-, Land- en Volkenkunde 59. The Hague: Nijhoff, 1971.

Brown, D. E. *Brunei: The Structure and History of a Bornean Malay Sultanate.* Vol. 2, no. 2. Brunei: Brunei Museum, 1970.

Colpe, C. "Syncretism and Secularization: Complementary and Antithetical Trends in New Religious Movements?" *History of Religions* 17 (1977): 158–176.

Dahm, B. *Sukarnos Kampf um Indonesiens Unabhängigkeit.* Frankfurt am Main: Metzner, 1966.

Dengel, H. H. *Darul-Islam: Kartosuwirjos Kampf um einen islamischen Staat Indonesien.* Wiesbaden: Steiner, 1986.

Dijk, C. van. *Rebellion under the Banner of Islam: The Darul Islam in Indonesia.* The Hague: Nijhoff, 1981.

Djamour, J. *The Muslim Matrimonial Court in Singapore.* London: Athlone, 1966.

Draguhn, W., ed. *Der Einfluß des Islams auf Politik, Wirtschaft und Gesellschaft in Südostasien.* Hamburg: Institut für Asienkunde, 1983.

Fatimi, S. Q. *Islam Comes to Malaya.* Singapore: Malaysian Sociological Research Institute, 1963.

Forbes, A. D. W., ed. *The Muslims of Thailand.* 2 vols. Gaya, India: Centre for South East Asian Studies, 1988–.

Funston, J. *Malay Politics in Malaysia: A Study of UMNO and PAS.* Kuala Lumpur: Heinemann, 1980.

Gort, J., H. Vroom, R. Fernhout, and A. Wessels, eds. *Dialogue and Syncretism: An Interdisciplinary Approach.* Grand Rapids, Mich.: Eerdmans, 1989.

Gowing, P. G. *Muslim Filipinos: Heritage and Horizon.* 2nd ed. Quezon City: New Day Publishers, 1979.

Gowing, P. G., and R. D. McAmis, eds. *The Muslim Filipinos: Their History, Society, and Contemporary Problems.* Manila: Solidaridad Publishing House, 1974.

Grossmann, B., ed. *Studien zur Entwicklung in Süd- und Ostasien: Neue Folge.* Vol. 4. *Malaysia.* Frankfurt am Main: Metzner, 1966.

——. *Southeast Asia in the Modern World.* Wiesbaden: Harrassowitz, 1972.

Hall, D. G. E. *A History of South-East Asia.* 3rd ed. London: Macmillan, 1968.

Hooker, M. B., ed. *Islam in South-East Asia.* Leiden: Brill, 1983.

Hund, B., ed. *Bumiputra-Politik in Malaysia.* Hamburg: Institut für Asienkunde, 1981.

Israeli, R., ed. *The Crescent in the East: Islam in Asia Major.* London: Curzon, 1989.

Jocano, F. L., ed. *Filipino Muslims: Their Social Institutions and Cultural Achievements.* Quezon City: University of the Philippines, Asian Center, 1983.

Kartodirdjo, S. *The Peasants' Revolt of Banten.* The Hague: Nijhoff, 1966.

——. *Protest Movements in Rural Java: A Study of Agrarian Unrest in the Nineteenth and Early Twentieth Centuries.* Singapore: Oxford University Press, 1973.

Kitingan, J. G., and M. J. Ongkili. *Sabah Twenty-five Years Later: 1963–1988.* Kota Kinabalu: Institute for Development Studies, 1989.

Koentjaraningrat. *Javanese Culture.* Singapore: Oxford University Press, 1985.

Kraus, W., ed. *Islamische mystische Bruderschaften im heutigen Indonesien.* Hamburg: Institut für Asienkunde, 1990.

Lacar, L. Q. "The Emerging Role of Muslim Women in a Rapidly Changing Society: The Philippine Case." *Journal of Muslim Minority Affairs* 13, no. 1 (January 1992): 80–98.

Larousse, W. *A Local Church Living for Dialogue: Muslim-Christian Relations in Mindanao-Sulu (Philippines), 1965–2000.* Rome: Pontificia Università Gregoriana, 2001.

Lee, Hock Guan, ed. *Civil Society in Southeast Asia.* Singapore: 2004.

Lee, R. L. M. "The Globalization of Religious Markets: International Innovations, Malaysian Consumption." *Sojourn* 8, no. 1 (February 1993): 35–61.

Lev, D. *Islamic Courts in Indonesia: A Study in the Political Bases of Legal Institutions.* Berkeley: University of California Press, 1972.

Li, T. *Malays in Singapore: Culture, Economy, and Ideology.* Singapore: Oxford University Press, 1989.

Lim Kit Siang. *Malaysia: Crisis of Identity.* Petaling Jaya: Democratic Action Party, 1986.

Magnis-Suseno, F. *Javanische Weisheit und Ethik: Studien zu einer östlichen Moral.* Munich: Oldenbourg, 1981.

——. *Neue Schwingen für Garuda: Indonesien zwischen Tradition und Moderne.* Munich: Kindt, 1989.

Majul, C. A. *Muslims in the Philippines.* 2nd ed. Quezon City: University of the Philippines, Asian Center, 1973.

——. *The Contemporary Muslim Movement in the Philippines.* Berkeley: Mizan, 1985.

Man, W. K. Che. *Muslim Separatism: The Moros of Southern Philippines and the Malays of Southern Thailand.* Singapore: Oxford University Press, 1990.

——. "The Thai Government and Islamic Institutions in the Four Southern Muslim Provinces of Thailand." *Sojourn* 5, no. 2 (August 1990): 255–282.

McAmis, R. D. *Malay Muslims: The History and Challenge of Resurgent Islam in Southeast Asia.* Grand Rapids, Mich.: Eerdmans, 2002.

Means, G. P. *Malaysian Politics: The Second Generation.* Singapore: Oxford University Press, 1991.

Mohamad, Mahathir bin. *The Malay Dilemma.* 4th ed. Singapore: Times Books International, 1979.

——. *The Challenge.* 3rd ed. Petaling Jaya: Pelanduk Publications, 1989.

Mutalib, H. *Islam and Ethnicity in Malay Politics.* Singapore: Oxford University Press, 1987.

——. *Islam in Malaysia: From Revivalism to Islamic State?* Singapore: Singapore University Press, 1993.

Muzaffar, Ch. *Islamic Resurgence in Malaysia.* Petaling Jaya: Fajar Bakti, 1987.

——. *Challenges and Choices in Malaysian Politics and Society.* Penang: Aliran Kesedaran Negara, 1989.

Nasution, H. "Der islamische Staat: Ein indonesisches Konzept." In *Indonesiens verantwortliche Gesellschaft,* edited by R. Italiaander, 107–21. Erlangen: Verlag der Evangel.-Lutherischen Mission, 1976.

Noer, D. *The Modernist Muslim Movement in Indonesia, 1900–1942.* Singapore: Oxford University Press, 1973.

Ongkili, J. P. *Modernization in East Malaysia, 1960–1970.* Kuala Lumpur: Oxford University Press, 1972.

——. *Nation-Building in Malaysia, 1946–1974.* Singapore: Oxford University Press, 1985.

Pitsuwan, S. *Islam di Muangthai: Nasionalisme Melayu Masyarakat Patani.* Jakarta: 1989. (Originally "Islam and Malay Nationalism: A Case Study of the Malay Muslims in Southern Thailand" [Ph.D. diss., Harvard University, 1982]).

Ranjit Singh, D. S. *Brunei, 1839–1983: The Problems of Political Survival.* Singapore: Oxford University Press, 1991.

Rinkes, A. D. *Nine Saints of Java.* Kuala Lumpur: Malaysian Sociological Research Institute, 1996.

Rothermund, D., ed. *Islam in Southern Asia: A Survey of Current Research.* Wiesbaden: Steiner, 1975.

Santa Maria, L. "L'Indonesia negli anni 70." *Oriente Moderno,* n.s., 10 (1991): 103–161 (pt. 1), 393–462 (pt. 2).

Saunders, G. *A History of Brunei.* Kuala Lumpur: Oxford University Press, 1994.

Schumann, O. "Christians and Muslims in Search of Common Ground in Malaysia." *Islam and Christian-Muslim Relations* 2 (1991): 242–268.

———. "Staat und Gesellschaft im heutigen Indonesien." *Die Welt des Islams* 33 (1993): 182–218.

Suffian, T. M., et al., eds. *The Constitution of Malaysia: Its Development, 1957–1977.* 3rd ed. Kuala Lumpur: Oxford University Press, 1979.

Syukri, I. *History of the Malay Kingdom of Patani.* Translated by Conner Bailey and John N. Miksic. Athens, Ohio: Ohio University, Center for International Studies, 1984.

Teeuw, A., and D. K. Wyatt. *Hikayat Patani: The Story of Patani.* 2 vols. The Hague: Nijhoff, 1970.

Tregonning, K. G. *A History of Modern Malaya.* London: London University Press, 1964.

Trinidade, F. A., and H. P. Lee. *The Constitution of Malaysia: Further Perspectives and Developments; Essay in Honour of Tun Muhammad Suffian.* Singapore: Oxford University Press, 1986.

Turnbull, C. *A History of Malaysia, Singapore, and Brunei.* Sydney: Allen and Unwin, 1989.

Wawer, W. *Muslime und Christen in der Republik Indonesia.* Wiesbaden: Steiner, 1974.

Wertheim, W. F. *Indonesian Society in Transition.* 2nd ed. The Hague: W. van Hoeve, 1969.

Weyland, P. "International Muslim Networks and Islam in Singapore." *Sojourn* 5, no. 2 (August 1990): 219–254.

Wiesner, G., ed. *Synkretismusforschung: Theorie und Praxis.* Wiesbaden: Harrassowitz, 1978.

Yegar, M. *The Muslims of Burma: A Study of a Minority Group.* Wiesbaden: Harrassowitz, 1972.

10. Maghreb *(Franz Kogelmann)*

Abun-Nasr, J. M. *A History of the Maghreb in the Islamic Period.* Cambridge: Cambridge University Press, 1987.

al-Ahnaf, M., B. Botiveau, and F. Frégosi. *L'Algérie par ses islamistes.* Paris: Karthala, 1991.

Bonner, M., M. Reif, and M. Tessler, eds. *Islam, Democracy and the State in Algeria: Lessons for the Western Mediterranean and Beyond.* London: Routledge Curzon, 2005.

Camau, M., and V. Geisser. *Le syndrome autoritaire: politique en Tunisie de Bourguiba à Ben Ali.* Paris: Presses de Sciences Po, 2003.

Chaarani, A. *La mouvance islamiste au Maroc: du 11 septembre 2001 aux attentats de Casablanca du 16 mai 2003.* Paris: Karthala, 2004.

Désiré-Vuillemin, G. *Histoire de la Mauritanie: des origines à l'indépendance.* Paris: Karthala, 1997.

al-Fasi, ʿA. *The Independence Movements in Arab North Africa.* Translated by H. Z. Nuseibeh, New York: Octagon Press, 1970. (Original Arabic edition, *al-Harakat al-istiqlaliyya fiʾl-Maghrib al-ʿarabi* [Cairo, 1948].)

Ferrié, J.-N. *La religion de la vie quotidienne chez les Marocains musulmans.* Paris: Karthala, 2004.

Green, Arnold H. *The Tunisian Ulama, 1873–1915: Social Structure and Response to Ideological Currents.* Leiden: Brill, 1978.

Kogelmann, F. "Muhammad al-Makki an-Nasiri alias Sindbad der Seefahrer: Networking eines marokkanischen Nationalisten in den dreißiger Jahren des 20. Jahrhunderts." In *Die islamische Welt als Netzwerk: Möglichkeiten und Grenzen des Netzwerkansatzes im islamischen Kontext,* edited by R. Loimeier, 257–286. Würzburg: Ergon, 2000.

——. "Islamische Stiftungen und 'religiöse Angelegenheiten' im Algerien des 20. Jahrhunderts." *Orient* 42, no. 4 (2001): 639–658.

——. "Islamische Stiftungen und andere wohltätige Einrichtungen in Nordafrika. Algerien." In *Islamische Stiftungen und wohltätige Einrichtungen mit entwicklungspolitischen Zielsetzungen in arabischen Staaten,* edited by S. Faath, 121–133. Hamburg: Deutsches Orient-Institut, 2003.

——. *Islamische Stiftungen und Staat: Der Wandel in den Beziehungen zwischen einer religiösen Institution und dem marokkanischen Staat seit dem 19. Jahrhundert bis 1937.* Würzburg: Ergon, 199).

Laroui, A. *The History of the Maghrib: An Interpretative Essay.* Princeton: Princeton University Press, 1977.

——. *Les origines sociales et culturelles du nationalism marocain (1830–1912).* Casablanca: Centre Culturel Arabe, 1993.

Loimeier, R. *Säkularer Staat und islamische Gesellschaft: Die Beziehungen zwischen Staat, Sufi-Bruderschaften und islamischer Reformbewegung in Senegal im 20. Jahrhundert.* Münster: LIT, 2001.

Martinez, L. *The Algerian Civil War.* New York: Columbia University Press, 1999.

Merad, A. *Le réformisme musulman en Algérie de 1925 á 1940: essai d'histoire religieuse et sociale.* Paris: Mouton, 1967.

Moussaoui, A., ed. *Espace et sacré au Sahara.* Paris: CNRS, 2002.

Munson, Henry, Jr. *Religion and Power in Morocco.* New Haven: Yale University Press, 1993.

Pennel, C. R. *Morocco since 1830: A History.* New York: New York University Press, 2000.

Perkins, K. J. *A History of Modern Tunisia.* Cambridge: Cambridge University Press, 2004.

Stewart, C. C. *Islam and Social Order in Mauritania: A Case Study from the Nineteenth Century.* Oxford: Clarendon, 1973.

Ruedy, J. *Modern Algeria: The Origins and Development of a Nation.* Bloomington: Indiana University Press, 1992.

Tamimi, A. S. *Rachid Ghannouchi: A Democrat within Islamism.* Oxford: Oxford University Press, 2001.

Tozy, M. *Monarchie et Islam politique au Maroc.* Paris: Presse de la Fondation Nationale des Sciences Politiques, 1999.

Traoré, A. "L'Islam en Mauretanie." In *Introduction à la Mauritanie,* ed. D. G. Lavroff, 155–166. Paris: Centre National de la Recherche Scientifique, 1979.

Vermeren, P. *Le Maroc en transition.* Paris: La Découverte, 2001.

Volpi, F. *Islam and Democracy: The Failure of Dialogue in Algeria.* London: Pluto, 2003.

Willis, M. *The Islamist Challenge in Algeria: A Political History.* New York: New York University Press, 1996.

11. The Independent States of Sub-Saharan Africa
(Jamil M. Abun-Nasr and Roman Loimeier)

Abun-Nasr, J. M., ed. *Muslime in Nigeria: Religion und Gesellschaft im Wandel seit den 50er Jahren.* Hamburg: LIT, 1993.

Adeleye, R. A. "The Sokoto Caliphate in the Nineteenth Century." In *History of West Africa,* vol. 2, ed. J. F. A. Ajayi and M. Crowder, 57–92. London: Longman, 1974.

Anderson, J. N. D. *Islamic Law in Africa.* London: Cass, 1978.

Armah, Ayi Kwei. *Two Thousand Seasons.* London: Heinemann, 1973.

Bates, M. "Social Engineering, Multi-racialism and the Rise of TANU: The Trust Territory of Tanganyika." In *History of East Africa,* vol. 3, ed. D. A. Low and A. Smith, 168–169. Oxford: Oxford University Press, 1976.

Behrman, L. *Muslim Brotherhoods and Politics in Senegal.* Cambridge: Harvard University Press, 1970.

Bosaller, A., and R. Loimeier. "Radical Muslim Women and Male Politics in Nigeria." In *Gender and Identity in Africa,* ed. M. Reh and G. Ludwar-Ene, 61–70. Münster: LIT, 1995).

Brenner, L. *Controlling Knowledge: Religion, Power, and Schooling in a West African Muslim Society.* Bloomington: Indiana University Press, 2001.

Clayton, A. *The Zanzibar Revolution and Its Aftermath.* Hamden, Conn.: Archon Books, 1981.

Cruise O'Brien, D. B. *The Mourides of Senegal.* Oxford: Oxford University Press, 1971.

Delval, R. *Les Musulmans au Togo.* Paris: Centre des Hautes Études sur l'Afrique et l'Asie Modernes, 1980.

Faath, S. *Algerien: Gesellschaftliche Strukturen und politische Reformen zu Beginn der neunziger Jahre.* Hamburg: Deutsches Orient-Institut, 1990.

Fage, J. D. *A History of Africa.* New York: Cambridge University Press, 1979.

Froelich, J. C. *Les Musulmans d'Afrique Noire.* Paris: Éditions de l'Orient, 1962.

Günther, U. "Lesarten des Islam in Südafrika: Herausforderungen im Kontext des soziopolitischen Umbruchprozesses von Apartheid zur Demokratie." *Afrika Spectrum* 37, no. 2 (2002): 159–174.

Harrison, C. *France and Islam in West Africa, 1860–1960.* Cambridge: Cambridge University Press, 1988.

Hock, K. *Der Islam-Komplex: Zur Wahrnehmung des Islams und der christlich-islamischen Beziehungen in Nordnigeria während der Militärherrschaft Babangidas.* Hamburg: LIT, 1996.

Holt, P. M. *The Mahdist State in the Sudan, 1881–1898.* Oxford: Oxford University Press, 1958.

Hopkins, J. F. P., and N. Levtzion. *Corpus of Early Arabic Sources for West African History.* Cambridge: Cambridge University Press, 1981.

Kaba, L. *The Wahhabiyya, Islamic Reform and Politics in French West Africa.* Evanston: Northwestern University Press, 1974.

Kane, O. *Muslim Modernity in Postcolonial Nigeria: A Study of the Society for the Removal of Innovation and Reinstatement of Tradition.* Leiden: Brill, 2003.

Klein, M. *Islam and Imperialism in Senegal, Sine-Saloum, 1847–1914.* Stanford: University of California Press, 1968.

Lacunza Balda, J. "Translations of the Quran into Kiswahili, and Contemporary Islamic Revival in East Africa." In *African Islam and Islam in Africa,* ed. D. Westerlund and E. Evers-Rosander, 95–126. London: Hurst, 1997.

Lewis, I. M. *A Modern History of Somalia.* Boulder, Colo.: Westview Press, 1988.

Loimeier, R. *Islamic Reform and Political Change in Northern Nigeria.* Evanston: Northwestern University Press, 1997.

———. *Säkularer Staat und islamische Gesellschaft Die Beziehungen zwischen Staat, Sufi-Bruderschaften und islamischer Reformbewegung in Senegal im 20. Jahrhundert.* Hamburg: LIT, 2001.

———. "Gibt es einen afrikanischen Islam? Die Muslime in Afrika zwischen lokalen Lehrtraditionen und translokalen Rechtleitungsansprüchen." *Afrika Spectrum* 37, no. 2 (2002): 175–188.

———. "Patterns and Peculiarities of Islamic Reform in Africa." *Journal of Religion in Africa* 33, no. 3 (2003): 237–262.

Ludwig, F. *Church and State in Tanzania: Aspects of a Changing Relationship, 1961–1994.* Leiden: Brill, 1996.

Mattes, H. "Algerien." In *Wuqūf*, vol. 6. Hamburg: Deutsches Orient-Institut, 1992.

Monteil, V. *L'Islam noir: une religion à la conquête de l'Afrique.* Paris: Seuil, 1980.

Mrina, B. F., and W. T. Matoke. *Mapambano ya ukombozi Zanzibar.* Dar es-Salaam: Tanzania Publishing House, 1980.

Müller, H. *Zur Lage der Muslime im nachkolonialen Ostafrika: Überblick und Bibliographie.* Würzburg: Ergon, 2000.

Peters, R. *Islamic Criminal Law in Nigeria.* Ibadan: Spectrum Books, 2003.

Pouwels, R., and N. Levtzion. *The History of Islam in Africa.* Oxford: Oxford University Press, 2000.

Ranger, T. "The Invention of Tradition in Colonial Africa." In *The Invention of Tradition,* edited by E. Hobsbawm and T. Ranger, 211–262. Cambridge: Cambridge University Press, 1983.

Rivière, C. *Guinea: The Mobilization of a People.* Ithaca: Cornell University Press, 1977.

Sheriff, A., and E. Ferguson, eds. *Zanzibar under Colonial Rule.* London: James Currey, 1991.

Skinner, E. P. *African Urban Life: The Transformation of Ouagadougou.* Princeton: Princeton University Press, 1974.

Villalon, L. A. *Islamic Society and State Power in Senegal: Disciples and Citizens in Fatick.* Cambridge: Cambridge University Press, 1995.

Wegemund, R. "Die Rassenunruhen in Senegal und Mauretanien 1989." *Afrika Spectrum* 89 (1989): 255–274.

Westerlund, D. "Ahmed Deedat's Theology of Religion: Apologetics through Polemics." *Journal of Religion in Africa* 33, no. 3 (2003): 263–279.

12. The Islamization of Sub-Saharan Africa *(Hans Müller)*

Blanckmeister, E. B. *Dīn wa dawla: Islam, Politik und Ethnizität im Hausaland und Adamawa.* Emsdetten: A. Gehling, 1989.

Clarke, P. B. *West Africa and Islam: A Study of Religious Development from the 8th to the 20th Century.* London: E. Arnold, 1982.

Cuoq, J. M. *Les Musulmans en Afrique.* Paris: Maisonneuve et Larose, 1975.

———. *Recueil des sources arabes concernant l'Afrique occidentale du VIIIe au XVIe siècle (Bilād as-Sūdān).* Paris: CNRS, 1975 (reprint, 1985).

———. *L'Islam en Éthiopie des origines au XVIe siècle.* Paris: Nouvelles Éditions Latines, 1981.

———. *Histoire de l'islamisation de l'Afrique de l'ouest des origines à la fin du 16e siècle.* Paris: Geuthner, 1984 (reprint, 1985).

———. *Islamisation de la Nubie chrétienne, VIIe—XVIe siècle.* Paris: Geuthner, 1986.

Forstner, M. "Der Islam in der westafrikanischen Sahel-Zone: Erscheinungsbild—Geschichte—Wirkung." *Zeitschrift für Missionswissenschaft und Religionswissenschaft* 71 (1987): 25–84 and 97–120.

Froehlich, J. C. *Les Musulmans d'Afrique noire.* Paris: Orante, 1962.

Haron, M. *Muslims in South Africa: An Annotated Bibliography.* Cape Town: South African Library, 1997.

Hiskett, M. *The Development of Islam in West Africa.* London: Longman, 1984.

———. *The Course of Islam in Africa.* Edinburgh: Edinburgh University Press, 1994.

Hopkins, J. F. P., and N. Levtzion, eds. *Corpus of Early Arabic Sources for Western African History.* Cambridge: Cambridge University Press, 1981.

Insoll, T. *The Archeology of Islam in Sub-Saharan Africa.* Cambridge: Cambridge University Press, 2003.

Kritzeck, J., and W. H. Lewis, eds. *Islam in Africa.* New York: Van Nostrand, 1969.

Levtzion, N., and R. L. Pouwells, eds. *The History of Islam in Africa.* Athens: Ohio University Press, 2000.

Lewis, I. M., ed. *Islam in Tropical Africa.* 2nd ed. Bloomington: Indiana University Press, 1980.

Monteil, V. *L'Islam noir: une religion à la conquête de l'Afrique.* 4th ed. Paris: Éditions du Seuil, 1986.

Moreau, R. L. *Africains musulmans: des communautés en mouvement.* Paris and Abidjan: Présence africain and Inadès, 1982.

Müller, H. *Zur Lage der Muslime im nachkolonialen Ostafrika: Überblick und Bibliographie.* Würzburg: Ergon, 2000.

Nicolas, G. *Dynamique de l'Islam au sud du Sahara.* Paris: Publications orientalistes de France, 1981.

Ofori, P. E. *Islam in Africa South of the Sahara: A Select Bibliographic Guide.* Nendeln: KTO Press, 1977.

Otayek, R., ed. *Le radicalisme islamique au sud du Sahara: Da'wa, arabisation et critique de l'Occident.* Paris: Karthala, 1993.

Pouwels, R. L. *Horn and Cresent: Cultural Change and Traditional Islam on the East African Coast, 800–1900.* Cambridge: Cambridge University Press, 1987.

Reusch, R. *Der Islam in Ost-Afrika, mit besonderer Berücksichtigung der muhammedanischen Geheim-Orden.* Leipzig: Klein, 1930.

Rosander, E. E., and D. Westerlund, eds. *African Islam and Islam in Africa: Encounters between Sufis and Islamists.* London: Hurst, 1997.

Trimingham, J. S. *Islam in the Sudan.* London: Frank Cass, 1949 (reprints, 1965 and 1983).

———. *Islam in Ethiopia.* London: Frank Cass, 1952 (reprints, 1965 and 1976).

———. *Islam in West Africa.* London: Oxford University Press, 1959 (reprint, 1961–1978).

———. *A History of Islam in West Africa.* London: Oxford University Press, 1962 (reprint, 1963–1982).

———. *Islam in East Africa.* London: Oxford University Press, 1964 (reprints, 1971 and 1980).

———. *The Influence of Islam upon Africa.* London: Longman, 1968 (2nd ed. 1980).

Willis, J. R., ed. *Studies in West African Islamic History.* Vol. 1. *The Cultivators of Islam.* London: Frank Cass, 1979.

Zoghby, S. M., ed. *Islam in Sub-Saharan Africa: A Partially Annotated Guide.* Washington, D.C.: Library of Congress, 1978.

13. Horn of Africa *(Hans Müller)*

Africa South of the Sahara. London: Europa Publications, 1971 (1st ed. 1971, 32nd ed. 2003).

Alwan, D. A., and Y. Mibrathu. *Historical Dictionary of Djibouti.* Lanham, Md.: Scarecrow, 2000.

Braukämper, U. *Islamic History and Culture in Southern Ethiopia: Collected Essays.* Hamburg: LIT, 2002.

Cuoq, J. M. *Les Musulmans en Afrique.* Paris: Maisonneuve et Larose, 1975.

Dilger, K. "Die Rolle des islamischen Rechts im ostafrikanischen Raum. Ein Beitrag zur Rechtsentwicklung in Somalia, in der Volksrepublik Jemen und in Äthiopien." In *Jahrbuch für Afrikanisches Recht,* vol. 2, 3–42. Heidelberg: C. F. Müller, 1981.

Erlich, H. *The Cross and the River: Ethiopia, Egypt, and the Nile.* Boulder, Colo.: Lynne Riener, 2002.

Haberland, E., and Straube, H. "Nordostafrika." In *Die Völker Afrikas und ihre traditionellen Kulturen.* Vol. 2. *Ost-, West- und Nordafrika,* ed. H. Baumann, 69–156. Wiesbaden: Franz Steiner, 1979.

Helander, B. "Somalia." In *Islam Outside the Arab World,* ed. D. Westerlund and I. Svanberg, 37–55. Richmond, Surrey: Curzon, 1999.

Institut für Afrika-Kunde, ed. *Afrika Jahrbuch, 1987–.* Opladen: Leske und Budrich.

Killion, T. *Historical Dictionary of Eritrea.* Lanham Md.: Scarecrow, 1998.

Laitin, D. D., and S. S. Samatar. *Somalia: Nation in Search of a State.* Boulder, Colo.: Westview, and London: Gower, 1987.

Lewis, I. M. *Peoples of the Horn of Africa: Somali, Afar and Saho.* London: Lowe and Brydone, 1955 (reprinted with supplementary bibliography 1969).

——. "Sufism in Somaliland: A Study in Tribal Islam." *Bulletin of the School of Oriental and African Studies* 17 (1955): 581–602 and 18 (1956): 145–160.

——. *A Modern History of Somalia: Nation and State in the Horn of Africa.* London: Longman, 1980.

Metz, H. C., ed. *Somalia: A Country Study.* 4th ed. Washington, D.C.: Federal Research Division, Library of Congress, 1993.

Mohamed-Abdi, M. "Un multipartisme non démocratique: la montée des intégrismes musulmans en Somalie." In *Religion et transition démocratique en Afrique,* edited by F. Constantinet and C. Coulon, 163–185. Paris: Karthala, 1997.

Mukhtar, M. H. *Historical Dictionary of Somalia.* Lanham Md.: Scarecrow, 2003.

Nelson, H. D., and I. Kaplan, eds. *Ethiopia: A Country Study.* 3rd ed. Washington, D.C.: Headquarters, Department of the Army, 1981.

Prouty, C., and E. Rosenfeld. *Historical Dictionary of Ethiopia and Eritrea.* 2nd ed. Metuchen N.J.: Scarecrow, 1994.

Trimingham, J. S. *Islam in Ethiopia.* London: Cass, 1952 (reprints, 1965 and 1976).

Waal, A. de, ed. *Islamism and Its Enemies in the Horn of Africa.* London: Hurst, 2004.

14. Libya *(Hanspeter Mattes)*

Ayoub, M. M. *Islam and the Third Universal Theory: The Religious Thought of Mu'ammar al-Qadhdhafi.* London: KPI, 1987.

Evans-Pritchard, E. E. *The Sanusi of Cyrenaica.* Oxford: Oxford University Press, 1949.

Kooij, C. *Islam in Qadhafi's Libya: Religion and Politics in a Developing Country.* Amsterdam: Antropologisch-Sociologisch Centrum, Universiteit van Amsterdam, 1980.

Mattes, H. *Islam und Staatsaufbau: Das theoretische Konzept und das Beispiel der Sozialistischen Libyschen Arabischen Volksgamahiriyya.* Heidelberg: Forschungsstätte der Evangelischen Studiengemeinschaft, 1982.

——. *Die innere und äußere Mission Libyens: Historisch-politischer Kontext, innere Struktur, regionale Ausprägung am Beispiel Afrikas.* Mainz: Grünewald, 1986.

——. "Qaddafi und die islamistische Opposition in Libyen: Zum Verlauf eines Konflikts." *Deutsches Orient-Institut:* Mitteilung no. 51 (Hamburg, 1995).

976 *Bibliography*

Mayer, A. E. "A Survey of Islamifying Trends in Libyan Law since 1969." *Society for Libyan Studies: Seventh Annual Report* (1975–76): 53–55.
———. "Islamic Resurgence or New Prophethood: The Role of Islam in Qadhdhafi's Ideology." In *Islamic Resurgence in the Arab World,* edited by H. Dessouki, 196–220. New York: Praeger, 1982.
Scarcia Amoretti, B. "Libyan Loneliness in Facing the World: The Challenge of Islam?" In *Islam in Foreign Policy,* edited by A. Dawisha, 54–67. Cambridge: Cambridge University Press, 1983.
Ziadeh, N. A. *Sanusiyah: A Study of a Revivalist Movement in Islam.* Leiden: E. J. Brill, 1968.

15. Egypt *(Alexander Flores)*

Anawati, G., and M. Borrmans. *Tendances et courants de l'Islam arabe contemporain.* Vol. 1. *Égypte et Afrique du Nord.* Munich: Kaiser, and Mainz: Grünewald, 1982.
al-Ashmawy, M. S. *L'islamisme contre l'islam.* Paris: La Découverte, and Cairo: Al-Fikr, 1989.
Büttner, F., and J. Klostermeier. *Ägypten.* Munich: Beck, 1991.
Carré, O., and G. Michaud. *Les frères musulmans (1928–1982).* Paris: Gallimard/ Julliard, 1983.
Crecelius, D. "The Course of Secularization in Modern Egypt." In *Islam and Development,* edited by J. L. Esposito, 49–70. Syracuse: Syracuse University Press, 1980.
Damir-Geilsdorf, S. *Herrschaft und Gesellschaft: Der islamistische Wegbereiter Sayyid Quṭb und seine Rezeption.* Würzburg: Ergon, 2003.
Eccel, A. C. *Egypt, Islam, and Social Change: Al-Azhar in Conflict and Accommodation.* Berlin: Klaus Schwarz, 1984.
Forstner, M. "Auf dem legalen Weg zur Macht? Zur politischen Entwicklung der Muslimbruderschaft Ägyptens." *Orient* 29 (1988): 386–422.
Hopwood, D. *Egypt: Politics and Society, 1945–1990,* 3rd ed. London: Routledge, 1993.
Jansen, J. J. G. *The Neglected Duty: The Creed of Sadat's Assassins and Islamic Resurgence in the Middle East.* New York: Macmillan, 1986.
Kepel, G. *Le prophète et pharaon.* Paris, 1984. (In English: *Prophet and Pharaoh: Muslim Extremism in Egypt.* Translated by Jon Rothschild. London: Al Saqi Books, 1985.)
Kogelmann, F. *Die Islamisten Ägyptens in der Regierungszeit von Anwar as-Sādāt (1970– 1981).* Berlin: Klaus Schwarz, 1994.
Krämer, G. *Ägypten unter Mubarak: Identität und nationales Interesse.* Baden-Baden: Nomos, 1986.
———. *Gottes Staat als Republik: Reflexionen zeitgenössischer Muslime zu Islam, Menschenrechten und Demokratie.* Baden-Baden: Nomos, 1999.
Lemke, W.-D. *Maḥmūd Shaltūt (1893–1963) und die Reform der Azhar: Untersuchungen zu Erneuerungsbestrebungen im ägyptischen Erziehungssystem.* Frankfurt am Main: P. D. Lang, 1980.
Lüders, M., ed. *Der Islam im Aufbruch? Perspektiven der arabischen Welt.* Munich: Piper, 1992.
Mitchell, R. P. *The Society of the Muslim Brothers.* London: Oxford University Press, 1969.
Pawelka, P. *Herrschaft und Entwicklung im Nahen Osten: Ägypten.* Heidelberg: UTB/ C. F. Müller, 1985.
Reuter, B. *Gelebte Religion: Religiöse Praxis junger Islamistinnen in Kairo.* Würzburg: Ergon, 1999.

Sagiv, David. *Fundamentalism and Intellectuals in Egypt, 1973–1993*. London: Frank Cass, 1995.

Schamp, H., ed. *Ägypten: Das alte Kulturland am Nil auf dem Weg in die Zukunft.* Tübingen: Erdmann, 1977.

Schulze, R. *Islamischer Internationalismus im 20. Jahrhundert.* Leiden: Brill, 1990.

Sivan, E. *Radical Islam: Medieval Theology and Modern Politics.* New Haven: Yale University Press, 1985.

Vatikiotis, P. J. *The History of Egypt.* 2nd ed. London: Weidenfeld & Nicholson, 1980.

Zakariya, F. *Laïcité ou islamisme: les arabes à l'heure du choix.* Paris: La Découverte, and Cairo: Al-Fikr, 1991.

16. Sudan *(Hanspeter Mattes)*

Abdelsalam, S. E. *A Study of Contemporary Sudanese Muslim Saints' Legends in Sociocultural Contexts.* Ann Arbor: University Microfilms International, 1983.

Affendi, A., el-. *Turabi's Revolution: Islam and Power in Sudan.* London: Grey Seal, 1991.

Bashier, Z. *Islamic Movement in the Sudan: Issues and Challenges.* Leicester: Islamic Foundation, 1987.

Burr, J. M., and R. O. Collins. *Revolutionary Sudan: Hasan al-Turabi and the Islamic State, 1989–2000.* Leiden: Brill, 2003.

Daly, M. W., ed. *Al Majdhubiyya and al Mikashfiyya: Two Sufi Tariqas in the Sudan.* Khartoum: Garnet Publishing, 1985.

Fluehr-Lobban, C. *Islamic Law and Society in the Sudan.* London: Routledge, 1992.

Gallab, A. A. The First Islamist Republic: Development and Disintegration of Islamism in the Sudan. Aldershot: Ashgate, 2008.

Grandin, N. "Al-Sayyid Muhammad al-Hasan al-Mīrghanī (Soudan)." *Islam et Sociétés au Sud du Sahara, Paris* 3 (1989): 107–118.

Jok, J. M. Sudan: Race, Religion and Violence. Oxford: Oneworld, 2007.

Karrar, A. S. *The Sufi Brotherhoods in the Sudan.* Evanston: Northwestern University Press, 1992.

Köndgen, O. *Das islamierte Strafrecht des Sudan: Von seiner Einführung 1983 bis Juli 1992.* Hamburg: Deutsches Orient-Institut, 1992.

Na'im, A. A. an-. "Mahmud Muhammad Taha and the Crisis in Islamic Law Reform: Implications for Interreligious Relations." In *Muslims in Dialogue,* edited by L. Swidler, 59–86. Lewiston, N.Y.: Mellen, 1992.

Osman, A. A. M. *The Political and Ideological Development of the Muslim Brotherhood in Sudan, 1945–1986.* Betchworth: The University of Reading 1989.

Taha, M. M. *The Second Message of Islam.* Syracuse: Syracuse University Press, 1987.

Trimingham, J. S. *Islam in the Sudan.* 1945. London: Chapman & Hall, 1965.

17. Israel and the Occupied Territories *(Thomas Philipp)*

Abu-ʿAmr, Z. "Hamas: A Historical and Political Background." *Journal of Palestine Studies* 22 (Summer 1993): 5–19, 122–134.

——. *Islamic Fundamentalism in the West Bank and Gaza.* Bloomington: Indiana University Press, 1994.

Berger, E. *Peace for Palestine: First Lost Opportunity.* Gainesville: University Press of Florida, 1993.

Beaupain, A. *Befreiung oder Islamisierung? Hamas und PLO: Die zwei Gesichter des palästinensischen Widerstands.* Marburg: Tectum, 2003.

Cobban, H., "The PLO and the Intifada." *Middle East Journal* 44 (Spring 1990): 2, 207–233.

Darwaza, M. I. *Al-Qadiyya al-filastiniyya fi mukhtalif marahiliha.* 2 vols. Beirut and Sidon, 1951.

Freund, W. *Looking into Hamas and Other Constituents of the Palestinian-Israeli Confrontation.* Frankfurt am Main: Peter Lang, 2002.

Heilberg, M., G. Ovensen et al. *Palestinian Society in Gaza, West Bank, and Arab Jerusalem: A Survey of Living Conditions.* Oslo: FAFO, 1993.

Höpp, G. "Religion im Konflikt: Gibt es eine islamische Lösung für Palästina?" In *Die Welt nach dem Ost-West-Konflikt: Geschichte und Prognosen,* edited by M. Robbe and D. Senghaas, 249–265. Berlin: Akademie Verlag, 1990.

Hroub, K. *Hamas: A Beginner's Guide.* Ann Arbor: Pluto, 2006.

Israeli, R. *Muslim Fundamentalism in Israel.* London: Brassey's, 1993.

Landau, D. *Piety and Power: The World of Jewish Fundamentalism.* London: Secker & Warburg, 1993.

Legrain, J.-F. "Islamistes et lutte nationale palestinienne dans les territoires occupés par Israël." *Revue française de Science Politique* 36, no. 2 (April 1986): 227–247.

———. "The Islamic Movement and the Intifada." In *Intifada: Palestine at the Crossroads,* edited by J. R. Nassar and R. Heacock, 175–189. New York: Praeger/Greenwood, 1990.

Legrain, J.-F., and Chenard, P. *Les voix du soulèvement palestinien.* Cairo: CEDEJ, 1991.

Lustick, I. *For the Land and the Lord.* New York: Council on Foreign Relations, 1988.

Mayer, T. "Pro-Iranian Fundamentalism in Gaza." In *Religious Radicalism and Politics in the Middle East,* edited by E. Sivan and M. Friedmann, 143–155. Albany: SUNY Press 1990.

Migdal, J. S. *Palestinian Society and Politics.* Princeton: Princeton University Press, 1980.

Mishal, S., and S. Sela. *The Palestinian Hamas.* New York: Columbia University Press, 2000.

Moseley Lesch, A. *Arab Politics in Palestine, 1917–1939.* Ithaca: Cornell University Press, 1979.

Porath, Y. *The Emergence of the Palestinian-Arab National Movement, 1918–1929.* London: Cass, 1974.

———. *The Palestinian Arab National Movement: From Riots to Rebellion, 1929–1939.* London: Routledge, 1977.

Roy, S. "Hamas and the Transformation(s) of Political Islam in Palestine." *Current History* (January 2003): 13–20.

Sahliyeh, E. F. "The West Bank and the Gaza Strip." In *The Politics of Islamic Revivalism,* edited by S. T. Hunter, 88–100. Bloomington: Indiana University Press, 1988.

Shadid, M. K. "The Muslim Brotherhood Movement in the West Bank and Gaza." *Third World Quarterly* 10, no. 2 (April 1988): 658–682.

Sicherman, H. *Palestinian Autonomy, Self-Government, and Peace.* Boulder, Colo.: Westview, 1993.

Smith, C. D. *Palestine and the Arab-Israeli Conflict.* New York: St. Martin's, 1988.

Stein, K. W. "The Intifada and the Uprising of 1936–1939: A Comparison of the Palestinian Arab Communities." In *The Intifada: Its Impact on Israel, the Arab World, and the Superpowers,* edited by R. O. Freedman, 3–36. Miami: University Press of Florida, 1991.

Steinberg, M. "The PLO and Palestinian Islamic Fundamentalism." *Jerusalem Quarterly* 52 (Autumn 1989): 37–54.

Sunderbrink, U. *Die PLO in der Krise? Genese, Strukturmerkmale und Politikmuster der Palästinensischen Befreiungsorganisation und deren Herausforderung durch den politischen Islam in der Intifada.* Münster: LIT, 1993.

18. Syria *(Andreas Christmann)*

Böttcher, A. *Syrische Religionspolitik unter Asad.* Freiburg: Arnold Bergstraesser Institut, 1998.

——. "Official Sunni and Shi'i Islam in Syria." *EUI Working Papers.* Robert Schuman Centre for Advanced Studies, Mediterranean Program Series, Florence, 2002.

Christmann, A. "An Invented Piety? Subduing Ramadan in Syrian State Media." In *Muslim Traditions and Modern Techniques of Power,* edited by Armando Salvatore, 243–263. Yearbook of the Sociology of Islam 5. Münster, Westphalia: LIT, 2001.

de Jong, F. "The Naqshbandiya in Egypt and Syria: Aspects of Its History, and Observations Concerning its Present-Day Condition." In *Naqshbandis: Historical Developments and Present Situation of a Muslim Mystical Order,* edited by M. Gaborieau, A. Popovic, and T. Zarcone, 589–602. Istanbul, 1990.

Pinto, P. "The Limits of the Public: Sufism and the Religious Debate in Syria." In *Public Islam and the Common Good,* edited by D. Eickelman and A. Salvatore, 181–204. Leiden: Brill, 2004.

Teitelbaum, J. "The Muslim Brotherhood and the Struggle for Syria, 1947–1958." *Middle Eastern Studies* 40 (2004): 134–158.

Wedeen, L. *Ambiguities of Domination: Politics, Rhetoric, and Symbols in Contemporary Syria.* Chicago: University of Chicago Press, 1999.

19. Iraq *(Henner Fürtig)*

Aziz, T. M. *The Islamic Political Theory of Muhammad Baqir al-Sadr of Iraq.* Ann Arbor: University of Michigan Press, 1993.

Bahjat, S., *Die politische Entwicklung der Kurden im Irak von 1975 bis 1993 unter besonderer Berücksichtigung von Saddam Husseins Kurdenpolitik.* Berlin: Schwarz, 2001.

Batatu, H. *The Old Social Classes and the Revolutionary Movements of Iraq: A Study of Iraq's Old Landed and Commercial Classes and of Its Communists, Ba'thists, and Free Officers.* Princeton: Princeton University Press, 1978.

Bremer, L. P. *My Year in Iraq: The Struggle to Build a Future of Hope.* New York: Simon & Schuster, 2006.

Brown, N. J. *Post-election Iraq: Facing the Constitutional Challenge.* Washington, D.C.: Carnegie Endowment, 2005.

Buchta, W. *Schiiten.* Kreuzlingen: Hugendubel, 2004.

Cole, J. "The United States and Shi'ite Religious Factions in Post-Ba'thist Iraq." *Middle East Journal* 57, no. 4 (2003): 544–566.

Fürtig, H. *Kleine Geschichte des Irak.* Munich: C. H. Beck, 2003.

Gunter, M. M. *The Kurdish Predicament in Iraq: A Political Analysis.* New York: St. Martin's Press, 1999.

Ibrahim, F. *Konfessionalismus und Politik in der arabischen Welt: Die Schiiten im Irak.* Münster: LIT, 1997.

International Crisis Group. "Iraq's Shiites under Occupation." In *Middle East Briefing* 8. Brussels, 2003.

——. "The Next Iraqi War? Sectarianism and Civil Conflict." In *Middle East Report* 52. Brussels, 2006.

Jabar, F. A. *Ayatollahs, Sufis and Ideologues: State, Religion and Social Movements in Iraq.* London: Saqi Books, 2002.

Kehl-Bodrogi, K., ed. *Syncretistic Religious Communities in the Near East.* Leiden: Brill, 1997.

Mallat, C. *The Renewal of Islamic Law: Muhammad Baqer as-Sadr, Najaf and the Shi'i International.* Cambridge: Cambridge University Press, 1993.

Mufti, M. *Sovereign Creations: Pan-Arabism and Political Order in Syria and Iraq.* Ithaca: Cornell University Press, 1996.

Nakash, Y. *The Shi'is of Iraq.* Princeton: Princeton University Press, 1994.

Rahe, J.-U. *Irakische Schiiten im Londoner Exil: Eine Bestandsaufnahme ihrer Organisationen und Untersuchung ihrer Selbstdarstellung, 1991–1994.* Würzburg: Ergon, 1996.

Rahimi, B. "Ayatollah Ali al-Sistani and the Democratisation of Post-Saddam Iraq." *Middle East Review of International Affairs* 8, no. 4 (2004): 12–19.

Sluglett, P., and M. Farouk-Sluglett. *Der Irak seit 1958: Von der Revolution zur Diktatur.* Frankfurt am Main: Suhrkamp, 1991.

Soeterik, R. *The Islamic Movement of Iraq (1958–1980).* Amsterdam: Middle East Research Associates, 1991.

Tripp, C. *A History of Iraq.* Cambridge: Cambridge University Press, 2000.

Wiley, J. N. *The Islamic Movement of Iraqi Shi'as.* Boulder, Colo.: Lynne Rienner, 1992.

20. Jordan *(Renate Dieterich)*

Boulby, M. *The Muslim Brotherhood and the Kings of Jordan, 1945–1993.* Atlanta: Scholars Press, 1999.

Dieterich, R. "'To raise one's tongue against His Majesty'—Islamist Critique and Its Response in Jordan: The Case of Laith Shubeilat." In *Encounters of Words and Texts,* edited by L. Edzard and C. Szyska, 159–176. Hildesheim: Georg Olms Verlag, 1997.

Messara, A. "La régulation étatique de la religion dans le monde arabe: le cas de la Jordanie." *Social Compass* 40, no. 4 (1993): 581–588.

Schwedler, J. M. *Faith in Moderation: Islamist Parties in Jordan and Yemen.* Cambridge: Cambridge University Press, 2006.

Wiktorowicz, Q. *The Management of Islamic Activism: Salafis, the Muslim Brotherhood, and State Power in Jordan.* Albany: State University of New York Press, 2001.

21. Lebanon *(Axel Havemann)*

Abu-Izzeddin, N. M. *The Druzes: A New Study of Their History, Faith, and Society.* Leiden: Brill, 1984.

Ajami, F. *The Vanished Imam: Musa al Sadr and the Shia of Lebanon.* Ithaca: Cornell University Press, 1986.

Bar, L.-H. de. *Les communautés confessionelles du Liban.* Paris: Éditions Recherche sur les civilizations, 1983.

Betts, R. B. *The Druze.* New Haven: Yale University Press, 1988.

Chalabi, T. *The Shi'is of Jabal 'Amil and the New Lebanon: Community and State, 1918–1943.* New York: Palgrave Macmillan, 2006.

Firro, K. M. *A History of the Druzes.* Leiden: Brill, 1992. (*Handbuch der Orientalistik.* Section 1. *Der Nahe und der Mittlere Osten.* Supplementary vol. 9.)

———. *Inventing Lebanon: Nationalism and the State under the Mandate.* London: I. B. Tauris, 2003.

Goria, W. R. *Sovereignty and Leadership in Lebanon, 1943–1976.* London: I. B. Tauris, 1985.

Halawi, M. *A Lebanon Defied: Musa al-Sadr and the Shi'a Community.* Boulder, Colo.: Westview Press, 1992.

Hanf, T. *Erziehungswesen in Gesellschaft und Politik des Libanon.* Bielefeld: Bertelsmann Universitätsverlag, 1969.

———. *Coexistence in Wartime Lebanon: Decline of a State and Rise of a Nation.* London: I. B. Tauris and Centre for Lebanese Studies, 1993. (Original German version: *Koexistenz im Krieg: Staatszerfall und Entstehen einer Nation im Libanon.* Baden-Baden: Nomos, 1990.)

Havemann, A. *Geschichte und Geschichtsschreibung im Libanon des 19. und 20. Jahrhunderts: Formen und Funktionen des historischen Selbstverständnisses.* Beirut and Würzburg: Ergon, 2002.

Johnson, M. *Class and Client in Beirut: The Sunni Muslim Community and the Lebanese State, 1840–1985.* London: Ithaca Press, 1986.

Norton, A. R. *Amal and the Shi'a: Struggle for the Soul of Lebanon.* Austin: University of Texas Press, 1987.

Perthes, V. *Der Libanon nach dem Bürgerkrieg: Von Ta'if zum gesellschaftlichen Konsens?* Baden-Baden: Nomos, 1994.

Rosiny, S. *Islamismus bei den Schiiten im Libanon: Religion im Übergang von Tradition zur Moderne.* Berlin: Das Arabische Buch, 1996.

Salibi, K. S. *The Modern History of Lebanon.* London: Weidenfeld and Nicholson, 1965.

———. *A House of Many Mansions: The History of Lebanon Reconsidered.* London: I. B. Tauris, 1988.

Schenk, B. *Kamāl Ǧunbulāṭ: Das arabisch-islamische Erbe und die Rolle der Drusen in seiner Konzeption der libanesischen Geschichte.* Berlin: Klaus Schwarz, 1994.

———. *Tendenzen und Entwicklungen in der modernen drusischen Gemeinschaft des Libanon: Versuche einer historischen, politischen und religiösen Standortbestimmung.* Berlin: Klaus Schwarz, 2002.

Shehadi, N., and D. H. Mills, eds. *Lebanon: A History of Conflict and Consensus.* London: Centre for Lebanese Studies and I. B. Tauris, 1988.

22. Saudi Arabia *(Guido Steinberg)*

Buchan, J. "The Return of the Ikhwan 1979." In *The House of Saud: The Rise and Rule of the Most Powerful Dynasty in the Arab World,* edited by David Holden and Richard Jones, 511–526. London: Holt Rinehart & Winston, 1981.

Commins, David. *The Wahhabi Mission and Saudi Arabia.* London: I. B. Tauris, 2006.

Ende, W. "Religion, Politik und Literatur in Saudi-Arabien: Der geistesgeschichtliche Hintergrund der heutigen religiösen und kulturpolitischen Situation, I–IV." *Orient* 1, no. 22 (1981): 3, 377–390; 2, no. 23 (1982): 1, 21–35; 3, no. 23 (1982): 3, 378–393; and 4, no. 23 (1982): 4, 524–539.

Fandy, M. *Saudi Arabia and the Politics of Dissent.* London: Macmillan, 1999.

Glosemeyer, I. "Saudi-Arabien: Wandel ohne Wechsel?" In *Elitenwandel in der arabischen Welt und Iran,* edited by V. Perthes, 172–188. Berlin: Stiftung Wissenschaft und Politik, 2002.

Habib, J. S. *Ibn Sa'ud's Warriors of Islam: The Ikhwan of Najd and Their Role in the Creation of the Sa'udi Kingdom, 1910–1930.* Leiden: Brill, 1978.

Okruhlik, G. "Islamism and Reform in Saudi Arabia." *Current History* (January 2002): 22–28.

Peskes, E., and W. Ende. "Wahhabiyya." In *The Encyclopaedia of Islam,* vol. 11, 39–47. Leiden: Brill, 2002.

al-Rasheed, M. *A History of Saudi Arabia.* Cambridge: Cambridge University Press, 2002.

Reissner, J. "Saudi-Arabien und die kleineren Golfstaaten." In *Der Islam in der Gegenwart,* 4th ed., edited by W. Ende and U. Steinbach, 531–543. Munich: Beck, 1996.

Schulze, R. *Islamischer Internationalismus im 20. Jahrhundert: Untersuchungen zur Geschichte der Islamischen Weltliga.* Leiden: Brill, 1990.

Steinberg, G. *Religion und Staat in Saudi-Arabien: Die wahhabitischen Gelehrten (1902–1953).* Würzburg: Ergon, 2002.

——. "The Shiites in the Eastern Province of Saudi Arabia (al-Ahsa'), 1913–1953." In *The Twelver Shia in Modern Times: Religious Culture and Political History,* edited by R. Brunner and W. Ende, 236–254. Leiden: Brill, 2001.

Teitelbaum, J. *Holier Than Thou: Saudi Arabia's Islamic Opposition.* Washington, D.C.: Washington Institute for Near East Policy, 2000.

Vogel, F. E. *Islamic Law and Legal System: Studies of Saudi Arabia.* Leiden: Brill, 2000.

Winder, R. B. *Saudi Arabia in the Nineteenth Century.* London: Macmillan, 1965.

23. The Small Gulf States *(Katja Niethammer)*

Alqudsi-Ghabra, T. "Kuwait: Striving to Align Islam with Western Values." In *Teaching Islam,* edited by E. Abdella Doumato and G. Starrett, 89–101. Boulder, Colo.: Lynne Rienner, 2007.

Anthony, J. D. *Arab States of the Lower Gulf: People, Politics, Petroleum.* Washington, D.C.: Middle East Institute, 1975.

Badry, R.: "Marja'iyya and Shūrā." In *The Twelver Shia in Modern Times: Religious Culture and Political Culture,* edited by R. Brunner and W. Ende, 188–206. Leiden: Brill 2001.

Bahry, L. "The Socioeconomic Foundations of the Shiite Opposition in Bahrain." *Mediterranean Quarterly* (Summer 2000): 129–143.

Brown, N. *The Rule of Law in the Arab World: Courts in Egypt and the Gulf.* Cambridge: Cambridge University Press, 1997.

——. *Pushing toward Party Politics? Kuwait's Islamic Constitutional Movement.* Carnegie Paper no. 79, Carnegie Endowment, February 2007.

Byman, D., and J. Green. *Political Violence and Stability in the States of the Northern Persian Gulf: Prepared for the Office of the Secretary of Defense.* Santa Monica: Rand, 1999.

Byman, D., and J. Wise. *The Persian Gulf in the Coming Decade: Trends, Threats, and Opportunities; Prepared for the United States Air Force.* Santa Monica: Rand, 2002.

Crystal, J. *Oil and Politics in the Gulf: Rulers and Merchants in Kuwait and Qatar.* Cambridge: Cambridge University Press, 1990.

Dabbous-Sensening, D. "To Veil or Not to Veil: Gender and Religion on Al-Jazeera's 'Islamic Law and Life.'" *Westminster Papers in Communication and Culture* 3 (July 2006): 60–85.

Dazi-Héni, F. "Bahrein et Koweit: la modernisation des dynasties Al Khalifa et Al Sabah." In *Monarchies arabes: transitions et dérives dynastiques,* edited by R. Leveau and A. Hammoudi, 215–238. Paris: Les études de la documentation française, 2002.

Eickelman, D. "Kings and People: Information and Authority in Oman, Qatar, and the Persian Gulf." In *Iran, Iraq, and the Arab Gulf States,* edited by J. A. Kechichian, 193–209. New York: Palgrave, 2001.

Findlow, S. *The United Arab Emirates: Nationalism and Arab-Islamic Identity.* Abu Dhabi: The Emirates Center for Strategic Studies and Research, 2000.

Gause, F. III: "The Persistence of Monarchy in the Arabian Peninsula: A Comparative Analysis." In *Middle East Monarchies: The Challenge of Modernity,* edited by J. Kostiner, 167–186. Boulder, Colo.: Lynne Rienner, 2000.

——. *Political Opposition in the Gulf Monarchies.* EUI Working Papers, RSC 2000/61.

Hamzeh, N. "Qatar: the Duality of the Legal System." *Middle Eastern Studies* 30, no. 1 (January 1994): 79–90.

Herb, M. *All in the Family: Absolutism, Revolution, and Democracy in the Middle Eastern Monarchies.* Albany: State University of New York Press, 1999.

——. "Princes and Parliaments in the Arab World." *Middle East Journal* 58, no. 3 (2004): 367–384.

——"Subordinate Communities and the Utility of Ethnic Ties to a Neighboring Regime: Iran and the Shi'a of the Arab States of the Gulf." In *Ethnic Conflict and International Politics in the Middle East,* edited by L. Binder, 155–180. Gainesville: University Press of Florida, 1999.

Khalaf, A. "What the Gulf Ruling Families Do When They Rule." *Orient* 44, no. 4 (2003): 537–554.

Khuri, F. *Tribe and State in Bahrain: The Transformation of Social and Political Authority in an Arab State.* Chicago: University of Chicago Press, 1980.

Kostiner, J., ed. *Middle East Monarchies: The Challenge of Modernity.* Boulder, Colo.: Lynne Rienner, 2000.

Lawson, F. "Economic Liberalization and the Reconfiguration of Authoritarianism in the Arab Gulf States." *Orient* 46, no. 1 (2005): 19–43.

Leveau, R., and F. Charillon, eds. *Monarchies du Golfe: les micro-états de la péninsule arabique.* Paris: La documentation française, 2005.

Limbert, M. "Oman: Cultivating Good Citizens and Religious Virtue." In *Teaching Islam,* edited by E. Abdella Doumato, 103–124. Boulder, Colo.: Lynne Rienner, 2007.

Louer, L. "Les reconfigurations du chiisme politique au Moyen-Orient." In *Afrique du Nord–Moyen Orient: espace et conflict,* edited by R. Leveau, 187–201. Paris: La documentation française, 2004.

Nasr, V. *The Shia Revival.* New York: W. W. Norton & Company, 2006.

Niethammer, K. "The Paradox of Bahrain: Authoritarian Islamists through Participation, Pro-Democratic Islamists through Exclusion?" In *Moderate Islamists as Reform Actors: Conditions and Programmatic Change,* edited by M. Asseburg, 45–54. Berlin SWP Research Paper 4, April 2007.

Nonneman, G. *Political Reform in the Gulf Monarchies: From Liberalisation to Democratisation? A Comparative Perspective.* Sir William Luce Fellowship Paper no. 6, Durham Middle East Papers no. 80, Durham, June 2006.

Onley, J. "Britain's Informal Empire in the Gulf, 1820–1971." *Journal of Social Affairs* 22 (2005): 29–45.

Peterson, J. E. "What Makes the Gulf States Endure?" In *Iran, Iraq, and the Arab Gulf States,* edited by J. Kechichian, 452–460. New York: Palgrave, 2001.

Sager, A. "Political Reform Measures from a Domestic GCC Perspective." In *Constitutional Reform and Political Participation in the Gulf,* edited by A. Khalaf and G. Luciani, 17–32. Dubai: Gulf Research Center, 2006.

Smith, K. "The Kuwait Finance House and the Islamization of Public Life in Kuwait." In *The Politics of Islamic Finance,* edited by C. Henry, 168–190. Edinburgh: Edinburgh University Press, 2004.

Tétreault, M. *Stories of Democracy: Politics and Society in Contemporary Kuwait.* New York: Columbia University Press, 2000.

Walbridge, L., ed. *The Most Learned of the Shi'a: The Institution of the Marja' Taqlid.* New York: Oxford University Press, 2001.

Wright, S. *Generational Change and Elite-Driven Reforms in the Kingdom of Bahrain.* Sir William Luce Fellowship Paper no. 7, Durham Middle East Papers, Durham, June 2006.

Zahlan, R. *The Making of the Modern Gulf States: Kuwait, Bahrain, Qatar, the United Arab Emirates and Oman.* London: Hyman, 1989.

24. Yemen *(Iris Glosemeyer)*

Bruck, G. vom. *Islam, Memory, and Morality in Yemen: Ruling Families in Transition.* New York: Palgrave Macmillan, 2005.

Carapico, S. *Civil Society in Yemen.* Cambridge: Cambridge University Press, 1998.

Daum, W., ed. *Yemen: 3000 Years of Art and Civilization in Arabia Felix.* Innsbruck: Pinguin-Verlag, 1987.

Douglas, L. *The Free Yemeni Movement, 1935–1962.* Beirut: American University of Beirut, 1987.

Dresch, P. *Tribes, Government, and History in Yemen.* Oxford: Oxford University Press, 1989.

——. *A History of Modern Yemen.* Cambridge: Cambridge University Press, 2000.

Glosemeyer, I. *Politische Akteure in der Republik Jemen.* Hamburg: Deutsches Orient-Institut, 2001.

Halliday, F. *Arabia without Sultans.* Harmondsworth: Penguin Books, 1974.

Lackner, H. *P.D.R. Yemen: Outpost of Socialist Development in Arabia.* London: Ithaca Press, 1985.

Leveau, R., F. Mermier, and U. Steinbach, eds. *Le Yémen contemporain.* Paris: Éditions Karthala, 1999.

Peterson, J. E. *Yemen: The Search for a Modern State.* Baltimore: Johns Hopkins University Press, 1982.

Weir, S. *A Tribal Order: Politics and Law in the Mountains of Yemen.* London: British Museum Press, 2007.

Wenner, M. W. *Modern Yemen, 1918–66.* Baltimore: Johns Hopkins University Press, 1967.

Würth, A. *Ash-Sharī'a fī Bāb al-Yaman: Recht, Richter und Rechtspraxis an der familienrechtlichen Kammer des Gerichtes Süd-Sanaa (Republik Jemen), 1983–1995.* Berlin: Duncker & Humblot, 2000.

V. The Islamic Diaspora

1. Western Europe and 2. France, Great Britain, the Netherlands, and Germany *(Nico Landman)*

Abdullah, M. S. *Geschichte des Islams in Deutschland.* Graz: Verlag Styria, 1981.

——. "Muslims in Germany." In *Muslim Minorities in the West,* edited by Z. Sardar and S. Z. Abedin, 67–77. London: Institute of Muslim Minority Affairs, 1995.

Allievi, S. "Islam and Society: Public Space and Integration, the Media." In *Muslims in the Enlarged Europe: Religion and Society,* edited by B. Maréchal, S. Allievi, F. Dassetto, and J. S. Nielsen, 289–329. Leiden: Brill, 2003.

Allievi, S., and J. S. Nielsen, eds. *Muslim Networks and Transnational Communities in and across Europe.* Leiden: Brill, 2003.

Andézian, S. "Migrant Muslim Women in France." In *The New Islamic Presence in Western Europe,* edited by T. Gerholm and Y. G. Lithman, 196–204. London: Mansell Publishing, 1988.

Ansari, H. *The Infidel Within: The History of Muslims in Britain from 1800 to the Present.* London: C. Hurst & Co., 2004.

Azimi, A., and M. Brückner. "Muslim Communities in German Webspace." Paper presented at the conference "The Impact of Information and Communication Technologies on Religious, Ethnic and Cultural Diaspora Communities in the West," University of Göteborg, Sweden, 2003.

Binswanger, K., and F. Sipahioglu. *Türkisch-islamische Vereine als Faktor deutsch-türkischer Koexistenz.* Benediktbeuren: Riess, 1988.

Boyer, A. *L'islam en France.* Paris: Presses universitaires de France, 1998.

Bundeszentrale für politische Bildung. "Muslime in Europa." *Politik und Zeitgeschichte,* no. 20 (2005).

Canatan, K., C. H. Oudijk et al. *De maatschappelijke rol van de Rotterdamse moskeeën.* Rotterdam: Centrum voor Onderzoek en Statistiek, 2003.

Canatan, K., M. Popovic et al. *Maatschappelijk actief in moskeeverband: Een verkennend onderzoek naar de maatschappelijke activiteiten van het vrijwilligerswerk binnen moskeeorganisaties en het gemeentelijk beleid ten aanzien van moskeeorganisaties.* Utrecht: Ihsan, 2005.

Cesari, J. "Muslim Minorities in Europe: The Silent Revolution." In *Modernizing Islam: Religion in the Public Sphere in Europe and the Middle East,* edited by J. L. Esposito and F. Burgat, 251–269. London: Hurst, 2003.

Clark, P. "Van fantasie naar geloof: islamitische invloeden op de openbare ruimte in Groot-Brittanië." In *Naar een Europese Islam? Essays,* edited by D. Douwes, 163–186. Amsterdam: Mets & Schild, 2001.

Dassetto, F. *La construction de l'islam européen: approche socio-anthropologique.* Paris: L'Harmattan, 1996.

Feindt-Riggers, N., and U. Steinbach. *Islamische Organisationen in Deutschland: Eine aktuelle Bestandsaufnahme und Analyse.* Hamburg: Deutsches Orient-Institut, 1997.

Goldberg, A. "Islam in Germany." In *Islam, Europe's Second Religion,* edited by S. T. Hunter, 29–50. Westport, Conn.: Praeger, 2002.

Haut Conseil à l'Intégration. *L'Islam dans la République.* Paris: La Documentation française, 2000.

Heimbach, M. *Die Entwicklung der islamischen Gemeinschaft in Deutschland seit 1961.* Berlin: Klaus Schwarz Verlag, 2001.

Höpp, G., and G. Jonker. *In fremder Erde: Zur Geschichte und Gegenwart der islamischen Bestattung in Deutschland.* Berlin: Verl. Das Arabische Buch, 1996.

Hussain, D. "The Holy Grail of Muslims in Western Europe: Representation and Their Relationship with the State." In *Modernizing Islam: Religion in the Public Sphere in Europe and the Middle East,* edited by J. L. Esposito and F. Burgat, 215–250. London: Hurst, 2003.

Johansen, B. "Staat, Recht und Religion im sunnitischen Islam: Können Muslime einen religionsneutralen Staat akzeptieren?" In *Religion in fremder Kultur: Religion als Minderheit in Europa und Asien,* edited by M. Pye and R. Stegerhoff, 12–81. Saarbrücken-Scheidt: Dadder, 1987.

Jonker, G. "Religiosität und Partizipation der zweiten Generation: Frauen in Berliner Moscheen." In *Der neue Islam der Frauen: Weibliche Lebenspraxis in der globalisierten Moderne; Fallstudien aus Afrika, Asien und Europa, R. Klein-Hessling,* edited by S. Nökel and K. Werner, 106–123. Bielefeld: Transcript Verlag, 1999.

———. *Eine Wellenlänge zu Gott: Der Verband der Islamischen Kulturzentren in Europa.* Bielefeld: Verlag für Kommunikation, Kultur und soziale Praxis, 2002.

Kepel, G. *A l'ouest d'Allah.* Paris: Seuil, 1994.

Khedimellah, M. "Aesthetics and Poetics of Apostolic Islam in France." *ISIM Newsletter* 11, no. 2 (2002): 20–21.

Khosrokhavar, F. "Terrorism in Europe." *ISIM Newsletter* 14 (2004): 11.

Kroissenbrunner, S. "Islam in Austria." In *Islam, Europe's Second Religion,* edited by S. T. Hunter, 141–156. Westport, Conn.: Praeger, 2002.

Landman, N. *Van mat tot minaret: De institutionalisering van de islam in Nederland.* Amsterdam: VU-Uitgeverij, 1992.

Lemmen, T. *Islamische Organisationen in Deutschland.* Bonn: Friedrich-Ebert-Stiftung, 2000.

Lopez Garcia, B. "A. Planet Contreras: Islam in Spain." In *Islam, Europe's Second Religion,* edited by S. T. Hunter, 157–174. Westport, Conn.: Praeger, 2002.

Malik, J., ed. *Muslims in Europe: From the Margins to the Center.* Münster: LIT, 2004.

Manço, U., and M. Renaerts. "Lente institutionnalisation de l'islam et persistance d'inégalités face aux autres cultes reconnus." In *Voix et voies musulmanes en Belgique,* edited by U. Manço, 83–106. Brussels: Publications des Facultés universitaires Saint-Louis, 2000.

Maréchal, B., ed. *L'islam et les musulmans dans l'Europe élargie: radioscopie.* Louvain-la-Neuve: Academia Bruylant, 2002.

——. "Institutionalization of Islam and Representative Organizations for Dealing with European States." In *Muslims in the Enlarged Europe: Religion and Society,* edited by B. Maréchal, S. Allievi, F. Dassetto, and J. S. Nielsen, 151–182. Leiden: Brill, 2003a.

——. "Islam and Society: Public Space and Integration, the Economic Dimension." In *Muslims in the Enlarged Europe: Religion and Society,* edited by B. Maréchal, S. Allievi, F. Dassetto, and J. S. Nielsen, 415–448. Leiden: Brill, 2003b.

——. "Modalities of Islamic Instruction." In *Muslims in the Enlarged Europe: Religion and Society,* edited by B. Maréchal, S. Allievi, F. Dassetto, and J. S. Nielsen, 19–78. Leiden: Brill, 2003c.

Masud, M. Kh. "Islamic Law and Muslim Minorities." *ISIM Newsletter* 11 (2002): 17.

Matar, N. *Islam in Britain, 1558–1685.* Cambridge: Cambridge University Press, 1998.

Modood, T. "De plaats van de moslims in het Britse seculier multiculturalisme." In *Naar een Europese Islam? Essays,* edited by D. Douwes, 51–76. Amsterdam: Mets & Schild, 2001.

Oebbecke, J., ed. *Muslimische Gemeinschaften im deutschen Recht.* Frankfurt am Main: Lang, 2003.

Ramadan, T. *Être Musulman européen: étude des sources islamiques à la lumière du contexte européen.* Lyon: Tawheed, 1999.

Rath, J., R. Penninx et al. *Nederland en zijn islam: een ontzuilende samenleving reageert op het ontstaan van een geloofsgemeenschap.* Amsterdam: Het Spinhuis, 1996.

Rex, J. "Islam in the United Kingdom." In *Islam, Europe's Second Religion,* edited by T. Hunter, 51–76. Westport, Conn.: Praeger, 2002.

Roald, A. S. *Women in Islam: The Western Experience.* London: Routledge, 2001.

Rohe, M. "Islam und deutsche Rechtsordnung: Möglichkeiten und Grenzen der Bildung islamischer Religionsgemeinschaften in Deutschland." *Der Bürger im Staat* 51, no. 4 (2001): 233–240.

——, ed. "Sharī'a in Europe." *Die Welt des Islams* 44 (2004): 321–431.

Roy, O. *Vers un Islam européen.* Paris: Esprit, 1999.

——. *L'islam mondialisé.* Paris: Le Seuil, 2002.

Schiffauer, W. *Die Migranten aus Subay: Türken in Deutschland; Eine Ethnographie.* Stuttgart: Klett-Cotta, 1991.

——. *Die Gottesmänner: Türkische Islamisten in Deutschland.* Frankfurt am Main: Suhrkamp Verlag, 2000.

Seidel, E., C. Dantschke et al. *Politik im Namen Allahs: Der Islamismus; Eine Herausforderung für Europa.* Rüsselsheim: Ozan Ceyhun, 2001.

Seufert, Günter. "Die Türkisch-Islamische Union (DITIB) der türkischen Religionsbehörde: Zwischen Integration und Isolation." In *Turkish Islam and Europe: Europe and Christianity as Reflected in Turkish Muslim Discourse and Turkish Muslim Life in the Diaspora,* edited by G. Seufert and J. Waardenburg, 261–294. Stuttgart: Steiner, 1999.

Spuler-Stegemann, U. *Muslime in Deutschland: Nebeneinander oder Miteinander?* Freiburg: Herder, 1998. (New edition: *Muslime in Deutschland: Informationen und Klärungen.* Freiburg: Herder spektrum, 2002.)

——. "Muslime in Deutschland: Organisationen und Gruppierungen." *Der Bürger im Staat* 51, no. 4 (2001): 221–225.

Sunier, T. "Disconnecting Religion and Ethnicity: Young Turkish Muslims in the Netherlands." In *Post-migration Ethnicity,* edited by T. Sunier and G. Baumann, 58–77. Amsterdam: Het Spinhuis, 1995.

Tezcan, L. "Inszenierungen kollektiver Identität, Artikulationen des politischen Islam, beobachtet auf den Massenversammlungen der türkisch-islamistischen Gruppe Milli Görüs." *Soziale Welt* 53 (2002): 301–322.

——. "Das Islamische in den Studien zu Muslimen in Deutschland." *Zeitschrift für Soziologie* 32, no. 3 (2003): 237–261.

Vertovec, S., and R. Alisdair, eds. *Muslim European Youth Reproducing Ethnicity, Religion, Culture.* Research in Ethnic Relations Series. Aldershot: Ashgate, 1998.

Werbner, P. "Public Spaces, Political Voices: Gender, Feminism and Aspects of British Muslim Participation in the Public Sphere." In *Political Participation and Identities of Muslims in Non-Muslim States,* edited by W. A. R. Shadid and P. S. van Koningsveld, 53–70. Kampen: Kok Pharos, 1996.

——. "The Place Which Is Diaspora: Citizenship, Religion and Gender in the Making of Chaordic Transnationalism." *Journal of Ethnic and Migration Studies* 28 (2002): 119–133.

3. Eastern and Southeastern Europe *(Hermann Kandler)*

Asmussen, J. *"Wir waren wie Brüder": Zusammenleben und Konfliktentstehung in ethnisch gemischten Dörfern auf Zypern.* Münster: LIT Verlag, 2003.

Axt, H.-J. "Zypern: der Annan-Friedensplan und sein Scheitern." *Südosteuropa-Mitteilungen* 44 (2004): 48–66.

Axt, H.-J., and Brey, H., eds. "Cyprus and the European Union: New Chances for Solving an Old Conflict?" *Südosteuropa aktuell* 23 (1997): 247–255.

Calic, M.-J. "Kosovo: Krieg oder Konfliktlösung?" *Südosteuropa-Mitteilungen* 38 (1998): 112–123.

Calotychos, V., ed. *Cyprus and Its People: Nation, Identity, and Experience in an Unimaginable Community, 1955–1997.* Boulder, Colo.: Westview Press, 1998.

Glenny, M. *The Balkans: Nationalism, War, and the Great Powers, 1804–1999.* East Rutherford, N.J.: Penguin, 2001.

Goffman, D., ed. *The Ottoman Empire and Early Modern Europe.* Cambridge: Cambridge University Press, 2002.

Kandler, H. "Die anatolische 'Bruchlinie': Chance für ein neues Fremdbewusstsein bei Türken und Griechen." *Orient* 41 (2000): 65–82.

——. "Sadık Ahmet (1947–1995): Politischer 'Spaltpilz' Griechisch-Thrakiens." *Orient* 39 (1998) 285–307.

Malcolm, N. *Bosnia: A Short History.* New York: New York University Press, 1996.

Nonneman, G., T. Niblock, and B. Szajkowski. *Muslim Communities in the New Europe.* Reading, Berkshire: Ithaca Press, 1997.

Poulton, H. *The Balkans: Minorities and States in Conflict.* London: Minority Rights Group, 1994.

Seewann, G., ed. *Minderheiten als Konfliktpotential in Ostmittel- und Südosteuropa.* Munich: Oldenbourg, 1995.

Steindorff, L. "Von der Konfession zur Nation: Die Muslime in Bosnien-Herzegowina." *Südosteuropa-Mitteilungen* 37 (1997): 251–264.

——. "Der lange Weg zum Kosovo-Krieg." *Südosteuropa-Mitteilungen* 37 (1997): 193–206.

Suttner, E. C. "Das religiöse Moment in seiner Bedeutung für Gesellschaft, Nationsbildung und Kultur Südosteuropas." *Südosteuropa-Mitteilungen* 37 (1997): 1–9.

Todorova, M. *Die Erfindung des Balkans: Europas bequemes Vorurteil.* Darmstadt: Wissenschaftliche Buchgesellschaft, 1999.

Troebst, St. "Die albanische Frage: Entwicklungsszenarien und Steuerungsinstrumente." *Südosteuropa-Mitteilungen* 40 (2000): 124–137.

——. "Kommunizierende Röhren: Makedonien, die Albanische Frage und der Kosovo-Konflikt." *Südosteuropa-Mitteilungen* 39 (1999): 215–229.

Voss, C. "Der albanisch-makedonische Konflikt in der Republik Makedonien in zeitgeschichtlicher Perspektive." *Südosteuropa-Mitteilungen* 41 (2001): 271–281.

4. The Americas *(Monika Wohlrab-Sahr)*

Abdo, G. *Mecca and Main Street: Muslim Life in America after 9/11.* Oxford: Oxford University Press, 2006.

Essien-Udom, E. U. *Black Nationalism: A Search for an Identity in America.* Chicago: University of Chicago Press, 1962.

Haddad, Y. Y. *A Century of Islam in America: The Muslim World Today.* Occasional Paper no. 4. Washington, D.C.: Middle East Institute, 1986.

Haddad, Y. Y., and J. L. Esposito, eds. *Muslims on the Americanization Path?* Atlanta: Scholars Press, 1998.

Köszegi, M. A., and J. G. Melton, eds. *Islam in North America: A Sourcebook.* New York: Garland, 1992.

Malcolm X (with the assistance of A. Haley). *The Autobiography of Malcolm X.* New York: Grove Press, 1966.

McCloud, A. B. *African American Islam.* New York: Routledge, 1995.

Melton, J. G. *Encyclopedia of American Religions.* Detroit: Gale Research, 1993.

Moses, W. J. *Black Messiahs and Uncle Toms: Social and Literary Manipulations of a Religious Myth.* University Park: Pennsylvania State University Press, 1993.

Muhammad, E. *Message to the Blackman in America.* Chicago: Nation of Islam, 1965.

Schmidt, G. *Islam in Urban America.* Philadelphia: Temple University Press, 2004.

Wohlrab-Sahr, M. "Conversion to Islam in Germany and the United States." In *Embracing Islam: Gender and Conversion in the West,* edited by Karin van Nieuwkerk, 71–92. Austin: University of Texas Press, 2006.

——. *Konversion zum Islam in Deutschland und den USA.* Frankfurt am Main: Campus, 1999.

VI. The Discussion within Islam on Secularism, Democracy, and Human Rights *(Alexander Flores)*

al-Ashmawy, M. S. *L'islamisme contre l'islam.* Paris: La Découverte, and Cairo: Al-Fikr, 1989.

an-Naʿim, A. A. *Toward an Islamic Reform.* Cairo: AUC Press, 1992.

Bielefeldt, H. "Schwächlicher Werterelativismus?" In *Der Islam und der Westen,* edited by K. Hafez, 56–66. Frankfurt am Main: Fischer Taschenbuch, 1997.

Ferjani, M.-C. *Islamisme, laïcité, et droits de l'homme.* Paris: L'Harmattan, 1991.

Flores, A. "Rutschpartie in den Gottesstaat?" In *Festschrift Prof. Dr. Detlef Schumacher,* edited by W. E. Rossig and J. Prätsch, 69–84. Bremen: Hochschule Bremen, 2003.

——. "Die säkulare Dimension." *Entwicklungspolitische Korrespondenz* 5–6 (1987): 44–47.

——. "Säkularismus und Islam in Ägypten." In *XXV. Deutscher Orientalistentag, Vorträge*, edited by C. Wunsch, 174–182. Stuttgart: Franz Steiner, 1994.

——. "Secularism, Integralism, and Political Islam." In *Political Islam: Essays from Middle East Report*, edited by J. Beinin and J. Stork, 83–94. Berkeley: University of California Press, 1997.

Khoury, P. *L'Islam et l'Occident: Islam et Sécularité*. Neckarhausen: Deux Mondes, 1998.

Krämer, G. *Gottes Staat als Republik: Reflexionen zeitgenössischer Muslime zu Islam, Menschenrechten und Demokratie*. Baden-Baden: Nomos, 1999.

Müller, L. *Islam und Menschenrechte: Sunnitische Muslime zwischen Islamismus, Säkularismus und Modernismus*. Hamburg: German Orient Institute, 1996.

Rasoul, F. "Islam und Säkularismus: Protokoll einer Diskussion." In *Kultureller Dialog und Gewalt*, edited by S. Rockenschaub-Rasoul, 139–201. Vienna: Junius, 1991.

Schölch, A. "Säkularistische Traditionen im Vorderen Orient." In *Jahrbuch 1985–86 des Wissenschaftskollegs zu Berlin*, 191–201. Berlin: Siedler, 1987.

Schulze, R. "Integration der Menschenrechtskonzeption in die islamische Ideologie." In *Menschenrechte im Vorderen Orient: Eine Auswahlbibliographie*, edited by I. Otto and M. Schmidt-Dumont, vii–xxiii. Hamburg: German Orient Institute, 1991.

——. "Der politische Islam im 20. Jahrhundert." *Entwicklungspolitische Korrespondenz* 5–6 (1987): 7–11.

Steppat, F. "Der Muslim und die Obrigkeit." In *Islam als Partner: Islamkundliche Aufsätze, 1944–1996*, 109–127. Beirut: Orient Institute, 2001.

Trautner, B. J. *The Clash within Civilizations: Islam and the Accomodation of Plurality*. Bremen: University of Bremen, Institute for Intercultural and International Studies, 1999.

Zakariya, F., *Laïcité ou islamisme: les Arabes à l'heure du choix*. Paris: La Découverte, and Cairo: Al-Fikr, 1991.

VII. The Situation of Women in Islamic Countries *(Wiebke Walther)*

Abadan-Unat, N., ed. *Women in Turkish Society*. Leiden: Brill, 1981.

al-Munajjed, M. *Women in Saudi Arabia Today*. London: Macmillan, 1997.

Amirpur, K. *Gott ist mit den Furchtlosen: Schirin Ebadi und der Kampf um die Zukunft Irans*. Freiburg: Herder, 2003.

Badran, M. *Feminists, Islam, and Nation: Gender and the Making of Modern Egypt*. Princeton: Princeton University Press, 1995.

Badran, M., and M. Cooke, eds. *Opening the Gates: A Century of Arab Feminist Writing*. London: Virago, 1990.

Baron, B. *The Women's Awakening in Egypt: Culture, Society, and the Press*. New Haven: Yale University Press, 1994.

Beck, L., and N. R. Keddie, eds. *Women in the Muslim World*. Cambridge: Harvard University Press, 1978.

Davis, F. *The Ottoman Lady: A Social History from 1718 to 1918*. Westport, Conn.: Greenwood Press, 1986.

Dennerlein, B. "Islamisches Recht und sozialer Wandel in Algerien: Zur Entwicklung des Personalstatus seit 1962." Berlin: Schwarz, 1998.

Donohue, J. J., and L. Tramontini, eds. *Crosshatching in Global Culture: A Dictionary of Modern Arab Writers*. 2 vols. Beirut: Ergon, 2004.

Ebert, H. *Das Personalstatut arabischer Länder: Problemfelder, Methoden, Perspektiven.* Frankfurt am Main: Peter Lang, 1996.

Fernea, E. W., ed. *In Search of Islamic Feminism: One Woman's Global Journey.* New York: Doubleday, 1998.

Haddad, Y. Y., and J. L. Esposito, eds. *Islam, Gender, and Social Change.* New York: Oxford University Press, 1998.

Haeri, S. *Law of Desire: Temporary Marriage in Iran.* London: Tauris, 1989.

Hijab, N. *Womanpower: The Arab Debate on Women at Work.* New York: Cambridge University Press, 1988.

Jabbra, J., and N. Jabbra, eds. *Women and Development in the Middle East and North Africa.* Leiden: Brill, 1992.

Joseph, S., ed. *Encyclopedia of Women and Islamic Cultures.* 6 vols. Leiden: Brill, 2003–2007.

——, ed. *Intimate Selving in Arab Families: Gender, Self, and Identity.* Syracuse: Syracuse University Press, 1999.

Kandiyoti, Deniz, ed. *Gendering the Middle East.* London: Tauris, 1996.

——, ed. *Women, Islam, and the State.* London: Macmillan, 1991.

Kuske, S. *Reislamisierung und Familienrecht in Algerien.* Berlin: Schwarz, 1996.

Milani, F. *Veils and Words: The Emerging Voices of Iranian Women Writers.* Syracuse: Syracuse University Press, 1992.

Mir-Hosseini, Z. *Islam and Gender in the Muslim World: The Religious Debate in Contemporary Iran.* Princeton: Princeton University Press, 1999.

Moghadam, V. M., ed. *Gender and National Identity.* London: Zed Books, 1994.

——. *Modernizing Women: Gender and Social Change in the Middle East.* Boulder, Colo.: Rienner, 1993 (reprint, 2003).

Moghissi, H. *Feminism and Islamic Fundamentalism: The Limits of Postmodern Analysis.* London: Zed Books, 1999.

——, ed. *Women and Islam.* Vol. 1, *Images and Realities;* Vol. 2, *Social Conditions, Obstacles and Prospects;* Vol. 3, *Women's Movements in Muslim Societies.* London: Routledge, 2008.

Mutahhari, M. *The Rights of Women in Islam.* Tehran: World Organization of Islamic Services, 1980 (also available at www.al-islam.org).

Naggar, M., and K. al-Maaly, eds. *Lexikon arabischer Autoren des 19. und 20. Jahrhunderts.* Heidelberg: Palmyra, 2004.

Nashat, G. *Women and Revolution in Iran.* Boulder, Colo.: Westwood Press, 1983.

Paydar, P. *Women and the Political Process in 20th Century Iran.* Cambridge: Cambridge University Press, 1995.

Poya, M. *Women, Work and Islamism: Ideology and Resistance in Islam.* London: Zed Books, 1999.

Saktanber, A. *Living Islam: Women, Religion and the Politicization of Culture in Turkey.* London: Tauris, 2002.

Sanasarian, E. *The Women's Rights Movement in Iran: Mutiny, Appeasement, and Repression from 1900 to Khomeini.* New York: Praeger, 1982.

Sedghi, H. *Women and Politics in Iran: Veiling, Unveiling, Reveiling.* Cambridge: Cambridge University Press, 2007.

Shaarawi, H. *Harem Years: The Memoirs of an Egyptian Feminist.* Translated, edited, and introduced by M. Badran. London: Virago, 1986.

Shahidian, H. *Women in Iran: Emerging Voices in the Women's Movement.* Westport, Conn.: Greenwood, 2002.

——. *Women in Iran: Gender Politics in the Islamic Republic.* Westport, Conn.: Greenwood, 2002.

Sullivan, E. *Women in Egyptian Public Life.* Cairo: American University in Cairo Press, 1986.

Tekeli, S., ed. *Women in Modern Turkish Society: A Reader.* London: Zed Books, 1995.

Tellenbach, S. *Einführung in das türkische Strafrecht.* Freiburg im Breisgau: Ed. juscrim, 2003.

———, trans. and intro. *Strafgesetze der Islamischen Republik Iran.* Berlin: de Gruyter, 1996.

Walther, W. *Die Frau im Islam.* 3rd rev. ed. Leipzig: Edition, 1997.

———. "Die Frau im Islam." In *Der Islam: Religion, Ethik, Politik,* by Peter Antes et al., 98–124. Stuttgart: Kohlhammer, 1991.

———. *Women in Islam.* Princeton: Marcus Wiener, 1993. (A revised and updated edition is forthcoming.)

Webb, G., ed. *Windows of Faith: Muslim Women Scholar-Activists in North America.* Syracuse: Syracuse University Press, 2000.

Yamani, M., ed. *Feminism and Islam: Legal and Literary Perspectives.* London: Ithaca Press, 1996.

Zaydan, J. *Masadir al-adab al-nisa'i fi al-'alam al-'arabi al-hadith, 1800–1996.* Beirut: al-Mu'assasa al-'arabiyya li-l-dirasat wa-l-nashr, 1999.

VIII. Islamist Groups and Movements
(Guido Steinberg and Jan-Peter Hartung)

Arjomand, S. A. *The Turban for the Crown: The Islamic Revolution in Iran.* New York: Oxford University Press, 1988.

Ayubi, N. N. *Political Islam: Religion and Politics in the Arab World.* London: Routledge, 1991.

Damir-Geilsdorf, S. *Herrschaft und Gesellschaft: Der islamistische Wegbereiter Sayyid Quṭb und seine Rezeption.* Würzburg: Ergon, 2003.

El Affendi, A. *Turabi's Revolution: Islam and Power in Sudan.* London: Grey Seal, 1991.

Hartung, J.-P. "Reinterpretation von Tradition und der Paradigmenwechsel der Moderne: Abūl-A'lā Maudūdī und die Jamā'at-i Islāmī." In *Sendungsbewußtsein und Eigennutz: Zu Motivation und Selbstverständnis islamischer Mobilisierung,* edited by D. Reetz, 107–126. Berlin: Das Arabische Buch, 2001.

Kepel, G. *Jihad: The Trail of Political Islam.* London: I. B. Tauris, 2001.

———. *Muslim Extremism in Egypt: The Prophet and Pharaoh.* Reprinted with new preface, Berkeley: University of California Press, 2003.

Krämer, G. *Gottes Staat als Republik: Reflexionen zeitgenössischer Muslime zu Islam, Menschenrechten und Demokratie.* Baden-Baden: Nomos, 1999.

Lia, B. *The Society of the Muslim Brothers in Egypt: The Rise of an Islamic Mass Movement, 1928–1942.* Reading, Berkshire: Ithaca Press, 1998.

Lobmeyer, H. G. *Islamismus und sozialer Konflikt in Syrien.* Berlin: Das Arabische Buch, 1990.

Lübben, I., and F. Issam. "Ein neuer islamischer Parteienpluralismus in Ägypten? *Orient* 41, no. 2 (2000): 229–281.

Metcalf, B. D. *Islamic Revivalism in British India: Deoband, 1860–1900.* Princeton: Princeton University Press, 1982.

Mitchell, R. P. *The Society of the Muslim Brothers.* Reprint, New York: Oxford University Press, 1993.

Nasr, S. V. R. *The Vanguard of the Islamic Revolution: The Jama'at-i Islami of Pakistan.* Berkeley: University of California Press, 1994.

———. *Mawdudi and the Making of Islamic Revivalism.* New York: Oxford University Press, 1996.

Pirzada, S. A. S. *The Politics of the Jamiat Ulema-i-Islam Pakistan: 1971–1977.* Oxford: Oxford University Press, 2000.

Rashid, A. *Taliban: Islam, Oil and the New Great Game in Central Asia.* London: I. B. Tauris, 2000.

Reetz, D., ed. *Sendungsbewußtsein oder Eigennutz: Zu Motivation und Selbstverständnis islamischer Mobilisierung.* Berlin: Das Arabische Buch, 2001.

Reissner, J. *Ideologie und Politik der Muslimbrüder Syriens: Von den Wahlen 1947 bis zum Verbot unter Adīb aš-Šīšaklī 1952.* Freiburg: Klaus Schwarz, 1980.

Riexinger, M. *Sanā'ullāh Amritsarī (1868–1948) und die Ahl-i-Hadīs im Punjab unter britischer Herrschaft.* Würzburg: Ergon, 2004.

Rosiny, S. *Islamismus bei den Schiiten im Libanon.* Berlin: Das Arabische Buch, 1996.

Roy, O. *L'échec de l'Islam politique.* Paris: Seuil, 1992.

Schulze, R. *Islamischer Internationalismus im 20. Jahrhundert: Untersuchungen zur Geschichte der Islamischen Weltliga.* Leiden: Brill, 1990.

Sikand, Y. *The Origins and Development of the Tablighi-Jama'at (1920–2000): A Cross-country Comparative Study.* New Delhi: Orient Longman, 2002.

Sivan, E. *Radical Islam: Medieval Theology and Modern Politics.* Enlarged ed. New Haven: Yale University Press, 1990.

Wiktorowicz, Quintan. *Radical Islam Rising: Muslim Extremism in the West.* Lanham: Rowman & Littlefield, 2005.

IX. Mystical Brotherhoods and Popular Islam *(Frederick De Jong)*

Akhmisse, M. *Médicine, magie et sorcellerie au Maroc.* Casablanca: Eddar El Beida, 1985.

Bannerth, E. *Islamische Wallfahrtsstätten Kairos.* Schriften des Österreichischen Kulturinstituts Kairo 2. Wiesbaden: Harrassowitz, 1973.

Blackman, W. S. *The Fellāhīn of Upper Egypt.* London: George Harrap, 1927.

Curtiss, S. I. *Ursemitische Religion im Volksleben des heutigen Orients.* Leipzig: J. C. Hinrichs, 1903.

De Jong, F. "Turuq and Turuq-Opposition in 20th-Century Egypt." In *Proceedings of the Sixth Congress of Arabic and Islamic Studies,* 84–95. Filologisk-filosofiska series 15. Stockholm: Almqvist & Wiksell International, 1975.

———. "Cairene Ziyāra-Days: A Contribution to the Study of Saint Veneration in Islam." *Die Welt des Islams* 17 (1976–77): 26–43.

———. "The Sufi Orders in Nineteenth- and Twentieth-Century Palestine." *Studia Islamica* 58 (1983): 191–223.

Dermenghem, E. *Le culte des saints dans l'Islam maghrébin.* Paris: Gallimard, 1954.

Donaldson, B. A. *The Wild Rue.* London: Luzac, 1938.

Einzmann, H. *Religiöses Volksbrauchtum in Afghanistan: Islamische Heiligenverehrung und Wallfahrtswesen im Raum Kabul.* Beiträge zur Südasien-Forschung. Wiesbaden: Franz Steiner, 1977.

Fodor, A. "Types of Shi'ite Amulets from Iraq." In *Shi'a Islam, Sects, and Sufism: Historical Dimensions, Religious Practice, and Methodological Considerations,* edited by F. De Jong, 118–143. Utrecht: Houtsma Stichting, 1982.

Goldziher, I. *Muhammedanische Studien.* 2 vols. Halle: Max Niemeyer, 1889–1890.

Horten, M. *Die religiöse Gedankenwelt des Volkes im heutigen Islam.* 2 parts. Halle: Max Niemeyer, 1917–18.

Krawietz, B. "Islamic Conceptions of the Evil Eye." *Medicine and Law* 21 (2002): 339–355.

Kriss, R., and H. Kriss-Heinrich. *Volksglaube im Bereich des Islam.* Vol. 1, *Wallfahrtswesen und Heiligenverehrung;* Vol. 2, *Amulette, Zauberformeln und Beschwörungen.* Wiesbaden: Otto Harrassowitz, 1960–1962.

Loeffler, R. *Islam in Practice: Religious Beliefs in a Persian Village.* Albany: State University of New York Press, 1988.

Reysoo, F. *Pèlerinages au Maroc: fête, politique et échange dans l'islam populaire.* Neuchâtel: Institut d'Ethnologie Neuchâtel, 1991.

Schimmel, A. *And Muhammad Is His Messenger: The Veneration of the Prophet in Islamic Piety.* Chapel Hill: University of North Carolina Press, 1985.

Seligmann, S. *Der böse Blick und Verwandtes: Ein Beitrag zur Geschichte des Aberglaubens aller Zeiten und Völker.* 2 vols. Berlin: Hermann Barsdorf, 1910.

Trimingham, J. S. *Islam in the Sudan.* London: Oxford University Press, 1949 (reprint 1965).

———. *The Sufi Orders in Islam.* New York: Oxford University Press, 1971.

Wallis Budge, E. A. *Amulets and Superstitions.* New York: Dover, 1978.

Winkler, H. A. *Siegel und Charaktere in der muhammedanischen Zauberei.* Berlin: Walter de Gruyter, 1930.

———. *Bauern zwischen Wasser und Wüste: Volkskundliches aus dem Dorfe Kimān in Oberägypten.* Stuttgart: Kohlhammer, 1934.

———. *Die reitenden Geister der Toten: Eine Studie über die Besessenheit des ʿAbd al-Rādī und über Gespenster und Dämonen, Heilige und Verzückte, Totenkult und Priestertum in einem oberägyptischen Dorfe.* Stuttgart: Kohlhammer, 1936.

Zbinden, E. *Die Djinn des Islam und der altorientalische Geisterglaube.* Bern: Paul Haupt, 1953.

X. Sects and Special Groups *(Werner Schmucker)*

Ben-Dor, G. *The Druze of Israel.* Jerusalem: Magnes Press, 1979.

Cole, J., et al. "Bahai Faith or Bahaism." In *Encyclopaedia Iranica,* vol. 3, 438–475. London: Routledge and Kegan Paul, 1989.

Custers, M. H. *Ibadis of the Mashriq.* Maastricht: Custers, 2006.

Daftary, F. *The Ismāʿīlīs: Their History and Faith.* Cambridge: Cambridge University Press, 1990.

The Encyclopaedia of Islam. 2nd ed. 12 vols. Leiden: Brill, 1960–2004. (Entries [by various authors] "Ahl-i Ḥaḳḳ," "Aḥmadiyya," "Bahāʾīs" "Al-Ibāḍiyya," "Ismāʿīliyya," "Nuṣayriyya," "Yazīdī.")

Friedmann, Y. *Prophecy Continuous: Aspects of Ahmadi Religious Thought and Its Medieval Background.* New Delhi: Oxford University Press, 2003.

Hodgson, M. *The Order of Assassins.* The Hague: Mouton, 1955. (Reprint, New York: AMS Press, 1980.)

Holley, H., ed. *Bahāʾi Scriptures: Selections from the Utterances of Bahāʾuʾllāh and ʿAbduʾl-Bahāʾ.* New York: Brentano's, 1923–1928.

Karolewski, J. "What Is Heterodox about Alevism?" *Die Welt des Islams* 48 (2008): 434–456.

Kreyenbroek, P. G. *Yezidism*. Lewiston, N.Y.: Mellen, 1995.
Lewis, B. *The Origins of Ismāʿīlism*. Cambridge: Cambridge University Press, 1940–1975.
Makarim, S. N. *The Druze Faith*. Delmar, N.Y.: Caravan Books, 1974.
Momen, M. *Islam and the Bahá'i Faith*. Oxford: G. Ronald, 2000.
Müller, K. E. *Kulturhistorische Studien zur Genese pseudo-islamischer Sektengebilde in Vorderasien*. Wiesbaden: Franz Steiner, 1967.
Ourghi, A.-H. *Die Reformbewegung in der neuzeitlichen Ibadiya*. Würzburg: Ergon, 2008.
Schmucker, W. *Krise und Erneuerung im libanesischen Drusentum*. Bonn: Selbstverlag des Orientalischen Seminars der Universität Bonn, 1979.
White, P. J., and J. Jongerden. *Turkey's Alevi Enigma: A Comprehensive Overview*. Leiden: Brill, 2003.

XI. Islam and Non-Islamic Minorities *(Johanna Pink)*

Betts, Robert B. *Christians in the Arab East: A Political Study*. Atlanta: Knox, 1978.
Courbage, Y., and P. Fargues. *Christians and Jews under Islam*. London: Tauris, 1997.
Fattal, A. *Le statut légal des Non-Musulmans en pays d'Islam*. Beirut: Imprimerie catholique, 1958.
Khuri, F. I. *Imams and Emirs: State, Religion and Sects in Islam*. London: Saqi Books, 1990.
Krämer, G. *The Jews in Modern Egypt, 1914–1952*. Seattle: University of Washington Press, 1989.
——. "Minorities in Muslim Societies." In *The Oxford Encyclopedia of the Modern Islamic World*, edited by J. L. Esposito, vol. 3, 108–111. Oxford: Oxford University Press, 1995.
——, ed. *Anti-Semitism in the Arab World. Die Welt des Islams* 46, no. 3 (2006) (special theme issue).
Lewis, B. *The Jews of Islam*. Princeton: Princeton University Press, 1984.
Noth, A. "Möglichkeiten und Grenzen islamischer Toleranz." *Saeculum* 29 (1978): 190–204.
Pink, J. "The Concept of Freedom of Belief and Its Boundaries in Egypt: Jehovah's Witnesses and the Baha'i Faith between Established Religions and an Authoritarian State." *Culture and Religion* 6 (2005): 135–160.
Sanasarian, E. *Religious Minorities in Iran*. Cambridge: Cambridge University Press, 2000.
Shatzmiller, M., ed. *Nationalism and Minority Identities in Islamic Societies*. Montreal: McGill–Queen's University Press, 2005.
Stillman, N. A. *The Jews of Arab Lands in Modern Times*. Philadelphia: Jewish Publication Society, 1991.

XII. International Islamic Organizations *(Johannes Reissner)*

Bouteiller, G., de. "Après Taef 1981: la Nation Islamique?" *Défense Nationale* (April 1981): 97–105.
Deutsches Orient-Institut (T. Koszinowski and H. Mattes), ed. *Nahost Jahrbuch, 1987–*. Opladen: Leske & Budrich, 1988–.
Gibb, H. A. R. "The Islamic Congress at Jerusalem in December 1931." *Survey of International Affairs, 1934* (1935): 99–109.

Hartmann, R. "Zum Gedanken des 'Kongresses' in den Reformbestrebungen des islamischen Orients." *Die Welt des Islams* 23 (1941): 122–132.

Kramer, M. S. *Islam Assembled: The Advent of the Muslim Congresses.* New York: Columbia University Press, 1986.

——. *An Introduction to World Islamic Conferences.* Occasional Papers 63. Tel Aviv: Shiloah Center for Middle Eastern and African Studies, 1978.

Kupferschmidt, U. M. "The General Muslim Congress of 1931 in Jerusalem." *Asian and African Studies* 12 (1978): 123–157.

Landau, J. M. *The Politics of Pan-Islam: Ideology and Organization.* Oxford: Clarendon, 1990.

Schöne, E. *Islamische Solidarität: Geschichte, Politik, Ideologie der Organisation der Islamischen Konferenz (OIC), 1969–1981.* Islamkundliche Untersuchungen Band 214. Berlin: Klaus Schwarz, 1997.

Schulze, R. *Islamischer Internationalismus im 20. Jahrhundert.* Leiden: Brill, 1990.

Sékaly, A. "Les deux Congrès généraux de 1926: le Congrès du Khalifat (Le Caire, 13–19 mai 1926) et le Congrès du monde musulman (La Mecque, 7. juin—5. juillet 1926)." *Revue du monde musulman* 64 (1926).

Part Three
Present-Day Islamic Culture and Civilization

I. "Orientalistics" and Orientalism *(Reinhard Schulze)*

Abaza, M., and G. Stauth. "Occidental Reason, Orientalism, Islamic Fundamentalism: A Critique." *International Sociology* 3, no. 4 (1988): 343–364.

Abdel-Malek, A. *La dialectique sociale.* Paris: Éditions du Seuil, 1972.

——. "L'orientalisme en crise." *Diogène* 44 (1963): 109–142.

al-Azmeh, A. "The Articulation of Orientalism." In *Orientalism, Islam, and Islamists,* edited by A. Hussain et al., 384–402. Brattleboro, Vt.: Amana Books, 1984.

Ammann, L. "Islamwissenschaften." In *Phänomen Kultur: Perspektiven und Aufgaben der Kulturwissenschaften,* edited by E. Klaus, 71–96. Bielefeld: Transcript, 2003.

——. *Östliche Spiegel: Ansichten vom Orient im Zeitalter seiner Entdeckung durch den deutschen Leser 1800–1850.* Hildesheim: Olms, 1989.

Arberry, A. J. *British Orientalists.* London: W. Collins, 1943.

Arkoun, Mohammed. "L'Islam moderne vu par le professeur G. E. von Grunebaum." *Arabica* 11 (1964): 113–124.

——. "La perception arabe de l'Europe." *Awraq* (Madrid) 10 (1989): 25–39.

——. *Pour une critique de la raison islamique.* Vols. 1 and 2. Paris: Maisonneuve et Larose, 1984.

Bartol'd, V. V. *La découverte de l'Asie: histoire de l'orientalisme en Europe et en Russie.* Paris: Payot, 1947.

Behdad, Ali. "The Discursive Formation of Orientalism." *L'orientalisme: Interrogations, Peuples méditerraneens* 50 (1990): 163–170.

——. "Orientalist tourism." *L'orientalisme: Interrogations, Peuples méditerraneens* 50 (1990): 41–58.

Behrmann, G. *Hamburgs Orientalisten.* Hamburg: Persiehl, 1901.

Benfey, T. *Geschichte der Sprachwissenschaft und orientalischen Philologie in Deutschland seit dem Anfang des 19. Jahrhunderts mit einem Rückblick auf die früheren Zeiten.* Munich: J. G. Cotta, 1896.

Binder, L. "Deconstructing Orientalism." In *Islamic Liberalism: A Critique of Development Ideologies,* 85–127. Chicago: University of Chicago Press, 1988.

Bobzin, Hartmut. "Geschichte der arabischen Philologie in Europa bis zum Ausgang des achtzehnten Jahrhunderts." In *Grundriß der arabischen Philologie.* Vol. 3, 155–187. Supplement. Wiesbaden: Reichert, 1992.

Bourel, Dominique. "Die deutsche Orientalistik im 18. Jahrhundert: von der Mission zur Wissenschaft." In *Historische Kritik und biblischer Kanon in der deutschen Aufklärung,* ed. H. Reventlow, W. Sparn, and J. Woodbridge, 113–126. Wiesbaden: Harrassowitz, 1988.

Büren, R. *Gegenwartsbezogene Orientwissenschaft in der Bundesrepublik Deutschland.* Göttingen: Vandenhoeck und Ruprecht, 1974.

Burke, Edmund, and David Prochaska. *Genealogies of Orientalism: History, Theory, Politics.* Lincoln: University of Nebraska Press, 2008.

Büttner, F., et al. "Die Entdeckung des Nahen Ostens durch die deutsche Politikwissenschaft." In *Dritte Welt-Forschung: Entwicklungstheorie und Entwicklungspolitik,* edited by F. Nuscheler, 416–435. Opladen: Westdeutscher Verlag, 1985.

Charnay, Jean Paul. *Les Contre-Orients ou comment penser l'Autrui selon soi.* Paris: Sindbad, 1980.

———. "Méthodologie et Islamologie." *Studia Islamica* 54 (1981): 183–196.

Daniel, Norman. "Edward Said and the Orientalist." *MIDEO* 15 (1982): 211–222.

———. *Islam, Europe and the Empire.* Edinburgh: Edinburgh University Press, 1966 (1st ed. 1960).

———. *Islam and the West: The Making of an Image.* Edinburgh: Edinburgh University Press, 1960.

Darmesteter, J. "De la part de la France dans les grandes découvertes de l'orientalisme moderne (1879)." In *Essais orientaux,* 1–103. Paris: A. Lévy, 1883.

Djait, Hichem. *Europe and Islam: Cultures and Modernity.* Berkeley: University of California Press, 1985.

Dugat, G. *Histoire des orientalistes de l'Europe du XIIe au XIXe siècle précédée d'une esquisse historique des études orientales.* Vols. 1 and 2. Paris: Maisonneuve et cie, 1868–1870.

Eigler, Friederike. *Reassessing Orientalism in German Studies.* Toronto: University of Toronto Press, 2005.

Endress, G. *Der Islam: Eine Einführung in seine Geschichte.* Munich: Beck, 1991.

Ess, Josef van. "From Wellhausen to Becker: The Emergence of Kulturgeschichte in Islamic Studies." In *Islamic Studies: A Tradition and Its Problems,* edited by Malcolm H. Kerr, 27–51. Malibu, Calif.: Undena Publications, 1980.

Falkenstein, A. *Denkschrift zur Lage der Orientalistik.* Wiesbaden: Franz Steiner, 1960.

Fück, J. "Die arabischen Studien in Europa vom 12. bis in den Anfang des 19. Jahrhunderts." In *Beiträge zur Arabistik, Semitistik und Islamwissenschaft,* edited by R. Hartmann and H. Scheel, 85–253. Leipzig: O. Harrassowitz, 1944.

———. *Die arabischen Studien in Europa bis in den Anfang des 20. Jahrhunderts.* Leipzig: O. Harrassowitz, 1955.

Fudge, Bruce. "Qur'anic Exegesis in Medieval Islam and Modern Orientalism." *Die Welt des Islams* 46, no. 2 (2006): 115–147.

Gabrieli, F. "Apologie de l'orientalisme." *Diogène* 50 (1965): 128–136.

Grandguillaume, Gilbert. "Le langage de l'orientalisme." *L'orientalisme: Interrogations, Peuples méditerraneens* 50 (1990): 171–176.

Grossir, Claudine. *L'Islam des Romantiques*. Vol. 1. *1811–1840: du refus à la tentation*. Paris: Maisonneuve et Larose, 1984.

Haarmann, U. "Die islamische Moderne bei den deutschen Orientalisten." In *Araber und Deutsche: Begegnungen in einem Jahrtausend*, edited by F. H. Kochwasser and H. R. Roemer, 56–61. Tübingen: Erdmann, 1974. (Reprint, *Zeitschrift für Kulturaustausch* 24 [1974]: 5–18.)

Hafez, Kai. *Orientwissenschaft in der DDR: Zwischen Dogma und Anpassung, 1969–1989*. Hamburg: Deutsches Orient-Institut, 1995.

Hanafi, Hassan. "De l'orientalisme à l'occidentalisme." *L'orientalisme: Interrogations, Peuples méditerraneens* 50 (1990): 115–120.

Hanisch, L. *Die Nachfolge der Exegeten: Deutschsprachige Erforschung des Vorderen Orients in der ersten Hälfte des 20. Jahrhunderts*. Wiesbaden: O. Harrassowitz, 2003.

Hentsch, Thierry. *L'Orient imaginaire vision politique de l'Est méditerranéen*. Paris: Édition de Minuit, 1988.

Horten, M. "Die Probleme der Orientalistik." *Beiträge zur Kenntnis des Orients* 13 (1916): 143–161.

Johansen, B. "Politics and Scholarship: The Development of Islamic Studies in the Federal Republic of Germany." In *Middle East Studies: International Perspectives of the State of the Art*, edited by T. Y. Ismael, 71–130. New York: Praeger, 1990.

Kolluoglu-Kirli, Biray. "From Orientalism to Area Studies." *CR: The New Centennial Review* 3, no. 3 (2003): 93–111.

Kračkovskij, I. J. *Die russische Arabistik: Umrisse ihrer Entwicklung*. Leipzig: O. Harrassowitz, 1957.

Kraemer, J. *Das Problem der islamischen Kulturgeschichte*. Tübingen: M. Niemeyer, 1959.

Kramer, Martin S. *Ivory Towers on Sand: The Failure of Middle Eastern Studies in America*. Washington, D.C.: Washington Institute for Near East Policy, 2001.

——, ed. *The Jewish Discovery of Islam*. Tel Aviv: The Moshe Dayan Center, Tel Aviv University, 1999.

Kusnecova, Nina A. *Iz istorii sovetskogo vostokovedeniya, 1917–1967*. Moscow: Izd. Nauka, 1970.

Laroui, A. "Fora Methodology of Islamic Studies: Islam as Seen by G. von Grunebaum." *Diogenes* 81–84 (1973): 12–39.

Laurens, Henry. *La Bibliothèque Orientale de Barthélemy d'Herbelot: aux sources de l'orientalisme*. Paris: G.-P. Maisonneuve et Larose, 1978.

——. *Les origines intellectuelles de l'expédition de l'Egypte: l'orientalisme islamisant en France (1698–1798)*. Istanbul: Éditions Isis, 1987.

Mahrad, A. "Wiederbelebung der Orientalistik an deutschen Hochschulen nach dem Zweiten Weltkrieg." *Hannoversche Studien über den Mittleren Osten* 4 (1987): 227–279.

Marr, Timothy Worthington. "Imagining Ishmael: Studies of Islamic Orientalism in America from the Puritans to Melville." Ph.D. dissertation, Yale University, 1997.

Migdal, Joel S. Review of Martin Kramer, *Ivory Towers on Sand: The Failure of Middle Eastern Studies in America*. *International Journal of Middle East Studies* 35 (2003): 1, 201–203.

Monroe, James T. *Islam and the Arabs in Spanish Scholarship (16th Century to the Present)*. Leiden: Brill, 1970.

Nagel, Tilman. "Die Ebenbürtigkeit des Fremden: Über die Aufgaben arabistischer Lehre und Forschung in der Gegenwart." *Zeitschrift der Deutschen Morgenländischen Gesellschaft* 148 (1998): 367–378.

——. "Gedanken über die europäische Islamforschung und ihr Echo im Orient." *Zeitschrift für Missionskunde und Religionswissenschaft* 62 (1987): 21–39.

Nanji, Azim, ed. *Mapping Islamic Studies: Genealogy, Continuity, and Change.* Berlin: Mouton de Gruyter, 1997.

Nieuwenhuijze, C. A. O. van. "Oriental Studies as Intercultural Studies." *Orient* 22 (1981): 113–120.

Owen, Roger. "Studying Islamic History." *Journal of Interdisciplinary History* 4 (1973): 187–198.

Paret, R. *Arabistik und Islamkunde an deutschen Universitäten: Deutsche Orientalisten seit Theodor Nöldeke.* Wiesbaden: F. Steiner, 1966.

Preissler, H. "Deutsche Orientalisten und die Öffentlichkeit um die Mitte des 19. Jahrhunderts." In *Norm und Abweichung: Akten des 27. Deutschen Orientalistentages (Bonn, 28. Sept. bis 2. Okt. 1998),* edited by S. Wild and H. Schild, 777–784. Würzburg: Ergon, 2001.

Reeves, M. *Muhammad in Europe: A Thousand Years of Myth Making.* With a biographical contribution by P. J. Stewart. New York: New York University Press, 2000.

Reig, Daniel. *Homo orientaliste: la langue arabe en France depuis le XIXe siècle.* Paris: Maisonneuve et Larose, 1988.

Rodinson, Maxime. "Das Bild im Westen und westliche Islamstudien." In *Das Vermächtnis des Islam,* edited by J. Schacht and C. E. Bosworth, vol. 1, 24–81. Munich: Artemis 1980.

——. *La fascination de l'Islam.* Paris: François Maspero, 1981.

——. "Orientalisme et ethnocentrisme." In *XXI. Deutscher Orientalistentag vom 24.3. bis zum 29.3. 1980 in Berlin; Vorträge,* edited by F. Steppat, 77–86. (ZDMG Supplement 5.) Wiesbaden: Steiner, 1983.

Roemer, Hans Robert, ed. *Deutsche Orientalistik der siebziger Jahre: Thesen, Zustandsanalyse, Perspektiven.* Wiesbaden: Deutsche Morgenländische Gesellschaft, 1972.

——. "Spezialisierung, Intergration und Innovation in der deutschen Orientalistik." *Die Welt des Islams* 28 (1988): 475–495.

Rosenthal, F. "Die Krise der Orientalistik." In *XXI. Deutscher Orientalistentag vom 24.3. bis zum 29.3. 1980 in Berlin; Vorträge,* ed. F. Steppat, 10–21. (ZDMG Supplement 5.) Wiesbaden: Steiner, 1983.

Rousillon, Alain. "Le débat sur l'orientalisme dans le champ intellectuel arabe: l'aporie des sciences sociales." *L'orientalisme: Interrogations, Peuples méditerraneens* 50 (1990): 740.

Said, Edward W. *Covering Islam: How the Media and the Experts Determine How We See the Rest of the World.* New York: Pantheon Books, 1981.

——. "Orientalism Reconsidered." *Race and Class* 27, no. 2 (1985): 1–15.

Salvatore, A. "Beyond Orientalism? Max Weber and the Displacements of 'Essentialism' in the Study of Islam." *Arabica* 43 (1996): 457–485.

Schipperges, H. *Ideologie und Historiographie des Arabismus.* Wiesbaden: Steiner, 1961.

Schluchter, W., ed. *Max Weber's Sicht des Islams.* Frankfurt am Main: Suhrkamp, 1987.

Schmidt, Jan. "The Joys of Philology Studies in Ottoman Literature, History, and Orientalism, 1500–1923." *Analecta Isisiana* 60, vol. 1: *Poetry, Historiography, Biography, and Autobiography.* Istanbul: Isis Press, 2002.

Schöller, M. *Methode und Wahrheit in der Islamwissenschaft: Prolegomena.* Wiesbaden: O. Harrassowitz, 2000.

Schulze, R. "Gibbons Muhammad." In *Der Sieg des Islam,* by Edward Gibbon, 321–363. Frankfurt am Main: Eichborn, 2003.

Shaban, Fuad. *Islam and Arabs in Early American Thought: Roots of Orientalism in America.* Durham, N.C.: Acorn Press, 1991.

Sivan, Emmanuel. "Edward Said and His Arab Reviewers." *Jerusalem Quarterly* 35 (1985): 11–23.

——. "Orientalism, Islam and Cultural Revolution." *Jerusalem Quarterly* 5 (1977): 84–94.

Stauth, G., and B. Turner. *Nietzsche's Dance: Resentment, Reciprocity and Resistance in Social Life.* Oxford: Blackwell, 1988.

Steppat, F., ed. "Der moderne Vordere Orient als Aufgabe an deutschen Universitäten." *Zeitschrift der Deutschen Morgenländischen Gesellschaft* 126 (1976): 1–34.

Stover, Dale. "Orientalism and the Otherness of Islam." *Studies in Religion* 17 (1988): 27–40.

Syndram, K. U. "Der erfundene Orient in der europäischen Literatur vom 18. bis zum Beginn des 20. Jahrhunderts." In *Europa und der Orient, 800–1900,* edited by G. Sievernich and H. Budde, 324–341. Gütersloh: Bertelsmann Lexikon Verlag, 1989.

Thomson, Ann. *Barbary and Enlightenment: European Attitudes towards the Maghreb in the 18th Century.* Leiden: Brill, 1987.

Tibawi, A. L. "English-Speaking Orientalists: A Critique of Their Approach to Islam and Arab Nationalism." *Muslim World* 53 (1963): 185–204, 298–313.

Turner, Bryan S. *Marx and the End of Orientalism.* London: Allen and Unwin, 1978.

——. "Orientalism and the Problem of Civil Society in Islam." In *Orientalism, Islam, and Islamists,* edited by A. Hussein et al., 23–42. Brattleboro, Vt.: Amana Books, 1984.

——. *Weber and Islam.* London: Routledge & Kegan Paul, 1974.

Varisco, Daniel Martin. *Reading Orientalism: Said and the Unsaid.* Seattle: University of Washington Press, 2007.

Waardenburg, J. D. J. *L'Islam dans le miroir de l'Occident: comment quelques orientalistes se sont penchés sur l'Islam et se sont fermés une image de cette religion; I. Goldziher, C. S. Hurgronje, C. H. Becker, D. B. Macdonald, L. Massignon.* Paris: Mouton, 1962.

——. "Islamforschung aus religionswissenschaftlicher Sicht." In *XXI. Deutscher Orientalistentag vom 24. bis 29. März 1980 in Berlin,* edited by Fritz Steppat, 197–211. (*Zeitschrift der Deutschen Morgenländischen Gesellschaft,* Suppl. 4.) Wiesbaden: Steiner, 1983.

——. "Mustashrikun." In *The Encyclopaedia of Islam,* new ed., vol. 7, 735–753. Leiden: Brill, 1993.

Wirth, E. "Orientalistik und Orientforschung: Aufgaben und Probleme aus der Sicht der Nachbarwissenschaften." In *Deutscher Orientalistentag 1975 in Freiburg im Breisgau: Vorträge,* edited by W. Voigt, 55–82. (*Zeitschrift der Deutschen Morgenländischen Gesellschaft,* Supplement 3). Wiesbaden: Franz Steiner, 1977.

Yamanaka, Yuriko, and Tetsuo Nishio. *The Arabian Nights and Orientalism Perspectives from East and West.* London: I. B. Tauris, 2006.

II. Islam and Cultural Self-Assertion *(Rotraud Wielandt)*

Abdel-Malek, A. *La pensée politique arabe contemporaine,* 2nd ed., chaps. 1–4. Paris: Éditions du Seuil, 1975.

Arkoun, M. "L'identité islamique." In M. Arkoun and L. Gardet, *L'Islam hier–demain,* 199–218. Paris: Buchet/Chastel, 1978.

Binder, L. *Islamic Liberalism: A Critique of Development Ideologies.* Chicago: University of Chicago Press, 1988.

Boullata, I. *Trends and Issues in Contemporary Arab Thought.* Albany: State University of New York Press, 1990.

Cooper, J. et al., eds. *Islam and Modernity: Muslim Intellectuals Respond.* London: I. B. Tauris, 1998.

Djait, H. *La crise de la culture islamique.* Paris: Fayard, 2004.

Gaebel, M. *Von der Kritik des arabischen Denkens zum panarabischen Aufbruch: Das philosophische und politische Denken Muhammad ʿAbid al-Jabiris.* Berlin: Klaus Schwarz, 1995.

Gershoni, I. "Reconstructing Tradition: Islam, Modernity, and National Identity in Egyptian Intellectual Discourse, 1930–1952." *Tel Aviver Jahrbuch für deutsche Geschichte* 30 (2002): 155–212.

Gottstein, K., ed. *Islamic Cultural Identity and Scientific-Technological Development.* Baden-Baden: Nomos, 1986.

Haarmann, U. "Die 'Persönlichkeit Ägyptens': Das moderne Ägypten auf der Suche nach seiner kulturellen Identität." *Zeitschrift für Missionswissenschaft und Religionswissenschaft* 62 (1987): 101–122.

Hoffmann, G. "'at-turāth' und 'al-muʿāṣara' in der Diskussion arabischer Intellektueller der Gegenwart." *Asien afrika lateinamerika,* special volume 2 (1990): 50–54.

Kreile, R. "Geschlechterordnung als Schlüsselelement in islamistischen Authentizitätsdiskursen." *Orient* 40 (1999): 253–266, 356–357.

Laroui, A. *La crise des intellectuels arabes.* Paris: La Découverte, 1974.

———. *L'idéologie arabe contemporaine.* Paris: Maspéro 1967 (revised eds. 1977, 1982).

Lee, Robert D. *Overcoming Tradition and Modernity: The Search for Islamic Authenticity.* Boulder, Colo.: Westview Press, 1997.

Meijer, Roel, ed. *Cosmopolitanism, Identity and Authenticity in the Middle East.* London: Curzon Press, 1999.

Roussillon, A. "Les 'nouveaux fondamentalistes' en colloque: 'Authenticité et modernité'; les defies de l'identité dans le monde arabe." *Maghreb-Machrek* 107 (1985): 5–22.

Scheffold, M. *Authentisch arabisch und dennoch modern? Zaki Najib Mahmud's kulturtheoretische Essayistik als Beitrag zum euro-arabischen Dialog.* Berlin: Klaus Schwarz, 1996.

Thompson, M. J., ed. *Islam and the West: Critical Perspectives on Modernity.* Lanham, Md.: Rowman & Littlefield, 2003.

III. Islam and Local Traditions

1. The Concept of Syncretism *(Olaf Schumann)*

Berner, U. "Heuristisches Modell der Synkretismusforschung (Stand 1977)." In *Synkretismusforschung: Theorie und Praxis,* edited by G. Wiessner, 11–26. Wiesbaden: Harrassowitz, 1978.

Colpe, C. "Syncretism and Secularization: Complementary and Antithetical Trends in New Religious Movements." *History of Religions* 17 (1977): 158–176.

———. *Theologie, Ideologie, Religionswissenschaft.* Munich: Kaiser, 1980.

Geertz, C. *Islam Observed: Religious Developments in Morocco and Indonesia.* New Haven: Yale University Press, 1968.

Gort, J., et al., eds. *Dialogue and Syncretism: An Interdisciplinary Approach.* Grand Rapids, Mich.: Eerdmans, 1989.

Lanczkowski, G. *Begegnung und Wandel der Religionen.* Düsseldorf: Diederichs, 1971.

Wiessner, G., ed. *Synkretismusforschung: Theorie und Praxis.* Wiesbaden: Harrassowitz, 1978.

2. Indonesia as a Case Study *(Lode Frank Brakel)*

Akkeren, Ph. van. *Een gedrocht en toch de volmaakte mens.* The Hague: Excelsior, 1951. (Contains the Serat Gatholoco.)

Beatty, A. *Varieties of Javanese Religion: An Anthropological Account.* Cambridge: Cambridge University Press, 1999.

Bechert, H., ed. *Buddhism in Ceylon and Studies on Religious Syncretism in Buddhist Countries: Symposium zur Buddhismusforschung.* Vol. 1. Göttingen: Vandenhoek und Ruprecht, 1978.

Benda, H. J. *The Crescent and the Rising Sun: Indonesian Islam under the Japanese Occupation, 1942–45.* The Hague: W. van Hoeve, 1958.

Boland, B. J. *The Struggle of Islam in Modern Indonesia.* Verhandelingen van het Koninklijk Instituut voor Taal-, Land- en Volkenkunde 59. The Hague: Martinus Nijhoff, 1971.

Bonneff, M. "Le renouveau d'un rituel royal, les Garebeg à Yogyakarta." *Archipel* 9 (1974): 119–147.

Bowen, J. R. *Muslims through Discourse: Religion and Ritual in Gayo Society.* Princeton: Princeton University Press, 1993.

Brakel, L. F. "*Hamza Pansuri*: Notes on Yoga Practices, Lahir dan Zahir, the 'Taxallos,' Punning, a Difficult Passage in the *Kitab al-Muntahi*, Hamza's Likely Place of Birth, and Hamza's Imagery." *Journal of the Malaysian Branch of the Royal Asiatic Society* 52, no. 1 (1979): 73–98.

——. "Der Islam und lokale Traditionen: Synkretistische Ideen und Praktiken. Indonesien." In *Der Islam in der Gegenwart. Entwicklung und Ausbreitung, Staat, Politik und Recht, Kultur und Religion,* edited by W. Ende and U. Steinbach, 570–582. Munich: C. H. Beck, 1984. (Fourth revised and enlarged edition 1996, 736–748.)

Brakel-Papenhuyzen, C. "In memoriam Lode Frank Brakel." *Indonesia Circle* 28 (1982): 45–46.

——. *The Bedhaya Court Dances of Central Java.* Leiden: E. J. Brill, 1992.

——. "Sandhang Pangan for the Goddess: Offerings to Sang Hyang Bathari Durga and Nyai Lara Kidul." In *Goddesses and Female Spirits in South-East Asia,* edited by R. Wessing. *Asian Folklore Studies* 56, no. 2 (1997): 253–83.

——. "The Tale of the Skull, an Islamic Description of Hell in Javanese." *Bijdragen tot de Taal-, Land- en Volkenkunde* (BKI) 158 (2002): 1–20.

Damais, L.-C. "Études javanaises: les tombes musulmans datés de Tralaya." *Bulletin de l'École Française d'Extrême-Orient* 48 (1956): 353–415.

Doorenbos, J. *De Geschriften van Hamzah Pansoeri.* Leiden: Batteljee & Terpstra, 1933.

Drewes, G. W. J. "The Struggle between Javanism and Islam as Illustrated by the Serat Dermagandul." *Bijdragen tot de Taal-, Land- en Volkenkunde* 122 (1966): 309–366.

——. "Javanese Poems Dealing with or Attributed to the Saint of *Bonan.*" *Bijdragen tot de Taal-, Land- en Volkenkunde* 124 (1968): 209–241.

——. "New Light on the Coming of Islam to Indonesia?" *Bijdragen tot de Taal-, Land- en Volkenkunde* 124 (1968): 433–460.

——. "Further Data Concerning 'Abd as-Samad al-Palimbani." *Bijdragen tot de Taal-, Land- en Volkenkunde* 132 (1976): 267–292.

——. *An Early Javanese Code of Muslim Ethics.* Koninklijk Instituut voor Taal-, Land- en Volkenkunde, Bibliotheca Indonesica 18. The Hague: Martinus Nijhoff, 1978.

Drewes, G. W. J., and L. F. Brakel. *The Poems of Hamzah Fansuri.* Koninklijk Instituut voor Taal-, Land- en Volkenkunde, Bibliotheca Indonesica 26. Dordrecht: Foris, 1986.

Ensink, J. "Siva-Buddhism in Java and Bali." In *Buddhism in Ceylon and Studies on Religious Syncretism in Buddhist Countries,* edited by H. Bechert, 178–198. Göttingen: Vandenhoek und Ruprecht, 1978.

Ferrand, S. G. *Relation de voyages et textes géographiques arabes, persans et turks relatifs à l'Extreme-Orient du VII au XVIIIe siècles.* 2 vols. Paris: Leraux, 1913.

Geertz, C. *The Religion of Java.* Glencoe: Free Press, 1960.

——. *Islam Observed: Religious Development in Morocco and Indonesia.* New Haven: Yale University Press, 1968.

Hamonic, G. "Travestissement et bisexualité chez les *bissu* des Pays Bugis." *Archipel* 10 (1975): 121–135.

Hefner, R. W. *Hindu Javanese: Tengger Tradition and Islam.* Princeton: Princeton University Press, 1989.

Hidding, K. A. H. Review of Zoetmulder: *Pantheïsme en monisme in de Javaansche soeloekliteratuur. Djawa* 16 (1936a): 222–226.

——. *Tweeërlei geestesstructuur.* Solo: De Bliksem, 1936b.

Hooker, M. B., ed. *Islam in Southeast Asia.* Leiden: E. J. Brill, 1983.

Israeli, R., and A. H. Johns. *Islam in Asia.* Vol. 2. *Southeast and East Asia.* Jerusalem: Magnes Press, 1984.

Juynboll, Th. W. *Handleiding tot de kennis van de Mohammedaansche wet.* 4th ed. Leiden: E. J. Brill, 1935.

Kähler, H. "Die Kultur des Islams in Indonesien und Malaysia." In *Handbuch der Kulturgeschichte.* Part 2. *Die Kultur des Islams,* 333–437. Frankfurt am Main: Athenaion, 1971.

Koentjaraningrat. *Javanese Culture.* 2nd ed. New York: Oxford University Press, 1989.

Kraemer, H. *De wortelen van het syncretisme.* The Hague: Boekcentrum, 1937.

Leeuw, G. van der. *Phänomenologie der Religion.* 2nd ed. Tübingen: Mohr, 1956.

Levtzion, N. "Islamisierungsmuster: Die Begegnung des Islam mit 'Achsenzeitreligionen.'" In *Kulturen der Achsenzeit,* edited by S. N. Eisenstadt, vol. 2, part 3, 226–41. Frankfurt am Main: Suhrkamp, 1992.

Mulder, N. *Mysticism and Everyday Life in Contemporary Java.* Singapore: Singapore University Press, 1978.

Naguib al-Attas, Syed Muhammad. *The Mysticism of Hamzah Fansuri.* Kuala Lumpur: University of Malaya Press, 1972.

Noer, Deliar. *The Modernist Muslim Movement in Indonesia, 1900–1942.* Singapore: Oxford University Press, 1973.

Noorduyn, S. J. "De islamizering van Makassar." *Bijdragen tot de Taal-, Land- en Volkenkunde* 112 (1956): 247–266.

Pigeaud, Th. *Java in the Fourteenth Century.* 5 vols. The Hague: Martinus Nijhoff, 1960–1963.

Ricklefs, M. C. "Islamization in Java: An Overview and Some Philosophical Considerations." In *Islam in Asia.* Vol. 2. *Southeast and East Asia,* edited by R. Israeli and A. H. Johns, 11–24. Jerusalem: Magnes Press, 1984.

Ricklefs, M. C. *A History of Modern Indonesia.* London: Macmillan, 1990.

Rinkes, D. A. 1996. *Nine Saints of Java.* Kuala Lumpur: Malaysian Sociological Research Institute, 1990.

Robson, S. O. *The Wédhatama.* KITLV Working Papers 4. Leiden: KITLV Press, 1990.

——. *Desawarnana (Nagarakrtagama).* Leiden: KITLV Press, 1995.

Skeat, W. W. *Malay Magic.* 2nd ed. New York: Dover Publications, 1967.

Snouck Hurgronje, C. *The Achehnese.* 2 vols. Leiden: E. J. Brill, 1906.

Stöhr, W., and P. Zoetmulder. *Die Religionen Indonesiens.* Stuttgart: W. Kohlhammer, 1965.

Winstedt, R. O. *The Malay Magician: Being Shaman, Saiva and Sufi.* Rev. ed. London: Routledge & Kegan Paul, 1961.

Zoetmulder, P. J. *Pantheïsme en monisme in de Javaansche soeloekliteratuur.* Nijmegen: Berkhout, 1935.

——. "Iets omtrent de naam 'Serat Tjentini.'" In *Het Triwindoegedenkboek Mangkoenagoro,* vol. 7, 82–86. Soerakarta: Het Comite, 1939.

——. "Bekroonde vertaling 'Serat Wedatama.'" *Djawa* 21 (1941): 182–198.
——. "Een merkwaardige passage in de onuitgegeven Tjentini." *Djawa* 21 (1941): 73–84.
——. *Pantheism and Monism in Javanese Suluk Literature: Islamic and Indian Mysticism in an Indonesian Setting,* edited and translated by M. C. Ricklefs. Leiden, KITLV Press, 1995.

IV. Is There an Islamic Linguistic Sphere? *(Otto Jastrow)*

Abraham, R. C. *The Language of the Haussa People.* London: University of London Press, 1959.
Atsız, B., and H. J. Kissling. *Sammlung türkischer Redensarten.* Wiesbaden: Harrassowitz, 1974.
Bailey, T. G. *Teach Yourself Urdu.* London: English Universities Press, 1950.
Baldauf, I. *Schriftreform und Schriftwechsel bei den muslimischen Russland-und Sowjettürken, 1850–1937.* Budapest: Akadémiai Kiadó, 1993.
Chehabi, I. *Deutsch-persischer Sprachführer.* Wiesbaden: Harrassowitz, 1965.
Erwin, W. M. *A Basic Course in Iraqi Arabic.* Washington, D.C.: Georgetown University Press, 1969.
Ferguson, C. A. "Root-Echo Responses in Syrian Arabic Politeness Formulas." In *Linguistic Studies in Memory of Richard Slade Harrell,* edited by D. G. Stuart, 37–45. Washington, D.C.: Georgetown University Press, 1967.
Fischer, A. "Vergöttlichung und Tabuisierung der Namen Muhammads bei den Muslimen." In *Beiträge zur Arabistik, Semitistik und Islamwissenschaft,* edited by R. Hartmann and H. Scheel, 307–339. Leipzig: Harrassowitz, 1944.
Fischer, W., and O. Jastrow, eds. *Handbuch der arabischen Dialekte.* Wiesbaden: Harrassowitz, 1980.
Harrell, R. S. *A Basic Course in Moroccan Arabic.* Washington, D.C.: Georgetown University Press, 1965.
Harrell, R. S., L. Y. Tewfik, and G. O. Selim. *Lessons in Colloquial Egyptian Arabic.* 2nd ed. Washington, D.C.: Georgetown University Press, 1963.
Jungraithmayr, H., and W. J. Möhlig. *Einführung in die Hausa-Sprache.* 2nd ed. Berlin: Reimer, 1981.
Kähler, H. *Grammatik der Bahasa Indonésia.* Wiesbaden: Harrassowitz, 1956.
Lambton, A. K. S. *Persian Grammar.* 4th ed. Cambridge: Cambridge University Press, 1961.
——. *Persian Vocabulary.* Cambridge: Cambridge University Press, 1954.
Laut, J.P. *Das Türkische als Ursprache? Sprachwissenschaftliche Theorien in der Zeit des erwachenden türkischen Nationalismus.* Wiesbaden: Harrassowitz, 2000.
Lewis, G., "The Ottoman Legacy in Language." In *Imperial Legacy,* edited by L. C. Brown, 214–223. New York: Columbia University Press, 1966.
——. *The Turkish Language Reform: A Catastrophic Success.* Oxford: Oxford University Press, 1999.
Penzl, H. *A Grammar of Pashto.* Washington, D.C.: American Council of Learned Societies, 1955.
Perrot, D. V. *Teach Yourself Swahili.* London: Teach Yourself Books, 1976.
Piamenta, M. *Islam in Everyday Arabic Speech.* Leiden: Brill, 1979.
Polomé, E. C. *Swahili Language Handbook.* Washington, D.C.: Center for Applied Linguistics, 1967.

Qafisheh, H. A. *A Basic Course in Gulf Arabic.* 3rd ed. Tucson: University of Arizona Press, 1977.

Scharlipp, W. E. *Türkische Sprache, arabische Schrift.* Budapest: Akadémiai Kiadó, 1995.

Spies, O., and E. Bannerth. *Lehrbuch der Hindustani-Sprache.* Leipzig: Harrassowitz, 1945.

Steuerwald, K. *Untersuchungen zur türkischen Sprache der Gegenwart.* Vols. 1–3. Berlin: Langenscheidt, 1963–1966.

Tarbiat, G. A. *Gespräche des täglichen Lebens in persischer und deutscher Sprache.* Tehran: Fardin, 1960.

Thackston, W. M. *An Introduction to Persian.* Bethesda, Md.: Iranbooks, 1993.

Wexler, P. "Problems in Monitoring the Diffusion of Arabic into West and Central African Languages." *ZDMG* 130 (1980): 522–556.

Wild, S. "Arabische Eigennamen." In *Grundriß der arabischen Philologie,* vol. 1, edited by H. Gätje and W. Fischer, 154–164. Wiesbaden: Reichert, 1982.

V. Islam Reflected in the Contemporary Literature of Muslim Peoples *(Johann Christoph Bürgel)*

Abramson, G., and H. Kilpatrick, eds. *Religious Perspectives in Modern Muslim and Jewish Literatures.* London: Routledge, 2006.

al-ʿAqqad, ʿA. *ʿAbqariyyat Muhammad.* Cairo: Al-istiqama, 1943; Dar al-Islam, 1972.

Alavi, B. *Geschichte und Entwicklung der modernen persischen Literatur.* Berlin: Akademie Verlag, 1964.

al-Sharqawi, ʿA.-R. *Muhammad rasul al-hurriyya.* Cairo: Al-Hilal, 1962.

Anthologie de la littératture arabe contemporaine. 3 vols. Vol. 1, R. and L. Makarius, *Le roman et la nouvelle.* Vol. 2, A. Abdel-Malek, *Les essais.* Vol. 3, L. Norin and E. Taraby, *La poésie.* Paris: Seuil, 1964–1967.

Badawi, M. M. "The Lamp of Umm Hashim: The Egyptian Intellectual between East and West." *Journal of Arabic Literature* 1 (1970): 145–161.

——. "Islam in Modern Egyptian Literature." *Journal of Arabic Literature* 2 (1971): 154–177.

——. *The Saint's Lamp and Other Stories.* Leiden, 1973.

——. *A Critical Introduction to Modern Arabic Poetry.* Cambridge: Cambridge University Press, 1975.

——, ed. *Modern Arabic Literature.* Cambridge: Cambridge University Press, 1992.

Baljon, J. M. S. *Modern Muslim Koran Interpretation (1880–1960).* Leiden: Brill, 1961.

Bellamy, J. A., E. N. McCarus, and A. I. Yacoub, eds. *Contemporary Arabic Readers.* Vol. 4. *Short Stories.* Ann Arbor: Ann Arbor Publishers, 1963–64.

Brockelmann, C. *Geschichte der arabischen Litteratur.* 3rd supplementary vol. Leiden: Brill, 1942.

Bürgel, J. C. "Verstand und Liebe bei Hafis." In *Drei Hafisstudien.* Berne: Lang, 1975.

——. "Rückkehr aus Europa: Zu einem zentralen Motiv im Werk Djamalzadehs." In *Zeitschrift der Deutschen Morgenländischen Gesellschaft,* supplement 3, no. 2, 1042–1048. Wiesbaden: Steiner, 1977.

——, ed. *Iqbal und Europa: Vier Vorträge.* Berne: Lang, 1980.

——, ed. *Steppe im Staubkorn: Texte aus der Urdu-Dichtung Muhammad Iqbals.* Freiburg, Switzerland: Universitätsverlag, 1982.

——, trans. *"Der Damm (as-Sudd): Ein modernes arabisches Drama von Maḥmūd al-Masʿadū."* *Die Welt des Islams* 21 (1981): 30–79.

——. "Muhammad oder Galen: Das Doppelgesicht der Heilkunst in der islamischen Kultur." In *Die Blütezeit der arabischen Wissenschaft,* edited by H. Balmer and B. Glarus, 41–68. Zurich: Verlag d. Fachvereine, 1990.

——. *Allmacht und Mächtigkeit: Religion und Welt im Islam.* Munich: Beck, 1991.

——. "Tradition and Modernity in the Work of the Tunisian Writer al-Mas'adi." In *Tradition and Modernity in Arabic Language and Literature,* edited by J. R. Smart, Richmond, Surrey: Curzon Press, 1996.

Cachia, P. "Themes Related to Christianity and Judaism in Modern Egyptian Drama and Fiction." *Journal of Arabic Literature* 2 (1971): 178–194.

Cooke, M. "Zaynab al-Ghazali: Saint or Subversive?" *Die Welt des Islams* 34 (1997): 1–20.

Dolinina, A. A. *Ocherki istorii arabskoy literatury novogo vremeni: Egipet i Siriya.* Moscow: Nauka, 1973.

Donohue, J. J., and L. Tramontini, eds. *Crosshatching in Global Culture: A Dictionary of Modern Arab Writers; An Updated English Version of R. B. Campbell's "Contemporary Arab Writers."* 2 vols. Beiruter Texte und Studien 101. Beirut: Ergon, 2004.

El-Enany, R. *Naguib Mahfouz: The Pursuit of Meaning.* London: Routledge, 1993.

Enginün, I. "Turkish Literature under the Republic." In *The Turks.* Vol. 5. *Turkey,* edited by H. C. Güzel et al. Ankara: Yeni Türkiye Publications, 2000.

Furrer, P. "Propaganda in Geschichtenform: Erzählstrukturen und Handlungsanweisungen in islamischen Frauenromanen aus der Türkei." *Die Welt des Islams* 37 (1997): 88–111.

Grunebaum, G. E. von. "Das geistige Problem der Verwestlichung in der Selbstsicht der arabischen Welt." In *Studien zum Kulturbild und Selbstverständnis des Islams,* 229–272. Zurich: Artemis, 1969.

Hedayat, S. *The Myth of Creation.* Translated from the Persian by M. R. Ghanounparvar. Costa Mesa, Calif.: Mazda, 1998.

Hussein, T. *The Future of Culture in Egypt.* Translated by S. Glazer. Washington, D.C.: American Council of Learned Societies, 1954.

——. *'Ala hamish al-sira.* Cairo, Ma'arif, 1958.

Jamalzadeh, M. A. *Once Upon a Time.* Translated by Heshmat Moayyad and Paul Sprachman. Delmar, N.Y.: Caravan Press and Bibliotheca Persica, 1985.

Kamshad, H. *Modern Persian Prose Literature.* Cambridge: Cambridge University Press, 1966.

Ibn Khaldun. *The Muqaddimah: An Introduction to History.* Translated from the Arabic by F. Rosenthal. Princeton: Princeton University Press, 1967.

Karimi-Hakkak, A. *Recasting Persian Poetry: Scenarios of Poetic Modernity in Iran.* Salt Lake City: University of Utah Press, 1996.

Khouri, M. *Poetry and the Making of Modern Egypt.* Leiden: Brill, 1971.

Kotsarev, N. K. *Pisateli Egipta: XX vek.* Moscow: Nauka, 1975.

Kraemer, J. *Das Problem der islamischen Kulturgeschichte.* Tübingen: Niemeyer, 1959.

Landau, J. M. *Arabische Literaturgeschichte der neuesten Zeit: 20. Jahrhundert.* Part 2 of *Arabische Literaturgeschichte,* edited by H. A. R. Gibb and J. M. Landau. Zurich and Stuttgart: Artemis, 1968.

Lewis, B. *The Emergence of Modern Turkey.* 2nd ed. London: Oxford University Press, 1968.

Manzalaoui, M., ed. *Arabic Writing Today: The Short Story.* Cairo: American Research Center in Egypt, 1968.

Massignon, L. *La passion de Hallaj.* Paris: Gallimard, 1975.

Mikhail, M. N. "Broken Idols: The Death of Religion in Two Stories by Idris and Mahfuz." *Journal of Arabic Literature* 5 (1974): 147–157.

Milani, F. *Veils and Words: The Emerging Voices of Iranian Women Writers*. Syracuse: Syracuse University Press, 1992.

Moayyad, H., ed. *Stories from Iran: A Chicago Anthology, 1921–1991*. Washington, D.C.: Mage, 1991.

Nasr, A. A. "Popular Islam in Al-Tayyib Salih." *Journal of Arabic Literature* 11 (1980): 88–104.

Paret, R. "Zur Frauenfrage in der arabisch-islamischen Welt." 1934. Reprinted in *R. Paret: Schriften zum Islam*, edited by J. van Ess, 135–205. Stuttgart: Kohlhammer, 1981.

Pedersen, C. V. *World View in Pre-revolutionary Iran: Literary Analysis of Five Iranian Authors in the Context of the History of Ideas*. Wiesbaden: Harrassowitz, 2002.

Sadiq, M. *A History of Urdu Literature*. London: Oxford University Press, 1964.

Schimmel, A. *Gabriel's Wing: A Study into the Religious Ideas of Sir Muhammad Iqbal*. Leiden: Brill, 1963.

——. *Al-Halladsch: Märtyrer der Gottesliebe*. Cologne: Hegner, 1968.

——. *Mystical Dimensions of Islam*. Chapel Hill: University of North Carolina Press, 1975.

——, ed. and trans. *M. Iqbal: Botschaft des Ostens*. Tübingen: Erdmann, 1977.

Semaan, K. *Murder in Baghdad*. Leiden: Brill, 1972.

——. "Islamic Mysticism in Modern Arabic Poetry and Drama." *International Journal of Middle East Studies* 10 (1979): 517–531.

Siddiqi, I. A., ed. *Kulliyyat-i nazm-i Hali*. Vol. 2. Lahore: Majlis Taraqqi-yi Adab, 1968–.

Simon, R., ed. *Erkundungen: 17 arabische Erzähler*. Berlin: Volk und Welt, 1971.

Somekh, S. *The Changing Rhythm: A Study of Najib Mahafuz's Novels*. Leiden: Brill, 1973.

Spuler, C. U. "Das türkische Drama der Gegenwart." *Die Welt des Islams* 11 (1968): 1–220.

Starkey, P. "Philosophical Themes in Tawfiq al-Hakim's Drama." *Journal of Arabic Literature* 8 (1977): 136–152.

Steppat, F. "Gott, die Futuwwat und die Wissenschaft: Zu Najīb Maḥfūẓ: Aulād ḥāratnā." In *Correspondance d'Orient*. 1975. Reprinted in *Islam als Partner*, 215–228. Beirut: Ergon, 2001.

Szyska, C. "On Utopian Writing in Nasserist Prison and Laicist Turkey." *Die Welt des Islams* 35 (1995): 95–125.

——. "Najib al-Kilani on His Career, or: How to Become the Ideal Muslim Author." In *Conscious Voices: Concepts of Writing in the Middle East; Proceedings of the Berne Symposium*, edited by S. Guth et al., 221–235. Beirut: Steiner, 1999.

Taymur, M. *Al-Nabi al-insan wa-maqalat ukhar*. Cairo: Makt. al-Adab, n.d.

Talattof, K. *The Politics of Writing in Iran: A History of Modern Persian Literature*. Syracuse: Syracuse University Press, 2000.

Walther, W. "Das Bild der ägyptischen Gesellschaft in einigen Werken von Najīb Mahfūẓ aus den sechziger Jahren." In *Asien in Vergangenheit und Gegenwart: Beiträge der Asienwissenschaftler der DDR zum XXIX. Internationalen Orientalistenkongress 1973 in Paris*, 239–258. Berlin: Akademie-Verlag, 1974.

——. "Mittel der Darstellungskunst und des Stils in einigen Romanen von Najīb Mahfūẓ aus den sechziger Jahren." In *Problemy literatur orientalnych: Materialy II Miedzynarodowego Sympozjum Warszawa-Kraków, May 22–26, 1972*, 199–212. Warsaw: Polska Akademia Nauk, 1974.

Wessels, A. "Najīb Maḥfūẓ and Secular Man." In *Humaniora Islamica*, vol. 2, 105–119. The Hague: Mouton, 1974.

Yavuz, K., *Der Islam in Werken moderner türkischer Schriftsteller.* Freiburg im Breisgau: Schwarz, 1974.

Ziock, H., ed. *Der Tod des Wasserträgers.* Herrenalb: Erdmann, 1963.

VI. Contemporary Painting and Graphic Art in the Islamic World *(Peter Heine)*

al-Azzawi, D. *The Influence of Calligraphy on Contemporary Arab Arts.* London: Saqi, 1980.

Encyclopaedia of Islam. 2nd ed. Leiden: E. J. Brill, 1960–2005. "Khaṭṭ," vol. 4 (1978), and "Taṣwīr," vol. 10 (2000).

Faath, S., H. Mattes et al. *Muhammad az-Zwawi: Ein libyscher Karikaturist.* Scheessel: Mattes, Edition Wuqûf, 1984.

Goody, J., ed. *Literalität in traditionellen Gesellschaften.* Frankfurt: Suhrkamp, 1981.

Gosciniak, H.-T. *Kleine Geschichte der islamischen Kunst.* Cologne: Du Mont, 1991.

Heine, P. "Malerei." In *Der Nahe und Mittlere Osten,* vol. 1, edited by U. Steinbach and R. Robert, 617–624. Opladen: Leske, 1988.

Heyberger, B., and S. Naef, eds. *La multiplication des images en pays d'Islam.* Würzburg: Ergon, 2003.

Ipşiroğlu, M. S. *Das Bild im Islam: Ein Verbot und seine Folgen.* Munich: Scholl, 1971.

Khatibi, A., and M. Sijelmassi. *Die Kunst der islamischen Kalligraphie.* Cologne: Du Mont, 1977.

Knopp, H.-G., and J. Odenthal, ed. *DisOrientation: Contemporary Arab Artists from the Middle East; Literature, Films, Performance, Music, Theatre, Visual Arts.* Berlin: Haus der Kulturen der Welt, 2003.

Kühnel, E. *Die Arabeske.* Graz: Akademie-Verlag, 1976.

Naef, S. *Y a-t-il une "question de l'image" en Islam?* Geneva: Téraèdre, 2004.

Sijelmassi, M. *L'art contemporain au Maroc.* Paris: ACR Édition, 1989.

Sourdel-Thomine, J., and B. Spuler. *Die Kunst des Islam.* Berlin: Propyläen, 1973.

VII. Contemporary "Islamic" Architecture and Representational Art *(Mohamed Scharabi)*

Abu-Lughod, J. L. *Cairo.* Princeton: Princeton University Press, 1971.

Al-Qahira fi alf 'am. Cairo, Ministry of Culture 1969.

Azzam, O. A. "The Development of Urban and Rural Housing in Egypt." Dissertation, ETH, Zurich, 1962.

Bianca, S. *Hofhaus und Paradiesgarten: Architektur und Lebensformen in der islamischen Welt.* Munich: Beck, 1991.

Bonine, M. E. et al., eds. *The Middle Eastern City and Islamic Urbanism: An Annotated Bibliography of Western Literature.* Bonn: Dümmler, 1994.

Elsheshtawy, Y., ed. *Planning Middle Eastern Cities: An Urban Kaleidoscope in a Globalizing World.* London: Routledge, 2004.

Fathy, H. *Architecture for the Poor.* Chicago: University of Chicago Press, 1973.

Gray, B. *Persian Painting.* Geneva: Skira, 1961.

Haarmann, U. *Geschichte der arabischen Welt.* 4th ed. Munich: Beck, 2001.

Hillenbrand, R. *Islamic Architecture: Form, Function, and Meaning.* New York: Columbia University Press, 2004.

Jadarji, R. K. "Nahw uslub ʿarabi fi fann al-ʿimara." *Hiwar* 24–25 (1966): 88–100.

Kultermann, U. *Architekten der Dritten Welt: Bauen zwischen Tradition und Neubeginn.* Cologne: DuMont, 1980.

Myntti, C. *Paris along the Nile: Architecture in Cairo from the Belle Epoque.* Cairo: American University Press, 2003.

Naef, S. *À la recherche d'une modernité arabe: l'évolution des arts plastiques en Egypte, au Liban et en Irak.* Geneva: Slatkine, 1996.

Naef, S. *Y a-t-il une "question de l' image" en Islam?* Paris: Téraèdre, 2004. (Revised and enlarged German ed.: *Bilder und Bilderverbot im Islam.* Munich: C. H. Beck, 2007.)

Naguib, E. *Themen der ägyptischen Malerei des 20. Jahrhunderts.* Cologne: Böhlau, 1980.

Nippa, A. *Haus und Familie in arabischen Ländern: Vom Mittelalter bis zur Gegenwart.* Munich: Beck, 1991.

Raafat, S. *Cairo, the Glory Years: A Guide.* Alexandria: Harpocrates, 2003.

Scharabi, M. "Einfluß der Pariser École des Beaux-Arts…" Dissertation, Technische Universität, Berlin, 1968.

——. "Civic Centre in Djeddah, Saudi Arabien." *Deutsche Bauzeitung* 7 (1974): 653–656.

——. "Die deutsche Architektur des Expressionismus." *Architectura* 11, no. 1 (1981): 66–82.

——. *Der Bazar: Das traditionelle Stadtzentrum im Nahen Osten und seine Handelseinrichtungen.* Tübingen: Wasmuth, 1985.

——. *Kairo: Stadt und Architektur im Zeitalter des europäischen Kolonialismus.* Tübingen: Wasmuth, 1989.

——. *Industrie und Industriebau in Ägypten: Eine Einführung in die Geschichte der Industrie im Nahen Osten.* Tübingen: Wasmuth, 1992.

Schölch, A. *Egypt for the Egyptians! The Socio-Political Crisis in Egypt, 1878–1882.* London: Ithaca Press, 1981.

Serageldin, I. *Architecture of the Contemporary Mosque.* London: Academy Editions, 1996.

Wirth, E. *Die orientalische Stadt im islamischen Vorderasien und Nordafrika.* 2 vols. 3rd ed. Mainz: von Zabern, 2002.

About the Authors

Jamil M. Abun-Nasr, b. 1932, studied Middle Eastern history in Beirut and oriental studies at Oxford. Between 1979 and 1997 he held the chair of Islamic studies at Bayreuth University, with a special focus on Africa. Selected publications include *The Tijaniyya, a Sufi Order in the Modern World* (1965) and *A History of the Maghrib* (1987).

Munir D. Ahmed, b. 1934, studied political science, Islamic studies, and comparative education in Lahore and Hamburg. He received his Ph.D. in 1967 and between 1967 and 1999 served as a research associate at the German Orient Institute and adjunct professor at Hamburg University. He has published numerous works on sociocultural developments in the Middle East and several volumes of narrative prose in Urdu. Recent publications include an autobiography (2005) and his correspondence with the Urdu writer Agha Babur (2005).

Lode Frank Brakel, 1941–1980, studied Semitic and Austronesian languages and literature and, before his death, served as executive director of the Department of Indonesian and Pacific Languages at Hamburg University. Selected publications include *The Hikayat Muhammad Hanafiyyah* (1975) and *The Story of Muhammad Hanafiyyah* (1977).

Johann Christoph Bürgel, b. 1931, majored in Islamic studies at the Universities of Frankfurt am Main, Bonn, Göttingen, and Ankara. Between 1970 and 1995 he was a professor of Islamic studies at Bern University. Selected publications include *Die Hofkorrespondenz ʿAdud ad-Daulas und ihr Verhältnis zu anderen historischen Quellen der frühen Buyiden* (1965); *Hafis: Gedichte aus dem Diwan* (2nd ed., 1977); *Dschalaluddin Rumi: Gedichte aus dem Diwan* (2003); *Nizami: Chosrou und Schirin* (1980); *Steppe im Staubkorn: Texte aus der Urdu-Dichtung Muhammad Iqbals* (1982); *Der Islam im Spiegel zeitgenössischer Literatur der islamischen Welt* (1985); *Allmacht und Mächtigkeit: Religion und Welt im Islam* (1991); *Nizami: Das Alexanderbuch* (1991); *Nizami: Die Abenteuer des Königs Bahram und seiner sieben Prinzessinnen* (1997); and *Tausendundeine Welt: Klassische arabische Literatur* (2007).

Heribert Busse, b. 1926, studied classical philology, Islamic studies, history, and geography in Mainz and London. He completed his habilitation in Islamic studies in 1965 and worked as a professor and director at the Department of Oriental Studies in Kiel until his retirement. Selected publications include "Die arabischen Inschriften im und am Felsendom in Jerusalem" (in *Das Heilige Land* 109, 1977); *Die theologischen Beziehungen des Islams zu Judentum und Christentum* (1991); "Die Versuchung Muhammads: Die Satanischen Verse in der islamischen Koranexegese" (in *Festgabe für H.-R. Singer*, edited by M. Forstner, 1991); and "Geschichte und Bedeutung der Kaaba im Licht der Bibel" (in *Zion: Ort der Begegnung*, 1993).

Andreas Christmann, b. 1965, studied Islamic studies, Arabic studies, and the history of religion in Leipzig and Leeds. After receiving his Ph.D. in 1999, he was appointed lecturer on contemporary Islam at the University of Manchester and a member of the editorial committee of the *Journal of Semitic Studies*. He has published widely on modern Islam in Syria, particularly on the works of the Kurdish scholar Muhammad Saʿid Ramadan al-Buti (1998, 2003, 2005, 2007) and the writings of the intellectual Muhammad Shahrour (2003, 2005, 2008). He has also examined the functional transformation of religious practices and their presentation in the Syrian mass media (1999, 2001, 2006).

Renate Dieterich, b. 1963, studied Islamic studies, political science, and geography in Bonn. In 1989 she began the first of several research fellowships in Jordan. She received her Ph.D. in 1998 and between 1999 and 2004 worked as a research associate in the Department of Oriental Studies at the University of Bonn. Selected publications include *Transformation oder Stagnation? Die jordanische Demokratisierungspolitik seit 1989* (1999); *Türkische Literatur in deutscher Sprache: Dokumentation einer Recherche* (2001); "Zum Verhältnis von Staat und Religion in der Türkei und im Iran" (in *Islam und Homosexualität*, edited by M. Bochow and R. Marbach, 2003); and *Gefährliche Gratwanderung: Jordaniens prekäre Lage angesichts von Wirtschaftskrise, Irakkonflikt und Palästinaproblem* (2004).

Hans-Georg Ebert, b. 1953, studied Arabic studies and law in Leipzig. He received his Ph.D. in 1982, completed his habilitation in 1990, and has served as professor of Islamic law at the University of Leipzig since 1998. He is the editor of *Leipziger Beiträge zur Orientforschung* and a board member of the Gesellschaft für arabisches und islamisches Recht. Selected publications include *Die Interdependenz von Staat, Verfassung und Islam im Nahen und Mittleren Osten in der Gegenwart* (1991); *Das Personalstatut arabischer Länder* (1996); and *Das Erbrecht arabischer Länder* (2004).

Werner Ende, b. 1937, studied Arabic studies, Islamic studies, history, and sociology in Halle, Hamburg, and Cairo. He served as a professor of Islamic studies at Freiburg University between 1983 and 2002. Ende is editor of the series *Freiburger Islamstudien* and co-edits the journal *Die Welt des Islams* and other periodicals. Selected publications include *Arabische Nation und islamische Geschichte* (1977); *The Nakhāwila, a Shiite Community in Medina* (1997); and *The Twelver Shia in Modern Times* (co-editor, 2001).

Alexander Flores, b. 1948, studied sociology, Arabic studies, and Islamic studies in Münster. He completed his habilitation in 1993 and has served as a professor at the Bremen University of Applied Sciences since 1995, with a focus on Arabic as a business language. Selected publications include *Nationalismus und Sozialismus im arabischen Osten* (1980); *The Palestinians in the Israeli-Arab Conflict* (1984); *Intifada: Aufstand der Palästinenser* (2nd ed., 1989); and *Die arabische Welt: Ein kleines Sachlexikon* (2003).

Rainer Freitag-Wirminghaus, b. 1948, studied Islamic studies, Turkish studies, ethnology, political science, and education. He received his Ph.D. in 1983, and between 1989 and 2006 served as a research associate at the German Orient Institute in Hamburg. Selected publications include *Geopolitik am Kaspischen Meer: Der Kampf um neue Energieressourcen* (1998); "US-Politik im Südkaukasus" (in *DOI-Focus*, April 2005); "Armeniens Außenpolitik zwischen den Ansprüchen der Mächte: Grundlagen und Grenzen des Konzepts der Komplementarität" (in *Orient* 1, 2005); and "Vom Panturkismus zum Pragmatismus: Die Türkei und Zentralasien" (in *Osteuropa, Machtmosaik Zentralasien* 8–9, September 2007).

Henner Fürtig, b. 1953, studied Arabic studies and history in Leipzig. He received his Ph.D. in 1983 and completed his habilitation in 1988. Between 1976 and 1993 Fürtig worked as a research associate and assistant professor at Leipzig University. In 1993 he joined the staff of the Center for Modern Oriental Studies in Berlin, and in 1996 he was named research group director. Since 2002 he has worked at the German Orient Institute in Hamburg. Publications include *Iran's Rivalry with Saudi Arabia between the Gulf Wars* (2002); *Die irakische Opposition und der 11. September* (2002); *Kleine Geschichte des Irak* (2003); *Der Irakkrieg: Katalysator für Demokratisierung in Nahost?* (2003); and "Iraq: How Severe Is the Threat?" (in *Iraq: Threat and Response*, edited by G. Beestermöller and D. Little, 2003).

Iris Glosemeyer, b. 1964, studied political science, Islamic studies, and history in Münster, Hamburg, and Berlin. She earned her Ph.D. in 2000 and since 1993 has worked on a freelance basis for German and international organizations, institutions, and institutes. Between 2001 and 2005 she was a fellow at the German Institute for International and Security Affairs. Selected publications include *Liberalisierung und Demokratisierung in der Republik Jemen 1990–1994* (1995); *Politische Akteure in der Republik Jemen* (2001); "Jemen: Staatsbildung mit Hindernissen" (in *States at Risk*, edited by U. Schneckener, 2004); and "Saudi Arabia: Dynamism Uncovered" (in *Arab Elites*, edited by V. Perthes, 2004).

Hans Harder, b. 1966, majored in Indian studies at Hamburg, Heidelberg, and Halle-Wittenberg. He earned his Ph.D. in 1997 and between 1995 and 2007 lectured on Bengali, Hindi, and modern South Asian literatures at Martin Luther University in Halle-Wittenberg. He holds the chair in modern South Asian languages and literatures at Heidelberg University. Selected publications include *Die mystische Säge: Gedichte aus dem Bengalischen* (edited and translated with C. Weiß, 1999); *Der verrückte Gofur spricht: Mystische Lieder aus Ostbengalen* (2004); *Bankimchandra Chattopadhyay's Srimadbhagabadgita: Translation and Analysis* (2001); and *Looking at the Coloniser: Cross-Cultural Perceptions in Central Asia and the Caucasus, Bengal, and Related Areas* (co-edited with B. Eschment, 2004).

Jan-Peter Hartung, b. 1969, studied Indian studies, Central Asian studies, and philosophy in Leipzig. He received his Ph.D. in 1983 and is a lecturer in the Department of the Study of Religions at the School of Oriental and African Studies, London. Publications include *Viele Wege und ein Ziel: Leben und Wirken von Sayyid Abū l-Ḥasan ʿAlī al-Ḥasanī Nadwī, 1913–1999* (2004).

Axel Havemann, b. 1949, studied Islamic, Iranian, and Byzantine studies in Berlin. He received his Ph.D. in 1983 and completed his habilitation in 2001. In 1976–1981 and 1985–1991 he served as a research associate at the Free University of Berlin and in 1981–1985 at the Saarland University. He became a Privatdozent in 2001. Selected publications include *Riʾāsa und qaḍāʾ: Institutionen als Ausdruck wechselnder Kräfteverhältnisse in syrischen Städten vom 10. bis zum 12. Jahrhundert* (1975); *Rurale Bewegungen im Libanongebirge des 19. Jahrhunderts* (1983); and *Geschichte und Geschichtsschreibung im Libanon des 19. und 20. Jahrhunderts* (2002).

Thomas Heberer, b. 1947, studied ethnology, political science, and sinology in Frankfurt am Main, Göttingen, Mainz, and Heidelberg. He received his Ph.D. in 1977 and finished his habilitation in political science in 1989. In 1991–92 Heberer was a professor of business sinology at the University of Bremen, and between 1992 and 1998 he served as professor of political science at Trier University. Since 1998 he has been a professor of political science at the University of Duisburg-Essen. Selected publications include *Private Entrepreneurs in China and Vietnam: Social and Political Functioning of Strategic Groups* (2003); *Why Ideas Matter: Ideen und Diskurse in der Politik Chinas, Japans, Malaysias* (with C. Derichs and N. Sausmikat, 2004); *Rural China: Economic and Social Change in the Late Twentieth Century* (with Fan Jie and W. Taubmann, 2005); *Power of Ideas: Intellectual Input and Political Change in East and Southeast Asia* (with C. Derichs, 2005); and *Ethnic Entrepreneurs in Southwest China: Nuosu (Yi) Entrepreneurs and their Impact on Social Change in Liangshan Prefecture* (2005).

Peter Heine, b. 1944, studied philosophy, Islamic studies, and ethnology in Münster and Baghdad. He completed his habilitation in 1978 and from 1994 until 2009 he was professor of Islamic studies at the Humboldt University of Berlin. Selected publications include *Konflikt der Kulturen oder Feindbild Islam* (1996); *Halbmond über deutschen Dächern: Muslimisches Leben in unserem Land* (1997); *Der Islam auf dem Weg in das 21. Jahrhundert* (1998); *Handbuch Recht und Kultur des Islams in der deutschen Gesellschaft* (with A. T. Khoury and J. Oebbecke, 2000); *Terror im Namen Allahs: Extremistische Kräfte im Islam* (2001); and *Der Islam* (2007).

Otto Jastrow, b. 1942, studied Semitic studies, Islamic studies, phonetics, and phonology in Saarbrücken and Tübingen; Turkish studies in Istanbul; and Arabic studies in Beirut. He received his Ph.D. in 1967 and completed his habilitation in 1974. Jastrow has worked as a research fellow (1971–1980) and professor (1980–1990) at the University of Erlangen-Nuremburg and a professor of Semitic studies at the University of Heidelberg (1990–1996). Since 1996 he has been a professor of oriental philology at the University of Erlangen-Nuremburg. Together with Werner Arnold, he co-edits the journal *Zeitschrift für arabische Linguistik* and is editor of the series *Semitica Viva* and *Semitica Viva: Series Didactica.* He has carried out numerous field studies in the Middle East and published works based on them, including *Handbuch der arabischen Dialekte* (editor, 1980); *Die mesopotamisch-arabischen qeltu-Dialekte* (2 vols., 1978 and 1981); *Der arabische Dialekt der Juden von ʿAqra und Arbil* (1990); *Lehrbuch der Turoyo-Sprache* (1992); *Lehrgang für die arabische Schriftsprache der Gegenwart* (with W. Fischer, 5th ed., 1996); *Arabische Texte aus Kinderib* (2003); and *Glossar zu Kinderib* (2005).

Frederick de Jong, b. 1944, studied Arab studies, Islamic studies, sociology, and ethnology in Leiden and Cairo. Since 1987 he has been a professor of Islamic languages and cultures at Utrecht University. Selected publications include *Turuq and Turuq-Linked Institutions in Nineteenth-Century Egypt* (1978); *Names, Religious Denomination and Ethnicity of Settlements in Western Thrace* (1980); *Shīʿa Islam, Sects and Sufism: Historical Dimensions, Religious Practice and Methodological Considerations* (editor, 1992); *Islamic Mysticism Contested: Thirteen Centuries of Controversies and Polemics* (edited with B. Radtke, 1999); and *Sufi Orders in Ottoman and Post-Ottoman Egypt and the Middle East* (2000).

Hermann Kandler, b. 1963, studied Islamic studies, Islamic philology, and geography in Mainz. He received a Ph.D. in Islamic studies in 1993 and completed his habilitation in 2001. In 1998 Kandler held an EU professorship in Komotini. He is currently a research associate at the Department of Oriental Studies in Mainz. Selected publications include *Die Bedeutung der Siebenschläfer (Ashāb al-kahf) im Islam* (1994); *Die Bedeutung des Mercator-Atlas für die islamisch-geographische Literatur* (1995); *Sadık Ahmet (1947–1995): Politischer "Spaltpilz" Griechisch-Thrakiens* (1998); and *Die anatolische "Bruchlinie"* (2000).

Franz Kogelmann, b. 1965, studied Islamic studies, ethnology, and African history in Bayreuth, where he earned his Ph.D. Between 1992 and 1996 he worked as a research fellow in the "Identity in Africa" research program at Bayreuth University. Between 2000 and 2004 he was a research associate at the German Orient Institute in Hamburg. In 2005 he collaborated on the special research project "Local Action in Africa in the Context of Global Influences." In 2006 he was appointed director of the project "Sharia Debates and Their Perception by Christians and Muslims in Selected African Countries." Publications include *Die Islamisten Ägyptens in der Regierungszeit von Anwar as-Sadat, 1970–1981* (1994); *Islamische fromme Stiftungen und Staat* (1999); and *Comparative Perspectives on Shari'ah in Nigeria* (with P. Ostien and J. M. Nasir, 2005).

Nico Landman, b. 1958, studied theology, religion, and Arab studies in Utrecht and Amsterdam. Landman received his Ph.D. in 1992 and since 1993 has worked as a lecturer at the Institute of Middle Eastern Studies at Utrecht University. Publications include *Van mat tot minaret: De institutionalisering van de islam in Nederland* (1992).

Roman Loimeier, b. 1957, studied Islamic studies, religion, ethnology, and African history in Freiburg, London, and Bayreuth. Between 2000 and 2005 he directed the research project on Islamic education in East Africa at the University of Bayreuth. Since 2008 he has been an assistant professor at the Center for African Studies at the University of Florida, Gainesville. Selected publications include *Islamic Reform and Political Change in Northern Nigeria* (1997); and *Säkularer Staat und islamische Gesellschaft: Die Beziehungen zwischen Staat, Sufi-Bruderschaften und islamischer Reformbewegung in Senegal im 20. Jahrhundert,* 2001.

Hanspeter Mattes, b. 1951, studied economics, political science, and development economics in Heidelberg and Arabic in Tunisia (1976–1978). He received a Ph.D. in political science in 1982 and since 1983 has been a research fellow at the German Orient Institute in Hamburg. Mattes has served as editor of *Nahost-Jahrbuch* since 1987 and with S. Faath he co-edits the academic series *Wuqûf: Beiträge zur Entwicklung von Staat und Gesellschaft in Nordafrika.* Publications include *Tradition vs. Moderne: Die ambivalente Rolle staatlicher Religionspolitik in Nordafrika, Nah- und Mittelost* (2005).

Hans Müller, b. 1927, studied economics, Islamic studies, ethnology, and sociology in Mainz, Munich, and Heidelberg. He holds both a master's in economics (Diplom-Volkswirt) and a Ph.D. Until retiring in 1992 he served as academic director and associate professor of Islamic studies at Freiburg University. Müller has published on a wide range of topics, including Persian history; Islamic economic and social history; Turkish literature; the didactics of Arabic, Persian, and Turkish; literary relations between East and West; and Islam in Black Africa. His works include *Zur Lage der Muslime im nachkolonialen Ostafrika* (2000).

Volker Nienhaus, b. 1951, studied economics in Bochum. He completed his habilitation in 1985 and between 1990 and 2004 served as a professor of economic history at Ruhr University in Bochum. He has been president of Marburg University since 2004. Fields of specialization include regulatory and structural policy, foreign trade and European economic policy, collaborative development policy, Islamic economics, and the economies of Islamic countries.

Katja Niethammer, b. 1971, studied communication and Islamic studies at both the Free University of Berlin and Birzeit University. She took her Ph.D. at the Free University in 2007 and in August 2008 became a postdoctoral fellow at the Center for International and Regional Studies at the Georgetown University School of Foreign Service in Qatar. Selected publications include *Political Reform in Bahrain: Institutional Transformation, Identity Conflict and Democracy* (forthcoming); and "Bahrainisches Paradox: Autoritäre Islamisten durch Partizipation, pro-demokratische durch Exklusion?" (in *Politische Reformen und politischer Islam,* edited by Muriel Asseburg, 2007).

Rudolph Peters, b. 1943, studied law and Islamic studies in Amsterdam and Leiden. He completed his habilitation in 1979 and has been a professor of Islamic and Middle Eastern law at Amsterdam University since 1991. Selected publications include *Jihad in Mediaeval and Modern Islam* (1977); and *Islam and Colonialism: The Doctrine of Jihad in Modern History* (1979).

Thomas Philipp, b. 1941, studied Arabic studies, sociology, and modern Arab history in Berlin, Jerusalem, and Los Angeles. From 1988 until 2008 he served as professor of the politics and contemporary history of the Middle East at the University of Erlangen-Nuremburg. Selected publications include *Al-Jabarti's History of Egypt* (with G. Schwald, 1994); *The Mamluks in Egyptian Society and Politics* (co-edited with U. Haarmann, 1998); and *The Syrian Land: Infrastructures and Communication; Processes of Integration and Separation in Bilad al-Sham from the 18th Century to the Mandatory Period* (co-edited with B. Schäbler, 1998).

Johanna Pink, b. 1974, studied Islamic studies and law in Erlangen and Bonn. She earned her Ph.D. in 2002 and between 2002 and 2006 held various research grants. Since 2006 Pink has been a research associate at the Department of Islamic Studies at the Free University of Berlin. Publications include *Neue Religionsgemeinschaften in Ägypten* (2003).

Abbas Poya, b. 1967, studied Islamic studies, political science, and comparative religion in Hamburg and Damascus. After receiving his Ph.D., Poya served as an adjunct professor at Hamburg University between 2002 and 2004. In 2003 he worked as a research fellow at the Afghanistan Academy of Sciences. Since 2004 he has been a research associate at the Department of Middle Eastern Studies of Freiburg University. Selected publications include *Anerkennung des Iğtihād—Legitimation der Toleranz: Möglichkeiten innerer und äußerer Toleranz im Islam am Beispiel der Iğtihād-Diskussion* (2003); and "Perspektiven zivilgesellschaftlicher Strukturen in Afghanistan: Ethische Neutralität, ethnische Parität und Frauenrechte in der Verfassung der Islamischen Republik Afghanistan" (in *Orient* 44, 2003).

Bernd Radtke, b. 1944, studied Islamic studies, Semitic studies, psychology, and Slavic studies in Hamburg and Basel. He completed his habilitation in 1985 and has been an assistant professor of Arabic and Persian at Utrecht University since 1992. Selected publications include *Weltgeschichte und Weltbeschreibung im mittelalterlichen Islam* (1992);

Drei Schriften des Theosophen von Tirmidh (1992–1996); *The Exoteric Aḥmad Ibn Idrīs: A Sufi's Critique of the Madhāhib and the Wahhābīs* (with J. O'Kane, K. S. Vikør, and R. S. O'Fahey, 1999); *Neue kritische Gänge: Zu Stand und Aufgaben der Sufikforschung* (2005); and *Pure Gold from the Words of Sayyidī 'Abd al-'Azīz al-Dabbāgh: Al-Dhahab al-Ibrīz min Kalām Sayyidī 'Abd al-'Azīz al-Dabbāgh by Aḥmad B. al-Mubārak al-Lamaṭī* (translated with John O'Kane, 2007).

Johannes Reissner, (1947–2009, studied Islamic studies, philosophy, and religion in Berlin and Vienna. He received his Ph.D. in 1978 and has been a research associate at the German Institute for International and Security Affairs in Berlin since 1982. Selected publications include *Ideologie und Politik der Muslimbrüder Syriens, 1947–1952* (1980); and "Europe's 'Critical Dialogue' with Iran" (in *Honey and Vinegar,* edited by R. N. Haass and M. L. O'Sullivan, 2000).

Mohamed Scharabi, b. 1938, studied architecture and philosophy in Berlin. He received a Ph.D. in engineering in 1967 and completed his habilitation in 1981. From 1988 until 1995 he was a professor of architectural history and the foundations of design at the Darmstadt Institute of Technology. Scharabi has co-designed several large housing developments and cultural/business centers in Egypt, Kuwait, Saudi Arabia, and the Sudan. Selected publications include *Zur deutschen Architektur des Expressionismus* (1981); *Der Bazar: Das traditionelle Stadtzentrum in Nahen Osten und seine Handelsbeziehungen* (1985); *Kairo: Stadt und Architektur im Zeitalter des europäischen Kolonialismus* (1989); *Industrie und Industriebauten in Ägypten* (1992); and *Architekturgeschichte des 19. Jahrhunderts* (1993).

Werner Schmucker, b. 1940, studied Islamic and Mongolian studies as well as comparative religion in Bonn. Between 1983 and 2005 he served as a professor of the Islamic languages of the Middle East at Bonn University. Selected publications include *Die maltesischen Gefangenschaftserinnerungen eines türkischen Kadi aus dem Jahre 1599* (1970); *Untersuchungen zu einigen wichtigen bodenrechtlichen Konsequenzen der arabischen Eroberungsbewegung* (1972); and *Krise und Erneuerung im libanesischen Drusentum* (1979).

Reinhard Schulze, b. 1953, studied Middle Eastern and Islamic studies and Arabic studies as well as Romance studies in Bonn. He completed his habilitation in 1987 and in 1992 was appointed professor of Islamic and Arabic studies at Bamberg University. Since 1995 Schulze has held a professorship at Bern University. Selected publications include *Islamischer Internationalismus im 20. Jahrhundert* (1990); *A Modern History of the Islamic World* (2002); "Das Böse in der islamischen Tradition" (in *Das Böse in den Weltreligionen,* edited by J. Laube, 2003); "'Talibanisierung' der islamischen Welt? Der Islamismus und der Irak-Krieg" (in *Der Irak,* edited by K. Hafez and B. Schäbler, 2003); "Islamismus im Kontext der Globalisierung" (in *Religion, Kultur und Politik im Vorderen Orient,* edited by P. Pawelka and L. Richter-Bernburg, 2004); and "Islamische Solidaritätsnetzwerke" (in *Transnationale Solidarität,* edited by J. Beckert et al., 2004).

Olaf H. Schumann, b. 1938, studied Protestant theology in Kiel, Tübingen, and Basel and Islamic studies in Tübingen and Cairo. He was a lecturer in German language at Assiut University in Egypt between 1966 and 1968 and served as a research fellow at the Council of Churches in Jakarta between 1970 and 1981. Schumann served as a professor of religion and missionary studies at Hamburg University between 1981 and 2004, and from 1989 to 1992 held a guest professorship at the Jakarta Theological Seminary in Indonesia. Selected publications include *Der Christus der Muslime* (2nd ed., 1988; in English, *Jesus the Messiah in Muslim Thought*, 2002); *Dialog antar umat Beragama* (2 vols., 1980, 1982); *Pemikiran Keagamaan dalam Tantangan* (2nd ed., 1998); *Hinaus aus der Festung* (1997); *Selbstverständnis und Fremdwahrnehmung* (1999); *Zentrale Texte des Glaubens* (2002); and *Menghadapi Tantangan, memperjuangkan Kerukunan* (2nd ed., 2006).

Riem Spielhaus, b. 1974, studied Islamic and African studies in Berlin and earned her Ph.D. in 2008. In 2002–3 she served as a specialist on Islam on the Task Force of the Federal Commissioners for Integration, Migration, and Refugees. She has been a research fellow at the Humboldt University of Berlin since 2002. Selected publications include *Islam auf Sendung: Islamische Fernsehsendungen im Offenen Kanal* (co-edited with Anke Bentzin, Jeanine Dagyeli et al., 2007); *Islamisches Gemeindeleben in Berlin* (co-edited with Alexa Färber, 2006); "Religion and Identity: How Germany's Foreigners Have Become Muslims" (in *Internationale Politik*, Spring 2006); and "Cooperation between Muslim Organizations and State Institutions: Obstacles und Opportunities" (in *Muslim Philanthropy and Civic Engagement*, edited by Peter Heine and Aslam Syed, 2005).

Ursula Spuler-Stegemann, b. 1939, studied Middle Eastern studies, comparative religion, modern German literature, and Semitic studies. Spuler-Stegemann holds a Ph.D. and has been an honorary professor of the history of religion at Marburg University since 1995. Selected publications include *Muslime in Deutschland: Informationen und Klärungen* (3rd ed., 2002); and *Feindbild Christentum im Islam: Eine Bestandsaufnahme* (editor, 2003).

Udo Steinbach, b. 1943, studied Middle Eastern studies and classical philology in Freiburg and Basel. He received his Ph.D. in 1970 and served as director of the German Orient Institute in Hamburg between 1976 and 2007. Steinbach has published widely on politics and society in the Near and Middle East (with a focus on Turkey); on the status of the Middle East in international politics; and on Islam in Germany. Selected works include *Politisches Lexikon Nahost/Nordafrika* (co-edited with R. Hofmeier and M. Schönborn, 3rd ed., 1994); *Geschichte der Türkei* (3rd ed., 2003); *Zentralasien: Geschichte, Politik, Wirtschaft: Ein Lexikon* (co-edited with M.-C. von Gumppenberg, 2004); *Autochthone Christen im Nahen Osten: Zwischen Verfolgungsdruck und Auswanderung* (editor, 2007); and *Der Kaukasus: Geschichte, Kultur, Politik* (co-edited with M.-C. von Gumppenberg, 2008).

Guido Steinberg, b. 1968, studied history, Islamic studies, and political science in Cologne, Bonn, and Damascus. He received his Ph.D. in 2000, and in 2001 was named academic coordinator of the interdisciplinary Social History of the Middle East center of the Free University of Berlin. Between 2002 and 2005 he served as a terrorism expert at the Federal Chancellery, and since 2005 he has been a research fellow at the Institute for International and Security Affairs in Berlin. Steinberg is also an adjunct professor at the Otto Suhr Institute for Political Science at the Free University of Berlin. Selected publications include *Religion und Staat in Saudi-Arabien: Die wahhabitischen Gelehrten (1902–1953)* (2002); *Saudi-Arabien: Politik, Geschichte, Religion* (2004); and *Der nahe und der ferne Feind: Die Netzwerke des islamistischen Terrorismus* (2005).

Wiebke Walther, b. 1935, studied Middle Eastern studies in Halle. She received her Ph.D. in 1966 and completed her habilitation in 1980. She served as a guest professor at the Ain Shams University, Cairo, between 1989 and 1991, and since 1999 she has been an adjunct professor at the University of Tübingen. Selected publications include *Die Frau im Islam* (1980); *Erkundungen: 28 Erzähler aus dem Irak* (editor and translator, 1986); *Tausendundeine Nacht: Eine Einführung* (1987); "The Beginnings of the Realistic School of Narrative Prose in Iraq" (in *Quaderni di Studi Arabi* 18, 2000); "The Arabian Nights in Modern Arabic Literature" (in *The Arabian Nights Encyclopedia*, edited by U. Marzolph and R. van Leeuwen, 2004); and *Kleine Geschichte der arabischen Literatur* (2004), Polish translation 2008.

Rotraud Wielandt, b. 1944, studied Islamic studies, Turkish studies, comparative religion, and philosophy in Munich, Tübingen, and Istanbul. She completed her habilitation in 1982 and has been a professor of Islamic and Arabic studies at Bamberg University since 1985. Selected publications include *Offenbarung und Geschichte im Denken moderner Muslime* (1971); *Das Bild der Europäer in der modernen arabischen Erzähl- und Theaterliteratur* (1980); *Das erzählerische Frühwerk Mahmud Taymurs* (1983); and "Wurzeln der Schwierigkeit innerislamischen Gesprächs über neue hermeneutische Zugänge zum Korantext" (in *The Qur'an as Text*, edited by S. Wild, 1996).

Monika Wohlrab-Sahr, b. 1957, studied Protestant theology and sociology in Erlangen and Marburg. She received a Ph.D. in sociology in 1991 and completed her habilitation in 1999. She has served as a professor of the sociology of religion (1999–2006) and professor of cultural sociology (since 2006) at Leipzig University. In 1996 she was a visiting scholar at the Department of Sociology at the University of California, Berkeley, and in 2007–8 a Fernand Braudel Fellow at the European University Institute, Florence. Selected publications include *Konversion zum Islam in Deutschland und den USA* (1999); *Atheismus und religiöse Indifferenz* (co-edited with C. Gaertner and D. Pollack, 2003); and *Konfliktfeld Islam in Europa* (co-edited with L. Tezcan, 2007).

Translated by Adam Blauhut

Name Index

Page numbers followed by letter *t* refer to tables.

Subject Index

Page numbers followed by letters *f* and *t* refer to figures and tables, respectively.

Geographical Index

Page numbers followed by letters *f* and *t* refer to figures and tables, respectively.

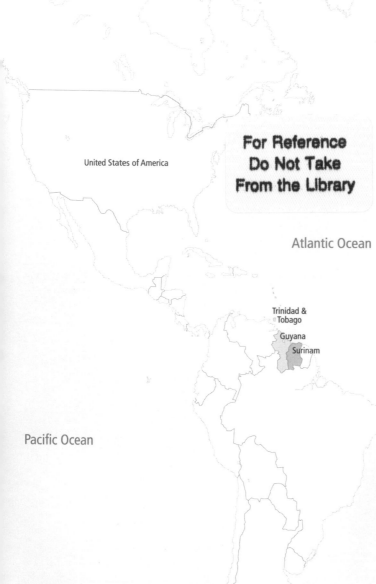

Norway

Great Nether-
Britain lands
Belgium Germa

Switzerland
France
Italy
Spain Bosnia

Tunis

Morocco

**For Reference
Do Not Take
From the Library**

Algeria

Western Sahara

United States of America

Atlantic Ocean

Mauritania Mali Niger

Senegal Burkina
Gambia Faso Nigeria
Guinea-Bissau Guinea Ghana
Côte
Sierra Leone d'Ivoire
Liberia Togo Camer
Benin

Trinidad &
Tobago

Guyana
Surinam

Pacific Ocean

Muslim Population

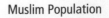

| | 90 – 100% |
| 50 – 89% |
| 20 – 49% |
| 5 – 19% |
| 1 – 4% |
| under 1% |